WORK PSYCHOLOGY

Understanding Human Behaviour in the Workplace

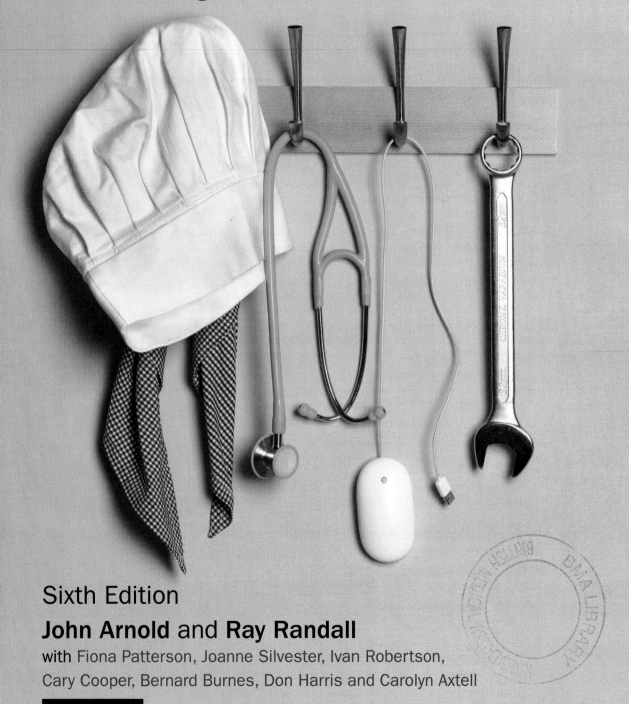

Sixth Edition

John Arnold and Ray Randall

with Fiona Patterson, Joanne Silvester, Ivan Robertson,
Cary Cooper, Bernard Burnes, Don Harris and Carolyn Axtell

PEARSON

Harlow, England • London • New York • Boston • San Francisco • Toronto • Sydney • Auckland • Singapore • Hong Kong
Tokyo • Seoul • Taipei • New Delhi • Cape Town • São Paulo • Mexico City • Madrid • Amsterdam • Munich • Paris • Milan

Pearson Education Limited
Edinburgh Gate
Harlow CM20 2JE
United Kingdom
Tel: +44 (0)1279 623623
Web: www.pearson.com/uk

First published 1991 (print)
Second edition published 1995 (print)
Third edition published 1998 (print)
Fourth edition published 2005 (print)
Fifth edition published 2010 (print)
Sixth edition published 2016 (print and electronic)

Pearson Education is not responsible for the content of third-party internet sites.

The Financial Times. With a worldwide network of highly respected journalists, The Financial Times provides global business news, insightful opinion and expert analysis of business, finance and politics. With over 500 journalists reporting from 50 countries worldwide, our in-depth coverage of international news is objectively reported and analysed from an independent, global perspective. To find out more, visit www.ft.com/pearsonoffer.

ISBN: 978-1-292-06340-9 (print)
     978-1-292-06342-3 (PDF)
     978-1-292-14418-4 (ePub)

British Library Cataloguing-in-Publication Data
A catalogue record for the print edition is available from the British Library

Library of Congress Cataloging-in-Publication Data
A catalog record for the print edition is available from the Library of Congress

10 9 8 7 6 5 4 3 2
20 19 18 17 16

Front cover: Getty Images

Print edition typeset in 9/11.5 pt Stone Serif ITC Pro by Lumina Datamatics

Print edition printed and bound by L.E.G.O. S.p.A., Italy

NOTE THAT ANY PAGE CROSS REFERENCES REFER TO THE PRINT EDITION

BRIEF CONTENTS

CONTENTS

PREFACE

Work psychology is about people's behaviour, thoughts and emotions related to their work. It can be used to improve our understanding and management of people (including ourselves) at work. By work, we mean what people do to earn a living. However, much of the content of this book can also be applied to study, voluntary work and even leisure activities.

All too often, work organisations have sophisticated systems for assessing the costs and benefits of everything except their management of people. It is often said by senior managers that 'our greatest asset is our people', but sometimes the people do not feel that they are being treated as if they were valuable assets. People are complicated, and their views of themselves and their worlds differ: you will see a great many references to individual differences throughout this book. People do not necessarily do what others would like them to do. One reaction to all this is for managers to focus on things that don't talk back, such as profit and loss accounts or organisational strategy. Another is to adopt a highly controlling 'do as I say' approach to dealing with people at work. Either way, the thinking behind how people in the workplace function, and how they might be managed, tends to be rather careless or simplistic. Work psychologists seek to counter that tendency by carefully studying people's behaviour, thoughts and feelings regarding work. As well as developing knowledge and understanding for its own sake, this also leads to insights about motivation, leadership, training and development, selection and many other people-related aspects of management. Work psychologists are also concerned about the ethical use of psychological theories and techniques, and their impact on the well-being and effectiveness of individuals, groups and organisations.

This book is designed to appeal to readers in many different countries, especially in Europe and Australasia. Judging by the feedback and sales figures for previous editions, we seem to have generally been successful in appealing to a range of people in a range of places. We have tried to make the book suitable both for people encountering the subject for the first time and for those who already have some familiarity with it. Specifically, and in no particular order, we intend that this book should be useful for:

- undergraduate students in psychology, taking one or more modules with names such as work psychology, work and organisational psychology, business psychology, organisational psychology, occupational psychology, and industrial–organisational psychology;

- undergraduate students in business and management taking one or more modules that might have titles such as organisational behaviour, managing people or human resource management;

- postgraduate (MSc, MBA, MA) and post-experience students in psychology or business/management taking one or more modules with any or all of the titles listed above;

■ students taking professional qualifications, particularly (in the United Kingdom) those of the Chartered Institute of Personnel and Development (CIPD);

■ students on undergraduate or postgraduate courses in other vocational subjects such as engineering, whose curriculum includes some elements to do with managing people at work.

We aim to give clear and straightforward – but not simplistic – accounts of many key areas of contemporary work psychology. More specifically, we try to achieve several objectives in order to make this book as useful as possible to its readers.

First, we seek to blend theory and practice. Both are important. Without good theory, practice is blind. Without good practice, theory is not being properly used. We therefore describe key theories and evaluate them where appropriate. We also discuss how the concepts described can find practical application. We provide case studies and exercises to which material in the book can readily be applied. These can be used as classroom exercises, or as assignments for individual students. Some guidance and suggestions about how to use these are included on the website for this book.

Second, we try to present material at a level the reader should find intellectually stimulating, but not too difficult. It is all too easy to use a slick, glossy presentation at the expense of good content. There is always the temptation to resort to over-simple 'recipes for success' that insult the reader's intelligence. On the other hand, it is equally easy to lose the reader in unnecessarily complex debates. We hope that we avoid both these fates (and that you will let us know if we do not!).

Third, we try to help the reader to gain maximum benefit from the book by providing several more aids to learning. Each chapter begins with clearly stated learning outcomes, and concludes with some short self-test questions and longer suggested assignments that reflect these outcomes. At the end of each chapter we provide a small number of suggestions for further reading. Throughout the text we specify key learning points that express succinctly the main message of the preceding sections of text. We include a number of diagrams as well as text, in recognition that pictures can often express complex ideas in an economical and memorable way. We highlight key controversies and debates because it is not uncommon for research findings to point in different, apparently contradictory, directions. To help the reader, we weigh up the arguments. Because no topic in work psychology sits in isolation from others, we also point towards some of the most natural connections between different parts of the book. At the end of the book there is a comprehensive glossary explaining in a concise way the meaning of lots of key words and phrases. There is also a very long list of references, to enable interested readers to find more material if they wish – for more advanced study for example.

Fourth, we have chosen topics that we judge to be the most useful to potential readers of this book. Some usually appear in organisational behaviour texts, whereas others are generally found in books of a more specifically psychological orientation. We believe we have found a helpful balance between these two overlapping but different worlds, so that there should be plenty of relevant material both for people who want to be psychologists and those who do not. The topics we cover in chapters or parts of chapters include individual differences, employee selection, assessing work performance, attitudes at work, training and development, teamwork, work motivation, stress and well-being at work, designing work and work equipment, managing diversity, leadership, careers, organisational change and culture, dispersed working, the nature of work psychology as a discipline and profession and how to design, conduct and understand research studies in work psychology.

Fifth, we provide up-to-date coverage of our material. There are currently exciting advances in many areas of work psychology, and we try to reflect these. At the same time, where the old stuff is best and still relevant, we include it. There is nothing to be gained by discussing recent work purely because it is recent, especially if that comes at the expense of better quality and more useful material.

Sixth, we attempt to use material from many different parts of the world, and to point out cross-national and cross-cultural differences where these seem particularly important. Much of the best research and practice in work psychology originate from North America, but it is possible to go too far and assume that nowhere else has contributed anything. No doubt we have our own blinkers, but we try to include perspectives from places other than North America, especially the UK and other European countries. Nevertheless, the USA and Canada provide much valuable material. We therefore also make use of research and theory originating in those countries.

Developments from the fifth edition

Readers familiar with the fifth edition of this text, published in 2010, may find it helpful if we describe the changes we have made. These are more evident in some parts of the book than others. Readers familiar with previous editions will readily recognise this book as a direct descendant of the others, but will also notice quite a few differences. As the book has grown over the years, so has the workload involved during its revision. We say this every time, but it has taken us longer than we (and our families) would have liked. As ever, we apologise for this. If you have been waiting for this new edition you might justifiably have been losing patience with us.

The changes from the fifth edition reflect the fact that quite a lot has happened in work psychology over the last few years. Reviewers commissioned by the publisher (plus users' comments made direct to us) helped us to see where rethinks were required.

I (Ray Randall) worked on Chapters 1, 2, 6, 10 and 11. John Arnold is now the contributor of three chapters (7, 12 and 13). As with the fifth edition, Fiona Patterson (Chapters 3 and 4) and Joanne Silvester (Chapters 5 and 9) also took a major role. Bernard Burnes has once again contributed the chapter on organisational change and culture. Don Harris (Chapter 8) and Carolyn Axtell (Chapter 15) handled a chapter each. Ivan Robertson and Cary Cooper have taken more of a back seat this time but their contributions can be seen in various parts of the text, most notably in Chapter 10. All contributors are excellent researchers with an international reputation in their field. Importantly, all are also practitioners, with extensive experience of intervention in organisations and this allows them to describe how theory can be put into practice. We are proud of this edition, but as with all preceding editions, your opinion is the one that really matters!

Feedback from readers of previous editions clearly indicated that they appreciated the clarity of style and the combination of theoretical and practical considerations. They also very much valued the substantial list of references, many quite recent. Naturally, we have tried to preserve these features. The style remains the same and the reference list has been revised and updated. We are grateful for the feedback we have received and wherever possible we have reflected it in this edition.

We have chosen to include some new learning features in this edition that we hope prove useful. The 'Research methods in focus' feature is designed to give readers a deep and detailed insight into how work psychologists go about their business (whether it be research or practice). Hopefully, it helps to demystify research methods by showing how these 'come to life' when applied to investigate or solve important issues. Reading about research methods and statistics can be daunting and difficult so we hope that this feature makes the activity more accessible and enjoyable. After much deliberation, we have chosen to retain the more generic material about research methods in Chapter 2. This is designed to give readers the 'lenses' needed to make sense of a wide range of published research. When read in conjunction with the Research methods in focus features it is designed to help readers to develop a solid knowledge base that can be used to interpret, use and critique any other research they encounter.

Psychologists often disagree about theories, the meaning of research findings, what constitutes good data and too many other things to list in this preface without doubling the length of the book. This can be confusing. Who are we to believe? Is the weight of evidence in favour of one side or the other? We use the new 'Key debate' feature to help these debates stand out from the rest of the text. Without appointing ourselves as judge and jury, we use this feature to present the arguments as we see them and to comment on the amount and quality of evidence available. We can't always solve the controversy, but we try to describe why it exists and how it might one day be resolved. We feel these issues have important implications for practice: too often promises are made about interventions before uncertainties about the underlying research have been adequately resolved.

As work psychologists progress in their careers, they often become more specialised, focusing on particular topics, organisational problems or research methods (it's one of the reasons why we need so many contributors for this text). There's nothing wrong with this and it certainly helps us to avoid overloading ourselves or attempting to practise in areas we know too little about. That said, we feel it is very important to understand and appreciate the linkages and connections between different topics in our field. A simple question demonstrates the point. Is it worth training someone to do a job if a good selection process would identify somebody who is already adequately skilled? The answer to this question is not a simple one (excuse us for sitting on the fence, just this once) but it does involve considering the research on both selection and training. To keep the book neatly organised and easy to navigate we keep these topics separate. We simply couldn't do justice to them unless a chapter is devoted to each. The Points of integration feature is designed to give the reader a quick insight into how these connections work – both in terms of research and theory. We also use them to show how people from different fields of expertise can be brought together to develop effective interventions.

From positive feedback provided by reviewers we have kept the large number of exercises and case studies. The majority of case studies have been updated to highlight the relevance that psychology has when dealing with contemporary issues in the workplace. We have kept several of the exercises that are familiar to instructors, but many are updated to ensure their relevance to, and resonance with, our intended readership. Where we feel the case studies from earlier editions still have a strong relevance these have been retained.

In the fifth edition we significantly increased the number of meta-analyses and systematic reviews we used and this seems to have been well-received. We are aware that this emphasis can carry with it a risk. We could omit the important details and 'colour' that come with the discussion of specific studies carried out in interesting organisational contexts. This time around we have tried to do justice to both the 'big data' studies and the smaller-scale, well-designed, interesting and important pieces of research. It is, after all, the latter that make up the 'bread and butter' activities of many researchers and practitioners. We offer commentary throughout designed to help readers to avoid falling into the trap of overestimating the importance of the results of either studies of 'big data' or isolated research findings.

We have retained the Stop to consider boxes. There are two to four of them in most chapters. These are designed to encourage students to pause to reflect on their learning. Their content is designed to foster critical thinking and cement learning. We hope these prove useful for students who wish to go beyond an understanding of content to attempt further analysis of the issues described.

Chapter 1 retains much of the introductory material of previous editions. We feel that this is particularly useful for those new to the study of psychology. It is also designed to illustrate how the basic assumptions made by psychologists, and the approaches they follow as a result, find their way into work psychology. This chapter is now considerably shorter than before. The feedback we received indicated that the content on workplace trends was better left to the relevant parts of the book. We still provide a brief introduction to important cross-cutting themes including culture and diversity, but these are now dealt with more comprehensively by considering them throughout the book. Contemporary issues are integrated into the content of each chapter (including in the Exercises and Case studies) in order to provide clearer illustrations of how research and theory can be applied.

We thought long and hard about removing the material on research methods in Chapter 2, and decided not to. In order to make use of the latest research we make reference to a large number of journal articles in the book. Therefore, we feel that this chapter does a reasonable job as a 'quick reference' guide to help readers make sense of the source material that we used and as an aid for interpreting research they encounter in the future. Its content is designed to be just 'technical enough' to give the reader a basic understanding of why different methods of data collection and analysis are used to deal with various theoretical and practical questions. In this edition we also include some discussion of evidence-based management to go alongside discussion of the notion of the scientist-practitioner and a detailed analysis of the academic–practitioner divide. These sections are designed to help readers to cement their understanding of how the transition can be made between theory and practice, a recurrent theme in the book. This is not a research methods book, but we hope that Chapter 2, along with the Research methods in focus features throughout, orientate students to many of the ways data are collected, analysed and used in our discipline.

Thanks to the considerable effort made by Fiona Patterson, Chapter 3 changed a lot for the fifth edition. Generally, it was seen as more accessible as a result, and better integrated with the rest of the text. This time around the focus has been on expanding the coverage of some of the more difficult and controversial issues associated with the study of individual differences. Fiona has included a more detailed discussion of the issues of bias and fairness when using psychometrics tests to measure individual differences. New research on emotional intelligence, creativity and innovation receives considerable coverage to reflect the growing importance of these topics for researchers and organisations alike. Some important questions are now being asked about the structure and nature of personality: these challenges to established theories are examined in some detail.

Chapter 4 is now one (rather large) chapter covering all aspects of personnel selection. Fiona Patterson's chapters on selection have always been very well received. This time around we gave her the rather tough job of joining them together. The idea was to enable readers to better appreciate the connections between different elements of this complex and diverse topic. The coverage is similar to previous editions, but has been extensively updated. Selection has always been a rapidly developing area of research and practice. New and important advances such as the promise offered by situational judgements tests and the more widespread use of online testing get increased coverage to reflect their growing importance. Candidates' reactions to their experiences of selection are dealt with in more detail.

Chapter 5, by Jo Silvester, on assessing performance at work retains much of the structure from the fifth edition. There are many important technical issues that are covered in detail: it was important to keep this content and to update it in line with the changing needs of work organisations. As multisource feedback has become more popular, this approach to measuring and managing performance is discussed in considerable detail. Given the changing nature of work, there are now many jobs for which good (and bad) performance is difficult to define. In the chapter, Jo uses some of her own research with politicians as an example of this challenge and how it can be addressed. Performance that is outside of contractual obligations (e.g. proactive helping behaviours) is discussed, along with its causes and consequences. The updated chapter contains a more detailed analysis of the use of electronic performance monitoring. The way such data are perceived sets an important research agenda for psychologists that also has significant practical implications.

Chapter 6 on attitudes at work has been refocused. It is never an easy decision to cut content for the fear that some readers might be disappointed. In the fifth edition, there were still some remnants of the basic social psychology material that dominated this chapter in early editions. The section on the basic psychology of attitude change has gone: the factors that change key workplace attitudes such as job satisfaction and organisational commitment are now weaved into the core content. The section on the psychological contract has expanded considerably to better reflect the diversity and quantity of research on the topic. We also took the decision that topics associated with employee relations (e.g. participation at work, management of careers, management of change) now receive good coverage elsewhere in the text. This left us with more room to give additional space to work-related attitudes and the associated concepts of employee turnover, unemployment and underemployment. As we have done before, when lots of material has been removed from a chapter, we have placed Chapter 7 from the fifth edition on the website accompanying this book.

Chapter 7 (work motivation and work design) has been extensively updated. Strong coverage of established theories of motivation do remain. John Arnold has given additional coverage to developing research agendas (e.g. perceptions of justice) that offer great promise. Research is also examined that has identified ways of enhancing the effects of established theories of motivation such as goal-setting. The impact of individual differences on motivational processes is now discussed in detail across the chapter. Emerging concepts including purposeful work behaviour are examined in depth. The chapter includes consideration of new approaches to the topic of work design and their relevance to various contemporary working practices and work environments.

Chapter 8, Design at work by Don Harris, was a new addition in the fifth edition. Its relevance may not be obvious to all readers. We strongly feel that the contribution that psychologists can make to the design and improvement of physical work environments and work equipment deserves a prominent place in this text. These contributions have been substantial, not least in the design of various types of displays and these are discussed in depth in new material for this edition. The proper management of end-user input into design is a recurrent theme in the chapter. The complex psychological processes that humans use to process the information at work are also discussed throughout. These are just two aspects of workplace design where psychologists will continue to make very significant contributions to research and practice.

Jo Silvester's chapter on training and development (Chapter 9) retains the extensive coverage of the various elements of the training cycle and theories of learning from previous editions. The mechanisms for delivering training and development in work organisations now receive much more attention. There is a detailed section on team-based training that taps into a growing research agenda regarding the effectiveness of delivering training in this way. Mentoring as an intervention, and the challenges associated with mentoring a diverse workforce, are now discussed. Leadership is covered in many chapters and here Jo examines the psychological processes that are important when implementing leadership development. This is an activity that represents a significant investment for many organisations.

Chapter 10 on stress and well-being at work was well-received in the fifth edition. For some time now we have wanted to include more balanced coverage in this chapter so that the benefits of 'good work' are as apparent as the risks associated with 'bad work'. This time around there is much more coverage of theories that describe how employees thrive and develop through their experiences at work. Concepts from positive psychology are examined in detail. There is more breadth and depth in the discussion of individual differences to include concepts such as resilience and psychological capital. The detailed section on interventions has been retained, but expanded to provide a more in-depth treatment of how these can be used to help employees develop their psychological resources.

Chapter 11 on teamwork has been trimmed a little as some of the content we felt was better positioned elsewhere (e.g. participation in decision-making is covered in several places in the text). The basic psychological research on groups is retained but shortened so that the chapter now moves a little more quickly into the topic of work teams. We also felt this was a good place to focus on the issue of diversity and how it relates to work performance and other important outcomes. Implementing teamwork is generally seen as being a good idea with potential benefits for the organisation and for the employee. In this edition we give more consideration to the research that helps us to identify what can be done to increase the chances that these good outcomes will occur.

John Arnold has revised the chapters on careers and leadership. There are many changes in both. Chapter 12 on leadership covers more ground than before. Leadership research throws up many contentious issues and the chapter includes an enhanced critical analysis of the key established theories. The links between leadership and the use of participation and empowerment now feature prominently in this chapter (and less so than in the chapter on teams). Gender and leadership and leading across cultures get increased coverage to reflect the importance of these research agendas to modern organisations. Throughout the chapter there is commentary on the 'dark side' of leadership including, for example, the misuse of transformational leadership behaviour and the ethical issues that arise when employees become highly susceptible to their leader's influence.

The revisions in Chapter 13 (Careers and career management) include: more detailed analysis of the boundaryless career that taps into a rich vein of recent research; increased breadth and depth of coverage of career interventions (both at an organisational and individual level); and more detailed consideration of how career success is defined and achieved. The key elements of this chapter have been retained from previous editions: the chapter is seen as one of the defining features of the book. However, there is enhanced coverage of mentoring, the connections between gender and career development, and the development of career preferences. This is a very comprehensive chapter that delves deep into many areas where theory and practice come together.

Bernard Burnes' chapter on change (Chapter 14) retains its structure from the fifth edition. It has been very well-received in the past as an authoritative review of the field. The updates reflect innovative and important new thinking around the topics of change and culture. In several parts of the chapter the updated material provides new insights about how existing theories and models can be put to better use. The chapter also identifies where new approaches might be needed to deal with the situations and pressures being faced by modern work organisations. Several promising emerging theories are identified, discussed and evaluated.

Carolyn Axtell's chapter on the psychology of dispersed working (Chapter 15) is the final chapter because it integrates many of the issues discussed throughout the text. It is a good demonstration of the relevance and utility of psychological theory in contemporary work settings. The chapter shows that if we are to make the best use of new ways of working, research from various different areas of work psychology need to be applied. This topic also has its own research agenda and presents new challenges for work psychologists. These have produced innovative and exciting approaches to research and intervention.

As with every iteration of this book, the average length of each chapter is greater (with the exception of Chapter 1). We hope that the coverage is contemporary and more integrated than before. Lecturers using the book may want to recommend parts of certain chapters, rather than whole chapters, to support a particular lecture topic, so it is worth having a close look at the contents pages to check what is where.

As before, we welcome feedback and dialogue about this book. Please direct it to Ray Randall, School of Business and Economics, Sir Richard Morris Building, Loughborough University, Leicestershire, Leicester, LE11 3TU, UK (r.randall@lboro.ac.uk). Thank you for reading this preface, and please now carry on into the rest of the book!

ABOUT THE AUTHORS

John Arnold is Professor of Organisational Behaviour at the School of Business and Economics, Loughborough University, UK.

Ray Randall is a Senior Lecturer at the School of Business and Economics at Loughborough University, UK.

Fiona Patterson is Founder Director of the Work Psychology Group, Principal Researcher the University of Cambridge and Visiting Professorship at City University, London, UK.

Joanne Silvester is Professor of Psychology, Cass Business School, City University London, UK.

Ivan Robertson is Founder Director of Robertson Cooper Ltd and Emeritus Professor of Work and Organizational Psychology, Manchester Business School, UK.

Professor Sir Cary Cooper CBE is 50th Anniversary Professor of Organizational Behaviour and Health, Alliance Manchester Business School, and President of the British Academy of Management.

Bernard Burnes is Professor of Organisational Change, Stirling Management School, UK.

Don Harris is Professor of Human Factors in the Centre for Mobility and Transport, Coventry University, UK.

Carolyn Axtell is Senior Lecturer at the Institute of Work Psychology, Sheffield University Management School, UK.

ACKNOWLEDGEMENTS

We thank Donna Goddard and Eileen Srebernik at Pearson Education for their immense patience in waiting for the manuscript, and for doing everything they could to help it along without putting the authors under too much pressure, even when we thoroughly deserved it. Ray Randall would like to thank his wife Kirsty, children Izzy and Owen, and his parents Lal and Bob for their patience, advice, understanding and support. He would also like to thank Sue Harrington for her contribution to the material on workplace bullying and Danny Sharples for his help with some of the material on rater bias in Chapter 5. John Arnold would also like to thank his parents Ann and Rev, and his wife Helen, for their love, wisdom and support.

Publisher's acknowledgements

We are grateful to the following for permission to reproduce copyright material:

Cartoons
Cartoons on pp. 185 and 192 from Randy Glasbergen, Glasbergen Cartoons, www.glasbergen.com

Photos
Figure 9.1 (left) Allan Cash Picture Library/Alamy Stock Photo, (right)

Figures
Figure 2.2 adapted from *Organizational Effectiveness: The Role of Psychology*, Wiley-Blackwell (Robertson, Ivan T., Callinan, M., Bartram, D. 2002) pp. 48–9, © 2002 by John Wiley & Sons, Ltd; Figure 4.1 from Identifying critical success factors for designing selection processes into postgraduate specialty training: the case of UK general practice, *Postgraduate Medical Journal*, vol. 86, p. 324 (Plint, S. & Patterson, F. 2010), reproduced with permission from BMJ Publishing Group Ltd; Figure 4.6 from The general factor of personality: A meta-analysis of Big Five intercorrelations and a criterion-related validity study, *Journal of Research in Personality*, vol. 44, pp.315–27 (Van der Linden, D., te Nijenhuis, J. and Bakker, A.B. 2010), reprinted with permission from Elsevier; Figure 6.1 from Prediction of goal-directed behavior: Attitudes, intentions, and perceived behavioral control, *Journal of Experimental Social Psychology*, vol. 22(5), pp. 453–74 (Ajzen, I. and Madden, J.T. 1986), copyright (1986), with permission from Elsevier, reprinted with permission from Elsevier; Figure 6.4 adapted from *Psychological Contracts in Organizations*, Sage (Rousseau, D.M. 1995) Figure 5.1, p. 118, © 1995 by Sage Publications, reprinted by permission; Figure 8.2 from Using SHERPA to predict design-induced error on the flight deck, *Aerospace Science and Technology*, Vol. 9(6), pp. 525–32 (Harris, D., Stanton, A., Marshall, A., Young, M.S., Demagalski, J.M. and Salmon, P. 2005), reprinted with permission from Elsevier; Figure 8.4 adapted from Flight decks and free flight: Where are the system boundaries?, *Applied Ergonomics*, vol. 38, pp.409–16 (Hollnagel, E. 2007), Reprinted with permission from Elsevier; Figure 8.5 from *Human Factors for Civil Flight Deck Design*, Ashgate

(Harris, D. 2004) p. 76; Figure 10.1 from The Job demands-resources model: The state of the art, *Journal of Managerial Psychology*, vol. 22, pp. 309–28 (Bakker, A. and Demerouti, E. 2007), © Emerald Group Publishing Limited, all rights reserved; Figure 11.3 from Eurofound, Fifth European Working Conditions Survey, Publications Office of the European Union, Luxembourg, 2012. http://www.eurofound.europa.eu/publications/report/2012/working-conditions/fifth-european-working-conditions-survey-overview-report Cited in: OSHwiki. Figure 1 (Oeij, P., Kraan, K., and Dhondt, S.) http://oshwiki.eu/wiki/Work_teams_and_psychosocial_risks_and_work_stress#cite_ref-fifth_9-1; Figure 11.5 adapted from What a mess! Participation as a simple managerial rule to 'complexify' organisations, *Journal of Management Studies*, vol. 39(2), pp.189–206 (Ashmos et al 2002), reproduced with permission of Wiley; Figure 13.2 from Organisational boundaries and beyond: A new look at the components of a boundaryless career orientation, *Career Development International*, vol. 19, p. 656 (Gubler, M., Arnold, J. and Coombs, C. 2014); Figure 13.7 adapted from *On the Move: The psychology of change and transition*, Wiley (S. Fisher, S. and Cooper, C. (eds) 1990), reproduced with permission of Wiley.

Tables

Table 2.1 from Evidence-Based Management: Concept Cleanup Time?, *Academy of Management Perspectives*, vol. 24(4), 9.21 (Briner, R.B., Denyer, D. and Rousseau, D. M. 2009); Table 3.1 from *The AH5 Test*, The Association for Science Education (Heim, A.W.) © 1968 A.W Heim, reproduced with permission of the publisher, ASE, The Association for Science Education, College Lane, Hatfield, Herts, AL10 9AA, UK; Table 4.9 from Fairness reactions to personnel selection techniques in France and the United States, *Journal of Applied Psychology*, vol. 81(2), pp. 134–41 (Steiner, D.D. and Gilliland, S.W. 1996), reproduced with permission of Wiley; Table 6.1 adapted from Experiencing work: values, attitudes and moods, *Human Relations*, vol. 50, pp.393–416 (George, J.M. and Jones, G.R. 1997), © 1997, reprinted by permission of Sage Publications; Table 6.3 from *Occupational Stress Indicator: The manual*, NFER/Nelson (Cooper, C.L., Sloan, S. and Williams, S. 1988); Table 7.1 adapted from The management of organizational justice, *Academy of Management Perspectives*, vol. 21(4), p. 36 (Cropanzano, R., Bowen, D.E. and Gilliland, S.W. 2007); Table 8.1 adapted from *Human Factors Integration: Implementation in the onshore and offshore industries (HSE Research Report 001)*, HSE Publications (Widdowson, I. and Carr, J. 2002) p. 4, Contains public sector information licensed under the Open Government Licence (OGL) v3.0.http://www.nationalarchives.gov.uk/doc/open-government-licence; Table 8.2 adapted from *Human Factors Integration: Implementation in the onshore and offshore industries (HSE Research Report 001)*, HSE Publications (Widdowson, I. and Carr, J. 2002) p. 9, Contains public sector information licensed under the Open Government Licence (OGL) v3.0.http://www.nationalarchives.gov.uk/doc/open-government-licence; Table 8.3 from *Human Factors for Civil Flight Deck Design*, Ashgate (Harris, D. 2004) p. 77; Table 10.1 from Validating abbreviated measures of effort-reward imbalance at work in European cohort studies: The IPD-Work consortium, *International Archives of Occupational and Environmental Health*, vol. 87, pp.249–56 (Siegrist, J., Dragano, N., Nyberg, S. et al. 2014), Copyright 2014, With permission of Springer; Table 10.3 adapted from *Stress Management Interventions. Performance and Well-being*, CIPD (Donaldson-Feilder, E. 2007) with the permission of the publisher, the Chartered Institute of Personnel and Development, London (www.cipd.co.uk); Table 12.2 from Transformational leadership and performance across criteria and levels: A meta-analytic review of 25 years of research, *Group and Organisational Management*, vol. 36(2), pp. 223–70 (Wang, G., Os, I-S., Courtright, S. H., and Colbert, A. E. 2011), © 2011, reprinted by permission of Sage Publications; Table 13.1 adapted from *Careers In and Out of Organizations*, Sage Publications (Hall, D.T. 2002) Table 11, © 2002 by Sage Publications, Ltd, reprinted by permission; Table 13.3 adapted from *Understanding Careers*, 2nd edn, Sage (Inkson, K., Dries, N. and Arnold, J. 2014) pp. 337–8, Copyright © 2014 by Sage Publications Ltd, reprinted by permission; Table 13.4 from Career success across 11 countries: Implications for international human resource management, *International Journal of Human Resource Management*, vol. 26(13), p. 1762 (Shen, Y., Demel, B., Unite, J., Briscoe, J.P., Hall, D.T., Chudzikowski, K. 2015), reprinted with permission from Taylor & Francis Ltd; Table 13.5 adapted from An empirical investigation of the predictors of career success, *Personnel Psychology*, vol. 48, Table 3, pp. 485–519 (Judge, T.A., Cable, D.M., Boudreau, J.W. and Bretz, R.D. 1995), reproduced with permission of Wiley.

Text

Extract on p. 17 adapted from *Code of Ethics and Conduct Guidance published by the Ethics Committee of the British Psychological Society*, British Psychological Society (Ethics Committee 2009); Extract on pp. 15–16 adapted from *Standards for the Accreditation of Masters and Doctoral Programmes in Occupational Psychology* British

Psychological Society (Partnership and Accreditation Team 2014) pp. 24–6; Case study on pp. 112–13 adapted from Give in to temptation and fail in life, *The Sunday Times*, 02/11/2008 (Allen-Mills, T.), © The Sunday Times 2008; Case study on p. 210 adapted from Vicars report greatest job satisfaction while publicans are least happy, *The Guardian*, 21/03/2014 (Addley, E.), copyright Guardian News & Media Ltd 2016; Case study on pp. 261–3 from ONS survey reveals scale of zero-hours contracts, FT.com, 30/04/2014 (Groom, B), © The Financial Times Limited, All Rights Reserved; Exercise 6.5 adapted from Keep staff happy with a 'duvet day', *The Sunday Times*, 08/07/2007 (Hofkins, D.), © The Sunday Times 2007, www.nisyndication.com; Example 7.4 adapted from One Company's New Minimum Wage: $70,000 a Year, *New York Times*, 13/04/2015 (Cohen, P.); Case study on p. 344 adapted from So Much Training, So Little to Show for It, *Wall Street Journal* (Silverman, R.E.), reprinted with permission, © 2012 Dow Jones & Company, Inc. All Rights Reserved Worldwide. License number 3806110888168; Case study on p. 377 adapted from Working longer hours increases stroke risk, major study finds, *The Guardian*, 20/08/2015 (Bosely, S.), Copyright Guardian News & Media Ltd 2015; Case study on pp. 441–3 adapted from Helplines prosper as more workers feel the strain, *Financial Times*, 17/02/2014 (Plimmer, G. and Jacobs, E.), © The Financial Times Limited. All Rights Reserved; Case study on pp. 446–7 adapted from Keeping body and soul together: why NHS teamwork is critical to patient outcomes, http://www.lancaster.ac.uk/lums/research/research-showcase/nhs-teamwork/; Case study on pp. 493–4 adapted from X-teams swing the axe at team bonding, *Financial Times*, 11/05/2009 (Ancona, D.), © The Financial Times Limited. All Rights Reserved; Case study on p. 537 after A life after redundancy, *Financial Times*, 24/09/2008 (Clegg, A.), © The Financial Times Limited. All Rights Reserved; Case study on pp. 581–2 adapted from Charities: Passion and skills in aid of a good cause, *Financial Times*, 13/10/2008 (Murray, S.), © Sarah Murray, © The Financial Times Limited. All Rights Reserved; Exercise 13.2 from The cleaner who soared all the way to the board, *Financial Times*, 05/01/2015 (Clegg, A.), © The Financial Times Limited. All Rights Reserved; Exercise 13.3 adapted from Young people are having to take career decisions too early, *The Guardian*, 26/07/2013 (Lane, A.), copyright Guardian News & Media Ltd 2013; Case study on p. 586 adapted from Serco set to clear out senior UK team, *Financial Times*, 18/10/2013, p. 25 (Plimmer, G. and Smith, A.), © The Financial Times Limited. All Rights Reserved; Exercise 14.1 adapted from Women stuck in executive slow lane, *Financial Times*, 11/12/2013, p. 22 (Groom, B.), © The Financial Times Limited. All Rights Reserved; Exercise 14.2 adapted from Supplier development: A study of Nissan Motor Manufacturing (UK) and its suppliers, *Proceedings of the Institution of Mechanical Engineers Part D: Journal of Automobile Engineering*, vol. 208(1), pp. 63–8 (Lloyd, A., Dale, B. and Burnes, B. 1994), reprinted by permission of Sage Publications Inc.; Exercise 14.3 adapted from Nuclear meltdowns are bad for returns, *Financial Times*, 02/05/2011, p. 6 (Le Floc'h, M and Thamotheram, R), © The Financial Times Limited. All Rights Reserved; Case study on pp. 627–8 adapted from From a distance, *People Management* (Axtell, C., Wheeler, J., Patterson, M. and Leach, A.), reproduced by permission of Dr Carolyn Axtell and Dr Jo Kandola.

CHAPTER 1

Work psychology
An initial orientation

LEARNING OBJECTIVES

After studying this chapter, you should be able to:

1 describe five areas of basic psychology;

2 examine the relationship between basic psychology and work psychology;

3 describe the key features of each of the following traditions in psychology:

   psychoanalytic

   trait

   phenomenological

   behaviourist

   social cognitive;

4 identify the main similarities and differences between the traditions;

5 specify how each tradition contributes to work psychology;

6 specify the topics covered by work psychologists;

7 describe the employers of, and roles adopted by, work psychologists;

8 specify ethical issues in work psychology;

9 describe the main sources of information about work psychology research and practice;

10 outline why diversity and culture are cross-cutting themes in work psychology

11 identify some of the significant changes in the world of work that psychologists need to consider.

Introduction

In this chapter we aim to help the reader gain a broad understanding of the nature of work psychology and the context within which it operates before tackling more specific topics later in the book. We start with a brief description of the discipline of **psychology** as a whole and discuss the links between what we call basic and applied psychology, with work psychology positioned as one branch of applied psychology. Then we provide a brief analysis of images of the person offered by five traditions within basic psychology. These are psychoanalytic, **trait**, phenomenological, behaviourist and social cognitive. Each of these traditions has influenced work psychology: in some respects they contradict each other and in some circumstances they complement each other. As you read this text you will see that some of the issues we know most about have been examined using a variety of traditions and approaches and this can help to enrich greatly our understanding. The nature of their contribution is briefly outlined in this chapter and the portions of this book that examine those contributions in more detail are identified. We then recount briefly some history of work psychology before moving to coverage of work psychology today. Here we give an account of the different labels sometimes given to work psychology, the topics it covers, what work psychologists do and ethical issues that arise in practice. We also alert readers to the best sources of good knowledge about work psychology (apart from this book of course!). In the latter part of this chapter we look briefly at some cross-cutting themes in work psychology: **diversity** and cultural differences. The British Psychological Society (2014) specifies these as themes relevant to all aspects of work psychology: we have done our best to reflect these in each chapter of the book so that you can see how they 'come to life' in practice. We also point out some ways in which the world of work is changing: again these are covered in much more detail in the relevant chapters.

Basic psychology and work psychology

Psychology has been defined in various ways. Perhaps the simplest yet most informative definition is that provided long ago by Miller (1966): 'the science of mental life'. Mental life refers to three phenomena: behaviours, thoughts and emotions. Most psychologists these days would agree that psychology involves all three.

The notion that psychology is a **science** is perhaps rather more controversial. Science involves the systematic collection of data under controlled conditions, so that theory and practice can be based on verifiable evidence rather than on the psychologist's intuition. The aims are to describe, explain and predict behaviours, thoughts and emotions (see Chapter 2 for more on psychological theory). Not everyone agrees that it is appropriate to study behaviours, thoughts and emotions in a scientific manner. Some argue that human behaviour is too complex for that, and anyway people's behaviour changes in important ways when they are being observed or experimented upon (see also Chapter 2). The scientific approach has a large influence on most courses and **training** in psychology, and is perhaps most evident in the emphasis given to research design and statistical analysis in many university psychology courses.

The discipline of psychology can be divided into several subdisciplines, each with its own distinctive focus. Collectively they can be termed *basic psychology*. There are several ways of splitting psychology. Perhaps the most helpful of these is as follows:

■ **Physiological psychology** concerns the relationship between mind and body. For example, physiological psychologists might investigate the activity in the brain associated with particular behaviours, thoughts and emotions, or they might be interested in the bodily changes associated with feeling stressed at work.

- **Cognitive psychology** focuses on our cognitive functioning; that is, our thought processes. This includes topics such as how well we remember information under various conditions, how we weigh up information when making decisions, or how quickly and accurately we deal with questions in a **psychometric test**.

- **Developmental psychology** concerns the ways in which people grow and change psychologically. This includes issues such as how and when children become able to understand particular concepts, and how they learn language. Also, developmental psychology is beginning to pay more attention to change and growth throughout adult life.

- **Social psychology** concerns how our behaviours, thoughts and emotions affect, and are affected by, other people. Topics include how **groups** of people make decisions, and the extent to which a person's **attitudes** towards particular groups of people influence his or her behaviour towards them.

- **Personality psychology** focuses on people's characteristic tendency to behave, think and feel in certain ways. It is concerned with issues such as how people differ from each other psychologically, and how those differences can be measured. It also increasingly recognises that situations as well as personality influence a person's behaviour, thoughts and emotions. Hence some attention is also paid to defining how *situations* differ from each other.

Work psychology is defined in terms of its context of application (see Figure 1.1), and is not in itself one of the subdisciplines of psychology defined above. It is an area of applied psychology. As you will see throughout this book, work psychologists use concepts, theories and techniques derived from all areas of basic psychology. These areas are not mutually exclusive: studying people at work from a number of different perspectives is often necessary in order to understand fully the issue being examined. The same is true of psychologists working in other applied contexts such as education and health.

As shown in Figure 1.1, areas of applied psychology use ideas and information from basic psychology. Conversely, they can also contribute ideas and information to the development of basic psychology. Sometimes theory from basic psychology can directly contribute to the solution of real-world problems, and conversely those problems can also stimulate developments in basic psychology. More often, applied psychology rather than basic psychology offers

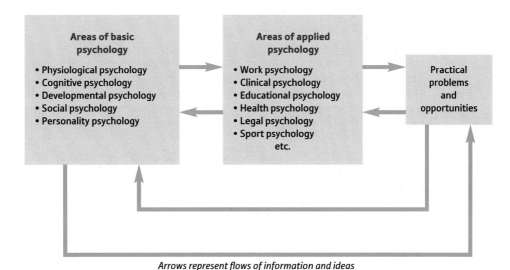

Arrows represent flows of information and ideas

| Figure 1.1 | The relationship between areas of psychology |

theories and techniques directly applicable to practical problems and real-life situations. In fact, it might be argued that some applied psychologists are more interested in solving practical problems than in theory and ideas from basic psychology (see Chapter 2 for a discussion of the academic–practitioner divide within work psychology). Thus there may be a danger that the areas of applied psychology will fail to reflect advances in basic psychology. It might also be the case that some more theoretically inclined psychologists fail to take sufficient account of work in applied psychology, or of current real-world issues. Schönpflug (1993) argued that applied psychology has not benefited much from basic psychology. Applied psychologists are interested in solving problems, while basic psychologists are driven by a love of knowledge for its own sake. The development of psychology as a profession that can be put to good use depends upon the information flows shown in Figure 1.1.

Key learning point

The five areas of basic psychology all contribute ideas and techniques to work psychology.

Whatever the strength of these diverse and sometimes contradictory viewpoints, it can be said that work psychology, as one branch of applied psychology, does have its own theories and techniques. The following chapters will demonstrate this. Some draw upon basic psychology a lot, others less so.

It would be dishonest to pretend that psychology is a well-integrated discipline with generally accepted principles. Underlying it are several competing and quite different concepts of the person. These are most apparent in personality psychology – not surprisingly since personality psychology is the subdiscipline most concerned with the essence of human individuality. These competing conceptions of humanity will now be examined briefly. The interested reader can find much fuller coverage of each in texts such as Ewen (2010) and Schultz and Schultz (2001). Table 1.1 summarises some of the differences and similarities between the five traditions reviewed in the next section.

Table 1.1   Key characteristics of five theoretical traditions in psychology

	Behaviour	Emotion	Thinking/ reasoning	Self-actual-isation	The un-conscious	Biologically based needs/ drives	Personal change	Self-determi-nation
Psychoanalytic (Freud)	0	✓	✗	✗	✓	✓	✗	✗
Trait	✓	✓	✓	✗	✗	✓	✗	✗
Phenomenological (Rogers)	0	✓	0	✓	0	0	✓	✓
Behaviourist (Skinner)	✓	✗	✗	✗	✗	✗	✓	✗
Social cognitive	✓	0	✓	0	0	✗	0	✓

✓ = Emphasised   0 = Acknowledged but not emphasised   ✗ = De-emphasised or considered unimportant

> ### Key learning point
>
> Psychology is a discipline that includes many different views of what a person is. Some of these views contradict each other. However, in studying people at work, drawing on a variety of traditions can help to increase the depth and breadth of knowledge about an issue.

Five traditions in psychology

The psychoanalytic tradition

This approach, also sometimes known as *psychodynamic*, was developed by Sigmund Freud (1856–1939). He developed a completely new approach to human nature which has had a great influence on many areas of pure and applied social science, literature and the arts. Perhaps in reaction to the stilted Viennese society in which he spent much of his life, Freud proposed that our psychological functioning is governed by instinctive forces (especially sex and aggression), many of which exert their effect outside our consciousness. He developed his ideas in a series of famous published works (e.g. Freud, 1960). Freud identified three facets of the psyche:

1   The **id**: the source of instinctual energy. Prominent among those instincts are sex and aggression. The id operates on the *pleasure principle*: it wants gratification and it wants it now. It has no inhibitions, and cannot distinguish between reality and fantasy.

2   The **ego**: this seeks to channel the id impulses so that they are expressed in socially acceptable ways at socially acceptable times. It operates on the *reality principle*. It can tolerate delay, and it can distinguish between reality and fantasy. However, it cannot eliminate or block the id impulses, only steer them in certain directions.

3   The **superego**: the conscience – the source of morality. It develops during childhood and represents the internalised standards of the child's parents. It defines ideal standards and operates on the principle of *perfection*.

According to Freud, these parts of the psyche are in inevitable and perpetual conflict. Much of the conflict is unconscious. Indeed, Freud's concept of the psyche has often been likened to an iceberg, of which two-thirds is under water (unconscious) and one-third above water (conscious). When conflicts get out of hand we experience **anxiety**, though often we cannot say *why* we feel anxious.

Because anxiety is unpleasant, people try to avoid it. One way to do this is to distort reality and push unwelcome facts out of consciousness. Freud proposed a number of **defence mechanisms** that accomplish this. For example, *projection* occurs when we see in other people what we do not like in ourselves. It is easier to cope with righteous indignation about somebody else's faults than to come to terms with our own. *Denial* is when we pretend things are not as they really are.

Defence mechanisms consume energy, and impair realism. They therefore detract from a person's capacity to live a full life. When asked what a psychologically healthy person should be able to do, Freud replied 'love and work'. Even many people who have little time for his general approach regard this as a valid point.

For Freud, the key to understanding a person is to uncover unconscious conflicts. Most of these have their origins in childhood and are very difficult to change. They are revealed most clearly when the person's guard is down – for example, in dreams or in apparently accidental slips of the tongue ('**Freudian slips**') where the person expresses what they *really* feel. Freud believed that virtually no behaviour is truly accidental, but that people can rarely account for it accurately. Some psychologists working from other perspectives in psychology would agree that people cannot report accurately the causes of their own behaviour (Nisbett and Wilson, 1977). If correct, this would make a mockery of current work psychology, much of which is based on self-reports, e.g. using **questionnaires** (see Chapter 2) which are taken more or less at face value. Fortunately, there are research methods that allow us to examine the quality of self-report data.

Key learning point

The **psychoanalytic tradition** places a high emphasis on unconscious psychological conflicts which can reduce personal effectiveness at work.

Some psychologists who initially followed Freud subsequently broke away from him, though they remained within the psychoanalytic school of thought. Their biggest quarrels with Freud were that the drives he proposed were too few and too negative, and that the ego was more powerful than he gave it credit for. They tended to place greater emphasis than Freud on social behaviour, and believed that strivings for ideals reflect something more noble than rationalisation of instincts. Perhaps the best known of these post-Freudian psychoanalytic psychologists is Carl Jung. He extended the concept of the unconscious to include the collective unconscious as well as the personal unconscious. Jung saw the collective unconscious as an inherited foundation of personality. It contains images that have never been in consciousness such as God, the wise old person and the young hero. Jung (1933) also examined the ways in which different people relate to the world. He distinguished between **introversion** (a tendency to reflect on one's own experiences) and **extroversion** (a preference for social contact). He identified sensing, intuition, feeling and thinking as other ways of experiencing the world. Some of these concepts have been taken up in trait-based approaches to personality (see next section and Chapter 3).

Within psychology as a whole, the psychoanalytic school of thought lost its earlier domination around the 1950s, and has never regained it. Critics complain that it is highly interpretative, incapable of being proved or disproved, and therefore unscientific. They argue that Freud was a product of his time (but aren't we all?), and was over-influenced by hang-ups about sex. Many also claim that he does not account for women's psychological functioning nearly as well as men's.

Nevertheless, the psychoanalytic approach is far from dead. Freudian terms and concepts (e.g. defence mechanisms) have found their way into common parlance, and some psychologists have used psychoanalytic concepts in the world of work. Much work of this kind seeks to demonstrate that individual and collective behaviour in business is not driven by straightforward pursuit of profit but by the conflicts, defence mechanisms and personal concerns of the people involved. Fotaki et al. (2012) point to several examples of the application of these theories to understand workplace phenomena including: the diversity and complexity of emotional experiences at work (e.g. why some people enjoy a particular work situation while others are distressed by it); the unconscious processes that are linked to workers' respect for and response to those in positions of power; the reasons why we make irrational choices; leadership behaviour as an expression of the type of person the **leader** would like to be (i.e. a person's leadership style might provide us with some insights into their unconscious wants, **needs** and desires). Schneider and Dunbar (1992) analysed media coverage of hostile takeover bids, where one business makes an unwelcome attempt to take over another business. They identified several different themes in media accounts of these events (e.g. growth, control, dominance and synergy) and related these to developmental themes identified by psychoanalytic psychologists, including dependency, control, mastery and intimacy. Also, Vince (2002) applies psychoanalytic ideas to the ways in which major organisational change was understood and managed in a large company.

> ## Key learning point
>
> The psychoanalytic tradition tries to explain why behaviour at work can often seem irrational, hostile or self-defeating.

The trait tradition

This approach is essentially concerned with measuring a person's psychological characteristics. These characteristics, which include intellectual functioning, are generally assumed to be quite stable. That is, a person's personality is unlikely to change much, especially during adulthood (McCrae and Costa, 1990). Some theorists have developed personality types, or 'pigeonholes', in which any individual can be placed. One good example dates back to ancient Greek times when Hippocrates wrote of four types: phlegmatic (calm); choleric (quick-tempered); sanguine (cheerful, optimistic); and melancholic (sad, depressed).

These days psychologists more often think in terms of traits than types. A trait is an underlying dimension along which people differ one from another. Hence rather than putting people into a pigeonhole, trait theorists place them on a continuum, or rather a number of continua. Trait psychologists such as Eysenck (1967) and Cattell (1965) did pioneering work by identifying specific traits through much careful experimental and statistical investigation (some of this work is covered in more detail in Chapter 3). Favoured assessment devices of trait psychology are personality questionnaires, which consist of a number of questions about people's behaviour, thoughts and emotions. The better questionnaires are painstakingly developed to ensure that the questions are clear and responses to them are stable over short and medium time periods (see also Chapters 3 and 4). Of course, ideally one would collect information about a person's actual behaviour rather than *reports* of their behaviour. Indeed, Cattell among others did just this. However, normally that would be too time-consuming. Personality questionnaires are the best alternative and are used quite extensively in selection and assessment at work.

Most trait psychologists argue that the same traits are relevant to everyone, though for any individual some traits (usually those on which they have extreme scores) will be more evident than others in their behaviour. However, some trait psychologists have taken a rather more flexible approach. Allport (1937) long ago argued that for any given person, certain traits may be *cardinal* (that is, pervasive across all situations), *primary* (evident in many situations) or *secondary* (evident only in certain quite restricted situations). So if we wanted to predict a person's behaviour, it would be important to identify their cardinal traits. These traits would be different for different people.

In recent years there has been a growing consensus among trait theorists that there are five fundamental dimensions of personality – the so-called 'Big Five' or five-factor model (FFM) (Digman, 1990; see also Chapter 3). These are:

1   extroversion, for example sociability, assertiveness;
2   emotionality, for example anxiety, insecurity;
3   agreeableness, for example conforming, helpful to others;

4   **conscientiousness**, for example persistent, organised;

5   **openness to experience**, for example curiosity, aesthetic appreciation.

Key learning point

Research by trait theorists suggests that there are approximately five fundamental personality dimensions.

Most advocates of the trait approach argue that traits are at least partly genetically determined, which is one reason why they are stable. Research comparing the personalities of identical and non-identical twins tends to support this conclusion, though it is very difficult to separate the effects of environment from those of genes. This has been a somewhat controversial topic. Bouchard and McGue (1990) argued that around one-quarter of personality variations are due to inherited factors. This of course means that three-quarters of the variation is due to other factors. Much research on this issue comes from twin studies. Most recently, Power and Pluess (2015) carried out some extremely innovative research using genetic profiling. The links between variations in these profiles and variations in self-report personality data were tested. They found that genetic variations were only significantly linked to two of the Big Five: **neuroticism** and openness to experience. Genetic variations explained 15 per cent of the former and 21 per cent of the latter.

Trait theory carries the danger of circularity. Advocates of **behaviourism** (see the behaviourism section below) have always been keen to point this out. How do we know somebody scores highly on a particular personality trait? Because they behave in a certain way. Why does the person behave in that way? Because they score highly on that personality trait. Behaviour is therefore taken as a sign of certain traits, which is all very well so long as the underlying traits not only exist but also determine behaviour. There is plenty of evidence that situations, as well as personality, influence behaviour (see Cervone and Mischel, 2002). In situations where social rules are strict and widely understood, personality will influence behaviour less than in unstructured situations that lack clearly defined codes of behaviour. For example, in selection interviews usually the candidate must answer questions fully, and avoid interrupting the interviewer. Thus the demands of this situation dictate the candidate's behaviour to a considerable extent. This makes it more difficult for the interviewer to make inferences about the candidate's personality (although they are likely to do so anyway).

In spite of such caveats, the **trait tradition** has had a great influence in work psychology. This is particularly evident in selection (see Chapter 4) and vocational guidance (see Chapter 13), where the aim is to match individuals to work they will enjoy and in which they will work effectively. Salgado (2003), among others, has produced some evidence that people's scores on personality tests based on the FFM are linked to their work performance.

Key learning point

The trait tradition emphasises the importance of stable and measurable psychological differences between people which are frequently reflected in their work behaviour.

Large sums of money are spent on the development and marketing of personality measures such as the NEO PI-3 (published in the UK by Hogrefe), the 16PF (Oxford Psychologists

Press; see also Cattell and Cattell, 1995), the Hogan Personality Inventory (Hogan Assessment Systems) and the Occupational Personality Questionnaires (CEB SHL Talent Management). The latter was originally developed specifically for use in work settings with the backing of many large organisations. Such ventures testify to the continuing prominence of the trait approach in work psychology.

The phenomenological tradition

Phenomenology concentrates on how people experience the world around them. It emphasises our capacity to construct our own meaning from our experiences (Spinelli, 1989). With roots in philosophy as well as psychology, phenomenologists assert that our experience of the world is made up of an interaction between its 'raw matter' (i.e. objects) and our mental faculties. Thus, for example, a piece of music exists in the sense that it consists of a series of sounds, but has meaning only when we place our own interpretation on it.

Phenomenologists argue that what appears to be objectively defined reality is in fact merely a widely agreed *interpretation* of an event. They also assert that many interpretations of events are highly individual and not widely agreed. Thus phenomenology places a high value on the integrity and sense-making of individuals. That general sentiment underlies many somewhat different perspectives that can loosely be called phenomenological. Several of these perspectives also portray the person as striving for personal growth or self-actualisation; that is, fulfilment of their potential. This optimistic variant of phenomenological theory is often called humanism.

A good example of humanism is provided by Carl Rogers (e.g. Rogers, 1970). He argued that if we are to fulfil our potential, we must be *open to our experience*. That is, we must recognise our true thoughts and feelings, even if they are unpalatable. Unfortunately we are often not sufficiently open to our experience. We may suppress experiences that are inconsistent with our self-concept, or that we feel are in some sense morally wrong. Rogers has argued that often we readily experience only those aspects of self that our parents approved of when we were children. Parents define conditions of worth – in effect, they signal to children that they will be valued and loved only if they are a certain sort of person.

For Rogers, the antidote to conditions of worth is unconditional positive regard (UPR). In order to become a fully functioning person, we need others to accept us as we are, 'warts and all'. This does not mean that anything goes. Rogers argues for a separation of person and behaviour, so that it is all right (indeed desirable) to say to somebody 'that was not a sensible thing to do', and if necessary punish them for it. But it is not all right to say 'you are not a sensible person', because that signals disapproval of the person, not just their behaviour. Only when people realise that their inherent worth will be accepted whatever their actions can they feel psychologically safe enough to become open to their experience. Further, since Rogers believes that people are fundamentally trustworthy, he has argued that they will not take advantage of UPR to get away with murder. Instead, UPR encourages more responsible behaviour.

Key learning point

The phenomenological tradition puts high emphasis on personal experience and the inherent potential of people to develop and act responsibly.

As far as work psychology is concerned, the basic point that people's *interpretations* of events are crucial has been heeded to some extent. As you will see throughout this text, many questionnaire-based measures of people's experiences at work have been developed. On the other hand, people's responses on such questionnaires are often taken as approximations of an objective reality rather than as a product of the individual's interpretative faculties, which rather contradicts the humanist position.

Phenomenological approaches find expression in some theories of work stress, work motivation and the design of jobs (see Chapters 7 and 10). The idea that people strive to express and develop themselves at work is quite a popular one, though by no means universally held. Trends in management towards empowerment of employees and total quality management (TQM) are based on the assumption that people can and will use their skills to help their organisation, not sabotage it. Phenomenology has also contributed to career development (see Chapter 13). Many counsellors make extensive use of Rogers' ideas when working with clients on career decisions and other work-related issues. They work on the assumption that showing a client unconditional positive regard will allow them to bring true career interests and ambitions into consciousness. By and large, though, phenomenological approaches are not currently dominant in work psychology. Chapter 2 includes some further discussion of how phenomenological approaches can be brought to life in organisational research.

The behaviourist tradition

In its more extreme forms, behaviourism makes no inferences whatever about what is going on inside the organism. It is concerned only with observable behaviour and the conditions (situations) that elicit particular behaviours. A person, and their personality, is a set of behaviours; nothing more and nothing less. There is no need to invoke invisible concepts such as traits or defence mechanisms when what we are really interested in – behaviour – can be observed directly. A leading advocate of the behaviourist tradition was B.F. Skinner (1904–1990) (see, for example, Skinner, 1971). He and other learning theorists argued that our behaviour is environmentally controlled. He used the concept of *reinforcer* to refer to any favourable outcome of behaviour. Such an outcome reinforces that behaviour, i.e. makes it more likely to occur again in a similar situation. Punishment is where a behaviour is followed by an unpleasant outcome. This theory can be applied to the management of performance at work, although this is a very simplistic way of influencing human behaviour (see Chapter 5).

Behaviourists therefore argue that the behaviour a person performs (which is their personality) is behaviour that has been reinforced in the past. If a child is consistently reinforced for being polite, they will behave in a polite manner. Abnormal behaviour is the result of abnormal reinforcement. If a child's parents pay attention to them only when they misbehave, the child may learn to misbehave because parental attention is a reinforcer. Behaviour problems can also rise from *conflicts*. One is an *approach–avoidance conflict*. This occurs when a particular behaviour is associated with both reinforcement and punishment. For example, a person may find that volunteering to take on extra tasks at work is reinforced by a pay rise, but also punished by the disapproval of workmates.

The behaviourist approach to personality implies that behaviour (and therefore personality) can be changed if reinforcement changes. The introduction of a reward for arriving at work on time is likely to lead to greater frequency of staff arriving on time. This change in behaviour would *not* mean that staff had changed their position on a personality trait of punctuality or conscientiousness. Behaviourists do not believe in traits. The change would simply be the result of events.

Of course, when we ask *why* a particular outcome reinforces a particular behaviour, it becomes difficult to avoid reference to a person's internal states. We might say a person liked or wanted that outcome, and then we would probably enter a debate about *why* they liked or wanted it. Some behavioural psychologists have acknowledged the necessity of taking internal states into account, and have suggested that biologically based drives or needs are the bases for reinforcement (Hull, 1952). Skinner's reliance solely on observable behaviour may perhaps have been viable for the rats and pigeons with which he performed many of his experiments. Most psychologists these days agree that it is insufficient for human beings, though there are also some claims that Skinner made more allowance for cognitive processes than he was given credit for (Malone and Cruchon, 2001).

Key learning point

Behaviourism focuses on what people do, and how rewards and punishments influence that.

A major development of behaviourist theory is *social learning* (e.g. Bandura, 1977b). This differs from traditional learning theory in a number of ways, and is one basis of the social cognitive tradition described in the next section. Briefly, advocates of social learning theory stress our capacity to learn from the reinforcements and punishments experienced by other people as well as ourselves. Other people may *model* certain behaviours, and we notice the reinforcements that follow for them. They also point out that we do not necessarily *immediately* do something that will obtain reinforcement. We may choose to delay that behaviour if we would prefer to be reinforced at some other time. In short, social learning ideas portray people as much more self-controlled and thinking than traditional behaviourist theory.

Concepts from learning and social learning have been used quite a lot in work psychology. In training, rewards can be used to reinforce the desired behaviours when trainees perform them. Trainees can also learn appropriate behaviours if they are performed (modelled) for them by a competent performer. More generally, in organisational behaviour modification rewards are used to reinforce behaviours such as arriving for work on time or taking appropriate safety precautions. Some organisations make extensive use of mentoring in their career development, based partly on the social learning idea that the experienced mentor will model desirable behaviours that the less experienced young employee will learn. Some motivation theories draw upon social learning theory. Social learning has in recent years developed further into what is now termed social cognition (see next section).

The social cognitive tradition

From around the mid-1970s, psychology has become increasingly influenced by a fusion of ideas, chiefly from social psychology and cognitive psychology but also from behaviourism and to a lesser extent phenomenology. *Social cognition* focuses on how our thought processes are used to interpret social interaction and other social–psychological phenomena such as the self. There is also a recognition that our thought processes reflect the social world in which we live, as well as formal logic. As noted in the previous section, one major root of the social cognitive tradition is social learning. Advocates of social cognition see the person as motivated to understand both self and the social world in order to establish a sense of order and predictability. The existence of other people (whether or not they are actually physically present) affects the nature of thought processes.

Bandura (1986) among others has argued that although the person is partly a product of their environment (including reinforcement history), the person can also influence that environment. This is the principle of reciprocal determinism. It can apply to groups of people and whole societies as well as to individuals. For example, we can administer our own rewards and punishments rather than relying on the environment to do it. Thus I might decide that

I will allow myself a cup of coffee when I have finished writing this section, and not before. In the process of observational learning, we notice the behaviour of other people and the reinforcement that follows, but we do not necessarily copy them even if the reinforcement is positive. Instead, we consider our own goals and our values (for example, concerning what reinforcements we most want, or what we consider acceptable behaviour) before acting.

Advocates of the social cognitive tradition also pay a great deal of attention to *information processing* (Schneider, 1991). High emphasis is placed on memory, and it is assumed that the ways in which people process information are general – that is, the same across different kinds of situation. It is assumed that how we store new information depends partly upon how our existing knowledge is structured, and that we are biased towards preserving existing cognitive structures. In other words, although we can assimilate new information, we are normally unwilling to let it change our general outlook.

Also, conceptions of the *self* work as a filter through which information is processed. For example, we tend to process information about ourselves which is consistent with our self-concept more readily than inconsistent information. We also remember it better. Indeed the *self* is seen by some social cognitive psychologists as playing a very important regulatory role in behaviour. Our ideas about the type of person we are, and about our goals and interests (i.e. our self-concept), influence the type of situations we seek and the behaviours we choose to perform. One especially important concept here is **self-efficacy** (Bandura, 1997a), which concerns the extent to which a person believes they can perform the behaviour required in any given situation. Self-efficacy is frequently a good predictor of behaviour. People with a high sense of self-efficacy are more likely than others to set challenging goals for themselves, and to keep trying in the face of setbacks. For example, in the text we discuss how it might help us when we are facing difficult or stressful situations.

The **schema** is another key concept in social cognition. It is a knowledge structure that a person uses to make sense of situations. An example of a schema is a **stereotype** of what members of a certain group of people are like. If, for example, we believe soccer fans are violent thugs, we will interpret their behaviour accordingly, and behave towards them in certain ways. Schemas are in effect ready-made frameworks into which one's experiences can be fitted. Schemas that involve sequences of actions are termed **scripts** (Abelson, 1981). For example, we might have a script of the sequence of events we expect to happen when we enter a restaurant. Scripts guide our own behaviour and also enable us to develop expectations about the behaviour of other people in any given type of situation. Events that cannot be accommodated within our schemas and scripts are experienced as puzzling, and may lead us to revise them. This is analogous to scientists changing their theories in the light of new evidence (Kelly, 1951).

Key learning point

Social cognition examines the ways in which people think about and regulate themselves and their behaviour.

The impact of social cognition on work psychology is growing. As a general rule, work psychology is slow to incorporate new theoretical perspectives (Webster and Starbuck, 1988). This is partly because it usually takes some time to identify how new theories can be applied. In the case of social cognition, however, there is also the 'problem' that its relative complexity limits its capacity to generate straightforward 'off-the-shelf' techniques that can be applied across a range of situations.

Nevertheless, ideas from social cognition are certainly highly relevant to the world of work. In several chapters, this can be seen in the context of the way people are perceived (for example in selection and **performance appraisal**) and the processes that underpin people's responses to work situations (e.g. when faced with stress). Gioia and Manz (1985) argued that scripts play a key part in learning behaviour from others (vicarious learning) at work. Akgün et al. (2003) discuss how concepts drawn from social cognition can help us understand how whole organisations learn, as well as individuals and groups. Social cognition is becoming more prominent in work psychology, especially when coupled with social learning.

The origins of work psychology

Work psychology has at least two distinct roots within applied psychology. One resides in a pair of traditions that have often been termed 'fitting the man [sic] to the job' (FMJ) and 'fitting the job to the man [sic]' (FJM). The FMJ tradition manifests itself in employee selection, training and vocational guidance. These endeavours have in common an attempt to achieve an effective match between job and person by concentrating on the latter. The FJM tradition focuses instead on the job, and in particular the design of tasks, equipment and working conditions that suit a person's physical and psychological characteristics. You will see the influence of both approaches throughout this text.

Much early work in these traditions was undertaken in response to the demands of two world wars. In the UK, for example, there was concern about the adverse consequences of the very long hours worked in munitions factories during the First World War and again in the Second World War (Vernon, 1948). The extensive use of aircraft in the Second World War led to attempts to design cockpits that optimally fitted pilots' capacities, and the processes used in designing military equipment have found their way into the design of other work environments (as Chapter 8 shows). In both the UK and the USA, the First World War highlighted the need to develop methods of screening people so that only those suitable for a post were selected for it. This need was met through the development of tests of ability and personality. One major source of such work in the UK was the National Institute of Industrial Psychology (NIIP), which was established in 1921 by the influential psychologist C.S. Myers and a business colleague named H.J. Welch, and survived in various forms until 1977. The brief of the NIIP was 'to promote and encourage the practical application of the sciences of psychology and physiology to commerce and industry by any means that may be found practicable'. The UK Civil Service began to employ a considerable number of psychologists after the Second World War. Their brief was, and largely still is, to improve civil service procedures, particularly in selection and training. Especially in the 1960s and 1970s, some other large organisations also employed psychologists. Organisational and labour market trends since the 1980s have reduced the proportion of work psychologists employed in large organisations, and increased the proportion who are self-employed or employed by small consultancy firms.

Key learning point

Two important traditions in work psychology concern how jobs can be fitted to people and how people can be fitted to jobs.

The FMJ and FJM traditions essentially concern the relationship between individuals and their work. The other root of work psychology can be loosely labelled *human relations* (HR). It is concerned with the complex interplay between individuals, groups, organisations and work. It therefore emphasises social factors at work much more than FMJ and FJM. The importance of human relations was highlighted in some famous research now known as the

Hawthorne studies. These were conducted in the 1920s at a large factory of the Western Electric Company at Hawthorne, near Chicago, USA. The studies were reported most fully in Roethlisberger and Dickson (1939). Originally, they were designed to assess the effect of level of illumination on productivity. One group of workers (the experimental group) was subjected to changes in illumination, while another (the control group) was not. The productivity of both groups increased slowly during this investigation; only when illumination was at a small fraction of its original level did the productivity of the experimental group begin to decline. These strange results suggested that other factors apart from illumination were determining productivity.

This work was followed up with what became known as the *relay assembly test room study*. A small group of female assembly workers was taken from the large department, and stationed in a separate room so that working conditions could be controlled effectively. Over a period of more than a year, changes were made in the length of the working day and working week, the length and timing of rest pauses, and other aspects of the work context. Productivity increased after every change, and the gains were maintained even after all conditions returned to their original levels.

Why did these results occur? Clearly, factors other than those deliberately manipulated by the researchers were responsible. For example, the researchers had allowed the workers certain privileges at work, and had taken a close interest in the group. Hence some factor probably to do with feeling special, or guessing what the researchers were investigating, seemed to be influencing the workers' behaviour. The problem of people's behaviour being affected by the knowledge that they are being researched has come to be called the *Hawthorne effect*. The more general lessons here are: (i) it is difficult to experiment with people without altering some conditions other than those intended and (ii) people's behaviour is substantially affected by *their interpretation* of what is happening around them (Adair, 1984).

These conclusions were extended by a study of a group of male workers who wired up equipment in the bank wiring room. A researcher sat in the corner and observed the group's activities. At first this generated considerable suspicion, but apparently after a time the men more or less forgot about the researcher's presence. Once this happened, certain phenomena became apparent. First, there were social *norms*; that is, shared ideas about how things should be. Most importantly, there was a norm about what constituted an appropriate level of production. This was high enough to keep management off the men's backs, but less than they were capable of. Workers who either consistently exceeded the productivity norm or fell short of it were subjected to social pressure to conform. Another norm concerned supervisors' behaviour. Supervisors were expected to be friendly and informal with the men: one who was more formal and officious was strongly disapproved of. Finally, there were two informal groups in the room, with some rivalry between them.

The bank wiring room showed clearly how social relationships between workers were important determinants of work behaviour. These relationships were often more influential than either official company policy or monetary rewards.

Key learning point

The human relations tradition in work psychology emphasises individuals' experiences and interpretations at work.

There has been much criticism of the experimental methods used by the Hawthorne researchers and considerable debate about the exact reasons for their findings. However, subsequent research by other social scientists confirmed and extended the general message that human relations matter. For example, a seminal study by Trist and Bamforth (1951) carried out in British coalmines, showed that if technology is introduced that disrupts existing social groups and relationships, then there are serious consequences for productivity, industrial relations and employee psychological well-being. Their work gave birth to the *socio-technical systems* approach to work design (see also Chapters 7 and 10).

Work psychology today

What is work psychology?

One source of confusion is that work psychology has a lot of different names. In the UK and the USA, the old-established term (still sometimes used) is *industrial psychology*. The newer label in the USA is *industrial/organisational psychology* (or *I/O psychology* for short). In the UK, it is often called *occupational psychology*, but this term is uncommon in most other countries. Throughout Europe, increasing use is made of *the psychology of work and organisations* and *work and organisational psychology* to describe the area. Just to confuse things further, some specific parts of the field are given labels such as *vocational psychology*, *managerial psychology* and *personnel psychology*. Meanwhile, there are also some bigger areas of study to which psychology contributes greatly. These include *organisational behaviour* and *human resource management*.

Our advice for the confused reader is: don't panic! The differences between these labels do mean something to some people who work in the field, but should not unduly worry most of us. The main distinction mirrors that made in the earlier section between individually oriented versus group- or organisation-oriented topics. In the UK, the label 'occupational psychology' is most commonly applied to the first, and 'organisational psychology' to the second (Blackler, 1982), but many psychologists in the workplace regularly cross this rather artificial boundary. We use the term *work psychology* because of its simplicity, and because to us it encompasses both the individual and organisational levels of analysis.

A reading of this chapter so far should have given the reader a reasonable idea of what work psychology is. In order to be more specific, we now list five of the areas (or knowledge domains) in which work psychologists operate as teachers, researchers and consultants. This list is adapted from the Standards for the Accreditation of Masters and Doctoral Programmes in Occupational Psychology published by the **British Psychological Society (BPS)** in 2014 (available via http://www.bps.org.uk). With each heading is a summary of the BPS's overview description of the content:

1 *Psychological assessment at work.* This covers a range of aspects and stages in the assessment of people already in or being selected to join work settings. These range from analysis of the job and the attributes required to perform it effectively, through to the eventual wider impact on organisations. It includes coverage of the nature and effectiveness of different assessment methods, including consideration of issues such as fairness, diversity and candidate reactions.

2 *Learning, training and development.* This covers the ways in which individuals learn and develop in the context of their work and the wider organisational context. It includes cognitive **theories of learning** and skill development and coverage of how these inform our understanding of learning processes. Theories of occupational and career choice form part of this domain. This also encompasses the practices of **coaching** and training, their psychological underpinnings and likely effectiveness. The organisational perspective is also included: for instance the links between development activities and succession planning (including how these can facilitate **innovation** and **creativity**).

3 *Leadership, engagement and motivation.* This domain examines theories of work motivation, and their relationship with different approaches to performance appraisal/performance management. It also includes the popular concepts of leadership, power and influence and how these connect to psychological concepts such as employee **engagement**, commitment and perceptions of fairness. This domain covers both negative and

positive responses to work experiences. It also includes consideration of working in groups and **teams**.

4   *Well-being and work*. The BPS indicates that this includes four key components: (a) how work links with individual and organisational well-being; (b) how work is structured and continues to evolve including the interface of work and non-work; (c) any negative effects of work including various theories of stress and pressure and the role of emotions; and (d) positive and preventative approaches to employee well-being.

5   *Work design, organisational change and development*. This covers the design of working environments and the associated risks and benefits. It also includes the widely researched topics of organisational change and development. The agenda for this domain is long and includes the consideration of how economic issues, globalisation and consumer perspectives impact on organisations.

These are the content areas of work psychology. In addition, the common and important themes of diversity, gender, fairness and **culture** need to be addressed in each content area. The BPS describes two other areas that integrate with all domains. First, students and practitioners in occupational psychology need good knowledge of research design, data gathering and analysis. Second, it is expected that qualified work psychologists will understand a range of specific techniques they are likely to use in their practice. This involves the development of generic skills such as questionnaire design, **interviewing**, report writing, presentation skills and data analysis methods, hence much of the content of Chapter 2 of this text and the Research methods in focus feature throughout.

Key learning point

Work psychology concerns all aspects of human behaviour, thoughts, feelings and experiences concerning work.

The qualifications and roles of work psychologists

How can one tell whether somebody who claims to be a work psychologist is, in fact, appropriately qualified? In the United Kingdom, the British Psychological Society (BPS) oversees the professional practice of psychologists. To become a **Chartered Psychologist (CPsychol)** a person must possess not only an approved degree in psychology (or the equivalent) but also several years of appropriate training and/or work experience. It is also possible to be an *Occupational* Psychologist: this is a person eligible for full membership of the Division of Occupational Psychology of the BPS. This means obtaining the Qualification in Occupational Psychology (QOP (Stage 2)) or the International Qualification in Occupational Psychology (IQOP (Stage 2)). Obtaining these doctorate-level qualifications involves demonstrating *practical expertise* and both breadth and depth of supervised experience in several of the areas listed above – *knowledge* is not enough. Certain tests of ability and personality can be administered only by Chartered Psychologists or (in some cases) by people who have been awarded a BPS Certificate of Competence in Occupational Testing (or equivalent) after training from a Chartered Psychologist. In August 2009 in the UK, the Health and Care Professions Council began to keep the register of psychologists in the UK. As a consequence of this, the title of Occupational Psychologist is now protected in law in the UK, meaning that only appropriately qualified persons can use the title *occupational psychologist*.

Chartered Psychologists and Occupational Psychologists in the UK are bound by BPS ethical guidelines and disciplinary procedures. Information on all of these matters, including lists of Chartered Psychologists, can be obtained from the BPS via their website.

The ethical code of conduct produced by the BPS (British Psychological Society, 2009) covers a range of topics. It includes the ways in which work psychologists are allowed to advertise their services, guidelines for the use of non-sexist language, and guidelines on conduct in professional practice and in psychological research. The code of conduct requires practising psychologists to be guided by four principles:

1   *Respect*: Psychologists value the dignity and worth of all persons, with sensitivity to the dynamics of perceived authority or influence over clients, and with particular regard to people's rights including those of privacy and self-determination.

2   *Competence*: Psychologists value the continuing development and maintenance of high standards of competence in their professional work, and the importance of preserving their ability to function optimally within the recognised limits of their knowledge, skill, training, education, and experience.

3   *Responsibility*: Psychologists value their responsibilities to clients, to the general public, and to the profession and science of Psychology, including the avoidance of harm and the prevention of misuse or abuse of their contributions to society.

4   *Integrity*: Psychologists value honesty, accuracy, clarity, and fairness in their interactions with all persons, and seek to promote integrity in all facets of their scientific and professional endeavours.

(From BPS Code of Ethics and Conduct, 2009)

In practical terms, this means that psychologists are required to consider, among other things, the following:

■   *Consent*: Those who participate in the research should normally be made aware beforehand of all aspects of it that might reasonably be expected to influence their willingness to participate.

■   *Deception*: Deception of those who participate in the research should be avoided wherever possible. If deception is necessary for the effective conduct of the research, it should not be the cause of significant distress when **participants** are debriefed afterwards.

■   *Debriefing*: After participation, the participants should be given any information and other support necessary to complete their understanding of the research, and to avoid any sense of unease their participation might have engendered.

■   *Withdrawal from the investigation*: The psychologist should tell participants of their right to withdraw from the research.

■   *Confidentiality*: Subject to the requirements of legislation, including (in the UK) the Data Protection Act, information obtained about a participant is confidential unless agreed otherwise in advance. This is in some ways especially important in work psychology where, for example, a senior member of an organisation may put pressure on the researcher to reveal what a junior member has said.

■   *Protection of participants*: The investigator must protect participants from physical and mental harm during the investigation. The risk of harm should normally be no greater than that posed by the participant's normal lifestyle.

Key learning point

Work psychologists are required to demonstrate their academic and practical competence, and also to adhere to ethical principles. This is partly to protect the rights and well-being of people who pay for their services and/or participate in their research.

Work psychologists can be teachers, researchers and consultants. Many are found in academic institutions, where they tend to engage in all three activities, especially of course the first two. Work psychologists in academia are now much more often employed in departments of business and management than in departments of psychology. This reflects both a tendency for work psychology to be used primarily to achieve management goals, and a mixing of psychology with other disciplines in a subject that has come to be called organisational behaviour (OB). Other work psychologists operate as independent consultants, advising organisations and individuals who seek their services on a fee-paying basis. There are also some specialist firms of psychologists and/or management consultants. Some psychologists are employed full-time by such firms. Others work for them on an occasional basis as independent associates. Still other psychologists are employed by larger organisations to give specialist advice, in effect acting as internal consultants. In the UK, the Civil Service, the Armed Forces and manufacturing, information technology and communications industries have been prominent in this regard.

Another issue concerns the influence of work psychologists on organisations which purchase their services. Many tend to see themselves as technical experts (Blackler and Brown, 1986), able to advise on the detail of specific procedures – for example, psychometric tests, stress management training, ergonomics and so on. On the other hand, human resource managers are attempting to play an increasingly central and strategic role in their organisations. If work psychologists are to influence organisational functioning, they need to move away from a technical specialist role toward that of a general business consultant (Anderson and Prutton, 1993). They must understand the organisational impact of their techniques, be able to work on 'macro' issues such as organisational change and human resource planning, and be able to demonstrate the likely financial impact of their recommendations. They must be able to speak the language of business, and to communicate with a wide range of people. They need to be open to new ideas and techniques, including those originating outside psychology (Offerrmann and Gowing, 1990). They need to recognise the politics of doing work psychology – that is, the power relationships between individuals and organisations involved in it. Regarding research, this means being able to 'sell' a research proposal so that practical benefits for the potential sponsoring organisation are apparent (and exceed the costs), to be prepared to negotiate and renegotiate on how the research will be conducted, and to develop and maintain contacts within the organisation. All of this must be done without contravening the ethical guidelines described earlier. Some would, however, argue that ethical and practical issues go deeper than this. Who, exactly, is the psychologist working for? Many see occupational psychologists as working partners with senior managers. Effectiveness and efficiency (concepts related to profitability) are often seen as the key deliverables of an occupational psychologist's work (rather than, for example, employee satisfaction). This is *not* to argue that psychologists' intentions and effects are malign, only that their agendas are often most heavily influenced by concerns that might be described as managerial.

Reading about work psychology

Where can one find out about advances in work psychology? Some can be found in books. General texts such as this give a necessarily brief account of major developments. Other specialist books are devoted to particular topics and sometimes even to particular theories. Many new theoretical developments, and also tests of established theories, can be found in certain academic journals. Leading journals of work psychology include *Journal of Occupational and Organizational Psychology* (published in the UK), *Journal of Applied Psychology* (USA), *Journal of Occupational Health Psychology* (USA), *Journal of Organizational Behavior* (USA/UK), *Applied Psychology: An International Review* (The International Association of Applied Psychology), *Organizational Behavior and Human Decision Processes* (USA),

Personnel Psychology (USA), *Human Relations* (UK), *Work & Stress* (EU), *European Journal of Work & Organizational Psychology* (EU) and *Journal of Vocational Behavior* (USA). There are also other prestigious journals which include work psychology along with other disciplines applied to work behaviour. These include *Academy of Management Journal* (USA), *Academy of Management Review* (USA), *Administrative Science Quarterly* (USA), *Organizational Research Methods* (USA) and *Journal of Management Studies* (UK). Some other journals concentrate more on the concerns of practitioners; that is, people who earn their living by supplying work psychology to organisations (e.g. *The Industrial–Organizational Psychologist* [USA]).

This is a long list of journals, and plenty more could be added to it, but there are subtle differences among journals in content and approach, which soon become evident to the observant reader. This makes information search easier if one has carefully defined the topic one wishes to explore. Also, online literature searches can be accomplished through commercially run databases such as ISI Web of Science, PsycINFO, ingentaconnect and EBSCO. It is worth noting that more authors are now making their articles available to all through open access (sometimes through their online profiles or through services such as ResearchGate). Most of the journals listed above publish reports of carefully designed evaluations of theories or psychological techniques. They also publish review articles summarising the current position and perhaps proposing new directions: recent reviews can be an excellent starting point for those wishing to know more about a particular topic. For example, the *Annual Review of Psychology* contains many such articles that can provide a quick insight into the key issues.

Sometimes people feel that when they read about work psychology what they get is common sense dressed up with jargon. Indeed, one of the better jokes about psychologists is that they tell you what you already know, in words that you do not understand. Like most good jokes, it has a grain of truth – but only a grain. To see why, let us look a little more at the notion of common sense.

Common sense is sometimes expressed in proverbs such as 'look before you leap'. Yes, one says, that is common sense – after all, it would be stupid to proceed with something without checking first to see if it was wise. But the reader may already have called to mind another proverb: 'He who hesitates is lost.' Well, yes, that is common sense too. After all, in this life we must take our chances when they come, otherwise they will pass us by. This example illustrates an important characteristic of common sense: it can be contradictory. Interestingly, one research study found that students sometimes endorsed pairs of contradictory proverbs of this kind as both having high 'truth value' (Halvor Teigen, 1986). And so they should. Both *are* true – sometimes, and in some circumstances. Psychologists are in the business of working out when, and in what circumstances. For example, when do high levels of job demands become a problem and for whom, and under what circumstances? Even so, psychologists' claims about common sense can sometimes undermine their credibility. Kluger and Tikochinsky (2001) suggest that, over the years, psychologists have often too readily claimed that their research findings on specific topics contradict common sense, only to find later that they have overgeneralised from the results of a single study. Approaches to the use of theory such as the scientist-practitioner approach, evidence-based management and pragmatic science attempt to overcome this problem and are discussed in more detail later (in Chapter 2).

Key learning point

Work psychology seeks to go beyond 'common-sense' views of work behaviour, thoughts and feelings.

Because most research, training and consultancy in organisations are paid for by senior managers, it is likely that the agenda will be driven by their perspectives and priorities.

Obtaining the informed consent of people at lower levels of the organisation does not really get round that reality. An alternative is to work only on behalf of individuals or groups and communities with low power and resources. Decisions such as this have obvious links with the psychologist's own values and political stance, and equally obvious consequences for the level of financial rewards they enjoy. Most work psychologists take the view that usually organisations are sufficiently unitarist (that is, united in objectives and values) to permit all constituencies within them to gain from the psychologist's interventions, or at least not lose. Some might argue that this is a convenient assumption, as opposed to a carefully considered and justified position, and that ensuring that a person or group is not harmed by the work psychologist's activities is not the same as actively working for their interests.

Key learning point

Many work psychologists wish to influence top managers, but they may be seen as technicians, not strategists. Also, it is important for the work psychologist to consider their impact on all parties, not just senior managers.

The changing world of work

It is probably true to say that nobody has ever lived at a time when they felt that not very much was happening or changing in their world. Even without the seismic economic events that characterised the last few years, there is a lot of consensus that the last 20 years have seen some quite radical changes in the nature of work. Some of the more notable changes are outlined in Table 1.2. There is no doubt that many work psychologists have been keen to investigate the consequences of some of the workplace changes described above. This is shown by the number of articles on, for example, work-related stress, diversity in teams, dispersed working, balancing work with non-work demands, agency workers, the psychological contract and women in management, among other topics. The changing nature of the workplace implies wide and deep changes of emphasis across most areas of work psychology. In Table 1.2 we note some of the world of work changes and suggest some consequences for what are, or should be, hot topics within work psychology. Without highlighting them using 'bells and whistles' throughout this text, you will notice that research and practice of direct relevance to these issues can be found throughout this book.

Many of these changes arise from a combination of technological advances and demographic and economic trends. These go hand in hand to some extent. Improved communication and information technologies mean that, for example, it is now much easier than it used to be to work away from a physical location. Chapter 15 focuses on the issues generated by dispersed working. Some companies now provide customer services from call centres in countries far away from their main markets. This can bring some problems, such as when the call centre staff perhaps do not know enough about the culture and people of the country or countries they are dealing with. For some time, many companies have been reducing their workforces, partly by outsourcing functions such as catering, premises' security and sometimes human resources, IT and other functions, too. In some companies (though by no means all), only staff who are core to the company's business have full-time employment contracts with the company. Others come and go, often employed short-term via an agency or as independent contractors. The psychological contract that companies have with their employees is very different as a result of some of these changes (see Chapter 6).

Table 1.2	World of work changes and their implications for work psychology
World of work changes	**Implications for work psychology (i.e. topics of increasing importance)**
Ageing working population	Learning, performance, satisfaction and engagement with work of older people
Increasing labour market participation and equality for historically disadvantaged groups, including ethnic minorities and people with a disability	Further development of fair selection procedures; the work experiences of members of disadvantaged groups; impact of diversity on workplaces and organisational performance; diversity policies; inter-group relations at work
Increasing workloads for people in work	Stress and pressure at work; burnout and mental health; balance between work and other aspects of life; effects of workload on thinking and behaviour
More people working remotely (e.g. at home) using information and communication technologies (ICT)	Selection of people suited to home working; supervision and leadership of people not physically present; impact of isolation on work performance and satisfaction; effective virtual communication and teamwork; recruitment and selection via the Internet
Pressures on organisations both to cut costs and to use knowledge well	Impact of these competing pressures (including new technology) on the design of jobs; organisational learning and knowledge management; stress and pressure at work; innovation and creativity; organisational change
Downsized, delayered and outsourced organisations	Fewer and more ambiguous organisational career paths; individuals coping with change and uncertainty; relations between 'core' and 'peripheral' workers; working life in small organisations; entrepreneurship
(Slow) increase in women's participation in traditionally male-dominated high-status work	The experience of being a woman in a man's world; gender stereotypes; women's career success, rewards and costs relative to men's; 'feminine' ways of working
Reduction in availability of manual work; growth of low-skill service-sector jobs; growing divide between those with marketable skills and qualifications and those without	The psychological and societal impact of income and wealth differences; the experience and consequences of unemployment and underemployment
Increasing internationalisation of organisations and markets	Cross-cultural comparisons of workplaces; working abroad; interpersonal and intercultural influence; the appropriateness of selection, etc. procedures across cultures

Key learning point

The world of work is changing rapidly because of technological advances, global competition, and societal demographic and cultural trends. Work psychology can be used to examine the human consequences of these changes.

A longer-term trend is the relocation of manufacturing operations from developed countries to developing ones where wages are lower. This means the export of some jobs (predominantly, but not only, relatively low-skilled work) from rich countries to poorer ones. In many organisations employees need to be able to work effectively with colleagues from different cultural backgrounds. In order to find ways of competing, governments and companies in northern and western Europe, Japan, Australasia and North America are emphasising both cost-cutting and the need to stay ahead of the game in advanced skills and knowledge. Again, in order to cut costs and improve performance, some Western governments have privatised some public services and industries. These changes have led to what is sometimes referred to as the intensification of work in developed countries: increasing work hours and pressure, the need for lifelong learning, the ability and willingness to change the type of work one does, perhaps several times in one career. Some people who, during the middle-to-late part of the 20th century, were able to jog along in seemingly secure jobs without much need to change or work very hard, now find themselves in a far less comfortable position (see also Chapter 13, on careers). It is important to recognise that these changed demands can have both positive and negative effects (see Chapter 10).

Many people adopt a fairly fatalistic approach to technology, feeling they have to adapt to the new and different demands placed on them by it. One of the best-known examples of how technology has changed work is call centres. These have been defined by Holman (2003: 116), drawing on the Health and Safety Executive (1999), as a work environment in which the main business is mediated by computer- and telephone-based technologies that enable the efficient distribution of incoming calls (or allocation of outgoing calls) to available staff, and permit the use of display-screen information when customer–employee calls are in progress. Worries have been expressed that call centre work is likely to be alienating because it is designed to minimise costs and skill requirements, i.e. so-called Taylorism (see Chapter 7). Often the workers have to stick to a script and a call time limit, and their adherence to both is monitored closely. This can make for stressful and unfulfilling work (Holman et al., 2002). However, it is also clear that it is possible to give workers more freedom about how they deal with such demands (Bond et al., 2008) and to make interactions more like relationships than encounters (Gutek, 1995). Although customer resistance to this can occur when they perceive that a sales pitch is masquerading as a relationship, on the whole people (both customers and call centre workers) seem to prefer being treated as individuals rather than in a standardised way. It also seems to be possible to use monitoring systems in ways that support the development of workers, rather than as a disciplinary device to catch workers who deviate from the script and/or deal with calls too slowly (Aiello and Kolb, 1995).

Thus it seems that, in call centres, the technology does not have *inevitable* consequences. It does not necessarily deskill and dehumanise people who work there. This should not surprise us, because exactly the same conclusion was drawn by work psychologists investigating the impact of changes in manufacturing technology (especially computer-controlled machine tools) in the 1970s and 1980s (Wall et al., 1987). How new technology affects jobs, well-being and individual and organisational performance depends not just on how clever the technology is, but also on the motives of those who introduce it, the processes by which it is introduced, and how well it fits with existing social systems in the workplace (Blackler and Brown, 1986; Burnes, 1989). Chapters 8 and 15 tackle these issues head-on by examining how the design and implementation of new technology can be best managed (using a human-centred approach to design). Such approaches tend to produce good results (see Chapter 8) because they make use of the knowledge of system operators and have the best chance of securing their commitment (because workers have been involved in the process).

Key learning point

Recent research on new technology at work reinforces earlier conclusions that the introduction of new technology does not inevitably deskill jobs. However, the impact of new technology on organisational success is often less positive than anticipated because the technology is not well-suited to the psychological characteristics of individuals, nor to the patterns of social interaction in the workplace.

Diversity and culture

The trends described in the previous section indicate that diversity and culture are cross-cutting themes that need to be considered in every aspect of work psychology. They are all closely connected to issues of fairness. Rather than treat them extensively as 'stand-alone' topics we have chosen to integrate coverage of these issues where they are relevant in each chapter. Below we outline briefly just some of the overarching reasons why these issues are important and need to be considered. In this section we focus on gender, ethnicity, disability and culture as prominent aspects of diversity and why they are important. However, as we hope to illustrate throughout this text this diversity is much broader than this:

> The basic concept of managing diversity accepts that the workforce consists of a diverse population of people. The diversity consists of visible and non-visible differences which will include sex, age, background, race, disability, personality and workstyle. It is founded on the premise that harnessing these differences will create a productive environment in which everybody feels valued, where their talents are fully utilised and in which organisational goals are met.
>
> (Kandola and Fullerton, 1994: 19)

Ever since major civil rights legislation was enacted in the USA, the UK and many other European countries in the 1960s and 1970s, considerable attention has been devoted in work psychology to fairness in selection and other organisational procedures, especially regarding women and ethnic minorities. Work psychologists are seen (or at least, see themselves) as having a lot to offer in the systematic evaluation of techniques (such as selection interviews) and instruments (such as psychometric tests), including how to make them free from bias (see Chapters 3 and 4). Managers in organisations were said to be motivated to implement equal opportunities by (i) support for the ethical principle of fairness (Kandola and Fullerton, 1994) and (ii) fear of prosecution (Werner and Bolino, 1997). From around the late 1980s onwards, however, the thinking and language began to change somewhat. The term 'managing diversity' became popular. The motivation for this is still partly ethical and partly to avoid prosecution, but now it is also argued that diversity is good for business, and that it makes for good publicity for the organisation.

In many developed countries there are also changes in the working population brought about by demographic trends. For example, for some years there have been trends toward smaller families which means that now there are relatively smaller numbers of people starting work and in early career than there were in some earlier times. In contrast, in the UK more than one million people over the age of 65 are now working since the abolition of enforced retirement (Department for Work and Pensions, 2014). Hence the average age of the working population is increasing. Life expectancy is also on the rise in most developed countries. It is likely that this will increase the retirement age (how lucky we are!) and changes in pension provision.

Other changes to workforce diversity arise from changing views about the rights and roles of various groups within societies. Often these views are backed up with legislation to try to ensure that those rights are upheld. During nearly all of the 20th century many countries saw sustained moves towards equality of provision and treatment for men and women. Many would argue that there is still a long way to go on that score. For example, in the UK in 1971 around 53 per cent of women were economically active; in 2014 it was nearer 67 per cent (Office for National Statistics, 2014). This change has several interrelated causes, including many women's wish to be employed, changing expectations about the roles of women in society, the introduction of legislation to promote equal opportunities, legislation supporting maternity leave (etc.), a wish for higher material standards of living for households, and a realisation in many organisations that competitiveness depends on having the right people in the right jobs, whatever their gender (Cassell, 2000). Less optimistically, there is still a clear tendency for women to be over-represented in certain kinds of work (e.g. caring, teaching, secretarial), under-represented in others (e.g. only a handful of women are CEOs of large companies). Although progress has been made, there is still some way to go, even to conform to legislation, let alone to transform social attitudes.

Women's earnings are lower than men's too, in spite of equal pay for equal work legislation. In the UK, average earnings for women are between 70 and 80 per cent of those for men, depending on occupation. The pay gaps are bigger than that in some other European countries, and smaller in yet others, but the gap is always present. They cannot be explained away by women being in less skilled employment than men. Even if they could, it is necessary to ask why women (whose educational achievements are on average higher than men's) are in less highly skilled and/or highly paid employment than men. According to the UK government's Labour Force Survey, men achieved their highest weekly wage between the age of 40 and 49 years. However, while women achieved their highest weekly wage somewhat sooner (between 30 and 39 years), the average wage was much lower. The picture is similar in the USA. As an aside (rather depressingly for this author) salaries rose up to these age ranges, but dropped afterwards.

In terms of what people are capable of doing in the workplace, these findings appear unjust. Most gender-related differences in ability and personality are really quite small, or even non-existent. In Chapter 4 we discuss, among other things, ways of assessing people for selection and appraisal that avoid biases that may stem from assessors' beliefs about how men and women differ. In Chapter 12, on leadership, we comment briefly on how leaders might be perceived as different as a result of their gender, and the consequences of that. So it might be a mistake to focus purely on a person's biological sex (i.e. their genes) or their gender (i.e. whether they live as a man or a woman). There are some sources of stress that because of wider societal factors are more relevant to women than to men. Women are more likely to experience sexual harassment than men. Often women feel work–life balance issues more keenly than men. Women are more likely than men to suffer from anxiety and depression, and this is sometimes attributable to stresses at work. On the other hand, men are more likely to suffer from more life-threatening stress-related illnesses such as heart problems (see Chapter 10 for more on stress).

Key learning point

Although it is clear that women are still paid less and have lower-status jobs than men, arguments rage about whether women are oppressed, or whether they are free to make choices never previously available to them.

Gender is not the only basis for potential discrimination. There are numerous statistics and specific incidents which show clearly how people with ethnic minority affiliations tend to get a raw deal in the labour market. Legislation to promote equality of opportunity has been introduced, of course, and strong cases have been made for the value to organisations of having an ethnically diverse workforce (see Chapter 11). These measures have arguably reduced bias against people with ethnic minority affiliations, but they have not eliminated it. The issues underlying this are complex, and include not just overt prejudice, but also more subtle phenomena of social perception of individuals and groups (see also Chapter 11).

Many anecdotal reports, 'fly on the wall' television programmes and research studies indicate clearly that people from ethnic minorities in any given country are at a disadvantage relative to members of the majority when it comes to getting jobs and other opportunities. High-quality reviews such as Huffcutt and Roth (1998), McKay and McDaniel (2006) and Dean et al. (2008) offer confirmatory scientific evidence of this. These impressive studies show that the mean ratings for black candidates in employment interviews, assessments of job performance and assessment centre ratings are lower than those for whites. The authors of these reviews cite many reasons for these differences that reside in problems with the way performance is measured (in general) and specific biases that operate in the assessment of people at work. Given research findings such as these, perhaps it is not surprising that members of ethnic minorities seem less likely to enter high-prestige occupations than members of the majority, and even if they get there, they often do not progress as far. This is in spite of legislation in many countries to ensure equal rights.

Key learning point

Members of ethnic minorities tend to be at a disadvantage in the labour market relative to the majority. This is mostly due to aspects of person perception and identity that lead majority and minority groups to hold certain opinions about themselves and each other, sometimes without realising it.

The kinds of social networks that people build up are also probably partly a consequence of their identities, as well as the opportunities that they are given. People in minorities tend to form networks that consist of other members of minorities, and members of the majority also stick together. Usually, members of the majority hold most of the powerful positions, and the people who get to know them also tend to be from the majority. To the extent that decisions such as who gets which job are made on the basis of the decision-maker knowing the people concerned, then these social networks will become self-perpetuating (Ibarra, 1995). One way round this is to institute mentoring or other schemes where members of the (powerful) majority take some responsibility for the development of one or more members of a minority. There is more about the roles of social networks and mentoring (among other things) in Chapter 13 on careers.

Another potential basis for discrimination is disability, and again many countries now have legislation to protect and promote the rights of people with a disability. In many countries, legislation now puts an onus on workplaces and educational institutions to take on and then cater properly for people with a disability, even though this may mean some additional cost and effort in providing appropriate equipment and adjustments to physical layout. Again, though, much depends on how individuals (especially those who have power in a workplace) perceive people with a disability.

Barnes (1991) defines disability as 'the loss of opportunities to take part in the normal life of the community on an equal level with others due to physical and social barriers'. This definition highlights the social element of disability – it is not simply a physical phenomenon. How disability and disabled people are viewed by society as a whole affects the opportunities available to people with disabilities (McHugh, 1991). It is clear that, although the lot of people with a disability in the workplace is improving, they are still at a disadvantage compared with people with no disability. The introduction in many countries of laws protecting and enhancing the rights of people with a disability has reduced the gap, but not eliminated it. It seems that the image of disabled people as ill, dependent on others, child-like and asexual does persist, even though much of the medical and other provision for people with a disability has moved away from treating people in that way (Oliver, 1990). Yet many of the technological advances outlined earlier make it easier for people with a disability to work productively, because they compensate for any limitations people may have in physical coordination and mobility. Much of the provision required to make workplaces usable for people with a disability is hardly rocket science, which is one reason why the UK Disability Discrimination Act, which came into force in 1995, insists that employers make 'reasonable accommodations' where the working arrangements and/or physical features of the workplace put people with a disability at a significant disadvantage.

Even so, the UK Labour Force Survey in 2012 recorded 46 per cent of disabled people as being in employment compared with 76 per cent of people without a disability. Of course, some of this difference may be due to fewer disabled than non-disabled people looking for work, but that is not the whole story because the UK unemployment rate (which includes only those seeking work) is nearly twice as high for disabled people than non-disabled ones.

As is the case with other diversity issues, legislation does not in itself override human perceptions, beliefs and prejudices about people with a disability. So it is likely to remain difficult for disabled people to rise to the top of their professions. Numerous studies in the 1980s confirmed that disabled people tend to be concentrated in lower-status occupations and if they did get into higher-status occupations, they tended to be at junior levels within them (Walker, 1982). There is now much more concern than there used to be with identifying ways in which disabled people can be supported in achieving independence. Furthermore, this is increasingly being done by finding out the experiences of disabled people themselves, rather than simply implementing what able-bodied people think would be good for them (Hendey and Pascall, 2001).

Key learning point

The talents of people with a disability are being increasingly recognised in employment and education, and this is supported by laws upholding their rights in many countries. However, there is still some disadvantage relative to people without a disability.

The persistent difficulties of disabled people in the labour market are neither due only to real limitations in their capabilities nor to unreasonable employers. It also seems clear that gender, ethnicity and social class play their parts, through the ways in which children with a disability are socialised. In fact, in some respects, these factors may be more important than disability in shaping what disabled people expect of themselves. Shah et al. (2004a) for example have shown that, among a group of disabled professionals who had achieved considerable career success, those raised in middle-class professional households recalled rarely being allowed to use their disability as an excuse for failure. Education is also a key factor. Some people with a disability are educated in separate schools whereas others are in mainstream schools. Which of these two forms of schooling is more successful has been debated at length over many years (e.g. Jenkinson, 1997), and it is likely that much depends on the personal resources of the young person in dealing with whichever environment they are in. As a generalisation, it seems that mainstream schools offer a relatively challenging curriculum, but sometimes not much social support, while segregated schools tend to be the other way round (Shah et al., 2004b).

Work psychology has quite a lot to offer to theory and practice in managing diversity. Problems in managing diversity often stem from perceptions of dissimilarity between individuals and/or groups. On the whole, people tend to feel more attracted to people who are similar to themselves than to those who are dissimilar. They also tend to be more generous towards them, and happier to cooperate with them. These and other findings about interpersonal perception and inter-group relations are well-established ones within psychology. The identification of these tendencies, and the analysis of the circumstances in which they occur and their consequences for behaviour, have wide implications for many aspects of working life. Following on from this, work psychology should also offer the tools to evaluate the impact of attempts to manage diversity. Common forms of diversity management in organisations are:

■ workshops designed to improve understanding and communication among members of different groups;

■ support groups, mentoring and networks for minority and/or disadvantaged groups;

- organised and recognised groups of employee representatives reporting on issues of diversity to top management;

- rewarding managers for their development of members of minority and/or disadvantaged groups;

- fast-track developmental programmes and special training opportunities for minority and/or disadvantaged groups.

However, one of the main reasons for focusing on diversity so early in this text is that it is an issue that weaves throughout this book. Enhancing the management of diversity is often about following best practice that has been identified in a number of aspects of work psychology. These include:

- Ensuring that selection processes are based on the proper job analysis so that the criteria for selection are related to the potential, or ability, to do the job (and not irrelevant factors such as age or gender). This includes training employees in the use of fair selection techniques and methods (see Chapters 4 and 9) and has implications for career development (Chapter 13). In addition, organisations wishing to transform their culture (see Chapter 14) by recruiting tolerant employees, need to communicate clearly that they value diversity (Kim and Gefland, 2003).

- Designing physical work environments that allow people to perform to their full potential (see Chapter 8).

- Establishing and developing teams that include people with the skills, knowledge, abilities and attitudes that are needed to get the job done (rather than a group of people who are all good friends because they are similar in some way – see Chapter 11).

- Ensuring that training and development interventions allow a diverse workforce to develop (see Chapter 9).

- Ensuring that the criteria for measuring performance advancement are open to all employees and having formal induction processes for all employees (see Chapter 9).

- Allowing flexible working for all employees (and not just for working mothers), and introducing interventions to tackle harassment and discrimination (see Chapter 10).

Of course, there are significant dangers in attempts to manage diversity. There is some evidence that attempts to increase contact and understanding can sometimes backfire, and make stereotypes more entrenched (Nemetz and Christensen, 1996). Also, it is important not to equate being a minority group with being disadvantaged in all respects. For example, there is evidence that Asian Americans achieve more in education and earn more than European Americans, though on the other hand the average boost to earnings provided by education is less for Asian Americans than European Americans, which shows the complexity of the phenomena involved (Friedman and Krackhardt, 1997). As discussed in the next section on culture, perhaps the biggest danger is of treating individuals as if they were identikit members of one or more groups. Even if different groups (for example men and women) are different on average, this does not mean that all men are the same. Nor are they different from all women in the same way.

Key learning point

Work psychology has a lot to offer the management of diversity, particularly in understanding how individuals and groups perceive, and relate to, each other.

To summarise then, for all three group differences discussed, it is noticeable that:

■ the position of women, ethnic minority groups, and people with a disability in the labour market is improving somewhat (e.g. ability to get jobs, the types of jobs they get, how successful they are in their occupation);

■ their position still does not match that of the majority group (in this case, white able-bodied males);

■ this appears not to be entirely attributable to possibly legitimate factors such as differences in qualifications and experience;

■ their disadvantage has not been entirely eradicated by legislation; it is probably due partly to subtle or not-so-subtle prejudice and/or discrimination;

■ in some instances, people's sense of identity (i.e. how they see themselves) may matter as much as their objective group membership.

Chapter 13, on careers, explores some of the factors that affect the extent and nature of career success that people experience. It is highly relevant to this section, particularly regarding the career success experienced by women.

Key learning point

Women, ethnic minorities and people with a disability are all seeing moves towards better recognition in the labour market, but still do not enjoy equality, and legislation to protect them is not always fully effective.

An important aspect of diversity is nationality. This is associated with ethnicity, of course, but is not always the same. Hofstede (2001) and Trompenaars (1993), among others, have found systematic cultural differences between people from different countries. Cross-national differences crop up quite a lot in this book, most notably in Chapters 7 (motivation), 11 (groups and teams), 12 (leadership) and 13 (careers). Students of occupational psychology are often confused by the array of different populations and research settings that they encounter when studying the academic literature. Inconsistencies in research findings are often difficult to fathom or explain (just take a look at the discussion section of many research papers to see how baffling these can be for even the most experienced academics). One very important issue that drives some of these inconsistencies in work psychology is that of cultural differences.

Gelfand and colleagues (2007) provide a neat summary of the meaning of culture, drawing together a range of definitions. They state that culture is the human-generated part of the environment that is transmitted across time and generations; culture results in people from the same culture having a set of shared meanings (they see things in a similar way and share similar patterns of thinking); culture gives us 'standard operating procedures' or ways of doing things.

In other words, the culture we grow up in, or spend some time in, gives us a 'lens' through which we see and interpret the world around us. Culture can have many different dimensions: it may be a national culture, a historical religious culture, or it may even be an organisational culture (see Chapter 14). As far as possible we have tried to give this text an international feel, to subtly raise the issue of culture as you study each topic. Still it is worth noting early on in your reading of this text that various dimensions of culture can have a quite profound impact on the way people think and behave in the workplace.

Extensive research has consistently shown that people from different national cultures look for different things in the environment. People from different cultural backgrounds also have different interpretations of the same events or situations and culture determines our norms and standards. What is seen as right in one culture might be seen as wrong in another, and different cultures have different sources of self-worth (what makes us feel worthwhile and valued is highly affected by the culture we develop and live in). These norms provide a number of very useful functions. For example they help us to manage our anxiety. If we know a course of action is acceptable within a cultural norm we are less anxious about acting in that way.

Key learning point

The culture that a person develops within, or lives in, has a strong impact on what they notice, how they make sense of what they notice, and the impact that external events have on them.

Chapter 12 gives an in-depth description of a number of different dimensions of culture and how they relate to leadership (e.g. what is important for people from different cultures). For now we will look at one of the most frequently studied cultural dimensions: individualistic vs. collectivistic (Hofstede, 1980, 2001). The former reflects a belief that individuals should be self-sufficient while the latter emphasises people's belongingness to groups in which there is mutual support.

Two reviews published in the *Annual Review of Psychology* provide elegant summaries of the importance of culture for anyone using psychology in organisational settings. Reviewing a wide range of research (only a small amount of it drawn from work psychology), Lehman et al. (2004) identify a number of important effects of culture that have an obvious relevance for work psychology. Their review focused on comparing the East Asian culture (collectivistic) and the European/North American culture (individualistic). Gelfand et al. (2007) looked more closely at how some of these effects translate into important differences in the workplace (the words in italics). A summary of the key findings is presented in Table 1.3.

At this stage it is important not to read too much into the content of Table 1.3. There are huge individual differences within cultures and neither cultural perspective is inherently right or wrong. For example, there are circumstances where it is helpful to investigate and attribute personal responsibility for work problems. In other situations it might be better to identify systematic causes for problems, but culture means that the environment shapes employees' preferences to some degree.

Peter Warr (2008) looked at a different dimension of culture, that of historical religious values. Almost 21,000 employees were asked what they valued about their job. Although good pay was important across various cultures, it seems particularly important in historically communist cultures. Having pleasant people to work with, or a job with high levels of responsibility, was seen as important by significantly fewer people in communist countries than it was in Catholic and Protestant countries.

All of this might have you thinking that cultural differences threaten the idea that good psychological theories can generalise across cultures (the idea of *psychological universals*). They may, but to simplify things a little, what we generally find is that similar issues affect most cultures. There is evidence that the Big Five personality factors exist across cultures but that culture influences the way people respond to questionnaire items that measure them (Thompson, 2008). Job satisfaction, motivation, leadership and so on are clearly important to some extent to the vast majority of the global working population. However, culture

Table 1.3	The impact of a national cultural difference

Individualistic culture European/North American	Collectivistic culture East Asian
Tend to develop an analytical thinking style, focusing on the 'hard facts'. They tend to be troubled when logic fails to make accurate predictions *Employees tend to seek facts and figures on which to base their efforts to solve work problems*	Tend to use holistic thinking styles, using subjective impressions to solve problems, rather than relying on formal logic *Employees tend to seek and use a range of different information (e.g. hard facts and subjective impressions) in decision-making*
Prefer to attribute causes of events to individuals rather than to situational factors *Employees tend to attribute personal blame to others when others fail (and personal credit for others' successes)*	Prefer to attribute causes of events to a wide range of environmental, group and social factors *Employees take a complex and multifaceted view when looking at reasons for success and failure*
View themselves and others as independent beings (i.e. people are independent, self-contained and autonomous) *Employees highly motivated by jobs that provide autonomy*	See people as being interdependent (i.e. people have value in society as part of a group) *Employees highly motivated by jobs that involve co-dependency with colleagues*
Tend to seek knowledge for its own sake, with their motivation for learning being to fulfil their own potential *Employees tend to value job demands, training and development that helps them as an individual*	Knowledge is sought that will serve the 'wider good' with personal development being less important *High value is placed on job demands and training that will help the employees to make a stronger contribution to team or company performance*
Individual, positively focused feedback tends to be important *Employees likely to be motivated by feedback about their own performance rather than by feedback about the performance of the group they work in*	Feedback on poor performance, and how it impacts on those around them tends to be a powerful motivator *Negative feedback likely to create a strong response, especially if it is about group performance*
Life satisfaction tends to be quite dependent on self-esteem, personal freedom and pursuit of individual goals *Employees are likely to be motivated by goals that they choose themselves that help them realise their own potential*	Social standing/reputation tends to be closely linked to person's feelings of self-worth. Group failures tend to be ego-threatening and pursuit of team goals and good interpersonal relationships contributes strongly to self-worth *Employees are likely to be motivated by the goals set for the work group they are in, especially when these goals are set for them by figures of authority and when achievement is measured in terms of contribution to a group*
Biases such as unrealistic optimism and self-enhancement are common *Self-perceptions/appraisals might present an overly positive estimate of performance and this need to be validated with other sources of information*	Tend to be quite self-critical, getting their self-esteem instead from being a valued member of the group and being connected to other group members *Self-appraisals may be overly harsh, but optimistic biases may operate when employees evaluate the performance of the group they are in*

might play an important role in determining the factors that have an impact on these issues. For example, Warr (2008) shows that, in general, job satisfaction is determined by a range of different factors that are all relevant across different cultures. It is the relative importance of these factors that becomes different because of cultural influences. In a similar vein, motivation tends to be related to job performance but what motivates people may differ from one culture to another. This helps to explain why some working practices with their origin in Asian cultures have proved difficult to implement in Europe.

Culture may sometimes force us to re-examine the meaning of some of the concepts we use. Meyer et al. (2002) found that outside of the USA, organisational commitment (see Chapter 7) may be more about perceived support from the organisation than it is to do with age and tenure (age and tenure have stronger relationships with organisational commitment in the USA than they do elsewhere).

Lehman et al. (2004) also argue that there is ample evidence to indicate that developing cultural experience is a bit like a building a toolkit. When we experience different cultures we grow to appreciate a wider range of normative values, and we gather up more 'lenses' (tools) which we can then use to see the world in different ways. It seems that travel really does broaden the mind. The authors called this 'contextual priming' and it is a principle already being put to use by companies whose workers operate across cultures. Many organisations use cultural acclimatisation periods to prepare their employees for work overseas. Employees who have experienced the culture they are working in are more likely to understand the cultural norms that are operating and appreciate how their actions will be viewed by others.

Summary

Modern psychology can be divided into several subdisciplines which reflect different facets of human psychological functioning. Cutting across these divisions are competing theoretical traditions in psychology. These are the psychoanalytic, trait, behaviourist, phenomenological and social cognitive traditions. None of them can be described as correct, though the social cognitive tradition is the most recent, and makes most use of other traditions. The traditions make some contradictory assumptions about the fundamental nature of the person. Their differences and similarities are summarised in Table 1.1. Each tradition finds some expression in work psychology. The differences between them emphasise that any apparent coherence of work psychology is due to the fact that it always take place in the work setting. It does not possess a generally agreed view of human nature.

Work psychology concerns both the interaction between an individual and their work, and the relationships between people in the work setting. This includes issues such as: psychological assessment; learning, training and development; leadership, engagement and motivation; employee well-being; work design; and organisational change and development. Work psychologists act as researchers, teachers and consultants in these areas. In the UK, the British Psychological Society and the Health and Care Professions Council oversee the professional qualifications and conduct of work psychologists. Many other countries have equivalent bodies.

We also believe it is important to examine the context in which work psychology is operating. Changes have been occurring over the past two decades or so which mean that many work organisations are more pressured than they were, with flatter structures, fewer employees and more varied terms and conditions. Employees may well be required to be flexible to suit employers' needs, but there is also often a chance for them to work flexibly to suit their own needs. It is clear that new technology in the workplace does not have inevitable consequences – its effects on people, jobs and organisations depend a lot on how it is introduced and subsequently used. The changing mix of people in the labour force in terms of their gender, ethnic affiliation, (dis)ability, religion, nationality, age, sexual orientation and other factors presents both challenges and opportunities for work psychology. So does the increasing awareness of diversity issues, independent of the changing nature of the workforce. Work psychology should be analysing and answering questions such as 'How do different groups at work relate to each other?', 'How can fairness be achieved at work?', 'How can the potential value of a diverse workforce be made a reality?' and 'How can small organisations with limited resources make use of what work psychology can offer?'

Test your learning

Short-answer questions

1   What are the areas of basic psychology, and what kind of issues does each area address?
2   Draw a diagram to show the relationship between basic psychology and work psychology.
3   In psychoanalytic psychology, what are (i) the id, (ii) the ego, (iii) the superego and (iv) defence mechanisms?
4   What is a trait? Briefly describe two key features of the trait approach to personality.
5   In behaviourism, what is reinforcement? Why do behaviourist psychologists think that personality can be changed?
6   In phenomenological psychology, what are (i) conditions of worth, (ii) unconditional positive regard and (iii) self-actualisation?
7   Why is the self an important concept in the social cognitive tradition?
8   What were the key lessons learned by work psychologists from the Hawthorne studies?
9   Name and briefly describe five areas of work undertaken by work psychologists.
10 If you were a manager considering buying the services of a work psychologist, what would you want to know about the psychologist's qualifications and experiences?
11 How would you evaluate whether the research undertaken by a work psychologist was ethical?
12 Specify five ways in which workplaces tend to be different now from 30 years ago.
13 Choose one of these (from question 12), and comment on what work psychology can contribute to understanding its impact.
14 Suggest three ways in which work psychology should be able to help in the management of diversity.

Suggested assignments

1   Compare and contrast any two approaches to personality.
2   Select any two traditions in personality. Imagine two managers. One believes one tradition is correct; the other supports the other tradition. Examine the probable impact of their beliefs on the way they deal with other people at work.
3   Examine whether the ethical codes of practice governing work psychologists adequately reflect all the ethical issues that can arise in work psychology research and practice.
4   How can work psychology help to ensure that workplace diversity is healthy and productive?
5   What role does culture play in understanding workplace behaviour?

Relevant websites

Professional psychology associations offer considerable information about the theory and practice of psychology, including work psychology. Three good ones are the International Association of Applied Psychology (IAAP) at http://www.iaapsy.org; the European Association of Work and Organizational Psychology (EAWOP) at http://www.eawop.org/ and the British Psychological Society at http://www/bps.org.uk/. For those wishing to be an occupational psychologist in the UK the Health and Care Professions Council is also relevant (http://www.hcpc-uk.co.uk)

The Chartered Institute of Personnel and Development (CIPD) has an excellent website that provides access to reports and surveys on a range of important workplace issues. It is at http://www.cipd.co.uk

One of a number of websites devoted to supporting people who experience disadvantage in the workplace is http://www.wideplus.org/. This is a European network for women, with a particular interest in training and development.

The UK's Equality and Human Rights Commission has a broad mission to support equality in all aspects of life. The organisation is taking increasing interest in workplace issues, and you can find out about current activities, including advice for employers, at http://www.equalityhumanrights.com/

Suggested further reading

Full details for all references are given in the list at the end of this book.

1 Two papers from the *Annual Review of Psychology* are accessible and useful. These are the articles on (i) culture (Gelfand et al., 2007) and (ii) diversity (Van Knippenberg and Schippers, 2007).

2 The seventh edition of Robert Ewen's book *An Introduction to Theories of Personality* provides a thorough but readable account of different traditions in psychology, particularly concerning how each tradition has construed the nature of the person and personality. Although Ewen majors on the psychoanalytic tradition, his coverage of the other traditions is clear and informative.

3 The 2004 book edited by David Holman and colleagues called *The Essentials of the New Workplace: A guide to the human impact of modern working practices*, published by John Wiley and Sons, offers a really good detailed look at the human side of nearly every technology-driven workplace change.

4 Binna Kandola's book titled *The Value of Difference: Eliminating bias in organisations* (Pearn Kandola, 2009) provides a down-to-earth but not overly simplistic account of some of the practical issues in managing a diverse workforce, and is written by the UK's leading consultant in this area.

CHAPTER 2

Theory, research and practice in work psychology

LEARNING OBJECTIVES

After studying this chapter, you should be able to:

1 describe the main elements of a psychological theory, and explain the links between those elements;

2 distinguish between two opposing philosophies in the conduct of psychological research;

3 describe the various methods of data collection used in research by work psychologists;

4 describe the key features, advantages and disadvantages of different research designs used by work psychologists;

5 define the null and alternative hypotheses in psychological research;

6 explain the concept of statistical significance;

7 explain the concepts of power and effect size in statistical testing;

8 define in words the circumstances in which the following statistical techniques would be used:

t-test

analysis of variance

chi-square

correlation

multiple regression

meta-analysis

structural equation modelling;

9 describe how qualitative data can be collected and analysed;

10 describe how interventions can be evaluated;

11 describe the divide that can sometimes occur between researchers and practitioners.

Introduction

In this chapter we build on the previous one by looking more closely at how theories in work psychology can be developed, evaluated and used. We start with an examination of the nature of theory and we provide a concrete example to show the factors that a good theory needs to take into account. Then we turn to the relationship between theory and practice. We argue that good practice requires good theory, and we discuss the problem that all too often theory-oriented and practice-oriented work psychologists find it difficult to communicate with (and learn from) each other. Then we take a look at the ways in which work psychologists conduct research, from the point of view of the overall strategy (research design) and also specific techniques (research methods). We consider how work psychologists' assumptions about the nature of knowledge and theory influence how they go about their research work, the kinds of data they obtain and how they interpret their data. Finally, we explain how statistical and qualitative techniques for analysing data can be utilised in order to draw conclusions about what the data mean. Many complex issues are involved in the appropriate use and interpretation of research data, and psychologists sometimes ignore them. This chapter attempts, hopefully in a straightforward way, to help the reader avoid some of the more common pitfalls.

The nature of theory in work psychology

A theory in psychology can be defined as an organised collection of ideas that serves to describe, explain or predict what a person will do, think or feel. To be successful, it needs to specify the following five elements (see also Figure 2.1):

1   The particular behaviours, thoughts or emotions in question. These should have significance for human affairs.

2   Any differences between people in the degree to which they characteristically exhibit the behaviours, thoughts or emotions in question.

3   Any situational factors that might influence whether or when the behaviours, thoughts or emotions in question occur.

4   Any consequences of the interaction between 2 and 3 for the behaviours, thoughts or emotions.

5   Any ways in which the occurrence of particular behaviours, thoughts or emotions might feed back to produce change in 2 and 3.

To take an example, let us suppose that a psychologist wishes to develop a theory to explain and predict the occurrence of arriving late for work. Relevant individual characteristics might include a person's job satisfaction and stable traits such as the extent to which they tend to be well organised. Relevant past experiences might include punishments for being late. Situational features might include the distance from home to work, the simplicity or complexity of travel between home and work, and the expectations of the person's workmates. They may also include factors that change day by day such as the weather. These might all directly affect the person's actual incidence of arriving late for work, but so might the *interaction* between person and situation. For example, a well-organised person may have no difficulty making complex travel arrangements between home and work. For such a person, complexity of travel arrangements might *not* have much effect on time of arrival at work. A poorly organised person may be able to cope with straightforward travel arrangements but not complex ones. For that person, the complexity of travel to work could make a big difference to punctuality. This is an example of an *interaction effect* – the travel between work and home affects the lateness of some people but not others. In this case the interaction appears to be between the person and the environment.

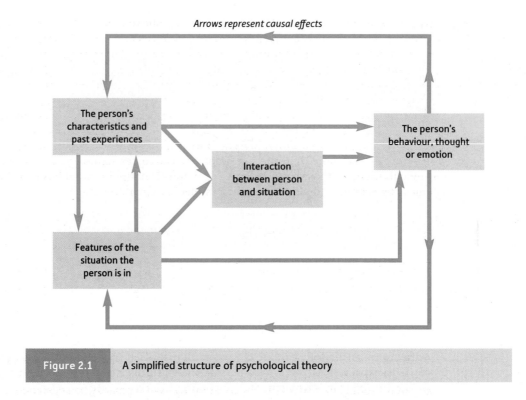

Figure 2.1	A simplified structure of psychological theory

Just to make things more complicated, it is likely that person and situation influence each other (this is sometimes referred to as the person–environment *transaction*). This can occur in at least three ways. Two of these will have happened before the specific events of interest to the psychologist. First, people's characteristics can affect the types of situation they expose themselves to. In this example, a badly organised person might not think carefully about travel to work when deciding where to live. Second, people may be able to change features of their situation, or features of their situation may change them. Third, a person's behaviour right now may lead him or her to change ('I'm late again; I must become a better organised person') or may cause a change in their situation (in an extreme case, being dismissed for being late once too often).

Naturally, it is possible to suggest many other personal characteristics and situational features that could influence lateness for work. The choice of which to investigate might itself be guided by theory. Testing and applying a theory of lateness for work would also require sound methods for assessing personal characteristics, situational features and lateness for work. As you might imagine this could result in a very complex piece of research, and it is sometimes the case that a researcher chooses to focus on a smaller range of factors and leave some variables unmeasured.

It is important to note that good theories are not conjured out of thin air. The concepts and proposed relationships between them are based on past research and theory, and the psychologist's reflections upon them. Many branches of science are characterised by this iterative pattern of steady developments that stem from previous research. Cassell and Symon (2004) point out that researchers are often quite conservative in this respect, 'adding a variable here or there, trying the model out in a different context or with a different sample etc.' (2004: 4). The choice of what to study in the first place can also be influenced by current events and public opinion. In fact, a frequent criticism of psychology (including work psychology) is that it takes insufficient account of broader factors such as social class, power structures in society and economic conditions (Pfeffer, 1991). Sociologists, economists and political scientists, among others, focus on those phenomena much more than psychologists do. Others argue that researchers need to keep a close eye on how the organisational setting impacts upon their findings. Rousseau and Fried (2001) talk about the importance of three neglected factors – 'location, location, location' – when attempting to make sense of research findings. This leaves work psychology open to accusations of: (i) naivety in failing to recognise the 'real' causes of human behaviour; (ii) overemphasis on the importance of characteristics of individual people; and (iii) acting as agents of the powerful rather than the powerless (see also Chapter 1 for an account of some related issues). Psychologists usually respond by arguing that individuals do have some control over what they think, feel and do. Each of us is more than the sum total of social forces acting upon us. To avoid bland generalisations, or those based on naive or simplistic notions of what it is to be human, it is crucial to examine individuals and their immediate environments.

Key learning point

The conventional view of good theory in work psychology is that the theory should be precise in specifying the behaviour, thoughts or feelings it is designed to predict, and the individual and situational characteristics which influence them.

The point was made in Chapter 1 that psychology is not a united or unified discipline. The multiplicity of views certainly extends to what research and theory are about and how research should be conducted. The most fundamental polarity has been described nicely by, among others, Easterby-Smith et al. (2002: Chapter 3) as positivism versus social constructionism. Each of these positions has distinct and very different philosophical roots. Easterby-Smith and colleagues stress that in practice nowadays much research includes a bit of both, and that they represent two extremes.

Positivism assumes that the social world exists objectively, i.e. that it has an objective reality. This usually (but not always) implies measuring things using quantitative (i.e. numerical) data. Science is seen as advancing by making hypotheses about laws and causes of human behaviour and then testing those hypotheses, preferably by simplifying the problem of interest as much as possible. Progress is often made by ruling out alternative explanations for findings or for data that might disprove a theory. In the absence of such findings and data we can be more confident that a theory is at least approximately correct or at least useful. To draw upon an often used example: if you want to prove all swans are white then it's better to look for non-white swans than to spend your time identifying even more white ones. It is also assumed that the researcher can investigate without influencing what is being investigated: that is, their presence and actions are assumed not to alter how people would naturally behave, think or feel.

The other extreme is labelled social constructionism by Easterby-Smith et al. It might also be termed phenomenological (see Chapter 1). This viewpoint suggests that reality is not objective. Instead, the meaning of events, concepts and objectives is constructed and interpreted by people, through their thought processes and social interactions. The discussion of cross-cultural issues in Chapter 1 shows how different people can interpret similar events in different ways. Research conducted on the basis of this philosophy will aim 'to understand and explain why people have different experiences, rather than search for external causes and fundamental laws to explain their behaviour' (Easterby-Smith et al., 2002: 30). So instead of measuring how often certain behaviours occur, the aim of research is to examine the different ways in which people interpret and explain their experience. The data produced by such research tend to be harder to obtain and to summarise than those produced by positivist research, but tend to be richer in meaning, detail and explanation.

To extend this principle one step further, if we collect data on people's interpretations of things, then we as researchers do some interpreting as well. We interpret our participants' interpretations and readers of our interpretations then interpret them: this is a sentence that is probably not best read late at night! In other words, we cannot really gain direct access to the way participants view things because we have to interpret others' views. If we are going to collect data about someone's view of the world we will need to interact with them and interpret what they say. This means that the data produced are always an interpretation of the participants' experience, and hence the term interpretative phenomenological analysis (IPA) (Willig, 2008). Reflexivity is an important concept in phenomenological research: researchers often go to great lengths to reflect upon their own point of view and how it has influenced the way they tackled the research question and interpreted research findings. Therefore, data are not viewed as some objective reality that exists independent of the view of the researcher or the views of the research participants.

Many topics in work psychology can be investigated from both perspectives and all points in between. To continue the example of arriving late for work, a positivist research project (which was the sort implied in the example given earlier) would assess the frequency of this behaviour and try to link it with objective factors such as distance from work as well as perhaps more subjective factors such as job satisfaction. The assumption would be that such factors may *cause* lateness for work, irrespective of the sense individuals might make of their situation. On the other hand, social constructionist research on lateness at work would focus much more on how individuals thought and felt about being late for work, and how they explained their own behaviour in this area. The general theoretical framework outlined in Figure 2.1 would still have some relevance, but aspects of the person and situation to be examined would be treated as part of people's ways of understanding and/or explaining their own behaviour rather than as objectively verifiable forces causing it. Ways of understanding and explaining might be researched by asking people about them directly, or alternatively by observing their behaviour and making inferences from the observations. For example they might look at what distance to work *meant* to the employee (did they see it as a challenge to be tackled through planning, or as a good source of excuses for being late?). The researcher might also consider how their own views on lateness had impacted upon the data collection and analysis.

Work psychology research published in academic journals (such as those listed in Chapter 1) is mostly positivist. This probably reflects psychology's attempts to position itself as a science subject, with consequences for the ways in which work psychologists are trained, as well as the kinds of people it attracts in the first place. Some psychologists (e.g. Johnson and Cassell, 2001) have, however, criticised the highly positivist and quantitative orientation of work psychology. They argue strongly that phenomenological studies have many advantages over positivist ones, and deserve a more prominent place in work psychology. Cassell and Symon (2004) state that qualitative non-positivist studies 'hold out the promise of new insights by adopting a critical stance on accepted practices and approaching research topics with different objectives' (2004: 4). As far as possible we try to reflect both positivist and non-positivist research in this text as it is clear that both have something to offer our understanding of work-related issues.

Key learning point

There is an important philosophical disagreement in psychology between positivism and phenomenological approaches. The former emphasises objectively verifiable causes of behaviour, thoughts and emotions; the latter focuses more on people's subjective explanations and accounts.

Theory and practice in work psychology

Some might argue that theory has little to offer practice. There are various reasons for advancing that argument. Theories in a particular area may not be very good, in the sense that they do not adequately or accurately specify the phenomena portrayed in Figure 2.1. A psychologist may find that a particular technique seems to work well, and not be concerned about theoretical reasons *why* it works. Work psychology is predominantly problem-centred. There is no single dominant theoretical perspective, and (again as noted earlier) work psychology has sometimes been somewhat isolated from theoretical developments in mainstream psychology. Sparrow (1999), for example, criticised work psychologists for ignoring theoretical developments in social psychology in their study of people at work. The present authors firmly believe that a good theory is essential to *good* practice. It is incorrect to say, as people sometimes do, that an idea is good in theory but not in practice. A good theory does a good job of describing, explaining and predicting behaviour, thoughts or emotions which have important outcomes. Basing practice on good theory *is* better than basing it on superstition, guesswork or an inferior theory. As the distinguished social psychologist Kurt Lewin (1945) long ago argued, there is nothing so practical as a good theory.

In an excellent article, Gary Johns (1993) analysed why techniques advocated by work psychologists (e.g. in personnel selection or job design) are not always adopted in organisations. This can happen if they are be based on good research and have potential to save (or make) money. He argued that work psychologists often neglect the political and social contexts of organisations. Organisational context can be defined as 'situational opportunities and constraints that affect the occurrence and meaning of organizational behaviour as well as functional relationships between variables' (Johns, 2006: 386). Context considerations (such as 'I am under pressure to make money') loom larger in managers' minds than the finer points of a psychologist's arguments concerning the technical merit of, for example, a particular personality measure. You won't often hear lay people asking questions like, 'Are you sure this measure has sufficient construct validity?', and if they do you can always refer to the Glossary of this text. Managers are likely to respond to factors such as how rival companies do things, what legislation requires and what their bosses are likely to find readily acceptable. Evidence for the effectiveness of a psychological theory or technique is often derived from quite complex, abstract research, where the social and political context in which the research was carried out is either not adequately reported or non-existent. The sorts of contextual variables Johns (2001, 2006) has in mind include an organisation's recent history, the state of the labour market (e.g. how much unemployment there is) and cultural influences on what constitutes appropriate behaviour at work.

Johns (1993) argued that if work psychologists want to influence management practice, they should also be prepared to publicly name organisations that adopt good practice, since permission to do so is usually granted, and managers are more impressed by information about named organisations than unnamed ones. Of course, the permission of the organisation involved would be needed before 'going public' with the findings. Perhaps this is one reason why articles in popular management journals have more impact within organisations than those published in psychology journals. Work psychologists should also actively seek to publish their work in managers' journals as well as academic ones. Unfortunately, many academics are not accustomed to writing for manager audiences. In addition, the reward system in academia that values publication of research in academic journals rarely gives them sufficient encouragement to do so.

In recent years work psychologists and their professional bodies have become increasingly concerned about an apparent lack of communication between those who produce new knowledge (scientists and researchers) and those who might put it to use in real workplaces (consultants and managers). It seems that researchers often believe that consultants and managers fail to make proper use of existing knowledge, preferring instead to follow

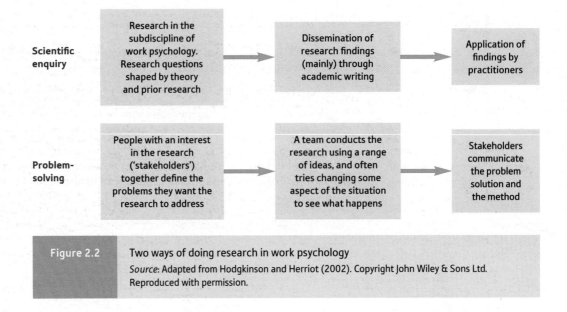

| Scientific enquiry | Research in the subdiscipline of work psychology. Research questions shaped by theory and prior research | → | Dissemination of research findings (mainly) through academic writing | → | Application of findings by practitioners |

| Problem-solving | People with an interest in the research ('stakeholders') together define the problems they want the research to address | → | A team conducts the research using a range of ideas, and often tries changing some aspect of the situation to see what happens | → | Stakeholders communicate the problem solution and the method |

Figure 2.2   Two ways of doing research in work psychology
Source: Adapted from Hodgkinson and Herriot (2002). Copyright John Wiley & Sons Ltd. Reproduced with permission.

their 'gut feeling' or established practice. Managers and consultants commonly think that researchers fail to produce information that is relevant to their day-to-day concerns, and even if they do, they fail to communicate it well. The complexity of psychological theories means that instant 'off the shelf' solutions are few and far between: knowledge and skill is often needed in order to apply theory in a useful and appropriate way.

Hodgkinson and Herriot (2002) distinguish between two ways of doing research in work psychology: scientific enquiry and problem-solving. These are shown in Figure 2.2. It can be seen that the latter involves much more engagement than the former with people in the workplace(s) being researched. However, Hodgkinson and Herriot also argue for the importance of conducting problem-solving research rigorously using careful methods and relevant theory, rather than just chatting to a few people or 'getting the feel of things'.

Much has been made of an 'academic–practitioner' divide that seems to exist in work psychology. What this is divide is, and how such a gap can be bridged, has been the subject of much debate from both sides of the divide. By now you might have formed your own views about psychology as a science. Certainly, there are some aspects of psychology that are like the 'hard sciences' (such as physics or chemistry) where variables are carefully measured and manipulated in controlled settings. Experimental studies of visual and auditory perception are examples of this. When we use psychological theory in organisations, things are generally less clear-cut. As Johns (2006) and Cox et al. (2007) argue, work psychologists often practise in fairly chaotic environments, where there are a number of different influences on what is achievable and acceptable. This leads many psychologists who come from an experimental background to question the scientific rigour of research carried out in organisational settings.

Anderson et al. (2001b) provide a useful categorisation of four types of enquiry that work psychologists might engage in. In *popularist science* the relevance of the research is very high: it addresses a pressing organisational problem. However, in the dash to solve the problem, scientific rigour is sacrificed. The latest fads in organisational research might fall into this category. There is always a risk that organisations will be drawn to practitioners of this type of science, because of its perceived relevance. Academics worry that concepts developed in this way often fail to deliver on the promises made by those who develop them. Researchers often complain that managers and consultants are far more keen on management fads (i.e. the latest popular ideas about how to do management) than on the findings of rigorous research. Academics tended at one time to be very dismissive of so-called fads such as business process re-engineering (BPR), total quality management (TQM) and emotional intelligence (EI), because they were not based on good research showing their **validity**. More recently, though, academics have become more interested in understanding how management fads start, are sustained and then fade away. There is now more acknowledgement that fads do meet some needs and concerns of managers, that they are sometimes broadly consistent with research findings and that even when they have gone out of fashion, they may well leave a lasting mark on management practices (Jackson, 2001).

In other words, the task for researchers is not to moan about fads, but to understand them. Many would add that the existence of management fads may partly be a consequence of researchers' failure to produce and communicate findings that are perceived to be useful. One possible reason for this is that theories most favoured by academics are in fact not very easy to apply. However, Miner (2003) has found that theories perceived to be valid by senior academics in organisational behaviour and strategic management also tended to be seen as usefully applicable in work organisations. This suggests that, at least to some extent, academics do indeed see good theory as linking with good practice. Miner sees this as a positive trend, and one that is considerably more evident now than when he conducted a rather similar study 20 years earlier.

More recently the term **evidence-based management (EBMgt)** has been used to describe better how theory and practice can be connected. There remains some debate about the precise nature of EBMgt and what it entails, but it is certainly more than just knowing about the latest research and then making some clumsy attempt to apply it in an organisation. Briner et al. (2009) provide an excellent summary of what EBMgt often means in practice (see Table 2.1).

Table 2.1	What is evidence-based management?
Evidence-based management is . . .	**Evidence-based management is not . . .**
Something managers and practitioners do	Something management scholars do
Something practitioners already do to some extent	A brand-new way of making decisions
About the practice of management	About conducting particular types of academic research
A family of related approaches to decision-making	A single decision-making method
A way of thinking about how to make decisions	A rigid, one-size-fits-all decision-making formula
About using different types of information	About privileging evidence from academic research
About using a wide range of different types of research evidence depending on the problem	About using only certain types of research evidence irrespective of the problem
Practitioners using research evidence as just one of several sources of information	Scholars or research evidence telling practitioners what they should do
A means of getting existing management research out to practitioners	About conducting research only about management practices
Likely to help both the process and outcome of practitioner decision-making	The solution to all management problems
About questioning ideas such as 'best practice'	About identifying and promoting 'best practice'

Source: Briner, R.B. et al. (2009) *Academy of Management Perspectives*, 23(4), 19–32

There is a lot to think about in Table 2.1 but it provides an excellent insight into some of the pitfalls that can face well-intentioned academics and practitioners alike. Put a little more simply, Briner and colleagues argue that effective decisions in organisations need to combine:

■ Evaluated good quality evidence. Research findings that have been subjected to critical review by independent experts, for example through systematic reviews of findings from numerous studies, can provide a solid evidence base for decisions. The use of results from single studies to inform practice in new settings would be especially risky.

■ The experience and judgements of practitioners who have some reliable insight into the issue being addressed.

■ Input from those likely to be affected by the decision (stakeholders), including what is important to them and what they prefer.

■ Information drawn from the organisational context, for example data held by the organisation about the issue being tackled, information about the pressures and opportunities facing the organisation and so on.

These features of EBMgt indicate clearly that no matter how knowledgeable or qualified the psychologist appears to be, they will need to work with a range of stakeholder groups if their advice and interventions are to have the best chance of success. The term scientist-practitioner is often used to describe people who integrate research and practice to good effect. Lowman's (2012) article indicates that these are people who work with important issues and measure important outcomes of their interventions. They are also good at sharing their knowledge. This sounds relatively straightforward, but as Lowman points out, 'the needs of clients do not necessarily derive from what research has chosen to study nor does the path of science always focus on practical applications' (2012: 153). Collaborative working as suggested by EBMgt might go some way to address this divergence. We return to this issue later.

Key learning point

The terms evidence-based management and scientist-practitioner emphasis the need for psychologists to not only make good use of quality research but also to connect with the various end-users of their work and other knowledgeable professionals.

At the other extreme Anderson et al. (2001b) identify two other approaches to science: *puerile science* and *pedantic science*. These forms of research have limited use because they fail to address problems that have practical relevance. Pedantic science addresses issues well enough to satisfy the hard-nosed academic through well-designed and executed research, but the results are of limited use because there are few opportunities to apply them. An excellent study about the relationship between scuba-diving experience and the performance of bee-keepers in a call centre environment might constitute pedantic science. This is an extreme (and to the best of our knowledge hypothetical) example. In puerile science the methodological rigour is poor (perhaps only one bee-keeper was studied and a poorly designed questionnaire was used) and the issue being addressed is unimportant. Fortunately, such information rarely finds its way into the work psychologist's toolkit.

The approach that many work psychologists aim for is what Anderson et al. (2001b) refer to as *pragmatic science*. This type of work addresses problems of practical importance and does so using rigorous methodology. We have tried to ensure that, where possible, the vast majority of the material cited in this text falls into this category. It refers to research that is done well, that has been subject to review and critique, and stood up to tests of its quality.

At the same time, the research is useful and relevant: it helps organisations. Linley (2006: 3) summarises the benefits of this approach:

> Good research questions have the potential to bridge the academic-practitioner divide very effectively, because they catalyse the interests, needs, and aspirations of both parties through delivering findings that are not only academically sound and valued, but that also offer practical application and advancement.

Key learning point

Pragmatic science gives us the best of both worlds: good research that has clear practical relevance.

In pragmatic science good research and practice are almost indistinguishable. Bond et al. (2008) report an excellent example of pragmatic science. They implemented an intervention designed to improve working conditions in a call centre. The study had a **control group** (that did not receive the intervention, so the effects on the group receiving the intervention could be adequately examined) and collected data over a reasonably long period of time. The study examined the impact of the intervention on issues that were important to the organisation (e.g. absence levels). From a theoretical perspective the study was also strong because it looked at how changes in perceptions of working conditions and individual differences (and the interactions between them) are linked to employee well-being.

There are many tensions that can draw researchers and practitioners away from pragmatic science and EBMgt or from the scientist-practitioner model. The vast majority of research published in academic journals is carried out by academics (written by academics for academics). One might suspect that academics do not always have an intimate understanding of the issues that are currently vexing managers and practitioners. The organisational context can also ration the opportunities for carrying out rigorous work in organisations. In intervention research it is often difficult (though not impossible) to persuade organisations to use control groups. Managers might sensibly ask why, if an intervention is likely to be effective, should it be denied to a large proportion of employees through the use of a control group? Managers might also be concerned that if there is a need for a control group, there might be some doubt as to whether the intervention is effective at all. Rigour in real-world research is more difficult to establish and maintain, meaning that talented academics also need to develop strong consultancy skills in order to carry out pragmatic research. It is also the case that ethical considerations mean that some manipulations are not possible in functioning organisations. For example, it would not be ethical to attempt the controlled manipulation of the information provided to a manager about their employees' performance because this could result in irrecoverable damage to manager–subordinate relationships. This is one of the reasons why many controlled investigations into the dynamics of performance appraisals are carried out in simulated appraisal settings (quite often using **samples** of willing undergraduate students). Of course, there is likely to be some debate as to whether such findings will be valid in the 'real world' (i.e. whether the results demonstrate *ecological validity*).

Rynes et al. (1999) have examined how research projects can have an impact on practice within work organisations. They found that the amount of time spent by the researcher on site and whether the organisation contracted the research (as opposed to simply helping a work psychologist conduct their research) both appeared to influence whether the research findings were implemented. Both of these factors are consistent with a scientist practitioner and EBMgt rather than 'scientific enquiry'. Yet there is still much work psychology research that relies upon the use of questionnaires designed using the researcher's knowledge and interests and completed by employees with minimal researcher involvement in the organisation. We should not be surprised if this research has little practical impact.

Key learning point

If work psychology is to have a substantial influence on organisational and public policy, work psychologists must get involved in the organisations they research, and address the political acceptability as well as the technical merit of their recommendations.

Finally in this section, we should note that the effective application of theory and research is rarely straightforward. It depends on many broader factors such as policy priorities, values and demographics. Two examples illustrate this well. First, Gardner (2003) points out that the finding that it is difficult to change intelligence as measured by psychometric tests (see Chapter 3) could mean that (i) it is not worth trying or (ii) we need to try extra hard and devote lots of resources to the effort. The choice depends on many factors, including what we think intelligence test scores say about an individual's behaviour and quality of life, and what value we ascribe to those potential consequences of intelligence.

The second example arises from the work of one of this text's authors (Arnold). He and colleagues conducted research for the UK Government's Department of Health, investigating why people did or did not want to work for the UK's National Health Service (NHS) as nurses, radiographers or physiotherapists. Two of the findings were as follows:

1   People who were already qualified in one of those three professions and had chosen to leave the NHS were unlikely to return.

2   After allowing for factors such as whether someone is already qualified, and their perceptions of NHS work, older people were less inclined to work for the NHS than younger people.

On the face of it, two implications for employers attempting to raise NHS staffing levels might be: do not target already-qualified people, and target younger people more than older ones. However, it is possible to draw quite different conclusions. On the first point, it can be argued that already-qualified people are quite easy to find (for example via professional associations) and do not require extensive training, so even a low success rate in attracting them back to the NHS might be a worthwhile investment. On the second point, given that the general population of the UK (like most countries) is ageing, it would be unwise to stop trying to recruit older people. Instead extra efforts and new strategies should be devised to attract older people.

Key learning point

A schematic summary of some key points of this section is shown in Figure 2.3. The formulation, conduct, output and utilisation of research in work psychology are all part of a complex process.

Research methods in work psychology

Work psychologists use a variety of techniques in their research on human behaviour, thoughts and emotions in the workplace. In considering these techniques, it is helpful to

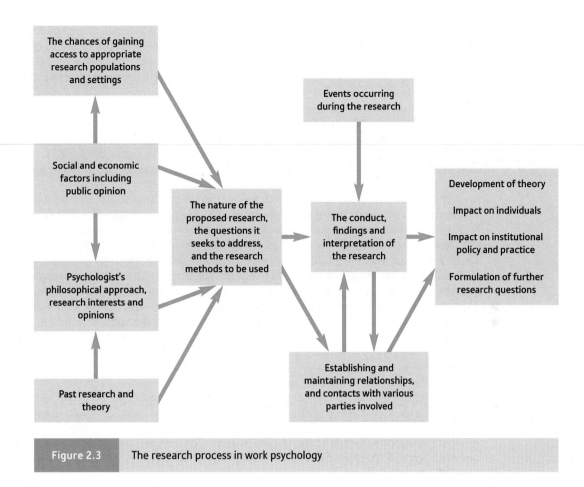

| Figure 2.3 | The research process in work psychology |

distinguish between research *designs* and research *methods*. The former concern the overall research strategy employed. This strategy depends on the researcher's beliefs about scientific investigation as well as the nature of the phenomena being researched. Research methods are the specific ways in which information is gathered within the overall research strategy. There is more than one way of carrying out each design and each method. We have included Research methods In focus sections throughout this book to give you a flavour of how a range of both designs and methods are applied in work settings. The designs are discussed later in this chapter. First, it is necessary to make a few points about each of the research methods.

Key learning point

Research design refers to the overall strategy in conducting research, whereas research methods are the procedures by which information is collected.

Questionnaires and psychometric tests

Many research projects in work psychology, especially surveys, use one or both of these. Questionnaires are often used to assess a person's attitudes, values, opinions, beliefs or experiences (see also Chapters 3 and 4). Psychometric tests are normally employed to measure ability or personality (see also Chapters 3 and 4). Questionnaires and tests normally require a person to answer a series of written questions presented on paper or on a computer screen. Answers are often multiple choice; that is, the person has to select the most appropriate response from a choice of several. This kind of questionnaire is often referred to as *structured*, because both the questions asked and the response options available to the person completing it have been predefined by the researcher. Unstructured questionnaires, where questions are broader and people respond in their own words, are much rarer. Responses are usually expressed as a number representing, for example, a person's intelligence, extroversion or job satisfaction. Some questionnaires and tests need to be administered by the researcher in person or in a tightly controlled way (such as psychometric testing). Others are designed to be self-explanatory and can be filled in by the respondent without supervision. Increasing use is being made of online administration of questionnaires and tests. Structured questionnaires are easily the most commonly used research method in work psychology. They have the advantage of providing large quantities of data with relatively little hassle for researcher or respondents. Also, the data are usually relatively easily subjected to statistical analysis. They are often used in a positivist way. This means that they may fail to reflect important aspects of respondents' experiences, and be (mis)used by the researcher as a way of getting quick and easy information rather than truly engaging with people in the setting being researched (see also the previous section of this chapter).

Interviews

A work psychologist may conduct one or more interviews, normally with an individual, but sometimes with a group of people. Group interviews are often designed to encourage discussion among interviewees about one or more topics, and are often referred to as focus groups. The work psychologist asks questions and records responses, either by making notes and/or using a voice recorder. The questions may be specified in advance, in which case it is a *structured interview*. On the other hand, the interviewer may define only the general topic they wish to investigate and permit respondents to talk about whatever they wish within that topic. This is an *unstructured interview*. Somewhere between the two extremes is a semi-structured interview: questions are designed before the interview and used to guide the discussion but the interviewer may ask follow-up probe questions or adjust the schedule in response to what the interviewee says or how they behave.

Interview data, and some forms of archival data (see below), are particularly open to alternative forms of analysis. The type of analysis that is to be carried out should be reflected in the design of the interview. Content analysis usually involves assigning interviewee responses to one or more categories or themes, according to what the interviewee said when asked a particular question. This is probably the most common way of analysing interview data in work psychology. One of the authors of this text and colleagues used this form of analysis to understand better how employees working in elderly care adapted to working more closely together in work teams (Nielsen et al., 2015). Discourse analysis and conversation analysis involve a closer look at sequences of interviewee statements, often including information about the length of pauses, voice intonation and perhaps (if videotaped) other aspects of non-verbal behaviour. The aim here would usually be to show how the interviewees are seeking to present themselves in certain ways, and/or to construct plausible accounts. The researcher might also be interested in how the normal rules of conversation are reflected (or not) in the interviewees' talk. An example of how interview data can be analysed appears later in this chapter. Grounded theory (see Lansisalmi et al., 2004) is a technique that is used to generate new theories from data. In this approach to data analysis, the researcher seeks to identify categories or concepts within qualitative data and take this a step further by examining the linkages and relationships between those categories.

Psychophysiological and psychophysical measures

Psychophysiological and psychophysical measures involve assessing a person's neurological, biological, physical or physiological state or performance. So, for example, in a study of work stress, blood samples may be taken to gauge the concentration of cortisol in a person's bloodstream. Other types of measures include muscle activity, eye movements and electrical activity in the brain (by electroencephalogram [EEG]). These methods of data collection are less common in work psychology than in some other areas of psychology. This is partly because collecting such data is invasive, and organisations and their employees are often reluctant to engage in such research. Moreover, although research of this type yields 'hard data', organisations are rarely concerned about blood cortisol levels, and much more concerned with issues such as performance, absence and turnover.

Observation

Work psychologists may observe people's behaviour by stationing themselves as unobtrusively as possible, and recording the frequency, source and timing of behaviour. This can be termed structured observation. Alternatively, work psychologists may participate in the events they are studying. For example, King (1992) investigated innovations on a hospital ward while also working as a nursing assistant. This is participant observation. Observations are often used in the development of competency frameworks for use in selection and training. Patterson et al. (2008) describe how observations of doctors were used to help choose and design appropriate selection methods and to identify the knowledge, skill and attitudes that needed to be assessed during selection. Where people are being observed in their workplace, they are normally informed, or asked about it in advance. Their awareness may itself affect their behaviour (see Chapter 1), but that is usually preferable to the alternatives of secrecy or even deception. Observation may also include observing the consequences of behaviour; for example, a person's work productivity. Silverman (2001) emphasises that observation is not simply seeing and hearing what is 'out there'. The researcher's observations will inevitably be influenced by their theoretical orientation and the focus of their research. This is not bad in itself, but needs to be acknowledged: *reflexivity* is often used to describe this process of introspection whereby the researcher analyses how their own perspectives influence on the way the data were collected and recorded. Observation without some focus or goals will in any case lead to an unmanageable amount of uninterpretable data. Clearly, a strength of observation is that it allows the researcher to form impressions of what is said and done in a workplace at first hand (without having to rely upon *potentially* biased data from employees). It also allows access to everyday mundane events, not just 'big' events, and not just the kind of summary of a person's opinions and perceptions that is usually obtained from questionnaires and interviews. One possible disadvantage of observation is that if people know they are being observed, they may behave, think or feel differently from how they otherwise would.

Key learning point

Observational data should not be interpreted as 'hard facts'. This is because employees are likely to be aware that they are being observed, and the observer will have their own perspective on what they are observing.

Diaries

People may be asked to keep a diary of key events and/or their behaviour, thoughts and feelings. It is normally necessary to give people a fair amount of structure to help them to focus their written comments, and to stay in contact with them as an encouragement to keep up the diary-filling. For example, in a study of the impact of achieving goals on people's sense of emotional well-being, Harris et al. (2003) obtained diary data from 22 call centre workers twice a day for 12 days. Most of these data consisted of workers' responses to questions about their goals and their mood – in effect, a questionnaire in diary form. Respondents were e-mailed each day to remind them to complete their diary. One important advantage of the diary method is the ability to track the detailed and fast-moving developments of people's day-to-day lives. One disadvantage is that, almost inevitably, some people on some occasions will forget to complete their diary, or simply not bother.

Experience sampling methodology (ESM) is a mixture of questionnaire and diary methods. Often ESM studies use electronic hand-held devices that are issued to participants or through smartphone applications. Typically software will trigger alarms on these devices a number of times during the day: when the alarm sounds the participant answers questions presented on the electronic device. This approach helps researchers to investigate the subtle sequential relationships between variables (for example, if a person reported feeling happy at work at lunchtime, might it be that their experiences at work in the morning offered an explanation for their happiness?). Because data collection is more 'instant', arguably less invasive and disruptive, and less affected by biases and flaws associated with human memory, the data collected may be more accurate than data collected once a day (see Daniels et al., 2009).

Archival sources

As Bryman (2001) has pointed out, archival sources are a potentially rich but sometimes neglected form of data. This is, strictly speaking, a source of data rather than a method of collecting it. Archival information is anything that exists in organised form before, during or after the work psychologist's investigation. Examples include absenteeism data, company accounts, productivity records, human resource policy documents, accident statistics, minutes of meetings and many others. Data from archival sources are most often used either to provide a context for a particular research project, or to investigate the impact of an event on the functioning of an organisation.

Archival sources are important in pragmatic science. Research that shows how interventions impact upon 'hard' organisational outcomes such as absence, performance or turnover are seen as providing good evidence to support theories and as having a direct (often monetary) benefit to organisations. Archival sources often yield **quantitative data** such as how much a workgroup has produced or how many people were promoted in a particular year. There is a temptation to view such data as being inherently free from bias and as objective criteria upon which to judge the validity of a theory or success of an intervention. However, this is not always the case. In Chapter 5 we discuss the difficulties in obtaining reliable, valid and fair objective measures of performance. Unfortunately, organisations do not always keep accurate records of absence (e.g. is someone who is 'working at home' actually absent from work?). We also know that turnover is a very complex phenomenon and extremely difficult to influence through a single intervention (see Chapter 6). The same could also be said of absence and performance data. Nonetheless, if such measures can be shown to be accurate, explaining and influencing them is often seen as the 'holy grail' of pragmatic research.

Archival methods can also produce qualitative data, which may be the main focus of a particular research study. For example, when looking at how decisions were discussed in board meetings many years ago, minutes of those meetings are an important source of data. A researcher may wish to examine what kinds of narrative structures are present in the minutes, what issues were discussed, in what order, what disagreements and conflicts arose and so on.

Research methods and philosophical stances

We noted earlier that there is a broad distinction between two kinds of research in work psychology (Easterby-Smith et al., 2002). One (easily the most common in published work psychology research) is based on the proposition that the data collected reflect (albeit imperfectly) an objective reality. This research is sometimes referred to as positivist research. The other kind is based on the assumption that most or all of what work psychologists study is best seen as *socially constructed* – that is, it reflects subjective experience that is made sense of by individuals and groups through their own thought processes and social interactions.

In work psychology, most of the first kind of research tends to use questionnaires and tests because these tend to produce the most 'ready-made' quantitative data, and because the researchers believe that they will yield data that approximate to an objectively verifiable reality. There is also some use of psychophysical and psychophysiological methods – these are quite rare in most areas of work psychology, but where they are used, they are almost always in research of the positivist kind. The other methods listed above may also be used in that kind of research, but tend not to be. Qualitative researchers tend to use interviews, observations and/or archival material, and possibly unstructured questionnaires and recorded naturally occurring conversations.

The same method may be viewed in different ways by researchers from the two traditions. It is important to note that a particular approach to science is not wedded to particular research methods. For example, a positivist researcher who uses interview data will aim to obtain facts about the interviewee's behaviour, thoughts or emotions. If there is some other information that appears to contradict what the interviewee said, or if researchers analysing the interview data do not agree on what an interviewee's response means, the validity of the data is seen as being open to question. Positivist researchers will often use qualitative methods to gather information about an issue that is poorly understood: the qualitative data will then be used to design a questionnaire so as to understand the issue better (e.g. Randall et al., 2009). For example, Nielsen, Abildgaard and Daniels (2014) used interview data to design a bespoke questionnaire to measure the demands faced by postal workers in a way that reflected the idiosyncrasies of their particular work setting. They report that this approach was better than using a standardised questionnaire as, among other things, it provided richer and more meaningful information to inform the design of interventions that were helpful to the study participants.

Non-positivist researchers, on the other hand, are more likely to treat the interviewee's talk as reflecting their authentic experiences, or as something mutually constructed in conversation with the interviewer. For example, Millward (2006) used interpretative phenomenological analysis to explore women's experiences of maternity leave through to their return to the organisation. Shepherd (2006) used an interpretative approach to explore how the implementation of technology was described in organisations as a means of understanding how such changes could be successfully implemented.

In this type of research, the existence of other information which contradicts what the interviewees said (possibly even other information from the interviewees themselves) may be seen as interesting or as inconsequential, but not usually as a problem (see Silverman, 2001: Chapter 4).

A work psychologist's research data can be obtained using questionnaires, psychometric tests, interviews, observation of behaviour, measurement of bodily activity and data routinely collected by organisations.

Research designs

The survey design

The key distinguishing feature of a **survey** is that it does not intervene in naturally occurring events, nor does it control them. It simply takes a snapshot of what is happening, usually by asking people about it. The aim is usually to gather (mostly) quantitative information about certain phenomena (for example, events, attitudes) from a large number of people. On occasions this will be done simply to ascertain the frequency of occurrence of a certain event, such as feeling anxious at work. More commonly, a survey will be used to discover the relationships of variables with each other – for example, whether anxiety at work tends to be accompanied by low job satisfaction (this does not mean that anxiety causes satisfaction, but just that the two tend to occur together).

The survey design could involve use of any of the methods described above. Most commonly these involve questionnaires. Questionnaires cannot be just thrown together (as they are in some popular magazines) if they are to do a proper job. Consistent with the positivist research philosophy, they must be carefully devised so that they unambiguously measure what they are supposed to measure – i.e. so that they are *valid* (see Chapter 4). It is important to ask the right people to participate in the survey. Ideally, the respondents should be a *representative sample* of all those people to whom the survey is relevant. Sometimes random sampling is used along with checks and balances to ensure that the random sample is representative of the group being studied. This means that everyone to whom the survey was relevant would have an equal chance of participating in it. In practice, of course, this is rarely the case.

This leads to another point: exactly what information should be collected in the survey? Questionnaires set the boundaries for the data collection: if the question is not asked, the employee cannot respond to it. What is included in the questionnaire and the way questions are worded are often driven by the researcher's interpretation of theory. The work psychologist might ask about any number of things. If we were interested in the relationship between the type of work a person did and their job satisfaction, then age, sex, work experience, educational attainment, abilities required by work, job status, supervision, friendships at work, wage levels and working conditions are just a few of the things we might ask about. There is always the possibility that some *third variable* (a factor we had not considered and measured), such as prior work experience, determined *both* a person's job satisfaction *and* the kind of work he or she did. Unless we knew about their prior experience, we could not examine its importance.

Thus the survey has both advantages and disadvantages (see Bryman, 2001). It can be used with people directly involved in the issues to be investigated. It can investigate their experiences in their day-to-day setting. It is normally fairly easy to conduct, and makes relatively low demands on people's time. On the other hand, the survey does not involve any manipulation of the variables being investigated. This makes it very difficult to establish cause and effect. The survey takes the world as it is – often a 'snapshot'. The world is complicated, and unless the survey takes all relevant factors into account, it may lead the psychologist to draw incorrect conclusions. Various sophisticated data analysis techniques (see later in this chapter, especially the section on regressions and the description of **structural** equation modelling) can reduce this danger, but not eliminate it entirely. Having said all of that, surveys often provide a good jumping off point for further research. They provide quick tests of relationships between variables that can then be examined more rigorously with more complex research designs.

Key learning point

Surveys are relatively easy to conduct and they investigate the real world in which people work. However, it is often difficult to be sure about causes and effects.

Longitudinal surveys can provide some insight into cause and effect relationships. In a longitudinal survey, data are gathered on more than one occasion. This contrasts with *cross-sectional* surveys, where data are collected on one occasion only. Longitudinal data can help to tease out possible causal connections for further investigation. Conditions pertaining at time 1 may cause those at time 2 but not, presumably, vice versa. Again, though, there remains the danger of key information not being collected. Also, even if event A happens before event B, that does not necessarily mean that A *causes* B, just that it happens first: our research design would also need to gather data on other possible causes of B and examine their effects.

Sometimes survey research involves collection of information from sources other than the people concerned (for example, archival data from the personnel records of a company), but often *all* the data consist of people's *self-reports* of their behaviour, thoughts and/or emotions. These may not be accurate or complete, and in any case the questions asked of respondents may not reflect what matters most to them. Data that are entirely self-reported are also subject to a problem called common method variance, which is where the relationship between variables is artificially high simply because all of the data are obtained by the same method. For example, if we found that having lots of control at work was linked to high job satisfaction, this relationship could be partly due to the fact that the respondents responded to all questionnaire items in a similar way, rather than there being some psychological mechanism that linked control at work and job satisfaction. To avoid this problem, researchers suggest that where possible more than one source of data should be used to capture information.

Finally, survey information can be collected using interviews (see previous section). Market researchers and social researchers often conduct them. The interview is in effect often used as a talking questionnaire. It can also be employed to explore issues with respondents in more depth than a questionnaire allows. Conducting research interviews is a skilled business. From a positivist point of view, care must be taken to gain the trust of the respondent, to explore issues to the extent required and to avoid accidentally influencing the respondent's answers. All these are in order to maximise the accuracy of the data and reflect the true state of affairs. Of course, work psychologists who are not sympathetic to positivist research would say that there is no absolute truth out there to find, and that while establishing a good relationship with the interviewee might be ethically desirable, it inevitably influences what is said in the interview.

The experimental design

One key advantage of an experiment is that it allows the psychologist *control* over what happens and rules out alternative explanations for the research findings. This in turn permits inference about causes and effects. On the other hand, there are some disadvantages too. These are discussed below, but first let us examine a concrete example.

The most controlled environment is the psychologist's laboratory. For example, the psychologist might set up a conveyor belt in the laboratory. They would probably choose a task typical of conveyor belt work – perhaps checking that boxes of chocolates have been properly packed. The boxes travel along the conveyor belt at a set speed, and the worker has to remove any faultily packed ones. People might be asked to work on this task for a period of several weeks, and to indicate their job satisfaction at various points during that period.

All of this would, of course, cost a lot of money. A large research grant would be required. The psychologist would probably also take the opportunity to record other things apart from job satisfaction, such as work performance (proportion of incorrectly packed boxes identified) and perhaps some physiological measures of stress (e.g. heart rate, blood cholesterol levels).

This would not be enough on its own. It would also be necessary to include a *control group* as well as the *experimental group* already described. People in the control group should as far as possible do the same job as the experimental group, except that their task would not be machine-paced. Hence, the control group would perhaps be given piles of boxes of chocolates, and instructed to check them. Data on job satisfaction, etc. would be collected from members of the control group in the same way and at the same times as from the experimental group.

The work psychologist would try to ensure that the conditions experienced by the experimental and control groups differed *only* in whether or not their task was machine-paced. The two groups have the same task. They perform it in the same laboratory (though the groups may not see each other or even be aware of each other's existence). They can be paid the same amount with the same pay rules, and be supervised in the same way, though the difference between paced and non-paced work may make these last two similarities difficult to achieve in practice. The groups can be given the same opportunities (or lack of them) for interaction with other workers. It would not be easy to ensure that the two groups did the same *amount* of work. The control group could be told that they had to check the same number of boxes per day or week as the experimental group. This would introduce some degree of pacing, though not nearly as much as a conveyor belt running at a constant speed.

Two key terms in experimental jargon are as follows. The independent variable is what the psychologist manipulates in order to examine its effect on the dependent variable. In this example, therefore, the independent variable is whether or not the work is machine-paced, and a dependent variable is job satisfaction. More complex experiments often have more than one independent variable (in the example above we might also adjust the volume of work to examine its effects), and more than one dependent variable (in the example above we could look at job satisfaction, self-reported well-being, blood pressure, etc.).

Another important point concerns the people who undertake the work for the sake of the experiment (the *participants*). Ideally, they would be typical of people who do that kind of work. If so, this would increase the confidence with which experimental results could be applied to the 'real world'. An attempt to recruit such people to the experiment could be made by advertising online or in local newspapers. This might not be successful, however. Since most researchers work in higher education, they would be tempted to recruit students because they are easy to find – and they usually need the money or course credits that often follow in return for participation in experiments! But because students are unlikely to work at conveyor belts for much of their careers, their reactions in the experiment might not be typical of those who do. Whoever participates in the experiment, individuals would normally be *assigned at random* to either the experimental group or the control group. This random assignment helps to ensure that the people in the two groups do not differ in systematic ways.

It should now be clear that the laboratory experiment allows the psychologist to make unambiguous inferences about the effects on job satisfaction of machine-paced work. Or does it? The psychologist's control necessarily makes it an artificial situation because the real world is rarely so neat and tidy. Unless the psychologist indulges in a huge (and unethical) deception, the experimental participants will know that they are not in a real job, and that the experiment will last only a few weeks. This could crucially affect their reactions to the work. So could the guesses they make about what the psychologist is investigating. These guesses will be influenced by unintentional cues from the experimenter via (for example) tone of voice and body posture. Such cues are termed demand characteristics. Every experiment has them. In running experiments something is gained – control – but something is lost – realism. Arguments rage over the use of experimental approaches to investigate organisational phenomena. Some argue that it is only by finding out things in controlled settings first that one can begin to study them in more applied settings. Others argue that the experimental situation produces results that wouldn't be discovered in the 'real world' because they do not exist there.

Key learning point

Laboratory experiments allow the work psychologist to control and manipulate the situation in order to establish whether there are causal relationships between variables, but it is often not clear whether the same relationships would occur outside of laboratory situations.

Sometimes it is possible to conduct a *field experiment* instead. *Quasi-experiments* (see Cook and Campbell, 1979) of varying degrees of sophistication are often used in work psychology. For a work psychologist these experiments would take place in a real work setting, probably with the people who worked there. Such experiments rarely have 'perfect' designs. Even if managers and union officials at a factory were prepared to allow the psychologist to create an experimental and control group on the factory floor, they would probably not allow random assignment of subjects to groups. Also, they probably could not arrange things such as identical supervision and identical opportunities to interact with co-workers, even if they wanted to. And even if they did, it would be unlikely that the researcher could maintain control over these things throughout the whole study.

Occasionally, it is possible for psychologists to conduct a field experiment using events that are occurring anyway. This is sometimes called a *natural experiment*. For example, some groups may engage in interventions to improve their working conditions while other groups who will get the intervention some time later act as a 'waiting list' control. For example, a chocolate factory may be changing some, but not all, of its chocolate inspection from self-paced work to conveyor belts (see Kemp et al., 1983, for a rather similar situation). The psychologist could use this profitably, especially if they were able to obtain data on job satisfaction, etc. both before and after the change was made. Here again, though, the gain in realism is balanced by a loss of control and the consequent presence of confounding factors. For example, the people working at the factory might have some choice of which form of work they undertook. This immediately violates the principle of random allocation to groups. On the other hand, one might argue that if this is the way the world works, there is nothing to be gained by trying to arrange conditions that do not reflect it. Random allocation of established groups of employees to interventions is sometimes possible (e.g. department A gets the intervention while department B does not).

Key learning point

It is occasionally possible to conduct experiments in real-world settings, though usually the work psychologist has far less control over the situation than in laboratory experiments.

Evaluating interventions

One of the key aims of work psychologists as a scientist-practitioner or as a pragmatic scientist is to make a difference in organisations (as well, of course, as coming up with interesting and exciting new theories). **Quasi-experimental research designs** are often used to help us identify whether an intervention works or not. For example, we might be interested in whether training employees to use a new piece of equipment helped them to develop more knowledge about how that piece of equipment worked. The simplest solution would be to train all employees and to see if their knowledge changed (i.e. to measure knowledge before the training, and then again after the training).

Could we be sure that it was the training that had an effect? Could it be that by just working with the new equipment their knowledge had developed? What if completing the knowledge test before the training sparked some employees' interest and they went to do some of their own research about the new equipment, and it was this that helped them to develop new knowledge?

Research designs of varying degrees of sophistication are used to evaluate interventions, and as a general rule of thumb, the more sophisticated the design, the more alternative explanations for change are tested. Table 2.2 shows some of the designs available to researchers.

A very strong design for organisational interventions is known as the **Solomon four-group design** as shown in Table 2.2. This design is the 'gold standard' in quasi-experimental research. It is well known that the process of being observed can impact on intervention outcomes (see Chapter 1). The Solomon four-group design can identify whether this is occurring.

Table 2.2	Some research designs for the evaluation of interventions		
Pre–post single intervention group, no control group design			
	Measure before intervention?	**Intervention delivered?**	**Measure after intervention?**
Group 1	Yes	Yes	Yes
Pre–post single control group intervention design (for an example see Bond et al., 2008)			
	Measure before intervention?	**Intervention delivered?**	**Measure after intervention?**
Group 1	Yes	Yes	Yes
Group 2	Yes	No	Yes
Solomon four-group design (for an example see Jackson, 1983)			
	Measure before intervention?	**Intervention delivered?**	**Measure after intervention?**
Group 1	Yes	Yes	Yes
Group 2	Yes	No	Yes
Group 3	No	Yes	Yes
Group 4	No	No	Yes

If there are changes that occur independent of the impact of the intervention, repeated tests without intervention (Group 2) will show significant change over time. If measuring before the intervention was having an effect then the after-intervention measure for Group 2 would be different from the after-intervention scores for Group 4 (no pre-intervention measure). By the same logic, pre-testing would also be having an impact if the after-intervention scores for Group 3 were different from the after-intervention scores for Group 1 (i.e. the change was biggest in an intervention group that had been measured before the intervention).

Clearly, establishing such a design requires a considerable degree of goodwill and flexibility on the part of the client organisation and a favourable organisational context. The rarity of this design in intervention research shows how infrequently such opportunities present themselves to researchers. As a result, in our view students should not be critical of organisational research that does not follow this design.

The simple pre–post design without a control group (see Table 2.2) is used often. Unfortunately, the lack of a control group means that it is not possible to rule out alternative explanations for change without gathering more data (Cook and Campbell, 1979). Studies that use a single control group are, in many cases, the most complex that can be achieved. Fortunately, such studies can still be extremely informative since data analysis techniques and the measurement of a range of variables allow for some alternative explanations for change to be tested. In the training example mentioned above, if we only have one control group we might gather additional data about whether employees had previous experience of the equipment they were being trained on and we might also investigate whether variables such as self-confidence were related to training outcomes.

One often-cited criticism of the use of quasi-experiments to evaluate organisational interventions is that they focus on measuring what changes, at the expense of looking at why something changed (Griffiths, 1999; Randall et al., 2005). This is especially problematical if an intervention fails because we don't know whether (i) the intervention is useless or (ii) the intervention is fine, it's just that it was poorly implemented. Returning to our earlier example, the training might fail because the trainer delivered the course in a very bland and uninteresting way. Cook and Shadish (1994) point out that if we are interested in why interventions work or fail then we need to gather more data about the *processes* of change (e.g. we might collect some data about what the trainees thought of the trainer's style of delivery and the course content). This might involve the use of a range of data collection methods, but qualitative methods have often been used to carry out process evaluation. Qualitative methods offer a flexibility and breadth of data collection that can be useful when the researcher is not sure what process factors might have influenced intervention outcomes (Randall et al., 2007). A more detailed discussion of process evaluation in relation to stress management interventions can be found in Chapter 10.

Key learning point

Quasi-experiments can be used to evaluate interventions in the workplace. These focus on the outcomes of change so additional data collection and analysis are often needed to examine the processes of change.

Qualitative design

Both surveys and experiments normally express data using numbers (i.e. quantitatively). They allow the people participating in the research little chance to express their opinions in their own words, since the work psychologist investigates a limited number of variables of their own choice, selected in advance. Hence surveys and experiments do not obtain a detailed picture of any individual's world. They both involve the psychologist in a fairly detached, quasi-scientific role, and tend to reflect the positivist research philosophy described earlier. As discussed later in this chapter, the strength of findings from quantitative research is usually governed to some extent by the number of research participants. It is generally agreed that qualitative methods produce more data per participant than quantitative methods, and that smaller samples of participants support rigorous data analysis. This is not just of theoretical concern: small organisations may not be able to make use of methods that rely upon huge participant samples.

Qualitative research often (though not always) involves a much greater emphasis on seeing the world from the point of view of the people who participate in it (Cassell and Symon, 2004). That is, it tends to more often reflect the phenomenological research philosophy described earlier. This normally means collecting detailed information using observation and/or unstructured interviews from a fairly small number of individuals or organisations – perhaps only one. This information is intended to paint a picture rather than measure a limited number of specific phenomena. Therefore, rather than *testing hypotheses*, qualitative methods deal with *research questions*. Drawing on Gubrium and Holstein (1997), Silverman (2001: 38–9) has identified four kinds of qualitative research:

1   *Naturalism*: The emphasis is on observing what goes on in real-life settings. This tends to produce rich descriptions of behaviour and events, but little insight into how those things are understood by the people involved.

2   *Ethnomethodology*: Focuses on a close analysis of interactions between people and how these maintain and reflect social order. This can show how social groups and cultures work, but runs the risk of neglecting the role of broader contextual factors such as economic conditions.

3   *Emotionalism*: Here the primary interest is in establishing a close rapport with the people being researched, and finding out about their experiences and feelings. This differs from the previous two categories in giving priority to people's personal opinions, rather than the researcher's frame of reference, but runs the risk of overemphasising emotion.

4   *Postmodernism*: Rejects the notion that there is an objective truth, focusing instead on how people portray themselves and their contexts in order to achieve personal goals and/or affirm their sense of identity.

Rather than testing a pre-specified theory, a work psychologist who conducts qualitative research may well begin the research with some loose theoretical ideas, and then develop and perhaps later test theory in the light of the data obtained during the course of the research. Data collection should also be influenced by developing theoretical ideas as the research proceeds (as in *grounded theory*).

Returning to our earlier example, a work psychologist engaging in qualitative research would most likely be interested in how people working on paced and/or unpaced inspection of boxes of chocolates made sense of their situation, and how they coped with it. The psychologist might work on the task as a participant observer, and might also interview individuals or groups about it.

Key learning point

Qualitative research often involves an attempt to describe and analyse how individuals make sense of the situations they are in. The focus may be on behaviour, social interaction, personal experience or self-presentation.

Qualitative research usually produces a large amount of data, which requires some editing and interpretation by the researcher. It is time-consuming and difficult to carry out. Even obtaining the necessary access to people in their workplace can prove impossible. It leaves researchers vulnerable to the accusation that they have simply discovered in the data what they expected to find. Because this research is usually conducted with relatively small numbers of people, it is often not clear whether the findings would be repeated with a bigger, different sample. These are some of the reasons why there are relatively few articles reporting qualitative research in leading work psychology journals. On the other hand, many qualitative researchers reject positivist criteria for evaluating research (such as generalisability and objectivity). They argue that the results of qualitative research are often intended to resonate with others in similar situations (rather than to generalise in the traditional scientific sense of the word). They point out that qualitative work has the advantages already outlined in this section. It is becoming more popular as dissatisfaction with the shortcomings of surveys and experiments slowly grows.

There is a wide variety of qualitative research methods. Cassell and Symon's (2004) text provides an excellent description of many such techniques, including 'worked examples'. Some have already been mentioned. Other techniques include:

■ Case study research, which involves the collection of data from a number of teams, organisations or individuals in order to better understand how the research context influences the research findings. Case studies can be aggregated in order to identify some of the general findings that apply across different research settings.

■ Ethnography where the researcher participates in the research setting in order to collect data that reflect the meaning of events, behaviours or activities in the research setting (rather than the meaning that might be attached to things by some 'detatched' observer). For example, one of the authors of this text spent some time with various sewage workers in order to better understand their working conditions (and who said the work psychologist's life wasn't very glamorous?).

■ Repertory grid technique, which is sometimes used to identify the knowledge, skills and competencies of effective (and ineffective) employees in job analysis (see Chapter 4).

■ Attributional coding, which can be used, for example, to analyse how people describe the causes of the events that occur in their working lives (see Chapters 3 and 10).

By far the most commonly used technique is the qualitative interview and this is discussed in some detail later in this chapter.

Action research design

Lewin (1946) coined the term action research to describe research where the researcher and the people being researched participate jointly in it. Action research is intended both to solve immediate problems for the people collaborating with the researcher, and to add to general knowledge about the topic being researched. It involves not only diagnosing and investigating a particular problem, but also making changes in a work organisation on the basis of research findings, and evaluating the impact of those changes. Increasingly, it also involves the development of an organisation's capacity to solve problems without external help in the future (Eden and Chisholm, 1993).

Action research can involve any of the research methods described earlier but, like qualitative research, is most likely to use interviews and participant observation (see Meyer, 2001). Much more than other research designs, it focuses on a specific problem in an organisation and what to do about it. It abandons the detachment of survey and experimental designs. Like qualitative research, it seeks to examine how people participating in the research see things, and it usually covers fairly long periods of time. Unlike much qualitative research, it involves attempting to solve a problem, and monitoring the success of that attempt.

From the point of view of the researcher, action research can be exciting, difficult and unpredictable. Because of its problem orientation, it requires close involvement with an organisation. This in turn requires careful **negotiation** and renegotiation of the researcher's role in the organisation, particularly concerning who in the organisation (if anyone) the researcher is 'working for'. Also, people in the organisation may reject the researcher's recommendations for dealing with a problem. This creates obvious difficulties for the evaluation of attempts to deal with the problem, though the researcher may be permitted to evaluate the success of any alternative strategy produced by organisation members. In action research, therefore, the process of conducting the research can become as much a focus of interest as the problem it was originally designed to address.

Key learning point

In action research, the psychologist and the people involved in the situation being researched work together to define the aims of the research and solve practical problems.

Mixed methods approaches

An increasing amount of research in work psychology is beginning to draw upon a number of methods used in combination, or sequence, to strengthen research designs. This **mixed methods** approach is used to make the best of both worlds, drawing on the advantages of a number of different techniques to offset the disadvantages of each. It is common that this 'mixing' refers to the use of both qualitative and quantitative methods in the same study. Bryman (2006: 105, citing Greene et al., 1989) describes a number of ways this can be done and the benefits of each:

1 *Triangulation*: Convergence, corroboration, correspondence or results from different methods.

2 *Complementarity*: 'Seeks elaboration, enhancement, illustration, clarification of the results from one method with the results from another' (Greene et al., 1989: 259).

3 *Development*: 'Seeks to use the results from one method to help develop or inform the other method, where development is broadly construed to include sampling and implementation, as well as measurement decisions' (Greene et al., 1989: 259).

4 *Initiation*: 'Seeks the discovery of paradox and contradiction, new perspectives of [sic] frameworks, the recasting of questions or results from one method with questions or results from the other method' (Greene et al., 1989: 259).

5 *Expansion*: 'Seeks to extend the breadth and range of enquiry by using different methods for different inquiry components' (Greene et al., 1989: 259).

Key principles in hypothesis testing using quantitative data

Much research in work psychology, particularly in the positivist tradition, examines one or both of the following questions:

■ Do two or more groups of people differ from each other?

■ Do two or more variables *covary* (that is, go together, or are related to each other) within a particular group of people? Often we test linear relationships (e.g. as one thing goes up so does the other), although as you will see throughout this text, relationships between variables are often not quite as simple as that.

Work psychologists ask these questions because the answers to them enhance our understanding of human behaviour in the workplace. For example, a researcher might be interested in the relationship between machine-paced work and job satisfaction. They would obtain job satisfaction data from each individual within the experimental group (which experienced machine-paced work) and the control group (which experienced self-paced work). Clearly, to establish the effect of machine-pacing on job satisfaction, it is necessary to compare the job satisfaction scores of the two groups. This could be done using a statistical technique called a *t*-test (which is described later in this chapter).

To move on to the second question, a psychologist might conduct a survey in order to establish whether or not people's age is associated with the amount of job satisfaction they experience. It would be possible to divide people into age-groups (e.g. 20–29, 30–39, etc.) and compare pairs of groups. But this would lose information about people's ages – for example, 29-year-olds would be lumped together with 20-year-olds (variance, as discussed later in this chapter, would be lost). Also, the age groupings would be arbitrarily defined. It would be better to see whether age and job satisfaction go together by means of a correlation. This essentially plots each person's age against their job satisfaction on a graph, and assesses the extent to which as age increases, job satisfaction either increases or decreases age is connected to reported job satisfaction. Correlation is discussed further below.

Key learning point

Work psychologists use statistics to assess whether two or more groups of people differ psychologically in some way, or whether two or more aspects of people's psychological functioning tend to go together.

Psychologists often test *hypotheses* in their research. An important concept here is the null hypothesis (H_0). Essentially, this is the hypothesis that there is 'nothing going on' (or at least what the researcher predicted would happen, did not happen!). Thus, if a psychologist is investigating whether two or more groups differ in their job satisfaction, the null hypothesis would be that they do not. If the psychologist is investigating whether age and job satisfaction tend to go together, the null hypothesis would be that they do not. That is, knowing someone's age would tell you nothing about their level of job satisfaction, and vice versa. Trying to break a theory by testing alternative explanations for observations is sometimes referred to as *falsification*. The well-known philosopher of science Karl Popper argued that science advances better if researchers focus their efforts on looking for the limits of their theories instead of seeking ever more confirmatory evidence.

In each case, we can also make an *alternative* or experimental hypothesis (H_1). This can either be directional or non-directional. For example, a directional alternative hypothesis would specify whether people doing machine-paced work would experience higher or lower job satisfaction than those doing self-paced work, or whether job satisfaction increases or decreases as age increases. Non-directional hypotheses would be less specific. They would simply state that there was a difference between groups in levels of job satisfaction (but not which group was higher) or that age and job satisfaction do go together (but not whether older people are more satisfied or less satisfied).

Hypotheses refer to the *population(s)* from which the sample(s) of people who participate in research are drawn. They do *not* refer to those samples alone. In essence, then, when doing research, a psychologist is asking: 'Given the data I have obtained from my research sample, is the null hypothesis or the alternative hypothesis more likely to be true for the population as a whole?' Note that 'population' does not mean everyone in the whole world, or even in a particular country. It should refer to those people to whom the psychologist wishes to generalise the results. This might be, for example, 'production line workers in Denmark' or 'people currently employed in the Netherlands'.

Interestingly, researchers are sometimes not very specific concerning what population they wish to draw conclusions about. Also, they sometimes use *samples of convenience* – that is, people they can get data from easily. Ideally, from a statistical point of view, those who participate in the research should be a random sample of the population of interest (see 'The survey design' section earlier in this chapter). Surveys may involve questionnaires being sent to a random sample of people from a given population, but of course not everybody replies. One inevitably wonders whether responders differ in important ways from non-responders. Responders may, for example, be more conscientious/conforming, or simply have more time on their hands: sometimes researchers attempt to test whether there is any systematic bias underpinning failure to respond.

Therefore, rather than attempting to obtain a random sample, it is more common for researchers to try to show that their inevitably non-random sample is reasonably *representative* (for example in age, sex, type of employment, location) of the population as a whole. Even when random sampling is used the researcher needs to check that the sample obtained is representative. Put another way, the proportions of people of each age, sex and so on among those participating in the research should not differ much from those in the wider population. But it is still possible that participants differ from non-participants in other respects, including those of interest in the research. So, for example, it may be that people high on the conscientiousness dimension of personality are more likely to respond than others. This obviously matters if, for example, the research concerns overall levels of conscientiousness in the population.

Statistical analysis of data in work psychology most often involves assessment of *the probability of accepting the alternative hypothesis when the null hypothesis is in fact true for the population*. The lower this probability, the more confident the psychologist can be that the alternative hypothesis can be accepted, and the null hypothesis can be rejected. This probability is also called statistical significance – a crucial concept in psychology. Typically, psychologists are not prepared to accept the alternative hypothesis (thus rejecting the null hypothesis) unless there is only a probability of 0.05 (a 5 per cent or 1 in 20 chance) or less that the null hypothesis is true, given the data the psychologist has collected. Erroneously rejecting the null hypothesis is sometimes called type I error.

Key learning point

The concept of statistical significance refers to the probability of the null hypothesis being true, given the data obtained.

The psychologist is therefore saying, 'I must be at least 95 per cent sure that I can reject the null hypothesis before I am prepared actually to do so.' This might be considered pretty conservative – perhaps *too* conservative. After all, how many of us wait until we are 95 per cent certain of something before we act on the basis of it in our day-to-day lives? Would 94 per cent certainty then not be enough? There is also the other side of the coin, less often considered by psychologists: the probability of accepting the null hypothesis when the alternative hypothesis is in fact true. Erroneously accepting the null hypothesis is sometimes called type II error (in other words, concluding something is not significant when in fact it is).

If the psychologist finds that, on the basis of their data, there is less than a 0.05 (i.e. 1 in 20) chance of mistakenly rejecting the null hypothesis, they will usually declare that the result is *statistically significant at the 0.05 level*. If the probability is less than 0.01 (i.e. 1 in 100), the result is *statistically significant at the 0.01 level*. A similar rule applies for a probability of 0.001 (1 in 1000). These are, of course, arbitrary cut-off points but many make the mistake of interpreting them as absolute thresholds. For example, some are quick to dismiss something significant at the 0.06 level because it does not meet the 0.05 'cut-off'. Many interesting results have probably been missed in this way. Basically, the lower the probability, the more confident the psychologist is in rejecting the null hypothesis. Notice also that the lower the probability, the more 'highly statistically significant' the result is said to be.

Something you need to remember when looking at any piece of research is that a highly statistically significant finding does not necessarily imply that a big effect is occurring (Smith and Morris, 2015). Highly significant findings can translate into very small effect sizes, particularly when the sample size is very large. For example, there is considerable debate about the significance of the link between personality and performance. In general, statistically significant effects have been found in sophisticated studies of large groups of people. However, debate rages about whether these are large enough to make any meaningful difference to work performance – especially since other significant predictors such as intelligence show both significant and large effects. Effect size is considered in more detail later in this chapter.

As an aside (albeit quite an important one) there is another less well-known error to be aware of. The type III error can occur in intervention research. When interventions fail it is easy to conclude that the intervention is ineffective. However, the intervention might not have been implemented as it should have been, or something about the organisational context might have prevented it from working as it should. Erroneously concluding that an intervention is ineffective when there are other explanations for a lack of change is a type III error. This is discussed further in Chapter 10.

But how do psychologists calculate statistical significance given their research data? They use one or more techniques referred to collectively as *statistical tests* of the data. We now briefly examine some of these in general terms. Doing worked examples with a calculator is an excellent way of understanding the principles of statistical testing – but it can be tedious! There are several commercially available software packages for conducting statistical analyses, and normally these are used. The most commonly used is called SPSS – the Statistical Package for the Social Sciences.

Some common statistical tests

In this section we look at some of the most common tests used in work psychology. They are discussed briefly here in order that you may gain an understanding of their purpose. We begin by examining the *t*-test in some detail: not because it is the most important test, but because it helps us to describe the principles that apply across a range of statistical tests.

The *t*-test

Suppose for a moment that a psychologist is interested in seeing whether production managers are more or less numerate than accountants. They administer a test of numeracy to (say) 20 of each and obtain a mean score of 25 for the production managers and 30 for the accountants. Clearly, the accountants score higher on average, but what other information is required before deciding whether to accept or reject the null hypothesis that the populations of production managers and accountants do not differ in their numeracy? No measure of ability is 100 per cent accurate, so we need to know if there is enough 'clear blue water' between the two scores so that we can be more comfortable that other factors (such as errors in the measures used) do not account for all of the difference between scores. Typically, in order to assess whether two mean scores show a statistically significant difference, psychologists use a *t*-test.

First, we need to consider whether the difference between sample means is large relative to the overall range of scores. After all, if scores in the sample ranged from 10 to 50, a difference of 5 between the two means might not mean very much. However, if scores ranged only from (say) 20 to 35 that difference of 5 might seem quite large in comparison.

The most commonly used numerical measure of the spread of scores is the standard deviation. The bigger the standard deviation, the more variable the individual scores are. The standard deviation is a function of the differences between each individual score and the overall mean score, and of the sample size. Hence if all scores were exactly the same as the mean, the standard deviation would be zero because there would be no differences between individual scores and the mean. This would mean there was not much spread in the data. Apart from this exceptional case, we can normally expect much more spread than this: about 68 per cent of all individual scores to be within one standard deviation either side of the mean (as one might expect on a lot of measures, most people are about average). About 96 per cent of scores are within two standard deviations of the mean.

Sample size is also important in evaluating the significance of a difference between two means. Suppose for a moment that the null hypothesis was in fact true. If a psychologist repeatedly took samples of 20 production managers and 20 accountants, they would *on average* expect their mean scores to be equal, but of course in small samples it takes only one or two exceptional scores to make quite a big difference between the two group means. Thus, although on average the mean scores for the samples should be equal, in some samples there could be quite big differences. If the psychologist repeatedly took bigger samples (say 100 production managers and accountants), then the influence of a few extreme scores would be more diluted. If the null hypothesis was in fact true, we would again expect the difference between the two group means to be zero, but this time there would be less variation from that figure between samples.

So, to evaluate the statistical significance of a difference between two mean scores in a research study, we need to consider not only the magnitude of that difference, but also the *standard deviation* and the *sample size*. For any given difference between means, the smaller the standard deviation, and the larger the sample size, the more likely it is that the psychologist could reject the null hypothesis. The result of the number-crunching behind the *t*-test is a single number (the bigger it is the more likely it is to be significant).

Key learning point

The *t*-test assesses the significance of a difference between two group mean scores, taking into account the sample sizes and the amount of variation in scores within each group.

Of course, the *t*-test requires that the data are *quantitative*. That is, the data should reflect scores on a dimension along which people vary, not different types, or pigeonholes, into which they fall. Strictly, the data should also be such that a difference of a given number of units between two scores should reflect the same amount of difference no matter what the absolute level of the scores. So, a score of 100 should be the same amount more than 90 as 20 is more than 10. This may seem straightforward, but with many self-report measures (e.g. job satisfaction) we cannot strictly be sure whether it is the case (although in practice in work psychology we often assume that it is). Further, scores should approximate to a normal distribution (see Figure 2.4). This is a technical term for a bell-shaped distribution of scores, which peaks at the mean, and drops off at equal rates on either side of it, with that rate being linked to the standard deviation, i.e. 68 per cent of scores within one standard deviation of the mean.

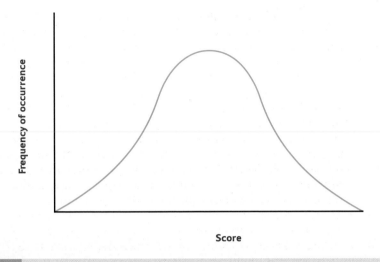

| Figure 2.4 | The normal distribution |

Fortunately, the *t*-test is not usually invalidated if the data do not approximate a normal distribution (Sawilowsky and Blair, 1992). In the jargon, it is a *robust* test. This is just as well, because the research data obtained by psychologists are often very unlike the normal distribution. Some data are not very 'spread' at all. For example, in employee performance appraisals it is common to find that almost all employees get high scores. This is not by accident because if selection and management processes are working well very able staff are selected and then trained and developed to a high standard. The *restriction of range* we find in some data makes life a little more difficult – but not impossible – for researchers. The reason for raising this issue is that many students skim over the topic of the normal distribution, thinking it to be of only statistical importance. However, it can tell us quite a lot about what is going on in work organisations.

A somewhat different version of the *t*-test can be employed if we wish to see whether the means of two sets of scores from the *same* people differ significantly. So, for example, we might be interested in assessing people's performance at a task before and after training. The formula is somewhat different, but most of the principles for this *t*-test for *related samples* are the same as those for the independent samples *t*-test described earlier.

Analysis of variance

What happens when the scores of more than two groups are to be compared? In this situation, another very common statistical test is performed – it is called analysis of variance. Essentially, it is an extension of the *t*-test procedure. The resulting statistic is called *F*, and the principles concerning statistical significance are applied to *F* in the same way as to *t* (see above). The same limitations to the use of *t* also apply to *F*. *F* can also be used instead of *t* to compare just two means.

F reflects the ratio of variation in scores between groups to variation in scores within groups. The greater the former relative to the latter, the higher the *F* value, and the more likely it is that the population means differ (i.e. there is a low probability of obtaining our results if the null hypothesis is in fact true for the population). If a statistically significant *F* value is obtained, we can reject the null hypothesis that the population means are identical. If we wish, we can then use a modified form of the *t*-test to identify which particular pair or pairs of groups differ significantly from each other.

Data from more complex research designs can be analysed using analysis of variance. Suppose, for example, the psychologist was interested in the effects of both machine-paced work *and* style of supervision on job satisfaction. They run an experiment with four groups of people. One group does machine-paced work under close supervision. Another does the same work under distant supervision. The third does self-paced work under close supervision, and the fourth performs self-paced work under distant supervision. Analysis of variance can be used to examine the statistical significance of the separate effects of each factor (pacing of work and style of supervision) on job satisfaction. It can also identify *interaction effects*. For example, the impact on job satisfaction of close versus distant supervision might be greater when work is self-paced than when it is machine-paced. This type of effect is often referred to as moderation; in this example the way work is paced moderates the relationship between job satisfaction and supervision. Given the complexity of many psychological processes, it is often important to look out for such nuanced effects.

Key learning point

The statistical technique called analysis of variance extends the principles of the *t*-test to more than two groups and can be used to identify interaction effects.

Chi-square

As indicated earlier, data are sometimes qualitative rather than quantitative. Suppose, for example, that a psychologist wishes to examine whether women are more likely or less likely than men to be unemployed. The psychologist cannot use *t* or *F* because the data are *categorical*. The psychologist is therefore interested in determining whether there is a statistically significant difference in employment status that could be linked to gender. The statistical test employed in this instance is known as **chi-square** (χ^2). The more the groups differ, the higher the chi-square figure for the data, and the less likely it is that the null hypothesis is true. As with *t* and *F*, critical values of chi-square at various levels of statistical significance can be checked in tables in most statistics texts. Unlike *t* and *F*, these critical values do not depend directly on sample size. Instead, they depend on the number of rows and columns in the data when tabulated. In the above example, the table would contain four cells altogether: 2 (gender) × 2 (employment status). The figure in each cell would be the number of participants falling into that category. The chi-square procedure compares the observed numbers with those that would be expected if the proportions reporting unemployment/employment were the same for each gender.

Key learning point

The statistical technique called chi-square is used to test differences between groups in the frequency with which group members fall into defined categories.

Correlation

The second question posed at the start of this section concerned whether two or more variables tend to go together. Correlation is commonly used in survey research. Thus, for example, a psychologist might wish to find out whether job satisfaction and intention to leave one's job are connected. Alternatively, they might be interested in seeing whether self-esteem and salary are connected. In other words, the researcher wishes to find out whether the two variables correlate (co-relate).

There are several different but similar statistical tests of correlation, each of which produces a *correlation coefficient*. The most common of these is *Pearson's product–moment correlation coefficient*, or *r* for short. Correlation coefficients cannot exceed a value of 1, and cannot be lower than –1. A Pearson's *r* of 1 would mean that when scores on the two variables of interest were plotted on a graph, a straight line could be drawn that would go through all of the plotted points (see Figure 2.5a). This line would rise from left to right, indicating that as the value of variable *A* increased, so did the value of variable *B*. This line would not need to be at any particular angle, nor would it necessarily go through the origin. An *r* of –1 would also mean that a straight line could be drawn through all of the plotted points, but this time it would slope the other way, so that as *A* increased, *B* decreased (see Figure 2.5b). An *r* of 0 would mean that there was no tendency whatever for scores on either of the two variables to rise or fall with scores on the other one (see Figure 2.5c).

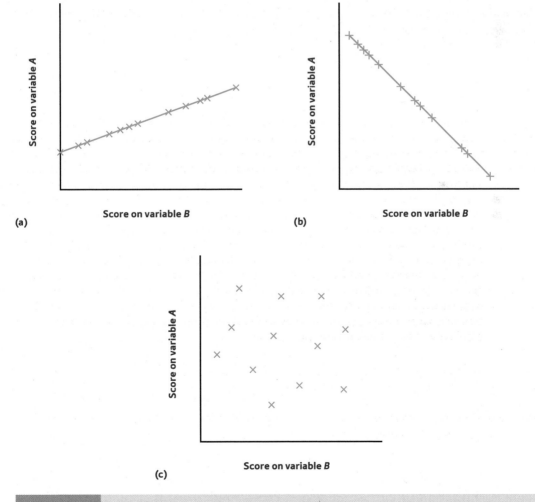

(a)	(b)
	(c)

Figure 2.5   Correlation: (a) a correlation of 1; (b) a correlation of –1; (c) a correlation of 0 (each x represents data collected from one person)

The psychologist therefore typically asks, 'Does the correlation coefficient I have obtained with my sample differ sufficiently from 0 for me to reject the null hypothesis?' Just as with other statistics, for any given sample, size dictates the point at which a correlation becomes significant. Thus, for example, with a sample size of 20, the critical value of *r* for significance at the 0.05 level is ±0.444. Corresponding values at the 0.01 and 0.001 levels are 0.590 and 0.708 (we got these values from hideously long statistical tables at the back of dusty textbooks, but most statistics software packages will do this leg work for you).

Another form of correlation is the *Spearman rank correlation (rho, ρ)*. This is used when the data do not reflect absolute scores, but only a rank order. This would mean that we know, for example, that score *x* is greater than score *y*, but not by how much. The formula for calculating *rho* looks different from that for *r*, but in fact it boils down to the same thing. *Rho* can also be useful when the data deviate a great deal from the normal distribution (see Figure 2.4) and when there are a few scores hugely different from the others.

Key learning point

The statistical technique called correlation tests the extent to which scores on two variables tend to go together (i.e. covary).

Whatever the exact correlation technique, it is important to remember the old maxim, *correlation does not imply causality* (see also the earlier section on survey design). Often, a psychologist would like to infer that the reason why two variables are correlated is that one causes the other. This may seem plausible, but it is hard to be sure. Suppose that a psychologist finds a highly significant positive correlation between self-esteem and salary. If both are measured at the same time, there is no basis on which to decide whether self-esteem causes salary or salary causes self-esteem. It is fairly easy to think of possible explanations for either causal direction. It is also possible that some other variable(s) (e.g. social status, educational attainment) cause both self-esteem and salary, but unless we have measured them, we can only speculate. There is one slight caveat to this and it applies when one of our variables is a demographic. For example if we find that age correlates with self-esteem, it would be difficult to argue that self-esteem causes age, but we would still need to be cautious because other variables that correlate with age might be the things that are driving self-esteem. A good example of the difficulties in establishing causality can be found in the research into job satisfaction (see Chapter 6).

As noted earlier in this chapter, obtaining data over time (a *longitudinal study*) can help, in so far as it may uncover whether scores on one variable at time 1 predict scores on the other at time 2, but even then, the fact that phenomenon A happens before B does not necessarily mean that A *causes* B: more evidence and good theory would be needed before such conclusions could be drawn.

Multiple regression

Just as analysis of variance is an extension of the *t*-test for more than two groups, so multiple regression is an extension of correlation for more than two variables. In other words it is a 'posh correlation'. Suppose a psychologist wishes to assess the correlation with self-esteem of each of salary, educational attainment and social status. They might well find that the latter three variables are all correlated with each other, and also with self-esteem. In this case, the psychologist might wonder which one(s) really matter in predicting self-esteem.

Multiple regression is a statistical technique that allows the social scientist to assess the *relative* importance of each of salary, educational attainment and social status as predictors of self-esteem. It involves estimation of the correlation of each of the three with self-esteem *independent of the other two* (the technique can, of course, be extended to larger numbers of variables). In this way the researcher can end up with an equation that specifies the weighting to be given to each predictor variable in predicting self-esteem, as well as an overall indication of just how predictable self-esteem is using all of the predictor variables. But note: just because variables are designated 'predictors' in multiple regression analyses, it does not mean that they are necessarily 'causes' of the variable to be predicted.

Another advantage of multiple regression is that it allows demographic variables to be included in the analysis (usually within a hierarchical multiple regression). To continue with the example given above, the social scientist might want to examine the effects of age and gender on self-esteem before considering the other variables. These demographics could then be entered in a 'block' before a second block of variables in a hierarchical regression (salary, educational attainment and social status). The social scientist could then make things even more complicated if they so wished by including a third block of variables that looked at the interactions between the variables entered in the first two blocks (for example whether social status was less of a predictor of self-esteem for older people). This type of interaction is often called a moderating effect: a moderator variable is one that alters the strength of the relationship between two other variables.

Regressions are also used to test for mediated relationships. For example, we may find that machine-paced work is linked to low job satisfaction. But is it machine-paced work per se, or the fact that machine-paced work results in fewer opportunities for the employee to exercise control at work (i.e. control at work mediates, or acts as a 'bridge', in the relationship between machine-pacing and low job satisfaction)? If we find that it is control that is mediating the relationship we might look for ways of introducing more control into the employees' work (rather than abandoning machine-paced work altogether).

Because it can test so much, multiple regression is a much-used technique in work psychology. It is quite complex. Its intricacies are beyond the scope of this book, but the interested reader can find out more by consulting Baron and Kenny (1986), Licht (1997) or Cohen *et al.* (2003). Factor analysis is also based on correlational techniques, but rather than testing relationships between variables it looks to find structures within data (e.g. it was used extensively to identify the five clusters of personality variables, the 'Big Five'). Kline (1993) provides a good description of this technique.

If regression is a posh correlation, then structural equation modelling (SEM) is positively regal. This method of data analysis has gained popularity because it enables researchers to disentangle the many different relationships between multiple variables in applied settings. Essentially it works by asking the researcher to plot what they think might be going on in the data, by specifying a model that they feel should provide an adequate explanation of the data. Statistical software then tests whether this model does indeed explain or 'fit' the data. If the fit is good then there is evidence for theories used to make the predictions. If the fit is not good enough then the theory may need to be modified. Results of SEM analysis contain lots of information but it is the path coefficients that are usually the focus of researchers' attention as these indicate the direction, strength and significance of the connections between variables (higher coefficients indicate stronger connections). SEM is also a powerful way of testing for mediating effects. For example, it has been used to identify whether the link between leadership behaviour and employee well-being is mediated by the impact that leaders have on their subordinates' working conditions.

The sophisticated analysis provided means that SEM can provide very robust results with their complexity reflecting the complex nature of workplace phenomena. This, however, does not offset any limitations associated with the study design (even if you use SEM it does not mean that you can identify cause and effect relationships from a cross-sectional study). The technique is not for the faint-hearted, but fortunately most researchers who use it provide clear explanations of the meaning of SEM results in research papers.

Other phenomena in statistical testing

Effect size

The reader may have wondered whether statistical significance is necessarily the same as significance for practical purposes. At least one behavioural science statistics text (Rosenthal and Rosnow, 1984) repeatedly reminds its readers that statistical significance depends on the size of the effect (e.g. the difference in means between two groups relative to the standard deviation; or the value of *r* for two variables) *multiplied by* the size of the study. Thus, when research uses large samples, quite small effect sizes can lead us to reject the null hypothesis – probably correctly, of course, *but* if the effect is so small, albeit detectable, are we going to worry about it? For example, a psychologist might find that, in a large sample, marketing managers score on average 58 out of 100 on a numeracy test whereas production managers score on average 59.5 out of 100, and that this difference is highly statistically significant. So what? How much does this tell us about, for example, the relative effectiveness of marketing and production managers? Clearly, although production managers do slightly better, there are many marketing managers who score higher than many production managers. One way of addressing this issue is to assess the relationship between numeracy and work performance, focusing particularly on the extra work performance one could expect given a specified increase in numeracy, and then translating this into practical benefits (see Chapter 4 concerning utility analysis).

However, it is also useful to consider effect size in more abstract terms. We can think of it as *the degree to which the null hypothesis is false*. For *t*, we can consider the difference between group means as a proportion of the standard deviation of scores (*d*) to be a measure of effect size. For *r*, we can use the proportion of variance in scores common to both variables. This is r^2. Thus, a correlation of 0.60 indicates that $0.60 \times 0.60 = 0.36$, or 36 per cent of the variance in one variable is 'accounted for' by scores in the other. With large samples, it is often possible for a correlation of only 0.2 or less to be statistically significant. In this case, the variables share just 4 per cent of variance. This sounds small, but Rosenthal and Rosnow (1984: 207–11) have demonstrated that it can nevertheless reflect practical outcomes of real importance. For example, if one form of treatment for depression is 4 per cent better than another, over a whole nation that could amount to a lot more happy people.

Key learning point

Effect size goes beyond statistical significance by assessing the magnitude of the relationship obtained, rather than how confident one can be that the relationship is not zero.

For *F*, one often-used indicator of effect size is called *eta* (η). It reflects the proportion of total score variation that is accounted for by group membership. Like r^2, *eta* can be considered an indicator of the proportion of total variance accounted for. Cohen's *d* (see below) indicates the size of the effect when differences between groups are significant. For example if we compared an intervention and a control group on their levels of well-being, and found a Cohen's *d* of 0.5 then 69 per cent of the members of the intervention group report well-being that is above the average score for the control group; with a Cohen's *d* of 1.0 this becomes 84 per cent, a bigger effect. There is *nothing* mysterious about indices of effect size. They are often quite simply derived, and are sometimes even routinely calculated on the way to a test of statistical significance.

Statistical power

Statistical power refers to the probability of rejecting the null hypothesis when it is indeed false and therefore should be rejected. It is, in other words, the probability of avoiding making a type II error. Like all probability estimates, it can vary from 0 to 1. The level of power operating in any particular research study depends on the level of statistical significance the psychologist wishes to work at, the size of the sample and the size of the effect under examination. The chief practical lesson to be learned is that small sample sizes have very low power – that is, a high probability of missing a relationship that does exist in the population from which the sample is drawn.

Cohen (1977) has produced tables that specify the sample sizes required to achieve certain levels of power for particular statistical tests at specified significance levels and effect sizes. These tables are a useful guide for researchers wondering how many participants they need for their study.

These observations about statistical power are very important. Often in research, one investigator reports a statistically significant finding with a moderate to large sample size. Then another researcher attempts to replicate the result with a smaller sample, fails to find a statistically significant effect, and declares that the original finding must have been a fluke. Close examination shows that the *effect size* in the second study is as large as the first – it is just that the smaller sample prevents statistical significance being achieved.

Key learning point

There is a high probability that small-scale studies will fail to find effects which exist in the population of interest.

Meta-analysis

Some published research articles report a **meta-analysis** of findings from a number of studies. This type of article is quite common, especially in topic areas where a lot of research has been conducted. The aim of meta-analysis is to provide an overview and summary of what general conclusions can be drawn from a body of research. Using concepts such as effect size and statistical power (see the previous section of this chapter), a researcher conducting a meta-analysis extracts (and if necessary adjusts) measures of association (usually correlation) between variables of interest from each relevant research study, and weights them according to the sample size. The technique is powerful because it focuses on looking at the average effect size and the spread of effect sizes. For example, it will show if it is common to find a big effect size or whether smaller effect sizes are more typical. This can help us to avoid the pitfalls associated with basing our practice on findings from single, possibly unrepresentative, studies.

Other information may well also be recorded – for example whether the people studied were managers or blue-collar workers, how variables of interest were measured, and whether the study was an experiment or a survey. Then the person conducting the meta-analysis is in a position to make some general statements about the extent to which two or more variables are statistically associated with each other, and whether the strength of the association depends partly on factors such as the measures used and the populations studied. For example in Chapter 11 we highlight the findings from several meta-analyses indicating that results from studies of teamwork in the laboratory differ from those found in real-life work teams.

Meta-analysis has been criticised by some as being something of a blunt instrument that cannot capture important details of how particular research studies were carried out.

There is a risk we may lose sight of some of the important contextual nuances that impact on the variables we are interested in. Imperfect studies are often excluded from the research analysed, even though these may contain interesting and important findings. Others have defended meta-analysis. Rosenthal and DiMatteo (2000) have reviewed these arguments and conclude that many of the criticisms are invalid if meta-analysis is properly conducted. An example of meta-analysis that gives some insight into its usefulness is that reported by Kivimäki and colleagues (2015) into the links between long working hours and a serious illness, the experience of a stroke (see Chapter 10). Their meta-analysis gathered up data from 25 studies from across the world containing an eye-watering total of 528,908 participants. It would be difficult if not impossible to conduct a single study of this size into such an important issue with such a diverse participant group.

Systematic reviews sometimes use meta-analysis in order to provide a commentary on the consistent and reliable findings that have emerged from a body of research. These can also be useful when there is not quite enough evidence to support a full-blown meta-analysis. In such circumstances a body of sufficiently good quality research is gathered according to stringent selection criteria (e.g. a set of minimum standards relating to the quality of research methods and study designs used). Features of each study are then coded/evaluated by experts. The links between these features and research findings can then be evaluated so that the consistent and secure findings from within the literature can be identified. Bambra et al. (2007) used this approach to identify some of the active ingredients of work redesign interventions that have been used to improve employee well-being.

Analysing qualitative data

Just as there are many techniques for analysing numerical data, so the same is also true for qualitative data. Just as statisticians sometimes disagree about which statistical techniques are appropriate in which circumstances, so qualitative researchers sometimes disagree about the best ways to analyse qualitative data. But statistical arguments are usually about technical issues, whereas disagreements over how to analyse qualitative data are more often to do with the researcher's philosophical and theoretical position. Much qualitative data analysis is conducted by hand, but here, too, there are computer packages (e.g. NVivo) available to help locate and code data according to categories nominated by the researcher.

Table 2.3 shows an extract from a research interview conducted by one of the authors of this text. The interview was one of 80 conducted by one of the authors and colleagues as part of an investigation of how lawyers and architects see their work, and in particular how they, as professionals, view management and being managed. In this extract, the interviewer (I) and respondent (R) (a lawyer working for a large firm of solicitors) discuss how the respondent's work is evaluated.

First of all, notice that this is not a highly structured interview. To some extent the interviewer follows up what the respondent says, for example when he asks, 'But it doesn't sound like you feel that way about your PDR?' A highly structured interview would not include such a specific question based on what the interviewee just said, since all or virtually all of the questions would be specified in advance. However, the interview was semi-structured rather than unstructured because there was a list of topic areas to be covered, but also scope to adjust the depth in which each was covered. Second, notice how the interviewer to some extent adopts what Silverman (2001) terms an 'emotionalist' position. This is evident in the question mentioned a few sentences back. Also, in his first question of this extract he is clearly interested in the respondent's opinion as well as trying to elicit what might be thought of as factual information about the way the respondent's work performance was evaluated. On the other hand, the interviewer also wants to use the interview to go beyond the interviewee's own experiences. This is demonstrated by his observation, 'There's a

Table 2.3	An excerpt from a research interview

A lawyer discusses assessment of work performance

Note: I = Interviewer, R = Respondent

I: How is your performance evaluated here and what do you think of that?

R: They have an annual PDR, which is Personal Development Review. You are given a form to complete a short time before and then you meet with whoever's undertaking it generally – the partner that you report to – and you sit in a room and discuss it.

I: And is that a fruitful discussion or is it going through the motions?

R: For me it was fruitful because I think the . . . the difficulty I have with these is that more senior people can see the benefit and the relevance of them. When you get down to the secretaries, they view it very, very much as a . . . almost as a disciplinary matter. It's their annual kicking from the boss because they haven't been up to standard.

I: But it doesn't sound like you feel that way about your PDR?

R: No. I think it's the only true way of finding out your own standing and seriously expressing ambitions and what you have to achieve to reach those.

I: And is it sufficiently candid and open to achieve that?

R: It was for me, yes.

I: There's a couple of indications that it might not be for everybody. Is that true? Or am I reading too much into that?

R: No, you're right. There are some people who I've been told on the quiet have reached as far as they will go, but having spoken to those individuals – not directly about their PDRs, but you know, just generally – I don't think they've actually been told that clearly.

I: Okay.

R: I think that's more a function of whoever's actually doing the PDR because I had two very forthright speakers who will tell you exactly whereas others are a little bit more political.

I: Okay. There would have been a time when having your performance assessed and working in a managed system was a bit of an insult for a professional person, but it sounds like that comes with the territory now.

R: It does. I've only had them since I've been here. It was a new concept to me. And yes, I was very nervous before it. But unless you do get some form of independent view, I don't think you're the best judge of your own performance.

couple of indications that it might not be for everybody.' That could be seen as an attempt to gain a more general picture of performance assessment in that firm, but it could also arguably be an extension of the emotionalist position because the interviewer is seeking to access indirectly the experiences of other people in the firm.

How might these data be analysed? What general statements can be made, and conclusions drawn, on the basis of data such as these? This depends heavily both on the research questions being asked (together with the theoretical and/or practical basis for considering those questions important), and on the philosophical assumptions of the researcher. Excellent coverage of the range of methods available for analysing qualitative data (including interviews) can be found in the texts by Cassell and Symon (2004) and Symon and Cassell (2012).

One way of analysing this transcript would in effect involve turning qualitative data into quantitative data. The researcher could attempt to assess how positively the interviewee felt about the firm's methods for assessing the work performance of employees, perhaps on a numerical scale. Another researcher could be asked to do the same, partly in order to check that the scoring of the interviewee's opinion about the performance assessment showed interrater reliability.

Table 2.4	An example of content analysis categories
Respondent's name: Content category	Coding option (tick as applicable)
1 Frequency of assessment	Less frequently than annual Annual More frequently than annual
2 Prior preparation	Thinking only Some written None specified
3 Who does the assessment?	Boss Other more senior person(s) Peer(s) Other

While such a scoring procedure might be useful, it would of course be a huge waste of information if that was all that was done with these data. Another approach would be to conduct a *content analysis* of what the interviewee says. Bryman (2001: 180) defines content analysis as 'an approach to the analysis of documents and texts that seeks to quantify content in terms of predetermined categories and in a systematic and replicable manner'. So in this case, the researcher might have prepared the content categories shown in Table 2.4 based on prior theory and research.

The researcher would study the interview transcript and decide, for each content category, which response option(s) were evident in what the interviewee said. Probably another researcher would do the same, in order to establish interrater reliability. Notice that agreement between raters is normally considered a sign that their 'scoring' of the interview is getting at objective truth, though it might also be argued that such agreement simply means the two raters share similar perceptions (sometimes referred to as *intersubjective agreement*).

Sometimes the categories for a content analysis are specified in advance of the data being gathered. This is consistent with the idea that the categories are 'systematic' and 'predetermined' (see the definition above). However, it is usually very difficult to anticipate the kind of responses interviewees will offer. Categories are therefore defined in some studies by the researchers doing an initial reading of interview transcripts and then devising content categories that reflect as much as possible the things the interviewees chose to focus on. Template analysis (King, 2004b) is one method whereby a predetermined set of codes can be reviewed and changed in response to the analysis of data. This can achieve a good balance between deductive reasoning (that is, deducing what types of response are important on the basis of prior theory and research) and inductive reasoning (that is, starting with the data and trying to develop theory on the basis of it). Some themes that might be recorded in this example are:

- description of personal experience of the performance assessment system;
- differences in perception between staff at different levels;
- belief that PDRs have value;
- variation in PDR process and outcome according to who conducts it;
- existence of 'off-the-record' communications about people's performance.

These themes would probably do better than a very detailed content analysis at capturing the meaning of what was said in the interview. On the other hand, the themes, in themselves, might miss some of the more precise points made.

It might also be said that thematic analysis still does not get at the complex and dynamic nature of what is going on in talk and text. Some researchers might use *discourse analysis* (Potter, 1997; Dick, 2004) to try to access this. Researchers have used several different approaches to discourse analysis. They have in common a desire to analyse in detail the versions of reality offered by a person, and their purposes in presenting themselves and their worlds in the way they do. Often this endeavour requires quite a lot of interpretation. It rests partly on subtle elements of what is said, and indeed what is not said. Some versions of discourse analysis use features such as voice intonation and the existence and length of pauses, as well as what is actually said. Researchers who use discourse analysis frequently (though not always) take the view that reality is entirely defined by people through their talk, interaction and thought (social constructionist rather than positivist). Most now consider their own interpretation of what is said to be an important factor in shaping the analysis (reflexivity).

An analysis of the discourse in Table 2.3 might lead to the following conclusions about what the interviewee is trying to do: through expressing appreciation of the PDR (some methods might note facial expressions, such as if the person smiles or nods when they mention something and attach meaning to these), they are showing themselves as loyal and believe they are valued by the firm, and who is concerned to perform well and advance his career. His depiction of himself as initially nervous about the PDR could be taken to indicate an attempt to show how the firm's benevolence had convinced a sceptic about the integrity of the performance assessment system, to the benefit of both parties. His points about how secretaries experience PDR might serve to emphasise the difference in status between them and him, yet also show his good-hearted concern for their situation. Being the recipient of 'on-the-quiet' information about the performance of others could be offered as a sign that he is well-placed in informal company social networks.

This is, of course, quite speculative and focused more on the motives and purposes that could lie behind what was said than on the content of what was said. This analysis, then, entirely avoids the kinds of conclusions that might be reached by positivist or realist researchers, particularly if a number of interviewees and not just this one come up with the same point. These conclusions might be that the PDR is experienced as disciplinary by secretaries but as developmental by lawyers, and that nevertheless PDRs still, on occasion, fail to deliver open and honest feedback. Instead, the discourse analyst draws conclusions about the broad nature of the realities offered by interviewees and about their reasons for presenting those realities in the way they do.

All of this points to interviews being a very flexible and data-rich technique. Sometimes students use them in their research because they see interviews as the 'easy option' when it would take time and effort (and lots of reading around) to identify variables of interest and source questionnaires. Many late nights spent transcribing and analysing qualitative data eventually persuade them that this is not the case. Interviews are time-consuming (but generally enjoyable) for participants, so care needs to be taken over recruitment and retention (King, 2004a).

Summary

Research designs used by work psychologists include surveys, experiments, qualitative research and action research. These designs vary in the amount of control exerted by the work psychologist, the degree of difficulty in carrying out the research, the

74 Work Psychology

role of theory and the nature of the data obtained. Perhaps most importantly, work psychologists using different designs often have different philosophical positions about the nature of knowledge and the existence (or not) of an objective reality. Research designs can be distinguished from methods of data collection. Methods include questionnaires, tests, interviews, observation, psychophysiological measures and archival sources.

Statistical techniques are available to help draw appropriate conclusions from quantitative data. Collectively, these techniques are intended to address two general situations. First, where there are comparisons between two or more groups of people (*t*-test; analysis of variance; chi-square), and second, where two or more variables are being examined within a participant group to see whether they tend to go together (correlation, multiple regression). The concept of statistical significance is important in interpreting the results produced by statistical tests. So is the notion of effect size. Techniques for analysing qualitative data are many and varied and offer a degree of flexibility that can be attractive when dealing with a number of issues in work psychology.

Test your learning

Short-answer questions

1 Briefly describe a psychological study of your own invention and specify a null hypothesis and an alternative hypothesis suitable for that study.
2 Explain the concepts of statistical significance, statistical power and effect size.
3 Explain (in one sentence) the type of data and research question to which each of the following techniques can be applied:
   - *t*-test
   - correlation
   - chi-square
   - regression
   - content analysis
   - discourse analysis.
4 Imagine that you are trying to develop a theory to explain successful performance in telephone sales work. For each box in Figure 2.1, suggest at least two possible factors.
5 List three important differences between positivist research and social constructionist research.
6 How do work psychologists tend to evaluate interventions?
7 List five methods by which work psychologists obtain research information.
8 Write a short paragraph on the differences between experimental, quasi-experimental and survey research in work psychology.
9 What is action research?
10 What are the advantages and disadvantages of the interview as a research method?

Suggested assignments

1 Choose any issue in work psychology that interests you. Examine how different research designs (both qualitative and quantitative) might be used to tackle that issue. Is any one design better than the others?
2 'It is not worth distinguishing between research designs and research methods in work psychology because the choice of research design dictates the choice of method.' Discuss why you agree or disagree with this statement.

3 Find an article in an academic work psychology journal. Check that it reports research in which some kind(s) of data were collected. Identify the underlying research philosophy (e.g. was it positivist?), the research design, methods and data analysis techniques used and discuss (i) whether these were appropriate given the research hypotheses or questions specified, and (ii) whether you think the research hypotheses/questions were appropriate.

Relevant websites

The publisher SAGE produces many books on research methods in psychology and the social sciences more generally. There are both general books about a range of methods, and specific books about one or a small number of similar methods. Check out the following address for their latest offerings: http://www.sagepub.com/ and go to the section on research methods and evaluation.

To do with the results of research more than method, the American Psychological Association (APA) publicises recent research in various fields of psychology. To see recent research on psychology, much of it applied, go to http://www.apa.org/monitor/

Statistics at Square One provides descriptions and worked examples of a variety of common statistical methods including many of those mentioned in this chapter. Although aimed at medical researchers, the examples given are clear and useful: http://www.bmj.com/about-bmj/resources-readers/publications/statistics-square-one

The colourfully titled http://www.statisticshell.com/ maintained by Andy Field is an excellent site for those a little nervous about statistics (don't let the name put you off).

If you are feeling more adventurous you might also want to visit David Kenny's site at http://davidakenny.net/index.htm, which looks at some of the more advanced methods mentioned in this chapter (such as regression and SEM).

Suggested further reading

Full details for all references are given in the list at the end of this book.

1 The book by Sylvia Shimmin and Don Wallis, *Fifty Years of Occupational Psychology in Britain* (BPS, 1994), provides a well-written description of how work psychology has evolved in the UK and the topics it focuses on. Although the historical details are of course specific to the UK context, much of the content of this book can be generalised to other countries.

2 Cathy Cassell and Gillian Symon's books *Essential Guide to Qualitative Methods in Organizational Research* (Sage, 2004) and *Qualitative Organizational Research: Core methods and current challenges* (Sage, 2012) are superb, focused introductions to a wide range of qualitative methods and how they are used in organisational research.

3 Although about management rather than work psychology, the book by Mark Easterby-Smith et al., *Management Research: An introduction,* 4th edition (Sage, 2012), gives a clear and practical guide to key issues in formulating and doing research.

4 Alan Bryman's book, *Social Research Methods* (Oxford University Press, 2001) includes detailed discussion of important conceptual and practical issues that are relevant to the way work psychologists collect and analyse data. Bryman's 2006 article 'Integrating quantitative and qualitative research: How is it done?' in *Qualitative Research* is also very useful.

5 The book by Adamantios Diamantopoulos and Bodo Schlegelmilch, *Taking the Fear out of Data Analysis* (Dryden Press, 1997), is a gentle and entertaining introduction for those who feel they are not particularly numerate but want to understand how to apply basic statistics appropriately. The examples used are not confined to psychology.

6 *Discovering Statistics Using SPSS* (Introducing Statistical Methods series) by Andy Field (Sage, 2009) is a very accessible text that shows how to understand and use the SPSS software package. It is peppered with a good amount of humour to lighten the load.

CHAPTER 3
Individual differences

LEARNING OBJECTIVES

After studying this chapter, you should be able to:

1 outline contemporary theories of human intelligence and intelligence testing;

2 compare conventional approaches to intelligence with system models;

3 describe the main theories and models of emotional intelligence;

4 describe the research evidence for emotional intelligence and how it is assessed;

5 define the 'Big Five' personality constructs;

6 describe the characteristics and behaviours associated with innovation at work;

7 discuss how innovation might be assessed;

8 describe socio-cognitive approaches to understanding behaviour at work.

Opening case study

Soft skills, hard outcomes: the effects of emotional intelligence in two international companies

In recent years, there has been an explosion of interest in the concept of emotional intelligence (EI) in both the media and academic literature. The term 'emotional intelligence' was coined by American psychologists Dr Peter Salovey and Dr John Mayer as 'a type of social intelligence that involves the ability to monitor one's own and others' emotions, to discriminate among them, and to use the information to guide one's thinking and actions'. Their research led them to assert that EI is a quantifiable form of intelligence that can be measured and taught.

The American management guru Daniel Goleman, who developed and popularised the concept, has suggested that applying it can bring dramatic improvements in the workplace. He believes the contribution of EI to 'effective performance' is 66 per cent for all jobs and 85 per cent in leadership roles. Another leading EI figure, Reuven Bar-On, is more cautious. His research suggests that the difference EI brings to effective performance is an average of 27 per cent across all jobs and sectors.

Between 2013 and 2014, two well-known international companies – FedEx Express and Amadori (a supplier to McDonald's and one of the leading companies in the Italian food sector) – took heed of this and attempted to teach their employees new EI skills after recognising a need to achieve better communication processes and develop stronger people-leadership skills. Both companies partnered with Six Seconds, the Emotional Intelligence Network, to develop, implement and measure new EI training programmes based on the Six Seconds Model of Emotional Intelligence (see Figure 3.1).

The model is divided into three areas: 'Know Yourself', based on self-awareness; 'Choose Yourself', based on self-management; and 'Give Yourself', based on self-direction. Within these areas, there are eight core competencies that form a learnable skillset, providing managers with new insights that enable them to manage a changing workforce. These are: enhancing emotional literacy, recognising patterns, applying consequential thinking, navigating emotions, engaging intrinsic motivation, exercising optimism, increasing empathy, and pursuing noble goals.

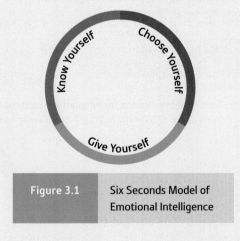

Figure 3.1	Six Seconds Model of Emotional Intelligence

Amadori

In this company a three-year-long study assessed the links between EI and measures of performance and employee engagement. It was found that:

• Emotional intelligence predicted 47 per cent of the variation in managers' performance management scores.

- Emotional intelligence was massively correlated with employee engagement (EE), and predicted 76 per cent of the variance in EE.
- Higher bottom-line results were achieved via a link between EI and employee engagement and, in turn, performance.
- Employee turnover decreased by 63 per cent over the three years.

Of the EI program, HR director Paolo Pampanini said:

> The feedback we received from the participants was extremely positive ... We were impressed by the pragmatism of the training – the results are measurable and that created a clear return on investment for the project. It is possible to say that within a few years of using the performance and talent management system we have witnessed an improvement of the managerial competencies of the whole structure ... This is a not a negligible result, it affects both corporate culture and the management approach towards change and complexity.

FedEx Express

FedEx Express is one of the world's largest cargo airlines, with almost 300,000 employees moving seven million packages per day. In such a fast paced, task-focused environment, founder Fred Smith has always believed that people are the key to business. In such an environment, it would be easy to lose sight of the relational dynamics that sustain team performance. To build a team where people give their 'discretionary effort', task-based management is not enough. Managers must form connections with their employees at an emotional level – emotional intelligence provides the insight and skill to enable this strategic use of feelings.

FedEx Express employees underwent a five-day course, followed by a six-month follow-up coaching process built around the Six Seconds Emotional Intelligence Assessment. Results showed that:

- Over half of the training participants experienced large improvements in key EI skills and leadership outcomes.
- 75 per cent experienced increases in effective decision-making.
- 60 per cent reported improvements in quality of life.

In the words of one program participant:

> I learned how to apply different leadership styles to meet specific situations, apply consequential thinking, and continue to improve my emotional intelligence. I am already applying this new-found knowledge in my day-to-day work environment as well as my personal life.

> *Source*: White Paper: Linking bottom line performance to emotional intelligence and organizational climate, 3 April 3, 2013; http://www.6seconds.org/2013/04/03/amadori-case-engagement-emotional-intelligence/

Case Study: Emotional Intelligence for People-First Leadership at FedEx Express, 14 January, 2014; http://www.6seconds.org/2014/01/14/case-study-emotional-intelligence-people-first-leadership-fedex-express/

Introduction

The case study demonstrates that there is a growing interest in intelligence, personality and emotion in relation to job performance and other organisational outcomes. This is happening in many different organisational settings. However, it also raises some important questions: Does emotional intelligence exist? Do different types of intelligence exist? What do tests of intelligence actually measure? How does an individual's personality relate to performance at work? In this chapter we explore theories of intelligence and personality, and provide a brief historical overview of the research literature in these areas. Traditionally, studies of intelligence and of personality have been treated separately but more contemporary theories of individual differences have begun to integrate these approaches in order to explain behaviour. As the opening case study illustrates, recent research explores whether emotional intelligence is a critical factor in explaining performance at work. This has been a topic of fierce debate and current research evidence is reviewed in this chapter.

Point of integration

Individual differences are an important feature of theories and research across the various chapters of this text. For example, they can be linked to how employees respond to stress (Chapter 10) and how they form attitudes (Chapter 6). Here we focus on ability and personality, but there are many other individual differences such as cognitive styles (or typical ways of thinking) that are explored elsewhere in this text.

Key debate

Are people or situations more important in predicting behaviour?

Historically, in attempts to explain personality, psychologists have tended to emphasise the role of either internal (person) factors or external (situational) factors. The debate about the relative importance of people and situations in determining behaviour is a long-standing and controversial issue within psychology. Many approaches have focused on the structure and measurement of individual differences without emphasising the role of situational factors in determining behaviour. It would be a mistake, however, to conclude that the approaches described do not recognise the potential for situations to influence how people behave.

Recent theoretical and research work has led to the development of sophisticated theories of how various individual differences and characteristics of the work environment come together to shape workplace behaviour. Given recent global economic uncertainty, the topic of innovation at work has become an increasingly important part of the research agenda for many work psychologists. In this chapter we examine the individual-level resources such as intellect and personality that are important in predicting innovative working. However, what evidence shows is that innovation is multifaceted and is influenced by a wide range of personal resources (also including motivation, mood states and values) and social resources such as teamworking. Later in the chapter we examine innovation research in detail to show how and why both the people-level resources and work situations are important.

Key learning point

Personal and situational factors interact to determine behaviour. In some theories the situation is more important than personal factors. In other theories personal factors are dominant. More recently, integrative theories have aimed to provide more complete insights into the determinants of behaviour.

Traditional models of cognitive ability

Some people are better at processing information than others. These differences can have a significant impact on how they perform when faced with various tasks. We are constantly exposed to evidence that, when it comes to cognitive (thinking) ability, there are significant and relatively stable variations among people. Thanks to good quality research it is equally clear that some of these differences in intelligence are the result of differences in opportunities to learn: they are, in part, situationally or environmentally determined. A recent review of the research evidence concluded that the importance of environment for the development of IQ (intelligence quotient) can be seen in an average six-point increase in IQ for children adopted from a working-class environment to a middle-class environment (Nisbett et al., 2012). Psychologists have invested a great deal of time and effort into trying to understand and measure differences in cognitive ability. One approach to the issues involved has a long history and is particularly relevant to personnel selection and assessment: this is the use of carefully designed tests to assess people's levels of cognitive ability.

Point of integration

Measures of cognitive ability are widely used to select people for work roles (see Chapter 4). This is because there is evidence that cognitive ability is linked to work performance.

In the early years of the 20th century, two French psychologists, Alfred Binet and Theodore Simon, developed what is generally accepted as the first satisfactory test of human intelligence. France, in common with other industrialised nations, had introduced compulsory education. Most of the children entering schools seemed well able to benefit from the regular mainstream approach to education. Some seemed to require extra help, but could still prosper in the regular system. A third group, however, did not benefit from the regular system but it was not always easy to identify these children who were in need of more specialised educational interventions. The test developed by Binet and Simon was intended to help in identifying these children by assessing their intellectual capabilities in a reliable and standardised way.

The approach adopted by Binet and Simon is still the basis for contemporary intelligence tests. In essence, they considered that intelligence could be measured by assessing a person's ability to answer a carefully selected collection of questions. Although the questions in modern tests (see Table 3.1) differ from the type of questions used by Binet and Simon, the principle of sampling test-takers' behaviour on a carefully selected set of tasks is still at the core of most tests. Such tests need to be administered under standardised conditions and require people to attempt to answer written questions, all of which have been evolved through a highly technical process of trialling and analysis (see Table 3.1 for illustrative questions). The standardisation of tests is achieved through careful and consistent administration (e.g. the time allowed and instructions given should be exactly the same for all test-takers) and test content (all test-takers answer the same questions). This means that, in theory, everyone is given the same opportunity to perform. The need for standardisation also brings some disadvantages: this approach cannot assess people on their capacity to conduct everyday, real-life tasks. This is seen by some psychologists as a serious weakness, and is a criticism that is gaining support within the recent literature.

Key learning point

Traditional tests of cognitive ability and intelligence usually need to be administered in a standardised way. This allows for differences between individuals to be measured as all individuals are deemed to have been given an equal opportunity to answer the questions because they all completed the test under the same conditions.

Sternberg (2006, Sternberg et al. 2007) studied the concept of 'practical intelligence', which refers to the ability to solve real-life problems using information that is not necessarily contained within a problem statement. In these measures of intelligence there are many possible solutions as opposed to the one 'correct answer' per problem as is the case for the majority of intelligence tests. Practical intelligence has been found to be only moderately correlated with traditional IQ tests, yet it is predictive of significant amounts of variance in academic and occupational achievement and above and beyond that explained by IQ tests alone (in other words, it shows incremental validity).

This has led several authors (see, for example, Hunt, 2011) to conclude that measuring practical intelligence could significantly improve the predictive power of intelligence testing. Another important, but often overlooked, issue is that cognitive ability is often tested within a maximal performance paradigm: test-takers are instructed to do the *very best they can do* within a set time frame. This is in contrast to the typical performance paradigm in which information is gathered about what test-takers *tend to do*. Clearly, by sampling behaviour in the maximal performance paradigm alone, one runs the risk of drawing false conclusions about a person. Perhaps because of the particular questions asked, the circumstances in which the test is taken, or various other reasons the person's test performance may not reflect their underlying abilities: we look at this issue in more detail throughout the chapter. It is worth pointing out that Binet and Simon certainly recognised that test scores alone were not enough and they proposed that, before any decision about a child's education was taken, other types of assessment should also be made.

Intelligence testing

Since the pioneering work of Binet and Simon, psychologists have carried out a considerable amount of work in their attempts to measure intelligence and to understand its structure. So far we have managed to discuss the underlying structure of intelligence without directly confronting the problem of what intelligence actually is! Defining intelligence presents problems for psychologists, and to this day there is no universally accepted definition. Many psychologists will settle for the definition first proposed by Boring (1923: 35): 'Intelligence is what intelligence tests measure.' In fact, this definition is not as meaningless as it seems at first sight. Tests of general intelligence (which Spearman, 1927, labelled 'g') are designed to examine the innate ability of people to carry out various *mental operations*. These include

Table 3.1	Some example questions from an intelligence test

Q7	Mountain is to molehill as valley is to . . . 1 2 3 4 5 hollow chasm hill plain mound
Q8	The third member of this series is omitted. What is it? 0.1, 0.7, . . . , 34.3, 240.1
Q9	Which one of the five words on the right bears a similar relation to each of the two words on the left? 1 2 3 4 5 Class; shape Rank Grade Analyse Size Form
Q10	Here are five classes. Write down the number of the class which contains two, and two only, of the other four classes: 1 2 3 4 5 Terriers Mammals 'Scotties' Dogs Canines
Q11	Sniff is to handkerchief as shiver is to . . . 1 2 3 4 5 blow fire catarrh burn sneeze
Q12	How many members of the following series are missing? 1, 2, 5, 6, 7, 11, 12, . . . , 20, 21, 22, 23
Q13	Which one of the five words on the right bears a similar relation to each of the two words on the left? 1 2 3 4 5 Stream; tolerate Brook Contribute Bear Support Pour
Q14	Working from the left, divide the fourth whole number by the fifth fraction: 8, 6, 5/7, 3, 9, 2/9, 3/8, 1, 17/31, 4/9

Source: The AH5 Test. Copyright © 1968, A. W. Heim. Reprinted by permission of the publisher ASE, College Lane, Hatfield, Herts, AL10 9AA, UK.

the ability to manipulate data, solve problems, interpret information and so on as shown in the examples in Table 3.1: don't worry if you find them difficult – they are! The various tests of general intelligence are all interrelated and people tend to obtain similar scores in different well-constructed tests: this is thought to be because to some extent the same underlying construct, 'g', has an impact on performance across different tasks and tests. Thus, it has been widely argued that 'g' is a quality that can be measured reliably and with some precision. Regardless of whether the available tests measure what we think of as intelligence or some other qualities, several factor analyses of models of intelligence have shown that the existence of 'g' is difficult to dispute (Bickley et al., 1995).

There is a wide range of different tests available to measure 'g'. A widely used test of 'g' which requires minimal special experience or training is Raven's Progressive Matrices: this test measures 'g' through a series of abstract diagrammatic problems (Raven et al., 1996). There is also plenty of evidence to indicate that 'g' determines performance across different job roles. However, it is important to recognise that 'g' does not provide a perfect prediction of performance regardless of the type of task. Far from it. Specific abilities have been shown to also influence performance with their impact being dependent on the particular types of information being handled or the specific tasks being completed. For example, in addition to 'g', the ability to work quickly and accurately with numbers would be linked to test-takers' success in dealing with problems involving money, weights, distances and other concepts expressed in a numerical way. These core specific 'primary' ability factors tend to predict performance when they are 'matched' to the demands of the job role. For example, verbal ability may predict the performance of a journalist, while numerical ability may more reliably predict the performance of an accountant. Other primary factors include spatial reasoning, verbal ability, word fluency and perceptual speed and accuracy. Indeed, measures of these primary abilities appear to predict variability in task performance that is not predicted by 'g' alone (i.e. they offer some additional and useful predictive information). Tests of both 'g' and more specific abilities have been used with some success in personnel selection (see Chapter 4 for a more detailed discussion).

Key learning point

General intelligence 'g' has been linked to performance across a range of work-related tasks. Other more specific abilities also appear to influence performance. The specific abilities required vary according to the demands of the task.

Tests of intelligence have been criticised on various grounds. One criticism is based on the argument that intelligence tests do not measure pure underlying intelligence, but a mixture of intelligence and of taught or acquired knowledge (sometimes referred to as crystallised intelligence). For example, the questions in Table 3.1 require the test-taker to have knowledge of the English language (although it could be argued that the vast majority of test-takers would possess enough knowledge of the English language to engage in the mental processes required to tackle the questions).

Unfortunately, it is one thing to make such a distinction in writing but quite another to put it into practice by developing tests that are 'pure' tests of one or other factor. Proponents of intelligence tests believe that this can be done; others consider that it has not been done properly and is probably impossible. Furthermore, tests that focus more heavily on one or another form of intelligence might pose difficulties for certain age groups due to differences in the rate of decline of each type of cognitive ability. For example, measures such as Raven's Progressive Matrices (RPM Raven et al., 1996, 2003) that focus on fluid intelligence – i.e. the capacity to think logically in new situations and without acquired knowledge – will have scores that decline with age at a faster rate than measures that focus on crystallised intelligence. While there is recent evidence that fluid intelligence can be enhanced through training to delay decline (Salthouse, 2010) it is worth noting that age differences may occur dependent on the type of test used.

Key debate

Are cognitive tests culturally biased?

In the personnel selection context, tests are also criticised because they are biased in favour of certain ethnic or cultural groups. The argument of cultural bias asserts that the intellectual development that takes place naturally is dependent on the specific environmental and cultural background in which a person develops. This means that perfectly bright and intelligent people from certain socio-economic or ethnic backgrounds will have experiences that impact (either positively or negatively) on the development of the qualities assessed in the tests. The consequence will be that the test results will not accurately reflect their underlying intelligence.

The criticism that intelligence tests are biased against certain ethnic groups is, at least in part, based on the frequently replicated research finding that some ethnic minority groups obtain lower scores on cognitive tests than others (see Sackett et al., 2008 for a review of evidence). This has led to much discussion and heated debate in the scientific community. Despite the subgroup differences, many have argued that it is not unfair to use such tests for selection decision-making. In essence, this conclusion is based on the finding that although there are consistent differences between subgroups in mean scores, the accuracy of prediction of the tests (i.e. the prediction of future levels of work performance) is the same for different ethnic groups.

There is now some evidence to the contrary. A recent meta-analysis examined ethnic differences in the criterion-related validity of cognitive ability tests. This research examined lots of different high-quality studies of the correlations between test scores and criterion measures such as task performance. The results showed that compared with the average correlations for White individuals, correlations between test scores and performance were lower for Blacks and Hispanics, but similar for Asians. This suggests that despite their standardisation, cognitive ability tests may not provide a fair assessment of potential for every ethnic group (Berry et al., 2011). This is particularly important in selection scenarios, where test scores result in job offers or promotions. In such settings, the validity of intelligence tests is vital, and therefore the finding that validity favoured white over black and Hispanic test-takers across the majority of studies in Berry et al.'s (2011) meta-analysis is very important.

Encouragingly, there is a consensus throughout the literature that there is no evidence of gender differences in overall measures of 'g'. Having said that, the sexes may have different propensities towards certain aspects of intelligence: males may display an advantage towards visuospatial abilities (our ability to process visual information about the location of objects) and females towards verbal abilities (Nisbett et al., 2012). Of course, there are also many wider, societal issues to consider when examining the various influences on test performance. These include any links between demographic factors and access to educational opportunities and any connections between socio-economic factors and opportunities for intellectual development: these are complex and important societal issues but fall outside the remit of this book.

A final criticism of intelligence tests is that while individual differences in ability are assumed to exist, there is little research examining differences in test-taking motivation. Duckworth et al. (2011) argue that although intelligence tests operate on a maximal performance paradigm, they do not always succeed in maximising effort. A common assumption is that test-takers are alert, motivated, and fully focused on the task, and thus can do their very best within the time limit. While this is truer of high-stakes settings, research has indicated that for lower-stakes settings, this is unlikely to be the case. This poses the question: are intelligence tests really measuring a person's best performance?

Recent studies indicate not. Findings have shown that IQ scores can be increased by heightening motivation through material incentives (tangible rewards) in low-stakes conditions. Self-reported motivation has been found to be higher in high-stakes settings (e.g. when the result is very important to the test-taker). It is worth noting that this is typically measured after the test, so it is possible that responses are clouded by test subjects' estimates of their performance as opposed to an unfettered and honest reflection of how hard they tried. Stress can also influence performance on intelligence measures, since high levels of stress hormones can affect areas of the brain that are important for regulating attention and memory. As discussed earlier, the maximal performance paradigm has been favoured over a typical performance paradigm in testing: perhaps the typical paradigm would reflect a truer representation of test-takers' intelligence in the absence of stress and with optimal motivation. It is noteworthy that long-term stress can also impact intelligence more generally, and may partially explain some of the ethnic group differences reported in a number of research studies. For example, Sharkey (2010) studied the effects of exposure to various stressors on children's intelligence. It was found that Black children living in Chicago scored significantly lower (between 0.50 and 0.66 standard deviations) on tests after experiencing stressful events. Research suggests that the IQ gap between ethnic groups may be explained by the finding that children from some groups are more likely to live in stressful environments (for various reasons unconnected to their ability) where they are consistently exposed to stressors. This is a relatively new avenue of research and is an important area for future study.

Key learning point

There are consistent differences in the general mental ability test scores obtained by different subgroups. These may occur for a number of reasons and may not be linked to future job performance.

Systems models of intelligence

Unlike previous structural models of intelligence, systems models expand the concepts underlying intelligence to include concepts other than cognitive abilities. Three prominent approaches are Gardner's theory of multiple intelligences (Gardner, 1983), the triarchic theory of intelligence (Sternberg, 1985), and the three-stratum theory of cognitive ability (Carroll, 1993). An emerging approach is that of emotional intelligence (see Goleman, 1995; Bar-On, 2000; Mayer et al., 2001; Joseph and Newman, 2010).

Gardner's multiple intelligences

Drawing on studies of giftedness and brain injury deficits, Howard Gardner (1983) proposed a theory of multiple intelligences (MI). Gardner argued that there is more than a single, general factor of intelligence. His theory has attracted a great deal of attention, particularly in the media, and it has some intuitive appeal. Gardner proposes seven different types of intelligence as follows:

1   *linguistic* – a mastery of language, the ability to effectively manipulate language to express oneself;

2   *spatial* – ability to manipulate and create mental images in order to solve problems;

3   *musical* – capability to recognise and compose musical pitches, tones and rhythms;

4   *logical-mathematical* – ability to detect patterns, reason deductively and think logically;

5   *bodily kinaesthetic* – ability to use one's mental abilities to coordinate one's own bodily movements;

6   *interpersonal* – ability to understand and discern the feelings and intentions of others;

7   *intrapersonal* – ability to understand one's own feelings and motivations.

Each of these seven intelligences is derived from Gardner's subjective classification of abilities based on a set of scientific criteria such as neuropsychological evidence (e.g. speech and language functions appear to reside in the left cerebral hemisphere in the brain), and support from experimental psychology. There is also evidence from psychometric testing that some individuals may perform very poorly on IQ tests, yet demonstrate exceptional talent in other domains such as music. Gardner claims that although the seven intelligences are anatomically separated from each other, they rarely operate independently. In other words, the intelligences are hypothesised to operate concurrently thereby complementing one another as individuals develop skills or solve problems. For example, the theory suggests that a dancer can perform well only if they have (i) strong musical intelligence to understand the rhythm of the music, (ii) interpersonal intelligence to understand how they can inspire their audience, and (iii) bodily-kinaesthetic intelligence to provide them with the dexterity and coordination to complete the movements successfully.

Although many educationalists have used Gardner's theory in schools, MI theory has been criticised by many academics. Critics have argued that MI theory is subjective, and is incompatible with the well-established concept of 'g' and with the likely impact of environmental influences on the development of intelligence. Gardner (1995) has vehemently defended MI theory by referring to various laboratory and field studies for support, arguing that researchers should be more interested in understanding intellectual processes that are not explained by the concept of 'g'. Matthews et al. (2003b) argue that there are some potentially serious omissions in MI theory. For example, the well-established primary mental abilities associated with intelligence such as word fluency, inductive reasoning, memory and perceptual speed cannot be classified in his system. They also argue that MI theory has some limitations:

> [F]or example, assuming bodily kinaesthetic intelligence is a distinct domain, do we take it that one should also distinguish tennis intelligence, athletic intelligence, football intelligence, dance intelligence, and golf intelligence? If not, one might assume that an individual who turns out to be highly proficient at football might equally have turned that talent to performing in a classical ballet production.

(2003b: 121)

Sternberg's triarchic theory of intelligence

Robert Sternberg's triarchic theory (Sternberg, 1985, called *Beyond IQ: A triarchic theory of human intelligence*) builds on Spearman's 'g' and the underlying information processing components of intelligence. The theory consists of three parts (also known as subtheories) used to describe and measure intelligence. The three facets (or subtheories) are: *analytical* (componential), *creative* (experiential) and *practical* (contextual). Each is defined as follows:

■   *Analytical (componential) subtheory:* Analytical intelligence refers to academic problem-solving (such as solving puzzles) and reflects how an individual relates to their internal world. Sternberg suggests that analytical intelligence (problem-solving skills) is based on the joint operations of 'metacomponents', 'performance' components and 'knowledge acquisition' components of intelligence. Metacomponents control, monitor and evaluate cognitive processing. These are the executive functions that help to organise strategies for performance and the process of knowledge acquisition. In other words, metacomponents are heavily involved when we are deciding what to do. Performance components are the basic operations that execute the strategies governed by the metacomponents. They are the cognitive processes that enable us to encode information, hold information in short-term memory, perform mental operations and recall information from long-term memory. Knowledge acquisition components are the processes used in gaining and storing (memorising) new knowledge (i.e. the capacity for learning).

- *Creative (experiential) subtheory:* Creative intelligence involves the insights people have, their ability to synthesise (e.g. have new ideas) and their ability to react to novel situations and stimuli. Sternberg suggests that this experiential aspect of intelligence reflects how an individual associates their internal world to the external world. Creative intelligence comprises the ability to think creatively and the ability to adapt creatively and effectively to new situations.

- *Practical (contextual) subtheory:* Practical intelligence involves the ability to understand and deal with everyday tasks. It is referred to as 'real-world intelligence'. This contextual facet of intelligence reflects how the individual relates to the external world. People with high levels of this type of intelligence can adapt to, or shape their environment. Sternberg and Wagner's test of Practical Managerial Intelligence includes measures of the ability to write effective memos, to motivate people, to identify when to delegate and so on. In contrast to structural models of intelligence, measures of practical intelligence go beyond mental skills and include assessment of attitudes and emotional factors (Sternberg et al., 2000). In this way, one of Sternberg's most important contributions to intelligence theory has been the redefinition of intelligence to incorporate practical knowledge. Sternberg's discoveries and theories have influenced cognitive science, and have resulted in the rethinking of conventional methods of evaluating an individual's intelligence.

Carroll's three-stratum theory of cognitive ability

John Carroll proposed a three-stratum theory of cognitive ability, based on a re-analysis of over 450 datasets of cognitive ability test results. He used factor analysis (see Chapter 2 for an explanation of this analytical technique) to identify consistent patterns across test-takers' performance to see if there were clusters of components of 'g' arranged in a hierarchy. His analyses showed that cognitive ability could be reliably clustered into three layers (strata), defined as representing narrow, broad and general cognitive ability (see Figure 3.2). Stratum III most closely resembles 'g', reflecting one factor of 'general intelligence'. Stratum II splits this general factor into broad abilities such as fluid or crystallised intelligence, general memory and visual perception. Stratum I even further narrows these into specific abilities such as picture recognition and word fluency: each of these are aspects of the general factors in Stratum II. This model has been described as 'the most viable description of human abilities' (Bickley et al., 1995: 311), and can be thought of as a unifying model since it combines and extends the dimensions of other established theories.

Key learning point

Sternberg's triarchic theory of intelligence redefines intelligence to incorporate a practical knowledge component. Carroll's three-stratum theory of cognitive ability unifies and extends earlier theories by conceptualising intelligence using a three-layered model of general, broad and specific intelligence.

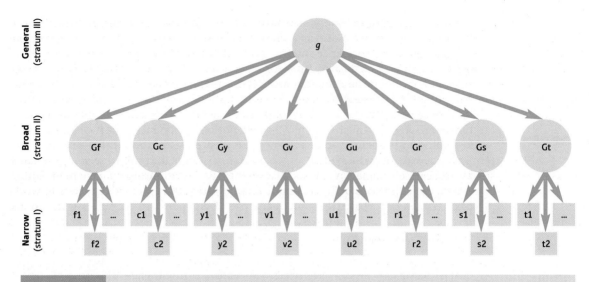

| Figure 3.2 | The three-stratum theory of cognitive ability |

Emotional intelligence

As described in the opening case study in this chapter, emotional intelligence (EI) is a concept that has generated a great deal of interest. Since Daniel Goleman's book *Emotional Intelligence* was published in 1995, many researchers have initiated studies of EI, believing that EI fills a gap in knowledge. Not surprisingly, this has led to heated debate among researchers and practitioners who are keen to define EI. This has prompted questions about how it differs from established theories of intelligence and how it is best measured. For practitioners, a key question is whether EI predicts aspects of job performance that cannot be predicted by measuring cognitive ability alone (see Chapter 4 for a discussion of validity in assessment).

Point of integration

Testing whether a measure of an individual difference predicts subsequent performance is not a simple task. Lots of data are required and there are various technical and practical issues to overcome. A detailed discussion of these is provided in Chapter 4.

Early research led to three main conceptualisations of EI appearing in the literature: one proposed by Goleman, one by Bar-On and the third by Mayer and Salovey (e.g. Bar-On, 2000; Goleman, 1995, 1998; Mayer and Salovey, 1997). More recently, Joseph and Newman (2010) conducted a meta-analysis of existing research: this led them to propose a 'cascading model' of EI that explains the progressive effect of the different facets of EI on job performance. Although there is some obvious commonality, there exists some significant divergence of thought in these approaches. We now briefly review each in turn.

Goleman defined EI as:

> abilities such as being able to motivate oneself and persist in the face of frustrations; to control impulse and delay gratification; to regulate one's moods and keep distress from swamping the ability to think; to empathize and to hope.

(Goleman, 1995: 34)

Goleman's conceptualisation has been criticised on the basis that the definition is over-inclusive and that it is 'old wine in new bottles'. In other words, some have argued that EI is a repackaging of previous literature on personality and intelligence and nothing 'new' has been identified (Chapman, 2000). Matthews et al. (2003b) suggest that Goleman's conceptualisation of EI rests on gathering up various aspects of what psychologists today would describe as cognition, motivation, personality, emotions, neurobiology and intelligence.

Goleman has responded by insisting that EI is an ability that differs from other more established abilities (although there is limited scientific evidence to support some of his claims). In later publications, Goleman (1998, 2001) suggests how his EI theory represents a framework of an individual's potential for mastering the skills in four key domains: self-awareness, self-management, social awareness and relationship management. Unlike other conceptualisations of EI, Goleman's framework (2001) specifically refers to workplace behaviours and is based on content analyses of competencies in several organisations. Rather than being purely an innate ability, he defines an emotional 'competence' as 'a learned capability based on emotional intelligence that results in outstanding performance at work'. Each of the four domains is viewed as a competency. For example, in considering self-awareness, this is the extent to which an individual is accurate (competent) in their self-assessment of their personal strengths and limitations.

Equally influential in this area is the work of Reuven Bar-On (1997, 2000). He defines EI as 'an array of non-cognitive capabilities, competencies and skills that influence one's ability to succeed in coping with environmental demands and pressures' (1997: 14). He produced the first commercially available measure of EI, based on a self-assessment instrument called the *Emotional Quotient Inventory* (EQi). Bar-On (2000) presents his model as an array of traits and abilities related to emotional and social knowledge: these influence our ability to cope effectively with environmental demands. In this way, it is a model of *psychological well-being and adaptation*. His model includes four domains, including the ability: to be aware of, to understand and to express oneself (intrapersonal intelligence); to be aware of, to understand and relate to others (interpersonal intelligence); to deal with strong emotions and control one's impulses (stress management); and to adapt to change and to solve problems of a personal or social nature (adaptability). Bar-On has reported several validation studies of the EQi and there is reasonable evidence that it predicts academic success and the diagnosis of some clinical disorders. However, as with Goleman's work, one of the main criticisms centres around the question of whether it captures any construct that is unique and is not already captured in existing personality measures (see Mayer et al., 2000). Further research is clearly warranted in this area to explore whether the EQi is measuring personal qualities beyond personality as it is currently understood (see the discussion of personality later in this chapter).

The research of Jack Mayer and Peter Salovey (1997) has perhaps been the most influential: they were first to publish their accounts of EI in scientific peer-reviewed journal articles. Unlike other approaches, they describe EI as extending traditional models of intelligence. They define EI as 'a concept of intelligence that processes and benefits from emotions. From this perspective, EI is composed of mental abilities, skills or capacities' (Mayer et al., 2000: 105). They suggest that traditional measures of intelligence fail to capture effectively individual differences in the ability to perceive, process and manage emotions and emotional information. Their approach defines EI as the ability to perceive emotions, to access and generate emotions to assist thought, to understand emotions and emotional knowledge and to reflectively regulate emotions to promote emotional and intellectual growth (Mayer and Salovey, 1997). For measurement purposes Mayer et al. (1999) have produced a Multifactor Emotional Intelligence Scale (MEIS) to assess facets of EI, comprising 12 subscales (e.g. feeling biases, managing self and managing others), all of which are connected to a single underlying factor (an 'emotional "g"'). Unlike other approaches, this model attempts to measure EI as a *distinct concept*, i.e. something that is not captured in established measures of personality. Vernon et al. (2008) found evidence to support the possible existence of a genetic component of EI. However, the evidence on the validity of the MEIS as a distinct concept is mixed.

One of the most recent models of EI was proposed by Dana Joseph and Daniel Newman (2010). Their meta-analysis aimed to clarify the theoretical basis for EI, and generated a *cascading model of emotional intelligence*, in which a causal chain exists between three subfacets of EI: emotion perception, emotion understanding, and emotion regulation; and job performance. The model also includes personality (specifically, conscientiousness and emotional stability) and cognitive ability as important antecedents of various stages of the EI process. Emotion perception refers to *the ability to identify emotions in oneself and others*; this influences emotion understanding, which refers to *understanding how emotions evolve over time, how emotions differ from each other,* and *which emotion is most appropriate for a given context*; this then influences emotion regulation, which is concerned with *the process by which individuals influence which emotions they have, when they have them,* and *how they experience and express these emotions*. It is then emotion regulation in turn that influences job performance (alongside aspects of personality and ability). Joseph and Newman (2010) suggest that emotion regulation is theoretically related to job performance through the generation of affective (mood) states that are beneficial to job performance (such as pleasure or excitement). Positive affective states have been linked to favourable work behaviour, and those with a greater ability to regulate their emotions would be more likely to create and maintain these states over time and across situations. Similarly, they would be less likely to use ineffective emotion regulation strategies such as 'suppression' of negative affect or 'surface acting'. In other words, the behaviour does not match the emotions being felt: these strategies cover up rather than actually change a negative emotional state. Emotional stability is proposed as an antecedent of emotion regulation since individuals reporting high levels of neuroticism have been found to regulate their emotions less effectively than those with high levels of emotional stability. Gross and John (2003) found that individuals with a high level of neuroticism do not engage in effective emotion regulation strategies as often as emotionally stable individuals (e.g. by re-appraising or re-interpreting the meaning or significance of events).

Key learning point

Specific aspects of personality and ability are linked to some of the emotional regulation processes in the cascading model of EI.

The cascading model also suggests that conscientiousness is positively related to emotion perception since conscientious individuals (described as methodical, cautious and careful) have shown above average levels of interpersonal functioning and an increased capacity for self-conscious emotions (the emotions linked to how we see ourselves and how others see us, such as pride). This means that conscientious individuals may be in a better position to use emotional cues (such as facial expressions) to guide their need for controlled behaviour. For example, they will be able to quickly and effectively determine when various behaviours are appropriate or inappropriate. Cognitive ability has been linked to the emotion understanding phase: those with high levels of cognitive ability would have greater knowledge of how to understand their own and others' emotions. Meta-analyses drawn from lots of different research projects and diverse research populations have shown a good fit with this cascading model.

Clearly there are some similarities, but also some important differences, between the four approaches. Bar-On has tried to develop a general measure of social and emotional intelligence associated with psychological well-being and adaptation. Mayer and Salovey attempted to establish the validity of a new form of intelligence, whereas Goleman's approach is specific to behaviour in work organisations based on the ability to exhibit social and emotional competencies. Joseph and Newman took a more integrative approach and explored the relationships between established aspects of EI and different factors including personality, intelligence and job performance.

Emmerling and Goleman (2003) argue that EI is something unique that helps to explain performance over and above measures of intelligence and cognitive ability. This kind of reasoning has led practitioners to believe that EI is a useful concept in assisting decisions about promotion to leadership positions, for example. However, Locke (2005) argues that EI cannot strictly be classed as a type of intelligence: he suggests that the vast number of factors found in definitions of EI renders it too broad a concept to be properly measured, understood and used in a meaningful way.

Key debate

Do measures of emotional intelligence work?

Just how good are the measures of EI? Not surprisingly, those who develop the measures tend to be confident about their quality and utility. Conte (2005) reviewed the research evaluating the most prominent measures of EI, including Goleman's Emotional Competence Inventory (ECI), Bar-On's Emotional Quotient Inventory (EQi), and Mayer and Salovey's Multifactor Emotional Intelligence Scale (MEIS). He concluded there were 'serious concerns' regarding all three measures, for example with the way ability-based EI tests were scored (can there be unequivocally correct and incorrect answers for questions about the awareness and regulation of emotions?) and the discriminant validity of self-report EI measures (i.e. more data were needed about how these measures correlated with established concepts in order to evaluate whether the EI measure captured a new and unique construct). As a result of his findings, Conte (2005) cautioned against the use of EI measures for selection purposes, until further research has shown EI to be a valid concept.

Point of integration

Measures used in work psychology need to demonstrate a number of important properties such as reliability, validity and fairness. These are considered in detail in Chapter 4.

One of the most important contributions of Joseph and Newman's recent work is that it has shed some light on some of the burning questions surrounding the utility of EI: is EI a unique and valid concept? Does it add anything unique over and above personality and ability measures? According to their meta-analysis, the answer is: probably not. Joseph and Newman studied EI in two senses. One in relation to ability-based EI – that is, EI as a narrow set of constructs pertaining to the recognition and control of personal emotion, and another in relation to mixed EI – an umbrella term for a broad range of relevant constructs. Ability-based measures of EI were more theoretically grounded than mixed EI measures. However, scores on ability-based EI measures did not predict job performance across job types: predictive validity was localised to specific professions. Nevertheless, where they were predictors of performance, these EI measures added significantly to the level of prediction offered by the Big Five personality traits and by cognitive ability. It is important to note that although statistically significant, this incremental predictive validity was small: this may not translate into differences in performance that significantly influence important work outcomes. Subgroup differences were also found, with women and White individuals achieving the best scores on ability-based EI measures. Considering these findings, it seems that the value of EI measures is yet to be established and there is a risk that these measures may create adverse impact for certain groups.

Moreover, large differences in predictive validity and subgroup differences were found between the different types of EI measures. Unlike ability-based EI measures, results for mixed EI measures such as the EQi (Bar-On, 2000) show significant overlap with the Big Five dimensions and largely support critics' claims that the measure does not capture anything not already captured by existing personality measures. Despite this, recent research has found EI to be a predictor of success in medical school, over and above conscientiousness and cognitive ability (Libbrecht et al., 2014).

Key learning point

The existence of emotional intelligence as a new construct, distinct from other established constructs, has been vigorously debated. Although there is an acceptance that EI is multifaceted, there is still disagreement about what these facets are. Recent research does not support the widespread use of EI measures in job selection processes due to their lack of practical utility and the inconsistencies in sub-group differences between measures that may lead to adverse impact.

In line with Joseph and Newman's findings, Zeidner et al.'s (2008) review argues that EI has traditionally been viewed as a *trait* and measured using self-report methods, or as an observable *ability* and assessed using objective methods. This has fuelled even more debate about which assessment methods *should* be used to measure EI. It can be argued that responses to self-report measures can be faked, coached and manipulated by individuals. Zeidner et al.'s conclusion is that the different measures of EI do not converge: different measures have been found to be measuring different concepts.

If we look back to the concept of EI we can see that it is appealing to organisations who want to recruit employees who can work effectively with colleagues and customers. However, Zeidner et al. (2008) highlight three key problems with EI research in occupational settings. These are:

1   The approach to measuring EI in occupational settings has been generic (i.e. it has not been specific to particular occupations). Different jobs have different emotional demands (e.g. compare demands faced by a palliative care nurse to those faced by an accountant). Generic measurement means that the emotional demands of various jobs are not well understood, and therefore it is difficult to identify how the various aspects of EI relate to performance in a variety of different job roles. Indeed, recent research has found the predictive validity of EI measures to be limited across different professions.

2   Few measures of EI have extensive norm (comparison) groups which show how EI varies across different occupational groups. If we do accept that EI exists, then we might reasonably assume that different jobs require different 'levels' of EI.

3   Perhaps most important of all, besides Joseph and Newman's work, at present there is a lack of evidence that shows measures of EI are linked to future job performance (although more evidence may emerge with time).

In order to address some of these highlighted problems, Zeidner et al. (2008) call for the use of 'emotional task analyses'. This is rather like job analysis (see Chapter 4) but focuses on the emotional demands in the workplace. This would help us to understand exactly which emotional demands are made by particular occupations and organisational contexts. Such analyses would make it possible for us to identify which aspects of EI are required in different occupational settings.

More research is required to answer many questions about EI. There is no doubt that the debate associated with EI has begun to challenge previous assumptions of what leads to success in organisations, and indeed, many organisations have seen positive results come from focusing on EI. Perhaps the concept is better used in a developmental context than from a selection and assessment perspective?

Key learning point

Emotional intelligence is seen by many as an exciting concept because it encompasses thought, emotion and interpersonal awareness more than earlier models of intelligence. While there is some evidence from specific workplaces that improving EI can improve organisational outcomes like performance, researchers tend to advise caution around using EI measures for selection.

Trait views of personality

Psychoanalytic theories of human personality (e.g. the work of Freud that you may well have heard something about) are often criticised by other psychologists. They argue that these theories often lack scientific rigour, or fail to clearly define their key concepts (i.e. the main ingredients of the theory). From a scientific perspective, the most fundamental criticisms are that these theories either do not generate testable predictions about human behaviour or, if they do, when predictions are made they do not work out in practice. Trait theories perhaps come closest to describing the structure of personality in a way that matches our everyday use of the term personality. Trait theories use words such as *shy, outgoing, tense* and *extroverted* to describe the basic factors of human personality. These basic elements – traits – represent predispositions (or tendencies) to behave in certain ways, in a variety of different situations.

Point of integration

Trait-based theories have been prominent in leadership research. These indicate that certain levels of particular personality traits help people to become, and function as, effective leaders. This approach has attracted a great deal of criticism (see Chapter 12). There is considerable evidence that personality traits such as neuroticism are linked to the experience of work stress: here the evidence of a link is consistent. However, the extent to which personality is linked to stress when compared to the effects of working conditions remains controversial (see Chapter 10).

Over several decades' academic debate, research has produced some fairly consistent evidence of the existence of five – the so-called Big Five – major personality factors. A fairly high degree of consensus has emerged and investigators have agreed that a five-factor structure represents an almost universal template for describing the basic dimensions of personality (Digman, 1990; McCrae and Costa, 1990; Costa and McCrae, 1992). The Big-Five dimensions of personality are described below. Costa and McCrae's work found that within each of these dimensions there appear to be a number of facets (or subdimensions). These facets help us to understand the breadth of each of the Big Five and to appreciate how the model attempts to measures the richness of individual differences in personality. These facets are also listed after each of the Big Five labels below:

Openness to experience – fantasy, aesthetics, feelings, actions, ideas, values. People who report themselves to have high levels of O tend to like working with ideas and possibilities (as opposed to established methods), and they are ready to re-examine their attitudes and values.

Conscientiousness – competence (i.e. feeling capable), preference for order, dutifulness, achievement striving, self-discipline, deliberation (e.g. giving thorough and careful thought to tasks). People who report themselves to have high levels of C tend to describe themselves as being highly organised and thorough in their approach to tasks, implying a desire to do things well.

Extroversion – warmth, gregrariousness, assertiveness, activity (energy), excitement-seeking and the experience of positive emotions. People who report themselves to have high levels of E tend to describe themselves as outgoing, gregarious, lively and sociable.

Agreeableness – trust, straightforwardness, altruism, compliance, modesty, tender-mindedness. People who report themselves to have high levels of A tend to describe themselves as being helpful to others and mindful of others' feelings, and as preferring cooperation to competition. A typically manifests itself in behavioural characteristics that are seen as kind, sympathetic and cooperative.

Neuroticism – anxiety, angry hostility, depression, self-consciousness, impulsiveness and vulnerability. People who report themselves to have high levels of N tend to describe themselves as prone to worry and self-doubt, and being highly affected by their emotions in stressful situations.

Key learning point

The Big Five has become a widely accepted template for understanding the structure of human personality. Tip: you can remember the Big Five dimensions using the acronym OCEAN.

Substantial evidence exists that the Big Five structure is consistent across various national groups. For example, McCrae and Costa (1997) reported results comparing six diverse samples (German, Portuguese, Hebrew, Chinese, Korean and Japanese) showing all to have substantial similarity in a Big Five structure when compared with a large American sample. This and other evidence suggests very strongly that the Big Five structure is a useful general framework although, as McCrae and Costa acknowledge, this may be limited to modern, literate, industrialised cultures. It also seems that the Openness to experience dimension is less well defined than the others (Ferguson and Patterson, 1998). Lee and Ashton (2004) suggest that there may be a sixth factor called honesty-humility (with facets of sincerity, fairness, greed avoidance and modesty), a measure of which is found in their HEXACO personality questionnaire.

The identification of the Big Five personality factors is an important development in the trait-factor analytic approach. It is important to realise, though, that the establishment of the Big Five does not mean that other conceptualisations of personality become redundant (Hough and Oswald, 2000). The Big Five provide a useful view of the minimum factors that must be included in any description of human personality. In many circumstances it may make sense to use a more detailed set of dimensions. Hough and Ones (2001), for example, make an important distinction between the use of personality variables for *description* and their use for *predicting job performance*. In other words, while the Big Five may be a useful framework for describing the different aspects of personality, they may not be as accurate when predicting job performance. A number of studies and meta-analyses have therefore examined the relationship between the broad Big Five factors and job performance, but debate still persists regarding their suitability for predicting job performance.

Research methods in focus

Lower-order personality trait

Recently researchers have aimed to provide a more comprehensive review of the role of personality in job performance by focusing on lower-order traits as opposed to the broad factors (the Big Five). Judge et al. (2013) argue that weak overall relationships with job performance may be masking significant relationships at the facet level, perhaps because some subtle facets of personality are particularly important for effective work performance. As such, using DeYoung et al.'s (2007) widely cited typology, they conducted a comprehensive test of all of the recognised lower-order Big Five personality facets. Each of the Big Five dimensions were divided into two distinct lower-order traits that in turn represented the six facets of each dimension described earlier (see the middle column of Figure 3.3 – you could call these the 'Big 10').

Conscientiousness was divided into *industriousness* – which represented the facets: achievement striving, competence and self-discipline, and *orderliness* – representing deliberation, dutifulness and order. Agreeableness comprised *compassion* and *politeness*, which represented the facets of tender-mindedness, altruism and trust; and compliance, modesty and straightforwardness respectively. Neuroticism consisted of *volatility* – made up of angry hostility and impulsiveness, and *withdrawal* – characterised by anxiety, depression, self-consciousness and vulnerability. The lower-level traits of openness to experience were *intellect* – representing the desire to work with ideas and possibilities, and *aesthetic openness*, made up of: actions, aesthetics, fantasy, feeling and values. Finally, Extraversion contained *enthusiasm* – reflecting gregariousness, positive emotions and warmth, and *assertiveness* – containing the facets activity and assertiveness. Both lower-order traits shared an interest in the facet excitement seeking.

This meta-analysis yielded a number of interesting and rather intricate findings about the links between personality and work performance. Conscientiousness and its facets showed the highest correlation with performance, with industriousness correlating slightly higher than orderliness. At the facet level, achievement-striving, dutifulness and self-discipline showed the strongest correlations with job performance. Agreeableness overall had a weaker correlation than conscientiousness with job performance, though still relatively high. Its lower-level traits did not diverge much in their correlations with performance, but at the facet level there were larger differences, particularly with regard to modesty and tender-mindedness (tender-mindedness correlated more highly with job performance). Rather expectedly, Neuroticism overall had a weak correlation with job performance (since one might reasonably expect the frequent experience of negative emotions to adversely impact on performance). At the lower-order trait level, however – although still weak – withdrawal correlated slightly higher than volatility. In terms of Extraversion, the broad trait correlated quite highly with job performance, and lower-order traits showed little difference in their correlations with job performance. At the facet level, there was distinctly more variation, with very small effects for excitement-seeking but larger, albeit modest ones for positive emotions.

▶

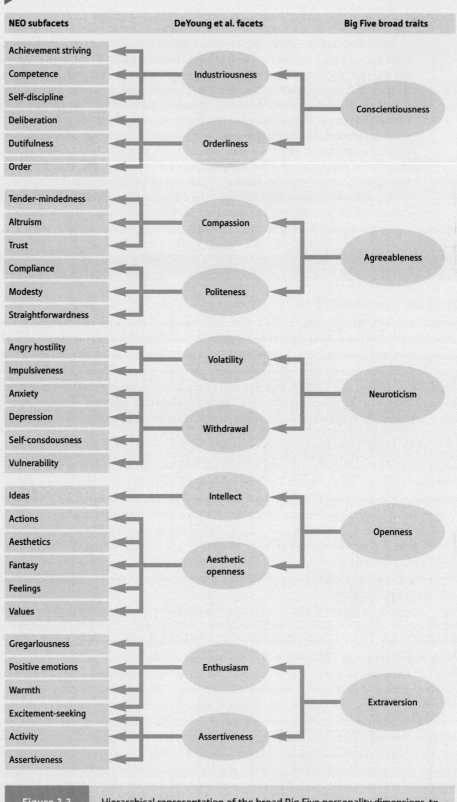

NEO subfacets	DeYoung et al. facets	Big Five broad traits
Achievement striving		
Competence	Industriousness	
Self-discipline		Conscientiousness
Deliberation		
Dutifulness	Orderliness	
Order		
Tender-mindedness		
Altruism	Compassion	
Trust		Agreeableness
Compliance		
Modesty	Politeness	
Straightforwardness		
Angry hostility		
Impulsiveness	Volatility	
Anxiety		Neuroticism
Depression		
Self-consdousness	Withdrawal	
Vulnerability		
Ideas	Intellect	
Actions		
Aesthetics		Openness
Fantasy	Aesthetic openness	
Feelings		
Values		
Gregarlousness		
Positive emotions	Enthusiasm	
Warmth		Extraversion
Excitement-seeking		
Activity	Assertiveness	
Assertiveness		

Figure 3.3   Hierarchical representation of the broad Big Five personality dimensions, to DeYoung et al.'s lower-order traits, to the six subfacets of each dimension.

Source: Judge et al. (2013).

Such findings indicate that personality-to-performance relationships at the facet level can be obscured if the broad Big Five dimensions are examined alone. At the facet level, the Openness to experience facets displayed the most variation of all of the Big Five traits. Overall it correlated moderately with job performance, and at the lower-order trait level intellect correlated higher with performance than aesthetic openness. This research provides fairly convincing evidence that lower-order traits and facets can help us to predict organisational-relevant behaviours. The evidence is that the facets of each of the Big Five have different links to job performance.

Key learning point

The lower-order traits and facets of the Big Five have links to job performance that might be obscured if we only examine the links between the Big Five broad traits and performance (see Figure 3.4).

Recent research has also indicated a role for personality in other organisational-relevant behaviour such as organisational citizenship behaviours (OCBs – see Chapter 5 for a fuller description of OCBs). As you might expect, high levels of conscientiousness and agreeableness have frequently been found to be linked to OCBs. However, Chiaburu et al. (2011), in a meta-analysis of 87 independent samples, found emotional stability (that is, the opposite of neuroticism), extraversion and openness to experience also predicted OCBs, even after accounting for the effects of conscientiousness and agreeableness. Additional analyses compared the sizes of the relationships between each of the Big Five dimensions and both OCBs and task performance. Findings showed that conscientiousness, emotional stability and extraversion relate similarly to OCBs and task performance, but openness and agreeableness relate more strongly to OCBs than to task performance. This suggests that certain personality traits may be more (or less) important for specific organisational behaviours and facets of work performance.

Point of integration

The links between personality and performance may depend upon the particular type of performance being examined. Performance of core job tasks may be related to elements of personality that are not as closely linked to organisational citizenship behaviour (and vice versa). Understanding the different aspects of work performance (see Chapter 5) is important when making predictions about how individual differences may impact on behaviour at work.

Key debate

Does personality change through life?

Is our personality enduring and stable? Much of the research into personality has concluded that it is. However, research is starting to emerge that challenges this assumption. Roberts et al. (2006) conducted a meta-analysis of longitudinal studies which included a total of around 50,000 participants drawn from 92

▶

▶

different studies in order to investigate the changeability of mean levels of personality traits throughout their lives. Findings showed that as people grew older social dominance (an aspect of Extraversion), emotional stability (an aspect of Extraversion) and Conscientiousness all increased (this trend was most notable between the ages of 20 and 40). Rantanen et al. (2007) conducted a meta-analysis into Big Five trait stability in an adult sample, using structural equation modelling (see Chapter 2). Their findings show that between the ages of 33 and 42, there was a significant increase in mean levels of Extraversion, Openness to experience, Agreeableness and Conscientiousness. Levels of Neuroticism fell between ages 33 and 42. In the same study it was found that Extraversion and Neuroticism changed less over time in the male sample, compared to the female sample. Such findings may indicate that job performance could be impacted by changes in self-reported personality over the lifespan but more research is needed before firm conclusions can be drawn.

Point of integration

The role of personality in personnel selection decision-making is discussed further in Chapter 4. For the moment it is sufficient to recognise that the Big Five provide a level of description for personality that dominates the research literature.

Personality measures

Although several studies have shown that the factors measured by many personality measures can be related to the Big Five, the tests themselves provide data on a variety of personality dimensions. Table 3.2 gives some information on the better-known personality questionnaires available.

As with all kinds of psychological measures, personality questionnaires need to satisfy various well-established psychometric criteria before they can be considered to be acceptable measuring instruments. These criteria are concerned with assessing the extent to which the test measures what it is intended to measure (the issue of validity) and the precision or consistency of measurement that the test achieves (reliability). The way personality data are collected does seem to have implications the predictive validity of measures. Salgado and Táuriz (2014) examined the criterion-related validity of various measures of the Big Five. They specifically looked into forced choice (FC) measures and examined these in comparison to single stimulus (SS) response measures. FC measures require the respondent to compare a number of options and pick the one that is most or least preferred, dependent on the context. This often presents the respondent with a choice between desirable alternatives meaning they are 'forced' to prefer one over the other(s). For example, you might be asked which word best describes you: 'cheerful' or 'organised'? In contrast, SS measures require respondents to rate statements as they occur. Respondents do not need to choose between desirable alternatives (for example, you would be given the opportunity to describe yourself as both 'cheerful' and 'organised'). Results showed that validity is slightly higher when personality is assessed with

FC measures than with SS measures. This suggests that perhaps responses from FC measures are more closely linked to actual work behaviour than data from SS measures. This may be because FC measures are more resistant to respondents' efforts to manage the impression they give of themselves. This means FC measures may be more suitable for use in a selection context where they form all or part of the basis for academic and occupational decisions.

As a light-hearted illustration, Table 3.3 provides descriptions of the 16 Personality Factor (16PF) scales together with examples of historical or literary figures who are supposed to exemplify the personal qualities described. You may want to think of some other famous (or infamous) individuals who display such qualities!

Table 3.2	Personality questionnaires
Instrument	**Personality characteristics measured**
Eysenck Personality Questionnaire (EPQ; Eysenck and Eysenck, 1964)	Extraversion, neuroticism (or emotional stability), psychoticism.
The Sixteen PF5 (16PF; Cattell et al., 1970). Several versions of short/long forms are available and measure second-order personality factors etc., in addition to the 16 factors mentioned here	Sixteen personality factors, e.g. submissiveness (mild, humble, easily led, docile, accommodating); self-assurance (placid, serene, secure, complacent); tender-mindedness (sensitive, clinging, over-protected).
The Occupational Personality Questionnaire (OPQ32r)	Thirty two personality dimensions are measured using forced-choice questions in the most detailed version of the OPQ (the OPQ32r). The questions have their origins in descriptions of people's behaviour in the workplace. Other versions/models of the questionnaires are available. Illustrative personality dimensions are: sociability (including the specific personality characteristics outgoing, teambuilding and socially confident) dynamism (vigorous, competitive, achieving, decisive) and empathy (modest, democratic and caring).
The Hogan Personality Inventory	Its seven primary scales are: adjustment, ambition, sociability, agreeability, prudence, intellectance and scholarship. It was designed specifically for use in occupational settings and hence questionnaire responses can also be scored on six occupational scales: service orientation, stress tolerance, reliability, clerical potential, sales potential and managerial potential. The measure is based on the Big Five model, but also socio-analytic theory. This means that the questionnaire's items are designed to measure how people present themselves to others (rather than how they would describe themselves).
The International Personality Item Pool (IPIP; Goldberg, 1999). A short version – the mini IPIP – is also available (see Donnellan et al., 2006).	The IPIP is a 50-item measure based on the Five Factor Model of personality. It measures each of the Big Five dimensions of: openness, conscientiousness, extraversion, agreeableness, and neuroticism with ten items each, and has been found to be a reliable and valid measure of these dimensions. A mini 20-item version was developed in 2006, designed for use in time-critical situations. Research has showed reliability and validity to be comparable to the parent measure, thus establishing the mini IPIP as a useful measure of the Big Five dimensions.
The revised NEO Personality Inventory (NEO PI-R, Costa and McCrae, 1992)	The Big Five personality factors, plus facet scores for six subscales within each of the Big Five domains. This measure is designed for a wide range of purposes (e.g. clinical, research and occupational uses). Descriptions of each factor and their subfacets can be found in Table 3.4.

▷

Table 3.2	(continued)
Instrument	**Personality characteristics measured**
The Myers-Briggs Type Indicator (MBTI)	This measure is based on a very different theory from the Big Five. It uses Jung's theory of psychological types, which discusses fundamental differences between people in terms of *dichotomies* rather than positions on a scale. Research shows that while the MBTI does not have a direct measure of Neuroticism, its constituent parts do correlate with the Big Five. Extroversion–Introversion (EI) correlates with Extraversion but also taps into elements of openness); Sensing–Intuition (SN) correlates with Openness to experience; Thinking–Feeling (TF) correlates with Agreeableness; and Judging–Perceiving (JP) correlates with Conscientiousness and Openness to experience (Costa et al., 1991). It is important to remember that although there are correlations with the Big Five there are some qualitative differences in what the MBTI measures because it is based on a different underlying theory.

Stop to consider

In reading about the Big Five you may have reached the conclusion that some personalities are more 'desirable' than others. However, this is a dangerous assumption as so much depends upon the social context within which the person is behaving. Most personality measures used in occupational settings are measures of 'normal' personality: questionnaire responses not an absolute indicator of a problem (e.g. people may score high on the Big Five Neuroticism scales without having a psychiatric disorder). Costa and McCrae (2006) discuss the advantages and disadvantages of various scores on the Big Five. They say about Conscientiousness: 'On the positive side, high C is associated with academic and occupational achievement; on the negative side, it may lead to annoying fastidiousness, compulsive neatness or workaholic behaviour' (2006: 17).

Have another look at the Big Five. Try to think of jobs in which low E, low O, high N, low A (etc.) might be advantageous (hint: there are some). What personality might be well suited to being a librarian, an elite track and field athlete, a lawyer, a CEO, a counsellor/therapist (insert some more of your own examples here)? Think about the lower-level facets as well as the broad dimensions. This will help you to think about whether certain personality profiles really are inherently advantageous/disadvantageous. As you will see, much depends upon the demands of the situation. The evidence about the relationships between the Big Five factors/scales and job performance is discussed in Chapter 4.

Creativity and innovation

Over the past two decades there has been an explosion of interest in innovation as organisations have recognised that creating new processes, products and procedures is vital for productivity and growth in all sectors. With more dispersed and virtual working, **role innovation** is essential, since clearly defined job descriptions no longer exist for many jobs. The research literature on creativity and innovation is immense. The case study exercise below (Exercise 3.1) illustrates the 'business case' for enhancing innovative working in organisations.

Table 3.3	The personality traits assessed by the 16PF with examples of famous individuals exemplifying the traits			
Factor	**Trait descriptions**		**Famous individuals**	
	High	**Low**	**High**	**Low**
A	Outgoing Warm-hearted	Reserved Detached	Falstaff	Greta Garbo
C	Unemotional Calm	Emotional Changeable	George Washington	Hamlet
E	Assertive Dominant	Humble Cooperative	Genghis Khan	Jesus
F	Cheerful Lively	Sober Taciturn	Groucho Marx	Clint Eastwood
G	Conscientious Persistent	Expedient Undisciplined	Mother Teresa	Casanova
H	Venturesome Socially bold	Shy Retiring	Columbus	Sylvia Plath
I	Tough-minded Self-reliant	Tender-minded Sensitive	James Bond	Robert Burns
L	Suspicious Sceptical	Trusting Accepting	De Gaulle	Pollyanna
M	Imaginative Bohemian	Practical Conventional	Van Gogh	Henry Ford
N	Shrewd Discreet	Forthright Straightforward	Machiavelli	Joan of Arc
O	Guilt prone Worrying	Resilient Self-assured	Dostoyevsky	Stalin
Q1	Radical Experimental	Conservative Traditional	Karl Marx	Queen Victoria
Q2	Self-sufficient Resourceful	Group-dependent Affiliative	Copernicus	Marilyn Monroe
Q3	Controlled Compulsive	Undisciplined Lax	Margaret Thatcher	Mick Jagger
Q4	Tense Driven	Relaxed Tranquil	Macbeth	Buddha

Note: Dimension B (intelligence) is omitted.
Sources: From Conn and Rieke (1994); Matthews and Deary (1998).

Table 3.4	Descriptions of the NEO PI-R facets
NEO facet	**Description**
Conscientiousness	
Competence	Sense that one is adept, prudent and sensible
Order	Neat, tidy and well organised; methodical
Dutifulness	Governed by conscience; ethical, fulfils moral obligations
Achievement-striving	High aspirations and works hard to achieve goals; driven to succeed
Self-discipline	Ability to begin and carry out tasks; self-motivating; persistent
Deliberation	Ability to think carefully before acting; cautious and deliberate
Agreeableness	
Trust	Belief that others are honest and well intentioned; not sceptical
Straightforwardness	Sincere; unwilling to manipulate through flattery or deception
Altruism	Active concern for others' welfare; helpful, generous and considerate
Compliance	Cooperative; seeks to inhibit aggression; forgiving; mild-mannered
Modesty	Humble and self-effacing
Tender-mindedness	Sympathy for human side of social policies; concerned for others
Neuroticism	
Anxiety	Apprehensive, fearful, prone to worry, tense, jittery
Hostility	Quick to anger; easily frustrated and irritated by others; bitter
Depression	Depressive affect, guilt, sadness, hopelessness; prone to dejection
Self-consciousness	Shame and embarrassment, sensitive to ridicule
Impulsiveness	Inability to control cravings or urges; susceptible to temptation
Vulnerability	Susceptibility to experience stress; easily panicked

Table 3.4	Descriptions of the NEO PI-R facets (*continued*)
NEO facet	**Description**
Openness to experience	
Fantasy	Active imagination; tendency toward daydreaming; lost in thought
Aesthetics	Appreciation for art and beauty, moved by poetry and music
Feelings	Receptive to inner feelings and emotions; empathetic
Actions	Willingness to try different activities; preference for variety to routine
Ideas	Intellectual curiosity; willingness to consider new ideas
Values	Readiness to re-examine values; liberal; anti-tradition and anti-authority
Extraversion	
Warmth	Affectionate and friendly; informal and unreserved around others
Gregariousness	Sociable; preference for company of others; 'the more the merrier'
Assertiveness	Dominant, forceful and socially able; takes charge and assumes leadership
Activity	Prefers fast-paced life; high energy level; vigorous
Excitement-seeking	Craves excitement and stimulation; sensation-seeking
Positive emotions	Experiences joy; laughs easily; cheerful and optimistic; high-spirited

Source: Judge et al. (2013).

Exercise 3.1   Creativity pays, and not just financially

A recent paper, published by Cornell University in 2013, highlights the important organisational and individual benefits of innovation. It reports the story of Nottingham University Hospitals Trust (NUH), a public healthcare provider in England, set up in 2006.

In recent times, the public healthcare sector in the UK has faced pressures to find new ways of working to decrease costs. Based on evidence that innovation can be driven by a bottom-up employee process, efforts were made to create changes with the goal being to become England's best acute teaching trust by 2016. This was an ambitious agenda and would involve:

- providing services that are good value for money
- being the best in: clinical outcomes, patient experiences, staff satisfaction, teaching, training, and research.

▶

As a result, the National Health Service (NHS) Institute for Innovation and Improvement designed and implemented the 'Productive Ward' programme, with the purpose of providing tools 'specifically developed to engage frontline staff in the initiation and implementation of change'. The programme was initially rolled out on a voluntary basis over three years; the results now speak for themselves. The Trust is one of the largest and busiest trusts in England, with 13,000 staff providing services to over 2.5 million residents. The innovation programme has also resulted in several other individual and organisational improvements, including:

- new opportunities for staff involvement – at least 50 per cent of staff are now involved in implementing change;
- more opportunities to offer feedback – monthly meetings include the discussion of ideas for change, which managers have said is good for encouraging them to think about and challenge old ways of thinking, leading to the implementation of better working strategies;
- staff development – delegating implementation responsibilities resulting in more active engagement, increased confidence and enhanced CVs;
- improvements in teamworking;
- more efficient patient care and working practices such as the ordering of equipment;
- improved experience and safety of patients;
- an overall improvement in performance at the hospital;
- organisational culture change – the organisation now listens to employees, breaks down hierarchy and allows staff to be change agents.

(Based on Foley and Cox, 2013)

Suggested exercise

Evidently, there is a business case for innovation. The above case study has illustrated how implementing an innovation program has helped this organisation to develop an effective and efficient workforce, enabling them to overcome challenges such as spending cuts and new health threats. Imagine you were the chief executive of NUH. How would you ensure that creativity and innovation are valued by employees and managers? How would you encourage creative thinking in your employees? Do you think there are some individuals who are more predisposed to innovate? And how might you attract, select and hire these creative thinkers? What challenges might there be in managing creative people?

So, what is known about the individual-level resources associated with innovative working? The concepts of creativity and innovation are often confused and used interchangeably in the literature. The main distinction can be seen as novelty. Creativity is concerned with generating new and entirely original ideas. Innovation is a broader concept because it also encompasses the application and implementation of new ideas to produce something new and useful (in the context of groups, organisations or societies). Innovation is often referred to as a process, because implementing new ideas necessarily involves influencing others (whereas creativity could be achieved in isolation).

One of the most widely accepted definitions of innovation is that of West and Farr (1990), emphasising the positive nature of innovation; 'the intentional introduction and application within a role, group or organization of ideas, processes, products or procedures, new to the relevant unit of adoption, designed to significantly benefit the individual, the group, the organization or wider society' (1990: 9). Authors commonly agree that innovation in organisations is a complex, iterative process. Numerous approaches and process models have been proposed, but two main stages are common to all. First, there is a suggestion phase and second, an implementation phase. Innovation is not a linear process: it involves several cycles of activities such as initiation, reappraisal, adaptation, implementation and, finally, stabilisation. Innovation is a result of both person-level resources and various environmental factors such as feedback, leadership style, resource availability and organisational climate. In terms of the measurement of innovative potential, there are various measures available that claim to assess the propensity to innovate, such as Patterson's (2002) Innovation Potential Indicator.

Innovation involves multiple components at the individual level. In her reviews on individual differences, Patterson (2002, 2004) suggests that the research literature can be classified into studies of the links between innovation and intelligence, knowledge, motivation and personality. Later research indicated a role for additional factors including emotional intelligence, mood states and values.

Key debate

Is creativity equivalent to genius?

Is creativity determined by or even equivalent to high intelligence? The best-known researcher in this field is Guilford. In his theory of the Structure of Intellect (SI), first published in the 1950s (see Guilford, 1996), he claimed that creative thinking was a mental ability, involving *divergent production (i.e. thinking that goes off in different directions)*. Many researchers followed Guilford's work by producing evidence that ideational fluency (i.e. the quantity of new ideas) underlies divergent thinking test scores. This is akin to Edward De Bono's 'lateral' thinking concept. However, review studies have cast doubt on this conclusion: divergent thinking scores often fail to correlate significantly with various indices of innovation. Some authors doubt whether divergent thinking tests are adequately measuring the abilities actually involved in creative thinking as it is the quantity, not quality, of ideas that are considered. Since innovation can only be useful if it adds value to an organisation, it is idea *quality* that is of the highest importance (Wycoff, 2004).

Other authors suggest that *genius*, as the most obvious manifestation of high intelligence, is closely tied to the propensity for innovation. However, despite the large amount of research carried out, there has been a substantial lack of evidence to support a direct relationship between innovation and intelligence. Recent studies conclude that intelligence and innovation potential are moderately related, but once IQ scores go over 115 the relationship is near zero. This finding has been described as 'threshold theory': once intelligence reaches a certain point, its relationship to innovation breaks down. It seems that instead of being twin or even sibling constructs, intelligence and innovation potential may be more like 'cousins'.

Finke et al. (1992) suggest that in order to understand the role of cognitive abilities in idea generation, we must draw upon cognitive psychology. These researchers have used experimentally based observations of the processes that underlie generative (creative) tasks. Their work follows a framework called the '*geneplore model*'. The model proposes that many creative activities can be described in terms of:

• an initial generation of ideas or solutions; *followed by*
• an extensive exploration of those ideas.

They suggest that individual differences in idea generation occur due to variations in the use and application of these two generative processes, together with the sophistication of an individual's memory and knowledge in the domain they are working in. In summary, findings showed that the capacity for creative cognition is normally distributed among the general population (see Chapter 2) and therefore, highly creative people do not have minds that operate in any fundamentally different way from other individuals.

Exercise 3.2   Test your creative thinking

Task 1: The nine dots puzzle

Look at the nine dots below. Draw no more than four straight lines (without lifting the pencil from the paper) which will cross through all nine dots.

Task 2: One-minute idea generator

Your task is to ask yourself the following question: *How many uses are there for a teaspoon?*
Go for quantity not quality of ideas. Write down every idea. Do not judge or criticise! Stay relaxed, playful, even silly. Adapt your point of view. For example, look at the teaspoon as if you were an insect or as a designer or as an electrician or in the middle of the desert. Ask yourself 'What if . . .?' questions. What if the teaspoon was flattened out and one end was sharpened to a point? What if several of them were linked together somehow? Time yourself for one minute.

Stop to consider

After reading the section on creativity and innovation and trying the two tasks above, ask yourself the following questions:

1   What individual-level factors do you feel influenced your performance on the above tasks?
2   What group-level factors may have influenced your performance if you had been working as part of a team in an organisation to complete the tasks?
3   Do you think these are robust tests to assess an individual's creativity? If not, why?

A common criticism of intelligence research is that traditional measures of intelligence (that is, IQ) do not fully explain 'real-world' intelligence. Part of the issue here has been that intelligence (similar to innovation) is often viewed as a unitary concept. Previous theories of intelligence have tended to overemphasise cognitive abilities and underestimate the role of knowledge-based intelligence (Silvia, 2008). However, knowledge is a key variable in both generative thinking and innovation. An essential condition for innovation is being immersed in domain-specific *knowledge*, as one must develop an accurate sense of the domain before one can hope to change it for the better. For example, it might be difficult to design the world's best car if you did not know what a car was! However, on the other hand, the literature highlights that too much expertise in one area can also be a block to innovation within that domain. This is illustrated by research by Simonton (2004), who studied the lives of over 300 eminent people to explore lifespan development of innovation. They found that both a lack of, and an excess of, familiarity within a subject domain, can be detrimental to innovation. It seems that knowing too much can stifle innovation.

Most studies on the motivation to innovate rely on the well-established typology of human motivation which differentiates between intrinsic and extrinsic motivation. Motivation is said to be intrinsic if an activity is valued and performed for its own sake and the individual has a genuine passion and interest in innovation itself. By contrast, a person performing a task with the aim of obtaining a reward separable from the task (e.g. pay) is said to be extrinsically motivated. Research has generally found that extrinsic motivators are related to innovation only under certain circumstances. Intrinsic motivators can therefore be said to have a stronger and more consistent relationship with innovation (Hammond et al., 2011). It should not be ignored, however, that constructive evaluation (i.e. feedback that is informative, supportive and recognises accomplishment) can enhance innovation. In related studies, results showed that individuals who received positive feedback given in an informational style, and who worked in a high task autonomy environment, generated the most innovative solutions (see Zhou and Shalley, 2008). Research has also suggested that intrinsic and extrinsic motivators may be important at different stages of the innovation process.

In the 1980s, Amabile suggested a *componential model* of innovation that involves three components: intrinsic task motivation, domain-relevant skills (i.e. expertise) and innovation-relevant process skills (cognitive skills and work styles conducive to novelty). The model includes a five-stage description of the innovation process – task presentation, preparation, idea generation, idea validation, and outcome assessment – where the roles of the three components vary at each of the stages. According to Amabile (1988), intrinsic motivation is particularly important in tasks that require novelty, and extrinsic motivators may be a distraction during the early stages of the innovation process. Later in the innovation process, where persistence and evaluation of ideas is required, synergistic extrinsic motivators may help innovators persist in solving the problem within the domain.

From several decades of research on the association between innovation and *personality*, a consistent set of characteristics has emerged. Innovative people tend to be imaginative, inquisitive, have high energy, a high desire for autonomy, social rule independence and high self-confidence. Research suggests that (of the Big Five) Openness to experience is perhaps the most important personality dimension to predict the propensity for innovation. Research also shows that *low Conscientiousness* is associated with innovation. Defined by terms such as fastidious, ordered, neat and methodical, the evidence shows that individuals high on Conscientiousness are more resistant to changes at work, and are more likely to comply with current organisational norms. The literature suggests that the relationships between the five personality domains and innovation are more complex at the facet level, and although this requires further research, it seems that assessing personality at the facet level could prove more useful than assessing at the domain level in terms of predicting innovation.

The emergence of EI as a popular concept more generally has been discussed earlier in this chapter. Recently, interest has shifted to the role of EI in innovation at the organisational, leadership, team and individual levels. For example, in a review of the role of emotions in transformational leadership behaviour, Ashkanasy and Tse (2000) suggested that EI involves the ability to use emotions in a way that allows flexible planning and creative thinking. Similarly, leaders' levels of EI are likely to accentuate the employees' inclination to engage in the innovation process. From a team perspective, Barczak et al. (2010) found that emotionally intelligent teams create both cognitive and affective team trust, which in turn builds a collaborative culture and facilitates higher levels of creativity and innovation. For individual employees, it has been found that those who show high levels of EI also display higher levels of readiness to create and innovate (Suliman and Al-Shaikh, 2007), and are likely to benefit more from both positive and negative creativity-related feedback. Furthermore, it is thought that EI may be beneficial when innovative employees have to persuade others to support them during the implementation phase of innovation. Specifically, being able to perceive others' emotions and to regulate them appears to be important in the persuasion process.

Point of integration

Leadership behaviour may have a significant impact on employees' propensity to innovate (see Chapter 12). It is a good example of the interactions that occur between individual differences and the situation. In this case leader behaviour can moderate (i.e. turn up or down) the 'volume' of employees' potential to innovate.

Examining the relationship between emotions, mood states and innovation is a new but rapidly growing research area. When referring to emotions and mood states, the most commonly used terms are *affect, mood* and *emotion*. Affect refers to a subjective feeling that involves both general (and long-lasting) states such as cheerfulness or depression, and more specific ones such as happiness or anger. Mood and emotion can then be seen as subtypes of affect, with emotions typically being directed toward a specific stimulus (e.g. a person, object or event) and moods tending to lack this directedness. Research findings have been quite conflicting in this area – some studies suggest that positive moods facilitate innovation, while others suggest that negative mood states are more conducive to innovation. A meta-analysis of 102 independent samples and over 7,000 research participants (Baas et al., 2008) aimed to alleviate some of the inconsistency found in the literature on the association between mood states and innovation. With regard to causality, it was concluded that when compared with neutral moods, positive moods generally produce more creativity. Further, while negative moods are not inclined to produce creativity over and above neutral moods, they do not tend to produce *less* creativity. In the case of positive versus negative moods, no statistically significant differences were found between the two in relation to creativity, suggesting that one is no more important than the other in influencing innovative behaviour. Therefore, it might be that different mood states are relevant to different stages of the innovation process.

Point of integration

The expression of traits in behaviour can be influenced by psychological states, such as attitudes (see Chapter 6). In contrast to traits, attitudes can change quickly (but not as quickly as moods) and for this reason there is a considerable literature on the factors that can bring about change in work attitudes. As we have already seen in this chapter there is relatively little research looking at the factors that influence personality traits.

Recently, the impact of one's values in innovation has become a topic of research. Values are learned beliefs that serve as guiding principles about how individuals ought to behave (Parks and Guay, 2009). They provide directions for action and serve as standards for judging and justifying action, therefore they may provide a basis for innovative actions. Indeed, Dollinger et al. (2007) found that a central element in innovation is the desire to be creative, implying creativity as a core value. That being said, empirical research has been inconsistent in terms of the exact values that facilitate innovation – some studies have found that self-directedness and stimulation facilitate innovation, and values such as tradition and security stifle innovation; yet other studies have found conservation (the respect for tradition, security and conformity) to be a predictor of innovation. Clearly, more research in this area is warranted.

Exercise 3.3	Assessing the propensity to innovate at work

A long-standing problem for HR managers has been how to select and develop innovative individuals effectively. Getting the right raw material in the first place is a critical issue. The propensity to innovate is often listed as a key competency in person specifications, but there has been little available material to assess it in a reliable way. Traditional measures of creative thinking have been of the kinds that ask, 'How many uses for a paper clip can you think of?' in, say, three minutes. Such measures may indicate some level of conceptual thinking, but are of limited use in identifying individuals who are innovative in the workplace.

Previous literature has been confused as to whether the propensity to innovate is predicted by an individual's level of intelligence or whether it is more concerned with personality. Early research suggested that innovative potential was an aspect of general intelligence. However, many authors have demonstrated that aspects of intelligence may be a necessary, but not a sufficient, condition for innovation to occur. Later research focused on the propensity to innovate as an aspect of personality. More recently, researchers have noted that motivation and job-specific knowledge are key components in predicting the propensity to innovate at work. While there has been a vast amount of work examining these characteristics, this has lacked an integrative model with which to understand how all these aspects interrelate – although more recent theories are beginning to integrate the literature (see Patterson et al., 2009; Sears and Baba, 2011)

The technology and consulting company IBM recently spoke out about the problem of assessing innovation potential, agreeing that identifying innovative individuals in a recruitment process is one of the most difficult responsibilities of HR professionals. Nevertheless, based on their expertise in sophisticated HR tools and practices, they propose a number of strategies for assessing and recruiting innovative individuals. First and foremost, the use of behavioural assessments that can identify desirable individual differences is key. Trait-based measures that directly assess the propensity to innovate, such as the Innovation Potential Indicator (IPI; Patterson, 1999) can be invaluable for assessing one's capability of implementing ideas in specific contexts. Other behavioural assessments include: measures of personality variables associated with innovation such as novelty, creativity and initiative; intelligence; motivation; biographical data; and situational judgement tests (SJTs). According to IBM, ability tests that focus on assessing things like word fluency (see Carroll's three stratum theory, 1993) are more appropriate indicators of innovation potential than measures of general intelligence. Other methods like SJTs can assess one's innovative approach to various situations, and behaviour-based interviews can be an indicator of individuals' previous innovating experiences.

Suggested exercises

1   Create a list of the person-level variables that might influence the propensity to innovate at work. How do you think these variables interrelate?

2   Suggest how these person-level variables might be best measured. What further research could be conducted to learn more about innovation at work?

3   Do you think innovation potential is more useful in a selection context or for employee development? Why is that?

Socio-cognitive approaches to individual differences

The beginnings of the socio-cognitive approach were evident in the debate about whether it is individual differences or the situations that people find themselves in that determine people's behaviour. To most of us it is clear from everyday experience that our behaviour is not completely at the mercy of situational influences. There is some cross-situational consistency in how we behave from one setting to another, particularly in terms of key features of our psychological make-up, such as extroversion, agreeableness and anxiety. On the other hand most people will behave quite differently at a lively party and at a very important formal business event. The relative influence of person and situation variables has been a topic of considerable controversy. Some people have argued very strongly for the predominance of situational influences, suggesting that stable individual differences in psychological make-up have a relatively small role to play (e.g. Mischel, 1968). Despite these historical differences of opinion, it is clear that modern psychology allows for the influence of *both person and situation variables*. Eysenck captured the essential futility of trying to identify a single cause by writing:

> Altogether I feel that the debate is an unreal one. You cannot contrast persons and situations in any meaningful sense . . . No physicist would put such a silly question as: which is more important in melting a substance – the situation (heat of the flame) or the nature of the substance?

(Quoted by Pervin, 1980: 271)

Situations influence our behaviour because we think about how we should respond to them. We could argue that work psychologists are equally guilty of ignoring the thought processes that underlie behaviour. For example, most selection research has sought to determine *whether* various selection methods predict job performance, rather than *why* these methods predict. For example, we know that personality traits predict work performance (see Chapters 4 and 5), but we know much less about how personality traits influence behaviour. Moreover, it is highly unlikely that there is a direct relationship between personality traits and behaviour (Skarlicki et al., 1999). After all, individuals will have their own way of *appraising* the situation that they find themselves in and *deciding* how they should best respond.

Point of integration

Cognitive appraisal of working conditions is an important element of theories of work-related stress (see Chapter 10) and features in many theories of career choice (Chapter 13). These theories help us to explain why different individuals have different responses to the same situation.

Hodgkinson (2003) found that senior managers, particularly CEOs and senior executives, all have their own way of explaining key organisational events (such as company performance) and this way of thinking influences strategic decisions (Sparrow and Hodgkinson, 2002). This is just one example of how individual differences in cognitive style may play a significant role in job performance. A number of cognitive-based personality characteristics have been developed and investigated over the years, including proactive personality, personal initiative, self-efficacy, attributional style, and locus of control (e.g. Bandura, 1982; Frese et al., 1997; Silvester et al., 2003). Interestingly, all of these appear to relate to motivation – a construct that has been notoriously difficult to explain in terms of personality traits. Kanfer and Ackerman's (2002) work on motivational traits acknowledges the importance of cognition in motivation. This raises the intriguing possibility that the impact of personality traits on work performance will be mediated by individual differences in cognitive style. Evidence for this can be found in work examining the relationship between attributional style and the performance of sales personnel. For example, Corr and Gray (1996) found that male insurance sales agents who attributed positive outcomes (such as making a sale) to internal, stable and global causes (such as their own personality) were more successful than individuals who externalised the cause to more unstable causes (e.g. luck, or being in a good mood that day).

Silvester et al. (2003) also found that individuals who perceived themselves to have more control over sales outcomes (both successful and unsuccessful) were rated as more successful by their managers. These findings indicate that even in the case of failure, individuals who attribute the outcome to more *internal controllable causes* (e.g. using the wrong sales strategy) will be more likely to maintain a higher level of motivation and effort than sales staff who typically put the failure down to external uncontrollable causes (e.g. the customer had seen a cheaper version of the product elsewhere). Clearly, there is tremendous potential for selection researchers to explore how individual differences in sense-making and cognition impact upon work performance.

Key learning point

Stable individual differences in cognitive style represent another potential source of variance in job behaviour.

Summary

Individual differences in personality and cognitive ability have been the subject of much psychological research. Research has uncovered stable, underlying structures for both cognitive ability (a general factor and specific abilities) and personality (five major factors). Measures have been developed for cognitive ability and personality. To be of value in work psychology, such measures need to be both reliable and valid (see Chapter 4). At the moment there is a great deal of interest in exploring the concept of emotional intelligence and whether it might offer something new in terms of our understanding of behaviour at work. There has been an increase in research into possible biological, neurological and physiological correlates of intelligence. For example, McDaniel (2005) conducted a meta-analysis of 37 participant samples encompassing 1530 individuals and found a modest positive correlation of 0.33 between individuals' intelligence and the volume of their brain, a finding that was consistent across all gender and age groups in the sample. Beaujean (2005) conducted a meta-analysis of studies that have investigated the relationship between individuals' genetics and the speed at which they are able to process information: this showed that genetics played a role in mental processing speed, with the impact of genetics being most important when tasks were difficult. The closing case study illustrates the growing interest in neuroscience and exploring the biological aspects of brain functions and how these relate to behaviour. However, there is also increasing recognition that understanding individual differences means that we also need to understand how factors such as learned patterns of social interaction and features of the situation impact on work behaviour.

Closing case study

Give in to temptation and fail in life: the secret of how some of us can resist temptation may soon be unlocked

A psychologist who found he could predict children's prospects by testing whether they could resist eating a marshmallow, is to scan their brains to find the neurological roots of temptation. The 'marshmallow test', one of the world's simplest and most successful behavioural experiments, was developed by Professor Walter Mischel. He proved conclusively that the longer a four-year-old child was able to wait before taking a sweet, the better were their chances of a happy and successful life. Mischel has been monitoring the lives of dozens of his subjects since he started the marshmallow experiments at a nursery on the campus of Stanford University, California, in the 1960s.

His findings have proved so compelling that 40 of his original subjects, now in their forties, are preparing to undergo scans in the hope of answering a perplexing human question: why are some of us better than others at resisting temptation? 'Brain imaging provides a very exciting and important new tool,' said Mischel, who now works at Columbia University in New York. By examining the differences between the brains of subjects who turned out to be good at controlling their impulses and those who wolfed down the marshmallow the moment it was offered, researchers hope to come up with new ways of teaching the benefits of delayed gratification. Mischel's marshmallows have become a cornerstone of research into what is now known as emotional intelligence (EI), a human quality more to do with feelings than education and rationality.

His experiments began with a simple proposition. He placed a marshmallow on a plate in front of his subjects and told them they could eat it if they wanted to. But if they could wait while he left the room for a few minutes, he would give them a second marshmallow. Mischel would then leave the room for 10 to 15 minutes. He found that about a third of his subjects would grab the marshmallow immediately, a third would wait for his return to claim two marshmallows and the rest would try to wait but give up at varying times. It was not until 14 years later, when his earliest subjects were leaving school and going on to university or to work, that Mischel began to confirm a dramatic correlation between marshmallow munching and success in life. The children who grabbed the sweets immediately turned into teenagers who lacked self-esteem and experienced difficult relations with their peers. Those who waited for a second marshmallow turned out to be more socially competent, self-assertive and academically successful. In their school exams, the 'waiters' scored an average of 210 points more than the 'grabbers'.

Mischel continues to monitor the progress of his original subjects and his broad findings have entered American academic lore – the ability to delay gratification turns children into successful adults. This lesson has since been embraced in all walks of American life. Preachers refer to the marshmallow test when urging worshippers to suppress sinful impulses. Business gurus cite marshmallows when telling chief executives to resist short-term strategies that boost the share price but risk long-term problems. Sceptics have suggested Mischel might have had different results had he replaced the marshmallow with a more tempting treat, such as a Jelly Tot or a toffee. Many others, however, cite Mischel's work as evidence that EI – or what some refer to simply as 'grit' – plays a crucial role in child development.

One study by Martin Seligman and Angela Duckworth concluded that an individual's IQ, or intelligence quotient, accounts for only a third of any difference in academic performance when compared with peers. The rest has to do with qualities such as perseverance, self-discipline, hard work, creativity and luck. One impediment to developing grit, another study concluded, was a parent's overindulgent praise of a child. For Mischel and other researchers, the question now is whether neuroscience can identify the part of the brain that processes marshmallow desire.

Source: The Sunday Times, 2 November 2008 (Allen-Mills, T.),
© The Sunday Times 2008, www.nisyndication.com

Suggested exercises

1   What factors are important to consider in exploring the reliability of Mischel's research findings?

2   If the researchers are successful in identifying the 'neurological roots to temptation', what does that imply for interventions by work psychologists?

3   Do you agree with Seligman and Duckworth that an individual's IQ accounts for 'only a third' of any difference in academic performance when compared with peers?

Test your learning

Short-answer questions

1   Give examples of how cognitive ability can be assessed.
2   Are a person's scores on tests of different cognitive abilities likely to be similar? Explain your answer.
3   What are Gardner's multiple intelligences?
4   What are the Big Five personality factors?
5   What is emotional intelligence?
6   What are Joseph and Newman's subfacets of emotional intelligence?
7   Suggest three general reasons why a person's scores on personality and intelligence tests might influence their work performance.
8   What tools are available to assess creative thinking at work? Are they reliable?

Suggested assignments

1   What evidence is there that emotional intelligence is distinct from traditional conceptualisations of personality and intelligence?
2   Discuss the extent to which the Big Five provide a comprehensive picture of human personality.
3   What are the individual-level resources associated with innovation in organisations?

Relevant websites

A very useful site for learning about psychometric testing from the points of view of both the tester and the person being tested is provided by the British Psychological Society at http://ptc.bps.org.uk/

If you are interested in intelligence testing, Indiana University, USA, hosts a site with material you may find helpful. It is not specifically about the workplace, but much here is relevant to the workplace. Find it at http://www.intelltheory.com/index.shtml

The MBTI is a widely used personality measure in work psychology. A good source of information about the measure can be found at http://www.myersbriggs.org/my-mbti-personality-type/mbti-basics/

The International Personality Item Pool at http://ipip.ori.org/ contains lots of questionnaire items designed to measure the Big Five personality domains (including the facets).

Suggested further reading

Full details for all references are given in the list at the end of this book.

1 Paul Kline's book *Handbook of Psychological Testing* (Sage, 1999) provides a good overview of the theoretical underpinnings of personality and intelligence and how it translates into measurement. Also see *The New Psychometrics: Science, psychology and measurement* (Routledge, 2000) by Paul Kline.

2 Matthews et al.'s book on *Personality Traits* (Cambridge University Press, 2003a) provides an excellent overview of the research literature in personality and provides a summary of evidence relevant to work psychology.

3 Matthews et al.'s book called *Emotional Intelligence: Science and myth* (MIT Press, 2003b) provides an in-depth analysis of the evidence on emotional intelligence.

CHAPTER 4

Personnel selection
Analysing jobs, competencies and selection methods

LEARNING OBJECTIVES

After studying this chapter, you should be able to:

1 outline the personnel selection design and validation process;

2 name and describe different job analysis techniques, including advantages and disadvantages of each;

3 define competencies and competency models, and describe how the outputs are used as assessment criteria;

4 in the context of personnel selection, define reliability and five different types of validity: (i) faith, (ii) face, (iii) content, (iv) construct, (v) criterion-related validity;

5 outline the criterion problem and some practical difficulties associated with conducting validation studies in organisations;

6 list and describe several personnel selection methods;

7 state the major evaluative standards for personnel selection procedures;

8 specify advantages and disadvantages of several selection methods, including: (i) interviews, (ii) psychometric tests, (iii) situational judgement tests, (iv) assessment centres;

9 specify which selection methods tend to be (i) most valid and (ii) most acceptable to applicants;

10 explain how some selection techniques could lead to bias and unfairness to some subgroups;

11 explain some of the advantages and challenges associated with the increasing use of technology in personnel selection.

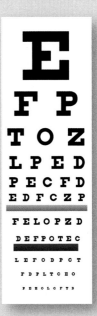

Opening case study

Selection into general practice training: a complete overhaul

Imagine you are living in the UK. You've just graduated from medical school, and next on your list is beginning your postgraduate specialty training. Let's say you want to become a general practitioner (GP, or sometimes termed 'family doctor'). What would the selection process for your training programme look like? Well, if you asked that question a few years ago, the answer would have been: it depends where in the country you apply for the training. But not anymore.

The recruitment process for GP speciality training in the UK has been completely overhauled in recent years. In the past it consisted of a number of independent and inconsistent processes that were applied across deaneries (a deanery is a regional office in the UK responsible for the education and training of junior doctors). Now there is a new robust, reliable, valid and fair process that has been rolled out nationally.

As you can imagine, developing this process was a big task, and as such, it had to be broken down into a number of important stages. The first stage was conducting a thorough job analysis. This was a key step as it involved systematically collecting information about the job, including the tasks, responsibilities, work context, and the knowledge, skills, abilities and other attributes (KSAOs) required to do the job well. The output from the job analysis informed all of the subsequent stages in the process, so it was important to get it right! This specific job analysis was done using a multi-method, multi-level approach, consisting of critical incident focus groups and interviews with experienced GPs and a diverse range of patients, and observations of GP–patient consultations (more information on the specifics of each method, as well as other methods not included in this process, can be found later on in this chapter).

The output from these methods revealed that there were a number of key competencies for the GP role, including empathy and sensitivity, clinical knowledge and expertise, and conceptual thinking and problem solving. This data informed the development of a competency model (see Figure 4.1), with behavioural indicators for each competency that applicants could be assessed against. It also formed the basis of job and person specifications (detailed descriptions of the behaviours and personal attributes necessary for the job). These can also help to improve self-selection as they provide candidates with a realistic perception of what the job entails, helping them to make an informed choice about whether or not to apply for the job.

When deciding on the actual methods used to select doctors for GP training, the job analysis is again a key feature in ensuring that the methods chosen are those that can most appropriately assess the important competencies. The current GP selection process now includes low-fidelity clinical problem-solving situational judgement tests (SJTs), as well as high-fidelity selection centres, where applicants participate in tasks such as group and written exercises, and simulated consultations with patients.

A number of empirical validation studies have now been completed. These have shown that candidates' performance in low-fidelity simulation-type methods like SJTs and high-fidelity assessment centres are both predictive of performance in the GP role. Candidates also report satisfaction with the new process. However, it is important not to become complacent – job roles change over time and new validation studies and job analyses are needed to ensure the continued relevance and suitability of the selection process. Particularly in recent years, structural and policy changes have meant that there have been significant changes to the roles and responsibilities of GPs.

In 2013, this was addressed with a new job analysis. Output revealed a new competency domain – leading for continued improvement, illustrating that the role had increased in breadth and therefore updates to the selection criteria are now needed to take this change into account.

This case example shows that selection processes are not (or at least should not be) one-offs. It is important that they are iterative in nature, and that they follow the process outlined in Figure 4.1. Continued research is needed to inform changes to selection criteria in order to make sure that the correct people are matched to the correct competencies using the correct selection methods. Job analysis should be at the heart of any selection process, as recruiting without knowing a) what should be assessed, and b) whether what is assessed is important for the job, is always going to be a stab in the dark! A thorough job analysis, however, helps to ensure that candidates have a realistic job preview and can self-select into roles that suit them; that recruiting organisations will benefit from the recruitment and retention of the most suitable employees; and that future job performance can more accurately be predicted. Everyone's a winner!

Sources: Patterson, F. et al. (2013). *A new competency model for general practice: implications for selection, training, and careers.*

Plint, S. and Patterson, F. (2010). *Identifying critical success factors for designing selection processes into postgraduate specialty training: the case of UK general practice.*

Introduction

The research and practice of work psychology have important contributions to make in many areas of organisational life, but personnel selection and assessment probably constitute the area where the biggest and most consistent contribution has been made. Given the centrality of psychological measurement to psychological science in general, psychologists are recognised as experts in the design and validation of technically sound selection processes.

Two main principles underlie the roles that personnel selection and assessment procedures play in organisational settings. The first principle is that there are individual differences between people in aptitude, skills and other personal qualities. This simple principle leads to the very important conclusion that people are not equally suited to all jobs, and suggests that procedures for matching people and jobs could have important organisational benefits. The second principle is that future behaviour is, at least partly, predictable. The goal of selection and assessment activities is to match people to jobs and use procedures (e.g. interviews, psychometric tests) to provide means of estimating the likely future job performance of candidates; the belief that *future job performance* can be estimated is an important facet of this principle.

This chapter focuses on different aspects of selection and related processes. We examine the aspects of psychological theory and practice that underlie the successful application of personnel selection procedures in relation to the two principles given above. First, since personnel selection has traditionally involved the matching of people to the requirements of jobs, job analysis is covered (individual differences between people were discussed in Chapter 3). The next part of this chapter concentrates on topics concerned with the development of procedures for predicting future job aptitudes; specifically, validation studies and associated issues regarding the practicalities of conducting research in organisations. We then describe the main personnel selection procedures that are used frequently in organisations and examine their relative accuracy at determining who is 'the best person for the job'. After examining the evidence concerning the validity of each of the main methods, this chapter explores the extent to which the various methods are used and how fair they are perceived to be by applicants. There is a growing need to understand issues regarding fairness and how adverse reactions could lead to challenges in the law courts. Finally, we focus on the role of technology in selection and discuss some of the advantages and challenges technology may bring to the recruitment process.

The design and validation process in selection

Figure 4.1 provides an outline of the main elements involved in designing and implementing a personnel selection procedure. The process begins with a *job analysis* to define a *competency model* and create a *person specification*. This information is used to identify the *selection and assessment criteria* and may also be used for *advertising* the job role. The job analysis information is used to decide which *selection methods* to use to access applicant behaviour related to the selection criteria. Selection methods can then be *piloted* and where possible validated and candidate reactions assessed. In attracting a pool of applicants, prospective candidates will engage in *self-selection* where they can make an informed judgement about whether the particular role suits their skills and abilities. Once candidates have applied, a

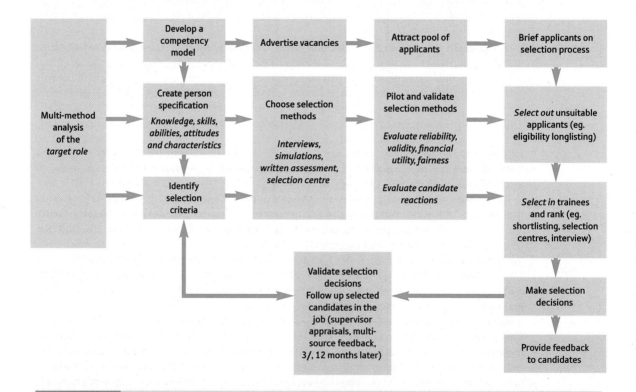

Figure 4.1	The personnel, selection, design and validation process

Source: Plint and Patterson (2010: 324).

selecting out process may take place based on eligibility (e.g. essential criteria such as educational qualifications are checked) before the *selecting in* process is undertaken using the chosen selection methods. Following the selection decisions, the accepted applicants enter the organisation (assuming they accept the organisation's offer).

After some time has elapsed, information on the work performance of job holders (i.e. measures of performance related to the original competency model) can then be used to examine the *validity* of the selection methods and decisions (i.e. whether high and low scores on the selection instruments are associated with good and poor work performance respectively). Results from validation studies can be used to reassess the original thinking behind the job analysis and choice of selection methods, and can help to inform changes to the original competency model. Best practice selection is an iterative process whereby feedback is used continually to improve the selection system and enhance accuracy and fairness. Feedback to candidates (both successful and unsuccessful), which is useful for development, may also be provided – although many organisations have practical and legal reasons for not always giving detailed feedback.

Point of integration

The results of a selection process can be used to identify training needs (Chapter 9). This is relatively rare in organisations and represents a missed opportunity, particularly as it could be used to help smooth the process of integrating new employees into the organisation.

Key learning point

Most selection processes require candidates to go through a number of stages before selection decisions are made. There is typically first a selecting out phase, where candidates who do not meet essential criteria (e.g. academic qualifications or experience) are filtered out of the process. The subsequent stage(s) then select in to the organisation using the chosen selection methods.

A thorough job analysis is the foundation of an effective selection process and is used to guide choice of selection methods. The outputs from a job analysis should detail the tasks and responsibilities in the target job and also provide information about the particular behavioural characteristics required of the job holder. The analysis may suggest, for example, that certain personality and **dispositional characteristics** are desirable, together with specific previous work experience, technical qualifications and levels of general intelligence and specific cognitive abilities (e.g. numerical ability).

The next stage in the process is to identify selection instruments (e.g. psychometric tests, work simulation exercises, interviews, application forms) that can be used to examine the extent to which candidates display the required characteristics. These instruments are then used to assess candidates and selection decisions are made.

Empirical validation studies are needed to monitor the quality of the selection process. Here, the psychologist is focusing on how useful (and accurate) the selection procedure was in identifying 'the right person for the job'. In addition, it is important to assess the candidates' reaction to the process too. Poorly run selection processes are likely to result in candidates having a negative first impression of the organisation. As a consequence, the best candidates for the job could decide to work for another (possibly competing) organisation. Historically, selection has tended to be a 'buyers' market'. Recently, there has been a recognition in some organisations that selection is a two-way process: in order to attract the best candidates, being seen to have professional and effective selection procedures is very important.

Although we have outlined the core elements in the selection process, in practice there are two elements in the process that are often not conducted effectively. First, often there is no thorough job analysis to identify precisely the key knowledge, skills and behaviours associated with successful performance in the target job role. As we saw from the opening case study, conducting a thorough job analysis is the most important part of the selection process since it informs all of the following stages. It is especially important when job roles change frequently or when new job roles are created.

Point of integration

There are some significant overlaps between the methods used for job analysis and those used for training needs analysis (Chapter 9). The objectives may be different but information about the job or the personal qualities (competencies) required to do the job are collected in both activities.

Unfortunately, many organisations are choosing to opt out of conducting job analysis, and rely on educated guesses to decide which competencies are important. Part of the problem is that job analysis techniques require specialist training, and few human resources departments have this expertise within the organisation. Second, validation studies are rarely conducted in organisations because they can be difficult to do well, and are time-consuming and costly. Validating a selection process often means tracking the performance of new recruits over several months or years. Validation studies are usually only possible with large-scale recruitment programmes and many organisations do not recruit large numbers of people into one specific job role to provide enough data for statistical validation. The result is that the best-practice methodology of (i) conducting a thorough job analysis, (ii) designing selection tools based on job analysis output, and (iii) validating the process, tends to be reserved for large organisations and is near impossible for small to medium-sized enterprises (SMEs) to achieve (Wyatt et al., 2010). Organisations therefore often draw upon research evidence from other organisations by employing work psychologists to advise on best practice procedures in selection.

Key learning point

Best practice personnel selection is an iterative process. It involves thorough job analysis and using feedback from validation studies to continually improve accuracy and fairness. Validation can be difficult to achieve practically.

Job analysis

Job analysis procedures are designed to produce systematic information about jobs, including the nature of the work performed, responsibilities, equipment used, the working conditions and the position of the job within the organisation. The outputs from a job analysis are often used to generate a job description and/or a person specification for the job role. It is worth noting that satisfactory job analyses are prerequisites for many decisions and activities that have a crucial influence on the lives of employees within the organisation (including the design and validation of selection procedures, training and career development schemes, job design or job redesign, job evaluation and safety). There is a wide range of techniques and procedures available. Pearlman and Sanchez (2010) and Morgeson and Dierdorff (2011) provide accounts of job analysis research and examine the principal techniques that will be introduced in this chapter.

Although not always clear-cut, there is an important distinction between *job-oriented* and *worker-oriented* job analysis procedures. As the term suggests, job-oriented (or task-oriented) procedures focus on the work itself, producing a description in terms of the equipment used, the end results or purposes of the job, resources and materials utilised. In contrast, worker-oriented (or person-oriented) analyses concentrate on describing the psychological or behavioural requirements of the job, such as communicating, decision-making and reasoning (see Brannick et al., 2007). With the rapid pace of change in modern organisations future-oriented job analyses are now commonly used for newly created job roles, focusing on the knowledge, skills and abilities associated with these new roles. The reason for this is because many organisations are, or have been, involved in business process re-engineering where downsizing and reorganising job roles is commonplace. In this way, many jobs are now 'newly created job roles' (NCJs) where there are no pre-existing job descriptions nor indeed current job holders who can provide information during the job analysis. The challenge for psychologists is to find new ways of conducting future-oriented job analysis techniques (see Sanchez and Levine, 2012).

Although there has been a recent decrease in job-analytic research (Morgeson and Dierdorff, 2011), the research that does exist has highlighted a distinction between *task performance* (focusing on specific responsibilities in the job) and *contextual performance* (for example organisational citizenship behaviours such as courtesy, prosocial behaviour and being altruistic towards others at work). Each of these might imply using different selection criteria and related techniques to assess them. In general, there still tends to be more emphasis on the discrete *task performance*-oriented analyses rather than considering the contextual aspects in job analysis research and practice (although Sanchez and Levine, 2012, argue that contextual performance is an important part of *three* building blocks of successful job analysis: work [or task] factors, worker factors, *and* contextual factors).

Traditional job analysis approaches in personnel selection are aimed at 'fitting the person to the job'. With recent changes in the nature of work and employee work patterns, this approach is becoming less relevant and other techniques are being introduced including the suggestion for a more proactive and strategic approach to job analysis. There has even been talk of renaming job analysis to 'work analysis' to reflect the boundary-less nature of people's work roles that may no longer fit the confines of a 'job' (Sanchez and Levine, 2012).

Key learning point

Job analysis procedures are generally either worker-oriented or job-oriented. Newer research highlights the role of the work context, and much research now focuses on the future requirements of the job role.

Competencies and competency analysis

Traditionally, job analyses have aimed to identify the tasks and responsibilities associated with a job role. In general, job analysis is an umbrella term for many different analyses and involves analysing *job tasks*. In practice, it is sometimes difficult to translate the information into describing observable behaviours that underpin the tasks and responsibilities. For example, it is difficult to describe the behaviours associated with writing a complex financial report. As a result, competency analysis has become very popular in organisations to help define the person-focused assessment criteria. A *competency* can be defined as the cluster of specific characteristics and behaviour patterns a job holder is required to demonstrate in order to perform the relevant job tasks with competence. Many organisations now use competency analysis to identify the required knowledge, skills and behaviours that are essential to perform a specific job role. The main aim of competency analysis is to derive a *competency model* for the target role. A competency model comprises a comprehensive list of all the relevant competencies associated with a given job role. For more detailed discussions see Sparrow and Hodgkinson (2002) and Schippman et al. (2000).

To illustrate the use of competency analysis, imagine you are examining the person-focused requirements for the job of a sales assistant, in a large retailing company. A key competency of a sales assistant might be called 'customer service'. The observable behaviours (or behavioural indicators) that underlie this competency could be:

- actively listens to customers and attempts to understand their needs;
- proactively seeks feedback and involvement of customers in decision-making processes;
- ensures that customers feel at ease and in control of a sales interaction.

Note that these are all *positively* associated with job performance. Many competency models also detail the negative behavioural indicators, i.e. what job holders are expected to avoid doing. Competency analysis is used to build a competency model for each job role, where a model may define several competencies with associated behavioural indicators. In practice, a specific job may have between six and twelve competencies in a competency model, although there is wide variation depending on the target job role.

Point of integration

Competencies can be used as assessment criteria which have a variety of different applications including selection, but also performance appraisal, management development, careers counselling and so on, as you will see in several chapters in this book. One of the key advantages in using competencies as assessment criteria is that competencies can become a common language shared by employees in the organisation to describe the desired (and undesirable) behaviours during performance appraisal and career development activities. In this way, the competency analysis outputs can directly inform the design of the assessment criteria in selection.

For example, if demonstrating positive communication skills is a key job requirement for sales assistants, the researcher could design a competency-based interview question for selection purposes such as: 'Describe a time when you have encountered an angry customer and had to use your communications skills to deal with the situation. What did you do and what was the outcome?' An applicant's response could then be assessed on predefined behavioural criteria derived from the competency model. Exercise 4.1 provides further opportunities to explore the use of competencies and behavioural indicators in defining assessment criteria.

Exercise 4.1   Competency analysis and defining behavioural indicators

A key competency for the job of a teacher is communicating with clarity. An initial job analysis indicates that a teacher must be able to impart accurate information and be receptive to others. Some example behavioural indicators for this competency are:

- listens effectively and checks to ensure understanding;
- communicates accurately and without ambiguity;
- shows a genuine interest in other people's views;
- is always approachable and receptive.

Example negative behavioural indicators are:

- withholds or provides inaccurate information;
- is unapproachable;
- uses inappropriate language or tone;
- tends not to listen to others.

Suggested exercise

Think about your own experiences in education. What do you remember about your good teachers and your not-so-good teachers? Describe other competencies that might be associated with the job role of a teacher. For each, suggest some example positive and negative behavioural indicators.

Although the use of competencies and competency modelling has become commonplace in organisations, there is considerable confusion about what competencies actually are and how they differ from other job analysis outputs. As we have seen, competency models define behavioural indicators or behaviour patterns that impact on performance. However, in many organisations competency models for a job role have been developed *without* using appropriate psychological techniques to identify precisely the requirements in terms of behavioural indicators. This is important because it is these indicators that can be targeted for measurement purposes in selection, and other contexts. Further, in some organisations a generic *competency framework* has been developed: this often comprises a set of core competencies relevant to many job roles in the organisation. Although this approach is appealing for ease of interpretation, generic competency frameworks often lack sufficient behavioural specificity for many job roles. In other words, the behavioural indicators in a competency model should be directly relevant to the job role and the context within which the employee operates. By adopting a tailor-made approach, the assessment criteria can be more accurately defined, which in turn may optimise their use at selection.

Although many companies have found off-the-shelf competency frameworks to be cost-effective and sometimes a valuable starting point, Campion et al. (2011) warn against using them without conducting some evaluation of their suitability for the organisation's unique environment. The more specific the competency analysis is to the target job, the more useful (and potentially more accurate) the behavioural indicators are as assessment criteria. In Table 4.1 we provide an example of three competencies in a competency model for a family doctor (a general practitioner in the UK, see the opening case study). In the example, each competency heading is defined by a series of behavioural indicators. Note that the behavioural indicators (assessment criteria) associated with communication skills share some similarities with those of the teacher, but the content is qualitatively (and significantly) different. Similarly, recent research evidence demonstrates that when comparing communication skills output from job analyses *across* different medical roles and specialties, the content is reflective of the context of the specialties. Different medical specialties exhibit slightly different, context-specific, behavioural indicators of the same competency (Patterson et al., 2008).

Key learning point

Competency models define the key behaviours associated with performance in the target job role. While off-the-shelf competency frameworks may be a tempting and cost-effective option, bespoke is best as every job role (however similar they may appear) has context-specific behavioural indicators that could be missed on a generic framework.

Table 4.1   Three competencies from a competency model for family doctors

Competency	Definition	Example positive behavioural indicators
1 Empathy and sensitivity	Patient is treated with sensitivity and personal understanding, asks patient about feelings. Doctor is empathetic, in control but not dominating, and creates atmosphere of trust and confidence. Focuses on the positive rather than negative, works to involve the patient, shows interest in the individual, gives reassurance and checks patient needs are satisfied.	Generates an atmosphere where the patient feels safe Patient is taken seriously, treated confidentially Picks up on patient's emotions and feelings Encourages patient, gives reassurances Use of 'I understand what you're saying' Focuses on the positive Is sensitive to feelings Treats people as individuals Checks patient needs are satisfied Demonstrates a caring attitude
2 Communication skills	Active listening to patients, understands and interprets body language. Able to use different questioning styles and probe for information to lead to root cause. Matches patient language, uses analogy to explain, engages in social conversation, confident style. Clarity in both verbal and written communication.	Demonstrates active listening skills Is not patronising Confident in approach Able to form relationships with people and build rapport easily Uses analogy to explain problems/complex issues Re-states information for understanding Open body language and direct eye contact Matches patient's language Allows patients time to talk Engages in social conversation Refers to the patient by name
3 Clinical expertise	Able to apply and trust their judgement (and others') in diagnosing problems. Fully investigates problem before prescribing, able to anticipate rather than just react and to maintain knowledge of current practice. Does not allow patient to develop a dependency.	Trusts in their clinical judgement Clinical competence Provides anticipatory care Guards against dependency Has courage to make decisions Seeks to update clinical skills Gives clear decision and diagnosis Prescribes and checks medication Provides clear explanation of facts and systems Gets to the root of the problem Encourages patient compliance

It is important to note that competency models are not static documents: as we learned in the opening case study, best practice personnel selection is characterised by a continuous improvement cycle. Over time, as the needs of the organisation evolve (possibly in response to a range of external influences such as changes in legislation or customer demand), the job requirements and competencies required for a specific role may also change. For example, in the UK general practitioners have experienced significant changes in their role: familiarity with information technology, financial acumen and legal awareness are now core requirements for the job of running an effective medical practice. The evidence suggests that competency models and outputs from job analyses should be regularly reviewed (especially after a selection programme has been implemented) to evaluate the original assessment criteria. There are now legal reasons for ensuring accurate selection procedures are used and it is essential for compliance with current employment law. Organisations could be asked to demonstrate that they have used fair and accurate selection processes that assess candidates on competencies that are relevant to the job role.

Job analysis data

Sources of job analysis data may be divided into four categories: written material, job holders' reports, colleagues' reports and direct observation.

Written material and existing documentation

Until the 1990s, many organisations held written job descriptions available for many job roles, which provided the researcher with useful information, particularly for blue-collar job roles. Unfortunately, in many organisations existing job descriptions are rarely up to date, comprehensive or detailed enough, especially given the rapid pace of organisational change. The assessment criteria for use in selection procedures must reflect these changes, and must be updated regularly.

In some organisations, rather than having precise job descriptions, job holders may have 'performance contracts' that detail the broad objectives and responsibilities for the job that are to be fulfilled within a prescribed time frame. Where this approach is used for appraising job performance, expectations are documented and an employee is assessed on the extent to which they have met the specified objectives. In general, published analyses of jobs may provide useful leads but are of limited value: jobs analysed elsewhere are likely to be similar but not identical to the one under consideration. An accountant's, secretary's or production manager's job will vary considerably from one organisation to another, perhaps in ways that are crucial to the selection process. Other written material such as production data, organisation charts, training manuals, job aids and so on may also provide useful additional information.

Job holders' reports

Interviews in which job holders are asked, through careful questioning, to give a description of their main tasks and how they carry them out, provide extremely useful information and are seen as an essential element in any job analysis. It can be difficult to be sure that all of the important aspects of the job have been covered by the interview and that the information provided by the job holder is not too subjective, biased (owing to faulty memory, perhaps) or even deliberately misleading. For example, there has been a substantial amount of recent research into the role of 'carelessness' (e.g. Morgeson et al., 2014; Sanchez and Levine, 2012), which occurs when job holders are indifferent to the job analysis task, not reading items closely enough, being deliberately obstructive, or failing to make important distinctions between questions about their job. This has been studied using bogus items that represent work tasks job incumbents cannot perform in their roles – despite this, it has been found that many job holders endorse the importance of such items. In other words, people make judgements on tasks they have never done. Therefore, it is usual that several job holders are interviewed to get a consistent picture of the target job role. However, this can be problematic for newly created jobs that have no incumbents to interview: in this case it is likely that senior personnel would be consulted to describe the key responsibilities and performance indicators for the target job role, using a future-oriented approach.

Where there are existing job holders, reports may be obtained by asking them to complete a diary or activity record. This can be done on a regular basis as the job is being carried out to avoid problems associated with faulty memory and so forth. The advantage here is that the psychologist can gain an insight into the temporal components to the job (e.g. the sequences in which different tasks occur), and the information can offer a useful level of detail on the job activities. Work diaries, however, are a difficult and time-consuming procedure, for both the job holder and the analyst. The diaries have to be constructed in such a way as to provide the appropriate level of detail. For example, Exercise 4.2 illustrates a hypothetical work diary for a finance manager working in a large manufacturing company. The diary is a record of daily events and is only structured through time spent on different tasks. In this example, the information gathered is limited as it lacks specificity and can be difficult to translate into behavioural indicators that could be used in the selection process.

Exercise 4.2   Excerpt from an unstructured work diary

8.00–8.20	Examined e-mail and related correspondence.
8.20–8.30	Met with secretary to plan priorities and responses to correspondence. Organised diary of events and had to reschedule two meetings.
8.30–10.00	Attended strategy meeting with the Executive. Presented a 15-minute summary of the new product launch and projected impact report. Responded to technical questions about calculation of the key performance indicators and profit margin.
10.00–12.00	Analysed data tables of departmental expenditure for first quarter and sketched out a draft report to go to senior management for the forthcoming business process re-engineering review. Involved calculating spend versus income and forecasting total year spend, both for staff salaries and associated costs. Highlighted key figures in the report and illustrated in graphical format.
12.00–12.20	Grabbed sandwich!
12.20	Made telephone call to key supplier to negotiate pricing of materials for product launch.
12.30–1.30	Chaired a team meeting with my staff. Presented news update and business figures. Discussed implications of restructure of job roles.

Suggested exercises

1   Examine the extract from the work diary shown above and create a list of behaviours that appear to be associated with successful performance in this finance manager's job role. (Hint: you may find it useful to highlight particular words that refer to behaviours, e.g. 'prioritise' or 'negotiate'.)

2   Having created your list, comment on how the information you have gathered can be used. Suggest ways in which the work diary could be improved to provide additional information in order to design relevant assessment criteria.

To improve the collection of data from job holders, Flanagan (1954) developed a procedure known as the critical incident technique (CIT). In brief, using this technique involves asking the interviewee to recall specific incidents of job behaviour that are characteristic of either highly effective or highly ineffective performance in the job. A critical incident is defined as 'any observable human activity that is sufficiently complete in itself to permit inferences and predictions to be made about the person performing the act'. By describing the behaviours and characteristics that led to the incident, the analyst can get an excellent insight into the relevant job behaviour(s) that are important. Not only will this information enable the analyst to differentiate between good and poor job holders, it can provide some contextual information that might be helpful in designing the actual selection methods. CIT is a versatile technique that can be conducted either during interviews with individuals or with groups of job holders. A group-based CIT can be very useful to get initial 'cross-validation' of information, where job holders might have experienced or witnessed similar incidents (see Patterson et al., 2000, 2008, 2013). One potential drawback with using this method is that it might lead to job holders focusing on the extreme behaviours (good or bad) that influence performance, at the expense of a detailed analysis of the more routine but important elements of job performance. However, a skilled practitioner can use CIT in a way that avoids this problem.

The position analysis questionnaire (PAQ) produced by McCormick et al. (1972) remains an oft-mentioned example of a structured, and standardised, questionnaire approach to job analysis. The elements in the questionnaire are worker-oriented in that they focus on generalised aspects of human behaviour and are not closely tied to the technology of specific jobs. This means the questionnaire can be used, without being tailored, to analyse a wide variety of jobs. The PAQ consists of nearly 200 items organised into six broad categories. These questions ask about what the job involves, including: (i) the information input components of the job; (ii) the mediation processes (i.e. the mental processes of reasoning, decision-making, etc.) involved in the work; (iii) work output; (iv) interpersonal activities associated with the work (i.e. relationships with colleagues); (v) the work situation and job context; (vi) miscellaneous aspects of the job (i.e. things not covered by i–v). The results of the PAQ then point directly to specific abilities and skills the job holder would require. One problem with the PAQ is that it requires a fairly high level of reading ability on the part of respondents (some of the questions are quite complex). Nevertheless, the PAQ is a well-researched and valuable means of analysing jobs using a standardised and well-established technique.

Key learning point

Generic job analysis questionnaires are available. They can be used to analyse a wide variety of jobs in a standardised and thorough way.

McCormick and others carried out the original development work for the PAQ in the USA. There has also been development of British job analysis questionnaires such as that by Banks and colleagues (Banks et al., 1983; Banks, 1988) who produced the job components inventory (JCI). This inventory focuses on both the job and the worker, and, as with the PAQ, the outputs from the analysis include quantified profiles of the skills required for the job under investigation. Another British questionnaire is the Work Profiling System (WPS) (produced by UK occupational psychology consultants SHL). This consists of a set of over 800 items. A subset of about 200 items is usually used for any particular job, depending on the level of complexity of the job being analysed.

Functional job analysis (FJA) is job-oriented rather than worker-oriented (Fine and Wiley, 1974; Fine and Cronshaw, 1999). This approach makes use of standardised language to describe what job holders do and provides a means of examining both the complexity and the *orientation* of the job. Orientation here is described as the extent to which the job is directed towards 'data', 'people' or 'things': as a result of analysis, this orientation can be expressed in percentage terms. The basic unit of analysis in FJA is the task – that is, an action or action sequence organised over time and designed to contribute to a specific end result or objective. FJA draws a sharp distinction between what gets done and what workers actually do to get the task done. Using a very similar definition of the task, Annett and others (Annett et al., 1971; Shepherd, 1976) have developed a means of analysis known as hierarchical task analysis (HTA): this is described in more detail later (Chapters 8 and 9). A more recent development is the use of flexible, large-scale, computer-driven databases that contain information not just about work behaviours but also associated worker attributes, including information on the personality, behavioural and situational variables (see Hough and Oswald, 2000).

Research methods in focus

Repertory grid technique

A procedure for collecting job analysis information that still remains popular involves the use of Kelly's (1955) *repertory grid technique*. This approach provides systematic worker-oriented data. It has an advantage over other means of obtaining worker-oriented data such as the PAQ in that it does not limit the responses of the job holder by providing a predetermined set of categories. The repertory grid technique is based on Kelly's personal construct theory and works by eliciting an individual's personal constructs. Kelly describes a personal construct as 'a reference axis, a basic dimension of appraisal, often unverbalised, frequently unsymbolised'. Metaphorically, the theory suggests that individuals view the world through their own personal 'lenses', and hold a set of mental models and beliefs about how the world works. Using repertory grid in job analysis aims to get job holders to reveal and describe their mental models of the work they do and what is required to perform the job effectively. This involves a highly structured interviewing process to elicit mental models.

The theory assumes that behind any act of judgement (conscious or unconscious) lies an *implicit theory* about the domain of events within which the individual is making the judgement. In addition, it is assumed that these implicit theories are unique to an individual but that similar constructs may occur between individuals (so there may be common mental models about what is required for effective job performance among a group of workers doing a similar job).

For job analysis purposes, the repertory grid technique is often used to interview job holders about the knowledge, skills and abilities involved in the target role and provides a rich source of qualitative data (Fransella and Bannister, 1977). It has a powerful advantage over many other techniques in that job holders may describe constructs that they have never verbalised before, perhaps allowing them to describe tacit knowledge. In practice, the repertory grid technique is most useful as a starting point in a job analysis because it helps to explore the breadth of the job domain (particularly if the range of activities and tasks involved in the job is not well known). In this way, the technique avoids predetermining the domain of questioning, unlike structured work profiling questionnaires. It is also a useful technique for analysing the cognitive components of the job (e.g. expert decision-making processes) that are opaque to someone observing the worker doing the job.

Colleagues' reports

In addition to gleaning information directly from job holders, it can be useful to obtain data from direct reports, peers and supervisors. For example, when collecting critical incident data, the views of a job holder, a direct report and a supervisor on the nature of such critical incidents might provide for interesting comparisons. It might also be useful to gain information from customers or the *user group* of the intended job holders. In a job analysis of family doctors (Patterson et al., 2000), information was collected not just from the doctors themselves, but also from patients. An important part of this study was to compare the patient perceptions to doctor perceptions of the job role (i.e. it identified aspects of job performance that were important from the perspective of established experts, but also from those for whom they provided care). In this way, the user group perspective can be reflected in the assessment criteria in both selection and performance management applications. In another study Patterson et al. (2008) collected information from other healthcare professionals who worked alongside doctors: this significantly increased the accuracy of the job analysis.

Direct observation

In any job analysis some direct observation of the job being carried out is invariably helpful. It is, of course, possible that the presence of the researcher may alter the job holder's behaviour, and as with the approaches described earlier the data obtained cannot be perfect. Yet data derived from observation, perhaps even from participant observation (where the analyst does all or some of the job) can provide insights that no other method can. Observation is most useful for jobs where there is a manual or visible component such as a factory line worker, as the tasks conducted can be viewed clearly. For managerial jobs however, where there are extended periods of time spent working on a computer or on the telephone, or simply thinking about decisions, observation may not add a great deal of useful information for the job analysis.

A variety of different techniques for job analysis have been introduced and it is often useful to conduct an analysis using a variety of methods rather than just one. On this basis, as well as being useful for personnel selection, the outputs may be helpful in other applications, such as training and development or job evaluation.

Key learning point

No single method of job analysis is perfect. Job analyses are usually best developed by using as many different approaches and means of data collection as possible and pooling the results.

Little recent research has been conducted that compares the relative effectiveness of the different job analysis methods (Morgeson and Dierdorff, 2011). Levine et al. (1980) did conduct an early study to compare the PAQ with CIT, **task analysis** and job elements, and found that while the PAQ was the least costly to implement, it was not highly rated by participants. CIT seemed to generate more data than other methods, but overall the different methods did not have much differing impact on the quantity of data gathered. This indicates that there is probably no one best way to conduct a job analysis. Indeed, it is generally recommended that using multiple methods is the best way of capturing the most comprehensive range of perspectives on the target job role. When deciding which approach (or approaches) to adopt in conducting a job analysis in practice, Table 4.2 provides a checklist of questions or criteria that you may wish to consider when deciding which methods to use in a given setting.

Using job analysis information

The job analysis information is used in a number of ways. A job description can be prepared from the job analysis data to give an outline of the key responsibilities. The job analysis also

Table 4.2	A checklist of considerations for conducting a job analysis

- Is my purpose to conduct a task-oriented or worker-oriented analysis (i.e. precise tasks and responsibilities or primarily psychological factors)?

- What level of expertise is required for the analyst?

- What is the level of job proximity in using this technique (direct observation versus remote analysis of self-report on a questionnaire)? How will this influence the quality of data I collect?

- What type of data does this technique provide and how will this be analysed?

- How can I best validate my initial findings?

- What is the capacity of using this technique to generate usable outcomes?

- What is the cost (both in terms of time and resource) of using this technique?

- Are there issues regarding employee sensitivity and access to job holders that need to be addressed?

provides information that might be used when recruitment advertisements and so forth are prepared to attract candidates for the job (and so that candidates can decide whether the job will suit them before they decide to enter the selection process). Naturally, it is essential for designing and/or choosing appropriate selection tools.

A personnel specification represents the demands of the job translated into human terms. It involves listing the essential criteria that candidates must satisfy and also those criteria that would exclude candidates from consideration. As described earlier, job analysis information may also be used to define a competency model for the job role. However, moving from a job analysis to a clear specification of the psychological qualities thought to be required by a successful job holder is a difficult process. Various procedures have been suggested and used to make this step, but it is important to remember that none of them are entirely objective and that some inferences and judgements are required.

The inferential steps needed and the nature of these inferences are different, depending on whether one is designing a *sign-* or *sample-based* selection procedure. Wernimont and Campbell (1968) made this important distinction between what they described as *signs* and *samples* of behaviour. Consider, for example, how a candidate for a sales position may react to being asked to complete a personality questionnaire, containing questions such as 'Do you often wish that your life was more exciting?' Consider also how the same candidate may react to being required to conduct a role-play exercise in which they are expected to persuade a client to make a purchase. The relevance of the role-play exercise is obvious due to its potential to provide the selection decision-makers with a realistic *sample* of the candidate's behaviour. Although it may not be so obvious to the candidate, the results of the personality questionnaire may also provide important *signs* relating to job-relevant psychological characteristics. For example, success in sales jobs may be more likely when someone is extraverted (high extraversion), emotionally stable (low neuroticism) and seeks to avoid conflict and help others (high agreeableness).

Job analysis data may be used in two broadly different ways in the design of selection procedures depending on whether the selection procedure will be used to assess samples or signs of behaviour.

Job analysis information may be used to design sign- or sample-based personnel selection procedures.

The more traditional use of job analysis involves moving from the analysis to make inferences about the kind of psychological characteristics (signs) needed for successful job performance. By contrast, the sample approach involves focusing on the job tasks and designing selection procedures that stimulate the actual behaviour needed for successful jobs. There are also challenges and opportunities in using technology to collect and inform the job analysis process. McEntire et al. (2006) and Reiter-Palmon et al. (2006) describe how Web-based job analysis processes and applications (such as O*NET) can be more flexible and less resource-intensive than traditional job analysis methods. They argue that there are benefits of this approach that meet the needs of today's dynamic workforce. Sometimes conducting an in-depth job analysis with multiple techniques will provide excellent information, but unfortunately it may take so long that the job role which was analysed is no longer needed by the organisation.

Stop to consider

In the preceding section we have looked at job analysis in quite a lot of detail. What are the possible consequences of not carrying out a thorough job analysis before designing and implementing a new selection process? Do you think that these offset the costs of carrying out the job analysis? Why?

You may also have noticed that many jobs change quickly and the boundaries of many job roles are not clearly defined. Are there some job analysis techniques that might be better than others for these types of jobs? What might be some of the advantages of using more than one technique/method to analyse a job?

Validation processes

The pivotal stage in the personnel selection process occurs when the selection decision is taken and a candidate is either offered a position within the organisation, or turned away. At this point various pieces of evidence concerning the current or past performance of candidates (e.g. behaviour at an interview, psychological test scores or references), usually referred to as **predictors**, are used to decide whether or not a candidate is suitable for the job in question. Although a job analysis may suggest that certain candidate characteristics might be desirable, on its own the job analysis data cannot *prove* that candidates with these characteristics will do better than others on the job. This evaluation of the accuracy of the selection methods is obtained by assessing the *criterion-related validity* of the predictors. Validation is about finding out whether the various parts of the selection process were effective. There are a number of ways of examining the effectiveness of a selection process.

Criterion-related validity

This is the strength of the relationship between the predictor (e.g. psychological test scores or interview ratings) and the criterion (e.g. subsequent work behaviour). Criterion-related

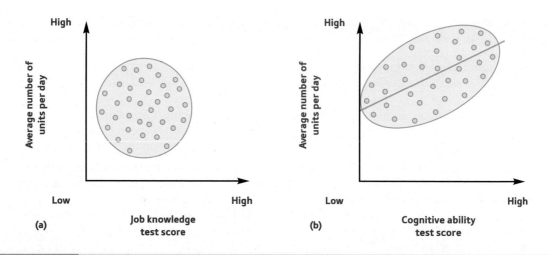

Figure 4.2   Some hypothetical predictor and criterion scores: (a) job knowledge test; (b) a cognitive ability test

validity is high if candidates who obtain high predictor scores obtain high criterion scores *and* candidates who obtain low scores on a predictor also obtain low criterion scores. Figure 4.2 shows a scatter plot of some hypothetical data obtained by using two predictors:

1   a job knowledge test score; and

2   a cognitive ability test score;

and one criterion: an average number of units produced per day.

Inspection of the scatter plot in Figure 4.2b shows that the criterion-related validity of the cognitive ability test appears to be quite good. Participants' scores in this test correspond closely with the number of units produced. It is also worth noting that the correspondence is not perfect. For perfect correspondence all of the points would lie exactly on the diagonal line drawn in on Figure 4.2b. For the job knowledge test there is no correspondence at all. Figure 4.2a shows that the points are distributed more or less in a circle and high scores on one variable can be associated with either high or low scores on the other variable.

Key learning point

The criterion-related validity of a selection procedure is normally indicated by the magnitude of the validity coefficient (the correlation between the predictor and criterion scores).

The ideal way to collect criterion-related validity data is to use a predictive (or follow-up) design. This design involves collecting predictor information for candidates during the selection process and then following up the candidates (e.g. during their first year of employment) to gather work performance criterion data (see for example Patterson et al., 2005). What might be assessed as the predictor criterion needs careful consideration (Sackett and Lievens, 2008; Rotundo and Sackett, 2002). Task performance, citizenship performance and counterproductive work behaviour are the three major domains of job performance. Cognitively loaded predictors (e.g. cognitive ability test scores) tend to be the strongest correlates of task performance and non-cognitive predictors tend to be the best predictors in the citizenship and counterproductive behaviour domains. This indicates that careful attention needs to be paid to the criterion of interest to the organisation: this should

The meaning of correlations

The strength of the relationship between predictor scores and criterion scores is usually expressed as a correlation coefficient (referred to as a validity coefficient). Perfect positive correlation between two variables will produce a correlation of 1. No correlation at all, as in Figure 4.2a, will produce a coefficient of zero.

When the correlation between two variables is high it is possible to predict the score of one when supplied with the score on the other. Consider, for example, Figure 4.3, where the predictor–criterion relationship is perfect (i.e. a validity (correlation) coefficient of +1.0). In the case of a new candidate, it would be possible to obtain their score on predictor A and thus predict a score on the criterion. If the organisation wished to select staff who would produce an average of at least 75 units per day, what should be done?

As Figure 4.3 shows, if only people who obtained a score of above 80 on selection test A were offered jobs by the organisation, all future employees would be very likely to produce at least 75 units per day. In practice, selection can rarely be conducted in such an idealised and clear-cut fashion and there are several practical problems that must be considered.

Research has shown that it is most unusual in practical situations to obtain validity coefficients much in excess of +0.5, let alone the coefficient of +1.0 that will allow perfect prediction (e.g. Patterson and Ferguson, 2007; Salgado et al., 2001). Nevertheless, validity coefficients of considerably less than +1.0 can provide a basis for improved selection.

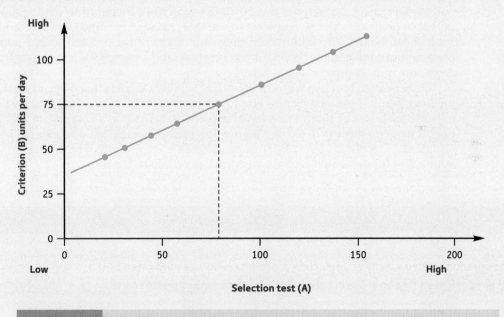

Figure 4.3	Prediction of criterion scores from selection test scores

be a critical determinant of the eventual make-up and success of a selection system (Sackett and Lievens, 2008). Clearly it would be unwise to have a selection system that predicted perfectly aspects of performance that were irrelevant to the organisation.

Similarly, the role of the human raters in the measurement of performance is also an important consideration. Viswesvaran et al.'s (2005) meta-analysis compared correlations between ratings on various different performance dimensions made by different raters with those made on various performance dimensions by the same rater.

This analysis showed the positive impact of rater training and experience within the organisation on the quality of performance measurement, and hence predictive validity (especially when the selection process has been running for more than one year). When selection processes are new, the way performance measures are identified and designed improves predictive validity, but as the selection process matures, the qualities of the rater tend to become increasingly important. There is now some research into the effects of interventions designed to standardise and quality assure rater involvement. In a high-stakes selection process Patterson et al. (2014) developed competency models for the role of the assessors. These can be valuable for (i) recruiting suitable assessors, (ii) measuring the performance of assessors and highlighting areas for development, and (iii) training assessors; all of which are likely to raise the validity and reliability of the process they are assessing.

An alternative design for conducting criterion-related validity studies is the *concurrent* design. In the concurrent design, predictor data are obtained from existing employees on whom criterion data are already available. Ideally, scores on selection tasks should not be used to take selection decisions until after a validation study has been conducted. This creates a difficulty: until the relationship between predictor and criterion is firmly established, candidates should be offered employment regardless of their performance on the predictors. If job analysis data and other information suggest that the use of certain predictors should improve their selection decisions, in many organisations managers would not be willing to permit candidates with low scores on these predictors to enter employment. Sometimes it is possible to convince them not to use the results of potential predictors and to continue to use their existing methods while a validation study is carried out. Often, however, they cannot accept the constraints of a complete predictive validity design (because it takes considerable time to follow up enough candidates) and some compromise is needed.

Another design problem with the predictive validity design is that of ensuring that the predictor results obtained by new employees are not revealed to other members of the organisation before a validity study has been conducted. Obviously a supervisor who is allocated a new employee with either a high or low predictor score could be affected by these results. The supervisor's behaviour towards the new employee might be influenced and/or estimates of the new employee's work performance could be biased.

Key learning point

Predictive validity designs are more rigorous than concurrent validity designs but their implementation usually presents a number of practical problems.

One advantage of the concurrent design is that the organisation is not required to collect predictor data from job applicants and then somehow ignore that data during selection decision-making. Predictor data are collected from existing employees only. A second advantage of the concurrent design is that there is no time delay between the collection of predictor and criterion data. Existing employees' predictor scores are correlated with their criterion performance. The criterion data are likely to be readily available. There is certainly no need to wait for the lengthy follow-up period. Figure 4.4 compares the two designs in a hypothetical situation and indicates the considerable differences in timescales and data collection effort that can occur.

However, this approach has disadvantages. The workers presently employed by an organisation provide a population that may be very different from the population of job

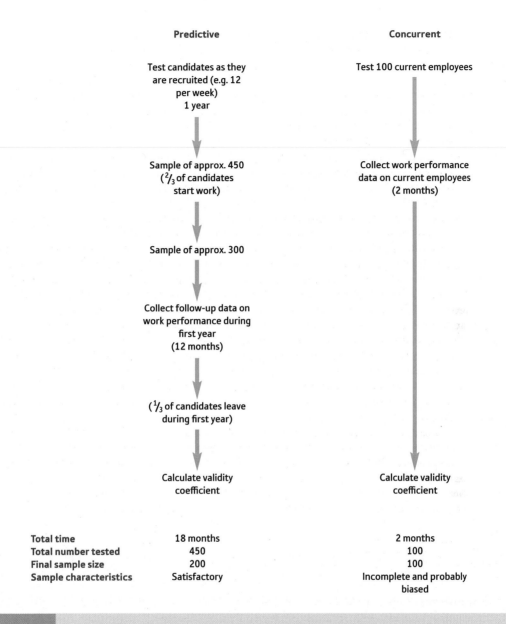

	Predictive	Concurrent

Predictive

Test candidates as they are recruited (e.g. 12 per week) 1 year

↓

Sample of approx. 450 ($^2/_3$ of candidates start work)

↓

Sample of approx. 300

↓

Collect follow-up data on work performance during first year (12 months)

↓

($^1/_3$ of candidates leave during first year)

↓

Calculate validity coefficient

Concurrent

Test 100 current employees

↓

Collect work performance data on current employees (2 months)

↓

Calculate validity coefficient

	Predictive	Concurrent
Total time	18 months	2 months
Total number tested	450	100
Final sample size	200	100
Sample characteristics	Satisfactory	Incomplete and probably biased

Figure 4.4   A comparison of predictive and concurrent validity study designs

applicants. Current job holders have already been selected in using existing company selection procedures and represent a preselected group of people who have been with the organisation for some time. No data are available on people who were not hired by the company, or on those who were hired but have subsequently left. It is very likely that the concurrent sample is incomplete and not representative of the potential workforce. If, as a result of a concurrent validity study, a link between, say, scores in an arithmetic test and job performance is established, it is difficult to be sure if the people tested came to the job with such skills or whether arithmetic skills are acquired as a result of training and job experience. It would not be fair or informative to test new applicants for skills that could only be acquired through training and experience within the company. Such problems make it hard to be certain about the actual predictive value of results derived from a concurrent validity study.

As we have already seen, once people are in the job their performance may be measured across a number of different criteria. Therefore, validation studies can quickly become very complex in practical terms because organisations rarely use one single predictor to make selection decisions. Given the multifaceted nature of job analysis information, recruiters are likely to design multiple selection tools to assess these criteria. Therefore, recruiters must decide whether a job applicant must score highly on all assessment criteria (a *non-compensatory approach* to selection) or whether high scores on some criteria can make up for low scores on another (a compensatory approach). In practice, recruiters might assign different weightings to various assessment criteria, depending on the nature of the job role (e.g. it might be decided that customer service skill is the most important criterion and applicants who do not achieve a certain score will not be considered further).

Most selection systems combine several predictors such as an applicant's score on an interview and on a situational judgement test. In validation studies, a key question is how much does adding another predictor increase the predictive power of the selection process? This is known as *incremental validity*. In other words, recruiters might want to know how much accuracy is improved as a result of adding a psychometric test to the process. Information on the incremental validity of a specific selection tool is extremely valuable as it allows organisations to conduct a cost–benefit analysis of using additional tools. Research including meta-analysis has attempted to estimate the incremental validity of one predictor over another (almost a league table of selection methods). This research attempts to better understand the relationships among predictors and dimensions of job performance to enhance the practical choice of selection methods (see Sackett and Lievens, 2008, for a summary of incremental validity studies and limitations to these). The typical levels of predictive validity for various selection methods are examined later in this chapter.

Another significant practical difficulty in today's organisations is that of accessing an adequate sample size in order to perform certain statistical analyses on the data. Most organisations are not involved in large-scale recruitment programmes and usually it is sizeable recruitment initiatives (e.g. graduate recruitment schemes) that are the focus of validation studies involving several hundred applicants from which at least a hundred begin working for the organisation.

One important point to make about any validity study is that the initial validity study should always be followed by a 'cross-validation' study on a second sample of people to cross-check the results obtained. For studies that involve relatively few predictors this requirement is perhaps not essential and represents a 'counsel of perfection'. However, when a study has investigated many possible predictors and those with the strongest predictor–criterion relationship are to be used for selection purposes, cross-validation is more important. The more potential predictors are used, the more likely it becomes that random or chance variations will produce apparent but spurious predictor–criterion relationships. Relationships due to chance would be unlikely to occur again in the cross-validation sample.

Key learning point

Cross-validation is necessary to be confident of the results from a validation study, unless the sample is very large.

Stop to consider

In this section we have discussed how we can examine whether test scores at selection are related to job performance. Now consider how well the performance measures used by organisations (e.g. manager appraisals, sales performance, number of mistakes, etc.) provide a true reflection of job performance. Is the care taken in the design and use of selection measures matched by the care taken in the design and use of performance measures?

Also consider the challenges facing small organisations (e.g. of fewer than 25 employees) when they attempt to validate their selection processes. How would their situation differ from that faced by large organisations carrying out high-volume recruitment? What implications might this have for small organisations seeking to improve their selection processes?

Other types of validity

Criterion-related validity is the most important type of validity as far as selection is concerned because the main purpose of selection procedures is to select people who are likely to perform well in the role. However, there are also other important types of validity. The first two are not 'real' forms of validity, in the sense that they refer to appearance rather than substance, but can be important for things like candidate perceptions.

Faith validity

Sometimes organisations might believe that a selection method is valid because a reputable company sells it, and it is packaged in a very expensive-looking way (**faith validity**). However, Cook (2009) suggests that money spent on 'gloss' could mean less money has been spent on research and development of the instrument. He suggests that organisations must be wary of blindly accepting the validity of an instrument without thorough inspection of all supporting data and documentation.

Face validity

A selection test or procedure displays **face validity** if it 'looks right'. For example, requiring an applicant for a carpenter's job to make a T-joint from two pieces of wood would show face validity. On the other hand, asking the applicant to carry out a test of general intelligence would probably have much less face validity for the candidate, since the link between that test and job performance would probably be less obvious to the candidate. One key advantage of face validity is the positive impact it has upon user acceptability: candidates are less likely to feel unfairly treated and challenge the outcomes of selection processes if they believe that the selection process looks relevant to the job role.

Content validity

Content validity is established on a logical basis rather than by calculating validity coefficients or following other technical statistical procedures. A predictor shows content validity when it covers a representative sample of the behaviour domain being measured. For example, a content-valid test of car-driving ability would be expected to cover all of the essential activities of a competent driver. A test that did not include an emergency stop and a reversing exercise would be lacking in content validity (and most likely result in higher car insurance premiums and more work for accident compensation lawyers!).

Construct validity

This involves identifying the psychological characteristics (or constructs) such as intelligence, emotional stability or manual dexterity that underlie successful performance of the task (such as a test or performance on the job) in question. Since **construct validity** involves relationships between predictors and characteristics that are not directly observable (e.g. cognitive processes), it can be assessed only by indirect means. Often this is achieved by correlating a well-established measure of a construct with a new measure of the same construct. For example, if a new measure of extraversion had been developed, one would expect that scores on this new measure would be highly correlated with scores on other well-established measures of extraversion (we might also reasonably expect that correlations between the new measure and other, very different constructs, should be low). Exploring the construct validity of any psychological instrument is an important facet of understanding what the instrument actually measures (i.e. 'does it do what it says on the tin?').

Exercise 4.3 gives an opportunity to reflect upon your own experiences of selection processes, particularly in relation to your perceptions of the validity of the process.

Point of integration

Validity – and the various types of it – is an important property of all measures and methods used in work psychology, not just in selection. For example, considerable time and effort goes into the validation of attitude measures and measures of leadership behaviour. The same applies to the issues of reliability, fairness and candidate perceptions discussed later in this chapter.

Exercise 4.3   The validity of selection processes

In this exercise you are asked to reflect upon your own experience(s) of selection and recruitment processes. Think about a job in which you have been, or are currently, employed (whether full time or part time) and consider the following issues:

Suggested exercises

1   What are the key responsibilities of the role?
2   Describe the elements of the recruitment process. From your perspective as the applicant, did the selection procedures display face validity and content validity at each stage?
3   In general, what is your impression of the accuracy of the selection process?
4   What recommendation would you make to improve the likely validity of this selection process?

Reliability

Any measuring instrument used in a selection procedure must be both valid and reliable. The reliability of a selection instrument is an extremely important characteristic and refers to the extent to which it measures *consistently under varying conditions*. If the same candidate produces very different scores when they take a test on two different occasions, the reliability of the test must be questioned. In technical terms, if a selection tool has high reliability it is relatively free from errors of measurement (i.e. the score that we obtain is close to the *true* score). Of course, this means that a test cannot be valid unless it is reliable. There are a number of different types of reliability.

If we want to assess the reliability for an ability test we could calculate the *test–retest reliability* (where participants are administered the same test on two separate occasions with a significant time lag between administrations). If the test was reliable we would expect the scores not to change very much over time. In other words, if the test had high reliability we would expect a strong positive correlation between scores at time 1 and time 2 administrations. In assessing this form of reliability it would be very important to ensure that the testing conditions were the same on both occasions, and that the construct being measured was thought to be relatively stable.

Another form of reliability is *parallel forms*, where test developers might design two tests to be equivalent, including items of similar content and equal difficulty. Test publishers might develop 50 high-quality questions for a test and use 25 in version A and the other 25 in version B. For example, organisations involved in graduate recruitment often use similar psychometric ability tests. In order to prevent practice effects, test publishers produce parallel forms of the same ability test. In designing parallel forms of the same test, the test developers assess the external reliability between scales, where high reliability is characterised by a strong positive correlation between participant scores on both tests. Not all tests will have parallel forms because of the increased costs involved in development (i.e. developing double the number of test items than are actually needed).

Test–retest and parallel forms can both be described as *external* forms of reliability, because scores on the measure in question are compared with an external reference point, even if that reference point scores on the same measure at a different time.

The *internal* reliability of a scale can be assessed by a variety of different statistical methods and formulae (see Smith and Robertson, 1993; Kline, 1999, for relevant formulae and further technical information). Internal reliability always concerns the extent to which different parts of the same measure produce results consistent with each other. In essence it is a measure of the extent to which questions designed to measure the same thing produce similar, consistent, results. The type of scale and its content determine the specific approach to assessing internal reliability. Common approaches to assessing the internal reliability of scales include Cronbach's coefficient alpha, the 'split half' method (where the researcher can examine the association between scores on two halves of a test, for example) and KR20 (which is used for questions that have right or wrong answers). Clearly, it is desirable to find consistency across different items that are measuring the same thing: as a rule of thumb high internal consistency reliabilities (e.g. Cronbach's coefficient alpha of 0.7 or above) are desirable. However, if internal consistency reliability is too high (above about 0.95) then the test may be inefficient because it is essentially asking the same questions (and therefore gathering the same data) over and over again.

Key learning point

To be effective, personnel selection methods must be both valid and reliable.

Financial utility

Like many organisational practices, personnel selection procedures cost money to implement. Using selection procedures with good predictive validity is always important but, unfortunately, procedures with good predictive validity alone do not guarantee that a selection procedure will be cost-effective. Two important factors determining cost-effectiveness (usually referred to as **utility**) are:

1   the selection ratio, i.e. number of jobs/number of candidates;

2   the financial benefit of improved job performance.

Let us now examine in a little more detail the role that validity, **selection ratio** and the other factors play in determining utility. Figure 4.5a shows the situation for

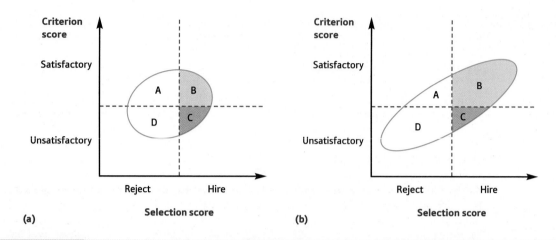

Figure 4.5   The effect of different validity coefficients on the proportion hired: (a) validity coefficient = 0.1; (b) validity coefficient = 0.5

a validity coefficient of 0.1. The shaded areas (B and C) identify people who will be hired by the organisation. Notice, however, that although all of these people achieve the minimum acceptable score on the predictor (the cut-off score), only a proportion of them (B) also show satisfactory work performance. Similarly, although all of the people in the unshaded areas (A and D) fail to achieve the cut-off score on the predictor, some of them are capable of satisfactory work performance (those in area A). Areas B and D represent correct selection decisions; area D contains people who have justifiably been rejected, known as true negatives. Area C contains the false positives; that is, people who would be hired but produce unsatisfactory work performance. Area A contains the false negatives; that is, people who would not be hired but are capable of satisfactory work performance. Areas A and C represent errors in the selection process. Note that unless the validity coefficient is 1.0 there will *always* be errors of selection.

As Figure 4.5b shows, when validity increases (0.5), the proportions in areas A and C decrease and the proportion of correct decisions (areas B and D) increases. Thus, as validity increases, the quality of selection decisions also increases.

The financial benefit of improved job performance can be calculated by applying a value of 40 per cent of salary to each standard deviation of performance. Then, the cost of the selection procedure needs to be subtracted and account taken of the expected tenure of recruits and the number of people selected.

Personnel selection and assessment methods

There is over a century's research literature exploring how best to select a person for a job. Work psychologists have had a major influence on the way selection processes are designed and implemented across many organisations in all sectors of industry across the world. Over the past three decades, the research shows that although there are a variety of personnel selection methods available to use in organisational settings, not all of the methods are equally useful or appropriate in some selection processes.

An overview of personnel selection methods

Table 4.3 shows the major personnel selection methods that are available for use and also gives a brief explanation of what the methods involve. Most of the methods are well known, and many readers will have first-hand experience of some of them.

Table 4.3	Personnel selection methods
1	**Interviews**
	Many involve more than one interviewer. When several interviewers are involved, the term panel interview is used. The most important features of an interview are the extent to which a pre-planned structure is followed and the proportion of questions that are directly related to the job.
2	**Psychometric tests**
	This category includes tests of cognitive ability (such as general intelligence, verbal ability, numerical ability), self-report measures of personality* and situational judgement tests.
3	**References**
	Usually obtained from current or previous employers, these are used often in the final stages of the selection process. The information requested may be specific or general and open-ended.
4	**Biodata**
	Specifications of biographical information about a candidate's life history. Some biodata inventories may contain many (e.g. 150+) questions and ask objective questions, such as which professional qualifications are held by the applicant, and more subjective ones, such as preferences for different job features.
5	**Work-sample tests**
	Such tests literally use samples of the job in question (e.g. the contents of an in-tray for an executive position, specific kinds of typing for a secretarial post or interacting with a customer for a sales position). The applicant is given instructions and then a specific amount of time to complete the tasks.
6	**Handwriting analysis (graphology)**
	Inferences are made about candidates' characteristics by examining specific features of their handwriting (e.g. slant, letter shapes). Obviously, a reasonably lengthy sample of the candidate's normal writing is required.
7	**Assessment centres**
	This procedure involves a combination of several of the previously mentioned techniques (e.g. psychometric tests, interviews, work samples). Candidates are usually dealt with in groups and some of the techniques used require the candidates to interact (e.g. in simulated group decision-making exercises or group presentations).
8	**CVs/résumés**
	These are written descriptions of the applicant's professional experiences, education, and any other relevant information.
9	**Application form**
	A form or collection of forms that an applicant must fill out as part of the process of informing an employer of their availability and desire to be employed. They will usually ask for information on the applicant's background and why they believe they are suited to the job they have applied for.

*The term personality test is used here for simplicity. However, measures of personality are not really tests because they do not have 'right or wrong' answers. Personality questionnaire and personality measure are also appropriate terms.

When using predictors such as interviews, psychometric tests or work-sample tests, the specific areas to be investigated in the interview or test should be derived from job analysis data. The information from the job analysis provides a basis for deciding which factors (e.g. numerical ability, communication skills, organisational skills) might be important for job success.

Biographical data are often developed in a different way. When candidates apply for a job with an organisation it is likely that they will complete an application form and other documents in which they are expected to provide certain verifiable biographical information concerning factors such as previous employment, personal career history and education. The main purpose of collecting biographical data is that information can be gathered on a number of candidates and correlated with subsequent job performance. Items of information that predict subsequent performance can then be identified and perhaps used in selection decision-making. Items of information chosen on this basis do not necessarily have any obvious link with the job; it has merely been demonstrated, on a statistical basis, that they predict future performance.

In most practical situations it is not sensible to base selection decisions on the use of one predictor only or even on one type of predictor. As you will see in this chapter, each predictor has its own strengths and weaknesses. When several different predictors are used together, the aim should be to ensure that the various predictors *complement* one another rather than duplicate each other. One successful method of selection that makes use of many different predictors is the 'assessment centre'. Assessment centres typically include interviews, psychological tests, in-tray exercises and group discussions. The assessments may go on for as short as a few hours or as long as a week. Candidates are usually assessed by trained assessors, who are often senior managers in the organisation. A typical assessment centre might involve groups of 12 candidates being assessed by 6 assessors. Assessment centres are also used frequently to evaluate people who already work within an organisation and can be used to help take decisions concerning promotion and career development (i.e. it becomes a **development centre**).

Key learning point

In most situations it is best to use a combination of several personnel selection techniques to ensure fairness and accuracy.

How well do selection methods work?

Before it is feasible to consider how well selection methods work it is necessary to be clear about what it means for a selection method to work. Earlier in the chapter, we introduced the concept of criterion-related validity and demonstrated how this could be evaluated by means of validation procedures. Obviously, criterion-related validity is an essential requirement for a selection method but other features are also important; Table 4.4 lists a number of these features. In the interests of clarity and simplicity, the evaluation of selection methods that follows concentrates on criterion-related validity.

Key learning point

One of the key evaluative standards for personnel selection methods is criterion-related validity (i.e. to what extent is performance at selection linked to job performance?).

Table 4.4	Major evaluation standards for personnel selection procedures
1	**Discrimination**
	The measurement procedures involved should provide for clear discrimination between candidates. If candidates all obtain similar results (i.e. scores, if a numerical system is used), selection decisions cannot be made. Of course, this discrimination should be based on job-relevant criteria and not irrelevant factors such as gender or ethnicity.
2	**Validity and reliability**
	The technical qualities of the measurement procedures must be adequate.
3	**Legality and fairness**
	The measures must not discriminate *unfairly* against members of any specific subgroup of the population (e.g. ethnic minorities).
4	**Administrative convenience/practicality**
	The procedures should be acceptable within the organisation and capable of being implemented effectively within the organisation's administrative structure. Those administering the procedures are likely to need appropriate training.
5	**Cost and development time**
	Given the selection decisions (e.g. number of jobs, number of candidates, type of jobs) involved, the costs involved and the time taken to develop adequate procedures need to be balanced with the potential benefits. This is essentially a question of utility.
6	**Applicant reactions**
	Applicant reactions have important consequences for an organisation. If the best candidates reject the job offer, then the utility of the selection system is reduced. The best candidates may decide to work for competitor organisations and speak negatively about their treatment. In addition, dissatisfied candidates at selection are more likely to take legal action to challenge the outcome.
7	**Generates appropriate information for feedback**
	When using selection tools such as psychometric tests, it is good practice to ensure that candidates receive appropriate and useful feedback. Sometimes, giving detailed feedback is difficult to achieve in high-volume recruitment. However, most candidates will expect some level of feedback after the selection process, especially those who have reached the latter stages of the selection process.

Estimating the validity of personnel selection procedures

Predictive or concurrent validation processes may be used to estimate the criterion-related validity of a selection procedure. Most of the selection procedures mentioned so far in this chapter have been examined in this way: investigators have conducted a huge number of validation studies on many selection procedures in many industries. However, any single validation study is unlikely to provide a definitive answer on the validity of a selection method. This is because any particular study can be conducted on only a sample of relevant people and, of course, has to be conducted in a specific organisation, at a particular time, using particular measures. There may be specific factors – to do with the sample of people used, the measures, the timing of the study and so on – which influence the study and bias the results in some way.

It is obvious, then, that to estimate the validity of a particular selection procedure more than one study is needed, so that any bias due to specific features of any particular study will not have an unduly large influence on the findings about that selection procedure overall. An example will help to illustrate the way in which the results of validation studies may be cumulated and summarised to more accurately estimate validity. A researcher may be interested in the extent to which a particular individual difference characteristic, such as intelligence, achievement motivation or verbal ability (call this factor X) is predictive of managerial performance. As already noted, any individual study, using a particular sample of managers, will not give a definitive result for the validity of factor X (see Table 4.5 for explanations of some factors that influence the accuracy of the results of any specific study). As Table 4.5 makes clear, some of the problems are caused by sampling error (item 1), imperfect reliability in the selection method or the criterion measure (item 2), and range restriction in the selection method scores (item 3). Consider these sources of error in relation to our example of the predictive validity of factor X. The sources of error are usually referred to as *artefacts* because they are not part of the natural relationship under investigation, but are a consequence of the particular investigative procedures used in the study (carrying out research in functioning organisations is very different from carrying out research in the laboratory setting). If the researcher in our example was able to identify 10 studies of the predictive validity of factor X, each study would have inaccuracies due to the artefacts that impacted upon that study. Sampling error would be present because in each study the sample involved would not be perfectly representative of the population (although studies with larger samples would of course be less prone to sampling error, because the sample is a bigger percentage of the available population).

As far as unreliability and range restriction are concerned, these artefacts will adversely affect observed validity coefficients (i.e. the validity will appear to be less than it actually is). Test reliability may be calculated and expressed in a numerical form, with zero indicating total unreliability (e.g. in a totally unreliable test someone's score on a second

Table 4.5	Major sources of distortion in validation studies
1	**Sampling error**
	The small samples (e.g. 50–150) used in many validation studies mean that the results obtained may be unduly influenced by the effects of small numbers of people within the sample whose results are unusual. As sample size increases, these irregularities usually balance each other out and a more reliable result is obtained.
2	**Poor measurement precision**
	The measurement of psychological qualities at both the predictor (i.e. selection method) and criterion (i.e. job performance) stage of the validation process is subject to unsystematic error. The result we get from a selection method comprises the candidate's true score *plus* error. The error (unreliability) in the scores obtained will *reduce* the maximum possible observed correlation between predictor and criterion: the error is unsystematic and random, thus this element of the predictor or criterion score will not correlate systematically with anything. This means that as reliability decreases, the maximum possible correlation between predictor and criterion will decrease.
3	**Restricted range of scores**
	The sample of people used in a validation study may not provide the full (theoretically possible) range of scores on the predictor and /or criterion measures. This occurs in practice because data are collected on predictors in a *restricted* population, i.e. individuals that have already been selected. The results are then generalised to the whole applicant pool, i.e. an *unrestricted* population. This has a straightforward statistical effect: it limits the size of the linear correlation between two variables. So, just like unreliability, range restriction in a sample serves to reduce the magnitude of the observed correlation coefficient, making the predictor appear less valid than it actually is.

administration could not be predicted with any accuracy from his or her score on the first). To illustrate the impact of even modest deviations from reliability (0.8 is usually taken as the ideal, acceptable lower limit), Table 4.6 shows how the confidence interval for estimating an individual's *true* score on the test gets wider and wider as test reliability decreases.

Key learning point

Studies with larger sample sizes are less prone to sampling error and more likely to give reliable results. This is because they represent a larger proportion of the population than a smaller sample would.

Even with good reliability, two apparently quite different observed scores such as 94 and 112 could, because of a lack of measurement precision, have identical true scores. When data from unreliable tests are used to calculate correlation coefficients, the effect is clear. An unreliable test contains a large amount of random error. Hence, as the reliability of a measure decreases, the opportunity for the measure to correlate with any other variable also decreases. The reliability of a measure sets a precise limit on its correlation with any other variable (the square root of the reliability is the maximum possible level of correlation; see Moser and Schuler, 1989). Similarly, the availability of only a restricted range of scores will set an artificially low ceiling on the magnitude of any observed correlation.

Consider what tends to happen in a predictive validity study. The candidates who score badly on the selection tests are (quite sensibly) not offered employment. If these low-scoring candidates were offered jobs (i.e. if the organisation was inexplicably benevolent!) they would be expected to perform badly. This link between people with low selection test scores producing low job performance scores is an important element in producing high validity coefficients. Of course, we almost never get to collect the performance scores from those who do badly at selection: the low scorers are excluded from the sample in the validation study because they were not offered the job. The resulting validity coefficient can be based only on high and average scorers, where differences in job performance will be much less extreme. The resulting validity coefficient will thus be limited in magnitude.

The main strategy for managing this problem of *range restriction* is to apply a statistical correction using formulas to estimate the correlation in the population of interest (see Sackett and Yang, 2000, for a detailed summary). This issue has been debated recently and the most accurate estimates of range restriction occur when the researcher can identify the mechanism by which restriction occurred (e.g. *direct* restriction is due to the use of the test for selection versus *indirect* restriction due to use of another predictor that is correlated with the test as the basis for selection; see Hunter et al., 2006, for a detailed review). In other

Table 4.6	The impact of different reliabilities on an estimated true score		
	Reliability		
	0.9	0.8	0.6
Observed score	100	100	100
Probable (95% confidence) range for candidate's true score	91–109	87–113	81–119

words, if the researcher has information about the spread of test scores in the population of interest (e.g. the applicant pool where there will be low, average and high scores) as well as in the restricted sample, estimates can be made of the correlation in the population of interest. This correction for restriction of range is often needed in validation studies: it usually raises the validity. However, Hunter and colleagues (2006) concluded that, in general, corrections for restriction of range may produce conservative *underestimates* of the actual validity of selection methods.

It has recently been found that correcting for indirect range restriction (IRR) may be a more accurate course of action than trying to deal with direct range restriction (DRR). While DRR correction has been used in the majority of studies relating test scores to subsequent job performance, Sjöberg et al. (2012) argue that most predictive validity studies would inevitably have some kind of IRR, and therefore using the DRR correction method may result in at least partially inaccurate results. By looking at lots of previous research, they were able to conclude that correcting for IRR was the more accurate method and that by applying this method of correction, the effect of individual difference variables (e.g. scores on personality and intelligence measures) in predicting job performance increased substantially compared with DRR. The authors point out that in a practical setting, this knowledge is invaluable as even a minor increase in validity can provide a substantial increase in utility that may be overlooked if an inappropriate correction method is used.

Key learning point

Restriction of range in scores will artificially limit the size of validity coefficients and give misleadingly low results. Failure to take range restriction into account can dramatically distort research findings, often underestimating the predictive validity of selection methods.

Research methods in focus

Meta-analysis

The statistical procedures of meta-analysis aggregate the results from many separate studies in order to obtain a more stable indication of the effect under investigation. This makes it especially useful for trying to identify the methods of selection that typically work best. Meta-analysis is carried out using statistical methods that estimate the amount of sampling error in a set of studies. Taking this error into account then allows for the calculation of a more accurate estimate of the validity coefficient in question. More complex meta-analysis formulae also allow the estimation of validity coefficients corrected for unreliability and range restriction (Hunter and Schmidt, 2004). Notice that removing the effect of sampling error does not change the magnitude of the validity coefficients; it changes the estimated variance (i.e. the spread) in observed coefficients and hence narrows the confidence interval around the average coefficient (i.e. we can be more confident about what the true coefficient actually is).

As you might expect, correcting for unreliability and range restriction will increase the size of the mean validity coefficients. The development and use of meta-analytic procedures have had a considerable impact on personnel selection. Research findings from meta-analyses have allowed researchers to see past the problems associated with conducting research on a single functioning selection process and isolate the extent to which different personnel selection methods predict job performance across different selection processes.

Hermelin and Robertson (2001) demonstrated that around 50 per cent of variance in the meta-analytic validity coefficients was explained by the correctable experimental artefacts of sampling error, direct range restriction in the predictor variable and criterion unreliability. Therefore, when interpreting results from meta-analytic studies, remember that statistical corrections are likely to have been applied so that the 'operational' or 'true' validity coefficients are reported. Because it is such a useful way of drawing together the results of different and varied studies, you will see many examples of meta-analyses referred to throughout this book.

Key learning point

Meta-analysis has been used extensively to derive estimates of the validity of personnel selection procedures. This allows us to isolate the true extent to which job performance is predicted by different selection methods with less interference from artefacts that impact on the results of each individual validation study.

One of the most oft-referenced meta-analysis studies reported is by Schmidt and Hunter (1998), who based their results on 85 years of research in personnel selection. This study separated the results of selection studies into two categories: (i) training performance used as criteria and (ii) overall job performance used as criteria to examine employee performance. The results showed that the predictive validity for each selection method is broadly similar in predicting both training and overall job performance criteria. Since this study there have been several other meta-analytic studies on the relative accuracy of different selection methods. The significant research evidence on each of the techniques listed in Table 4.7 is discussed next in this chapter. Also included is an estimate of the extent of usage, and likely applicant reaction to, each technique.

Stop to consider

Have a close look at Table 4.7. You will see that the best selection methods are not always the most widely used. Also, there are some quite weak methods that are widely used. Why do you think this might be? Think about how different stakeholders in the selection process might view the various selection methods (e.g. might there be some that managers prefer to use?). Table 4.7 lists some practical issues that might also help you with this task. Is it always practical or necessary to use the selection methods with the highest validity – and if not, why not?

Extent of use

Despite evidence that they have predictive validity, work-sample tests are rarely used in the USA, whereas lower-utility methods like graphology are relatively more widely used in France. In Germany, general mental ability (GMA) testing is rare and declining still, few assessment centres (ACs) are used in Scotland, and in Australia, situational interviews have been found to be a little-used method. In Switzerland, CVs/university reports, references and interviews (mostly semi-structured) are the most-used methods; personality tests, ACs and work-sample tests are moderately used; and biographical questionnaires are rarely used (König et al., 2010). In the UK, Zibarras and Woods (2010)

Table 4.7	A summary of studies on the validity of selection procedures		
Selection method	Evidence for criterion-related validity	Applicant reactions	Extent of use*
Structured interviews	High	Moderate to positive	High
Cognitive ability tests	High	Negative to moderate	Moderate
Personality measures	Moderate	Negative to moderate	Moderate
Situational judgement tests	High	Moderate to positive	Low to moderate
Biodata	Can be high	Moderate	Moderate
Work-sample tests	High	Positive	Low
Assessment centres	Can be high	Positive	Moderate
Handwriting	Low	Negative to moderate	Low
References	Low	Positive	High

*Note that there are international differences in the extent of usage for various techniques. For example, assessment centres are used more frequently in the UK than in the USA.

examined selection method use across organisation sizes and industry sectors and found that CVs, application forms, interviews and references were generally the most widely used methods. Formalised methods (i.e. methods developed by psychologists that have a clear methodological underpinning) like ACs were used less.

These findings seem somewhat counterintuitive – we can see from Table 4.7 that methods like references have typically been found to have low criterion-related validity, yet they are highly used. Similarly, work-sample tests and ACs are high on criterion-related validity, but are not used as much. There is a significant scientist-practitioner gap when it comes to the choices organisations are making regarding their selection procedures. In spite of a wealth of research on the utility of different selection methods, organisations are continuing to use methods with low predictive validity and ignoring those that are more valid (Schuler and Jackson, 2007). But why is this? To date, König et al. (2010) are some of only a handful of researchers that have begun to answer this question (see also Wilk and Cappelli, 2003). In their Swiss study, they investigated the reasons organisations have for using (or not using) certain selection methods. Five selection methods (semi-structured interviews, ability tests, personality tests, ACs and graphology) were evaluated against six predictors of their use:

1 *Diffusion* – the extent to which the selection method is widely used in the organisation's field.
2 *Legal defensibility* – does the organisation believe the selection method to be legally defensible if necessary?

3   *Applicant reactions* – the extent to which applicants believe the selection method to be fair and acceptable.

4   *Organisational self-promotion* – the extent to which the selection method will allow the organisation to present itself in a positive light. This is separable from applicant reactions as it involves the organisation actively using the selection situation to present positive information about itself (as opposed to trying to give candidates a positive experience).

5   *Predictive validity* – will the selection method predict future job performance?

6   *Costs* – the costs involved in implementing the selection method. While highly valid methods are cost-efficient in the long term (because of things like higher retention), the immediate costs do precede the gains and may sway an organisation's decision.

It was found that applicant reactions, costs and diffusion were the most important predictors of selection method choice overall. Legal defensibility only had a minor role in organisations' decision-making – as Myors et al. (2008) pointed out, there are only a few countries in which organisational psychology is affected by legal considerations (e.g. Canada, South Africa), whereas employers in countries such as Switzerland feel much less legal pressure. Rather surprisingly (from a research perspective at least – but perhaps unsurprisingly from a practical standpoint), predictive validity only modestly predicted selection method choice – in other words, it is a relatively unimportant factor in organisations' decision-making.

Interviews

Interviews have long been the most popular form of personnel selection (e.g. Dipboye et al., 2012; Keenan, 1995; Macan, 2009; Ryan and Ployhart, 2014). They are used by nearly every organisation and for selecting employees at all levels. Recent authors have even gone as far as to say that it would be 'rare, even unthinkable, for someone to be hired without some type of interview' (Huffcutt and Culbertson, 2010: 185). Despite this popularity, interviews have been criticised for being subjective, unreliable and vulnerable to bias. This was probably fair criticism 30 years ago, when interviews were often little more than an informal chat between an interviewer and a prospective employee. We now know considerably more about how selection decisions are reached, and the potential sources of error and bias, so there is the potential to design and execute better interviews. There have been several reviews of the literature on selection interviews in recent years (e.g. Dipboye, 2005; Posthuma et al., 2002; see Levashina et al., 2014 for a summary and critical analysis of the last two decades' research on the selection interview). These reviews show that interviews can be structured, and interviewers trained, in ways that considerably enhance their validity. Therefore a critical point to remember is that the employment interview can represent an extremely important and valid means of selecting employees *if* it is structured to ensure that (i) interviewer questions are based on a job analysis, (ii) questions are consistent across interviewers and interviewees, and (iii) the interviewers use a consistent set of criteria to evaluate interviewees' responses. Meta-analytic data have consistently found strong evidence for the superiority of structured versus unstructured interviews. In fact, a meta-analysis by Huffcutt et al. (2001) found that criterion-related validities for interviews compared favourably with other forms of personnel selection such as cognitive ability tests. Structured interviews in particular show incremental validity over personality and cognitive ability tests (e.g. Berry et al., 2007).

While there is considerable evidence to support the use of structured interviews in selection, there is much less agreement as to *why* selection interviews predict work performance. In his review, Dipboye (2005) notes that the majority of previous research on interviews has focused on (i) analysing the way interviewers process information, (ii) the social processes involved in the interaction between the interviewer and the candidate, and (iii) the quality of interviewer assessments. In their review of the last century of selection, Ryan and Ploy-hart (2014) highlight that there has been little research into the structure and content of interviews, apart from how one might improve structured interviews (e.g. Melchers et al., 2011). Instead, research has continued to focus on issues like impression management (e.g. Kleinman and Klehe, 2011; Swider et al., 2011). Investigations of these issues have found that non-verbal and verbal cues and impression management can play an important role in determining the evaluation that a candidate receives in the interview. These issues are discussed a little later. However, what this research suggests is that great care needs to be taken in the design and execution of interviews for them to have a chance of exhibiting good reliability and validity.

The two most common forms of structured interview used in selection are behavioural interviewing (e.g. Janz, 1989) and situational interviewing (e.g. Maurer et al., 1999). Also known as Behavioural Pattern Description Interviews (BPDIs), behavioural interviewing involves asking interviewees to describe previous behaviour in past situations that are relevant to the job they are being interviewed for. This type of interviewing is based upon the premise that past behaviour predicts future behaviour. In essence, interviewers are looking for evidence that an individual has demonstrated behaviour that would suggest they are capable of similar behaviour in a job situation. This type of interviewing forms the foundation of much of the competency-based interviewing that is popular today. For example, an interviewer may ask an interviewee: 'Can you please describe a time when you have been able to persuade someone to do something that they had initially been unsure about?' This could provide an opportunity to demonstrate behavioural indicators for a competency concerned with *persuasion and negotiating skills*. In both competency and BPDI interviews, interviewers use a behaviourally anchored rating scale (BARS; see Table 4.8) to rate interviewee responses. This helps to ensure consistency of rating across interviews, increase job relatedness since anchors are based on job-relevant behaviours and requirements, and reduce bias by providing interviewers with objective behaviour standards (Reilly et al., 2006). Interviews rated using BARS have been found to have higher validity and reliability (Taylor and Small, 2002).

Key learning point

Situational interviews and behavioural structured interviews produce good criterion-related validity.

In contrast, situational interviews are based on goal-setting theory. These interviews present interviewees with hypothetical job-related situations and ask them to indicate how they would respond. They are based on the assumption that *intention to behave predicts future behaviour*. The interviewer will compare your response with those provided by a group of experts who have been asked to indicate the type of responses they would expect from good, average and poor performers in this role. Interviewers will often use a behaviourally anchored rating scale to rate a response and compare it with those provided by others. Table 4.8 provides an illustration of a situational interview question and a scoring key using behavioural indicators.

A key problem with situational interviewing, however, is that it takes no account of different levels of experience. For example, there may be recent graduates with no relevant previous experience who are competing alongside other applicants with several years' experience. One might therefore expect the experienced applicants to have a better understanding of what is required in terms of a 'good' answer. Individuals with little experience

Table 4.8	Example situational interview question and response anchors to assess initiative

'You are the new personnel officer in a large car manufacturing plant and the boiler is not working properly. The temperature has dropped below the legal minimum and the shop floor workers are threatening to walk out at any minute. The trade union representative is demanding an urgent meeting with the managing director. The managing director is playing golf with the chairman today (they are using the opportunity to discuss a hostile takeover of a competitor organisation). Production is way behind schedule for the week and the costs of stopping the line could be enormous. What would you do in this situation?'

Behavioural indicators and score points

Poor	Stop the line immediately.
	Send the workers home.
	Call the managing director on her mobile phone to ask advice.
	Tell the union representative that the meeting will have to wait.
Satisfactory	Ask the employees to stop work immediately.
	Call all employees together, including the union representative, for a public meeting.
	Arrange for the technicians to repair the boiler on emergency call-out.
	Text the managing director asking her to get in touch when she finishes playing golf with the chairman.
Excellent	Ask the employees to continue working on the line and arrange for portable heaters to be installed immediately. Ask catering to provide free hot drinks for all employees.
	Meet the union representative to discuss your actions and arrange a time later that day to review the situation.
	Log the incident and actions you took and leave a note on the managing director's desk to discuss when she comes into the office.

Note: The indicators reflect an excellent, average and poor response reflective of initiative. They were previously agreed by the personnel department in the car manufacturing company. Note that what constitutes poor, satisfactory or excellent responses may be quite highly organisation-specific.

yet great potential to learn may be disadvantaged. A further potential problem, which besets both behavioural and situational interviewing, is the criticism that what interviewees *say* in selection interviews may bear very little relation to what they actually *do* once in the job.

Nevertheless, meta-analytic research has found both types of interview to have good criterion-related validity, i.e. interview performance is predictive of job performance (Klehe and Latham, 2006). Factors such as job complexity, however, have been found to influence the validity of situational interviews. In a study by Huffcutt et al. (2004), job complexity influenced the validity of situational interviews but not behavioural interviews. Similarly, Krajewski et al. (2006) found that behavioural interviews significantly predict job performance for complex jobs, but situational interviews do not. In examining whether the two types of interview show incremental validity, findings have been mixed. Some research shows that situational interviews display incremental validity over behavioural interviews, while other research shows the opposite pattern. Despite this, both still display good validity and can both be used with confidence, although Levashina et al. (2014) suggest that behavioural interviews may be slightly better for more complex jobs. Perhaps actual experience becomes more important as job complexity increases? Research has also indicated that the different types of interview may be more or less suited to assessing different types of performance. For example, because situational interviews *force* candidates to think about how they would behave in certain situations, they can predict maximal as well as typical performance. On the other hand, behavioural interviews focus only on candidates' actual experiences and therefore are likely to predict only typical performance.

Key debate

Are selection interviews worthwhile?

While no personnel selection will demonstrate absolute comparability between what is assessed during selection and subsequent work behaviour, interviews are particularly vulnerable to criticism. Interviewers are often worried about being deceived by candidates engaging in impression management: those appointed may demonstrate altogether different patterns of behaviour once in the job. It assumes that the task of the interviewer is to peel away layers of impression management in order to uncover the true person underneath. This may be an overly simplistic notion. Indeed, certain researchers have argued that personality is itself socially constructed, and that there is no 'true' persona hiding beneath layers of presentation waiting to be discovered. As such, individuals adapt proactively to different situations and people according to needs. Research has suggested that impression management may be heightened in high-stakes settings where there is a lot to lose if applicants do not make a good impression. However, Levashina and Campion (2007) advise that deceptive impression management (i.e. lying or embellishing) should be separated from honest impression management (framing genuine achievements in a self-promoting way).

Research suggests that self-promotion is the type of impression management that has the largest impact on interviewer ratings (Levashina et al., 2014). It could be argued that this ability to understand different contexts and adapt one's behaviour to meet their varying needs is an exceptionally useful skill, and one that can be useful in helping an individual to navigate their work environment successfully (Rosenfeld et al., 2002). However, other research suggests that the way in which individuals choose to present themselves during interviews (their impression management) may reflect cognitive personality characteristics associated with motivation. For example, Silvester et al. (2002) found that more successful applicants demonstrated an attributional style also found in higher performers at work. Individuals who explained past behaviour in terms of causes that they were able to control tended to be rated more favourably by interviewers (e.g. 'I didn't do well in the exam because I left my revision until too late') than those who explained performance in terms of uncontrollable causes (e.g. 'The lecturer didn't like us so she made the examination question too difficult'). Interestingly, the interviewer's own attributional style was also important in determining how they evaluated the attributions made by the interviewee (i.e. impression management is the result of an interaction between what the interviewer sees as desirable behaviour and what the interviewee sees as desirable behaviour). Research has shown that the effects of impression management can be reduced by implementing a more tightly structured interview. Barrick et al. (2009) found that the relationship between verbal impression management and interview ratings was lower for high-structure than for low-structure interviews. This is because the nature of structured interviews is that specific competencies are looked for and assessed against specific evaluative criteria, thereby narrowing the interviewer's focus and directing them to job-relevant information only. Other research has found that coaching interviewees to perform in interviews can influence scores. Maurer et al. (2008) examined coaching interventions designed to help interviewees focus on interview-relevant content and to help them convey the content accurately (as opposed to interventions designed to teach interviewees to manipulate their scores). Using a predictive validation study of a situational panel interview, Maurer et al. (2008) showed that the predictive validity of interview performance was higher in a sample of coached interviewees compared to a sample of uncoached interviewees.

Psychometric tests and measures of personality

In the 1980s, Cronbach described psychometric tests as providing 'a standardized sample of behaviour which can be described by a numerical scale or category system'. In other words, psychometric tests offer a quantitative assessment of some psychological attribute (such as verbal reasoning ability, general intelligence, numerical reasoning ability, etc.). Psychometric tests can be indicative of either maximal performance, i.e. how people perform at their peak, or typical performance – how people typically behave. For personnel selection purposes psychometric tests may be divided into two categories: cognitive ability tests (e.g. general intelligence, spatial ability, numerical ability) and personality measures (see Chapter 3 for more information on specific cognitive and personality tests). Cognitive ability tests tend to measure maximal ability, whereas personality tests are measures of typical performance – they indicate preferences.

Cognitive ability tests in selection

In the past 30 years, there has been an explosion in the use of cognitive ability tests for selection purposes. For many practitioners conducting large-scale recruitment programmes, ability tests are relatively cost-effective selection tools. Unlike most other selection techniques, to purchase and administer psychometric tests in many countries you have to demonstrate a specific level of competence in administration, scoring tests and interpreting test scores (e.g. the British Psychological Society's Test User qualifications).

In the 1970s, particularly in the USA, cognitive ability testing became increasingly unpopular and it was common for people to argue that such tests had no useful role in personnel selection. The meta-analytic work and the evidence for validity generalisation (i.e. the generalisation of validity across different types of jobs and different organisational settings) caused work psychologists to revise these views. In general, cognitive ability tests have been shown to be the single best predictor of job performance (e.g. Sackett et al., 2008; Ones, 2005; Gottfredson, 2002; Salgado et al., 2003; Schmidt and Hunter, 1998) with validity coefficients generally shown to be approximately 0.50 (i.e. explaining an impressive 25 per cent of the variance in the test-taker's future job performance).

Large-scale research has demonstrated consistently that cognitive ability accurately predicts future job performance across almost all occupations and organisations. In her large-scale review of many meta-analytic studies (a meta-analysis of the meta-analyses), Ones (2005) shows that the evidence for the validity of cognitive ability tests in predicting job performance is overwhelming. In this respect, many researchers argue that cognitive ability tests are perhaps the best and most widely applicable predictor in personnel selection because all jobs require some cognitive ability to learn the job and perform effectively. Ones and Viswesvaran (2003) suggest that the predictive validity of cognitive ability tests tends to be higher for high-complexity jobs (0.58) than for low-complexity jobs (0.23), but is still significant regardless of the level of complexity. A high-complexity job (such as, believe it or not, a professor in work psychology) involves *denser* processing of information than a lower-complexity job (we have deliberately avoided offering an example to avoid the risk of causing unintended offence!).

In addition to tests developed to assess general cognitive ability ('g') (see Chapter 3), sometimes referred to as general mental ability (GMA), there are tests tailored to assess specific abilities such as mechanical comprehension or spatial ability. Such tests measure 'g' to some extent, but also have a specific ability component which means that tests of cognitive-specific abilities could be more predictive for specific jobs. Ones and Viswesvaran (2003) suggest that the predictive validity of specific abilities stems from their assessment of a general information-processing ability (i.e. the general ability required to perform well on the test). Thus, if the general cognitive ability is held constant, most of the predictive power of specific ability tests disappears. On the other hand, in considering the practical

Individual difference in ability can be described in many different ways (see Chapter 3). Measures of 'g' and specific cognitive abilities have been extensively used in selection processes. As a result there is a great deal of evidence about their effectiveness.

application of tests in organisations, specific ability tests may have more face validity and generate positive candidate reactions in a selection context.

Bertua and colleagues (2005) report a meta-analysis that compares the validity of tests of GMA and specific cognitive abilities when predicting job performance and training success in the UK. The analyses were based on a data set of 283 independent samples with job performance as the criterion, and 223 with training success as the criterion: by any standard this is an impressive number of studies. The results showed that GMA and specific ability tests are valid predictors of job performance and training success, with validity coefficients in the region of 0.5–0.6. As anticipated, the highest validities were found between cognitive tests and various performance criteria (i.e. job performance and training success) in occupational groups with greater job complexity. Similar studies that use data from a number of different countries and cultures have found similar results. Salgado and colleagues (2003) examined the validity of GMA and other specific cognitive abilities, including verbal, numerical, spatial–mechanical, perceptual and memory across 10 European countries (with N ranging from 946 to 16,065). Once again, GMA and specific cognitive ability were found to be very good predictors of job performance and training success across Europe.

Key learning point

Cognitive ability tests produce good criterion-related validities for a wide range of jobs in various countries and cultures.

Key debate

Is using cognitive tests an unfair way of making personnel selection decisions, especially as they are not particularly liked by the candidates themselves?

The evidence on this issue is reviewed briefly in a separate section on fairness later in this chapter. In overview, the evidence suggests cognitive ability testing does not provide differentially 'unfair' predictions for people from different ethnic minority groups (see Ones et al., 2007b; Berry et al., 2014), although it may not be appropriate to use ability tests for all selection purposes. A second argument against the use of cognitive tests is that candidate reactions to them can be less than positive. Both test publishers and users would agree that how the tests are used is critical to their effectiveness as selection tools. Port and Patterson (2003) suggest that best practice guidelines in using tests in selection are not always followed, and some test users are 'less than thorough' in their use of tests in selection (e.g. they may neglect to explain why tests are being used or fail to provide full feedback on the test results). Therefore, the way tests are used, rather than the tests themselves, might be responsible for candidates' negative reactions to them.

Research on the validity of cognitive ability testing has been scarce in recent years, possibly due to cognitive ability having been so firmly established as a predictor of job performance in earlier research (Ryan and Ployhart, 2014). However, there is merit for expanding the focus of cognitive ability to include procedural knowledge (i.e. domain-specific knowledge) and declarative knowledge, for example, in addition to the traditional 'g'. Indeed, meta-analyses have found knowledge tests to be one of the best predictors of job performance (Schmidt and Hunter, 1998), a finding that has been confirmed by more recent high-quality research (e.g. Lievens and Patterson, 2011).

In summary, the research findings clearly demonstrate the validity of cognitive ability tests for selection purposes. However, there are two main issues to consider for future research. First, while selection research is focusing on a unitary trait of general mental ability, research into intelligence itself is moving away from this simple conceptualisation and developing multifaceted models of intelligence (see Chapter 3). Second, in the last decade, the amount of research investigating the use of new technology in personnel selection procedures (particularly Internet testing) has dramatically increased. The widespread use of the Internet is likely to transform personnel selection procedures in the future. In their review, Lievens and Harris (2003) suggest that although Internet recruitment is now being used on a global basis, the research literature cannot keep pace with its proliferation (see also Sackett and Lievens, 2008). The limited evidence available suggests that applicants have more positive reactions to cognitive ability tests administered via the Internet than they do to 'pencil-and-paper' equivalents. The issues surrounding the impact of technology on selection procedures is discussed in more detail later in this chapter.

Personality measures

The personality measures used in selection activities are usually based on some kind of trait-factor analytic model of personality (described in Chapter 3). For more than two decades the status of personality measures as predictors of performance was low. However, some authors have argued persuasively that personality is an important determinant of behaviour at work and there has been a resurgence of interest in personality assessment in the past three decades.

Results from various meta-analytic studies (see Salgado et al., 2003) suggest that conscientiousness is a valid predictor of performance across most jobs and organisational settings, with an average criterion-related validity of 0.23. Ones et al. (2007a) report that particular facets of conscientiousness are predictive of job performance, for example, the facet 'achievement' is predictive of 'overall job performance' and 'task performance' ($r = 0.18$ and $r = 0.22$, respectively). Openness to experience tends to be positively correlated with training performance across many job roles. Emotional stability has been shown to be positively associated with job performance across many organisational settings. Extroversion is generally found to correlate positively with performance in jobs such as sales, where performance is judged within an interpersonal environment.

Hough and Furnham (2003) highlight that validity of personality variables varies according to the type of performance being measured and job type. For example, conscientiousness correlates most highly with overall job performance, compared to all other Big Five personality dimensions. However, conscientiousness may be negatively correlated with creativity (a competency for many job roles). In this way, depending on the job, the facets of conscientiousness are *differentially* important. Hough and Furnham (2003) report that the dependability facet of conscientiousness correlates 0.18 with overall job performance in sales jobs and 0.03 with overall job performance in managerial jobs. In addition, when comparing the validity for facets of conscientiousness for managerial jobs, results show that the achievement facet correlates 0.17 with overall job performance but the dependability facet only correlated 0.03 (more or less zero, or no relationship) with overall job performance. In other studies, research suggests that agreeableness is positively associated with job performance in some job roles, but chief executives of organisations tend to be low on agreeableness (as you might have noticed).

Point of integration

Personality seems to play a role in several aspects of leadership behaviour, despite the very strong criticisms levelled at trait theories of leadership (see Chapter 12).

To provide a more comprehensive review of the role of personality in job performance, researchers have begun to focus on lower-order traits as opposed to the broad factors (such as the Big Five). Judge et al. (2013) argue that weak overall relationships with job performance may be masking significant relationships at the facet level of personality. Their meta-analysis revealed that while the broad Big Five factors followed the typical pattern (i.e. conscientiousness, extraversion, and agreeableness being highly correlated with job performance, openness correlating moderately with job performance, and neuroticism having a low correlation with job performance), things were more complex at the facet level. For example, achievement striving, dutifulness and self-discipline were highly correlated with job performance, but other conscientiousness facets like deliberation were not. Similarly, intellect was highly correlated with job performance, but the more aesthetic facets of openness did not correlate as highly; and the excitement-seeking aspect of extraversion had a much lower correlation with job performance than the positive emotions facet. This suggests that there is some basis for the argument that the facets of the Big Five dimensions may differentially predict job performance.

Other research suggests that rather than looking deeper at the facet level, we should perhaps be looking more broadly at the relationship between personality and job performance. It has recently been suggested that a general factor of personality (GFP) exists that sits at the top of the hierarchical structure of personality, and in personality terms is comparable to Spearman's 'g' – the general intelligence factor. Empirical evidence in favour of the existence of this GFP has been growing (e.g. Musek, 2007; Rushton and Irwing, 2008), and for the first time, was linked to job performance by Van der Linden et al. (2010) (see Figure 4.6). Their research showed that the Big Five factors loaded onto two factors – stability (or α), consisting of conscientiousness, agreeableness and neuroticism; and plasticity (or β), consisting

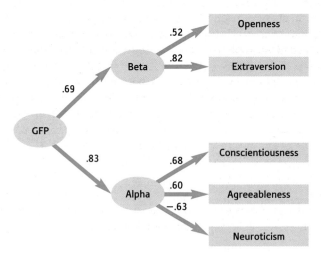

Figure 4.6	Model of GFP
	Source: Van der Linden et al. (2010).

of openness and extraversion. These two factors then loaded on to one single factor – the GFP. Following this, Van der Linden et al. (2010) found that the GFP had a significant relationship with performance indicators, namely supervisor-rated job performance.

Research has also indicated that the relationships between personality factors and job performance may not be straightforward. Curvilinear relationships have been found between both conscientiousness and extraversion and three measures of performance: task performance, organisational citizenship behaviours, and counterproductive work behaviours (see Le et al., 2011). Such findings indicate that in terms of the links between personality and performance, there can be 'too much of a good thing'.

Key learning point

Conscientiousness tends to predict overall job performance over a range of occupational settings. However, when exploring validity at the facet level, results are criterion dependent. For other personality factors, their relationship with job performance tends to depend upon the nature of the job being carried out.

Key debate

Is personality assessment worthwhile in selection?

In a recent debate, Ones et al. (2007a) cited meta-analytic data to suggest that, in contrast to ability testing, the predictive validity of personality measures for 'overall job performance' is not seen across all occupational areas and settings. Instead, only the trait of conscientiousness is predictive of 'overall job performance' over a range of occupations; the predictive traits for other occupations vary along with the occupations themselves. For example, for managerial roles, it is the 'achievement' and 'dependability' facets of conscientiousness that predict job performance. Morgeson et al. (2007a) contributed to the debate by expressing concern over the lack of consistent evidence for the predictive validity of personality measures in the selection context. Ones et al. (2007a) responded to Morgeson et al. (2007a), arguing that there is supporting evidence from many meta-analytic studies for the predictive validity of personality measures for various organisational outcomes, including 'overall job performance' ($r = 0.27$), 'individual teamwork' and 'leadership criteria'. Ones and colleagues concluded that the evidence is 'substantial' and that the valid use of personality measurement in selection is confirmed. Tett and Christiansen (2007) also responded to the concerns of Morgeson et al. (2007a), suggesting that the individuality of different measures of personality (i.e. they are all a bit different) and each measure's relationship to relevant organisational behaviour (i.e. different jobs have different performance criteria) should be considered: therefore, the predictive validity of personality measurement is often underestimated. Tett and Christiansen (2007) argue that research should focus on identifying the specific circumstances that yield strong (or weak), and positive (or negative) relationships between personality traits and job performance. Morgeson et al. (2007b) responded by arguing that the statistical correction methods applied to the ('very low') validity coefficients for personality measures (remember such corrections tend to raise the validity coefficient) are not appropriate, meaning that evidence for the validity of personality measures is poor. They also suggest that only the 'job proficiency' outcomes (i.e. measures of how good someone is at their job) are relevant, thus arguably rendering Ones et al.'s (2007a) inclusion of outcomes such as 'leader emergence' unimpressive.

Researchers have also found that criterion-related validity may differ as a result of the type of personality measure used. A recent meta-analysis by Salgado and Táuriz (2014) examined the criterion-related validity of various measures of the Big Five. They specifically looked into forced choice (FC) measures and examined these in comparison to single stimulus (SS) response measures. FC measures require the respondent to compare a number of options and pick the one that is most or least preferred, dependent on the context. In contrast, SS measures require respondents to rate statements as they occur. Results showed that validity is slightly higher when personality is assessed with FC measures than with SS measures. This suggests that perhaps FC measures are more suitable for use in a selection context where they form all or part of the basis for academic and occupational decisions. Salgado and Táuriz's meta-analysis also distinguished between three types of FC measures – ipsative, quasi-ipsative, and normative:ipsative measures: the sum of the scores obtained across all of the attributes measured (i.e. the Big Five dimensions) is constant; allowing for intra-individual comparisons.

- Quasi-ipsative measures: these do not meet the criteria for pure ipsivaty. This could be due to a number of reasons, for example scales having different numbers of items.
- Normative measures: items representing different scales, for example a Conscientiousness scale and an Extraversion scale, would not be paired. This means that scores on each scale are independent of any other scores the assessed individual may have, and are statistically dependent on other individuals in the population to determine whether a specific score is high/low.

Their results indicated that ipsative measures were more valid than normative measures, and quasi-ipsative measures were more valid still. In examining the validity of the different types of measure in predicting job performance, it was found that Conscientiousness assessed using quasi-ipsative measures was the single best predictor of job performance and almost double that of the validity found in past meta-analyses. This illustrates the previously underestimated utility of quasi-ipsative personality measures as predictors of job performance.

Point of integration

Workers' responses to questionnaire measures of attitudes (Chapter 7) can also be affected by their desire to present a positive, or socially acceptable impression of themselves through the answers they give. Ipsative approaches to measurement may blunt this effect.

There is much ongoing debate about using personality measures in selection: you might therefore find it difficult to reach conclusions. It would be fair to say that the research indicates that personality variables can be useful in predicting job performance. Perhaps it is more important to recognise that their predictive accuracy is increased when the predictor and criterion variables are closely matched (e.g. in terms of their complexity, or job type).

Key learning point

Personality measures used in selection can add significant incremental validity for some job roles, particularly when predictor and criterion variables are carefully matched.

A common concern for practitioners involved in recruitment is whether job applicants could fake (or intentionally distort) their responses on a personality measure and present themselves in a socially desirable manner. Morgeson et al. (2007a) questioned whether the potential for applicant faking in the completion of personality measures limits their usefulness for selection purposes. Many authors have debated this issue of faking and response distortion (e.g. Landers et al., 2011; Sackett, 2011; Tett et al., 2012). Hough and Furnham (2003) suggest that when instructed to do so (in a laboratory setting, for example), people can distort their responses to self-report personality measures in either a positive or negative direction, depending on the instruction they are given. However, in real-world settings, the majority of the evidence suggests that intentional distortion *does exist but it does not have a substantial influence on the criterion-related validity of personality measures*. The research suggests that in real-life settings distortion is reduced when warnings about the detection of faking and the potential negative consequences of faking are included in the administration instructions to applicants. In practice, most personality measures used in selection will include a scale to assess social desirability and intentional distortion. Ones et al. (2007a) argue that experimental manipulation of conditions in laboratory-based studies of faking is very likely to exaggerate the actual effect of faking on validity (as seen in the real world): they urge researchers to conduct more studies of faking in real-life settings. Tett and Christiansen (2007) suggest that of those predictive validity studies conducted in real-life settings, results demonstrate that faking might have an effect on validity, but does not remove validity entirely.

In overview, the literature suggests that when used appropriately, personality measures can add significant incremental validity in a selection process because they measure something unique that also predicts performance. We illustrate here the ongoing debate. Morgeson et al. (2007b) cite Guion (1965): 'In view of the problems … one must question the wisdom … of using personality as instruments of decision in employment procedures' (2007b: 1046), but Ones et al. (2007a) argue that the abandoning of personality measurement in selection would be senseless, as evidence proves its value. Future research is likely to consider cross-cultural differences in personality testing. With an increasingly global marketplace there is much work to be done to explore the use of personality testing on an international basis.

Exercise 4.4   Personalities and jobs

Think about the five different jobs listed below:

- a sales job in a large international advertising agency;
- a teacher in a secondary school;
- a plumber running a business independently;
- a pharmacist working in a small shop in the local community;
- a financial controller in a large manufacturing organisation.

Suggested exercise

For each role, suggest which personality factors might be important in performing the job. Using the information from Chapter 3 on personality, discuss the personality factors that might help or hinder effectiveness in each role. You may also like to think of how people with very different personalities could do a job equally well – but in very different ways.

Assessment centres

An assessment centre (AC) is a popular and effective method of recruitment consisting of a multifaceted assessment process. An AC is not a place, as the name suggests, but instead is a term used to describe the setting of multiple assessments of individuals using different methods, and involving multiple observers called assessors. In a typical AC, numerous applicants are invited together for between half a day and three days of assessment. Assessment methods can include: work sample exercises, group exercises, presentations, in-tray exercises, role plays, practical skills, interviews and psychometric tests; the particular combination depends on the target job role. ACs profile an applicant's ability across a range of competencies and job-related contexts. The appeal of ACs lies in their generally good levels of criterion-related validity and face validity (Hough and Oswald, 2000). Although there has been much debate regarding the predictive validity of ACs, meta-analytic studies show the average validity of AC studies to be very good.

Point of integration

Development centres (DCs) that are used to train employees (Chapter 9) bear a close resemblance to assessment centres. The key difference is that the experience of participating in a DC is designed to foster personal development (e.g. through experiential learning and the provision of feedback). Detailed information about participants' performance can also be used as part of a training needs analysis.

There are certain criteria that an assessment process must fulfil in order to be defined as an AC. These include: (i) explicit dimensions (now more commonly referred to as competencies; see earlier in this chapter) derived from a job analysis which defines the key knowledge, skills and abilities required by a candidate in order to perform the role they are being assessed for; (ii) multiple techniques (methods) to provide information relevant to the dimensions to be assessed and the context in which those dimensions are to be demonstrated (e.g. different aspects of the role); (iii) multiple, trained assessors to observe and evaluate each candidate; and (iv) a systematic procedure to record and rate specific behaviours as they occur. Independent assessor ratings and reports are then brought together to form an overall rating for each candidate at what is often referred to as the 'wash-up' session or moderation session: this is where candidates' performance is discussed and selection decisions are made.

Key learning point

Assessment centres assess an applicant on multiple competencies using multiple job-related exercises and multiple trained assessors.

The design of an AC reflects the need to assess the extent to which applicants can demonstrate a range of competencies. Consequently a series of exercises and assessment tools are developed that: (i) are able to elicit the required behaviours; (ii) reflect the actual content of the role; (iii) assess applicants' performance in a variety of job-related situations; and (iv) allow for different assessors to assess these competencies over different exercises.

Typically, competencies are assessed multiple times within each AC, using different exercises. Typically, each exercise assesses multiple competencies. For instance, a group exercise may be assessing leadership skills and communication skills. However, exercises should never attempt to assess *all* of the competencies, as this would overload assessors with too much information (Sackett and Tuzinski, 2001); there are limits to their cognitive abilities. Certain exercises are best suited to assessing particular competencies. For example, a communication skills competency can be better assessed in a presentation exercise and a group exercise, rather than in a psychometric test.

Key debate

What do assessment centres actually measure?

Do ACs measure stable, underlying traits that influence performance across situations, or do they identify candidates' ability to do well in the specific situations that are part of the AC? There is a substantial body of research debating the traditional assumptions that dimensions (competencies) are central to how ACs work. Lance (2008) conducted a review of the last 25 years of research into this so-called '*construct validity problem*'. This problem has plagued the AC literature and is as follows. It has generally been assumed that assessors look for evidence that candidates can or cannot demonstrate competence in each of the dimensions across the varying work-related situations in different exercises. Unfortunately, a common finding is that performance ratings on individual AC component exercises often reflect factors associated with the *exercises, as opposed to the traits*, or 'constructs' that the AC is designed to measure. This relates to the problem of convergent validity versus discriminant validity: performance tends to be more consistent across competencies within an exercise, than it is within a competency across different exercises (Lance, 2008).

The problem can be illustrated as follows. If dimensions are of central importance in assessor decision-making, one would expect relatively high correlations between different assessors' ratings of a candidate for the same competence (say communication skills) across different exercises. This would mean that the applicant demonstrates good communication skills in a presentation, in a group exercise and in an in-tray exercise. However, they may not score highly for all competencies within a particular exercise. Cross-situational consistency across exercises rather than within exercises indicates that the AC has discriminant validity, i.e. that different competencies are evaluated separately in each exercise. However, researchers have found that in most ACs assessors are more likely to provide similar ratings for an individual across different dimensions within the same exercise, rather than for the same competency across different exercises (Robertson and Smith, 2001). This represents *convergent validity* and suggests that exercises, not dimensions, are the important construct behind candidate ratings. Another recent meta-analysis of 24 studies into the construct validity of ACs was conducted by Bowler and Woehr (2006), who found that AC exercises explain more variance in candidate performance than do AC dimensions. Similar results have continued to be found in more recent research (e.g. Petrides et al., 2010).

This poses a problem: are ACs measuring what they are supposed to measure (i.e. a dimension or competency that drives performance across a range of situations)? If not, does it matter as long as they predict job performance? What other mechanisms might contribute to the validity of ACs? Some argue that the tasks that assessors have to undertake when observing and rating a candidate's behaviour are complex and demanding and that in general it is easier to provide an overall evaluation of effectiveness in a particular exercise. There has been much recent discussion around the construct validity problem. Arthur and colleagues (2008) responded to Lance (2008), suggesting that dimension-based AC construct validity should not be abandoned. Instead, a more representative sample of constructs must be taken to represent the job content. They argue that the AC is theoretically sound and that the construct validity of AC dimensions may still stand up if the appropriate constructs

▶

▶

(i.e. competencies that are relevant to the job role) are measured in the AC, and they are defined in the appropriate way. This is an important point as it represents a possible explanation for the problems associated with AC construct validity. Rather than viewing construct validity as problematic for ACs, there may be good reasons why performance on the same dimension can differ between exercises. A person may be much more effective at communicating on a one-to-one basis than presenting information in a public-speaking context: a competency/dimension such as communication skills might be assessed in both contexts, with the same individual achieving different scores in the two different contexts. It may be that defining the competency differently (e.g. defining *presentational* communication skills and *individual* communication skills as two separate dimensions) might lead to greater consistency across exercises.

Kuncel and Sackett (2014) proposed the argument that the construct validity problem may not actually be the big deal it has been conceived to be over the past three decades! According to their research, we are forgetting that competency scores for each exercise are only a *step* towards an overall final AC rating for each competency. They argue that if we shift our focus to this overall AC competency rating, we will see that when ratings for each competency across all of the AC exercises are combined, we can see from the data that exercise-specific effects are no longer the dominant source of final AC ratings. This may be because variations of competency performance and rating errors do not unduly influence the process of arriving at an overall evaluation for each competency.

Key learning point

When designed appropriately, assessment centres are valid predictors of job performance. Construct validity is enhanced by ensuring the content is directly relevant to the target job role.

The AC is generally assumed to have good predictive validity because assessment is based upon direct observation of job-relevant behaviours. This enables assessors to predict how candidates will behave in the job by observing them engaging in job-relevant behaviour. Hermelin et al. (2007) conducted a meta-analysis of 26 studies into the predictive validity of ACs with performance ratings provided by participants' supervisors as the criteria. They found a correlation of 0.28 between 'overall assessment ratings' and ratings of performance by supervisors. Another explanation for why ACs work is that incremental validity is achieved by using many different methods that assess separate and distinct aspects of performance. This makes an AC a better predictor because each of its components adds something unique to the predictive power of the process. Research has been conducted into the predictive validity of particular assessment methods used within ACs. Slivinski (2008) investigated the predictive validity of AC pencil-and-paper tests compared with the predictive validity of AC situational test measures: both tests were equally valid, but used together, both types of measures added incremental validity over and above each other. Meriac et al. (2008) conducted a meta-analysis of 38 studies to find out whether seven particular AC dimensions (organising and planning, influencing others, drive, problem-solving, stress tolerance, consideration/awareness of others and communication) were distinct from cognitive ability and personality. They found that although there was some overlap between performance on the AC dimensions and cognitive ability and personality, the relationship was small, showing that AC dimensions are, in the main, distinct from cognitive ability and personality.

In terms of the cost-effectiveness of ACs, Crail (2007) reported on the research findings of a survey carried out by *Employment Review*, which contacted individuals in personnel roles within 91 different private and public sector organisations. Although ACs are known for being a very expensive method of recruitment, 53 per cent of those surveyed felt this level of cost was 'justified'. Furthermore, Crail's results showed that over nine out of ten employers felt that ACs are effective for use in recruitment, and 47 per cent of employers surveyed felt that ACs are 'very effective' in recruiting new employees.

Situational judgement tests

An example of an assessment method with lower physical fidelity is where applicants are presented with paper-based scenarios in a written exercise. Here, applicants might be asked to indicate how they would respond in the situations described, and to justify their decisions. These types of assessments are sometimes referred to as *situational judgement tests* (SJTs). SJTs are designed to assess an applicant's judgement regarding situations where hypothetical work-based scenarios are presented to applicants, who make judgements about possible responses, and these responses are then assessed against a predetermined scoring key (Lievens et al., 2008). Following best practice (Lievens et al., 2008), SJT scenarios are based on a thorough analysis of the relevant work role in order to assess the key attributes and competencies that are associated with successful performance in the role. This ensures that the content of the SJT reflects work-related situations that candidates are likely to face in the job.

Applicants can be required to make their judgements in the format of choosing the best option, worst option, or asked to rate the effectiveness of alternatives. Their responses are typically scored by comparing them to the judgements of experts in the respective field (Bergman et al., 2006). Some similarities can be seen between SJTs and situational interviews, assessment centre exercises and work samples, but there are key differences in terms of presentation (usually because SJTs are written), how options are presented and how options are scored (i.e. SJT predetermined scoring from a set of pre-determined options), and the type of responses given. Research shows that SJTs can be used reliably in selection to identify a range of non-academic or professional attributes (Clevenger et al., 2001; Patterson et al. (2015; 2016); Wyatt et al., 2010).

Over the last 20 years, SJTs have become increasingly popular (see Weekley and Ployhart, 2006; Lievens et al., 2008; Whetzel and McDaniel, 2009 for reviews), though they actually date back to at least 1926, in the form of the George Washington University Social Intelligence Test. The popularity of SJTs is seen most in large-scale selection, often at the shortlisting stage (Patterson et al., 2009). SJTs are relatively easy and cost-effective to develop, administer and score. SJTs are also versatile in their presentation, and can be written, Internet- or video-based (Lievens et al., 2008). However, although SJTs have become popular for practical reasons, their construct validity has remained elusive (and there remains uncertainty over how SJTs work and what they actually measure, although recent research has attempted to classify SJT constructs; see Christian et al., 2010). That said, there is an emerging consensus that they are a measurement method for job-relevant attributes that reflect complex situations and events, are tailored to the particular context, and can be designed to measure a variety of cognitive and non-academic constructs This is important because it means that their content and format can be amended to fit the job and specification of the test (Lievens et al., 2005).

Point of integration

There is some evidence to suggest that SJTs can be used to measure the way people tend to make use of their traits and abilities (see Chapter 3).

Correlations between SJTs and personality are to be expected, due to the types of situations included in SJTs (e.g. many situations include interpersonal aspects of situations and tap into work preferences/styles). McDaniel and Nguyen (2001) conducted a meta-analysis and found that SJT scores are significantly related to the Big Five personality traits ($r = 0.31$ between SJTs and Emotional stability; $r = 0.26$ for Conscientiousness; $r = 0.25$ for Agreeableness). Other researchers have found similar but not entirely consistent patterns (Clevenger et al., 2001). This is likely to reflect the wide variation in content of the SJTs and the range of contexts in which they are used. In relation to cognitive ability, the McDaniel et al. (2001) meta-analysis shows a mean correlation of $r = 0.34$ with SJTs, although they note that this masks a wide variation of results. McDaniel et al. (2007) more recently highlighted the importance of the type of response instructions in determining the link between SJT scores and cognitive ability, i.e. whether the test has knowledge or behavioural tendency related questions.

With regards to predictive validity, meta-analyses show moderate to good criterion-related validity of SJTs. Research evidence suggests that SJTs are able to predict job performance across a range of different occupations such as in sales performance (Wyatt et al., 2010), the military (Borman et al., 1993) and in medical education and training (Patterson et al., 2013). Importantly, SJTs have incremental validity over ability and personality measures (e.g. Oswald et al., 2004; McDaniel et al., 2007). However, most of this research was not conducted in operational (real-life) settings, although in two key studies, Patterson et al. (2009) and Lievens et al. (2005) have found evidence of both the predictive and incremental validity of SJTs in operational settings.

Exercise 4.5   **Designing an SJT to recruit doctors (see Patterson et al., 2009)**

The following question comes from a research study to develop a new SJT for recruiting doctors. An example question using a multiple best-answer response format is:

You are looking after Mrs Sandra Jones, who is being investigated in hospital. You are asked by her family not to inform Mrs Jones if the results confirm cancer.

Choose the three most appropriate actions to take in this situation:

(a) ignore the family's wishes
(b) agree not to tell Mrs Jones
(c) explain to the family that it is Mrs Jones' decision
(d) ask Mrs Jones whether she wishes to know the test results
(e) ask Mrs Jones whether she wishes you to inform the family
(f) inform Mrs Jones that her family do not wish her to have the results
(g) give the results to the family first
(h) give the results to the next of kin first.

Suggested exercises

1   What do you think this question is testing?

2   Could anyone answer this question? What does a candidate need to know before they can answer the question?

3   Try to create another question that is relevant for recruiting doctors. What is difficult in developing the question? What skills do you need to write the question?

In terms of fairness and adverse impact, findings show there are generally smaller sub-group differences when using SJTs than when using cognitive ability tests (Jensen, 1998, as cited in Lievens et al., 2008). Research also shows that fairness and adverse impact may vary with the way that constructs are measured, for example it may vary in accordance with the presentation format. Kanning et al. (2006) also found that multimedia SJTs are more face valid, more enjoyable and tend to invoke better applicant reactions.

One area that SJTs have been particularly useful in is values-based recruitment. You will see in the closing case study that hiring candidates whose values are aligned to those of the organisation can be very important for certain roles. But since values are non-academic factors, they are difficult to assess with traditional selection methods. For example, panel interviews are often criticised for their potential to be biased or for their lack of standardisation, while personality tests offer lower face validity and are less acceptable to candidates as a selection tool. SJTs offer significant advantages over these methods as they are a standardised way of objectively assessing a broad range of attributes for large numbers of applicants, while being face valid to candidates since scenarios used in SJTs are based on job-relevant situations. Indeed, there is good evidence to show that SJTs are a useful methodology to evaluate a range of professional attributes for selection into fields such as medicine and dentistry (see Patterson et al. 2015 for a review). Long-term follow-up studies have shown an SJT measuring empathy, integrity and resilience (used to select candidates applying for training in UK general practice) to be the best single predictor of subsequent job performance compared with other selection methods (Lievens and Patterson, 2011). This is likely due to SJTs being constructed differently using different formats depending on the requirement of the role. SJTs are designed to assess an applicant's judgement regarding situations encountered in the workplace (or in education settings), targeting professional attributes rather than knowledge.

Key learning point

Situational judgement tests are a valid selection method. Applicant reactions tend to be positive. Further research is needed to explore the construct validity of SJTs.

Other methods

Biodata

The use of biographical data (referred to as biodata) as a selection procedure is an interesting and sometimes controversial topic. The underlying principle in the use of biodata is that past behaviour is a good predictor of future performance. Biodata items can be described as 'hard' or soft' items. A hard item might include verifiable information such as educational qualifications, whereas a soft item might be an applicant's preferred interests or hobbies. The fundamentals of the biodata approach involve identifying correlations between items of biographical information and criterion measures (e.g. work performance, absenteeism). These correlations are established empirically by conducting a predictive or (more often) concurrent validation study.

Biodata items that predict the criterion are then combined into a questionnaire which may be administered to applicants. Information from the prior validation stage can then be used to provide a scoring procedure. For example, items may be assigned weights based on their ability to predict the relevant criterion. It should be stressed at this point that the correlations observed between biodata items and the criterion could be influenced by chance factors that only occur in a single data set. It is not uncommon for one source of biodata (e.g. educational qualifications) to show predictive validity in one recruitment process, but not in another (this is sometimes referred to as 'shrinkage' in the validity coefficient). Before using the results of a biodata validation study for selection purposes, cross-validation, preferably using a second sample, is needed. It is also clear from empirical research that the validity of biodata items is not always stable over time and it is advisable for them to be revalidated from time to time. Despite this, results from meta-analytic studies report good predictive validity of biodata in general with validity coefficients of approximately 0.48.

Key learning point

The uncritical use of empirically derived items in biodata questionnaires can lead to problems with equal opportunities. Rationally derived items are a safer option.

References

Reference reports are widely used methods for obtaining information on candidates, although it seems likely that in many situations potential employers take up references only when they are about to make a job offer. In general, the validity evidence for reference reports is not particularly good and there has been no analysis of whether reference reports add any incremental validity over cognitive ability tests, for example.

Work sample tests and job simulations

Work sample tests and job simulations provide examples of alternatives to the 'sign-based' approach to personnel selection exemplified by psychometric testing. Examples include the in-tray tests mentioned earlier in this chapter. Results from various meta-analytic studies show that work sample tests have high criterion-related validity (an average of approximately 0.55). Given that they have high face validity, applicants respond favourably to work sample tests in selection.

Work sample tests and job simulations can be expensive to develop since they have to be tailored. Many selection methods are criticised on the grounds that they have limited fidelity to the job role. Work sample tests build realism into the selection methods by simulating as much as possible the genuine conditions under which individuals have to perform their work. They test how well individuals perform in those simulations. Simulations can differ in the extent to which there is psychological and physical fidelity to reality. For example, in her development of an assessment centre to recruit doctors, Patterson et al. (2005) designed a GP–patient consultation exercise, where medical actors play the role of patient and follow a script.

Stop to consider

In the preceding sections we have considered the properties of a range of different selection methods. What do the best selection methods have in common? What do the worst methods have in common? Is good selection just about the predictive validity of measure? If not, what other factors contribute to the effectiveness of a selection method?

The impact of selection procedures on applicants

Fairness

Until recently, there has been relatively little work in personnel selection which has looked at the issues involved from the perspective of candidates. The main area of work concerns the extent to which selection procedures are fair to different subgroups (such as ethnic minorities or women) of the population. This issue has stimulated a large amount of research. A variety of terms such as bias, adverse impact, fairness and differential validity are used in the literature on this issue, and a clear grasp of the meanings and definitions of some of these terms is crucial to an understanding of the research results.

First, it needs to be made clear that a test is not unfair or biased simply because members of different subgroups obtain different average scores on the tests. Men and women have different mean scores for height; this does not mean that rulers are unfair measuring instruments. However, it would be unfair to use height as a selection criterion for a job, if the job could be done by people of any height, since it is important for selection criteria to be job-related.

Unfortunately, it is possible for tests to appear to be valid and yet be biased against some subgroups. This may happen if the relationship between the test score and job performance is not the same for the two subgroups. For example, it is possible to imagine that the link between job performance and certain personality or ability factors could be different for two subgroups of the population (e.g. the personality factor predicts performance for men but not for women). A validity study based on a mixed sample of people would produce results that were somewhat incorrect for both subgroups; if the results were used to develop a selection procedure the predictions of candidates' work performance would be in error. For example, significant differences were found in criterion-related validity between members of minority and majority ethnic groups that applied for training with the Dutch police (de Meijer and Born, 2009). Of course, the situation would be even worse if the validity study was based on only one subgroup but was then used to select members of another. Unfair direct discrimination is where the selection process treats an individual less favourably because of their gender or ethnic group, for example. Indirect discrimination is usually unintended and difficult to prove. It occurs when an employer applies a requirement for applicants (e.g. score on a test) which one group (defined by gender/race/socio-economic background, etc.) finds it considerably harder to comply with, i.e. a larger proportion of one group cannot meet this requirement. This is known as *adverse impact*.

> ### Key learning point
>
> Indirect discrimination occurs when an employer applies a requirement for applicants (e.g. score on a test) which one group (defined by demographic variables finds it considerably harder to comply with. A procedure is biased or unfair when it shows different validity for different groups.

In using a selection test, the test designers would need to ensure that the difficulty level of items (percentage of applicants getting the item right) is not significantly different across different ethnic groups sitting the test. If differences are found, then there is said to be *differential item functioning*. There are sophisticated statistical procedures that can be applied to assess differential item functioning for tests. In general, the research evidence suggests that for professionally developed selection tests there is little or no evidence of differential item functioning across ethnic groups. The fact that the scientific research provides little evidence of differential validity for well-established selection procedures does not imply that all selection methods are unbiased, nor does it imply that unfair discrimination does not take place. For example, cognitive ability testing is the method that has created the most frequent problems with adverse impact in selection processes. Large-scale meta-analytic research has shown that there are significant ethnic subgroup differences in validity of cognitive ability tests, with validity favouring White candidates over Black and Hispanic candidates (Berry et al., 2011). This holds true even after correcting for statistical issues such as range restriction – criterion-related validity coefficients were 11.3–18 per cent lower for Black and Hispanic applicants than their White counterparts (Berry et al., 2014).

Other selection methods such as SJTs have also been found to be biased towards certain subgroups. Whetzel and colleagues (2008) found that Whites scored better than African Americans, Asians and Hispanics, and women perform better than men. Racial subgroup differences become even larger when the SJT is more cognitively loaded. Bobko and Roth (2013) reported larger white/African American subgroup differences for SJTs than was found in previous research after taking into account the limitations of statistical analysis and the context in which the research was conducted.

ACs make use of several selection methods and this may minimise the impact of bias in one component. Dean et al. (2008) conducted a meta-analysis with 27 research studies to explore adverse impact in ACs. They looked at 'standardised subgroup differences' produced by ACs for three particular subgroups (namely Black people, Hispanic people and females). They found a subgroup difference of 0.52 between Black and White individuals, showing that in contrast to the traditional assumption of low subgroup difference effects in ACs, there is still a significant difference between the ratings of Black and White individuals in ACs. In the same study, a lower level of subgroup difference was found between Hispanic and white individuals than between Black and White individuals. There was also evidence of a negative subgroup difference between female and male individuals, as females tended to receive higher performance ratings in ACs. Anderson et al. (2006) conducted a study into gender differences in AC performance using a military sample, and found that females achieved higher ratings than males on interpersonal leadership-style traits, including 'oral communication and interaction' and 'drive and determination'. The studies conducted by Dean et al. (2008) and Anderson et al. (2006) can be taken alongside other studies of diversity and fairness to illustrate the mixed picture of evidence that exists regarding potential discrimination arising from the use of ACs. It is also worth remembering that candidates taking part in an AC are a small proportion of the general population, that is they have chosen to apply for the job and have been selected for the AC based on the information provided in their application form (and perhaps some other pre-AC assessments). Therefore, it might be that some of the effects observed at ACs are a result of events that occur before the AC. For example, it may be that only very able female candidates apply for the job and make it through the pre-AC assessments. In contrast, males of all levels of ability may apply for the job and some of the pre-AC assessments may favour males, thus resulting in males from across the ability spectrum being assessed at the AC.

Applicant reactions

In recent years, there has been more emphasis placed on applicants' decision-making where selection is now viewed as a two-way process. Attracting applicants to apply for a job is the first important step. If offered the job, an applicant with a negative reaction is likely to refuse a job offer (and the best applicants could work for a competing organisation). In an extreme case, an applicant who has a negative reaction to a selection procedure could make a legal challenge on the basis of unfair discrimination. Applicants who have negative experiences with an organisation's selection system could boycott the organisation's products and encourage their friends and acquaintances to do the same.

Exercise 4.6   Adverse impact in selection

A large organisation was found to have discriminated against ethnic minority applicants after an employment tribunal. Following a restructuring of the organisation, 100 new middle management posts were created. Approximately 30 per cent of employees are of ethnic minority origin, and currently, 3 per cent of management are of ethnic minority origin. The personnel department decided to use a structured interview and two cognitive ability tests (a measure of verbal reasoning and a measure of numerical reasoning).

Of the 600 employees who applied for management posts, 30 per cent were of ethnic origin. However, only 10 per cent of the job offers were made to ethnic candidates. The tribunal ruled that the tests were inappropriate in terms of the time allowed, the level of difficulty, the skills tested and the content covered. There was evidence of adverse impact and unlawful discrimination. The organisation conceded there was unintentional and indirect discriminatory impact on ethnic minority candidates and suggested compensation.

Suggested exercises

1   What is the difference between fair and unfair selection testing?

2   How can unfair discrimination be recognised?

3   What needs to be considered in evaluating the fairness of the test?

Research has tended to explain the different factors that affect applicant reactions using theories of organisational justice. Distributive justice focuses on perceived fairness regarding equity (where the selection outcome is consistent with the applicant's expectation) and equality (the extent to which applicants have the same opportunities in the selection process). Procedural justice refers to the formal characteristics of the selection process such as the level and quality of information and feedback offered, job-relatedness of the procedures and methods and recruiter effectiveness.

Point of integration

Procedural and distributive justice have their origin in research into employee relations and worker motivation (see Chapter 7). They have provided a useful framework for investigating the factors that influence worker satisfaction with a range of human resource management processes and interventions.

For an early review of these theories see Anderson et al. (2001a) and Gilliland (1993). Anderson et al. (2001a) suggest that four main factors seem to account for positive or negative applicant reactions to selection methods. These are: (i) the selection method is based on a thorough job analysis and appears more job-relevant; (ii) the selection method is less personally intrusive; (iii) the method does not contravene procedural or distributive justice expectations; and (iv) the method allows applicants to meet in person with the recruiters. Other literature suggests that applicants prefer multiple opportunities to demonstrate their skills, that they prefer assessment that allows them to talk about their potential, and that the selection system is administered consistently for all applicants.

Of course, perceptions of injustice can depend partly on whether the person is successful in the selection process. For example, Robertson and Smith (2001) suggest that if the selection decision is in the candidate's favour, then the procedure is likely to be viewed as fair. However, 'if the decision goes against the candidate, it is unlikely to be viewed as fair ... it seems that the concepts of fairness and self-interest are closely entwined!' (2001: 452). Hausknecht et al. (2004) conducted a meta-analysis of the applicant reactions literature, using 86 studies, providing a summary of their main findings as follows. The organisational outcomes of: intentions to accept a job offer; intentions to recommend the organisation to people; and positive opinion of the organisation are more likely to be reported by those individuals who perceived the selection process in a positive light. Applicants' perceptions of the selection process were found to be related to their actual level of performance *and* the level of performance they believe they had achieved. Hausknecht et al. (2004) reported that applicants' perceptions of predictive validity and the face validity of the selection method were strongly linked to many aspects of candidates' perceptions of the selection process (e.g. predictive and distributive justice and applicant attitudes towards selection and its component tests). In terms of the relative popularity of different types of selection tests, Hausknecht et al.'s (2004) meta-analysis showed that applicants held favourable perceptions of interviews, CVs, work sample tests and references.

Many studies have used a measure originally developed by Steiner and Gilliland in 1996 to assess applicant reactions to ten widely used selection methods (see Table 4.9 for an overview of each method). To date, 18 known samples have been studied using this measure in countries across Europe, America, Asia and the Middle East. The general consensus is that interviews, CVs, and work-sample tests are among the most favourable methods, and graphology and honesty tests are among the least favourable methods. In an age in which many companies operate internationally and must extend their selection systems beyond their home countries, however, it has become increasingly important to investigate the hypothesis that applicant reactions may vary as a result of cross-cultural differences. In 2008, Anderson and Witvliet assessed the procedural and distributive justice of the 10 selection methods outlined in Table 4.9 using Steiner and Gilliland's (1996) measure on a Dutch sample. Their results mirrored the general trend of the most and least favourable methods found in previous studies, however, in order to investigate whether there were any cross-cultural differences in applicant reactions, they conducted international comparisons between their Dutch sample and the six other samples that existed at the time of publication. Results indicated a basis for the notion that cross-cultural variations in applicant reactions are minimal, as high correlations were generally observed between the applicant reactions of all six countries. A study conducted in the UK (St Ledger and Zibarras, under review) took this one step further by comparing the UK sample with every single existing sample studied using the Steiner and Gilliland (1996) measure (excluding papers not published in English). This study is the largest cross-cultural comparison of applicant reactions to date, and includes samples from Vietnam, Saudi Arabia, Turkey, Romania, the Netherlands, Greece, Italy, Spain, Portugal, France, the USA and Singapore.

Results supported the notion that there may be a core component in applicant reactions that is stable across countries. Practically, this is particularly useful for large multinational companies that must extend their human resource management practices internationally. Since authors such as Moscoso and Salgado (2004) and Bertolino and Steiner (2007) proposed that applicant reactions may differ as a result of cultural differences, there has been a degree of uncertainty regarding whether the same human resource practices can be applied in multiple countries and be perceived just as favourably. The body of literature on applicant reactions shows that there seems to be a general consensus that the methods viewed as favourable in one country will also be favourable in another. Consequently, companies will be able to extend their selection practices across countries without having a differing impact on applicant reactions.

Table 4.9	Selection methods and descriptions (Steiner and Gilliland, 1996)
Selection method	**Description**
Interviews	Face-to-face interactions in which employers ask you a variety of questions about your background and qualifications.
Résumés/CVs	A written description of information on all of your professional experiences, your education, etc.
Work-sample tests	Tests in which you actually perform a part of the job so that your success in doing that part of the job can be determined.
Biographical information	Forms requesting very specific information about your work experience, education, and skills. They often include questions about your hobbies, interests, and past accomplishments. The questions are frequently in multiple-choice format where you check the appropriate answer.
Ability tests	Tests that evaluate your intelligence on your reasoning, verbal or mathematical skill.
Personal references	In this method, you must request letters of reference or provide the names of your prior employers so that the employer can obtain information about your suitability for the job.
Personality tests	Tests that ask you questions about your opinions and past experiences to assess your personality traits.
Honesty tests	Tests that ask you about your thoughts on theft and experiences related to your personal honesty.
Personal contacts	Knowing someone influential in the company whose connections can help you get the job.
Graphology	The analysis of aspects of your handwriting, including style and form, to determine personal characteristics.

It is important to acknowledge, however, that research on applicant reactions tends not to be conducted during live selection processes, and because of the lack of studies focusing on important organisational outcomes (e.g. applicants actually choosing to withdraw from selection processes, or refusing to take the job offer), there are some weaknesses in this field of research, especially when it is applied to real selection settings.

Key learning point

Organisational justice theories are used to understand applicant reactions to selection methods. Applicant reactions to selection methods are generally stable across countries.

Stop to consider

It might be argued (although not by the authors of this textbook) that if a selection method predicts job performance then applicant reactions are of little importance. From what you have read in the preceding sections, what is it about a selection method that shapes candidates' perceptions of it? You might want to consider your own experiences of selection processes to help you think about this question.

▶ Is it possible that a selection method that generally prompts positive candidate reactions might, if it is not delivered in a professional manner, provoke negative candidate reactions? When delivering a selection process, what needs to be done in order to ensure that candidates do not have negative reactions to it?

The use of technology in selection

The rapid advances that have been made in the world of technology and telecommunications have presented selection practitioners and researchers with new opportunities and challenges. No least is how to balance the tremendous potential of technology to increase the pool of potential applicants to an organisation, with the possibility that technology itself may influence the decisions that are reached (Anderson, 2003). Let us take the example of Internet-based application forms. There has been a dramatic increase in the number of organisations advertising via the Internet and expecting applicants to complete and submit online application forms. The advantages for the organisation include:

- the ability to create interactive application forms;
- the possibility of providing additional information to potential applicants by signposting other relevant webpages;
- the capacity to request information from applicants in a standard format that can be processed and assessed by computer technology.

For example, it is now possible for the first stage of a selection process involving analysis of biodata to be completed by computer without any member of the organisation gaining sight of the application form.

Some applicants may approve of online application forms, which could be perceived as easier and faster to complete and send (even up to seconds before the deadline). Others may experience technical difficulties that may lead to negative applicant reactions. In this topic, researchers have been left trailing in the wake of advances that have been made in practice. For example, Internet-based forms are often cited as a way of improving international recruitment in global organisations. However, we do not know as yet whether cultural differences and familiarity with technology will impact upon the way in which applicants present themselves in these applications. Certainly, by restricting application to Internet-based procedures, those with reduced access to computer technology, or who are less familiar with it, will be at a disadvantage.

In his review of applicants and recruiter reactions to the use of technology in selection, Anderson (2003) identifies three main themes to consider including (i) applicant reactions, (ii) equivalence (e.g. is an applicant's score on a selection test administered online equivalent to the same test administered using paper and pencil?) and (iii) adverse impact. For some selection methods there has already been extensive research (e.g. cognitive ability testing via computer), but for others there is very little evidence yet available (for a detailed review of this literature see Lievens and Harris, 2003). It is possible that interviews conducted using technology such as telephones or videoconferencing could result in negative applicant perceptions and could even put potential applicants off applying (Sackett and Lievens, 2008).

Considering applicant reactions to technology-based selection methods is of increasing importance. A salient feature of the selection experience not identified by Gilliland (1993) is the role of technology (Anderson, 2003; Zibarras and Patterson, 2015). Applicant reactions to up-to-date methods are now being investigated: these include video interviewing (Guchait et al., 2013; Chapman et al., 2003), video résumés (Hiemstra et al., 2012), interactive situational judgement tests (Weekley and Ployhart, 2006) and online selection systems (Konradt et al., 2013), in addition to the more traditional methods. Lievens and Sackett (2006) found video-based SJTs to have high predictive validity, and incremental validity over written SJTs. Although there were no differences in face validity between the video and written SJT, candidates did react favourably to the video version. Video interviews have also been found to be favourable to candidates (Toldi, 2011); this is discussed in more depth in the closing case study. Konradt et al. (2013) suggest that the very nature of technologically based selection means that applicant reactions towards these methods may be influenced in a different way than traditional methods of selection. For example, there is usually no personal contact until the latter stages of selection; online tests are highly standardised, which could influence applicants' perspective of their opportunity to perform; and applicants generally use their own equipment when completing Web-based exercises, meaning that the experience may not be the same for every candidate due to differences in working environment and Internet speed.

The concept of equivalence is a critical question since there is increasing usage of the Internet for use in recruitment in general, and legal concerns are of importance. Research investigating the equivalence across different selection methods has produced mixed results. Sackett and Lievens (2008) report that using Internet-based testing produces 'lower means (average scores), larger variances (more spread in the data), more normal distributions, and larger internal consistencies (i.e. internal reliability)' (2008: 1619). Potosky and Bobko (2004) argue that one advantage of tests delivered via the Internet is that they do not allow candidates to flick through the test items and make strategic decisions about the way they distribute their time across the test items.

Key learning point

Applicant reactions, equivalence and adverse impact are key themes in investigating the use of technology in selection. Recruiter characteristics may also impact upon the choice to use new technologies in selection.

Sackett and Lievens (2008) recommend that future research should explore the utility of technology-based selection methods, and uncover if and how Internet-based selection may impact upon the type of candidates completing these tests, and the predictive validity of these tests. As you may imagine, there are potential dangers involved with the use of 'unproctored Internet testing' (which is Internet-based testing without a person physically administering the test to candidates). These dangers include the possibility that the identity of candidates may be revealed and the test may not be securely stored. Some suggest that the latter may be overcome but the former will present a problem until more advanced identification technology enters mainstream use. Tippins et al. (2006) suggest that given these concerns, unprotected Internet testing should be restricted to use on 'low-stakes' selection.

Oostrom et al. (2013) have made the argument that recruiter characteristics may affect whether new technology is incorporated into selection practices. They found that recruiter characteristics were significantly related to perceptions of the usefulness and ease of use of technology, and in turn, this related to intentions to use new technologies. Recruiter characteristics were also found to be more important in determining whether recruiters will use new technologies than perceived face and predictive validity and fairness.

In summary, a great deal of further research is needed to explore the various ways in which technology can influence the personnel selection process from both the organisation's and the applicant's perspective.

Exercise 4.7   Video interviewing

Video interviewing – the next big thing? Video interviewing has recently become quite a buzz in the world of recruitment and selection. To give a high-level overview of the concept, video interviewing essentially involves conducting an interview through the use of technology – namely a webcam and a set of speakers – as opposed to being conducted over the telephone or face to face. Video interviews can either be live or non-live – the difference being that in a live interview, the interviewee and interviewer(s) exchange dialogue in real time through a video link. Non-live interviews typically present a set of standardised questions (either written, recorded or both), appearing on-screen one by one, that the candidate must answer. Their answers are recorded and sent to the recruiting organisation for consideration.

In 2013, Qatar Airways partnered with Sonru, an international recruitment partner, to implement a new video interviewing process. In their case, the video interview is used as a preliminary measure to filter applicants before the actual face-to-face interview. Just like a traditional interview, the candidates who sit Qatar Airways' video interview do not see any questions in advance – they follow an online link and are presented with each question one by one, with instructions and rehearsal time included. Candidates cannot stop, pause or restart an interview once they begin. Qatar Airways can set the maximum read and answer times for each question. Hiring managers can then view the responses in their own time and record their feedback on each candidate.

Of the new process, chief HR officer Elizabeth Johnston said:

> Video interviewing has allowed us to accomplish a much higher conversion rate of interviewees to placed candidates by zeroing in on those who met those initial requirements – both technically and interpersonally. We seized an opportunity to reduce the size of our applicant funnel relative to hires, reduce costs of travel and stabilise recruiter headcount. What we have found is that we are able to interview a higher number of candidates in less time, allowing us to optimise the recruitment process. This approach [also] allows us to very much standardise questions asked of candidates so comparisons really help our assessment consistency and also adds a level of transparency and diligence that would be otherwise hard to build.

Suggested exercises

1   List the possible advantages of using video interviewing for recruiters and applicants. To what extent do you think these outweigh the possible challenges?

2   What advice and practical recommendations would you offer organisations thinking of implementing video interviewing?

3   Are there any instances where video interviewing wouldn't work?

Summary

Selection processes are designed on the assumption that there are job-relevant, individual differences between people, which can be assessed. The cornerstone of effective selection processes is the job analysis, which defines the assessment criteria that form the basis for many human resource activities in organisations, and it is particularly important in personnel selection. More recently, organisations have used competency analysis to define the key behaviours that underpin successful performance in the target job role. A range of approaches to job analysis are available, including qualitative and quantitative techniques. Job analysis information may be used to develop sign- or sample-based selection procedures.

Given significant changes in the nature of work and work patterns in recent years, many jobs do not have specific, prescribed job descriptions. This presents a variety of challenges for the job analyst, particularly in deciding which job analysis techniques to employ. Since the reliability and validity of such procedures determine the quality of personnel entering the organisation it is crucial that selection procedures provide valid assessments of future work behaviour. Several different (e.g. predictive or concurrent) validation processes are available for assessing validity.

Various personnel selection procedures are available for use in organisational settings. Research over the past three decades has provided a much clearer picture of the criterion-related validity of these procedures. Some of the methods, such as cognitive ability tests, seem to have broad applicability across a range of situations. As well as examining the validity of personnel selection procedures, research has also concentrated on the impact of the procedures on candidates. One area that has been reasonably well researched involves an examination of the fairness (to different subgroups) of the various techniques.

Closing case study

Recruiting for values: the value of values-based recruitment

The notion of values-based recruitment – that is, assessing and selecting suitable candidates based on the appropriateness of their values for the job for which they have applied – has gained both research and practical interest in recent years. Values are guiding principles about how individuals ought to behave; they govern one's choices and are predictive of behaviour. But how valuable are values to selection? Research suggests that they can be a useful part of a selection process, particularly in an era where success at work is increasingly based on factors beyond ability alone (although a bit helps, of course!).

One sector that has recently drawn public attention to the importance of values at work is the healthcare sector. It is widely agreed that irrespective of job suitability 'on paper', a set of values including compassion, empathy, respect and dignity are also important for all healthcare professionals; these have been linked with high-quality care and favourable patient outcomes, and are held in the National Health Service (NHS) constitution in the UK. The absence of these values, however, can have disastrous consequences.

The Francis Report (2013) reported findings from an inquiry into a failing UK NHS hospital trust. Shockingly, the inquiry uncovered a severe lack of compassion, care and committed nursing that resulted in the appalling suffering of many of the hospital's patients. The same year, the Cavendish Review was published, which focused heavily on the importance of making sure healthcare workers have core values in place that ensure the safety of patients and the success of workers (Cavendish, 2013). In fact, the key recommendation was that employers must define a thread of values common to all healthcare professionals, and this must be considered a core attribute in recruitment if cases like that of the Francis inquiry are to be avoided.

Other hospitals and private healthcare organisations have thankfully been more successful. The Cavendish Review revealed that a core theme across top-performing healthcare providers was

▶

▶

an emphasis on values in addition to traditional selection measures. For patients, values-directed care provides that 'something extra' over and above good job performance; for organisations in the UK and the USA, lower staff turnover and sickness absence, and higher performance and quality of patient care are just some of the many benefits of values-based recruitment.

But how do we assess values? Recent research has examined the utility of a number of selection methods for assessing non-academic attributes, including interviews, CVs, personal statements and situational judgement tests (SJTs). Generally, multiple mini interviews (MMIs) and SJTs are effective for values-based recruitment, while personal statements and CVs are less effective. SJTs in particular stand out as being a good addition to any selection process that wishes to assess values, as they have been found to have high face, content and predictive validity, even over methods like personality tests. SJTs assess applicants' judgements about various work-related scenarios by asking them to identify appropriate responses to a number of written or video-based scenarios. The advantage is that SJTs can be extremely versatile – they can be constructed using different formats and can capture several different domains dependent on the requirements of the role.

Clearly, in the healthcare sector at least, there is definite 'value' (pardon the pun!) in values-based recruitment. But this is not unique to healthcare recruitment – recruiting based simply on academic ability or test scores is becoming a thing of the past, while non-academic attributes are becoming increasingly important. Values-based recruitment can provide a reliable and valid indication of the underlying motivations behind candidates' behavioural choices and ensures that they are in line with those desirable for the organisations to which they apply.

Is it more important to assess values than any other aspect during recruitment? Perhaps not. But are they an important addition to a selection process that is predictive of both organisational and individual success? Most definitely.

Sources: Francis, R. (2013) Report of the Mid Staffordshire NHS Foundation Trust Public Inquiry: Executive Summary (vol. 947).

Cavendish, C. (2013) An Independent Review into Healthcare Assistants and Support Workers in the NHS and Social Care Settings, London: Department of Health.

Test your learning

Short-answer questions

1 Why is it important to conduct a thorough job analysis?
2 What are competencies and competency analysis?
3 What are behavioural indicators in competency models and how are they used?
4 What are the differences between face, content and construct validity, and how is each type of validity assessed?
5 What selection methods can be used in assessment centres?
6 How does sampling error distort validation studies?
7 What is an adverse impact in personnel selection?
8 What stages are involved in developing a situational judgement test?
9 What can be done to ensure that selection interviews are as effective as possible?

Suggested assignments

1 Given recent changes in the nature of work and the increasing number of newly created job roles in organisations, discuss the relative effectiveness of job analysis techniques and suggest how psychologists might improve them.

2 Outline the key stages in the selection process. Discuss the practical problems associated with validating selection procedures in organisations.

3 Critically review the validity evidence for three of the following contemporary personnel selection methods: personality assessment, tests of cognitive ability, interviews, assessment centres.

4 Discuss the advantages and disadvantages of using technology for personnel selection and assessment.

5 What do situational judgement tests measure? What are their advantages and disadvantages compared to other selection methods?

Relevant websites

The British Psychological Society has recently published a set of Standards that describe best practice in the use of assessment centres http://www.bps.org.uk/networks-and-communities /member-microsite/division-occupational-psychology/assessment-centre-standards

A guide to the application of selection methods published by SHL Ltd can be found at http:// www.cebglobal.com/shl/assets/whitepaper-shl-approach-to-selection-assessment_us.pdf

Suggested further reading

Full details for all references are given in the list of references at the end of this book.

1 For more depth on the issues raised in this chapter, consult a comprehensive text on personnel selection, such as Evers et al.'s *The Blackwell Handbook of Personnel Selection* (Blackwell Publishing, 2005) or Cook's *Personnel Selection: Adding value through people* (Wiley, 2004), or Schmitt and Chan's *Personnel Selection: A theoretical approach* (Sage, 1998).

2 A very detailed treatment of validity and reliability is given in Anastasi's book, *Psychological Testing* (Macmillan, 1988), or Kline's *Handbook of Psychological Testing* (Sage, 1999).

3 Sackett and Lievens's (2008) article presents an excellent review of the state of the art in personnel selection. Some of the language used is a little complex but it is an excellent source for use throughout your study of personnel selection.

4 Patterson et al. (2009) 'Evaluation of three short-listing methodologies'. This article shows how important it is that shortlisting is done well. It provides a good analysis of the impact on selection decisions of using different shortlisting methods.

5 Schmidt and Hunter's (1998) review article explores the validity and utility of selection methods over 85 years of research. It analyses a huge amount of data to examine the links between performance during selection and in the job itself.

6 Ryan and Ployhart's (2014) 'A century of selection' presents a discussion of recent advances in designing, implementing and evaluating selection systems.

CHAPTER 5

Assessing performance at work

LEARNING OBJECTIVES

After studying this chapter you should be able to:

1 understand the importance of defining work performance;

2 recognise different methods of measuring and rating performance;

3 identify how different sources of bias can influence the various interpersonal judgements being made when performance is being assessed;

4 compare different methods of assessing performance in the workplace;

5 understand the qualities of different performance rating scales;

6 recognise how knowledge of human psychology can be used to inform good practice in the design and execution of performance appraisals;

7 identify how the changing nature of work poses challenges for managers engaged in performance assessment;

8 describe the properties of multi-source feedback systems and understand the strengths and weaknesses of these systems;

9 be aware of the current issues and future directions in performance assessment research.

Opening case study

Professor Edward E. Lawler III, July 2012

Writing for *Forbes Magazine* Professor Lawler, an expert in performance management, describes performance appraisals as 'one of the most frequently criticized talent management practices'; criticisms ranging from appraisals being 'an enormous waste of time' to claims that they even have 'a destructive impact on the relationship between managers and their subordinates'. Despite acknowledging that many potential flaws can affect many performance management systems, Professor Lawler argues that appraisals are vital to effective people management and therefore should not be abandoned any time soon. He says, 'I cannot imagine a company doing a good job of managing its talent without gathering information about how well individuals perform their jobs, what their skills and knowledge are, and what their responsibilities and performance goals are for the future. These types of data are simply fundamental to the effective management of the talent of any organization.'

Pointing to findings from a survey of 100 large US companies he conducted, Professor Lawler said that all stated they had performance management systems and only six were considering getting rid of appraisals. The survey also found that while companies were no more satisfied (or dissatisfied) with their performance management systems than they had been a decade previously, 85 per cent considered their system to be 'at least moderately effective'. On this evidence Professor Lawler argues that we are unlikely to see the death of appraisals any time soon.

Source: http://www.forbes.com/sites/edwardlawler/2012/07/12/
performance-appraisals-are-dead-long-live-performance-management/
(accessed 27 April 2015)

Introduction

Assessment of performance at work can be a contentious topic that has important implications for individuals and their employers. Yet it is also a complex and fascinating activity that has generated many interesting challenges for researchers and practitioners. As the opening case study suggests, there are many potential flaws that can threaten the validity of systems and procedures organisations use to assess employees, but there is also a substantial body of research findings that can help inform how assessment can be made more reliable, accurate and fair. Not surprisingly, performance assessment is a core area of research and practice for work psychologists. This chapter sets out to describe important challenges (e.g. what is work performance and how do we measure it?) and discusses some practical solutions (e.g. multi-source feedback).

The purpose of performance assessment is to evaluate how employees are performing relative to their colleagues and managers' expectations, provide feedback about how performance can be improved, and to provide managers with information that can be used to guide strategic decisions about investing in personnel or work design that can enhance individual and team and, ultimately, help to achieve business goals. Therefore performance assessment is a critical part of many complex organisational systems including those governing performance management and human resource management (HRM).

HRM is the core business function concerned with recruiting, developing and managing employees. The HRM philosophy typically views employees as an essential business resource (often referred to as 'human capital') that requires monitoring and careful management in order to achieve the best return on investment (ROI). In order to successfully align HR strategy with business strategy management, systems are needed that can reliably and accurately assess the performance of individuals at work, ensuring good decision-making about how best to develop, reward and manage personnel (Guest, 1997).

These systems are important for individual employees, because they impact on opportunities like career progression and reward. For example, 'talent pipelines' are used by many large organisations to identify individuals at junior levels (e.g. recent graduate recruits) with potential to achieve future senior leadership positions. Identifying these individuals at an early stage means that the company can provide additional support and development opportunities to facilitate skill development and progression through the 'pipeline' to more senior roles. Of course, ensuring these initial judgements of potential are accurate is vital to avoid resources being directed inefficiently and, perhaps more importantly, to ensure that people with potential are not overlooked and potentially lost to the company if they leave and move to a competitor. Accurate and fair assessment is therefore essential to ensure that employees receive the most appropriate reward, support and development, and ensure that human capital is not wasted.

Data from performance assessment systems can also inform strategic decision-making: performance data collected from different parts of a company can be useful when making decisions about investing in, or supporting, human capital. For example, if there are reliable data that employees in an important part of the company are not performing well then remedial interventions (e.g. training or improved selection processes) can be prioritised. Advances in information technology have made it possible to collect large quantities of performance data electronically. This allows performance to be tracked over time, and comparisons to be made about performance across different work groups, different parts of an organisation and sometimes between different companies. We explore this in more detail later in the chapter. However, despite electronic monitoring becoming easier and more prevalent, most performance assessment still relies on the interpersonal ratings made by managers about the work of the people they supervise. The psychological processes influencing the quality of these ratings have been extensively studied.

This chapter aims to provide an overview of key areas where work psychology has contributed to the understanding and practice of performance assessment at work. It explores why, for example, performance appraisals continue to receive such criticism, and the methods that can be used to improve the delivery and effectiveness of performance assessment procedures. Consequently, we begin by considering what is meant by work performance, how it can be defined and how it can be measured. Next, the chapter explores how interpersonal assessment of performance can be subject to bias and distortion, and how work psychology has contributed to the development of performance assessment and performance management systems that contribute to more reliable and valid decisions. The chapter concludes by looking at future challenges for researchers and practitioners in this area.

Defining work performance

Understanding what constitutes work performance and how it can be assessed is one of the most important challenges facing work psychologists (Campbell, 2012). Assessing work performance is a surprisingly complex activity. At its core lie two fundamental questions (i.e. 'what do we mean by performance at work?' and 'how do we measure it?'). Together these have come to be known as the 'criterion problem' and have generated a substantial body of research and discussion (Austin and Crespin, 2006; Bennett et al., 2006).

Good measurement requires a good definition of what is being measured (it is impossible to carry out accurate measurement without first determining what needs to be measured).

In the case of work performance this is more difficult than it may first seem. Take the case of three people with different jobs: an actor who is playing a lead role in a stage production of Macbeth, a high-school mathematics teacher and a journalist working for an online newspaper. It may seem obvious that good performance for the actor is being able to act well, but what exactly do we mean by 'act well'? For example, what criteria would we use to indicate someone is acting well and how would we assess these? We might refine our definition of 'good performance' further by describing it as the actor behaving in ways that lead audience members to see a character that is believable and engaging, but this in turn relies on subjective evaluations by different members of the audience and arguably by theatre critics too. For the journalist good performance might be defined in terms of writing articles that motivate readers to click subsequently on further online news articles in the newspaper. Good work performance for the teacher may involve marking homework assignments, providing feedback to students on time, and preparing well-structured lessons that help students to understand and learn new information.

Not only do these examples indicate that there are often many different ways that job holders can demonstrate good and poor work performance, performance judgements may also vary according to the subjective views of different observers (Murphy and Jackson, 1999). The potential variety and complexity of judgements involved in assessing performance means that it is very important to have clarity for workers *and* managers about what a job holder is expected to do and the standards they are expected to achieve.

Exercise 5.1	Rating your lecturer

Most universities routinely ask students to rate their lecturers as a way of capturing information (feedback) about the relative quality of different courses and teachers. Think about the questions that you are asked about your lecturers' performance. Now consider whether these questions capture all aspects of the work of a university lecturer. What other areas of performance are likely to be important and how might these be assessed? What other performance criteria might be used to provide a comprehensive assessment of how well a lecturer is performing his or her work?

Generic models of work performance

One way in which researchers have sought to deal with the complexity of work performance as a construct has been to investigate whether there are underlying components of work performance that are common to all job roles. According to Campbell (1990), attempts to map this 'latent structure' of work performance are just as important as past efforts by psychologists to understand the latent structure of intelligence and personality. For example, personality theorists have identified five traits that appear to help us make sense of much of the rich diversity of human personality (see Chapter 3). In a similar way, work psychologists have undertaken research to identify common components of job performance that can inform the development of the theory and design of performance assessment tools. One of the first large-scale investigations by Campbell and his colleagues (1993) identified eight general factors of job performance, each of which is made up of several more specific factors (see Table 5.1, and Campbell et al., 1996). According to the researchers, all eight general factors are useful to a greater or lesser extent in describing performance across different types of work, but three factors (i.e. core task proficiency, demonstrating effort and maintaining discipline) are relevant for *every* job role. As an aside, this is consistent with the research (discussed in Chapters 3 and 4) showing the links between conscientiousness and job performance. Subsequent studies have found evidence for this eight-factor model

Table 5.1	Job performance factors		
Campbell		**Bartram**	
1 Job-specific 'core' task proficiency*		1 Enterprising and performing	
2 Non-job-specific proficiency		2 Interacting and presenting	
3 Written and oral communication		3 Analysing and reporting	
4 Demonstrating effort*		4 Creating and conceptualising	
5 Maintaining discipline*		5 Adapting and coping	
6 Facilitating peer/team performance		6 Supporting and cooperating	
7 Supervision/leadership		7 Leading and deciding	
8 Management/administration		8 Organising and executing	

*Important for all job roles.

of job performance. Therefore, it is a useful framework but more precise definitions of the individual factors are often needed when attempting to apply the model to performance assessment in organisations.

Bartram (2005) takes a somewhat different approach in his research to map the latent structure of work performance. His starting point was to examine competency frameworks developed by many different companies for different and similar jobs (in other words a deductive approach). Competencies relate to the observable skills or abilities that an individual requires in order to perform a task or role effectively. Competency frameworks describe the behaviours associated with good and poor performance for each competency (see Chapter 4). By comparing the competencies that many different companies had produced for similar and different jobs, Bartram was able to identify whether there was any congruence – or common factors – across these independent sources. Interestingly, his meta-analysis of 29 validation studies that used line managers' ratings of performance ratings also found evidence for eight 'great' factors of job performance. Listed next to Campbell's eight factors in Table 5.1 it can be seen that while both researchers identify the same number of factors, there are some intriguing differences. For example, unlike Campbell, Bartram does not identify factors associated with core task performance, effort or motivation. However he does identify 'creativity' (innovation), 'conceptualising' and 'analysing' (cognitive ability), none of which were identified by Campbell, but factors that

Key learning point

It is clear that different work roles have different performance requirements, but there appear to be several common categories of work activity that are found in the majority of work roles.

have become increasingly recognised by practitioners as important to job performance. As Table 5.1 shows, used together these two models provide a comprehensive description of the breadth and depth of work performance.

Key debate

Is there a 'g' factor of work performance?

Although researchers have sought to identify various different core components of work performance, other researchers take a different view (Scullen et al., 2000). In their research Viswesvaran et al. (2005) were able to find evidence for 25 conceptually distinct categories of job performance. Importantly, however, they argue that statistical analysis of these data identifies a single underlying factor of job performance. In other words, there may be one underlying competency that is reliably linked to overall job performance across many different work roles in different organisational contexts. Therefore, rather than an eight-factor model, they claim that job performance is better understood in terms of a single overarching 'g' factor in much the same way as cognitive ability (see Chapter 3). This would certainly simplify many selection, training and performance appraisal procesess! Others maintain that it is important from both a theoretical and practical perspective to understand the differences between competencies so that interventions can be focused and precise. Even though good workers might tend to be good at sticking to their tasks and exhibit strong social skills, might the psychological processes that underpin the perseverance be very different to those that drive effective interacting with others? No doubt debate about the underlying structure of work performance is likely to continue.

Point of integration

The techniques and methods used to investigate and analyse work performance are very similar to those used in the early stages of the design of a selection process (see Chapter 4). Indeed, results from competency analysis are often used to shape both performance assessment and selection processes.

Extra-role performance

So far we have focused mostly on job performance as defined or expected by managers, which might be described in a role description. However, in the early 1980s Organ and his colleagues coined the term 'organisational citizenship behaviour' (OCB) to describe what might be considered as extra-role performance demonstrated by workers. Smith et al. (1983) asked supervisors to describe the types of behaviour they might expect from good workers, but which they could not reward or force them to do. They found that managers typically listed behaviours like employee helpfulness, conscientiousness, courtesy, sportsmanship (i.e. tolerating impositions without complaining), and civic virtue or positive political behaviour at work. These were all actions not requested directly by managers, and not listed on job descriptions or appraisal forms, yet all were identified as important in helping to make the workplace a better environment (Organ, 1997). For example, whereas one employee might fulfil traditional performance expectations by producing accurate and detailed reports on time, a second might do the same but in *addition* offer to help other colleagues who might be struggling (providing discretionary help to others is sometimes referred to as *prosocial behaviour*). OCB has been defined as 'individual behaviour that is discretionary, not directly or explicitly recognised by the formal reward system, and that in the aggregate promotes the effective functioning of the organisation' (Organ, 1988: 4). OCB may be of benefit to the organisation as whole (e.g. when an employee provides advance notice of a planned absence from work) or targeted more towards individual colleagues (e.g. helping with the induction of a new member of staff).

Point of integration

OCBs are a recurrent theme in work psychology. In this text you will also find them mentioned as features of engagement at work (Chapter 10) and as outcomes in theories of motivation (Chapter 7). Perceptions of justice appear to play a particularly important role in motivating OCBs. There is little evidence that pay incentives increase OCBs.

From its definition it is easy to see why OCB might be important for creating positive work climates and improved group performance, prompting interest in other aspects of job performance not usually captured in traditional job descriptions or conceptions of work performance. For example, Borman and Motowidlo (1997) draw a useful distinction between 'task' performance (defined as the effectiveness with which an employee completes a set of technical or role-specific objectives) and 'contextual' performance (which impacts indirectly on organisational climate and improved work satisfaction). They argue that while task performance contributes to the organisation's technical objectives, contextual performance is important for broader organisational performance because it impacts indirectly on work climate and perceived support. Borman and Motowidlo identify seven types of behaviour associated with contextual performance, including volunteering to take on responsibilities not formally part of one's role, supporting and defending organisational decisions, persisting with enthusiasm, and following rules even when they may be personally inconvenienced. This work helps to identify performance-related behaviours that have hitherto been neglected. But extra-role behaviour can also prove a challenge for performance assessment: if extra-role behaviour goes beyond what managers expect it may not be possible to include it on traditional rating scales because by doing so it becomes expected behaviour!

Work by Griffin and his colleagues has built on the distinction between task and citizenship performance in an effort to develop a generic taxonomy of work role performance. Arguing that changes in the nature of work over the past 30 years have resulted in a need for a broader range of role behaviours required for work performance, Griffin et al. (2007) identify two new forms they believe are particularly important: (i) the need for employees to demonstrate *adaptivity* (i.e. the extent to which an individual adapts to change in work systems or roles), and (ii) the need for employees to be *proactive* (i.e. the extent to which an individual takes self-directed action to anticipate or initiate change in work systems or roles). Together with a third component, *proficiency* (i.e. the extent to which an individual meets the formal requirements of his or her role), they propose a model that describes nine dimensions of work performance achieved by cross-classifying these components with three different levels at which behaviour can be demonstrated (individual, team and organisational). One important advantage of this model is that it can be used to investigate and describe in more detail how worker behaviour can be assessed in terms of its contribution to performance at these three different levels (Neal et al., 2012). This level of complexity shows that there is still much to be explored in relation to defining and operationalising work performance. As Hanson and Borman (2006) argue, neither core task performance nor OCB in isolation is likely to provide a sufficient framework for understanding. As jobs change, future research needs to look at broadening both our conceptualisations of job performance and our methods of measuring.

Key learning point

For performance assessment to be successful in any work context, two questions need to be answered: (i) what constitutes good and poor performance, and (ii) how can it be measured? It is useful to distinguish between core task performance and organisational citizenship behaviours.

Measuring work performance

Our ability to define work performance is important because it impacts on how performance is measured and assessed. In the case of the actor mentioned earlier, if audience perception is used as a criterion of good or poor performance, we need to ask the audience to rate the actor. We also need to consider what rating scales might be used and how we can be sure that different members of the audience are rating the actor's performance in a similar way. There are many different criteria that can be used to assess performance, and some are easier to quantify than others. For example, performance criteria for a retail sales person might include the number of successful sales they achieve, their customer satisfaction ratings, their absence from work (days/year) or the number of errors or mistakes they make. These types of information are often viewed as more objective measures of performance than ratings by managers, which can be influenced by bias or insufficient opportunity to observe a worker. It is important to recognise that no performance criterion – even if it is represented by a number – is likely to be a perfectly reliable and valid indicator of performance. Volume of sales can be influenced by the product area for which an employee is responsible (for example, in a retail pharmacy store there may be fewer opportunities to sell foot spas than to sell hair products), or whether an employee is working in a store located in a relatively deprived or economically vibrant area. In order to overcome problems associated with any one type of performance data, data from several different performance criteria can be collected and the findings triangulated (i.e. examined together) to build a more comprehensive picture of how an individual or work group is performing. To date, however, the most common form of performance data is still generated from managers' direct or indirect observation of individuals in the workplace (Arvey and Murphy, 1998).

"I always give 110% to my job.
40% on Monday, 30% on Tuesday, 20% on
Wednesday, 15% on Thursday, and 5% on Friday."

'Real performance is going beyond what is expected; it is setting one's own highest standards, invariably standards that surpass what others demand or expect' (Whitmore, 2004: 97). John Whitmore defines 'real' work performance as that which exceeds what managers expect. This presents something of a difficulty for those developing rating scales. Can or should extra-role behaviour be included as something to be reviewed as part of an appraisal process? Does this mean that the unexpected becomes an expected part of an employee's contribution to the workplace?

Observing and judging performance

Managers routinely observe and informally judge the performance of their subordinates on a day-to-day basis, but there is considerable evidence that these interpersonal judgements can be selective and biased. There is a substantial body of literature in social psychology and work psychology concerned with common forms of bias that influence managers' (and others') interpersonal judgements. They include 'halo and horns', where individuals tend to make generally favourable or unfavourable evaluations of people based on the limited information initially available to them. The 'halo' effect can happen in a job interview when the interviewer reads an applicant's CV and identifies something they like about them (e.g. that they attended the same university), which subsequently sensitises the interviewer to other positive features of the applicant. The opposite occurs with the 'horns' effect, when for example, an interviewer is sensitised to negative things about the applicant (e.g. after hearing the applicant answer a question in a way they don't like). Managers can also be vulnerable to primacy and recency effects, where information presented early or late in a sequence dominates memory and judgement. For example, observations made by a manager about how a new employee performs in their first few days can play an overly significant role in shaping the manager's expectations about the employee's long-term potential. Another common bias is the **fundamental attributional error**: individuals habitually attribute the behaviour of others to more internal dispositional causes (e.g. personality or ability) than situational causes. This can lead managers to underestimate the importance of environmental factors on individual performance, including the impact of their own actions on the performance of others.

Several different unconscious biases can undermine the reliability and validity of performance ratings made by others (e.g. colleagues, managers, clients).

The biases discussed are likely to apply to whomever managers are rating, but certain sources of bias can have a detrimental effect on certain groups of employees compared to others. For example, the similarity–attraction theory (Byrne, 1971) predicts that the more similar to themselves an observer (e.g. manager) perceives another person (e.g. subordinate) to be in terms of personality, attitudes, values or demographic characteristics, the more prone they are to like, trust and interact with them. This means that employees who are similar to their line manager may be rated more favourably and allowed more opportunities to work on important assignments, thereby increasing their potential to progress (Wyatt and Silvester, 2015).

Point of integration

Biased performance ratings can have an impact on the career development opportunities available to employees (see Chapter 13).

These types of bias often result from unconscious cognitive shortcuts (better known as cognitive **heuristics**). These we use to make sense of, and respond quickly to, complex situations, people and surroundings. Another example is stereotyping, which arises when we rely on automatic processing of cognitive schemata that develop over time from experience and cultural learning (Klimoski and Donahue, 2001). While these stereotypes can be useful in speeding up the way we make decisions about people and actions, this comes with very significant costs: accuracy and fairness. Stereotypes are too simple and can reduce the accuracy of judgements about performance (Barnes-Farrell, 2001). For example, a manager might hold a stereotype of new graduates as 'clever but poor at understanding client needs'. This stereotype might lead to the manager prioritising training in client liaison, but it could mean that the manager is more likely to attribute a client's complaint to a graduate's lack of experience while overlooking the failure of their more experienced colleagues.

In many organisations performance judgements are used to make decisions about whether an individual has potential to achieve future leadership roles, and biased performance evaluation can have important implications for employees from minority groups (Kraiger and Ford, 1985; Stauffer and Buckley, 2005). According to Lord and Maher (1991), becoming a leader depends on being perceived to be a leader by others. But as Virginia Schein's work on 'think manager – think male' (Schein, 1975; Schein et al., 1996) has shown, women and members of minority groups can be disadvantaged because leadership prototypes are typically white and male. As people judged to have leadership potential are usually singled out for additional training and development and greater access to mentors and networks (Maume, 1999), it is therefore important to train managers so that they are aware of and motivated to address different sources of bias. Another way to make managers more careful and less likely to engage in automatic stereotypic thinking is by holding them to account for the assessment decisions they make. For example, evidence shows that simply asking assessors to record their observations and explain their decisions results in them engaging in more controlled processing of information (Pendry and Macrae, 1996).

Key learning point

To maximise fairness and validity, raters need to be aware of the ways in which biased heuristics can influence the way they perceive and rate the performance of others. This awareness may help them to manage the impact of such biases.

Rating performance

The last section focused on naturally occurring sources of bias during interpersonal decision-making, but another equally significant source of variation in assessment occurs when there are no clear or shared criteria regarding good and poor performance (Graves and Powell, 1988). This can be one of the reasons why ratings are frequently influenced by non-performance related factors. This section considers an area where work psychologists have made an extremely important contribution, namely the design of rating scales for performance assessment.

Stop to consider

Work by David Kipnis and Susan Fiske reveals the importance of power in interpersonal decision-making. Their research shows that power-holders often fail to take account of how their own power and status can influence other people's behaviour (e.g. Kipnis et al., 1980). For example, leaders tend to think that subordinates agree with them, because the subordinates think the decisions are good. In doing so leaders often overlook other potential reasons for agreement such as subordinates' fear of a leader, or their desire to curry favour with a leader who has the power to determine their future success. Fiske (2001) developed earlier work by Kipnis in her power-as-control theory. She identifies three reasons why powerful people stereotype less powerful people at work. First, she argues that as power-holders already have influence and resources, they may have less need to expend the cognitive effort required to overcome stereotypes and individuate others. Second, Fiske suggests that managers at higher organisational levels are often responsible for large numbers of people, which generally requires a lot more effort to pay individual attention to everyone and therefore may not happen given competing demands on managers' attention. Third, she suggests that people selected into positions of power may be more likely to have personal characteristics that make them less interested in those lower in a hierarchy, or motivated to expend the effort needed to individuate them.

Suggested exercise

How might these findings be used to design training to improve the performance assessment and performance management skills of leaders?

Figure 5.1 shows several graphical rating scales that vary in their effectiveness at eliciting performance appraisal data. Like many forms of psychological measurement, key issues concern problems of reliability and validity. For example, scales should provide a clear indication of the meaning that can be assigned to each point on the scale (validity) so that the rater, and anyone who needs to interpret the rating on the scale, can make a valid inference. Of course, clear and unambiguous interpretation is impossible with the scale in Figure 5.1a, since it provides so little information (e.g. what does 'very good' actually mean?). It is also important that scales are used consistently, either by different raters, or by the same rater on different occasions. The scale in Figure 5.1b poses problems, because with so much subjective judgement required, judgements may well vary from rater to rater or from one day to the next. Although the scale in Figure 5.1c provides a better basis for validity and reliability, such graphical rating scales are still vulnerable to many possible sources of error. One of these, leniency, is a characteristic of the person doing the rating. Some people appear to be 'easy' raters and tend to provide a greater proportion of high scores (positive leniency). Others can be harsh or severe raters (negative leniency). Leniency effects can often be observed when the results of two or more assessors are compared. Although leniency effects may be the result of unconscious bias on the part of the rater, there is also a potential for motivated leniency, which occurs when a rater is motivated to favour one assessee over another. Motivated leniency might occur when a manager wishes to promote a particular employee rather than another. Rating individuals in a group situation can increase the likelihood of motivated leniency, particularly when there is competition between managers for finite resources to reward their staff such as financial bonuses or access to leadership development

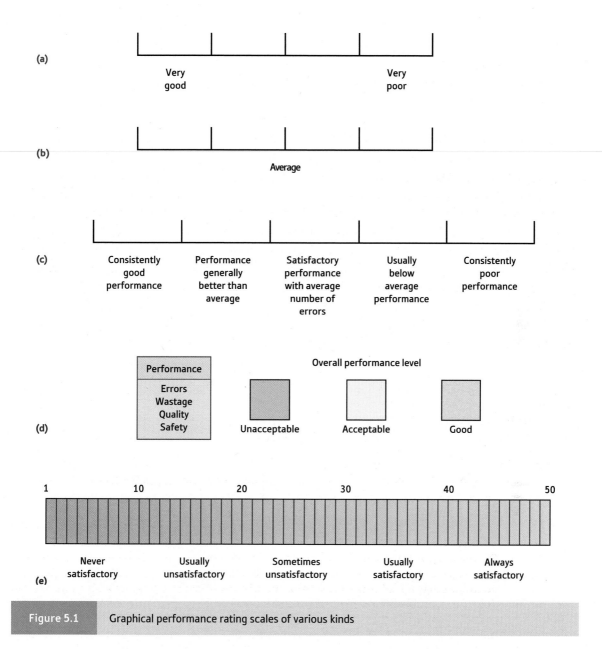

| Figure 5.1 | Graphical performance rating scales of various kinds |

opportunities. Leniency may also be linked to individual differences between raters. Those who describe themselves as high on the personality trait agreeableness have a preference for avoiding conflict and maintaining harmonious relationships and this has been shown to increase leniency, thus elevating performance ratings. It is perhaps therefore unsurprising that managers with a high level of agreeableness tend to be significantly more lenient in their ratings of others than those with a low level of agreeableness (Harari et al., 2015). The same authors also found that making raters accountable for their ratings (i.e. asking them to offer justifications for their evaluation alongside the numerical ratings) tended to moderate, or blunt, this effect somewhat.

As well as unconscious biases, deliberate manipulation of performance ratings may occur.

Other sources of error include the halo error, which is a tendency for raters to allow their assessment of an individual's performance in one area influence the evaluation of that person on other specific traits (if we believe that someone is outstandingly good in one important area of performance, we might rate him or her high in all areas, regardless of their true performance). Finally, the central tendency error occurs when raters are reluctant to provide ratings at the extremes of a scale and as a consequence ratings tend to group around the mid-point of the scale resulting in a potential restriction of range. All of these can influence the accuracy and fairness of decisions that result from ratings made using scales, but one straightforward way of helping to minimise the error in any type of rating scale is to use multiple questions (items) for each of the performance areas being rated. As any individual item is open to some degree of misinterpretation by the rater a set of items that are relevant to the construct being rated will help to reduce overall error. This is because the misinterpretations and errors related to each item will probably be random in their effect and will therefore balance each other out (although an exception to this will be the case of motivated bias). A score based on the average of all items will almost certainly be more reliable than a score derived from a single item: longer measures are more reliable (see Figure 5.2 for an example of a multiple item scale).

Point of integration

Many of the biases that impact on the accuracy of performance ratings can also impact on the evaluations assessors make of candidates during selection processes (see Chapter 4). This means that training provided to those administering selection processes can share many features with the training provided for those carrying out performance appraisals.

Key learning point

Using multiple items will help to improve the reliability of rating scales.

Behaviourally anchored rating scales (BARS)

As we have seen, a common problem with unsatisfactory rating scales concerns the failure to define sufficiently the 'anchors' points. Broad, generalised descriptions of anchors such as 'average', 'good' or 'excellent' make it impossible to be sure that everyone who uses the scales will interpret them similarly. Inter-subjectivity is the term used to describe these individual differences in interpretation. One popular means of providing unambiguous anchor points on a scale is to use *behaviourally anchored rating scales* (BARS; see Figure 5.2), where anchors describe a specific behaviour which is

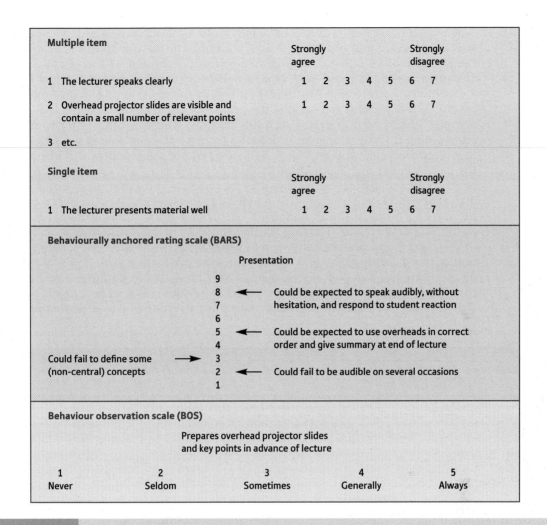

Figure 5.2 Multiple item BARS and BOS rating scales

critical in determining a particular level of job performance (Smith and Kendall, 1963). BARS are developed using a four-step procedure:

1   With the aid of a group of 'experts' (these are people who understand the role in detail, for example employees, supervisors or senior managers), define the factors needed for successful job performance.

2   Use a second group of 'experts' to provide examples of specific behaviour associated with high, average or low performance on the factors.

3   A third group takes the examples from step 2 and independently matches them with the factors from step 1. This 'retranslation' acts as a cross-check on the two previous steps. Examples that are not assigned correctly to the aspect for which they were written do not provide unambiguous behavioural anchors for that aspect of job performance and should not be used.

4   The final step involves using more 'experts' to assign scale values to the surviving items, which then serve as the behavioural anchors for the scale.

Research suggests that BARS produce results that are only slightly better than well-constructed graphic rating scales, leading some people to question whether the effort involved in constructing BARS is worth the trouble. However, two points are worth bearing in mind here. First, a well-constructed graphic scale may require an amount of effort equal to that involved in constructing BARS. Second, with planning, it is possible to combine the process of eliciting information required to compile a BARS with undertaking a job analysis, which minimises both cost and effort. Other scale development procedures include *behaviour observation scales* (BOS) (e.g. Weirsma and Latham, 1986). BOS development procedures will also ensure the development of reasonably sound scales. In essence BOS, like BARS, are based on examples of critical behaviour, i.e. those behaviours that make a significant difference in terms of job performance outcomes. With BOS the rater assesses the ratee in terms of the frequency of occurrence of the relevant behaviour (see Figure 5.2). Some research has shown that there is a preference among users for BOS in the case of appraisal. BOS are seen as better for providing feedback, determining training needs, setting goals and overall ease of use (see Latham et al., 1993). Somewhat disappointingly, however, no procedures have been able to produce scales that are completely immune to rating errors. Rating behaviour still remains one of the most difficult tasks that managers must undertake when assessing employee performance.

Key learning point

Rating scales can be improved by using behavioural anchors that define the types of behaviours that raters might expect someone to demonstrate for each point on the rating scale.

"Before we begin your performance review, I took the liberty of ordering you some comfort food."

Rater training

One of the oldest methods of improving the quality of performance ratings is to train those people who are providing ratings (Spence and Baratta, 2015). Of all the forms of training used with raters, most support can be found for Frame of Reference (FOR) training (Woehr and Huffcutt, 1994). This aims to provide raters with: (i) an effective theory of performance by explaining the dimensions of performance along which behaviours coincide or group together; (ii) an understanding of how to rate these behaviours in terms of their effectiveness; and (iii) how to combine these judgements into performance ratings. It is argued that by providing raters with a theory about why and how behaviours may vary, they are less susceptible to the various types of bias that were discussed earlier. Recent research by Roch et al. (2012) provides additional support for FOR training. Expanding on earlier work by Woehr and Huffcutt (1994), Roch et al. found clear evidence in their meta-analysis that FOR significantly improved rater accuracy across different work situations. They suggest that it has become the method of choice for rater training.

Performance assessment in practice

Having considered efforts by work psychologists to define and measure work performance, the next section explores how this knowledge has been applied in practice to design and implement performance assessment systems. We begin by examining traditional performance appraisal systems, before examining how changes in the nature of work and technology have resulted in new challenges and opportunities for managers involved in performance assessment.

Performance appraisal

Performance appraisal is probably the most common means by which organisations require managers to formally assess how well their staff are performing. Performance appraisal usually involves an annual or six-monthly process where individual employees are evaluated according to predetermined performance dimensions (Spence and Baratta, 2015). In broad terms, the process exists to determine how well an individual is performing in relation to the requirements of their role, and in comparison to other colleagues in their work group or the wider organisation.

As part of the performance appraisal cycle, managers may be expected to observe and record how well an employee is performing over a period of time and, where available, to collate their observations with those from other sources capable of viewing the employee's work (e.g. other managers, team members and clients). The manager will then evaluate these observations against pre-determined job-related performance criteria (e.g. performance objectives and standards). They then meet with the employee to provide feedback, examples of how the employee has demonstrated good or poor performance to support their assessment, and identify and agree areas for improvement. In many performance appraisal systems, employees are also asked to reflect on their own performance and development needs, and to discuss these with their manager during the meeting. The appraisal meeting is particularly important because it provides an opportunity for two-way dialogue about how to achieve high levels of performance, identify future goals and improve employee engagement. In fact, performance appraisal can serve many different purposes including:

1   providing feedback to an employee about how he or she has performed;

2   determining an employee's development needs;

3   identifying areas where performance can be improved;

4   establishing future performance goals or objectives;

5   identifying individuals with potential to move to more senior or challenging roles;

6   determining reasons for poor performance;

7   comparing individual performance with that of other employees;

8   making appropriate performance-related rewards.

Importantly, performance appraisal is an opportunity for managers to help employees understand how their personal objectives contribute to the overall business strategy, helping to build a shared understanding about wider organisational needs and how they can be achieved (Williams, 2002). Clearly, therefore, an important advantage of performance appraisal is its versatility of purpose. However, Fletcher reminds us that perhaps the most important question for those intending to develop and implement an appraisal process is 'what is the aim?' He argues that getting this bit wrong means that it is almost inevitable that 'the appraisal system will not run smoothly – if at all' (Fletcher, 2008: 5). Indeed, one-third of the people in Kluger and DeNisi's (1996) study experienced reduced performance following their appraisal; an important reminder that, if not done properly, appraisal also has the ability to de-motivate employees.

Key learning point

If not done well performance appraisal processes can have a negative impact on employee motivation and subsequent performance.

One of the most common problems with performance appraisal is when a system is designed for both development *and* reward. **Performance-related pay (PRP)** or 'merit pay' is a difficult and contentious area for managers, and discussing reward alongside employee developmental needs can compound this difficulty still further. Few individuals are likely to be open and frank about areas they need to improve if they also know that information from the performance appraisal process will be used to determine their pay. Moreover, while many people might like the idea of linking pay to performance, we also tend to believe our own performance is better than most of our peers (Fletcher, 2008) and this perception can increase with increasing seniority (Wright, 1991): something that may help to explain the prevalence of 'fat cat' bonuses at executive levels! For these reasons, most performance appraisal systems strive to keep assessment for the purposes of employee development separate from those concerned with reward.

Providing appropriate feedback is crucial if individuals are to understand what and how they need to change, but this can be a stressful activity for managers and a source of considerable dissatisfaction for managers and employees. Managers sometimes find it difficult to deliver feedback to an under-performing employee, or meet the expectations of those performing very well. However, providing feedback to employees of a different gender or ethnicity can prove a further challenge for some managers, with research suggesting that managers often 'hold back' from providing critical feedback to Black and Minority Ethnic (BME) employees and women, for fear of appearing racist or sexist (Croft and Schmader, 2012; Wilson, 2010).

Performance appraisal can therefore suffer from potential flaws. Importantly, performance ratings and decisions in many cases are usually heavily reliant on the judgement of a single source (the manager). As managers often observe only a small fraction of the work performed by an employee (and this fraction may not be typical of their overall performance), performance appraisal can be particularly vulnerable to bias and error. Managers' ratings can be influenced by whether they have worked with an employee previously, whether they like the person, and how valuable the individual is considered to be for the team and the manager's own performance in the future (Randall and Sharples, 2012). Thus a performance appraisal can entail a complex social interaction between people with different and often competing needs and it is perhaps not surprising that both parties can seek to actively distort the outcomes of appraisals, presenting a favourable impression of themselves in order to achieve their needs (Longenecker et al., 1987). According to Frink and Ferris (1998), evaluation systems where employees set performance goals are particularly prone to the effects of impression management. Rosenfeld et al. (2002) argue that some people are more skilled at managing impressions than others, and this may reduce the validity and accuracy of managers' decisions. However, managers can also distort performance appraisal procedures for their own needs, for example, when they are keen to retain a valuable team member or even lose a difficult or poor performer (Gioia and Longenecker, 1994). In fact, performance appraisal settings have been identified as one of the work settings most vulnerable to political activity (Ferris and King, 1991); leading Murphy and Cleveland (1995) to suggest that political factors may exert an even stronger influence on performance ratings than the capabilities and limitations of those doing the appraising. Certainly the impact of power and politics in assessment deserves further attention from work psychologists (Silvester and Wyatt, 2016).

Key learning point

There are numerous contextual factors that can influence the performance appraisal process: many of these are linked to the importance and value employees place on their working relationships with others.

Improving performance appraisal

In light of the potential problems that can affect performance appraisal, Villanova and Bernadin (1991) summarise the practical implications of research for the assessment process:

1 Ensure that the performance criteria used by managers in performance appraisal are relevant to the job, and essential – or at least important – to job performance.

2 Provide clear definitions for performance criteria so that managers and employees have a shared understanding of what is being assessed.

3 Train appraisers and those being appraised so they know how to use the system.

4 Ensure that appraisal happens frequently to avoid managers relying too much on memory or generic impressions.

5 Aggregate individual performance to a group or team level when the performance of employees is co-dependent on others.

6   Increase the number of people who provide performance ratings and statistically combine ratings from these raters.

7   Hold appraisers accountable for their ratings.

Another method that has been used to improve performance appraisal ratings involves forced distribution rating systems (FDRS; Scullen et al., 2005). Also known as 'forced ranking', FDRS address the fact that managers typically show a central tendency (where more employees than expected receive a middle ranking) or positive bias when rating their staff. Thus, although performance may be normally distributed, managers will tend to rate most employees as '4' (where 1 = low performance and 5 = high performance), with very few if any employees rated '1' or '2' (see Figure 5.3). FDRS require that a manager rates individual employee performance in a way that ensures it is directly compared with that of other workers in a group. More specifically, managers must identify the 20 per cent of their staff who are 'top performers', 70 per cent who are 'average performers' and the bottom 10 per cent who are 'low performers'. Managers are also expected to act on these ratings by rewarding top performers (e.g. with increased wages or promotions) and dealing with under-performers by setting explicit expectations regarding improved performance or potentially by firing the bottom 5 to 10 per cent.

FDRS are seen as a way of encouraging managers to take a more critical look at the people who work for them, but it can be unpopular. A common complaint from managers is that, because they can allocate top grades to only 20 per cent of their staff, the system forces them to downgrade other excellent performers and make them appear as mediocre performers. There may well be situations where it is not valid to assume that the performance of a group of employees is normally distributed – for example when there are relatively few people in a group it may be that they are all performing at a very similar level. It can also be very difficult to implement FDRS when the performance of one group member depends on the performance of others. Consequently, FDRS may be better suited to situations where managers supervise larger numbers of relatively independent employees.

Performance appraisal and the modern manager

While appraisal remains a popular method for assessing employee performance, technological advances, together with changes to the way we work, have prompted work psychologists

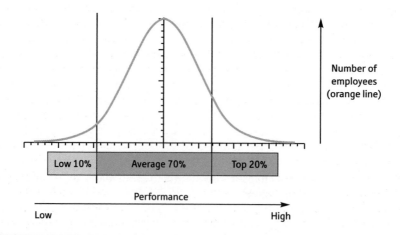

| Figure 5.3 | Typical bell curve distribution for FDRS |

to investigate new ways of assessing work performance that can accommodate many of the new challenges facing modern managers. These challenges include managers being required to supervise people working in diverse and geographically distant locations (e.g. different countries and time zones). Employees today may have roles that require them to be highly mobile, or they might work at home supported by computer and information technology. In fact, managers can find that they spend very little time interacting directly with their direct reports – and even then conversations could be via e-mail, telephone, video- or tele-conference (Dambrin, 2004). In such cases managers are unable to observe how these employees interact with clients or colleagues directly. They also have less opportunity to build relationships, which may increase the likelihood of managers de-individualising those they supervise (i.e. losing the sense that each employee has their own distinct individual identity). These types of changes to working arrangements mean that there is a growing need for new methods capable of capturing diverse performance-relevant information, and for managers to understand how distance can impact on ratings and feedback.

Point of integration

The growth of dispersed working has had a significant impact on the type of information available to managers about the performance of those they supervise. Chapter 15 describes these changes in the type and amount of information available.

For many employees, work, and therefore work performance, have also become increasingly co-dependent, with many working as part of teams or wider organisational work systems (Griffin et al., 2007). In these types of settings it may not be clear who has contributed what to a team's work outcome, or the nature and quality of their specific contribution. Here performance outcomes can depend as much on the actions of others as they do on an individual's own efforts, and the challenge for those assessing performance is to determine how the efforts of different individuals can be isolated in order to decide how individuals might be rewarded or developed.

Further challenges include the 'flattening' of organisations, which has involved the reduction of middle management layers, with remaining managers now having a broader span of control and responsible for a larger numbers of direct reports to assess (London and Tornow, 1998b). A faster pace of change at work also means that employees are regularly required to move between assignments and managers, reducing the time available for a manager to get to know an individual employee's strengths and development needs. Therefore while the chance to participate in interesting and challenging projects can provide employees with a valuable opportunity to develop their knowledge and experience, it may come at a cost if changing managers also means a loss of continuity in understanding the individual needs of employees. Consequently, modern assessment systems are required that are capable of monitoring performance and development over time.

Finally, globalisation provides another important challenge for modern managers. Most global companies are keen to ensure that their performance management and talent development procedures are fair and consistent across different areas and regions. This means that managers need to be able to appraise direct reports who can be from different cultural backgrounds to their own accurately and reliably. They may also have direct reports from multiple cultural backgrounds. This diversity can substantially increase the complexity of the assessment process and often requires that managers are trained to be aware of the potential for cultural bias alongside other forms of bias.

Clearly, there is a need to build a theoretical and practical evidence base capable of supporting the development of assessment systems for these 21st-century challenges, and although work psychologists have begun to explore how these challenges can be addressed, there is still much work to be done. One of the most promising areas draws on technological innovations to shape assessment systems able to collect and analyse performance data across large numbers of employees over periods of time.

Exercise 5.2 — Assessing and rewarding team members

You are the manager of a team of 16 software specialists responsible for designing new software for client-owned mobile phone networks. The team represents the end-point in the design process. Team members interface with client users and help them to implement the new technology. They are ultimately responsible for making sure that there are no problems or glitches with the new software, and that implementation occurs smoothly. Most of the work involves final stage testing of the software and client liaison, either remotely, or by travelling to the client's location, which can be anywhere in the world. While there are some very good team members, who consistently put in extra effort, others are less committed and 3 to 4 frequently under-perform. One of the under-performers has been suffering from depression and as a result has had to take several weeks off work (although the reason is unknown to the team). You have also received complaints from some of your team that another team that is responsible for getting a virtually finished product to your team to work on have often produced poor work or missed deadlines. This year the company has decided to allocate a bonus of £30,000 to be divided between you and your team.

Your task is to decide how to divide this bonus up and explain why you have reached your decision. How would you make the process fairer next year?

Stop to consider

There are many situations where an individual worker performs well because of situational factors rather than their own efforts. A good example of this is the case of equity traders who buy and sell shares on stock markets. It is usually easier to make a profit buying and selling shares in a 'bull market' (where the price of shares is moving up) than in a 'bear market' (where prices are falling). Yet, the bonus payments made to traders in bull markets are higher than those made in bear markets. Why might this be the case, and can anything be done to separate the effects of the market on individual trader performance?

Multi-source feedback (MSF)

Multi-source feedback emerged in response to criticisms levelled at a traditional performance appraisal (PA). It is often referred to as 360-degree feedback, because the performance of a target individual is rated anonymously by many different people who are able to observe different aspects of their work behaviour. These raters typically include the target's manager, their work colleagues, the people they supervise (direct reports) and, potentially, clients who are internal or external to the organisation (see Figure 5.4). The '360-degree' label therefore derives from the fact that raters can be above the target in terms of their seniority, at the same level, or at lower levels where they effectively provide upward feedback on performance. While MSF was scarcely heard of prior to the 1980s, its popularity grew rapidly

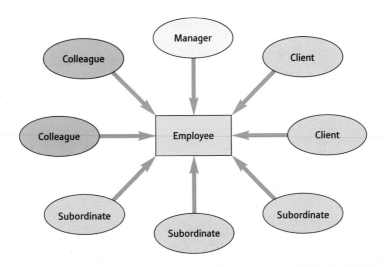

| Figure 5.4 | Feedback sources for multi-source feedback |

in the 1990s to the extent that most large US and UK organisations have incorporated it as a part of their performance management systems (Fletcher, 2015). One important reason for this success is that by collating feedback from many sources into a report for the target individual, MSF can provide a more rounded, and therefore potentially more accurate, picture of an individual's performance (London and Smither, 1995). This is because, unlike a manager, who may get to see only a selective part of an individual's performance, soliciting feedback from many different people makes it possible to capture ratings from people who may each observe a slightly different aspect of the person's work. Arguably this enhances both reliability and validity because a larger sample is behaviour and is observed more often. For example, work colleagues may be better able to judge how well someone engages with team members, customers can provide a perspective on service interactions, and direct reports can comment on their manager's ability to supervise others.

Most MSF is collected via an online questionnaire, which means that it is possible to collect and collate feedback from many different raters and rater groups, and translate these data into feedback reports quickly and with relatively little effort (Stanton, 2000). Individuals providing feedback are asked to rate a series of behaviours that are relevant to different competencies that the target individual is required to perform in their job (e.g. 'responds quickly to customer needs' or 'provides clear instructions to colleagues').

Figure 5.5 illustrates how feedback from different sources (self, manager, colleagues and subordinates) might be summarised and presented in a report. Each horizontal bar indicates how a different person or group has rated the target individual on the questions relating to a particular competency: in this case the competency is managing performance. Here the 7-point rating scale ranges from 1 'well below average' to 7 'well above average'. The bottom bar shows that the individual has rated themselves at 4.7. The other bars represent the mean scores of the combined responses provided by members of different rater groups. For example, the second bar up represents the mean score from the target's three senior managers (i.e. 4.3). The bar above this is the mean score from colleagues (i.e. 5.5) and the top bar is the mean score of ratings from the target's direct reports (i.e. 5.2). The horizontal lines on the bars also show the highest and lowest ratings from members of each group, and therefore help to illustrate the range of ratings received.

The aim of these reports is to provide target individuals with anonymous feedback from different groups in order to help them understand how they might need to change their

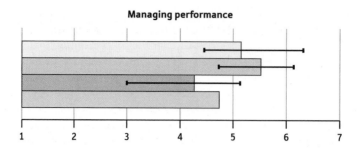

Figure 5.5	Comparison of ratings from different sources

behaviour. For example, if a target rates themselves high on 'listens to customers' needs' but their rating is much higher than the rating provided by clients the individual is alerted to the need to improve in this area. Thus feedback can lead to a change in behaviour. It can also help to improve an employee's confidence and motivation when they find that others rate them higher than the employee has rated him or herself (Johnson and Ferstl, 1999). These discrepancies between self- and other-ratings can occur because individuals lack self-awareness (Atwater et al., 1998), therefore feedback enables them to calibrate their own efforts and performance more effectively against the expectations of others.

Although feedback is particularly powerful when a consistent pattern emerges from all feedback groups, patterns are not always consistent (Hoffman et al., 2010). In such cases interpreting differences between ratings provided by different groups can be challenging. For example, who is to say that one particular rater is 'correct'? As we have already seen, there are plenty of reasons why performance ratings might be biased. Take the example of someone who is rated high on customer service by their colleagues and customers, but not by their manager: which ratings should be believed? This raises questions about the validity of multiple assessments. While correlations between ratings from different sources are generally low (Conway and Huffcutt, 1997), it is quite possible that each set of ratings is an accurate reflection of the views of that particular group, but each group has a slightly different understanding about what constitutes good performance in that particular performance area. For example, a manager's view of excellent customer service might be influenced by broader organisational requirements that good customer service is that which produces sales. Yet, customers might view excellent customer service as the target helping them to understand that a particular product may not be suited to their needs. Clearly, there is no single 'right' view of what good customer service looks like. That said, certain sources of feedback may be viewed by targets as more powerful or legitimate. Thus source credibility determines what feedback employees are most likely to pay attention to and relates to both trust in, and perceived level of influence of, a particular feedback source (Kluger and DeNisi, 1996). Perhaps not surprisingly, Bailey and Fletcher (2002) found that although feedback from direct reports was the most accurate, targets paid most attention to the feedback that came from their boss!

Key learning point

Multiple performance ratings from different sources can provide a more rounded picture of an individual's work performance, but care must be taken not to assume that any one source provides the most accurate or correct rating.

Key debate

Does multi-source feedback work?

A key question concerning MSF is, does it work? More specifically, is there any evidence that the feedback received by targets using MSF results in improved work performance? Dai et al. (2010) report positive findings from their longitudinal study, which found that competencies identified for development using successive rounds of MSF improved significantly more than competencies not identified for development. According to Smither et al. (2005), however, evidence is mixed; they found only modest improvements in employee behaviour and attitudes following the introduction of MSF systems in their meta-analysis of 24 longitudinal studies. However, further work has sought to understand the factors that impact on the success of MSF systems. For example, Atwater et al. (2007) suggest a number of factors including whether the purpose of MSF is clear to others (i.e. is it being used for development or evaluation?), the level of trust participants have in the system, individual characteristics of feedback recipients, and organisational factors like the availability of post-feedback support.

Importantly, it appears that MSF is most successful if implemented first as an employee development tool, rather than as a tool for evaluation. For this reason London (2001a) suggests that the first two to four rounds of MSF should be used for developmental purposes and that, at least initially, individuals should not be expected to share their feedback with their bosses. This helps foster trust in the system, a factor identified as important by Bolton et al. (2004) who also found that online feedback helped to promote anonymity for raters. This anonymity increased the level of trust that individuals had in the system.

In addition, employers might pay attention to individual differences among employees that can determine reactions to feedback. Smither et al. (2005) found that subsequent improvements in ratings provided by direct reports, peers and supervisors were greater among individuals with a positive orientation to feedback, who perceived a need to change and believed that change was possible, and set realistic goals for themselves. Colquitt et al. (2000) also found that individual differences moderated the impact of MSF: individuals with high conscientiousness and self-efficacy, low anxiety and an internal locus of control were more motivated to use feedback for personal development. Interestingly, Smither et al. (2005) found that although leaders who received unfavourable feedback reacted negatively at first, after six months this group had set more performance goals than other leaders who had received more favourable feedback. This suggests that MSF may have a delayed effect on performance, with recipients taking a little time to process and respond to the feedback: researchers and practitioners need to consider this time-lag when evaluation data are collected in order to properly evaluate impact.

Finally, it appears that follow-up support also enhances the likelihood that performance will improve among feedback recipients. Mabey (2001) found that individuals who believed that co-workers and supervisors supported their development reacted more positively towards feedback, and that simply discussing their feedback with managers resulted in significantly greater improvement over five years (Walker and Smither, 1999). Providing post-MSF coaching has also been found to increase the benefits of feedback through improved job satisfaction and reduced intentions to leave the organisation (Tyson and Ward, 2004). Clearly, MSF systems provide an opportunity to collect, analyse and compare large volumes of performance data relatively quickly and easily, and as such they are likely to continue as popular methods of performance assessment. Future research is therefore needed to further our understanding of factors that influence successful use of MSF with different groups and in different organisational settings.

Key learning point

MSF can lead to improvements in employee performance provided there is trust in the process, and support is provided post-feedback to help individuals understand and act on identified development needs.

Using mixed methods to define work performance

In many work roles it is not easy to define good work performance when different observers may have different points of view. And if we can't agree on what good performance is, how do we measure it? Recent mixed methods research into the performance of politicians illustrates how work psychologists have attempted to pull together data from a range of different sources and to analyse it with a range of different methods to tackle such difficult questions (Silvester, 2008; Silvester et al., 2014).

Although political scientists often use election performance as a proxy for role performance, voters can choose whatever criteria they like when they decide whether to vote for a candidate (e.g. whether they find them likeable or personable). We also know that electoral performance can be subject to a variety of factors including how well a candidate's political party is performing nationally, or the traditional strength of the support for a political party in that particular location. Electoral performance also takes no account of how well, when elected, a politician performs the day-to-day aspects of their role in government or their local constituency (e.g. when working on a parliamentary committee or helping an individual constituent). Silvester et al. argue that unlike in other work roles, where performance is normally defined by managers according to organisational objectives, political performance is a contested construct. This is because (i) different people and groups vary in what they think a particular politician should do in office, and (ii) as democratically elected representatives politicians, unlike employees, have a legitimate right to define their own work roles.

In their study Silvester et al. examined whether politicians shared a latent mental model of political performance (in others words, whether politicians had a shared common understanding of what good performance was). They developed behavioural indicators of performance from semi-structured critical incidents technique interviews with 32 local government politicians. These interviews elicited examples of specific behaviours that the interviewees believed were important indicators of good performance in different aspects of the politicians' role (e.g. when working with political colleagues, the public and local government workers). These incidents were analysed using thematic analysis to group the behaviours into several themes (or competencies). The coding of the final themes was then checked with a group of subject matter experts (the politicians themselves and people who worked closely with them).

These results were used to develop two versions of quantitative questionnaire measures of political performance (a self-rating and an other-rater version). These questionnaires were used to collect 360-degree feedback, i.e. self-ratings from the politicians and anonymous other-ratings from their political colleagues and the non-elected local government employees they worked alongside. Factor analysis was then used to identify clusters in the ratings, i.e. groups of behaviours that were rated in a similar way. The exploratory factor analysis of the data from the self-ratings revealed five common dimensions, or clusters, of performance-related behaviours: representing people, resilience, politicking (reversed as integrity), analytical skills, and relating to others.

But did this set of clusters just reflect the view of the politicians themselves? To test this, confirmatory factor analysis of the ratings from the other-rating version (completed by political colleagues and civil servants) was carried out. This revealed a similar cluster of performance dimensions. In other words, the different rating groups tended to hold a common view of the underlying factors that were important when considering the overall effectiveness of a politician. The authors argued that analysis of 360-degree feedback data provides an important method for determining whether there are underlying shared latent constructs of performance in roles where stakeholders can hold very different and potentially conflicting views about what constitutes good and poor performance.

Electronic performance monitoring

Most of this chapter has been devoted to performance assessment that is conducted by managers who are able to directly observe and interact with the people they are rating, but technological advances have made electronic performance monitoring (EPM) increasingly widespread (Bhave, 2014). EPM is defined as electronic technologies that are used to observe, record and analyse information on employee performance (Stanton, 2000). The most common setting for EPM is call centres, where work involves employees using computers and information technology to engage with customers and clients (Holman, 2005). Most of us are likely to have talked to someone being monitored by EPM when we have called a helpline to enquire about banking services, insurance or a new mobile phone contract.

Although there are different forms of EPM, most assess performance continually by collecting and analysing information like keystrokes made by individual call centre workers as they respond to customer enquiries, the time they spend working and not working, and even how often employees take comfort breaks and for how long! Telephone calls can also be monitored to check whether employees follow proscribed scripts when talking to customers, the accuracy of the information they provide or their level of helpfulness, enthusiasm and empathy during interactions. Managers can also use EPM to make 'spot checks' on the quality of an employee's work by listening in to conversations between workers and customers. In fact, Holman (2005) reports that one-third of call centres typically monitor the conversations of individual workers once a week and another third monitor conversations at least once a month.

EPM provides advantages over traditional performance monitoring by managers because it enables employers to collect and compare performance data from large numbers of workers over periods of time. This makes it easier to answer questions like, 'Do workers who have been working for longer periods of time respond less well to difficult customers?', or 'Does the performance of employees improve after a training programme?' Data collected from EPM are therefore an important source of information for making business decisions such as whether to invest in training and development or redesign selection procedures.

While EPM has prompted concerns about potential negative impact on employees, including claims that it may be overly intrusive and stressful (e.g. Bates and Holton, 2005), contrary arguments propose that EPM may actually benefit employees. More specifically, researchers point to evidence that performance data collected over time is generally more reliable, resistant to rater error or manager bias, and less vulnerable to the effects of one-off events like employee illness or a problem at work. Studies investigating the impact of EPM on employees have yielded mixed findings, with Bakker et al. (2003) finding that performance feedback from electronic monitoring actually reduced emotional exhaustion among employees – possibly because it helped them to understand how to improve their performance and develop new skills. However, Holman et al. (2002) found that these positive effects were wiped out if monitoring was perceived as intense or intrusive. More recently, Bhave (2014) has investigated whether EPM has positive or negative consequences in two longitudinal field studies of organisations using EPM. The first field study revealed that employee task performance increased with more frequent use of EPM to assess performance. The second field study also revealed organisational citizenship behaviour was higher among employees whose managers used EPM to monitor performance. Ending on a cautionary note, however, Bhave argues that organisational use of EPM is not always matched with providing managers with sufficient resources (e.g. time and training) to enable them to make the most of these data and to avoid information-overload. Clearly, more can be done to explore the responsibilities and skills required by managers in order to engage in EPM effectively.

Key learning point

Electronic performance monitoring can yield reliable, dynamic and sensitive data about employee performance, but it may not be welcomed by employees and may add to the cognitive complexity of a manager's work role.

Improving performance

A key purpose of performance assessment is to provide information that can help identify the best strategies to improve individual and, ultimately, organisational performance. As part of wider HR systems performance assessment procedures in many organisations require managers to identify the development needs of those being assessed as a routine part of the process (see Chapter 9). Another important function of performance assessment is to determine how individual employees are best motivated in order to achieve the highest levels of performance. As we have discussed, there are disadvantages to using performance appraisal for development and reward, but the performance appraisal meeting can provide a useful opportunity for managers to learn about what motivates staff and, perhaps, how they can be rewarded in ways that do not involve increased pay (see Table 5.2).

Table 5.2	Examples of rewards		
Social context	**Job-related**	**Personal**
Private office	Flexible working hours and/or breaks	Saying 'thank you'
Desk near a window	Job with more responsibility	Compliments on work in progress
Company parties	Control over work content (e.g. choice of clients, projects)	Friendly greetings
Club privileges	Access to a mentor or coach	Soliciting advice, views or suggestions
Access to personal learning opportunities (not job-related)	Home-working	Non-verbal recognition (smile)
Introduction to senior personnel	Job rotation	Formal recognition of achievement (letter, in-house journal)
Membership of 'high potential' group		

Behaviour modification

These types of rewards can also feature as an important component of behaviour modification (OBMod), the theory and practice of which has been used as part of behaviour change programmes for several decades (Hellervik et al., 1992). The essence of behaviour modification involves focusing on critical behaviours that are important for satisfactory work performance and the application of reinforcement principles to strengthen desired behaviour patterns. According to Luthans and Kreitner (1975), the first step is to identify the desired behaviour and then specify the critical behaviours that need changing and how. This can be done in a number of ways, such as through discussion with relevant personnel, systematic observation or via focus groups. The second component of OBMod involves creating a baseline measure of the frequency of critical behaviours, either by direct observation or recording, or perhaps from existing company records. This is important for two reasons: the baseline provides an objective view of the current situation and acts as a basis for examining any change that may take place. The third step involves a functional analysis that identifies (i) the cues or stimuli in the work situation (antecedent conditions) that trigger the behaviour, and (ii) the contingent consequences (i.e. the consequences in terms of reward or punishment etc.) that are maintaining the behaviour. This step is important because changing target behaviour depends on understanding the situational triggers that cause it, as well as the factors that reinforce or could potentially extinguish it.

Once the functional analysis has been completed, an intervention strategy can be designed to modify the target behaviours by strengthening desirable behaviour and weakening undesirable behaviour using reinforcement. Positive reinforcement works by increasing the frequency of the desired behaviour when the reinforcement is introduced. For example, a manager who e-mails to say thank you for a report that an employee has worked extremely hard to produce is using a social reinforcer to increase the likelihood that the employee will demonstrate similar levels of effort in future. Another example of positive reinforcement would be the introduction of flexible working hours for employees who have demonstrated a high level of commitment and punctuality. In contrast, the effects of negative reinforcement appear when the negative reinforcement is removed. An example of this would be when performance levels increase after employees are told that they are no longer required to complete time-sheets recording how they spend their day. Punishment works by extinguishing a behaviour (e.g. a manager issuing a formal warning to an employee for inappropriate language towards a colleague). Some people argue that this approach underestimates the extent to which workers interpret and makes sense of their environment (i.e. their cognitive processes), reducing their behaviour to simple stimulus-response relationships. However, this approach to intervention has been found to be effective in changing several types of work behaviour, for example in increasing compliance with health and safety requirements.

Key learning point

While it may be effective in some circumstance, behaviour modification does not take account of the many cognitive processes and individual differences that can impact on work performance.

Stop to consider

In a letter printed in the *Financial Times* on 8 January 2009, a manager describes being so fed up with people turning up late to weekly team meetings that, with the team's agreement, he decided to fine any individual who arrived more than five minutes late. They were each asked to pay £1 into a kitty that would be used at the end of the year to buy bottles of wine for the office party. The manager writes that this proved so popular that punctuality increased to 100 per cent and they failed to buy even a single bottle. How was this manager drawing on principles of behaviour modification?

Summary

This chapter has explored the contribution of work psychology to the field of performance assessment at work. As Professor Lawler noted in the opening case study, there are many potential flaws with performance assessment. These can occur because performance measures have been badly designed, or the flaws may be caused by the unconscious or conscious biases of those evaluating employee performance. The good news is that research has provided some excellent insights into how these issues can be managed. The bad news is that such problems are unlikely to be eliminated entirely through the proper design of measures and the use of effective rater training.

It is therefore unlikely that any one assessment method in isolation (e.g. performance appraisal, 360-degree review, electronic monitoring) will be sufficient to overcome all potential threats to validity and reliability. However, each method has particular strengths and there is now a substantial body of research and evidence that can inform evidence-based decisions about which systems are most suited to different contexts. More importantly, such knowledge can be used to improve understanding among managers and employees about how to make performance assessment more effective.

As the section about challenges facing modern managers illustrates though, there are still many ways in which assessment can be improved and adapted for new work settings. Advances in technology are likely to play a continuing and prominent role in performance assessment – prompting a further need to understand how the use of technology can enhance and/or detract from valid, reliable and fair assessment. There is also a need for further research investigating ratee reactions to performance assessment, and how these reactions can impact on employee motivation and performance over time (Spence and Baratta, 2015). One particular area that deserves further attention from work psychologists concerns potential ethical risks associated with collecting and storing vast amounts of performance data about individual employees. While Big Data provides big opportunities for analysis and research, there is also a need for clear guidelines about appropriate ways to store, use and potentially sell performance data. Work psychologists will need to explore how these complex ethical issues can be incorporated into best practice.

Closing case study

Assessing performance in investment banking

In the London headquarters of an international investment bank it is time for the annual assessment of performance for all junior-level investment bankers. Fifteen middle managers are meeting to compare and rate the 75 junior managers who work for them. As this information will be used by the bank to decide who should be promoted and what bonuses will be paid, senior management are keen that middle managers are consistent and fair in their ratings. These middle managers are responsible for different market sectors. Some of their direct reports sit at the same trading desk in London, while others work remotely in Paris, Tokyo, Singapore, Frankfurt, New York, Beijing and Moscow.

The atmosphere in the meeting is buoyant today. The bank's global headquarters have announced pre-tax profits of $7 billion. However, the rest of the banking sector has done well too and managers are aware that their top performers are likely to be actively courted by their competitors with lucrative deals to move jobs. They also know that their own bonuses depend on how well their teams have performed.

Before they met today, the middle managers were asked to rate 10 per cent of their juniors as 'under-performing', 70 per cent as 'performing as expected' and 20 per cent as 'performing above expectation'. They are here to discuss their ratings and ensure consistency across different managers. The first manager is asked to run through his three juniors. After consulting his notes he begins by describing Junior A as 'a safe pair of hands, somebody who is technically excellent, and who does a lot behind the scenes'. Junior B is described as 'delightful, helpful to colleagues, has an exceptional focus on detail, not always aggressive and tends to avoid risks'. Finally, Junior C is described as 'a rock star, one of the best juniors I've ever seen, unbelievable presence, someone who kicks ass and is undoubtedly a future leader'. After asking for comments from other managers who might have come across these individuals, the managers decide to rank Junior A as 'performing', Junior B as 'under-performing' and Junior C as 'performing above expectation' and someone who should be promoted.

The meeting as a whole lasts six hours and managers argue competitively for their personal favourites. At one point, a representative from HR suggests that the managers try to identify behavioural examples to support their ratings, but she is ignored. At the end of the meeting, 35 per cent of the juniors are rated 'performing above expectations' 60 per cent are rated 'performing as expected' and 5 per cent as 'under-performing'.

Suggested exercise

As the HR director responsible for ensuring fairness and consistency in performance assessment across the bank, what would you identify as the key problems with this process and what steps might you take to improve it?

Test your learning

Short-answer questions

1   Define job performance.
2   What is organisational citizenship behaviour?
3   What is the fundamental attribution bias and why might it influence interpersonal ratings?

4   How would you create a behaviourally anchored rating scale?

5   What steps can be taken to improve performance appraisal?

6   What does FDRS stand for?

7   Define 'electronic monitoring'.

8   What are the potential advantages of MSF over traditional performance appraisal?

9   Why might different sources rate an individual's performance differently?

10 List five ways that managers can reward staff, which don't involve money.

Suggested assignments

1   What approaches have researchers taken to map the latent structure of job performance?

2   What are the sources of bias that raters need to be aware of when judging others' performance, and why are these important?

3   'Performance assessment is rife with politics.' Discuss.

4   What are the potential advantages and disadvantages of electronic monitoring?

5   How have changes to the way we work influenced the design and use of performance assessment?

6   Should performance assessment be linked with reward?

Relevant websites

The O*NET program is the primary source of occupational information for job roles in the USA. The O*NET database is a free resource that contains information on hundreds of standardised and occupation-specific descriptors: http://www.onetonline.org/

The CIPD publishes a range of free resources relating to performance assessment, including the following on performance review: http://www.cipd.co.uk/hr-resources/factsheets/performance-appraisal.aspx

Suggested further reading

Full details for all references are given in the list at the end of this book.

1   The recent text by Kurt Kraiger and colleagues, *The Psychology of Training, Development and Performance Improvement* (John Wiley, 2015) provides an outstanding and detailed overview of how psychological theory and research can be used effectively in organisations.

2   Michael Harris' *Handbook of Research in International Human Resource Management* (Lawrence Erlbaum Associates, 2013) gives an excellent insight into the many practical issues associated with the implementation of theory into the assessment of work performance.

CHAPTER 6

Attitudes at work

LEARNING OBJECTIVES

After studying this chapter, you should be able to:

1 briefly describe two ways in which attitudes have been divided into three components;

2 specify two functions of attitudes for the person who holds them;

3 describe the theory of planned behaviour;

4 explain why attitudes and behaviour are not always consistent;

5 describe three features of attitudes that increase the probability that they will influence behaviour;

6 define job satisfaction and identify three general propositions about what affects it;

7 describe the evidence indicating that a person's job satisfaction is not simply a function of the nature of their work;

8 define organisational commitment and its component parts;

9 specify the factors that appear to strengthen a person's organisational commitment, and outline its consequences;

10 understand the main causes of employee turnover;

11 describe different explanations of why unemployment has negative consequences;

12 explain the psychological contract and understand what influences it and how breaches of it affect employees and employers.

Opening case study

Vicars report greatest job satisfaction while publicans are least happy

Overall job satisfaction has little to do with salary, figures drawn from Office for National Statistics data show.

Want to be happy in your work? Go to theological college and avoid a career pulling pints. That would seem to be one conclusion to draw from a new study into wellbeing and public policy, which found that employees reporting greatest job satisfaction were vicars, while publicans – who on average earn almost £5,000 a year more – were the least happy in their work.

Overall job satisfaction, in fact, has little to do with salary, according to the figures drawn from Office for National Statistics data. While company chief executives, earning £117,700 a year on average, were found to be the second happiest employees (mean clergy income by contrast is a mere £20,568), company secretaries, fitness instructors and school secretaries, all earning less than £19,000 a year, emerged among the top 20 most satisfying careers.

Slumped with pub landlords at the bottom of the list of 274 occupations were construction workers, debt collectors, telephone sales workers and care workers, all earning significantly below the national average salary of £26,500. But chemical scientists, earning almost £10,000 more, only scraped into the top 200, while quantity surveyors, on £38,855, could do no better than 234th place.

The data has been used to help inform a report, published on Friday by the Legatum Institute, an independent thinktank that examines wellbeing as a core part of national prosperity, alongside wealth.

"Not only does GDP fail to reflect the distribution of income, it omits intangibles, or feelings, that are not easily reducible to monetary values," note its authors, who were chaired by Lord O'Donnell, formerly the head of the civil service. "There is a growing recognition that the measures of a country's progress need to include the wellbeing of its citizens."

The government has taken some steps towards measuring and incorporating the nation's happiness into policymaking – the ONS was asked to include four questions in its annual population study relating to life satisfaction, while [UK Prime Minister] David Cameron has said: "If you know ... that prosperity alone can't deliver a better life, then you've got to take practical steps to make sure government is properly focused on our quality of life as well as economic growth."

The director of communications at the Legatum Institute, Shazia Ejaz, said: "A lot of careers advisers will tell you, 'If you become a doctor you will earn this much, as a teacher you'll earn this much. But perhaps people should also know what different careers can do in terms of their life satisfaction."

Top 10

1. Clergy
2. Chief executives and senior officials
3. Managers and proprietors in agriculture and horticulture
4. Company secretaries
5. Quality assurance and regulatory professionals
6. Healthcare practice managers
7. Medical practitioners
8. Farmers
9. Hotel and accommodation managers and proprietors
10. Skilled metal, electrical and electronic trades supervisors

Bottom 10
265. Plastics process operatives
266. Bar staff
267. Care escorts

268. Sports and leisure assistants
269. Telephone salespersons
270. Floorers and wall tilers
271. Industrial cleaning process occupations
272. Debt, rent and other cash collectors
273. Elementary construction occupations
274. Publicans and managers of licensed premises

Esther Addley, 21 March 2014 http://www.theguardian.com/money/2014/mar/
21/vicars-greatest-job-satisfaction-publicans-least-happy

Introduction

The opening case study is just one example of many surveys that point out the links between our occupation and how satisfied we are with life in general. Taking the results of this survey at face value indicates that this might not be determined just by how much we get paid for doing the job. The article highlights some important issues that we will examine in detail in this chapter. Is it something about the job we do that at least partly determines our levels of satisfaction? Or is it something about the person doing the job? There may well be some joyful publicans to be found. Or might it be a mixture of the two with some other factors thrown into the mix as well? Overall, the article indicates that our satisfaction is not neutral and is subject to change according to the choices we make and the circumstances we encounter.

Surveys such as those summarised in the case study are a common feature of 21st-century life. The questions asked often require us to provide a subjective evaluation of how we feel about things. This might include measuring whether we feel very satisfied, very dissatisfied or somewhere between the two extremes. Or it might focus on how much we like or dislike something or someone. This means that our responses also include an element of emotion. Arguably, such measures tap into our attitudes: to simplify a little, these are how positively or negatively we feel about something (there's a better definition at the start of the next section). Attitudes have both strength and direction. As the case study indicates, governments are becoming increasingly interested in the causes and consequences of our attitudes. Might it be that more satisfied workers behave in a way that means they are more productive or that they lead healthier lives? If so, such survey data could be used to inform powerful interventions and have significant implications for government policy. Could it be that knowing how satisfied (or not) others are in a particular job influences our own attitudes towards that type of work? Did reading the opening case study change your feelings about the attractiveness of the careers/work roles listed?

You may have noticed that the information in the case study does not allow us to identify what it is about some jobs that might make them less satisfying than others. Nor does it tell us much about the individual differences that might be involved. Work psychologists have taken a close interest in these issues. Attitude surveys more detailed and complex than that described in the case study are needed to deal with such questions. A great deal of research has focused on obtaining good data about employees' attitudes towards specific features of their job or towards the employing organisation. It is well over half a century since attitude surveys become a standard tool for managers to check on what employees thought of their work and their workplace (Schneider et al., 1996). Theoretically minded academic social psychologists have developed some sophisticated analyses of the nature of attitudes, how they change and how they predict behaviour (or fail to). In this chapter we first discuss attitudes as psychological constructs. Second, we briefly describe the ways in which attitudes can be measured. Then we will look at two of the attitudes that are particularly important in work psychology – job satisfaction and organisational commitment. We will also take a broader look at what work means to people by examining the issues of turnover and unemployment.

Then attention turns to the question of what factors affect the formation and change of attitudes at work. A particularly important concept in work psychology is the psychological contract, so we look at this in some detail. Attitude change might not be very important if it is not reflected in behaviour change, so the connection between attitudes and behaviour is a recurrent theme in this chapter.

What is an attitude?

Attitudes were defined by Secord and Backman (1969) as 'certain regularities of an individual's feelings, thoughts and predispositions to act toward some aspect of his [sic] environment'. Feelings represent the *affective component* of an attitude, thoughts the *cognitive component* and predispositions to act the *behavioural component*. Attitudes are evaluative; that is, they reflect a person's tendency to feel, think or behave in a positive or negative manner towards the object of the attitude. Evaluative dimensions of attitudes include good–bad, harmful–beneficial, pleasant–unpleasant and likeable–dislikeable (Ajzen, 2001). Attitudes refer to a particular *target*, or *object* – a person (e.g. boss), group of people (e.g. close colleagues, senior management), object (e.g. work equipment) or concept (e.g. performance-related pay). Because of this, attitudes are different from personality which reflects a person's predispositions across a range of situations. Everyone holds attitudes, not least because it seems that we usually attach an evaluation to our perceptions of people and things around us (Ajzen and Fishbein, 2000). However, some people hold some attitudes more strongly than others. This is because the strength of the tendency to evaluate is partly an individual difference variable (Jarvis and Petty, 1996).

The affective component of an attitude (how we feel about something) is reflected in a person's physiological responses (e.g. blood pressure might rise when the computer crashes – again) and/or in what the person says about how they feel about the object of the attitude. The cognitive component refers to a person's *perception* of the object of the attitude, and/or what the person says they believe about that object (e.g. that computers are unreliable). The behavioural component is reflected by a person's observable *behaviour* toward the object of the attitude and/or what they say about that behaviour (e.g. furiously clicking the mouse button in frustration!). In practice, the term 'attitude' is usually taken to mean the cognitive and/or affective components. Behaviour is most often construed as an outcome of attitudes (see below, Attitudes and behaviour).

Key learning point

Attitudes are a person's predisposition to think (cognitive component), feel (affective component) or behave (behavioural component) in certain ways towards certain defined targets. Attitudes are different to personality because they focus on a particular object/target.

It is worth noting that there can be some differences between these three components (Breckler, 1984). Hence, it is possible for a person to feel positive about their job (affective component) but to believe that the job has few attractive elements (cognitive component). Depending upon how it is worded, responses to a questionnaire measure of an attitude could be influenced more by affect than cognition, or vice versa (Schlett and Ziegler, 2014). For example, 'How do you feel about your computer?' and 'How reliable do you believe your computer to be?' are two very different questions that could elicit different responses. Which attitude is expressed, and which one will influence behaviour on any given occasion, may therefore depend on whether the person is concentrating on emotions or on cognitions at that time (Millar and Tesser, 1989). Later in this chapter we look at employee turnover and you will see that because someone does not like a job, it does not mean that this will be the strongest influence on their behaviour, especially if there are few alternatives in the labour market.

It is also important to distinguish attitudes from other related concepts. George and Jones (1997) analyse the relationships between attitudes, values and moods. Values are a person's

Table 6.1	Values, attitudes and moods		
	Values	**Attitudes**	**Moods**
Time perspective	Future (how things should be)	Past (my past experience of a target)	Present (how I feel right now)
Dynamism	Stable (little change over long periods)	Evolving (slow or steady change)	Fluctuating (substantial change over short periods)
Focus	General (guides approach to life)	Specific (directed towards a specific target)	General (how I feel about everything right now)

Source: Adapted from J. M. George and G. R. Jones (1997) 'Experiencing work: values, attitudes and moods', *Human Relations*, 50, 393–416. Adapted with permission.

beliefs about what is good or desirable in life. They are long-term guides for a person's choices and experiences. It might be that a worker does not like their boss but what they value the most are the money and security that the job provides, and that a harmonious working relationship with their boss is relatively unimportant to them. Moods, on the other hand, are 'generalized affective states that are not explicitly linked to particular events or circumstances which may have originally induced the mood' (George and Jones, 1997: 400).

Values, attitudes and moods differ in terms of: (i) whether they concern the past, present or future; (ii) their stability over time; and (iii) whether they are general or specific. These differences are summarised in Table 6.1. The three concepts are linked. Engaging in work activities that are congruent with one's own values (*self-determined behaviour*) has been shown to be linked to more positive work attitudes (Glomb et al., 2011). In the long run, attitudes can change values. For example, being dissatisfied with one's job for a long time may cause a person to re-appraise the importance or centrality of work in their life. A consideration of values and moods also helps to explain why attitudes do not always predict behaviour at work. A person may have negative attitudes towards their job and colleagues but still help out others at work because they place a high value on being responsible and cooperative. The link (or lack of it) between attitudes and behaviour is discussed further later in this chapter.

Exercise 6.1	Attitudes to this book

Consider your attitude (if any) to this book. How positively or negatively do you feel about it (affective component)? How positive or negative are your thoughts about it (cognitive component)? How positively or negatively do you behave towards it, e.g. how often do you read it and for how long (behavioural component)? In each case, describe what your feelings, thoughts and behaviours are. Consider whether the extent to which you use this book is influenced by your values, attitudes and moods. What other factors affect your behaviour towards the book?

Pratkanis and Turner (1994) and Cialdini and Trost (1998), among others, asked why we have attitudes – in other words, what purposes do they serve? There seem to be three general answers to this:

1   Attitudes can help us to make sense of our environment and act effectively within it. For example, people who are dissatisfied with their job are more likely than others to believe that ambiguous events are sure to end in disaster.

2   Attitudes can help us to define and maintain our sense of self-identity (who we are) and self-esteem (a sense of personal value). It seems to be important to most people to have a clear sense of who they are, and to feel reasonably positive about it.

3   Attitudes can help us maintain good relations with other people, particularly those who have the power to reward or punish us. By holding and expressing attitudes similar to another person, we can often make ourselves more attractive to them, and more able to understand and empathise with them.

Key learning point

Attitudes are related to, but distinguishable from, values, moods and personality.

Point of integration

Understanding our own attitudes and those held by others helps us to categorise people into groups. The causes and consequences of this categorisation process are discussed in detail in Chapter 11.

Pratkanis and Turner (1994) have argued that an attitude is stored in memory as a 'cognitive representation', which consists of three components:

1   An object label and rules for applying it. For example, if one is concerned about attitudes to colleagues, it is necessary to be clear about who counts as a colleague.
2   An evaluative summary of that object, i.e. whether it is broadly 'good' or 'bad'.
3   A knowledge structure supporting the evaluative summary. This can be simple or complex, and may include technical knowledge about the domain, arguments for or against a given proposition, or a listing of the advantages and disadvantages of a target.

Key learning point

Attitudes are cognitive representations which help us to structure our social world and our place within it.

As an example of some research on attitudes, let us take an article by Furnham et al. (1994). They used their academic contacts in 41 countries to obtain a total sample of more than 12,000 young people, who completed a questionnaire concerning their attitudes to work and economic issues. Furnham et al. assessed, among other things, the following attitudes, each of which was measured with several statements and a Likert response scale (see next section) asking the respondent to what extent they agreed or disagreed with each statement.

■   Work ethic – Example statement: 'I like hard work.'
■   Competitiveness – Example statement: 'I feel that winning is important in both work and games.'
■   Money beliefs – Example statement: 'I firmly believe money can solve all my problems.'

They found quite marked differences between countries in the extent to which young people held these attitudes. Work ethic was higher in America than in Europe, the East and Asia. The reverse was true for competitiveness. Money beliefs were highest in the East and Asia, lower in America and lower again in Europe. At the level of individual countries, those with high economic growth tended to score higher on both competitiveness and money beliefs. However, it is not clear whether the attitudes caused the economic growth, were caused by it, both or neither. This illustrates one of the problems of the survey method, as discussed in Chapter 2.

Measuring attitudes

Attitudes are almost always assessed using self-report questionnaires. In other words, attitude measurement usually depends upon what people say about their feelings, beliefs and/or behaviour towards the particular object in question. Thurstone scaling and Likert scaling are frequently used to measure attitudes. Likert scales are easier to understand and use, and tend to be more widely used in research, so we will concentrate on those.

Research methods in focus

Measuring attitudes using Likert scales

The *Likert technique* is sometimes known as the summated scale. In this approach, the psychologist selects a large number of statements that relate to the attitude object concerned. They should either be clearly in favour of the object, or clearly against it. Respondents indicate their agreement or disagreement with each statement. Statements are included in the final scale only if they (i) tend to be responded to in the same way as others covering apparently similar ground, and (ii) elicit the same responses on two occasions. A five-, seven- or ten-point response scale is utilised for each statement, usually in terms of strongly agree to strongly disagree.

For example, with a five-point response scale, respondents might have the options 'strongly agree' (score 4), 'agree' (score 3), 'neither agree nor disagree' (score 2), 'disagree' (score 1) and 'strongly disagree' (score 0). Scores are reversed (i.e. 4 changes to 0, 3 to 1, etc.). Some statements are worded negatively to check that the respondent is not simply agreeing or disagreeing with everything for the sake of it, or perhaps not reading the items properly. For example in a questionnaire to measure attitudes to overtime, a positively worded item could be 'overtime is the best part of my job' and a negatively worded item could be 'overtime is a real nuisance'. The person's overall attitude score is the sum or mean of their responses to the statements. In the case of the overtime example used above, because the scores for negatively worded statements have been reversed, a high score indicates a favourable attitude.

One difficulty with using questionnaire measures of attitudes is that they are subject to the social desirability effect – that is, to respondents giving the socially desirable answer, such as, for instance, 'Of course, I have never driven faster than the speed limit' when, in fact, they have (actually, almost everyone has). There are techniques available to minimise this effect. *Social desirability scales* contain questions that almost everyone responds to in the same way *if* they are telling the truth. To return to the example, almost everyone who drives has broken a speed limit at least once, so the vast majority of people who drive say they have broken the speed limit if they are telling the truth. Therefore if the responses a person gives to a series of questions like this consistently goes against that of the majority, there is an increased likelihood they are trying to present in a socially desirable way on the questionnaire. Another way of dealing with the problem is given in the questionnaire in Table 6.2. One of the authors wanted to find out what people thought about male and female managers. Instead of asking them directly, he devised two questionnaires that were exactly alike, except that in each version a single word was different – 'man' and 'woman'. The two versions of the questionnaire were distributed among a random sample of the general public and the differences between the two forms were assessed, without the issue of male versus female stereotypes ever being raised on the questionnaire. Forced choice items can also be used to address the problem. In these questions, the respondent chooses between two desirable responses. An example would be: 'Is it better to be (a) helpful to colleagues or (b) well-organised in your approach to work?'

Point of integration

Forced choice items are also sometimes used in measures of personality to deal with the problem of socially desirable responding or faking (see Chapters 3 and 4).

Table 6.2	Stereotyped attitudes towards male versus female managers

Description of a character you may know:

Is 21 years old
Graduate
Trainee manager
Woman/man*
Unmarried
Enjoys films

Whereabouts on these scales would you place this character? Please put a tick in the appropriate box according to where you think she/he* would most probably be best described on the scale.

Will be a high flyer								Will not necessarily be a high flyer
Is inclined to be bossy								Is inclined to be meek
Is a good mixer socially								Is rather shy socially
Is very studious								Is not very studious
Would assume leadership in groups								Would not assume leadership in groups
Contains emotions								Expresses emotions freely
Is self-confident								Is not self-confident
Is ambitious								Is not particularly ambitious
Is assertive								Is not particularly assertive

How much do you think he/she* will be earning	(a) when he/she* is 30? £ ...../p.a.
	(b) when he/she* is 60? £ ...../p.a.

*One or the other given on each form.

The result of attitude measurement is normally a measure of how *extreme* a person's attitude is: for example, whether they strongly like, mildly like, are indifferent towards, mildly dislike or strongly dislike studying work psychology. Petty and Krosnick (1992) have argued for the more general concept of attitude *strength*. As well as extremity, this includes the amount of certainty people feel about their attitude, its importance to them, how intensely they hold the attitude and how knowledgeable they are about it. Petty and Krosnick suggested that consideration of these factors will improve the predictability of behaviour from attitudes. Along the same lines, Pratkanis and Turner (1994) have referred to attitude *salience*, which concerns the extent to which an attitude is clearly relevant to the situation at hand. Their definition of a strong attitude is one that comes easily to mind.

This definition seems quite appropriate because research suggests that beliefs that are important to a person are remembered more completely and more quickly than those that are not (Van Harreveld et al., 2000). In fact, some psychologists believe that the speed with which a person reacts to a stimulus could be the most valid indicator of their attitude because attitudes are outside of conscious awareness and control (Greenwald et al., 1998). In experimental psychology, Implicit Association Tests (IATs) are often used to measure this speed of reaction. It may be that responses to IATs and explicit questionnaire measures of attitudes measure different things. Karpinski and Hilton (2001) suggest that IATs are a measure of what people have been exposed to in their environment (a product of environmental association) rather than a measure of their own views. Take, for example, somebody who frequently saw their female colleagues being discriminated against because of their gender. Environmental association could mean that an IAT would show that they have subconscious negative attitudes towards female colleagues. Your implicit attitudes towards the book might be heavily influenced by how many people you see using a copy or how popular it is as a loan item in the library. However, based on their laboratory studies, Karpinski and Hilton pointed out that it was the conscious attitudes revealed by explicit measures rather than the subconscious ones that were the strongest predictors of behaviour.

This difference between implicit and explicit attitudes raises an important question: to what extent are attitudes measurable? Verkuyten (1998) argues that it is a mistake to see attitudes as quantitatively measurable phenomena that in some sense exist inside a person's head independent of the situation the person is in or, for example, what they would like to gain by expressing that attitude. Like other discursive social psychologists, Verkuyten argues that explicit attitudes are expressed in conversation as part of an attempt to achieve the personal goals of the speaker. These might be to convince others of one's correctness, morality, acceptability, rationality and so on. They might be very transient and heavily influenced by the context in which they are expressed.

Our explicit attitude to something depends very much on the meaning we attach to it, or how it fits into our lives. Your explicit attitudes toward this book are most likely the result of your seeing it as an aid to your studies (well, that's what we hope!). For the publishers of this book, their explicit attitudes towards it are more likely to be the result of their seeing it as a product. Senior management attitudes towards a trade union representative might develop from a view of the representative as an adversary. Employees' attitudes toward the same representative are more likely to be based upon the view that the representative is an advocate. What all of this means is that the complexity of attitudes can be difficult to pin down with a high level of precision using a questionnaire survey.

Attitudes and behaviour

So far we have looked at what attitudes are and hinted that they might be important in organisational settings, but it could be argued that attitudes only matter if they influence actual behaviour. For example, racial prejudice in the workplace is damaging to the extent that it finds expression in discrimination or other negative behaviour towards minority groups. Research shows that attitudes predict behaviour to some extent, but not always and not often by very much.

Going back to the opening case study, if true, this would mean that people who say they like their job do not necessarily work harder or better, work longer hours or relate better to customers than people who say they do not like their job. It would also mean that all the many attitude surveys conducted in workplaces were a waste of time.

A number of possible reasons have been suggested for this lack of correspondence. One is social pressures of various kinds: laws, societal norms and the views of specific people can all prevent a person behaving consistently with their attitudes. So can other attitudes, limitations on a person's abilities, and, indeed, a person's general activity levels. There has also been some suggestion that the research on this issue was badly designed, and therefore failed to find correspondences that did in fact exist between attitudes and behaviour. In particular, it has been argued that measures of attitude were often general (e.g. attitudes about law-breaking) whereas measures of behaviour were specific, reflecting only one of many elements of the attitude (e.g. committing motoring offences). Also, behaviour was assessed on only one occasion or over a short time period in the contrived setting of a psychologist's laboratory. Longer-term assessments of multiple instances of the behaviour would be a fairer test of whether attitudes predict behaviour.

In their influential work, Pratkanis and Turner (1994) identified four of the factors they suggest will increase the correspondence between attitudes and behaviour:

1   When the object of the attitude is both well-defined and salient. An example of a poorly defined object would be where a person was not sure whether their immediate supervisor should be classed as a colleague or as a member of the management team. This would make it uncertain whether that person's attitudes to management would affect their behaviour towards the supervisor. Salience concerns the extent to which the object of the attitude is perceived as relevant to the situation at hand.

2   When attitude strength is high – that is, when the attitude comes easily to mind.

3   When knowledge supporting the attitude is plentiful and complex. This increases a person's certainty about what they think, as well as their ability to act effectively towards the object of the attitude.

4   When the attitude supports important aspects of the self. For example, an account-ant may have positive attitudes towards other accountants because they believe that accountants (and therefore by extension themselves) perform an important role in the national economy.

Key learning point

The lack of correspondence between attitudes and behaviour found in much research is due partly to poor research design, and partly to a neglect of cognitive processes concerning attitudes.

Ajzen and Fishbein (1980) developed a model of the relationship between attitudes and behaviour designed to overcome these difficulties. This model was called the *theory of rea-soned action*. It includes an extra step in the attitude–behaviour link: intention. It assumed that actions are best predicted by intentions, and that intentions are in turn determined by a person's attitude and their perception of social pressure. For example, in the work context, we might look at how well intention to leave predicted actual staff turnover.

The theory of reasoned action was then adapted by Ajzen and Madden (1986), and its name was changed to the theory of **planned behaviour** (Figure 6.1). It now includes the concept of **perceived behavioural control**. This reflects the extent to which the person believes that they can perform the necessary behaviours in any given situation. It can affect both intention and the extent to which intention translates into actual behaviour.

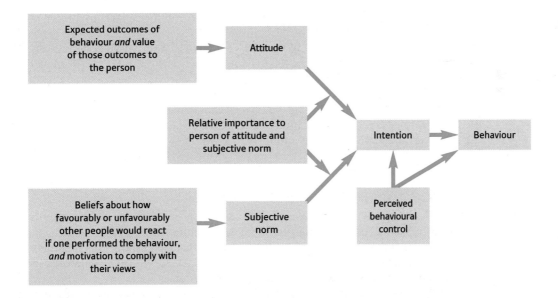

Figure 6.1	Theory of planned behaviour

Source: Reprinted from Ajzen, I. and Madden, J.T., 'Prediction of goal-directed behavior: Attitudes, intentions, and perceived behavioral control', *Journal of Experimental Social Psychology*, 22, 453–74. Copyright (1986), with permission from Elsevier.

Note that in the theory of planned behaviour, 'attitude' is defined in precise and rather unusual terms – it concerns beliefs and personal values about the consequences of a specific behaviour, and not general beliefs or feelings about an object or person. This is similar to expectancy theories of motivation (see Chapter 7). Note also that 'subjective norm' takes into account both the opinions of other people and the person's wish (or lack of it) to comply with those opinions. Therefore this model allows us to consider the influence of factors such as culture in determining thought and action (see Chapter 1). The theory of planned behaviour also acknowledges that people vary as to whether their attitude or the subjective norm is the key driver in determining their intentions. The theory has proved quite successful in predicting behaviour in a wide range of settings. However, relatively few of these directly concern work behaviour (though many concern consumer behaviour). This is perhaps an example of how work psychology sometimes neglects theoretical advances in social psychology.

Point of integration

The theory of planned behaviour takes ideas from cognitive theories of motivation (see Chapter 7) in proposing that actions are the product of attitudes, social pressures and intentions. It is effective in explaining both intentions and actual behaviour.

Ajzen (1991) has provided a thorough account of the theory of planned behaviour and research on it. He pointed out that, as the theory suggests, intentions to perform particular behaviours are often accurately predicted by attitudes towards the behaviour, subjective norms and perceived behavioural control. Also, intentions, together with perceived behavioural control, are quite good at predicting a person's actual behaviour. Ajzen also draws attention to some additional points. First, the relative importance of the various factors in predicting intention might be expected to vary with different behaviours and different situations, but little is known beyond this very general proposition about how particular situations/behaviours might exert such an influence. Second, perceived behavioural control really does matter – so the theory of planned behaviour is an improvement on the theory of reasoned action. However, the usefulness of perceived behavioural control will be limited if the perception is wildly inaccurate. If a person believes that they are in control of a situation, but is mistaken, then no amount of belief will translate an intention into behaviour. Third, the influence of subjective norms on intentions and behaviour is often quite weak. Ajzen suggests that some people may be more responsive to their own perceptions of moral obligations than to the opinions of other people, at least in individualistic Western cultures. These observations suggest areas in which the theory of planned behaviour may be improved in future. Also, comparison of the theory of planned behaviour with material presented earlier in this chapter shows that it ignores factors such as the salience of the attitude, the extent to which it is supported by knowledge and any possible influences of unconscious influences on behaviour.

Reviews of the theory of planned behaviour by Ajzen (2001) and Armitage and Conner (2001) have reinforced many of the points already made. Armitage and Conner conducted a meta-analysis of tests of the theory. Based on a total sample of nearly a million people across many research studies, they found that the combination of attitude, subjective norm and perceived behavioural control correlated 0.63 with behavioural intention. They also found that intention plus perceived behavioural control correlated 0.52 with actual behaviour. These are impressive findings. A more recent systematic review by McEachan et al. (2011) looked at the results of 237 longitudinal studies that used the theory to predict health-related behaviours (such as smoking, alcohol consumption and healthy eating). The authors found some, but not unequivocal, support for the theory. Overall, the theory accounted for just under 20 per cent of the variation in measures of health-related behaviour. In common with many other tests of the theory, intention was the strongest predictor of behaviour and the theory worked best for short-term studies. It did not predict long-term behaviour particularly well, especially outside of controlled laboratory settings. When data on behaviour were collected using objective or observational measures rather than self-report measures there was less evidence that the theoretical mechanisms worked as described. Sniehotta et al. (2014) also point out that the theory does not include any feedback loops: it is reasonable to expect that a person's behaviour and its outcomes might have an influence on their subsequent attitudes.

Many studies have shown that subjective norm may not be as potent an influence as Ajzen suggested. Armitage and Conner considered that this was partly due to a tendency to measure it with only one question, but there may also be other reasons. For example, in Western culture we may be unwilling to admit that the opinions of other people influence us, even if they really do. Also, we may surround ourselves with people who generally agree with us, so that subjective norm is not much different from attitude. Another issue concerns the evaluation of alternative courses of action. In a research study, a person may score quite high on intention to pursue action A, but what we do not know (because we did not ask) is that they score even higher on intention to pursue action B. Finally, there is considerable debate about the nature of perceived behavioural control. Is it, in effect, self-efficacy, or does it include external factors such as lack of opportunity?

The theory of planned behaviour can be applied to a number of workplace issues and situations. For example, a person may have the opportunity to apply for promotion. Their attitude to doing so will be determined by an assessment of the potential consequences of doing so (both good and bad), the probability that those consequences might include increased pay, a better car, a more interesting job, a requirement to work longer hours and the risk of being turned down. For a person with fragile self-esteem and/or a concern about personal image, this last possibility might be extremely important. Subjective norm would reflect whether other people (for example partner and colleagues) thought it was a good idea to apply for promotion, and how much the person cared about their opinions. Perceived behavioural control should not be a problem, since it

---

Exercise 6.2   A lunchtime drink

Jerry Lander felt that there was nothing wrong with drinking a glass or two of beer during his lunch break. He could afford it easily enough. He claimed that he had never seen any evidence that a lunchtime drink harmed his work performance during the afternoon. He found that it helped him feel more relaxed and happy at work. Nevertheless, he could do without a drink without much difficulty if he had to. Jerry liked the friendship and approval of other people, and at lunchtime the nearby bar was full of acquaintances he could chat to. Work was an important part of Jerry's life and he was keen to gain promotion.

Unfortunately, his boss did not approve of alcoholic drink at lunchtime – or indeed at any other time. Nor did most of his colleagues, with whom he had to work closely. They seemed to view it as a sign of personal inadequacy.

Suggested exercise

Use the theory of planned behaviour to decide whether Jerry Lander is likely to drink a glass of beer during his lunch break on most working days.

refers simply to the person's ability to apply for the promotion, not to do so effectively. Intention should lead fairly reliably to behaviour in this instance, unless for example the promotion opportunity is unexpectedly withdrawn.

What all of this means is that the link between attitudes and behaviour is often quite complex. Sniehotta et al. (2014) point to the obvious perils associated with trying to offer reliable explanations for behaviour using models and theories that contain a relatively small number of variables. Nonetheless, even given the frailties of models used to explain it, the link is there. Even if theories do not offer complete explanations of the attitude–behaviour links, they point to some important factors that influence both. So far in this chapter we have deliberately avoided discussing specific attitudes, in order to ensure that we cover the important general points. Now it is time to be more specific. We now look at two concepts of great importance in work psychology: job satisfaction and organisational commitment. In the first the object of the attitude is the job. The second reflects how attached the employee is to the employing organisation: the object of the attitude is the organisation. These have been the subject of much research and practical interest over many years.

Stop to consider

From what you have read so far, how concerned do you think managers should be about their employees' attitudes? To what extent might they be able to alter employee attitudes (and how could they do this)?

Job satisfaction

Job satisfaction has been seen as important for two main reasons. First, it is one indicator of a person's psychological well-being, or mental health. As such it is often used in stress research (see Chapter 10). As the opening case study suggests, a person who is unhappy at work is at an increased risk of being unhappy in general. So psychologists and others who are concerned with individuals' welfare are keen to ensure that high job satisfaction is experienced. Second, it is often assumed that job satisfaction will lead to motivation and good work performance. We have already noted that such simple connections do not necessarily occur. The link between job satisfaction and work performance is a good example of how it is often assumed that attitudes affect behaviour, but this is not easy to demonstrate.

What is job satisfaction?

Locke (1976) defined job satisfaction as a 'pleasurable or positive emotional state resulting from the appraisal of one's job or job experiences'. The concept generally refers to a variety of aspects of the job that influence a person's levels of satisfaction with it. These usually include attitudes toward pay, working conditions, colleagues and boss, career prospects and the intrinsic aspects of the job itself. Even as long ago as 1976, job satisfaction had been the topic of huge amounts of research. Locke found well over 3000 published studies. It is worth noting that some authors also now distinguish between expectation-based job satisfaction and performance-based job satisfaction. The former is the focus of many job satisfaction questionnaire measures and refers to whether a person's expectations are being met in their work role; the latter is a measure of the extent to which the employee is satisfied with their own level of performance (see Avery et al., 2015).

Judge and Hulin (1993), among others, have suggested that in the field of job satisfaction there are three different approaches. The first is that work attitudes such as job satisfaction are dispositional in nature; that is, they are 'stable positive or negative dispositions learned through experience' (Griffin and Bateman, 1986; Staw et al., 1986) or that they stem from a person's genetic inheritance (Judge et al., 2012). This hypothesis proposes that job satisfaction has more of the properties of trait than that of an attitude. This could then imply that attempts to improve satisfaction by changing jobs in the same way for every worker would be doomed to failure. Judge and colleagues (2012) suggest that the impact of genetic factors could mean that workers need to be given opportunities to shape their own work environments in line with their inherited preferences.

The second approach is the '*social* information processing' model, which suggests that job satisfaction and other workplace attitudes are developed or constructed out of experiences and information provided by others at work (Salancik and Pfeffer, 1978; O'Reilly and Caldwell, 1985). At least in part, job satisfaction is a function of how other people in the workplace interpret and evaluate what goes on: if colleagues show that they are satisfied at work then this might have an influence upon your own satisfaction levels.

The third approach is the information-processing model, which is based on the accumulation of cognitive information about the workplace and one's job. This argues that a person's job satisfaction is influenced most directly by the characteristics of their job (see also Chapter 7), and the extent to which those characteristics match what that person wants in a job.

Key learning point

Job satisfaction can be seen in three ways – as a function of: (i) a person's general personality or disposition; (ii) the opinions of other people in the person's workplace; or (iii) the features of a person's job. It may be the result of the interactions of all three.

Measuring job satisfaction

There have been many measures of job satisfaction in the workplace. Examples include the very widely used Job Description Index (JDI; Smith et al., 1969), the Job Satisfaction Scales of Warr et al. (1979), the Overall Job Satisfaction scale (Brayfield and Rothe, 1951); the Job Satisfaction Survey (Spector, 1985); and the job satisfaction scale of the Occupational Stress Indicator (OSI; Cooper et al., 1987). They all involve questions or statements asking respondents to indicate what they think and/or feel about their job as a whole (so-called global satisfaction) and/or specific aspects of it, such as pay, work activities, working conditions, career prospects, relationships with superiors and relationships with colleagues (facet-level satisfaction). Likert scaling (see earlier in this chapter) is usually employed. In Table 6.3 we provide an example of a measure of job satisfaction from the OSI, which contains all of the elements that usually make up a job satisfaction measure.

Table 6.3	A job satisfaction measure

How you feel about your job

Very much satisfaction	6	Much satisfaction	5
Some satisfaction	4	Some dissatisfaction	3
Much dissatisfaction	2	Very much dissatisfaction	1

1	Communication and the way information flows around your organisation	6 5 4 3 2 1
2	The relationships you have with other people at work	6 5 4 3 2 1
3	The feeling you have about the way you and your efforts are valued	6 5 4 3 2 1
4	The actual job itself	6 5 4 3 2 1
5	The degree to which you feel motivated by your job	6 5 4 3 2 1
6	Current career opportunities	6 5 4 3 2 1
7	The level of job security in your present job	6 5 4 3 2 1
8	The extent to which you may identify with the public image or goals of your organisation	6 5 4 3 2 1
9	The style of supervision that your superiors use	6 5 4 3 2 1
10	The way changes and innovations are implemented	6 5 4 3 2 1
11	The kind of work or tasks that you are required to perform	6 5 4 3 2 1
12	The degree to which you feel that you can personally develop or grow in your job	6 5 4 3 2 1
13	The way in which conflicts are resolved in your company	6 5 4 3 2 1
14	The scope your job provides to help you achieve your aspirations and ambitions	6 5 4 3 2 1
15	The amount of participation which you are given in important decision-making	6 5 4 3 2 1
16	The degree to which your job taps the range of skills which you feel you possess	6 5 4 3 2 1
17	The amount of flexibility and freedom you feel you have in your job	6 5 4 3 2 1
18	The psychological 'feel' or climate that dominates your organisation	6 5 4 3 2 1
19	Your level of salary relative to your experience	6 5 4 3 2 1
20	The design or shape of your organisation's structure	6 5 4 3 2 1
21	The amount of work you are given to do, whether too much or too little	6 5 4 3 2 1
22	The degree to which you feel extended in your job	6 5 4 3 2 1

Source: © 1988 Cooper, Sloan and Williams. Reproduced with permission of the publisher ASE, College Lane, Hatfield, Herts, AL10 9AA, UK.

It is generally assumed in attitude measurement that it is better to ask lots of questions than only one. The argument is that this increases accuracy, for example by including many different facets of the attitude concerned and by avoiding the possibility that a careless response to a single question will mess everything up. One problem with such an approach is that it focuses on the *cognitive component* of job satisfaction because people are asked to evaluate in detail various job conditions in a logical and rational manner. In contrast, shorter measures with more general questions may better capture the *affective component* of the attitude or how the person feels about their work overall (Thompson and Phua, 2012). Nagy (2002) has shown that having just one question to measure global job satisfaction, and/or one question to measure each facet of job satisfaction, can work well enough (it's the best of both worlds). Nagy's point is that people generally know how satisfied they feel, and do not need a whole set of questions to express this. Many definitions of job satisfaction do focus on its affective component so it would seem important to capture this. Thompson and Phua (2012: 301) have developed a four-item measure of job satisfaction designed to tap directly into this component:

1   I find real enjoyment in my job
2   I like my job better than the average person
3   Most days I am enthusiastic about my job
4   I feel fairly well satisfied with my job

Response categories: 1 = Strongly disagree, 2 = Disagree, 3 = Neutral, 4 = Agree, 5 = Strongly agree. Note: the measure also includes distractor items available in the article.

Sometimes detailed cognitions may need to be captured in order to answer a research question or to design an intervention. Can these then be used to calculate an overall measure of job satisfaction? Taber and Alliger (1995) have investigated the extent to which overall job satisfaction can be thought of as the total or average of people's cognitive evaluations of each task in their job. They asked over 500 employees of a US medical college to describe the tasks of their job, and to rate each task according to its importance, complexity, level of supervision, level of concentration required, how much they enjoyed it and the amount of time spent on it each week. They found that the percentage of time spent in enjoyable tasks correlated 0.40 with satisfaction with the work itself, and 0.28 with global job satisfaction. The importance of the task, closeness of supervision and concentration required did not have much impact on job satisfaction. The correlations show that the accumulation of enjoyment across the various tasks involved in the job did, not surprisingly, say something about overall job satisfaction, but the correlations were also low enough to indicate that other factors also matter. Many researchers have found that non-work factors (such as family problems) can influence overall job satisfaction and these are rarely measured directly in job satisfaction scales. In addition such a detailed 'adding up' approach to measurement might not capture very accurately an employee's overall feelings about a job. As the authors noted (1995: 118):

> Perhaps workers form a gestalt – a perception of pattern – about their jobs that is not a simple linear function of task enjoyment … a worker might perform 15 different enjoyable tasks; nevertheless, the worker's global job satisfaction still could be low if the 15 tasks were so unrelated to one another that the total job was not meaningful, or did not relate clearly to the mission of the organization.

The coverage of attitudes earlier in this chapter suggests that job satisfaction is likely to be used by people to help make sense of their work, and to define who they are, or are not. So in a brief reply to Taber and Alliger, Locke (1995) pointed out that job satisfaction will depend partly on how well people's tasks fit their long-term purposes, how much their self-esteem depends on their job and which job experiences are processed most thoroughly in their memory. One could add that the opinions of others, as discussed by O'Reilly and Caldwell (1985), will also influence a person's overall feelings about their job. These influences might play a role in determining workers' responses to less detailed overall measures of job satisfaction.

Key learning point

Job satisfaction is more than how much the person enjoys the job tasks. It also depends on how important the job is to the person, and how well it fits in with their long-term aims.

Another issue, particularly for global organisations, is whether questionnaire measures of job satisfaction (or indeed anything else) travel well across cultures. Possible problems are that translations between languages are imperfect, that people in different countries understand the same words in the questions (e.g. 'stress') in different ways, and that they interpret response scale options such as 'quite' or 'often' in different ways. These problems are difficult to identify, let alone solve, but they might matter to managers who want to know, for example, whether employees working in a factory in one country are more satisfied than those in a factory in another country. Ryan et al. (1999) give an example, using complex statistics, of how some of the problems of comparing across cultures can be investigated. They found only relatively minor differences between data obtained from employees of one large company in the USA, Spain, Mexico and Australia. If we accept that the measures do translate well enough then could it be that some aspects of people's jobs are more important drivers of job satisfaction in some countries than they are in others. In a study of 14,446 employees from 24 different and diverse nations, level of income, independence and good working relationships were found to be linked to job satisfaction to a similar extent across all of the cultures studied (Hauff et al., 2015). The same study showed that this was not true for every aspect of people's work. For example, national cultures seemed to moderate a little the strength of the links between job satisfaction and job security, and between job satisfaction and the extent to which the job was interesting. For workers in individualistic cultures interesting work was more strongly linked to overall job satisfaction than it was in collectivist cultures. This may be because their own – and not others' – experiences at work were most important to them. In cultures where status differences were marked (high power–distance) job security was more strongly linked to job satisfaction than it was in low power–distance cultures. Job security was also less important in determining job satisfaction in countries with high uncertainty avoidance. At first this may seem odd: a person who avoids uncertainty might seem likely to value job security. Hauff and colleagues argue that in these countries the prevailing culture means that there tends to be better support systems for people who find themselves without a job. Chapter 12 contains fuller definitions of the features of these cultures.

Causes and consequences of job satisfaction

The major determinants of job satisfaction seem to derive from all three of the theoretical approaches identified earlier. Thus, regarding the job itself, for most people the major determinants of global job satisfaction derive from the intrinsic features of the work. These are most commonly based on the Hackman and Oldham (1976) core constructs of skill variety, task identity, task significance, autonomy and feedback (see also Chapter 7). Hackman and Oldham (1976) defined their constructs as:

- *skill variety*: the extent to which the tasks require different skills;
- *task identity*: the extent to which the worker can complete a 'whole' piece of work, as opposed to a small part of it;
- *task significance*: the extent to which the work is perceived as influencing the lives of others;

- *autonomy*: the extent to which the worker has freedom within the job to decide how it should be done;

- *feedback*: the extent to which there is correct and precise information about how effectively the worker is performing.

In addition, as Griffin and Bateman (1986) observed, 'in general, most studies find significant and positive correlations between leader behaviours such as initiating structure and consideration, and satisfaction'. So leader behaviour is also important in satisfaction at work (see Chapter 12). Of course, it is also possible that job satisfaction causes these job perceptions. People who are obviously satisfied (e.g. they are working with a smile on their face) may be given the more interesting tasks to do by their bosses, and/or they may optimistically rate their job more favourably than those who are dissatisfied. Wong et al. (1998) collected data over a two-year period and found both that perceived job characteristics lead to job satisfaction and vice versa. Of course, leadership behaviours could also be linked to lower levels of job satisfaction. Mathieu et al. (2014) examined the so-called 'Dark Triad' of leadership traits (psychopathy, narcissism and Machiavellianism). These traits are thought to be linked to some particularly unpleasant leadership behaviours including deceit, engaging in manipulation and ridicule of others, unfairly blaming others for mistakes, and harassment. As one might expect, Mathieu and colleagues found that there was a strong and direct connection between workers' job satisfaction and their ratings of their supervisors' typical behaviours on this 'Dark Triad' (just to be clear, the 'Dark Triad' was linked to *dissatisfaction*). By way of a sharp contrast, Amundsen and Martinsen (2014) in their study of Norwegian workers found that satisfied employees tended to have leaders who were self-aware or who slightly under-estimated their own abilities. These more modest leaders, who are in touch with their own limitations, may be easier to get along with and trust.

Other social factors have more subtle influences on job satisfaction, as predicted by the social information processing approach. For example, Agho et al. (1993) found that perceptions of distributive justice (the fairness with which rewards were distributed in the organisation) predicted job satisfaction. O'Reilly and Caldwell (1985) demonstrated that both task perceptions and job satisfaction of workers were influenced by the opinions of others in their workgroups.

Key debate

Is a satisfied worker a productive worker?

This question has been of particular interest to researchers. Work and organisational psychologists have usually examined this in the form of whether job satisfaction (happiness) correlates with work performance (productivity). This research tests whether the happy people in a company tend to be productive and whether unhappy people tend to be less productive. For some years the general consensus was that there was little connection. Iaffaldano and Muchinsky (1985) conducted a meta-analysis and found a mean correlation of 0.17, which is pretty low, but Judge et al. (2001) have pointed out several things that were wrong with Iaffaldano and Muchinsky's analysis. They discovered that when unreliability in the measures was taken into account, the mean corrected correlation between job satisfaction and job performance was 0.30. As they point out, this still is not huge but is comparable to correlations between some of the more valid employment selection techniques and job performance. Correlations tended to be highest for complex jobs, i.e. those requiring a range of skills. Harrison and colleagues (2006) found that job satisfaction was not only linked to job performance but also with withdrawal behaviours such as absence and lateness: these effects were small to modest, but they were significant. If you think back to the description of attitudes earlier in this chapter, this makes sense. Job satisfaction is a non-specific attitude in terms of

▶

▶

action, so it would be expected to influence a wide range of unrelated work behaviours. It could be a *common cause* for a lot of different employee behaviours.

Of course, demonstrating that two variables are correlated is not the same as demonstrating that one *causes* the other. Riketta (2008) chose to re-examine the satisfaction–performance relationship but his meta-analysis included fewer (14) studies that used strong longitudinal research designs. After controlling for initial levels of performance, this revealed a much weaker link between job satisfaction and later performance than the relationship between job satisfaction and performance found by Judge et al. (2001). This may be because Judge et al. had included many studies with cross-sectional survey designs. There was also no evidence that good performance consistently caused higher job satisfaction as Judge had suggested. Interestingly, Riketta also found that the link between satisfaction and performance was strongest when there was a short time gap between the measurement of satisfaction and performance, indicating that any effect of satisfaction on performance could be instant but short-lived, perhaps helping to explain why correlations are higher in cross-sectional survey studies. This short-lived connection may occur because high performers develop higher expectations of the rewards that are due to them – when these are unmet, performance levels may soon drop. As Riketta acknowledges, meta-analyses do sometimes gloss over important effects within particular studies: in some situations the satisfaction–performance link might be strong, but it does not appear to be consistently strong across a range of different longitudinal studies.

More recent work has looked at the connection between collective levels of job satisfaction (to simplify a little the *shared* levels of it) among a group of employees and the performance of that group as a whole. This approach makes sense because most organisational outputs (e.g. productivity, customer satisfaction, absence, employee turnover) are consequences of employees' collective efforts. Instead of testing the 'satisfied worker–productive worker' hypothesis, this approach tests the 'satisfied workplace–productive workplace' hypothesis. Imagine if you were a high-performing and satisfied individual. It might be difficult to maintain your high levels of job satisfaction and performance if most of your colleagues frequently expressed a dislike of their own work situation and were performing badly. Over time you might end up sharing their perceptions and as a consequence their performance levels.

Whitman et al. (2010) carried out a meta-analysis of 73 studies to test the group-level links between satisfaction and various organisational outputs. They found a relatively strong connection between group-level satisfaction and composite measures of output including productivity, client satisfaction and absence. Interestingly, their results showed that the satisfaction–output links were strongest when there was good consensus among employees regarding their level of job satisfaction. This indicates that when a group of employees are in agreement with each other about their levels of job satisfaction, it is most likely to be linked to their collective outputs. One possible implication of this finding is that interventions should be aimed at lifting satisfaction for a group of employees as a whole and to a similar shared level.

It may also be that employees are likely to be more satisfied working for a company that is doing well. Ford and Wooldridge (2012) tested this hypothesis by looking at how much various sectors of US industry had grown their revenue over a three-year period leading up to a questionnaire survey. This survey included a brief measure of job satisfaction. Compared to those working in industries in decline, workers in growing industries reported more job enrichment. This included doing new and varied work tasks, getting good opportunities to be creative at work, having more autonomy and opportunities to use their skills, making more decisions and having good opportunities to grow and develop their competencies. The authors argue that job enrichment is more likely to be found in growing industries and has a positive impact on the satisfaction of those working within them. In other words, this enrichment *mediates* the relationship between company performance and job satisfaction. Although not tested in this study it is also feasible that job enrichment could be a cause of both job satisfaction and improved company performance.

Judge et al. (2001) identify six possible reasons why job satisfaction and job performance might be related. These are shown and briefly explained in Figure 6.2. The last of the six abandons the usual pattern of treating job satisfaction as the measure of happiness and reflects the idea that job satisfaction may partly reflect a person's disposition. This means that even if job satisfaction is related to performance, we cannot be sure that it is the cause of it. Wright and Staw (1999) reported two studies in social services settings that strongly suggest that people's characteristic tendency to experience positive emotion (i.e. happiness) does predict their subsequent work performance as assessed by supervisory ratings. These people would also have high job satisfaction because of their disposition, but these studies

1.    Job satisfaction causes job performance, i.e. people tend to work harder and/or better because they like their job

2.    Job performance causes job satisfaction, i.e. people tend to like their job because they are successful at it

3.    Job satisfaction and job performance cause each other, i.e. both 1 and 2 apply

4. 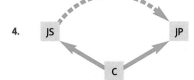   Job satisfaction and job performance are correlated, but only because of another variable (C) that affects them both. For example, the clarity of the job's requirements may help both satisfaction and performance

5. 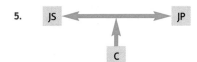   Job satisfaction and job performance may be causally linked, but the strength of this link depends on some other variable (C), for example, the extent to which successful performance is rewarded

6. 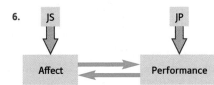   Job satisfaction and job performance are specific instances of more general constructs of positive feelings and personal effectiveness, and these have a causal impact on each other

Figure 6.2   Some possible relationships between job satisfaction (JS) and job performance (JP)
Source: Adapted from Judge et al. 2001. Copyright © 2001 by the American Psychological Association. Adapted with permission.

showed that the characteristic tendency to be happy was a better predictor of performance than more transient moods.

There is a good amount of evidence that some people are simply more satisfied than others by their nature. This is the dispositional approach to job satisfaction. As mentioned earlier, job satisfaction has both an affective and cognitive component. This means that for some people their stable disposition to feel happy or sad, or positive or negative, drives the affective component of job satisfaction. The cognitive component – the part more likely to be influenced by their experiences at work – becomes less important as a result. Recent evidence suggests that the job satisfaction levels of people with a high need for affect (a tendency to approach situations that are charged with emotions for themselves or others) tend to be determined more by their prevailing emotions than by their ratings of various features of their work environment (Schlett and Ziegler, 2014). There is also a good amount of evidence linking stable personality traits to the experience of job satisfaction. In general high levels of extraversion tend to be associated with high levels of job satisfaction (Avery et al., 2015). Arguably this is because extraverts tend to be more prone to experience positive mood, with the opposite being the case for those with high levels of neuroticism. Mindful individuals might also experience higher job satisfaction because they tend to view their experiences at work in 'a receptive, non-judgmental way, they observe stressful events more objectively and refrain from attaching a meaning or evaluation to it' (Hülsheger et al., 2013: 312). This can help people to interpret their experiences as challenges rather than sources of stress and hence enhance their job satisfaction.

Core self-evaluations (CSEs; see Chapter 10) have been found to predict job satisfaction in a number of studies (see for example Keller and Semmer, 2013). This relationship appears to work in both directions. Using data from a longitudinal study of almost 6000 workers, Wu and Griffin (2012) found that the experience of high levels of job satisfaction also predicted CSEs. For some workers at least, extended periods of high levels of job satisfaction could have a positive impact on the way they see themselves in terms of their effectiveness, sense of self-worth and capability.

Of course, individual differences and job characteristics might both influence job satisfaction, but what is the relative importance of each? Dormann and Zapf (2001) reviewed studies reported up to September 1997 and found that, on average, people's job satisfaction on one occasion was quite highly correlated (about 0.5) with their job satisfaction on a later occasion (on average, three years later). This finding might suggest that personality, being relatively stable, is linked to job satisfaction. However, in their own study of people in the Dresden area of Germany, Dormann and Zapf found a correlation for job satisfaction over five years of 0.26 among people who changed jobs during that time. When they adjusted statistically for changes in those people's job characteristics, the stability of job satisfaction scores fell virtually to zero.

Plenty of other studies do point to disposition and situational factors combining to determine job satisfaction. Bowling et al. (2006) found that job satisfaction was fairly stable (which suggests disposition is important), but that it changes when people change jobs (which suggests the situation is important). Perhaps more significantly they found that when people change jobs, people with a positive disposition tended to experience gains in job satisfaction, while those with a negative disposition tended to experience losses in job satisfaction. The researchers argue that this is because people with a positive disposition are more likely to look for, be aware of and remember positive experiences. In other words, some people are likely to seek and find jobs of certain kinds, and that the nature of these jobs then affects job satisfaction. Findings such as these suggest that the impact of a person's disposition on their job satisfaction is indirect. By studying young workers over a period of five years early in their careers, Keller and Semmer (2013) found that growth in both CSEs and an important job characteristic – job control – predicted job satisfaction. In this case the effects of both situational and dispositional factors were roughly similar. What they also found was that when CSE or job control was stable for a period, job satisfaction actually decreased. They argue that, at least among younger workers, sustained personal development and continuous improvements to work situation are significant influences on job satisfaction.

Point of integration

The 'fit' between a worker's personality and the demands of their work role can also influence job satisfaction. This is discussed in detail in Chapter 4. Christiansen et al. (2014) found that when workers were asked to carry out tasks requiring high agreeableness and conscientiousness, those with high levels of these traits experienced the highest levels of satisfaction.

Subjective well-being (how people feel about life right now) also appears to intervene in the links between disposition and job satisfaction. Judge and Hulin (1993) examined the linkages between affective disposition (that is, a person's tendency to feel positive or negative about life), subjective well-being, job satisfaction and job characteristics. Affective disposition not surprisingly had a substantial effect upon subjective well-being. That is, a person's tendency to take an optimistic and happy approach to life influenced how optimistic and happy they felt day to day. Subjective well-being (and therefore, indirectly, affective disposition) had a substantial impact on job satisfaction. Job satisfaction had almost as much effect upon subjective well-being. Intrinsic job characteristics affected job satisfaction, as one would expect, but scarcely more strongly than subjective well-being.

Point of integration

Relatively strong links have often been found between job satisfaction and subjective well-being. The two appear to exert a mutual influence on each other. This is one of the reasons why measures of job satisfaction are often used in research into work stress (see Chapter 10). Job satisfaction is sometimes labelled a measure of affective well-being.

Researchers have also attempted to go beyond self-reported disposition to isolate the genetic influences on job satisfaction. Studies of twins have proved extremely powerful and informative in this regard. Arvey et al. (1991) suggested that somewhere between 10 and 30 per cent of the variation in job satisfaction depends on genetic factors. They argued that 'there is less variability in job satisfaction between genetically identical people [i.e. identical twins] who hold different jobs than there is among genetically unrelated people who hold the same job' (1991: 374). More recent findings have tended to confirm these conclusions. In a sophisticated study of both identical and non-identical twins, raised either apart or together, Judge et al. (2012) found that 35 per cent of the variance in job satisfaction between these Swedish individuals appeared to be due to genetic factors. Until more research is available it is difficult to be sure about what proportion of job satisfaction is purely a function of a person's genetics and/or disposition. Twin studies offer strong insights because much earlier work construed that the effect of stable individual differences was what was left over when situational factors had been considered. This assumes that all of the important situational factors have been taken into account – surely an optimistic assumption.

Another angle on the idea that job satisfaction is more a feature of the person than the job is expressed in research on gender differences in job satisfaction. A number of studies have, for example, found that on average women's job satisfaction is lower than men's. Women might be less satisfied because gender biases in organisations and a host of other reasons might mean that they tend to have less good jobs than men. Indeed, this was what Lefkowitz (1994) found. Lefkowitz obtained a diverse sample of 371 men and 361 women from nine organisations. As predicted, men scored significantly higher on average than women on work satisfaction and pay satisfaction. However, these differences disappeared when variables such as actual income, occupational status, level of education and age were held constant.

Key learning point

It would seem that (i) the nature of the job really does matter for job satisfaction; (ii) so, indirectly, does a person's disposition and genetics; and (iii) job satisfaction has an impact on more general well-being – work does spill over, psychologically, into other areas of life. This issue is discussed in more depth in Chapter 10.

What about factors outside of work, might these spill over, psychologically, into work? Might a happy life event such as a marriage, or the birth of a child impact on job satisfaction? One possibility is that positive life events improve subjective well-being, something that, as discussed earlier, is linked to job satisfaction. It might also be that having good experiences outside of work offsets some of the negative experiences at work. Analysing data from almost 16,000 UK adults, Georgellis, Lange and Tabvuma (2012) examined some of these possibilities. They found that job satisfaction went up significantly prior to a person's first marriage and, to a lesser extent, prior to the birth of a first child. These results indicate that overall levels of life satisfaction can spill over into the work domain during the anticipation of these happy events. As the study included longitudinal data, the researchers were able to see if these effects were maintained. After the birth of the first child, job satisfaction levels were found to drop significantly with the researchers concluding that this could be due to added financial and time pressures and work–life conflict outweighing the boost to life satisfaction associated with starting a family. A smaller drop in job satisfaction was observed after a first marriage: increased work–life conflict might also account for this finding. It is also possible that culture plays a role in such findings. Haar et al. (2014) found that work–life balance had a bigger impact on job and life satisfaction in individualistic cultures than it did in collectivist cultures. The authors suggest that this could be because in individualistic cultures, responsibility for achieving a good balance falls very much on the individual worker and that it is a particularly critical aspect of their life. Those that achieve a good balance are therefore more likely to derive satisfaction from their achievement.

Does job satisfaction change over the lifespan?

Clarke et al. (1996) found in a sample of over 5000 UK employees that job satisfaction started fairly high in a person's teens, then dipped in their twenties and thirties, then rose through their forties (back to teenage levels) and further in their fifties and sixties. A more recent meta-analysis by Ng and Feldman (2010) identified that increases in job satisfaction with age were reliably observed in a wide range of different studies from across the globe. Why might job satisfaction tend to increase fairly steadily through working life? There are several possible reasons.

First, older people may be in objectively better jobs than younger ones, since they have had longer to develop their skills and to find a job that suits them. Second, older people may have changed their expectations of what is important to them over the years, so that they more readily draw satisfaction from what they experience at work. Ng and Feldman (2010) suggest that older workers may be inclined to focus on emotionally fulfilling work activities – and worry much less about acquiring new skills. This could be a result of them becoming increasingly aware that their remaining time at work is limited and a desire to 'make the most of it'. In both mechanisms, older workers are taking steps to adapt to and cope with changing circumstances. Truxillo et al. (2012) argue that mechanisms such as these are the result of *proactive self-regulatory processes*. As people age they may become more selective about what they do. The theory is that increasing age brings with it awareness that one's capabilities and goals are changing. Older workers may then adjust the way they work, or seek out different jobs that better fit with their capabilities and goals. For example, Truxillo and colleagues argue that older workers might seek out complex work tasks as these require the experience and knowledge that they have developed over time. By way of contrast, simpler jobs often come with physical demands that older workers might not feel that they can meet. The increased use of teamworking may also boost the job satisfaction levels of older workers as the autonomy and interdependence on offer allow them to be more selective about how they use their skills as well as providing the opportunities for social interaction that appear to be particularly valued by older employees (Truxillo et al., 2102).

Two other mechanisms might also come into play. Older people might always have been more satisfied than younger ones – a so-called **cohort effect**. Finally, dissatisfied older people may be more likely than younger ones to opt for early retirement or voluntary redundancy, so that those remaining in employment represent a biased sample of older people.

Key learning point

Job satisfaction is partly determined by a person's general disposition, but not so much so that it is constant over a person's working life.

Organisational commitment

What is organisational commitment?

The concept of organisational commitment has generated huge amounts of research from the 1980s onwards. This is no doubt partly because it is what some employers say they want from employees. It implies loyalty and the willingness to go the 'extra mile'. It has been suggested that commitment will lead to so-called organisational citizenship behaviours, such as helping out others and being particularly conscientious and hardworking (see Chapter 7). We look more closely at the validity of these claims later in this section. Commitment could be seen as being exceptionally one-sided: as Hirsh et al. (1995) have pointed out, what some employers now appear to want is totally committed but totally expendable staff. What, if anything, do employees get from being committed?

Organisational commitment has been defined by Mowday et al. (1979) as 'the relative strength of an individual's identification with and involvement in an organisation'. This concept is often thought to have three components (Griffin and Bateman, 1986): (i) a desire to maintain membership in the organisation; (ii) belief in and acceptance of the values and goals of the organisation; and (iii) a willingness to exert effort on behalf of the organisation. If a person is committed to an organisation, therefore, they have a strong identification with it, value membership, agree with its objectives and value systems, are likely to remain in it, and, finally, are prepared to work hard on its behalf. The concept of organisational commitment used in contemporary research is slightly differently from that described above. For example, with regard to point (ii), Ng (2015) draws a distinction between organisational commitment and *identification*, with the latter being a 'deep-level psychological phenomenon' (2015: 155) somewhat stronger than an attitude. This is characterised by the employee coming to believe that their values match those espoused by the employing organisation.

Allen and Meyer (1990) argued that there were three types of commitment. We use this very influential three-component model throughout this section as it remains widely used by researchers and practitioners:

- *Affective commitment*: essentially concerns the person's emotional attachment to their organisation or their liking for it ('I want to stay'). This type of commitment has received the most attention in the research.

- *Continuance commitment*: a person's perception of the costs and risks associated with leaving their current organisation ('I need to stay'). There is considerable evidence that there are two aspects of continuance commitment: the personal sacrifice that leaving would involve, and a lack of alternatives available to the person.

- *Normative commitment*: a moral dimension, based on a person's felt obligation and responsibility to their employing organisation ('I feel I ought to stay').

There is also good evidence that these three forms of commitment are distinct from each other (Dunham et al., 1994). Interestingly, they approximate respectively to the affective, behavioural and cognitive components of attitudes identified at the start of this chapter. Critics of the model have argued that this concept of organisational commitment is a little muddled because it combines an attitude toward a target (the organisation) with attitudes toward a behaviour (leaving or staying), and is therefore best used as a means of predicting turnover (Solinger et al., 2008).

Other observers have pointed out that people feel multiple commitments at work – not only to their organisation, but also perhaps to their location, department, work group or trade union (Reichers, 1985; Barling et al., 1990). Wasti and Can (2008) showed that employees distinguish between different targets of their commitment, i.e. commitment to the organisation, their colleagues and their supervisors. This is particularly important because the same study showed that the type of commitment determined its impact: commitment to the organisation predicted organisational outcomes (such as turnover), and commitment to the supervisor predicted citizenship behaviours (OCBs).

Point of integration

OCBs are frequently examined as important outcomes of organisational commitment. These are described in more detail in Chapters 5 and 7.

Becker et al. (1996) also found that commitment to the supervisor (especially when it goes deeper and the employee internalises the manager's values) is more highly correlated with job performance than is the less specific organisational commitment. Interactions between these different commitments can be important, too. Vandenberghe and Bentein (2009) found that low affective commitment to the supervisor was a good predictor of employee turnover, but that when coupled with low affective commitment to the organisation the chance of employee turnover was significantly increased. There is also a wider issue here: what exactly *is* the organisation that the employee is committed to? Complexities such as parent companies and franchises can make it difficult to identify exactly which organisation one belongs to. More than that, some psychologists (e.g. Coopey and Hartley, 1991) have been critical of the whole notion of organisational commitment because it implies that the organisation is unitarist – that is, it is one single entity with a united goal. A moment's thought reveals that most organisations consist of various factions with somewhat different and possibly even contradictory goals. Faced with these ambiguities, it seems that most people think of the term organisation as meaning top management when thinking about commitment, unless they are explicitly asked to consider other objects (such as their supervisor or work team).

Key learning point

Organisational commitment concerns a person's sense of attachment to their organisation. It has several components. As with any attitude commitment needs to have a specific object (e.g. supervisor, colleagues, senior management). The object of the commitment may be important in determining how commitment impacts upon their behaviour.

Measuring organisational commitment

A number of questionnaires have been developed to measure the various aspects or theories of commitment discussed above. The most widely used is that published by Allen and Meyer (1990). It contains subscales that measure affective, normative and continuance commitment, with each of the three components assessed by eight items. Although not perfect, this measure has stood up well to psychometric scrutiny. The Organisational Commitment Questionnaire (OCQ), which was developed by Mowday et al. (1979) is a 15-item questionnaire which has been used as a total commitment scale. It has also been broken down into subscales by various researchers (Bateman and Strasser, 1984). The OCQ comprises items such as, 'I feel very little loyalty to this organisation', 'I am willing to put in a great deal of effort beyond that normally expected in order to help this organisation be successful', and 'I really care about the fate of this organisation'. The OCQ was designed before the distinctions between different types of commitment were articulated in the literature. The OCQ chiefly reflects affective commitment. There are other scales in use as well. For example, Warr et al. (1979) developed a nine-item scale. An example item is, 'I feel myself to be part of the organisation'. This measure also tends to concentrate on affective commitment.

Exercise 6.3   Three different types of commitment

Example questions from Allen and Meyer (1990) include: 'I think that people these days move from company to company too often'; 'Right now, staying with my organisation is a matter of necessity as much as desire'; and 'I enjoy discussing my organisation with people outside it'. For each of these three items, try to identify which type of commitment is being measured.

All the commonly used measures of commitment are self-report: that is, a person indicates how committed they are. In many ways, this makes good sense. After all, the person is in the best position to comment on their own commitment. Yet perhaps we are biased. Perhaps other people could provide a more dispassionate view of how committed we are or at least how committed we appear to be. Goffin and Gellatly (2001) found that self-ratings of commitment were only moderately correlated with ratings given by supervisors and work colleagues. In line with much other research on self versus other ratings, ratings of people's commitment made by their supervisors and colleagues were more similar to each other than either was to self-ratings. This suggests that an external perspective is providing something over and above self-perceptions. Or it may be that commitment is a private psychological experience or that people are not keenly aware of how the commitment they feel translates into overt behaviour. It is also likely that the word commitment means different things to different people. Singh and Vinnicombe (2000) have shown that, for many people, it has more to do with taking a creative and assertive approach to one's work than with involvement in and loyalty to one's employing organisation. Research on attitudes suggests that these differences in perceived meaning could translate into different behaviours.

Key learning point

Like job satisfaction, organisational commitment is usually measured with questionnaires using Likert scaling.

Causes and consequences of organisational commitment

Much research has investigated how organisational commitment relates to other experiences, attitudes and behaviour at work. This is discussed below. Some of this has presented quite complex models indicating causal connections between commitment, satisfaction, motivation, job characteristics and other variables (see, for example, Eby et al., 1999). Figure 6.3 represents our attempt to summarise what is known, and what seems likely.

As with job satisfaction, there are several distinct theoretical approaches to organisational commitment. One of these, the behavioural approach, sees commitment as being created when a person does things publicly, of their own free will, and that would be difficult to undo (Kiesler, 1971). Rather like Bem's (1972) self-perception approach, it is suggested that people examine their own behaviour and conclude that since they did something with significant consequences in full view of others, when they could have chosen not to do so, they really must be committed to it. So if a person freely chooses to join an organisation, and subsequently performs other committing behaviours (e.g. voluntarily working long hours), they will feel more committed to it. This is a neat theory and there is a certain amount of evidence in favour of it (Mabey, 1986). In a more recent test of this type of mechanism, Flynn and Schaumberg (2012) looked at the effects of guilt-proneness on commitment. They found that people who experience high levels of guilt when they get things wrong tend to make extra efforts to put things right. It is well established that investment of effort is a predictor of affective commitment and that when employees invest lots of resources in a task they need to find a reason for doing so. Their results indicated that liking the employing organisation (reporting high affective commitment) makes it easier for guilt-prone employees to justify their extra efforts.

More commonly, however, it has been suggested that people's commitment can be fostered by giving them positive experiences. This reflects a kind of social exchange approach. The person is essentially saying, 'if this work organisation is nice to me, I will be loyal and

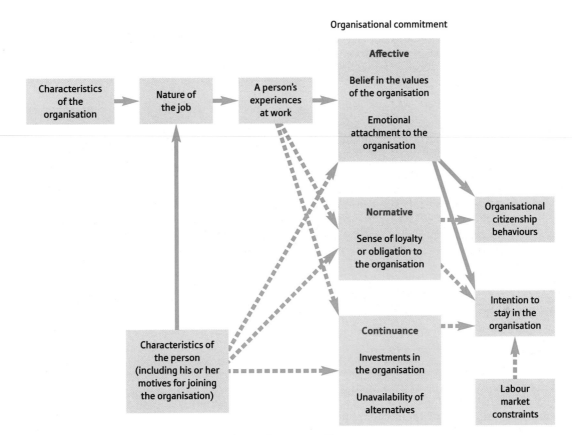

Organisational commitment

Note: Dotted arrows indicate weak effects; solid arrows indicate strong effects.

Figure 6.3	A model of organisational commitment

hardworking'. Many researchers have tried to identify exactly which pleasant experiences matter most for organisational commitment. Morrow (2011) summarises five categories of experiences that could, in theory, influence commitment:

- *Socialisation practices*. These occur around the point of entry to the organisation. High-quality selection processes designed to identify the right employees have been shown to foster good person–organisation fit something strongly linked to commitment. Giving new employees good experiences during induction and early tenure (e.g. clear work roles, challenging tasks and good support from a mentor) also fall into this category of experiences.

- *Organisational changes*. These include the introduction of teamwork, using technology to enhance worker autonomy (for example during automation of tasks), and the introduction of high worker involvement/participative management practices.

- *Human resource practices*. These include performance appraisal, performance management and training practices that are designed to develop and reward commitment.

- *Interpersonal relations*. These include experiences of working with inspiring and motivating leaders, good mentoring and being around co-workers who are helpful and courteous.

■ *Employee–organisational relations*. This category of experiences centres on the extent to which employees perceive that the organisation is supportive of their personal goals, values their work efforts and takes an interest in their well-being.

Morrow felt that more evidence was needed in order to draw firm conclusions about which of these experiences reliably leads to improvements in commitment. Even the results from the longitudinal studies reviewed could be affected by the organisational context and might not generalise. For some experiences (e.g. teamwork) there was evidence of both negative and positive effects on commitment. This may be a consequence of the way that the implementation of teamwork was handled (see Chapter 11). Perhaps unsurprisingly, the experience of changes such as downsizing and mergers usually had a negative impact on commitment. Some employers offer various accommodations and adjustments to employees according to their particular needs (e.g. additional training and development, special levels of pay, opportunities for promotion) in order to stimulate commitment. Ng and Feldman (2010) point out that these idiosyncratic deals are costly to employers but the 'special treatment' received may foster trust and excitement and, in turn, bolster affective commitment. By gathering data from 375 managers they tested this proposition and found that around 13 per cent of the variance in affective commitment reported after eight months could be attributed to contract idiosyncrasy. Such effects are not huge and it remains to be seen whether the benefits of increased commitment outweigh the costs of these tailored contracts.

Key learning point

It is usually assumed that organisational commitment is fostered by positive experiences at work, and to a lesser extent by the circumstances in which the person joined the organisation.

On the whole, it seems that factors intrinsic to the job (e.g. challenge, autonomy) are more important in fostering commitment than extrinsic factors such as pay and working conditions (Mathieu and Zajac, 1990; Arnold and Mackenzie Davey, 1999). This seems especially true for the affective component of commitment (i.e. commitment based on emotional attachment). On the other hand, continuance commitment (that is, the extent to which leaving would be costly for the person) is more influenced by the person's perception of their past contributions to the organisation and present likely attractiveness (or lack of it) to other employers (Meyer et al., 1989). Finegan (2000) reported an interesting study of how organisational values might affect commitment. The extent to which the organisation was perceived to value 'humanity' (e.g. courtesy, fairness) and 'vision' (e.g. initiative, openness) was correlated with affective commitment, while the value of 'convention' (e.g. cautiousness) was correlated with continuance commitment. It is also well established that overloading people at work can drive down commitment levels.

Fisher's (2014) huge study of over 6000 employees of a multinational company spread across 18 countries sheds some additional light on the factors that might protect commitment, even in the face of the very stressful working conditions associated with high workloads. He found that when employees reported working in a cooperative climate the negative impact of overload on commitment was less pronounced. This makes sense because when employees offer practical help to each other the effects of overload are likely to be less keenly felt. Empowerment also seemed to help but only in some cultures, namely those with *low power distance* where status differences are less pronounced. Sharing responsibility and power is the norm in such countries and this may explain why it helped to protect workers' commitment more in some locations than it did in others.

It also appears that it is not just what goes on inside the organisation that impacts on commitment. Employees' perceptions of how supportive the organisation is of their family also seem to be important. This support can be evidenced through the employer giving members of staff time to attend to family issues, allowing them to deal with personal issues during work time and not requiring employees to perform work roles that have a negative impact on their life outside of work. Wayne et al. (2013) found that when this support was high, employees were more likely to report that their family life had improved. They then attributed the cause of this good outcome to the source of the support (the work organisation) and it was this that strengthened commitment.

For some time it has been argued that experiences at work are only part of the picture and that commitment is also partly a function of the person (Bateman and Strasser, 1984). Perhaps some people are, through their personality or disposition, more prone to feel committed than others, just as some are more likely than others to feel satisfied with their job. Well-designed longitudinal studies have shown that organisational commitment is stable over long periods of time, which suggests dispositional factors are at play (Bowling et al., 2006). Factors such as positive and negative affect (defined in Chapter 10) show some relationship to organisational commitment. Positive affect tends to be associated with high levels of organisational commitment, and negative affect with low levels of commitment (Thoresen et al., 2003).

There is now also good evidence of some important and strong links between the Big Five personality traits and organisational commitment. Choi et al. (2015) carried out a powerful meta-analysis of these relationships and found agreeableness to be a particularly important factor in determining both affective and normative commitment. They suggest that this could be for a number of reasons. For example, those high in agreeableness are motivated to fulfil their need for trust and loyalty through committing to the organisation. They may also look to develop and maintain good close working relationships with colleagues, making their work more pleasant and enjoyable thus further strengthening their liking for their employer and their sense of moral obligation. It was perhaps not surprising then that the effects of agreeableness on commitment were stronger in collectivist cultures where group outcomes are valued more than individual ones. In the same analysis, those with high levels of emotional stability, extraversion and openness to experience tended to show lower levels of continuance commitment. Compared to most people, such individuals are likely to be less worried or apprehensive about moving to a new employer, more motivated to meet new work colleagues and keener to engage in new work activities or to adjust their values to fit with a new work setting.

Key learning point

A good amount of evidence indicates that several stable individual differences are linked to organisational commitment. This indicates that commitment is not just a result of what people experience at work.

Key debate

Is commitment linked to performance?

Early research indicated that the answer to this question may depend upon the type of commitment. Meyer et al. (1989, 1993) and Goffin and Gellatly (2001) found that workers high on affective commitment to their organisation tended to be better performers than those low on affective commitment. The opposite pattern of results was observed for continuance commitment. This

▶

▶

makes sense: high continuance commitment is based partly on a perceived lack of employment options, and one reason for people lacking options may be that they are not very good at their work! On the other hand, some other research has failed to find these links between commitment and performance. As with job satisfaction, it seems that many factors intervene between attitude and behaviour. One of these might be ability. A person is unlikely to perform well at a task that they are not able to do, even if highly committed to the organisation. Therefore, one might expect a stronger link between commitment and performance for aspects of performance that depend more on motivation than ability.

Consistent with this, Harrison et al. (2006) reviewed relevant longitudinal research and found a significant link between commitment and subsequent contextual performance (which is more or less organisational citizenship behaviours) of about 0.28, compared to 0.16 for focal (core) job performance. These correlations are quite small, but significant, and the evidence is mounting that organisational commitment predicts future performance. The research remains equivocal about the size and specificity of the relationship. A more recent meta-analysis of five longitudinal stud- ies (Riketta, 2008) suggests that the correlations are somewhat smaller than that found in earlier studies, with the links between organisational commitment on the one hand and focal and contex- tual performance on the other hand being about the same.

This brings us on to a relatively consistent finding in the research literature: a person who does not feel committed to their employing organisation is more likely to want to leave it, and actually to do so, than a person who feels more committed (Mathieu and Zajac, 1990). In fact, intention to leave the organisation is the strongest and most often reported correlate of low organisational commitment (Solinger et al., 2008). However, as we discuss next in this chapter, intention to leave does not necessarily translate into actual leaving.

Key learning point

Organisational commitment has only loose links with overall job performance. However, highly com- mitted people are more likely than less committed people to help others in the organisation.

Exercise 6.4   Satisfaction and commitment

Using your own experience of work, what factors most affect your job satisfaction? And what factors affect how committed you feel towards an employer? Are they the same things?

Consider the extent to which you think people can be 'made' more satisfied and/or committed by changing things in their work environment. In your experience, are some people just contented (or not) by nature, almost no matter what happens to them?

Employee turnover

For organisations employee turnover can have significant implications. There is the cost of hiring new staff, training new staff, disruption to teamwork, organising people to cover the work done by people who have left and so on. On the other hand, it can also lead to an influx of fresh talent, new ideas and enthusiasm. Depending upon the circumstances, employee turnover can have either good or bad outcomes for an organisation (Hausknecht and Holwerda, 2013). Therefore it is an issue that senior people within organisations like to be able to monitor and to try to control.

One of the problems with collecting data on turnover is that once employees have left the organisation, there is little that can be done to get them back. This is where measures of intention to leave become important. These can provide the organisation with some early warning signs. Thinking about leaving the organisation is something that has obvious links to eventual turnover (Mobley et al., 1978) and for a long time now research has shown this is often the case (Steers and Mowday, 1981). Of course, not everyone who considers leaving their job actually does leave their job, but such data can point to where intervention might be needed.

As we saw earlier in the theory of planned behaviour, intentions can sometimes be quite good predictors of behaviour. If the theory were correct, *attitudes to the act* of leaving would influence intention to leave the company. This would involve asking employees whether they agreed with statements such as 'leaving the organisation would be good for me'. *Subjective norms* would also come into the equation. This might mean finding out whether other people who were important to the employee (e.g. partner, colleagues, friends, etc.) thought it was acceptable for the employee to leave the job.

Breukelen and colleagues (2004) point out that the state of the employment market is an indicator of *actual behavioural control*. This is the essence of many *labour market theories* of turnover: these state that people are all essentially the same and turnover is mostly influenced by objective labour market conditions (Morrell et al., 2001). Psychological theories that have used the theory of planned behaviour include a person's perception of the amount of employment opportunities. This is an indicator of *perceived behavioural control* (i.e. an employee's view of their chances of getting another job in the labour market). A logical prediction from the model is that the better people see their chances in the labour market, the stronger their intention to leave *and* the more likely that their intention to leave will lead to them handing in their resignation. In an interesting study of workers in a Finnish hospital and university, De Cuyper et al. (2011) found that perceived employability was not significantly linked to turnover intention unless employees were dissatisfied with the level of control they had in their work. This is just one of many findings that suggests that that both 'push' and 'pull' factors interact to influence employees' intentions.

Key learning point

The theory of planned behaviour has been used to understand how intention to leave develops, and how this intention translates into actually leaving the organisation.

Although the theory of planned behaviour has some validity, plenty of research on turnover shows that factors that sit outside the theory have been implicated. Research has shown that intention to leave is not only influenced by attitudes towards the act of leaving, but also attitudes towards objects (whether the person likes the job itself and their employing organisation). By now, you can probably see where this is going: because they are attitudes toward very broad objects (the job and the organisation) it appears that organisational commitment and job satisfaction influence lots of organisational outcomes including turnover (Harrison et al., 2006). As discussed in the previous section, meta-analyses tend to indicate that there are some significant but modest links between organisational commitment and job satisfaction on the one hand, and turnover on the other hand (e.g. Griffeth et al., 2000).

> ### Key learning point
>
> To focus only on job satisfaction and commitment would seriously underestimate the complexity of employee turnover.

Breukelen and colleagues (2004) studied turnover intentions and actual turnover in part of the Netherlands' navy. They found that job satisfaction and organisational commitment had no significant direct effect on *actual* turnover. However, job satisfaction did have a significant effect on turnover intention (this was in addition to the influence of the factors set out in the theory of planned behaviour). This intention was then a significant predictor of actual turnover. They also found that tenure was important (as tenure increased, intention to leave weakened). This is probably because tenure is a measure of the strength of the relationship between the employee and the organisation. It could also indicate that they may have turned down many opportunities to leave: they might be particularly loyal or the job fits well with other aspects of their life. Results such as these point to turnover as a planned act. It also suggests that employees take into account lots of different factors when making a decision to leave or stay.

In a very comprehensive review of the turnover literature, Hom et al. (2012) found substantial evidence that not every employee's considered decision to leave is triggered by the same set of factors. They argue that employees can exhibit different 'proximal withdrawal states' (2012: 831) influenced by their own preferences, personal circumstances and their perceptions of choice and control. These motivational states can be used to place employees in four categories that help us to better understand the different mechanisms that drive turnover:

- *Enthusiastic leavers*. These are people who are dissatisfied with their work and actively seek employment elsewhere, or those who experience a significant change in life circumstances that leads to them looking for alternative employment (see external shocks below).

- *Reluctant leavers*. This category includes people who would like to stay but see themselves as potential candidates for being made redundant (e.g. if there was a downsizing or a merger). Those who are nearing retirement and those who leave a job they enjoy to fulfil caring responsibilities or to meet cultural expectations (e.g. to stay at home to look after children) also fall into this category.

- *Enthusiastic stayers*. These fall into two subcategories: 'engaged stayers' and 'slackers'. The former are people who enjoy the work and like being around their work colleagues; their competencies fit well with the demands of the work; they are loyal and engaged. The latter do not tend to enjoy the job but for them the benefits that come with the job such as security and financial reward are highly desirable; they do just enough work to get by. For these people it is only likely to be ill-health or retirement that precipitates leaving.

- *Reluctant stayers*. There are significant barriers to leaving for these people. 'Trapped stayers' do not enjoy their work, or do it particularly well, but feel that leaving would be disruptive to them or their family (e.g. they might have to relocate) or that there are insufficient opportunities in the job market. 'Contractual stayers' are those who feel that the job is not what was promised during recruitment. They perform the work well so as not to risk being fired or to harm their long-term prospects, but will stay only until the duration of the employment contract ends.

These different categories illustrate a number of important points. The antecedents and consequences of turnover are different for different people according to their motivational state. Some turnover is undesirable for all involved while other forms of turnover might represent a 'win–win'. For example, at the end of a 'reluctant stayer's' tenure they may move to a more satisfying role and be replaced by someone who is better suited to the role (an 'enthusiastic stayer'). These states may help to explain why the impact of turnover on company performance is not always negative or large (Hausknecht and Holwerda, 2013).

Key learning point

Different factors influence turnover for different employees. There are some common causes but also lots of idiosyncrasies that are linked to features of the person and the situation they find themselves in.

These categories show that employees might leave their job not because they are dissatisfied with their current work role or because of opportunities elsewhere, but for a host of other reasons including significant life events. Lee and Mitchell (1994) argued that these events were frequently powerful triggers for thoughts of leaving: this was their *unfolding model* of turnover. Morrell et al. (2004) examined turnover among nursing staff using this approach. They hypothesised that people have a relatively high degree of inertia when it comes to leaving their job, and that in order to leave they have to be 'shocked' out of this inertia. They use the concept of *image theory* to describe the turnover process. Image theory proposes that people develop habitual ways of perceiving events (schemas) and that we tend to see things in a way that fits with these schemas. For example, if you feel the organisation is a very good employer, but one of your colleagues says something at work that upsets you a little, it might not be enough to challenge your view of the company as a good employer. However, if something extreme happens, either at work or at home, this might be enough of a shock to break this habitual interpretation that you have a very good employer. For example, if you think your current employer pays a good salary, and you hear that a friend has a similar job that pays double your salary, that may be a significant enough shock to change the way you see things. This might then get you thinking about leaving your current employment (i.e. changing your habitual behaviour).

Morrell et al. (2004) found that negative shocks at work (e.g. a perceived unfairness after being passed over for promotion) tended to lead to people looking for other jobs. Positive shocks from outside the workplace (external shocks such as the opportunity for a new challenge elsewhere) were linked to people actually leaving the organisation. The implication of this is that organisations may be able to intervene to stop employees leaving as a result of some types of work-related shocks. It also tells us that in some cases turnover is the inevitable consequence of events that happen in people's lives. This type of effect might also derail employees' plans to develop their career outside the organisation. Positive career shocks such as an unexpected promotion, success in a work project or a salary raise have been shown to override employees' intentions to leave to pursue their ambitions in higher education (Seibert et al., 2013).

Key learning point

Events from within or outside of the organisation can jolt people out of their habitual way of thinking about their job and their employer. These shocks have been implicated as causes of turnover.

What about the content of the job itself? Chapter 10 discusses the issue of work stress in some detail, and stressful working conditions are often significant 'push' factors in an employees' decision to leave the organisation. Perhaps unsurprisingly, overall satisfaction with the characteristics of the job has frequently been found to link people's experiences at work and their intentions to leave (e.g. van der Aa et al., 2012). Podsakoff et al. (2007) carried out a meta-analysis of studies that had looked at the links between positive and negative aspects of jobs and employee turnover. Positive job characteristics are those that employees often interpret as challenges that give them opportunities to develop (*challenge stressors*). These include the level of attention required by the job, the demands of the role, having to work quickly and dealing with interesting tasks. These factors were largely *unrelated* to turnover intentions and actual turnover. The results were very different for *hindrance stressors* (the constraints that the work situation placed on employees, hassles, organisational politics, role conflict, role ambiguity and lack of resources (see Chapter 10). These were linked to both turnover intentions and actual turnover, as well as being linked to other predictors of turnover intention such as organisational commitment and job satisfaction. These results suggest that problems with job content are significant *push factors* for employee turnover. In team settings, it has been found that team leader and team member behaviours that support autonomy (e.g. by providing others with lots of choices and options in the work) and workers' feelings of empowerment help to lower voluntary turnover (Liu et al., 2011).

In terms of the *context* within which people work, a lack of fit between the values and needs of employees and what can be provided by the organisation also seems to play a small, but significant, role in employee turnover (Hoffman and Woehr, 2006). This can have some interesting consequences. For example, Pierce and Snyder (2014) argue that unethical employees tend to enjoy long tenure in companies when customers demand unethical services from those organisations. In other circumstances, unethical behaviour would tend to be linked to shorter tenure.

Point of integration

Changes in procedural justice (see Chapter 7) over time seem to have a particularly strong link to the development of turnover intentions (Hausknecht et al., 2011). This indicates that when it is particularly important to retain employees, organisational policies and procedures need to be implemented fairly and equitably.

As with most topics in work psychology, it is also worth considering the role of individual differences in determining employee turnover. Ng and Feldman (2009) present a huge meta-analysis of the relationship between age and turnover, finding a small but significant relationship between the two ($r = -0.14$) meaning that on average older workers are slightly less likely to leave a job than their younger counterparts. This relationship is a little stronger among those with few, or no, formal educational qualifications. Ng and Feldman argue that there could be a number of reasons for these findings, including:

- Age tends to be linked to tenure, and when tenure is higher the relationship between the employee and the employer tends to be stronger.
- Compared to younger adults, older adults tend to have less intense emotional experiences in the face of problems and, to coin a phrase, tend to 'accentuate the positive'.

■ For older adults, perceptions about job insecurity have only a weak link to turnover. This is probably partly because of anxiety about re-entering the job market and because they are not as skilled in moving between jobs as younger workers might be.

■ Older adults also tend to have lower self-efficacy than younger adults and hence have more doubts about their ability to adjust to a new job role.

■ Compared to younger adults, older adults strive for high-quality interpersonal relationships which might be provided by long-term employment. In other words, they are more focused on social needs and work fulfils some social needs.

These factors bring us back to an issue discussed earlier in this chapter: the relationship between age and job satisfaction. It might be that by comparing the job satisfaction of older workers with that of younger workers we are comparing apples with oranges: the two groups might be drawing their job satisfaction from very different elements of their work.

There is also plenty of research that shows another individual difference, personality, has an impact on both turnover intentions and actual turnover. In his meta-analysis, Zimmerman (2008) found a significant relationship between emotional stability (or neuroticism, see Chapter 3) and turnover intention: the higher emotional stability, the less likely the intention to leave. This is logical because people who report low levels of emotional stability experience more problems than most when dealing with stressful situations and experience and display more negative emotions than most. Almost always there is a certain level of stress involved in being a new employee, and a person's propensity to express negative emotions at work may also lead to a lack of support from colleagues. Interestingly, Zimmerman's analysis showed this effect of personality on *turnover intention to be direct*, meaning that the increased likelihood of turnover was not because people with low emotional stability were performing less well or were less satisfied with their job. Agreeableness and conscientiousness were related to *actual* turnover (the higher levels of these, the less likely people were to leave). Again, these relationships make sense. Those low on agreeableness are more likely to *act on impulse* and have less concern about the impact that their departure will have on others. People who have high levels of conscientiousness prefer to see things through and tend to make careful plans when decision-making. What was particularly interesting about Zimmerman's findings was that the link between agreeableness and conscientiousness and actual turnover was *not* dependent on turnover intentions. This indicates that those low on agreeableness and conscientiousness are more likely than most people to act on impulse and leave their job without planning. This challenges the theory of planned behaviour. The effects were not huge, but add an extra dimension to how we might think about the causes of employee turnover.

Rather less has been written about the links between cognitive ability and turnover. Individuals with high levels of ability may be in strong demand in the labour market and knowing this they may also be more likely to seek out more challenging and well-paid opportunities (i.e. be subject to strong 'pull' factors). The established links between cognitive ability and performance may mean that those with low levels of ability find themselves underperforming and 'pushed' out of work roles that demand higher ability. Taken together these findings suggest that turnover will be highest for those in low-ability and high-ability groups. Maltarich et al. (2010) found that this seemed to be broadly true for cognitively demanding work. It was also apparent that those with higher levels of job satisfaction were less likely to choose to leave cognitively demanding jobs. One practical implication of this finding is that using good job design to drive high satisfaction could be especially important when seeking to retain the most able employees to do very complex jobs. Things were not quite as simple as this for jobs with lower cognitive demands. Maltarich and colleagues found that those with high cognitive ability were less likely than might be expected to leave jobs that required low cognitive ability. They argue that choosing to do a job that matches one's values and circumstances can sometimes override any problems associated with doing work that is not intellectually fulfilling.

Unemployment

As we have seen there are a number of factors that influence a person's decision to leave an organisation. What about when this decision is made for them and they do not have an alternative job ready for them to go to? We have positioned unemployment in this chapter to highlight its contrast with voluntary turnover. We could have just as easily positioned it in Chapter 10: unemployment is often argued to be a far bigger source of stress than any of the problems people experience while at work.

Unemployment is a problem faced by many, from the unskilled to the professional worker, for those seeking their first job to those approaching retirement. Reviews of the research on the psychological experience of being unemployed (e.g. Winefield, 1995; Fryer, 1998; Wanberg et al., 2001) conclude that people who experience unemployment tend to suffer from lower levels of personal happiness, life satisfaction, self-esteem and psychological well-being than (i) people who are employed and (ii) when they themselves were in employment. They also tend to report increased depression, difficulty in concentrating and other minor to severe behavioural and physical problems. As discussed in Chapter 10, fear of losing one's job can have similar effects (e.g. Stansfeld and Candy, 2006). Some workers are in precarious roles, working on short-term contracts or with the constant threat of reductions in working hours or redundancy hanging over them. These are significant concerns for many people in work and have been shown to be linked to lower overall life satisfaction (e.g. Körner et al., 2012). As we discuss later, being in work provides people with many resources (such as money and social support) that can help to offset the effects of such concerns.

In what is one of the largest meta-analysis reported in this textbook, Paul and Moser (2009) analysed 323 studies that compared the mental health of employed people with unemployed people and 86 longitudinal studies (in total, data from around half a million people drawn from across a wide range of different countries). They found that the mental health of unemployed people was, on average, half a standard deviation lower (see Chapter 2) than that of employed people. In practical terms they conclude that this equates to 34 per cent of unemployed people reporting psychological health problems of clinical severity, compared to 16 per cent in the employed group. The size of this effect appears to be quite consistent across different people and different decades. Murphy and Athanasou (1999) conducted a meta-analysis of 16 longitudinal studies of unemployment published between 1986 and 1996. They found that moving involuntarily from employment to unemployment was associated with a fall, on average, of 0.36 standard deviations on measures of well-being. Regaining employment brought, on average, an improvement in well-being of 0.54 standard deviations. Paul and Moser (2009) found a similar effect: when people moved back into employment mental health improvements were bigger than the deteriorations associated with job loss. This suggests that, at least for a time, regaining employment may lead to better well-being than the person had experienced in their pre-unemployment job.

There is, of course, the possibility that poor mental health raises the likelihood of unemployment (i.e. reverse causality). Paul and Moser (2009) tested for this and found the effect of *mental health on unemployment* to be significant (i.e. those with impaired mental health were more likely to lose their job and find it more difficult to get another), but this effect was small in comparison to the impact of *unemployment on mental health*. One specific finding that supported this conclusion was the significant increase in school leavers' mental health when they found employment. In summary, there remains strong evidence that unemployment *causes* poor mental health.

Key learning point

Becoming unemployed tends to have a negative impact on a person's mental health, but the damage is often repaired when the person finds another job that is at least as satisfying as the one they left behind.

Although there are differences of opinion about the relationship between unemployment and mortality, evidence is emerging of a positive association, with studies indicating that long-term unemployment may adversely affect the longevity of the unemployed by as much as two to three years, depending on when the person had been made redundant. Milner et al. (2014) examined the results of several longitudinal studies (mainly conducted in Sweden and Denmark) into the links between unemployment and suicide. They found that people unemployed for 90 days or more who had experienced mental illness in the past were at significantly higher risk of death by suicide than those who had not experienced such illness. This may be because unemployment significantly worsens the situation of people who are already at a higher risk of suicide. Such findings indicate that people with a history of mental health problems are most in need of help and support soon after becoming unemployed. Even after taking past mental health into account, the same study found that the risk of suicide increased with unemployment albeit by a smaller amount. It is a common finding that this risk is higher for men than it is for women. Gunnell and colleagues (2009) summarise evidence from numerous studies carried out in several countries that show significant increases in suicide rates during economic recessions which resulted in high levels of unemployment.

The findings discussed above are large-scale reviews that seek to identify common effects. These rarely consider directly individual differences in the way an individual copes with the experience of unemployment. These could have a significant impact on its effects (Kinicki et al., 2000). It seems that problem-based coping (e.g. trying to find a job) rather than emotion-focused coping (e.g. telling oneself that employment is not very important) does not necessarily help people feel better at the time, but it does help them find a new job. As we have already noted, starting a new job often leads to a recovery of mental and physical health. Creed et al. (2009) carried out a longitudinal study of the predictors of the intensity of job search (i.e. the amount of time, effort and resources spent preparing CVs, contacting employers, looking for job advertisements, etc.). You will probably not be surprised to read that job search intensity is a good predictor of re-employment (and hence an increased likelihood of improved mental health). People who held a strong belief that their efforts would lead to self-improvement (a **learning goal orientation**) tended to also carry out the most intense job searches, much more so than those who believed their capabilities were fixed (**a performance goal orientation**). They also found that this relationship was mediated (see Chapter 2) by **self-regulation**. This meant that those who were goal oriented were more intense in their job search because they were more active in monitoring their own emotions and behaviour. They were also more active in critically evaluating whether how they were behaving, thinking and feeling was helping them to achieve their goals. It was learning goal orientation that led to more self-regulation, and this in turn led to more intense job searching.

Individual differences in self-control also seem to matter. In most countries, job search is a largely self-directed behaviour. The unemployed get advice and support but most of the effort they make to find a new job has to come from them. Careful preparation and controlling one's thoughts and actions may be particularly important during a job search process that could take a long time and contain many distractions and setbacks. Baay et al. (2014) tested the effects of self-control in a longitudinal study of 403 Dutch students seeking their first job after leaving school. They found that self-control was quite strongly linked to the level of pro-active job seeking behaviour reported by the students (e.g. doing some reading or talking to people about getting a job, or tracking down job opportunities by talking to others). These findings indicate that people who are good at retaining their focus and avoiding distractions might fare better when seeking work. As you might expect from the descriptions of the Big Five personality traits in Chapter 3, unemployed people with high levels of trait conscientiousness tend to keep a structured routine, stay organised and maintain high levels of persistence during periods of unemployment: these strategies may help them to maintain their well-being (Van Hoye and Lootens, 2013).

Key learning point

Individual differences appear to play a significant role in how a person responds to being unemployed and the way they approach seeking a new job.

Of course, some people experience more than average falls and rises in well-being when their employment status changes while others experience less. What determines this? Researchers have investigated a number of factors (Wanberg et al., 2001) and have mostly reported unsurprising findings. Greater financial hardship is associated with lower well-being, and so is the extent to which a person feels committed to the idea of being employed. High levels of social support and a high ability to structure time tend to reduce the impact of unemployment on well-being. Paul and Moser's (2009) analysis also revealed a number of other important moderators (see Chapter 2) of the relationship between unemployment and well-being:

- The effects of unemployment were felt most by men, those in blue-collar jobs and by people who had been unemployed for a long time. On average, poor mental health appeared to peak after about two years of unemployment, before getting still worse again for the very long-term unemployed.
- The context is important. Unemployment had more of an effect on mental health in less economically developed countries and those countries with less developed protection systems (e.g. unemployment benefits) for the unemployed. Gunnell et al. (2009)

present several pieces of evidence that show suicide rates have increased when spending on welfare provision for the unemployed has been cut in times of economic recession.

Key learning point

The impact, and length, of unemployment is determined by a number of individual differences and external factors such as labour market conditions and welfare support mechanisms.

Some psychologists have tried to identify exactly what it is about unemployment that leads people to feel psychologically bad. Jahoda (1979) wrote of the manifest function of employment (income), but also its latent functions – structuring of time, social contact outside the family, linkage to wider goals/purposes, personal status/identity and enforced activity. A person who becomes unemployed is deprived of both the manifest and the latent functions of employment, and it is this, Jahoda argued, that leads to negative psychological states. Others have seen Jahoda's approach as too limited. Warr (1987) pointed out that not all employment fosters mental health, and identified features of 'psychologically good' employment (see also the Vitamin model of work stress described in Chapter 10). These included money, variety, goals, opportunity for decision-making, skill use/development, security, interpersonal contact and valued social position. This pays more attention than Jahoda to characteristics of the job itself. Warr argued that becoming unemployed would have negative psychological effects to the extent that it led to loss of these features in day-to-day life.

Point of integration

Hobfoll's (1989) Conservation of Resources (COR) model (see Chapter 10 for a detailed description) provides a plausible and well-developed framework to help us understand some of the effects of unemployment (i.e. because it can result in the loss of significant resources).

Huffman et al. (2015) argue that the resources lost through unemployment (arguably these are very similar to the latent benefits described above) can sometimes be replaced by resources supplied by other parts of the unemployed person's life. For example, friends and family can help to replace some of the social support resources lost by not being at work. Social interactions may help an individual to maintain structure in the daily activities when the structure provided by work is lost. COR may also help to explain the frustrations that some people feel while unemployed. Fryer (1998) argued that the psychological effects of unemployment are the result of frustrated attempts to create a better future rather than memories and regrets about loss of a more satisfying past. COR suggests that people strive to develop and protect resources – something that may become more difficult when unemployed – and that unsuccessful attempts to do so can place well-being at risk. In COR terms, financial resources (such as money saved or income from other family members) can also help to buffer the effects of unemployment as these help people to conserve and obtain other resources, including their social life (Huffman et al., 2015).

Returning to Warr's earlier argument, it is important to remember that not all jobs are psychologically enriching (see Chapter 7), so it is possible that unemployment is a less bad experience than some of the least pleasant jobs. There is also the issue of what happens when people return to work, but take less rewarding jobs than the ones they had before, or jobs that demand of them something that is much below their full capacity. This is sometimes referred to as *underemployment*. McKee-Ryan and Harvey (2011) identify a host of factors that can contribute to a sense of underemployment. These include some that have likely and obvious financial implications for the individual: being paid less than one would like, working at what are perceived to be low levels in the organisational hierarchy or working a limited number of hours. Others reflect more psychological elements of person–job fit: being in jobs where skills, education, qualifications or experience are under-utilised, a lack of prestige, undemanding or monotonous work, or inadequate opportunities for personal development and career progression. McKee-Ryan et al. (2009) and McKee-Ryan and Harvey (2011) point out that these issues mean that unemployment has an important subjective dimension: losses and recovery of well-being may hinge on how favourably or unfavourably the employee views the changes in their situation. If people perceive themselves to be underemployed then various pieces of research show that there is an increased risk of undesirable outcomes such as poor well-being, low job satisfaction, poor job performance, a lack of discretionary effort and derailed careers. McKee-Ryan and Harvey (2011) identify various psychological theories that could underpin these effects including:

- *Human capital theory*: People tend to invest their psychological resources in situations where they feel they are likely to be adequately rewarded.

- *Person–job fit theories:* The greater the level of fit the better the chance of good outcomes for both the employee and their employer.

- *Relative deprivation theory*: Underemployed individuals harbour the belief that they should be in better jobs, a belief that might be driven by comparing themselves to others with similar skills, qualifications and so on.

- *Coping and control theory of reemployment*: Well-being may be at risk until people who were unemployed return to jobs that are at least as good as the ones they had before.

Key learning point

People may make comparisons between their new job and the one they lost when they become unemployed. If the new job does not compare well, satisfaction and well-being can be adversely affected.

It does seem that those on contingent contracts (e.g. part-time workers, those on short-term contracts, agency workers etc.) report, on average, lower job satisfaction than those on permanent contracts (Wilkin, 2015). The differences are not especially large overall and it is important not to see contingent workers as a homogenous group. Wilkin's analysis included a huge amount of data drawn from many different studies and showed that although agency workers do, on average, experience lower job satisfaction than permanent workers, the job satisfaction of contractors is roughly equivalent to that of permanent employees. Wilkin suggests that this may be because some contingent workers do not always compare their circumstances to that of permanent workers. It may be that they interpret the nature of the work they do and the rewards they get from it in different ways (e.g. by focusing on what is important to them at the time).

Point of integration

Theories of work-related stress (Chapter 10) offer some insight into the reasons why underemployment could be an unpleasant experience for people. These theories also indicate that individual differences are important and suggest that not every individual will react to underemployment in the same way.

One other interesting theoretical perspective on unemployment comes from Paul and Moser (2006) who describe the experience of being unemployed as a source of *value incongruence*. This theory suggests that people in many societies value having a job, but these values are incongruent with the reality of being unemployed. This incongruence is a source of significant emotional distress, which is, in turn, related to the various problems with mental health that are consistently associated with unemployment. Paul and Moser (2009) argue that while the effects of unemployment are well researched, much more research is needed to test the specific mechanisms that underpin those effects.

The psychological contract

So far in this chapter we have looked at what attitudes are, how they form, and why they are important in the workplace. By looking at turnover and unemployment we have also explored what work means to people and why it is important to them. In this section we bring these various issues together by looking at the *psychological contract*. The body of work on this topic has much to say about why employees hold certain attitudes towards their employer, why these attitudes might be linked to their behaviour, and how attitudes and behaviour are linked to what people want from their working lives.

A quite large research literature on the psychological contract has been produced in only a short time. Although there have been some debates about its usefulness (more of that later), it is currently a very important topic in work psychology. Much of the interest in the psychological contract is recent, but its roots go back a long time, it having originally been discussed by Argyris (1960). The psychological contract has been defined in several slightly different ways. We will use the following definition (Robinson and Rousseau, 1994: 246):

> An individual's belief regarding the terms and conditions of a reciprocal exchange agreement between that focal person and another party ... a belief that some form of a promise has been made and that the terms and conditions of the contract have been accepted by both parties.

To add a little more detail to this definition, 'psychological contract comprises subjective beliefs regarding an exchange agreement between an individual and, in organizations typically, the employing firm and its agents' (Rousseau, 2001: 512).

One of the reasons that the concept has been so useful is that it helps us to understand the combined effects of a lot of different psychological processes that influence employee behaviour and performance. Herriot (1992) describes psychological contracting between an individual and the organisation as 'the invisible glue which binds individuals to the organisation over time. It incorporates the parties' beliefs, values, expectations and aspirations' (1992: 6).

The psychological contract should not be confused with the legally binding employment contract (although inevitably there is some overlap between the two, especially around issues such as pay and working hours). It is of much interest to work psychologists because it is subjective. Just because it is generally not written down, this does not make it any less important. Many researchers in this field put the psychological contract at the heart of the relationship between the employee and the employer. This means that when it is working well for both parties good things happen – but when the contract breaks down, there are likely to be significant problems.

In the psychological contract there is a belief that the agreement is mutual and binding. From the employees' point of view, this is the agreement that they think they have with their employer about what they will contribute to the employer via their work, and what they can expect in return. So if the employee believes that working late will help them in the next round of promotions, they might expect that the number of times they had worked late would be viewed favourably by those making the decisions about promotions. When an employee makes these efforts they expect the employer to stick to the rules: they perceive the employer to have an obligation to give something back, to reciprocate their efforts. The word *promissory* appears quite a lot in psychological contract research. The contract is about making and keeping promises through exchanges between the employee and the employer. The employee does something based on the employer's promise to them, and gets something back in return. As you might expect, broken promises can have a serious negative impact on any relationship.

Types of psychological contracts

Of course, not everyone wants the same thing from their employment. Money might be more important to some than it is to others. Some people might take a job for the training opportunities it offers. Older workers might be especially interested in the social aspects of work. The same applies to the motives and needs of the employing organisation. Short-term contract workers might be hired to just do the job without being given any of the training or other benefits that went with being a permanent employee. The work of Rousseau (1990, 1995) and Herriot and Pemberton (1995) defines four different types of psychological exchanges/contracts commonly in operation in organisations. These are also widely used in contemporary research:

- *Relational contracts* offer the most mutual trust and stability. Employees offer loyalty, conformity to requirements, commitment to their employer's goals and trust in their employer not to abuse their goodwill. In return, the organisation offers security of employment, promotion prospects, training and development, and some flexibility about the demands made on employees if they were in difficulty. The harsh reality of the economic environment and fierce global competition are not always conducive to establishing and maintaining this type of exchange.

- *Transactional contracts* are based more on money and well-defined specific performance terms (for both parties). These are much more like a short-term economic exchange. The employee offers longer hours, broader skills, tolerance of change and ambiguity and willingness to take more responsibility. In return the employer offers (to some) high pay, rewards for high performance and, simply, a job. This type of exchange is more common in harsh economic conditions when people are aware that they have little security of tenure.

Key learning point

Different employees want different things from their work. By the same token, different employers want different things from their employees. The psychological contract describes what each party promises and expects from the relationship and this contract can change and develop over time.

There are quite clearly some major differences between transactional and relational exchanges. Two other types of exchanges, transitional and balanced exchanges, sit somewhere between the two. *Transitional contracts* are typical of an eroding relationship between the employer and the employee. This can happen when the company can no longer offer promises about future employment (i.e. it is moving away from a relational contract). In a *balanced contract*, mutual expectations are flexible and dynamic, and there is a mutual understanding that performance expectations are likely to change. In this type of contract the employer will make efforts to train and support the employee when things change. This is a bit like the relational contract being enacted when things are less stable for all involved.

All of these types of exchanges can be satisfying, if they are mutually understood, accepted and everyone sticks to the deal. If you took a job thinking it offered excellent training opportunities, but the employer thought that you wanted the job just for the money, this is unlikely to result in a satisfactory outcome for either you or your new employer.

The development of the psychological contract

The psychological contract starts to be formed at the very early stages of the relationship between the employee and the employer, probably as soon as a prospective employee hears about a company or a job opportunity for the first time. It starts to become even more crucial during recruitment and selection as this gives both parties a chance to find out a lot more about each other. Robinson and Morrison (2000) found that problems with the psychological contract were more likely when an employee had less interaction with the employer before being hired. Many researchers have found that giving prospective employees a *realistic job preview* has helped reduce levels of employee turnover near the beginning of tenure. This can be achieved through using good recruitment and selection procedures that allow prospective employees to get a good insight into the job role and the nature of the organisation they are considering coming to work for. Work sample exercises in assessment centres or situational judgement tests (see Chapter 4) are very good ways of giving employees some early (pre-employment) experiences of what it might be like to work for the company. Proper induction processes can also help to avoid problems with the psychological contract.

Key learning point

The early stages of contact between the employee and the employer – even before the employee starts work – can play a role in the formation of the psychological contract.

If the psychological contract is not to their liking, new employees may take it upon themselves to take action to try to put things right, rather than waiting for managers or colleagues to try to repair the situation. Bankins (2015) identified many different actions that newcomers took in response to feeling that their psychological contract had been breached. In her study she found that newcomers could sometimes feel that they were given tasks that were too simple for them. To deal with this, several approached their manager to identify opportunities for being involved in more challenging work (they self-initiated remedies for a breach). More often, however, newcomers enacted psychological coping strategies. For example, several coped by focusing on the future, and reappraised the problems as transient ones. In other words, they coped by accepting the less than challenging work as a temporary situation that would soon improve.

While important, these early interactions are not everything when it comes to establishing the psychological contract. Taris et al. (2006) examined the expectations of 1500 newcomers to an organisation. They found that unmet expectations did have an impact on important outcomes such as turnover and motivation. However, the newcomers' expectations changed over time, with some of the unmet expectations becoming less important to them as time went by after they joined the company. This shows that although a psychological contract is formed at recruitment it is fluid, often referred to as an 'unfolding process'. Employees and employers' expectations tend to change over time. One implication of this is that the contract needs to be frequently reassessed and managed, and we will return to this issue later in this section.

Key learning point

Psychological contracts change or 'unfold' over time. What people expect and what an employer can offer are both very dynamic.

Much of the research into the psychological contract has looked at what happens when it is broken, or breached, or when one party 'rats' on the deal. These *breaches* can be quite common. For example, in their early work Robinson and Rousseau (1994) found that 70 of their sample of 128 managers thought that their employer had *breached* their psychological contract (i.e. what they thought they had been promised) in the first two years of employment. Breaches most commonly concerned failure to deliver on promises about training and development, pay and benefits, and promotion opportunities. There are five items below adapted (slightly) from Robinson and Morrison's (2000) measure. These give a more detailed description of how employees might perceive a breach (employees would be asked to what extent they agreed with these statements):

1   Almost all the promises made by my employer during recruitment have been kept so far (agreement = no breach).
2   I feel that my employer has come through in fulfilling the promises made to me when I was hired (agreement = no breach).
3   So far my employer has done an excellent job of fulfilling its promises to me (agreement = no breach).
4   I have not received everything promised to me in exchange for my contributions (agreement = breach).
5   My employer has broken many of its promises to me even though I've upheld my side of the deal (agreement = breach).

Key learning point

The psychological contract concerns an individual employee's perceptions of their rights and obligations with respect to the employing organisation. When promises are broken, this is referred to as a breach of the psychological contract.

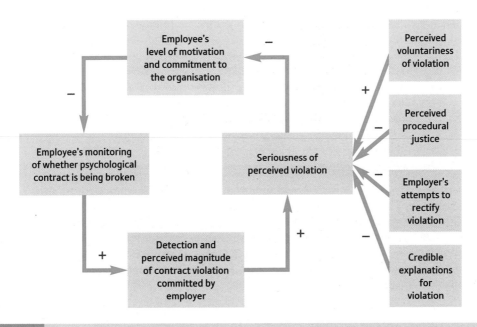

<table>
<tr><td>Figure 6.4</td><td>The process of psychological contract violation
Source: Adapted from Rousseau (1995: 118), reprinted with permission.</td></tr>
</table>

The apparent frequency with which psychological contracts are breached has led psychologists to try to clarify what is coming to be called the 'violation process' (e.g. Robinson and Morrison, 2000). Figure 6.4 illustrates this. One important issue here concerns the distinction between contract breach and contract violation. The former is often thought of as the realisation that what has been promised has not materialised (i.e. a perceived discrepancy). *Violation* is often used to describe the *negative emotional reaction to a breach*. Violation is more emotionally charged than the more neutral notion of unmet expectations, and more complicated than simply asking how pleasant a person's experiences have been within a work organisation. This distinction is important because it means that a breach could occur without there being a negative emotional reaction to it. Most researchers agree that violations occur when there is a perception that the breach was deliberate, purposeful and reflected unfair treatment (Robinson and Morrison, 2000) and carries with it a clear implication of a broken promise.

The effects of breaches and fulfilment of the psychological contract

Herriot and Pemberton (1995) describe typical behavioural reactions to violation of the psychological contract as get out, get safe or get even – or, to put it another way: to leave, to stay and keep your head below the parapet, or to stay and take your revenge. In terms of attitudes to their employer, when employees felt that their employer had violated the psychological contract, they were not surprisingly inclined to feel less sense of obligation and less commitment to their employing organisation. This means that we might look at behaviours such as performance, turnover and organisational citizenship and attitudes such as job satisfaction and organisational commitment when examining the impact of violations of the psychological contract.

Staff happy with a 'duvet day'

Sandwell Community Caring Trust looks after 350 adults and children with learning and physical dis-abilities, older people and their families. It is a 24-hour-a-day business. Staff agree their hours when they join, and are invited to request changes as their circumstances alter. 'If staff feel unable to cope with a specific task, they are encouraged to tell their manager,' the report said.

It's easy to see why Sandwell, based in the West Midlands, was second in this year's *Sunday Times*' '100 Best Companies to Work For' list. It came first nationally in the work–life balance category. Sandwell's employee turnover is only 4 per cent, compared with 20 per cent or more across the care sector. Since 1997, the number of staff has gone up from 60 to 280 and business turnover has increased from £1m to £9.5m. The average time taken as sick leave is only 0.6 days a year.

Teresa Aitken, founder director of PI Costing, a niche company based in Doncaster undertaking legal services on behalf of solicitors, said trust and good communication were essential. The company offers 'duvet days'. At the discretion of the manager, staff who have worked extra hard can spend an extra hour in bed. Aitken also says if someone has finished their work in the minimum time, she is happy for them to go shopping.

Most of Aitken's 20 employees are young women. Some have had babies and want to work shorter hours, or to work several days a week from home. Homeworkers, she has found, are 20–50 per cent more productive. It can be difficult ensuring that homeworkers feel involved in the company. Small firms such as PI Costing have regular staff meetings and maintain communication in other ways. Both are also able to offer less competitive salaries because people like working for them.

In all these firms, standards are high. 'This has demonstrated to all employees management's zero tolerance on breaching the trust placed on them,' the report said. And at Sandwell, where the clients are vulnerable adults and children, there is no question of shifts going uncovered.

Source: The Sunday Times, 8 July 2007 (Hofkins, D.),
© The Sunday Times 2007, www.nisyndication.com

Suggested exercise

Describe the nature of the 'typical' psychological contract that seems to be operating within these organisations. Do you think violations of the psychological contract are likely or unlikely to occur – why?

Conway et al. (2011) found that the consequences of a breach on attitudes such as job satisfaction and organisational commitment were bigger than the consequences of fulfilment. They argue that this could be because broken promises cannot easily be 'unbroken'. While this study suggested that there might be less to be gained from fulfilling psychological contracts, the effort and care required could be justified by the costs that are avoided. If different outcomes are examined a slightly different picture seems to emerge. Conway and Coyle-Shapiro (2012) carried out a complex longitudinal study of sales advisors and collected data on changes in performance over time. Stronger links between fulfilment and performance developed over time. This indicated that when employees had been with the organisation for some time, when they performed well they were more likely to experience fulfilment of their psychological contract (and vice versa). However, earlier on in their tenure the support they received from others appeared to help them to feel their psychological contract had been fulfilled, even if they were less than successful at achieving performance targets. The fluctuating state of the psychological contract over time is a common theme in longitudinal studies. As relationships develop and change between the employee, their supervisor and others in the organisation, perceptions of promises change. In Conway and Coyle-Shapiro's study, as time passed it appeared that performance loomed larger in people's evaluations of the promises being made.

The evidence for the impact of violations of the psychological contract continues to mount. In a meta-analysis of the research Zhao et al. (2007) looked at 51 well-designed studies of the consequences of psychological contract breaches and violations. The analysis revealed that the strongest links between the psychological contract and organisational outcomes occurred when employees had a strong emotional response (e.g. feelings of violation or mistrust) to the breach. As with many other issues examined in this book, how employees perceive and react to events is as important as the event itself. These reactions were particularly strongly linked to turnover intention, organisational commitment and job satisfaction. There were weaker, but significant, links to job performance and organisational citizenship behaviours. However, there was no significant link to actual turnover, most likely because turnover is a very complex, multi-causal phenomenon (as already discussed in this chapter). The type of contract breached did not seem to make too much difference to the outcomes, except that breaches of transactional contracts had stronger links to organisational commitment than breaches of relational contracts. Something that may be a concern for organisations is that employees who experience a breach stay in their jobs but are less effective.

Key learning point

Breaches and violations of the psychological contract appear to have a significant negative effect on employee attitudes such as job satisfaction and organisational commitment.

In their longitudinal study, Ng et al. (2010) found that organisational commitment was harmed by breaches and that this had knock-on detrimental effects on levels of innovation. They also found that after initial perceptions of breaches, employees held stronger perceptions about the breach – providing evidence that without some form of intervention there is a risk that the effects of breaches can grow over time.

Breaches, whether caused by the manager or not, seem to have a particularly damaging effect on line manager–employee working relationships with this, in turn, leading to long-term detrimental effects on employees' career success (Restubog et al., 2011). In Chapter 10 we look in more detail at the concept of engagement at work and how this is something that many employers want to foster in their organisation. Perhaps unsurprisingly, breaches of the psychological contract have also been linked to an increased likelihood that employees will report working with less vigour and energy after a breach then they did before it (Rayton and Yalabik, 2014). Drops in levels of job satisfaction seem to play an important role in the link between contract breaches and engagement.

Some of what you have read so far may leave you thinking that breaches of the psychological contract are an inevitable feature of most people's working lives. This is probably true as many organisations are faced with and respond to changing circumstances. As a result researchers have started to look at what factors determine whether a breach triggers an emotional response (violation or mistrust), and whether the negative outcomes of breaches can be averted. There is a lot of scope for individual interpretation in this process. For example, a person who starts out favourably disposed towards their employer might be less likely to notice breaches than somebody who already mistrusts the employer. They might also be less likely to construe breaches as violations or at least have less strong psychological reactions to them. The intensity of psychological responses to breach is the focus of a lot of research. For example, in a study of over 6000 British Royal Air Force personnel, Clinton and Guest (2014) found that it is the important *felt consequences* of breach that appear to drive its links to turnover. Their results suggest that if breach resulted in a perception that trust in the employer had been significantly damaged, or that the employee felt that their exchange with the employer was unfair (e.g. they got out less than they put in) then breach would be linked to turnover.

Individual differences and the psychological contract

One thing that is starting to emerge from recent research is that numerous individual differences seem to be important in the mechanisms linking breaches and violations to outcomes that are important to individual workers and their employers. There is some evidence that age moderates the impact of a breach. Are older workers perhaps a little more relaxed about breaches when they occur? Recent evidence from longitudinal research indicates that older workers react less intensely than younger workers to breaches with less impact on their job satisfaction and performance (Bal et al., 2008, 2013). This effect appears not to be a consequence of tenure and more likely to be linked to age-related differences in emotional regulation (more constructive regulation may be practised by older workers). It is well established that older people tend to have a wider repertoire of strategies for coping with and appraising the meaning of their emotions.

It also appears that psychological breaches can leave employees with some 'baggage' that they take forward into future employment. Robinson and Morrison (2000) found that experiences of breaches of the psychological contract with former employers were linked to the likelihood of breaches occurring with the current employer. Karagonlar et al. (2015) have found that some employees remain more wary than others of the promises made by employers, even if their experiences indicate that psychological contracts are fulfilled. The implication is that for some employees the impact of psychological contract fulfilment on their work-related attitudes and their performance might be less than it is for others.

There is a small amount of evidence that under certain circumstances, breaches may have positive consequences for some of those involved. Kiazad et al. (2014) examined the impact of breaches on innovation among university employees in Australia and found that some employees actually reacted positively to a breach by engaging in more innovative behaviours. They argue that such apparently surprising findings start to make sense if we consider how innovation can help people recover some of their losses associated with the breach. This involves looking at psychological contracts through the lens of conservation of resources theory (see Chapter 10 for a detailed discussion) rather than as a 'social exchange'. Kiazad and colleagues argue that innovation can involve strengthening existing collaborative links with colleagues, taking on more challenging tasks and a re-appraisal of the significance of their work situation (i.e. because of the breach they have 'little to lose' by innovating). All of these actions help with the development of resources than can offset the loss of resources associated with the breach. This might also indicate that workers take proactive steps to build up resources in the expectation that another breach might occur. This is a new line of research but does suggest that problems with the psychological contract might not always have predictable outcomes.

Of concern for many organisations is the possibility that those who feel that promises have been broken might engage in deviant or counterproductive work behaviours. These can include stealing, being rude to clients or colleagues, choosing not to collect revenue due to the organisation, or aggressive or hostile acts. Restubog et al. (2015) studied workers in the hospitality industry to examine the links between breach and these damaging behaviours. To do this they measured 'revenge cognitions': workers may consider exacting revenge but not actually act on their thoughts – they also hypothesised that if the organisational culture was aggressive then such thoughts might be more likely to translate into actions. Their findings confirmed this prediction, indicating that organisational culture needs to be managed carefully if some of the more unpleasant effects of breaches are to be minimised. This is just one of many examples of research showing that running an aggressive organisational culture carries with it significant risks. Their findings also highlighted the importance of an individual difference variable. Those higher in self-control felt the effects of psychological contract breaches as keenly as anyone else but, compared to those with low self-control, they were less likely to attempt to exact revenge through their behaviour at work.

What is most important to people in their psychological contracts can vary quite a bit from one person to the next. Restubog et al. (2007) found that breaches have bigger effects for people who attach high value to the tangible benefits of employment such as money (outcome-oriented people, or *entitled*) than it does for those who attach high value to the benefits of relationships at work (relationship-oriented people, or *benevolent*). When experiencing a breach, outcome-oriented employees tended to attempt to 'even the score' by extracting revenge. This was far less likely to be the case among the relationship-oriented employees, probably because these employees did not want to place at risk relationships with co-workers and supervisors.

Key learning point

Even within the same working environment, there are likely to be very significant differences between individuals in the kind of promises they expect to be kept, and the value they place on the rewards they might receive for their efforts.

Lambert (2011) argued that the way most people see their psychological contracts can be broken down into four components: promised inducements, promised contributions, delivered inducements and delivered contributions. Her results showed that much depends upon how each of these elements fulfils the specific needs of each employee at any given time: elements proximal (close) to personal need fulfilment appear to matter more than those distal from it. For some (e.g. those who have a personal need to pay next month's rent) it might be very important to receive, quite quickly, delivered inducements (pay) for their work. By contrast, for others their needs might be closely linked to their desire to achieve long-term goals and therefore promised inducements could be more likely to match their needs (e.g. the promise of a well-defined path to a top job sometime in the future). In this case they might be happy to exert effort in return for a promise from the employer.

Importantly for organisations, research also shows that how a breach is handled is important in determining whether it turns into a violation. Lester et al. (2007) found that open communication with employees about the nature of the psychological contract was important to keeping the contract fulfilled. As long as employers give credible, legitimate and consistent reasons for breaches then employees appear less likely to have strong emotional reactions to breaches (i.e. they are less likely to feel the contract has been violated or to develop feelings of mistrust). Zhao et al. (2007) argue that employers need to guard against breaches by making efforts to keep abreast of their employees' needs. The main point underlying all this is that contract breach does not necessarily lead to reduced employee loyalty and commitment. If it is felt that the breach was neither the employer's fault, nor intended, then the impact on the employee's loyalty is likely to be small, particularly if it is put right quickly.

Key learning point

Interventions can stop breaches of the psychological contract leading to feelings of violation or mistrust.

Criticism of the psychological contract

The concept of the psychological contract has not been accepted fully by all researchers. Some have argued that there is a danger that it is overused and that other important variables are ignored as a result (Arnold, 1996). In addition, an organisation is not a person, and therefore cannot be a party to a psychological contract. Organisations consist of many different individuals and groups, and each employee may have quite specific expectations about their rights and obligations vis à vis those individuals (e.g. supervisor) and groups (e.g. departments). However, Rousseau (1998) argued that the psychological contract provides a framework for better understanding some of the important psychological processes that influence individual attitudes and as a result organisational performance. It also represents a very flexible approach to understanding employee attitudes and behaviour: any aspect of the working relationship and a whole host of individual differences can shape the psychological contract. You may also think that there is some overlap with concepts of job satisfaction and organisational commitment, but if you look carefully, the underlying processes of the psychological contract are quite different (particularly the concepts of promises and reciprocity). Guest (1998) also argued that the concept is consistent with the spirit of the times (i.e. the changing nature of employment relationships); it helps to make sense of current employment relationships, and helps to highlight who has power. Perhaps the clincher is that the state of the psychological contract is linked to a range of important organisational outcomes (see Zhao et al., 2007). By capturing important aspects of people's experience of work, the concept offers considerable possibilities for understanding work attitudes and behaviour.

Exercise 6.6	Mark Reason's 'tyred' psychological contract

When Mark Reason started work as a tyre-fitter for Nice New Tyres Ltd he thought he would only be working there for a few months just to earn some money until something better came along. He didn't really know much about tyre-fitting, or the company, but the interview was easy enough, he got some training and after a short probationary period he was given a permanent contract. Months turned into years because filling in job application forms and going for interviews wasn't really his thing. Mark took on more and more responsibility, managing some junior staff and running the depot when the manager wasn't there. He worked hard at what he did, and although the pay wasn't overly generous it was fair and his colleagues were good people to be around. His manager sent him on some management training courses, telling him that he was 'clearly management material' and that he would be running a depot very soon.

Now, seven years after he started work for the company, many of his former colleagues have moved on to bigger and better things. Since the company started to struggle financially the managerial role is no longer discussed. All the training courses have stopped, too. Mark often finds himself wondering what he did wrong. True, he is still paid good money for just fitting tyres, but he also gets asked to do lots of the paperwork around the place to help out his manager. He isn't paid for this and finds that he doesn't get a lot of thanks for it either, so sometimes he 'deliberately forgets' to do it. All that keeps him coming to work now is the friendly chats with customers and the fact that he has a secure job when lots of people are struggling to find work.

Suggested exercises

1   How has Mark's psychological contract changed over the course of his employment with Nice New Tyres Ltd?

2   What breaches of the psychological contract can you see in the story described above?

3   What impact might these breaches have on Mark and his relationship with his employer?

4   Could Mark's employer have done anything different to stop these breaches or to manage the impact of the breaches?

Stop to consider

Think about some people you know well, and who have a job at the moment. Do you think that the concept of the psychological contract would make sense to them? If you have time, talk to one or two of these people about the psychological contract they have with their employer, and examine whether what they say fits with what you have read in this chapter.

Summary

In this chapter we have taken a close look at attitudes. In particular, we have focused on what they are, how they can be measured, how they can be changed and their links with behaviour. Like most social psychological phenomena, attitudes are more complicated than they seem at first sight. They have several different components which may or may not fit together nicely. A person's attitudes may predict their behaviour quite well in some circumstances, if the right attitude is assessed, and if the person's perceptions of social pressures and their own capabilities are also taken into account. Two key work attitudes are job satisfaction and organisational commitment. Job satisfaction concerns a person's evaluation of their job, while organisational commitment refers to the extent to which a person feels attached to their employing organisation. They can both be measured satisfactorily, both are influenced by the nature of the person's job, and both appear to have quite complex connections with a range of behaviours and other attitudes at work. However, they may both say more about whether a person stays in their employing organisation than about their job performance. Of course, employee turnover is complex and many other factors aside from attitudes influence this important aspect of employee behaviour. The psychological contract provides a useful framework for understanding how the employment relationship develops and is maintained. It also tells us quite a lot about how attitudes develop and what work means to people. The impact that unemployment has on people shows that work fulfils a number of important psychological needs.

Closing case study | ONS survey reveals scale of zero-hours contracts

Unions and politicians have called for action to curb employment on a "zero-hours" basis after official data showed that UK employers are using about 1.4m contracts that do not guarantee a minimum number of hours.

Most of the contracts – accounting for about 4 per cent of all jobs – were zero-hours, the Office for National Statistics said. About 13 per cent of employers reported some use of these contracts, including almost half

▶

▶

of tourism, catering and food-sector businesses. More than one in five employers in health and social work reported using them, although they were found to be relatively rare in finance, professional services, manufacturing, energy and agriculture.

The ONS surveyed 5,000 employers. Its previous estimates, based on surveys of employees, found that 583,000 people, or 2 per cent of the workforce, were on zero-hours contracts, though that was widely regarded as an underestimate. Some workers could have more than one contract, the ONS said. The Chartered Institute of Personnel and Development has put the number of people on zero-hours contracts at 1m, or 3.1 per cent of the workforce. Their use is thought to have increased sharply since the recession and some economists see it as a factor in the UK's poor productivity performance.

John Philpott, director of the Jobs Economist consultancy, said: "The ready supply of workers for low-paid, low-skilled jobs means employers are able to operate on a business model that has a high turnover of staff and compete on low cost and low value. But this business model is holding back productivity and the economic recovery."

The ONS study showed the average number of hours worked on zero-hours contracts was 25 a week. Women, under-25s and those over 65 were more likely to be on the contracts; and larger employers were more likely to use them.

Frances O'Grady, general secretary of the Trades Union Congress, said: "Insecure work with no guarantee of regular paid hours is no longer confined to the fringes of the jobs market. It is worrying that so many young people are trapped on zero-hours contracts, which can hold back their careers and make it harder to pay off debts like student loans."

Employers say the contracts offer flexibility for both staff and companies. Controversy over their use grew last summer after it emerged that some employers, including McDonald's, Cineworld and Sports Direct, used them for nearly all their staff. McDonald's has used zero-hours contracts in the UK since it opened its first restaurant in

1974. It says many of its employees are parents or students who are looking to fit flexible, paid work around childcare, study and other commitments.

Vince Cable, business secretary, last year proposed a ban on exclusivity clauses that tie workers on zero-hours contracts to one employer. He also proposed issuing advice and guidance about zero-hours contracts for employers and employees in an effort to stamp out abuses.

Labour plans to give staff the right to demand a fixed-hours contract when they have worked regular hours for more than six months with the same employer and the automatic right to such a contract after a year. The party would also offer protection against attempts by employers to force workers to be available at all hours, to insist they cannot work for anyone else or to cancel shifts at short notice without compensation.

Chuka Umunna, shadow business secretary, said the "shocking figures show that since David Cameron became prime minister, there has been a huge increase in the number of people on zero-hours contracts".

Mr Cable said the analysis "shows that these types of contracts can provide important and flexible employment opportunities that suit most people in these jobs". However, he said action was needed to tackle abuses and promised to publish the results of his consultation shortly.

Neil Carberry, director for employment and skills at the CBI employers' group, said: "Arbitrary attacks on the existence of flexible contracts would cost jobs and damage growth."

Figures add to debate on slack in labour market

The number of people on zero-hours contracts, which do not guarantee a minimum number of hours, appears to have grown strongly since the recession, writes Brian Groom. The question is: will this start to recede as the economy recovers or is this type of employment contract here to stay?

The term began to be used after the early 1990s recession, but the practice probably dates from well before then. Attempts to pin down the scale of the phenomenon have been dogged by problems of definition.

Employers say they offer flexibility for both staff and companies, and are popular with students, older workers and those with caring duties. But others say they have a damaging impact on workers who do not know what they will earn from one week to the next.

The ONS puts the number of zero-hours and similar contracts at 1.4m, or about 4 per cent of UK jobs, based on a survey of employers. Its previous estimate of the number of people on zero-hours contracts, based on surveying employees, was 583,000, though many considered that an underestimate.

In those earlier surveys, the number of workers saying they were on zero-hours contracts rose slowly from 2004 but doubled in 2013, possibly because of increased awareness of the term as a result of media coverage.

The new figures will fuel debate about the amount of slack in the labour market but are unlikely to completely explain the UK's poor productivity. Output per hour has not improved as expected since the economic recovery began but this may have more to do with problems in industries such as finance and North Sea oil.

If productivity starts to recover and real wages grow, zero-hour contracts could fall. But, says Professor Kim Hoque, of Warwick Business School: "They may represent a structural shift in the labour market."

 Source: Financial Times, 30 April 2014; http://www.ft.com/cms/s/0/eaf5d8d2-d045-11e3-af2b-00144feabdc0.html#axzz3krf3jj00

Suggested exercises

1 What does the research on job satisfaction, organisational commitment and the psychological contract tell us about the likely impact of zero-hours contracts on those employed in this way?
2 Having looked at this research, to what extent do you agree with the quotes and opinions in this article?
3 What factors might mean that zero-hours contracts have different effects on different people?
4 To what extent, if at all, do you think that taking a job with a zero-hours contract might impact on someone who is currently unemployed?

Test your learning

Short-answer questions

1 Define three aspects of an attitude.
2 Why are attitudes useful for a person?
3 Draw a diagram to show the theory of planned behaviour, and define its key concepts.
4 Briefly describe three general phenomena that can influence job satisfaction.
5 Define organisational commitment and its component parts.
6 List the factors that can influence employee turnover.
7 What factors might lessen, or worsen, the impact of unemployment?
8 What is the psychological contract?
9 Explain what is meant by a breach of the psychological contract. How is this different from a violation of the psychological contract?
10 Outline the individual differences that can impact on the way people respond to breaches or violations of the psychological contract.

Suggested assignments

1   In what circumstances do attitudes determine behaviours at work?
2   Examine how much is known about what factors determine either job satisfaction or organisational commitment.
3   To what extent does the research evidence about organisational commitment suggest that managers in organisations should care about how committed their staff are?
4   'The concept of the psychological contract tells us much about the causes of problems with employee attitudes and behaviour at work.' Discuss.

Relevant websites

www.jisc.ac.uk provides links to many sites about attitudes, and indeed to most other topics covered in this book.

National Health Service Trusts in the UK now carry out annual staff attitude surveys. The surveys used and summaries of results can be found at http://www.nhsstaffsurveys.com

A good example of how public opinion survey companies work and present their findings can be found at http://www.yougov.co.uk/ Here you can find a summary of opinion surveys carried out recently about attitudes to a very diverse range of topics.

Suggested further reading

Full details for all references are given in the list at the end of this book.

1   Ajzen's 2001 article in the *Annual Review of Psychology* describes the influential theory of planned behaviour, as well as other research on how attitudes work. Not an especially easy read, but very informative about attitude theory.
2   The paper by Pratkanis and Turner (1994) in the journal *Human Relations* is an excellent example of how the study of attitudes has profited from the social cognitive tradition in psychology.
3   The paper by Harrison et al. published in 2006 in the *Academy of Management Journal* does a good job of summarising the various possible links between attitudes, individual behaviour and subsequent organisational outcomes. The introduction is particularly useful.
4   The book *Understanding Psychological Contracts at Work: A critical evaluation of theory and research*, by Neil Conway and Rob Briner (Oxford University Press, 2005), provides an accessible and in-depth discussion of a high-profile topic in work psychology.

CHAPTER 7

Approaches to work motivation and work design

LEARNING OBJECTIVES

After studying this chapter, you should be able to:

1 define the meanings and components of motivation;

2 describe three common-sense approaches to motivation;

3 describe Maslow's hierarchy of needs;

4 identify the strengths and weaknesses of need theories;

5 define need for achievement and explain why it could affect productivity at work;

6 define valence, instrumentality and expectancy as factors in motivational processes;

7 define and describe three forms of organisational justice;

8 outline the features of goals that usually enhance motivation;

9 draw a diagram describing the main features of goal-setting theory;

10 suggest how material rewards can affect motivation;

11 list and define the different forms of motivation specified in self-determination theory;

12 list four techniques of job redesign;

13 draw a diagram to show the job characteristics model (JCM);

14 identify the ways in which theory and research about the motivational features of jobs has moved beyond the JCM;

15 describe three links between different motivation theories that can help to build up an overall picture of motivation.

Opening case study

Do you employ Australia's laziest worker?

By Caroline James, 3 December 2014

Is one of your team – possibly even a high-flyer – a serial skiver? They openly spend hours each week planning their weekend, and go AWOL when it's time to refill the photocopier. Conversely, you may have employees who clock more hours than you but regularly miss performance targets.

"Being 'lazy' and being 'unproductive' are two different things," explains Anne-Marie Orrock from Corporate Canary HR consulting. "You can have a person who is not looking lazy due to [evident] busyness and they'll still be unproductive."

Gavin Sharp of Psychology Melbourne agrees, advising small business bosses to "take care in diagnosing the lazy employee".

We are all at times prone to laziness; "What we are really looking for are patterns, not one-offs," the corporate psychologist says. Staff members may appear lazy when actually fatigued, ill, suffering stress, thinking or resting, he says.

According to Sharp, tell-tale signs of a deliberately lazy worker include:
- A blatant disregard for the efforts and plights of others;
- Absenteeism such as days off, long lunch breaks, increased use of internet for non-work-related matters;
- Non-attendance of meetings or no contribution in meetings;
- Regularly distracts others with non-work-related matters or work that is not necessarily a priority;
- Weak excuses as to why they did not meet a deadline such as "I didn't realise it was important", "it was so-and-so's fault" or "I thought someone else was doing it";
- A poor attitude and lack of engagement.

Employees who are unproductive but not intentionally lazy may be:
- Deficient in skills/knowledge/training;
- Misunderstanding the urgency of a task;
- Overloaded and/or under-resourced;
- Coping with personal life stress.

"In all cases, with a first conversation do not make the mistake that you have 'diagnosed the issue' and that the worker must be lazy," Sharp says. "It is imperative to assume this is not the case and ask if there is any help they need, identify barriers to completing work and advise of the resources/ people available to assist."

If the problem cannot be fixed with a quick chat in the tearoom, bosses should adopt "a holistic approach", says director of HR on Call, Melissa Behrend.

Ask yourself; are there any issues with your style of management or leadership? Do you provide the right motivational drivers for that employee?

Ask if there is anything external sapping work motivation, Behrend says, and explain how their lack of input is affecting the team and/or customers.

"Set down your expectations and ensure that you have regular communication and feedback with that employee. Set targets for the employee. If their performance is not meeting the expectations of the role, you may have to move into a formal performance management process."

Source: Adapted with permission from the Sydney Morning Herald website: http://www.smh.com.au/small-business/trends/do-you-employ-australias-laziest-worker-20141203-11wch5.html (accessed 1 May 2015)

Introduction

As the opening case study illustrates, motivation and how to manage it is a major concern for many managers. In this chapter we examine the concept of motivation and explore some of its implications. We look at some conflicting so-called 'common-sense' ideas about motivation. The chapter then turns to a description and evaluation of some enduring approaches to motivation, including need theories, expectancy theory, justice theories and goal-setting. Textbook discussions of motivation theories are sometimes described as 'a walk through the graveyard of psychology', in the sense that many of the theories are both old and lacking life. However, as we will see, in recent years many elements of these theories have been brought together to produce new understandings of motivation at work that stand up to scrutiny. The roles of the self and personality are also considered. Both theoretical and practical issues are covered. The idea that jobs can be designed to be motivating is also examined: this suggests that motivation is as much a feature of the job as it is of the person.

The topic of motivation has received huge attention from work psychologists over very many years, so it is not possible to cover every relevant theory. The earlier ones were often designed to be 'big theories' of human nature, whereas later ones have tended to confine themselves to specific aspects of motivated behaviour, with many focusing directly on the work setting. In fact, some recent approaches scarcely have the label 'motivation' at all. So although motivation continues to be a very significant concept in work psychology, its boundaries are not easy to define.

Overview of motivation

As with many important concepts in psychology, there is no single universally accepted definition of motivation. Nevertheless, the word itself gives us some clues. To use a mechanical analogy, the motive force gets a machine started and keeps it going. In legal terms, a motive is a person's reason for doing something. As Locke and Latham (2004: 388) put it: 'motivation refers to internal factors that impel action and to external factors that can act as inducements to action'. Clearly, then, motivation concerns the factors that push us or pull us to behave in certain ways. Specifically, it is made up of three components:

1 *Direction*: what a person is trying to do (sometimes called choice).

2 *Effort*: how hard a person is trying (sometimes called intensity).

3 *Persistence*: how long a person continues trying (sometimes called duration).

Some key points should be remembered:

■ People are usually motivated to do *something*. A person may try hard and long to avoid work: this is motivated behaviour! Hence we should always remember the 'direction' component. When someone is considered lazy at work (as in the opening case study) it normally means that they appear not to be motivated to do what their job description and their boss prescribe. They may however be highly motivated to do other things.

■ It is easy to make the mistake of thinking that motivation is the only important determinant of work performance. Other factors, such as ability, quality of equipment and coordination of team members' efforts also affect performance. Again, the opening case study illustrates this nicely. However, motivation matters. For example, Zhao and Chadwick (2014) show that the motivation to develop new products is a stronger predictor of companies' success in doing so than the capabilities of the staff.

■ Like most concepts in work psychology, motivation is abstract. It cannot be observed directly. Quite often a person's work performance is used as a measure of their motivation, but as we have just seen, many factors other than motivation influence performance. Individuals' reports of how hard they are trying (i.e. effort) are sometimes used as an indicator of motivation, but direction and persistence rarely feature (Ambrose and Kulik, 1999). This needs to change. Many people have jobs that offer choices in what to do and pay attention to (i.e. direction), and in many jobs it is necessary to keep trying over a long period (i.e. persistence) in order to succeed.

A distinction is often made between content theories and process theories of motivation. The former focus on *what* motivates human behaviour at work. The latter concentrate on *how* the content of motivation influences behaviour. In fact, most theories have something to say about both content and process, but they do vary considerably in their relative emphasis.

Key learning point

Motivation concerns what drives a person's choice of what to do, how hard they try and how long they keep trying. It is important, but is not the only factor that influences work performance.

Common-sense approaches to motivation

McGregor (1960), Argyris (1964), Schein (1988) and others collectively identified three broad common-sense approaches to motivation which are endorsed by different individuals or even by the same individual at different times. McGregor (1960) termed two of the three theory X and theory Y, though the reader should be clear that in neither case is the word 'theory' used in its formal academic sense. Schein (1988) added what can be called the social approach. In all three cases, we are essentially uncovering a general perspective on human nature. Briefly, they are as follows:

- *Theory X*: People cannot be trusted. They are irrational, unreliable and inherently lazy. They therefore need to be controlled and motivated using financial incentives and threats of punishment. In the absence of such controls, people will pursue their own goals, which are invariably in conflict with those of their work organisation.

- *Theory Y*: People seek independence, self-development and creativity in their work. They can see further than immediate circumstances and are able to adapt to new ones. They are fundamentally moral and responsible beings who, if treated as such, will strive for the good of their work organisation.

- *Social*: A person's behaviour is influenced most fundamentally by social interactions, which can determine their sense of identity and belonging at work. People seek meaningful social relationships at work. They are responsive to the expectations of people around them, often more so than to financial incentives.

As you can probably see, theory X and theory Y are in most respects opposites, with the social approach different from both theory X and theory Y. Which of these common-sense approaches do you find most convincing? The authors' experience with business/management undergraduates is that, if forced to choose one, about half go for the social approach, about 40 per cent for theory Y and about 10 per cent for theory X. Among practising managers, the overall distribution in our experience is about the same, but tends to differ between industries. The more physical the industry (i.e. the extent to which the industry relies on physical effort to make tangible things), the higher the proportion of theory X adherents. Managers' beliefs in theory X and theory Y seem to be reflected in their behaviour: theory X adherents are less participative (Russ, 2011), and less liked by their subordinates (Gürbüz et al., 2014).

In Chapter 1 we noted that humans are excellent at constructing plausible explanations of events after they have happened, and assuming that their explanation is 'common sense'. These 'common-sense' views of motivation are a good example of this.

None of these three 'common-sense' accounts is universally correct. However, as Schein (1988) pointed out, over time people may be socialised into their organisation's way of thinking about motivation. Up to a point, managers can perhaps influence their staff to see motivation their way. Of course, they may also attract and select staff who are already inclined to see things their way. Although each of these approaches finds some expression in theories of motivation, the match between theory and common sense is not particularly close. This means either that motivation theories are missing the point, or that they are going beyond common sense. See which you think is the case as you read though this chapter.

Common-sense views of motivation contradict each other, but all have some truth.

So what are the theories? Let us now examine some of the most widely known and extensively researched. Bear in mind that several of the theories originated more than half a century ago. That does *not* mean they are useless. They contain ideas that have found expression in subsequent work, and some practising managers insist they are helpful in managing their staff.

Need theories

Need theories are based on the idea that there are psychological needs, probably of biological origin, that lie behind human behaviour. When our needs are unmet, we experience tension or disequilibrium which we try to put right. In other words, we behave in ways that satisfy our needs. Clearly, the notion of need reflects the *content* of motivation as opposed to process, but most need theories also make some propositions about how and when particular needs become salient, so in a way they also refer indirectly to motivational processes. The notion of need has a long history in general psychology. It has, for example, formed the basis of at least one major analysis of personality (Murray, 1938). Two major traditions have been evident in the work setting. First, there are models based on the notion of psychological growth. Second, there are various approaches which focus on certain quite specific needs.

Need theories based on psychological growth

Easily the best known of these theories is that of Abraham Maslow (1943, 1954). Maslow was a humanistically oriented psychologist who offered a general theory of human functioning. His ideas were applied by others to the work setting.

Maslow proposed five classes of human need. Briefly, these are:

1 *Physiological*: need for food, drink, sleep, suitable ambient temperature etc., i.e. the most fundamental biological needs.

2 *Safety*: need for physical and psychological safety, i.e. a predictable and non-threatening environment.

3 *Belongingness*: need to receive support, affection, love and interpersonal warmth.

4 *Esteem*: need to feel valued and respected. There are two components: self-esteem and the respect, recognition and esteem of other people.

5 *Self-actualisation*: need to fulfil one's potential, to develop one's capacities and express them.

Maslow proposed that we strive to progress up the hierarchy shown in Figure 7.1. When one need is satisfied to some (unspecified) adequate extent, the next one up the hierarchy becomes the most important in driving our behaviour.

Other psychologists produced rather similar analyses. For example, Alderfer (1972) proposed three classes of need: existence, relatedness and growth. Existence equated to Maslow's physiological and safety needs. Relatedness can be matched to belongingness and the esteem of others. Growth is equivalent to self-esteem and self-actualisation. Both

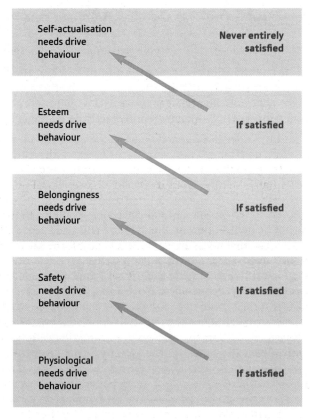

Note: start at the bottom!

Figure 7.1   Maslow's hierarchy of needs

Maslow and Alderfer made propositions about how particular needs become more or less important to the person (i.e. process), but need theories are often thought of as examples of content theories because of their emphasis on describing the needs in some detail.

For some years, need theories (especially Maslow's) dominated work motivation. Unfortunately, evaluations of them (e.g. Wahba and Bridwell, 1976; Salancik and Pfeffer, 1977; Rauschenberger et al., 1980) revealed a number of significant flaws, such as:

- needs did not group together in the ways predicted;
- the theories did not offer reliable predictions of when particular needs would become important;
- there was no clear relationship between needs and behaviour, so that (for example) the same behaviour could reflect different needs, and different behaviours the same need;
- needs were generally described with insufficient precision;
- the whole notion of need as a biological phenomenon is problematic. It ignores the capacity of people and those around them to construct their own perceptions of needs and how they can be met. Some (e.g. Cooke et al., 2005) have argued that Maslow's whole theory is a product of the context of the Cold War, with the tensions between religion and secularism, and between individualism and conformity that existed at the time the theory was constructed.

Key learning point

Need theories have intuitive appeal and provide possible explanations for some human behaviour, but research suggests that they are difficult to apply successfully to the work context.

Despite these limitations, in our experience many managers feel that the hierarchy of needs is helpful in understanding the behaviour of people who work for them, and that it gives important clues about how to motivate those people. Also, some research does support key aspects of the theory. For example, Taormina and Gao (2013) have developed a robust questionnaire measure of need satisfaction using Maslow's hierarchy. They demonstrated that satisfaction of a need went hand in hand with satisfaction of the need immediately below it in the hierarchy, just as the theory predicts. In their synthesis of different approaches to motivation (about which there will be more in this chapter), Locke and Latham (2004) argue that needs are the starting point for motivation, even if not necessarily the most useful focal point for research and practice.

Maslow's ideas still enjoy some support, and some research claims to support some of his predictions, though often the connections between what is measured in the research and Maslow's original concepts looks rather weak (e.g. Reiss and Havercamp, 2005). In our experience students can often relate to his theory. Even some of those who want to amend his theory believe that it says something profound about human nature. For example, Rowan (1998: 81) said, 'I am merely trying to tidy up the Maslow theory, which seems to me extraordinarily useful in general.' As well as emphasising the importance of distinguishing between the two types of esteem, Rowan proposed that a need for competence should be added to the hierarchy, probably between safety and belongingness. This need reflects our desire to master certain skills and do something well for the pleasure in being able to do it. As we will see shortly, the need for competence has also featured in some other motivation theories. Rowan also argued that there may be two kinds of self-actualisation. The first is where a person is able to express their real self. The second is something more mystical – a sense of closeness with God or humanity as a whole which goes beyond (transcends) the self. This distinction was evident in some of Maslow's later work, which drew upon ideas from Asian psychology and religion including Taoism and Zen Buddhism (Cleary and Shapiro, 1996).

Need for achievement

Several alternative need-based approaches to motivation have been developed over many years. They concentrate on a small number of specific needs. Like Maslow's hierarchy, they are rooted in general personality theory. **Need for achievement** is the one most often considered in work contexts. It is one of the 20 needs underlying behaviour proposed by Murray (1938). It concerns the desire 'to overcome obstacles, to exercise power, to strive to do something difficult as well and as quickly as possible' (Murray, 1938: 80–81, quoted by Landy, 1989: 73). Typically, people with high need for achievement seek tasks that are fairly difficult, but not impossible. They like to take sole responsibility for them, and want frequent feedback on how well they are doing.

Need for achievement formed the basis of McClelland's (1961) theory of work motivation. McClelland argued that a nation's economic prosperity depends partly on the level of need for achievement in its population. He based this argument on a statistical relationship between the economic performance of countries and the prominence of themes of achievement in popular children's stories in each country. He also believed that people could be trained to have a high need for achievement. As for personal success, Parker and Chusmir (1991) found that people with high need for achievement tend to feel more successful regarding status/wealth, professional fulfilment and contribution to society than those with lower need for achievement.

Need for achievement has attracted considerable attention in both theoretical and applied contexts (e.g. see Beck, 1983). It is not a simple construct, however, and several attempts have been made to identify its components (e.g. Cassidy and Lynn, 1989). Sagie et al. (1996) argued that it is important to restrict analysis to the level of tasks, as opposed to wider considerations of status and power. They proposed six task preferences that signal high need for achievement:

1   Tasks involving uncertainty rather than sure outcomes.
2   Difficult tasks rather than easy ones.
3   Tasks involving personal responsibility, not shared responsibility.

4   Tasks involving a calculated risk, rather than no risk or excessive risk.

5   Tasks requiring problem-solving or inventiveness, rather than following instructions.

6   Tasks that gratify the need to succeed, rather than ensuring the avoidance of failure.

Exercise 7.1   Need for achievement – always a good thing?

Take a close look at the six task preferences associated with need for achievement. In what respects is need for achievement a good thing in your kind of work or study, and in what respects could it be a bad thing?

Sagie et al. (1996) reported a five-country study of levels of achievement motivation. People from the USA generally scored highest on most components, followed by people from the Netherlands and Israel, with those from Hungary lower and those from Japan lower again, except on the first component, where Japanese people scored close to Americans. However, it is important to remember that need for achievement is not the only route to successful work performance. Also, need for achievement may be a very Western and individualistic concept, of little relevance to some other cultures. In fact, the link that McClelland claimed between achievement themes in children's stories and national prosperity has often been questioned. For example, an analysis of economic growth over 50 years by Beugelsdijk and Smeets (2008) found no relationship between growth and a country's need for achievement score based on McClelland's data from the mid-20th century. Of course, this may be because the need for achievement data were out of date, or indeed were inaccurate from the start.

A person's need for achievement is often assessed using *projective* tests, which involve the person interpreting ambiguous stimuli. For example, a person may be asked to make up a story about what is happening in a short series of pictures. It is assumed that people *project* their personality onto the stimuli through their interpretations. Need for achievement can also be assessed in a more straightforward manner using questions about the person's behaviour, thoughts and feelings as in a personality questionnaire. Spangler (1992) reviewed the relevant literature and found that scores on most assessments of need for achievement are indeed correlated with outcomes such as career success. Also, despite the generally poor record of projective tests in psychology, projective measures of need for achievement correlated more highly with outcomes than did self-report questionnaire measures.

Key learning point

At least in Western contexts, need for achievement is a sufficiently specific and valid construct to explain some aspects of work behaviour, including managerial behaviour.

One criticism of McClelland's work is that it was always unclear exactly how need for achievement eventually translated into economic success. McClelland himself thought that it was partly through high levels of successful entrepreneurial activity. There is mixed evidence on this. For example, Hansemark (2003) did not find that people with a high need for achievement were more likely than others to start up their own business. However, Rauch and Frese (2007) did find that high need for achievement was modestly associated with success among people who were already entrepreneurs. More generally, it is likely that if a person does not have much control over his or her situation, then high need for achievement is likely to be a source of frustration. In turn, this can lead a person to adopt an authoritarian approach to managing others as an attempt to regain control (Winter, 2010). Winter also argues that in politics and perhaps also in high level management, need for *power* is a better predictor of success than need for achievement. This is because the key to these roles is not so much to complete tasks yourself, but to ensure that decisions are acted upon by others.

Expectancy theory: what's in it for me?

Whereas need theories place heavy emphasis on the content of motivation, expectancy theory concentrates on the process. Originally proposed by Vroom (1964), expectancy theory (also sometimes called VIE – valence, instrumentality, expectancy – theory, or instrumentality theory) aimed to explain how people choose which of several possible courses of action they will pursue. This choice process was seen as a cognitive, calculating appraisal of the following three factors for each of the actions being considered:

1 *Expectancy*: If I tried, would I be able to perform the action I am considering?

2 *Instrumentality*: Would performing the action lead to identifiable outcomes?

3 *Valence*: How much do I value those outcomes?

Vroom (1964) proposed that expectancy and instrumentality can be expressed as probabilities (from zero to one), and valence as a subjective value. He also suggested that force to act is a function of the product of expectancy, instrumentality and valence: in other words, V, I and E are multiplied together to determine motivation. This would mean that if any one of the components was zero, overall motivation to pursue that course of action would also be zero. This can be seen in Figure 7.2, where, for example, the instrumentality question is not even worth asking if a person believes they are incapable of writing a good essay on motivation.

Notice how little attention VIE theory pays to explaining *why* an individual values or does not value particular outcomes. No concepts of need are invoked to address this question. VIE theory proposes that we should ask someone how much they value something, but not bother about *why* they value it. This is an illustration of VIE theory's concentration on process, not content.

If correct, VIE theory would have important implications for managers wishing to ensure that employees were motivated to perform their work duties. They would need to ensure that all three of the following conditions were satisfied:

1 Employees perceived that they possessed the necessary skills to do their jobs at least adequately (*expectancy*).

2 Employees perceived that if they performed their jobs well, or at least adequately, they would be rewarded (*instrumentality*).

3 Employees perceived the rewards offered for successful job performance to be attractive (*valence*).

Key learning point

Expectancy theory proposes that people's choice of course of action depends upon their beliefs about: (i) their own capabilities; (ii) whether the course of action will lead to rewards; and (iii) how valuable the rewards are.

Motivation to write an essay on motivation

Expectancy	X	Instrumentality	X	Valence
Question: How likely is it that I am capable of writing a good essay on motivation?		*Question:* How likely is it that I will receive rewards for writing a good essay on motivation?		*Question:* How much do I value those rewards?
Considerations: General self-efficacy Specific self-rated abilities Past experience of essay writing		*Considerations:* The weight attached to the mark in the assessment system The accuracy of the marking Likelihood of intrinsic rewards such as learning or satisfaction		*Considerations:* Importance of passing the course Interest in the subject Extent of commitment to self-development

Figure 7.2   An example of VIE theory in action

Exercise 7.2   Applying expectancy theory

Go back to the opening case study and look at the list of reasons why someone who appears unmotivated might actually not be 'lazy'. Which of those reasons reflect V, I or E? Can you use these three concepts to add to that list of possible reasons?

Although it looks attractive, VIE theory has not done especially well when evaluated in research. Like need theories, it has rather gone out of fashion as a free-standing theory. Van Eerde and Thierry (1996) found 74 published research studies on VIE theory prior to 1990 but only 10 subsequently. Van Eerde and Thierry (1996), and also Schwab et al. (1979), summarised the available research and drew the following conclusions. The first four reflect badly on VIE theory as a whole. The other two are more to do with limitations of research design rather than the theory itself.

- Research studies that have not measured expectancy, or have combined it with instrumentality, have accounted for effort and/or performance better than studies that assessed expectancy and instrumentality separately. This means that expectancy might not operate in the way specified in the theory.
- Behaviour is at least as well predicted by adding the three components V, I and E as it is by multiplying them.
- The theory does not work where any of the outcomes have negative valence (i.e. are viewed as undesirable) (Leon, 1981).
- The theory works better when the outcome measure is an attitude (for example an intention to act or a preference) than when it is a behaviour (performance, effort or choice).

■ Self-report measures of V, I and E have often been poorly constructed, so we cannot be sure that V, I and E are actually being measured and perhaps other variables might be coming into play.

■ Most research has compared different people with each other (i.e. between-participants research design), rather than comparing different outcomes for the same person (i.e. within-participants design). The latter enables a better test of VIE theory because the theory was designed to predict whether an individual will prefer one course of action over another, rather than whether one person will favour a course of action more than another person does. Where within-participant designs are used, results tend to be more supportive of the theory.

Key learning point

Expectancy theory may over-complicate the cognitive processes involved in motivation, but is a helpful logical analysis of key factors in the choices made by individuals.

Nevertheless, expectancy theory is still sometimes used in analysing motivation. Like Maslow's hierarchy, some managers like it because it gives a clear list of the different components of motivation, some of which they may be able to do something about. For example, Chiang and Jang (2008) found that expectancy, instrumentality and valence all made separate contributions to the motivation of hotel employees. Vansteenkiste et al. (2005) found that, among unemployed people, the value they placed on employment (valence) increased their distress at being unemployed, while their belief that they could get a job if they wanted to (expectancy) decreased their distress. Reinforcing Van Eerde and Thierry's (1996) conclusion that attitudes are better predicted by expectancy theory than behaviours are, Renko et al. (2012) found that while valence, instrumentality and expectancy all predicted intention to put a lot of *effort* into starting a business among potential entrepreneurs, none of them predicted the *completion of activities* required to set up a new company.

Justice and citizenship theories: am I being fairly treated?

Justice theories are like expectancy theory, in that they focus on the cognitive processes that govern a person's decision whether or not to expend effort. However, unlike expectancy theory they suggest that people want fairness above all. Some students and managers find it hard to believe that people might not always seek to maximise their gains, but let us suspend disbelief for the moment and consider the propositions of the original justice theory: **equity theory**.

Equity theory was derived from work by Adams (1965), originally in the context of interpersonal relationships. Huseman et al. (1987: 222) described the propositions of equity theory like this:

■ Individuals evaluate their relationships with others by assessing the ratio of their outcomes from and inputs to the relationship against the outcome:input ratio of a comparison other.

■ If the outcome:input ratios of the individual and comparison other are perceived to be unequal, then inequity exists.

■ The greater the inequity the individual perceives (in the form of either over-reward or under-reward), the more distress the individual feels.

■   The greater the distress an individual feels, the harder they will work to restore equity. Equity restoration techniques include altering or cognitively distorting inputs or outcomes, increasing or decreasing the amount of effort devoted to the task, acting on or changing the comparison other, or terminating the relationship.

In other words, a person is motivated to maintain the same balance between their contributions and rewards as that experienced by salient comparison person or persons. Research way back in the 1960s and 1970s provided some support for equity theory (e.g. Pritchard, 1969), especially in laboratory-based studies where the key constructs of the theory could be controlled and measured. However, perhaps unsurprisingly, the predictions of equity theory are less often supported by research when people receive more than their share as opposed to when they receive less (Mowday, 1991). In other words, we are more likely to do something in response to feeling under-rewarded than over-rewarded. Furthermore, rather like need theories, equity theory offers only vague predictions about exactly what people will do when they are dissatisfied. They might adopt any or all of the equity restoration devices listed above, and they might choose any of a number of comparison others. Equity theory is not good at specifying which restoration devices and which comparison others will be used (Greenberg, 2001).

Key learning point

The equity theory of motivation asserts that people are motivated by the fairness of the rewards they receive relative to the contributions they make, in comparison with other people.

Equity theory has been broadened into theories of organisational justice from the late 1980s onwards (see, for example, Cropanzano et al., 2001; Greenberg and Colquitt, 2013). These theories focus on perceptions of fairness in the workplace. They have become very popular and widely researched, perhaps because organisational change processes such as mergers and downsizing have brought issues of fairness to the fore. Equity theory refers mainly to what is called *distributive justice*: that is, whether people believe they have received (or will receive) fair rewards. However, this is only one kind of justice. There have been debates about how many different kinds of workplace justice can be identified (see Colquitt et al., 2001), but most work psychologists would say there are at least two more. *Procedural justice* reflects whether people believe that the procedures used in an organisation to allocate rewards are fair. Interactional justice refers to whether people believe they are treated in an appropriate manner by others at work, especially authority figures. The three forms of justice are depicted in Table 7.1.

If people believe that they are poorly paid relative to people doing similar jobs in other organisations, they may perceive distributive injustice. If at the same time they think their employing organisation is making available as much money for pay as possible, and operating fair systems to distribute them, then they may perceive procedural justice. If their bosses discuss pay openly and courteously, they may perceive interactional justice. Their satisfaction with pay would probably be low, but their commitment to their employer might well be high (McFarlin and Sweeney, 1992; Olkkonen and Lipponen, 2006).

Key learning point

The role of fairness and justice in motivation is becoming more prominent, and concerns a person's perceptions of the fairness of: (i) who gets what; (ii) the systems used to decide who gets what; and (iii) the courtesy and openness of interpersonal behaviour.

Table 7.1	Three forms of justice at work		
Distributive justice (appropriateness of outcomes)	**Procedural justice (appropriateness of the allocation process)**	**Interactional justice (appropriateness of the treatment received)**	
Appropriateness can be judged in various ways: *Equity* (as in equity theory) means that employee outcomes depend on their contributions. Alternatives include *equality* (everyone gets the same reward) and *need* (people get what they require).	This is said to depend on a number of factors: *Lack of bias* for or against any individual or group, i.e. consistent process. *Accuracy of information* used to make decisions. *Representation* for all stakeholders. *Correction of errors* or injustices via appeal or review procedure. *Ethical* codes of conduct are followed.	This has two components, which are sometimes considered two separate forms of justice: *Interpersonal* refers to the extent to which people are treated with dignity, courtesy and respect. *Informational* concerns the extent to which relevant information is shared with employees.	

Source: Adapted with permission from Cropanzano et al., 2007: 36.

Ideas about workplace justice have now been prominent for long enough to attract some close scrutiny. Helpful reviews of this field have been offered by Colquitt et al. (2005) and Fortin (2008). From the perspective of motivation, it is important to ask whether justice affects the direction, effort and persistence of work behaviour, and if so why? Starting with why, some people argue that justice is a moral virtue in itself, requiring no further justification other than to point out that it upholds human dignity. An alternative perspective is that being treated fairly signals that you personally are a valued member of a community, thus validating your personal and social identity. A more instrumental interpretation is that fairness enables you to control and predict what will happen to you in the future. Cropanzano and Stein (2009) argue that studies of organisational justice, including their own, don't pay enough attention to the moral dimension.

Point of integration

A key area in which perceived justice is important is the assessment of work performance (see Chapter 5). If assessment methods are not thought to be accurate or fairly administered, they are likely to be considered unfair. You may also notice some similarities with effort-reward imbalance models of work-related stress (see Chapter 10) that describe how increases in effort in an attempt to obtain reward can place worker well-being at risk.

A lot of evidence indicates that the three forms of justice are associated with motivation and performance, with motivation being the route through which justice leads to performance (see for example Zapata-Phelan et al., 2009). Notice that equity theory predicted that people would be motivated to achieve justice, whereas it seems here that the perception of justice leads to motivation. Why might that be? The most common explanation is based on social exchange – a person feels grateful to the organisation for doing things fairly, and responds by working harder, almost as a 'thank you'. However, social exchange may not be the only route. Aryee et al. (2015) argue that justice also improves people's opportunities to exercise self-determination at work, and that this motivates good work performance. We will revisit the concept of self-determination a little later in this chapter.

Another important consequence of perceived justice is a willingness to be 'good citizens' at work (see for example Liden et al., 2003; Brebels et al., 2014). This, too, is consistent with a social exchange explanation for the effects of justice. Since the early 1990s, psychologists have shown a lot of interest in what have become known as organisational citizenship behaviours (OCBs) (for a recent review see Podsakoff et al., 2014). OCBs include the following:

- *Altruism*: helping another person with a work task or problem.
- *Conscientiousness*: going well beyond minimum role requirements.
- *Civic virtue*: participation and involvement in the life of the organisation.
- *Courtesy*: preventing interpersonal problems through polite and considerate behaviour.
- *Sportsmanship*: willingness to tolerate less than ideal circumstances without complaining.

The interest in OCBs partly reflects a realisation that successful work organisations need people who help each other out in addition to doing the core tasks of their jobs well. OCBs are an interesting area for scholars of motivation, because they are usually thought to be discretionary – that is, a person has choice over whether they perform them – and OCBs have beneficial effects on organisational performance (Podsakoff et al., 2009).

The presence of one form of justice can at least partially offset the negative effects of the lack of another form (Cropanzano et al., 2007). For example, if your annual performance review does not lead to the bonus you feel you deserve (distributive injustice), but if you perceive the review process as meeting the criteria for procedural justice shown in Table 7.1, your motivation will be less (or not at all) adversely affected than if you also thought the process was unjust. Another plus would be if you were given the chance to state your views (interactional justice). In fact, there is some long-established evidence that this chance to have a say seems to help even when it cannot make a difference to the outcome (Folger et al., 1979). On the other hand, if people feel that in the past they have been repeatedly asked for their views and then ignored, being asked again can be more demotivating than not being asked, because it seems to be a sham and therefore a violation of interactional (and possibly procedural) justice (Folger, 1977). For example, this can be a problem in employee participation processes that are poorly executed (see Chapters 10 and 11).

Stop to consider

From your experience of the workplace, to what extent do you think that people care about the three forms of justice shown in Table 7.1? Do they care about it when other people are victims of injustice, or only when they themselves are? Do they ever believe they have been treated unfairly generously, and if so what, if anything, do they do about it?

How generalisable is fairness as a motivator across different parts of the world? Bolino and Turnley (2008) have presented an interesting analysis of how equity theory (see above) might affect behaviour differently across cultures. For example, they suggest that in collectivist cultures people are likely to choose a group (e.g. people in my occupation) as their comparison other, whereas people in individualistic cultures are more likely to choose individuals (e.g. a person who started working here at the same time as me). Li and Cropanzano (2009) applied somewhat similar reasoning in a meta-analysis of cross-cultural research on organisational justice, and concluded that the effects of organisational justice tend to be greater in the individualist culture of North America than the collective cultures of East Asia, where injustice might feel less personal, and where there is a cultural norm of social harmony that might inhibit complaint.

Key learning point

The motivation to perform 'good citizen' behaviours is currently a topic of considerable interest to psychologists. This motivation is enhanced by a sense of justice.

Cropanzano et al. (2007) offer some helpful though not particularly novel suggestions to managers about how to use insights from justice theory in managing people. For example, they highlight the importance of giving people every opportunity to show what they can do during selection and promotion processes. It is probably important both practically and morally that justice is implemented because it is valued, and not simply as a manipulation to increase employee compliance:

> Organizational justice allows managers to make tough decisions more smoothly ... power will be used in accordance with normative principles that reflect the dignity of all involved. This is sound business advice. It is also the right thing to do.

> (Cropanzano et al., 2007: 45, emphasis in original)

It is important not to get too starry-eyed about justice. At any given time, even in the best-run workplaces, there will always be some people who think something is unfair. That is partly because, although people often distinguish between what is good for them and what is fair, there is some overlap between outcome favourability and distributive justice (Fortin, 2008). In other words, we tend to be more tolerant of being over-rewarded than under-rewarded. Also, the various forms of justice do tend to go together. In the performance review example above, if we do not get the outcome we think we deserve (i.e. distributive injustice), we will probably explain it in terms of something wrong with the system (i.e. procedural injustice).

Key learning point

Perceived justice has significant consequences for people's work motivation and performance.

Goal-setting theory: how can I achieve my aims?

The theory

This approach to motivation was pioneered in the USA by Ed Locke and his associates, starting in the 1960s. It continued with increasing strength and sophistication – so much so, that by the 1990s well over half the research on motivation published in leading academic journals reported tests, extensions or refinements of goal-setting theory.

As Locke et al. (1981: 126) put it, 'A goal is what an individual is trying to accomplish; it is the object or aim of an action. The concept is similar in meaning to the concepts of purpose and intent.' Locke drew on both academic writing on intention (Ryan, 1970) and the much more practical 'management by objectives' literature in formulating his ideas. Figure 7.3 represents goal-setting theory, and provides the key concepts for this section.

The most fundamental proposition of goal-setting theory is that in most circumstances goals that are difficult but not impossible, and that are expressed in terms of a clearly defined performance level, produce higher levels of performance than other kinds of goals, or an absence of goals. In particular, goals of this kind produce better performance than vague

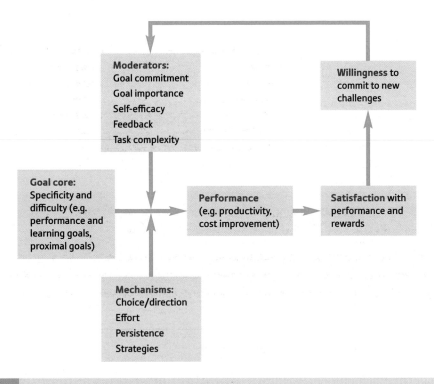

| Figure 7.3 | Essential elements of the goal-setting cycle |

'do your best' goals. Difficult and specific goals have this effect by focusing a person's attention on the task, increasing the amount of effort they put into it, increasing the length of time they keep trying, and encouraging the person to develop strategies for goal achievement. These fundamental ideas of goal-setting theory have, of course, found expression in popular management practice, particularly in the form of so-called 'SMART' – specific, measureable, agreed, realistic and time-based – goals.

Over the years it has been recognised that the goal-setting process can't always be quite that simple, for two main reasons. First, people and circumstances vary, sometimes in ways which affect the goal-setting process. Second, although the words and ideas in goal-setting theory are clear enough, applying them to any work situation is more complex than it initially seems. This is not a weakness of the theory, it's just how life is!

Some of these complexities have been incorporated into the goal-setting framework, and are shown as 'moderators' in Figure 7.3. **Goal commitment** and *goal importance* both signal that the effect of goals on behaviour and performance is likely to be much greater if the goals matter greatly to a person than if they do not. Goal commitment can be defined as an unwillingness to abandon or lower the goal (Wright et al., 1994). *Self-efficacy* reflects the point from expectancy theory that a person's belief that they are capable, or can become capable, of performing the necessary behaviours is an important component of motivation. There is good evidence that self-efficacy affects the level of difficulty of goals a person will be willing to feel committed to (Wooford et al., 1992), which shows that these moderators inter-relate. It also seems to be the case that people with high self-efficacy are better than those with low self-efficacy at developing new strategies in response to failure or difficulty (Latham and Pinder, 2005). The provision of *feedback* on progress towards the goal enables a person to refine their strategies.

While a person might well derive some satisfaction from successful task completion, attaching tangible rewards such as a cash bonus to that achievement will substantially increase the satisfaction, and consequently willingness to take on new challenges, perhaps even more difficult than those before. Locke and Latham (1990) reported that the impact of monetary reward for performance occurs either through raising goal level, or through increasing commitment to a goal – so long as the amount of money on offer is considered significant, and not tied to goals perceived as impossible. In turn, willingness to take on new challenges can affect how committed the person is to a new goal and, of course, over time successful performance is also likely to influence a person's sense of self-efficacy (Bandura, 1997a), hence the feedback loop in Figure 7.3.

Key learning point

The setting of performance goals that are specific and difficult (but not impossible), and to which the person feels committed, is likely to improve their work performance. This is especially the case if the person receives feedback on progress, and rewards for successful performance.

What does research say about goal-setting? Many of the main features of the theory are now well established, having been researched thoroughly (some would say exhaustively) in the 1970s to 1990s. Reviews by Locke and Latham (1990) and Mento et al. (1987) arrived at a number of conclusions, most of which fully or substantially supported goal-setting theory. Locke et al. (1981) reported that in goal-setting field experiments, the median improvement in work performance produced by goal-setting was 16 per cent. Locke and Latham (2002: 708) concluded that:

> With goal-setting theory, specific difficult goals have been shown to increase performance on well over 100 different tasks involving more than 40,000 participants in at least eight countries working in laboratory, simulation and field settings. The dependent variables have included quantity, quality, time spent, costs, job behavior measures, and more. The time spans have ranged from one minute to 25 years. The effects are applicable not only to the individual but also to groups, organizational units, and entire organizations. The effects have been found using experimental, quasi-experimental, and correlational designs. Effects have been obtained whether the goals are assigned, self-set, or set participatively. In short, goal-setting is among the most valid and practical theories of employee motivation in organizational psychology.

Point of integration

A key role of effective leaders (Chapter 12) is in the setting of challenging goals and the creation of conditions in which they can be achieved.

Key learning point

Goal-setting theory is strongly supported by research. The impact of difficult and specific goals on a person's work performance occurs through the focusing of their strategies and intentions, and the mobilisation of their knowledge and ability.

Learning goals and performance goals

Locke (2000: 409) proposed that one way in which goals work is by unlocking or mobilising existing knowledge and skills that are relevant to the task in hand: 'It is a virtual axiom that human action is a consequence of . . . knowledge (including skill and ability) and desire'. This is a reminder of the point made near the start of the chapter that motivation does not provide a complete explanation of performance. Of course, if a person does not have the necessary knowledge or skill, then setting a performance goal is unlikely to be successful, at least in the short term. This is particularly likely when the task is complex (see Figure 7.3). Instead, it is better to set a learning goal (e.g. find five different ways in which the quality of the production process can be monitored) rather than achieving a specific level of performance (e.g. make sure that the production process produces no more than 1 per cent substandard products). Research has shown that on complex tasks with which people are not familiar, setting performance goals hinders their learning of the best strategies, because they are too focused on the outcome itself, and not enough on figuring out the best way to achieve it (e.g. Kanfer and Ackerman, 1989). Seijts and Latham (2012) point out that the purpose of a learning goal is to improve task-relevant knowledge and skills, whereas the purpose of a performance goal is to mobilise already acquired skills and knowledge. A learning goal makes it clear that learning is required before performance can be achieved, and it focuses attention on developing an effective strategy and taking the opportunity to search for better ones.

Point of integration

When employees engage in training and development (see Chapter 9) it is important that they set aside performance goals and adopt learning goals in order to maximise the benefit they derive.

It seems also that people differ in their preferences for learning or performance goals. Dweck (1986) developed a theory of motivation and learning which distinguishes between *learning-goal orientation* and *performance-goal orientation*. A learning goal, which is also sometimes called a mastery goal, 'involves seeking to acquire knowledge or skills, to master or understand something new' (Dweck and Elliott, 1983: 645) while a performance goal concerns obtaining favourable judgements of one's competence, and avoiding unfavourable judgements of one's competence (Dweck and Elliott, 1983: 645). Elliot and Harackiewicz (1996) suggested that the performance-goal orientation should be split into performance-approach (seeking favourable judgements of one's competence) and performance-avoidance (avoiding unfavourable judgements of one's competence). Research has often found that mastery goals are better for performance improvement and psychological well-being than performance goals are, particularly performance-avoidance goals (Elliott et al., 2005). However, much of the relevant research has been conducted in educational settings, so we must be cautious in assuming these findings apply to the workplace. Farr et al. (1993) suggested that there is an increasing and ironic tendency in work organisations for goals to be set which are defined in terms of performance relative to other people, thus encouraging performance-goal orientation rather than learning-goal orientation. Worse, a performance goal is more likely than a mastery goal to lead a person to cheat (Van Yperen et al., 2011).

Point of integration

Learning-goal orientation seems to help people who are searching for a new job. It can be a more positive process for job seekers when they recognise and embrace the opportunities to learn and develop that occur in the job search process, rather than focusing only on the desired outcome of getting a job (see the discussion in Chapter 6).

There is quite a lot of evidence that the processes outlined in goal-setting theory do indeed apply more strongly to people with a learning-goal orientation than those with a performance-goal orientation (e.g. VandeWalle et al., 2001). However, although goal orientations were originally conceived as a fairly constant feature of a person, akin to a personality characteristic, this has been questioned (DeShon and Gillespie, 2005). It seems that a learning-goal orientation is quite easily induced in a given situation, even in those who score high on measures of dispositional performance-goal orientation (Seijts and Latham, 2001).

Stop to consider

Consider the extent to which you use goal-setting to manage and improve your own performance in employment or study. Could you use it more, or better? What special issues arise when goal-setting is used on oneself, rather than being administered by someone else?

Other issues in goals and goal-setting

As noted above, the notion of goal commitment has become very important in goal-setting theory. It is argued that if individuals do not feel commitment to a goal they will not exert effort in pursuit of it – even a difficult and specific one. Commitment is construed as more than simple acceptance of a goal. On the other hand, perhaps the notion of commitment is just another word for motivation – if I am committed to a goal, then that could be another way of saying I am motivated to achieve it. This means that a key focus, perhaps *the* key focus, of goal-setting theory should be how to foster goal commitment. At one time it was argued that the best way to ensure goal commitment is to allow people to participate in discussions about what goals to set (e.g. Erez, 1986). Subsequently, some research has suggested that often participation is not necessary as long as the goal is seen as challenging but not impossible by the person who is expected to achieve it (Locke and Latham, 1990). Then again, where a task is complex the goal assigner may find it difficult to specify a challenging but attainable goal without consultation with those who are to try to achieve it (Haslam et al., 2009). Effective goal-setting requires accurate assessment of whether a task is complex in the perception of the individual doing it, and what level of performance is difficult but not impossible for that person. If the person has a very low level of self-efficacy, even what seems to his/her boss to be only a moderate level of performance can seem too difficult. That is probably why some research still finds that collaborative goal-setting as opposed to assignment of goals helps to raise goal commitment, because participation is perceived to increase procedural fairness (e.g. Sholihin et al., 2011). This is a good example of how elements of different theories can be combined to help explain motivation.

Despite the clarity of goal-setting theory, it is not necessarily simple to implement in the workplace. In most organisations there are multiple goals to be achieved. For whole organisations, and for individuals and groups within them, there may be some conflict between goals. Achievement of one may be at the expense of another. For example, achievement of reductions in staff costs may be at the expense of quality of customer service. So when a manager is given goals to reduce costs by 10 per cent and to increase customer service by a similar amount, each goal on its own may be achievable but in combination they are not. This may well negate the positive effect of goal-setting. Also, a focus on goal achievement may lead to the neglect of ethical practice or increases in risk-taking as a person or team tries to achieve the goal at almost any cost (Barsk, 2008).

In some situations it is not easy to define what is a challenging but attainable goal. Miles and Clenney (2012) use the example of negotiation, where a lack of knowledge of the opposing negotiator's opening position means that what counts as a good outcome is unclear. They found that performance in negotiations was better where the initial goal was impossibly high than when it was challenging but (on the evidence of past similar negotiations) attainable.

Sometimes it takes considerable time and trouble to provide feedback on progress towards the goal, and to link rewards reliably with performance. In this respect there are important dilemmas such as what reward, if any, to use if a person just misses a goal, or if circumstances change part-way through the process, making the goal either easier or harder to achieve. Locke and Latham (2004) offer an interesting analysis of these issues. Shaw (2004) provides a practical illustration of how goals can easily become vague aspirations rather than clear performance targets, and how this problem was addressed at Microsoft.

Key learning point

Although goal-setting theory is well specified and uses well-defined concepts, successful implementation in the workplace still requires skill and sensitivity.

Recently there has been increasing interest in subconscious influences on goal-setting processes. This is partly because goal-setting theory has placed high emphasis on conscious self-regulation and reasoning, possibly at the expense of the unconscious (Latham, 2007: Chapter 9). For example, it seems that a person's achievement motivation and work performance can be influenced by briefly seeing (a few hours earlier) a photograph showing someone winning a race, even though the person is not aware of the connection (Shantz and Latham, 2009; Latham and Piccolo, 2012).

Research methods in focus

A field experiment testing motivation

Gary Latham and Ronald Piccolo (2012) conducted a field experiment to examine the motivation and performance effects of subconscious goal priming. Fifty-eight part-time employees in a US university's fund-raising call centre were divided at random into three groups. In one group, the fact sheet that employees kept in front of them when making calls had a photograph of a woman winning a running race added to the top left of the sheet. The second group had a photo of call centre employees (nobody they knew) looking cheerful and purposeful. It was anticipated that both photos would prime achievement goals without the employees being aware of it, with the call centre photo more effective than the race-winning photo because it was more relevant to the setting. The third group was a control group which had no photo added to the fact sheet.

▶

▶

Numbers of calls made and amounts of money solicited from contacts were recorded in the week before the introduction of the photos and in the week after. Also, immediately after the fact sheets were distributed, employees were asked to write a story about a neutral photograph of a tree or a stationary car. They were told this was a test of imagination, but in fact it was a projective test of achievement motivation (see earlier in this chapter). Their stories were scored for the number of achievement words they contained, such as accomplish, succeed. The employees were also asked after the experiment whether they thought there was any connection between the photo and their work performance. None thought that there was, and many barely noticed the photographs at all.

Results showed that both groups of employees who had a photo on their fact sheet wrote more achievement words than the control group, so it appeared that achievement goals were being subconsciously primed. Both experimental groups achieved an increase relative to the control group in the number of contacts who pledged a donation, and the group with the call centre photo (but not the group with the race-winning photo) achieved an increase in the total amount of money pledged. The authors concluded that achievement goals can be enhanced subconsciously, and that this can lead to better performance, especially if the subconscious prime is relevant to the work setting.

Suggested exercises

1   In the Latham and Piccolo study, what elements of good research design can you see?

2   Can you see any practical or ethical limitations? How confident are you about the generalisability of the findings, and why?

Exercise 7.3   Increasing sales at GoFarAway Holidays

GoFarAway Holidays is a phone- and Internet-based holiday company which is struggling in a competitive market. Each staff member has monthly targets for both number of telephone sales and the value of those sales, and they receive a 5 per cent salary bonus for achieving each of these, so 10 per cent for both. New staff are trained carefully in how to maximise sales and the value of each sale, including extras such as travel insurance and hotel parking. Company attitude surveys indicate that the call centre staff believe they have the skills and knowledge to do the job, but that the sales targets are unrealistically high. They were set several years before, when the market was better, and have not been revisited since. At the time, the targets were slightly above average performance, and sales increased after they were introduced. However, the call centre staff argue that because they deal with incoming calls only, they cannot control the overall potential for sales, only maximise returns from the people who call. Also, GoFarAway offers some holidays at reduced 'special offer' prices. This makes the sales value target even harder to achieve. Staff can use the automated sales system at any time to check their sales figures so far that month. Their calls are not closely scripted, so staff have some freedom to adopt styles that work for them, although calls are monitored and supervisors put a stop to anything they regard as outside company style. One current concern for the company is that although customers like their holidays with GoFarAway, some find the staff they deal with on the phone rather pushy in trying to encourage them to buy more expensive holidays than they intended. In a few extreme cases, this appears to have led to lost sales as potential customers resist this approach.

Suggested exercise

Use goal-setting theory and research to identify the strengths and limitations of GoFarAway's use of goal-setting. How could it be better?

Self-concept and individual differences in motivation

Many approaches to motivation have focused on how our sense of who we are, i.e. our self-concepts, personalities and values, influence the direction, effort and persistence of our behaviour (Leonard et al., 1999). To some extent this is reflected in research on the role of self-efficacy and goal orientation in goal-setting described earlier in this chapter.

However, some work in this area draws on other areas of social psychology, particularly self-categorisation and social identity (Turner and Onorato, 1999; Haslam, 2004). For example, it is proposed that a person does not have just one self-concept (i.e. set of perceptions about their own nature), but many. One distinction is between personal identity, which represents how we see ourselves relative to others in the same social groups, and social identity, which is those aspects of self-concept we think we have in common with others in the same group, and which differentiate us from members of other groups. We have many different personal and social identities, depending on which social group is most salient to us at any given time. Furthermore, we are motivated to behave in ways that are consistent with our identity, or perhaps in some cases our ideal self (how we would *like* to be). In a work context this might mean that if our social identity as (for example) a member of the marketing department is most salient, then we will be motivated to perform behaviours that support the value of marketing as a work activity and perhaps also the value of our marketing colleagues. On the other hand, if our personal identity as an ambitious young manager is most salient, we are more likely to pursue behaviours that we see as being in our own interest, such as concentrating on our own work or making ourselves look good in front of the boss in case there is a promotion opportunity on the horizon (Haslam et al., 2000; Van Knippenberg, 2000). Lewis (2011) argues that taking into account social identities is an important development in motivation theory because it gets away from seeing motivation purely as an individual phenomenon, and because it may reflect how people think, especially in more collectivist societies.

Intrinsic motivation, extrinsic motivation and self-determination theory

Studies have found that when asked what motivates them at work the majority of people give answers such as variety, responsibility, recognition for achievements, interesting work and job challenge rather than pay or working conditions (e.g. Herzberg, 1966). Herzberg's work has been influential in steering managers towards altering people's jobs rather than pay regimes in order to increase motivation. It relates closely to a broad distinction between *intrinsic motivation* and *extrinsic motivation*, which is often used in discussions about motivation. Ryan and Deci (2000: 56) defined intrinsic motivation as 'the doing of an activity for its inherent satisfactions ... a person is moved to act for the fun or challenge entailed rather than because of external prods, pressures, or rewards'. In contrast, extrinsic motivation 'pertains whenever an activity is done in order to obtain some separable outcome' (Ryan and Deci, 2000: 60).

Essentially then, Herzberg argued that intrinsic motivation is more reliable and powerful than extrinsic motivation as a way of influencing behaviour at work. Intrinsic motivation has clear links with Maslow's esteem and self-actualisation needs. Analysis of extrinsic and intrinsic motivation has been greatly advanced by Ryan and Deci (2000) and Gagné and Deci (2005) who have developed self-determination theory (SDT) and applied it to the workplace (see Figure 7.4).

In SDT, it is assumed that all individuals have a drive towards achieving *competence, relatedness* and *autonomy*, with autonomy playing a particularly important role in motivational processes. According to this theory, where there are no extrinsic or intrinsic rewards, then

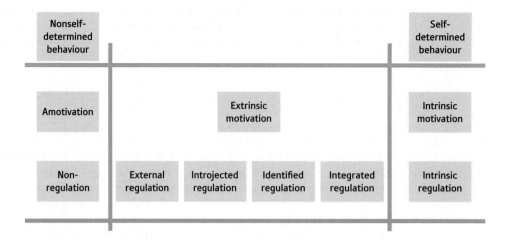

| Figure 7.4 | Self-determination theory |

there is no basis for regulation of behaviour, and no motivation, or *amotivation*, to use the technical term. The presence of extrinsic rewards leads to controlled motivation, where a person's behaviour is governed by rewards other than the joy of the task itself. One of the major contributions of SDT is to break down extrinsic motivation into several different forms. It is important to take a close look at extrinsic motivation because in the workplace the use of extrinsic rewards is very prevalent. In order of increasing feelings of autonomy, these are as follows, with a sample question from a recently developed measure of motivation at work based on SDT (Gagné et al., 2014) as an illustration.

■ *External regulation*: A person performs behaviour in order to satisfy an external demand, and experiences this as externally controlled and not what they would do by choice. The external demands can be social ('because others will respect me more') or material ('because I risk losing my job if I don't put enough effort in it').

■ *Introjected regulation*: Similar to external regulation, except that the person has internalised the external demand enough for it to matter to their sense of self-esteem ('because it makes me feel proud of myself').

■ *Identified regulation*: A person accepts an external demand or reward as being of personal importance, and therefore also uses self-regulation in order to perform the required behaviours ('because putting effort into this job has personal significance to me').

■ *Integrated regulation*: Similar to identification, but the person not only accepts external rewards or requirements as important, but also as an expression of self ('because my work is a big part of who I am' – this item not from Gagné et al., but from Moran et al., 2012, instead).

Rather similar to Maslow's concept of self-actualisation, *intrinsic motivation* is seen as the most desirable outcome, most reflective of development of competence, relatedness and (especially) autonomy. A sample item from Gagné et al. (2014) is 'because I have fun doing my job'.Recognising that few of us work only because it's fun, psychologists have made a broad distinction between autonomous motivation (intrinsic, integrated and identified) and controlled motivation (external, introjected). The autonomous motivations generally lead to better levels of performance and well-being than the controlled ones (e.g. Bono and Judge, 2003; Welters et al., 2014). This is consistent with the idea that, as Maslow said, we strive towards self-expression in our work. Still, Gagné et al.

(2014) found that even though forms of autonomous motivation were consistently predictive of good performance and well-being, controlled motivation was not on the whole harmful. Only amotivation was strongly associated with poor performance and poor well-being.

Key learning point

The distinction between intrinsic and extrinsic motivation is important conceptually, but in practice it is blurred. Over time, people can incorporate extrinsically rewarded behaviour into their views of themselves at work.

Pay as a motivator

The most obvious extrinsic reward is, of course, pay. In the case of external regulation, a person might do the work required simply because they need the pay to live. If it was a case of introjected regulation, then the person would also feel that what they earned was to some extent a reflection of their personal worth in the organisation and/or society. Identification would mean that the person viewed him or herself as someone who cared quite a lot about money (and would therefore work for it), while in the case of integrated regulation, money earned would be a central part of the person's self-concept and getting it would be an absolute necessity to retain not only a way of life but also a self-image.

Herzberg (1966) and others tend to argue that pay is not a key motivator at work, though it is acknowledged that this conclusion depends on some basic level of pay being provided in order to meet basic needs. Self-determination theory and research support the conclusion that when a person views pay as a mechanism for controlling their work behaviour, it will be less motivating than a set of circumstances in which they feel they want to perform the required behaviours for their own sake. For Maslow, pay would be a motivator only for people functioning at the lower levels of the hierarchy of needs. Advocates of need for achievement point to the fact that pay and other material rewards often signal that a person is successful. So from this perspective pay is a motivator if and when it indicates that the person has succeeded in their work tasks. In expectancy theory, pay will be an effective motivator to the extent that it is desired by the person, *and* they can identify behaviours that will lead to high payment, *and* they feel capable of performing those behaviours. Locke and Latham (2002) provide a useful analysis of the advantages and disadvantages of different ways of achieving these connections.

From the perspective of organisational justice, people will be concerned with whether their pay is a fair reward relative to the rewards received by others. They will also want to see fair procedures for allocating pay. A common problem for performance-related pay is that these procedures are often *not* seen as fair. Bloom (1999) studied the pay of North American baseball players over the years 1985 and 1993 and found that the more equal the pay of the different players in the team, the better individuals and teams performed. This suggests that the pay of others matters as well as our own, and that having a small number of highly paid 'superstars' is not a good move.

Goal-setting theory normally involves goals that are defined in terms of a person's behaviour and/or accomplishments, not pay. Nevertheless, if there is a very clear and direct link between a person's accomplishments and pay, then specific, difficult goals defined in terms of earnings may be motivating. On the other hand, when pay is an indicator of how well a person is doing *compared with others*, we can expect it to encourage a performance-goal orientation rather than a learning-goal orientation. As noted above, this may encourage some dysfunctional behaviour.

Rynes et al. (2004) have argued forcefully that the importance of pay as a motivator is often underestimated by human resource managers. This is partly because of the work of Herzberg and Maslow, and partly because other research (e.g. Jurgensen, 1978) has asked people what motivates them at work and consistently found that pay is reported to be less important than many other things, such as job challenge, interesting work and opportunities for promotion. Rynes et al. argue that people's behaviour suggests that pay is more important to them than they say it is. Perhaps people do not realise the reasons for their own behaviour, or perhaps they do but are embarrassed to admit that pay matters a lot. Rynes et al. argue on the basis of some past research that carefully designed performance-related pay schemes can be shown to enhance performance very effectively, and that people's decisions about which job to take are often made on the basis of pay level. The importance of pay is due to its being what in behaviourist terms is called a 'generalised reinforcer'. As a Beatles song long ago pointed out, money cannot buy love, but it can buy a lot of other things, and people can use it in ways that suit them. This might include non-acquisitive purposes such as giving it away to good causes, using it to pay other people to do things you don't want to do yourself (such as home maintenance), or accessing desired leisure activities (such as joining a sports club).

Key debate

How useful is pay as a motivator?

One controversial idea arising from self-determination theory is that extrinsic rewards such as pay or prizes can actually undermine intrinsic motivation by focusing a person's attention on how much they are being paid for the task rather than how much they enjoy it (Deci and Ryan, 1980). There have been numerous analyses of this issue (see for example Eisenberger et al., 1999) with differing views. In an attempt to bring clarity to the question of how intrinsic and extrinsic rewards interact to affect outcomes, Cerasoli et al. (2014) have conducted a meta-analysis of no fewer than 183 studies reporting data from over 200,000 people. They find that:

1   As one would expect, intrinsic motivation is positively related to performance, especially where performance is measured in terms of quality of work rather than quantity.
2   Where extrinsic incentives are closely tied to work performance levels (for example, performance-related pay), the effect of intrinsic motivation on performance is less strong (but still significant) than when financial incentives are only loosely tied to performance levels (e.g. a salary).
3   Financial incentives and intrinsic motivation had separate and equal effects on overall performance. Where performance was measured in terms of quantity, financial incentives were slightly more important than intrinsic motivation, but where performance was measured in terms of quality, the intrinsic motivation was considerably more important than financial incentives.

Exercise 7.4	New minimum wage: $70,000 a year

Dan Price, C.E.O. of Gravity Payments, surprised his 120-person staff by announcing that he planned over the next three years to raise the salary of every employee to $70,000 a year.

The idea began percolating after Price read an article on happiness by Angus Deaton and Daniel Kahneman, a Nobel Prize-winning psychologist. They found that what they called emotional well-being — defined as "the emotional quality of an individual's everyday experience, the frequency and intensity of experiences of joy, stress, sadness, anger, and affection that make one's life pleasant or unpleasant" — rises with income, but only to a point. And that point turns out to be about $75,000 a year.

His idea bubbled into reality on Monday afternoon, when Mr. Price surprised his 120-person staff by announcing that he planned over the next three years to raise the salary of even the lowest-paid clerk, customer service representative and salesman to a minimum of $70,000.

If it's a publicity stunt, it's a costly one. Mr. Price, who started the Seattle-based credit-card payment processing firm in 2004 at the age of 19, said he would pay for the wage increases by cutting his own salary from nearly $1 million to $70,000 and using 75 to 80 percent of the company's anticipated $2.2 million in profit this year.

The paychecks of about 70 employees will grow, with 30 ultimately doubling their salaries, according to Ryan Pirkle, a company spokesman. The average salary at Gravity is $48,000 a year.

"The market rate for me as a C.E.O. compared to a regular person is ridiculous, it's absurd," said Mr. Price, who said his main extravagances were snowboarding and picking up the bar bill. He drives a 12-year-old Audi, which he received in a barter for service from the local dealer.

"As much as I'm a capitalist, there is nothing in the market that is making me do it," he said, referring to paying wages that make it possible for his employees to go after the American dream, buy a house and pay for their children's education.

Hayley Vogt, a 24-year-old communications coordinator at Gravity who earns $45,000, said, "I'm completely blown away right now." She said she has worried about covering rent increases and a recent emergency room bill.

"Everyone is talking about this $15 minimum wage in Seattle and it's nice to work someplace where someone is actually doing something about it and not just talking about it," she said.

Source: Adapted with permission from the *New York Times* website: http://www.nytimes.com/2015/04/14/business/ owner-of-gravity-payments-a-credit-card-processor-is-setting-a- new-minimum-wage-70000-a-year.html?_r=0 (accessed 19 April 2015)

Suggested exercise

The wage rise to $70,000 might indeed make employees happier, but will it also motivate them to work harder? Use the theories you have encountered so far in this chapter to address this question.

Motivation through job redesign

Much of the discussion so far in this chapter has suggested that motivation is a property of the person. An alternative view is that motivation (or lack of it) is inherent in the nature of jobs. This viewpoint means that we need to look less closely at the person and more closely at what it is about work that can make it motivating.

Early recommendations for how to design jobs focused on efficiency and cost reduction rather than motivation. This usually meant minimising skill requirements of jobs, maximising management control and minimising the time required to perform a task. This may appear to make good sense, especially against economic criteria. Unskilled or semi-skilled labour costs less than skilled labour, and productivity is enhanced if tasks are done quickly. However, as we shall see, jobs designed in this way frequently have human costs, and perhaps economic ones too.

This 'traditional' approach to job design stems from a philosophy called scientific management, or Taylorism, after its creator, F.W. Taylor. Taylor (1911) formulated his ideas in the United States in the early 20th century. As a machine-shop foreman, he felt that workers consistently under-produced, and that the way to prevent this was to:

■ systematically (or 'scientifically') compile information about the work tasks required;

■ remove workers' discretion and control over their own activities;

■ simplify tasks as much as possible;

■ specify standard procedures and times for task completion;

■ use financial (and *only* financial) incentives;

■ by the above methods, ensure that workers could not deceive managers, or hide from them.

This, of course, bears a strong resemblance to the theory X view of human nature (described near the start of this chapter). Observers agree that jobs in many, perhaps most, organisations are implicitly or explicitly based on Taylorism. Some argue that some call centres are the most recent kind of organisation to exhibit Taylorism in a strong form (e.g. Bain et al., 2002).

Key learning point

Scientific management, also known as Taylorism, emphasises standardised methods and minimisation of costs in the design of work.

Taylorism might make for a well-ordered world, but is it a happy and productive one? As long ago as the 1960s, a number of studies seemed to show that work organised along scientific management principles was associated with negative attitudes towards the job, as well as poor mental and/or physical health (e.g. Kornhauser, 1965; Turner and Lawrence, 1965).

These studies of simplified work led to considerable concern about what came to be called *quality of working life* (QWL). Several theoretical perspectives were brought to bear on QWL. One was *job enrichment* – a concept developed through the work of Herzberg (1966) (see also the previous section of this chapter). Herzberg proposed a basic distinction between *hygiene factors* and *motivators*. Hygiene factors included pay, conditions of employment, the work environment and other features extrinsic to the work activities themselves. Motivators included job challenge, recognition and skill use – that is, features appealing to growth needs. On the basis of his data, Herzberg proposed that hygiene factors could not cause satisfaction, but that dissatisfaction could result if they were not present. On the other hand, motivators led to satisfaction: their absence produced not dissatisfaction, but a *lack of satisfaction*. Although Herzberg's data and conclusions can be criticised on several grounds, his recommendation that motivation and/or satisfaction can be enhanced by increasing skill use, job challenge etc. is consistent with much subsequent work.

Another relevant theoretical tradition is *socio-technical systems* (Cherns, 1976, 1987; Heller, 1989). Arising from studies in the immediate post-1945 years, socio-technical theory emphasises the need to integrate technology and social structures in the workplace.

Too often, technology is introduced with scant regard for existing friendship patterns, work groups and status differentials. Socio-technical theory attempts to rectify this, but it also makes wider propositions. For example, it states that job activities should be specified only in so far as necessary to establish the boundaries of that job. It also emphasises that boundaries should be drawn so that they do not impede transmission of information and learning, and that disruptions to work processes should be dealt with at source wherever possible, rather than by managers further removed from the situation. Such principles may seem self-evident, but close examination of many organisations will demonstrate that they are not adhered to. Socio-technical job design therefore emphasises autonomy, decision-making and the avoidance of subordinating people to machines.

Point of integration

The design of workspaces and equipment is also part of job design (see Chapter 8). Job re-design interventions are also used to tackle work-related stress (see Chapter 10).

Whatever their exact theoretical origin, until the early 21st century most attempts to redesign jobs centred on increasing one or more of the following (Wall, 1982):

- *variety* (of tasks or skills);
- *autonomy* (freedom to choose work methods, scheduling and occasionally goals);
- *completeness* (extent to which the job produces an identifiable end result which the person can point to).

This may be attempted in one or more of the following ways:

- *Job rotation*: People rotate through a small set of different (but usually similar) jobs. Rotation is frequent (e.g. each week). It can increase variety.
- *Horizontal job enlargement*: Additional tasks are included in a person's job. They are usually similar to tasks already carried out. This, too, can increase variety.
- *Vertical job enlargement*: Additional decision-making responsibilities and/or higher-level challenging tasks are included in the job. This increases autonomy, variety and possibly completeness. An increasingly commonly used term for this is *empowerment*: a person does not necessarily achieve an increase in formal status, but they are given more freedom to take decisions and implement them according to the needs of the situation at the time (Wang and Lee, 2009).
- *Semi-autonomous work groups*: Similar to vertical job enlargement, but at the level of the group rather than the individual. In other words, a group of people is assigned a task and allowed to organise itself to accomplish it. Semi-autonomous workgroups have been introduced in some car factories.
- *Self-managing teams*: More often composed of managers and professionals than semi-autonomous work groups, these teams are often given considerable freedom to accomplish a group task, and perhaps even to define the task in the first place.

Key learning point

Job redesign can take a variety of forms and arise for many reasons (see Figure 7.5), but it has normally involved an attempt to increase the amount of variety, autonomy and/or completeness inherent in the work of one or more people.

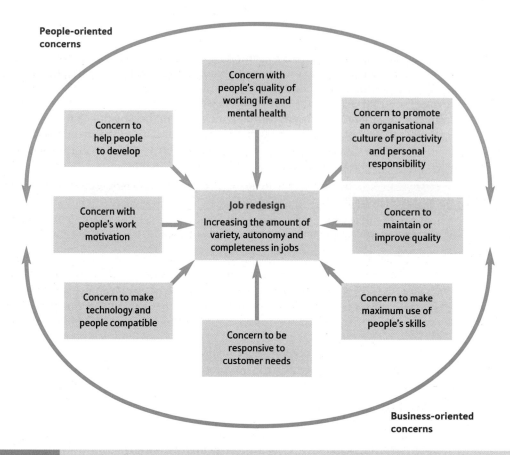

Figure 7.5	Concerns leading to job redesign

Interest in job redesign has been stimulated in more recent years by a mixture of concerns (see Figure 7.5), including the quality of products and services, and the needs for innovation and customer responsiveness. It is argued that well-motivated staff are particularly important for the delivery of outcomes like these (e.g. Shipton et al., 2006). In other words, job redesign is part of hard-headed business strategy rather than (or as well as) a philanthropic concern with the quality of working life. At the same time, cost-cutting and efficiency are also important for organisational competitiveness, so there is much attention to practices such as the use of new technology and so-called 'just in time' and 'lean' production methods. These may not be consistent with the creation of motivating jobs, though they can have benefits for organisational productivity (Birdi et al., 2008; De Treville and Antonakis, 2006).

The question of whether it is possible to design jobs that are both efficient and motivating has been investigated by Morgeson and Campion (2002). They conducted a detailed analysis of a set of jobs in one part of a pharmaceutical company and then redesigned some of them to include more 'scientific management' efficiency-based elements, some to include more variety and autonomy, and some to include more of both. They found that it was possible to increase both elements at the same time, and that this produced some small benefits for efficiency and satisfaction.

The job characteristics model

The *job characteristics model* (JCM) of Hackman and Oldham (1976, 1980) has been very influential. It is depicted in Figure 7.6, which shows that Hackman and Oldham identified five **core job characteristics:**

1   *Skill variety (SV)*: the extent to which the job requires a range of skills.
2   *Task identity (TI)*: the extent to which the job produces a whole, identifiable outcome.
3   *Task significance (TS)*: the extent to which the job has an impact on other people, either inside or outside the organisation.
4   *Autonomy (Au)*: the extent to which the job allows the job holder to exercise choice and discretion in their work.
5   *Feedback from job (Fb)*: the extent to which the job itself (as opposed to other people) provides information on how well the job holder is performing.

The core job characteristics are said to produce '**critical psychological states**'. The first three core job characteristics are believed to influence experienced meaningfulness of the work. Autonomy affects experienced responsibility for outcomes of the work, and feedback from the job impacts on knowledge of the actual results of the work activities. Collectively, the critical psychological states are believed to influence three outcomes: motivation,

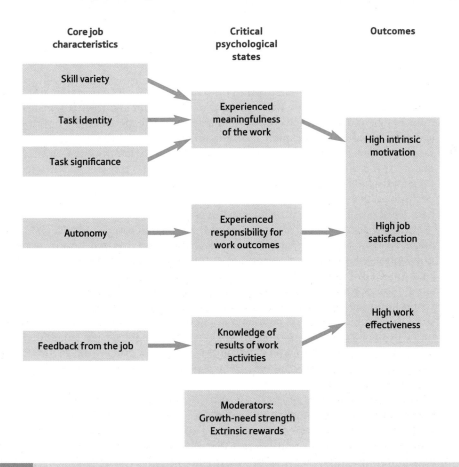

| Figure 7.6 | Hackman and Oldham's job characteristics model |

satisfaction and work performance. This whole process is said to be moderated by several factors (see Figure 7.6). The most often investigated of these is growth-need strength. This refers to the importance to the individual of Maslow's growth needs (see earlier in this chapter). The model is said to apply more strongly to people with high growth needs than to those with low ones.

Key learning point

The job characteristics model specifies five features of jobs that tend to make them intrinsically motivating and satisfying.

The JCM provoked a huge amount of research, especially in the USA. This is not surprising, since it provides specific hypotheses about exactly which job characteristics matter, how they affect people's psychological states, what outcomes they produce, and which individual differences affect the whole process. Also, Hackman and Oldham produced a questionnaire called the Job Diagnostic Survey (JDS) which assesses the constructs shown in Figure 7.6. The JDS is completed by job holders.

A number of helpful observations about the JCM were made in review articles (see, for examples, Fried and Ferris, 1987; Kelly, 1993). In summary, the job characteristics identified by Hackman and Oldham did indeed usually correlate with motivation and satisfaction, though not so clearly with the performance of individuals or organisations. However, there were few studies in which attempts were made to *change* jobs so that they had more of the core job characteristics (which is, after all, the whole point of job redesign). So the correlations between job characteristics and motivation and satisfaction may not have reflected a *causal* relationship. There was also quite a lot of doubt about whether the effects on attitudes and behaviour of each core job characteristic were mediated by the critical psychological states specified by Hackman and Oldham. Indeed, in general the core job characteristics seemed to have more effect on people's attitudes to their work than on their work performance. It was also recognised that additional job characteristics may matter. Warr (1987) suggested availability of money, physical security, interpersonal contact and valued social position as likely contenders. More recently, yet more job characteristics have been identified. These are discussed a little later in this chapter.

Ambrose and Kulik (1999) pointed out that research interest in the JCM decreased very markedly from about the mid-1990s. They argued that this may be appropriate, since it is now quite well understood. Nevertheless, the JCM has stood empirical testing reasonably well, especially considering the relatively large number of connections between specific variables it proposes. Even the more recent reviews acknowledge that the JCM specifies much that is important about jobs and job redesign (Humphrey et al., 2007), despite a clear need to broaden the range of job characteristics beyond those specified in it. The JCM continues to be the foundation of some empirical research on job design (e.g. Millette and Gagné, 2008; DeVaro et al., 2007), and extensions of it to suit virtual working have been proposed by Gibson et al. (2011).

21st-century approaches to work design

The need for employees to be responsive to customers and willing to change and learn is said to be much greater now than it used to be. So is the need to acquire new information rapidly and share it with others who can use it. Some argue that it is better to use the term 'work', because the word 'job' implies a fixed and stable set of duties. Such constancy is rarer than it used to be. This is partly because of the pace of change in the workplace, and partly because people are often encouraged to engage in 'job crafting' (Wrzesniewski and Dutton, 2001), i.e. emphasise some parts of the job at the expense of others in order to maximise their contribution and their fit with their organisation. Clegg and Spencer (2007) offer a helpful analysis of how job crafting and relationships with supervisors can lead to informal job redesign as the incumbent shapes it to what they want and wins the trust of the boss in doing so.

Although it was quickly recognised that the JCM's list of job characteristics was not wide-ranging enough, it took some time for well-developed alternative analyses to appear. The leaders in this respect are Fred Morgeson and Stephen Humphrey in the USA (Morgeson and Humphrey, 2006; Humphrey et al., 2007). They argued that work redesign theory and practice need to take into account all aspects of jobs in order to provide a sound basis for maintaining and improving the motivation, satisfaction and performance of individuals and organisations. Specifically, they make the case that:

- While the JCM focuses mainly on the nature of tasks, it is also necessary to consider the *knowledge* requirements. For example, does a person's work require deep specialist knowledge of an area? Does it require problem-solving, and are there a lot of factors to consider simultaneously? Also, while the JCM characteristic skill variety is important, so is task variety, and the two are not the same.

- Work is not only about tasks and knowledge. It is, for most people, also an intensely *social* activity. Therefore, a complete analysis of the nature of a person's work must include factors like the extent to which they receive social support and feedback from others, and have work which requires interaction and interdependence with others.

- The *context* in which work is carried out is also likely to be important. For example, is a person's workplace well-designed ergonomically (see Chapter 8)? What are the working conditions like in terms of noise, hazards etc.?

Humphrey et al. (2007) have reported a meta-analysis of studies that have tested the statistical relationships of work characteristics with motivation, performance and other outcomes. To the extent that they were able, they used the set of work characteristics developed by Morgeson and Humphrey (2006) for their analysis. Table 7.2 shows some of their results.

Note first of all that there are a lot of empty cells in the table, meaning that as yet there is no evidence about the associations of some of the work characteristics with outcomes. Second, note that the five JCM core job characteristics (autonomy, skill variety, task identity, task significance and feedback from the job) are all quite strongly associated with motivation, job satisfaction and organisational commitment, but not with performance (with the partial exception of autonomy). Again, this illustrates the fact that motivation and performance are not always as closely connected as one might think – other factors matter, too. Third, the strong relationships between information processing and job complexity on the one hand and satisfaction on the other suggest that these two knowledge components may also be significant for motivation. Fourth, there is clear evidence that social factors are related to motivation and (even more) to satisfaction and commitment. Hence it seems that we do indeed need to move beyond the core job characteristics in order to understand how work influences motivation and other outcomes.

Key learning point

The core job characteristics, knowledge requirements and social features of jobs are associated with motivation. Improvements in job performance do not necessarily occur as a direct consequence of changes in job characteristics, even if motivation and/or satisfaction do improve.

Table 7.2 Mean correlations of job characteristics with motivation, satisfaction, performance and commitment

	Work motivation	Work satisfaction	Work performance	Organisational commitment
Task characteristics				
Autonomy	0.27	0.37	0.14	0.30
Task variety		−0.35	−0.03	
Task significance	0.30	0.31		0.34
Task identity	0.17	0.23	0.05	0.18
Feedback from job	0.29	0.33	0.09	0.29
Knowledge requirements				
Information processing		0.31		
Job complexity	0.32	−0.06		
Skill variety	0.30	0.32	−0.03	0.23
Social factors				
Interdependence	0.21	0.23		0.34
Feedback from others	0.22	0.32		
Social support	0.11	0.41		0.56
Interaction outside organisation	0.05			
Work context				
Physical demands		−0.15		
Work conditions		0.20		

Source: Adapted with permission of American Psychological Association from Humphrey et al., 2007: 1342–3.

Of course, these statistical associations do not prove that the work characteristics *cause* the so-called outcomes. Also, even if there is a causal relationship, it is not clear how it works, or whether it does so more strongly for some people than for others. Hackman and Oldham thought that their JCM would apply to some people more strongly than others – for example, those high in 'growth need strength' were expected to respond more favourably to the core job characteristics than those not so high. Pierce et al. (2009) have suggested that at least some work characteristics create a sense of psychological ownership, which in turn leads to the outcomes. Truxillo et al. (2012) argue that, for older workers, some job features such as skill variety become less valued, while others such as task identity may become more so. This is because with age comes increasing desire to use existing skills and fulfil a socially valued role which contributes to coactive well-being.

Making a positive contribution that benefits others has also been the basis of some other recent thinking about work design. Arguing for the importance of social as well as task factors, Grant (2007) uses the term 'relational job design' to reflect this emphasis. Grant proposes that an important part of work motivation is, or can be, the motivation 'to make a prosocial difference' – in other words, to do things that benefit other people. In order to increase this form of motivation, Grant advocates the design of work to include frequent and in-depth contact with beneficiaries, and the opportunity to find out a lot about them. This, he says, will increase the person's perceptions of their impact on beneficiaries, and also foster a sense of commitment to them. These factors will then affect motivation to make a prosocial difference. Grant acknowledges that the notion of impact on beneficiaries overlaps with the JCM core job characteristic of task significance, but argues that his analysis is much more specific about (i) the social aspects of it and (ii) the implications for how relationships at work can and should be designed just as tasks are.

Indeed, the term 'McJob' has entered everyday language. The *Oxford English Dictionary* defines the term as 'an unstimulating, low-paid job with few prospects, especially one created by the expansion of the service sector'.

On the one hand, jobs at McDonald's are in some ways highly controlled, and described by some as robotic. There are strict targets for how long it should take to serve customers. There are strict rules too, down to exactly how many pieces of diced onion there should be with a burger (17). Each person's job is narrow and repetitive. It is often done under considerable pressure due to the volume of customers and the fact that a minority of them behave badly when very small things go wrong.

The wages are low, and in recent years there have been strikes by McDonald's workers striving for what they regard as a living wage. Many employees are not able to get the number of hours they would like at the times that fit in with their other commitments. There are frequent references to how managers earn only a little more than the base-level workers – not nearly enough to compensate for the stress of running a restaurant and ensuring that staffing, hygiene, profit margins and everything else are satisfactory. The McDonald's Workers' Resistance group describes working for the company as 'degrading and dehumanising', with employees' words, actions and interactions with customers all being specified by the company.

Yet there is another way to look at it. For a start at least career progression is possible, even if the manager's job is unappealing to some. McDonald's say that 95% of restaurant managers started out as crew members. Many current and former workers say that McDonald's takes training very seriously in order to ensure that the work is done well and the workers feel confident in their skills. There are eight major training centers around the world. Qualifications are offered from basic skills in maths and English right up to foundation degrees. Awards are given for skills acquired.

Many people who are familiar with McDonald's say there is a strong sense of teamwork amongst staff. Certainly reviews of McDonald's as an employer frequently mention this, and the camaraderie of working together to achieve good customer service sometimes in difficult circumstances. Shifts are referred to as 'crews' to encourage this ethos. There is also a sense that the pace and volume of work helps to avoid boredom.

McDonald's is experienced by many as an inclusive employer, where age, ethnic identity and other individual differences do not get in the way of opportunity. By working at a restaurant you get to see the same colleagues quite frequently, but there is enough variation in shift times to ensure that it's not exactly the same faces day in day out. For many employees, the flexible and perhaps variable hours are not a problem, and may even be convenient. McDonald's say on their website 'The benefits we offer our crew members who work in our restaurants include free meals, 28 days' paid holiday per year, offers with over 1,600 leading retailers including discounts on driving lessons and holidays and the chance to gain a nationally-recognised qualification such as an apprenticeship'.

Suggested exercise

Applying theories of job design to the content of this case study (and to any direct experience of McDonald's you may have) examine the ways in which jobs at McDonald's are likely to be motivating. Are there any factors evident in this case study that are not taken into account by job design theory?

Wider perspectives on work design

Parker (2014) points out that although the long tradition of research and practice in job/work design is rooted in the question of how work can be motivating, the importance of work design is much broader than that.

Work can be more or less good at preserving cognitive capacities, fostering development of skills, supporting work–life balance, stimulating creativity and proactivity, promoting health and well-being, and enabling people to try out alternative roles and identities. There is also evidence that some forms of bureaucracy and work which is either too routinised or (conversely) too cognitively taxing can all impair moral judgement. To a considerable extent, the job characteristics identified in the theories described in this section of the chapter are likely to be relevant to all of these outcomes, but which are most important for which outcomes, and whether more features of jobs need to be identified are unclear.

The processes by which jobs affect people may well not be confined to motivational ones, as assumed by traditional job redesign theories (Parker et al., 2001). For example, autonomy may increase the extent to which a speedy response to events is possible, and also whether employees are able to use their local knowledge to solve problems as and when they arise. Similarly, a much greater range of factors than those suggested in the JCM may affect the impact of job characteristics (and changes in them) on outcomes. For example, the extent to which tasks within an organisation are interdependent affects whether it is best to design work at the individual or group/team level. Parker (2014) rightly points out that in increasingly knowledge-based economies there is a difficult balance to be struck between on the one hand quality control processes that guarantee consistent performance standards and flexibility, and on the other hand the capacity to innovate and exercise expert judgement. This 'ambidexterity' requires skilful handling to ensure that reliability of performance is high while also offering jobs that highly skilled people want to do, and which make use of their expertise.

The outcomes of job redesign should be evaluated at individual, group and organisational levels. As well as motivation, satisfaction and profitability, relevant outcomes might include creativity, innovation, customer satisfaction, accident rates, absence and turnover. Regarding creativity, Elsbach and Hargadon (2006) have argued that, at least for busy professionals, a spell of 'mindless' work during a day may help creativity because it gives them space to think. This interesting suggestion highlights the possibility that it may not be desirable for people to have 'enriched' work all day every day.

Although the terminology differs from what you see in this chapter, some human resource management techniques also relate to work design. A good example is empowerment (Wilkinson, 1998), which refers to attempts to transfer more responsibility and scope for decision-making to people at low levels in an organisation. As Wall et al. (2002) have pointed out, empowerment often means increases in job control, performance monitoring, cognitive demands and possibly role conflict and social contact. It is likely to be embraced most wholeheartedly by people with a proactive personality, and perhaps have most impact in conditions of environmental uncertainty, where it is more likely that local quick decisions will be needed. Another recent management trend is towards 'high involvement work practices', which cover a mixture of human resource initiatives such as teamwork, participation in decision-making and suggestion schemes (Mohr and Zoghi, 2008). Using these practices may well have the effect of altering job characteristics (for example, feedback, task complexity and interdependence) but not explicitly under the label of work/job redesign. Parker (2014) argues that where it is difficult to design jobs that have motivational features such as discretion over when tasks are done, participation in decision-making (for example, about what the system for organising work should be) is a good back-up way of offering people a sense of control over their work.

These broader perspectives on work design take us beyond the focus of this chapter (motivation, in case you had forgotten!) and touch on the content of other parts of this book, particularly stress and well-being. Although inconvenient for this chapter, this more holistic view of what work can do to people and for people is helpful. A good example is provided by Holman (2013), who has analysed a huge amount of data from the 2005 European

Working Conditions Survey across 27 countries in order to create profiles of different kinds of job. Across a range of criteria, Holman identified the following job types:

- *Active*: Complex jobs in terms of demands, but also high autonomy and social support, and with a manageable workload; good opportunities for skill development, job security and working flexibly; high wages.
- *Saturated*: Similar to active, but higher workload and non-standard working hours.
- *Team-based*: High team autonomy and individual job autonomy; above average wages, moderate skills and development opportunities, pre-set and conventional working hours; high job security.
- *Passive-independent*: Low autonomy and social support, but also relatively low demands; high security but low wages and skills/development; pre-set and conventional working hours; high job security.
- *Insecure*: Low work complexity, skills development, pay and job security; few opportunities for flexible working; volume of work moderate.
- *High-strain*: Low work complexity but high workload and often non-standard working hours; high job security, average wages, and low to moderate skills and development.

Point of integration

Analyses of job quality such as Holman's help to tell us about how jobs can foster health or alternatively stress. This is examined further in Chapter 10.

As one might expect, active jobs tend to be the best for job satisfaction and psychological well-being. The others line up in descending order as in the list above, so high-strain jobs tend to be the worst, even worse than insecure ones. Results are a little different for physical well-being. Active jobs are again best and high-strain worst, but insecure and passive jobs are somewhat better than saturated and team-based ones. Holman, and others, argue that country-level institutional and economic factors as well as more local ones can affect jobs. In support of this argument, countries classified by Holman as 'social democratic' (Denmark, Finland and Sweden) had the highest proportion of active jobs (29 per cent). 'Liberal' countries (UK, Ireland) had 17 per cent. Lowest were the 'transitional' countries, mostly those in Eastern European, such as Bulgaria, Hungary and Poland.

Stop to consider

Think about a job you do, or have done. Alternatively, think about the job of someone you know well. Which of Holman's categories would you say it falls into? How motivating would you say it is, and why?

Key learning point

There are many criteria apart from motivation for evaluating whether a job is 'good' or not. These criteria reflect a wide range of indicators of individual, team and organisational performance and well-being.

Integration of motivation theories

There is nowadays general agreement that while some motivation theories get more support from research than others, (i) nearly all of them have something to offer, and (ii) in many respects they are compatible, or at least not contradictory. As Latham and Pinder (2005: 507) put it:

> the antagonisms among theorists that existed throughout much of the twentieth century have either disappeared or have been minimized. Much of the energy expended on theory destruction has been replaced by theory construction aimed at building upon what is already known.

To illustrate this point, Steel and Konig (2006) have proposed temporal motivation theory (TMT), which is designed to integrate a number of theories (some covered in this chapter and some not), including some from behavioural economics. Locke and Latham (2004) attempt a similar job, mostly using theories covered in this chapter. An adaptation of their model is shown in Figure 7.7. Needs are seen as the underlying basis of motivation, they find their expression in personality, which in turn affects the kinds of goals and incentives that are likely to be important to the person, as well as aspects of self-concept like self-efficacy. These factors as well as the core features of goal-setting theory help explain how motivating goals are and whether they lead to performance. Locke and Latham argue that most of the links in their model have at least some research to support them, and some of the links have a great deal of research support. It would take an ambitious programme of research to test the entire model, but if the field is to make progress then such endeavours will be necessary. Some aspects of their model can be queried. For example, work characteristics are portrayed as affecting satisfaction at the end of the process but not motivation or performance. There is also a surprising lack of feedback loops – one might expect performance, rewards or satisfaction to affect goal choice and goal behaviour as well as self-efficacy. However, it is always possible to question some elements of a model as complex as this. The real challenges are to test it, improve it and use it in work settings.

Barrick et al. (2013) have proposed another model which attempts to integrate some different aspects of motivation. They call it the theory of **purposeful work behaviour**. This is illustrated in Figure 7.8. Their starting point is personality, and they use the Big Five personality characteristics to capture the most fundamental individual differences. They

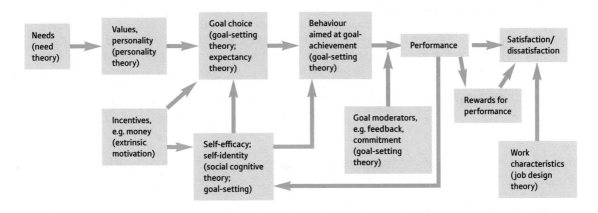

| **Figure 7.7** | An integrated model of work motivation |

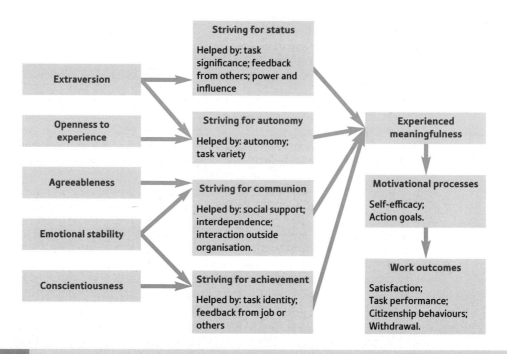

Figure 7.8   The theory of purposeful work behaviour

Source: Derived from Barrick et al. (2013) 'The theory of purposeful work behavior: The role of personality, higher-order goals, and job characteristics', *Academy of Management Review*, 38, 132–53.

argue that personality affects the type of purposes people strive for, and they identify four such strivings: for communion (i.e. companionship, harmony), status, autonomy and achievement. So, for example, they propose that extravert people will tend to strive for status and/or autonomy. To the extent that their work fits with their strivings, people experience meaningfulness (similar to the job characteristics model). Different job characteristics are important in supporting different strivings. In turn, the meaningfulness leads to motivational processes and work outcomes, including various kinds of work performance. This is an innovative theory, and the authors suggest a number of testable propositions and hypotheses arising from it. As they point out, instead of seeing work characteristics as key motivational drivers with personality as a moderator (i.e. something which affects the impact of work characteristics) as work design theory tends to, they see personality as the origin of motivation, expressed in the goals a person thinks are most important. Job characteristics are a moderator – i.e. they help or hinder the achievement of these personality-based goals.

Key learning point

Recent attempts to produce integrative theories of motivation start with individual differences in needs or personality and consider how these play out in the kinds of goals and job characteristics people want.

Summary

Work motivation is a wide-ranging topic of considerable practical and theoretical importance. It concerns the direction, intensity and persistence of work behaviour. Some psychologists view motivation as a product of innate human needs. Others see it as a calculation based on the question, 'How can I maximise my gains?' Still others take the view that we are motivated to achieve what we perceive as a fair outcome relative to that experienced by other people. Perhaps the most effective approach to motivation is goal-setting. It is based on the premise that intentions shape actions. If work goals (e.g. target levels of performance) are specific and difficult, and if they are accompanied by feedback on how well one is doing, work performance is usually enhanced. There are some circumstances, however, in which goal-setting in terms of levels of performance is less effective, especially if the task is novel and complex. Self-determination theory analyses the different ways in which external requirements to do tasks may be incorporated into people's sense of self, thus blurring the distinction between extrinsic motivation (doing something for the rewards it brings) and intrinsic motivation (doing something just for the joy or interest in doing it).

The most recent analyses of motivation focus on bringing together elements of various older theories, recognising that the practical 'nuts-and-bolts' approaches like goal-setting have their origins in personality, needs and values, which partly determine the kinds of goals and incentives that matter to a person. Another approach that has enjoyed some success is viewing motivation as something that is elicited by the right kinds of task. Here motivation is positioned as a property of the job, not the person. So the task for managers is to make jobs more motivating, not people more motivated. Early versions identified the extent to which jobs had variety and autonomy as being crucial for motivation. More recent theory and practice have broadened the range of work characteristics to include knowledge acquisition and use, the nature and extent of social interactions, and the physical conditions in which work takes place, as well as their impact on a wider range of outcomes for individual and organisation. Overall, motivation theories have done quite a good job of advancing our understanding of behaviour at work. But it is sometimes difficult to be sure about which theory is most helpful in any individual case. Recently, there have been signs that an overall theory may be developed which encompasses ideas from many of the existing ones.

Closing case study

An unmotivated building inspector

Nobody at Kirraton Local Authority planning department knew what to do about Simon Lucas. Simon was a building inspector. It was his job to approve proposals for small alterations to buildings (such as extensions and loft conversions) which did not need formal planning permission, and to check that the building work carried out was consistent with the approved plans. The trouble was, he didn't – at least, not often and not quickly. There had been a number of complaints about delays in approval of plans that were Simon's responsibility (each incoming application was assigned to one of the building inspectors for them to deal with independently). He did not seem to keep up to date with the frequent changes in building regulations, which meant that he sometimes made decisions that contradicted them. This had led to some appeals by builders and homeowners, and on three occasions the Local Authority had been forced to change its decision.

▶

▶

This was embarrassing and costly, and it was Simon Lucas's fault. He only rarely carried out site inspections, and even more rarely spoke directly with applicants or local residents who could be affected by a planning application. This meant that some of the less scrupulous builders got away with unauthorised changes to plans, and others who genuinely wanted his advice did not get it. This damaged the Local Authority's reputation and also increased the chances of a structurally unsound building being constructed.

However, it was difficult to point to specific rules that Simon Lucas was breaking. Local Authority guidance was vague: plans should be dealt with 'within a few weeks'; site inspections conducted 'as and when necessary', and decisions made 'within the spirit', not the letter, of some of the less vital regulations. In any case, it wasn't always clear which of the regulations, if any, could be treated as less vital.

Simon's boss, Katherine Walker, decided that she would check his records and unobtrusively observe him at work – it was an open-plan office, so this was feasible. She discovered that Simon was 26, and had qualified as a building inspector two years earlier. Simon had been recruited by Katherine's predecessor, apparently partly because Simon had 'come up the hard way'. Rather than attending college full time to obtain the necessary qualifications, he had worked for several years as an architect's draughtsman and attended college night classes. In fact, he had been almost the last person to qualify in that way. The building inspectors' professional institute had subsequently decided that part-time study could not develop the necessary skills and knowledge for work as a qualified building inspector. Katherine knew that the part-time route was often seen as 'second class'. She heard it said that this had prevented Simon from getting a job in another area of the country where he very much wanted to live. Few senior building inspectors held the view of Katherine's predecessor that Simon's route into the profession was superior to full-time study. Simon was certainly sensitive about this himself. He frequently mentioned how difficult it had been to combine study with work, but at the same time also remarked that he did not know enough about some things because his training had been 'too basic'.

Katherine observed that Simon often seemed not to be doing very much. He sat at his desk doodling quite a lot. He sometimes had to phone people more than once because he had forgotten to check something the first time. He seemed to have difficulty finding things on his shelves and desk. Sometimes he would give up after only a short and not very systematic search. He also sometimes jumped from one task to another without finishing any of them. As far as she could tell, his home life was not a particular problem. Simon was married, apparently happily, and seemed to participate in many social and leisure activities judging from his lunchtime conversations, not to mention his phone calls to squash clubs, campsites, etc. during work time! He was especially keen on long-distance walking, and could often be seen at lunchtime reading outdoor magazines and carefully planning his walking club's next expedition. He joked to Katherine that he should have her surname because it described what he liked most.

In general, Simon seemed to Katherine quite a cooperative person who wouldn't create conflict for conflict's sake. Despite some worries about his status in the organisation, he seemed generally calm and not given to emotional ups and downs. When she asked him what kept him in the job, he said that he needed a reliable income to support his home life, and that to be gainfully employed was the duty of every citizen capable of contributing unless they were at home bringing up children.

Simon's job was relatively secure. Ultimately, he could be dismissed if he demonstrated continuing incompetence, but he had successfully completed his probationary period (Katherine wasn't sure how). Because Kirraton Local Authority covered only a small area, and because Simon's job was a specialist one, he could not be moved to another town or department. Building inspectors' pay depended on age and length of service, with slightly higher rates for those with a relevant college degree. Outstanding performance could only be rewarded with promotion, and this was extremely unlikely for anyone with less than 10 years' service. Katherine established that Simon would like promotion because of the extra money it would bring rather than the status, but he correctly perceived that he had virtually no chance of achieving it. Apart from the fact he had been at Kirraton for a relatively short time, he thought he was not scoring very well on Katherine's recently implemented building inspector performance criteria. These were no lost appeals, high client satisfaction, at least 15 complete projects per month, and acknowledgement of receipt of plans within four working days. His poor (though not catastrophic) performance on these criteria was bad for him, and also bad for the department as a whole because it affected its overall performance statistics.

The other four building inspectors were quite a close-knit group of building sciences graduates who had worked together for several years before Simon's arrival. Simon didn't really see himself as a member of the group, preferring instead to emphasise how he, unlike them, was 'on the same wavelength' as the local people served by Kirraton Local Authority. He had found it hard to establish a relationship with his colleagues, and now it was even harder because they felt his apparently poor performance reflected badly on them all. They did not involve him much in their activities, nor did they appear to respect him. Simon was afraid that the others thought he wasn't doing his job properly and Katherine suspected that secretly he agreed with them. Katherine knew something had to be done, but what, and how?

Suggested exercises

1 Review the motivation theories discussed in this chapter. Pick two. How would each one describe and explain the problems with Simon Lucas's motivation?

2 To what extent does each theory provide guidance to Katherine Walker about what she should do? What actions would they recommend?

3 How motivating is Simon's job? Is this an inherent feature of the job, or a consequence of how he approaches it?

Test your learning

Short-answer questions

1 Describe the key features of the theory X and theory Y 'common-sense' views of motivation.
2 Suggest three ways in which Maslow's hierarchy of needs theory might helpfully be amended.
3 What kind of work appeals to people who have a strong need for achievement?
4 Define valence, instrumentality and expectancy. According to Vroom, how do they combine to determine motivation?
5 Name and define three kinds of perceived justice at work.
6 Draw a simple diagram that shows the key elements of goal-setting.
7 What are the key differences between performance-goal orientation and learning-goal orientation?
8 Name and define five types of motivation that vary along the extrinsic–intrinsic continuum.

9   Draw a diagram that represents the main features of the job characteristics model (JCM).

10   Suggest three limitations of the JCM as a framework for job redesign.

11   Describe five characteristics of jobs *not* in the JCM that have been identified as being important in work redesign.

12   List and define the six types of job identified by Holman (2013).

Suggested assignments

1   Examine the usefulness of need theories in understanding and predicting behaviour at work.

2   In what ways, if any, do academic theories of motivation improve upon so-called 'common sense'?

3   It is often claimed that goal-setting is a theory of motivation which works. Examine whether it works better in some circumstances than others.

4   When and how is pay a motivator?

5   Discuss this statement: 'The job characteristics model was a useful start as a guide to how to redesign jobs, but it was no more than a start.'

6   How can motivation theories be combined to get the best ideas from each?

Relevant websites

There are very many sites that describe training courses in motivational techniques (for managing self or others) and provide very brief accounts of some well-known motivation theories, usually the oldest and most straightforward ones. Here are a few examples: http://humanresources.about.com/od/motivationsucces3/a/lead_motivation.htm is part of a managers' self-help site. This particular item encourages managers to take on responsibility for the motivation of the people who work for them.

http://changingminds.org/explanations/theories/a_motivation.htm gives an index of different theories of motivation. Clicking on a theory brings you a little more information about it.

https://www.mindtools.com/ offers a long list of motivation topics which you can find by typing motivation into the search facility. To access the full articles you need to join mindtools.

Suggested further reading

Full details for all references are given in the list at the end of this book.

1   Gary Latham's book *Work Motivation* (Sage, 2007) presents an historical, theoretical and practical analysis of work motivation. If this chapter has interested you, then Latham's book will be a real treat.

2   Ed Locke and Gary Latham's 2004 article attempts to specify an integrated theory of motivation. It is quite heavy going but well written nevertheless, and a good way of expanding both your knowledge of theories and your understanding of how they might fit together.

3   Sharon Parker's 2014 review of how thinking on the design of work can help improve not only motivation but also a range of other desirable outcomes is a great source of ideas and references to other helpful research.

CHAPTER 8
Design at work

LEARNING OBJECTIVES

After studying this chapter, you should be able to:

1 understand the role that ergonomics has to play alongside other organisational systems (such as employee training);

2 appreciate the principles of Human Factors Integration (HFI);

3 describe the principles and process of human-centred design (HCD);

4 describe joint cognitive systems and distributed cognition;

5 understand the human factors issues at the various stages of the design process;

6 understand and apply the basic principles of display design across the various sensory modalities;

7 appreciate the changing role of the ergonomist during the various stages of work and task design.

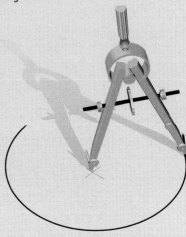

Opening case study

The importance of end-user input into design

User involvement in development programmes is vital for both reducing cost and ensuring success. The Chaos Report (Standish Group, 1995) established that early user involvement was the most important factor for the success of IT projects. It was found that the highest-rated reason for why IT projects succeeded was users' involvement during the development process. Conversely, the most commonly cited reason for IT projects failing was a lack of user involvement.

An excellent example of what can go wrong was provided by the failure of the IT system responsible for allocating London's ambulances to incidents. The system was designed to improve call handling and to improve the dispatch of ambulances while also gathering data to perform several other management auditing functions, such as monitoring how the availability of resources changed over time and tracking response times. The system comprised an automatic vehicle locating system and data terminals to enable dispatch staff to communicate with ambulance crews.

As the system entered service it became apparent that there were many technical and ergonomic issues resulting in severe communication difficulties. As a result, often the dispatch system could not establish the location or the status of the ambulances under its control. The system sometimes made incorrect allocations of ambulances to incidents or failed to allocate an ambulance at all. The software responded very slowly, causing an increase in telephone and radio traffic from both frustrated ambulance crews and members of the public. On 26 and 27 October 1992 this resulted in the system slowing even further, to a completely unacceptable level. On 4 November 1992, the system failed completely due to a minor programming error.

The report from the subsequent inquiry by the Communications Directorate of the South West Thames Regional Health Authority (1993) reported that the factors underlying the failure included inadequacies in training; understaffing in the control centre; poor processes and procedures; inadequate working practices and interface problems affecting system usability. The overall management of the specification, design and procurement of the IT system was also heavily criticised.

Modern ergonomics addresses all aspects of the work system design, not just the user interface: it takes a systemic approach. Problems in all of the areas criticised in the report could have been avoided with the implementation of a proper Human Factors Integration (HFI) programme. The findings of the inquiry stated that, 'The next CAD [computer-aided dispatch] system must be made to fit the Service's current or future organisational structure and agreed operational practices. This was not the case with the current CAD.' The report concludes that users were not sufficiently involved in the system's development.

Sources: Communications Directorate,
South West Thames Regional Health Authority (1993);
Johnson (2001); Ministry of Defence,
Human Factors Integration Defence Technology Centre (2006).
Case study by chapter author.

Suggested exercise

As you read this chapter you might want to try to identify specific actions that could have been taken to avoid some of the problems identified in this case study.

Introduction

There is no one accepted definition of this discipline. One that seems to capture the essence of the activities involved is offered by the International Ergonomics Association:

Ergonomics (or human factors) is the scientific discipline concerned with the understanding of interactions among humans and other elements of a system, and the profession that applies theory, principles, data and methods to design in order to optimise human well-being and overall system performance

(Source: http://www.iea.cc/whats/)

Ergonomics has evolved to be concerned with the design of whole systems of work. It is not simply about the design of work equipment that is comfortable or easy to use. This means that there is a great deal of overlap between what work psychologists do and what ergonomists do. Their commonalities are probably more pronounced than their differences. As you will see in this chapter, ergonomics draws upon many aspects of human psychology but also elements of human physiology, anatomy and engineering system design. Don't be alarmed, we'll focus mainly on the psychological aspects but along the way will also explain the links to other relevant disciplines and topics. As both the definition offered above and the opening case study indicate, optimising the design of equipment and work environments requires the integration of knowledge from across specialisms. Furthermore, consideration must also be given to supporting processes such as worker training. The analysis of activities carried out in work roles is an important part of ergonomics: but it is just one step in the process of defining, designing and testing of work equipment and work systems.

Key learning point

Ergonomics and human factors are not just about the physical aspects of work equipment and environments – they encompass the design of all aspects of work systems and process.

Human Systems Integration – HSI (also referred to in the UK as Human Factors Integration – HFI) is the name often given to the contemporary approach to the specification, design and development of major equipment acquisitions, and their subsequent operational deployment. HSI/HFI is used extensively by the military and other complex, safety critical industries (e.g. the nuclear, oil and gas industries).

The UK Ministry of Defence (MoD) specifies seven domains of HSI/HFI (Ministry of Defence, 2001) – see Table 8.1. You will notice that many aspects of HSI/HFI are also addressed in other chapters of this book (such as selection, teamwork and training to name just a few). This shows that HSI is not a product that sits in isolation from the organisational context. Rather, HSI is best seen as a process that considers a wide range of issues beyond the design of specific tasks and the equipment needed to carry them out (i.e. it is a process that best resides within a systems engineering context).

Clearly, this makes the whole of HSI far too broad and complex to be adequately covered in a single chapter. Therefore, in this chapter we also identify the ways in which HSI might be influenced by the issues covered in much more detail elsewhere in this book. The focus will be placed on a key component of the HSI: the human-centred design (HCD) process. This embraces the design of tasks and equipment for humans, and some of the basic design considerations of the user interface, particularly concerning the design of displays. The HCD process makes extensive use of research and theory from various branches of psychology.

No attempt will be made to outline the whole range of design solutions possible. As we discuss throughout the chapter, each solution is bespoke to the application area, task, user and the environment. For example, there is no such thing as 'the best type of visual display'; there is only the best type of display for certain types of information in a certain context. The same can be said for the design of controls: the design of this aspect of the user interface also depends upon the nature of the task to be undertaken. In work settings, all design is a compromise driven by such things as the space available at the work location; the available budget; national and local regulations (which sometimes mandate something of lower quality than the optimum design solution) or the requirement for a particular type of user interface. You need only think of a laptop computer; a trackpad is less than a good option for many control tasks (try using it for doing detailed graphical design work). It does, however, make the laptop easy to package up, and is a reasonable all-round multifunctional control device for the majority of tasks a user wants to carry out with a portable computer. It's a good enough compromise for most users.

Key learning point

Human-centred design does not necessarily result in a perfect work system because it usually involves making compromises as a result of practical and cost constraints.

Many modern machines can help to make us more effective both in terms of how we think about and carry out our work. Some argue that our use of machines had led to fundamental changes in our use of cognitive strategies and preferred ways of working. The frequently held view that ergonomics is about bending, lifting and twisting; lower back pain; comfortable chairs; and knobs and dials is a long way behind us. Modern ergonomics is about work systems and cognitive engineering.

Table 8.1	The domains of HFI	
HFI domain	**Example issues**	**Example topics**
Staffing	How many people are required to operate and maintain the system?	Staffing levels Team organisation Job specifications
Personnel	What are the aptitudes, experience and other human characteristics?	Selection, recruitment and career development Qualifications and experience required General characteristics (e.g. size, strength, eyesight)
Training	How to develop and maintain the requisite knowledge, skills and abilities to operate and maintain the system	Identifying requirements for new skills Training courses Requirements for specialist training facilities Individual and team training Skill maintenance (e.g. refresher courses)

Table 8.1	*(continued)*	
HFI domain	**Example issues**	**Example topics**
Human factors engineering	How to integrate human characteristics into system design to optimise performance	Equipment design Workstation/console design Workplace layout Ease of maintenance User interface design Function allocation
Health hazards	What are the hazards resulting from normal operation of the system?	Exposure to: Toxic materials Electric shock Mechanical injury Musculoskeletal injury Extreme heat/cold Optical hazards
System safety	How to avoid the safety risks caused by operating or maintaining the system abnormally	Sources of error Effects of misuse or abuse External and environmental hazards
Organisational and social	What is the optimum organisational configuration?	Organisational and national culture Information sharing

Source: Widdowson and Carr (2002), with permission.

Point of integration

Designing work equipment requires knowledge of various aspects of work psychology covered elsewhere in this text. Two examples are: selection and training (as these topics consider the assessment and development of knowledge, skills and abilities); and workers' motivation, attitudes and stress level (as these can be affected by the way work equipment changes the nature of their work tasks). As you read this chapter you will see various connections to other topics.

Design in a socio-technical context

All design takes place within a wider context. Simply focusing on the user interface without considering users, task requirements, organisation and/or the environmental context will usually result in substandard equipment being developed, which is also difficult to use. The Human Factors National Advisory Committee for Defence and Aerospace (2003) describes some examples of the benefits of taking a wider socio-technical/HSI approach to equipment design. For instance, the developer of an aircraft engine who adopted an HSI approach reduced the number of tools required for line maintenance of a new turbine from over 100 to just 10; fewer specialist skills were needed allowing a consolidation in the number of maintenance trades required, which also resulted in a reduction in training time. What this example illustrates is that organisations can realise significant economic benefits by actively considering the wider organisational context of impact equipment redesign.

A little more recently, in a structured analysis of Human System Integration programmes undertaken by the Australian Defence Science and Technology Office (DSTO, 2010) it was observed that early implementation of HSI activities could result in extremely large returns on investment across the lifespan of the equipment. Booher (1997) and Booher and Minninger (2003) report extremely impressive returns on investment from HSI programmes in US helicopter and armoured fighting vehicle programmes of between 22 and 33:1. US Air Force studies (2009) suggest that if HSI comprises between about 2.5 and 4 per cent of acquisition costs, a return in investment of 40–60:1 will be realised. Within the maritime domain the US Navy reported that the application of HSI principles allowed for an 11 per cent reduction in staffing of its aircraft carriers. However, these cost savings were not at the price of capability or the quality of life for those working on the ship. Similar cost savings attributable to early Human Factors analysis have been calculated by the French, Canadian and British Royal Navy.

One approach to characterising the wider context within which design and operations take place is described in the five Ms model (Harris and Harris, 2004; Harris and Thomas, 2005). This model shows how the operation of any commercial piece of equipment is not just about the integration of the user (*[hu]man*) and equipment (*machine*) to perform a particular task (or *mission*) within constraints imposed by the physical environment (*medium*), but that the societal environment (a further aspect of the *medium*) also needs to be considered, as does the role of *management* (see Figure 8.1).

Taking an HCD approach, the (hu)*man* component is the ultimate design forcing function: the ergonomist must operate within abilities of the human operator. The (hu)*man* and the *machine* components come together to perform a *mission*. However, designers must not only work within the constraints of the technology, end-users and the physical aspects of the *medium,* they are also bound by the rules and norms of society (a further aspect of the *medium*). Performance standards for human–machine systems are primarily determined by societal norms (such as health and safety regulations). It is important to note that these requirements set only the minimum level of performance required and may therefore not stimulate design solutions that fully utilise what we know about human psychology. This can mean that designers are more concerned with minimising operator error in the design of the controls of a nuclear reactor than they are when designing an office telephone. There may also be formal standards of user competence, such as that required to obtain a licence: most of us will be reassured to know that pilots are trained to an internationally agreed level of competence before they are allowed to fly an aeroplane with passengers aboard. As a result, a certain level of competence when designing flight deck equipment may be assumed (however, always remember that licensing only ever specifies the *minimum* level of user competence at one point in time). What the model shows is that it is not just the designer who plays an important role. *Management* must also work within these rules. The management prescribes secondary performance standards, for example through the proper selection and training of personnel who will be carrying out the task. Thus *management* is the key link between the (hu)*man, machine, mission* and *medium* which promotes safe and efficient operations.

Key learning point

Human resource management processes, including employee selection and training processes, need to be effective to ensure that equipment design is appropriate for the intended users.

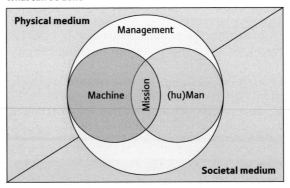

Figure 8.1	The five Ms framework

Stages in design

All design has several identifiable stages. These will differ slightly in every situation, but typically cover issues such as:

- *Concept formulation.* This focuses on the identification of the need for the equipment. (What is it going to do? What are the requirements for it?)

- *Functional specification.* This focuses on the question: how is it going to do it? Typically this involves a process of breaking down the larger task that the system will perform into smaller, more manageable tasks.

- *Detailed design.* Here the functional specifications of the individual components are operationalised (or brought to life). From an HSI perspective this involves designing the user interface and identifying the logic underlying any automation of tasks. It will also involve design and implementation of other aspects of the wider system, for example the design of training for employees and logistical support, such as making plans for maintenance of the equipment or technology.

- *Commissioning.* Putting together all the individual components into a representative system (system integration) and establishing that it performs to the standard required. At this stage the support infrastructure (e.g. delivering training to the personnel for its operation and maintenance) also needs to be established.

Key learning point

The early stages of design are particularly crucial. There is a 1:10:100 rule for design costs (Pressman, 1992). For every £1 to fix a problem identified in the early design stages it will cost £10 to fix it during detailed design and development, and £100 to fix it once the system is operational. Put simply: don't skimp on front-end design activities.

Human-centred design

Table 8.2 describes the **human-centred design (HCD)** activities within the HSI approach. As you can see, the actual design of the equipment itself occurs relatively late in the process. Table 8.2 shows that the important early activities include understanding the system requirements, its end users and the context in which it will be used. There are two very important aspects of HCD. First, it actively involves the end users of the system. Second, it is an iterative process (it is unlikely that your first design solution will be your final design!). Constant testing and refinement during the design process are essential.

Point of integration

Some of the methods used in HCD are similar to those used to design selection and training processes (see Chapters 4 and 9).

All design starts with a requirements analysis. Not only does this specify what the equipment must do, it will also form the basis for verifying if the final design performs to the standards required. Get the requirements analysis wrong (or incomplete) and, as everything else builds upon this, so everything else is subsequently mis-specified. Many major projects fail as a result of incomplete requirements analyses and/or a failure to include end users throughout the design process (Standish Group, 1995).

Table 8.2	HCD activities
Activity and objective	**Example activities**
Plan the human-centred process Ensure that specific HF activities are built into project plans and are sufficiently resourced.	HFI planning Requirements analysis
Understand and specify the context of use Identify the users and what they will be doing. Ensure that descriptions of users and tasks are considered as the basis for design.	Target audience description Scenario identification Task identification
Specify the user and organisational requirements Specify the characteristics required of the system which affect users and their wider organisation.	Task analysis Function allocation Ergonomics standards and guidelines User performance specification
Produce design solutions Apply HF expertise to generate design options which meet user requirements. Design iteratively using part-prototypes and prototypes as required.	Workstation design Workspace design Job/team design
Evaluate designs against user requirements Test designs against requirements by involving target users and HF specialists.	User interface prototyping User trials Human reliability assessment/formal error prediction

Source: Widdowson and Carr (2002), with permission

In HCD there are three types of requirement:

1   *Product requirements.* These are the attributes of the equipment itself (e.g. any applicable design standards regarding display formats; limitations on weight if it is a person-transportable piece of equipment; integration requirements with other existing pieces of equipment etc.).

2   *Performance requirements.* These specify the performance of the equipment and should be verifiable (e.g. usability; time taken from the start to the end of a task; acceptable error rates etc.).

3   *Process requirements.* These define the processes to be followed during the design and development process and are a critical part of any HSI plan. Typically these will specify such things as the human factors methods to be used for undertaking the formal requirements analysis; the format for reporting data; the required availability of subject matter experts and members of the target user population for undertaking design evaluations etc.

Understanding and specifying the context of use

Formally specifying the requirements for a piece of equipment raises two important issues in the design process:

1   What are the skills, knowledge and abilities required of its end users?

2   What is the context of its use (both operational and organisational)?

To address such issues, an early HCD task is the production of the **target audience description (TAD)**. This document contains information such as the physical characteristics of end users (e.g. users' body size and dimension and physical strength requirements); sensory characteristics (e.g. visual and auditory capabilities); psychological characteristics (e.g. particular aptitudes and abilities; reasoning and/or decision-making skills); social and cultural characteristics (e.g. age and gender); and specific skills and qualifications (overview of target audience descriptions) (these are published in the *Overview of Target Audience Descriptions*; MoD, 2000).

The TAD is a forward-looking document, anticipating demographic and cultural changes (if necessary). This is because many major pieces of hardware and equipment may be in service for many years (it is not uncommon for large or expensive pieces of military equipment, for example an aircraft carrier, to be in service for up to half a century). Therefore the modern ergonomist needs to be part scientist, part clairvoyant! Any TAD also needs to incorporate consideration of issues relating to initial and continuing training requirements. However, in the HCD process it is easy to concentrate entirely on the primary end user (i.e. the operator) but this can be a mistake. Good HCD is about the performance of the *whole* system. This means it is also vital to consider secondary use (and users) of the product (e.g. cleaning, maintenance and storage).

Appreciation of context is essential for successful system design, build and operation. To illustrate, as a 'rule of thumb', equipment is built from the inside outward but is maintained from the outside inward. Because of these different contexts, the requirements for efficient error-free assembly are quite different from those ensuring the maintainability of the system. Such conflicts of priority must be resolved at an early stage. If the equipment will be in service for an extended period, maintenance may take priority. If the equipment is relatively cheap to purchase, has a short service life or is likely to be single-use (or disposable), error-free assembly will be of more importance.

There is no such thing as a recipe for characterising context of use. Referring back to the five Ms model (Figure 8.1), context can include the physical and societal mediums, and the domain of management. Within this latter category issues such as organisational structure, team structure and operating autonomy and independence should be considered (e.g. will the equipment be operated by a team or by an individual?). The wider aspects of the medium may include protecting the user from extremes of temperature, a hostile atmosphere, poor illumination or noise and vibration. Furthermore, the equipment may be used for protracted periods of time, at a high tempo and/or when the user is under considerable stress, for example much of the equipment used by anaesthetists in the modern operating theatre or by a communications operator on site at a major incident. Such issues have a profound effect on the appropriate task structure and user interface.

Key learning point

Actively engaging users in the design process is a crucial part of HSI and the HCD processes.

Exercise 8.1   Different perspectives on design

When designing the wards in the new buildings of University College Hospital, London, cleaners were actively engaged in the process. Although one might immediately expect doctors and nurses to be involved in such a process, the role of cleaners is less clear. However, the input of cleaners resulted in several design changes. For example, their input led to a design decision that walls would not meet the floor at a sharp, 90 degree angle. Instead there is a large radius curve, stopping dirt gathering in the crack which harbours bacteria causing infection. As a result of this simple design modification, these wards are easier to clean and show lower reinfection rates in patients.

Suggested exercise

Think about the design of a lecture theatre. If lecturers were asked to input into the design process, what issues might they raise? As a student, what issues would you raise? Compare how the two are different and consider whether both sets of requirements could be accommodated in a single design.

Point of integration

End-user involvement in design is a recurrent theme in this text. For example, it has also been shown to be useful when designing stress management interventions (Chapter 10), performance appraisal systems (Chapter 5) and workers' goals (Chapter 7).

Specifying user and organisational requirements

So far in this chapter the context of use and potential users have been considered, but not the actual tasks that they will perform. This is the domain of task analysis, i.e. analysing, in detail, the various operations that are required for the execution of a task. Many excellent texts are available describing task analysis in all its major forms (e.g. Diaper and Stanton, 2004; Hollnagel, 2003; Crandall et al., 2006). However, as an analytical approach it can be broken down into two principal genres: behavioural and cognitive. Behavioural forms describe the tasks and subtasks that need to be performed and their organisation. Generally, these are observable, discrete operations (e.g. pull lever, push switch, turn handle, write down data etc.). Cognitive forms describe the underlying cognitive skills and processes for performing a task. These aspects of human behaviour are more difficult for a third partly to observe directly but can be identified through the careful application of knowledge elicitation techniques.

The outputs from both forms of task analysis perform several functions in addition to providing a basis for HCD. They are also useful for: specifying the attributes of personnel that might need to be identified during recruitment and selection; forming the basis of training needs analyses and training design; informing staffing and job organisation decisions and providing a basis for performance assessments and appraisals (Kirwan and Ainsworth, 1992).

Hierarchical Task Analysis (HTA) is the most common behavioural form of task analysis. HTA is based upon the principle that all large tasks can be decomposed (or deconstructed) into smaller tasks capable of being organised into a hierarchy (Stanton, 2004). Since its original conception by Annett et al. (1971), the method has been extended and expanded to incorporate other features, such as making plans and decision events, and now also allows for the incorporation of more detailed information (e.g. by including tabular analyses specifying interface or performance requirements). These changes have allowed HTA to give a more complete analysis of the events occurring in the execution of a task (beyond those that can easily be observed). An example HTA is included in Figure 8.2 (from Harris et al., 2005). However, HTA can only identify task requirements and information flows. The designer must interpret this information and make decisions based upon it, for example when devising the user interface.

Many modern jobs are largely cognitive in nature, for example the supervisory control of highly automated systems, or other professions not involving high-technology equipment, such as accountancy or the law, customer services and banking. In such cases HTA may be of limited utility as it is only a formal description of the behavioural task requirements.

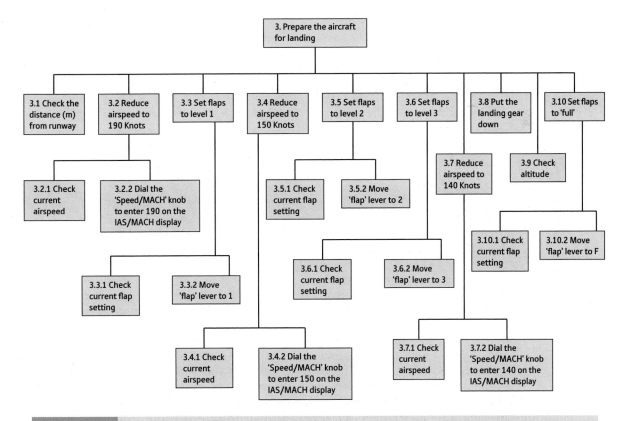

Figure 8.2   Extract from the HTA describing the task of preparing an Airbus A320 for a CAT III autoland
Source: From Harris et al. (2005).

Work activities in these highly automated or cognitive situations are most likely associated with situation assessment, risk management, planning, decision-making and selecting an appropriate strategy. Cognitive forms of task analysis describe the underlying cognitive skills and processes for performing a task. Crandall and colleagues (2006) suggest that cognitive task analysis (CTA) comprises three distinct stages: knowledge elicitation (extracting information to provide information on events, structures or mental models); analysis of the data (to provide structure and explanation of the cognitive processes); and knowledge representation (to depict the nature of the relationships and to help inform design and operational processes). These aspects of human functioning are difficult for a third party to observe directly. The outputs from both forms of task analysis perform several functions in addition to providing a basis for HCD. They are also useful for specifying the attributes of personnel, forming the basis of training needs analyses and training design, informing staffing and job organisation decisions and providing a basis for performance assurance (Kirwan and Ainsworth, 1992). To some extent, CTA can be conceptualised as just one component of a larger cognitively based analytical system, work domain analysis. For example, cognitive work analysis (Vincente, 1999) is a conceptual framework to analyse both cognitively based tasks and their context.

Point of integration

HTA and CTA are also commonly used in the design of training interventions (see Chapter 9). This shows that data gathered as part of HCD processes can also be used in the design of other interventions.

Key learning point

'Task analysis can get too detailed, and be too late [in the design process] to have an effect. Think about how much detail is needed for the people who will use the results. With a hierarchical description you can readily add detail later' (taken from HFI Practical Guidance for IPTs, Ministry of Defence, 2001).

As in the case of HTA, CTA only provides an analysis of the cognitive work of the system operator. Again, it does not, in itself, provide design solutions. Function allocation (FA) can be thought to be the beginning of this design process. FA is the attribution of functions to either the machine or its operator. FA should be performed while the system functions are still defined at a high level of abstraction (i.e. emphasis should be firmly placed upon defining what the system is attempting to accomplish and not *how* it is going to accomplish it). Traditionally, FA has proceeded on the simple basis of assigning a particular function to either the human operator or the machine based upon their relative strengths and weaknesses when performing this task. Parasuraman and colleagues (2000) describe automation as 'the full or partial replacement of a function previously carried out by the human operator' (2000: 287). However, Hollnagel (1999) has labelled this approach 'function allocation by substitution'. Dekker and Woods (2002) have suggested that designers need to get away from this practice as it falls into the 'electric horse' trap.[1]

By using this approach the automation does the same job as the human but in a slightly different way (i.e. substitution), and thus it can limit innovation. Greater benefit can often be gained by questioning some of the initial assumptions upon which the design is predicated and delivering the required capability in a different manner. Take the simple example of the airline ticket. The low-cost carriers questioned the basic assumption that a physical ticket was required. Now, all that is required is proof of identification at the point of check-in (if indeed you do now physically check in as this now is often done remotely and boarding passes are issued online). The function of check-in has largely been changed to that of a 'bag drop'. The function of the identification of the traveller is usually done at the point of departure. The function of the printed airline ticket has become redundant as have the functions of many of the check-in processes. Examples like this illustrate why it is important for work psychologists to examine underlying assumptions about the importance or necessity of a work activity before looking at interventions that might improve the way it is performed.

Key learning point

Automation is not simply about replacing human activity with a machine performing the same job. Smart design looks at the whole system and asks, 'Can we do it better'? It then analyses which aspects are best done by a human and which are best performed by a machine.

Ergonomists need to be aware of already proven options for the various system components when undertaking initial design iterations. Many standards exist for HCD, ranging from very simple things (such as the arrangement of the pedals in your car) to vastly more complex standards (such as those for the design of primary flight instruments in an aircraft). To help there are internationally recognised standards (e.g. ISO 13407, 1999) for the design processes for interactive systems. These activities largely mirror those described by Widdowson and Carr (2002) but have a greater focus on software design. The operation of the software interface and its 'look and feel' (i.e. the product) may be based around other 'unofficial' standards, such as the Microsoft® Office System User Interface Design Guidelines. The military have extensive standards for all aspects of human design. One of the most comprehensive is the UK Ministry of Defence DEF-STAN 00-250 (Ministry of Defence, 2008).[2] This standard runs to well over 1000 pages and contains information about the HF design process, interface options, Human-Computer Interaction (HCI), etc. It is more comprehensive and contains more practical advice than any textbook on the market, and is updated relatively frequently to reflect changes in technology and the underpinning science base. Other excellent, freely available Internet resources are Understanding Human Factors – a guide for the railway industry (Rail Safety and Standards Board, 2008: http://www.rssb.co.uk/Library/improving-industry-performance/2008-guide-understanding-human-factors-a-guide-for-the-railway-industry.pdf); and the Federal Aviation Administration Human Factors Design Standard (Ahlstrom and Longo, 2003: http://hf.tc.faa.gov/hfds/). Compliance with standards and guidelines may be specifically written into the system design contract or may be indirectly implied via compliance with rules and regulations. All of these regulatory requirements mean that the ergonomist involved with the design of a user interface does not necessarily have a completely free hand. What should always be remembered, though, is that regulation only specifies the minimum performance level of the human–machine system; when done effectively HCD can help achieve far better overall system performance and produce more satisfied users.

Producing design solutions

It should be evident by now that the design and evaluation of human–machine interfaces (HMI) is only one component of the ergonomist's task. However, if you are looking for the HMI as an entity in itself, you won't find it – it doesn't really exist! Figure 8.3 shows why this is the case. On the machine output–human input side of the interface, 'images' on the displays (hopefully) convey data/information to the operator (Figure 8.3). These images are interpreted and their content should be transformed into knowledge and understanding that allow control of the machine. On the human output–machine input side of the control loop, control intent from the operator needs to be translated into the desired machine output. A good control system will translate operator intent into system output in the manner desired and with minimal effort (physical or mental). A 'high-quality' HMI consists of a good 'fit' between the skills, knowledge and ability of the user and the controls and displays of the machine.

Ackoff (1989) suggested that there are five broad categories of information. These are described below, with an example to illustrate each (i.e. controlling the process in a nuclear reactor):

1   *Data.* Basic building blocks/symbols (e.g. the temperature in the primary cooling circuit in a nuclear reactor).

2   *Information.* Data that have been combined and processed to provide answers to questions concerning 'who', 'what', 'where' and 'when' (e.g. if the primary cooling circuit temperature is high, and the pressure in the steam generator is high and there is a high neutron count, then without intervention the level of criticality in the nuclear reactor will become unstable in 10 minutes).

3   *Knowledge.* This applies information to questions concerning 'how' (e.g. lowering control rods into the reactor will instantly reduce the reactivity of the reactor core and begin to lower the temperature and pressure).

4   *Understanding.* Begins to give an appreciation concerning 'why' questions (e.g. control rods (made of neutron-absorbing material) slow the processes occurring in the reactor, thus allowing the reactor temperature to fall).

5   *Wisdom.* This provides an evaluated understanding (e.g. without the close monitoring of the position of control rods and reactor temperatures and pressures, things could go very badly wrong!).

What can be seen from Figure 8.3 is that the HMI only provides 'data' and/or 'information' (perhaps 'knowledge') but what the user requires is 'understanding'. This illustrates the importance of considering the wider design context: users often need training and

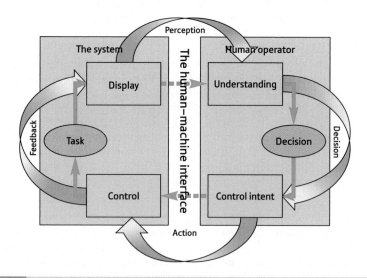

Figure 8.3   The concept of the human–machine interface superimposed over a representation of the classical 'perception-decision-action-feedback' control loop

supervision in order to develop the understanding and wisdom to work most effectively with the technology.

Key learning point

Good HCD provides the user with information. For example, the airworthiness regulations require aircraft flight decks to display fuel quantity and fuel flow rates. However, these data are of little use: what the pilot requires is information concerning what the remaining amount of fuel represents in terms of range or endurance (e.g. how many miles before the engines stop work because of lack of fuel). Information requirements are derived from the user requirements and task analyses.

Automation, autonomy and joint cognitive systems

The human control of many systems has changed greatly over the last half-century. Pilots do not fly the aircraft manually from London to New York (the autopilot and flight management system does large amounts of the work). Nuclear power plant operators do not continually control the rod positions in a reactor in response to data about the state of the reactor. Even driving a car is becoming more automated with the advent of cruise control, intelligent (distance-keeping) cruise control and automatic lane-keeping systems. Few systems are now controlled 'manually'. Most are now under some degree of supervisory control. The supervisory controller is an outer-loop controller (a setter of high-level system goals) rather than a 'hands-on', inner loop controller. However, 'automation' is not an 'all or nothing' thing.

At lower levels of automation the computer offers cognitive support. This might include the integration of various pieces of data in an easy-to-understand format or be achieved by presenting to the user the advantages and disadvantages of various decision alternatives. These lower levels can be characterised as automation that augments human cognition but the human still has overall control. For example, in financial markets traders may set up their computerised trading systems to monitor the price of certain stocks and shares and trigger an alert when a price reaches a certain level but the decision to buy (or sell) may still be made by a human (although as computer systems improve this is increasingly not the case). Higher levels of automation result in the control of some work activities by the technology and fewer by the operator. This may be necessary when the task is so complex that all of the cognitive demands are unmanageable by the worker without some assistance. Highly automated (or autonomous) systems can also interact with their wider environment in an intelligent way. They can respond to environmental demands, hence they are to some degree 'outward looking': the way the system responds is not just based on user activity but also determined by other performance-related events.

Even in these more advanced systems, the ultimate goals of the task are still set and managed by human operators in a human–machine system. This also means that operators decide upon which functions need to be automated and when these are activated. These systems work well when there is a reciprocal relationship between what the worker knows about the environment (i.e. their schemata) and the information held by the machinery. In this way the interaction between the worker and the machine directs the exploration of the environment either by the person or machine. New information is gathered, which leads to the modification of the worker's schemata (e.g. their knowledge) and the information held by the machine. This is an ongoing, cyclical process; Neisser (1976) referred to this as a 'perceptual cycle'. The awareness generated through this human–machine system influences several components of the worker's activities including what it is they choose to attend to.

This subsequently dictates how data (or information) are perceived, interpreted and what further information is subsequently actively sought. Hollnagel (2007) has described these components of activity as being either part of the worker's 'inner view' or part of their 'outer view'. The inner view is the knowledge or cognition of issues such as the management of workload, the need for attention to tasks, situation awareness (SA) and decision-making. The outer view includes the worker's understanding of the job context, the boundaries of the human–machine system, the nature of the task, their responsibility for outcomes and their level of autonomy or control.

Key learning point

Effective automated work systems involve reciprocal relationships between the information held by the user and the information stored in and made available by the technology. Transactions occur during work activities that lead to the development of both these knowledge bases.

This type of reciprocal interaction between person and machine is referred to as a **joint cognitive system (JCS)**. To make such systems effective, understanding the function of individual components is less important than the understanding of how the system as a whole operates. This means that we might not need to be too concerned about the knowledge level of the operator if the machine provides usable and accurate information to the operator and the operator is aware of the need to attend to this information. JCSs have several distinguishing features: they are goal orientated (i.e. designed with specific outcomes in mind), adaptive and respond to the changes in the environment (i.e. are outward looking). Hollnagel (2007) suggested that the JCS relating to an airliner could be characterised in a similar manner to the skins of an onion (see Figure 8.4). Here you can see that the crew's JCS sits within several 'wider' JCSs so is naturally responsive to, but also influences, the wider environment. These overlapping and reciprocal JCSs are essential if the pilot is keen to be

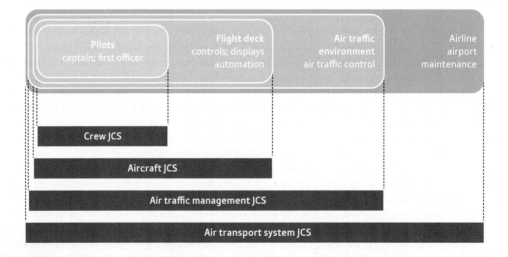

Figure 8.4	The many bounds of a JCS for the air transport system
	Source: Adapted from Hollnagel, E. (2007). Flight decks and free flight: Where are the system boundaries? *Applied Ergonomics*, 38, 409–16.

well-informed about the aircraft's location and condition, while at the same time being in control of a well-maintained aircraft in busy flight paths. In practical terms this means that pilots' knowledge of mechanical problems are passed into systems operated by maintenance staff and information about pilot behaviour is tracked and acted upon by air traffic controllers. Figure 8.4 implies that mechanical inspection schedules for some parts of the aircraft may change in response to the reporting of frequent problems, or that guidance to pilots may be updated and cockpit instrumentation updated if there is a 'near miss' detected by air traffic controllers. Note that this is in contrast to 'traditional' HMI described in Figure 8.3, which does not look far beyond the inner features of the machine itself.

Higher levels of automation ultimately conclude in complete machine autonomy (Sheridan and Verplank, 1978). There are degrees of delegation of authority and autonomy to the machine, from simple *management by delegation* (boss/slave type of relationship – 'I say, you do') through *management by consent* (where the machine suggests various options but the operator still retains ultimate control) to *management by exception* where the machine is operating almost autonomously; the operator is only informed of major deviations from normal operations by the system (Billings, 1997).

Stop to consider

The content of this chapter has concentrated primarily upon commercial equipment where the users are selected and trained by the organisation. However, joint cognitive systems are also active when we use consumer products (such as cars, mobile phones, computer software, games consoles and even washing machines). There is great diversity of knowledge, experience and competence found within the general population. What implications might this have for the design process and the final design solution?

The design of such highly automated processes carries with it a great deal of 'up-front' investment. In return, the obvious benefit of automation is lowering the operator's workload. When the system is running well the operators are relieved of large amounts of their minute-to-minute cognitive workload. When things go wrong, the operator can be faced with a high level of unfamiliar and challenging cognitive demands as they attempt to intervene in host processes that are usually automated. Automation can make the operator less aware of what the system is doing (i.e. its 'inner workings') and the operator may become somewhat de-skilled. For example, automatic systems are often used to keep oil tanker support ships in their correct position (dynamic positioning system). If this fails, then the person at the helm needs to: (i) recognise that the system has failed; (ii) step in and take control; (iii) immediately become familiar with the strength and direction of the local sea currents to maintain the position of the vessel; and (iv) secure or restore the automated system. These ships, weighing thousands of tonnes, will often be only a few metres away from an oil production platform: if the vessel is not in the correct place then there is a significant risk of collision and with extremely serious consequences. If the person at the helm had been controlling the vessel manually, they would have implicitly been aware of the direction and strength of the current and would have developed a 'feel' for the situation. Furthermore, they would not have needed to take the actions required to secure and restore the malfunctioning automated system. However, automation is probably essential because a human could not perform such a control task to the same degree of accuracy usually achieved by the automated dynamic positioning system, nor would they have the psychological and physical endurance to do so for long periods. This example shows that the skill set required to control an automated system is often quite different from that required for manual control.

Automation can also mean that manual control skills are still required in the event of a system failure, but also that they are rarely practised (see Bainbridge, 1987, for a discussion of more of these 'ironies of automation').

Automation allows some tasks to be completed more reliably and to a higher standard than might be possible for a human user working without the aid of technology. However, such systems can create additional workload for the user when things go wrong. In such situations the user may not have the knowledge and skills required to step in to resolve the problem.

Displays

Modern computerised display systems offer the HMI designer many new opportunities. They are essentially 'blackboards' onto which can be drawn and animated almost any display format of the designer's choosing. Computers can also integrate many data sources to provide the user with information. The ultimate objective of display design is to enhance users' situation awareness (SA). SA is a difficult construct to define but in this context Endsley's (1988) definition serves quite well: SA is 'the perception of elements in the environment within a volume of time and space, the comprehension of their meaning, and the projection of their status in the near future'. Endsley describes three levels of SA. Level one is based on the perception of *data*. Level two requires these *data* to be combined to provide a 'bigger picture' (*information*). Level three is achieved when the operator has *knowledge*, fully *understands* their current situation and can project ahead into the future. There are many texts that outline options for display formats: some are generic in nature (e.g. McCormick and Sanders, 1992) and others are dedicated to specific operational contexts (e.g. Rajan, 1997; Harris, 2004; Wickens *et al.,* 2004). Many of the standards cited previously contain excellent information on these topics. Displays need to be designed so that they meet users' requirements for data and information.

Stop to consider

Do you agree with the statement that 'data are of little use: what users require is information'. Is this always true? Data are flexible (they can be used to answer many questions by being utilised in novel ways). Information reduces workload and error but can only answer an explicit question (it is much more task specific). It all depends upon your user and your task. Can you think of some examples of work roles in which supplying users with data might be more helpful than supplying them with information (and vice versa)?

Types of display

Displays convey data or information to the operator regarding the status of equipment and/or the progress of a task. You probably think first of visual displays. Two other commonly used displays are auditory display systems (mostly used for conveying alerts and warnings) and haptic displays. Haptic systems transmit information via our mechanoreceptors (these detect touch, pressure, vibration and tensioning of the skin). You may have found that such displays are quite useful during lectures when you have your mobile phone set to its vibration mode. Our sense of smell is also used in some displays: natural gas has an artificial odour introduced into it to alert us to leaks.

Key learning point

Three types of display are commonly used in work equipment: visual, auditory and haptic displays. Each makes use of different human senses to convey information to the user. There are many variations of each type of display. Each has its own advantages and disadvantages.

Displays exist for a purpose and part of the art of display design is selecting the correct display format for the requirements of the task. This includes identifying the senses (i.e. the sensory modalities) that are most appropriately involved given the needs of the user and constraints of the work situation. But before any of this can be done, the function of the display, i.e. what it actually needs to do, must be defined. Buck (1983) identified six categories of these display functions: instructions, commands, advisory messages, answers to enquiries, historical displays and predictive displays.

Instructions guide behaviour: they support performance by prompting the user what to do and when to do it. A simple example is an emergency exit sign over a doorway. More complex examples include dialogue messages such as those provided on automated cash machines or prompts that appear when installing applications on computers or mobile phones. In contrast, *command* messages give a straightforward instruction, for example 'do not enter', and 'do not smoke'. Command displays may be more complex than this. In warehouse environments 'pick and pack' instructions are sometimes used to tell workers what to select from and the specific location and route to take to and from that location. Such commands can significantly increase productivity, but perhaps at the expense at the worker's sense of autonomy. There is often only a very fine distinction between commands and instructions. As a rule of thumb, commands are more often referring to high priority/important behaviours. *Advisory* messages are a less extreme form of command. These may include such things as recommendations to avoid a situation (e.g. warnings about heavy traffic that appear on some satellite navigation systems) or information that supports the preparation or planning of an activity.

Point of integration

Some of the information provided in displays can reduce a worker's perceptions of autonomy and control. Low levels of autonomy may increase the risk of work-related stress (see Chapter 10).

Answers are a response to a specific user enquiry or are available when the user is uncertain about some aspect of the task. The need for answers is typical of an interactive information-handling work situation. Usually 'questions' are not posed directly to the system in a way that prompts a direct response. Instead, displays make answers available and it is up to the user to find them and then make use of them. The majority of the information sought from displays is of this type. For example, if we want to know how fast we are going in a car or what level of fuel we have, we look at the speedometer or the fuel gauge respectively. The display (answer) is always there but it is up to us to look at it. Of course, our interrogation of the displays is usually done for a reason: we have a question in mind. In the previous example, the underlying question may be, 'Do I have enough fuel to reach my destination'? The displays would not provide the answer directly because the driver would need to also know the distance to the destination and the rate at which the car uses fuel (satellite navigation systems do now make this calculation a little easier). Therefore, when designing displays we also need to bear in mind that users will often need to combine various pieces of useful data (*answers* from displays) in order to derive the *information* to find the solution to a problem or to deal with a question.

Historical displays are used to look back at the value of a variable over time. This can be useful when trying to interpret trends or patterns in data. This function shows that displays are not just transmitters of information: they can also reduce long-term memory load and as a consequence can help to reduce errors. For example, monitoring temperature fluctuations is an important job in many chemical production processes. Therefore, the temperature trends exhibited over an extended period of time may be important. Recalling such information in enough detail would be a very difficult task and potentially reduce the cognitive resources available to a worker to focus on the tasks at hand. However, information about trends could be critical to the task at hand. If the temperature levels begin nearing a pre-determined 'unsafe' level, the worker may be tempted to intervene. Historical displays may reveal that the temperature has been near that value for several weeks and that this is not an immediately critical event requiring action. On the other hand, it may have reached that value only in the last few hours indicating an acute problem. In cases like this, looking back at the trends in the information reduces both cognitive load and uncertainty. The critical 'unsafe' value can also be marked on the display (the big red 'danger area' that you see in many James Bond films). This effectively transfers the memory load for this value from the operator to the display. This is a simple example of distributed cognition that we cover in more detail later.

Predictive displays are specialised displays increasingly found in the control of complex processes. Predictive information estimates future values to support performance when making a judgement based on the current value. These displays offer particularly important support to the operator when they are attempting to make smoother transitions from one state to another. For this reason they are used in slow response (high inertia) systems. Examples include the control of large aircraft flying at slow speed or a supertanker loaded with crude oil. In high inertia systems it is difficult for the operator to detect on their own the immediate effect of their actions. Predictive displays are driven by a real-time computer model of the system which predicts its future state based on a series of assumptions (e.g. the situation if the operator does nothing or if the operator continues with their current actions). The distance into the future that the computer predicts depends upon a variety of factors including such things as how long it takes for the user input to take effect (the time lag) and inertia (how much input is needed to cause some effect). As you may have guessed, these factors mean that these displays are not perfect and are only as accurate as the algorithms from which they are computed. This leads to a 'catch-22' situation. The further you look into the future with the algorithm the more beneficial this type of display becomes. Unfortunately, this also means the more inaccurate the predictions become as a result of the increased number of assumptions that need to be made in the calculations and the increased influence of other unpredictable and uncontrollable environmental factors.

Key learning point

Displays can serve a variety of different functions. In designing a display an essential first step is to identify the purpose it will serve.

Having considered the various functions of displays we will now look at how the different display modalities fulfil these functions.

Visual displays

Modern computerised flexible display surfaces allow for visual displays to be presented in an almost infinite number of ways, limited only by the designer's imagination. That said, there are still only three basic formats for conveying quantitative data or numerical values in a visual form. These are: digital counters, fixed-index moving-pointer displays; and fixed-pointer moving-index displays (see Figure 8.5). In terms of the way they are perceived and used by humans, each format has strengths and weaknesses (Table 8.3). To understand the relative merits of each type of display, it is important to consider the two types of data/information that they provide to the user. *Rate information* allows the user to estimate the speed at which a certain value is changing. *State information* conveys information concerning a specific value at a given point in time (i.e. when the user looks at the display).

Fixed-index moving-pointer and fixed-pointer moving-index instruments come in two common formats: circular dials and vertical or tapes (although there are others). Fixed-pointer moving-index scales can also come in either a *full-scale* (displays that always show the user the full range of possible values) or a *windowed* format (displays that show a limited range of relevant values around the current value). These design choices mean that when designing visuals, a series of questions need to be addressed in order to identify the appropriate display format:

- Is the priority rate information or state information?
- What range of values needs to be displayed (all values or windowed)?
- Will the display be used in conjunction with others, for example by a user comparing the status of two systems?

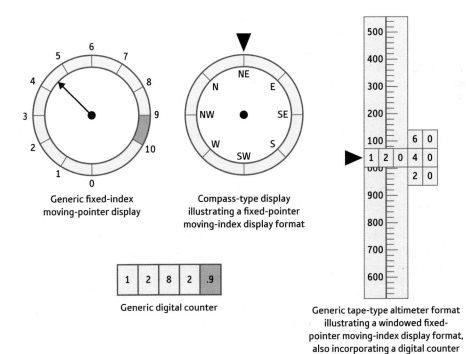

Generic fixed-index
moving-pointer display

Compass-type display
illustrating a fixed-pointer
moving-index display format

Generic digital counter

Generic tape-type altimeter format
illustrating a windowed fixed-
pointer moving-index display format,
also incorporating a digital counter

Figure 8.5	The basic visual display types for conveying quantitative information
	Source: Harris (2011).

Table 8.3	The relative merits of digital counters; fixed-index moving-pointer displays; and fixed-pointer moving-index displays

Situation	Preferred display format		
	Analogue		Digital
	Fixed-index moving-pointer	Fixed-pointer moving-index	Counter
Reading accuracy is very important	✗	✗	✓
Reading speed is important	✓	✗	✓
Values change quickly or frequently	✓	✗	✗
User requires rate of change information	✓	✗	✗
User requires information about deviations from a nominal value	✓	✗	✗
Minimal space is available	✗	✓	✓
User required to set a quantitative value	✓	✗	✓

Source: Harris (2011).

- Are the values being displayed likely to change slowly or rapidly?
- What degree of precision is required and how quickly must the user read them? In many systems there is a speed-accuracy trade-off: it might not be possible to display information in its most accurate and detailed form if the user needs to read it quickly. A combination of dials and counters can provide the best balance of both speed and accuracy.

The position of an individual display in relation to other displays is also important. If the user needs to make a comparative check reading between several systems, it often helps to have an easily recognisable nominal (or reference) value that has significant meaning to the operator in a consistent position. For example, a value at 12 o'clock on the dial can be easily interpreted by a user seeking to find out if the value is to the right or to the left of that nominal position. This enables a faster scan of the various pieces of data because at a glance the operator can see if the value is above or below or close to the reference value. This also helps the user to mentally integrate data from various dials into an emerging 'whole' picture of what is going on. Arranging the display elements in close proximity to one another further facilitates the mental integration of different pieces of data: this is the proximity compatibility principle (see Barnett and Wickens, 1988).

Flexible electro-optical display surfaces (such as LED, LCD and gas-plasma screens) allow the depiction of more complex processed data (information) using a range of formats not possible using earlier electro-mechanical ('clockwork') instruments. An example is a moving map display, now common in car satellite navigation systems and smartphones. The display options used in these devices allow the depiction of information that requires much less interpretation and re-coding by the user when compared to the use of static maps or charts. Navigation displays (NDs) in modern commercial aircraft demonstrate such advantages, especially when combined with high levels of control automation. For many years, answering a pilot's navigational questions (such as 'Where am I?'; and 'Which way am I going?') required interpretation of information sent by ground-based beacons to the aircraft. Modern NDs provide a moving 'God's-eye' view of the planned and actual progress of the journey (see Figure 8.6). The position of airports and beacons are clearly recognisable but – as you can see – a degree of knowledge is still required to interpret the display. It is also current practice to overlay the weather radar picture and Traffic Alert and Collision Avoidance System information on the NDs. Such systems allow pilots to better anticipate poor weather and plan an alternative route around it (i.e. the ND aids long-term decision-making) or avoid conflicting traffic (i.e. the ND also aids short-term decision-making). In an example you may be more familiar with when driving a car, traffic congestion may be displayed. Displaying these critical pieces of information in such a way allows a rapid assimilation of information about the situation.

Key learning point

If they are designed to convey information, visual displays can help to significantly reduce the cognitive load associated with specific work tasks (e.g. those involving the integration and analysis of various pieces of data).

| Figure 8.6 | Boeing 737 Navigation Display (ND) in map mode (God's-eye view). Navigation information is 'track oriented', not North oriented, as you would see in most maps |

Many modern process control displays (e.g. in those large petrochemical plants) utilise synoptic display formats. The *Oxford English Dictionary* defines 'synoptic' as 'taking or affording a comprehensive mental view'. This type of display is particularly useful for showing information about the status of relatively stable processes (rapidly changing values can be difficult to incorporate into such displays). The synoptic display depicted in Figure 8.7 is for an industrial coffee roaster. The advantage of this type of display is that the information is presented in a manner compatible with the operator's own mental model and/or the physical configuration of the system they are supervising and how it works. Numerical data (e.g. values about the temperature in different parts of a production process) and the system status (e.g. the green line indicating good flow of materials through a pipe) can be presented simultaneously. This helps the user to identify and diagnose any problems quickly.

If the system to be displayed is complex it may not be possible to depict all of the necessary information at once (partly because it would require a large screen and partly because it would be very confusing). *Interactive synoptic displays* take things one step further. Using cursor-positioning devices (e.g. a mouse, track ball, touchpad, etc.) users can interact directly with the display to focus in on particular elements of a process. This means the distinction between what constitutes a control and what constitutes a display becomes increasingly blurred: skilled operators will need to develop knowledge about which parts of the display to focus on through their control of the system. Indeed, most modern multifunctional interfaces now hide more information than they display. With old-style mechanical instruments this was impossible: each system parameter needed a dedicated display. Now many systems share the same display space, i.e. displays are 'moded'. For example, in the past it was typical for operators controlling chemical production processes to be faced with monitoring a plethora of mechanical gauges

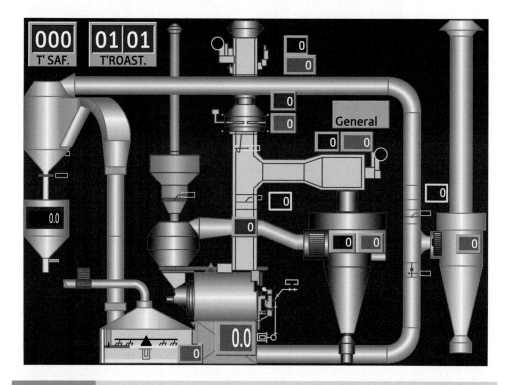

| Figure 8.7 | Synoptic display showing the Scolari Engineering Industrial Coffee Roaster process control (http://www.scolarieng.com) |

and dials, some of which were not even in the central control room. Today, it is common for all such data to be accessed by skilled and knowledgeable operators from a small number of computer screens cited in a central control room.

With moded displays critical system parameters are often monitored automatically and failures are only drawn to the attention of the operator as required. In a system under supervisory control, targets for performance are set using one part of the interface and then hidden while the tasks needed to achieve them are executed (their display being replaced with another component associated with system monitoring). While the manner in which the information is now conveyed may be superior to the old instrumentation, the operator now requires a great deal more knowledge about how to use the computerised HMI in addition to the knowledge needed to manage the system or work processes they are trying to control. For example, the chemical process operators discussed earlier now need to remember which pieces of data are hidden (e.g. the mix of chemicals in the reactor) while they are accessing information (e.g. about the temperature of the chemicals entering the reaction vessel). There is an apt, old saying: 'out of sight, out of mind'. If you can't see it, you have a good chance of forgetting about it. On an aircraft flight deck, for exactly this reason, it is mandated that certain primary flight data (e.g. altitude) must be displayed at all times.

Key learning point

Workers need to develop new knowledge and skills to work with some types of visual displays as important information can be hidden until the user requests it.

Auditory displays

As already discussed, visual displays can be quite complex and provide the user with a potentially bewildering array of information. Workers are now being asked to monitor and manage increasingly complex systems. There is a risk that the cognitive processes linked to the visual senses can become overloaded. This has made the design of auditory warning systems even more important. As an aside, when two or more display modes (e.g. auditory and visual) are combined it becomes a multi-modal design.

The auditory sensory channel has various advantages and disadvantages over the visual channel. Its main advantage is that it is not dependent on the user's direction of gaze, which makes it particularly suitable for alerting functions. Aside from somewhere to situate a speaker, auditory displays do not require significant space. One potential limitation is that the information they convey is transient (it lasts for only a short time) and can be lost against a background of other noise. Whenever the auditory channel is used, the phonological loop of human working memory (WM) will be involved. This has inherent limitations as we may not recall all of the sounds that we hear. All of this means that the auditory modality is best used just to grab a user's attention (e.g. an alarm signal) and direct them towards a particular situation or towards an element of a visual display which contains relevant non-transient data (e.g. a temperature level that would have triggered the alarm). Specifically, Sanders and McCormick (1993) suggest the auditory channel is best used when:

- the message is simple and short and will not need to be referred to later;
- the message deals with events in time (i.e. it indicates when an event is occurring such as warning the user when a temperature reaches a certain critical value);
- the message calls for immediate or urgent action;
- the user's visual system is overburdened with data and information from other displays;

- the lighting level (e.g. bright sunshine) limits use of visual displays;
- the user is moving around when operating the system because this can make it difficult to use visual displays and location of auditory signals can be detected by the user.

As with any display, it is important to identify the function of an auditory warning before it is used. Noyes et al. (2004) identified four common functions of these types of auditory displays:

- *Monitoring*: Assessing a situation by indicating deviations from pre-determined fixed limits or a threshold value. These deviations may not require any action on the part of the user. For example, a monitoring function is fulfilled when a device automatically monitoring a patient's blood pressure beeps to indicate that a reading is currently being taken;
- *Alerting*: Drawing the operator's attention to a hazardous or potentially hazardous situation. In the example of the blood pressure measuring device, an auditory display may alert a nearby nurse that there had been a significant drop in a patient's blood pressure;
- *Informing*: Providing information about the nature and criticality of a problem to facilitate a response (e.g. when the pitch of the sound is high this may indicate that the patient's blood pressure has dropped to a dangerously low level, requiring intervention by the nurse);
- *Advising*: Supporting decision-making activities when addressing an abnormal situation (e.g. a specific alarm signal indicating that additional specialist needs to be contacted as a matter of urgency so that the patient can be resuscitated).

For an auditory display system to be effective, the information that it transmits must first be heard by the user. The background noise within which the signal needs to operate means that a noise spectrum analysis of the operating environment needs to be completed across all audible frequencies. This allows the identification of appropriate amplitudes and frequencies into which to insert a warning signal. This helps to ensure that the warning signal is loud enough but also that it doesn't share its frequency components with those found in the background noise, making it easier for the user to differentiate the signal from other ambient noise. This is just a starting point in designing the signal. As described shortly, manipulating other features of the signal can help to ensure that the operator can discriminate it from the other potential warnings and identify its meaning. Auditory warnings come in two basic types: *non-speech warnings*, comprised of sounds alone, and *speech warnings*, which use a combination of introductory warnings tones followed by a short spoken message. Edworthy and Patterson (1985) listed four features that aid in the discrimination of non-speech auditory warnings. These may be applied either singly or in combination:

- The *pitch* of the signal (e.g. a very high-pitched signal is very often used for security or fire alarms because it is unpleasant to listen to, so people are motivated to take action to distance themselves from the noise).
- Its *harmonic* qualities. These can manipulated by mixing several frequencies to produce a single chord-like sound: the 'start up' signals associated with different brands of personal computers are easily recognisable chord-like signals.
- Its *timbre*. This is the sound wave shape/quality that gives sound its 'colour', often indicating how it was produced or where it came from. For example, it remains relatively simple to distinguish between most artificial computer-generated voices and human voices because vocal chords help to produce signals with a recognisable timbre; timbre is the quality that serves to distinguish a guitar from a piano.
- The *rhythm* (or cadence) of the signal.

Key learning point

There are numerous ways that an auditory signal can be manipulated to ensure that it conveys pertinent and useful information in a way that is noticed by the user.

The use of auditory icons may be one way of enhancing auditory signals (Gaver, 1989). These are acoustically complex, environmental sounds which represent in the mind of the user the event(s) linked to the warning. Ulfvengren (2003) produced a prototype suite of auditory icons for use as warnings in vehicles: high temperature was represented by the sound of sizzling hot water and low battery voltage by the sound of an engine failing to start. These were significantly more effective than simple, meaningless warning sounds (such as bleeps). Perry, Stevens and Howell (2006) found similar results for auditory icons in aircraft. You may have already anticipated a potential drawback of this approach: these icons can become hidden in the background noise as they are specifically designed to mimic those produced by events occurring frequently in the work environment.

Integrating both tone and speech warnings can be a useful way of attaching meaning to a tone, but these also have great potential for getting lost in the environmental background noise. To avoid this problem the warning message can be preceded by an introductory alerting sound (as you often hear when associated with announcements made at railway stations). This can also be used to convey the priority of the message: on Airbus aircraft, the highest priority warnings are introduced by a single chime; cautions are introduced by two chimes and advisories by three (naturally, the highest priority warning is presented first). Research in auditory perception indicates that when a speech warning is introduced by an alerting sound, it is essential to leave a gap of around 0.5 seconds between the alert and the speech message. Without this gap a phenomenon known as 'forward masking' will occur, with psychological processes becoming cluttered with information and obliterating the first part of the speech message. The human information-processing system needs time to re-focus the subject of its attention and to allow new information through the sensory register. Research also shows that speech messages should be kept short: the function of the warning system is only to gain the attention of the operator and orientate them to other displays where other, less transient information can be found. Messages that are too long and/or too complex will overburden the working memory and as a consequence may not be acted upon.

Key learning point

An understanding of the limits of human information-processing facilitates the effective design of displays.

Haptic displays

There has been increasing interest in the last decade about the use of haptic display devices (i.e. those that use our ability to sense touch, pressure and vibrations). The haptic channel has several benefits:

■ It is omnidirectional (it can receive signals from all directions) and is not blocked by the high levels of background noise or low light levels that are found in some workplaces or in many emergency situations.

- It can be used to convey spatial information indicating where the signal is coming from. Research shows that this is superior to auditory localisation – we can locate the source of a signal very accurately through touch.

- The haptic sense cannot be 'switched off' by either the users themselves or by the impact of the environment. This makes it particularly useful for providing warnings. Sometimes it can be blocked by other features of the work setting (e.g. if the user wears thick gloves or various items of protective work equipment).

- Warning information delivered through the haptic sense is noticeable, but is less distracting when the user is engaged in other tasks and for those around them. It also tends not to be prone to evoking the startle reaction often associated with auditory displays which can distract users' attention away from critical elements of their core work tasks.

- It has a longer short-term memory trace/effect than the other major senses. Research shows that it lasts ten times longer than the visual sense and at least three times longer than that received through the auditory sense.

In its simplest form we can use haptic signals by providing them with a distinctive shape or edge to make them distinguishable without having to look at them or need illumination. Courtney and Chow (2001) described how blind people could use their feet to discriminate shape symbols on pavements. Such markings are now common and found adjacent to pedestrian crossings, often designated by raised bumps.

The haptic sense has been used for some time in the design of aircraft warning systems in the form of a device that vibrates key controls (a 'stick shaker') used to warn pilots that, without intervention, the aircraft is about to stall. Similar systems have been developed for road cars (see Ho and Spence, 2008) sending vibrations through the seat to warn drivers of such things as lane departure (the Lane Departure Warning System, introduced by Citroën) or of the presence of potentially conflicting traffic in their blind spot (found in BMW cars). More complex haptic display devices have been developed for military aviation applications. These are used when visual workload is high and there is a strong requirement for keeping the pilot alert to visual signals (in military terms this is rather colourfully referred to as 'head up and eyeballs out'). This may occur when the pilot is controlling a hovering rescue helicopter searching for a person or a boat in the sea near a cliff face. The Tactile Situational Awareness System (TSAS) is made up of a vest worn beneath the flying suit, lined with vertical rows of 'tactors' (vibrating pads). These tactors vibrate to indicate to the pilot the directional drift, the type of target being sought and its target direction. A similar system of tactors worn under a wetsuit has been developed for use by navy bomb disposal divers: they often work in very restricted visibility with the tactors acting as an aid to guide them when swimming to their target.

Distributed cognition

Using any automated or highly computerised system requires semantic, syntactic and lexical knowledge. Semantic knowledge refers to having some idea of what the system can do (e.g. we know that a computer can be used to store data, retrieve data, manipulate data). Syntactic knowledge encompasses the lower-level operating concepts and grammars needed to operate a system (when using a PC this includes pointing and clicking, dragging and dropping, 'opening' and 'closing' files etc.). At an even lower level, lexical knowledge is required to learn the particular sequence of low-level actions to perform a task (Schneiderman, 1998). This means that a user's mental model of the computerised system is needed to realise the potential for the equipment to improve work performance. This is a product of experience and training, so it needs to be recognised that HCD does not progress in isolation. Within the HSI philosophy there are intimate links between the design of equipment and the physical work space and the provision of education and training. As we will see, not only have computers and automation changed the nature of the control of systems, they have also changed the nature of human cognition.

Key learning point

The concept of distributed cognition illustrates that the ultimate goal in HCD is to offer better control of the work process and to improve work outcomes, not just to manage the user interface. Very 'usable' systems are not always good at helping the user to achieve their goal.

Human information-processing theories underpin a great deal of HMI/HCD, but on their own are not enough to explain human cognition during work tasks. We need to look beyond the psychological and physical capabilities of the human operator. Hutchins (1995a) developed the concept of *distributed cognition*, a concept which became one of the underlying principles in JCSs. Hutchins argued that cognitive psychology (see Chapter 1) was not wrong, but was limited, focusing only on the individual and not on them interacting in their environment. JCSs help us to understand better how workers benefit from using 'things that make us smart' (Norman, 1993). Everyone, either knowingly or unknowingly, uses artefacts around them to enhance their cognitive abilities. Understanding how this works helps us to design work equipment and work environments in ways that would not be possible through the application of principles of cognitive psychology alone.

Distributed cognition is the coordination and collaboration between users, the artefacts they use and the wider environment. It is probably best explained through a few examples. At a very basic level, using a pencil and paper improves human memory, either in the long term (e.g. when keeping a diary) or in the shorter-term working memory context (as we might do when doing a mathematics task involving long division, we use the pencil and paper to free up space in our working memory). In other words, a pencil and paper makes us smarter. When doing long division with the aid of a pencil and paper, the main information-processing limitation is now not the size of our working memory but rather the accuracy with which we can recall and execute the procedure for doing such a calculation. The role and function of memory is now distributed between a human and a non-human component (in this case, the pencil and paper).

Key learning point

Looking at the cognitive capabilities of humans provides us with some insight into how good design can be achieved. But more can be done if we consider how human cognitive process capabilities are altered by the way we use work equipment.

Salomon (1993) proposed two general categories of distributed cognition: shared cognition and off-loading. Shared cognition describes interactions between different people engaged in a common activity. In this situation, cognition across a group changes as their interactions progress: there are changes in individual workers' representations of the task and the group's shared representations of the task (their mutual understanding of what needs to be done). Off-loading describes cognitive tool use (also described as 'external cognition'; Scaife and Rogers, 1996). This is more pertinent to the design of HCD. The technology being used serves as a 'cognitive amplifier' (Pea, 1985). It enhances the user's abilities by distributing a task (or tasks) between the technology, equipment and the user. It also simultaneously changes the nature of the cognitive tasks carried out by the user. Modern technology can transform data on behalf of the human, a process that would previously be done either in working memory or via a series of processes and calculations using rudimentary technology. The work done by architects is a good example: much of their work now involves computer-aided design. This changes the skills and knowledge needed to exploit the properties of the artefact(s) that, in turn, enhances the user's cognitive system. To make the best of the capabilities of a word-processing package you need the skills and knowledge to use the computer. Being a creative and knowledgeable wordsmith is not now enough if you want to exploit the additional functionality. The skill sets required to search for information on the Internet are very different to those needed to locate information in a library. Early aircraft were flown using stick and rudder; modern aircraft are managed using the on-board automation. The effects of high degrees of automation and computerisation go on and on, but it is now essential to realise that tasks are distributed between the user and the computer; this *dialogue* with the computer makes us smarter. It is no longer a 'boss and slave' relationship ('I say – you do') as in early machines. Technology changes the nature of cognition *and* of the work itself.

Hutchins (1995b), in the paper 'How a cockpit remembers its speeds', examines the manner in which the pilot's cognitive representation of speed and the processes for calculating target speeds is distributed across human and machine agents on the aircraft flight deck. Calculations of air speeds draw upon the pilot's long-term memory, information displayed on air speed indicators, speed reference cards and the use of established prescriptive flight deck procedures. This example shows that speed calculation and speed awareness are *not* simply a product of the pilot's working memory (which is rather reassuring for all passengers given the limitations and frailties of human working memory). Instead, it is a task distributed across the whole flight deck that ultimately results in a smarter flight crew and a more resilient system.

Research methods in focus

Evaluating human–machine interfaces (HMIs) using multiple methods

Evaluating designs against user requirements is a complex task that cannot be satisfactorily completed using a single research method. It shows how different methods can be combined to deal with difficult evaluation issues. The evaluation of the human–machine interface (HMI) falls into two distinct stages. *Formative evaluation* addresses individual interface components, usually as part prototypes. These are functional prototypes of discrete parts of the HMI process. *Summative evaluation* assembles all the components into a full implementation of the user interface to assess its usability as a whole. *Summative evaluation* occurs at the end of the detailed design stages. *Formative evaluation* takes place during the design evaluation/commissioning stages. These two stages require quite different approaches to data collection and analysis.

Early stage *formative evaluations* often use a simple design walk-through. This utilises a simple paper-based, page-by-page representation of the interface, presented to typical users for comment. For example, Morley and Harris (1994) presented experienced pilots with simple paper-based, PowerPoint mock-ups of a new terrain awareness display, depicted in various ways. These were very quick and cheap to produce and pilots were able to freely annotate these paper-based representations, giving the researchers a lasting record of points of concern to modify in the next design iteration, before progressing to the time and expense of producing a computer-based animated prototype system. This approach is ideal as an initial 'coarse filter' for assessing the design and operating logic of an interface. If the interface passes this test, then prototypes of the various components can be developed.

This stage of formative evaluation typically uses one (or more) of three approaches. *Experimental approaches* are the most sophisticated. These are most useful when evaluating several competing design solutions for one aspect of the HMI using a part-prototype. If the system is implemented on a computerised, rapid prototyping system then quantitative data such as keystrokes, time taken, errors etc. may be logged automatically (see Card et al., 1980). This approach provides objective ('hard facts') information about *what* people did but not *why* they did it. In other words, the focus is on the use and the outcomes achieved when using the HMI, but would yield little data about the underlying cognitive mechanisms of the process. For example, we might see that design Option A led operators to make two errors per minute, whereas design Option B led operators to make 10 errors per minute, and often of a certain type. We can see Option A is better, but we can only guess at why. To evaluate the cognitive component it is necessary to supplement the experimental approach with structured questionnaires, subjective workload scales or with a full user debrief.

Observation and qualitative interviews provide data concerning which aspects of the interface users find difficult and why, but in contrast to experiments provide little hard performance data. However, this approach often produces the most useful data for the first design iterations of a system. These are an excellent adjunct to experimental evaluations. *Questionnaires* are the best way to evaluate the user's affective response to a system in a structured manner (e.g. to capture data about levels of frustration, perceived workload, perceptions of autonomy etc.). Again, these are especially useful when used in conjunction with other approaches. Several textbooks describing the full range of evaluation approaches are available (e.g. Stanton et al., 2013). There are also compendia describing the range of subjective measures available (e.g. Gawron, 2000).

Summative evaluation is the evaluation of the whole system in its (almost) final form. The whole system is not just the user interface, software and hardware. It also encompasses supporting material such as manuals and training courses. The tasks undertaken during summative evaluation are representative of the tasks carried out using the whole system in everyday operation. For example, when evaluating an aircraft's flight management system, summative evaluation may be based around setting it up in flight or defining and inserting a new mid-flight. Benchmarking tests of software are also summative evaluations. These also comprise a series of representative tasks, usually undertaken by expert users so that comparisons between systems are not compounded by the effects of expertise.

There are other forms of summative evaluation. Large, safety-critical systems (e.g. nuclear power plants or petrochemical plants) may be subject to error analyses and probabilistic risk assessments at various stages in their design cycle using a variety of formal techniques. Probabilistic risk analysis techniques (e.g. THERP – technique for human error rate prediction, Swain and Guttman, 1983; HEART – human error assessment and reduction technique, Williams, 1986) model a range of likely normal and non-normal scenarios that may occur when the system is in use. Typically they integrate the procedures to be followed, the quality of the interface, the users' characteristics (experience, fatigue etc.) and their working environment (noise, vibration, temperature etc.) within a single analysis to produce an estimate of the likelihood of various anticipated types of failure. Human error identification methods (e.g. SHERPA – systematic human error reduction and prediction approach, Embrey, 1986; HET – Human Error Template, Stanton et al., 2006) only predict the likely types of errors. These latter methods are better used during early design stages where it is quicker and cheaper to correct any HMI or procedural design flaws. Full-scale probabilistic risk-assessment techniques (e.g. THERP or HEART) need a relatively mature, near operational interface and operating concept to support good estimates.

▶

▶ No matter how good they are, these formal methods cannot identify all problems that reside in the depths of the systems that lie dormant until someone tries to use them. It is essential to follow up the performance of a piece of equipment when it enters service, for example using formal reporting procedures. This information will be useful when producing mid-life updates or designing the next generation of the system. Summative evaluation does not stop on release to service. For example, many software companies ask users to send program-generated error reports over the Internet when software fails or crashes.

Key learning point

To evaluate against performance requirements these criteria need to be operationalised. This is sometimes not easy; for example, how would you operationalise 'promoting user understanding'? When developing performance criteria they need to be measurable in some way.

Summary

The modern concept of ergonomics is quite different from the old approach which was concerned only with the user interface. Ergonomics is about work systems. Although this chapter has concentrated largely on the HCD process, it should be evident that this cannot be separated from other activities such as selection, training and other organisational and economic imperatives (such as the requirements to reduce staffing levels or outsource). Ergonomists who restrict themselves to the design of the user interface without considering the wider context are more likely to contribute to the problem rather than its solution. In Chapter 15 we focus on one such situation: the use of communications technology at work.

Psychological research and theory allow us to design displays that 'work with us' when we are carrying out work tasks. They allow us to gather and process much more information than might be possible without them. The concepts of joint cognitive systems and distributed cognition allow us to identify and capitalise upon the many synergies between human and machine capabilities. They also highlight how we might need to rethink the limits of human capabilities now that there is so much equipment that makes us 'smarter'. None of this comes without some drawbacks. Might we risk overloading workers with information? When automated systems fail, workers may not have the necessary skills to get things up and running again. However, without these systems it might not be possible to complete work tasks to the required standard. Therefore, systems, designers need to go through a rigorous design and evaluation process to achieve the right balance between user and machine control.

Ergonomists are often members of a larger design team and there is usually great pressure to produce 'product' – clients like to see something. However, there is an old, cautionary saying: 'there is never enough money available to design it right first time but there is always enough money to redesign it'. If the early stages of the design process (the requirements) are not right, no matter how brilliant the designer is, the rest will be of poor quality. Investing money in the early stages of the design process will ultimately save money in the later stages. Therefore it appears that being an ergonomist is one of the least rewarding jobs in the world: if you get it right, no one will notice.

Closing case study

Driving (and stopping) on autopilot

Many modern cars have cruise control installed in them, but a more advanced form of the technology, adaptive cruise control (ACC), is now available in several makes of luxury car. ACC not only controls the speed of the vehicle but when in traffic moving more slowly than the driver's selected free-traffic speed, the system keeps station (at a set following distance) from the vehicle in front. It does this with the aid of a low-powered radar system. ACC systems also have limited authority over the vehicle's brakes.

However, an even more advanced technology is now available. Honda's advanced driver assistance system (ADAS) links ACC with a lane-keeping assistance system (LKAS). This combination keeps the vehicle centred in the roadway following a vehicle in front at a set distance without driver input to the steering wheel or throttle – almost analogous to an aircraft's autopilot system. In the ADAS system, three levels of automation are available to the driver: simple cruise control (automation has authority over the throttle); ACC (automation has authority over the throttle and brakes to keep station with the leading vehicle) and ADAS (where the vehicle has authority over throttle, brakes and steering). These modes are arranged hierarchically.

Not all automatic protections (lane keeping and/or following distance) are available in all modes and the ADAS system automatically transitions between modes at set speeds, hence protections that the driver may think are in place are actually not available. Automatic mode transitions were one of the principal concerns identified in the implementation of automation on the flight deck and have been implicated in several aviation accidents and incidents. Furthermore, these new driver aids may be supplemented with collision warning and avoidance systems (CWS/CAS).

With these systems the nature of the primary guidance of the car has changed from one of percep-tual motor control to that of hazard surveillance and automation management.

Source: Don Harris (chapter author), using Young et al. (2007).

Suggested exercise

Taking a systemic HSI approach to analysing the problem, the technology and the driver interfaces may be adequate for the job. However, have the requirements for driver training and the regulatory overview for the performance and maintenance of these highly automated systems kept pace? Is there a better way of implementing automation of this type?

Test your learning

Short-answer questions

1 Provide brief definitions of the following: human factors; human-centred design; the socio-technical context of design; hierarchical task analysis; functional allocation.
2 Provide a brief description of the key stages in the human-centred design process.
3 What are the three types of requirement in human-centred design?
4 Describe Ackoff's (1989) categories of information.
5 In the human-centred design process, how are the user and organisational requirements specified?
6 What are distributed cognition and joint cognitive systems?
7 List the advantages and disadvantages of a) visual displays; b) auditory displays; and c) haptic displays.

Suggested assignments

1   How can information about end-user requirements be collected during the design process? What are the strengths and weaknesses of the various methods you have identified?
2   How can the eventual success (or failure) of a human-centred design process be evaluated?
3   Discuss the impact that the wider organisational context has on the human-centred design process.
4   Why might the automation of tasks be desirable and what are its drawbacks? How might these drawbacks be minimised?
5   Discuss the ways in which different types of displays can be integrated to ensure effective task performance.

Relevant websites

The website of the Chartered Institute of Ergonomics & Human Factors provides an excellent starting point for exploring the various issues associated with designing work and work environments. It can be found at: http://www.ergonomics.org.uk/

The US National Institute for Occupation Safety and Health (NIOSH) publishes a number of documents about the impact of the physical aspects of work design on employees. These can be found at: http://www.cdc.gov/niosh/topics/Ergonomics/

The User Experience Professionals Association website http://uxpa.org/ provides some useful definitions and examples of human-centred design. http://www.usabilitynet.org also provides some good descriptions of key elements of the human-centred design process.

Suggested further reading

Full details for all references are given in the list at the end of this book.

1   Excellent introductions to the use of psychology in the design of work and work environments are provided in Noyes' *Designing for Humans (Psychology at Work)* (Psychology Press, 2001) and Grandjean and Kroemer's *Fitting the Task to the Human: A textbook of occupational ergonomics* (Taylor and Francis, 1997, 5th edition).

2   The topic of human factors is covered in both breadth and depth in Stanton et al.'s *Human Factors Methods: A practical guide for engineering and design* (Ashgate, 2013, 2nd edition).

Notes

1   If you want to travel faster and carry a heavier load, making a mechanical horse is not the best way of achieving these aims – a different approach to solving the problem is required, for example designing a car!

2   Many other standards also exist (e.g. the US military MIL-STD-1472: Department of Defence, 1999; or US Nuclear Regulator's NUREG-0700 Design at work: US Nuclear Regulatory Commission, 2002).

CHAPTER 9
Training and development

LEARNING OBJECTIVES

After studying this chapter, you should be able to:

1 identify and explain the three components of the learning cycle;

2 describe and explain the purpose of three different levels of training needs analysis;

3 explain how learning theories can inform training design;

4 recognise how individual differences can impact upon trainee learning;

5 identify barriers to learning transfer and how these can be addressed;

6 explain why teams have specific training needs;

7 understand the importance of training evaluation for determining cost effectiveness and utility of training interventions;

8 describe differences between formal and informal learning;

9 outline how leaders engage in training and development;

10 describe how training activities form part of a learning organisation.

Opening case study

Wall Street Journal interview with Professor Eduardo Salas

When a journalist from the Wall Street Journal asked Professor Eduardo Salas – one of the most influential researchers in the field of corporate training – what surprised him most about the way in which companies conduct training for staff, his response was 'How little organisations rely on the science of learning and training'. He says that most companies have a myth about training – that if you send an unskilled employee to training, there will be an immediate improvement when the employee returns to work. Drawing on decades of research, Professor Salas lists the following as the biggest mistakes made by companies in relation to training:

1 Companies failing to take the time to analyse what their training needs are, who needs training and what kind.

2 Not evaluating how well employees have learned, or relying on reaction data – whether employees have enjoyed the training.

3 Believing that technology can solve all training problems – that a mobile app or computer game will solve everything, when in reality learners need precise learning objectives, clear feedback, a form of measurement or assessment of how well they are doing, and regular opportunities to practice and get feedback.

4 Failing to set the conditions, so that when trainees go back to work they have the right support from supervisors to apply and sustain their new skills in their job.

5 Work psychology, he suggests, provides a scientific framework, empirical evidence and a clear rationale for how employee training can be developed and implemented by companies to achieve maximum return on investment.

Source: Wall Street Journal from: http://online.wsj.com/news/articles/
SB10001424052970204425904578072950518558328 (accessed 26 October 2014)

Introduction

Training and development activities have the potential to benefit individuals, organisations and society as a whole. Engaging in training means that employees are able to develop a portfolio of skills that can improve their earning potential, chances of promotion and opportunities to engage in more interesting work. Now regarded as a core business activity, training and development is recognised as an important contributor to employee performance and organisational success: US organisations spend more than $160 billion annually on employee learning (American Society for Training and Development, 2013), and similar patterns of investment are repeated across the world. In China, for example, businesses historically had to rely on government to allocate labour, but profound economic changes have prompted a dramatic growth in investment targeted at equipping employees with the core skills and abilities for business success (Warner and Goodall, 2010).

National economic competitiveness is linked to a country's skill base: the existence of a substantial pool of skilled workers is not only important for local business, but also essential for attracting inward investment from international sources like global companies. An example of this was investment by Japanese companies in the British car market in the 1980s and 1990s, which was prompted in part by the existence of a skilled workforce. More recently, India has been able to attract considerable inward investment because of the existence of a large pool of employees with IT and computing knowledge and skills.

Just as companies compete on a global level for the best 'talent', national governments are therefore increasingly focused on implementing policies and strategies designed to improve the employability and productivity of future workers in their countries (Ashton and Felstead, 2000; Bacon and Hoque, 2010; Grugulis, 2007).

Work psychology has played a very important part in the development of the science of training and development. There is research to show that skilled individuals perform work faster and more safely, make fewer errors, produce higher quality work, and that training can lead to improved job performance and other benefits like improved efficacy and lower stress among employees (Arthur et al., 2003; Frayne and Geringer, 2000). There is also a great deal of research and theory that provides us with good insight into how employees learn, the training methods likely to result in successful transfer of learning to the workplace, and how training can be evaluated to ensure maximum return on investment (Aguinas and Kraiger, 2009; Salas et al., 2012). In this chapter we draw on this evidence base to introduce core concepts (i.e. the training cycle, training-needs analysis, training design and **training evaluation**) and describe some of the methods used to support employee learning. We also reflect on the emergence of **learning organisations** and consider future opportunities and challenges for the science of training. To begin with, however, it is important to clarify what we mean by training and how it compares to the concept of learning.

Point of integration

The learning organisation is an important concept in organisational change (see Chapter 14). This underlines the importance of training and development before, during and after episodes of organisational change.

Learning is a much broader concept than training. We learn all the time by observing and listening to others, particularly when we take on a new role or join a new company. For example, organisational newcomers often spend a lot of time watching and listening to others in order to learn the social norms and values that influence how people work in that setting. This learning is described as 'informal', because what is learnt is not structured by the organisation: the learner has more influence over what he or she considers important and therefore what he or she will learn. In contrast, training is a *subcategory* of learning that depends on structured activities that are designed by an organisation in order to achieve learning and development that is desired by the organisation because it meets specific business needs. Therefore, unlike training, informal learning does not necessarily result in improved performance: for example, a newcomer might learn by observing a colleague whom they like, but who may not be working in a way that is desired or rewarded by the organisation.

In this chapter we draw on the definition provided by Salas et al. (2012: 77), which describes training as 'planned and systematic activities designed to promote the acquisition of knowledge (i.e., need to know), skills (i.e., need to do) and attitudes (i.e., need to feel)' that have the goal of creating 'sustainable changes in behaviour and cognition so that individuals possess the competencies they need to perform a job'. We also follow Aguinas and Kraiger (2009) in using 'training' to refer to training and development activities.

How training has changed

There have been many changes to the ways in which people work over recent decades, which have also impacted on how training has evolved (Cascio and Aguinis, 2008; Salas et al., 2012). The photographs in Figure 9.1 illustrate a few of these changes. The group of 1950s engineering apprentices with their tutor in photograph A illustrate one of the most common means by which workers were trained by companies until the early 1970s: the

Figure 9.1	The changing context of training (left: c.1950; right: modern day)
	Source: left: Allan Cash Picture Library/Alamy Stock Photo

apprenticeship. Most apprentices spent several years with a company learning a particular skilled 'craft'. Typically, they remained with the company when their apprenticeship ended, often in a 'job for life'. As job tasks and demands did not change very much and apprentices stayed with the company that had trained them, businesses could afford to invest time and money in lengthy and relatively expensive training programmes, because there was a high likelihood that their investment would be repaid.

However, today's workers are far more likely to work in offices and have jobs related to service or knowledge work. They are more likely to use computers and information technology and, as the employees in photograph B, they may be expected to monitor and respond to continual streams of information from different sources simultaneously while also communicating with colleagues and customers who might sometimes be located in another part of the world. Whereas traditional training often focused on teaching the manual skills needed to produce 'something' (e.g. on a manufacturing production line), modern-day training is much more likely to involve developing cognitive and social skills necessary for performing customer service work or data analysis. Advances in technology have also led to more innovation and shorter product cycles, which in turn have meant that organisations often need to operate in more competitive and volatile markets. One response has been the introduction

Point of integration

The way that workers shape their careers (see Chapter 13) has changed significantly over recent years. This has consequences for the way that employers make decisions about the type of training made available. Employee attitudes such as organisational commitment and job satisfaction can also be heavily influenced by the availability of training.

Suggested exercise

Think about your own training and development learning. What training have you received from employers, and how is the course you are studying likely to contribute to your learning for future jobs? Looking ahead, what other training might an employer expect you to engage in?

of flatter organisational structures (i.e. fewer levels of management and multi-skilled employees) that allow for greater flexibility. This has led to a focus on enabling employees to develop a portfolio of skills and a commitment to continual learning that makes it easier for them to undertake different roles as demands change. However, as employees develop marketable knowledge and skills, they are also able to move between employers, which makes it less financially viable for companies to invest in long periods of training.

The training cycle

Training has the potential to deliver many benefits, but it is important to note (as Salas does in the opening case study) that training per se may not necessarily be beneficial. Too little, too much or the wrong type of training can all cause problems. In fact, training that is misdirected or inappropriate for the specific needs of those involved can be worse than no training at all (Davies, 1972). Training is only beneficial if it is based on a needs analysis and is designed in a way that ensures this need is met. We can only know if training is beneficial if we evaluate its success. These three components – training needs analysis (TNA), training design (TD) and training evaluation (TE) – constitute the training cycle (see Figure 9.2). Together they form a tripod that supports effective training. All three are equally important: if one leg of the tripod is poorly constructed or is missing then the training is likely to fail. As Figure 9.2 shows, the training and development process moves from assessment of need (TNA), which provides the information needed to design and implement appropriate development activities (TD), to an evaluation of what has taken place (TE). This is described as a cycle, because information gained through TE should be used as feedback to improve future training activities. Each of these elements (TNA, TD and TE) is considered in more detail in the following sections.

Key learning point

Training needs analysis (TNA), training design (TD) and training evaluation (TE) constitute the three stages of the training cycle.

Training needs analysis

Before starting any systematic training or development activity, those responsible should satisfy themselves that it will produce worthwhile results. Unfortunately, detailed TNA does not always happen. It may be that managers believe that training (any training) is a 'good thing'. On occasions, training programmes can take on a life of their own; occurring regardless of any clear and established need for them, and employees may find themselves

| Figure 9.2 | The training cycle |

on a training course simply because their manager has been given a performance target to ensure that staff participate in a pre-determined number of training days per year. Alternatively, those with power over budgets or resources may prefer to rely on personal 'instinct' rather than undertake what is perceived as a costly TNA. Yet, poorly constructed training programmes can be substantially more costly for an organisation. Money and time are needed to develop, implement and manage the training, and there is often a decline in productivity while employees are away from their work. Not surprisingly, senior managers are likely to ask for a justification of expenses in terms of return on investment (ROI).

Point of integration

There is frequently a trade-off between the need for training and selection activities. If well-qualified and appropriately skilled employees already exist then good selection processes may off-set the need for extensive TNA activities. If, however, there is a shortage of ready-equipped workers then TNA takes on greater importance, and individuals' potential to benefit from training (their trainability) takes on added importance.

A training needs analysis (TNA) is the important first step in developing a training programme. Its primary aim is to identify the **training objectives (TOs)** or in simple terms, what the training needs to achieve. Training objectives can be diverse and range from individual to organisational level. For example, an *organisational-level* training objective might be that all employees should receive basic training in health and safety procedures, or that all newcomers should participate in a two-day corporate induction programme.

Examples of *individual-level* training objectives for, for instance, taxi drivers at a particular company include being able to identify the quickest route between two locations, and knowing how to access up-to-date knowledge of roadworks and other disruptions within their city. As TNA is used for identifying what the important outcomes of a training programme should be, the more precisely a training need can be specified, the more focused the training can be. Thus TNA has an important impact on how the training is designed, delivered and evaluated. However, assessing training needs is not a mechanistic procedure; it involves a significant amount of judgement and, in order to properly identify the training need, it is useful to distinguish between three basic levels of needs analysis: (i) **organisational analysis**, (ii) job/task/role analysis, and (iii) **person analysis**.

1 Organisational analysis

The purpose of undertaking a TNA at the organisational level is to understand where training activities fit into wider organisational systems and how they relate to organisational strategy. In broad terms, the question being asked is: 'What are the training needs of the whole organisation?' A first step might be to examine a company's strategic aims and policy statements, then discuss these with senior personnel in order to identify and prioritise the organisational objectives likely to have a training solution. For example, a manufacturing company in Sweden might have the strategic aim of increasing sales of their computerised drilling technology in a new market: Argentina. This could generate a need to train existing sales and marketing staff in how to work in an unfamiliar business setting. But strategic objectives only relate to training needs if they are best resolved through training, rather than another solution like providing additional resources. Training is not a panacea for the challenges facing organisations; for example, it may be more cost-effective or faster for this Swedish manufacturer to recruit local sales and marketing staff in Argentina, or outsource these activities to a firm with local knowledge. Other strategic aims may be more efficiently delivered by redesigning roles (Chapter 7) than by training.

Point of integration

Various interventions discussed in other parts of this text might increase or reduce the need for training.

Organisational TNA is also necessary to determine whether investment in training provision in different parts of an organisation is appropriate for its needs. Senior managers usually control investment in training and development: this includes access to finance, the number of people dedicated to the delivery of training, and their power to make decisions about the training. In order to justify an investment, senior managers are likely to need to know why the training is needed, how much it will cost, and how it will help the organisation achieve key performance indicators. In larger organisations, HR managers are often responsible for an annual review of training needs across different business areas, to ensure that resources are available to deliver training provision. Information pertinent to an organisational review is also routinely collected as part of other HRM systems, including performance management, succession planning and recruitment.

Occasionally, there is a need for a 'global review' of training needs and activities across the whole of an organisation. This involves examining *every* job category in a company in order to create or revise job specifications, then an assessment of *every* employee against the new specifications for their role, with a shortfall indicating a potential training need. This exhaustive form of organisational review is comparatively rare, not least because it can be extremely costly and time consuming. It is most likely to be worthwhile if a company is undergoing radical change, such as a sudden need to downsize or restructure.

Not all organisations are large enough to have big HR functions, and smaller firms and new start-up companies often require more responsive and focused methods of organisational TNA. One such method is Critical Incident Analysis. This involves initial interviews with members of the core management team to prioritise their aims and establish how and where training can help to achieve business objectives. Critical incident analysis also helps key stakeholders visualise how training can benefit their organisation, and to identify likely barriers and facilitators to implementing training successfully. This method is also useful in larger organisations when there is a need to understand how future training activities might need to adapt to changing business objectives and unpredictable business environments.

2 Task analysis

In many ways TNA at the task level is similar to a job or role analysis (see Chapter 4). But whereas job analysis is concerned with defining the knowledge, skills and abilities (KSAs) an employee needs to perform a particular role, task analysis identifies the training needs associated with the role or task. It is used to produce a specification of what training is needed in order to develop the requisite KSAs, breaking down tasks into separate 'operations'.

Task analysis has a long history. Researchers from the scientific management movement originally began to investigate the best methods to train workers in the early 1900s, and interest in task analysis was stimulated further by the emergent field of ergonomics in the 1950s (Stanton, 2004). This work led to the development of *hierarchical task analysis* (HTA: Annett and Duncan, 1967), which is one of the most well known and widely used methods of task analysis. HTA provides a flexible method of analysing work tasks that creates a hierarchy of goals and subgoals by breaking work down into increasingly specific operations, defined by Annett et al. (1971) as 'any unit of behaviour (no matter how long or short in duration, or how simple or complex its structure) that can be defined in terms of its objective'.

HTA begins with a general description of the main operations involved in a job or job components being analysed. These operations are then divided into sub-operations, which in turn may be subdivided. By way of illustration, consider a new barista in a coffee shop who is learning to use a traditional expresso machine to make a cappuccino. The overall task can be considered 'making a cappuccino to the required standard'. Sub-operation one might be 'preparing the milk', and this can be subdivided further into: (i) pouring milk into a metal jug until it is a third full, thereby allowing space for foam to fill; (ii) giving the steam wand a purge (i.e. releasing steam for one to two seconds); (3) placing the jug under the steam wand so that the tip of the steam wand is just in the milk; (iv) turning the steam wand on carefully to begin heating the milk; (v) moving the steam wand towards the sides and bottom of the jug as the milk starts to get warm; (vi) turning the steam off; (vii) removing the jug and tapping the bottom gently on the bench (i.e. to disturb any bubbles at the bottom of the jug); and finally (viii) wiping off the steam wand.[1]

HTA is particularly useful for tasks that have clear observable components and are relatively unchanging (e.g. production line work or routine call-centre work). The method is less suited to analysing tasks involving high levels of cognitive work – which by its very nature is difficult to observe – or where demands are diverse and changing. For example, design work, journalism, investment banking and midwifery all require employees to apply knowledge and cognitive skills in order to solve novel, unpredictable and complex problems.

While HTA might be useful for analysing subtasks, like teaching midwives to administer pain relief during childbirth, it is less effective at breaking down more complex tasks like counselling new parents whose child has significant health problems. In these types of role, several other methods can be used. Questionnaires are useful for collecting job-related information from large numbers of people, including those with different perspectives such as new or experienced job-holders, managers and customers. One example is the Position Analysis Questionnaire (PAQ; www.paq.com), which has been used to analyse more than 300,000 job roles in the USA over the past 30 years. The PAQ is described as a classification process rather than a job analysis, because the full questionnaire contains more than 300 characteristics of job roles, making it possible to analyse and compare different roles in terms of their training needs. Another method involves using interviews and other discussion-based data (e.g. focus groups) to capture information about job processes and their relevant importance. Observation of job holders performing a role may sometimes also be necessary to fully understand how tasks are performed in different work settings. In addition, certain methods have been developed specifically to investigate cognitive processes involved in performing a job. For example, cognitive task analysis (CTA; Zsambok and Klein, 1997) and probed-protocol analysis (Kraiger et al., 1993) both involve taking subject-matter experts through a series of detailed and systematic steps where they are asked to verbalise how they analyse information and make decisions in relation to a particular task. These methods are particularly useful in roles where most of the work is predominantly cognitive and cannot be directly observed, like computer programming.

3 Person analysis

Unlike task analysis, which determines the skills needed to perform a task, person analysis involves identifying *who needs training* and *what kind of training they require*. Person-level TNA occurs at different times and for different reasons. It may be in response to a specific business need, such as determining whether a group of employees possess a required skill level (e.g. when a company wants to ensure that all HR managers who use psychometric tests for staff recruitment have been trained to use the tests).

Point of integration

Person analysis is also an ongoing component of most performance review procedures, with managers and employees discussing current and future training needs during appraisal, often using feedback collected using 360-degree review (see Chapter 5).

Making managers responsible for identifying employee training needs is part of the broader philosophy of a learning organisation, where individual employees are encouraged to engage in continual learning and development with support from their line manager (see also Chapters 10 and 12). There are many advantages of this approach, including that it helps to ensure training remains central to dialogue about performance at work. That said, difficulties can arise if employees and managers disagree about the nature and importance of learning needs, or availability of appropriate training. For example, an employee might well believe that she needs coaching to develop her leadership skills, whereas her manager prefers that she attend a less costly assertiveness training course. Potential conflict between person-analysis, appraisal and rating future potential is one of the reasons why managers need training to conduct effective appraisal interviews and identify training needs.

Key learning point

TNA identifies the objectives of training, and can occur at three levels: organisational, job or task, and individual.

Exercise 9.1   What's the need?

Companies often fail to carry out formal training needs analysis (Salas et al., 2012). What arguments would you use to persuade senior managers in a retail organisation that it is worthwhile investing time and resources into a TNA before investing in customer service training for its employees? Why might the senior managers resist a TNA?

Training design

Training design (TD) is the second component of the training cycle. Salas et al. (2012) argue that training design is the single most important element of an effective training programme, because it involves asking questions about what methods will be used, how feedback will be provided to trainees, and how managers can support trainees when they return to the workplace. In practical terms, TD needs to: (i) set the training aims and objectives, (ii) determine an appropriate training strategy, and (iii) plan and implement the training.

Training aims and objectives

Training design (TD) builds on TNA by translating information about *why* the training is needed into what a training programme needs to achieve and how. Training aims involve general statements of intent such as: (i) 'This programme sets out to provide participants with "a grasp" of the basic principles of management accountancy' and (ii) 'The course aims to give trainees an awareness of the relevance of industrial psychology to the management process.' By contrast training objectives are much more specific and precise. They focus specifically on what trainees should be able to do at the end of training, and are crucial for determining whether or not the training has been effective at a later point. They can be expressed in the following three-component form:

1   *The criterion behaviour* is a statement of what the trainee should be able to do at the end of training. Because of this emphasis on criterion behaviour, objectives expressed in this way are often referred to as *behavioural objectives*. Importantly, they are not a description of training content, for example 'participants will gain experience of various personnel selection interviewing techniques' would *not* be acceptable as a behavioural objective, because it describes what happens during the training – not what the trainee will know or be able to do at the end. In this example, 'participants will be able to ask job-related questions in a structured selection interview scenario' could be an appropriate objective of the training.

2   *The conditions* under which the behaviour is to be exhibited. This might involve a specification of the equipment available to support the behaviour and the context within which it will need to occur. For example, after training, a mechanic trained to service a new computer-controlled engine will need the appropriate tools, the opportunity to practise on new engines and support from their manager to trial new patterns of working.

3   *The standard of performance* of the behaviour. This is important, because it provides guidance to trainees, managers and those providing the training about what is expected, and provides a means for evaluating whether the training has achieved its objectives.

Key learning point

Training objectives give a clear description of what the trainee should be capable of doing at the end of training.

Once the training aims and objectives have been identified, the next step in design is to decide how employees will be trained. This means considering what methods are likely to achieve the desired learning and performance in this particular context. Designing training can be complicated, as there are very many training methods (e.g. lecture-based, online and/or self-directed learning, role play and virtual simulations) as well as different ways of presenting, sequencing and rehearsing information. In addition, trainees can vary in their ability and motivation to engage in learning, and there are practical matters like cost, where trainees are located and the availability of qualified personnel. There are therefore many important considerations when determining what training should look like; fortunately work psychology research and practice provide theories and an evidence base to help us make these decisions.

Theories of learning

Understanding how people learn is a good place to start when thinking about how to design training. Theories of learning and skill development are important, because they help us to choose the most appropriate methods of instruction. Learning theories represent 'ideas' about how learning occurs; they are also an area where psychological research has been particularly influential. Although there is no single, universally accepted theory for the learning process, there are several widely accepted principles and points of agreement among psychologists. From a historical perspective, the most prominent approach to learning derives from the behaviourist tradition (see Chapter 1). According to this approach, learning results from strengthening stimulus (S)-response (R) links; reinforcing appropriate behaviour by trainees by giving rewards and, in some cases, 'punishing' inappropriate behaviour (something that in practice very rarely happens in the training environment for a host of very good reasons).

While the behaviourist tradition has played an important role in training, it does have some limitations. For example, learning is seen as occurring largely through trial and error, but clearly not all learning takes place by reinforcing S-R links as this would take too long. As such the approach ignores cognitive processes involved in learning, such as how the learner feels about what he or she is learning, or their understanding of new concepts and how their growing knowledge influences the choices they make. Social learning theory (SLT), which was developed by Bandura (1986), addresses many of these criticisms by allowing a bigger role for internal mental processes (e.g. trainees' expectancies about learning outcomes), and recognising the capacity of individuals to learn without direct experience (e.g. by observing someone else performing an activity). In terms of employee training, SLT emphasises the need for trainees to engage actively in the learning process and think about the training experience. One of the most important aspects of this theory is the emphasis it places on how experience of success helps the trainees develop belief in their ability to do the task. This is referred to as self-efficacy and we will discuss this in more detail later in this chapter.

SLT has had an important impact on the design of training. SLT-based training interventions have three stages. First, trainee *attention is focused* by using a 'model' to perform the target behaviour (e.g. demonstrating how to engage a customer effectively). Second, the trainee *observes* a sequence of behaviours where the model is rewarded for performing appropriate behaviour (i.e. interacting with customers in a desired manner) or punished for inappropriate behaviour (i.e. responding to a customer in an undesirable way). Third, trainee learning is *strengthened* by providing opportunities to rehearse and practice. The following example describes what might happen in a SLT-based training intervention to improve transfer of information between team members:

1   The trainer begins by emphasising the importance of communication skills for team-working success.

2   Trainees then watch a video of a model effectively listening and facilitating communication between team members in a group meeting.

3   The trainer draws out key points about the model's behaviour and encourages group discussion between trainees and trainer.

4   Trainees participate in a role-play exercise where they are required to perform a group task; they receive feedback post-exercise from the trainer and other group members.

5   Trainees return to work where they begin to practise their new behaviour with members of their own teams.

6   The trainer and trainees meet two weeks after training to discuss their experiences and how they dealt with them.

Thus trainees are told why effective communication is important, they observe the required skills, then practise and receive feedback; finally they attempt to generalise their learning to other situations when they return to work. A large body of research has documented the effectiveness of SLT as a training method (e.g. Davis and Yi, 2004). Importantly, SLT identifies straightforward and relatively easy ways to improve training success.

For example, we know that learning improves if the role models used for training are friendly, helpful, high status and of the same race or gender as the trainees (Bandura, 1977b). Similarly powerful role models who are able to control desired resources are also more effective – thus how managers behave is frequently an important source of learning for their direct reports. Modelled behaviour should also be vivid and memorable, sufficiently detailed and structured sequentially to allow the least difficult behaviours to be modelled first, followed by more complex behaviour. A good illustration of how principles of SLT have been applied to training can be found in the popularity of commercial 'off-the-shelf' training materials featuring films of well-known actors using humour to model how (and how not) to perform activities like appraisal interviews.

Stop to consider

Recent financial scandals have been blamed on unethical cultures that arise because employees observe unethical (and potentially illegal) behaviour by their managers being accepted or even rewarded by others in the company. It might be argued that this is an example of informal learning. Apply SLT to consider how informal learning could be taking place within these organisations – and why it might be important in determining some of the problematical workplace behaviour in this work context.

Baldwin (1992) makes an interesting and important observation in relation to SLT and the use of **modelling** in training. He argues that trainers providing trainees with examples of how tasks should be performed, ignores the fact that trainees may already be proficient in performing a task – *but in a different or less desirable way*. For example, a chef working for a chain of fast-food restaurants may be extremely proficient at cooking noodles, but not in the most cost-efficient, standardised way expected by their employer. In this case the chef may need to *unlearn* their old pattern of behaviour *before* she can learn the new way. More-over, because old learning can interfere with new learning, more experienced trainees can take longer to learn a task than novices. Therefore in order to be motivated to learn, the chef will need to be persuaded as to *why* her effort is worthwhile.

Although SLT is extremely useful in the design of training, it is unlikely to be useful for all training because not all tasks can be modelled (Gist, 1989). For example, an aspiring author is unlikely to learn very much by observing an experienced author writing a book – all they would see is someone typing a sequence of words! For this reason, learning theories derived from cognitive psychology have become important for training design, because these help training designers to understand factors that can impede learning. Using analogies from information technology, these theories propose that learning can be considered in terms of a 'signal' (i.e. the information provided to trainees), the transmission of information along different channels of communication (e.g. training materials, context for learning), 'noise' in the system (e.g. whether trainees receive contradictory information from different sources), and the need for regulatory systems to monitor whether learning has occurred (i.e. feedback for learners). Thus a cognitive approach emphasises the importance of clarifying communication, reducing 'noise' and facilitating feedback as part of training design.

Social constructivist theories of learning have also been helpful for training design, because these theories argue that trainees should not be treated as *passive* learners, but as *active* learners who proactively engage in learning to co-produce knowledge when they interact with other people to discuss, analyse and experiment with this new information and the world around them. A distinction can be drawn between 'surface learning', which typically involves a simple memorisation of facts (i.e. a common component of last-minute exam revision), and 'deep learning' that occurs when existing knowledge is applied to problems and modified in light of new learning and understanding. According to social constructionist theories learners on a training programme will need encouragement to make an effort to engage in higher-level information processing, as well as opportunities to try out and reflect on their learning with other people. Importantly, social constructionist theories also remind us that the co-production of knowledge creation often results in serendipitous and quite unexpected learning!

Skill development

Work psychologists generally distinguish between knowledge, skills and abilities (KSAs) when describing person- and job-level requirements. Knowledge concerns the recall and understanding of information, skills refer to the psychomotor movements required when performing practical activities (e.g. operating machinery or making a cappuccino) or to cognitive expertise (e.g. in designing a computer programme, or drafting a legal contract), and abilities concern an individual's affective or emotional response to the learning (e.g. enthusiasm, commitment or scepticism). In terms of training, KSAs are all important: a trainee might learn to operate a drilling machine (i.e. demonstrate skill), understand the safety procedures that must be observed (i.e. knowledge), yet still feel that the safety procedure is a waste of time and unnecessary (i.e. attitude). Training design therefore needs to take account of all three aspects of learning, but in this section we focus on skill development; an area where cognitive psychologists have made some of the most important contributions to training.

Over 50 years ago, Fitts (1962) proposed a theory that is still highly regarded by psychologists and practitioners (Table 9.1). In essence he suggested that skill development progresses through three distinct phases: (i) a cognitive phase where the learner gains an intellectual understanding of the tasks involved; (ii) an associative phase where the learner begins to practise and receives feedback; and (iii) an autonomous phase where, through further practice, the learner can demonstrate a skilled performance that is resistant to interference.

Table 9.1	Phases of skill development
Fitts	**Anderson**
Cognitive phase: learning the basic ingredients that make up skilled performance. Performance is prone to error and some lack of understanding of how to conduct task(s) may be apparent	Declarative stage: establishing the basic 'facts' about the tasks. The trainee is beginning to grasp what is involved in the task(s) (i.e. declarative knowledge)
Associative phase: establishment of the appropriate patterns of behaviour, underpinned by the knowledge acquired in the first phase. Initially, rather a lot of errors but improvement with repeated practice	Knowledge compilation stage: physical mechanisms are developed for transforming the declarative knowledge into procedural knowledge (i.e. knowing how to accomplish the task(s))
Autonomous phase: the task(s) are performed increasingly smoothly with relatively low demands on memory or attention. Performance is very resistant to interference or stress	Tuning stage: performance strengthens and generalises across tasks within the relevant skill domain

Sources: Fitts (1962); Anderson (1983, 1987).

If we use the example of a novice barista, the *cognitive* phase would involve the trainee learning about which ingredients, cups and utensils he should use, how to turn on the expresso machine and so on. But for skills that are not very easy to learn (and expresso machines can be quite challenging for the uninitiated), practice is the key feature of the next associative phase as the learner attempts to produce and reproduce skilful performance. During the *associative* phase there is less and less ponderous concentration on the steps involved, and the learner shows a gradual improvement in the smoothness and accuracy of their performance. The novice barista who had progressed to the associative stage would be practised in producing cappuccinos for customers; they would probably produce cappuccinos of a consistent standard and in less time. Finally, as the barista reaches the autonomous stage the skill becomes more and more automatic. In this phase, performance of the skill requires less in the way of psychological resources such as memory or attention, and is increasingly resistant to interference from distractions of competing activities. At this point our hypothetical barista might be able to hold a conversation with the customer as he makes a perfect cappuccino. He is also likely to be very capable of fulfilling an order for five cappuccinos, three with skimmed milk, one with soya and another with extra hot full-fat milk. In short, the expert barista makes the task look easy and risk free. At this stage, it is likely that even in the face of distractions from customers and colleagues, the barista would be able to make a good cup of coffee.

Key learning point

Learners pass through a series of stages when learning a skill, with each stage producing performance that is more and more automatic.

Fitts' ideas were developed further by Anderson (e.g. 1983, 1987) who drew on advances being made in contemporary cognitive psychology to propose a further theory of skill acquisition. This also has three stages, but a central feature is that it distinguishes between *declarative* and *procedural* knowledge, and explains how declarative knowledge is turned into procedural knowledge as skill development proceeds. Anderson defines declarative knowledge as that which can be stated (declared) and made explicit; an example would be instructions in a handbook that explain how to use a piece of machinery. By contrast, procedural knowledge is the basis for knowing *how* to perform a skilled behaviour like riding a horse. An individual may possess declarative knowledge (e.g. they may know what riding a horse involves: sitting in the saddle, holding the reins, and gripping with the knees to maintain balance) but not the procedural knowledge, which in this case is needed to know how to stay on a horse for any length of time.

Point of integration

The importance of some skills can be reduced (or raised) by redesigning work tasks and work equipment (see Chapters 7 and 8).

Anderson proposed that, in developing a new skill, a trainee first moves into the *declarative stage*, where they learn important facts and try to use them to work out how to conduct the tasks involved. At this stage there are considerable demands on the trainee's attention and memory, so in practical terms a trainee will need time to practise and little distraction. Next, learning proceeds through the *knowledge compilation stage* when the trainee develops better and better procedures for conducting the tasks involved. By the end of this stage procedural knowledge is in place, usually with guiding rules about application. Finally, the *tuning stage* is reached, where the underlying rules are refined and streamlined so that performance is increasingly efficient and automatic.

These theoretical ideas about skill development provide insight into the practical ways in which training content can be structured and designed. For example, motor skills require repeated practice and feedback to develop adequately. Training must also take account of the stage of skill development reached by trainees. It would be pointless to design a series of high-speed practice exercises for trainees at the first (declarative knowledge) stage of skill development. The theory also distinguishes between experts and novices; unlike novices, experts understand when to apply their knowledge and expertise, and how to adapt this to new and different situations. Researchers describe this as strategic knowledge and adaptive expertise (Koslowski et al., 2001). In terms of training design, this indicates that trainees need opportunities to apply knowledge and skills in different environments and to different problems in order to become an expert.

Training methods

Training methods are structured activities designed to bring about desired changes in trainee behaviour by facilitating acquisition of knowledge, skills and attitudes. There are many different ways to present learning materials that involve different training media (e.g. class-based, video or information handouts), instructional settings (e.g. lecture theatre, multi-media learning environment, or the learner's home) and ways of sequencing of material (e.g. learner-controlled pace, structured learning programmes). While theories of learning and skill development help us to understand how trainees learn, they can also help to identify what methods are most likely to bring about this learning. Similarly, training research provides an evidence base to inform decisions about what methods are likely to be most effective with different trainees, and in different settings. For example, a meta-analysis of studies investigating training effectiveness found that trainees' declarative knowledge and task performance ten days post-training were significantly increased simply by rehearsing tasks mentally (Arthur et al., 2003).

Possibly the biggest influence on training design over the last decade, however, has been the use of technology to support learning. Although there is no universally accepted definition of e-learning (which is also referred to as Web-based learning), researchers and practitioners broadly agree that it relates to learning that is enabled or supported using information and communications technology (ICT). E-learning can therefore involve material being provided to learners via a website that can be accessed via work or home computers, or via mobile technology. It can also involve learning using virtual reality simulations, or where trainers provide remote feedback to trainees by e-mail or video-link. While technology has generated many new ways to present training materials to learners, researchers have yet to fully explore and evaluate the benefits of e-learning over traditional face-to-face or class-based learning. For example, in their meta-analysis of studies comparing the effectiveness of Web-based and classroom-based instruction, Sitzman et al. (2006) found that Web-based and classroom-based methods were equally effective for learning procedural knowledge, but Web-based formats were slightly better for trainees learning declarative knowledge. 'Blended learning', which involves the combined use of e-learning and traditional face-to-face formats, may overcome potential disadvantages associated with using one method of training in isolation. This may be because such an approach offers more confident, independent learners more opportunity for self-directed learning, while less confident learners benefit from face-to-face learning and increased opportunities for support and feedback (Klein et al., 2006). Further research should help those involved in training design have a better understanding of the conditions likely to suit different forms of e-learning.

Designing for different needs

Although most learning theories tend to assume that all learners go through the same processes or stages when acquiring new information and skills, not all learners are alike and individual differences like intelligence, personality, motivation and confidence can all have an influence on whether training is successful. Different training methods are likely to suit different learners, and while it is not always possible to design training to meet the individual needs of every learner, it is still important to be aware of factors that can influence the trainee's experience of learning.

Point of integration

Individual differences (see Chapters 3 and 10) can have a significant impact on training outcomes. In their meta-analysis Colquitt et al. (2000) identified conscientiousness, anxiety, age and job involvement as trainee characteristics with significant impact on learning.

Many researchers have identified learner self-efficacy – a trainee's belief in their ability to complete tasks – as a particularly important influence on individuals' willingness to take part in training and learning. Stevens and Gist (1997) found that trainees with higher self-efficacy learnt skills more quickly, and were more likely to use the skills when they returned to the workplace. More recently, Sitzman and Ely (2011) found that the self-regulation constructs with strongest effects on trainee learning were goal level, persistence, effort and self-efficacy. In practical terms, these findings indicate that those designing training need to have a good understanding of the target group of trainees. Sometimes the training intervention may need to include additional support for those likely to be less confident in the training setting, perhaps by notifying managers and ensuring that they get extra support before and after the training programme.

Key learning point

In many countries companies have a legal responsibility to accommodate the needs of protected groups by designing training in a way that provides employees with particular needs with equal opportunities to learn. For example, this might mean providing employees with a special learning need like dyslexia with a quieter environment in which to learn, longer periods of time to practise or rehearse, and training materials in formats that are more accessible. Similarly, adjustments may be needed for employees with physical disabilities. Identifying these needs at an early stage (e.g. by using information collected during the person-level TNA) makes it much easier to include such adjustments in the training design.

Team-based training

A team is defined by Mohrman et al. (1995) as 'a group of individuals who work together to produce products or deliver services for which they are mutually accountable'. Although teams are one of the most popular methods used by companies to organise employees on projects and complex problems (see Chapter 1), they present specific challenges for training design. For example, teams are often comprised of members who play different roles. Teams are likely to include people from different professional backgrounds and with different amounts and types of work experience. As such team training can mean accommodating trainees with different skills and therefore different learning needs. A common feature of teams is that, while members often perform different roles, their performance is interdependent. This means that team members need to learn to coordinate their actions, communicate effectively, understand how others' roles impact on their own and who to go to for specific information or expertise.

Point of integration

Training design and training outcomes need to take into account key features of teamwork as this is the context in which many employees carry out work tasks.

Thus team training will often need to accommodate individual-level and team-level training needs. To complicate things further, teams are usually in a state of flux, changing over time as members leave, new members join and new working relationships are formed. Thus team training design has to accommodate this longitudinal and dynamic perspective.

Research on team training has evolved significantly in recent years, though most studies still tend to focus on teams involved in high-risk work (e.g. aviation, the military and medicine) where poor performance can have a critical impact on the safety and well-being of others (Edkins, 2002; Morey et al., 2002; Salas et al., 2006). In their meta-analysis, Salas et al. (2008) found that team training tends to have a positive impact on team performance across a variety of work settings, tasks and team types. This was moderated by team stability, such that training was more likely to result in increased performance for 'intact' teams that had an established history of working together. The size of the team also mattered, particularly in terms of the type of training effect that was achieved. Large teams showed general work performance increases following team training. In contrast, small teams were more likely to show specific improvements in team processes like internal coordination and communication. Research has also shown that behaviour modelling training (see the earlier discussion of SLT) can change team members' knowledge structures regarding what represents appropriate work behaviour in the team – with subsequent positive effects on work behaviour itself (Marks et al., 2002).

Cannon-Bowers and Salas (2001) argue that for teams to successfully coordinate action, each member must have common knowledge and a shared vision that enables the member to predict how other members of the team will behave based on shared performance standards. Put simply, every team member needs to know (i) what is to be achieved, (ii) how it is to be achieved, (iii) their individual responsibilities, and (iv) what performance checks and standards should be used. Although most recent research on team training has been undertaken in medical contexts, there are useful lessons that can be applied to the design of training for other teams. For example, those responsible for training teams need to be more aware of the multiple roles within a team and how these are likely to impact on the common training needs of those within the group and those specific to particular individuals. Similarly, training needs to take account of the different relationships that team members will have with one another, as well as the need to accommodate individual as well as team-level objectives. In broad terms, teams usually need an opportunity to learn and practise interdependent skills together. This means that training delivery through e-learning may be helpful to provide team members with declarative knowledge (e.g. facts and figures), but the development of procedural knowledge within teams is likely to require a different training medium. Time and space will be needed in order for members to develop a shared understanding of what they need to know and how they will implement it as a team, before coordinated action can be achieved.

Exercise 9.2   Training for teamworking

Members of surgical teams usually come from different professional groups (e.g. nurses, anaesthetists and surgeons) and have probably had many years of specialist skills training. However, new teams need time and support to learn to work together effectively as a team. How would you design training for a newly formed surgical team whose members do not know each other? What content might you cover and what training methods would you use? Are there any practised behaviours (such as those specific to their own professional groups) they might need to unlearn in order to work as effectively as possible in a team?

Transfer of learning

So far we have discussed the content of training and how it can be structured. However, in the opening case study Eduardo Salas points out that one of the most important responsibilities for people designing and delivering training is to make sure that trainees and managers understand why training is required, in order to increase successful transfer of learning from the training environment to the work context. Transfer of learning involves trainees translating their learning into behaviour change on the job, and this depends in part on managers creating a supportive climate to facilitate behaviour change, and improved job and organisational performance (Cheng and Hampson, 2008).

Baldwin and Ford's (1988) original model of learning transfer differentiates between three areas: (i) *learning and retention* – what the trainee learns and remembers from the training programme, (ii) *generalisation of learning* – the extent to which trainees can adapt what they have learned and apply it to the specific needs of their own workplace, and (iii) *maintenance* – trainees continuing to use and apply this learning over time. The model also provides some useful explanations of why individual, training and environmental factors can have different effects on trainee learning, and how learning transferred to the workplace eventually translates into improved performance. An important individual-level (i.e. trainee) factor is learning: 'positive transfer' occurs when a trainee possesses an 'old' skill that helps her acquire a new skill, and 'negative transfer' is when a previously learned skill interferes with learning or applying a new skill. An example of the latter is the need for trainees to sometimes 'unlearn' or 'unfreeze' old skills before acquiring new ones (Baldwin, 1992). As we discussed earlier in the chapter, the need to unlearn old patterns of behaviour can lead to an initial decline in trainee behaviour when they return to work and begin to practise their new skills. This is why it is so important for managers to understand the need to support newly trained employees through what can be a demotivating period (Birdi et al., 1997; Blanchard and Thacker, 2007).

Manager support can be viewed as an organisational-level factor. It might involve making sure that trainees have adequate resources to practise their skills when they return from training programmes, providing reminders about what they have learned, as well as frequent feedback and rewards for putting the new skills into practice. Managers may also need training in order to appreciate the importance of their role in facilitating others' development: this is why training programmes are often cascaded down organisations, with managers trained first so that they can understand what the training involves, model new behaviours and recognise how best to support new learners (Silvester et al., 1999).

In an effort to further understand how organisational-level factors impact on transfer, Tannenbaum and Yukl (1992) examined the post-training environment and found that certain elements encouraged (e.g. rewards, job aids, recognition), discouraged (e.g. ridicule from peers) or even prohibited (e.g. lack of the necessary equipment) application of new skills and knowledge. Tracey et al. (1995) examined transfer of learning in considerable detail by studying 505 supermarket managers taking part in a three-day off-site training programme to improve customer service and employee relations. They asked trainees questions about whether they had received relevant information before training, whether they knew they would be held accountable for their learning, and whether they perceived training as mandatory. Trainees were also asked to rate their manager's behaviour before and after the training. The study found that organisational climate and culture were directly related to post-training behaviours, with social support in the workplace playing a central role in the transfer of learning. More recently a meta-analysis of the results of 89 studies found that trainee characteristics such as self-efficacy and motivation, and environmental context become particularly important when training involves the development of *open* skills (i.e. where trainees have a high level of choice over how they use what they have learned in their training in their job). These factors were less important for the transfer of *closed* skills: these involve behaviours which are much more prescribed, giving employees less choice about how they use their newly acquired skills in the work environment (Blume, Ford, Baldwin and Huang, 2010). These studies are important because they help us to understand how training can be designed to achieve improved transfer of learning for different learners.

Key learning point

For training to be successful, employees must transfer their learning to the job; changing their behaviour by using their new KSAs, and maintaining this change over time. Managers play an important role in creating a supportive work climate for this transfer to take place – but some characteristics of the trainees are also important.

Training evaluation

The third component of the training cycle is training evaluation (TE). This is concerned with establishing whether or not the training has worked (i.e. that the learning objectives have been achieved), and the organisation's investment in training has been worthwhile. TE also collects information to explain *why* the training has or has not achieved its intended outcomes in order to show how future training can be improved. What is striking is that many companies do not evaluate their training programmes (Salas et al., 2012). Various surveys indicate that as few as 10 per cent of organisations evaluate post-training trainee behaviour change, and less than 5 per cent evaluate whether training has resulted in financial benefits (Patrick, 1992). One reason for these low figures is that TE can be difficult and expensive to undertake. Practical challenges can include trying to measure trainee behaviour change when trainees have dispersed to many different locations after training, and capturing data in sufficient quantity and quality to link trainee performance to organisational performance. There is evidence that companies with a significant commitment to employee learning and development also take training evaluation more seriously (Aguinas and Kraiger, 2009).

Models of training evaluation

Probably the most widely used model of training evaluation was developed by Kirkpatrick (1967) and involves four levels of data collection: (i) reaction, (ii) learning, (iii) behaviour, and (iv) results (see Figure 9.3). Collecting **reaction data** represents the first and minimal level of evaluation for a training programme. In Kirkpatrick's model this type of data relates to trainees' views about the training, and it is generally assumed that trainees need to have a positive reaction to the training experience for training to be effective. Collecting reaction-level data usually involves trainees completing post-training evaluation questionnaires asking questions about how they perceived the quality of the training and how enjoyable they found it (you may have come across something similar in the form of course feedback forms collected in universities to monitor the quality of teaching). Level two assumes that effective training depends on trainees acquiring the desired KSAs. **Learning data** are collected to determine whether trainees show evidence that they have attained the immediate level objectives of the programme. Kirkpatrick's third level of evaluation is concerned with changes in behaviour, specifically the extent to which trainees demonstrate the skills that they have learned on the training programme once they return to work. The fourth and final level of evaluation is described as 'results' and concerns the extent to which the training has had an impact on organisational effectiveness.

Level	Method of assessment
1 Reaction	Post-training feedback sheets (e.g. 'did you enjoy the training?'; 'was the training useful?')
2 Learning	Tests of knowledge acquired (e.g. a test of knowledge of the procedures for dealing with customer complaints)
3 Behaviour	Observation of skill performance and job behaviour, tests of speed and accuracy (e.g. observing an employee dealing with a customer complaint)
4 Results	Assessment of team performance, levels of absenteeism, overall organisational effectiveness, productivity and profitability (e.g. customer satisfaction with the way the employee dealt with a variety of complaints)

Figure 9.3   Kirkpatrick's model of training evaluation

Key debate

It is popular, but is Kirkpatrick's model a good one?

Criticisms of Kirkpatrick's model have focused on two aspects: (i) methods used to collect and assess data at each level, and (ii) the hierarchical assumptions of the model where success at one particular level is viewed as dependent on successful achievement of the previous level(s). Many training interventions rely on level one reactance data to evaluate training. While trainees' views are important, and post-training questionnaires provide a relatively easy and inexpensive source of information, this type of data can give a misleading impression of the value of a training programme and an incomplete view of training effectiveness. For example, trainees may be enthusiastic about a training programme, because it provided an enjoyable break from their work routine, or because they found the trainer likeable and engaging. Trainees may also provide poor reports for training when they needed to work harder than expected or where they had a less entertaining instructor. But none of this feedback tells us whether the training was effective at producing new learning. Reactance-level feedback is often dismissed as 'happy sheets', but studies show that there are relatively simple ways in which it can be improved (Brown, 2005). For example, Warr and colleagues (1999) found that including questions about how difficult and how useful trainees found the course increased the correlation between reactance-level data and subsequent learning.

Key learning point

Reaction-level (reactance) evaluation data can be improved by asking trainees how difficult and useful they found the training.

There are also different ways to assess the second level of Kirkpatrick's model (i.e. learning), including asking trainees to complete pre- and post-programme written tests of knowledge, or assessing how accurately or quickly trainees can perform new skills. These enable the trainer to check participants' understanding of the material covered during training. Although learning data are typically collected at the end or immediately after training, retention of material over a longer period is also important, and ideally learning should also be tested six months post-training. Just like reaction data, learning data are useful but incomplete; importantly, while trainees may have learned the relevant knowledge or skills there is still a question of whether they apply them when they return to work.

Point of integration

The methods used to collect and assess third-level data about behaviour change are similar to those used for assessing job performance (see Chapter 5).

A majority of these outcomes rely on managers' assessments of the trainee's performance once they return to work and can therefore be vulnerable to distortion and bias. For example, managers' ratings can be influenced by expectations that training will be effective (e.g. higher ratings if the training was the manager's idea) or ineffective (e.g. lower ratings if the manager believes the training is a waste of time). It is possible to collect more *objective assessments* of behaviour change such as changes in the number of mistakes an employee makes before and after training, changes in the quality of work produced, or even changes in the number of customer complaints. That said, this level concerns behaviour *change* so data are more difficult and time consuming to collect because it needs to happen both before and after the training. Moreover, as initial performance can decline when a trainee begins to practise a new skill, it may be important to assess post-training behaviour at several time points. It is therefore as important to decide *when* to collect behavioural data, as it is to decide *what* type of data to collect, for a training evaluation.

Finally, level four (i.e. results) concerns organisational performance. Although conceptually clear, results criteria are extremely difficult to assess in a controlled fashion. It can be almost impossible to determine with certainty that improved organisational effectiveness, even at a team or functional level, has been brought about by the effect of the training rather than a combination of other factors (e.g. a general improvement in the economy or the company's launch of a successful new product). No doubt the senior managers responsible for deciding to invest in a training programme will hope that it has an ultimate impact on company effectiveness or profitability, but in practice results-level data are the most difficult and expensive to collect and interpret (Mabey and Ramirez, 2005). In fact Alliger and Janak (1997) identified only two investigations that had attempted to collect such data and relate it directly to training effectiveness in their meta-analysis of evaluation studies. Their study investigated possibly the strongest of criticisms levelled at Kirkpatrick's model; that there is no evidence for his claim that the four levels are hierarchical, where successful learning (level 2) is seen as dependent on an individual enjoying the course (level 1). Similarly, behaviour change in the workplace (level 3) is seen as reliant on successful acquisition of knowledge (level 2). Consider the fact that while many students do not enjoy learning statistics, most usually learn enough during statistics lectures to pass their exam. Perhaps then enjoyment may be desirable but not necessary for learning. Alliger and Janak (1997) found that associations between the four levels were consistently low in their meta-analysis. The authors accept that Kirkpatrick's model provides an easy to understand, accessible and useful framework for training evaluation, but emphasise that by making implicit assumptions about the nature of learning the model also can lead to misunderstandings and over-generalisations when judging the success of training programmes.

Key learning point

Although important, results-level evaluation data are often difficult to collect and interpret. Information about trainees' performance in the workplace may be influenced by a range of factors unrelated to the impact of the training on their knowledge, skills and attitudes.

Kraiger et al. (1993) argue that because Kirkpatrick's model lacks specificity, it is not easy to identify which methods are best suited to assess different stages of learning. Focusing on the second level of 'learning' they propose a more detailed framework for evaluation based upon three broad, but conceptually different, categories of learning outcomes: (i) cognitive outcomes, (ii) skill-based outcomes, and (iii) affective outcomes (Figure 9.4). Kraiger et al. suggest that by identifying the specific changes that should result from these categories of learning at different stages of expertise, it is possible to identify the most appropriate assessment techniques. For example, in the compilation stage, skill-based learning can be assessed using methods such as targeted behavioural observation, hands-on testing and structured situational interviews. However, at the automaticity stage, skill-based learning outcomes are better assessed by looking at how trainees respond to interference problems (i.e. being asked to perform a secondary task simultaneously, like talking to a customer while serving them). Alternatively, affective learning outcomes can be assessed using self-report questionnaires measuring constructs such as trainees' confidence in their ability to demonstrate a particular skill before and after training. The advantage of this model is that it allows us to investigate the causes and processes of learning in much greater detail than we might gain from Kirkpatrick's model.

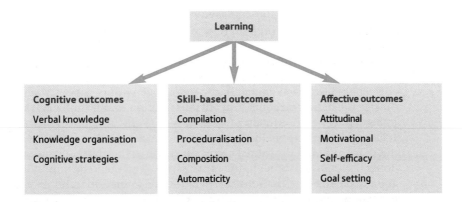

Figure 9.4	A classification for learning outcomes *Source:* Adapted with permission of American Psychological Association from Kraiger et. al., 1993: 311–328

Threats to accurate evaluation

As we have seen, training evaluation can be complex, and in general, no single method is capable of providing detailed and comprehensive information regarding all aspects of the effectiveness of a training programme. The most successful and useful evaluation requires a multi-method approach and different types of data to build up a picture of whether a training process has achieved its objectives and how it can be improved. Anderson (2007) claims that it is critical for trainers to demonstrate the value of learning in order to ensure the commitment of senior decision-makers to invest in training and development. Yet Anderson goes on to point out that only one-third of UK organisations seek to capture the effect of training and development on bottom-line business performance. There are important practical reasons for this. Individuals in the organisation may simply lack the skills required to conduct this type of analysis, or have little interest in collecting traditional evaluation data (Anderson, 2007). There can be substantial costs associated with allocating time and resources to training evaluation that may deter investment, and few managers responsible for spending large amounts of money on a training programme want to be associated with something that has not worked quite as well as they would have liked. Yet, only by evaluating training is it possible to determine how best to target future investment in learning and development activities.

The problem of establishing whether training, rather than some other factor, is responsible for causing observed changes is one that can make evaluation a technically complex and extremely time-consuming endeavour. The most thorough consideration of experimental designs that can be used by evaluators to examine the effectiveness of training programmes is presented by Cook et al. (1990). Fundamentally, the goal of training evaluation should be to provide the training designer with information about effectiveness that can be *unambiguously* interpreted and is *relevant* to the question of training effectiveness. To illustrate the problems involved in conducting good evaluation work, consider some of the common difficulties that may arise. These are usually referred to as internal or external threats to *validity*, since they affect (or threaten to affect) the validity of conclusions that can be drawn from the evaluation. The validity of training can be divided into two broad types: **internal validity**, which is concerned with the extent to which the training has brought about new learning, and **external validity**, which is concerned with the extent to which the effects of the training will generalise to subsequent groups of trainees and settings.

Threats to internal validity are concerned with the factors or problems that can make it appear that a training programme has been responsible for changes in learning, behaviour or results, when in fact the changes were caused by some other factors. For example, a group of new entrants to an organisation may be given a pre-training test of knowledge of the organisation's rules and procedures. After a period of induction training (e.g. one hour per day for their first week) they may be tested again. If their test scores have improved, does this mean that the induction training was responsible? Of course not: the improved knowledge could have been gained in the six or seven hours per day spent in the organisation outside the induction course. An obvious solution to this problem is to administer the tests immediately before and after training. Would any differences now be attributable to the training? It seems more likely now, but, for example, there is the possibility that trainees might benefit from the formal training only when they have spent some of the previous day doing their normal duties in the organisation. This could be important, for instance, if, for any reason, the organisation wanted to run the induction training in one block all at once, instead of spreading it over the first week. The question here is partly one of internal validity: did the training bring about the change? It is also partly a question of external validity: will the programme be effective for different trainees in different circumstances?

Designs for training evaluation

In an attempt to control the various threats to the validity of training, evaluation investigators will often make use of experimental designs. Most training evaluation has to be conducted within real organisational settings, and under these circumstances it is often not possible to obtain the conditions necessary for perfect experimental designs. In such circumstances it is common for what Campbell and Stanley (1963; see also Cook et al., 1990) have called quasi-experimental designs, to be utilised. Campbell and Stanley (1963) also described what they term **pre-experimental designs**. Such designs are not the strongest, but are commonplace in the training world: they produce results with so many threats to validity that they are uninterpretable and not capable of providing clear findings about training effectiveness (see Wexley, 1984: 538–9).

Research methods in focus

Pre-experimental, experimental and quasi-experimental designs

Two of the best known training pre-experimental training evaluation designs are shown in Figure 9.5, together with more complex designs that overcome some of the problems inherent in the pre-experimental designs.

Clearly, the single-group, post-test-only design controls for none of the possible threats to internal or external validity and it is quite impossible to interpret the data. It is impossible to tell whether scores are better after training than before – let alone whether training or some other factor is responsible for any changes. The one-group, pre–post measure design goes some way towards resolving the problems by making it possible to measure *change over time*. Nevertheless, it is not possible with this design to assess whether training may have caused any difference.

This may only be done if there is also an untrained control group, who are similar to the trained group and whose performance has also been measured at the appropriate times. To conduct a true experiment, trainees should be assigned to the experimental and control groups on a random basis since systematic differences between groups before the experiment could bias the results. Often this degree of control is impossible in field research and the kind of quasi-experimental design shown in the non-equivalent control group example of Figure 9.5 is the best that can be done. Typically pre-existing groups in the organisation, such as all of the members of a particular job group, region or unit, form the groups. This is administratively much more convenient than random assignment and does control for some of the main threats to validity. Even the pre–post measure control group design is subject to some threats to validity, and for totally unambiguous results more complex designs are needed (see Campbell and Stanley, 1963).

One group, post-measure only

X  M$_2$

One group, pre-measure/post-measure

M$_1$ ⟹ X ⟹ M$_2$

Pre-measure/post-measure control group

R ⟹ M$_1$ ⟹ X ⟹ M$_2$
R ⟹ M$_1$ ⟹ M$_2$

Non-equivalent control group

M$_1$ ⟹ X ⟹ M$_2$
M$_1$ ⟹ M$_2$

Key:
M$_1$ = pre-measure (administered prior to training)
M$_2$ = post-measure (administered after training)
X   = training programme
R   = random assignment of people to groups

Figure 9.5	Pre-experimental, experimental and quasi-experimental designs for training evaluation studies

Key learning point

Pre-experimental designs, such as the one-group post-test-only design, are common in the training world but they are not capable of providing clear, unequivocal results about training effectiveness. Practical constraints often make it difficult, or impossible, to execute the most complex evaluation study designs that have high levels of external and internal validity.

Training and development in practice

In this section we consider some examples of how training and development activities have been used to address specific business needs including (i) leader development, (ii) improving diversity and inclusion, and (iii) creating organisational learning cultures.

Training and development for leaders

Leadership development is an important area for many organisations. A huge amount of money is spent annually on efforts both to develop potential leaders, and enhance the skills of incumbent leaders. Indeed, leadership development is now often treated as a reputational benchmark for companies competing to hire the most talented people. The Hay Group conducts an annual survey to identify the top companies for leadership development. In the 2014 survey five features were identified as common among the most successful companies. First, these companies were highly likely to prioritise leadership development in good times as well as bad (i.e. they do not cut back on activities or funding when the economy is difficult, or company performance has suffered). Second, the most successful companies invested in leadership development for employees at all levels of the company, creating a leadership pipeline that allows them to nurture and develop leadership potential over time. Third, senior leaders in these companies (including chief executive officers) were more likely to be visibly involved in development activities, thereby championing their importance to others in the company. Fourth, the companies could demonstrate a commitment to leader development over the long term. Finally, there was evidence that the leadership beliefs and development model adopted by these companies remains consistent over time.

Point of integration

There is a debate about whether leaders are 'born or made' (see Chapter 12). Training and development research indicates that people can acquire some of the important knowledge, skills and other qualities that impact on leader behaviours.

Although leadership development generates considerable interest and receives much attention in practice, relatively little research has explored factors that contribute to its effective design and delivery. In their research on leadership development in Fortune 500 companies like GE, Motorola, PepsiCo, FedEx and Johnson & Johnson, Day et al. (2014) found that most organisations use a mixture of methods to develop leaders. These included formal training (the most popular), 360-degree feedback, executive coaching, job assignments, mentoring, networks, reflective learning, action learning and outdoor challenges. But gaining access to participants in learning at senior levels can be particularly challenging, and as such, most existing knowledge comes from qualitative research involving interviews and commentaries rather than more scientific studies capable of investigating causal relationships (as described in Figure 9.5).

Key learning point

Evaluating the impact of training on those working at senior levels can be difficult. There are few participants and these employees are likely to develop and learn through the impact of numerous inter-related diverse interventions and experiences. However, surveys show that leaders in successful organisations are engaged in lots of personal development activity.

As gaining access to a large number of senior leaders can be challenging, much of our existing knowledge about leader development comes from qualitative data drawn from interviews with them. For example, McCall (2010) interviewed successful business leaders and from these identified what he describes as 'seven sure bets of leadership development'. These are:

- Leadership is learned from experiences, and hardships and mistakes are just as important for learning as is the experience of success.

- Experiences are powerful because of the challenges they present.

- Certain experiences are more significant than others (i.e. experiences that are often unexpected, involve high stakes, complexity, or pressure, can all make for potentially powerful learning experiences);

- Different types of experience teach different lessons: therefore it is important for aspiring leaders to seek out, and take on, assignments and projects that are high-profile and that put them in contact with people from different parts of the organisation;

- There is an important responsibility on employers and managers to make jobs and projects more developmental (i.e. there are always opportunities to provide feedback on learning, as well as additional coaching and mentoring);

- Whoever decides who gets a particular job controls potential development opportunities and access to future leadership roles, therefore it is important to know who the decision-makers are for aspiring leaders to proactively seek them out to make them aware of their interest in future development and promotion opportunities.

- Learning is dynamic and occurs over time. Consequently, employees and their managers should be prepared for making the most of unexpected serendipitous learning opportunities, including experiencing (and coping) with hardships or mistakes at work.

McCall's findings point to an interesting potential disconnect between the more formal training activities described earlier in this chapter more typically available to employees at lower organisational levels. At senior levels, there may be a reluctance to engage in traditional training activities for fear of stigma – often because taking part in training implies a development need, which can be construed or revealed as a weakness to others (Silvester and Menges, 2011). For this reason, much of the development activity of senior personnel is likely to involve one-to-one bespoke learning activities such as coaching: this has the appeal of occurring in private 'behind closed doors' where potential development needs can be discussed without fear of prejudice. The coaching provided to organisational leaders often involves an external coach who works one-to-one with the leader to identify and help address a specific development need, frequently in relation to leadership ability and style (Stern, 2004).

Key learning point

Leaders' development often takes place outside of the formal training environment, for example through one-to-one coaching.

These types of development activities are extremely difficult to observe and learning objectives (if they exist) are much less likely to be formalised or measured compared with traditional training activities. As such there is less empirical evidence from studies capable of investigating causal relationships between the design of coaching and learning outcomes, but qualitative findings – and indeed the popularity of coaching – suggests that participants gain something worthwhile from the process. That said, the 2013 Coaching Survey undertaken by the Miles Group and Stanford University (Stanford, 2013) found that 66 per cent of CEOs surveyed received no coaching or leadership advice from external sources. They describe this as the 'loneliness of being at the top' and their findings certainly suggest that many CEOs continue to rely on self-directed informal learning, supported by advice from friends, peers and close advisors.

Mentoring and diversity

Although this chapter has focused on formal learning activities, and training in particular, it is important not to overlook other less structured and potentially more informal ways in which organisations seek to support and develop their staff. One such example is mentoring: this usually involves an interpersonal relationship between a more experienced individual (mentor) who provides guidance and support to a junior organisational member (protégé) in order to facilitate learning and career development (e.g. sponsorship, political understanding and exposure to senior decision-makers: Kram, 1985). Mentoring has become a popular means of supporting employee development in business (Allen and Eby, 2008; Payne and Huffman, 2005), with research documenting a variety of benefits, including improvements to on-the-job training, socialisation, career guidance and personal support (Lankau and Scandura, 2002). Mentoring is also frequently provided as part of leadership development programmes for employees considered to have the potential and ability to rise to more senior levels (Silvester and Menges, 2011).

Point of integration

Mentoring and coaching can extend beyond the discussion of job-related skills. These interventions often address wider career development agendas (see Chapter 13).

Most training programmes are designed to help trainees acquire *explicit* knowledge, which is defined as knowledge that can be written down or formalised in a set of instructions or procedures. Explicit knowledge therefore includes information provided in training manuals, or specified in the objectives and specifications for training programmes, as well as in training materials such as handbooks, slides and Web-based learning resources. However, it is generally thought that mentoring is particularly good at providing employees with an understanding of the social norms and cultural assumptions that define organisational environments and how they are expected to perform their roles. This type of knowledge is described as *tacit* knowledge, because it cannot be articulated or verbalised and is therefore rarely written down and can be very difficult to access. Tacit knowledge resides in intuition and is typically learned via shared, collaborative experiences (like mentoring) that require active participation from all those involved (Nonaka, 1994).

Key learning point

Tacit knowledge is difficult to verbalise and therefore not easily conveyed through formal training methods.

Mentoring can help employees access this hard-to-reach tacit information about 'how things really work' because mentors, who are more experienced in knowing how the organisation works, can share insights with their protégé about how decision-making occurs via informal rather than formal routes. For example, this may include information about who knows what and who has the power to make decisions within the organisation. In short, mentors can provide insight into the political side of organisations that is often hidden from newcomers or those outside privileged powerful groups (Silvester and Wyatt, 2016). Similarly, mentors can provide sponsorship or advocacy for their protégés by introducing them to other senior people in the organisation who can provide access to the types of influential projects that McCall identifies as important for learning.

Employees from minority groups often find it especially difficult to access the types of tacit, political information that can help facilitate career progression. This can be because they find it more difficult to access powerful role models who are willing to share information about successful ways to apply knowledge. For this reason, many organisations sponsor formal mentoring programmes aimed at improving inclusion and enhancing development for employees from minority groups. Formal mentoring involves mentoring relationships that are organised and/or facilitated by the organisation, rather than those that are initiated independently by a protégé or mentor. Formal mentoring to improve inclusion and career progression opportunities usually involves matching women and/or minority ethnic employees with senior organisational leaders to facilitate sharing of tacit hard-to-reach knowledge about organisational practices and decision-making (Wyatt and Silvester, 2015). While these efforts represent a positive advance to use development to overcome differential progression for employees from minority groups (Ragins, 2010), there is still evidence that some employees are much less likely to find powerful mentors who are racially similar (Blickle et al., 2009). Thus this group of employees may still find it difficult to find good-quality relationships with senior personnel able and willing to help them develop the knowledge and skills required to advance to higher levels (Blass et al., 2007).

Key learning point

Formal mentoring arrangements can be used to address differences in the rate and extent of career progression that sometimes exist between demographic groups.

Training and the learning organisation

Finally, although our discussion in this chapter has focused on training as an important activity in its own right, it is only proper that we end by discussing training as part of the wider organisational system of strategic human resource management, with relevance for concepts like organisational learning (OL) and knowledge management (KM). Generally speaking, OL and KM are more typically discussed in fields like organisational behaviour and change, and as such have received relatively little coverage in traditional work psychology texts on training and development. Two possible reasons for this could be that (i) work psychology training and development research has usually focused on individual learning and development, and (ii) research has been driven by an emphasis on positivist empirical approaches to the evaluation of the impact of training (our Research methods in focus earlier in this chapter). These approaches have enhanced our scientific understanding of learning and development. Unfortunately, neither has been as successful at explaining or predicting the complex dynamic learning systems that characterise successful organisations.

Point of integration

Organisational change can often be a stimulus for learning (see Chapter 14). Collaborative change processes often involve different groups of employees working together to plan change or to solve problems.

The past few decades have seen training and development increasingly recognised as core business functions, as well as the main mechanisms to create learning organisations. Driven by the need to cope with what seems like an ever-increasing pace of change and instability in economies and global markets, it has been argued that organisations must learn to thrive on (rather than simply react to) change. To do this they must become learning organisations capable of adapting flexibly to changing environments and needs. Central to the concept of the learning organisation is that organisations can only adapt if their employees are also flexible and adaptive to change; therefore, employees must view learning as an ongoing feature of their jobs (Burgoyne, 1999). Encouraging a positive attitude to the take-up of training opportunities can be seen as part of traditional approaches to training and development. However, what is new is the increasing focus on *capturing individual learning* ensuring that it is (i) passed on and shared by different organisational members and groups, and (ii) used to achieve organisational benefits.

This can be illustrated by the case of management consultancies and professional service firms where individual employees such as solicitors, consultants and financial advisors often develop considerable knowledge and expertise relating to specific clients or subject areas. As one CEO once commented, 'our most expensive assets walk out of the building every evening': this metaphor illustrates the dependency of such companies on the knowledge and expertise of key individuals. Although the company may control the content of corporate learning and development activities, it has little influence or control over the ability of the employee to learn from their experiences with clients and in different work environments. Yet this knowledge may be extremely important and valuable to the company. In such cases the employee can become more powerful and less dependent on their employer through the development of a unique knowledge base about particular clients and their needs. As a consequence, there has been growing interest in how learning and development systems can be 'turned on their head' to ensure that unstructured employee learning is transferred back to the organisation through KM systems where it can be shared and dispersed between different employees (e.g. Argote et al., 2000; Goh, 2002). For example, many consultancies ask employees to write up case studies and notes about their clients or specific projects: these are then made available on a central intranet for other employees to access and learn from.

Point of integration

Dispersed working (see Chapter 15) presents many challenges and opportunities for knowledge sharing, mentoring and personal development. The type of interactions between employees working at a distance from each other can have a significant impact on the amount and quality of information that is shared.

This illustrates a substantial shift in our thinking about learning and development activities. There has been a move away from seeing training as a top-down process where the organisation identifies the knowledge and skills required by an employee and controls access to them through formal, structured learning opportunities. Instead, there has been growing interest in knowledge as a *social construction*, co-created by individuals through their interactions with one another (or between mentor and protégé as we saw earlier) and the environment. Informal learning, driven by the interests and proactive engagement of an employee is recognised as an ongoing feature of working life. This is less controllable by management, but is still key to sense-making and creating a shared understanding among work colleagues (Currie and Kerrin, 2003). What this type of learning emphasises, however, is the inherently political nature of learning and development. Employees do not passively acquire learning, but exchange, barter and gift knowledge as a commodity in order to gain power and influence with colleagues and their employer (Konstantinou and Fincham, 2011). Although relatively unexplored by work psychologists, these political aspects of learning and development undoubtedly provide a fertile and fascinating area for future research (Silvester, 2008).

Point of integration

Opportunities for personal growth and development can help to reduce the risk of work stress and have a positive impact on employees, psychological resources (see Chapter 10).

Summary

Constant social and technological change provides a context for organisational life. This coupled with individual growth and career development means that training has an important, if not core, role to play in organisations. Effective training needs analysis (at organisation, task and person levels) provides the basis for the design and implementation of training activities. Although the analysis of needs, together with a clear statement of training aims and objectives, is important, there is still a certain degree of judgement involved in choosing appropriate training methods. This essential subjectivity can be checked and assessed by the application of systematic procedures for evaluating the effectiveness of training. Evaluation at reaction, learning, behaviour and results levels provides a way of determining the overall value of training and assessing necessary improvements. In general, research has shown that training is an effective way of bringing about behaviour change, although there are often problems in ensuring that the potential for change provided by training activities actually transfers to the work setting. In fact, organisations today are far more likely to see training as a continuous process of organisational learning that incorporates formal, structured training activities as well as informal learning opportunities, where employees are expected and encouraged to share their knowledge and learning with each other.

Closing case study

Welcome on-board!

Organisational socialisation is the area of study concerned with how newcomers adjust to their new surroundings and learn the behaviours, attitudes and skills necessary to function effectively in their roles and as organisational members (Saks et al., 2011). Also referred to as 'on-boarding' it involves the formal processes – including training – that exist to help new employees learn the knowledge, skills and behaviours they need to succeed in their new organisations (Bauer and Erdogan, 2011).

There is evidence that formal training for newcomers is becoming more important for organisations as individuals move more frequently between jobs and organisations, and companies need to increase the speed and efficiency with which new employees are brought up to speed about how the organisation works, important values and procedures and what is expected of new organisational members.

▶

▶

In 2005 figures indicated that approximately 25 per cent of US workers were undergoing organisational socialisation at any one time with individuals changing jobs an average of 10.2 times over 20 years (Bureau of Labor Statistics, 2005). It seems that training as part of socialisation is likely to become increasingly important as organisations strive to streamline procedures and achieve maximal levels of performance from employees in the shortest period of time.

Suggested exercise

What are the things that a newcomer to an organisation will need to know? In what ways might on-boarding differ from training?

Test your learning

Short-answer questions

1 What are the three key phases in the training system?
2 Why is training needs analysis important and what are the levels at which this can occur?
3 Explain the function of learning objectives in the design of training.
4 Describe Anderson's three stages of skill development.
5 Explain how a consideration of individual differences in learning capabilities can help in training design.
6 Name and explain (briefly) Kirkpatrick's four levels of evaluation data.
7 How can we improve reactance-level data?
8 Give a brief critical explanation of two designs that might be used for an evaluation study.
9 What can be done to enhance training in a very diverse workforce?
10 How might the training of top-level managers be best delivered?

Suggested assignments

1 Why is it important to position training as a central HR function linking with other selection and performance management systems?
2 Explain how you would review the training needs of an organisation and design relevant training programmes.
3 Consider what value and understanding the psychology of learning has for a training manager.

Relevant websites

The UK Health and Safety Executive provide detailed guidance for employers regarding training in the use of work equipment. This material provides a good insight into how research and theory in training can be translated into effective practical interventions: http://www.hse.gov.uk/work-equipment-machinery/training-competence.htm

The Chartered Institute of Personnel and Development provides a range of resources to help employers develop and implement effective training and employee development. Their Learning and Development Survey provides an excellent insight into the challenges being faced by employers: http://www.cipd.co.uk/hr-topics/learning-development.aspx

One of many examples of excellent online training courses for workers provided by the National Institute for Occupational Safety and Health (NIOSH) can be found at: http://www.cdc.gov/niosh/topics/violence/training_nurses.html. Their publication on training effectiveness is also useful: see http://www.cdc.gov/niosh/docs/99-142/pdfs/99-142.pdf

Suggested further reading

There are two particularly strong and accessible textbooks in this topic area. These are:

1 Noe (2012) *Employee Training and Development* (McGraw Hill, 6th edition).

2 Goldstein and Ford (2001) *Training in Organizations: Needs assessment, development, and evaluation* (Wadsworth Publishing, 4th edition).

Note

1 You can watch an expert explain the whole process online at 'How to make a cappuccino with a traditional espresso coffee machine' by caffesociety; http://www.youtube.com/watch?v=gc-sloCajV0. Alternatively, watch how your cappuccino is made next time you are in a coffee shop.

CHAPTER 10

Work-related stress and well-being

LEARNING OBJECTIVES

After studying this chapter, you should be able to:

1 define stress and work-related health;

2 describe some key structural models of work stress;

3 describe some key transactional models of work stress;

4 describe conservation of resources theory and the job demands-resources model;

5 compare and contrast the concepts of stress and positive well-being;

6 identify the workplace conditions that are linked to stress and health problems;

7 identify some of the individual differences that are linked to the experience of stress, positive well-being at work and employee health;

8 list measures of work-related health, well-being and stress;

9 distinguish between primary, secondary and tertiary interventions designed to improve work-related psychological well-being;

10 discuss the evidence relating to the effectiveness of different intervention strategies.

Opening case study

Working longer hours increases stroke risk, a major study finds. Danger highlighted by research suggesting those working a 55-hour week face 33% increased risk of stroke than those working a 35- to 40-hour week.

The likely toll of long working hours is revealed in a major new study which shows that employees still at their desks into the evening run an increased risk of stroke – and the longer the hours they put in, the higher the risk.

The largest study conducted on the issue, carried out in three continents and led by scientists at University College London, found that those who work more than 55 hours a week have a 33% increased risk of stroke compared with those who work a 35- to 40-hour week. They also have a 13% increased risk of coronary heart disease.

The findings will confirm the assumptions of many that a long-hours culture, in which people work from early in the morning until well into the evening, with work also intruding into weekends, is potentially harmful to health.

The researchers, publishing their findings in the Lancet medical journal, say they cannot state categorically that long hours cause people to have strokes – but their study shows that there is a link, and it gets stronger as the hours people put in get longer.

"Sudden death from overwork is often caused by stroke and is believed to result from a repetitive triggering of the stress response," they write. "Behavioural mechanisms, such as physical inactivity, might also link long working hours and stroke; a hypothesis supported by evidence of an increased risk of incident stroke in individuals who sit for long periods at work.

"Physical inactivity can increase the risk of stroke through various biological mechanisms and heavy alcohol consumption – a risk factor for all types of stroke – might be a contributing factor because employees working long hours seem to be slightly more prone to risky drinking than are those who work standard hours."

People who work long hours are also more likely to ignore the warning signs, they say – leading to delays in getting treatment.

Mika Kivimäki, professor of epidemiology at UCL, and colleagues looked separately at heart disease and at stroke. For coronary heart disease, they pulled together 25 studies involving more than 600,000 men and women from Europe, the USA and Australia who were followed for an average of 8.5 years.

They then pooled and analysed the data that had been collected. This produced the finding of a 13% increase in the chances of a new diagnosis of heart disease or hospitalisation or death.

For stroke, they analysed data from 17 studies involving nearly 530,000 men and women who were followed up for an average of 7.2 years. They found a 1.3 times higher risk of stroke in individuals working 55 hours or more, compared with those working a standard 35- to 40-hour week.

This association remained even after taking into account health behaviours such as smoking, alcohol consumption and physical activity as well as standard cardiovascular risk factors including high blood pressure and high cholesterol.

The longer the working week, the higher was the risk of stroke. Those working between 41 and 48 hours had a 10% higher risk of stroke and those working 49 to 54 hours had a 27% increased risk.

Kivimäki said the scale of the study allowed the team to be more precise about the health toll of long hours than ever before. He suggested that doctors should take note of the possible risks to their hard-working patients. "Health professionals should be aware that working long hours is associated with a significantly increased risk of stroke, and perhaps also coronary heart disease," he said.

In a commentary in the journal, Dr Urban Janlert from Umeå University in Sweden writes that the European Working Time Directive, meant to limit the week to 48 hours, is not in effect in all countries. "Long working

▶

▶

hours are not a negligible occurrence. Among member countries of the OECD, Turkey has the highest proportion of individuals working more than 50 hours per week (43%) and the Netherlands the lowest (less than 1%).

"Although some countries have legislation for working hours ... it is not always implemented. Therefore, that the length of a working day is an important determinant mainly for strokes, but perhaps also for coronary heart disease, is an important finding." Dr Tim Chico, reader in cardiovascular medicine at the University of Sheffield, said the study did not prove long working hours could cause stroke or heart disease. "It is almost certainly impossible to prove whether there is a direct link as this would require thousands of people to be randomly allocated to work more or less hours and followed up for years to see if this changes the risk of stroke, while keeping all other behaviours the same between groups," he said.

For many people, cutting down on working hours would be difficult or impossible, he said. "Most of us could reduce the amount of time we spend sitting down, increase our physical activity and improve our diet while working and this might be more important the more time we spend at work. We should all consider how the working environment could be altered to promote healthy behaviour that will reduce strokes, irrespective of how long we work."

Source: **http://www.theguardian.com/lifeandstyle/2015/aug/20/working-longer-hours-increases-stroke-risk**,
Sarah Boseley, The Guardian Online, 20 August 2015

Introduction

The health of people at work has been an important issue for psychologists for some time. As the opening case study demonstrates, the evidence that shows work can impact upon employee health continues to mount. The case study also points to consequences that are far from trivial. Over recent years the management of employee well-being has become a priority issue for all types of organisations.

The focus of this chapter is on the effects that work can have on people's health and well-being through a variety of different psychological mechanisms. It has been argued for some time that problems such as work stress can be very damaging to individuals and organisations alike. The opening case identifies a particularly serious potential consequence for individuals. Certain occupations, such as teachers, ambulance staff, police, social workers etc. are often believed to have the highest stress levels (Johnson et al., 2005). The case study shows that the consequences of work-related stress are not confined to certain types of jobs traditionally seen as 'highly pressured'. It also highlights that the way people respond to feeling stressed (e.g. by drinking alcohol) can mean that stress has an indirect effect on workers' health. One other finding to note: the effects of work stress on significant health outcomes might not always be large in comparison to other risk factors (such as smoking, obesity or lack of exercise).

Longitudinal studies have provided powerful information about the possible causal links between the workers' psychological responses to their job conditions and other serious illnesses such as heart disease (CHD). The 'Whitehall Studies' were carried out with a large sample of workers employed in the UK Civil Service (see Ferrie et al., 2005; Griffin et al., 2007; Kuper and Marmot, 2008). A consistent finding from this research was that employees reporting job strain (high job demands combined with a lack of opportunities to make decisions, or as they are often referred to as 'high strain' jobs) were at a significantly increased risk of developing CHD. As you might imagine problems with individual well-being can have consequences for organisations and the economy as a whole. All of this is in addition to the 'human costs' of the problem as people experience significant personal difficulties in their own lives.

These findings paint a rather negative picture: unless work is well managed, psychological processes can be activated that can damage employees' health. It is also worth remembering that very positive psychological processes can be activated through work. It is now well established that well-designed and managed jobs can have a significant positive impact on employees. Theories from positive psychology focus on issues such as engagement, personal development and the joy that people can experience at work. Much of the work in this area examines the experience of positive emotions at work and their roles in building well-being and changing the way people think and act in a healthy way (e.g. Fredrickson, 1998; Fredrickson and Joiner, 2002).

Point of integration

As you read this chapter, you may note that there are many connections between those factors that are linked to stress and those that are linked to positive work outcomes. For example, high levels of autonomy have been shown to be linked to positive emotions at work while low levels are well-documented sources of stress. Some of these positive outcomes (job satisfaction, organisational commitment and employee engagement) are also discussed in Chapter 6.

Much of this chapter covers research, theory and practice on a major topic in psychological well-being at work: work-related stress. However, we also discuss other markers of work-related health. In identifying organisational sources of stress we will look at a range of factors such as job demands, control at work, work-role problems, workplace bullying, relationships at work, career development, organisational climate and structure, and the work–home interface. We also discuss the positive aspects of work that can promote well-being. In doing so we consider a number of individual differences that play a role in determining how employees respond to their experiences at work. The chapter then discusses different forms of intervention for reducing stress and promoting well-being in the workplace.

Work-related stress

What is stress?

Stress is a word derived from the Latin word *stringere*, meaning to draw tight. Early definitions of stress drew on concepts used in physics and engineering: external forces (load) were seen as exerting pressure upon an individual, producing strain. Therefore, one could measure stress as an external stimulus to which an individual is subjected in the same way that the physical stress upon a machine could be measured (Hinkle, 1973).

In contrast, Cannon (1929) defined stress in terms of the internal physiological state of subjects exposed to threatening or exciting situations (e.g. the raised adrenalin secretion that can be observed in the well-known fight or flight reaction). Hans Selye (1946) provided a more elaborate model of the human response to stressors. This he called General Adaptation Syndrome. It has three stages:

1   Alarm reaction, in which an initial phase of lowered resistance is followed by counter-shock, during which the individual's defence mechanisms become active.

2   *Resistance*, the stage of maximum adaptation and, hopefully, successful return to equilibrium for the individual. If, however, the stress agent continues or the defence mechanism does not work, the individual will move on to a third stage.

3   *Exhaustion*, when adaptive mechanisms collapse.

These models are rarely used now in work psychology, although their influence is still felt in the way we understand the causes and consequences of work stress. For example, a stressor has been defined as any force that pushes a psychological or physical factor beyond its range of stability, producing a strain within the individual (Cooper et al., 2001). The term 'high strain' was used to refer to a combination of high workload and low control. Stress is no longer defined in terms of environmental pressures or its impact on physiological well-being. Stress is not really an illness, although people often use the term in this way.

Instead, contemporary theories of work-related stress describe it as the *intervening psychological processes that link exposure to work-related problems to the negative impact of those problem*s. Stress is a negative emotional state that results from the transactions between a person and their environment. It is something that is *caused or made worse* by work. The UK Health and Safety Executive's (www.hse.gov.uk/stress) definition of work stress does a good job of capturing the essence of many of the various scientific definitions: 'the process that arises where work demands of various types and combinations exceed the person's capacity and capability to cope'. Stress is not high workload or work-related absence, rather it is the negative emotional state that can arise from pressures at work (e.g. high workload is a potential cause of stress) and can contribute to a range of problems with psychological, physical health and organisational health (e.g. absence is a potential consequence of stress).

Before we look at different theories of stress, it is important to emphasise that individual perception or *appraisal* is important in most of them. This puts psychological processes at the heart of the topic. Two people exposed to similar working conditions can perceive them very differently. For example, some students enjoy examinations. Others (probably most readers) find exams immensely stressful. Returning to the HSE definition given above, stress occurs when an individual *perceives or appraises* that the various demands placed on them exceed their own view of the capacity they have to cope with them. Even if two people evaluate the demands as the same, they may each have different views on their own ability to respond to those demands. This is important because as we discuss later it has significant implications for how stress at work is measured and managed.

Key learning point

When perceived demands exceed the individual's perceived ability to cope, they can be said to be experiencing a negative and unpleasant emotional state that is referred to as stress.

Models of work stress

Most students of work psychology will encounter a rather confusing array of models and theories of work stress. Most describe stress as in some way resulting from a perceived lack of fit between an individual's capacity and the demands of their particular work environment. This allows us to understand better why one person seems to flourish in a certain setting, while another suffers. Some models also describe how the individual chooses and evaluates their responses to the problems they face (i.e. how they cope with pressure). Some include a description of the impact of individual differences. Contemporary theories offer quite detailed explanations of how workers' thoughts and behaviours result in them changing the way they respond to work demands (some of these changes might exacerbate their experience of stress while others might reduce it). Understanding these *transactions* has allowed researchers and practitioners to develop a range of intervention strategies.

In this section, the most influential models will be described and their key features identified. To simplify things a little, many of the models (but not all) can be split into three categories: *structural approaches*, *transactional approaches* and *resource-based models*.

Structural approaches

Structural approaches to stress focus on describing the features of work that are thought to be likely to lead to the negative emotional state of stress for most (although perhaps not all) workers. Research using these approaches has tended to focus on identifying the psychological aspects of work (often referred to as *psychosocial working conditions*) that are reliably linked to significant physical or psychological health problems. Initially, these models focused on a small number of factors such as demands and control. Over time many more have been found to be linked to employee health and are discussed in more detail later in this chapter.

The demand–control model (DCM; Karasek, 1979) was built around just two features of the work environment. Demands relate to the amount of work that a person does but also include factors such as time pressures and the amount of mental and physical effort involved in the job and its difficulty. In other words, demand has both *quantitative* (amount of work) and *qualitative* (type of work) elements. It would be surprising if any theory of work-related stress did not include workload: most people expect stress and workload to be positively correlated such that high workload equals high stress. Recent research shows that this is true, but only up to a point. A meta-analysis by Bowling et al. (2015) found that high perceived workload is consistently and strongly linked to impaired physical and psychological health. However, and importantly, it does not completely explain variations in employee health, in fact far from it. After analysing a huge amount of research, Bowling et al. (2015) found only weak links between workload and measures of depression. Tetrick and Winslow (2015) report that heavy workload is not in the top five sources of work stress reported by workers in the American Psychological Association's 2014 Work and Well-Being Survey. Even before such a large amount of research evidence became available, academics quickly realised that other aspects of work needed to be considered.

Karasek's original definition of control includes two components: *skill discretion* (the extent to which the job allows the employee to use their skills and capabilities) and *decision latitude* (the amount of control the employee has over their work situation). By combining demands and control, four categories of job were identified:

1   passive job (low demands – low control);

2   high-strain job (high demands – low control);

3   low-strain job (low demands – high control);

4   active job (high demands – high control).

Karasek and Theorell (1990) used strong longitudinal research designs to test their model and found that employees in high-strain jobs were at a particularly increased risk of developing various psychological and physical health problems. Numerous recent studies confirm these findings. The finding that those in active job roles tended to be less likely to develop health problems indicated that job control might have a positive impact on well-being beyond simply off-setting the effects of demands. Fox and colleagues (1993) argue that control is such an important psychological variable for two reasons. First, because it provides employees with *opportunities to deal better* with the demands they are facing. Second, because it fulfils *a basic human need* for control. For the same reasons, low levels of control can have serious consequences. According to Karasek and Theorell's model, a job with high demands might not be stressful because of the positive effects of control. An example of this 'active job' would be someone with a very high workload having the freedom to prioritise tasks and to use their skills to get the job done well in the most efficient way.

The model was expanded by Johnson and Hall (1988) to include social support (the demand–control–support model, the DCSM). Social support is the helpful interactions with supervisors and co-workers (Daniels et al., 2009). In this model, high levels of social support are thought to act as a *buffer* against the negative effects of work demands. Given similar levels of demands, jobs with higher levels of social support will tend to be healthier (this means that

Exercise 10.1   How stressful are these jobs?

Below is a list of job roles. Karasek and Theorell (1990) describe how a number of different jobs were categorised according to the levels of demands and control in each job. In which of the four categories of job is each job role likely to be most appropriately classified?

- Call-centre phone-call handler;
- Elite team sports athlete;
- Qualified medical doctor;
- Shopping centre security guard;
- Lifeguard at a swimming pool;
- Company chief executive;
- Supermarket checkout operator;
- Assembly line worker;
- Used car salesperson.

Suggested exercises

1   Do you think that some of these jobs could be inherently stressful and therefore likely to be seen as stressful by most people?

2   In your current work, or in your studies, how much does having control help you when you are faced with high demands?

demands, control and support might interact to predict well-being: see Chapter 2 for a description of interaction effects). The basic premise is that, like control, emotional support or practical help reduces the impact of high work demands on employees (O'Driscoll and Brough, 2010): this is the *strain hypothesis* (Daniels et al., 2009). High control and social support when accompanied by high job demands can also help employees to learn new skills in order to adapt to the demands placed on them and lead to improved motivation and satisfaction: this is the *learning hypothesis* (De Witte et al., 2007). It is worth noting that the benefits of this type of work may be at risk when other aspects of the job are not well-managed, for example when working hours are long and unpredictable active jobs can become *saturated* (Holman, 2013).

Reviews of these models examining the results of a large number of studies (e.g. De Lange et al., 2003) tend to show that high levels of control and support often exert positive effects and that high levels of demands exert negative effects on employee well-being, especially when control and support are low. However, the stress process does not seem to be quite as simple and predictable as the models propose. The evidence for *buffering* effects of social support and control in high demand situations is less consistent and clear. There is also a small amount of evidence that because of individual differences (such as **psychological flexibility** discussed later in this chapter) very high levels of control might not be utilised by everyone (Bond et al., 2008).

Karasek's four combinations of demand and control still make sense for lots of work roles. Of course, since it was published many jobs have changed beyond recognition and new types of jobs have emerged. By analysing the quality of working conditions reported by a large number of workers from across Europe, Holman (2013) identified several additional job categories (see also Chapter 7). Saturated jobs are similar to active jobs except they have a very high workload, high demands for interaction with others, long working hours and unusual working hours (e.g. frequent weekend and evening work). Senior managers and professionals are most likely to report these working conditions. Team-based jobs involve lots of collective decision-making (e.g. regarding the allocation of tasks to team members) coupled with lots of discretion and support from others, with the work being carried out during fixed, standard hours. Such work roles include craft and trade workers and those in technical support roles. Insecure jobs are low-paid roles in which employees are uncertain about the security of their tenure. These work roles typically have low levels of control and support, few opportunities for training and inflexible work hours. Workers in retail sales, construction trades (e.g. bricklayers) and cleaning are more likely than most to report such working conditions. This new taxonomy shows that it is not just demands, control and support that need to be considered when evaluating the likely impact of work on well-being. Note for example the importance of job insecurity: we return to this point later.

You may have noticed that these models focus on a limited range of working conditions (albeit important ones) and that some combinations of working conditions are consistently 'unhealthy'. Other models have looked at a wider range of sources of stress and also placed more emphasis on describing the impact of employees' appraisals of the 'fit' between their own skills, abilities and preferences and the demands of the job.

Key learning point

Demands, control and support at work are particularly important in structural models of work stress.

The Michigan model (Caplan et al., 1975) and the person–environment fit model (French et al., 1982) propose that each employee's skills, abilities, knowledge and attitudes need to be well matched to the demands of their job. Stress is likely to occur if there is a mismatch between the person and the job, and the bigger this mismatch, the greater the stress experienced. *Subjective perceptions* of work stressors are particularly important in these models and the Michigan model does include additional factors of increasing relevance such as job insecurity, lack of participation and role-related issues. The core concept of lack of fit has been particularly influential in stress research, partly because it allows us to consider the role of skills, ability, personality and other *individual differences* in the stress process. For example, the author of this chapter would find it very stressful to have to repair a broken-down car by the side of the motorway, but this is a task that a skilled mechanic with a calm approach to life would find much easier. There are so many factors that can influence person–environment 'fit' that it is difficult to make specific predictions from these complex models that can be tested using traditional scientific methods (Mark and Smith, 2008). With its more easily 'testable' predictions, it is perhaps understandable that the DCSM remains widely used in the research literature.

Tests of structural models of work stress show that working conditions such as control can have both positive and negative effects on the employee. This idea was extended in Warr's **vitamin model** (see Warr, 2009). In this model, working conditions, like vitamins, can have a positive impact on health, but 'mega-doses' are wasteful or in some cases harmful. This means that some working conditions will help to increase health up to some *threshold level*, at which point they will not have any more positive effects, but will not become harmful. These include factors such as levels of pay. Other factors become harmful if they are *excessive or absent*. These include factors such as demands, control and social support. Having lots of control at work might not be helpful for all employees, especially for employees who do not have sufficient knowledge, confidence or skill to exercise that control in a productive way. Being overwhelmed with unwanted support from colleagues might not be a good thing, as we discuss later.

Point of integration

Chapter 7 of this text describes one other model to consider – the job characteristics model (Hackman and Oldham, 1980). Although not a 'stress theory' per se, the links between job characteristics and measures of well-being can be quite strong.

The amount of 'fit' between the employee and their work environment plays an important role in determining how stressful the employee finds their job.

Transactional approaches

If you take time to observe an individual at work it is clear that they react to, respond to and *transact with* the work environment. In other words, they do things that change their situation and then respond to the changed situation through an ongoing series of transactions. If you have used this book for a while you might find you now use it in a very different way to how you did when you first purchased it – perhaps now as a handy quick reference guide rather than something to be immersed in during late-night revision. At the centre of these models are the worker's dynamic and ever-changing perceptions of the *balance between the demands they perceive and their evaluations of their own coping resources*. Transactional models highlight the importance of workers' perception of the success of their attempts to respond to demands (i.e. workers look for and evaluate feedback). Hence, these are sometimes referred to as cognitive theories of stress and coping. The dynamic nature of the stress process was highlighted by Cummings and Cooper (1979) who argued that:

- Individuals, for the most part, try to keep their thoughts, emotions and relationships with the world in a 'steady state' (sometimes referred to as homoeostasis).

- Each element of a person's emotional and physical state has a 'range of stability', in which that person feels comfortable. When forces disrupt one of these states beyond this comfortable range, the individual must act or cope to restore a perception of comfort.

- An individual's behaviour aimed at maintaining a steady state makes up their 'adjustment process', or coping strategies. These behaviours could include adjusting their approach to work tasks, withdrawing from work, seeking support from colleagues and so on. Research shows that it is not uncommon for individuals to do this in a proactive way that helps them to shape and manage their exposure to stressors. This is referred to as job-crafting (see resource-based models later in this chapter).

Transactional models of stress focus more on describing the *psychological mechanisms of the stress process*. These include employees' cognitive evaluation of their working conditions (e.g. 'Is my workload high?'), their emotional responses to their work ('Is the way I am feeling unpleasant?') and decision-making mechanisms relating to coping and behaviour (e.g. 'Is what I am doing helping me to deal with my workload?'). These individual differences in cognitive evaluations and coping styles were not considered in detail in structural models. The central role of employees' perceptions in these models means that many different aspects of work can be sources of stress because it very much depends upon what is important to the individual and how they make sense of their own experiences.

Lazarus and Folkman (1984) proposed that individuals evaluate the extent to which situations or events pose threats to them or present them with opportunities for gain: this is a *primary appraisal*. The appraisal might be that there is a problem (a *harm-loss* appraisal), could be a problem (a *threat* appraisal) or that the situation presents some potential for gain (a *challenge* appraisal). There is then a *secondary appraisal* where the person evaluates whether they can cope with the situation. If a person thinks they can cope with a situation they are less likely to appraise it as a threat and more likely to appraise it as a challenge. Together, these primary and secondary appraisals are the basis of what the person chooses to do in response to the situation (i.e. their *transaction* with the work environment). The appraisals are also linked to the person's emotional response and, in turn, their physiological responses (such as changes in blood pressure). If threat appraisals occur often, there are likely to be negative outcomes for the employee (such as anxiety). In contrast, challenge appraisals are likely to yield positive emotions and be quite motivating. As you can see, the meanings that people attach to events are extremely important in this model, and different people attach different meanings to similar events. The way people make sense of what is going on around them can be influenced by any number of individual differences (discussed later).

Cox and MacKay's transactional model of work stress (see Cox, 1993, and Mark and Smith, 2008, for summaries) also includes detailed consideration of how people evaluate the outcomes of the coping response/the action taken (sometimes referred to as a *tertiary appraisal*). If they feel their action was effective, then they may become immediately less anxious and perceive similar problems as being less stressful in the future. In this model the outcomes of the individual's responses feed back into all the preceding stages of the process (i.e. feedback shapes what stressors they are exposed to in the future, it informs how they appraise those stressors, and how they choose to respond to them). These *feedback loops* are particularly important in determining how people respond to working conditions over a period of time. This model does not suggest that the problem a person encountered is always solved by their coping responses. Some maladaptive coping responses (e.g. increased alcohol consumption) can be consequences of work stress. Some actions might help employees to reduce their exposure to stressors (e.g. by getting on with important job tasks). Coping responses are not always rational responses and are influenced by individual differences. Some people might have high levels of self-efficacy and therefore feel very able and just like to get on with things. Others may be less confident and tend to focus on dealing with unpleasant emotions like worry or fear. Feedback on the success (or otherwise) of the employee's actions might not always be accurate or available. For example, bosses and customers don't always tell an employee when they have done well or badly. Even if feedback is available people do not always interpret it correctly.

Key learning point

Transactional models of stress are more complex than structural models. These models have more to say about the role of perception, individual differences and coping in the experience of stress. Importantly, they also describe how the individual receives and responds to feedback from the environment.

Transactional approaches to work stress also give us some important insights into the possible causes of employee over-commitment. Siegrist (1996) argued that two factors are particularly important in many transactions: perceived *efforts and rewards*. According to this effort–reward imbalance (ERI) model, negative emotions are experienced when an employee perceives that their efforts are not reciprocated (in terms of money, esteem and recognition). Stress arises when efforts are not appropriately rewarded, and this yields perceived unfairness. Siegrist proposes that one way that employees might respond to this imbalance is to increase work effort, or *over-commit* in a desire to obtain reward and recognition. The individual then gets into a cycle of working harder and harder, experiencing more stress while at the same time reducing the quantity and quality of recovery. One implication of ERI is that some unscrupulous managers might be tempted to exploit this effect by withholding rewards from hardworking employees! Aspects of work such as career development, job security and promotion prospects can be powerful sources of stress (see Table 10.1). This model also places an individual difference, *self-esteem*, at the heart of the stress process. There is quite a lot of evidence to support the main predictions of this model (Siegrist et al., 2014; Tsutsumi and Kawakami, 2004).

Table 10.1	Questions from Siegrist et al.'s abbreviated measure of effort–reward imbalance

Effort questions

I have constant time pressure due to a heavy workload.

I have many interruptions and disturbances while performing my job.

Over the past few years, my job has become more and more demanding.

Reward questions

I receive the respect I deserve from my superiors.

My job promotion prospects are poor.

I have experienced or I expect to experience an undesirable change in my work situation.

My employment security is poor.

Considering all my efforts and achievements, I receive the respect and prestige I deserve at work.

Considering all my efforts and achievements, my job promotion prospects are adequate.

Considering all my efforts and achievements, my salary/income is adequate.

Suggested exercise

Some of these reward questions are 'reverse scored' such that disagreement with the statement would indicate a high level of reward. Can you identify these?

Note: Siegrist et al. use the ratio of efforts and rewards to estimate the level of imbalance.
Source: Adapted from Siegrist et al. (2014).

Resource-based models

Conservation of resources (COR) provides a very different explanation of how individuals interact with their work environment. It is based on the premise that employees are highly motivated to identify, protect and develop their resources and this process is instrumental in determining the amount of stress they experience (Hobfoll, 1989). Hobfoll describes these resources as the personal characteristics and environmental conditions that are valued by employees because they help them to cope with demands and sources of stress and, therefore, protect their well-being. While these can vary from one person to another, those often valued by employees include *conditions* (the situation a worker finds themselves in such as having good security of tenure or a valued senior role), *personal resources* (including the individual differences discussed later in this chapter and in Chapter 3 such as locus of control, optimism and self-efficacy) and *energies* (these include time, knowledge and skills). Hobfoll argues that social support is also important across these categories as it helps people to preserve their resources. For example, in the work context having a good network of friends can help people achieve promotion at work and bolster their self-esteem.

Employees are more likely to experience stress when these resources are lost or when they perceive that there is a threat that they might be lost – and that the loss is undesirable. COR suggests that very high workload might place well-being at risk for a number of possible reasons. Perhaps because it uses up resources, employees' perceive a threat to their resources or because it makes it more difficult to obtain or replenish resources (Bowling et al., 2015). Of course, stress is not just linked to workload. Drawing upon the examples above, loss of status, loss of confidence in one's ability to do the job, or increased time pressures could all be seen as lost resources. In fact, it could include anything that the employee perceives as being expended to help them to meet demands or anything that they value.

Arguably, the model provides an insight into proactive worker behaviour not offered by structural and transactional models. If a resource is lost, employees may act to *replace* that resource or rethink the importance of that resource (e.g. by appraising it in a different way). For example, after missing out on a promotion at work a worker might re-appraise the importance of career progression in their life. An important contribution of this model is that it offers an explanation of what employees do in situations when work is not stressful: they are motivated to gain resources to improve their current situation and also to shelter or protect them from stress that may occur in the future. Bakker and Demerouti (2007) argue that structural and transactional models emphasise the importance of a relatively narrow range of potential work stressors (they call this a 'laundry list' approach, 2007: 309) and do not take into account subtle differences in the nature of job demands. They cite the high level of information-processing demands faced by air traffic controllers with working with technology – a role which involves far fewer emotional demands than those faced by a nurse or a teacher. You may want to have a look back at Exercise 10.1: what are the differences in the types of demands people typically face in each work role? It is worth noting that non-work demands can also be incorporated into the model.

The job demands–resources (JD-R) model (Demerouti et al., 2001; Bakker and Demerouti, 2007) develops Hobfoll's ideas into a model that is focused on the demands and resources commonly found in workplaces. In the model, resources can be used to obtain work goals, reduce job demands and stimulate personal growth and development. Its key features are summarised in Figure 10.1.

The JD-R is a dual process model. Psychological *health impairment processes* deplete employees' resources and can lead to exhaustion. Demands can trigger this process, especially those that obstruct effective performance or prevent the worker from learning and developing (*hindrance demands*). *Challenge demands*, in contrast, provide workers with opportunities to succeed, learn and grow. Job resources can activate *motivational processes* because they help employees achieve work goals, and have a positive impact on employee attitudes and competencies. They can lead to high levels of work engagement, which has been described by Schaufeli et al. (2002) as having three components:

1   *Vigour*: Having high energy and mental strength to exert a high degree of effort and to do these things even in the face of difficulties.

2   *Dedication*: Holding the view that your effort 'means something'; feeling inspired, enthusiastic and welcoming new/persistent challenges.

3   *Absorption*: Being so engrossed that it is difficult to 'let go' of tasks; attachment to tasks at the exclusion of more mundane concurrent events (such as the passing of time).

Key learning point

The JD-R model helps to explain why some features of work environments can be linked to positive outcomes for employees.

Bakker and Demerouti (2007) also suggest that job resources help employees to fulfil the basic human needs described in self-determination theory (Ryan and Deci, 2000). These are autonomy, competence and belongingness (the need to be fond of others and for others to be fond of us). The crossed lines in the middle of Figure 10.1 indicate that demands can moderate the links between resources and motivation. The model proposes that in a job with very high demands, resources may not be as motivating as they might otherwise be. Similarly,

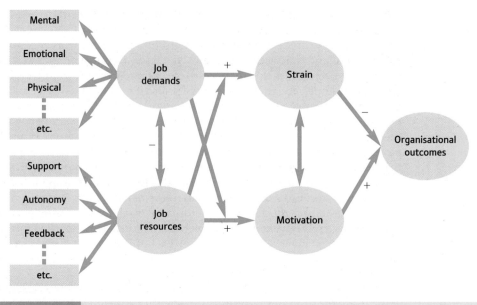

Figure 10.1	The job demands–resources model
	Source: Bakker, A. B. and Demerouti, E. (2007) 'The job demands-resources model: State of the art', *Journal of Managerial Psychology*, 22, 309–28.

when resources are very high, the link between demands and strain might not be particularly strong. Autonomy, feedback and social interaction have been identified as particularly important and common organisational resources (Crawford et al., 2010; Demerouti et al., 2001). According to Bakker and Demerouti (2007), these resources can also act as buffers against demands. Job autonomy might give employees opportunities to develop their own effective ways of responding to work demands without having to deplete their resources too much. Reliable and timely feedback on performance can help employees to adjust their work efforts so that they use their resources more efficiently to get tasks completed.

More recently, personal resources and non-work resources have also been added to the model (Bakker and Demerouti, 2008, 2013; Bakker et al., 2014). According to Bakker and Sanz-Vergel (2013) personal resources are a cluster of individual differences related to an individual's own perceptions of their ability to successfully control and to have an impact on their environment. The inclusion of personal resources in the model indicates that interventions to reduce health impairment and enhance motivation could be focused on both features of the work environment and the individual workers' psychological resources. Non-work resources include social support from family and friends.

The demand-induced strain compensation model (DISC; see de Jonge and Dormann, 2006; van Veldhoven et al., 2005) includes three categories of resources and demands (emotional, cognitive and physical). In this model, the matching of each type of resource to each type of demand is important – if an employee has high levels of cognitive resources this might not help them much if the physical demands of the job are very high. Tests of this model indicate that stress will occur if: (i) emotional demands at work are not matched by the available emotional resources; (ii) cognitive demands are not matched by the available cognitive resources; or (iii) that physical demands at work are not matched by the available physical resources.

The JD-R model also offers an explanation of how employees might make their own work environments less stressful. *Job-crafting* is 'the physical and cognitive changes individuals make in the task or relational boundaries of their work' (Wrzesniewski and Dutton,

2001: 179). Through job-crafting, individuals strive to shape a job role in which they can use their skills (Tims and Bakker, 2010) and to identify and use resources that are important to them (Demerouti et al., 2001). This can involve a range of different activities: it may involve shaping work activities in ways that reduce demands, enhance control or maximise available social support (Holman et al., 2010). In contrast to many other models of the links between work and well-being, this portrays workers as being proactive in the way they seek to adjust the content and context of their work (Petrou et al., 2012). Nielsen and Abildgaard (2012: 372) measured the prevalence of various job-crafting activities by asking employees to respond to statements such as: 'When there isn't much to do I offer to help my colleagues'; 'When there isn't much to do I see it as an opportunity to do things that need to be done, for example tidying up'; and 'When there is an opportunity to get involved I seize it'. Importantly, Nielsen and Abildgaard found that job-crafting was not just confined to high-powered professionals; it was something that blue-collar workers also enacted (they studied postal workers).

The model is also especially useful when we consider how employees might respond to changes at work, something that is often described as stressful or difficult. COR indicates that workers can only deal successfully with new demands if they already have or develop personal resources that are helpful in dealing with these new demands. This means that an employee who is given more responsibility (e.g. new management responsibilities as a result of downsizing) is faced with a new demand that requires new resources (e.g. leadership knowledge and skills).

Key learning point

Conservation of resources theory proposes that individuals are motivated to develop and protect various psychological, organisational and non-work resources that help them to meet the demands of work.

Key debate

Which model of stress is best?

Research has shown that all of the models of work-related stress listed in this section have something to offer. Structural models offer relatively simple, universal and mechanical predictions about the impact of work on employee well-being. This simplicity and the more intricate predictions from the models, such as the buffering effects of social support, are not always borne out by research findings. That said, there is plenty of strong research (see the opening case study) showing that features of work such as demand, control and support are consistently linked to employee well-being.

Transactional theories of stress give us a more complete account of the dynamic psychological mechanisms of the stress process, and point to the impact of individual differences on perceptions of, and responses to, sources of stress. This added complexity also makes them more difficult to test and validate using traditional quantitative research methods. Resource-based models have done much to further our understanding of how work can have a positive impact on the individual by providing workers with access to organisational resources and opportunities for psychological growth. These models help us to consider the many different stressors workers face and individual differences in their responses to work demands. It is noticeable that the JD-R model is increasingly influential as a basis for research and intervention in work psychology. This may be because it offers a flexible way to capturing the idiosyncrasies of the stress process in different work settings that provides insight into both the risks and benefits of work.

Most models of stress have contributed something to our current understanding of the issue. The models share many features but offer different descriptions of the stress process. The more complex transactional models are more difficult to test and validate as these incorporate a large number of variables that influence each other over time. The simpler models appear to underestimate the complexity of psychological processes associated with stress and the ways in which individuals cope with the demands placed on them. The most recent models offer a better insight into how employees are motivated to develop resources that can help them to tackle work demands.

The consequences and costs of work stress

The negative impacts of stress on physiological and psychological functioning can lead to a variety of negative outcomes. There is plenty of evidence of the immediate physiological effects of stress including high levels of activation of the sympathetic-adrenal-medullary system and the hypothalamic-pituitary-adrenal system of the brain (Nixon et al., 2011). These trigger elevated adrenaline levels, blood cortisol, heart rate and blood pressure (Sonnentag and Fritz, 2015). All of this can be very useful as it prepares the body for action (the 'fight' or 'flight' responses). However, if stress is chronic, these responses can become problematic. For example, prolonged high levels of cortisol can impair the physiological processes that help the body to repair itself and impact on cognitive performance (particularly learning processes). Given the chronic nature of many work stressors, such physiological processes lay behind many of the symptoms listed in Table 10.2. Many of the possible ramifications of stress listed tend to be apparent *before* the onset of illness in which the experience of stress may play a part. As you can see, some significant ailments may be brought on, or aggravated, by stress, but it is often difficult to isolate with precision the extent to which stress plays a part.

Looking at Table 10.2 it is all too easy to 'medicalise' stress as an illness and make some rather alarmist predictions about its impact. Many argue that to describe stress as a medical condition is unhelpful and inaccurate, and most influential stress researchers agree on this point (despite much media reporting to the contrary). Instead, it is the unpleasant emotion labelled work-related stress that can play a role in the development of a variety of important individual and organisational problems (EU-OSHA, 2014). The opening case study mentions some other very influential factors including exercise and alcohol consumption. Therefore, the relationship between the experience of stress and various outcomes is not a simple one. Many senior managers are interested in tackling work stress as it may be a cause of absence, but to argue that absence is just caused by stress would be absurd. Absence is a form of illness-related behaviour that is heavily influenced by a host of psychological, physical, societal and cultural factors including attitudes to how generally acceptable people believe it to be absent from work in their organisation (Johns, 2011; Whitfield, 2009). That said there are significant links between stressful working conditions and a variety of outcomes valued by both individuals and organisations.

The measures most frequently used to examine health and well-being at work can be grouped into four categories:

1   organisational measures (or measures that employers value/consider important: Bowling et al., 2015);

2   psychological and physical health measures;

3   physiological measures;

4   measures of health-related behaviours.

Table 10.2	Physical and behavioural symptoms of stress	
Physical symptoms of stress	**Behavioural symptoms of stress**	**Ailments with stress aetiology**
Lack of appetite	Constant irritability with people	Hypertension: high blood pressure
Craving for food when under pressure	Feeling unable to cope	Coronary thrombosis: heart attack
Frequent indigestion or heartburn	Lack of interest in life	Migraine
Constipation or diarrhoea	Constant or recurrent fear of disease	Hayfever and allergies
Insomnia	A feeling of being a failure	Asthma
Constant tiredness	A feeling of being bad or of self-hatred	Pruritus: intense itching
Tendency to sweat for no good reason	Difficulty in making decisions	Peptic ulcers
Nervous twitches	A feeling of ugliness	Constipation
Nail-biting	Loss of interest in other people	Colitis
Headaches	Awareness of suppressed anger	Rheumatoid arthritis
Cramps and muscle spasms	Inability to show true feelings	Menstrual difficulties
Nausea	A feeling of being the target of other people's animosity	Nervous dyspepsia: flatulence and indigestion
Breathlessness without exertion	Loss of sense of humour	Hyperthyroidism: overactive thyroid gland
Fainting spells	A feeling of neglect	Diabetes melitus
Frequent crying or desire to cry	Dread of the future	Skin disorders
Impotency or frigidity	A feeling of having failed as a person or parent	Tuberculosis
Inability to sit still without fidgeting	A feeling of having no one to confide in	Depression
High blood pressure	Difficulty in concentrating	
	The inability to finish one task before rushing on to the next	
	An intense fear of open or enclosed spaces, or of being alone	

Key learning point

The unpleasant emotion labelled stress has consequences. It can trigger physiological changes that can have an impact on how people think and behave. In turn, this can have an impact on individual well-being and outcomes valued in organisational settings.

You will also notice that the majority of these measures are designed to detect problems rather than to measure positive aspects of well-being. Recently this is changing, and measures of the positive impact of work on employee health are discussed later in this chapter.

There is evidence that these different measures correlate with each other. In a large-scale meta-analysis of good-quality research, Faragher et al. (2005) found quite strong correlations between job satisfaction on the one hand and depression and anxiety on the other, but weaker correlations between job satisfaction and physical health. The link between employee health and organisationally valued outcomes may be influenced by other factors including employee attitudes and the organisational culture. For example, Väänänen et al. (2008) found that a group of employees' tolerance for absence behaviour among their colleagues and their cohesiveness (or 'togetherness') influenced individual workers' attitudes towards taking absence. In the healthcare sector high levels of job satisfaction and low levels of absence have been found among groups of employees who report poor physical well-being

(Cox et al., 2002). Such findings indicate that employees can find their job satisfying and be reluctant to take time off (perhaps because of felt obligations to clients and colleagues) while still finding the job to be exhausting. Time away from work can also trigger improvements in psychological health because it allows the employee to escape from and to recover from the stressors impacting on their psychological health (Sonnentag and Fritz, 2015).

Organisational measures

Measures valued by organisations include absence levels, various measures of job performance, accidents or 'near miss' incidents and actual staff turnover. Absenteeism is one of the most widely researched because of the obvious associated costs to employers and because it provides a strong indication that an employee is experiencing a serious problem. Various causes of absence such as home and family responsibilities, personal problems, poor workplace morale, long working hours, lack of commitment and drug and alcohol problems may also be stress-related (EU-OSHA, 2014). There is a general consensus in the research literature that work stress is one of several trigger mechanisms for absence-taking behaviour because of its negative impact on employees' physical and psychological health, work-related attitudes and behaviour.

A combination of high demands and low control has been shown to place employees at significantly greater risk of developing common mental health problems and cardiovascular disease and these conditions typically cause prolonged absence (Ferrie, 2004; Stansfeld and Candy, 2006). Chronic exposure to poor working conditions can also have an adverse impact on worker attitudes (e.g. job satisfaction and commitment) and therefore reduce motivation to attend, even if employee health remains largely unaffected (Johns, 2011). These issues are also discussed in Chapters 6 and 7.

Inaccurate or inappropriate recording of absence as stress-related makes it difficult to be precise about how much absence is connected to work-related stress but rigorous investigations indicate that stress is likely to be closely linked to around 40 per cent of work days lost (CIPD, 2012). Stress-related absence also tends to be costly because employees can be absent for long periods and managing their return to work can be complex. The UK HSE estimates the typical cost to employers of a single case of work-related stress to be quite substantial (around £16,400). The total annual costs of stress, anxiety and depression in the UK have been estimated at £3.6 billion (EU-OSHA, 2014) with the annual cost of work-related depression across the EU-27 estimated to be €617 billion (Matrix, 2013). The links between stress and various diseases (e.g. heart disease, diabetes, depression) mean that stress is indirectly linked to absences from work or early retirements caused by these diseases (EU-OSHA, 2014). Such figures have prompted researchers to spend a great deal of time attempting to identify the factors linked to employee absence and to track changes in absence during intervention studies.

Perhaps an equally serious but more difficult to detect problem is presenteeism (Hemp, 2004; Hoel et al., 2003). This occurs when people are attending work when they are ill (Johns, 2010). Unlike recorded instances of absence, data on a subjective experience like presenteeism can only be collected by self-report via questions such as: 'Has it happened over the previous 12 months that you have gone to work despite feeling that you really should have taken sick leave because of your state of health?' (Aronsson and Gustafsson, 2005; Aronsson et al., 2000). Some authors also add productivity losses into the definition, with presenteeism being measured by asking employees to evaluate their current work ability compared with their lifetime's best. It could be that the underperformance associated with presenteeism is due to various stress-related outcomes including reduced commitment, motivation or satisfaction as well as health problems (Brun and Lamarche, 2006). Ahlstrom et al. (2010) found that presenteeism is a strong predictor of future absence, making it a useful early warning signal of more significant problems. The antecedents of presenteeism are not yet well understood and may include both *positive reasons* such as enjoyment of work, maintaining a good social network and helping colleagues, and *negative reasons* such as fear of losing one's job or loss of earnings (Johansen et al., 2014). One important finding is that the working conditions linked to presenteeism may be subtly different from those found in many models of work-related stress. Johns (2010) identifies *adjustment latitude* as a feature of some jobs that allows employees to modify the way they do their work or their work outputs when they are feeling unwell. The extent to which the work missed by an employee while absent accumulates and then has to be done upon their return (*ease of replacement*) and a strong sense of obligation to colleagues in a work team also appear to be linked to presenteeism (Johns, 2010).

Key learning point

Presenteeism may be more difficult to detect that absenteeism, but it may be an indicator of work stress that has an impact on worker performance.

Employee turnover has been shown to be linked to working conditions in a number of studies (see Bond et al., 2006, for an excellent review of this research). Estimates vary but there is reasonable evidence indicating that around one in five cases of turnover is stress-related. High rates of employee turnover can become quite expensive to a company – they raise training costs, reduce overall efficiency and disrupt other workers (EU-OSHA, 2014). It is thought that the cost of the loss of a member of staff is equal to about five times an employee's monthly salary (Quick and Quick, 1984). The issue of staff turnover is discussed in some detail in Chapter 6.

Taking data from many different organisations, Taris (2006) and Taris and Schreurs (2009) have found significant, but *modest*, negative correlations between employees' work-related exhaustion and their performance. This means that, in general, higher levels of exhaustion are associated with lower performance; but the modest correlation also means that the effect does not always appear strong or hold true for all workers. Cognitive performance has been used in a small number of studies of work stress (Parkes and Sparkes, 1998). This is often classed as an objective measure because it is difficult to fake. Experiments and studies have shown that, within certain limits, an individual's performance actually improves with increased levels of stress. Karasek and Theorell's early work also showed that too little demand is undesirable and the JD-R model indicates that some demands provide opportunities for growth: hence perhaps the argument that 'a little bit of stress is good for you'. This statement rather confuses the stress bought about by difficult working conditions with the opportunities for development associated with well-designed challenges. For a short time difficult working conditions might lead to increased performance (e.g. if employees perceive that their position is under threat if they do not perform or there is a pressing and important task to be completed). After reviewing the evidence, O'Driscoll and Brough (2010) argued that the relationship between stress and performance tends to be fairly linear: as jobs get more stressful, there is a greater impact on employee well-being and long-term productivity, and performance tends to drop.

Employers are also paying directly for stress-related illnesses through workers' compensation claims. In several European countries legal action has been taken by employees who have alleged they have been unnecessarily and/or knowingly exposed to known stressors. The law is constantly changing in face of new test cases, but one common specific type of compensation claim, 'gradual mental stress' (NIOSH, 1993), refers to 'cumulative emotional problems stemming mainly from exposure to adverse psychosocial conditions at work.' Note that emotional problems related to a specific traumatic event at work or to work-related physical disease or injury, such as witnessing a severe accident, are not included. This reflects the chronic nature of many work stressors and their long-term effects on employee health. For example, in a recent study of UK police officers working in custody environments, Houdmont (2013) found that chronic organisational stressors such as intense pace of work and low staffing were more strongly linked to burnout than acute operational stressors such as dealing with threats of violence or dangers posed by people under arrest.

Key learning point

Stress has a significant cost in industrialised economies (some estimates put the cost at 10 per cent of GNP), through sickness absence, ill-health, labour turnover, decreased performance/presenteeism and litigation. However, the links between individual well-being and outcomes valued by organisations (e.g. low absence) are not always clear.

Key debate

Should we use organisational measures in stress research?

Organisational measures are often thought to be good measures of the consequences of work stress because the data are 'objective' and are of value to the organisation. If absence and turnover rates are reduced, cost savings can be estimated. It is worth remembering that absence records are not always kept perfectly accurately. Take for instance the employee who feels unwell and informs their office that they are 'working from home'. Johns (1994) has argued that self-reports of absence can be accurate enough if people are asked the question in the right way, for example: 'People have many reasons for missing work. Most people miss an occasional day once in a while. How many times have you missed work in the last 6 months?' followed by, 'In total, how many days of work did you miss in the past 6 months?'

The assumption that stress levels are *always* associated with taking absence from work in every situation is simply not supported by the research evidence (Darr and Johns, 2008). It is also fairly obvious that employee absence behaviour is influenced by many factors aside from stress. This begs the question: does absence have sufficient construct validity when it is used as a measure of the impact of stress. Similarly, turnover is a complex issue that is not always a result of how stressed a person is in their current role (see Chapter 6). Problems with the reliability, validity and sensitivity of measures of employee performance are also well documented (see Chapter 5). All of that aside, these organisational outcomes can be important indicators of the costs of stress and the value of interventions: it is just that the quality of these data as indicators of differences in stress levels needs to be critically evaluated. On a more general note, it is common for work psychologists to underestimate the potential problems with the reliability and validity of organisational measures. It is unfortunate that such data are rarely subjected to as much scrutiny or scepticism as self-report data.

Point of integration

Psychological self-report data are sometimes referred to as being at the individual–organisation interface as they provide insights into workers' very subjective and personal psychological processes but are also valued by organisations. These include measures of job-related affect or mood (such as job satisfaction and motivation), and attitudes (such as organisational commitment and intention to leave the organisation). As these are discussed extensively in other chapters of this book they are not covered in detail here, but you will find measures of these variables widely used in stress research.

Psychological and physical health measures

In general terms, research has revealed links between psychological well-being and three major categories of physical health: cardiovascular disease (heart attack, stroke, blood pressure etc.); sugar/fat metabolism (diabetes, obesity etc.); and immune system functioning (minor infections and serious diseases). For example, Kuper et al. (2002) systematically reviewed all of the prospective studies that they could identify and concluded that, 'based on prospective epidemiological data, there was evidence for an association between depression, social support and psychosocial work characteristics and (coronary heart disease) aetiology and prognosis' (2002: 267). Similar research has also established links between psychological stress, obesity and diabetes (Brunner, 2007; Heraclides et al., 2009) and compromised functioning of the immune system (Cohen et al., 2001). Cooper and Quick (1999) contend that stress is indirectly involved in cancer, chronic liver disease and bronchial complaints such as emphysema. Stress may also play a role in the development of musculoskeletal problems through its impact on muscular tension and the body's repair mechanisms. The development of diagnosed serious disease is sometimes used in long-term population-based studies of the impact of work on health (such as the opening case study). Data on the incidence of disease may also be available at an organisational level in company records of staff absences (which sometimes contain data about the reasons for absence) or records of referrals to occupational health departments/company doctors.

The problem with these outcome measures is that they provide indications of the impact of stress only when the problem has already taken a significant toll on the individual, rather than a timely indication that problems may be about to occur. This is one of the main reasons why self-report questionnaire measures of physical and psychological *symptoms* are often used. Despite their drawbacks, these can be more sensitive and detect the early signs of poor health.

There are many self-report measures of well-being and health. These measures allow for a quick and convenient assessment of variations in employee health without the need for clinical diagnosis of disease. For example, these may reveal that symptoms of anxiety are more prevalent in a specific group of workers than they are in the general working population, even if few of these employees are absent from work because of stress. Some of these measures also have threshold scores: people scoring in excess of these levels are significantly more likely to already have a diagnosable psychological illness (e.g. clinical depression). The General Health Questionnaire (GHQ) (Goldberg and Williams, 1988) is a questionnaire that is commonly used in stress research: it measures symptoms of anxiety, depression, social dysfunction and loss of confidence. The Brief Symptom Inventory (BSI) (Derogatis and Melisaratos, 1983) assesses a wide range of physical and psychological symptoms, although it is not specifically designed to assess work-related well-being.

The World Health Organisation's Well-Being Index (WHO-5) is a brief (five-item) questionnaire measure of general psychological well-being that is increasingly widely used. It is available in many languages and is simple to complete. It also contains non-intrusive questions such as: 'I have felt cheerful and in good spirits' (responses range from 'all of the time' to 'at no time'). It was not specifically designed to assess the impact of work on well-being as it was originally designed as a measure of overall quality of life. However, it can be used to track the effects of interventions and scores from it have been shown to be reliably linked to more established and invasive measures of depression (Krieger et al., 2014). More specific work-related measures (e.g. work engagement) can provide an excellent insight into the positive outcomes of work (Salanova et al., 2014; Schaufeli et al., 2002). More specific symptom-reporting measures include the Beck Depression Inventory (BDI-II) (Beck, 1996), the State-Trait Anxiety Inventory (STAI) (Spielberger et al., 1970) and the Maslach Burnout Inventory (MBI) (see Maslach and Jackson, 1981).

The MBI is interesting because it measures psychological symptoms of emotional exhaustion and cynicism that are particularly important to those in the caring professions (e.g. nurses, doctors, social workers etc.), which are often regarded as high-stress occupations.

Maslach and Jackson (1981) identified three subscales of burnout that are measured using the inventory:

1   *Emotional exhaustion*: feelings of being emotionally over-stretched and exhausted by work.
2   *Depersonalisation*: an unfeeling and impersonal response to clients.
3   *Personal accomplishment*: feelings of competence and successful achievement at work.

Measures of recovery from work are also being more widely used in stress research (see for example, Oerlemans and Bakker, 2014). Recovery has been found to be important because it appears to help explain how it is that some people in very demanding jobs not only retain their health by reducing symptoms of strain but also continue to experience enjoyment and fun (Sonnentag and Fritz, 2015).

Key debate

Is it acceptable to use questionnaires in stress research?

The use of questionnaire measures in stress research has been the subject of much controversy. Some argue that although easily gathered, self-report data can be riddled with the errors and biases that impact on human memory and judgement. Some argue that personality factors such as neuroticism and negative affect can influence the reporting of symptoms of illness (Watson and Pennebaker, 1989). These problems are less likely to affect the quality of measures such as the number of days of absence, disease diagnoses and changes in observable behaviour and physiological systems. Therefore it is especially important to use good-quality measures questionnaires that have good reliability and validity.

Questionnaires capture useful data about the immediate emotional effects of the work environment on the individual such as negative emotional experiences, psychological distress and dissatisfaction. Self-report may be the only way of capturing these very personal and subjective experiences. It could also be argued that questionnaire measures are less contaminated by the multitude of factors that impact on organisational-level measures (e.g. absence and turnover) and measures of disease (Kompier and Kristensen, 2001). Self-report data become even more powerful if secured by triangulation and the use of longitudinal research designs (see Chapter 2). Longitudinal research designs can reveal problems with self-reported psychological health that are developing over a period of time. These designs can also show whether such changes are associated with fluctuations in levels of common work stressors (e.g. increased demands and lower control). If these variations in work conditions and well-being are also accompanied by, for example, increases in absence levels, then we might be more likely to accept that the self-reported psychological health data are correct and that intervention is needed.

Key learning point

Questionnaire measures are an extremely useful way of collecting information about physical and psychological symptoms. The presence of these symptoms can indicate that stress is a problem. It is vital that good-quality questionnaires are used that have been shown to yield reliable and valid data.

Physiological measures

Changes in our physiological functioning are some of the first things that many of us sense when we experience acute stress. As mentioned earlier in this chapter, these include elevated blood pressure, increased sweating and heart rate, elevated blood cortisol and muscular tension. These changes can be measured and provide relatively 'instant' indications that the body is responding to perceived stress. For the individual employee these changes help to support coping responses (e.g. by preparing the body for increased effort in response to increased demands). The downside is that prolonged or frequent demands on physiological systems are implicated as causes of more serious chronic health problems. Collecting data about these changes is not simple. Employees are more likely to be willing to complete a questionnaire about their health than they are to consent to having blood samples taken from them or even to have their blood pressure monitored for a 24-hour period. Collecting physiological data raises significant ethical issues associated with the invasive processes involved and the potential inconvenience and distress that participants may experience. The relatively infrequent use of these measures in stress research is an indication of these significant practical and ethical problems.

Health-related behaviours

Health-related behaviours include sleeping patterns, exercise levels and other maladaptive coping behaviours such as poor diet, smoking, drug and alcohol use. These data are usually captured through self-report/questionnaire measures or records from occupational health departments in organisations. Sometimes health-related behaviours are referred to as maladaptive coping patterns. For example, someone who drinks alcohol to excess in order to relax or to detach themselves from thinking about work at the end of a working day may be using alcohol as a means of coping with work stress, but this coping strategy itself causes harm. Moreover, these strategies do not help individuals develop organisational or personal resources.

The relationship between these behaviours and working conditions is not always obvious. In a study of over 3000 employees in the USA, Gimeno et al. (2009) found that those in passive jobs (i.e. jobs with low demands coupled with low control) were significantly more likely than others to engage in heavy drinking (but were not likely to drink more frequently than most). Sikora et al. (2008) carried out a longitudinal study of alcohol use and work stress during downsizing and found that alcohol use can also be a cause of work stress (through, for example, its impact on work performance) as well as a consequence of it.

The use of maladaptive coping strategies often indicates that an employee has already been 'damaged' in some way by their work. As such, these problems are often dealt with through tertiary interventions, which are examined later in this chapter.

Key learning point

Employees may attempt to cope with stress through behaviours that are harmful to them in the long term.

Stop to consider

Theories and models of work stress are designed to help explain the problems with organisational and individual health you have just read about. How could you test whether these theories did help to explain these problems? Have a look back at Chapter 2 and the Research methods in focus features of this text. Consider if any of the research methods described there could be of use. Thinking about this issue will help you to get a feel for how work-stress research is generally conducted.

From stress to positive well-being

Stress is a topic (or perhaps more accurately a word) that has generated huge amounts of research and media interest over many years. Yet not everyone agrees that the term is entirely helpful. This is for various conceptual and practical reasons. In common usage the word stress tends to refer to almost anything unpleasant that happens, and/or as anything that leads a person to feel negative emotion. Many would argue this is far too broad a domain for just one word, and risks hiding important differences between different kinds of emotions. In turn, this increases the difficulty of devising research and management practices that address key issues effectively.

Much of the literature seems to construe stress as entirely negative, yet in some circumstances it is possible for both stress and positive emotions to arise from the same experience. As mentioned earlier, healthcare workers are often faced with heavy pressure but also experience quite high job satisfaction. Indeed, it seems that some level of challenge may even be necessary in order for other more positive things to happen, such as personal development (see, for example, Nicholson and West's 1988 analysis of how people react to new jobs). So as Hart and Cooper (2001) argue, it is possible to experience what we might call satisfaction and stress at the same time. This means that looking at stress would get only half the picture of a person's current experience of work.

It is tempting to see stress as the negative end of the single dimension of well-being and/or emotion. Many psychologists argue that this is too simplistic. It seems that the extent to which a person is experiencing pleasant emotion (*positive affect*) is more or less independent of the extent to which they are experiencing unpleasant emotion (*negative affect*). So any individual at any given moment could be high on one and low on the other, or high on both, or low on both (Agho et al., 1992). It is also possible to distinguish between high arousal and low arousal. This creates four quadrants of emotion that can be experienced (see Figure 10.2). Again, this helps us gain a more complete picture of a person's work experience than simply examining 'stress'.

Positive psychology rallies against the notion of psychology existing just as a healing profession (Seligman and Csikszentmihalyi, 2000). The interest in enjoyment and excitement at work, and the opportunities it offers personal growth have been stimulated by the positive psychology movement. Positive psychology is partly about helping us to understand how people flourish when all is well (see for example the COR theory above) and also about helping us to understand how people develop and grow in difficult times. The use of positive psychology is therefore more about the study of what makes life better – rather than being focused on why people are struggling and what can we do to help them. The avoidance of the negative consequences of poor well-being is still an important driver for

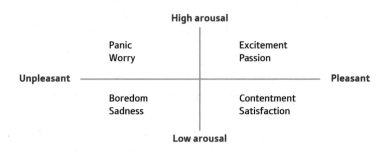

| | Figure 10.2 | Four types of emotion |

theory, research and practice. However, the benefits of positive psychological well-being are becoming increasingly important to researchers and practitioners alike.

Key learning point

Positive psychology points to the importance and value of positive emotions at work. It does not imply that we should ignore the negative outcomes.

You may have already noticed that some sources of work stress are the inverse of features of work that can be beneficial for employees (e.g. the positive motivational benefits of high levels of control at work). We have already described how positive well-being can result from experiences at work (e.g. see the JD-R model earlier in this chapter). Work linked to this more positive view of well-being has been boosted and supported by the growing evidence base that shows the benefits of positive psychological well-being and happiness, in particular, the role of positive emotions in building well-being and broadening people's thought-action repertoires (e.g. Fredrickson, 1998; Fredrickson and Joiner, 2002).

As well as providing a different perspective on psychological well-being, research in positive psychology has also produced a wide range of findings that indicate how positive psychological well-being and health may be built. In many cases these research results have shown that relatively small everyday experiences will bring about shifts in people's overall level of psychological well-being. In a series of studies, Sonja Lyubomirsky (2007, 2013) has demonstrated the improvements in psychological well-being, or 'happiness', that can flow from positive behaviours, such as committing acts of kindness for others, or expressing gratitude or optimism. Other research within the broad area of positive psychology has focused on techniques that might be used to develop people's resilience and their capacity to cope with adversity. One outstanding example of this work is the Penn Resiliency Program – a resilience training programme designed for young people (see Brunwasser et al., 2009 for a meta-analysis). Other researchers and training designers have designed similar resilience training programmes specifically targeted on the workplace. The design and the effectiveness of these interventions will be discussed later in this chapter.

Research in positive psychology has also made a major contribution to our understanding of the benefits that higher levels of psychological well-being (e.g. happiness) confer. These benefits cover life experiences, employment success and physical health. Lyubomirsky et al. (2005) conclude that those with higher levels of psychological well-being:

■   are more productive at work and more creative;

■   make more money and have superior jobs;

■   are better leaders and negotiators;

■   are more likely to marry and to have fulfilling marriages, and less likely to divorce;

■   have more friends and social support;

■   have stronger immune systems, are physically healthier, and even live longer;

■   are more helpful and philanthropic;

■   cope better with stress and trauma.

The relationship between psychological well-being and physical health has become increasingly clear as more research has emerged and it is now apparent that low psychological well-being has a detrimental impact on health – and positive psychological health has a beneficial impact. Such findings have also focused attention on the protective effects of positive psychological well-being: these include lower mortality rates, more healthy behaviour and better cardiovascular health. Boehm and Kubzansky (2012) reviewed research into the links between positive psychological well-being (PPWB) and cardiovascular disease (CVD). They concluded that, 'Findings suggest that PPWB protects consistently against CVD, independently of traditional risk factors and ill-being' (2012: 655). Chida and Steptoe (2008) reviewed prospective studies looking at mortality and positive psychological well-being. Their conclusions, which echoed those of Boehm and Kubzansky (2012), were that their review, 'suggests that positive psychological well-being has a favourable effect on survival in both healthy and diseased populations' (2008: 741).

Key learning point

There is evidence that the experience of positive emotions can have implications for our physical health, although this evidence is not yet as extensive as that linking negative emotions and health.

Robertson and Flint-Taylor (2008) point out that positive psychological well-being at work has two key components – a purposive (or *eudemonic*) element and an emotional (or *hedonic*) element. The distinction between eudemonic and hedonic components of well-being dates back to Aristotle (see Boniwell and Henry, 2007). The hedonic element associates well-being with the experience of positive feelings (moods and emotions) and factors such as overall life satisfaction. Even for the most committed hedonist, day after day lounging on the yacht in the tropical sun would not produce high levels of well-being – unless there was some purpose to it – at least that's what the theory says, but if you get the chance it's probably worth testing this out for yourself! Most people feel at their very best not when totally relaxing, but when something worthwhile has been achieved. For example, task significance is a key feature of the job characteristics model (see Chapter 7). This key principle of a worthwhile life being one that has a point or a purpose is the core of the eudemonic approach to well-being. The leading exponent of this approach is Carol Ryff (e.g. Ryff and Keyes, 1995). Her model includes six dimensions: autonomy; environmental mastery; personal growth; positive relations with others; purpose in life; and self-acceptance. At work, the eudemonic aspect of psychological well-being is exemplified by people feeling that their work activity has a clear sense of purpose.

Point of integration

Research in positive psychology (e.g. Fredrickson et al., 2003) has revealed the importance that meaningfulness and a clear sense of purpose can play in supporting psychological well-being. In the workplace, 'sense of purpose' is most obviously related to the immediate job role that people hold – and the goals and objectives of that role. Goal-setting theory (see Chapter 7) shows that when people are committed to goals that are clear, specific and challenging they tend to perform well. People also tend to experience higher levels of well-being when they have a clear sense of purpose, i.e. clear, specific and challenging work goals. The section of this chapter on the JD-R model also highlights the differences between hindrance and challenge demands.

The idea of purpose and positive emotion as the key ingredients of positive well-being is supported by research in the area of positive psychology. Fredrickson (1998) proposed a theory that states that the experience of positive emotions serves to broaden the scope of people's attention, thought processes and actions; furthermore it also serves to build physical, intellectual and social resources. Fredrickson (1998) referred to this as the 'broaden and build' theory. Research findings (e.g. Fredrickson, 1998; Fredrickson and Joiner, 2002; Seligman et al., 2005) lend some support to the theory. Further research has also shown that the broadening effect of positive emotions leads to an upwards positive spiral in which 'positive affect and broad-minded coping serially enhanced one another ... positive emotions initiate upwards spirals towards enhanced emotional well-being' (Fredrickson and Joiner, 2002: 172).

There is also research to support the idea that an overall *sense of purpose* enhances the impact that positive emotions can have on psychological well-being. In a study of people who were recovering from the trauma of the terrorist attacks on the USA on 11 September 2001, Fredrickson et al. (2003) observed the beneficial effect that positive emotions had and suggested that 'finding positive meaning may be the most powerful leverage point for cultivating positive emotions during times of crisis' (Fredrickson et al., 2003: 374).

Key learning point

Sense of purpose is a key concept when applying positive psychology to the work domain.

These findings lead to the view that a complete concept of well-being should include elements of both pleasure and purpose, leading Robertson and Flint-Taylor (2008) to define psychological well-being at work as 'the affective and purposive psychological state that people experience while they are at work'. They note that this is a view of positive psychological well-being that translates very well into the organisational domain. It implies that some part of well-being at work will be derived from positive feelings that are, in turn, derived from doing something that is seen as worthwhile.

The role of eudaimonic well-being in work settings provides an important link between motivation, performance and satisfaction. The need for meaningful experiences forms part of the models for healthy psychological well-being and it is clear that work can provide opportunities for people to experience high levels of eudaimonic well-being. As noted above, the best feelings of psychological worth, pleasure and satisfaction come from achieving something that was challenging and worthwhile. In general, there is a widespread and evidence-based view that work is good for people (Waddell and Burton, 2006). Unfortunately, not all work provides the employee with good opportunities to experience positive psychological well-being and there is a distinction between 'good' and 'bad' work. In reporting on the deliberations of the Good Work Commission, Parker and Bevan (2011) note that providing workers with meaning and purpose is one of the key ingredients in good work. As they point out, it is more or less impossible to think of work as 'good' if it appears meaningless to the job holder. Of course, the specific elements that make up good work will differ from one individual to the next but many of the aspects of work design, opportunities for job-crafting, management and leadership dealt with elsewhere in this book combine to determine the extent to which any specific job role provides a good basis for positive psychological health.

Another reason for the increased interest in positive well-being at work is its potential link with desirable behaviours and attitudes at work such as engagement, commitment and organisational citizenship. A great deal has been written about the importance to organisations of developing an engaged workforce. Engagement has been defined as 'an employee's willingness to put discretionary effort into their work' (MacLeod and Brady, 2008: 11) and as 'a positive, fulfilling, work-related state of mind that is characterised by vigour, dedication, and absorption' (Schaufeli et al., 2002: 74). Most of the work on engagement emphasises its potential links with beneficial organisational outcomes such as performance and reluctance to leave, and the results of research are promising in this respect (e.g. Halbesleben and Wheeler, 2008). The possible downsides of engagement could be workaholic tendencies –but several studies appear to provide evidence that refute this argument. It appears that engagement and workaholism are correlated but not very strongly, with the former reliably associated with positive work outcomes and the latter with negative outcomes (Shimazu et al., 2012)

Key learning point

The concept of engagement provides some clues as to why positive psychological well-being could influence work performance.

Engagement can also take on more extreme forms. Flow was first described as a psychological concept by Csikszentmihalyi (1990, 1999). Nielsen and Cleal (2010: 180) summarise it as 'a state of consciousness where people become totally immersed in a task and enjoy it immensely' and Schaufeli et al. (2002: 75) as 'effortless concentration, complete control, loss of self-consciousness'. It is more short-lived than engagement and tends to occur when people 'lose themselves' in highly skilled tasks. You might see it for example in a musician when they play the best concert of their life in front of an enthusiastic audience. Nielsen and Cleal (2010) argue that flow is more likely to occur when people are doing things they prefer doing, that are well suited to their specialist capabilities and when there is feedback and control inherent in the task itself and in the wider work context.

Engagement may also be linked to a set of constructs that are already familiar to psychologists. In a thorough and scholarly review of engagement, Robinson et al. (2004) note that the core constructs of engagement coincide very much with two established psychological constructs: commitment to the organisation and organisational citizenship. Broadly, organisational commitment relates to the obligation and emotional attachment that employees feel towards their organisation (see Chapters 5 and 7).

The other concept linked to engagement, organisational citizenship, was originally defined by Organ (1988: 4) as 'individual behaviour that is discretionary, not directly or explicitly recognised by the formal reward system, and that in the aggregate promotes the effective functioning of the organisation'. This, of course, is very close to the idea of discretionary effort that forms part of contemporary views of engagement (see MacLeod and Brady, 2008).

All of this means that as well as providing protective benefit for individuals' health, positive psychological well-being may also have important benefits for organisations. Research has indicated that psychological health is correlated with work performance. Ford et al. (2011) carried out a meta-analysis of 111 independent samples drawn from 98 different research reports. Their results showed that there is a moderate to strong relationship between psychological health and work performance. The correlations between health and independent supervisor/peer ratings of performance were very close to the correlations between health and self-ratings of performance (.42, .41 respectively). Other research has also linked psychological well-being with outcomes such as client/customer satisfaction. Taris and Schreurs (2009) reviewed results from 66 different organisations and found quite strong relationships between psychological health and client satisfaction. Donald et al. (2005) found that almost 25 per cent of the variance in reported levels of productivity was predicted by psychological well-being, the perceived commitment of the organisation to the employee and resources and communication.

In a meta-analysis of data collected from nearly 8000 separate business units in 36 companies, Harter et al. (2002) found relationships between scores on an employee questionnaire (combining elements of self-reported engagement, satisfaction and psychological well-being) and business unit level outcomes, including customer satisfaction, productivity, profitability, employee turnover and sickness/absence levels. Robertson et al. (2012) have explored the extent to which levels of engagement and positive psychological well-being are associated with improved indicators of performance. In summary, their findings, based on large samples from a variety of organisations, suggest that higher levels of psychological well-being strengthen the relationship between employee engagement and performance.

Key learning point

There is some evidence linking positive well-being to organisational outcomes, but more research is needed in this area to identify the psychological mechanisms involved.

Ford et al. (2011) note that more longitudinal research is needed for conclusive proof that positive psychological health has a causal role in determining work performance, since many of the studies that they reviewed were cross-sectional, but the evidence available so far suggests strongly that interventions are worth considering. Implementing policies and practices to address the psychological well-being of the whole workforce, not restricted to people experiencing psychological stress or mental health problems, represents a much more comprehensive and positive approach than traditional stress-orientated approaches. We include a discussion of such interventions later in this chapter.

Is this focus on positive well-being and performance appropriate? Wright and Cropanzano (2004: 348) noted that:

> Employee PWB has both theoretical and applied relevance in today's society. Using the Positive Psychology/Positive Organisational Behaviour (POB) framework, it seems evident that promoting employee PWB is an intrinsic good for which all should work. If this approach promotes better job performance, which the findings strongly suggest is the case, then so much the better.

Key learning point

The concept of stress may be a little too narrow to capture the wide range of emotions that are generated through experiences at work. Positive well-being is not simply the absence of ill-health.

Factors linked to employee stress and well-being

In this section we examine the various working conditions and individual differences that have been shown to be implicated in work stress and employee well-being. We describe the nature of each factor and for each present some example studies that provide evidence of its importance. The key factors that drive psychological well-being in the workplace may be very broadly grouped into factors that relate to the person, or *individual differences*, and factors that relate to the *situation* that the person is in. Individual differences include the attitudes, personality, coping strategies, and skills and abilities of the individual. Situational factors include everything that is part of the work situation that the person experiences.

The research literature on these factors is so large that we focus on those factors that meta-analyses, extensive literature reviews and large-scale research studies have shown to be significantly related to some of the various outcomes of work stress and well-being described

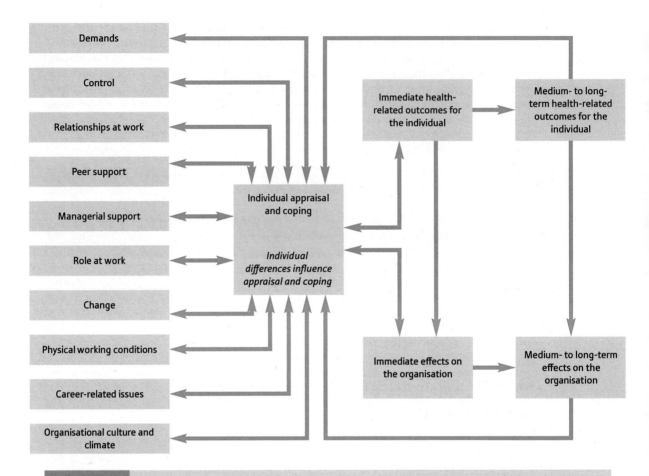

Figure 10.3	Dynamics of work stress

Note the use of two-way arrows in some parts of this figure, indicating that people transact with their environment. These arrows show that there is feedback into the individual appraisal throughout the process. They also show that people's perceptions/appraisals can result in them changing their environment.

earlier in this chapter (e.g. Bonde, 2008; Bond et al., 2006; Kivimäki et al., 2006; O'Driscoll and Brough, 2010; Ng et al., 2006; Podsakoff et al., 2007). Figure 10.3 gives an overview of the factors that receive the most frequent attention in studies of workplace stress.

It is important to remember that situational factors do not always cause problems for each and every worker. Figure 10.3 shows that individual differences are important in determining how individuals react and respond to their situation. For example, someone with the characteristics of resilience – the positive adaptation to previous experiences of adversity (see Fletcher and Sarkar, 2013) – could be better able to withstand various situational stressors than someone who is less resilient. Much can still depend on individual differences in personality, coping styles, ability and so on.

Key learning point

Aspects of the situation and individual differences are both important in determining the impact of work on individual employees.

In addition, these factors interact, or mix, with each other, giving each workplace a unique profile of working conditions. Contemporary models of work-related stress (such as the job demands–resources model: Bakker and Demerouti, 2007) indicate that a wide range of factors have the potential to be stressful. Whether they are or not depends upon an individual worker's personal resources and the resources available to them in their work setting. As already discussed, sources of stress can also be linked to good well-being (e.g. when high levels of demand occur in the context of high levels of autonomy and good support from colleagues). Therefore we will take a look at both the potential 'upsides' and the potential 'downsides' of the situational factors. Setting that complexity aside for a moment, it is clear that some working conditions are more likely than others to be sources of work stress.

Key learning point

If there is agreement among a group of employees that a particular aspect of work is a problem, then situational factors (rather than individual differences) are more likely to be an important source of stress.

Situational factors

Not all researchers agree on how situational factors should be grouped into categories. However, to use a culinary analogy, most cut the same 'cake', but choose to cut it into a slightly different number of 'slices'.

Demands

Job content and workload   There are several elements of the core content of jobs that can be significant sources of work stress, and these are probably the most familiar to the lay person. These include working at a fast pace, working intensively and having to meet frequent tight deadlines. Employees are often at risk of work stress if their work is often performed under pressure, and if it contains extended periods of hard physical work or concentration with very few breaks or respite. A simple but useful way of thinking about demands is to use the categories set out in the DISC model described earlier in this chapter: cognitive demands, emotional demands and physical demands. If demands are perceived as excessive by an individual then there is good evidence that problems tend to follow for both the individual and the organisation (Bowling et al., 2015).

Two different types of work overload have been described by researchers. Quantitative overload refers simply to having too much work to do. In this case, too much work often leads to working long hours and the problems that go with it. Qualitative overload often refers to work that is perceived by the individual to be too difficult for them (French and Caplan, 1972). People's perceptions of workload are used in research more often than objectives measures. Repetitive routines, boring and under-stimulating work can also be a problem as the work environment does not provide sufficient organisational resources for psychological growth (Bakker and Sanz-Vergel, 2013). Weinberg and Cooper (2007) have also described this as *underload*, or not being sufficiently challenged by work.

Certain workers, such as pilots, air traffic controllers and nuclear power workers, face a special aspect of work underload. They must deal with long periods of time in which they have little to do while facing the possibility that they may suddenly be required to spring into action in a crisis. On a smaller scale, this is also a problem for some workers with **advanced manufacturing technology** who (depending on how jobs are configured) may become relatively unskilled machine-minders but who nevertheless have to respond quickly if the machine malfunctions (Chase and Karwowski, 2003).

Point of integration

The automation of some work tasks has led to increased efficiency, safety and effectiveness in a number of work settings (see Chapter 8). This is not without its downside as workers may have less interesting work to do and their under-used skills may start to diminish.

Emotional labour is a concept that has received much attention in the stress research. This is relevant in jobs (such as many forms of customer service work) where an individual must manage their emotions and their responses to the emotions of others (Morris and Feldman, 1996). One particularly stressful element of this is *emotional dissonance* that has been found to have links with several measures of employee well-being (Zapf, 2002). This is when an employee has to use effort to mask or hide their emotions (for example it might be particularly taxing for an airline steward who needs to appear sympathetic to the unreasonable demands of an angry passenger). It is also worth noting that high workload may also be the consequence of other problems including lack of supervisory support and having unclear or overlapping work roles (Bowling et al., 2015). This means that problems with workload can sometimes be tackled by adjusting various other aspects of work design.

Key learning point

Unless the content of a job is well designed and managed, there is a risk that several types of demands become excessive and employees will then be more likely to experience work-related stress. It is important to note that underload may also be problematical as it may harm worker motivation and degrade of competencies.

Working hours   The long working hours required by many jobs appear to take a toll on employee health. One early research study linked long working hours and deaths due to coronary heart disease (Breslow and Buell, 1960). This seminal investigation of light industrial workers in the USA found that individuals under 45 years of age who worked more than 48 hours a week had twice the risk of death from coronary heart disease than did similar individuals working a maximum of 40 hours a week. It seems that in many Western countries the average number of hours worked per week is slowly reducing (partly due to legislation such as the European Working Time Directive). However, a recent large-scale survey of a diverse sample of the UK working population revealed that 11 per cent of employees reported working more than 48 hours per week and on average these workers were more likely than those with lower working hours to report work-related tension, worry or stress (van Wanrooy et al., 2014). Interestingly, the same survey revealed that 41 per cent of employees felt it necessary to work long hours to progress in their job. Of course, typical working hours in some developing countries can be twice those in some of the industrialised developed countries.

It is now commonly recognised that beyond 40 hours a week or 8 hours a day, time spent working is increasingly unproductive and increases the long-term risk of significant ill-health. Bannai and Tamakoshi (2014) argue that those working long hours need more time to recover, but that they are unable to have sufficient recovery time because they return to work before being fully recovered (and a 'vicious circle' is established). A meta-analytic investigation of a large number of international studies linking hours of health found that consistently working long hours damaged individuals' physical and/or psychological health – and 'long' was considered any hours over 40 (Sparks et al., 1997). In reviewing 19 of the most rigorous longitudinal studies, Bannai and Tamakoshi (2014) found that these long working hours were associated with poor psychological health (depression and anxiety), health-related behaviour (sleep patterns) and coronary heart disease, but the links to other outcomes such as diabetes and metabolic problems were less conclusive. Kivimäki et al. (2015) looked at health data from over 500,000 workers drawn from longitudinal studies across Europe. In comparison to a 35–40 hour week, doing up to 48 hours increased the risk of suffering a stroke by 10 per cent. Those working over 55 hours had a 33 per cent increased risk. The details of this research can be found in the opening case study of this chapter.

People who choose to work long hours may be especially driven individuals who are prone to health problems. Their jobs may be demanding in many different ways (for example overload, responsibility), which may lead the person to work long hours in order to complete their tasks (Burke and Cooper, 2008). Or it may be that work patterns and schedules (e.g. shift work) associated with long hours also play a role. This finding raises an important issue: many sources of work stress interact with and influence each other.

Sonnentag and Fritz (2015) describe quite neatly the importance of recovery from work and how this might be impeded by long work hours. Time away from work allows psychological strain and negative moods to dissipate, particularly if a worker engages in pleasurable or relaxing experiences. They argue that although this time away from work provides an important opportunity to unwind, it is also crucial that psychological detachment occurs in order to facilitate the recovery process. They define detachment as not being involved in work or work-related tasks and not thinking about the job. The implication is that people can be physically away from their workplace but not psychologically detached from it. They might find themselves at home in the evening checking work e-mails on their smartphone or struggling to get to sleep at night worrying about an unfinished work task. Sonnentag and Fritz summarise plenty of evidence that shows people in stressful jobs find it tougher to detach from work. They suggest that one way to foster detachment from work is to involve oneself in non-work tasks that are totally different to those carried out at work with people that you do not meet at work. It might also help to avoid checking work e-mails while at home.

Shift work   Many workers today have jobs requiring them to work in shifts, some of which involve working unusual or unsociable hours. Studies comparing shift- and non-shift workers doing the same work have found that shift work is a commonly reported source of stress. It has been demonstrated that shift work has quite a profound impact on physical functioning, bringing about changes in blood temperature, metabolic rate, blood sugar levels, in addition to having an impact on sleep patterns, family and social life, mental efficiency and work motivation. These changes can have significant long-term effects. Vyas and Garg (2012) reviewed data from over two million participants across 34 high-quality studies and found that workers engaged in various types of shift work were more likely to experience heart attacks and ischaemic stroke (it is worth noting that the increased risk was modest but statistically significant). Other studies focus on the more immediate impacts of shift work. Demir et al. (2003) examined the effects on nurses and found that working night shifts led to exhaustion, loss of energy and 'detachment' from patients. The most telling finding was that for nurses working night shifts these problems were significantly greater than for nurses doing the same amount and type of work on day shifts.

Of course, not all shift work is the same. Shifts can start and finish at somewhat different times, they can be different lengths, and there are variations in the extent and frequency with which staff are required to change shifts. The Vyas and Garg study (2012) found that only evening shifts were not associated with increased risk of heart attack and stroke. The longer the work shift – for example '28 days on, 28 days off' versus '14 days on, 14 days off' – the greater its impact on employee well-being (Sutherland and Cooper, 1987). The effects of longer periods of shift work tend to be particularly problematical for workers who have significant caring responsibilities. Fixed shifts (i.e. working just nights or just days) tend to be less unhealthy than rotating shifts (working some nights, some days, some evenings, etc.) because employees need to make less frequent and less significant changes to adapt to different working hours. However, Barnes-Farrell et al. (2008) in their study of shift work in healthcare workers from a number of different countries found that workers on fixed night shifts reported lower mental well-being when compared to workers on day shifts or rotating shifts (this was after the effects of age, marital status and working conditions had been controlled for). The researchers argue that the benefits of permanent night shifts may be apparent only for those employees who prefer such a work schedule: such findings indicate the importance of individual differences and perceptions.

This issue of shift length is quite complex. Shifts that are longer than the usual working day seem to have benefits for some. Hoffman and Scott (2003) found that nurses working 12-hour shifts experienced no more stress than those working 8-hour shifts. Barnes-Farrell et al. (2008) report similar results. Mitchell and Williamson (2000) reported that power station workers on 12-hour shifts experienced fewer problems in domestic life, and better sleep and mood, than those on 8-hour shifts. The explanation for these findings may lie in the opportunities for recovery from work that occur with longer shifts if such work schedules also provide the benefit of working fewer shifts with longer uninterrupted chunks of time away from the workplace. Korunka et al. (2012) found that railway controllers' psychological detachment from work was linked to lower levels of fatigue at specific points during both day and night shifts. Rather ominously, some aspects of work performance can suffer towards the end of long shifts, for example an increase in error rates towards the end of a 12-hour shift. Reviewing the studies of 12-hour shifts in nursing, a profession with high levels of cognitive and physical demands, Ball et al. (2014) found several examples where fatigue over this period could impact on core work performance. The various possible performance losses brought about by very long shifts are also discussed by Sparks et al. (2001).

Work–life interface   People have lives outside work (most of us anyway, even me when I am not writing this book). There are many reasons why the interface between home and work lives has become increasingly prominent in work psychology (Frone, 2002). The proportion of women in the workforce is steadily increasing: traditionally women have tended to shoulder most of the responsibility for managing the home and caring for children (Greenhaus and Parasuraman, 1999). The so-called boundaryless career (see Chapter 13) is now much more common: this is where work and home lives are thought of as intertwined and (ideally) existing in harmony with each other. Many surveys have noted the increasing pressure that some people feel to work harder and/or for longer hours than was formerly the case (van Wanrooy, 2014). There has also been a significant increase in the number of dual-career households, where the total burden of employment and domestic responsibilities tends to be high, and personal resources stretched.

It is clear that in many countries, individuals are becoming more aware of, and sometimes less satisfied with, the imbalance between the amount of time they spend at work and the amount of time they spend away from it. The interactions (or overlaps) between the work and non-work domains are at the heart of most work–life integration research. Kopelman et al. (1983) described the negative aspects of these interactions as 'inter-role conflict'. This occurs when the pressures and demands of one role *conflict* with the pressures and demands of the other. For example, working late because of an urgent deadline might conflict with an arrangement to socialise with friends or with childcare commitments. The individual's perception of a *problematic conflict* also plays a key role in determining the impact that the situation has on an employee's well-being and satisfaction (van Steenbergen et al., 2008).

Sometimes, however, *positive spillover* can occur. Some have argued that the skills or knowledge gained in one domain can positively enhance performance in the other domain (e.g. Grzywacz and Marks, 2000). For example, someone who is required to be very organised at work might use similar skills in planning their social or leisure activities, thus enhancing the quality of their non-work time. However, the evidence shows that poor work–life integration appears to be associated with stress and ill-health (Geurts and Demerouti, 2003; Hurst et al., 2009). Greenhaus and Beutell (1985) suggested that three types of conflict commonly occur:

1   *Time-based conflict*: Pressures from one domain (e.g. work) make it physically impossible to meet demands from the other domain (e.g. home). Time-based conflict might lead to guilt or anxiety that one is not fulfilling one's roles properly and consequently low satisfaction.

2   *Strain-based conflict*: The impact of engagement in one domain reduces the resources (e.g. energy) available for the person to meet demands in the other domain. The amount of cognitive, emotional or physical resources (energy) required to fulfil the demands of roles in one domain may mean that insufficient resources remain for roles (including tasks and relationships) in the other. This conflict can produce exhaustion and irritability (see Sonnentag and Niessen, 2008).

3   *Behaviour-based conflict*: In this type of conflict the person finds themselves taking on a different role at work from the one they take on at home (e.g. a hard negotiator at work, and a sensitive friend or spouse outside of it). For example, a salesperson may be expected to be aggressive and dominant at work, but gentle and cooperative at home. The kinds of values, attitudes and behaviours required in one domain may be different from (or clash with) those required in the other. This value-based conflict can lead to a sense of alienation and/or loss of self-identity.

Work psychologists have tended to concentrate on these problematic interactions between perceived work pressures and perceived family pressures. Inevitably, issues such as long working hours and working away from home have been the focus of the research. The impact of family life on work, such as sudden and unexpected family commitments demanding an employee's attention, can also be a source of stress (Gutek et al., 1991). Westman et al. (2008) highlighted this important distinction between the impact of work on the family (work–family conflict) and the impact of the family on work (family–work conflict). Therefore, thorough research on this topic captures the dynamics of employees trying to balance a wide range of work and non-work activities (Lewis and Cooper, 2005). Large-scale reviews of research on the topic tend to identify that satisfaction at home tends to influence satisfaction at work and vice versa: this means that stress at home can influence variables such as job satisfaction (Ford et al., 2007).

The impact of interventions designed to achieve better work–life integration may be determined by historical factors and social norms. For some groups in society (e.g. lower income families) the quality of work–life balance depends upon the availability of good childcare support among family and friends (Kossek et al., 2008). It might not always be that time away from family demands is stressful. For some women working away from home, it was the return home that was most stressful (Westman et al., 2008). Interestingly, this study found that during the business trip, female workers' psychological health improved, indicating that they were benefiting from some 'respite' from non-work demands during the trip. It may also be that the *role diversity* offered by engaging in a wide range of work and non-work commitments could enrich the lives of many people by exposing them to a wider range of experiences than they would experience either at work or at home.

One additional complicating issue for researchers in this field is, what does 'home' mean? Does it mean anything that is not work? If so, perhaps the term is too broad, and if not, maybe it would be more helpful to distinguish between various domestic and leisure commitments a person may have (e.g. parent, spouse, fitness fanatic, amateur photographer, etc.). Also, to some extent there are differences between cultures/countries in the importance typically assigned to work versus home roles, and in the extent to which work and home roles are typically seen as necessarily separate or compatible. As with all work stressors, a person's appraisal of their situation is important in determining whether they see it as a problem or not, and this might be influenced by whether they are made aware that there are positive benefits to be gained from balancing different work and non-work roles (van Steenbergen et al., 2008). Sonnentag and Niessen (2008) found that individuals high in trait vigour (those with high self-esteem, high extroversion and who follow a healthy lifestyle) tend to have the most energy to deal with non-work issues after a hard day at work.

Now that many employees use wireless technology (e.g. smartphone and tablet computers) to assist with core parts of their job, there is increasing interest in the impact of this technology on the management of the work–life boundary. It appears that this can be a double-edged sword with technology use supporting increased flexibility for workers and better efficiency and productivity for organisations (Yun et al., 2012). The possible costs include increasingly blurred work–life boundaries and the associated risks of conflicts (Kossek et al., 2012). It appears that people choose to manage the boundary between work and non-work in different ways and that some of these strategies are healthier than others. Kossek et al. (2012) found that some people identify very closely with their work (they called these people 'work warriors') and that some individuals ('overwhelmed reactors') value work and family equally, but have a tendency to *react* to demands to carry out work tasks in non-work time and vice versa. In contrast, others take a more *controlled and proactive* approach to managing the work–non-work boundary. These include 'high dividers' (who rarely allow a non-work task to interrupt work and vice versa) and 'fusion lovers' (who take a proactive approach to managing the extent to which they choose to work in non-work time). It may not surprise you that Kossek et al. found that those who controlled the boundary tended to experience less psychological distress.

In terms of interventions to help employees, changes to working practices include different working patterns such as part-time working or flexible hours. These may have a profound and positive impact on the psychological contract between the employee and the employer (see Chapter 6). Compressed hours/working weeks (e.g. working a small amount of extra time each day so that employees could have one day off work every two weeks), on-site provision for childcare, and maternity and paternity benefits have also all been used to help employees. As well as these formal arrangements, research suggests that a culture of flexibility (i.e. the availability of informal flexible working arrangements) is very important. De Menezes and Kelliher (2011) found that these practices tend to have a reasonably strong positive impact on employee attitudes, but there is less evidence of the impact on performance and productivity: this relationship might or might not exist but there is as yet insufficient evidence either way.

Personal resources and communications   To perform their job effectively, individuals need to feel they have the appropriate training, equipment and resources. As Bakker and Demerouti's (2007) JD-R model shows, these resources refer to the worker's personal resources including knowledge, skills, abilities, attitude, cognitive style and so on as well as the organisational resources they need to do the job. They also need to feel that they are adequately informed and that they are valued. A number of sources (e.g. NIOSH et al., 1999; Rothmann and Cooper, 2008) have associated all or some of these factors with stress. Good-quality training and selection are rarely mentioned as stress management interventions, but they can go a long way towards ensuring that the fit between the individual employee and the demands placed upon them.

Risk, danger and the physical work environment   A job that involves risk or danger can result in poor well-being (Clarke and Cooper, 2004). When someone is constantly aware of potential danger, they are prepared to react immediately. The individual is in a constant state of arousal, as described in the 'fight or flight' syndrome. The resultant adrenalin rush, respiration changes and muscle tension are all seen as potentially threatening to long-term health. On the other hand, individuals who face physical danger – such as police officers, mine workers, firefighters and soldiers – often appear to have reduced stress levels. Once again, training is important: those who are adequately trained and equipped to deal with emergency situations often find dealing with them a source of motivation and satisfaction. Our physical surroundings – noise, lighting, smells and all the stimuli that bombard our senses – can affect our moods and overall mental state, whether or not we find them consciously objectionable. Considerable research has linked working conditions to mental health. Kornhauser (1965) long ago suggested that poor mental health was directly related to unpleasant working conditions. Others have found that physical health is also adversely affected by repetitive and dehumanising work settings, such as those that often exist in fast-paced assembly lines (Weinberg and Cooper, 2007).

Each occupation has its own potential environmental pressures. For example, in jobs where individuals are dealing with close detail work, poor lighting can create eye strain. On the other hand, extremely bright lighting or glare presents problems for air traffic controllers. Again, control seems to play an important part in determining how problematical these environmental factors become. Ivancevich and Matteson (1980) noted that it was not the level of noise itself that was stressful. Rather it was when changes in noise were unexpected or unpredictable. These changes then elicited a stress response from employees.

The physical design of the workplace can be another potential source of stress. If an office is poorly designed, with personnel who require frequent contact spread throughout a building, poor communication networks can develop, resulting in role ambiguity and poor relationships.

Point of integration

Chapter 8 shows that many of the problems with the design of workplaces can be minimised or eliminated through use of a design process that involves workers and puts their needs as near to the top of the agenda as is possible.

Control

According to the Fifth European Working Conditions Survey a considerable proportion of the European workforce now has high levels of autonomy over how they work, the pace at which they work and the scheduling of work tasks (Eurofound, 2012). This is probably good news as autonomy and control feature prominently in many good theories of work-related stress. Control can apply to almost any aspect of work. In their widely used high-quality measure of control, Dwyer and Ganster (1991) include no fewer than 22 questions for employees to measure various different aspects of control. These include:

- control over the quality of work;
- control over work pace;
- how much influence the worker has over policies and procedures;
- how much control the employee has over when they can take holidays or time off;
- control over the variety of methods used;
- control over decision-making and so on.

As the opening case study shows, control is a particularly powerful predictor of employee health. In a large-scale longitudinal study of Australian workers, Bentley et al. (2015) found that those who experienced increases in the opportunities to decide how to use their skills and to make work-related decisions reported significant and meaningful improvements in their self-reported mental health. This effect was found even after other factors associated with mental health such as changing employment, age and gender were taken into account. In their meta-analysis, Bond and colleagues (2006) also found that high levels of control are also associated with higher levels of job performance and lower levels of absence. In the same review it was also found that improvements in control tend to underpin the effectiveness of many stress management interventions.

Whether the various aspects of control at work off-set or buffer other stressors is less certain (O'Driscoll and Brough, 2010). The effects of control may also depend on whether an individual prefers to be in control or not and whether they have the personal psychological resources to utilise the additional control. Meier et al. (2008) found that high levels of job control helped to buffer the impact of work stressors on well-being, but only for those people with an internal locus of control. Bond et al. (2008) found that those with a high level of psychological flexibility benefited the most from an intervention designed to enhance various aspects of control at work. Both of these individual differences are discussed in more detail later in this chapter.

Managerial support

There is a large body of evidence that shows lack of managerial support places employee well-being at risk. As with control, high levels of support can provide an important resource with significant benefits for employees. Reviews of numerous specific research studies testify to the importance of perceived supervisor support. Ng and Sorenson (2008) examined the results of 59 studies (containing a total of over 40,000 participants) and found strong relationships between this type of support and job satisfaction, commitment to the organisation and intention to stay with the organisation.

Donaldson-Feilder and colleagues (2008) have conducted a thorough analysis of managerial behaviours and how they impact on employee well-being. They say that these behaviours work through a number of mechanisms:

> Management behaviour has a direct impact on staff well-being – managers can prevent or cause stress in those they manage. Managers also act as 'gatekeepers' to their employees' exposure to stressful working conditions and are vital to the identification and tackling of stress in the workplace.
>
> (Donaldson-Feilder et al., 2008: 11)

As a result of this research, 19 categories of positive management behaviour have been identified. Four categories of behaviour are particularly important in helping employees to feel supported. They are:

1 *Accessible/visible*: has an open door policy and is in regular contact with those being managed by them.
2 *Health and safety*: takes the health and safety of the team seriously.
3 *Feedback*: provides feedback, showing gratitude and praising good work.
4 *Individual consideration*: provides regular one-to-one meetings with employees and is flexible with regard to issues affecting individual employees (e.g. work–life interface issues).

Sparks et al. (2001) pointed out that competitive pressures on organisations usually lead to increased pressure on individual managers. Skakon et al. (2010) argue that when leaders experience stress they are more likely to behave in ways that result in a negative work environment for their subordinates (e.g. by engaging in abusive behaviours or offering little in the way of support). Research showing the positive effects of worker control means that many managers now face a new challenge: learning to manage by participation. Some find this hard to cope with, and many respond by behaving in unpleasant ways towards their subordinates. A boss under stress may change the nature of a subordinate's job so that it becomes more stressful – for example by supervising the subordinate much more closely (Lobban et al., 1998). Management training and performance appraisal can be used to help managers recognise and manage better the impact of their behaviour on employees (Donaldson-Feilder et al., 2008). It may also be that by using more participative 'high-involvement' management approaches, line managers can increase subordinate workloads and change the nature of the demands placed upon them. This can even lead to a spike in short-term absence, but benefits in the longer term when things settle down (Böckerman et al., 2012).

The impact of leadership styles (see Chapter 12 for full definitions and descriptions) on employee well-being has received an increasing amount of attention in stress research, After reviewing a large of body of research, Skakon et al. (2010) concluded that there is enough evidence to state that leadership has significant and reliable links to employee well-being. In general, inspiring leadership can significantly reduce the amount of stress experienced by subordinates because it includes giving priority to the development needs of specific individuals, setting a personal example and establishing a clear mission for the work group or organisation. Care needs to be taken not to over-interpret the significance of leadership behaviour. In their study of public sector employees, Mellor et al. (2009) found only modest or weak links between transformational leadership behaviour and employee absence – but also that leaders could do much to create a positive work climate and this was something that had significant links to employee well-being.

Peer support

Our work colleagues can be major sources of both stress and support (Makin et al., 1996). Lazarus (1966) suggested that supportive social relationships with peers, supervisors and subordinates at work are less likely to create interpersonal pressures, and will directly reduce overall levels of perceived job stress. Poor relationships were defined by researchers at the University of Michigan as those which include low trust, low supportiveness and low interest in listening or trying to deal with problems that confront the organisational member. Most studies show that high levels of support help to maintain good employee well-being, but that they are not always strong enough to buffer workers against the effects of other stressors (Brough et al., 2009).

Stress among co-workers can arise from the competition and personality conflicts usually described as 'office politics' (this is discussed in various parts of Chapter 11). Adequate social support can be critical to the health and well-being of an individual and to the atmosphere and success of an organisation (Bernin and Theorell, 2001). Because most people spend so much time at work, the relationships among co-workers can provide valuable support or, conversely, can be a huge source of stress. Most reviews (e.g. Cooper et al., 2001) have concluded that mistrust of fellow workers is connected with high role ambiguity and poor communications. It also seems that some well-intentioned attempts to support colleagues can have a negative impact (Beehr et al., 2010). These include: talking to colleagues about the stressors they are facing as this can focus their attention on problems at work; offers of help and support might make someone feel they are inadequate because it suggest that others feel that they are unable to cope with demands; and providing help when it is not wanted because the worker then has an additional difficult demand because of the excess support (perhaps they have to engage in an awkward conversation in which they refuse the help on offer). Such interactions have been shown to be stressors in their own right.

In the meta-analysis by Ng and Sorenson (2008), one interesting finding was that peer support was particularly important when employees are in jobs that involve working with customers. This may be because employees in such roles share similar experiences of stressful interactions with customers and understand each other's sources of stress: this helps them to offer more effective practical help and emotional support. This camaraderie might be an important mechanism through which peer support exerts its effects.

Key learning point

Lack of support from managers and/or colleagues can place employees at a significantly increased risk of experiencing work-related stress. Unwanted support can be a stressor in its own right.

Relationships at work

Much attention has also been paid to what happens when relationships at work are damaging. Friction, anger and disagreements between people at work are all well-documented sources of work stress. For example sexual harassment damages organisational commitment, job satisfaction, productivity and individual psychological health (Willness et al., 2007). Violence (or the threat of violence) at work is similarly problematical (see Kessler et al., 2008).

Salin defines bullying as '*repeated* and *persistent negative acts* towards one or more *individual(s),* which involve *a perceived power imbalance* and create a *hostile work environment*' (2003: 1214, emphasis in original). Giga and colleagues (2008) put the annual cost of bullying-related absenteeism, turnover and productivity losses at approximately £13.75 billion (based on UK figures for 2007).

The self-reported figures of being bullied vary greatly. In Scandinavian countries, the prevalence tends to be around 10 per cent or less experiencing bullying in the previous year (Coyne, 2010). In the USA it is around 27 per cent (Namie, 2014). In a study of almost 3000 workers in the UK NHS, Carter et al. (2013) found that 20 per cent had been on the receiving end of bullying behaviour and over four out of ten reported witnessing such behaviour. Wider studies of UK workers such as that conducted by Fevre et al. (2011) found that 33 per cent of a diverse sample of 4000 workers interviewed reported experiencing unreasonable treatment, denigration or disrespect at work during a two-year period. As an important aside, it is typical in many of these surveys that more people report witnessing workplace bullying than report being a victim of it: witnessing such unpleasant behaviour can have its own effects. A significant proportion of witnesses of workplace bullying leave the organisation. Rayner et al. (2002) put this figure at around 20 per cent.

Acute bullying, even a single incident, is associated with strong negative emotions and the associated consequences for employee health (Keashly, 2001). Naturally, the effects can be even more serious if it is prolonged. At the individual level, impacts are: *physical,* for example loss of appetite, sleep problems (e.g. Einarsen, 1999); *psychological,* for example difficulty concentrating, anxiety, depression, suicidal thoughts (e.g. Mikkelsen and Einarsen, 2001); *social,* for example relationships outside of work with friends and family (e.g. Keashly and Jagatic, 2003); and *financial,* for example loss of employment, inability to secure another position (e.g. Einarsen and Mikkelsen, 2003).

Various individual characteristics are associated with being the target of bullying, for example: coping and conflict management skills (Einarsen et al., 1994); low independence, extroversion and stability; high conscientiousness and achievement (Coyne et al., 2000); high anxiety and low social skills (Zapf, 1999). Perhaps unsurprisingly, few studies collect data from bullies but Zapf and Einarsen (2003) argue that bullying can occur for three main reasons:

1 It acts as a self-regulatory process to protect or enhance self-esteem, for example when threatened by a high-performing subordinate.
2 The perpetrator has poor social competencies, for example low emotional control.
3 It is political behaviour to protect the individual's interests and improve their position relative to others.

Fevre et al. (2011) found that managers and supervisors were most likely to be reported as the sources of unreasonable treatment, incivility and disrespect at work, but also that co-workers were often also the source of incivility and disrespect. Contemporary organisational contexts may have a significant role to play in the emergence of bullying. Overly competitive cultures with excessive workloads and constant change can create a negative working environment. Autocratic management styles may be more common when conditions in an organisation are difficult (see Chapters 11 and 12). The inappropriate labelling of bullying as 'strong management' (Simpson and Cohen, 2004) may be one indication of this. A culture of victim blaming can also occur (Ferris, 2004). Willness and colleagues (2007) found that organisational climate played a significant role in the occurrence of sexual harassment at work. Managers and HR may see the behaviour as 'the way of life' and therefore respond inadequately to claims of bullying.

Interventions for dealing with bullying can address the problem from a number of different angles. This includes an understanding at all levels of an organisation that bullying has a range of negative consequences that greatly outweigh the short-term benefits of achieving aggressive day-to-day performance targets. A clear implication from the qualitative research on workplace bullying is the need for a clear and consistent understanding of what does and what does not constitute bullying. One way to achieve this is a publicised organisational policy on bullying that defines the behaviour and the informal and formal procedures for dealing with it. Support mechanisms need to be available to employees experiencing bullying, whether they are victims, witnesses or accused of bullying. Such support can include more recognised routes to help, for example human resources professionals, occupational health and trade unions, but also external sources of help such as **employee assistance programmes (EAPs)**. Implementing a clear policy that defines how people should treat others and expect to be treated can also be effective. Training for managers on dignity at work, managing conflict and mediation can significantly help to address bullying (CIPD, 2007). As discussed earlier in this chapter, the behaviour of line managers is a key element in tackling workplace bullying, and skills such as communication, leadership, conflict resolution, stress management and **team-building** are associated with managers' effective handling of bullying.

Key learning point

Problems such as workplace bullying, harassment and violence at work have particularly strong links to work stress. The impact of such problems on individuals and organisations is often very significant.

Role at work

When a person's role in an organisation is clearly defined and understood, and when expectations placed upon the individual are also clear and non-conflicting, stress can be kept to a minimum, but as researchers have clearly seen, this is not the case in many workplaces. Three critical factors – role ambiguity, role conflict and the degree of responsibility for others – are seen to be major sources of stress (O'Driscoll and Brough, 2010). Glazer and Beehr (2005) found that across a number of nations and cultures, role-related stressors in nursing were consistently linked with psychological health and organisational outcomes (such as commitment).

Role ambiguity   Role ambiguity arises when individuals do not have a clear picture about their work objectives, their co-workers' expectations of them, and the scope and responsibilities of their job. Often this ambiguity results simply because a supervisor does not clarify to the employee the exact nature of their role. In their meta-analysis, Tubré and Collins (2000) found that role ambiguity was significantly linked to low job performance. This could be because when the role is ambiguous, employees are not sure what they need to do to get the job done thus creating additional perceived workload (Bowling et al., 2015). They may not also then be able to recognise when they are doing the job well, robbing them of an important source of feedback. A wide range of events can create role ambiguity (Beehr, 1995). These include starting a new job, getting a new boss, the first supervisory responsibility, a poorly defined or unrealistic job description, a change in the structure of the existing organisation or starting to work in a new team – all of these events, and others, may serve to create a temporary state of role ambiguity.

Role conflict   Role conflict exists when an individual's attention is torn by conflicting, or irreconcilable, job demands or by doing things that they do not really want to do, or things which the individual does not believe are part of the job. Conflict situations can clearly act as stress factors upon the individuals involved. Workers may often feel themselves torn between two groups of people who demand different types of behaviour or who believe the job entails different functions. In their meta-analysis, Schmidt et al. (2014) found that there was a consistent and reliable link between role conflict and depression. The link was not especially strong, but strong enough to suggest that resolving role conflicts could result in significant benefits.

Responsibility   In an organisation, there are basically two types of responsibility: responsibility for people, and responsibility for things, such as budgets, equipment and buildings. Responsibility for people has been found to be particularly stressful. Studies in the 1960s found that this was far more likely to lead to coronary heart disease than was responsibility for things (Wardwell et al., 1964). Being responsible for people usually requires spending more time interacting with others, attending meetings and attempting to meet deadlines, and thus increases the volume of work demands and changes the nature of those demands. As Ivancevich and Matteson (1980) stated:

> Part of the reason responsibility for people acts as a stressor undoubtedly results from the specific nature of the responsibility, particularly as it relates to the need to make unpleasant interpersonal decisions. Another part of the reason … is that people in responsibility positions lend themselves to overload, and perhaps role conflict and ambiguity as well.

Key learning point

A person's position within an organisation (their role) can be a major source of work stress. This is especially true if their role is not clear, it brings them into conflict with others in the organisation, or if it means their job carries with it a high degree of responsibility for people or things.

Change

Organisational change can be a source of stress for many employees. Because it is covered in depth in Chapter 14 it will not be considered in detail here. What comes through from many studies of major organisational change is that organisations need to monitor how the change process impacts on a variety of working conditions, employee health and attitudes. Change can often make employees feel insecure about their future in the organisation.

It is very well established that the threat of losing one's job can have a significant impact on psychological well-being (Hellgren and Sverke, 2003) and work-related attitudes (Sverke et al., 2002). Schreurs et al. (2010) found that employees who had more control at work were less likely to experience the negative outcomes of job insecurity. Among many other pieces of research, this finding lends support to the view that the way that change is handled can make a significant difference to the impact of change. In this example, giving employees more autonomy can help to buffer the effects of insecurity.

It also appears that when employees perceive that change is planned they have a more positive response to it, and that when management offers support through the change process employees experience less unpleasant uncertainty (Rafferty and Griffin, 2006). Similarly, Swanson and Power (2001) showed that social support played a key role in helping employees through a major restructuring. Kawakami et al. (1997) showed that the negative effects of major sudden change could be reduced through open and honest communications with employees, and the provision of ongoing support (e.g. an employee helpline).

Point of integration

The introduction of new technology into the work environment has required all workers to adapt continually to new equipment, systems and ways of working. As well as the sheer amount of change, the introduction of new technology can also mean that jobs can become less fulfilling yet in some ways more demanding, thus damaging well-being, though these patterns are not inevitable (Chase and Karwowski, 2003; see also Chapters 8 and 15).

Key learning point

Change (especially mergers and downsizing that are often associated with feelings of job insecurity) has the potential to be very stressful for employees. However, there are ways of managing change and communicating change that can reduce its impact on individual well-being.

Career-related issues

Career-related issues are considered in considerable depth and breadth in Chapter 13. However, they are mentioned here because a host of issues can act as potential stress factors throughout one's working life. Lack of job security, fear of redundancy, obsolescence or retirement and numerous performance appraisals can cause pressure and strain. In addition, the frustration of having reached one's career ceiling or having been over-promoted can result in extreme stress. Being unfairly treated perhaps by not being adequately rewarded for one's efforts (see Chapter 7) can also be a major source of stress. These sorts of issues are particularly important in Siegrist's (1996) ERI model discussed earlier in this chapter.

For many workers, career progression is of overriding importance. Through promotion, people not only earn more money, but enjoy increased status and new challenges. In the early years in a job, the striving and ability required to deal with a rapidly changing environment is usually rewarded by a company through monetary and promotional rewards. At middle age, however, many people find their career progress has slowed or stopped. Job opportunities may become fewer, available jobs can require longer to master, old knowledge may become obsolete and energy levels can drop. At the same time, younger competition threatens.

The transition to retirement can in itself be a stressful event. While a job is a socially defined role, retirement has been described as the 'roleless role'. The potential vagueness and lack of structure of retirement can bring problems for the ill-prepared. For some individuals, becoming 'pensioners' or 'senior citizens' presents a situation in which they are uncertain about how to obtain the social rewards they value. In contrast, those individuals who have maintained balance in their lives by developing interests and friends outside their work can find retirement a liberating period. Hanisch (1994) found that people who have positive reasons for retiring (such as travel) rather than negative ones such as poor health or job dissatisfaction, were more likely to plan ahead for retirement and to enjoy it.

The process of being evaluated and appraised can be a stressful experience for all of us (Fletcher, 2008; see also Chapter 5). It must be recognised that performance appraisals can be anxiety-provoking, for both the individual being examined and the person doing the judging and appraising. Particularly when poor performance is being appraised there is significant potential for conflict and damage to ongoing working relationships.

Organisational culture and climate

Much has been written about organisational climate and culture (e.g. Schein, 1992; Ashkanasy and Jackson, 2001; Clegg and Cooper, 2009). There has also been quite a lot of argument concerning what is the most appropriate definition of each concept. Broadly speaking, organisational climate is about employees' perceptions of how their organisation functions, while organisational culture refers to the values, assumptions and norms that are shared by organisational members, and which influence individual and collective behaviour. Culture and climate can provide the conditions that lead to the growth of other problems such as bullying at work and an acceptance or expectation of long working hours.

An individual is likely to experience stress if they do not share the values inherent in the employing organisation. Several factors could cause this. For example, the mismatch between individual and culture may lead the person to feel isolated and unable to communicate effectively with colleagues. It may mean that the person's role includes activities that they find distasteful and that conflict with personal preferences (a form of role conflict – see above). Intervention research suggests that when employees see that their work activities are consistent with their own values and goals employee well-being is enhanced (Flaxman and Bond, 2010).

'Organisational climate' can be a source of stress if a person believes that the way the organisation functions is unfair, or perhaps unclear and unpredictable (which could lead to role ambiguity). Perceived organisational support (see Stamper and Johlke, 2003) is defined as the extent to which employees perceive that their contributions are valued by their organisation and that the company cares about their well-being. This has been shown to have a positive impact on working conditions by reducing role ambiguity and role conflict as well as intention to stay with the organisation.

The impact of participatory work cultures has been extensively researched. As early as the 1940s, researchers began reporting that workers who were allowed more participation in decision-making processes produced more and had higher job satisfaction (Coch and French, 1948). They also found that non-participation at work was a significant predictor of strain and job-related stress, relating to general poor health, escapist drinking, depression, low self-esteem, absenteeism and plans to leave work. Participation in the decision-making process on the part of the individual may help with the development of a number of personal and organisational resources. These include an increased alignment between their own goals and those of the wider organisation, improved communication channels and greater access to social support from managers and colleagues (Nielsen and Randall, 2012). The resulting sense of being in control seems vital for the well-being of the workforce (Bond et al., 2008).

Key learning point

A participative organisational climate has been shown to be healthy in many organisations.

Exercise 10.2   A stressful job?

Look back over the situational factors described in this section. Now think of a job you know something about. It might be a job you have done yourself, or a job that is done by someone you know well.

Suggested exercise

What are the most likely sources of work stress in that job role? Set aside individual differences for a moment and focus on the features of that job that might place someone doing that job 'at risk' of experiencing work-related stress. Then look at the same job in a different way. What aspects of the job are likely to be sources of satisfaction or positive well-being?

Individual differences

As mentioned several times in this chapter, individual differences can play a significant role in the experience of stress or positive well-being. To summarise, these differences have one or more of the following roles in the processes that determine the impact of work on employee health and well-being:

■ *A direct effect on stress outcomes* (e.g. anxious people may be more tense across all kinds of situations, which can lead to psychological and/or physical health problems).

■ *A moderating effect in the stressor strain relationship.* In other words, certain personality characteristics may mean that some people are more affected than others by an aspect of their work situation. So, for example, extroverted people may find a socially isolated job more stressful than introverts, confident people might relish the challenge of difficult work tasks and so on.

■ *A direct perceptual effect.* Individual differences may have some impact on a person's perceptions of what his or her job is like. For example, people with a high need for control may be very aware of limitations on their autonomy, and rate their work autonomy low – for most people a similar level of autonomy at work would be seen as sufficient.

There are many individual differences that are often investigated in stress research. Some of the most prominent are discussed below.

Personality

The Big Five model of personality (see Chapter 3) has provided a useful summarising framework for the key personality traits. One of the best-established direct relationships between personality and psychological well-being is that linking neuroticism with poorer psychological well-being. In an extensive meta-analysis, DeNeve and Cooper (1998) found direct relationships between neuroticism and life satisfaction, happiness and negative affect. Positive affect was predicted equally well by (high) extroversion and agreeableness. Grant and Langan-Fox (2007) found that the relationship between neuroticism and psychological strain was mediated by the perceived level of stress. This finding indicates that personality also plays a role in the perception of sources of stress, and that it is this perception that helps to forge the link between personality and poor psychological health.

Watson and colleagues (1988) identified two elements of persistent and pervasive mood that have been particularly influential in stress research. High negative affect (NA) refers to the propensity to feel emotions such as anger, guilt, fear and nervousness. It often correlates highly with neuroticism. High positive affect is the propensity to feel enthusiastic, energetic and alert. As you might expect, many researchers have found these variables to influence directly the perception of sources of stress and the reporting of the consequences of work stress. Bowling et al. (2015: 97) argue that those with high NA may be pre-disposed to:

■ self-select into an objectively stressful work environment;

■ unintentionally create objectively stressful work situations; or

■ perceive an otherwise innocuous work environment as being threatening.

More subtle and specific aspects of personality have also been linked to the experience of work stress. Some people tend to set themselves very high performance standards. *Perfectionism* can be driven by different underlying motives. In some cases it is about taking pride in a job well done. In other cases, it can result in a tendency to set excessively high standards and a very self-critical approach when reviewing performance against those standards. Flaxman et al. (2012) looked at how academics with high and low levels of this self-critical perfectionistic tendency differed in how they recovered from work during and after an Easter break. Recovery was less evident for those reporting high levels of self-critical perfectionistic tendencies. Interestingly, this seemed to be because this group of academics reported more worry and rumination during time away from work thus reducing the quality of their recovery from work demands. In the wider literature it appears that a tendency to reflect positively on one's work experiences during time away from work is far healthier than a tendency to ruminate about mistakes and errors (Binnewies et al., 2009).

Point of integration

As Chapters 3 and 4 show, personality has been linked to people's suitability for work roles. The links between personality and job performance are controversial, but theories of work stress indicate that where there is a poor fit between someone's personal resources and the demands placed upon them, stress is more likely to occur. Personality traits may act as resources in the work environment. For example, someone with high levels of conscientiousness might find this a useful personal resource in work roles that typically require them to be thorough, highly organised and persistent.

Key learning point

Individual differences play an important role in: (i) how people perceive their work environment and (ii) their psychological and physical well-being. They can also play an important role in determining how strong the link is between (i) and (ii).

Psychological flexibility

> A key implication of psychological flexibility – and hence its name – is that, in any given situation, people need to be flexible as to the degree to which they base their actions on their internal events or the contingencies of reinforcement (or punishment) that are present in that situation.
>
> (Bond et al., 2013: 332)

To simplify somewhat, psychological flexibility is the extent to which a person uses thinking strategies that allow them to focus on actions (i.e. doing their job) while at the same time recognising and accepting in a non-judgemental way the events going on in their mind – such as fear, worry and anxiety – are unhelpful thoughts. Bond and colleagues refer to this as taking a mindful approach to one's thoughts. The research base on psychological flexibility is rapidly expanding and is replete with good studies that show psychological flexibility predicts both good mental health and strong work performance. These effects appear to be underpinned by the link between employees' psychological flexibility and their utilisation of resources around them that help to get the job done. When workers are not expending resources wrestling with their emotions they are in a better position to pay more attention to the task at hand. This enables them to have a better chance of identifying the best ways of completing tasks, responding to demands as they arise, identifying and using sources of social support and so on. One important feature of psychological flexibility is that it can be increased through intervention – something we discuss later in this chapter.

Resilience

There is quite a bit of debate about the meaning of resilience and lots of different definitions have been offered (see Fletcher and Sarkar, 2013). A recurrent theme in the definitions is that it refers to the individual's capacity to respond positively to failure and set-backs. It is also strongly linked to the frequent experience of positive emotions as this helps individuals to respond positively to failure when it occurs. Resilience is particularly interesting because it is currently receiving a great deal of attention in work settings. Many theories of stress propose that the experience of difficult conditions or circumstances are likely to be damaging, but researchers have found that carefully managed exposure to adversity can help people to draw upon previously untapped psychological resources (Fletcher and Sarkar, 2013). The current thinking is that regardless of how it is defined resilience has some connection to stable traits but that it can be developed (Robertson et al., 2015).

Cognitive styles

There are a number of elements of cognitive style (the way people tend to think about things) that are important in the stress process. *Locus of control* refers to the extent to which a person believes they have control over their life. In many circumstances, having an internal locus of control (i.e. believing one is in control) is helpful because it encourages a person to do something about their stressful situation. This is fine unless there really is not anything a person can do, in which case an internal locus of control will simply increase his or her frustration. *Self-efficacy*, a person's belief that they are capable (Bandura, 1982), and *self-esteem* (a person's feeling of their own worth) are also important.

Exercise 10.3   Your self-efficacy

Self-efficacy is a measure of a person's own belief in their capacity to complete a task. It has been shown to improve when we experience repeated successes and to diminish when we experience repeated failures. Various pieces of research have shown that high levels of self-efficacy tend to be healthy and can help people to deal with life's difficulties.

One interesting feature of self-efficacy is that it can vary from one situation to another. So, after reading this chapter if you were asked by a friend to describe what work stress is and what causes it, hopefully your self-efficacy in relation to this task will be higher than it was before you read this text. But what if you were asked to give a presentation about work stress to 100 senior executives? Would your self-efficacy be as high in this situation?

Below is a measure of general self-efficacy. It is designed to measure a person's belief in their capacity to cope with what daily life throws at them. For each question responses are: 1 = not at all true; 2 = hardly true; 3 = moderately true; 4 = exactly true. High scores indicate higher self-efficacy. In research this scale is often adapted a little by rewording the items to measure self-efficacy in specified situations.

1 I can always manage to solve difficult problems if I try hard enough.
2 If someone opposes me, I can find the means and ways to get what I want.
3 It is easy for me to stick to my aims and accomplish my goals.
4 I am confident that I could deal efficiently with unexpected events.
5 Thanks to my resourcefulness, I know how to handle unforeseen situations.
6 I can solve most problems if I invest the necessary effort.

7 I can remain calm when facing difficulties because I can rely on my coping abilities.

8 When I am confronted with a problem, I can usually find several solutions.

9 If I am in trouble, I can usually think of a solution.

10 I can usually handle whatever comes my way.

Use the questionnaire to help you consider your own current level of general self-efficacy. Then consider how your self-efficacy varies from one situation to another in your life. Is it high in situations you find that you tend to deal with effectively, but lower for those you find stressful? The use of goal-setting theory (see Chapter 7) is one way in which self-efficacy can be developed.

Source: Schwarzer, R., and Jerusalem, M. (1995) 'Generalised Self-Efficacy scale' in J. Weinman, S. Wright, and M. Johnston (eds), *Measures in Health Psychology: A user's portfolio. Causal and control beliefs* (pp. 35–37). Windsor, UK: NFER-NELSON; http://userpage.fu-berlin.de/~health/engscal.htm

Clusters of individual differences

In recent years researchers have started to become interested in how various individual differences might combine and interact to help individuals deal with stressors. Some researchers have taken a positive psychology perspective to examine clusters of individual differences that help individuals to flourish and develop in response to work demands. One of the first of these was the notion of the 'hardy personality' which is made up of internal locus of control, self-esteem, self-efficacy and motivation (especially to recover from disappointments).

The concept of **psychological capital (PsyCap)** has been developed to encapsulate what are thought to be the underlying (or latent) human characteristics that explain many positive outcomes for individuals. Before describing each of these characteristics, it is important to note that most researchers in positive psychology propose that these can be significantly developed or eroded over time.

The four different characteristics that form PsyCap are hope, optimism, efficacy and resilience (see Luthans et al., 2008); the latter two we have already described above. *Hope* is will-power and determination combined with plans, or 'pathways' for achieving goals. In other words, effort alone is not enough to sustain hope without a clear mental model of how an outcome will be achieved. *Optimism* is about the way people tend to attribute causes to events. A tendency to attribute successful outcomes to one's own efforts (internal attribution) linked to enduring capability (stable attribution) that could help us to succeed in other tasks in the future (global attribution) would indicate optimism. Negative events would be attributed to external, unstable and specific causes. Some elements of PsyCap are influenced by traits (e.g. the links between conscientiousness and reported self-efficacy and between neuroticism and pessimistic attributional styles). Luthans et al. (2008) suggest that interventions and work activities that allow people to plan for and to experience success (e.g. goal-setting activities) can facilitate the development of PsyCap. The body of evidence is growing that high PsyCap is linked to positive outcomes for individuals and organisations.

Core self-evaluations (CSEs) are described by Judge (2009: 58) as 'a broad, integrative trait indicated by self-esteem, locus of control, generalised self-efficacy, and (low) neuroticism (high emotional stability)'. Judge argues that there is enough evidence of strong correlations between these components to conclude that these variables are all influenced by a single underlying individual difference factor (CSEs). He cites numerous studies linking CSEs to low stress and burnout. The jury is still out on whether CSE has the stability of a trait or the malleability of a psychological state.

Coping strategies

How individuals cope with stress has been the focus of quite a lot of research and practice (see for example Zeidner and Endler, 1996). Coping is usually defined as the efforts people make, through their behaviour and thoughts, to alter their environment and/or manage their emotions. Coping strategies include analysing the situation, planning a course of action, seeking information from others, seeking support and comfort from others, relaxation techniques, counselling and using alcohol, tobacco or other drugs. Some of these place the individual's health at risk: these are referred to as maladaptive coping strategies. Employee assistance programmes (see later in this chapter) are often used to help people who are placing their health at risk in this way.

One general distinction is between *problem-focused strategies* (dealing with the original cause of stress) and *emotion-focused strategies* (dealing with how one feels about the stressful situation). Logically, when it is possible to change the situation, problem-focused strategies would seem to be the better option, but research suggests that the results of coping are hard to predict, perhaps not only because of the coping strategy a person uses, but also because how effectively they use it matters a lot.

Many authors argue that coping is a bit more complex than this, with there being a range of avoidant coping strategies and a range of more active coping strategies. Carver and colleagues (1989) presented a measure of coping with no fewer than 16 different coping scales (including humour, denial, substance abuse, behaviour disengagement and the use of social support). This shows how many different ways of coping people use when faced with difficult situations. Of course, a person may have a wide range of coping resources but only use some of them. Some people may have certain resources, such as sympathetic close friends, but not use them. Underlying this is a debate about whether people choose coping strategies on the basis of the current situation, or their personality and prior learning. As you will see later in this chapter, many stress management training programmes are designed to have an effect by training the individual to think or behave differently so that they use healthy and productive coping strategies (in terms of the way they think and behave).

Demographic factors

A wide range of demographic factors (e.g. age, gender, tenure, etc.) have been considered in stress research. Relationships between these factors on the one hand, and the perception of stressors and employee well-being on the other hand, tend to vary from one study to another. Meta-analyses show that older workers tend to cope best with some sources of work stress (e.g. role ambiguity), and that they tend to have lower turnover and absenteeism in the face of sources of work stress than younger employees (Shirom et al., 2008). This may be because older workers have had more time and experience to develop job-related skills (thus it could be that tenure, or experience, may be more important than age per se).

Exercise 10.4   Your experience of stress

Review your experience of work so far in your life. Consider the stressors discussed in this chapter so far, and try to decide which two or three of them have been most stressful for you in your working life (not why they might be stressful for other people). Then think about why you found them stressful. Was it because: (i) the amount of the stressor was so great; (ii) the stressor stopped you achieving the most important goals of your work; (iii) the kind of person you are makes you vulnerable to that kind of stressor; or (iv) there were some other reasons why these experiences were so stressful?

From what you have read in this chapter so far (and without reading any further!), how do you think organisations could intervene to tackle work-related stress? What strategies are available? How effective do you think each of these strategies might be? Which do you think would be a popular choice with (i) employees and (ii) senior managers? Do you think these two groups would prefer different types of interventions? If so, why?

Interventions to tackle work stress and promote employee well-being

The costs of stress indicate that the case for intervention is strong. As you have seen, there is also a considerable body of research and theory on which interventions can be based. If we know what causes work stress, then we should be able to do something about it. Government guidance and legislation in many countries now require organisations to assess and manage risks to psychological well-being (in addition to dealing with physical risks to employee health).

There are different levels of interventions that have different objectives and target different parts of the mechanisms that link work and well-being. Murphy (1988) identified three levels of intervention: (i) primary (i.e. reducing the sources of organisational stress); (ii) secondary (e.g. stress management training); and (iii) tertiary (e.g. health promotion and workplace counselling). This taxonomy is widely used and remains a reasonably good way of identifying the underlying mechanisms of a wide range of intervention activities. Tetrick and Winslow (2015) point out that another good way to think about interventions in terms of the JD-R model is by considering whether they are designed to have an impact on resources, demands or both.

Key learning point

A useful way to view stress management is to think of interventions in terms of their objectives. These are primary prevention (e.g. dealing with the source of the stress), secondary intervention (e.g. stress management training), and tertiary rehabilitation (e.g. employee assistance programmes, or EAPs).

Primary interventions: changing the sources of workplace stress

Primary interventions change the design, organisation and management of work. In other words, they tackle the sources of work stress or attempt to 'design into the job' the sources of positive well-being. Most often they are designed to deal with problems identified by a significant proportion of employees, targeting a group rather than the individual employee. The logic is that this then prevents employee health being damaged by the problem, because the problem no longer exists (or is significantly reduced). In terms of the JD-R model the focus is on changing demands. A list of examples of primary interventions is shown in Table 10.3. In theory, these interventions could be more effective in the long term as they tackle stress at its source, meaning that personal coping strategies need to be used less often. As yet there is little long-term evaluation work to either support or contradict this claim (LaMontagne and Keegel, 2012; Montano et al., 2014; Richardson and Rothstein, 2008). We return to the issues of effectiveness later; for now we just focus on describing the nature of these interventions.

You probably won't be surprised by the content of Table 10.3. Primary interventions are often used to remove the many sources of work-related stress identified earlier on in this chapter. You may also notice a general theme of these interventions. Participative action research (PAR) is often the driver of primary interventions. PAR involves employees working with researchers or consultants to identify problems and design solutions. This process seems to help different stakeholders agree on the nature of the problems and to all contribute to the design of workable solutions (Heaney et al., 1993). Whether or not PAR is used, proper assessment of the problems workers experience is a crucial precursor to primary intervention. Without this assessment a suitable bespoke (tailored) intervention for tackling a problem cannot be designed (Nielsen et al., 2010; Elo et al., 2008).

Table 10.3	Examples of primary interventions

Tackling problems with job demands

- Jobs enrichment: the removal or automation of mundane tasks with the introduction of more complex or interesting tasks that allow individuals to make better use of their skills and abilities
- Setting up quick informal meetings to provide timely feedback and help with decision-making
- Improving the planning and forecasting of workload so that employees face more realistic deadlines
- Analysing employees' knowledge, skills and abilities to ensure that they are equipped to do the job and providing opportunities for them to develop further
- Adjusting staffing levels so that they reflect peaks and troughs in workload
- Increasing variety by, for example, allowing people to rotate around the different tasks carried out in their team
- Training specialist staff to deal with difficult or complex tasks that eat into the time, and increase the workload, of other team members
- Using information technology to reduce the cognitive load on staff, for example systems to help staff monitor the progress of tasks that are carried out over a number of days or weeks, or when they are dealing with many simultaneous tasks
- Allowing staff 'protected time' to deal with complex or difficult tasks that require concentration
- Setting fixed and protected break times
- Introducing flexi-time or compressed working weeks
- Establishing and communicating predictable shift patterns well in advance so that employees can be prepared for them and organise their home and leisure activities accordingly
- Allowing employees to make arrangements with colleagues whereby shifts may be swapped (but that the work is still being done)
- Ensuring that there is equity and fairness in the allocation of shifts, for example by allowing all staff the opportunity to, at some point, be involved in the construction of shift rotas
- Having particularly influential individuals act as role models (e.g. by having successful staff leave the office on time, or be seen to take regular breaks)

Tackling problems with control

- Reviewing, and perhaps changing, the guidance that staff are given about the completion of tasks so that they have more discretion and control about how they are completed
- Making performance feedback available quickly and in a form that can be readily used by employees to manage their own performance
- Increasing employee control over how work is allocated, for example through the use of self-managing teams (see Chapter 11)
- Giving staff the control and freedom to identify and rectify common problems quickly and without unnecessary approval from senior managers

Tackling problems with support

- Encouraging interaction between team members by providing them with tasks that require employees to work together with shared objectives
- Managing the workload of supervisors and managers to ensure they have adequate time to fulfil the supervisory element of their role
- Providing new employees with a proper induction, and ensuring that existing employees have easy access to information about the support available to them to help them do their job
- Introducing a mentoring process
- Ensuring that work schedules or the allocation of tasks do not result in individuals or groups being isolated from others in the organisation

Relationships

- Allowing staff to 'rotate' roles to experience different jobs or tasks within their team or the organisation
- Altering the physical layout of the workspace can have a positive impact on social relationships at work
- Ensuring appraisal processes are of a good quality and properly implemented
- Implementing and maintaining effective systems for dealing with bullying and harassment (see earlier in this chapter)
- Ensuring that staff are protected from risks of violence or threat from clients, and 'designing out' where possible elements of the job role that place them at risk
- Allowing staff to experience their colleagues' working conditions by work shadowing or job rotation so that staff appreciate the degree of interdependency that exists between them
- Introducing handover times or overlapping shifts/work schedules to increase contact between employees

Role

- Review, update and publicise job descriptions
- Include the active review and clarification of roles in the performance appraisal process
- Allow teams discretion and control over how roles and responsibilities are allocated
- Examination of roles in relation to the current needs of the organisation and the demands of employees' jobs
- Establish systems for employee participation in decision-making about the boundaries of job roles and responsibilities
- Minimise the potential for competing or conflicting demands in roles when designing and revising job descriptions
- Reallocate tasks within a team to ensure that conflicting demands do not coincide for individual employees
- Ensure that an employee's role does not result in their being in frequent conflict with colleagues, clients or members of the public – this may include job rotation – if some conflict situations are unavoidable, then the implementation of secondary and tertiary interventions is particularly important

Change

- Opening up new lines of communication, or using new communication media, to disseminate important information about change
- Giving a small number of staff the job of highlighting particularly important information and communicating it to staff (to avoid it being hidden within a large of amount of information routinely communicated to staff)
- Providing training in different styles of management (see Chapter 12)
- The use of newsletters and staff briefings to ensure that all staff get vital information about organisational goals, objectives and plans

Source: Adapted from Randall, R. and Lewis, R. (2007) 'Stress management interventions', in E. Donaldson-Feilder (ed.), *Well-being and Performance*. London: CIPD, with the permission of the publisher, the Chartered Institute of Personnel and Development, London (www.cipd.co.uk).

When compared to stress management training and counselling, managers may think that primary interventions are not the 'easy option' for tackling stress. Designing them may take some time and involve difficult dialogue with employees. Such perceptions may be wide of the mark. Bond et al. (2006) examined examples of primary interventions and concluded that they are usually not expensive and the change process, if handled correctly, need not be disruptive or lengthy. In addition, the process of involving employees in the design and implementation of primary interventions can lead to positive outcomes in itself because of its positive impact on perceptions of participation and control at work (Elo et al., 2008).

There are relatively few published studies of primary interventions and the number of good-quality available studies is not growing rapidly (Tetrick and Winslow, 2015). This may be because it is not seen as the strategy of choice: many managers may think that sources of stress are resident in the individual (i.e. the result of individual weakness, or lack of resilience) or that primary interventions are too difficult to implement. It may also be that many intervention studies do not meet the high standards of academic rigour required by publishers of academic journals. We now take a close look at three excellent intervention studies that tested the effectiveness of primary interventions using very rigorous research designs.

Research methods in focus

The use of quasi-experimental designs in stress intervention research

For the first study we have to go back some time. There is a good reason for this: arguably it has the strongest research design ever used in a study of a primary intervention. Susan Jackson (1983) tested whether allowing hospital employees to have more input into decision-making helped them to feel more involved at work and to develop a clearer understanding of the demands of their work role. The intervention was quite simple: regular staff meetings were introduced. Researchers examined organisational records to check that meetings were happening and were being used to discuss important and relevant issues. The study was particularly powerful because the Solomon four-group design (see Chapter 2) was used to help rule out various alternative explanations for change that might have impacted on the results of the study.

The analysis required to track the impact of the intervention through changes in working conditions to changes in well-being was very complex; structural equation modelling (again, see Chapter 2) was used. As stress theory would predict, the meetings led to increased perceived participation and reduced problems with work roles (i.e. role conflict and ambiguity). These changes led to less emotional strain and higher job satisfaction among those involved in the meetings. The researchers were also able to show that the reductions in emotional strain were linked to lower levels of absence and lower turnover intention. However, all of this did not happen straight away: significant changes were only apparent when the intervention had been in place for six months. Findings such as these indicate that the effects of primary interventions may take time to emerge, perhaps because they work by reducing long-term exposure to chronic work stressors. Primary interventions can take time to work because they require employees to adapt to different ways of working. At first, they might even raise stress levels because they create additional workload or uncertainty. Initial apprehension and concern about changes to working practices may need to dissipate.

Primary interventions can also work in unexpected ways. Susan Jackson had predicted that changes in communication and social support would be linked to improvements in employee health. In fact, it was the reduction in role conflict and role ambiguity, and the increase in perceived influence, that were the most important drivers of changes in employee well-being. This illustrates that stress theories do not always allow us to make precise predictions about how the psychological mechanisms through interventions will work.

In the second example of a primary intervention, Bond and Bunce (2001) looked at two groups (a control group and an intervention group) employed in a UK government department. They established a series of problem-solving committee meetings in the intervention group. These committees, with help from researchers, were tasked with using their expertise of the work setting to identify interventions that would increase job control. The rationale for the intervention was based on established stress theories: it was predicted that improving control would have a positive impact on employee health and satisfaction. The committees designed and implemented a cluster of interventions that led to employees having more input into decision-making and control over their workload, and put systems in place for getting quick advice from managers about difficult or vague tasks. There were some striking outcomes. Employees from the intervention group (but not those from the control group) reported less mental ill-health, lower sickness absence and higher job performance. Data analysis also revealed that changes in perceived control in the intervention group underpinned these positive organisational outcomes.

In extending this work in another organisation, but using a similar approach to intervention, Bond et al. (2008) have found that an individual difference (psychological flexibility – see the section on individual differences in this chapter) appears to interact with the changes in control sparked by the intervention. Bond and colleagues found that those with higher psychological flexibility tended to benefit more from the improvements to control generated by the intervention. What this shows is that individual differences can mean that the same intervention can lead to different outcomes for different employees.

Descriptions of other primary interventions can be found in reviews of intervention research such as Cooper et al. (2001), Egan et al. (2008), Giga et al. (2003), Montano et al. (2014), Parkes and Sparkes (1998), Richardson and Rothstein (2008) and Tetrick and Winslow (2015).

Earlier in this chapter we looked at job-crafting in the context of the JD-R model. A recent study examined how interventions might be used to get employees thinking about proactively designing and implementing their own primary interventions by shaping their own working conditions. van den Heuvel et al. (2015) used a one-day training intervention (with a control group and an intervention group) to provide participants with information about job-crafting and the possibilities it might offer. Participants then examined their own work situation and made plans for how they could craft their own environments over the coming month to better manage demands and to identify, obtain and protect resources. At the end of the training, participants went away to implement their plans and returned to the training environment to report on their progress. There was some initial evidence that this compact intervention had good results.

Key learning point

For tackling the sources of work-related stress, primary interventions could be effective in the long term – but more evidence is needed in order to evaluate fully the effectives of these primary interventions. It is important to involve employees in the design of such interventions so that the active ingredients of the intervention match the nuances of the problems identified.

Secondary interventions

Most workplace stress initiatives have been directed at helping employees as individuals learn to cope with any stressors that occur at work. This is achieved by improving the adaptability of individuals to their environment by changing their psychological resources. Inherent in this approach is the notion that the organisation and its working environment may not change, therefore the individual has to adjust their capacity to meet the demands placed on them. In other words, the focus is on the worker in these interventions, aimed at improving person-environment 'fit'.

Often the aim of secondary intervention is to change employees' psychological resources thus enabling them to make different, more productive, responses to difficult or stressful elements of their work. Through these changes the links between exposure to sources of stress and its negative outcomes can become weaker or disappear. The objective is to *reduce or eliminate the harm* that employees might experience without altering their exposure to sources of stress. The way employees appraise their situation is crucial in stress theories: these interventions are often designed to help employees develop the habit of appraising things more positively. A subtle potential risk of the widespread use of secondary Stress Management Interventions (SMIs) is that employees may conclude that they are somehow to blame for the problems they are experiencing.

Specialist expertise is often needed to deliver these interventions (e.g. qualified counsellors or therapists) because the quality of the delivery has been found to play an important part in determining their success (Hofmann et al., 2012). Secondary interventions are usually completed relatively quickly, with employees attending a number of short training sessions and practising their new skills between these sessions (interventions often last a few weeks). These interventions can also be used when primary prevention is not a viable option.

Stress management training (SMT) is the most common form of secondary intervention. Generic skills are often developed through these sessions so that employees can use them to deal better with lots of different sources of stress. This includes stressors which they do not face at the time of the training but that emerge in the future (Murphy and Sauter, 2003). Cognitive behavioural interventions directly target the way employees think about their work situation and the links between their perceptions, emotions and behaviour. For this training to be effective, trainees need to work quite hard at developing new skills. There are other more passive secondary interventions where the trainee gets a bit of an 'easier ride'. Meditation and relaxation interventions focus directly on the adverse consequences of employees' reactions to stress, helping the employee to achieve a mental state that is incompatible with the experience of negative emotions.

Cognitive behavioural training (CBT) is based on the concept that unhealthy human behaviour and the experience of negative emotions can be reduced by changes in cognition/appraisal. As such it is very closely linked to theories of work stress. It involves training people to think differently about their experiences, or to give different meanings to events. To illustrate this point, imagine you are awoken by a noise in the middle of the night. If you think that noise is a burglar then you would be anxious (and understandably so). If you heard the same noise but thought it was the neighbour's cat jumping onto your dustbin, then you might be somewhat less anxious.

Workplace CBT focuses on changing the way people perceive and attach meaning to their experiences of work (rather than to noises heard in the middle of the night). Usually this training will start by targeting situations that the employee has identified as being particularly stressful. In some training the employee develops the skill of attaching more positive meanings to events. This *relabelling* might involve training an employee to think of a difficult situation as a chance to deal with a *challenge* rather than as a *problem to be coped with*. Beck's CBT works by training employees to use evidence around them to critically evaluate the validity of negative thoughts (Beck, 1995).

Stress Inoculation Training (Meichenbaum, 1996) involves focused practice of healthy ways of thinking in response to stressful work events. During initial stages of the intervention, employees are encouraged to practise new strategies for thinking about and responding to stressors in response to carefully controlled simulations that get progressively more difficult. They then progress to work towards using their skills in situations that resemble more closely those stressful situations faced in the work environment. Fletcher and Sarkar (2013) suggest that these controlled experiences of adversity can help employees to develop psychological resources that make them more resilient.

In a wider systematic review of interventions designed to develop resilience, Robertson et al. (2015) note that there is a wide diversity of intervention practices being followed. This appears to be at least partly due to a wide range of different definitions of resilience – different definitions point to different interventions. Various intervention programmes included activities discussed elsewhere in this book including activities designed to develop self-efficacy, optimism, empathy, ACT (see below), mediation practices designed to develop compassion for self and others, relaxation, cognitive-behavioural training and biofeedback. Several interventions combined these active ingredients. The review found some evidence that resilience training did have a positive impact on mental health and self-reported well-being, but that more research was needed before the most effective interventions strategies could be identified.

Key learning point

There are a number of different approaches to secondary intervention. They work in different ways by focusing on different psychological processes.

Acceptance and commitment therapy (ACT; see Flaxman and Bond, 2010) is designed to enhance psychological flexibility by providing trainees with opportunities and techniques that allow them to practise focusing on the present moment. These can have meditative elements (e.g. some exercises involve an eyes-closed focus on the experience of breathing). In these interventions participants are also provided with ways of reducing their tendency to allocate cognitive resources to 'wrestling' with their emotions. This can include practising 'just noticing' these emotions and using techniques that refocus cognitive resources onto actions that contribute towards task completion. This is in contrast to some other approaches to intervention that require participants to engage 'head on' with their negative emotions in order to manage them. Parts of the training can involve the identification of participants' values: this is thought to help participants develop increasing commitment to actions that are congruent with their values. Mindfulness based stress-reduction (MBSR) works on a similar set of underlying principles and theoretical models.

Point of integration

Cognitive resources can also be developed through experiences in the work setting (see Chapter 7). Self-efficacy, for example, has been shown to increase when an employee experiences success, when they see the success of others or when they receive good feedback from a valued work colleague or manager. Efficacy can also be raised when an employee is 'warmed up' for a task through activities that raise psychological and physical arousal levels.

Relaxation training is designed to train the individual to recognise when the body is becoming tense and then to think or behave in a way that relieves that tension. Physical relaxation techniques include deep breathing exercises, muscle relaxation and stretching. These methods are relatively cheap and popular with organisations. Cognitively based relaxation techniques use imagery and meditation to clear the mind of external thoughts relating to life events. *Biofeedback* is sometimes used in conjunction with relaxation training. This uses measurement devices (e.g. heart rate or blood pressure monitors) to show people their physiological responses to stress. This allows people to see if they are using the relaxation methods effectively enough to make a tangible difference.

Other possible stress management interventions include job-related skills training on topics such as time management and assertiveness. These can help employees to deal with some of the most difficult and stressful aspects of their job role. It is also important to remember that training to carry out core components of the job can have a significant and positive impact on personal resources. For example, time management training can be used to help employees rethink their approach to organising their work activities. This can be thought of as a stimulus for employee-led primary intervention as it often works by helping them to reduce exposure to stressors such as intense periods of work or short deadlines. These interventions are often overlooked by organisations but they can be very effective (Richardson and Rothstein, 2008). As with primary interventions, these interventions are based on the theory that a better person–environment fit is healthier.

The packaging up of several secondary interventions is quite common in stress management training. Different techniques and methods are used concurrently after an initial awareness phase where participants learn about the causes and consequences of occupational stress. In contrast to primary interventions, Richardson and Rothstein's study indicated this might not be a good idea as different intervention components might interfere with each other or just give the employee too much to learn and practice. It is worth noting that in a recent review Tetrick and Winslow (2015) highlight several examples of primary and secondary interventions being combined with each other (multimodal interventions) to good effect. This could be because simultaneously enhancing resources and tackling demands simultaneously is an effective intervention strategy.

Key learning point

The various secondary interventions work in different ways. However, all are designed to weaken, or break, the link between exposures to sources of stress and problems with well-being.

Tertiary interventions

The aim of tertiary interventions is to help to rehabilitate those who have already been damaged by their work. Clearly, it is better if employees are not damaged by their work, but tertiary interventions are particularly important when primary and secondary interventions are impractical or when they are unlikely to be totally effective for every employee. Increasingly, these initiatives have been in the form of employee assistance programmes (EAPs) (Berridge et al., 1997). The original EAPs were designed to help employees who were suffering from problems of alcohol dependency, but they are now designed to help employees who are experiencing any one of a number of different problems. Berridge and Cooper (1993: 89) defined an EAP as:

> a programmatic intervention at the workplace, usually at the level of the individual employee, using behavioural science knowledge and methods for the control of certain work related problems (notably alcoholism, drug abuse and mental health) that adversely affect job performance, with the objective of enabling the individual to return to making her or his full contribution and to attaining full functioning in personal life.

Most EAPs offer psychological counselling of one type or another. Usually there is a self-referral route for the employees plus the possibility of referral by line managers (training is often given to managers as to how to identify sources and symptoms of stress). These referral routes may sometimes lead to primary or secondary interventions being developed for individual employees (e.g. an employee may work with the line manager and their counsellor to redesign their workload, or may be referred to stress management or job-related skills training).

EAPs usually include a telephone-based or Internet-based helpline and information service. This is often used for assessing individual employees' needs, referring employees to sources of help and sometimes for short-term counselling (Employee Assistance Professionals Association, 2003). One of the key features of EAPs is that they often provide employees with support and help for non-work issues (e.g. a legal advice helpline) that can be made available to employees' relatives and retired staff. Health promotion activities (such as on-site fitness facilities, dietary control, cardiovascular fitness programmes, relaxation classes or stress and health education) are another key feature of most stress management and EAP initiatives (Kinder et al., 2008).

> ### Key learning point
>
> Tertiary interventions are designed to repair the damage. There is widespread agreement that they should not be seen as a substitute for primary and/or secondary interventions.

The popularity and effectiveness of interventions

There are few examples of good research into the effectiveness of primary interventions. Establishing and maintaining good research designs can be very challenging in organisational settings (as discussed in Chapter 2). From a management perspective, exposing as many people as possible, as quickly as possible, to an effective intervention is the priority. This often prevents researchers from establishing control groups, making it difficult to isolate the effects of the intervention. Primary interventions have been far less widely used than stress management training (LaMontagne et al., 2007; Tetrick and Winslow, 2015). This situation is changing, partly because of changes in government legislation that puts the onus on employers to tackle the sources of work-related health problems. The relatively small number of good-quality intervention studies means that there remains considerable debate about the effectiveness of stress management interventions.

In an attempt to make sense of the available research, Richardson and Rothstein (2008) carried out a rigorous meta-analysis of the effectiveness of primary and secondary interventions. They reviewed 36 intervention studies, only five of which were primary interventions. It is worth noting that the criteria for including studies were very rigorous and the review may have excluded many 'less than perfect' primary intervention studies that contain interesting and important findings. Setting that concern aside for a moment, the largest effects on employee well-being were found for cognitive–behavioural secondary interventions *without* other interventions. Relaxation interventions were the second most effective type of intervention. With so few studies to examine, they were able to find little evidence of the effectiveness of primary interventions.

There is also a relatively small body of evidence as to the effectiveness of mindfulness-based interventions that improve psychological flexibility (e.g. ACT, MBSR). The results of these studies do indicate some very significant positive effects being associated with well-designed and delivered interventions – although more information is needed about the features of intervention that seem to be most effective (Hülsheger et al., 2015).

Key learning point

Studies of intervention effectiveness indicate that, on average, secondary stress management interventions with a cognitive-behavioural element are the most effective. There is a paucity of evidence regarding primary interventions.

Another recent review by Montano et al. (2014) examined a larger number of primary intervention studies (39 this time). They used a more liberal set of criteria than Richardson and Rothstein to identify studies to include. Nonetheless only good-quality studies were included in their review. The most striking finding of their review was that when different primary interventions were delivered in combinations the effects were larger than when single interventions were implemented in isolation. They looked at various combinations of ergonomic improvements, intervention to tackle work pressure and intensity, and other improvements such as increasing levels of social support. For example, the introduction of teamworking (see Chapter 11) is often a 'package' of changes that have a positive impact on control, support, demands and role-related stressors. Combining different primary interventions may increase their effects because different aspects of demands and resource interact with each other in the way that models such as the JD-R describe.

Key debate

How do we measure the outcomes of different stress management interventions?

Richardson and Rothstein (2008) note the majority of research into secondary interventions looks at the impact of intervention on psychological outcomes, which may explain why they appear to be so effective at least in the short term. Studies that have assessed the impact of psychological counselling (Allison et al., 1989; Cooper and Sadri, 1991) have shown significant improvements in the mental health of counselled employees, but little change in levels of organisational commitment. Van der Klink et al. (2001) found that secondary interventions have little impact on levels of job satisfaction. Murphy and Sauter (2003) argue that stress management training significantly reduces symptoms of poor health but this does not lead to changes in organisational outcomes. Counselling and stress management training may have short-term effects, particularly if employees return to an unchanged work environment and its indigenous stressors. If such initiatives have little impact on improving job satisfaction, then it is more likely that the individual will adopt a way of coping that may have positive individual outcomes, but less benefit for the organisation (Cooper and Sadri, 1991).

The choice of criteria used to measure intervention outcomes might explain at least some of the differences in intervention effectiveness. There is a small, but growing, number of studies showing primary interventions to have a significant impact on important outcomes such as absence and performance. These outcome measures can be influenced by many organisational factors unrelated to the intervention itself, which may go some way to explaining why meta-analyses show the 'average' effects for primary interventions to be small. By way of contrast, symptoms of anxiety and depression are often targeted directly in secondary interventions, and it is measures of these psychological variables that are also then used to determine intervention effectiveness.

This line of reasoning is supported by evidence that changes in self-report measures (in particular measures of working conditions) are larger than changes in other outcomes for the majority of primary intervention studies (Parkes and Sparkes, 1998). Just as secondary interventions tend to produce changes in psychological symptoms, Kompier and Kristensen (2001) and Nielsen et al. (2010) have argued it is only reasonable to expect primary interventions to have consistent impact on the variables they target directly, i.e. perceived working conditions. As most theories of stress would suggest, changes in working conditions do not automatically guarantee changes in well-being. Factors such as individual differences and coping have the potential to play a role. These factors can influence the way employees perceive change and determine the *strength* of the relationship between changes in working conditions and health: those coping well may experience less benefit from a primary intervention than those who are struggling.

There is also good evidence that some working conditions have a particularly strong link to organisational outcomes, and by changing these working conditions it is possible to have a significant impact on problems such as high absence and poor performance. Bond and colleagues (2006) found that even modest interventions to improve control tend to have a large impact especially on organisational outcomes such as job performance. In other words 'a little goes a long way' (2006: 10). This does not seem to be the case for all working conditions. The same authors found that problems with work roles were more closely linked to turnover intention. All of this means that it is difficult to provide a simple answer to the question, 'Are primary interventions effective?'; certainly they can be, but much depends upon the nature of the intervention and the criteria used to evaluate it.

Key learning point

Some secondary interventions, particularly CBT training, have been found to have quite a large short-term impact on individual psychological well-being. The impact of these interventions on long-term employee well-being and organisational health is less clear.

When reading intervention studies you will doubtless encounter many anecdotal accounts of how problems with implementing the intervention or disruptive events occurring in the organisation diluted the impact of the intervention. However, few studies use a rigorous approach to finding out how these factors might have influenced intervention outcomes (Egan et al., 2008). This raises the chance that *type III errors* (see Chapter 2) are being made in previous intervention research.

Process evaluation is designed to help the researcher answer questions such as 'Why did the intervention work well?' and 'Why did the intervention fail?' (Nielsen and Randall, 2013). Research into secondary intervention has shown that *session impact factors* such as the sense of comfort and belonging generated in training sessions can significantly influence intervention outcomes (Bunce, 1997). For primary interventions, process evaluation involves documenting the delivery of the intervention (implementation factors) and significant events taking place in the organisation (contextual factors). Contextual factors, such as problems with maintaining staffing levels, can make it difficult for people to find the time, energy or resources for primary intervention activities (Nielsen et al., 2010; Nielsen and Randall, 2012).

A number of process factors appear to be important in the implementation of primary interventions. These include:

■ good levels of employee involvement and participation in all aspects of the intervention process, with senior management commitment to primary intervention and a culture supportive of positive change (e.g. Kompier et al., 1998; Murphy and Sauter, 2003; Nielsen and Abildgaard, 2013);

■ actions being taken to ensure that employees are provided with the skills, resources and support they need to extract the maximum possible benefit from the intervention (Nytrø et al., 2000; Nielsen et al., 2015; Saksvik et al., 2002);

■ employees' readiness for change, line management support for the intervention, employee perceptions of their participation in intervention design and of the active ingredients of the intervention, i.e. whether they are aware of, or exposed to, the active ingredients of the intervention (Nielsen, 2013; Nielsen and Randall, 2012; Randall et al., 2009);

■ employees' perceptions of the quality of the intervention and the amount of information they are given about the intervention – for example why it is being implemented and what it is intended to achieve (Nielsen et al., 2007).

You may notice that many of these features can be found in the implementation of PAR as discussed earlier in this chapter. This may be one of the reasons why such interventions, when properly delivered, appear to be particularly effective.

Key learning point

Primary interventions can have an impact on both individual well-being and the health of organisations. However, the processes through which they are designed and implemented play an important role in determining whether or not they are effective.

EAPs have proved more popular with organisations than other types of intervention for several reasons:

■ Cost–benefit analysis of such programmes has produced some impressive results. For example, the New York Telephone Company's 'wellness' programme designed to improve cardiovascular fitness saved the organisation $2.7 million in absence and treatment costs in one year alone (Cartwright and Cooper, 1997).

■ The professional 'interventionists' – the counsellors, physicians and clinicians responsible for healthcare – feel more comfortable with changing individuals than changing organisations (Ivancevich et al., 1990).

■ It is considered easier and less disruptive to business to change the individual than to embark on an extensive and potentially expensive organisational development programme, the outcome of which may be uncertain (Cooper and Cartwright, 1994).

■ They present a high-profile means by which organisations can be 'seen to be doing something about stress' and taking reasonable precautions to safeguard employee health. This is likely to be important, not only in terms of the message it communicates to employees, but also to the external environment. This latter point is particularly important, given the increasing litigation fears that now exist among employers throughout the USA and Europe.

Increasingly, organisations are using EAPs as safety nets to deal with the minority of problems where primary or secondary interventions do not deal with the problem. It is generally seen to be a problem when organisations over-rely on EAPs. This could mean that efforts at preventing and managing work-related problems are not taking place, or not being as effective as they could be.

Large-scale reviews of the research evidence have found that **wellness programmes** (i.e. the provision of fitness facilities and health education) significantly decrease absence and increase job satisfaction (Parks and Steelman, 2008). There is a risk that such benefits may be relatively short term, particularly if individuals fail to maintain a long-term commitment to exercise habits and are likely to revert to their previous lifestyle. Many EAPs also offer employees secondary interventions of the type mentioned earlier in this chapter, and therefore similar concerns have been voiced that EAP counselling interventions offer short-term gains for the individual, but have less impact on job satisfaction and performance. Lifestyle and health habits appear to have a strong direct effect on strain outcomes, in reducing anxiety, depression and psychosomatic distress, but do not necessarily moderate the stressor–strain linkage (Baglioni and Cooper, 1988). EAPs are often underused by employees who are not aware of the services on offer, or who have concerns about confidentiality (some employees become suspicious when they perceive that the employer is taking on a dual role of both manager and counselling provider).

Drawing on reviews by Murphy (1988) and French et al. (1997), Randall and Lewis (2007) identify that a number of features of an EAP are linked to its success:

- visible commitment and support for the EAP from senior management;
- clear, well-publicised and written agreement on the purpose, policies and procedures of the EAP, including an explicit policy on confidentiality;
- cooperation with employee representatives (e.g. trade unions);
- training of line managers to identify problems;
- frequent communication and training for employees concerning EAP services and workplace policies to employees;
- programmes that offer long-term ongoing support and referral to other agencies if necessary;
- maintenance of records to allow for programme evaluation.

Key learning point

Properly designed and well-managed EAPs can provide organisations with an important safety net to help employees whose health is damaged by their experiences at work.

When looking at reviews of the effectiveness of interventions it is important to remember that academics are still working with a very small (albeit slowly increasing) number of intervention studies. The diversity of interventions delivered and outcomes evaluated makes it difficult to draw generalisable conclusions. Certainly, a 'one size fits all' approach to intervention is not yet available nor might it ever be. For example, Kompier and Kristensen (2001) and Flaxman and Bond (2010) point out that interventions will be most effective for employees who are experiencing a problem before the intervention. Van der Hek and Plomp (1997) noted that voluntary participation in interventions does not necessarily attract the workers who are at risk. What is clear is that organisations need to follow a process that identifies the problems employees are experiencing and designing/choosing interventions that fit the particular needs of the organisation and its employees.

Key learning point

Dealing with the sources of stress may require a variety of interventions: these need to be tailored to the specific problems facing the organisation within the specific organisational context.

Stop to consider

Organisations may often be faced with a choice between primary, secondary and tertiary interventions. What factors should be considered when they are making that choice? What, if anything, could prevent them from using their preferred intervention strategy?

Problem-solving approaches to intervention

The complexity of employee well-being often leaves organisations confused about what to do to tackle any problems they find. Many experts recommend that each organisation follows a *systematic problem-solving* approach to the management of employee well-being.

Helping employees to become aware of the sources and consequences of stress in their own work environment is often a first step in the design of interventions. Organisational systems should be in place to monitor trends in employee turnover and absence data, and more subtle indices such as error and accident rates, insurance claims, tardiness, dips in job satisfaction and deteriorating industrial relations. Organisations can also provide training in symptom recognition and basic counselling skills for their supervisors and managers to help them to be more responsive to employee stress (see Donaldson-Feilder et al., 2008). From a senior management level downwards it is important to acknowledge and communicate to employees that stress has a legitimate place on the organisation's agenda (Murphy and Sauter, 2003).

At the organisational level, an employee survey can be used to assess and monitor employee health and well-being. A range of measures can be used in such an audit. Measures of working conditions include the Job Content Questionnaire (see Karasek et al., 1998), the Job Diagnostic Survey (Hackman and Oldham, 1980), the UK Health and Safety Executive Indicator Tool (see Exercise 10.5), and the Work Organisation Assessment Questionnaire (Griffiths et al., 2006). Surveys can also be constructed from various reliable and valid measures of specific aspects of work such as work control (Dwyer and Ganster, 1991), supervisory support (Greenhaus et al., 1990), social support (Caplan et al., 1980), monotony (Melamed et al., 1995) and work–family conflict (Kopelman et al., 1983). Problems that are reported by large numbers of employees via a survey are more likely to be the result of situational factors rather than individual differences. These tools may be supplemented with measures of individual differences, coping, job satisfaction, self-reported absence, intention to quit and physical and psychological health. By using various data analysis methods (e.g. correlation, analysis of variance, etc.), it is then possible to establish whether problems with working conditions are linked to poor employee well-being.

Some authors (e.g. Cox et al., 2000; Bakker and Demerouti, 2007) have argued that because every job and workplace comes with its own idiosyncratic demands and resources, tailored (bespoke) measures of work characteristics might be needed. Nielsen et al. (2014) found that this approach was appreciated by employees and smoothed the path to subsequent intervention. In small organisations, stress-related problems can be identified through the introduction of regular workgroup review meetings or quality circle-type initiatives.

Some form of assessment of problems is important because different stressors are likely to suggest different organisational solutions (see Table 10.3). It may also be that different stressors operate in different parts of the organisation for different groups of employees.

At the individual level, stressor identification can be achieved by the maintenance of a stress diary. Experience of sampling methodology (see Chapter 2 and Daniels et al., 2009) has also been used to combine the strengths of questionnaire methods of assessment with the advantages of continuous data collection offered by diary methods. By recording on at least a daily basis the incidents, types of situation and person(s) involved that cause distress over a period of time (e.g. four weeks), this information will reveal any significant themes or common stressor patterns. It is also useful if the individual records show how they responded to the situation at the time, whether the strategy was successful in both the short and longer term, and how, on reflection, they might have handled it better. The individual can then move towards developing an action plan as to how they could either eliminate the source of stress or change or modify it. If the stressor cannot be changed, however, then the individual has to accept the situation and explore ways of coping with the situation as it is. By cataloguing current responses and ways of coping and reviewing these with the benefit of retrospection, the individual can (i) identify areas where their coping skills could be improved and (ii) develop a repertoire of successful contingency-based coping methods which can be applied to similar situations in the future.

| Exercise 10.5 | Can we set acceptable standards for stress at work? |

The UK HSE issues guidance on how organisations can identify and manage stress in several stressor areas (these are referred to as the Management Standard). These are:

- demands;
- control;
- support;
- role;
- relationships;
- change.

Brief summaries of how organisations can use these standards to assess and manage stress have been published. See 'How to Tackle Work Related Stress' on HSE's website at http://www.hse.gov.uk/pubns/indg430.pdf. Further guidance from the HSE about work-related stress can be found at http://www.hse.gov.uk/stress.

The HSE makes available an indicator tool (a questionnaire for employees) that organisations can use to measure the sources of work stress. This is available from the HSE website. An article by Edwards et al. (2008) presents an up-to-date evaluation of the HSE's Stress Indicator Tool. A further article by Houdmont et al. (2013) provides an evaluation of a brief version of this measure. Both are cited in the References.

Suggested exercise

Using the materials from the HSE website, and the articles by Edwards et al. and Houdmont et al., consider whether you think it is appropriate to specify acceptable standards for stress levels in an organisation. Is the HSE going about it in the right way? For example, do you think it is taking all major sources of stress into consideration? Is the guidance thorough and detailed enough? Aside from using the indicator tool, what other data should organisations collect as part of the problem analysis?

Generally, legal requirements mean that organisations should look to primary interventions as the preferred option to deal with the sources of stress identified. Involving various stakeholders (employees, managers, trade unions etc.) in the intervention decision-making process is crucial: this allows the practicalities of various intervention options to be examined properly and for an intervention action plan to be devised.

There are likely to be certain stressors which neither the individual nor the organisation is able to change, but which have to be 'coped with'. For example, employees working in the emergency services are likely to be faced with distressing or upsetting situations and these cannot be designed out of the job. Secondary and tertiary levels of intervention can then be designed. Not all of the stress that impacts on the workplace is necessarily or exclusively caused by the work environment (Tetrick and Winslow, 2015). Financial crisis, bereavement, marital difficulties and other personal life events create stress, the effects of which often spill over into the workplace. Tertiary-level interventions can be extremely effective in dealing with non-work-related stress. What is important is that the options for primary intervention are discussed before secondary intervention is considered. Tertiary interventions should not be used to replace primary and secondary interventions.

Stress audits can provide a baseline measure whereby the introduction of any subsequent stressor reduction technique implemented by an organisation can be evaluated. After some time, measuring again working conditions and employee well-being can show whether interventions are having the desired effect. In addition, the more successful the organisation is in eliminating or modifying environmental stressors, the less demand there would be for stress management training and employee assistance programmes. In effect, this evaluation work is another audit and its results should be used as the stimulus for new efforts to tackle any problems that remain, or any new problems that have emerged since the original audit. This sets up a process of continuous improvement.

Key learning point

Managing stress and well-being at work requires a stage-by-stage approach – identifying a problem, intervening to change it or find ways of coping with it, and monitoring and reviewing progress. This allows the intervention strategy to be tailored to the needs of the organisation, rather than it being determined by a generic theory that may or may not be valid in the organisation.

Exercise 10.6   Managing your stress

Here is your chance to engage in a bit of role play. Below is a description of a pretty stressful day. Imagine that you experience a day like this.

7.30 A.M.   The day starts badly. You forgot to set the alarm and you're running late. You have an important client meeting at 9.30 A.M. and you intended to get into the office early to reread the papers in preparation for the meeting. You have to stop for fuel on the way in, which further delays you. Traffic is heavy and there are roadworks on the motorway. You find yourself in a tailback of slow-moving traffic and it's at least seven kilometres until the next exit. As you're crawling along, you suddenly become aware that you have developed a flat tyre. You limp on to the hard shoulder and look at your watch. It's 8.50 A.M. and you're still some 15 kilometres from your office. You're not going to make that meeting!

Assuming a typical response to the previous scenario, the day might continue as follows:

9.45 A.M.   You eventually arrive at your office. You go to collect the file for the client meeting and the phone rings. A subordinate is having some problems accessing information on the computer; brusquely, you give hasty instructions. You then spend a further 10 minutes wading through the huge piles of paper stacked on your desk, searching for the right file. You notice a new pile of correspondence and phone messages on the desk, some marked 'urgent'. You contemplate dealing with these but you're now already 30 minutes late for this meeting. Suddenly, you realise that before you left last night your boss popped in and suggested a meeting at 10.30 A.M. You're going to be late for that one too.

Suggested exercise

What is the most effective way of handling the various problems in the above scenario? Discuss how you would have coped with each of the problems as they occurred. Try to identify a primary, secondary and tertiary intervention that could be used to improve your day, and perhaps help prevent you from having too many more days like this in the future.

Summary

Stress has become a major issue for organisations. It is unlikely to move off the agenda as international competition increases and organisations are faced with tougher market conditions. Work psychologists are in the fortunate position that there is a lot of good theory in this area that can be put to use in organisations. There is a solid body of knowledge that shows what the risks are to employee well-being, and a growing body of research that shows how the positive effects of work can be maximised. In this chapter you will have seen that much of the stress at work is caused not only by work overload and time pressures, but also by a lack of rewards and praise and, more importantly, by not providing individuals with the autonomy to do their jobs as they would like. An important point made throughout this chapter is that different jobs have different sources of stress that affect different people in different ways.

While more research is needed to establish the relative effectiveness of different interventions, a closer inspection of primary interventions shows that many of them are features of good management practices. Involving employees in decision-making about primary interventions appears to be particularly important. Training employees to help them deal with unavoidable challenges at work also appears to have good outcomes, but such training must be delivered by competent practitioners and draw upon the latest advances in research. Of course, some employees may still slip through the net and tertiary interventions can help them to repair the damage done.

The assessment and management of employee well-being are not simple tasks. There are many factors to consider and these interact with each other in complex ways. However, it appears that enough is already known for work psychologists to offer clear advice to organisations about the processes that they should follow to help them develop a healthy workforce within successful organisations.

Closing case study

Helplines prosper as more workers feel the strain

If you are anxious about work, you are not alone. Companies that supply counselling services to banks, law firms, IT companies and government say they are receiving more calls asking for help with stress.

Capita, an outsourcing company that provides employee support to more than 800 companies, said the number of calls for work-related stress rose by about 10 per cent last year and continued last month, with restructuring and redundancies a common theme. Atos, the French outsourcer, is another company that has seen an increase in calls to its helplines at its Help Employee Assistance division.

Meanwhile, Right Management, part of the ManpowerGroup, which provides a 24-hour counselling and support line to 400 businesses, has seen a rise in calls from managers asking how to cope with stressed staff.

Stress remains one of the largest causes of work absence, according to all three companies. The Chartered Institute of Personnel and Development confirms that among non-manual workers stress is the chief reason employees fail to turn up to work and any resurgence in economic sentiment has yet to feed into more optimism in the workplace.

Phil Cox, a chartered member the CIPD, and a workplace counsellor and coach, said: "Although [staff] have been working harder, many are not getting the recognition they feel they deserve and for some this can trigger stress and depression."

▶

▶

If stress in the recession was triggered by job losses, now people are anxious about the prospect of getting their pay and hours cut as well as fearing that their terms and conditions of work will worsen.

Although the number of jobs is increasing, real wages have been falling consistently since 2010, the longest period for 50 years, according to fresh figures from the Office for National Statistics.

Dr Nerina Ramlakhan, a therapist at Capio Nightingale hospital in London, has also seen an increased number of executives who feel overworked. "People have been under such stress for the last few years. As soon as they relax and are no longer running on adrenalin they feel burnt out."

Mr Cox said the increase in demand for executive coaching might also be tied to the need for more counselling. "The goalposts have changed for executives in the past five years, which means they are having to develop new skills."

Dr Mike Drayton, a business psychologist, says some of the stress is driven by employees' inability to say "no".

"People at senior levels have very fuzzy boundaries between work and home life. Work life is more salient and encroaches on their personal life," says Dr Drayton.

Increasing demands on senior executives may also encourage people to shun high-flying positions. Andrew Roscoe, partner at Egon Zehnder, the executive search company, said many internal candidates were not aspiring to more senior jobs because of the stress involved. "When we delve into it we find most people don't want the combination of stress and strain and risk and reward that goes with senior jobs," he said.

Capita said people were working longer hours to earn extra cash, but in some cases this had led to exhaustion. "They then have time off and either reflect on their lifestyle and don't want to return to work or become ill and returning to work is delayed," Capita said.

Dr Ramlakhan said concern about staff welfare was pushing wellbeing up the corporate agenda. She noted that a recent workshop she held at a City law firm was fully booked within five minutes.

In the public sector, fear over redundancy remains high. Andrew Kinder, clinical director of Atos's Help Employee Assistance division, said: "The ongoing state of uncertainty and threat of redundancy can be very stressful."

Jayne Carrington, managing director of Right Management adds: "There is work intensity ... as organisations try to do more with less, but the salient point is how stress is managed.

Often people want a manager to notice that they ... seem to be struggling ... and this needs a manager to be confident and competent to have this conversation."

Jill Miller, research adviser at the CIPD, highlighted that increased numbers of calls to helplines signified employers were improving the awareness of such programmes. However, she believed stress had increased as employers set tighter deadlines and vacant positions created by redundancies were not refilled.

 Source: *Financial Times*, ft.com, 17 February 2014

Suggested exercise

How do theories of work-related stress help us to explain some of the observations made in this article? Try to identify findings that relate to at least two theories (e.g. the ERI model of the JD-R model). For each of the sources of stress mentioned. identify some interventions at the primary, secondary and tertiary level that might have a good chance of success.

Test your learning

Short-answer questions

1 What are Hans Selye's three stages of stress?
2 What are structural models of work stress?
3 What are the key predictions made by the demands–control–support model of work stress?
4 What are transactional models of work stress?
5 Outline the main features of the job demands–resources model.
6 To what extent is absence increased by, and performance decreased by, work-related stress?
7 Which source of workplace stress, in your view, is the most damaging to the individual employee? Why?
8 Define the following: role ambiguity, role conflict and locus of control.
9 What is positive psychological well-being?
10 List three individual difference variables that are important in the stress process.
11 Define primary, secondary and tertiary interventions.
12 What is an EAP?
13 List at least five different primary interventions that could be used to tackle five different sources of work-related stress.
14 What is more effective for tackling work stress: relaxation training or cognitive behavioural training? Briefly explain your answer.
15 What is a stress audit and what useful data might it yield?

Suggested assignments

1 What are the major sources of stress at work? Why are they stressful?
2 Compare and contrast transactional, structural and resources-based theories of work stress.
3 Is the concept of stress a useful one?
4 Is it appropriate to describe stress as an illness? Explain your answer with reference to theory and research on work stress.
5 Might individual-level stress management programmes be more or less effective than organisation-orientated interventions? Explain your answer.
6 'The way a stress management intervention is implemented is just as important as the content of that intervention.' Discuss.

Relevant websites

The work on line management behaviour and work stress that is part sponsored by the CIPD can be found at http://www.cipd.co.uk/hr-resources/guides/line-management-behaviour-stress.aspx

Practical concern with how to manage (and/or reduce) stress at work is always high, and seems to be growing. One manifestation of that is the International Stress Management Association, which can be found at http://www.isma.org.uk. This site offers links to ideas and resources for managing stress, and although it is UK-based, there are also links to equivalent sites in some other countries.

The British Association of Counselling and Psychotherapy (BACP) has a Workplace Division that can be found at http://bacpworkplace.org.uk/. A selection of several interesting articles from their *Counselling at work* journal are available from here free of charge. Many focus on the use of counselling to tackle contemporary work issues.

The European Agency for Safety and Health at Work is running a campaign 'Healthy Workplaces Manage Stress'. There are lots of useful resources and interesting cases studies showing how various organisations have tackled work-related stress at https://www.healthy-workplaces.eu/en

A host of resources, including the Management Standards Indicator Tool and case studies of stress management interventions can be found at the UK HSE website: http://www.hse .gov.uk/stress/. A full research report on an interesting case study from Somerset County Council is available to download in full from the HSE website: www.hse.gov.uk/research /rrhtm/rr295.htm.

Suggested further reading

Full details for all references are given in the list at the end of this book.

1 *Organizational Stress Management: A Strategic Approach* by Ashley Weinberg, Valerie Sutherland and Cary Cooper (Palgrave Macmillan, 2010) provides a good insight into how organisations can take a pragmatic approach to the issue.

2 The analysis of the business case for managing work-related stress by Frank Bond and colleagues in 2006 is an excellent and accessible review of the links between sources of stress and important organisational outcomes. It can be downloaded free from the UK HSE website: http://www.hse.gov.uk/research/rrpdf/rr431.pdf

3 Richardson and Rothstein's (2008) review of stress management interventions is rather technical, but begins with some very useful information about the various interventions that are available to organisations.

4 *How to Deal with Stress* by Stephen Palmer and Cary Cooper (Kogan Page, 2007) explores how individuals can and should cope with stress.

5 *Positive Psychology: The science of happiness and human strengths* by Alan Carr (Routledge, 2011) provides a good introduction to a branch of psychology that is generating increasing levels of interest from academics and practitioners alike.

6 *Contemporary Occupational Health Psychology: Global perspectives on research and practice* (Volume 1), published by Wiley-Blackwell in 2010, and edited by Jonathan Houdmont and Stavroula Leka, covers numerous work-related health topics in considerable depth and detail. The same editors also produced the excellent textbook *Occupational Health Psychology* (Wiley-Blackwell, 2010) covering a range of issues related to health at work.

7 *Employee Well-being Support* by Kinder et al. (John Wiley and Sons, 2008) is a comprehensive review of all research on organisational employee support systems (e.g. EAPs) as well as a guide for human resource professionals about how to choose one, how to evaluate them and the costs/benefits of these for organisations.

CHAPTER 11
Groups, teams and teamwork

LEARNING OBJECTIVES

After studying this chapter, you should be able to:

1 describe the differences between groups and teams;

2 outline the main features of the 'groupthink' model of group decision-making, and suggest two ways in which it may not be entirely accurate;

3 define group polarisation and minority influence and explain why they occur;

4 explain why relations between groups at work depend partly on individuals' sense of personal identity;

5 define stereotypes and specify two reasons why they can affect relations between groups at work;

6 explain how some of the problems associated with working in teams and groups can be addressed;

7 describe the incidence of teamwork in various European countries and explain the importance of autonomy in team working;

8 summarise how teams function using the IPO and IMOI models and the concept of team climate;

9 explain the stages of team development;

10 discuss the impact of team working on team members;

11 describe the importance of team roles and a popular team role typology;

12 explain the ways in which the diversity within a team can affect team functioning;

13 discuss the effect of team members' skills, personality and ability on team performance;

14 describe the extent to which work teams influence different types of decisions in organisations.

Opening case study

Keeping body and soul together: why National Health Service (NHS) teamwork is critical to patient outcomes

How care processes are managed within the NHS and what quality of care patients can and should expect within Britain's hospitals is a recurrent concern, surfacing once again with the public inquiry into higher than expected death rates at the Mid Staffordshire NHS Trust. Just why such situations arise, and what measures can be taken to ensure better quality of care, is very much at the heart of the research agenda for Professor Michael West. Around 10 years ago West and his colleagues started exploring the links between human resource management (HRM) practices and patient mortality.

Since 2003 West and his team have been conducting the annual NHS staff survey on behalf of the Department of Health, and what they have found has emphatically corroborated their earlier findings. "With this more extensive data," says West, "we have exactly the same findings: that what staff experience at work is a really good predictor of patient mortality."

Despite wide divergences between NHS trusts – for instance, in how staff view their leaders, whether staff have clear goals, their level of engagement and commitment, or the extent of positive feelings – the relationship between patient satisfaction and staff experience is, says West, strong across the board.

One of the most striking findings to emerge from their latest analysis, he adds, is that the very best predictor of patient mortality is the percentage of staff working in well-structured teams. However, all is not what it seems.

"Although 90 per cent of NHS staff say that they work in teams, when we probe a little deeper we think the true figure is nearer 40 per cent – and that around half NHS staff are working not in real teams but in what we would term pseudo teams."

The distinction between these two is, he explains, relatively simple but nevertheless telling. "We ask questions about whether the team has clear objectives, whether they work closely together to meet those objectives, and whether they meet regularly to review performance and how it could be improved. We think those three simple elements are actually fundamental to any kind of team. So when people answer no to any of those areas, we define them as a pseudo team. What we find is that the more people who work in real teams, the lower the rates of injuries and errors at work – errors that could harm patients. Those teams experience less violence against staff by members of the public, and lower levels of patient mortality. Levels of staff wellbeing are also higher. The reverse is true for pseudo teams."

The teams that West and his colleagues have looked at cover all sectors of the NHS, involving both clinical and managerial staff. Yet once again, despite the differences in context, the findings are remarkably consistent: teams that have clear objectives and take time out to review their performance are far more effective, productive and innovative than those that don't.

As might be expected, team dynamics are not always easily managed, and status issues can be particularly problematic. Here West and his colleagues are providing practical interventions for a variety of NHS organisations, designed to promote more effective teamworking:

"There is tension relating both to diversity of disciplinary background and to status inconsistencies in teams, so what we do is to help teams create an ethos where they value diversity, whether that be cultural diversity or disciplinary diversity. Because again the evidence we have is that where there's a positive attitude to diversity – whether it's professional, cultural or gender diversity – the teams with that diversity outperform more homogenous teams."

In this and other areas there is still much to do, concedes West. He is particularly concerned that the current emphasis on cuts is causing senior managers to focus on productivity at the expense of innovation – something borne out by his current research on the board minutes of NHS trusts. He would also like to see the innovative approaches already evident within the NHS being better exploited through better sharing of good practice. Nevertheless, many of the essential messages are getting through, and making discernible impact.

Source: http://www.lancaster.ac.uk/lums/research/research-showcase/nhs-teamwork/

Introduction

The opening case study shows that teams and groups are often seen as a way of improving organisational performance. In the case of the NHS, it may even help to save lives and it is difficult to envisage a more important performance outcome. The case study paints a picture of teamwork as a win-win situation with benefits for patients and staff alike. It also shows that teamwork does not guarantee success and poorly managed attempts to implement it may not always be appreciated by employees. It also highlights the importance of setting objectives for teams, allowing team members to work closely together on everyday tasks and giving them the opportunity to discuss and solve work problems. Professor West is also clear about the value of diversity within teams and how this can drive improvements in work performance.

Fortunately, there is a large body of research we can draw upon that helps us to understand how the benefits of teamwork can be maximised and how some of the problems mentioned above can be avoided. In this chapter we will focus on the research that gives some important insights into the psychological processes that underpin behaviour in teams. For example we will examine the links between teamwork and work performance and other important outcomes for employees. We will look at what goes wrong in teams and why these problems occur. In this chapter we also examine how creativity and innovation develop in teams, and the role of diversity in team membership.

The chapter begins by considering research into how humans function in groups. There is a great deal of experimental and field research on groups that can be applied to help us study and understand work teams (teams are 'special cases' of groups with some specific features that will be discussed later). Of course, not all of these findings translate into the work setting. However, there are some extremely powerful, well-executed research studies in social psychology that examine important psychological mechanisms that are as likely to operate in real-world work teams as they are in carefully controlled laboratory studies. For example, numerous studies have shown that we perceive and behave towards members of our own group (e.g. the people in our office) in ways that are very different to how we behave towards members of other groups (e.g. the people in the neighbouring office). Some of the key findings from controlled experiments are included in this chapter because they help us to develop a stronger understanding of how work teams function and operate.

Group decision-making

Groups versus individuals

Human beings have always lived, loved and worked in groups ... over the course of evolution the small group became the survival strategy adopted by the human species.

(West, 2001: 271)

In work organisations most major decisions (and many lesser ones) are made by groups of people, and not by individuals. It is often argued that many work tasks are simply too complex for one person to deal with alone. Teamwork offers a way of capitalising upon and integrating the diversity of knowledge, skills, abilities and values in the workforce through the effective allocation and coordination of different work tasks (Richter et al., 2011). If handled in the right way, a decision made by a group can evoke greater commitment to it than one made by an individual: this is because more people feel a sense of involvement in the decision and have a personal interest in its implementation (Nielsen et al., 2015).

On the other hand, group decisions usually consume more time (and more money) than individual ones. As a result one oft-asked question is whether individual or group decisions are superior. Teams may lead to workers correcting each other's mistakes and building on each other's ideas. An opposing view is that 'too many cooks spoil the broth': the problems of communication, rivalry and conflict between group members more than cancel out any potential advantage of the increased pool of available talent and ideas. Many researchers identify features of teams that can cause problems (or *group process losses*) but at the same time be linked to other desirable outcomes (*group process gains*). Stahl et al. (2010) found that culturally diverse teams were likely to experience more conflict (a group process *loss*) but also to achieve higher levels of creativity and experience higher job satisfaction (group process *gains*) than those working in very homogenous teams. As Hackman (1990) argued some time ago, if tasks are relatively simple then they are likely to be completed more effectively by an individual than by a group. In such a situation the potential process gains offered by the diversity of the team do not outweigh the potential process losses. This does not contradict the arguments advanced in the opening case study: in the NHS, multidisciplinary teams of doctors, nurses and allied health professionals are working on very complex tasks requiring input from various perspectives.

Therefore, it is not surprising that research has shown that it is not possible to generalise about whether individuals or groups are universally better. It depends on a large number of factors that can vary from one group to another. As you might expect, these include the abilities and training of the individuals involved. Effectiveness is also determined in part by the kind of task being tackled, the context in which the task is being tackled and the way the group decides to, or is instructed to, tackle it (Kerr and Tindale, 2004).

McGrath (1984) identified eight different types of task that groups can face. Four of these directly concern group decision-making. These are:

1   generating plans (e.g. how many new employees to hire to support expansion);

2   generating ideas (e.g. for new ways of completing work tasks or new work methods);

3   solving problems that have 'correct answers' (i.e. where the answer can be identified with a degree of certainty, for example the costs of purchasing and installing a new piece of equipment);

4   identifying issues that do not have a 'correct answer' at the time the decision is made where there is considerable uncertainty over the answer (e.g. estimating the costs of recruiting new employees over the next five years when levels of staff turnover are uncertain and fluctuating).

If the aim to is to carry out a controlled test of the differences between individual and group performance, the second and third of these provide the best tasks because the outputs can be counted (as in the number of new ideas) and objectively 'scored' (by checking whether the correct answer was identified). These are now examined in more detail. **Brainstorming** was originally advocated by Osborn (1957), who argued individuals can think up twice as many ideas in a group as they can on their own. However, such gains only occurred if those in the group agreed that:

■   the more ideas they think of the better; and

■   members will be encouraged to produce even bizarre ideas, and not be ridiculed for them.

Some research has indicated that lone individuals who are encouraged to think of as many ideas as possible generate more ideas *per individual* than do groups (e.g. Lamm and Trommsdorf, 1973). This may be because of *evaluation apprehension*, where a person feels afraid of what others will think, and *free-riding*, where group members feel that other group members will do the work for them. It may not surprise you to hear that these are common complaints when students are required to complete group work assignments as part of their studies.

Experiments conducted by Diehl and Stroebe (1987) identified a third explanation: *production blocking*. Simply, only one person at a time in a group can talk about their ideas. In the meantime other members who are listening may not be able to devote enough attention to developing their own original ideas or they may lose their train of thought while using cognitive resources to listen to contributions from others (Kerr and Tindale, 2004). Nevertheless, there is also clear evidence that exposure to the ideas of other people enhances creativity, especially if people are exposed to a diverse group of others (Paulus, 2000).

Taken together, the research indicates that the best brainstorming is achieved by exposing individuals to a diverse group of others, but without incurring production blocking or other negative group effects. Advances in information and communication technology can help by transmitting information between group members in a clear and impersonal way. Computer-mediated communication can produce more ideas than face-to-face interactions, and also support greater equality of participation (Kerr and Tindale, 2004). However, groups communicating in this way tend to make more extreme decisions and have some hostile communications.

Point of integration

Dispersed working (Chapter 15) is supported by a number of different methods of communication that allow group members to work on creative tasks without face-to-face contact. Some of these methods may overcome the problems identified in research into group interactions – but new problems may emerge as important information (such as that conveyed through non-verbal behaviour) may be lost through text- or voice-only exchanges.

Key learning point

The production of new ideas tends to be greater when individuals brainstorm alone with information about other people's ideas, rather than in the physical presence of others.

Psychologists have conducted a number of experiments comparing individual and group performance on *problems with correct answers*. For example Vollrath et al. (1989) found that groups of people working together recognised and recalled information better than individuals. This may be because the distribution of information allows group members to share between them the considerable workload of important cognitive processes such as paying attention to information, encoding and storing that information in memory and retrieving it during discussion (Kerr and Tindale, 2004). This is helpful when the information being shared is in itself correct and unbiased. But to what extent can such information be 'correct' when discussing complex work-related matters?

McGrath (1984) pointed out that there are several different types of correct answers. The group problem-solving processes enacted appear to vary according to the extent to which the correct answer can be shown to be correct: this concept of 'correctness' is best explained by using a few examples. When the correct answer is mentioned in 'Eureka' tasks, everyone suddenly sees that it must be right. This might happen when the group is tasked with identifying a correct factual answer (such as the gross profit for the previous financial year) from a series of plausible alternatives. Then there are problems where the correct (or best) answer can only be defined by experts, but whose wisdom may be challenged by a lay person. An example could be the negative environmental impact of a manufacturing process.

There are also problems that stimulate discussion because the answer can be proved correct using logic and calculations, but its correctness is not necessarily obvious at first sight. These problems are often used to investigate the complexities of group decision-making processes because they invoke much debate and draw out differences of views among group members. An example might be the costs of borrowing large sums of money to take over a competitor organisation. In this type of task, group members generally are willing to begin sharing the processing of information because of the apparent complexity of the task. This can help but the sharing of incorrect information can have a significant impact on the quality of the decision made by the group. One task often used in research is the so-called 'horse-trading task':

> A person buys a horse for £60 and sells it for £70. Then they buy it back for £80 and again sell it for £90. How much money does the person make in the horse-trading business? Many people say £10, but the correct answer is £20, though strictly this assumes that the person does not have to borrow the extra £10 to buy back the horse, and it ignores the opportunity cost of using the £10 in that way rather than another.

For problems like these, it typically needs two correct people, not one, to convince the rest of the group. Put another way, on average *the group is as good as its second-best member*: when solving problems with correct answers, groups are on average better than individuals, but inferior to the *best* individual. Early research using problems of this kind (e.g. Maier and Solem, 1952) produced several possible explanations for this. Lower-status group members had less influence on the group decision than higher-status ones, even when the lower-status people were correct. Even when at least one person in the group knew the correct answer, the group decision was by no means always correct – a very clear demonstration that a group is not always better than an individual. Group discussion made people more confident that the group's consensus decision was correct; unfortunately, the discussion did not make a correct decision more likely!

Key learning point

For problems with demonstrably correct answers, group processes result in a group decision that is, on average, as good as that made by its second-best member. However, groups can do better or worse than this average depending on their membership and the way their discussion is managed/conducted.

Some of the findings discussed so far in this chapter have emerged from elegant and carefully controlled laboratory experiments. These have allowed researchers to isolate psychological processes and to rule out some alternative explanations for the behaviour being observed. In other words, we can be fairly sure that these group processes are real and likely to re-occur. Unfortunately, no laboratory study can capture fully the complexity of the work setting. In laboratory studies participants are rarely worried about upsetting other study participants (who are generally people they do not know) in the same way that they might be when discussing a work problem with close colleagues or managers.

Many decisions made in organisations involve uncertainties, or best guesses based on the available data, or do not have a provable correct answer, or even an answer that well-qualified experts can agree on. As a result, findings from laboratory studies gives us some clues as to what might be going in work groups but cannot automatically or easily be generalised to work organisations. For example, Bell (2007) found that teams' average levels of personality factors such as conscientiousness and agreeableness predicted team performance in organisational settings more strongly than they did in simulated laboratory tasks. This may be because planning, persistence in the face of difficulty and the maintenance of strong interpersonal relationships come to the fore in teams working in real-world settings over long periods of time. Improving group decision-making when the group is faced with complex real-life issues is the focus of the next section of this chapter.

Group deficiencies and overcoming them

Some social scientists have concentrated on identifying the contextual factors linked to group performance (e.g. Hülsheger et al., 2009; Larson and LaFasto, 1989; Richter et al., 2011). These key ingredients include: having team members who are knowledgeable about the problem faced; having a clearly defined and inspiring goal (see Locke's goal-setting theory in Chapter 7); having group members who are committed to solving the problem in the best possible way; providing employees with the skills that they need to work effectively in teams; and support and recognition from important people outside the group. Such findings suggest that a supporting framework of effective human resource practices is needed to support effective teamwork.

By analysing data from numerous studies of teams in work settings, Bell (2007) has found evidence for the importance of many individual differences in determining team effectiveness. These include factors such as openness to experience, conscientiousness, agreeableness, the average level of cognitive ability within the team and the preference that team members exhibited for teamwork activities. Findings such as these indicate that effective selection processes are likely to be needed when putting together work teams.

Other work has attempted to identify the roles that group members should adopt in order to function effectively together (see Belbin 1981, 1993a: this work is covered in detail later in this chapter). Others have concentrated more on procedural factors that become active during interactions between team members (e.g. Rees and Porter, 2001). These include the practices of the chairperson in facilitating discussion and summing it up, ensuring that everyone has their say and that only one person speaks at a time, and making sure that votes (if taken) are conducted only when all points of view have been aired, and with clearly defined options.

Social psychologists have noted many features of the group decision-making process that can impair decision quality. These findings provide an important insight into some of the interventions that can be implemented during the decision-making process. Hoffman and Maier (1961) noted a tendency to adopt 'minimally acceptable solutions', especially where the decision task is complex. Instead of seeking the best possible solution, group members often settle on the first suggested solution that everyone considers 'good enough'. This might sometimes be appropriate in a situation where a quick, workable decision is required, but on most occasions it is probably not a good idea. Hackman (1990) pointed out that groups rarely discuss what strategy (e.g. whether to go for a 'good enough' or 'best possible' solution) they should adopt in tackling a decision-making task but that when they do, they tend to perform better. It appears that discussion of the group's strategy has to be treated as a separate task if it is to be taken seriously and have an impact.

Motivational losses in groups can also be a problem that needs to be tackled. Experimental research has consistently shown that as the number of people in a group increases, the effort and/or performance of each one decreases: this is the so-called social loafing effect (e.g. Latane et al., 1979). This motivational loss can be avoided if individuals in the group feel that their contribution can be identified as their own, *and* that their contribution makes a significant difference to the group's performance (Williams et al., 1981; Kerr and Bruun, 1983). Hence a group leader would be well advised to ensure that each group member can see the connection between the efforts of individuals and group performance (both for each individual themselves and so that they can see the contribution of other group members). Interestingly, culture may play an important role in group motivation. There is some evidence that social loafing does not occur as much in collectivist societies. Earley (1989) found evidence of social loafing among American management trainees in a management task set in a laboratory, but not among trainees from the People's Republic of China (even in the identical task). In collective societies, a person's sense of shared responsibility with others may explain this difference. Moreover, Erez and Somech (1996) found that differences in individualism–collectivism even within one country (Israel) made a difference to the social loafing effect (with those closest to the individualism end of the continuum being most prone to social loafing). This is another example of the culturally specific nature of some findings in applied psychology. Stahl et al. (2010) found that conflict during the task and low levels of social interaction were more likely to occur in culturally diverse teams, but that this was accompanied by increased creativity and employee satisfaction. This link between diversity and conflict was strongest when tasks were complex, perhaps because such tasks elicited a wider range of alternative viewpoints. It also appears that in larger teams cultural diversity becomes more strongly linked to lower satisfaction. We discuss other elements of diversity in much more detail later in this chapter.

Throughout the research on groups, it is clear that the nature of real-world team tasks and work contexts have to be taken into account. Social loafing appears only to occur when groups lack specific goals. As Erez and Somech pointed out, most groups in the workplace have members who know each other, communicate with each other, and have team goals that matter to them and contribute to the team in a way that means that individual performance can be identified. Self-managing teams – teams with very high levels of autonomy in which team members rely heavily upon each other – are increasingly common. In these teams it is even more likely that employees will have strong, established working relationships with colleagues and have a strong commitment to the team and its objectives (Nijholt and Benders, 2010). Social loafing may not be as widespread in the real world as it is in laboratory-based experiments: it may be the exception, not the rule, even in individualistic cultures.

Key learning point

Group members tend to reduce their efforts as group size increases, at least in individualistic cultures. This problem can, however, be overcome by setting teams specific goals and making team members accountable for their actions. Such interventions are common practice in work organisations.

Groupthink

Janis (1972, 1982a, 1982b) arrived at some disturbing conclusions about how some real-life groups charged with making important decision can make extremely poor decisions that have serious repercussions. He analysed the major foreign policy errors of various governments at various times in history. One of these was the 'Bay of Pigs' fiasco in the early 1960s. Fidel Castro had recently taken power in Cuba. As a response, the new US administration under President John F. Kennedy launched an 'invasion' of Cuba by 1400 Cuban exiles, who landed at the Bay of Pigs. Within two days they were surrounded by 20,000 Cuban troops, and those not killed were ransomed back to the USA at a cost of $53 million in aid.

Janis argued that this outcome was not just bad luck for the United States. Instead, such an outcome could and should have been anticipated. He suggested that the consequence of various group processes could be seen in this, which collectively he called **groupthink**. This occurs when group members' motivation for unanimity and agreement (i.e. consensus) overrides their motivation to evaluate carefully the risks and benefits of alternative decisions. It is most likely to occur in highly cohesive groups where group members are friendly with each other, and respect each other's opinions. In such groups disagreement is construed (usually unconsciously) as a withdrawal of friendship and respect, rather than as a useful critical insight. When this is combined with (i) a group leader known (or believed) to have a position or opinion on the issues under discussion, (ii) an absence of clear group procedures for discussion and decision-making, and (iii) a difficult set of circumstances (e.g. time pressure, or high-stakes decision-making), then the group members tend to seek agreement. This leads to groupthink as shown in Figure 11.1. The symptoms can be summarised as follows:

- *Overestimation of the group's power and morality*: In groupthink, group members tend to have positive opinions of each other and these are not challenged.

- *Closed-mindedness*: This can be seen through group members' efforts to downplay warnings and to stereotype other groups as inferior to their own.

- *Pressures towards uniformity*: This manifests itself through the suppression of private doubts, leading to an illusion of unanimity and the development of 'mindguards' to shield group members (especially the leader) from uncomfortable information.

Key learning point

Groupthink is a set of malfunctioning group processes that occur when group members are more concerned (although they may not realise it) to achieve unanimity and agreement than they are to find the best available solution to a problem or situation.

Janis (1982b) has argued that certain measures can be taken to avoid groupthink. These include:

- establishing impartial leadership (so that group members are not tempted simply to follow the leader);

- instructing each person in the group to give high priority to airing doubts and objections;

- having subject matter experts in attendance to raise doubts about the group's discussions and decision-making;

- including 'second chance' meetings where members express their doubts about a previously made, but not yet implemented, decision.

An overarching theme of these interventions is that groupthink can be minimised if there is a known 'group norm' that disagreeing with another group member does *not* signal disrespect or unfriendliness towards them. Intervention studies that test these predictions are few and far between and those that exist tend to be carried out with students: the findings should be interpreted with caution. These studies tend to indicate that when those leading the discussion have low power, are open to ideas and suggestion and are non-directive

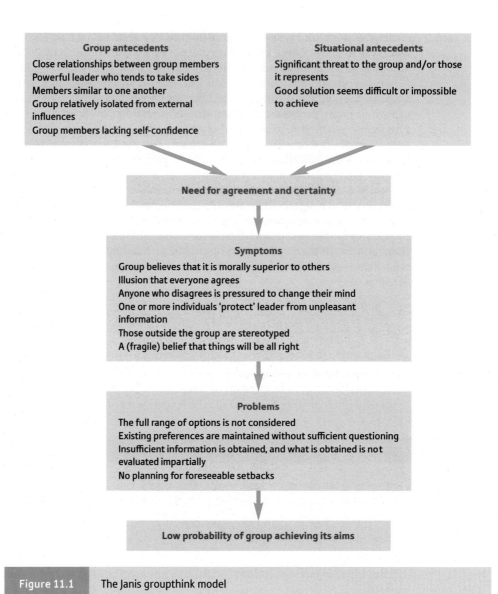

Group antecedents

Close relationships between group members
Powerful leader who tends to take sides
Members similar to one another
Group relatively isolated from external influences
Group members lacking self-confidence

Situational antecedents

Significant threat to the group and/or those it represents
Good solution seems difficult or impossible to achieve

Need for agreement and certainty

Symptoms

Group believes that it is morally superior to others
Illusion that everyone agrees
Anyone who disagrees is pressured to change their mind
One or more individuals 'protect' leader from unpleasant information
Those outside the group are stereotyped
A (fragile) belief that things will be all right

Problems

The full range of options is not considered
Existing preferences are maintained without sufficient questioning
Insufficient information is obtained, and what is obtained is not evaluated impartially
No planning for foreseeable setbacks

Low probability of group achieving its aims

| Figure 11.1 | The Janis groupthink model |

in their interventions, there is more discussion among the group and more ideas are put forward by group members (Rose, 2011).

Key learning point

It is possible for groups to use formal procedures to combat groupthink, even though these may mean that group discussion and decision-making takes more time, and may require more effort on the part of the group members.

Intuitively appealing as it is, Janis's work has not gone unchallenged. It has been argued that the groupthink syndrome is really simply a collection of separate phenomena that do not co-occur as neatly as Janis claims, and that these phenomena have already been separately investigated by other social scientists (Aldag and Fuller, 1993). Whyte (1989) argued that so-called groupthink is not itself a unitary phenomenon. Instead, it is a product of groups being inclined to accept risk when they perceive that losses are at stake, and of **group polarisation** (see below). Janis obtained much of his information and evidence for the theory from published retrospective accounts, which some argue may be inaccurate and or incomplete, especially if the outcome of the decision was known. Generally, scientists give more credence to theories developed through the rigorous testing of predictions and alternative hypotheses in a programme of carefully planned and executed research (see Chapter 2).

It is worth noting that studies which have failed to replicate groupthink have been laboratory-based studies of groups that do not have the 'history' implied by some of the antecedents listed in Figure 11.1. Park (2000) reviewed 28 tests of the groupthink model published between 1974 and 1998. Eleven of these tests were experiments using students, while most of the others were case studies of real-life events. Nine of the experiments produced partial support for the groupthink model, two produced no support and none was fully or almost fully supportive. The case studies did better: seven supported all, or nearly all, of the model, three offered partial support and three offered little or no support.

The greater support from case studies might be because the experiments were artificial situations without the historical antecedents needed for groupthink to occur. Or it could be because data from case studies are inherently more ambiguous and open to ad hoc interpretation in line with the groupthink theory. In another experiment, Park (2000) tested all the relationships between variables proposed by the groupthink model by collecting data from 64 groups of four students. Park found partial support for the groupthink model. Some of the key findings were as follows:

■ High group cohesiveness was associated with more symptoms of groupthink than low group cohesiveness.

■ Groups with members who had (on average) high self-esteem showed more symptoms of groupthink than where members had (on average) low self-esteem.

■ Group members' feelings of invulnerability and morality were associated with fewer symptoms of defective decision-making.

■ When the group discussion contained an incomplete survey of alternative solutions they tended to make poor-quality decisions.

You might find it helpful to refer back to Figure 11.1 and think about which of these findings are as Janis predicted, and which are not. For example, the groupthink model has little to say about the influence of the various individual differences, such as self-esteem, mentioned above.

Key debate

What is cohesion and is it really a bad thing?

At the heart of Janis' ideas is the potential for group cohesion to lead to negative outcomes. To many this seems counter-intuitive. Surely groups that are more tight-knit and 'together' produce better outcomes? Aldag and Fuller (1993) have pointed out that some research has found that group cohesiveness actually helps open discussion of ideas (rather than inhibiting it as Janis argued). Reviews of tests of the relationships between cohesion and performance tend to refute Janis's view of cohesion as inherently problematic. When Mullen and Copper (1994) reviewed 66 tests of the relationship between group cohesiveness and group performance, they found that cohesiveness was, on average, a significant (though not large) aid to performance, especially when groups were small. They also found that successful group performance tended to foster cohesiveness more than cohesiveness fostered performance – another finding that goes against Janis' argument that cohesion over-rides group members' concerns about performance.   ▶

▶

Some argue that researchers have confused matters by defining cohesion as a unidimensional construct when it is more accurately represented as a cluster of different, but related, components. Beal et al. (2003) looked at numerous studies of cohesion and found that measures of cohesion seemed to tap into three different things: the extent to which group members liked each other (interpersonal attraction, probably closest to Janis' original notion of cohesion); whether the task invoked individual and shared commitment to achieving shared goals (task commitment/cohesion); and whether group members liked the ethos of the group and valued being a member of it (group pride). This shows that cohesion appears to have both social and task-related elements. If we think of cohesiveness as a combination of interpersonal attraction, commitment to the task and group pride, we would reasonably expect all of these to help the group achieve its goals but also to increase when the group succeeds in its tasks. Meta-analyses tend to confirm these predictions.

Beal et al. (2003) also noticed that the effects of cohesion might have been misunderstood in previous research as group effectiveness was often measured using organisational performance outcomes. For example, it might be possible to measures changes in sales volumes after a group has devised and implemented a new sales strategy. But sales volume might depend on the quality of the product, the state of the wider economy, the location of the sales outlet and so on. Performance outcomes such as these cannot be entirely controlled by the actions of the group. Beal et al. found that when behaviours within the group were examined instead (e.g. the number of good answers or solutions produced), all the different facets of cohesion were linked to effective behaviours.

Chiocchio and Essiembre (2009) tried to understand better how the wider organisational context can influence the link between cohesion and performance. They found that the social elements of cohesion such as pride and interpersonal attraction influenced performance in many organisational contexts, something that did not seem to be found in laboratory settings (where task cohesion mattered more under the controlled conditions and with time-limited interactions, often among strangers). They suggest that cohesion tends to make a difference to performance in tasks where there is some uncertainty that provides room for discussion and debate among a diverse group of employees – but that there also needs to be enough correct and shared understanding among the group members to keep the group focused and working effectively. The links between team member attributes and performance are discussed more fully later in this chapter.

Although it has been an influential model, by no means all research into group decision-making has been designed to test the groupthink model. However, much of it has investigated phenomena similar to those identified by Janis. For example, Schulz-Hardt et al. (2002) found that groups of managers who had similar points of view even before they met, tended to seek yet more confirmatory information that supported their existing view. When there was genuine disagreement in initial points of view this led to the group carrying out a much more balanced search for information in their discussions. The presence of people instructed to be a 'devil's advocate' (i.e. to argue the opposite view of the group's preference whatever their own private opinion) also had some effect in reducing a group's preference for information that agreed with their initial opinions.

All of the criticisms of groupthink have some force. Nevertheless, Janis provided rich case studies which illustrate the many potential problems in group decision-making. There is now lots of well-designed research that dispels any comforting belief we might have that really important group decisions are always made rationally.

For example, Hodgkinson et al. (1999) demonstrated the tendency for people to be *risk-averse* when potential gains are highlighted, but *risk-seeking* when potential losses are highlighted (this is the so-called **framing bias**). In two experiments Hodgkinson and colleagues asked students and bank managers to consider what they would do about a business strategy decision, where the same possible profits were described in one of two ways: either in terms of cash (highlighting the positive) or relative to a target (highlighting the negative). Negative framing led people to favour decisions that had a *low probability of a big profit and a high probability of no profit* over decisions that had a *high probability of moderate profit and a low probability of no profit*. However, this tendency was virtually eliminated if people were asked to draw a diagram representing their thinking about factors relevant to the decision (causal mapping) before making it. This leads to the optimistic conclusion that by engaging in careful thought processes we can overcome more instinctive biases in our reasoning.

There is no particular reason to believe that groups of top managers responsible for strategic decisions will behave differently from other well-researched groups. This is reinforced by Forbes and Milliken's (1999) theoretical analysis of the behaviour of company boards of directors. They make a number of propositions that are very consistent with more general theorising about groups and teams, particularly concerning the impacts of team cohesiveness and diversity. For example, they suggest that board members feeling a sense of cohesiveness is a good thing up to a point, but that too much cohesiveness impairs decision-making. This is a similar prediction to that made by Janis in his groupthink model. Also, Forbes and Milliken predict that cognitive conflict (i.e. disagreements about the best solutions to problems) will increase the board's effectiveness, but reduce its cohesiveness.

Key learning point

Analyses of strategic decisions in organisations support the findings and perspectives of other less 'high-powered' research on groups and teams.

Exercise 11.1　　Group decision-making

Try to recall a time when you participated in a group that had to make a decision (for example, to choose between alternative courses of action). Bring to mind as much as you can about what happened, and then consider the following questions. If you can do so with someone else who was there, so much the better.

Suggested exercises

1　How cohesive was the group in terms of interpersonal attraction, group pride and task commitment? What consequences do you think these factors had for (i) the way the group went about its task and (ii) how you felt about participating?

2　If there was a leader of the group, to what extent were they admired and trusted by the other members? What was the impact of this on how the group conducted itself?

3　To what extent were alternative options carefully considered? Think about why.

4　Was the eventual decision actually implemented? Why (or why not)? Did the decision work out well, and if not, was that due to a poor decision being made by the group or the impact of external factors outside of the group's control?

5　Consider how well (or not) your observations match the theory and research discussed in this chapter so far.

Now consider the following hypothetical scenario:
Rudi Lerner was managing director of a medium-size soft drinks company. His father had founded and then managed the business for nearly 30 years before handing over to his son four years ago. Rudi felt he knew much more about the business than his colleagues on the top management team.

▶

▶

They agreed about that, and they liked and respected their boss as well as each other. They usually went out of their way to avoid contradicting him. On the rare occasions they did so, they received a friendly but firm reminder from the chairman that he had been in the business much longer than they had. That was true, but the team membership had not changed for five years now, so nobody was exactly ignorant. However, it was hard to argue – after all, the company had been successful relative to its competitors over the years. Rudi attributed this to frequent takeovers of competitors by people from outside the business. He rarely commissioned market research, relying instead on his 'gut feeling' and extensive prior experience. Now a new challenge faced the company: should it go into the low-calorie 'diet' drinks market, and if so, with what products? The demand for diet drinks was recent but might be here to stay.

Suggested exercise

How likely is it that Rudi and the rest of the management team will make a good decision about entering the 'diet' market? Explain your answer.

Key learning point

The groupthink model appears not to be entirely accurate, but it includes many ideas that have had a big impact on subsequent research on groups and teams.

Group polarisation

Research shows that groups tend to make more extreme decisions than we might expect given the initial preferences of group members (Bettenhausen, 1991). This is known as polarisation. This has most often been demonstrated with respect to risk. If the initial tendency of the majority of group members is to adopt a moderately risky decision, the eventual group decision is usually more risky than that. Conversely, somewhat cautious initial preferences of group members translate to even more cautious eventual group decisions.

Using systematic research, psychologists have reduced eleven possible explanations for group polarisation down to two (Isenberg, 1986). The *social comparison* explanation is that we like to present ourselves in a socially desirable way, so we try to be like other group members, *only more so*. The *persuasive argumentation* explanation is that information consistent with the views held by the majority will dominate the group discussion, and (so long as that information is correct and novel) have powerful persuasive effects. Both explanations are valid, though the latter seems to exert a stronger effect. Polarisation is not in itself inherently good or bad. In order to benefit from group decision-making, group members need to ensure that they share all relevant information and ideas. This means that all arguments rejecting the initially favoured point of view are heard. Group members also need to avoid social conformity. Chen et al. (2002) have shown that using a structured quantitative decision aid (e.g. a questionnaire) can reduce the impact of overly biased persuasive arguments on group members, albeit only slightly. It might also be that polarisation can be reduced by asking group members to engage in a bit of 'role-play' by making an effort to articulate the viewpoint of someone holding an opposing view while in their presence (Tuller et al., 2015).

Minority influence

Research has shown that minorities within groups only rarely convert the majority to their point of view. But how can they maximise their chances? Many people say that they should first gain the acceptance of the majority by conforming wherever possible, and *then* stick out for their own point of view on a carefully chosen crucial issue. However, research carried out by Moscovici and colleagues suggests otherwise (Moscovici and Mugny, 1983; Moscovici, 1985). They found that, if it is to exert influence, a minority needs to *disagree* consistently with the majority, including on issues other than the one that is of particular importance to the minority group. They demonstrated that minorities do not exert influence by being liked or being seen as reasonable, but by being perceived as consistent, independent and confident. Consistent with this, van Hiel and Mervielde (2001) found that group members believe that being *assertive and consistent is an effective strategy for minorities*, while being *agreeable is a better strategy for majority groups* than it is for minorities. If we think back to the previous section concerning group polarisation, we see that a minority can effectively limit the extent of group polarisation by expressing many arguments that oppose the majority point of view.

Much debate has centred on why and how minorities in groups exert influence (e.g. Nemeth, 1986; 2010; Smith et al., 1996; McLeod et al., 1997). Originally, it was thought that minorities needed to exert their influence through the use of persuasion. Now, the predominant view is that minorities and majorities exert influence in different ways. Nemeth (1986, 2010) suggested that majorities encourage convergent, shallow and narrow thinking. Consistent exposure to minority viewpoints stimulates deeper and wider consideration of alternative perspectives, or divergent thinking. Nemeth (2010: abstract) concluded that:

> Dissent, as has been repeatedly documented, 'opens' the mind. People search for information, consider more options and, on balance, make better decisions and are more creative. Dissenters, rather than rogues or obstacles, provide value: They liberate people to say what they believe and they stimulate divergent and creative thought even when they are wrong. The implications for group decision making, whether in juries or companies, have been considerable and there is increasing interest in research and in practice for the value of authentic dissent in teams and in creating 'cultures' of innovation.

This emphasises again that in order to reach good-quality decisions, groups need to encourage different points of view, not suppress them.

Wood et al. (1994) reviewed 143 studies of minority influence, and found that minorities do indeed have some capacity to change the opinions of people who hear their message.

This effect is even stronger if recipients of the message are not required to publicly acknowledge their change of opinion to the minority. Opinion change is also much greater on issues indirectly related to the message than it is on those directly related to it. These findings indicate that minority influences are significant and can often be subtle and not immediately obvious. Indeed, although the opinion of the majority usually has more effect than that of the minority, the minority exert greater influence on issues only indirectly related to the core message or viewpoint being conveyed by the minority. Ng and Van Dyne (2001) have found in an experimental study with students, that cultural issues also play a role. Group members who (i) value collectivist beliefs (i.e. act according to social norms that emphasise interpersonal harmony) and (ii) do *not* value individualist beliefs (i.e. *do not* focus on personal goals and perspectives) are less influenced than others by minority views. This means that they tend to be more influenced by the majority (or the collective viewpoint), something that according to Nemeth (2010) would hinder their decision-making. Ng and Van Dyne also found that the role in the group of the person holding the minority view makes a difference: when a one-person minority happens to be the leader of the group, they have more influence than when the one-person minority is not the leader.

One feature of work groups that might make a difference to the ways minority viewpoints are expressed is that its members might be motivated to hold back on sharing their views because they do not wish to damage their future working relationships with others. By manipulating the *expectation of future interaction* (EFI) with other group members, San Martin et al. (2015) found that minority groups were less likely to express dissenting views when there was a strong EFI. However, this effect was somewhat offset by strong EFI causing those with majority views to be more open to considering divergent minority viewpoints: it seems that majority groups are aware of the long-term value of harvesting minority viewpoints.

Point of integration

Minority viewpoints can significantly enhance decision-making processes but these can be suppressed by a number of factors. This suggests that organisations need to create a culture where minority views are aired. Features of organisational culture that can suppress or encourage the open exchange of views are discussed in Chapter 14.

Exercise 11.2   To expand or not to expand?

The management team of the Fastsave retail chain store company had a decision to make. Should they build a new store in Danesville, a medium-sized town in which the company owned a suitable patch of land? Fastsave was doing quite well, and had more than enough financial resources to make the necessary investment in a town that did not currently have a major supermarket. On the other hand, there were two existing large superstores within 25 kilometres. It was agreed that there was no significant danger of substantial losses: the question was more whether the time and effort involved in expansion would be worth the return.

The management team consisted of the general manager (GM), finance manager (FM), marketing manager (MM), operations manager (OM), personnel manager (PM) and company secretary (CS). Each member of the team had been supplied with reports on the demographic make-up of the town, a market research survey, detailed costings of building the store and the likely attitude of the local council planning authority.

Group members were accustomed to working together and there was rivalry (at present friendly) among them about which of them, if any, would succeed the GM when she retired in about three years. At the outset of the meeting, the GM made it clear that she would act as an impartial chairperson, and not reveal her own opinions until the end. In the past, however, she had usually been cautious about business expansions. The following extract is representative of the group's deliberations:

FM: I suspect the time is not right. We are currently upgrading six other stores, and to start a completely new one would run the risk of spreading our resources too thin. In purely financial terms we can do it, but would we do a good job?

OM: Yes, we've certainly got our hands full at present. In fact, I would be in favour of reviewing two of our already-planned store upgradings because I'm not sure they are really worth it either. Generally we're doing all right as we are – let's consolidate our position.

MM: I can't believe I'm hearing this! According to our market research report, the population of Danesville wants its own big supermarket, and what's more the 45+ age group particularly likes our emphasis on low price rather than super deluxe quality.

CS: Come on, as usual you're taking an approach which could possibly pay off but could land us in trouble…

MM: Like what?

CS: Well, there has been a lot of housing development in Danesville, and the local council is under pressure to preserve what it sees as the charm of the town. It would be very bad public relations to be perceived as undermining that. And having a planning application refused wouldn't be much better.

FM: That's right, and being seen as an intruder would probably reduce sales too.

PM: I can't comment on that last point, but as a general principle we should not stand still. Our competitors might overtake us. If resources are spread too thin, we can recruit more staff: we have the money, and experience suggests that the labour force in the region has the necessary skills.

FM: You've had a rush of blood to the head, haven't you? You're normally telling us how difficult it is to manage expansion of staff numbers. I must say I share the concern about a couple of our existing upgrading plans, let alone building an entirely new store. Do those stores really need refitting yet? They are doing all right.

CS: I notice that Danesville has an increasingly young, mobile population these days. In spite of the market research report, will they really be interested in a local store, especially with our position in the market?

MM: They can be made to be. Anyway, who says that a Danesville store should not go slightly more upmarket? Tesco seem to manage to have both upmarket and downmarket stores.

OM: Well yes, but I don't think we are big enough to be that versatile …

Suggested exercises

1. Examine this case study from the following perspectives:

    a. the likely attitude to risk;
    b. group polarisation;
    c. minority influence.

2. Given this examination, what do you think the group is likely to decide? What is your evaluation of that decision?

At this point in the chapter, think about how much the material you have read so far tells us about decision-making among groups of employees. Having read the sections on groupthink, polarisation and minority influence, how well can we explain decision-making in work groups using this body of knowledge? What are the issues that this literature has tackled successfully? What issues have been tackled? Also, consider the key question: under what circumstances do groups tend to make better decisions than individuals making decisions on their own?

Relations between groups

So far we have examined what goes on within groups that are attempting to generate ideas and/or solve problems. Another important perspective is what happens *between* groups. Most workplaces are composed of a large number of overlapping groups – for example different departments, committees, occupations, locations, project teams or hierarchical levels. Work organisations need groups to cooperate and relate well to each other, both for organisational effectiveness and for the well-being of people within them.

It is widely thought that our need for a clear and positive personal identity leads us, on occasions, to define ourselves in terms of our group membership(s): we evaluate those groups we are in positively (and more positively than other groups that we are not in). So in effect we use the groups we belong to, to give ourselves a positive sense of who we are. These are the fundamental ideas behind social identity theory (Tajfel and Turner, 1979) and self-categorisation theory (Turner, 1999).

A review of the inter-group literature by Hewstone et al. (2002) makes the following points:

- Usually, we tend to favour the group(s) we belong to (termed the 'in-group') more than we disparage out-groups, and this often happens without us even realising it.

- Successful inter-group bias enhances self-esteem, as predicted by social identity theory. When people's self-esteem is low or threatened, they might be even keener to evaluate their in-group positively. However, there is much less evidence for this.

- Groups of high status and numerical superiority tend to show more in-group bias than those of low status and low membership numbers. Such dominant groups may show generosity to out-group members when they see the status gap as being very wide. Low-status groups show high in-group bias when they have a chance of closing the gap and/or see their low status as unfair.

- Various methods have been tried to reduce in-group bias, on the assumption that this will improve relations between different groups. These include teaching people to suppress their biases; inducing them to behave positively towards out-groups so that they infer from their own behaviour that they must have a positive attitude; increasing people's knowledge about out-group members (so that they are seen as individuals more than group members); finding superordinate groups (for example, defining a group as everyone in the company) which allow people to recategorise from out-group members to in-group members.

- In some situations, and some cultures, people tend to define themselves in terms of their group memberships. In others they do so more in terms of their characteristics as an individual (Ellemers et al., 2002). So the nature and extent of in-group bias may change almost minute by minute.

Relations between groups at work are affected, often negatively, by group members' wishes to see themselves in a more positive light than members of other groups. This is a major challenge for organisations who wish to reap maximum benefits from having a diverse workforce.

An issue closely related to group membership concerns stereotypes. These are generalised beliefs about the characteristics, attributes and behaviours of members of certain groups (Hilton and Von Hippel, 1996: 240). Groups can be defined on any number of criteria. Obvious possibilities are race, sex, gender, occupation and age, but research suggests that most people do not have broad stereotypes (e.g. of all women, or all men, or all old people). Stereotypes tend to be based on rather more specific groups such as old men or old white women (Stangor et al., 1992). Some stereotypes held by a person refer to quite specific groups, as in the following hypothetical examples:

- 'Employee representatives are usually people who express the most extreme and militant views.'
- 'Most nurses are caring and conscientious.'
- 'Managers in this company never tell the truth.'
- 'Accountants are always more stimulating to talk to than anybody else in the company.'
- 'Production managers usually speak their mind.'

Clearly, then, stereotypes vary in their favourability. They also differ in their extremity. The third and fourth above do not allow for any exceptions, but the others do because they refer to 'most' rather than 'all'. Often stereotypes have some validity, in the sense that *on average* members of one group differ from members of another group. On average, senior managers may do better on some tests of cognitive ability than building site labourers. But there is equally certainly a large overlap – some building site labourers are more intelligent than some senior managers. In fact, one of the problems with stereotypes is that they lead to the overestimation of the differences between groups (Krueger, 1991). Persuasive arguments are put forward that stereotyping plays a significant role in the under-representation of females and ethnic minority groups in senior roles within organisations and in the pay disparities between different demographic groups (Kray and Shirako, 2011).

Stereotypes share some of the characteristics of attitudes (Chapter 6). They resemble attitudes towards groups of people that could be defined by some of their shared characteristics. They can be linked to the behaviour of both those being stereotyped and those who hold the stereotypical views.

Stereotypes of groups can develop from very limited information about them – perhaps confined to what we see on television. For example, our stereotypes about police officers may be heavily influenced by the latest television crime drama. Other stereotypes can arise when a generalisation is true of a very few people in one group and practically none in another group. Suppose for a moment that 1 in 500 trade union officials are members of revolutionary left-wing political groups, compared with 1 in 3000 of the general population. Would you then expect that a trade union official you were about to meet for the first time would be a revolutionary left-winger? Clearly not, as the chances of this are very small. While it is more probable that they hold such views than someone who is not a trade union official, it is still not very likely. In this example, it would be inaccurate then to define trade union officials by their membership of such political groups. Kray and Shirako (2011) in their review of the literature highlight many potential negative effects of stereotypical views in organisations. Those stereotyped might feel threatened by the views of others and this can result in, among other things, individual disengagement from work tasks in which their behaviour might confirm the stereotypical assumptions of others, the lowering of aspirations and a reluctance to seek and trust feedback on performance.

Some of the causes and consequences of stereotypes are shown in Figure 11.2. Devine (1989) argues that we cannot avoid starting out with stereotypes. As you can see, in several ways stereotypes help us to use up fewer cognitive resources when thinking about others (e.g. by not having to think so much about the differences between each person in the group as individuals and by helping us to make predictions about how others might behave). The difference between prejudiced and non-prejudiced individuals is that the latter *deliberately inhibit the automatically activated* stereotype and replace it with more open-minded thoughts (Devine, 1989: 15):

> [This] can be likened to the breaking of a bad habit … The individual must (a) initially decide to stop the old behaviour; (b) remember the resolution, and (c) try repeatedly and decide repeatedly to eliminate the habit before the habit can be eliminated.

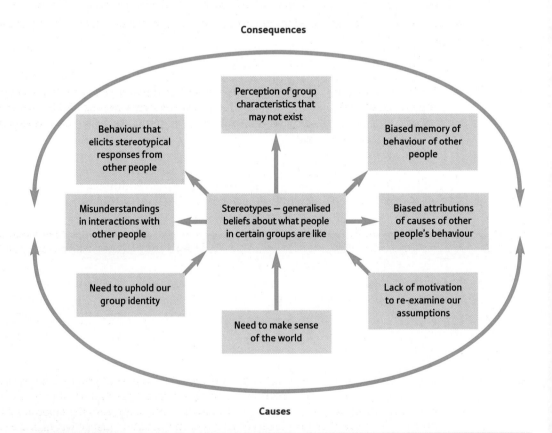

| Figure 11.2 | Some causes and consequences of stereotypes |

Other work has shown that simply instructing people to try to suppress stereotypic thoughts can actually be counterproductive. Ironically, this type of instruction itself leads people to be more conscious of the stereotype they are trying to suppress (Bodenhausen and Macrae, 1996). As Devine implied, what matters seems to be a personal commitment to changing one's perception or behaviour. Often this will involve changing one's assumptions about why a particular person is the kind of person they are – for example, by thinking about whether someone has a powerful position in an organisation because of their talent, drive and determination, rather than because they have been lucky.

Kray and Shirako (2011) suggest that the causes of stereotypes can also be tackled through organisational-level interventions. These include: emphasising the value of positive stereotypes (e.g. if women are stereotyped as more empathic than men, the benefits of high levels of empathy could be highlighted); focusing on the value of employee characteristics such as career aspirations and educational qualifications that over-ride more superficial characteristics often associated with stereotypes; providing equal access to training and development opportunities so that those individuals who are stereotyped develop greater self-efficacy; and valuing traits such as hard work and perseverance that are not associated with a worker's social identity (rather than gender, for example, something closely linked to social identities).

Key learning point

Stereotypes are generalised beliefs about what people in particular groups are like. They are often inaccurate, and we sometimes use them to devalue those that we perceive as being not in our own group.

There is no doubt that these theories from social psychology can help us better understand inter-group biases in the workplace. However, what goes on within groups (i.e. intra-group variables) also plays an important role in determining behaviour. As Hewstone et al. (2002: 594) acknowledge:

> It would be a mistake, however, to consider ethnic and religious mass murder as a simple extension of intergroup bias ... Real-world intergroup relations owe at least as much of their character to intra-group variables such as self-esteem, in-group identification ... and group threat.

In the following sections we will begin to focus less on research on groups and more on the research carried out within workplaces that has helped us to better understand teams in the context of functioning organisations.

Work teams

The team/group distinction

Much of the previous section focused on the effectiveness of groups, mainly focusing on how they make decisions. In order to isolate important psychological processes this often involves taking the group task out of the work context and into the laboratory setting. In this section we look at how teams function from a broader perspective, taking a closer look at the impact of the organisational context on teams.

Teamwork processes and their outcomes are examined in relation to numerous topics in work psychology. Research on leadership (Chapter 12) has a lot to say about how to manage teams, as do the sections in Chapter 15 that deal with dispersed working and how teams function when team members never meet or are based in different locations.

The words team and group are often used interchangeably and in some cases this distinction is unimportant, but for organisational research purposes it is important to define the things being studied and teams are no exception.

A *workgroup* is characterised by being made up of individuals who:

■ see themselves and are seen by others as a social entity, or unit;

■ are interdependent, i.e. they rely on each other because of the tasks they perform;

■ are embedded in one or more larger social systems (such as the organisation they work in);

■ perform tasks that affect others such as co-workers or customers (Guzzo and Dickson, 1996: 308).

Teams are different in the extent to which (i) members are interdependent (in teams levels of interdependency are very high) and (ii) the team as a whole (rather than the individuals in it) has performance goals (Sundstrom et al., 1990). As Mohrman et al. (1995: 39) have put it, a team is 'a group of individuals who work together to produce products or deliver services for which they are mutually accountable'. Hackman (2002) suggested that true teams are characterised by four essential features. You could think of these as the active ingredients of teamwork:

1 *Interdependence*: Team members are dependent upon each other to get things done, and the team members are not simply acting under the direction of a supervisor.

2 *Membership boundaries*: Team members know who is part of the team.

3 *Authority*: A defined and bounded authority so that the team can manage what it does without excessive interference from, or reference to, others outside of the team. Teams are often defined according to their degree of decision-making authority (e.g. self-managing teams, semi-autonomous work groups). The terms autonomy and empowerment often also used to describe this feature of teams.

4 *Stability*: A relatively stable membership for the lifetime of the team.

So, compared to a group, the composition of a team is relatively stable and the people within it depend upon each other to achieve shared goals with the authority to act within defined boundaries. As an aside, it is the level and scope of autonomy that is often used to determine whether employees are working in a 'real team' rather than a 'psuedo team' as mentioned in the opening case study. This is in contrast to assemblies of individuals (groups) where individuals rather than teams have work goals and there is much less close cooperation and interdependence and lower autonomy to make decisions that impact on team functioning and the outcomes for the team overall. An example of a group would be all of the students studying the same course, attending the same lectures. An example of a team would be hospital employees (e.g. surgeons, anaesthetists, nurses) working together on a regular basis in an operating theatre environment.

The prevalence of teamwork

Morita (2001) suggested that increased interest in teamworking in organisations has two distinct origins. The first grew out of concern for the quality of working life in Europe (especially during the 1960s and 1970s). Teamworking was thought to provide people with more satisfying work than either working alone or in a group. The second origin was an interest in the perceived advantages of Japanese management styles, with their emphasis on multifunctional employees, loyalty to the collective and collective responsibility for the quality and quantity of work (all features of work that are important in teams). We can supplement these origins with an increased interest in the characteristics of the high-performance workplace (HPWP). Teamwork is one of several practices usually associated with the HPWP (also known as the high-commitment workplace because work practices aim to instil high levels of employee commitment). High-performance practices are implemented in an attempt to get stronger levels of employee engagement and involvement in the way that work is designed as a way of reaching higher than average levels of performance. Alongside teamwork, HPWP practices include extensive training and development, multiskilling for flexibility and performance-related pay.

Key learning point

Teamwork has become an important and quite widespread way of organising employees.

So, if it is a good idea, how widespread is teamwork? The answer depends, of course, on how teamworking is defined, who is asked about it and exactly how the question is asked. Once they have established that people work together on tasks, most researchers have focused on the extent to which workers carry out collective tasks with a significant degree of autonomy. Of course, autonomy can take many forms and not all of them need to be exercised by workers in order for them to be considered a team. Benders et al. (2001) asked senior managers in nearly 6000 organisations in ten European countries to describe the extent to which people in the largest occupational group in their workplace worked in *teams which had the authority to make their own decisions in each of the following eight areas*:

1   allocation of work;

2   scheduling of work;

3   quality of work;

4   timekeeping;

5   attendance and absence control;

6   job rotation;

7   coordination of work with other internal groups;

8   improving work processes.

Benders et al. decided that, in order to qualify as a 'group-based workplace' (somewhat confusingly), this means lots of employees working in teams:

■   at least four of the eight decision areas should be assigned to teams; and

■   at least 70 per cent of core employees should work in such groups (i.e. teams).

When the research was carried out only 217 workplaces (about 4 per cent of the total) met both criteria. In fact, only 1404 (24 per cent) of the workplaces assigned *any* of the eight decision areas to teams. Significant differences between nations emerged with Sweden and the Netherlands at the top (the UK was fourth) and Spain and Portugal at the bottom. This paints a somewhat gloomy picture of the extent of teamwork in many countries.

A more recent survey carried out in 2010, the *Fifth European Working Conditions Survey* (Fifth EWCS: Eurofound, 2012) used a different method. Interviews were conducted across 34 countries with 44,000 workers of all types (not just managers). Given the potential benefits of teamwork discussed later in this chapter, it paints a somewhat more optimistic picture, at least in some countries. Compared to Benders et al., the survey used a slightly different and simpler way of identifying teamwork. First employees were asked if they were engaged in at least some collective tasks. Then the questions focused on three characteristics of those collective tasks. These were:

1   Autonomy to divide up tasks between group members.

2   Having the freedom to decide who was head of the team.

3   Autonomy over the timetabling of work activities.

If one or two of these features was present, employees were categorised as working in a team with moderate autonomy (no features = team without autonomy; one feature = low autonomy; three features = much autonomy, perhaps getting close to self-managing or autonomous work teams). If employees did not indicate that they worked on collective tasks then a finding of 'no teamwork' was recorded. Figure 11.3 displays the key findings.

Key learning point

Most European workplaces appear not to be predominantly organised in teams, but there is wide variation in this respect between countries.

The position of northern European countries (Sweden, Norway, Finland and Ireland) is perhaps unsurprising given the prevailing national cultures (see Chapter 14). For example Sweden has a tradition of participative democracy, sociotechnical work design (see Chapter 7) and high-profile examples demonstrating the success of teamworking (e.g. Volvo). The low incidence of teamwork and high incidence of teams with low autonomy reported in many southern European countries is consistent with evidence that these cultures tend to emphasise status and hierarchy. It is also interesting to note that only 11 per cent of all those surveyed reported that they worked in teams with much autonomy. Even in countries where teamwork was widespread this figure did not exceed 22 per cent. Of course, these findings may not just be due to culture but also the nature of the work that people do. The Fifth EWCS (Eurofound, 2012) showed that those working in the transport and retail sectors were least likely to report teamwork as these are sectors where there are many roles that require people to work alone (e.g. taxi driver, lorry driver, warehouse operative). In contrast it was only one in five of those working in healthcare who reported not working in a team: perhaps this goes some way to explaining why there is such a large amount of teamwork research that is carried out in healthcare settings.

Point of integration

Autonomy and control have been shown to be features of work that can have a significant impact on employee well-being and feature as key concepts in many theories of work-related well-being (see Chapter 10). The high levels of autonomy present in 'real teams' has been frequently cited as the main reason why those working in such teams often report high levels of satisfaction and well-being.

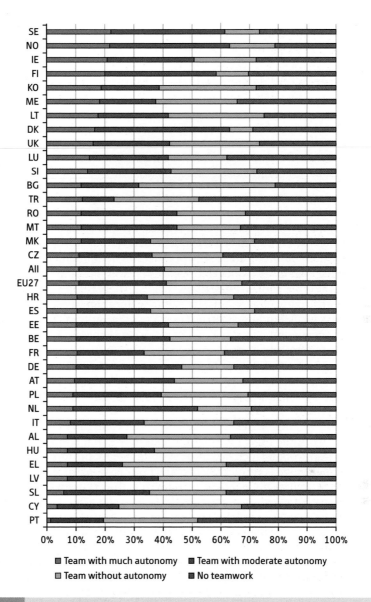

Figure 11.3   Percentage of employees in teamwork by degree of autonomy of the teams, in the EU27 and in other European countries
Source: http://oshwiki.eu/wiki/Work_teams_and_psychosocial_risks_and_work_stress#cite_ref-fifth_9–1

We have to go back to Benders et al.'s study to find out a bit more detail regarding which decisions teams made for themselves. From a senior manager perspective, improving work processes and scheduling were the most common, and job rotation, attendance and absence control the least common. 'Headline' figures from studies of teamwork in the USA are hard to obtain, but some suggest the prevalence of teamwork might be slightly higher there than in Europe (e.g. Gittleman et al., 1998; 32 per cent of workplaces using teamwork). On closer inspection it appears that this is partly because of differences in sampling methods and the way that questions were asked. If anything, teamwork seems to be more prevalent in Europe than in the USA. This is supported by more recent work (Blasi and Kruse, 2006: 572) which found that the level of adoption of self-managing teams in the 1990s was 'rather modest'.

Key learning point

In spite of a lot of enthusiasm for teamwork, true teamwork seems to be more the exception than the rule.

Perhaps the stringent criteria used to identify teams underestimates the extent of organisations' efforts to implement teamworking. The Workplace Employment Relations Survey (WERS, carried out in 2004 and 2011; see van Wanrooy et al., 2014) is a very large survey of tens of thousands of UK employees in various workplaces. It shows that teamwork is the most common of the HPWP practices to be implemented (Kersley et al., 2005). Around three-quarters of managers in UK workplaces report that at least some of their core employees 'work in formally designated teams'. There is some evidence in these surveys that teamwork is more common in the public sector than in private-sector workplaces. The various surveys also show that senior managers appear to retain a high level of control over team leader appointments, but that many other elements of teamwork are more readily devolved to the team members.

One conclusion from these surveys is that managers report high levels of teamwork if left to define teamwork for themselves: the extent of *real or true teamwork* seems considerably less when employees are asked about the level of autonomy their work group possesses. Scarbrough and Kinnie (2003) advise against the use of any stringent objective definition of teamworking because the many different configurations of teamworking reflect the different work and organisational contexts in which it is attempted. Influences upon the extent of teamworking include, but are not limited to, the industrial relations context, methods of management control, the size of the organisation, the production technologies used and the extent to which they allow teamworking, the imperative for change to teamworking and the focus on teamwork in the supply chain. Given that all organisations need to exert control over employees to some extent, teamwork can be seen as a way of getting employees to control themselves while they continue to work within a framework set out by management.

What happens in work teams?

The input–process–output model

The classic starting point for looking at team functioning is the input–process–output (I–P–O) model (McGrath, 1964). This recognises that for a given team, in a particular context, there are characteristics which can be seen as inputs that influence how the team performs (processes) and thus the final outputs. Inputs include team size, team-member diversity, structure and whether there are individual or group rewards for hitting targets. Other important input variables include the nature of the task(s) to be completed (e.g. physical or intellectual tasks, or both) and the organisational context the team is embedded in. These variables set the agenda for much of the research into the factors that are linked to work team effectiveness.

The interactions among the various inputs influence team processes. These include how cohesive team members feel, how well they communicate with each other and with stakeholders outside the team, how well they make decisions and how effectively team leadership occurs. Communication is influenced by the spontaneity and openness present at team meetings and may be enhanced if facilitating roles are shared rather than confined to a designated leader. While team leaders are usually appointed by the organisation, this does not prevent other team members from taking leadership roles – perhaps when their specialist knowledge or personal skills can be leveraged. Another key process is decision-making (discussed earlier in this chapter) which requires the team to focus on a problem or task and deconstruct the problem/task into its components for analysis.

Naturally, outputs vary depending upon what the team exists to do. A management team could be focusing on objective, measurable targets such as income growth or cost reduction. It may also focus on introducing changes to systems or improving the efficiency of processes. Product development or customer service teams will have more clearly defined targets (e.g. to reduce the number of customer complaints filed against members of the team). Beal et al. (2003) argue that this focus on outputs may have resulted in a criterion problem in research into group effectiveness: many of these outcomes are subject to a number of influences outside of the processes enacted by the team.

Key learning point

A simple model of how teams function is:

Inputs → Processes → Outputs

However, the I–P–O model falls short of fully describing the complex nature of teams when they are embedded in organisational settings. It also says little about the way that teams change and evolve over time. Criticisms of the I–P–O model (Ilgen et al., 2005) are as follows:

- Many factors that influence the conversion of inputs to outputs are not processes but 'emergent cognitive or affective states' (Ilgen et al., 2005: 520), i.e. how the team members think or feel about the problem is important, and not just the mechanics of what the team does.

- The I–P–O model implies linear paths throughout, even though there are many feedback loops present. For instance, analysis of performance outputs after some intervention is an input to subsequent team processes and cognitive states and hence an input to performance in the future.

- Relationships between the main effects in the model (e.g. the effect of team size on cohesion) are not linear as there are complex interactions between inputs and process. For example, changes in the size of the team may have an impact on team cohesiveness and small changes in team size may result in large increases in team diversity. There may also be interactions between different processes, if, say, the appointment, or emergence, of a new team leader could influence the openness of team meetings.

Beyond the I–P–O model

Kozlowski and Ilgen (2006) point out that the I–P–O model was not offered as a causal model but as a way of organising the research literature that had looked at different aspects of teams. It has, however, come to be seen as a useful working model. Ilgen and colleagues go beyond the I–P–O model by proposing an 'input-mediator-output-input' (IMOI) model. Processes have been replaced by mediators to capture a wider range of variables than processes alone: mediators encompass a whole range of factors within and outside of the team that influence what the team does and the results of its efforts. The addition of 'input' to the end of the model captures the influence of feedback loops. Most teams will know how they are performing and use these data to adjust their approach in the future. This sets up on-going cycles that can be represented as IMOIMOIMOI ... and so on.

Removal of the hyphens in IMOI is more than just a stylistic change: it deliberately signifies that causal paths are more likely to be non-linear than linear. This approach might better reflect the dynamic nature of teams. Cronin et al. (2011) argue that, among other things, any successful attempt to develop an understanding of team processes and outcomes needs to take into account changes in team composition, that people may leave or join at any time (and indeed may be involved in multiple teams), that relationships between team members may change over time and that outcomes may be different for different team members. This is in sharp contrast to the features of some of the very tightly controlled settings outlined at the start of this chapter that psychologists used to study group processes.

Ilgen et al. (2005) propose three main stages in team functioning. The early stages of team development they called *forming*, and are described by inputs and mediators (IM). The next stage they called *functioning* which captures mediators and outputs (MO). This is followed by a *finishing* stage which captures outputs and inputs (OI). These stages are summarised below.

Forming

Forming requires three activities: *trusting*, *planning* and *structuring*. Trusting is about team members, collectively, believing they have the wherewithal to be effective. It also requires that team members trust each other's intentions and motives: we can all think of how we guard ourselves in the presence of people that we do not trust, particularly when they have some power over us. Guarded contributions tend to impede team performance and so a climate of psychological safety is needed.

Planning involves gathering and using information. Communication needs to be open and information needs to be shared freely (and not only when people feel under pressure to do so). With information gathered the next step is to turn it into a strategy. This calls for goals to be articulated and shared.

Structuring represents the shared mental models held by team members. The concept of mental models has helped to advance team research: they describe how people see the inter-relationships that exist and who is responsible for particular outcomes. Where the mental models of team members are different, then teamwork will be compromised by differing views about how the task should be achieved (and there may be some differences about what the task actually is). Where mental models are similar then coordination is more efficient. Structuring also involves setting up a 'transactive memory': during this team members need to become aware of what is known within the team and of who knows what.

Functioning

Functioning involves *bonding, adapting* and *learning*. Bonding extends beyond trusting each other to reflect a genuine desire among team members to work together. It reflects concepts which have already been mentioned in this chapter including cohesion, commitment and social support. The extent of bonding can be influenced by the diversity within the team. However, the basis of the diversity matters; personality diversity may be counterproductive if, for example, members differ widely on agreeableness (i.e. there are some people who really like a good argument, and others who will do anything they can to avoid one!). The ability to manage conflict is therefore an important aspect of team bonding.

Adapting covers two distinct concepts; the ability of those in a team to recognise when conditions change from being routine to being novel (and to respond when they do) and the ability to share workload among the team through mutually supporting behaviour.

Learning relates to changes in the body of knowledge that a team draws upon. One aspect of this is learning from minority and/or dissenting team members (see also Minority influence). A minority in this context means people having minority views ('the lone voices'). At extremes, views that do not fit with the dominant paradigm can be suppressed to the point that the person holding them is isolated and treated as if they do not understand how complex the problem is (see also Groupthink above). However, teams need to hear minority opinions as they can challenge comfortable thinking. Likewise, teams need to learn from the 'best' member in the team. This is not necessarily the same person all the time, but as the team's needs change so may the most knowledgeable person on a particular topic.

Finishing

This phase of decline and winding-up of a team is not well understood and we currently know very little about what happens in the end game.

Key learning point

In reality, there are many feedback loops operating in teams. The complexity of interactions between inputs, processes, cognitive states and outputs is very difficult to model and test.

Factors associated with effective teamwork

The I–P–O and IMOI models describe how teams tackle tasks. They are descriptive and provide good insight into some of the variables that could impact on team effectiveness. They do not provide a detailed explanation of what effective teams do differently when compared to ineffective teams. The phrase 'we need good teamwork' is so often heard in organisations that it is important we understand what good and bad teamwork are and how to identify them.

Unfortunately, there are some rather pessimistic views about the extent to which theories have allowed us to understand the very dynamic and complex processes that influence team outcomes. Cronin et al. (2011) argue that the effects of many influential factors are poorly understood because research often fails to consider the evolution over time of team members' attitudes and beliefs, team roles and trust. The influence of contextual forces (such as the resources allocated to the team by senior managers, or the degree of competition between teams) may also vary over time, especially in groups that develop the capacity to influence their context (e.g. by obtaining new resources to help them complete tasks). This has important implications for practice since the determinants of team effectiveness might be different across time and organisational contexts.

However, all is not lost. We might get some insight into the key ingredients of effective teamwork through three different methods that are discussed over the next few pages:

1   By asking team members to describe various features of their teams and then testing whether their evaluations of these features correlate with measures of team performance.

2   By looking at what goes on in successful and unsuccessful teams to find out what differentiates the two.

3   Looking at lots of studies of teamwork to identify the average effects of different features of teams on team performance outcomes (a meta-analysis of team climate is presented as an example).

These methods do not give us much of an insight into the dynamic processes mentioned by Cronin and colleagues, but they do draw upon the expertise and experiences of those directly involved in work teams: some of those who would be in a good position to notice good team performance. In the following pages an example of each type of approach will be described in detail.

Using the first method, Hoegl and Gemuenden (2001) developed a theoretical model of the quality of teamwork (and an accompanying Teamwork Quality (TWQ) questionnaire) comprising six dimensions:

1   *Communication*: Good communication is frequent, spontaneous, direct between team members and open.

2   *Coordination*: Good coordination means that there is a shared understanding of who is doing what, for whom and when.

3   *Balanced contributions from members*: All team members are able to input what they know.

4   *Mutual support*: There is collaboration and cooperation (not competition) over tasks.

5   *Effort*: Whatever the level of effort required, it is important that team members know it and accept it.

6   *Cohesion*: This concerns the desire of team members to work together to stay together.

They tested this model with teams involved in innovative work projects. Their headline finding was that these features were reliably associated with three types of outcomes: team members' own views of the effectiveness and efficiency of the team; team leaders' evaluations of team effectiveness and efficiency; and senior manager's evaluations of team effectiveness and efficiency. All six facets of TWQ were roughly equally strongly linked to these outcomes and to the degree of job satisfaction and learning reported by team members. Interestingly, the links between TWQ and effectiveness and efficiency were strongest when the team member's own ratings of these outcomes were used: the links to managers' ratings of efficiency and effectiveness were far more modest. This raises an interesting methodological issue in team research: are those who have experienced the teamwork process really best placed to judge its success? Hoegl and Gemuenden speculated that when people have good experiences in a team situation they might want to attribute the success of the team to these good experiences. In other words, people can develop their own *implicit theories* of the predictors of good team outcomes and it is these that can emerge from the analysis of data collected from team members. Whether these implicit theories reflect some objective reality is another matter.

The second method is the subject of the feature below.

Research methods in focus

Repertory grid technique

To better understand the factors influencing team effectiveness, Senior and Swailes (2007) took the approach of comparing various successful and unsuccessful teams. They used a highly structured interview technique (repertory grid technique) that involved asking members of management teams to identify and discuss examples of poor-, average- and high-performing teams. This allowed them to identify the key differences (constructs) between teams performing at the three different levels. They found lots of these, 615 constructs in fact, perhaps reflecting the complexity and diversity of the team processes being discussed. To distil these into a more manageable form they looked for themes, or clusters, within the constructs. This was done as follows. Each interviewee, on average, produced about 10 constructs that they felt differentiated poor-, average- and high-performing teams. They were then asked to rate the extent to which each feature was true of their current work team (on a scale from 1 to 6). These data were then analysed using specialist software that identified a smaller number of clusters of constructs that correlated strongly with each other in participants' ratings. These could be logically grouped in seven themes, representing seven dimensions of team-work that participants had linked to team performance. These were:

1 *Team purpose*: goal clarity and acceptance by members.
2 *Team organisation*: allocation of roles, responsibilities and a structure for operating.
3 *Leadership*: the presence of appropriate leadership style and leader support for members.
4 *Team climate*: openness, professionalism, morale, respect for differences.
5 *Interpersonal relations*: care and support, healthy rapport, honesty and liking.
6 *Team communications*: constructive handling of conflict, frequency of contact, coordinated communications.
7 *Team composition*: the mix of personality and abilities and continuity of membership.

An eighth dimension reflecting the team's interaction with the wider organisation was added. This was based on previous research which shows how the impact of team is mediated by wider organisational factors such as respect for the team within the organisation, support for the team's development and the alignment of the team's objectives with organisational goals.

Point of integration

At this point you may also want to take a look at the closing case study ('X-teams swing the axe at team bonding'). This offers a critique of research into team effectiveness that ignores how team members interact with those outside of their own team (e.g. by developing relationships with other teams, publicising their successes and by seeking out new resources to help them become more effective).

West (2002) argued that teams at work are often required both to think of new ideas and to implement them. He refers to the former as creativity and the latter as innovation and these can be seen as performance outcomes. Because of the potential pay-off from creativity and innovation (i.e. better products, services and systems) both are highly prized by organisations. In light of the widespread use of work teams and the use of teams to deliver innovative solutions, Anderson and West (1998) developed a way of measuring the climate for innovation through a Team Climate Inventory (TCI). The theoretical basis of this is a four-factor model of the drivers of work group innovation. These are:

1   *Vision*: This embraces the idea that clearly defined objectives lead to behaviour focused on achieving the objectives. It is broadly defined and spans the extent to which the vision is understood, valued and shared by team members.

2   *Participative safety*: This embraces the idea that the team climate is conducive to raising and challenging ideas and information, and to making decisions without prejudice from others. For example, if a team member felt that another would bad-mouth them to their boss then the climate for innovation would be compromised.

3   *Task orientation*: This concerns staying focused on the task by allocating responsibility and by evaluating and changing performance in light of progress towards agreed targets that reflect excellent outcomes or high standards.

4   *Support for innovation*: The best ideas will struggle if team members do not feel that there is a genuine willingness in the workplace to change things. To be convincing, support needs to be visible (enacted) and not just articulated (for instance, by managers outside the team). This might be evidenced through messages that innovation is the norm, that openness to change is valued and through giving rewards for new ideas.

This theoretical model is the basis of the 86-item TCI (Team Climate Inventory). It can be used in surveys of organisational climate as a diagnostic tool to help understand team effectiveness. It can also be used at team development events as a way of helping team members to discuss issues touching upon innovation in their own work contexts.

But do these features of team climate make a difference to performance? Meta-analysis has been used to examine which of these team processes, and other potentially important factors such as diversity and cohesion factors, predict innovation across different types of teams and organisational contexts. Hülsheger et al. (2009) looked at the average effects of 15 different variables on innovation in team environments using data drawn from 104 good-quality studies. This analysis revealed that in terms of the I–P–O model it was indeed the processes that mattered most. The four features of processes with the strongest links to team innovation were:

■   Vision, support for innovation, and task orientation (see the TCI above).

■   External communication – the extent to which group members interact with others outside of their group. This appears to help teams identify new ideas and knowledge and to gain fresh perspectives that they can then bring to team innovation tasks. This is an aspect of teamwork that has received relatively little attention in teamwork research; the closing case study at the end of this chapter offers a critique of this situation.

■   Cohesion almost makes the list – it was shown to be linked to innovation but not as strongly as the factors listed above. Cohesion might not impede creativity as group-think theory might suggest, but the results of this study suggest that it also appears to do little to enhance it.

■   Similarly, one frequently researched input – job-relevant diversity – was also linked to innovation but not very strongly. We return to this issue later in this chapter.

Hülsheger and colleagues point out that the strongest effects were found when the outcome was innovation at the team rather than the individual level, so the factors listed above appear to impact most significantly on the effectiveness of collective efforts.

This body of research into teamwork is useful because it helps us to better understand not just what teams do, but how their activities are linked to their success (or failure). It helps us to understand the links between inputs, mediators and outputs. For example, measures of teamwork quality or team climate might help to explain why a diverse team fails to achieve its goals. Such measures can also be used in team development interventions in order to diagnose problems with team functioning (e.g. by getting people to reflect (in a structured way) on their own team and how it functions).

Selecting people for teams

Knowledge and skills

Stevens and Campion (1994) argued that there is a set of individual-level competencies that influence a person's performance in teams and thus the overall team performance. Team-work competencies, or knowledge, skills and attributes (KSAs), were proposed that covered two main areas: interpersonal knowledge and self-management. Interpersonal knowledge relates to the team member's competence when relating to others and responding to their emotions in order to release their ideas and to maximise team members' contributions to problem-solving. More specifically, this includes:

- *Conflict resolution*: a person's ability to recognise it, to discourage it and where possible to use disagreement positively, for example by finding a constructive way forward.

- *Collaborative problem-solving skills*: a person's skills which are used to overcome barriers and enable the team to use the resources of all members.

- *Communication skills*: which include listening without evaluating, communicating openly, awareness of non-verbal cues, and the ability to engage in social conversations.

Self-management KSAs relate more to goal-setting and the distribution of tasks within the team. More specifically, this includes:

- the team member's ability to set realistic and relevant goals for themselves, team members and for the team collectively; and

- the team member's ability to allocate work within the team to maximise the usage of the particular mix of personal skills and technical knowledge available.

Thus it follows that when selecting for teams, the extent to which potential team members already possess these KSAs needs to be considered. Fortunately, specific tests of these KSAs have been developed. The Teamwork KSA Test (Stevens and Campion, 1999) is a 35-item questionnaire embodying the KSAs listed above. However, research has shown that it had virtually the same power to predict team-related outcomes as general aptitude tests (and therefore added little extra). If we think of our own experience of teamwork we may remember work colleagues with potentially valuable contributions who were suppressed by their shyness, or of the dominant but not so able colleague whose bold assertions steered the team to its final destination (a very frustrating state of affairs!). This line of thinking led Miller (2001) to point out that it is not enough for team members to possess teamwork KSAs: it is the ability to put them into practice that really matters. Although the evidence is mixed, tests such as the Teamwork KSA Test show some potential to predict individual team member behaviour and thus predict individual-level effectiveness in teams (McClough and Rogelberg, 2003). Such KSAs may, therefore, be a necessary, not sufficient, requirement for effective individual performance in a team.

Team roles

Another concept of interest to teamwork theory and to the practical questions about selecting people for teams and team development programmes is that of team roles. Although several typologies of team roles exist, Meredith Belbin (1981, 1993a) developed a model that has been particularly influential and which is still widely used by organisations. He observed teams in action and concluded that teams made up of the brightest people did not necessarily produce the best outcomes. This led him to develop a theory of team roles: he argued that a key factor behind effective teams is the presence in the team of set people who each perform specified team roles. He argued that people taking different roles needed to be appropriately combined in a team in order to achieve high performance. He identified nine roles that team members need to fulfil if the team is to be successful. These are shown in Figure 11.4.

Of course, not all teams contain nine people, each of whom takes one role. Each of us, according to the theory, has one or two preferred roles and one or two roles that we are capable of doing if no one else in the team does them better. Hence, four or five people can possess all nine roles predicted by the theory. Most individuals are capable of playing more

Coordinator
Calm and tolerant
Keeps team focused on
goals and encourages
individuals to
contribute

Shaper
Energetic and extrovert
Wants to achieve task goals
High need for achievement

Technical specialist
Likes to be an expert
Provides team with
specialist knowledge
and experience

Plant
Innovative and
independent
Source of imaginative
new ideas

Completer finisher
Hardworking and orderly
Ensures that detailed
aspects of group tasks are
properly planned

Monitor evaluator
Detached and intelligent
Evaluates ideas with
logic and analysis

Resource investigator
Friendly and adaptable
Gets information from
outside the group

Teamworker
Caring and diplomatic
Maintains team spirit
and provides emotional
support

Implementer
Attends to detail
Hardworking, organises
practical matters and
routine jobs

Figure 11.4	Belbin's nine team roles

than one role and it is clear from Figure 11.4 that there are some roles that each of us would find it very difficult to fill effectively.

Key learning point

In theory, team members need to pool a range of different competences in order to optimise performance. However, empirical evidence for this hypothesis is limited.

Belbin developed a Team Role Self-Perception Inventory (TRSPI) and an Observer Assessment Sheet (OAS) to help identify a person's role preferences. The TRSPI gives a person's self-assessment of their role profile and should be used in conjunction with predictions from two or three others who know them, for example a supervisor and a colleague, via the OAS. The combined results should then be used for team development purposes. In practice, however, most situations usually only use the TRSPI, which curtails the amount of information used in development discussions.

The main value of the Inventory is to raise awareness and to provide a vocabulary with which people at work can appreciate the characteristics and strengths of others and thus talk about their teams and their roles in them. It may also allow people to extend their repertoire of team roles so that they are more effective in a wider variety of teamwork situations. As such, it has an important developmental role.

The TRSPI, however, has attracted some rather critical psychometric evaluations that cast doubt on the reliability of the nine scales and the differences between them: this in turn casts doubt on its ability to measure stable aspects of personality. Rather, it appears that people can take on a number of different roles in a team situation. Furnham et al. (1993) led the charge against it, but it is important to see Belbin's response to get both sides of the argument (Belbin, 1993b). Other critical assessments include Fisher et al. (2001) who questioned its lack of convergent and discriminant validity, i.e. that team roles did not show consistently high positive correlations with other similar constructs, or show consistently low correlations with different constructs. Anderson and Sleap (2004) questioned whether there are gender differences in the ways people respond to the Belbin questionnaire – for example women score significantly higher on the 'teamworker' scale. Some studies of the TRSPI have looked at reliability in different and arguably more appropriate ways, and are more supportive of its basic properties (e.g. Swailes and Aritzeta, 2006).

Key learning point

Team members can usually adopt two or three different roles and should appreciate the value of all the roles needed.

Cognitive ability

One of the reasons why Meredith Belbin felt moved to create the TRSPI was that, as a management trainer at the time, he noticed that teams comprising the most intelligent students did not necessarily perform better than other teams of more mixed abilities. His explanation for this drew upon the presence or absence of team roles as we have seen. While general intelligence is now thought to be a good predictor of individual performance in a job, it does not necessarily follow that high cognitive ability at the individual level translates directly into high performance at team level. As we have already seen, team tasks create a very different set of demands compared to individual tasks.

Meta-analyses of cognitive ability and team performance (e.g. Bell, 2007; Devine and Philips, 2001) tends to show that the intelligence of team members is positively correlated with team performance for a range of tasks. However, the relationships are much weaker in real work settings than in experimental (laboratory) conditions. Devine and Philips calculated that the average cognitive ability of team members explained just 8.6 per cent of variance in team performance. This means that 91.4 per cent (rather a lot!) is explained by other variables than the intelligence of team members. This finding gives some support to the rather intuitive conclusions that Belbin drew from his observations over 30 years ago. Stronger association between intelligence and performance may be found with complex tasks: when the team needs to be good at physical work (e.g. assembly or maintenance tasks) the association could be lower than when the task is more about planning and problem-solving. In addition, over time, the association between intelligence and performance diminishes as team members get more experience of what the task needs in order for it to be done successfully (see the IMOI model earlier in this chapter and the Stage of team development section later in this chapter). Overall, where tasks are relatively straightforward, familiar to the team and largely behavioural, intelligence and team performance are not strongly linked. This is another good example that illustrates the importance of organisational setting and context in explaining relationships among variables.

Point of integration

There is some evidence that the average level of emotional intelligence (EI) found in a team is linked to team performance (Bell, 2007). This is based on a small number of studies, but the key features of various models of EI (see Chapter 3) certainly suggest that EI could be useful during team tasks.

Key learning point

Smarter teams do not necessarily outperform the rest – but they do perform better when the task requires more intellectual ability.

Personality in teams

Peeters and colleagues (2006) and Bell (2007) have used meta-analysis to examine how personality variables are related to team performance. Given what we know about the nature of the Big Five personality factors and their impact on human behaviour, there is good reason to suspect that agreeableness, conscientiousness, emotional stability and openness to experience might be positively associated with team performance. Other researchers have found that in certain situations all can have significant, but modest, correlations with individual performance (see Chapters 3 and 4). Both of these meta-analyses revealed the expected correlation between performance and agreeableness: this is presumed to derive from 'interpersonal facilitation' within the team. Conscientiousness was also linked to team performance (perhaps because it is linked to persistence, thoroughness and attention to detail). Contrary to predictions, there were no correlations between emotional stability and it was only in Bell's analysis that the link between openness and performance was significant. In both studies strong positive links between personality and performance were only found in – yes, you guessed it – work teams and not in the student teams often studied by researchers. These results suggest that high agreeableness and conscientiousness could be viable criteria to use in the selection of team members but not at the exclusion of measures of skills and abilities.

More recent research by Livi et al. (2015) has looked at the link between a broader trait – positive orientation – and team performance. Positive orientation is a disposition to face tasks and experiences with a positive outlook, to feel pride in one's achievements and to have a positive view of the future. An interesting finding to emerge from this study of Italian workers was that those who had low levels of positive orientation benefited from being in a team where other team members had high levels of positive orientation. This illustrates that the 'collective' personality can make a difference to team performance.

Impacts on team members

What does teamworking do for members' work attitudes and performance? Allen and Hecht (2004) provide an interesting counter to the thrust of much of the literature on teams. They claim that 'current beliefs in the effectiveness of teams are out of proportion to the evidence regarding their effectiveness' (2004: 454). They go on to say that this state exists because teams tend to make people more satisfied at work and raise confidence. These psychological benefits are important and are good reasons in themselves for organisations to continue using teamwork as a way of organising. However, it is useful to ask what the evidence is for these enhanced psychological states.

Point of integration

Teamwork is often thought to be a positive intervention because it increases available social support, worker control and helps employees to manage better their work demands. The links between these resources and employee well-being are discussed in detail in Chapter 10 and are relevant when considering the likely impact of teamworking on employee well-being.

Rasmussen and Jeppesen (2006) reviewed 55 studies and found that teamwork generally does associate with psychological variables such as cohesion, organisational commitment and job satisfaction. These positive outcomes are found more often than not, but cannot be guaranteed. Van Mierlo et al. (2005) found that in the case of the implementation of self-managing teams it was only job satisfaction that was linked to the experience of this new way of working. The inconsistent effects of teamwork on employee attitudes might be linked to variations in the way teamwork is implemented (Bambra et al., 2007). As was found in the Fifth EWCS Eurofound (2012), discussed earlier in this chapter, just because people are working in something their manager calls a 'team' it does not mean they are experiencing the high levels of control and autonomy needed to influence work attitudes. Hollenbeck et al. (2012) point out that teams often differ in their authority differentiation – the extent to which all team members have a chance to get fully involved in decision-making. Not surprisingly, more involvement tends to be associated with better outcomes. West and Lyubovnikova (2013) argue that teams must engage in new activities such as reflecting on performance and the setting of shared objectives as these activities can significantly impact on worker satisfaction and the overall effectiveness of teamwork (see also the team processes identified by Hülsheger et al. (2009) discussed earlier in this chapter).

Some studies find little or no impact of teamworking because non-teamworkers in fact comprise two very different groups. One group is people who work in mundane jobs with low skill requirements and little discretion. The other is professional or craft workers who exercise both skill and discretion in pursuing their individualised un-teamlike work (i.e. their work tasks allow them ample opportunities to use skills and makes decisions, without needing to work in a team). In a survey of 800 Dutch workers, Steijn (2001) found that mundane jobs are less pleasant for the people who do them than both professional/craft work and for those involved in teamwork. In terms of how pleasant the jobs were, professional/craft work and those done in teams differed little from each other.

When teamworking reduces job satisfaction two conflicting forces may be at work. On the one hand, teamwork can reduce the amount of supervisor support that employees experience. On the other hand, teamwork can lead to more enriched jobs (e.g. multiskilling, responsibility). It can also be that implementing teamwork increases the autonomy of the team, while at the same time reducing the autonomy of some of the individual team members (e.g. if a worker cannot make a decision without checking first with colleagues). It is clear then that working in a team can bring with it some new demands. Harley (2001) points out that theorists from the 'critical management' school maintain that teamworking can lead to more work and less discretion for individuals, with senior managers effectively allowing pressure and scrutiny from other team members to substitute for formal supervisory control.

Some case-study-based work also suggests that teamwork may have multiple and complex meanings – a team in one organisation might look very different from a team in another. This makes the overall impact of teams difficult to discern. For example, Procter and Currie (2002) studied a local branch of the UK's tax collection system, Her Majesty's Revenue & Customs. It had reduced its layers of management during the 1990s and reorganised work so that tasks were allocated to teams rather than individuals. There was a general belief that teamwork was partly intended by management to elicit more workless resources. Procter and Currie note (2002: 304) that in some ways teamworking had meant little substantive change in job design, but that its impact was felt in other ways:

> The range of work is little changed; employees exercise little in the way of new skills; they appear reluctant to adopt responsibility for the work of others; and the performance management system operates on the basis of individual performance. Nonetheless, teamworking appears to work in the Inland Revenue. It does so by having a team rather than an individual allocation of work, and by encouraging individual identity with the team target.

Taking a slightly more optimistic perspective, it may sometimes be that those working in teams do not have the psychological resources to meet the new and different demands associated with teamwork (Nielsen and Daniels, 2012; Nielsen et al., 2010). Joint responsibility for completing tasks means that workers must interact with each other in different ways to support each other to complete tasks (Joiner, 2007). Team members may also be expected to have more of a say in decision-making with team leaders taking a back seat – this might be a daunting prospect for all involved. Nielsen et al. (2015) found some evidence that team members and team leaders alike benefited from training interventions designed to make them more aware of how to make the most of the new opportunities and resources available to them when working in a team. Training appeared to help those involved to develop a consistent shared view (or *mental model*) of what teamwork was and how it should work in practice. In the meta-analysis of the factors influencing team effectiveness, Richter et al. (2011) also found that teamwork had a stronger effect on performance and employee attitudes if its implementation was supported by appropriate human resource management practices such as team training.

Key learning point

Teamworking appears to have a complex association with work attitudes. This is partly because the introduction of teamworking may leave some work practices unchanged, improve others and also have a negative impact on some aspects of job design. It is also partly because people who do not work in teams have many different kinds of job – some of which already contain the beneficial features of job design that teamworking may introduce.

Workers' mental models of teams contain images and concepts that indicate quite a lot about, for example, what they expect from a team leader (see also Chapter 12) and their other colleagues within the team. Such images are also likely to vary somewhat between cultures. Gibson and Zellmer-Bruhn (2002) present an analysis of how employees in pharmaceutical firms in Europe, South East Asia, Latin America and the USA talk about teams. They invoke the concept of metaphor, which they define (2002: 102) as 'mechanisms by which we understand our experiences. We use metaphors whenever we think of one experience in terms of another. They help us to comprehend abstract concepts and perform abstract reasoning.'

From a careful analysis of how people talked about teams, Gibson and Zellmer-Bruhn identified five types of teamwork metaphor:

1   Sports metaphor: engage in specific tasks with clear objectives and performance measurement; members have clear roles; interaction between team members is largely confined to task-related matters; relatively little hierarchy; focus on winning and losing.

2   Military metaphor: similar to sports in that the team also engages in tasks with limited scope and clear objectives, but these teams have a clear and indisputable hierarchy; the focus of the metaphor is on life, death, survival and battle.

3   Family metaphor: these teams engage in broad-ranging tasks and interact across most domains of life; they have a relatively low emphasis on goals; clear roles (e.g. 'brothers' and 'sisters') and hierarchy ('father', 'mother').

4   Community metaphor: like families, communities are broad in the scope of interactions between members. However, roles are quite informal and ambiguous; goals sometimes quite ambiguous and the team quite amorphous.

5   Associates: these teams limit activity, with interactions only in the professional domain; little hierarchy; roles may be clear but can change; ties between group members quite loose.

Where a team leader holds a teamwork metaphor that differs from those held by other team members, problems are likely to arise. For example, if the leader tends to construe a team as a sports team but the others see it more like a community, the members may feel confused or alienated by their leader's concern with meeting targets and restricting interaction to task-focused activities. Managers need to be aware of the team members' metaphor in order to manage their team effectively.

DIfferences in national cultures (see Chapter 1) also have implications for multinational companies where managers are assigned to countries other than their own, and where teams are often made up of people of various nationalities. For example, as Gibson and Zellmer-Bruhn (2002) point out, Latin American countries tend to emphasise both collectivism and status differentials, which would tend to imply a *family team metaphor*. If a leader is from a highly individualist and low power distance culture such as the USA, they may find it easier to think in terms of a sports team metaphor or the associates metaphor.

Other factors influencing team performance

Teams have tasks to do and, at a simple level, team performance is simply the extent to which a task is achieved. The extent of task achievement does not tell us anything about how the team itself performed at team level. For instance, a team aiming to improve road safety in a region may be judged by the number of accidents, injuries and fatalities on certain roads over time. While these are good indicators of road safety, even if improvements do occur those statistics do not tell us anything about team-level performance, for example whether the team atmosphere fostered creativity and innovation, or whether it used all of the information available to it to tackle the problem. A significant thrust of team research is about understanding the links between teamwork and team outputs. Indeed, it is important to be clear about whether team performance is being used to describe *within-team processes* or the achievement of *objective output measures*.

With that caveat in mind, researchers have devoted considerable time and effort to understanding the factors that influence team performance and the conditions under which their influence occurs. There are too many to consider all of them here, so a selection of key factors is summarised below.

Stage of team development

Teams are not fully functional from the start: anyone who follows a sports team can see that they usually need time to reach their full potential. Over time there may be changes in personnel, and the team may change in terms of how team members approach their tasks and relate to each other. One early analysis (Tuckman, 1965) suggested that teams tend to go through a series of stages in their development:

1 *Forming*: This is the stage when a team first forms, when there is typically ambiguity and confusion. The members may not have chosen to work with each other. They may be guarded, superficial and impersonal in communication and unclear about the task.

2 *Storming*: This can be a difficult stage when there is conflict between team members and some rebellion against the task as assigned. There may be jockeying for positions of power and frustration at a lack of progress in the task.

3 *Norming*: In this stage it is important that open communication between team members is established. A start is made on confronting the task in hand, and generally accepted procedures and patterns of communication are established.

4 *Performing*: Having established how it is going to function, the group is now free to devote its full attention to achieving its goals. If the earlier stages have been tackled satisfactorily, the group should now be close and supportive, open and trusting, resourceful and effective.

Most teams have a limited life, so it is probably appropriate to add another stage that could be called *disbanding*. It would be important for team members to analyse their own performance and that of the group, to learn from the experience, agree whether to stay in touch and if so what that might achieve.

Understanding where a team is in terms of these stages of development might help us to understand team processes. However, not everyone agrees that these stages are either an accurate description or a desirable sequence. Teams composed of people who are accustomed to working in a certain way may jump straight to the norming stage. The members may already know each other. Even if they do not, they may be able to quickly establish satisfactory ways of interacting without conflict. In any case, many teams are required to perform right from the start, so they need to bypass the earlier stages, at least partially. West (1994: 98) has argued that key tasks in team start-up concern the establishment of team goals and individual tasks that are both meaningful and challenging, as well as setting up procedures for performance monitoring and review.

Point of integration

Some argue that different leadership behaviours are needed during the different stages of teamwork because the situation the leader is dealing with is different at each stage. To some extent contingency theories of leadership (Chapter 12) provide an insight into the type of leadership behaviour that might have the best chance of being effective given the defining features of each stage.

Key learning point

Some teams go through stages in their development, but many need to achieve high performance straight away, with these stages being very short-lived, or absent altogether.

Team-building

Team-building and development are widely practised by organisations from junior levels of new recruits to the most senior levels of top management. Activities might include 'away days' where teams take time away from the work setting to reflect on work issues in a more relaxed environment free from interruptions, social get-togethers, and physical activities (raft-building is used quite a lot!) that involve teamwork. This happens because organisations assume that team development is an antecedent of better team performance. Team-building is carried out on the assumption that optimal team performance occurs some time into the lifetime of a team: team development and team-building interventions are designed to move teams more quickly towards the latter stages of development. Therefore such interventions address, among other things:

- the respect for team members, their views and distinctive skills;
- team members' confidence to raise and to challenge views or information;
- the clarity of the team's goals and priorities;
- the allocation of work within the team and relationships with others outside the team.

We may ask, given the considerable costs of conducting it, whether there is any evidence that team-building actually has any impact on team performance. In some respects, this is a question for individual organisations to answer. If an employer is convinced that in their particular context their investments are being repaid then that is enough for them. Klein et al. (2009) carried out a meta-analysis of team-building research. Their main findings were as follows:

- Overall there was a significant but modest effect of team-building on various measures of team performance. This effect was strongest when looking at affective outcomes (such as trust) and team processes (e.g. coordination and communication). More modest effects were found for the development of competencies in the team, and with teams' task performance.

- There were various mechanisms at play that seemed to underpin the effects of team-building. The components of team-building that had particularly strong effects were dealing with role ambiguity through role clarification (see Chapter 10) and goal setting (see Chapter 7) such that the more these were part of team-building the stronger the effect on performance. Developing interpersonal relations and problem-solving were also effective active ingredients but did not have such strong effects.

- Team-building seemed to have beneficial effects for teams of all sizes, but the average benefits were larger for bigger teams.

In common with other meta-analyses the study aggregated different studies with different definitions of teams, different research settings and different measures of performance, all against a backdrop of diverse ways of attempting team-building with different development targets. This means that the findings do not necessarily apply to all team-building interventions, but they do represent interesting and discernible trends in the previous research.

Key learning point

Meta-analysis indicates that if team-building is attempted it is best focused on large teams where team processes and trust may need to be improved. Activities might be most effective if focused on role clarification and goal setting.

Team diversity

The basic concept of managing diversity accepts that the workforce consists of a diverse population of people. The diversity consists of visible and non-visible differences which will include sex, age, background, race, disability, personality and workstyle. It is founded on the premise that harnessing these differences will create a productive environment in which everybody feels valued, where their talents are fully utilised and in which organisational goals are met.

(Kandola and Fullerton, 1994: 19)

Work teams are often assembled by selecting a mix of individuals according to their specialist knowledge with little regard for the behaviour that they typically display. Over and above the mix of knowledge, skills and abilities that this produces, does team member diversity in itself have an influence on team performance? Homogeneous and heterogeneous teams may function differently through different social relations. A team of white males in their thirties is likely to function differently from a team of ethnically mixed women of different ages. Of course, as well as differences in these easily observable features, diversity also includes personality differences, team role variety, leadership skills and technical knowledge.

Similarity theory (see Tziner, 1985) says that groups and teams comprising people with similar characteristics will be the most productive. This is because of the mutual attraction held by people of similar demographics, for example working-class women relating more closely to each other than they would relate to middle-class men, but the key question is: even if ties are stronger does this translate into higher performance at team level? The alternative view says that where diverse backgrounds are combined the resulting tension will be constructive in terms of team outputs (e.g. more decision alternatives will be considered). However, equity theory describes how people adjust their inputs, up or down, to situations depending on their perceptions of their own rewards and the rewards given to others. In a team setting, individuals may lower their contribution if they see another team member as having more status due to their greater expertise or higher position in the organisation. Hence, if we accept this theory, in some circumstances heterogeneous teams could be less effective due to an unhelpful focusing on interpersonal differences. Van Knippenberg and Schippers (2007: 517) argue that there are two possible outcomes of diversity:

- Differences between work group members may engender the classification of others as either in-group/similar or out-group/dissimilar, categorisations that may disrupt group process (social categorisation perspective).

- Diversity may introduce differences in knowledge, expertise and perspectives that may help work groups reach higher quality and more creative and innovative outcomes. There is evidence that, in certain circumstances, such differences mean that diverse groups can outperform homogeneous groups (information/decision-making perspective).

Despite some of the potential drawbacks, the importance of role diversity in teams and the need for effective teams to have people with differing outlooks and strengths is now generally accepted. Konrad (2003) argues that because the workforce is becoming more diverse a team made up of the best available employees needs to contain people from a variety of demographic groups. In addition, a more diverse workforce might help organisations connect better with a more diverse client/customer base (especially as organisations sell their products and services in a global marketplace). As Shaw and Barrett-Power (1998: 1307) have put it: 'Diversity is an increasingly important factor in organisational life as organisations worldwide become more diverse in terms of the gender, race, ethnicity, age, national origin, and other personal characteristics of their members.'

Welbourne et al. (2007) found that gender diversity in top management teams had a direct association with financial performance of a large number of US-based companies. On the whole it seems that management teams with diverse membership do perform better than others, at least on tasks that require the generation and evaluation of ideas (Jackson and Joshi, 2001). This may be the case because diversity could help to avoid problems such as groupthink.

The problem is, of course, that we may devalue characteristics we happen not to possess ourselves. While diversity in terms of occupational or organisational roles is common in teams, diversity in terms of gender, nationality, ethnicity, age or personality is perhaps less often considered. It is also difficult to manage effectively, because team members may have quite different values and expectations of how to behave. So although teams with diverse members have the *potential* to be highly effective they often fail to achieve that potential (Kandola, 1995). Some time ago, Williams and O'Reilly (1998) found evidence that diversity had a negative relationship with performance, with damaging effects on relationships between employees and the cohesiveness of groups. Janssens and Zanoni (2005) argue that early reviews of diversity struggled to explain its inconsistent effects because diversity was reduced to the study of the impact of surface-level demographic differences without sufficient analysis of the impact that these differences had on human perceptions and interactions. In other words, they underestimated the impact of diversity on the deeper psychological processes active in teams.

Maznevski (1994) and Paulus (2000) have argued that teams need integration, and that this is more difficult to achieve as they become more diverse. Integration relies on a number of factors:

- a social reality shared by group members;
- the ability to 'decentre' – that is, see things from others' points of view;
- the motivation to communicate;
- the ability to negotiate and agree on norms of behaviour within the team;
- the ability to identify the true causes of any difficulties that arise (e.g. not blaming people for things that are not their fault);
- the self-confidence of all group members.

These are good guidelines for any team, but are harder to achieve in a diverse one. Teams with diverse members must be especially careful to establish integration. How to get the best out of team member diversity has, in recent years, attracted increasing research attention. Pelled et al. (1999), for example, refer to diversity in occupational backgrounds of team members. They suggest that functional diversity tends to lead to task-related conflict (that is, disagreement between group members about preferred solutions and methods) and that this (as long as it is handled well) helps group performance.

Jehn et al. (1999: 742) point out that, 'No theory suggests that a workgroup's diversity on outward personal characteristics such as race and gender should have benefits except to the extent that diversity creates *other diversity* in the workgroup, such as diversity of information or perspective.' Consistent with this assertion, Jehn et al. found that, among a sample of 545 employees, *informational diversity* in teams was associated with good group performance. Social *category diversity* (in the form of age and gender) made people more satisfied with their team, while *value diversity* (defined as disagreement about what the team's goals should be) tended to produce more relationship conflict within the team, and to undermine slightly the performance of the team.

Key learning point

There are different dimensions of diversity in teams, and each has different implications for team processes and team outputs.

Understanding better how diversity is perceived by employees has provided a much greater insight into the links between diversity and performance. Ely and Thomas (2001) re-examined the concept of diversity and identified three different perspectives on diversity that may be found in teams:

■ *The integration-and-learning perspective* perceives the different skills, knowledge, experiences and attitudes that accompany the demographic diversity in the team as being helpful to employees when they are working together.

■ *The access-and-legitimacy perspective* occurs when organisation's customers are culturally diverse. The perception is that having a diverse workforce helps the organisation gain access to a diverse market.

■ *The discrimination-and-fairness perspective* is based upon the perception that diversity is a moral issue to ensure fair treatment for all employees. This perception is often in evidence when the organisation focuses on equal opportunities and eliminating discrimination.

Ely and Thomas argue that when diversity is perceived within the integration-and-learning perspective, outcomes are more likely to be positive (i.e. there is improved task performance). When employees take the discrimination-and-fairness perspective, divisions and segregation are highlighted. Proudford and Smith (2003) conclude that if demographic differences have some salience to the job role and/or task itself then diversity is more likely to have a positive impact on the task. For example, young employees may assume that older workers have old-fashioned attitudes to work when compared to younger workers (i.e. diversity is perceived as a basis for separation). Or they may perceive that older workers have more knowledge, experience and wisdom than younger workers (i.e. diversity is associated with a perceived variety of skills and experience that could prove useful). This also suggests that the aspects of difference between people that matter may well vary a lot between contexts (Jackson and Joshi, 2001). In one workplace (e.g. a hospital serving a highly multi-ethnic local population) it might be team members' ethnicity could be important because of the associated knowledge and empathy with the client perspective it confers. In another (e.g. the research laboratory of a pharmaceutical company) it might be whether one's qualifications are in pharmacy, biochemistry or medicine.

This opens up the possibility that organisations might intervene to influence how employees perceive diversity in order to increases the chances of diversity interventions having positive outcomes. Harrison (2007) suggests that positive outcomes are more likely if employees see demographic differences as a source of variety (of skills, attitudes, values etc.) rather than as a basis for separation. Pettigrew (1998) suggests that contact between groups can improve relations, but only if the nature of the contact: (i) encourages *learning* about the other group as opposed to just co-existing; (ii) requires behaving differently towards the other group; (iii) creates positive emotions associated with the other group; and (iv) enables new insights about one's own group. This last point is interesting and important, because arguably empathy with members of other groups is possible only if one can appreciate that the worldviews of group(s) to which one belongs are just one way of looking at things rather than the absolute truth. Situations that meet these four criteria can sometimes be engineered in workplaces, and sometimes they occur naturally. Probably their key features are that they require members of different groups to work cooperatively towards a common goal, that goal-achievement is a real possibility and that nobody is allowed to opt out of the endeavour.

Key learning point

Effective management of diversity in teams requires attention to many kinds of differences between people, not just the obvious ones such as gender and ethnic origin. It is also involves understanding how differences are perceived by employees.

Lau and Murnighan (1998) have pointed out that how differences are distributed also matters. For example, suppose a six-person team consists of three middle-aged white male senior managers without university degrees who have all been production managers, and three young black female women managers with PhDs who have all been marketing managers. In this case, the many differences all stack up together and find expression in the same people. Lau and Murnighan refer to this as a 'faultline'. If, for example, seniority had been mixed up a bit so that one of the men was a middle manager and one of the women was a senior manager, then perhaps the dynamics of the group would have changed significantly. Although the group would be equally diverse, the distribution of the differences would have been different, and the 'faultline' less deep and wide.

As with many topics in this text, meta-analysis of a good number of different studies can help to resolve some of the debates about the impact of diversity. Horwitz and Horwitz (2007) found that in terms of explaining performance, the distinction between surface-level diversity and deep-level diversity was particularly important. Surface-level diversity refers to innate and observable differences such as age, gender and ethnicity. Deep-level diversity refers to underlying attributes such as knowledge, expertise and other cognitive resources. The latter have a more obvious connection with performance on the task at hand. In their analysis it was this deep-level diversity – and not the surface-level diversity – that was shown to be significantly and consistently related to team performance.

Key learning point

Research on diversity and team performance has shown some strong effects in individual studies. Meta-analysis tends to show that aspects of diversity directly related to the completion of the task (such as expertise, relevant experience and educational qualifications) show relatively consistent links to performance.

Exercise 11.3   Roles and diversity in a team

Recall your experience of working in a group or team that you used for Exercise 11.1. This time, consider the following questions:

Suggested exercises

1   How diverse were the team members in terms of (for example) age, sex, ethnic or religious affiliation, outlook, personality, past experience, social class? What consequences did the diversity (or lack of it) have for how the team went about its task, and for the final decision?

2   From the descriptions of Belbin's nine team roles, which do you think were most often displayed by team members? Consider whether this was helpful or not, and whether more (or less) of certain roles would have been helpful.

Stop to consider

We have now looked at a lot of different factors that can influence the performance of a team. At this point, to cement your knowledge of this diverse body of research, stop to consider the factors that contribute to effective/ineffective teamwork. Write a 'recipe' for a successful team, including as many factors as you possibly can. Now review the quality and quantity of the evidence presented so far: how confident can we be that if we follow this recipe we will get successful teamwork?

Participation in decision-making in organisations

Guzzo and Dickson (1996) have pointed out that improved group performance does not guarantee improved organisational performance. When we look at applying team research in its wider organisational context we need to consider the type of decision-making that teams are involved in, and at which phases of the decision-making process they have some involvement. As regards the types of decision, there are (i) operational decisions (usually with short-term effects and of a routine nature); (ii) tactical decisions (usually with medium-term effects and of non-routine nature but not going so far as reviewing the organisation's goals); and (iii) strategic decisions (usually with long-term effects and concerning the organisation's goals).

In line with leadership research (see Chapter 12), it is also possible to distinguish between people-orientated and task-orientated decisions within each type. The phases of decision-making include: (i) start-up, when it is realised that a decision is required; (ii) development, when options are searched for and considered; (iii) finalisation, when a decision is confirmed; and (iv) implementation, when the finalised decision is put into operation or fails (Heller et al., 1988).

Much attention has been focused on who in organisations really makes decisions, and how their influence is distributed across the decision types and phases described above (e.g. Mintzberg, 1983; Heller et al., 1988; Vandenberg et al., 1999). The concept of *power* is frequently invoked. Power concerns the ability of an individual or group to ensure that another individual or group complies with its wishes. The power a team has can be derived from a number of sources, including the ability to reward and/or punish, the extent to which a group is seen as expert and the amount of prestige or good reputation that is enjoyed by the group. These sources of power are distinct, though they tend to go together (Finkelstein, 1992). In the closing case study for this chapter you will see that the argument has been put forward that much of a team's effectiveness could be linked to how it manages the way it is perceived in the wider organisation.

Especially if they are in short supply, individuals and groups often use *organisational politics* to maximise their chances of getting their way. Politics consists of tactics such as enlisting the support of others, controlling access to information and creating indebtedness by doing people favours for which reciprocation is expected. In extreme forms politics can also involve more deceitful activities such as spreading rumours. In general, however, the effectiveness and morality of power and politics depend on their intended goals.

In many organisations, lots of decision-making power is still exercised by top management, particularly with regard to strategic decisions. Within tactical decisions, workers typically tend to have quite high influence at the start-up phase of people-orientated decisions but little thereafter. This consultation without true participation can be a source of frustration. For tactical task-orientated decisions, workers tend to have more influence in the finalisation phase when their expertise really comes into its own. Senior managers are often tempted to make decisions in quite an autocratic way, involving only a few senior colleagues with little or no consultation. This is not necessarily because those managers have autocratic personalities. In fast-moving environments it may be necessary to make decisions quickly, and passing those decisions on to groups can slow things down. However, Ashmos et al. (2002) have argued for a simple management rule: use participative styles of decision-making. Although this can be time consuming it can have a number of well-documented benefits (see also Nielsen and Randall, 2012). These include:

■ making use of the diverse skills and knowledge available in the organisation;

■ developing people's sense of involvement in the organisation, which can be especially helpful during change processes;

■ increasing the amount of energy and commitment people put into change (partly because they feel they have invested their time and effort so they want to make it work);

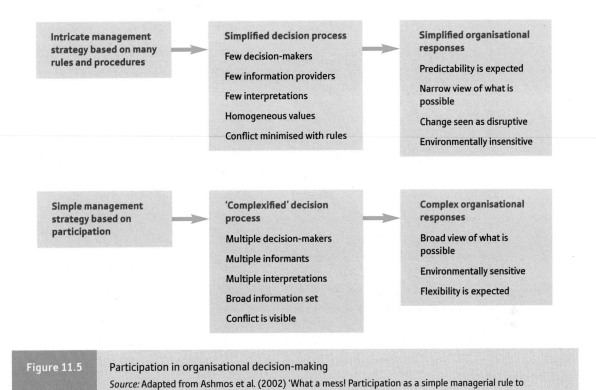

Intricate management strategy based on many rules and procedures	**Simplified decision process** Few decision-makers Few information providers Few interpretations Homogeneous values Conflict minimised with rules	**Simplified organisational responses** Predictability is expected Narrow view of what is possible Change seen as disruptive Environmentally insensitive
Simple management strategy based on participation	**'Complexified' decision process** Multiple decision-makers Multiple informants Multiple interpretations Broad information set Conflict is visible	**Complex organisational responses** Broad view of what is possible Environmentally sensitive Flexibility is expected

Figure 11.5   Participation in organisational decision-making

Source: Adapted from Ashmos et al. (2002) 'What a mess! Participation as a simple managerial rule to "complexify" organisations', *Journal of Management Studies*, 39(2), 189–206, Blackwell Publishing Ltd.

- increasing information flow and contacts among members of the organisation;
- making decisions that reflect the real (and changing) nature of the organisation's environment.

If the simple rule 'use participation' is followed, decisions are made and actions taken in less predictable and comfortable ways, but they could be better suited to the specific situation. Ashmos et al.'s ideas are summarised in Figure 11.5. They are consistent with the proposition in the Vroom–Yetton theory of leadership (see Chapter 12) and findings of intervention research that focus on tackling the sources of work-related stress (see Chapter 10).

Key learning point

The amount and type of workforce participation in organisational decision-making varies across cultures, between types of decision and between phases of the decision-making processes.

Finally, examinations of strategic decision-making by senior management have been undertaken (e.g. Forbes and Milliken, 1999). For example, Papadakis and Barwise (2002) found that the personalities and other characteristics of the chief executive officer and top management team had relatively limited impact on how decisions were made. Instead, the extent to which the decision would have an impact on the firm seemed to matter. Encouragingly perhaps, higher impact was associated with a more comprehensive process with more decentralisation (i.e. the involvement of a range of different people in the decision) and communication.

Dean and Sharfman (1996) used multiple in-depth interviews with senior managers involved in decision-making to investigate the process and outcomes of 52 strategic decisions in 24 companies. The most common types of strategic decision concerned organisational restructuring, the launch of a new product and organisational change. The procedural rationality of the decision-making process (that is, the extent to which relevant information was sought, obtained and evaluated) had a significant impact on decision effectiveness. This was particularly true when the business environment was changeable, requiring careful monitoring of trends. Even more important was the thoroughness and care with which the decision was implemented. However, not everything is under decision-makers' control. The favourability of the business and industrial contexts also had an impact on decision effectiveness. Political behaviour by those involved was usually bad for decision effectiveness. So, some of the problems associated with behaviour in groups and teams such as disguising one's own opinions, and complex and distracting negotiations between factions of the decision-making group need to be challenged. They impair organisational performance, though of course these things happen because they may serve the interests of individuals or subgroups.

Key learning point

Taking care over decision-making and implementation processes can often make a difference to organisational effectiveness.

Stop to consider

Participation in decision-making is often seen as one of the major benefits of implementing teamwork. Now that you have read about participation, consider the benefits and risks of increasing levels of participation in decision-making. As you read more of this book you might also want to consider how other bodies of research help us to understand why participation might be important and beneficial. In particular think about what theories of motivation (Chapter 7), work stress (Chapter 10) and leadership (Chapter 12) tell us about the possible risks and benefits of participation in decision-making.

Summary

Decisions by individuals and groups are influenced by many psychological phenomena. Groups are usually more effective than the average individual but less so than the best individual in decision-making tasks. Groups can make terrible decisions, especially if characterised by problems such as the groupthink syndrome. However, the research evidence about the 'typical' effectiveness of groups should not be viewed as the best that groups can do. Possible ways in which groups and teams can improve include more consideration in advance of the problem-solving strategy they wish to adopt, a clear expectation that members should challenge each other, and an understanding that such challenges do not signal hostility or disrespect. When such conditions exist, diversity within groups can have important benefits.

The extent to which employees are part of real teams with high autonomy seems to be relatively low overall, although it does vary from country to country. The processes that occur in teams are very complex with continuous cycles of feedback and adjustment occurring rather than a simple linear pathway. Teams pass through a life cycle that involves forming, mature functioning and then winding-down. Models of teamwork effectiveness emphasise the importance of factors such as goal clarity, balanced sharing of duties, open communication, good interpersonal relationships and the ability to manage conflict. Individual differences in personality and ability can influence team performance so selecting the right people to join a team is important but is only one of many factors that impact on team effectiveness. The concept that effective teams require a balance of different team roles is popular and is the basis of much of the team development that organisations carry out.

Many organisations rely on teamwork and use it to fuel creativity and innovation in the workplace. Aside of questions about whether teams actually perform better than individuals do, the evidence that being in teams leads to positive job-related attitudes (such as job satisfaction) contains some inconsistencies. This appears to be because teams are not always given high levels of autonomy to make decisions and change work practices. A long list can be made of the variables that have been used to predict team performance. They include: stage of development; climate inside the team; extent of team-building; diversity in terms of team roles, personality and gender; and cognitive ability. The nature of decision-making tasks, their importance and their subject matter all have implications for the way they are handled. The amount and type of employee participation in making decisions vary widely and the ways that decisions are made and implemented do link to organisational effectiveness.

Closing case study — X-teams swing the axe at team bonding

Perched on a shelf in Deborah Ancona's office at the MIT Sloan School of Management is a pair of purple high heels. The shoes – adorned with pink and pearly baubles at the toe – are a symbol of what Prof Ancona has taken to calling "career-limiting behaviours", or CLBs, for short.

When she first started out as an academic at a different institution, a male faculty member took her aside and told her that the purple pumps she had on were "not tenure track shoes". He was trying to be helpful, but the message was clear: if you want a future here, your footwear must change.

Prof Ancona moved on from that school. She has made a career out of determining what makes workers – from high-level managers to junior employees – successful within a given organisation. Her concentration is not on individuals' CLBs, rather she focuses on "distributed leadership" – the idea that a flatter, more flexible structure allows a

company to react better to fast-changing information and achieve its goals.

Specifically, she studies the characteristics of high-performing teams, or X-teams, a concept she helped develop, that describes externally orientated teams that drive innovation within large organisations.

Prof Ancona changed her major seven times before finally settling on psychology. "I loved it, I decided I wanted to do applied psychology in management," she says. She went on to earn her master's degree in psychology at Penn, and eventually enrolled in the PhD programme at Columbia University's Graduate School of Business. As a graduate student, she worked as a research assistant to David Nadler, a professor and founder of the Delta Consulting Group, a firm specialising in executive leadership and organisational change.

"[Nadler] was a huge influence on me," she says. "Before I was doing laboratory

▶

▶

experiments; as his research assistant, I started looking at organisations. I saw how organisational behavioural issues played out in the real world. My classes were great, but the biggest learning was by doing research."

The concept of X-teams emerged in the early 1980s when Prof Ancona was writing her dissertation. For her research on team dynamics, she worked closely with a company that sold communications systems to other businesses. She spent weeks with the company's sales force – attending their internal meetings, and going on their sales calls. She wanted to determine what made one team more profitable than another. Why was one team more effective at dealing with customers than another? And why did one team win the support of management, while another did not?

What she found ran counter to classic models: "There was this huge body of literature of what makes effective teams – clear goals, clear roles, cohesiveness, team spirit. But what I found is that these related to a team's satisfaction. It has zero relationship to revenue attainment," she says. High-performing teams are externally focused. They establish co-operative relationships with stakeholders and customers, seek out information from other teams and outside sources, and pursue support from senior management. She found that these characteristics are more correlated with success: X-teams come in on budget, and on schedule more often, and they receive better client ratings, and better ratings from top management.

The poorest-performing teams are inward-looking. "Because they're internally-focused, they build a wall between themselves and the world," Prof Ancona explains. "Because they aren't having an effective interaction with their environment, over time those teams become unhappy."

Her findings have been met with resistance. "Absolutely there was resistance, there still is," she says. "If you look at all the books on team building, there's very little mention of external activity." Indeed, the management mantras of the day are about trust-building exercises and group hugs. But Prof Ancona has other ideas about how a team ought to bond. "Rather than go on outward bound where you build cohesion, you break up into subgroups and talk to customers, talk to stakeholders, talk to competitors. You bond around what's going on in your environment," she says.

The creation of X-teams is critical to company success in today's trying economic times, according to Prof Ancona. "In a crisis, people are rigid, and unable to act, X-teams help to see the big picture," she says. Because they have their "pulse on what's going on in the environment", they can more effectively find new ways to cut costs, and they can better come up with ideas for new technologies and revenue generation, and can more easily figure out what customers want, she adds.

They are also an effective motivator for Gen X and Gen Y workers; younger employees stay engaged because they are able to interact with different people and different parts of the organisation. "It gives them a broader perspective on what it takes to create change," she says.

 Source: Adapted/abridged (shortened to highlight relevance) from *Financial Times*, 11 May 2009: http://www.ft.com/cms/s/0/cfa12710-3b64-11de-ba91-00144feabdc0.html#axzz3ov0YlnIU

Suggested exercise

1 Having read this chapter which of Professor Ancona's criticisms of teamwork research do you agree with? Why? Which do you disagree with and why?

Test your learning

Short-answer questions

1 What is groupthink?
2 What are the differences between a workgroup and a work team?
3 Summarise the I–P–O model of team functioning.
4 What is the IMOI model of team functioning?
5 Suggest three possible negative consequences of stereotypes in the workplace.
6 What strategies should minorities in groups use in order to maximise their chances of influencing a group decision?
7 What is group polarisation and why does it happen?
8 List the team roles identified by Belbin and explain why they are needed for team effectiveness.
9 Briefly outline three reasons why groups sometimes make poor decisions.
10 What is team diversity?
11 To what extent do the skills, personalities and intelligence of workers influence the effectiveness of teams?
12 Outline the main features of team climate.

Suggested assignments

1 Discuss the proposition that Janis's groupthink model adequately accounts for failures in group decision-making.
2 What gains can organisations make by organising their employees into teams? What are the risks for organisations that do this?
3 Discuss three different ways in which we might identify the factors that impact on team performance. Give an example of each, outlining the main findings of this research.
4 Examine the potential benefits and problems of diversity in teams.
5 To what extent has true teamwork become a normal feature of working life?

Relevant websites

A simple Google search for 'teamwork' or 'team development' leads you to many consultants' websites. They are interesting as they show how practitioners approach the topic.

Information about team roles and samples of the team role instruments are at http://www. belbin.com

Various documents relating to how a well-known measure of personality can be used in team development can be found at https://www.opp.com/en/tools/MBTI/MBTI-Step-I/MBTI-Team-Report

A resource pack for the measurement of team climate can be found at http://www.nrls.npsa. nhs.uk/resources/ (then search for 'team climate' in the directory). Although the measure is geared towards healthcare settings it provides a good example of how information about the key features of team climate can be obtained using a questionnaire measure.

An interesting report on the composition and effectiveness of top management teams is at http://www.idea.gov.uk/idk/aio/5028661

Suggested further reading

Full details for all references are given in the list at the end of this book.

1 Michael West's book *Effective Teamwork: Practical lessons from organisational research* (BPS Blackwell, 2012) gives an up-to-date and scholarly but accessible review of many team processes and outcomes.

2 R. Meredith Belbin's book *Beyond the Team* (Butterworth-Heinemann, 2000) is a good example of a genre that attempts to use everyday language to help people understand how to make teams work.

3 Steve Kozlowski and Daniel Ilgen provide a full review of team effectiveness in their paper in *Psychological Science in the Public Interest*, 2006.

4 For those who found the closing case study particularly interesting, Deborah Ancona's and Henrik Bresman's book *X-Teams: How to build teams that lead, innovate, and succeed* (Harvard Business School Press, 2007) will make for a good read.

CHAPTER 12

Leadership

LEARNING OBJECTIVES

After studying this chapter, you should be able to:

1 suggest reasons why leadership at work in the 21st century might be more challenging than ever before;

2 identify various criteria of leader effectiveness;

3 specify some common personality characteristics of leaders and their possible consequences;

4 define the terms consideration and initiating structure as they are used in leadership research, and summarise the extent to which they are associated with desirable outcomes;

5 specify features of situations that might require different leader styles;

6 define five leader decision-making styles (with varying degrees of participation), and six features of the problem situation identified by Vroom and Jago;

7 name and define four aspects of transformational leadership and two aspects of transactional leadership and examine the nature of charismatic leadership;

8 analyse the extent to which transformational and charismatic leadership influence performance at work;

9 identify some drawbacks of charisma and transformational leadership;

10 describe differences between women and men in leadership styles and effectiveness;

11 explain why and in what ways effective leader behaviour may differ between countries and cultures;

12 list ten cultural groupings across the world, and comment on whether they have distinctively different views of what constitutes effective leadership.

Opening case study

Leadership the Sir Richard Branson way

Sir Richard Branson is a British entrepreneur and corporate leader. He is best known as the founder of the Virgin Group, which now comprises more than 400 companies in a range of industries including aviation, mobile phones and perhaps in the future space tourism. He is also famous for making world record attempts in sailing and ballooning.

Branson is often criticised for his management style – or lack thereof. He holds no regular board meetings, has no business headquarters, and has no idea how to operate a computer. But, as his corporate empire has grown to gigantic proportions, Branson has had to develop the necessary leadership skills to ensure his survival.

"I've had to create companies that I believe in 100%. These are companies I feel will make a genuine difference," says Branson. "Then I have to be willing to find the time myself to talk about them, promote them and market them. I don't want to spend my life doing something that I'm not proud of." "Having a personality of caring about people is important," says Branson. "You can't be a good leader unless you generally like people. That is how you bring out the best in them." His overall leadership principle rests on the need to treat other people with respect.

Branson hires bright people, gives them a stake in his ventures so that they are motivated to be even more successful and then delegates. While his staff often takes care of the daily operations of a company, Branson focuses his time more on the end user experience, doing publicity and promoting his products.

Branson stresses the importance of time management skills, saying he spends roughly one third of his time on trouble shooting, one third on new projects – both business related and charitable – and one third on promoting and marketing his businesses. In between, he also makes time for his family and vacations. Part of being a good leader, according to Branson, is also the ability to know when to back away from a task. "As much as you need a strong personality to build a business from scratch, you also must understand the art of delegation," he says. "I have to be good at helping people run the individual businesses, and I have to be willing to step back. The company must be set up so it can continue without me." But, for Branson, the most important factor of good leadership is relating to other people. "If you're good with people … and you really care, genuinely care about people then I'm sure we could find a job for you at Virgin," he says. "The companies that look after their people are the companies that do really well. I'm sure we'd like a few other attributes, but that would be the most important one." Treating his employees as important team players is crucial to the success of Branson's Virgin Empires, putting employees first, customers second, and shareholders third. "A company is people … employees want to know … am I being listened to or am I a cog in the wheel? People really need to feel wanted."

Source: Adapted with permission from http://www.evancarmichael.com/ Famous-Entrepreneurs/592/Lesson-1-Be-A-Good-Leader.html. This includes a half-hour recording of a conversation where Branson talks a lot about his experiences of founding and developing businesses. It has some amusing anecdotes and at least one inaccurate prediction about future developments, which shows that even famous leaders aren't always right.

Introduction

Most corporate leaders have clear views about what constitutes good leadership, and understandably so because their approach has worked for them. Sir Richard Branson's views, to which we will return several times in this chapter, demonstrate both the complexity of leadership and the scope for different opinions about how to do it. The leader attributes and behaviours mentioned include caring about people, the ability and willingness to delegate, having a personal commitment to what the organisation does, representing the organisation, dealing with problems, spotting new business opportunities and recruiting the right people. Probably most people would agree that these things are desirable, but not everyone would give all of them the priority that Sir Richard Branson does. For example, it is often said that the customer always comes first, but for Branson it is employees first.

Many argue that demands on leaders in organisations are changing in their nature and also increasing. Work organisations are increasingly reliant upon rapid and skilful innovation to exploit changes in markets and technology while also being well organised and efficient in their current core business (Probst et al., 2011). Leadership based upon close monitoring and control of subordinates is often no longer appropriate or even possible. Subordinates and leaders sometimes work in different locations, which makes close supervision very difficult (see Chapter 15 for more on virtual teams and communication). The task of leaders, even at quite low levels in an organisation, is said to be managing continuous change and delegating responsibility while maintaining an overall sense of direction. Yet this may not come naturally to either leaders or followers. To quote an analysis of leadership from South African and American perspectives:

> What is killing us is the illusion of control: that things can be predictable, consistent and forever under control. What is also killing us is that followers require their leaders to be in control, on top of things, and to take the blame when things go wrong. Nearly all the new management programmes on TQM, re-engineering, right-sizing, just-in-time, this or that, are really old wine in new bottles – more efforts to design control systems that ask the workers to try harder, do better and be even more productive.

(April et al., 2000: 1)

Key learning point

Leadership is especially challenging nowadays because of the pace of change, the illusion of control and the high expectations of followers.

In this chapter we examine some of the many academic approaches to leadership. There is quite a long history of research in this area, and it would be impossible to cover all of it. Particularly influential work will receive most attention, along with applicability in 21st-century workplaces. In many of the early sections of this chapter you will see that we identify issues that will be discussed later in this chapter: this is because many early theories of leadership fail to account for important aspects of leadership behaviour. We also consider whether contemporary theories of leadership are successful in addressing these deficiencies. In accordance with the increasing internationalisation of the organisational realm, we will also examine the extent to which national cultures affect perceptions and the impact of leaders.

Some important questions about leadership

Leadership can be considered to be the personal qualities, behaviours, styles and decisions adopted by the leader. One attempt at defining leadership in a cross-culturally valid way comes from the Global Leadership and Organisational Behaviour Effectiveness (GLOBE) Project, to which we will return later. After ample discussion, scholars representing

56 countries defined leadership as 'the ability of an individual to influence, motivate, and enable others to contribute towards the effectiveness and success of the organisation of which they are members' (House et al., 2004).

A leader can be defined as the 'person who is appointed, elected, or informally chosen to direct and co-ordinate the work of others in a group' (Fiedler, 1995: 7). This definition acknowledges that the formally appointed leader is not always the real leader, but it confines the notion of leader to a group context. If we take the word 'group' literally, this definition *excludes* leaders of larger collectives such as nations, large corporations and so on (except in so far as they lead a small group of senior colleagues, such as a cabinet of government ministers, or other members of a board of company directors). You will probably notice that this goes against how we often view leaders; we also tend to see those who are indirect supervisors at much higher levels in organisations as leaders.

When most followers do not have direct contact with the leader, the dynamics of leadership may differ from those when they do. This is an important point because many leadership theories were developed for the situation of *close supervision* rather than more distant leadership. Waldman and Yammarino (1999) have argued that similar concepts can be used to describe leadership styles in these two situations, but the ways in which followers form impressions of the leader differ. For those close to the leader, impressions are derived from day-to-day interaction. For those distant from the leader impressions depend more on leaders' stories, vision and symbolic behaviours and on how well their organisations perform.

Key learning point

Leadership involves complex interpersonal processes, and is not simply telling people what to do. The real leader of a group may not be the person who was formally appointed to the role.

Over the years several distinct but related questions have been asked about leaders and leadership, including:

- Who becomes a leader and how do leaders differ from other people? In other words, can we predict the emergence of leadership?
- How can we describe their leadership?

It is difficult to consider these questions without bringing in the notion of effectiveness. So we can also ask questions like:

- What determines the effectiveness of leaders? What are effective leaders like (e.g. what characteristics do they possess, what do they do, what do they say?) and how do effective leaders differ from ineffective ones?
- What characteristics of the various situations that leaders find themselves in help or hinder a leader's effectiveness?

How can we tell whether or not leaders are effective? One method might be to assess the performance of their groups relative to other similar groups with different leaders. This assumes both that such comparison groups are available and that performance is easy to measure. However, some teams perform unique, new and knowledge-intensive tasks: this makes their performance harder to 'see'. Also, in many jobs, performance is difficult to define objectively and measure accurately in all aspects, especially in the long term. Then there is also the problem that performance is often determined by many things other than leadership. The current state of the employment market is an obvious example of such a factor affecting performance while not being directly under the leader's control. Employees may be aware that they can get better pay for doing a similar job elsewhere, and hence underperform despite good leadership. They might also leave when there are plenty of jobs available, rendering voluntary turnover an inaccurate measure of good leadership. Sometimes group members' satisfaction with the leader is used as a measure of leader effectiveness, but who is to say that high levels of satisfaction with the leader are always good? At times good leaders probably need to ruffle a few feathers. Although too much turnover tends to be harmful to the organisation, some turnover might be healthy because it can bring new people with new skills and ideas. In short, there is no perfect measure of leader effectiveness. Group performance is used most often, probably correctly, but we must remember not to expect an especially strong association with leadership: too many other factors come into play.

Key learning point

There is no one perfect indicator of leadership effectiveness, but the work performance of the leader's work group or organisation is probably the best (although the influence of other factors on work group performance also needs to be taken into account).

Before considering leadership theories, it is worth reflecting a little on why there is a chapter specifically about leadership in this book, and indeed in most others about work psychology or organisational behaviour. Should we automatically assume that leadership exists in an objective sense, or is it a concept we construct to help navigate a complex social world? Especially if it is the latter, what are our motives for using the concept of leadership so much? In an article entitled 'The romance of leadership', Meindl et al. (1985: 79) argued that:

> [W]e may have developed highly romanticised, heroic views of leadership – what leaders do, what they are able to accomplish, and the general effects they have on our lives. One of the principal elements in this romanticised conception is the view that leadership is … the premier force in the scheme of organisational processes and activities.

In some carefully designed research, Meindl et al. showed that we are inclined to explain major successes and failures as a success or failure of leadership, whereas if there is neither huge success nor failure, we tend to find other explanations for the average performance. It's as if leadership is a big concept that we use to explain big events. Gemmill and Oakley (1992) have argued that we use it to protect ourselves from anxiety brought about by uncertainty concerning what we should do ('no need to worry, the leader will decide'), and from various uncomfortable emotions and wishes that arise when people try to work together. They also argue that the cost of using the concept of leadership to organise our social world is *alienation* – that is, feeling distant from our true self and devoid of authentic relationships with others. This could be because we give too much responsibility to people we label leaders, and therefore find it difficult to view ourselves as purposeful, self-managing individuals.

All of this seems like good evidence for a romanticised view of leadership, where we tend to overestimate its importance, but this is not necessarily true. Meindl et al. (1985) did not demonstrate that we are wrong to make these attributions about leadership, only that we make them. Others, such as Yukl (2012), and the numerous sources of evidence cited in this chapter, argue that the quality of leadership really does make a difference to outcomes that matter in the real world.

The early leader-focused approaches to leadership

You will have noticed that for many of the chapters in this book we examine the simple ideas before moving to the complex theory and research. This is the approach we will take with leadership. Much theory and practice in leadership has had two key features:

1 Description of the leader in terms of their characteristics and/or behaviours rather than the dynamics of the leader's relationship with subordinates.

2 Attempts to identify the characteristics/behaviour of 'good leaders' *regardless* of the context in which they lead.

Leader characteristics

One of the questions early leadership research tried to answer was: which characteristics differentiate leaders from non-leaders, or effective leaders from ineffective ones? Some early work (reviewed by Stogdill, 1974; House and Baetz, 1979) found that leaders tended to be higher than non-leaders on:

■ intelligence;

■ dominance/need for power;

■ self-confidence;

■ energy/persistence;

■ knowledge of the task.

Many other personality traits (e.g. good adjustment, emotional balance and high integrity) were found in some early studies to be more common among leaders than non-leaders (e.g. Bass and Stogdill, 1990). Although this early search for what makes a leader did yield some interesting results, researchers did not find a definitive, consistent profile of characteristics among effective leaders. Also, this research was of variable quality which made it difficult to identify reliable findings.

More recently, meta-analysis has allowed researchers to isolate the common, reliable findings from the vast amount of previous research. Judge et al. (2004b) reviewed a large number of studies of leadership and discovered a modest but significant overall positive correlation ($r = 0.27$) between intelligence and leadership. Meta-analysis has also helped us to understand better the relationship between personality and leadership. Judge et al. (2002, 2009) have found that, overall, the Big Five model of personality (see Chapter 3) had a multiple correlation of 0.48 with leadership. This indicates that when traits are organised according to the five-factor model and they are all included, there is a moderate relationship between them and leadership. Looking at each of the Big Five in turn, this study showed that those who are more likely to emerge as leaders, and be more effective, tend also to be:

■ high in extroversion, openness to experience and conscientiousness (with there being relatively small positive correlations between these and the emergence of leadership and leadership performance);

■ low in neuroticism (with there being a small, negative correlation between this and leadership emergence and performance).

This comprehensive analysis of personality and intelligence concluded that no one trait stood out as the single most important determinant of effective leadership. One possible explanation that Judge et al. suggest for this is that traits may interact with each other to determine the quality of leadership. For example, high levels of intelligence may only lead to effective leadership if the individual also possesses the *other traits* that are also necessary to show effective leadership in any given context (Judge et al., 2004a):

> It is possible that leaders must possess the intelligence to make effective decisions, the dominance to convince others, the achievement motivation to persist, and multiple other traits if they are to emerge as a leader or be seen as an effective leader. If this is the case, then the relationship of any one trait with leadership is likely to be low.

(Judge et al., 2004a: 549–50)

Key learning point

Although no single characteristic or trait fully explains leadership, personal characteristics such as intelligence and personality appear to be important for the emergence of leaders and the effectiveness of leaders.

Point of integration

In Chapter 3 we discuss the role of personality and intelligence in explaining who are good performers at work. Leadership is an important component of many jobs, so you might like to compare general findings about personality and intelligence in Chapter 3 with those specifically about leadership in this chapter.

Therefore, there is enough reliable research evidence that intelligence and sociability play a role in determining which people emerge as leaders (although as we will see later they are only part of the story). However, these same characteristics that help leaders to reach the top may also subsequently prove their undoing, and lead to what is often called *derailment*, which is when things go very badly wrong. For example, a high level of dominance and need for personal power may help people reach leadership positions, but once there such traits may prevent a leader maintaining good relationships with their team or superiors, and this may precipitate their removal. Furnham et al. (2014) suggest that when leaders are selected for their roles, the selectors too rarely consider whether it is possible to have too much of a good thing. A leader who is, for example, highly extravert and dominant may talk all the time and alienate everyone by not listening to alternative points of view. There is increasing interest in so-called 'dark side' personality traits (Judge et al., 2009) that may be good in moderation but not in excess. An example is excitability, which at the extreme can produce a leader who is moody and has inconsistent concerns; is enthusiastic about something/someone and then suddenly becomes disappointed in them; and who has unstable and intense relationships. The Hogan Development Survey (Hogan, 2009) is a personality test designed to identify some of these danger signs before it is too late.

In addition, the characteristics of people who attain leadership positions have been found to depend partly on their motives for being leaders, and the acceptability of those motives to those who appoint them. Research in the Netherlands compared Chief Executive Officers (CEOs) in the 'not-for-profit' sector (e.g. organisations campaigning for children's rights or environmental protection) with CEOs in the commercial sector. Those in the not-for-profit sector scored *lower on the power motive and higher on the social responsibility motive* (De Hoogh et al., 2005; De Hoogh and Den Hartog, 2008). These pieces of research also showed CEOs in the voluntary sector were also generally seen as exhibiting more power-sharing leader behaviour and less despotic leader behaviour than those in commercial organisations. These findings fit with the idea that leaders are likely to be attracted to organisations that fit their personality and values (e.g. Schneider, 1987). People with a high concern for responsibility may be more attracted to jobs in not-for-profit organisations, as they feel these organisations have a social and morally responsible orientation. Therefore, when leaders use their power for purely personal goals in such organisations, they may be perceived to be acting against the organisation's altruistic values. Thus, the acceptability of leaders' motives is likely to vary in different contexts or for different 'audiences' and organisational contexts. We will return to this issue when we examine leadership in different cultures.

However, it should also be noted that some findings about leadership are applicable in many different organisational settings. House and Baetz (1979) have argued that the very nature of the leadership role must mean that sociability, need for power and need for achievement are at least somewhat relevant, across different organisations and organisational cultures. Two of their insights are generally accepted by many studying leadership:

1   A leader's personal characteristics must be expressed in their observable behaviour if those characteristics are to have an impact on others and their performance.

2   Different types of tasks may require somewhat different leader characteristics and behaviours.

Key learning point

The leadership characteristics that are desired and acceptable may vary across different organisational contexts. In any case, these characteristics only matter if they affect the leader's behaviour at work.

Task orientation and person orientation

Way back in the 1950s, one research team at Ohio State University and another at Michigan University launched independent projects on leader behaviour. Rather than focusing on the *characteristics* of leaders, they focused instead on how leaders *behaved*. They did this primarily by asking subordinates to describe the leader's behaviour. This produced a very long initial list of leaders' behaviours, within which there seemed to be two separate groups of behaviour (i.e. two general underlying dimensions). One focused on how leaders facilitate group maintenance and the other on what leaders do to ensure task accomplishment. These were described as follows (Fleishman, 1969):

1   *Consideration*: the extent to which a leader demonstrates that they trust their subordinates, respect their ideas and show consideration of their feelings.

2   *Initiating structure*: the extent to which a leader defines and structures their own role and the roles of subordinates towards goal attainment. The leader actively directs group activities through planning, communicating information, scheduling, criticising and trying out new ideas.

The Michigan team started by classifying leaders into two groups (as effective or ineffective) and then looked for behaviours that distinguished these two groups. Behaviours associated with relationships (consideration) and task orientation (initiating structure) differentiated the effective and ineffective managers: effective managers seemed concerned about both the task and their subordinates. Based on this, Blake and Mouton's (1964) managerial grid (still used in some management training courses) encourages leaders to examine their own style on these two dimensions: the suggestion is that it is usually best to be high on both consideration and initiating structure. Notice in the opening case study to this chapter how much Sir Richard Branson emphasises consideration as a key aspect of his leadership.

However, when trying to achieve different outcomes, might one style be more effective than another? Meta-analysis (Judge et al., 2004b) of leadership research has revealed that both consideration and initiating structure are positively related to desirable outcomes. There was a strong tendency for leader consideration to be associated with subordinates' satisfaction (correlation of 0.68, which is very high), which shows that followers want their leaders to be considerate. Leader consideration was less strongly associated with group performance (correlation of .23), but nevertheless there is a link: other things being equal, more consideration means better group performance. Initiating structure was less strongly associated with follower satisfaction than consideration is (.27) but it's still a positive correlation, meaning that more often than not followers like a leader who provides structure. Initiating structure has the same weak but positive association with group performance as consideration (.23).

Taking the comparison between consideration and initiating structure a step further, Lambert et al. (2012) examine whether it is not so much the amount of consideration and initiating structure the leader exhibits that matters, but how that amount compares with what the followers want. In two studies, they find that the fit between wanted and received consideration and initiating structure does indeed affect the satisfaction and commitment of followers. Interestingly, receiving more consideration than desired did not have negative effects, but in contrast receiving more initiating structure than desired did undermine followers' attitudes. It seems we would rather have an overly sympathetic boss than an overly controlling one.

In any case, structuring and consideration refer to quite specific styles of day-to-day behaviour. They give little indication of how *well* the leader structures tasks or expresses consideration. They also give no indication of how well the leader is thinking strategically about what the work group is trying to achieve, and by what routes. The extent to which leaders working at the highest levels of large organisations use structure and consideration with immediate subordinates may have little or no impact on the wider organisation. Later, we will return to the more strategic angle when we discuss providing an overarching vision as an important element of leadership.

Key learning point

Consideration and initiating structure are useful concepts that have stood the test of time in analysing leadership. However, they focus on the leader's day-to-day behaviour rather than their overall strategy.

Participation and empowerment

Another behavioural style that received much attention is participation. This concerns the extent to which the leader consults with his or her followers and takes their views into account before making decisions. Sharma and Kirkman (2015: 198) argue that empowering leadership incorporates participation, but also goes a step further in delegating decision-making to team members. This is in line with Gastil's (1994) conceptual analysis of **democratic leadership** where the leader: (i) distributes responsibility to ensure maximum involvement and participation of every group member in group activities and setting of objectives; (ii) empowers group members to make and implement decisions in order to achiever goals, and (iii) aids deliberation by playing an active part in the definition and solution of group problems, without dictating solutions.

Stop to consider

Referring back to the opening case study in this chapter, the importance Sir Richard Branson places on delegation is clear, but to what extent do you think he does the other things that empowerment requires?

In the aftermath of the Second World War it was hoped and believed that democratic or participative leadership was superior to autocratic leadership. In general this seems to be the case in work situations. Carmeli et al. (2011) for example found that empowering leadership at the top of a company improved company performance through increasing the self-belief of managers just below the top of the company and through the information-sharing and discussion that normally take place when teams make decisions collectively. There are also often benefits at the individual level as well, in terms of employee commitment, job performance and willingness to engage in good citizenship behaviours such as helping colleagues (e.g. Raub and Robert, 2010). Nevertheless, like many phenomena in the psychology of work, empowering leadership may not always be an unmitigated benefit. Sharma and Kirkman (2015) suggest that it may be possible to have too much of a good thing, particularly perhaps where team members are inexperienced or lack self-confidence. In this case participative leadership may lead to poor performance and also to stress (see Chapter 10) among team members. There is also evidence that participative leadership elicits a more positive response from some personality types than others. For example, in line with the point about stress, Benoliel and Somech (2014) have found that people who score high on neuroticism experience more psychological strain when they have a participative leader than when they have a more autocratic one. In contrast, their less neurotic colleagues experience less psychological strain in general, but especially when they have a participative leader. Results like this do not necessarily mean that in some situations leaders should be consistently autocratic. If they develop and support their subordinates, over time they can adopt a more empowering approach as the team members gain confidence.

Key learning point

Empowering leaders give decision-making responsibility to their subordinates but remain active in group affairs. They do not just sit back and let the rest of the group sort everything out.

Stop to consider

On the basis of what you have read so far in this chapter, which of your personality characteristics and preferred ways of behaving might help to make you a good leader?

Which might be a problem in leadership roles? Can you do something about this?

Contingency theories of leadership

Introduction and Fiedler's theories

The above approaches to leader behaviour contribute to our understanding of what leaders do and the effects of their behaviour. In their original forms these approaches have an important feature in common. They all describe leader behaviour without paying much attention to the situation or context in which the leader acts. To oversimplify a little, they are stating that in order to be effective, leaders need to perform certain behaviours regardless of the context or the particular demands of the situation.

However, it only needs a moment of thought to realise that leadership occurs in a wide variety of situations. Can it really be the case that the same leader characteristics and behaviours are required, whatever the situation? In fact we have already briefly considered an example of this in the previous section of this chapter. Empowering leaders may usually be what is wanted, but not when team members are inexperienced and/or lacking self-confidence. Contingency theories of leadership assume that optimal leader behaviour is contingent upon (i.e. depends upon) the situation. As a result, contingency theories are fairly complex. They specify not only which aspects of leader behaviour are crucial, but also which aspects of the situation matter most, and which behaviours are best suited to which situations. Just to complicate things a bit more, there is also the question of whether leaders are capable of changing their behaviours, or alternatively whether they have a style and they stick to it no matter what. Of course, all this leaves plenty of room for disagreement.

Key learning point

Contingency theories of leadership propose that different situations demand different leader behaviours.

The earliest well-known contingency theory was put forward by Fiedler (1967). He suggested that leaders are either person-orientated or task-orientated, and that this was reflected in how positive they were about the co-worker they liked least (least preferred co-worker, or LPC). The idea was that if a leader could be reasonably positive about even this person, then he or she must be person-orientated. Key aspects of the situation, according to Fiedler, were: (i) leader–member relations: whether or not subordinates trust and like their leader; (ii) task structure: whether the group's tasks, goals and performance are clearly defined; (iii) position power: whether the leader controls rewards and punishments for subordinates. His research found that person-orientated leaders were best in most situations, but task-orientated leaders were best when the situation was either very favourable (harmonious relations, structured task, high leader position power) or very unfavourable.

Fiedler's theory was much criticised for making some dubious assumptions, such as that leaders cannot change their style, and that a leader could not be both person-orientated and task-orientated. Some also argued that there was no convincing explanation for the results, and that (assuming extremely favourable and extremely unfavourable situations are rare) it would be simpler to say that leaders should be person-orientated because that works best most of the time. Despite these doubts, Peters et al. (1985) reported partial support for the theory in an extensive meta-analysis. Schriesheim et al. (1994) also found general support by reviewing studies comparing leader performance in different situations.

Fiedler built on his earlier work in his cognitive resource theory (CRT) which examined how the cognitive resources of leaders and subordinates affect group performance

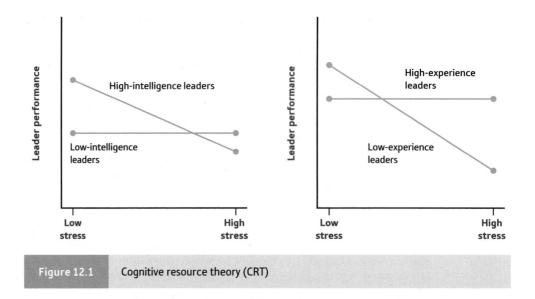

Figure 12.1   Cognitive resource theory (CRT)

Figure 12.1 — Cognitive resource theory (CRT)

(e.g. Fiedler, 1995). Some of the key predictions of CRT are shown in Figure 12.1. Fiedler argued that cognitive performance is inhibited in high-stress situations. That is, when leaders feel anxious or overloaded, they are unable to think clearly. In difficult situations they are likely to fall back on well-learned patterns of behaviour that result from their experience. Hence, in high-stress situations experience plays a more important role than intelligence in determining a leaders' performance. In low-stress situations there is more scope for clear thinking, so more intelligent leaders have an advantage that more than compensates for any lack of experience they may have. Sternberg (1995) has argued that experience is a disguised measure of so-called crystallised intelligence; that is, our store of know-how and knowledge about the world. This contrasts with fluid intelligence, which is the capacity to process new and complex information rapidly and accurately. When a lot of our cognitive resources (fluid intelligence) are being used in coping with a difficult situation, we use 'automatic' behaviour, which we can deploy without having to think too much about it (crystallised intelligence). CRT proposes that leaders' automatic behaviour in such situations is more likely to be appropriate and effective if it is based on long experience.

Key learning point

Fiedler's contingency theories treat leader characteristics and style as fixed features of the leader, and how stressful/difficult it is to be the leader as the key aspect of the situation to which a leader must be matched.

Point of integration

Fiedler used different aspects of intelligence to differentiate between different leaders and their likely effectiveness in different situations. For more on different approaches to intelligence and their relevance to work effectiveness, see Chapters 3 and 4.

Like Fiedler's earlier theory, CRT attracted considerable criticism (e.g. Vecchio, 1990). However, a more recent meta-analysis examining intelligence and leadership provides support for the two moderators suggested by CRT: fluid intelligence and leadership were more strongly related when leader stress was low and when leaders exhibited directive behaviours (Judge et al., 2004b).

Vroom and Jago's theory of leader decision-making

Vroom and Yetton (1973) proposed a contingency theory of leader decision-making (extended by Vroom and Jago, 1988). They took a different approach from Fiedler by focusing exclusively on specific decisions, big and small, that leaders have to make. In contrast to Fiedler, they suggested that leaders are able to adapt their behaviour from situation to situation. The theory identifies five styles of leader decision-making that leaders might choose to use. The options on this 'menu' range from autocratic styles to democratic styles (see also the section Participation and empowerment, above):

AI: The leader decides what to do, using information already available.

AII: The leader obtains required information from subordinates, then makes the decision about what to do. The leader may or may not tell subordinates what the problem is.

CI: The leader shares the problem with each subordinate individually, and obtains their ideas. The leader then makes the decision.

CII: The leader shares the problem with subordinates as a group, and obtains their ideas. The leader then makes the decision.

GII: The leader shares the problem with subordinates as a group. They discuss options together and try to reach collective agreement. The leader accepts the decision most supported by the group as a whole.

The **Vroom–Jago theory of leadership** (1988) identified some key features of a situation to consider that together indicate the style a leader should adopt in that particular situation. The situational features are shown in Figure 12.2. Also, Vroom and Jago argued that two further factors are relevant if the situational factors shown in Figure 12.2 allow for more than one recommended style to be used. These factors are (i) the importance to the leader of minimising decision time and (ii) the importance to the leader of maximising opportunities for subordinate development. Vroom (2000) provided some examples of this theory in action. Computer software has been developed that allows a leader to input answers to the questions listed in Figure 12.2. It then calculates an overall 'suitability score' for each possible style. The specific formulae are beyond our scope here, but general rules of thumb include the following:

- Where subordinates' commitment is important, more participative styles are better.
- Where the leader needs more information, AI should be avoided.
- Where subordinates do not share organisational goals, GII should be avoided.
- Where both problem structure and leader information are low, CII and GII tend to be best.

Key learning point

Vroom and Jago assume that leaders are able to alter their decision-making style to fit the situation they are in. Many factors in the situation can help determine appropriate styles, including time pressure, clarity of the decision parameters and attitudes of subordinates.

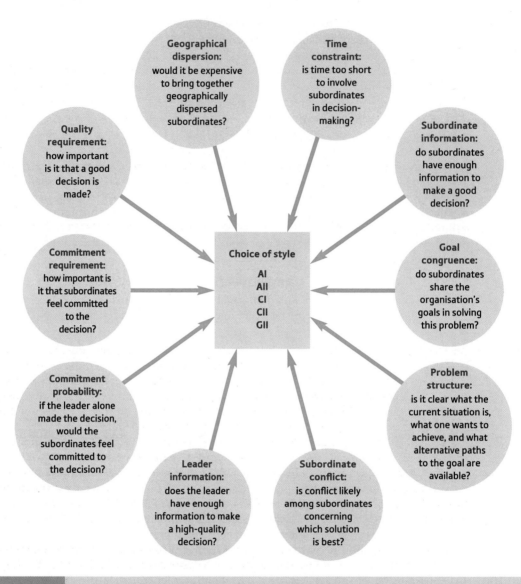

| Figure 12.2 | Vroom and Jago's features of leadership situations |

The model has not been examined much in the published research literature. There is some evidence that the skill with which leaders put their selected style into action is at least as important as choosing an appropriate style in the first place (Tjosvold et al., 1986). In practice, the model's complexity makes it difficult for leaders to use quickly and easily in their everyday decision-making. Due to their subjectivity, a leader's answers to the questions posed by the model (e.g. whether subordinates share organisational values) may say as much about the leader's personality and values (e.g. how they perceive the situation, or, remembering Fiedler, the leader's view of his or her least preferred co-worker) as about the reality of the situation itself. Vroom and Jago nevertheless suggested that knowledge of the general principles such as those presented here will often be useful, and sometimes even sufficient, for managers.

Leader decision style at Manchester United Football Club

Manchester United manager Louis van Gaal was reported in August 2015 as saying that he involved team captain Wayne Rooney in a range of decisions, including team selection. At the time Rooney was in his 12th season at the club, so he knew the club well. Van Gaal said he could trust Rooney to give honest and informed opinions about anything to do with the club. He felt there was mutual trust between the two of them, and he wanted to benefit from his team captain's knowledge. Van Gaal was quoted as saying 'When he comes to me and has remarks I always pay attention.' Van Gaal is also reputed to have consulted two leading players (Robin van Persie and Arjen Robben) about a change in team tactics when he was manager of the Dutch national soccer team.

In Vroom and Jago's terms, what decision style is Van Gaal using?

Considering the situational factors listed in Vroom and Jago's theory, identify the possible strengths and weaknesses of Van Gaal's approach.

Situational leadership theory

As Thompson and Vecchio (2009) have pointed out, there have been several versions of **situational leadership theory** (SLT). Two statements of it can be found in Hersey and Blanchard (1982) and Blanchard et al. (2013). This is another theory that contrasts two types of leader behaviour, in this case labelled directive and supportive. Directive behaviour is more or less the same as initiating structure. Supportive behaviour resembles a mixture of some elements of consideration and participation, and is mainly task-focused. SLT proposes that leaders can use both of these styles simultaneously, and can adjust their style to fit the situation. It proposes that what matters about the situation is the developmental maturity (sometimes also called readiness for self-direction) of the subordinates for the task(s) to be completed. This is construed as a combination of commitment to the task and competence to do it successfully. For the sake of simplicity, four levels of development and four leader styles are identified, based on combinations of the factors mentioned above.

SLT proposes that different leader styles are best suited to different developmental levels of subordinates. The predictions of the theory are outlined in Figure 12.3. During the early stages of employees' engagement with a task, leadership is mainly about orientating them to the task. They are enthusiastic about the task but probably unskilled in it. Therefore, the leader does not need to be supportive, but he or she does need to be directive. As employees gain maturity and start to cope with the task, their initial enthusiasm may wane a little but their competence increases somewhat. Therefore, the need for supervisory social-emotional support and development of employees increases, while the need for structuring decreases. At the highest levels of employee development in the task(s) required, supervisory behaviours (both task-related and social-emotional ones) become superfluous to effective employee performance. In other words, this approach suggests that once employees master both task and social relationships, they are perhaps best left to get on with it.

Vecchio (1987) and Thompson and Vecchio (2009) among others have tested SLT, although they argue that a strong test of it is difficult because levels of the key variables are difficult to specify (for example, how high does commitment have to be to be called high?) and it's not easy to differentiate between how leaders deal with individuals versus groups as a whole. Their general conclusion is that there is some support for SLT's prediction that at low levels of development a directive leadership approach is best. Perhaps this is similar to Fiedler's finding that task-orientated leaders are best suited to the most unfavourable situations. But beyond that, it is hard to find evidence for the theory's predictions. In particular, even with the most competent and committed employees, it is not a good idea for leaders to neglect both tasks and relationships. This echoes studies showing that a laissez-faire (or non-active) leader style is unlikely to be effective (e.g. Bass and Stogdill, 1990) and reminds us that when a leader delegates tasks this does not mean he or she can stand right back.

Despite some conceptual ambiguities and lack of support in research, SLT is used a great deal in leadership training. It is a commercial enterprise, and Blanchard and colleagues have registered a trademark for the term 'Situational Leadership'. A common academic response to this would be that the theory should not be used in this way unless there is clear support for it. It's true that there may be better ones, but it can also be argued that SLT is an excellent vehicle for leaders to consider their own behaviour and that of their team members. It specifies in an accessible way some key aspects of leaders and their team members, and encourages leaders to view their subordinates in the context of the tasks currently faced rather than making overall judgements about them. If leaders conclude, for example, that groups they lead do not necessarily progress through the development levels smoothly and in the order presented, this may help them consider why not and whether, in their context, adjusting their style in the way SLT recommends would be effective. It is important, however, that leaders do not passively accept the predictions of SLT, but instead actively consider whether they apply to their context.

Key learning point

Situational leadership theory is popular in leadership training. It encourages leaders to consider how directive and supportive they are, and to adjust this according to subordinates' competence and commitment to the tasks they face.

How does the situational approach work?

Employee's developmental level	Leader's leadership style
D1 — Low competence, High commitment	← S1 – Directing, High directive-low supportive
D2 — Some competence, Low commitment	← S2 – Coaching, High directive-high supportive
D3 — Mid-high competence, Low commitment	← S3 – Supporting, High supportive-low directive
D4 — High competence, High commitment	← S4 – Delegating, Low supportive-low directive

Figure 12.3   Predictions of situational leadership theory

General observations about contingency theories

Contingency theories have not been particularly successful in predicting and explaining the effects of leadership. However, that does not necessarily mean it is wrong to think that different situations require different styles of leadership. Contingency theories have a hard task because they have to specify what it is about leaders that matters, what it is about situations, and how the two fit together. That is a lot more difficult than, for example, identifying the components of transformational leadership. The scope of contingency theories also produces additional problems. Perhaps the most common problem is one which has long been identified in social and personality psychology: how can one separate the situation from the person? For example, in Fiedler's first theory, one of the situational factors is leader–member relations. Not only is this something that can change over time, but it is also something that the leader can perhaps play an active part in changing, for better or for worse. The styles and personality of the leader may affect not only the success of any attempt to improve relations, but also why they were bad in the first place. Separating the people from the situation is not easy, and in fact may, in any case, be a false distinction.

Another difficulty for contingency theories is that they tend to require the dividing up of reality into categories such as high competency, or low need for group acceptance. As noted in the discussion of SLT above, often it is not clear what counts as high or low, and therefore for leaders a decision about when to change their style is not made much easier by knowing the theory. How much easier, and how much more tempting, simply to try to be (for example) participative or charismatic. Finally, it is sometimes difficult to think about situations in a generalised and rather abstract way. As the following example of a research study suggests, it may be necessary to be very context-specific about the features of the situation that matter.

Research methods in focus

Using scenarios to examine effective leadership

Yun et al. (2005) reported a study of leadership in trauma resuscitation teams in the emergency department of a large hospital in the USA. These multidisciplinary teams deal with life and death every working day. They are led by an experienced surgeon and a somewhat different set of team members assembles for each patient who arrives, according to which staff are available at that moment. Often, the information available to the team about the nature of the patient's injuries when he or she arrives is very incomplete.

Yun and colleagues first conducted an ethnographic study of this environment for a year, observing what went on and interviewing (when it was safe to do so!) members of staff. This gave them an in-depth understanding of the context and how it was perceived by the people working within it. From this, they developed some hypotheses about the features of leader and situation that mattered most, and what leader approach was best in what situation. Specifically, they distinguished between empowering and directive leader styles, between more and less severe patient trauma severity, and more and less experienced trauma teams. They hypothesised that directive leadership is best when patient trauma is severe and team experience is low, and that team learning (very important for the saving of lives) is greater when the leader is empowering rather than directive.

The hypotheses were tested with staff at the hospital using a scenario approach. That is, staff were given several short but detailed fictional but realistic case studies of situations that the trauma teams typically faced. The leader style, team experience and severity of patient trauma described in the case studies were systematically varied, and staff were asked to indicate the likely

▶

▶

performance of the team and the learning opportunities that would arise from the situation. The authors also conducted manipulation checks – that is, they made sure that staff participating in the study perceived the leader style, team experience and patient trauma severity in the way the researchers intended.

The researchers found that, on average, empowering leadership was perceived to work better than directive leadership. However, as hypothesised, a directive leader was seen as more effective for the quality of healthcare provided when the patient was severely injured. This was especially the case when the team was inexperienced. Empowering leaders were perceived as better than directive ones for producing team learning opportunities.

The researchers note that the ethics and practicalities of the situation meant that they could not monitor real cases as they happened, so they had to rely on hypothetical cases, albeit ones judged very realistic by the staff. They also point out that the practical implications of the findings are that trauma team leaders need to appraise quickly and accurately not only the patient condition but also the experience of the team, and be able to adjust their style accordingly. Finally, they argue that the specific situational features of this and other work contexts matter a great deal. Although patient condition, team experience and the directive versus empowering dimension of leader style might seem fairly predictable key variables, they were chosen based on a long period of researcher engagement with the hospital, and obviously would not be applicable to most other work settings.

Exercise 12.2   General versus specific in contingency theories

Read carefully the above Research methods in focus box. The researchers argue that contingency theories need to be customised to different workplaces, but there are clear connections between the concepts they use and those suggested in some of the contingency theories. Go back through this section of the chapter and see if you can identify what these connections are.

Stop to consider

To what extent do you think that contingency approaches to leadership cover all of the possible important features of situations that a leader might face? Can you think of other aspects of the situation that might matter?

Transformational leadership and charisma

The theories already discussed in this chapter show that both task- and relationship-orientated behaviours are important for effective group leadership. However, as we have highlighted, these theories did not explain the effectiveness of leaders in all situations. An important leadership function was rarely considered: leaders often provide a uniting vision, or overarching goal, for followers to strive for. In essence, much of the early research on leadership viewed the leader as a *tactician*, not as an *inspirational figure* with a strategic role. If we consider successful leaders in business and politics they are frequently portrayed as heroes and heroines who unite, inspire and motivate their followers by offering attractive strategic visions of a better tomorrow. Thus, in the 1990s, many scholars turned their attention to qualities such as vision, charisma and other related concepts. These added an important new element to the study of leadership.

Theorists in this area make a clear distinction between transactional and transformational leadership (Burns, 1978; Bass, 1985, 1997). Transactional leaders try to motivate subordinates by observing their performance, identifying the rewards they desire and distributing rewards for desired behaviour. The underlying idea is that transactional leadership is based on exchanges, or transactions, with subordinates. Leaders define work goals and the behaviour deemed appropriate for reaching them. They offer clarity and the desired rewards, and in return subordinates contribute effort and skill.

Transformational leaders, on the other hand, try to go beyond this skilled use of inducements by developing, inspiring and challenging the intellects of followers so that they become willing to go beyond their self-interest in the service of a higher collective purpose, mission or vision. To be effective, this vision needs to be ambitious but realistic, and articulated clearly and in inspirational ways. Through formulating a vision a leader attempts to interpret reality for listeners and give meaning to events. The leader communicates this vision through deeds as well as words, modelling desired behaviours. Transformational leaders encourage followers by setting a personal example and followers become motivated and emotionally attached to the leader – at least, that's the idea (Bass, 1985, 1997). Bass (1985) developed a questionnaire called the Multifactor Leadership Questionnaire (MLQ) to assess the extent to which subordinates perceive their leader to exhibit different components of transformational and transactional leadership (as well as laissez-faire leadership). The measured components are described in Table 12.1.

Key learning point

Transformational leadership is about inspiring and challenging subordinates, providing an overarching goal and setting a personal example.

Table 12.1	Components of transformational, transactional and laissez-faire leadership

The four components of transformational leadership

1 *Individualised consideration*: The leader treats each follower on their own merits, and seeks to develop followers through delegation of projects and coaching/mentoring

2 *Intellectual stimulation*: The leader encourages free thinking, and emphasises reasoning before any action is taken

3 *Inspirational motivation*: The leader creates an optimistic, clear and attainable vision of the future, thus encouraging others to raise their expectations

4 *Idealised influence, or charisma*: The leader makes personal sacrifices, takes responsibility for their actions, shares any glory and shows great determination

The two components of transactional leadership

1 *Contingent reward*: The leader provides rewards if, and only if, subordinates perform adequately and/or try hard enough

2 *Management by exception*: The leader does not seek to change the existing working methods of subordinates so long as performance goals are met. They intervene only if something is wrong. This can be *active* where the leader monitors the situation to anticipate problems, or *passive* where the leader does nothing until a problem or mistake has actually occurred

Laissez-faire leadership

The leader avoids decision-making and supervisory responsibility, and is inactive. This may reflect a lack of skills and/or motivation, or a deliberate choice by the leader.

Although the components described in Table 12.1 can be theoretically distinguished in research, in practice this is harder. Leaders' MLQ scores on the four components of transformational leadership often co-vary. In other words, when leaders are seen to exhibit one of these, they also tend to be rated high on the others. For example, Den Hartog et al. (1997) found high correlations (of 0.61 to 0.75) between the different components of transformational leadership in ratings of their leaders by about 700 people in eight Dutch organisations. Geyer and Steyrer (1998) also report similar findings in their sample of over 1400 employees of Austrian banks, as did Tracey and Hinkin (1998) in their sample of hotel employees in the USA. This shows that the components of transformational leadership tend to 'hang together' in followers' perceptions of leader behaviour.

Furthermore, contingent reward, a component of transactional leadership, tends to go hand in hand with transformational leadership. In other words, transformational leaders also tend to administer contingent rewards. Such rewards can be tangible (e.g. money) but also intangible in nature (e.g. praise or symbolic appreciation). In some studies it seems that transformational leaders tend to also engage in active management by exception. This may be a matter of context: in a high-risk context 'good' leaders might need to or be expected to engage in monitoring.

It has often been argued over the years that transactional and transformational leadership are not mutually exclusive (e.g. Bryman, 1992), and that leaders can demonstrate one or the other, both or neither. Both and neither seem to be more common than one or the other. Therefore although they examine qualitatively different behaviours, measures of transformational and transactional behaviour are often highly correlated (e.g. Nielsen et al., 2008b). Transformational leaders also tend to be perceived as executing the transactional elements of their job effectively.

Not surprisingly, the extent to which a leader is transformational seems to depend partly on his or her personality. For example, Judge and Bono (2000) found that transformational leaders tended to score higher than others on the personality traits extroversion, agreeableness and openness to experience (see Chapter 3). This might seem to suggest that we have come full circle back to the old trait-based approaches to leadership. However, they concluded that the connections between personality and leadership style are not strong enough to consider transformational leadership a personality-based theory: transformational leadership also appears to be about learned behaviour.

Key learning point

In the behaviour of real leaders, the four components of transformational leadership tend to go together with (i) each other and (ii) elements of transactional leadership.

Other work has taken a closer look at one particular element of transformational leadership: *charismatic leadership* (Conger and Kanungo, 1998). Charisma, as you might imagine, has been a difficult construct for researchers to define. It tends to be viewed by researchers as a *perception of a leader held by followers* as well as a *characteristic of the leader*. Intuitively, we might think that charisma is something a leader is (or is not) born with. However, Frese and Beimel (2003) report a study which suggests that leaders can be trained to perform some of the behaviours associated with charisma. Also, as Gardner and Avolio (1998) put it, perceptions of charisma are in the eye of the beholder and thus do not always stem directly or only from the leader's behaviour. Most researchers agree that a leader is not charismatic unless described as such by their followers. Success plays a role in this: more successful leaders are often seen as more charismatic regardless of whether they had full control over getting there. For example, House et al. (1991) found that the perceived success of past US presidents was associated with how charismatic they were thought to be.

In order to construct a definition of charismatic leadership, Conger et al. (2000) collected data from about 250 managers on five aspects of charismatic leadership in a business context. They found that there were five key elements to charismatic leadership – you might like to consider which of these Sir Richard Branson demonstrates in the opening case study of this chapter.

1   The leader formulates a strategic vision, and articulates that vision.

2   The leader takes personal risks in pursuit of the vision.

3   The leader is sensitive to the opportunities and limitations provided by the environment (e.g. in terms of technology, money, people).

4   The leader is sensitive to others' needs.

5   The leader sometimes does unusual or unexpected things.

Although this is labelled charisma, it clearly has a wider meaning than the more specific charisma component of transformational leadership in Table 12.1. Sensitivity to others' needs resembles individualised consideration, and articulating strategic visions resembles inspirational motivation. So this model of charismatic leadership forms an alternative way of viewing transformational leadership. Rowold and Heinitz (2007) find a strong overlap between transformational leadership measured with the MLQ and charismatic leadership as measured with Conger et al.'s measure.

Key learning point

The components of charisma as defined by Conger and Kanungo go beyond the narrower charisma dimension of the Bass model. Combined, these components are similar to transformational leadership as a whole as defined by Bass.

Exercise 12.3   Uruguay bids farewell to José Mujica, its pauper president

Jose Mujica (born in 1935) was president of Uruguay from 2010 to 2015, and a very unusual politician. Nicknamed 'Pepe', he did not live in the palace he was entitled to, choosing instead to inhabit a small and very unglamorous single storey home on the outskirts of Uruguay's capital Montevideo. He also drove a battered old VW Beetle and gave away 90% of his salary to charities.

Mujica rarely wore formal clothes (though he was persuaded to switch from tattered old sweaters to smarter fleeces) and he was not too worried about sticking to the party line. 'Spin doctors' were not for him and he attracted some criticism as well as admiration for the unguarded things he sometimes said. He was described by some as the president that every country would like to have, for his down to earth 'man of the people' style which appeared genuine. Yet he appealed not only to the poorer people in Uruguay, but also to a substantial part of the middle class, which is something that very few politicians in South America or anywhere else manage to achieve. Mujica was a passionate advocate of humility, environmentalism, simple living, liberation from global markets and societies based on relationships rather than money.

Prior to being president Mujica had a tough, eventful and controversial life. He was a revolutionary in the 1960s and 1970s, and for some years was a member of the Tupamaros movement which engaged in sabotage and some violent acts. Imprisoned several times, he and comrades escaped on more than

▶

one occasion. When recaptured after a gun fight in a bar in which he was shot six times, he and several other leading revolutionaries were imprisoned for lengthy periods of time in solitary confinement and very poor conditions. For Mujica this included two years at the bottom of a horse trough. Deprived of everything and with physical health problems as a result of being shot, his mental health was also poor. He says that this gave him strength and an appreciation that every day is a new dawn, even though his new dawn was a very long time coming – he was in jail for 13 years.

Uruguay re-established a constitutional democracy in 1985 after some years of authoritarian rule. Shortly after that, Mujica and some other Tupamaros helped to set up the Broad Front political coalition which eventually gained power and enabled him to embark on a political career as a socialist. Inevitably some felt that he (and his wife Lucia Topolansky a fellow revolutionary) had abandoned their principles. However, much of the population loved his concern for their everyday lives.

At the end of his presidency, Uruguay was in good economic shape and politically and socially stable, partly thanks to trade with China. Inequality and poverty had been greatly reduced. Mujica was not afraid to make controversial decisions, such as the legalisation of marijuana. This was not because he thought marijuana was a good idea, but because users were at the mercy of drug traffickers and other criminals. He was acutely aware that Latin America is rich but wealth is very unequally distributed, and he argued that the region should work together in a more co-ordinated way for peace, prosperity and justice.

Mujica was dismissive of the admiration he received for his unusual approach to being president. For him, the fact that normal, humble ways of living were somehow seen as special was a sign of just how mad the world had become.

Suggested exercises

1   Consider the ways in which José Mujica appears to be a transformational and charismatic leader.

2   What evidence does this case provide for the effectiveness of transformational leaders?

3   Discuss whether the attributes and behaviours required to be perceived as transformational are likely to be different for leaders of thousands or even millions of people (corporate bosses; politicians) than for more 'local' leaders of smaller numbers of people who they regularly come into contact with.

Assessing and understanding the impact of transformational leadership

Of course, there is great interest in whether transformational and/or charismatic leadership measurably helps improve the work performance, satisfaction, attitudes and well-being of individuals, groups and organisations, and if so how. In other words, does transformational leadership 'work'? The simple answer seems to be yes. The extent to which leaders are perceived to use elements of transformational leadership is positively correlated with measures of individual satisfaction and performance, and also with more organisational measures of performance and effectiveness, especially in times of change (e.g. Bass and Avolio, 1994; Nemanich and Keller, 2007; Tims et al., 2011). Rowold and Heinitz (2007) also found that transformational leadership shows a stronger relationship to profit than transactional leadership does.

Geyer and Steyrer (1998) carried out a particularly well-designed study of the impact of transformational leadership. They took a careful look at the nature and measurement of transformational leadership and obtained objective measures of the performance of bank branches in Austria such as volumes of savings, loans and insurance products. They also took into account local market conditions for each branch (for example, the average income in the area). Staff then rated branch managers on the MLQ. Core transformational leadership (intellectual stimulation, inspirational motivation and charisma) was a significant predictor of branch performance. So was contingent reward, though to a lesser extent. In addition, Geyer and Steyrer found that core transformational leadership, individualised consideration and contingent reward were strongly associated with the effort that branch staff said they exerted. Passive management by exception was associated with less effort and lower branch performance. The correlations between ratings of leadership and branch performance were not especially high (around 0.25) but with a large number of branches and high volume of business, this small effect of transformational leadership could mean a big impact on profitability company-wide.

The impact of transformational leadership does not appear to be limited to financial outcomes. In a longitudinal study Nielsen et al. (2008a) found that transformational leadership has a positive impact on employee well-being, partly due to the influence that transformational leadership behaviour has on shaping the nature of the work carried out by employees. Research by Conger et al. (2000) found that when followers perceive their leader as charismatic, they form more of a sense of group identity, empowerment and reverence (i.e. awe or extreme admiration) for the leader. Using a range of different measures of transformational leadership, studies find that charismatic leadership is related to top team effectiveness (De Hoogh et al., 2004), followers' positive emotions (Bono and Ilies, 2006) and organisational citizenship behaviours (e.g. Den Hartog et al., 2007). In the USA, Waldman et al. (2001) and in the Netherlands, De Hoogh et al. (2004) found positive relationships between charismatic leadership of CEOs and financial outcomes, but only in dynamic and challenging market contexts.

Because so much research has been undertaken into the impact of transformational leadership, meta-analyses have been published which attempt to collate the results of all relevant studies, in order to see the big picture. Judge and Piccolo (2004) found that across 87 studies, there was a strong tendency for followers to be satisfied with the leadership of transformational leaders (correlation of .71) and a weaker but still significant association between transformational leadership and group performance (correlation of .26). As you might have noticed, these figures for transformational leadership are very similar to those for leader consideration reported by Judge et al. (2004a) described earlier in this chapter. The contingent reward component of transactional leadership was also positively associated with satisfaction and performance (correlations of .55 and .16 respectively), though somewhat less strongly than transformational leadership. Active management by exception was in general slightly positively associated with satisfaction and performance outcomes; passive management by exception and laissez faire were negative. Correlations of transformational leadership with outcomes were stronger in cross-sectional than longitudinal studies. Findings were fairly consistent across different sectors of the economy and level of leader (e.g. supervisor versus senior manager).

A more recent meta-analysis focusing more specifically on performance outcomes of transformational leadership has been reported by Wang et al. (2011). Across 113 studies (some of which were also covered by Judge and Piccolo, 2004) they found the correlations shown in Table 12.2.

This paints a consistent picture of moderately strong positive relationships between a leader's transformational leadership and various aspects of performance (contextual performance means doing things that are not strictly part of the job description, principally good citizen behaviours). The leader's use of contingent reward is also positively related to performance. Closer inspection shows that contingent reward is slightly more effective than transformational leadership for individual task performance, whereas transformational

Table 12.2	Correlations between leadership style and performance outcomes	
	Transformational leadership	Contingent reward
Individuals' task performance	0.21	0.28
Individuals' contextual performance	0.30	0.23
Team-level performance	0.33	0.24
Organisation-level performance	0.27	0.15

Source: Wang, G., Os., I-S., Courtright, S.H., and Colbert, A.E. (2011) 'Transformational leadership and performance across criteria and levels: A meta-analytic review of 25 years of research', *Group and Organisational Management*, 36, 223–70.

leadership is slightly more effective than contingent reward for individuals' contextual performance, team performance and (especially) organisation-level performance. Wang et al. found that these findings were on the whole generalisable across levels of leadership (supervisory versus mid/upper); location (North America versus East Asia); research design (cross-sectional versus longitudinal); questionnaires used (Bass' MLQ versus other); and sector (private versus public, though seem to be slightly stronger for public).

Point of integration

Quite a lot of attention is paid in the literature on transformational leadership to its potential effects on employees' willingness to be good citizens by seeking opportunities to help the collective and not just do their own job. This is sometimes referred to as organisational citizenship behaviour, which is discussed in the context of organisational justice in Chapter 7 on motivation.

More recent research on transformational leadership has focused less on whether it has effects, and more on why and how it has effects (e.g. Kovjanic et al., 2013; Zhu and Akhtar, 2014). In the language of research, this means searching for mediator variables: that is, factors that transmit the effect of transformational leadership on outcome variables such as performance and satisfaction. For example, given that one of the stated purposes of transformational leadership is to raise followers to a new level of morality, perhaps followers of transformational leaders are more willing to do things for the team that are not necessarily in their own individual interests (Effelsberg et al., 2014).

Figure 12.4 shows some of the possible processes by which transformational leadership operates, based partly on research findings and partly on the hypothesised but not yet empirically supported effects of transformational leadership. It is proposed that the most immediate effects of transformational leadership are on individual and team states such as feeling that they share the same values as the leader, a sense of competence, and willingness to think about how work is done and how it might be done better. Over time this leads on to more lasting changes in motivation and working practices (both group and individual), which in turn produce measurably more distal outcomes, including success at core tasks,

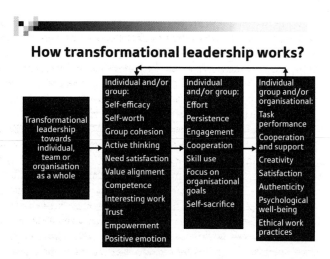

How transformational leadership works?

| Transformational leadership towards individual, team or organisation as a whole | Individual and/or group:
Self-efficacy
Self-worth
Group cohesion
Active thinking
Need satisfaction
Value alignment
Competence
Interesting work
Trust
Empowerment
Positive emotion | Individual and/or group:
Effort
Persistence
Engagement
Cooperation
Skill use
Focus on organisational goals
Self-sacrifice | Individual group and/or organisational:
Task performance
Cooperation and support
Creativity
Satisfaction
Authenticity
Psychological well-being
Ethical work practices |

Figure 12.4	A possible process for how transformational leadership influences individuals and organisations

Key learning point

Transformational and charismatic leadership tend to be associated with good performance of individuals, work groups and organisations. This is likely to occur through a variety of mechanisms to do with employee motivation, engagement, self-sacrifice and cognitive activity.

a cohesive and mutually supportive organisation, people who are mentally healthy and able to be themselves. These outcomes feed back into the more immediate day-to-day states shown in the second box from the left, thus helping the process to continue.

The limitations and ethics of transformational leadership

The concepts of transformational and charismatic leadership clearly represent an important advance in our understanding of how leadership can be described and of how to be an effective leader. In the complex 21st-century world many feel we need a leader we can believe in. However, even with all this evidence to support it, this approach too has several limitations. We highlight four of these.

First, researchers have speculated, but so far scarcely investigated, whether the type of situation in which leaders and followers find themselves affects the suitability of transformational leadership. A few exceptions are starting to show that contingency models may be needed for this form of leadership too. More challenging, uncertain contexts seem to offer more room for transformational leadership to have effects (e.g. Shamir and Howell, 1999). Li et al. (2013) have found evidence from Chinese organisations that where team members identify strongly with the team, and regard the leader as 'one of them', transformational leadership by the team leader does not affect team members' citizenship behaviour or their willingness to take charge. This suggests that in these circumstances, the leader does not need to be transformational because he or she is already accepted by the team and the team is cohesive. Interestingly, however, these very features may be things that a leader has created by being transformational in the past, which highlights the possibility that there may come a point where a transformational leader has influenced working practices and culture so thoroughly that things can work well without further injections of charisma.

Second, until recently, there seems to have been an implicit assumption that the leader is the source of most of what happens. The reality may be that followers have as much impact on the leader as the leader does on the follower. Barker (1997) noted that too much (transformational) leadership research ignores the fact that any workplace has conflict and competition. Leaders and followers do not necessarily have the same goals. Barker argues that the 'ship' in leadership has too often led to leadership being seen as a set of skills (as in craftsman*ship*) rather than a political phenomenon (as in relation*ship*).

Third, transformational leadership glosses over the issue of whether the leader is forming and articulating an appropriate vision of the future. History tells us that some transformational leaders fail, or even cause terrible harm. In any case, followers may reject the leader's vision as being inappropriate. These concerns coupled with recent ethical scandals and sustainable management issues fuelled research on different forms of authentic and ethical leader behaviour (e.g. Avolio et al., 2004; Brown and Treviño, 2006). Different theories that pay much more attention to the moral aspects of leadership emerged. Recently, researchers have begun to consider ethical leadership as a behavioural style in itself rather than focusing only on ethical aspects of other leadership styles (Brown et al., 2005; De Hoogh and Den Hartog, 2008).

Fourth, and most important, there are some significant dangers and ethical dilemmas around transformational leadership. Writers such as Tourish and Pinnington (2002) and Tourish (2013, especially Chapters 2 and 10) argue that the notion of transformational leadership moves too close to cult leaders who are revered by their followers as people who can do no wrong. Going back to the Conger et al. (2000) analysis of charisma, is it really a good idea to have faith, reverence and adoration for our leaders? These are quasi-religious words which seem to place the leader above the rest of humanity. Over a period of time, this may encourage authoritarianism, which is not helpful for democracy, nor for the development of employees as mature and responsible adults. Even without authoritarianism, Kark et al. (2003) and De Vries et al. (2011) have shown how transformational leadership relates both to followers' empowerment and to their dependence on the leader. Thus, although such leaders may intellectually stimulate followers and help them take responsibility, they may also (perhaps unintentionally) increase their need for leadership. Alimo-Metcalfe and Alban-Metcalfe (2005) among others argue that the concept of transformational leadership has become too heroic and individualistic, which means it is not surprising that it tends to create dependence among followers, despite the presence of intellectual stimulation as one of its components. They have developed a somewhat different version of transformational leadership which puts more emphasis on relationships between leaders and followers, including leaders valuing their followers, engaging in social **networking** and information-gathering to help resource the group and keep it in touch with its environment, and being accessible and approachable. None of these are contradictory to the standard model of transformational leadership, but on the other hand they are not really emphasised either.

So there is a danger that some parts of transformational leadership, especially 'charisma', are used by a leader but others are not. Partly because the details of what a leader has to *do* to be transformational are rather vague, we can think that a smooth-talking, energetic person with a clear view for the future must be truly transformational. But such a person may be imposing his/her own goals with scant regard for the well-being, development, intellects or values of the followers. Furthermore, they may exploit the willingness of followers to set aside their self-interest, and they may even start to believe that their cause is so right and just that they are exempt from the normal rules of morality. Christie et al. (2011) have used the term 'pseudo-transformational leadership' to reflect this scenario. This is exemplified by self-serving yet highly inspirational leadership behaviours, unwillingness to encourage independent thought in subordinates, and little caring for subordinates more generally. It is clearly important to be able to differentiate pseudo-transformational from genuinely transformational leaders. At first this may not be easy, but some of the tell-tale signs are described below.

The difference between transformational and pseudo-transformational leaders is largely a difference between ethical and unethical behaviour. Northouse (2015: Chapter 13) sums up a number of approaches to ethical leadership as requiring leaders to build community, respect others, serve others, act fairly and demonstrate honesty. This draws upon some other approaches to leadership not covered in this chapter, most notably servant leadership (Greenleaf, 1977). This is based on the idea that leaders are putting themselves forward to serve a community, which means they put the interests of that community before their own (a clear overlap with genuine transformational leadership here) and do all they can to facilitate the well-being, development and autonomy of that community, without disadvantaging others who are in a vulnerable position (Walumbwa et al., 2010). Brown et al. (2005) take a social learning approach to ethical leadership and focus on the exemplary behaviour of the leader. They define ethical leadership as 'the demonstration of normatively appropriate conduct through personal actions and interpersonal relationships, and the promotion of such conduct to followers through two-way communication, reinforcement, and decision-making' (2005: 120). They find a correlation between ethical and transformational leadership, but show the two do not overlap completely (i.e. they appear to be different concepts). Others have defined ethical leadership as something more than the perceived normative appropriateness of leadership behaviour. Factors such as the leader's social influence, the purpose of the behaviour of the leader and the consequences of that behaviour for the leader and others are also important in determining ethical leadership (e.g. De Hoogh and Den Hartog, 2008; Turner et al., 2002). For example, Kanungo (2001) states that the leader, in order to be ethical, must engage in virtuous acts or behaviours that benefit others, and must refrain from evil acts or behaviours that harm others.

Key learning point

Despite the evidence for its positive effects, transformational leadership can go wrong. In particular, a leader with charisma can either deliberately exploit followers or start to believe his or her own hype. Either way, the focus shifts from the success for the enterprise as a whole to the glory of the leader personally.

Exercise 12.4   The MBA Oath

In 2009, students taking the Masters in Business Administration (MBA) course at Harvard University in the USA developed what has come to be known as the MBA Oath. This was inspired by two events: the 100th anniversary of management education at Harvard and the financial crash that happened at the time, arguably partly due to poor leadership practice.

The MBA Oath can be found at http://mbaoath.org/. It consists of two statements about responsible management and leadership of business and seven promises about ethical behaviour in future when working in business.

Take a careful look at the MBA Oath now and consider whether you would like to sign up to it. Whether you do or not, evaluate which of the two statements and seven promises reflect a commitment to transformational (and avoiding pseudo-transformational) leadership.

What attributes of leaders really matter?

So far we have explored a range of leader characteristics and behaviours, most of which are associated to some extent in some cases with attitudinal and performance outcomes. Inevitably, the question arises of which of these characteristics and behaviours are most important. In an attempt to address this question, DeRue et al. (2011) have assembled a huge amount of evidence from many studies of leadership, combined the findings, and subjected them to sophisticated statistical analysis. They used gender, intelligence, and the Big Five personality characteristics (see Chapter 3) as leader characteristics, and consideration, initiating structure, transformational leadership and the components of transactional leadership as leader behaviours. Some of their findings are shown in Table 12.3.

The first thing to notice is how satisfaction with the leader is much more fully explained by leader characteristics and behaviours than group performance is. This is not surprising: it is easier to affect how people feel about us than how well they do something, or even how they feel about their job in general. Second, despite all the hype about transformational leadership, leader consideration is much more important in affecting follower satisfaction with the leader. Third, for group effectiveness, transformational leadership outperforms consideration, but still only explains 6 per cent of the variation in group effectiveness. Therefore it is necessary to be wary of people who imply that transformational leadership (or any other leader attribute) is the answer to performance issues. Fourth, the combination of initiating structure and conscientiousness explains 11 per cent of variation in group performance. This reinforces the importance of a leader who pays attention to organisation and deadlines – though leader conscientiousness seems to be mildly negative for follower satisfaction. Fifth, a leader who notices performance and rewards (contingent reward) is a very important factor in the job satisfaction of followers. Sixth, the supposedly negative aspects of leadership (passive management by exception and laissez faire) are indeed negatively associated with outcomes, but perhaps not quite as strongly as one might expect, especially in the case of passive management by exception.

Seventh, De Rue and colleagues note that leader behaviours overall had a stronger relationship with outcomes than leader characteristics did. This is consistent with our observation earlier in the chapter that the effects of personality are largely exerted through behaviour, and indeed DeRue and colleagues report further analyses which suggest that some personality characteristics link with leader behaviours, which in turn link with outcomes. For example, the data are consistent with the proposition that conscientiousness affects initiating structure, which in turn affects outcomes. Thus when one takes into account these indirect effects, leader characteristics are slightly more important than they appear to be in Table 12.3. Still, as an eighth observation, notice that leader intelligence and gender play a very minor role. That is not to say that it doesn't matter if a leader is very unintelligent – only that within the range of intelligence of people who become leaders, intelligence is not playing a major role in effectiveness and satisfaction. As Judge commented (noted earlier in this chapter), intelligence is more strongly associated with who becomes a leader than with how well they lead once in position. Finally, a big note of caution. Although the reporting of these findings has been expressed in terms of outcomes and therefore implicitly cause and effect relationships, the data are based on statistical associations, which do not in themselves prove causality.

Key learning point

Transformational leadership, consideration and contingent reward are all consistently associated with positive outcomes, though to different extents across different outcomes. Leader personality is on the whole less strongly associated with outcomes than behaviours, with conscientiousness being the most important of the Big Five personality characteristics.

Stop to consider

Based on the data shown in Table 12.3, what are the key observable differences between a leader who most cares about being liked versus a leader who most cares about improving team performance?

Table 12.3 The associations between leader characteristics and behaviours and indicators of satisfaction and performance

Leader characteristics and behaviours	Percentage of variation explained by leader characteristic/behaviour in:			
	Leader effectiveness	Group performance	Follower job satisfaction	Satisfaction with leader
Gender	0		0	0
Intelligence	1 (+)	0		
Emotional stability	2 (+)	2 (−)	0	0
Agreeableness	1 (+)	3 (+)	1 (+)	3 (+)
Conscientiousness	4 (+)	5 (+)	3 (−)	6 (−)
Extraversion	4 (+)	1 (+)	0	4 (+)
Openness to experience	4 (+)	1 (+)	0	0
Initiating structure	4 (+)	6 (+)	2 (+)	6 (+)
Consideration	7 (+)	3 (+)	8 (+)	39 (+)
Transformational	8 (+)	6 (+)	9 (+)	14 (+)
Contingent reward	9 (+)	2 (+)	22 (+)	8 (+)
MBE-active	1 (+)	1 (+)	1 (+)	2 (+)
MBE-passive	1 (−)	1 (−)	7 (−)	0
Laissez-faire	12 (−)		3 (−)	10 (−)
Total % of variance explained	58	31	56	92

Notes
Empty cells mean there was not enough data to provide an estimate.
(+) means effect of leader characteristic or behaviour on outcome is positive; (−) means it is negative.
MBE = management by exception.

Source: Derived from DeRue et al. (2011) 'Trait and behavioural theories of leadership: An integration and meta-analytic test of their relative validity', *Personnel Psychology*, 64(1), 7–52; p. 33.

Gender and leadership

Of course, one of the most evident and difficult to change personal characteristics is one's gender. It can be argued that most leadership roles are typically described in stereotypically masculine terms, which might mean that women have more difficulty in (i) being selected for leadership roles, and (ii) being seen as good leaders even when they are selected. This seems especially likely when one considers the continuing disadvantage women are at relative to men in getting promotion to higher levels of organisations and professions (Barreto et al., 2009). Yet we have already seen from DeRue et al's (2011) work above, that gender does not seem to be a major factor in leader performance or the satisfaction of followers with the leader. Based on gender stereotypes, one might at least expect gender differences in leadership style, with women being more interpersonally orientated than men, on average.

In reviews of the fairly extensive literature, Eagly et al. (1995) and Eagly and Carli (2003) found that women do *not* lead in a more interpersonally orientated and less task-orientated manner than men in organisations. However, on average women do use a more participative or democratic style than men, and their style tends to be more transformational than men's (especially charisma and individualised consideration). Women also tend to engage in more contingent reward behaviours than men, while men exhibit more 'management by exception' than women. Based on what has been discussed in this chapter about leadership success, we would expect that women will be more effective than men on average because they tend to adopt styles which are associated with effective performance and satisfaction of the teams they lead. A recent meta-analysis of 95 studies with robust data (Paustian-Underdahl et al., 2014) found that men rate themselves as significantly more effective than women rate themselves. This replicates an effect often found across a range of settings. In contrast, women are rated by others as significantly more effective than men, and this is not a recent phenomenon resulting from (slowly) increasing gender equality. Instead, it appears to have been the case since the 1980s. Women's advantage is most evident in business and education sectors; it does not occur in government or military ones. Also, women's advantage is present at middle and upper leadership levels, not junior ones. This may be because, as already noted, entry to higher level leadership roles is especially difficult for women and perhaps only the best women leaders reach those positions. On the other hand, given that in many organisations selection procedures leave something to be desired (see Chapter 4), one cannot assume that it is necessarily the most effective women leaders who reach those higher positions.

All this suggests that women overall have a slight advantage over men in leadership positions. This may be helped by not only the possibility that only the best women make it into leadership positions, but also changing perceptions of what is a good leader, which seem to be moving somewhat away from agentic, assertive stereotypically male characteristics to a more balanced view where relationships and empathy are also valued (Koenig et al., 2011). Nevertheless, women and men may still be perceived somewhat differently, and to the extent that leadership roles are still seen as masculine in character, women's behaviour may be interpreted as unsuitable, even if it is exactly the same as men's. An example of this can be seen in Lewis (2000). Lewis asked students to view videotapes showing a male or female company chief executive displaying anger, sadness or emotional neutrality in response to a company's poor performance. The students' ratings of the leaders' effectiveness tended to be *lower* if leaders expressed emotion than if they did not. However, displays of anger damaged the ratings of female leaders more than they damaged those of male leaders. Lewis suggested that this result showed the importance of followers' perceptions of leaders' behaviour. In this study it was suggested that whereas a man's anger might be perceived as assertiveness, a woman's anger may be perceived as aggression or instability.

> ### Key learning point
>
> Women tend to lead in more transformational and participative styles than men. To some extent these generally effective styles lead to slightly better evaluations of women's performance in leadership roles than men's, but women are still at a disadvantage in gaining access to higher-level leadership roles and in the way some of their behaviour is perceived.

Global leadership

The globalisation of markets brought about by communications technology and the mobility of production resources mean that more and more people work in countries and cultures that are novel to them. For many managers, this means leading people of different backgrounds and outlooks from their own. It is commonly argued that different leadership styles are required in different countries and cultures (note that most countries have multiple cultural subgroups, so country and culture are not quite the same thing). Especially in multinational companies a lot is invested in cross-cultural training for managers, a substantial proportion of which focuses on leadership. In general, it has some positive effects on managers' subsequent success in international assignments (Littrell et al., 2006). This approach to global leadership is a type of contingency approach (see earlier in this chapter for coverage of contingency theories) because it is saying that the best leadership style to adopt is contingent on (i.e. depends on) the cultural norms and expectations prevailing where the leader is working.

Of course, it's not enough to say that countries and cultures differ. We need ways of describing how they differ. Hofstede (1980, 2001) carried out pioneering work in this area. He collected data from employees of IBM across many countries and identified four cultural dimensions:

1 *Power distance*: the extent to which members of a society accept that there should be an unequal distribution of power between its members.
2 *Uncertainty avoidance*: the extent to which members of a society wish to have a predictable environment, and have set up institutions and systems designed to achieve this.
3 *Masculinity versus femininity*: a masculine society values assertion, success and achievement, while a feminine one is orientated more towards nurturing and caring.
4 *Individualism versus collectivism*: the former reflects a belief that individuals should be self-sufficient while the latter emphasises people's belongingness to groups in which there is mutual support.

Out of 52 countries, the USA scores the highest on individualism, and the UK third. In fact, the rankings for the two countries are quite similar on all four dimensions, yet of course there are still some cultural differences that are noticeable to those who are familiar with both countries. For example, the UK's loyalty to its National Health Service – a collectivist style of organisation – is strong, despite the country's overall individualist culture, and something of a mystery to many Americans. This signals that similarity on Hofstede's dimensions does not mean identical cultures in all respects. Still, the Hofstede dimensions are helpful in identifying just how cultures do and do not differ. For example, the UK and the People's Republic of China are similar on masculinity (quite high) and uncertainty avoidance (quite low) but very different on individualism-collectivism (the UK is much more individualistic) and power distance (China is much higher). Hofstede also later suggested a fifth dimension: long-term orientation versus short-term orientation, with China being the most long-term orientated country. Although Hofstede's databank has been extended subsequent to his seminal work, it is necessary to be cautious about the descriptions of countries because they are originally based on IBM employees working in those countries, who may not be typical of the country as a whole.

It would be strange if there were not differences between countries with respect to the preferred, most used and most effective leadership styles. Using Hofstede's cultural dimensions we might expect autocratic styles to be more effective in high power distance cultures than in low ones. Leaders whose style is high on structure will probably be most appreciated in high uncertainty-avoidance cultures. Dickson et al. (2003) provided a very informative review of research on cross-cultural leadership. They discussed in detail some of the reasons why the dimensions of culture identified by Hofstede and others might affect which styles of leadership are expected and effective. They argued that the search for leadership styles that work across the whole world is (or should be) accompanied by more research into indigenous models (i.e. models of how leadership works in specific culture, rather than across cultures) as well as exactly how culture and leadership affect each other.

Key learning point

Cultural differences between countries are likely to affect what people expect from their leaders. This can create problems for leaders who do not understand what these expectations are.

Dominating the field of cross-cultural leadership for some years is project GLOBE, which was a long-term study concerning how societal and organisational cultures affect leadership (House et al., 1999). Over 60 countries from all major regions of the world are represented in it, making it the most extensive investigation of cross-cultural aspects of leadership to date. The core quantitative study examined what the images of outstanding leadership are in different cultures, and included over 17,000 middle managers from some 800 organisations in the financial, food and/or telecommunications industries. These managers were asked to describe leader *attributes* and *behaviours* that they perceived to enhance or impede outstanding leadership in their respective organisations. Like many studies over the years, therefore, GLOBE majored on perceptions of and preferences for styles of leadership more than the performance outcomes of leadership.

What were the findings? Attributes reflecting integrity (i.e. *trustworthy, just* and *honest*) contributed to outstanding leadership in all cultures. Also, an outstanding leader in all studied cultures shows many attributes reflecting transformational leadership: these include the leader being described as *encouraging, positive, motivational, a confidence builder, dynamic* and *having foresight*. Team-orientated leadership is also universally seen as important (i.e. such a leader is effective in team-building, communicating and coordinating). Other universally endorsed attributes included *excellence-orientated, decisive, intelligent,* and a '*win–win*' *problem solver*. The GLOBE study also shows that several attributes are universally viewed as ineffective including: *being a loner, being non-cooperative, ruthless, non-explicit, irritable* and *dictatorial*. Interestingly, however, many different leadership attributes were found to be culturally contingent. In other words, a high positive rating was obtained in some and a low or even negative rating in other cultures. Examples include being *unique* (i.e. different from the 'norm'), *indirect, status-conscious, intuitive* and *habitual*. These are examples of attributes that are considered desirable for outstanding leadership in some cultures but impediments in others (Den Hartog et al., 1999).

The attributes seem to reflect underlying culture differences. For instance, country means for the attribute '*subdued*' range from 1.32 to 6.18 on a 7-point scale and for '*enthusiastic*' from 3.72 to 6.44. Thus, in some countries acting in a subdued manner is highly relevant to being an outstanding leader and in others such an approach is described as highly inefficient. Similarly, showing enthusiasm is relevant for outstanding leadership in some, but not in other cultures. This seems to reflect cultural rules regarding the expression of emotion. In some cultures, displaying emotion is interpreted as a lack of self-control and thus perceived as a sign of weakness: not showing one's emotions is the norm. In other cultures, it is hard to be an effective communicator and leader without showing emotions.

Other culture dimensions are also reflected. For instance, several of the differences in attributes seem to reflect different levels of uncertainty avoidance (see Hofstede's dimensions discussed above). People in uncertainty-avoidance cultures want things to be unambiguous, predictable and easy to interpret and in such cultures technologies, rules and rituals are used to ensure this. This is reflected in several of the cross-culturally varying attributes. For instance, the attributes *risk-taking, habitual, procedural, able to anticipate, formal, cautious* and *orderly* are seen to impede outstanding leadership in some countries and enhance it in others. Similarly, several attributes reflect high power distance versus egalitarianism in society. For example, *status and class-conscious, elitist, domineering* and *ruler* are attributes that fit a high power distance society, but are seen in a negative light in egalitarian societies. Also, several of the attributes reflect the cultural dimension of individualism, for instance, *autonomous, unique* and *independent* are more important for outstanding leaders in individualistic than in collectivist societies.

Table 12.4 summarises many of the key concepts and findings arising from the GLOBE project. These are discussed and analysed in more depth in several places, including Javidan et al. (2006), Dorfman et al. (2012) and House et al. (2004). Clear links can be seen between some of the cultural dimensions and Hofstede's work, and between some of the dimensions of leader style and the styles discussed earlier in this chapter. That's a good thing – it would be strange if GLOBE had identified dimensions that were quite different from what had gone before. There is a pleasing neatness to summaries like this, and of course some truth to them as well. However, as the GLOBE team acknowledges, there is much that is common across cultures in terms of leader preferences. Some examples are mentioned above. Also, the focus on preferences for different styles of leadership means that leaders are being advised what will be most readily culturally acceptable in a given location. That is important, but what is most acceptable is not necessarily the most effective way of being a leader. Also, one could argue that having a leader who behaves counter-culturally in some respects is good for learning and cross-cultural understanding. Two-way communication, feedback and experimentation between leader and team members is likely to be more helpful for effective and harmonious working than a leader trying to follow a pre-defined 'recipe' for how to behave (Chaney and Martin, 2013).

It is important not to over-state differences between parts of the world in desired leader attributes. GLOBE revealed a lot of similarity. For example, mean scores for the desirability of the team-orientated leader style on a 1–7 scale varied between 5.5 in the Middle East and 6.0 in Latin America. That is a statistically significant difference, but it's not very big relative to the available scale, and to confuse the picture further, the 5.5 mean for the Middle East was the highest given by people in that region to any of the six styles. A more fine-grained analysis of European countries reported by Brodbeck et al. (2000) also demonstrates the delicate balance between similarity and difference in leadership preferences. As part of the GLOBE project, they asked managers to indicate the extent to which 112 words (such as *foresight, honest, logical, dynamic, bossy*) were characteristic of outstanding leaders. The 112 words were grouped into 21 scales, which were given names such as visionary, diplomatic, administrative and conflict-inducer. The 21 scales were further combined to produce the six broad leader styles shown in Table 12.4. However, sticking with the 21 scales, Brodbeck et al. found that the top five of the 21 in terms of describing a good leader among people in Anglo countries (UK, Ireland) were, in descending order, performance, inspirational, visionary, team integrator, and integrity. For Latin countries (Italy, Spain, Portugal, Hungary) the top five were team integrator, performance, inspirational,

Table 12.4	A summary of some findings from the GLOBE project

Nine aspects of national culture

1 *Performance orientation*: the degree to which a collective encourages and rewards its members for performance excellence and improvement
2 *Assertiveness*: the degree to which people are assertive, confrontational and aggressive in their interactions with each other
3 *Future orientation*: the extent to which individuals plan and invest in the future, and delay gratification
4 *Humane orientation*: the degree to which a collective encourages and rewards people for being fair, generous and caring to others
5 *Institutional collectivism*: the degree to which societal institutional practices encourage and reward collective distribution of resources and collective action
6 *In-group collectivism*: the degree to which individuals express pride, loyalty and cohesiveness in their organisations or families
7 *Gender egalitarianism*: the degree to which the collective minimises gender inequality
8 *Power distance*: the degree to which people expect and support the idea that some people are more powerful than others
9 *Uncertainty avoidance*: the degree to which a collective uses social norms, rules and procedures to make future events as predictable as possible

Derived from data on national cultures, ten clusters of countries

1   *Anglo*: competitive and result-orientated
2   *Confucian Asia*: results-driven, encourage group over individual goals
3   *Eastern Europe*: forceful, supportive of co-workers, treat women with equality
4   *Germanic Europe*: value competition and aggressive approach to get results
5   *Latin America*: loyal and devoted to their families and similar groups
6   *Latin Europe*: value individual autonomy
7   *Middle East*: devoted and loyal to their own people, women afforded less status
8   *Nordic Europe*: high priority on long-term success, women treated with greater equality
9   *Southern Asia*: strong family and deep concern for their communities
10 *Sub-Saharan Africa*: concerned and sensitive to others, strong family loyalty

Six aspects of leader style – in descending order of desirability to respondents in the GLOBE studies

1 *Charismatic/value-based*: ability to inspire, motivate, expect high performance
2 *Team-orientated*: effective team-building and implementation of a common purpose
3 *Participative*: involving others in making and implementing decisions
4 *Humane-orientated*: support, consideration, compassion, generosity
5 *Autonomous*: independent and individualistic leader
6 *Self-protective*: concern with own safety, security and image.

integrity and visionary. This is the same five as the Anglo countries, just in a slightly different order. Probably it signals that being a team integrator is crucial for leaders in Latin countries, but that certainly does not mean leaders can forget about it when working in an Anglo country because it is still the fourth most desired of 21 leader styles.

It is helpful to know that, for example, it is important to be a team integrator in Latin European countries, but unfortunately the label 'team integrator' does not specify what leader behaviours will be interpreted in a given culture as supporting team integration. Some research (Smith et al., 1989; Peterson et al., 1993) has sought to discover whether similar leader styles are described using the same dimensions across different cultures. Using data from electronics firms in the UK, the USA, Japan and Hong Kong, Smith et al. (1989)

concluded that what they call maintenance and performance leadership styles (similar to the consideration and structuring dimensions described earlier in this chapter) do indeed exist in different cultures. However, they also stated that 'the specific behaviours associated with those styles differ markedly, in ways which are comprehensible within the cultural norms of each setting' (1989: 97). For example, one of the questions asked by Smith et al. was, 'When your superior learns that a member is experiencing personal difficulties, does your superior discuss the matter in the person's absence with other members?' In Hong Kong and Japan, this behaviour is seen as highly characteristic of maintenance (consideration). In the UK and the USA it is not: probably most Western subordinates would regard this as 'talking about me behind my back'. Such cross-cultural differences in interpretation also hold for other behaviours and attributes. For example, Bass states that 'Indonesian inspirational leaders need to persuade their followers about the leader's own competence, a behaviour that would appear unseemly in Japan' (Bass, 1997: 132). He goes on to say that, notwithstanding the fact that it can be expressed in different ways, the concept of inspiration appears 'to be as universal as the concept of leadership itself'.

Key learning point

The GLOBE project collected a vast amount of data about similarities and differences between nations in their cultures and their expectations about leaders. It has provided many useful concepts and information that help leaders in the workplace to understand what their team members are likely to expect from them.

Stop to consider

Look carefully at the six broad leader styles identified by the researchers in the GLOBE project. In what ways do they reflect well-established ways of describing leader style, and in what ways do they advance on them?

Summary

This chapter has explored many approaches to leadership. Personality, consideration, initiating structure, cognitive complexity/intelligence, empowerment, charisma, vision and contingent reward, among others things, have been identified as some key leader characteristics and behaviours. Other less discussed notions such as the extent of the leader's knowledge of the industry and organisation must not be overlooked. There is considerable overlap between the various leadership concepts, and some tidying up and increased precision is needed. The same is true of the various situational variables proposed by contingency theorists. It is therefore not surprising that several leadership theories are equally (and moderately) good at explaining leadership phenomena. Several approaches contain useful practical guidance about how to go about being an effective leader, and it is notable that the things about a leader that followers like are not necessarily the same as the things that make for an effective team. Transformational and charismatic leadership models present a significant step forward, but they are not the answer to everything and they carry some dangers if they are abused by a leader and if followers are not determined or powerful enough to put a brake on the leader's activities. Future theory and practice in leadership need to combine concepts from the better theories in a systematic way. There is also increasing recognition that leadership is not only about leaders. It also concerns followers and their preferences, characteristics and behaviours and cultural and individual perceptions of what leaders should be as well as about the relationships between leaders and followers. Greater attention to the question of whether and how leaders can be trained or selected not only to do the desirable things, but to do them well and in an ethical and sustainable manner, is also needed.

Closing case study

Leadership and policy implementation

It was a turbulent time in the health and safety department of SuperChem's Hamburg plant. The multinational chemical company had recently adopted a policy of developing managers by giving them international experience. A consequence of this policy had been that 32-year-old José Alonso, who came from Seville in Spain, had been put in charge of the department. José's German language skills were adequate for the task and improving all the time, but this was his first assignment outside Spain, a country seen by many in the company as peripheral to its operations. He had much to learn when he first arrived, especially about German health and safety legislation. He was, however, an experienced health and safety manager, having been head of health and safety at two plants in Spain for two years each.

After just a few months in the job, José was pitched into an interesting situation. Two major accidents at other plants had caused a high-level health and safety policy review. The resulting report had come out in favour of more stringent inspection and a tougher approach from company health and safety departments. The recommendations were clear and specific, and had quickly become company policy.

José knew that his presence was resented by his six staff, who had worked together for some time and tended to think alike. They felt they had more specialist knowledge than he did, which was true for this specific plant, but not in terms of a wider appreciation of SuperChem's operations. Most were older than him, and they could not understand why the deputy head, Gunter Koenig, had not been promoted. Koenig himself was understandably especially bitter. José felt that he could not follow his staff around as they inspected the plant: it would look too much like snooping. On the other hand, he needed to tap into his staff's knowledge of the plant and of how things had always been done there. Existing documents were too incomplete or too out of date to be of much help.

José had reason to believe that his staff were competent at what they did, and committed to health and safety in what was potentially a hazardous working environment. However, they typically adopted a collaborative approach with the plant managers whose areas they inspected. They preferred to use friendly persuasion and gentle hints rather than the precise written reports and threats for non-compliance that would almost certainly be required by the new policy. It had always worked at that plant, they said, and it would continue to do so. Yet José knew that exactly the same had been said at the plants where major accidents occurred. What was worse for José was that it was fairly clear that the plant manager privately agreed with José's staff.

José's position was all the more difficult because he was known to be on a 30-month secondment, after which the previous head (who had herself been seconded elsewhere) was expected to return in his place. Therefore he was not in a position to exert a long-term influence on the careers of his staff. His inclination would have been to intervene in his subordinates' work only when something was clearly wrong, but the new policy did not permit that approach. José himself was answerable not only to the plant manager but also to the company health and safety chief, who was the chief proponent of the new policy. Despite this tricky dual-reporting arrangement, he had considerable autonomy in deciding which of his team members should receive performance bonuses and other perks when these were reviewed every six months. He could also decide how to divide up the team's work. Some team members had clear preferences about which tasks and parts of the plant they preferred to deal with, so this was a significant matter. José devoted considerable time to ensuring that if his team members did a good job, they got more of the tasks they liked, as far as this was possible to arrange.

José knew that he was not a particularly creative or imaginative individual. He enjoyed the precision and rules and regulations of health and safety work. He preferred to focus on implementing the detail of policies rather than the big picture. He was usually inclined to draw up detailed plans of work for himself and others, and to keep a careful check on implementation of those plans. He liked to formulate work plans in a collaborative manner, encouraging his subordinates to think for themselves about what was required and how best to go about it.

José was, in a quiet way, quite a forceful and assertive person, and his staff were starting to notice this. He was conscious of deadlines and correct ways of doing things, and he expected himself and his team to play by the book. He was generally a calm person and rarely majorly worried by things, and although the possibility of a major accident which might be something he could have stopped was always at the back of his mind, it did not keep him awake at night. He was delighted to be working outside his home country for the first time and despite a few amusing and even embarrassing moments he was enjoying getting to grips with German culture and language.

José felt he could understand how his staff felt about his appointment as their head without their consent: he had been landed with an unwelcome boss himself a few years earlier. He did not blame them for their attitude, and, characteristically, he was always keen to emphasise what he genuinely saw as the many strengths of his subordinates. He took time to discuss their work with each of them individually and tried to assign them work that would broaden their skills. He even listened patiently to their grievances about his own appointment to his post.

Despite the complicated situation, a decision had to be made and implemented concerning exactly how the department's practices would need to change in order to implement the new health and safety policy. José knew that an uplifting speech from him about his and/or the company's vision for health and safety in its plants might help, but that wasn't really his strength. Anyway, as far as he was concerned, the position was simple: ensure that safe working practices were clearly defined, updated when necessary, and adhered to in all parts of the plant. He did not see how he could put it any other way. So, José was asking himself, given that company policy required some kind of more robust health and safety inspections by him and his staff: (i) what form should this take in this plant, (ii) how should he go about making decisions about this, and (iii) how could he ensure that his staff were motivated to work with whatever new inspection system was decided upon?

Suggested exercises

1   Analyse this case study using one or more of the contingency theories. What kind of situation is it? How well suited to it is José Alonso?

2   In what respects, if any, can José's leadership style be described as (i) transformational and (ii) transactional? What scope is there for him to change, and would it make any difference if he did?

3   How do you think José would score on the Big Five personality characteristics? What might be the consequences of this for his leadership style and success?

4   In what respects are national and cultural differences in perceptions of leadership relevant to this case study? (As well as the material in the previous few pages of this chapter, note that in Hofstede's data Spain is somewhat higher in power distance and uncertainty avoidance than Germany, and Germany is higher than Spain in masculinity.)

Test your learning

Short-answer questions

1 Describe the strengths and weaknesses of alternative measures of leader effectiveness.
2 What are major pressures facing corporate leaders in the early 21st century?
3 Why does leader personality tend to affect leader effectiveness less than the leader's behaviour does?
4 Define consideration and initiating structure.
5 Suggest why leader consideration is much more strongly associated with follower satisfaction than with work performance.
6 Describe the key features of empowering leadership.
7 What are the main features of contingency theories of leadership? Suggest two strengths and two weaknesses of the contingency approach.
8 Suggest why situational leadership theory is popular, even though not well supported by most research.
9 List the leadership styles and problem-situation features identified in Vroom and Jago's theory of leadership.
10 Name and define four aspects of transformational leadership and two aspects of transactional leadership.
11 Briefly describe three possible weaknesses or limitations of transformational leadership.
12 Provide some examples of universally appreciated leadership characteristics and of cross-culturally contingent ones.
13 Name and define six styles of leadership identified in the GLOBE studies.

Suggested assignments

1 Discuss the proposition that all of the aspects of leadership style identified in research essentially amount to person-orientation and task-orientation.
2 Examine the extent to which different contingency theories of leadership share the same key ideas.
3 Discuss what is known about the relationships between leadership styles and characteristics on the one hand and performance at work on the other. What can be learned from this?
4 It is often said that leaders need to change their behaviour when they move between countries. Is that really the case?
5 To what extent do women leaders get the credit they deserve?

Relevant websites

In the UK, the Council for Excellence in Management and Leadership has been working since 2000 to promote good practice – as indicated by its strap-line of 'Managers and Leaders: Raising our Game'. Its web address is http://www.managementandleadershipcouncil.org/. You can find quite a lot of useful information there, including reports prepared for the Council.

An example of how some consultancy firms offer leadership training and development can be seen at http://www.leadershipchallenge.com/home.aspx. There is no shortage of similar offers from many providers. This one is a little unusual in being founded by people who have also conducted a lot of academic research on leadership. Take a look at their model of leadership and see how it connects with ideas and theories presented in this chapter.

Other examples of how some organisations promote leadership knowledge, education and training can be found at http://www.ldl.co.uk/inspirational-leadership-management-training-course.htm and https://www.i-l-m.com/. These two organisations are very different, but they both show the connections between leadership and other topics, in this case motivation and management respectively.

One of the most influential and long-standing organisations promoting leadership research and practice is the Center for Creative Leadership, which is based in the USA but also has substantial operations in most parts of the world. Its home page is http://www.ccl.org/Leadership/index.aspx. There is a lot there to illustrate how ideas from theory and research are applied in management development. The CCL's approach to leadership specifically embraces leadership in the most specific situations (leaders working with individuals) to the most general (leaders influencing societies).

Suggested further reading

Full details for all references are given in the list at the end of this book.

1 Peter Northouse's very successful textbook *Leadership* is in its seventh edition (Sage, 2015) at the time of writing this chapter. It is a textbook that has a chapter on most of the topics contained within this chapter, and on some additional topics. It gives an overview of different approaches to leadership with a lot of practical examples and exercises.

2 *The New Psychology of Leadership* by Alex Haslam et al. was published in 2011 by Psychology Press. It uses the expertise of the authors in the theory and practice of social psychology and social identities. They focus on perceptions of leaders and what leaders do, and also pay more attention to the social processes of leadership than most writings on leadership do.

3 Gary Yukl is an experienced and distinguished scholar in organisational behaviour. He has produced a thorough text on many areas of the field called *Leadership in Organisations*. The eighth edition was published in 2012 by Prentice Hall.

4 The academic journal *The Leadership Quarterly* published by Elsevier is an important source for the latest research and theorising.

CHAPTER 13

Careers and career management

LEARNING OBJECTIVES

After studying this chapter, you should be able to:

1 define career and list three significant features of that definition;

2 describe and critique the key features of so-called 'boundaryless' and protean careers;

3 name and describe the career anchors identified by Ed Schein;

4 name and define Holland's six vocational personality types, and draw a diagram to show their relationship to each other;

5 identify the conclusions that can be drawn from research on Holland's theory;

6 describe the different approaches to career decision-making people can take;

7 name and briefly describe at least ten career management interventions that can be used in organisations;

8 explain the circumstances in which career management interventions are most likely to be successful;

9 distinguish between different conceptions of career success;

10 name and describe four kinds of variable that may affect career success;

11 describe what individuals and organisations can do to ensure that transitions into new jobs are successful;

12 discuss whether career theories apply as well to women as they do to men.

Opening case study   Careers in changing times

The stunned expressions of employees leaving Lehman Brothers were a grim reminder of the painful consequences of redundancy, particularly for those who have experienced unemployment. 'The overwhelming sense is one of being shell-shocked,' says Gavin Cullen, who lost his job as a senior associate in equity capital markets at Deutsche Bank in London during a wave of City downsizing six years ago. 'One minute you are working 80 hours-plus a week – then, suddenly, it's gone.'

Mr Cullen went on to build a successful career as an interim change manager, working on post-merger integration with investment banks, asset management firms and wealth managers. As a self-employed consultant he still puts in long hours, but his work is more varied and he has greater control over his life. 'In a full-time role you work to a line manager. As a freelance consultant, you effectively work for senior management. If you want to take time off between assignments, you can.'

His decision to embrace self-employment is not unusual. Across Germany, the Netherlands, the US and France, between 5 and 9 per cent of small business entrepreneurs begin their enterprises in response to redundancy, according to a survey by the specialist insurer Hiscox. In the UK, almost one-fifth of entrepreneurs start out in this way. Other displaced professionals use unemployment to travel or retrain for new careers.

However, while a change of profession or a venture into entrepreneurship creates opportunities, it also carries risks. The downturn multiplies these hazards. This makes it more important than ever for the newly unemployed to weigh their options carefully.

Life-stage plays a big part in how people respond to loss of employment. As an unencumbered 31-year-old, the reaction of strategy director Cathy Bryan to the collapse of her employer, Excite UK, during the dotcom clear-out, was to take herself off to the Himalayas, where she decided to retrain as a school teacher. 'I was earning lots of money and it was fun,' says Ms Bryan, who fell into new media while working as a parliamentary researcher. 'But it didn't feel particularly worthwhile. I made hay while the sun shone. When I was made redundant, I saw that as another opportunity.'

Despite age equality laws, older professionals with ideas to offer can still fall foul of bad practice. At the age of 54, Peter Smith lost his position as director of environmental risk consulting when Arthur Andersen collapsed. In spite of finding himself apparently in demand with several large companies, he failed to clinch a job offer. When a large insurance firm invited him to a fourth discussion, having interviewed him for 11 hours already, he concluded that he was being commercially exploited. 'I realised that firms were not really interested in employing me. They were systematically passing me from pillar to post to gain more and more information about what I had worked on at Andersen.'

Rather than suffer further disappointments, he used his experience to set up CSR-Evaluator, which markets a web-based tool to help companies assess the impacts of social, environmental and economic issues on their processes and people. Clients of the business include several large corporations such as British Nuclear Fuels and Portugal Telecom.

Do people who have used redundancy to change career advise others to follow suit? Ms Bryan, the strategy director turned teacher, admits freely that the strain of mastering a new profession, coupled with loss of income and a perceived loss of status, can be demoralising. The upside, she says, is that she now works in a profession of which she is genuinely proud. 'You will have dark days, because the first few years are really tough. My advice is to hang on in there.'

FT   Source: A life after redundancy, Financial Times, 24/09/2008 (Clegg, A.)

Introduction

This case study nicely illustrates a number of important themes in careers. Increasingly volatile labour markets mean that many people are likely to need to change jobs and occupations. In doing so, they will need to be durable, innovative and willing to do what they can to take control of their own careers. They may well need to seek advice and support throughout their working life (not just at the start), and to view a career as part of life as a whole rather than as a separate compartment. The case study also shows that there are different ways of evaluating career success (e.g. job satisfaction versus earnings), and that social contacts are important in gaining access to opportunities.

A distinction is often made between people who have careers and people who have jobs. Those with careers tend to be viewed as better educated, more highly paid and with better promotion prospects than those with jobs. However, this distinction between so-called careers and so-called jobs was never very helpful, and has become even less so. It can be argued that everyone has a career, but that those careers differ a great deal from each other.

In this chapter we examine alternative definitions of career, and also some of the contextual factors that affect the careers experienced by individuals. One common definition of career is an occupation or line of work. Most young people, and nowadays some older people too, are faced with decisions about what line of work to enter. Psychologists have been very interested in that, so in this chapter we also examine alternative approaches to career choice, and some of the practical applications arising from them. But careers are not just about choosing a type of work. They also concern what happens after that – particularly changes as a person moves between jobs and grows in experience and age. We will therefore also examine starting work and subsequent work-role transitions, how organisations play a part in people's careers, and some theories of human development over the lifespan. Overall the chapter aims to help readers to understand career theory and practice, and to apply key concepts to their own careers and also the careers of other people.

The context of careers

Definitions

Many definitions and meanings of career have been proposed (see Inkson et al., 2014: Chapter 1 for a brief discussion). Many of them, including dictionary definitions, tend to focus on the idea that a career necessarily means progression to something better, and/or working in an occupation with high skill and status. This notion of career is often contrasted with that of a 'job', which is considered to have neither of those characteristics.

Nowadays most social scientists favour a more inclusive definition of career: that is, one which makes as few assumptions as possible about the observable features of a person's sequence of work experiences. For our purposes, we can consider a career as *the sequence of employment-related positions, roles, activities and experiences encountered by a person*. Several points can be made about this definition:

- Careers are *not* confined to professional and managerial occupations, nor to 'conventional' career paths involving increasing seniority within a single occupation and/or organisation.

- The notion of *sequence* means 'more than one'. Instead of looking at a person's present job in isolation, we are interested in how it relates to their past and future.

- The inclusion of *experiences* emphasises that careers are subjective as well as objective. A sequence of jobs that looks haphazard to an outside observer may make a lot of sense in the narrative the person constructs about their own life (Inkson et al., 2014: Chapter 11). Also, as we will see later in this chapter, a person's subjective feeling of having been successful in their own career may differ from an objective assessment of success such as status or salary. One person may regard reaching deputy managing director as a great success, another as a disappointment.

■ The term *employment-related* means that activities such as training, education and voluntary work, as well as *un*employment, can be considered elements of a person's career. Employment includes self-employment and short-term contracts.

Key learning point

Careers include any sequence of work-related experiences, not just conventional or orderly ones.

Psychologists and careers

First, there is a long history of psychological theory and research in vocational guidance. This has particularly concerned helping people make good choices of occupation to enter (see Savickas and Baker, 2005), but has also included techniques of career counselling (Kidd, 2006). Second, psychologists have conducted a great deal of research on what predicts career success. Some of this has focused on the disadvantages often experienced by women relative to men, people deemed 'too old' or 'too young' (see the opening case study) and by ethnic minorities relative to ethnic majorities (Ng et al., 2005; Ng and Feldman, 2014). Third, attempts have been made to map out the sequence of a person's career in terms of ages and stages, each with their own characteristics (Kooij et al., 2011). A related body of work has focused on how people handle specific transitions from one role to another in the course of their career (Forrier et al., 2009). Fourth, psychologists have been interested in how careers in organisations are managed (Hall, 2002). Particularly close attention has been paid to personal and interpersonal phenomena such as mentoring (Haggard et al., 2011), and to a lesser extent to other techniques such as development centres and succession planning. Later in this chapter we will give some attention to all of the topics mentioned in this paragraph.

As you may have noticed, most of the psychological work on careers described above focuses on the individual person or the relationship between two people. This is typical of applied psychology more generally. It tends to neglect the impact on careers of the structure of economies and societies, including social class (Thomas, 1989). Similarly, although many careers occur in organisational settings, psychology has little to say about how organisational structures and other features can affect the careers of individuals (or indeed be affected by them) (Arnold and Cohen, 2013). This means that psychologists tend to be somewhat marginalised in some careers research and theory, to which sociologists, economists and others make major contributions (Moore et al., 2007). All of these areas of expertise offer something when examining careers: genuinely multidisciplinary thinking is needed in the analysis of careers (Arthur, 2008).

Key learning point

Careers lie at the intersection of individual lives and social structures. Therefore many different academic disciplines are relevant to careers.

Contexts

Many psychological research articles on careers start with statements something like these:

> Due to the changed and more volatile nature of careers, people are more often confronted with periods of unemployment.

(Vansteenkiste et al., 2013: 135)

> [W]idespread career uncertainty forces workers to take greater control over career management to remain employable in a highly competitive labour market.

(Direnzo et al., 2015: 538)

> In recent decades, successive generations of workers have witnessed economic and social changes that are altering the traditional psychological contract: employers no longer provide long-term employment guarantees.

(Lyons et al., 2015: 8)

Messages like this have been common since about 1990, and were reinforced once again by the financial meltdowns that occurred in many countries around 2008. The opening case study in this chapter is a good illustration of this. In the 1990s there was much concern about organisational delayering and downsizing, unexpected job insecurity and how people could cope with it (Herriot and Pemberton, 1995). Nowadays, many readers of this chapter may be surprised by how stable things apparently used to be.

The implication is that the world has become a lot tougher since an era when there was a predictable and safe environment where people made long-lasting career choices early in life, and found secure employment with prospects of promotion and personal growth until they chose to retire in perhaps their late fifties. Of course, that environment never applied to everyone, and historically it can be argued to have been quite fleeting, lasting perhaps from the early 1950s to the late 1980s. Conversely, some people do still experience relatively secure and predictable environments – the organisational career is not dead (Clarke, 2013), especially for employees identified as 'talent' (Dries, 2013). Although it is often asserted that people change jobs more often than they used to (due to necessity, career self-management and a more short-term attitude to work in general), evidence for this is hard to find (Rodrigues and Guest, 2010). That does not necessarily mean that people feel just as secure as they used to. Instead, they may be 'sitting tight' to avoid risk.

Many people who experienced a change from employment security and being looked after, to insecurity and a need to look after themselves, have now left the labour market through retirement. Nevertheless, images of careers as stable, privileged and predictable live on, so it's still important to understand the contrast of present with past. This is illustrated in Figure 13.1. To summarise, in current times:

1 It can be difficult to find time and energy to think about longer-term career issues, and to enjoy family and life outside work when you are working very hard and long hours.
2 Switching between types of work, organisations and locations is likely to occur during the course of a career.
3 Short-term contracts, flexible working, and 'portfolio' careers where a person is engaged in several projects at once are also likely experiences.

Key learning point

Careers take on varied forms, with multiple options and paradoxically multiple constraints on both people and organisations. This means that managing them is a challenge.

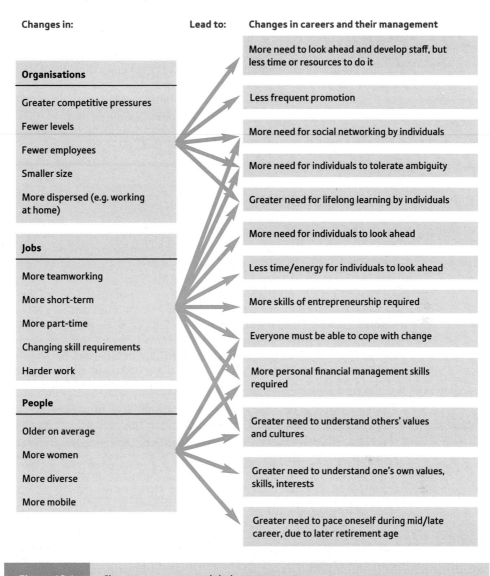

Changes in:	Lead to:	Changes in careers and their management

Organisations

Greater competitive pressures

Fewer levels

Fewer employees

Smaller size

More dispersed (e.g. working at home)

Jobs

More teamworking

More short-term

More part-time

Changing skill requirements

Harder work

People

Older on average

More women

More diverse

More mobile

More need to look ahead and develop staff, but less time or resources to do it

Less frequent promotion

More need for social networking by individuals

More need for individuals to tolerate ambiguity

Greater need for lifelong learning by individuals

More need for individuals to look ahead

Less time/energy for individuals to look ahead

More skills of entrepreneurship required

Everyone must be able to cope with change

More personal financial management skills required

Greater need to understand others' values and cultures

Greater need to understand one's own values, skills, interests

Greater need to pace oneself during mid/late career, due to later retirement age

Figure 13.1	Changes to careers and their consequences

Stop to consider

In what ways do you see your career as different from your parents'? Does this reflect the changed landscape described above?

Career forms

It is still tempting to view careers in the narrow sense of predictable moves to jobs of increasing status, usually within a single occupation or organisation. This is what Kanter (1989) has called the **bureaucratic career**, and indeed many people do still see career in that narrow way. Kanter (1989) also identified two other career forms. The first is *professional*, where growth occurs through development of competence to take on complex tasks rather than through promotion to another job. A person's status depends more on their reputation with other professionals or clients than on their level in an organisational hierarchy. Kanter's other career form is *entrepreneurial*, which rests on the capacity to spot opportunities to create valued outputs and build up one's own organisation or operation. The experience of many people is that careers are becoming more like the professional and/ or entrepreneurial form, and less like the bureaucratic form, because of the changing context discussed earlier in this chapter.

The boundaryless career

In recognition of the changing career landscape and the need for career theory to reflect it, Michael Arthur and colleagues (1999) refer to the boundaryless career. They define the boundaryless career in rather general fashion as '[a] range of career forms that defy traditional employment assumptions' (Arthur and Rousseau, 1996: 3). The term boundaryless career was coined as an extension of the idea of the boundaryless organisation, used by the then CEO of General Electric, Jack Welch. Since 1994 it has gained a lot of momentum and attention in career theory and practice. It clearly captures people's imagination, and resonates with what many see happening in their own careers and those of people they know. Nevertheless, the definition above is not entirely satisfactory because it says more about what the boundaryless career is not than what it is. Arthur and Rousseau (1996) therefore developed the concept by describing six features of the boundaryless career:

1   When a career draws validation – and marketability – from outside the present employer (e.g. academic, joiner).
2   A career that moves across the boundaries of separate employers (e.g. Silicon Valley career).
3   A career which is sustained through outside networks (e.g. estate agent).
4   When traditional organisational career boundaries, notably those involving hierarchical reporting and advancement principles, are broken (e.g. some matrix organisations, project work).
5   When a person rejects existing career opportunities for personal or family reasons ('downshifting').
6   Individual interpretation – when a person perceives a boundaryless future regardless of structural constraints (those who feel they have choices, freedom etc. notwithstanding organisational structures).

Careers are boundaryless in the sense that, either by choice or necessity, people move across boundaries between organisations, departments, hierarchical levels, functions and sets of skills. Movement across these boundaries is made easier by the fact that they are tending to dissolve anyway. Such movement is necessary for individuals to maintain their employability and for organisations to maintain their effectiveness. In some ways the boundaryless career is very similar to Kanter's notion of the professional career, because a person's marketability and affirmation are derived from outside their present employer and sustained through outside networks. Another boundary that is being broken down (in Arthur's opinion) is that between work and non-work. This is because people are increasingly likely to consider the impact of a job on their home life before taking it, and because more and more work is done at (or from) home. Arthur et al. (1999) found some evidence of boundaryless careers in action among a varied sample of people in New Zealand. They argue that career is a verb, not a noun: individuals are 'careering'.

All this might sound very individualistic, and certainly the concept of the boundaryless career is a product of individualistic Western culture, where many situations are what Weick (1996) calls 'weak' – that is, they have relatively few constraints and allow individuals to express themselves. Nevertheless, Arthur et al. (1999) point out that successful boundaryless careering does require communion (relating closely to others, recognising interdependence) as well as agency (individual action on the environment). Indeed, there is some suggestion that the boundaryless career favours women because they are more accustomed to having to change their work and balance multiple priorities (see for example Forret et al., 2010). Their orientation towards relationships, often termed 'communion', is said to be well suited to an era of networking and teamworking. Men's orientation is more towards problem-solving and acting upon the world (often called 'agency'), which may be useful but not sufficient in a complex world. Still, Fernando and Cohen (2014) among others have shown that agency is expected in careers, and women often find it difficult to be seen as both agentic and 'respectably' feminine.

Michael Arthur has done the field of careers a huge favour by developing the concept of the boundaryless career, and he continues to encourage its use as a way of shedding light on careers (Arthur, 2014). As he must have been aware it would, the boundaryless career has provoked many questions and some of these highlight possible weaknesses and ambiguities (see for example Arnold and Cohen, 2008; Inkson et al., 2012). Much of the thinking around the boundaryless career seems to be based upon the assumption that people can control their own fate, at least to a reasonable extent. This may be accurate for people with qualifications and marketable skills, but might be too optimistic for others. A good illustration of this is the contrast between migrants who choose to move between countries to further their careers in highly skilled work (e.g. Tams and Arthur, 2007) versus migrants who have moved between countries because of economic necessity or sometimes persecution (e.g. Pio, 2005).

Another set of questions concerns the nature and role of boundaries. It seems that in the literature on the boundaryless career, boundaries are thought of more as barriers. That is, they are more like high and sturdy walls than lines marking the edge of a sports field. Boundaryless careers occur when either these walls are dismantled, or when strong and purposeful individuals climb over them. Probably most of us could feel quite inspired by that, even though it is clear that barriers (in the form of people such as executive search consultants) do still place some constraints on the work opportunities people are and are not allowed access to (King et al., 2005). Still, barriers may not be entirely undesirable to everyone – it could depend on your perspective. For people on one side of a barrier, it keeps those on the other side out. Furthermore, boundaries (as opposed to barriers) are arguably very important to us, not expendable and undesirable. Boundaries help us understand where we are, where we have been and where we might go in the future. They contribute greatly to our cognitive maps (Hodgkinson and Healey, 2008) by which we make sense of and enact our careers. So even a career that is boundaryless in the sense that a person has worked in many different organisations derives its meaning from knowing what organisational boundaries have been crossed.

Key learning point

The concept of the boundaryless career is a popular one, but it might overestimate the power individuals have over their own careers as well as the extent to which career forms are changing.

Is the boundaryless career subjective, objective or both? Briscoe et al. (2006) have used the term 'boundaryless mindset', which refers to a person's construal of their career as being unrestricted by boundaries. However, while I might think that I can move across organisational and functional boundaries if I want to, and am certainly willing to consider it, I might choose not to because I like it where I am now. So despite my boundaryless mindset, my career might look very bounded from the outside. I would reflect the sixth component of the boundaryless career described above, but probably not the others. Sullivan and Arthur (2006) have attempted to deal with this by distinguishing between physical and psychological mobility, but further clarification of this distinction is required.

Underlying this is the point that the six aspects of the boundaryless career specified by Arthur and Rousseau (1996) do not necessarily work together. Indeed, Gubler et al. (2014a) have proposed a revised set of five components of the boundaryless career, based on extensive analysis of data from a large number of IT professionals in Europe. The five are preference for mobility between organisations; preference for mobility between geographical locations; preference for mobility between occupations; preference for working beyond organisational boundaries; and rejection of career opportunities for personal reasons. The IT professionals tended to fall into one of three groups, which Gubler and colleagues labelled work–life balancers, stay-puts and careerists (see Figure 13.2). Although much of the research literature on boundaryless careers focuses on moves between organisations, it is notable that preference for that kind of mobility did not distinguish between the three orientations. Instead, it was the preference for geographical mobility and the tendency to reject career opportunities due to personal reasons that were most notably different.

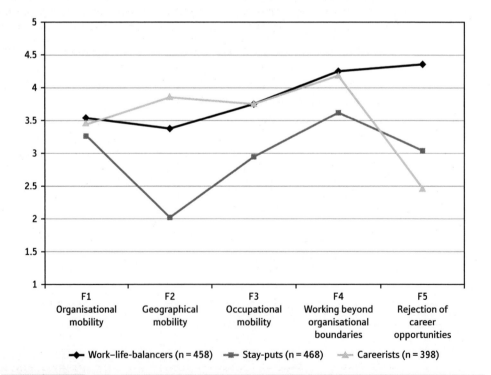

| Figure 13.2 | Three career orientations and how they score on five aspects of the boundaryless career |

Source: Reproduced from Gubler et al., 2014a: 656, by permission of Emerald Publishing.

Consider the five components of boundaryless careers identified by Gubler et al. (2014a). Would you expect all five to operate together, or are they quite independent of each other? To the extent that they are independent, what implications does this have for the concept of the boundaryless career?

The protean career

The protean career is a concept developed by American careers academic Tim Hall. Like the boundaryless career, it is intended to reflect the nature of careers today. However, its use is more overtly normative than the boundaryless career. That is, Hall and others appear to be not only describing an approach to career, but also arguing that it is the *best* way to approach one's career. Hall originally mentioned the protean career in his 1976 book *Careers in Organizations*, and he was well ahead of his time because he anticipated the trend towards self-driven careers that many people think has been necessitated by economic change. Hall developed the idea further in his 2002 follow-up book *Careers In and Out of Organizations* (note the change of title!). Also, in recent years Hall and colleagues, especially Jon Briscoe, have been researching the protean career further (e.g. Briscoe and Hall, 2006; Briscoe et al., 2006, 2012b).

The protean career has been defined as 'a career based on self-direction in pursuit of psychological success in one's work' (Hall, 2002: 23). The word 'protean' is derived from Proteus, a sea-god in Greek mythology who could change form at will. The idea is that people can (and should) both have a coherent sense of identity, but also be able to adapt to labour market conditions. Briscoe and Hall (2006) specify that a protean career is one where the person is:

1 *values-driven*, in the sense that the person's internal values provide the guidance and measure of success for the individual's career; and

2 *self-directed* in personal and **career management**, having the ability to be adaptive in terms of performance and learning demands.

Table 13.1 shows how Hall contrasts the protean with the traditional career. The traditional career is clearly similar to Kanter's bureaucratic career, and represents what Hall and others believe we have left (or should leave) behind. Hall (2002; Hall and Chandler, 2005)

Table 13.1	The protean career versus the traditional career	
	Protean	**Traditional**
Who is in charge?	Person	Organisation
Core values	Freedom, growth	Advancement, safety
Degree of mobility	High	Lower
Success criteria	Psychological success	Position, level, pay
Key attitudes	Work satisfaction Professional commitment	Organisational commitment

Source: Adapted from Hall (2002).

also speaks of the 'path with a heart', which develops the notion of vocation or calling in a career. This is an extension of the protean career idea to include a more explicit sense of (i) meaning to one's life and (ii) contribution to a community.

Gubler et al. (2014b) have suggested that being values-driven has two elements: being clear about one's self-concept (otherwise how can you know what your values are?) and using one's own values to measure one's career success. Likewise, they also suggest that being self-directed has two elements: being able and willing to learn and adapt, and believing that one is in charge of one's own career. Gubler and colleagues (2014b) also review the research on the protean career, and conclude that people who adopt a protean attitude to their career do tend to experience more success (for example in job search, number of promotions) than those who do not. However, the existing research is heavily biased towards American and managerial samples; it is often not clear that a protean career orientation actually causes the outcomes (only that it is associated with them), and the way that a protean career orientation is assessed is often not very true to the original concept.

As with the boundaryless career, the protean career has some limitations and tensions built in. Probably because the idea has been developed in a highly free-market economy, it seems to be assumed that the values that self-directed individuals will pursue are those of freedom and growth (though this is moderated somewhat in the 'path with the heart', which allows for more communal motives). What if an individual's values are to achieve secure employment in a large organisation, and not mind what kind of work they have to do? That person's value-driven career would look very different from the pursuit of freedom and growth, but still in a sense be protean.

Although the protean image is one of freedom and autonomy, in fact Proteus was constantly being pursued, and changed form only as a desperate measure to avoid capture. This presents a rather different image – of a person trying hard to stay ahead of the labour market (hence the element of adaptability mentioned by Hall) rather than doing what helps their personal growth and development. As if to reinforce this 'other side' of the protean career, Hall's approach is firmly rooted in corporate capitalism: 'we must consider both the person's path with a heart and the employer's path to profits' (Hall, 2002: 303).

Key learning point

The protean career is one that is driven by an individual in pursuit of their own values. Therefore it is defined more in terms of what motivates it, not what it looks like from the outside.

Career anchors

Another way to examine types of career is to concentrate on the subjective experience of the employee. Edgar Schein (1993) has used some research he carried out many years ago (Schein, 1978) to develop the concept of career anchors. This has become a very popular tool in practical career development work in recent years, though it has not sparked so much academic research. Schein defined a career anchor as:

> an area of such paramount importance to a person that he or she would not give it up. The person comes to define his or her basic self-image in terms of that concern and it becomes the over-riding issue at every stage of the career.

> (Schein, 1993: 20)

He felt that people's anchors develop and become clear during their early career, as a result of experience and learning from it. Schein's list of alternative anchors people hold is shown in Table 13.2. We might look at the list of anchors and feel that several or even all of them are important to us, but which would win if we had to choose? Schein argues that this 'winner' is our real anchor.

Key learning point

Career anchors are areas of the self-concept that a person would not give up, even if faced with a difficult choice.

Career anchors consist of a mixture of abilities, motives, needs and values. They therefore reflect quite deep and far-reaching aspects of the person. It is perhaps the career anchor that a person questions when they are in the transitional periods identified by Levinson (see later in this chapter). Notice that career anchors do not necessarily determine the type of work or occupation a person chooses. Within any given occupation, there can be people with different anchors. For example, Igbaria and Baroudi (1993) found that relatively few IT professionals prioritised the technical-functional competence anchor, which one might expect of 'techies'. Feldman and Bolino (2000) found in a sample of 153 self-employed people that autonomy was the most prevalent anchor, followed by entrepreneurial creativity and then security. Again, this shows that not too much should be assumed about people's career anchors: small business owners may be more concerned with doing things their own way and being able reliably to provide for themselves and their families than with growing their business.

Being able to identify one's career anchor is probably important for the effective management of one's own career. It is also important that people responsible for managing careers are aware of the prevalence of the various anchors in their organisation. This might inform human resource policies such as job placement and transfer, promotion hierarchies and control systems. For example, problems are likely if there is an attempt to impose standard working hours and methods on people who most value the autonomy/independence anchor. Also, a common issue in organisations is how far up the hierarchy specialists such as scientists and engineers can rise without becoming general managers. Often the answer is not very far, which may create a problem for some talented staff who subscribe to the technical/functional competence career anchor. People with a security anchor are likely to have quite a difficult time because security is now harder to attain than it was. The technical/functional competence anchor could be a

---

Table 13.2	Career anchors

1 *Managerial competence*. People with this anchor are chiefly concerned with managing others. They wish to be generalists, and they regard specialist posts purely as a short-term means of gaining some relevant experience. Advancement, responsibility, leadership and income are all important.

2 *Technical/functional competence*. These people are keen to develop and maintain specialist skills and knowledge in their area of expertise. They build their identity around the content of their work.

3 *Security*. People with a security anchor are chiefly concerned with a reliable, predictable work environment. This may be reflected in security of tenure – i.e. having a job – or in security of location – wanting to stay in a particular town, for example. So this might be considered two separate anchors.

4 *Autonomy and independence*. These people wish most of all to be free of restrictions on their work activities. They refuse to be bound by rules, set hours, dress codes and so on.

5 *Entrepreneurial creativity*. Here people are most concerned to create products, services and/or organisations of their own.

6 *Pure challenge*. This anchor emphasises winning against strong competition or apparently insurmountable obstacles.

7 *Service/dedication*. This anchor reflects the wish to have work that expresses social, political, religious or other values that are important to the individual concerned, preferably in organisations that also reflect those values.

8 *Lifestyle integration*. People who hold this anchor wish most of all to keep a balance between work, family, leisure and other activities, so that none is sacrificed for the sake of another.

problem in organisations with project-based multidisciplinary teams, while the lifestyle integration anchor is increasingly difficult to honour when workloads are increasing (Schein, 1996). There is some research evidence to suggest that people whose anchors are compatible with their work environments are happier than those whose anchors are not compatible (e.g. Feldman and Bolino, 2000; Tan and Quek, 2001), though again we must be cautious about making assumptions regarding what types of work environment nurture what kinds of anchor.

If you are familiar with the types of issues that repeatedly arise in applied psychology, you will not be surprised to hear that questions have been raised over the years about: (i) whether just one anchor emerges for each person, as Schein asserted; (ii) if so, whether it is constant through the remainder of the career; (iii) whether there are anchors other than those identified by Schein; and (iv) are the anchors just a list, or are they configured, so that for example some anchors are the opposite of others? On the whole, it seems that while if someone has to choose between anchors, they will, for most people it is not the case that at any given time one anchor is clearly more important than the others. Some researchers have suggested additional anchors such as variety, or separating the entrepreneurial anchor from creativity (Danziger et al., 2008), but in general the set of anchors seem to cover the ground quite well, and also to be relatively independent of each other, i.e. more like a list than for example a set of dimensions (Barclay et al., 2013).

Stop to consider

Career anchors are usually thought of as quite independent of each other, but is this realistic? Perhaps they work together in influencing a person's career priorities. Try to think of ways in which two or more anchors may simultaneously be important for a person.

Exercise 13.1   A medical career

Rashid Kassim has been appointed a consultant doctor at a general hospital. This is the fourth hospital he has worked in since qualifying as a doctor at the age of 25. The consultant grade is the most senior type of post available for doctors who continue to specialise in clinical work as opposed to taking on major managerial responsibilities. Rashid is delighted to have achieved this promotion because he believes that the status of consultant will allow him more freedom to shape his medical work in the ways he thinks most appropriate. Also, he is very active in his professional association and believes that having the status of consultant will help him make changes that he sees as necessary. It will also make him more visible to other senior doctors, with whom it might be possible to share ideas, experiences and knowledge. And who knows, perhaps one day one of them might offer him a job!

Even now, Rashid is thinking ahead a few years, and wondering how long it will be before he gets bored. He suspects that one day he will want to move to a higher-paid consultant post in a bigger hospital attached to a university medical school. This is mainly because he would be likely to see a wider range of medical conditions, to have better equipment available and be more closely in touch with the latest developments in medical research. Still, even without moving, he might well be able to work with eminent people based elsewhere. Another factor was that soon it would be hard to move for a few years because of the stage of education his children were at.

Suggested exercise

On the basis of the information given here, try to specify the career type(s) and anchor(s) that fit Rashid Kassim's career so far. How easy is this to do? Do your conclusions depend on whether you focus mainly on the observable moves he has made and hopes to make, or on his own personal motives?

Career management in organisations

Around the end of the 20th century, some organisations responded to the trends described so far in this chapter by giving up any attempt to manage the careers of employees. Because traditional career paths have disappeared and organisational structures are continually changing, some senior HR managers believed (and a few still believe) that there did not seem much point in attempting corporate management of careers. The term 'self-development' is now frequently used. As the words suggest, it means that individual employees are responsible for identifying their own development needs, and for doing something about them. Making the most of this necessity to look after your own career by using your own strategies is the idea behind what is sometimes called career self-management (see King, 2004). Refer back to the opening case study of this chapter for good illustrations of how some people approach this. However, self-development and self-management seem to mean slightly different things in different places. On the one hand, it can be quite an aggressive message: 'You're on your own; look after yourself.' Alternatively, it can be more supportive: 'Don't expect the organisation to tell you how you need to develop, but we can play a part in helping you to make and implement your own decisions.'

Hirsh and Jackson (2004) among others have argued that labour market uncertainties make it more, not less, important for organisations to participate in the management of employees' careers. There is evidence that organisations are again more involved in career management in order to retain their most valued people and to develop and deploy them in ways which meet organisational needs (CIPD, 2011). True, it's not easy to anticipate every future career step and when it will happen. But complete predictability is not required for career management to be useful. Hirsh and Jackson (2004: 6) argue that career management should matter to organisations because:

■ Careers are the way in which people accumulate skills and knowledge that are of use to the organisation.

■ Related to this, careers are how skills and knowledge are deployed and spread in organisations.

■ The movement of people around an organisation is how its culture and values are transmitted.

■ People want to know where they stand, and clear statements about how careers will be managed help in this.

■ Career development is a major way of attracting, motivating and retaining able employees.

An analysis of some of the techniques available and how they fit in with organisational human resource management strategies has been provided by Baruch (2004). Table 13.3 describes some of the interventions that can be used in organisations to manage careers. It is difficult to obtain accurate figures on which interventions are used most, though evidence from Baruch and Peiperl (2000) and De Vos and Dries (2013) is helpful. It looks as if internal vacancy advertising is nearly universal. After that, the picture is more mixed, though it seems that many organisations use a few of these interventions. Career conversations between supervisors and their subordinates seem to be common according to HR managers, but this may be wishful thinking on the part of the HR managers. De Vos and Dries' research indicates that coaching and cross-functional job moves are most commonly used for selected employees than for all of them, which draws attention to the tendency to restrict these interventions to people who are deemed to have particular talent or who are in some other way especially valuable to the organisation.

Several of the career management interventions shown in Table 13.3 (for example, mentoring, coaching and career action centres) can be used to support self-development rather than organisational control of careers. On the whole, the interventions are used to pursue organisational goals, and in some organisations the notion of managing careers has rather come back into fashion. This is partly a reaction to the fact that the choices people make about their self-development do not necessarily serve the needs of the organisation. For example, a company's IT specialists may tend to seek training on a popular software package which helps them to maintain their employability, but which happens to be of little use to that company.

It is neither possible nor desirable to use all of the interventions in the same organisation at the same time. Hirsh et al. (1995) pointed out that it is much better to do a few things well than a lot badly. It is also necessary to be clear about what an intervention is designed to achieve, and on whose behalf. Possible purposes are:

- filling vacancies – that is, selecting one or more people for specific posts;
- assessment of potential, competencies, skills or interests – this might help an organisation to assess its human resources, or individuals to know how well placed they are to obtain specific jobs inside or outside the organisation;
- development of skills and competencies – in order to help an organisation to function effectively in its markets, or individuals to be more effective in future jobs;
- identification of career options – that is, what types of work or specific posts might be obtainable for one or more individuals;
- action to implement career plans.

Any intervention might achieve more than one purpose, but it is important to be clear about what purpose(s) it is designed for. It is also necessary, according to Hirsh et al. (1995), to be clear about who in the organisation is eligible to participate in interventions – preferably everyone. The operation of a career management intervention must be consistent with its goals. So, for example, it would be inappropriate for detailed feedback about performance in a development centre to be withheld from participants if an aim of the development centre was to help people identify their career options. The success of an intervention is likely to depend not only upon its technical merit, but also on organisational processes supporting it, particularly the implementation of people's development plans and the willingness of people's line managers to participate in their career development when it may not be in their interests to do so (Arnold, 2002: Dick and Hyde, 2006). There are also some concerns about the fairness of interventions, for example in decisions about who is allocated a mentor (Lewis and Arnold, 2012).

Table 13.3	Career management interventions in organisations

1 *Internal vacancy notification.* Information about jobs available in the organisation, normally in advance of any external advertising, and with some details of preferred experience, qualifications and a job description.

2 *Induction and socialisation.* Programmes of instruction, training and work experience that enable a newcomer to become familiar with the organisation and prepare them for future roles within it.

3 *Career paths.* Information about the sequences of jobs that a person can do, or competencies they can acquire, in the organisation. This should include details of how high in the organisation any path goes, the kinds of moves that are possible and perhaps the skills/experience required.

4 *Career workbooks.* These consist of questions and exercises designed to help individuals to identify strengths and weaknesses, job and career opportunities, and necessary steps for reaching their goals.

5 *Career planning workshops.* Cover some of the same ground as workbooks, but offer more chance for discussion, feedback from others, information about organisation-specific opportunities and policies. May include psychometric testing.

6 *Online career management.* Various packages exist for helping employees to assess their skills, interests and values, and translate these into job options. Sometimes these packages are customised to a particular organisation.

7 *Training and educational opportunities.* Participation in courses (and/or financial support and information about courses), in the organisation or outside it. These can enable employees to update, retrain or deepen their knowledge in particular fields. In keeping with the notion of careers involving sequences, training in this context is not solely to improve performance in a person's present job.

8 *Secondments.* The opportunity to work in another context, usually in order to gain skills and experience not readily available in the organisation.

9 *Personal development plans (PDPs).* These often arise from the appraisal process and other sources such as development centres. PDPs are statements of how a person's skills and knowledge might appropriately develop, and how this development could occur, in a given timescale.

10 *Career action centres.* Resources such as literature, DVDs and perhaps more personal inputs such as counselling available to employees on a drop-in basis.

11 *Development centres.* Like assessment centres in that participants are assessed on the basis of their performance in a number of exercises and tests. However development centres focus more on identifying a person's strengths, weaknesses and styles for the purpose of development, not selection.

12 *Mentoring programmes.* Attaching employees to more senior ones who act as advisors, and perhaps also as advocates, protectors and counsellors.

13 *Coaching programmes.* Often similar to and overlapping with mentoring programmes, but usually with more of a focus on how an individual can improve his or her performance. The coach is often someone from outside the organisation who may 'teach' specific skills and/or use counselling and related techniques to help a person reflect on his/her own behaviour at work and find ways to improve.

14 *Individual counselling.* Can be done by specialists from inside or outside the organisation, or by line managers who have received training. May include psychometric testing. This overlaps with mentoring and coaching to some extent. The aim is usually to help a person solve his or her own career problems and/or take career opportunities, without imposing a solution.

15 *Job rotation schemes.* A group of people swap jobs periodically in order to develop their range of skills and their ability to cover for each other.

16 *Developmental job assignments.* Careful use of work tasks can help a person to stay employable for the future, and an organisation to benefit from the adaptability of staff. These can also be used as part of succession planning (see below) to get a person ready for a new role.

17 *Succession planning.* The identification of individuals who are expected to occupy key posts in the future, and who are exposed to experiences which prepare them appropriately. This can be done on a small scale for just one or a small number of senior posts and a small number of individuals, or on a large scale for a whole cohort of people and/or posts at lower levels of the organisation.

18 *Talent management.* This is defined in various ways but normally refers to the identification and systematic development of employees who are deemed to be of particular value to the organisation. It overlaps with several other interventions, especially succession planning, and utilises several others such as coaching and job rotation.

19 *Outplacement.* This may involve several interventions listed above. Its purpose is to support people who are leaving the organisation to clarify and implement plans for their future.

20 *Retirement and late career programmes.* When people approach an age where they are considering withdrawal from full-time work, organisations often provide workshops and training on matters like money management, adjustment to retirement living and considering various types of bridge or part-time work.

Source: Adapted from Arnold and Cohen (2013) and Inkson et al. (2014).

One reason why some HR managers are wary of these interventions is the fear that they may help people realise that they want to leave that organisation, and/or equip them to do so. A glib response to this is that if people truly do not fit with the organisation, it will be a good thing for both parties if they leave. However, given the cost and inconvenience of recruiting replacements for leavers, it is not easy to keep that in mind. Research has not yet produced a clear answer to whether the provision of career management by organisations more often increases employee commitment or on the other hand makes employees more willing to consider leaving. There is however some evidence for the former

(Sturges et al., 2010). It may also be the case that where organisations both encourage people to self-manage their careers and facilitate this via career management interventions, increased loyalty can result (De Vos et al., 2009).

Organisational career management interventions are part of human resource management, to which work psychologists make a substantial contribution. It has been argued that work psychologists need to be more than technical back-up to human resource management, and get more involved in strategic organisational issues (Briner et al., 2010 – see also evidence-based management in Chapter 2 of this book). Nevertheless, even as technical specialists, work psychologists can and do make a major contribution to these interventions. Examples include:

- design of exercises and questionnaires to assess abilities and personality in order to identify top performers in the organisation in the future, and/or identify people's development needs;
- training managers and specialists to assess employees;
- design of self-assessment tools to enable people to clarify their career preferences and plans for development;
- conducting feedback sessions with employees about their assessment results, and training others to do that;
- training managers in the skills required to be an effective mentor or coach, and also playing those roles themselves;
- use of counselling skills to help employees establish career plans;
- use of job analysis techniques to identify key organisational roles for the future;
- design of training programmes to develop organisational competencies and capability.

Point of integration

The skills and techniques used by work psychologists in organisational career management draw on many other chapters in this book, including those on psychometric assessment, training, employee selection and performance assessment.

Career success

In many respects, career success is an appealing topic for work psychologists. Why is this? First, it is to do with human performance. Second, there are many potential predictors of success that can be put into box-and-arrow models and tested statistically (you will have noticed that psychologists like this kind of thing). Third, some of those potential predictors of success concern individual differences in personality or ability – another favourite area of psychologists (Judge and Kammeyer-Mueller, 2007). Fourth, how to be successful in a career is a matter of personal importance for a lot of us. Finally, some of the potential predictors of success (e.g. gender, ethnic origin, age) may have implications for organisational and societal policies regarding equality of opportunity and diversity (Nicholson and de Waal-Andrews, 2005).

The nature of career success

How can we measure the success of a career? Perhaps the most obvious way is to see how high in a status hierarchy a person is, and/or how much they earn. We might also take a longer-term perspective and consider how much a person's earnings have grown over time, and/or how many steps they have risen up a hierarchy. Objectively verifiable indicators like these are indeed used in the majority of research on career success. Status and earnings are important to many people, and they reflect the distribution of material resources in societies. They are well geared to the traditional or bureaucratic concept of career. However, it is often argued that status and earnings are not centrally important to many people. Instead, subjective criteria such as career satisfaction, job satisfaction, work–life balance and feelings of personal accomplishment may be of more significance (Hall and Chandler, 2005). This is certainly consistent with protean and boundaryless careers, and of course with several career anchors. In any case, it is likely that subjective and objective success are somewhat related to each other. If we are objectively successful we will tend to feel successful (though not always), and perhaps if we feel successful we will be encouraged to take on more challenging goals that lead to greater objective achievements, as predicted by Hall and Nougaim's (1968) 'psychological success cycle'. Abele and Spurk (2009), in an interesting longitudinal study of professional workers, found that subjective career success led to objective career success more strongly than objective success led to subjective success.

Some time back, there was a tendency to view subjective success as satisfaction with various aspects of objective success such as pay and promotions (Greenhaus, 1971). In more recent years several studies have examined the different subjective meanings of career success that people may hold, which go beyond their satisfaction with objective measures. For example, Dries and colleagues (2008) interviewed people and asked them about how they saw career success. They used a technique called laddering to get at progressively more fundamental concepts of success. So, for example, if a person said that learning something new was significant to them, they were asked why it was significant. This process continued until the person could not say why something mattered to them, except that 'it just did'. All these fundamental criteria of success were reviewed by Dries and colleagues, and identical or near identical ones were eliminated. The remaining 42 were then sorted (using a Q-sort method) where career development experts were asked to sort them into piles, so that similar criteria were in the same pile. The experts were also asked to articulate what it was that criteria in the same pile had in common. These data were then pooled and subjected to multidimensional scaling (a technique that allows clusters of concepts to be identified).

Dries and colleagues found that the clusters of success criteria could be described in terms of their location on a two-dimensional diagram (see Figure 13.3). The affect versus achievement dimension reflects the distinction between positive feelings and factual accomplishments. The intrapersonal versus interpersonal dimension concerns on the one hand the person's self or inner world (particularly their goals, health or happiness), and on the other hand their relationships with the outside world. Using these dimensions as a framework, Dries and colleagues identified nine clusters (or regions as they called them). Some of these contained subclusters, so more than nine are shown in Figure 13.3.

Dries and her colleagues observed that salary is very difficult to place in their model. This is probably because money has many different meanings to different people. Hence salary might contribute to advancement, recognition, security and probably some other regions too. This raises the interesting possibility that as a quick measure of success, salary might be more versatile and generally applicable than it might appear. The intrapersonal achievement quadrant has been used relatively little in studies of career success. This is important, because some of the success constructs in that quadrant (such as career self-management) seem well suited to 21st-century careers, and should be used more.

Another examination of subjective meanings of career success has been reported by Shen et al. (2015). They interviewed 226 people from 11 countries across most parts of the world. The broad categories of success they derived from their data are shown in Table 13.4.

It is not easy to bring order to data derived from interviews, and Shen and colleagues have done a helpful job. Of course, as Shen et al. point out, many of their categories contain a lot of variety, so it would be a mistake to think that two people whose definition of success fell into the same category were necessarily thinking the same way. For example, within the job/task characteristics category, one person might see success as keeping a wide variety of tasks and skills, whereas another might value specialising in one thing in order to be a leading expert. The formidable task of combining a list like this with career anchors and perhaps

Interpersonal

Recognition, e.g. being recognised for one's accomplishments

Performance, e.g. going to great lengths to achieve good things

Cooperation, e.g. having a good understanding with one's employer

Advancement, e.g. getting promoted, climbing the ladder

Experienced contribution, e.g. realising that one person can make a world of difference in an organisation

Factual contribution, e.g. demonstrating that one is a valuable asset to the organisation

Affect ———————————————————————————————— **Achievement**

Security, e.g. experiencing job security

Creativity, e.g. accomplishing innovative, extraordinary ideas

Work–life balance, e.g. feeling healthy and happy, at home as well as at work

Goal attainment, e.g. accomplishing one's own goals

Achievement satisfaction, e.g. being proud of oneself and one's achievements

Career self-management, e.g. creating opportunities in life

Intrapersonal

| Figure 13.3 | A mapping of career success constructs |

a more general values framework such as that of Schwartz (1999) could lead to something approaching a definitive mapping of conceptions of career success that travels well across cultures. The beginnings of this are apparent in the wider project behind Shen et al.'s paper (see Briscoe et al., 2012a).

Key learning point

There are many different criteria of career success. They vary in their relative emphasis on objective achievements, personal feelings and perceptions, and recognition from other people.

Stop to consider

Take another look at Figure 13.3. Which quadrant of the graph contains the types of career success that matter most to you? Also take a look at Table 13.4. Which of those categories, if any, do you think are most important to you? Don't just give the answer you think sounds right – consider your career behaviour past and present and see what governs your behaviour.

Table 13.4	Eleven types of subjective career success
Category	**Brief description**
Achievement	Securing material and/or symbolic things such as financial rewards, promotion or company ownership
Job/task characteristics	Having work that contains features that one values, such as responsibility, autonomy or challenge
Satisfaction	Being pleased and content with how one's career is going so far
Learning and development	Continuous learning and/or growing as a person, whether or not it leads to formal qualifications
Making a difference	Feeling that one has contributed in some positive ways to other people or the world in general
Work–life context/balance	Successfully integrating or managing the interface between work and other parts of life
Survival and security	Feeling that one is secure, and at least 'getting by' without undue danger of being in difficulties
Social working environment	Experiencing positive relationships and/or climate at work
Recognition	Being formally and explicitly recognised for one's accomplishments, such as getting awards or positive feedback
Job performance	Doing one's job well, and/or better than others
Self-actualisation	Becoming a better or more complete person through one's career, perhaps by pursuing a calling or leaving a legacy to benefit others

Source: Shen et al., 2015: 1762.

Predictors of career success

Of course, there is great interest in identifying what factors help a person achieve career success. If we know what those factors are, we may be able to do something about some of them. On the other hand, we may not! A huge number of variables have been found to be related to career success in one or more of the many studies in this area. That is not surprising, because careers happen over extended periods of time, and are subject to many kinds of influences located in the person and in numerous different aspects of their environment. The challenge for work psychologists is to find helpful ways of classifying the array of potentially relevant variables and to develop a convincing theory about how and when these variables affect career success. Bearing in mind also that career success can be construed and measured in many different ways (see above), it quickly becomes obvious that this is a huge task.

Of course, simply identifying predictors of career success does not necessarily mean that the reasons why they predict become obvious. For example a study of nearly 1400 US executives by Judge et al. (1995) evaluated the impact on salary, status and career satisfaction of a large range of variables. Table 13.5 shows how some of those variables affected salary. Taking them together it can be seen that the highest earners were married men in the consumer durables industry with non-employed spouses who had a degree from a top-rated American university, who desired to progress further up the hierarchy and who worked extra hours.

Table 13.5	Which American executives are the best paid?
Predictor	**Salary value in US dollars (in mid-1990s)**
Working in consumer durables industry	54,195
Being a graduate of a top university	30,929
Being a law graduate	30,328
Being married	27,845
Having a non-working spouse	22,011
Having a high performance rating	11,816
Each seven years of age	10,262
Ambition (per level up the hierarchy aspired to)	9238
Being male	6575
Working extra (per evening per week)	3855

Note: The predictors' effects are not cumulative – for example, being a law graduate from a top university does not mean a salary advantage of over $60,000.

Source: Adapted from Judge et al. (1995), reprinted with permission.

Career satisfaction was correlated with salary showing that the subjective and objective careers are connected. Interestingly, whites were less satisfied than people from other ethnic backgrounds, and ambitious people were less satisfied than unambitious ones, presumably because those with ambition had not yet risen as far as they wanted to. Those in the consumer durables industry tended to be more satisfied than those in entertainment/leisure, high technology, industrial manufacturing and food and beverages.

We can probably generate possible explanations for these findings quite easily, but that's the point – all too easily! For example the degree from a top-rated university might have its impact because high-paying employers only recruit from top universities, or it might be because those universities provide the best teaching and learning thus making their graduates more employable, or it might be a kind of quality label that attaches to a person and that others interpret as an easy way of knowing that this person 'must be good'. And of course it might be none of those things. Perhaps highly able people get to the top universities, so although having attended a top university looks like a cause of success it is only a correlate of success. The real cause of success might be the person's intellectual ability and/or personality/experience and/or social background that got them to that university in the first place.

Ng and colleagues (2005) made a gallant attempt to bring this vast literature together. They report a meta-analysis of predictors of subjective and objective success based on 140 studies. As noted earlier, it is very difficult to find clear-cut and convincing ways of dividing up possible predictors into different types in order to bring order to chaos. Ng et al.'s approach is shown in Figure 13.4. They split predictors up into four groups. *Human capital* reflects experiences, skills, social contacts and motivations relevant to work. *Organisational sponsorship* concerns the resources invested in a person by the employing organisation.

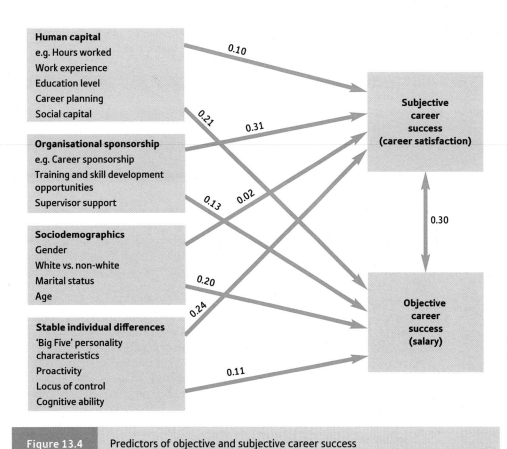

| Figure 13.4 | Predictors of objective and subjective career success |

Sociodemographics are inherent or at least stable features of a person's individuality. *Stable individual differences* refer to personality characteristics.

Ng et al. used salary and promotions as indicators of objective success and career satisfaction as an indicator of subjective success, but promotions proved quite difficult to predict, and have been omitted from Figure 13.4. Salary and career satisfaction correlated at $r = 0.3$, which supports the idea that they are connected but different. *Human capital* variables, especially education level, hours worked and work experience, were fairly good predictors of salary. They tended to be less good at predicting career satisfaction, though career planning, social capital and work centrality did so. *Organisational sponsorship* variables, on the other hand, predicted career satisfaction better than salary. However, training and development opportunities and career sponsorship predicted both, albeit more strongly for career satisfaction than salary. It is significant, and perhaps unexpected, that receiving support from one's employing organisation has a stronger impact on how one feels about one's career than on how much one earns. *Sociodemographics* predicted salary much better than they predicted career satisfaction. You might not be surprised to hear that white married older men tended to earn most. Slightly more optimistically, Ng et al. found that the salary advantage for men over women was smaller in more recent studies, suggesting that perhaps discrimination is reducing over time. *Stable individual differences* were fairly good predictors of career satisfaction. Extrovert, emotionally stable people who believed that they could influence what happened to them and were willing to take the initiative tended to be most satisfied. This suggests that there is a dispositional component to career satisfaction: some people are just more content than others. However, it does not prove the point, because this kind of person might be better than others at finding objectively better opportunities. Just one of the stable individual difference variables was a strong predictor of salary, and that was cognitive ability. This reinforces the consistent message that general intelligence is a strong predictor of performance in almost all domains (Schmidt and Hunter, 2004).

Key learning point

The stronger predictors of salary tend to be intelligence, work experience and effort, while the stronger predictors of career satisfaction are aspects of personality and signs of support from one's employer.

The Ng et al. (2005) meta-analysis provides a very helpful summary of a great deal of research. However, two important limitations should be noted. The first is that although some variables are labelled 'predictors' of career success, they are not necessarily causes of it (see the discussion above of the Judge et al. 1995 study). In fact, they may not even precede the career success variables. Much of the research reviewed by Ng et al. was cross-sectional. It is easy to imagine that, for example, people who experience career satisfaction will attract more support from their supervisors than less satisfied people because they seem more positive and congenial to work with. So in this case career satisfaction would lead to supervisor support, not vice versa. Second, it is likely that contextual variables such as economic climate, organisational history and industry and occupation characteristics affect what causes career success. These factors tend to be hidden or unmeasured, unless they are apparent in the original studies and used in the meta-analysis.

More recently, Ng has again contributed to our understanding of career success through another meta-analysis, this time of 191 research studies that have investigated subjective career success (Ng and Feldman, 2014). Importantly, demographic variables like social class of family of origin, gender, ethnic identity, marital status, number of children, educational performance and past job history had weak or non-existent relationships with subjective career success. This means that a feeling of success is possible for everyone, not just high fliers, and is consistent with the lack of impact of sociodemographic variables found in the earlier meta-analysis (see Figure 13.4). In contrast, many aspects of motivation and work attitudes (such as job dissatisfaction and low work engagement), personality (especially low self-esteem), social and organisational factors (such as lack of support from supervisor, lack of promotion opportunities) and job characteristics (such as unmet expectations, low job challenge) were all associated with low subjective career success. Here again, it is hard to be sure about the cause and effect, if any. A lack of support from the supervisor might make a person feel less satisfied with his or her career, but equally a clearly unsatisfied person might lead a supervisor to feel disinclined to give much support.

Mentoring as a means to enhance career success

Over many years, mentoring (and more recently coaching) has been extensively used in organisations, and equally extensively researched by psychologists. It is widely seen as, among other things, a way to enhance the career success of individuals being mentored (and also sometimes the mentor as well) and the overall effectiveness of an organisation using it. Mentoring has been defined in a number of ways (see Research methods in focus box below), but perhaps the most widely quoted definition is that of Kram (1985: 9):

> a relationship between a young adult and an older, more experienced adult that helps the younger individual learn to navigate in the adult world and the world of work. A mentor supports, guides and counsels the young adult as he or she accomplishes this important task.

Not all other definitions are quite as broad as this. They focus on the work context, not life as a whole, and often they assume that part of what the mentor does is to help the recipient of mentoring to progress up career hierarchies. However, most share Kram's assumptions that the mentor is older than the person being mentored, the person being mentored is in early career and that mentoring is a one-to-one relationship.

Mentoring can fulfil a number of specific functions for the person being mentored (who is normally called the protégé). Kram (1985) divided these into *career functions* and *psychosocial functions*. The career functions include sponsorship, where the mentor promotes the interests of the protégé by putting them forward for desirable projects or job moves; exposure and visibility to high-ranking people; coaching the protégé by sharing ideas and suggesting strategies; protecting the protégé from risks to their reputation; and (if the mentor is in a position to do so) providing challenging work assignments for the protégé. The psychosocial functions include acting as a role model for the protégé; providing acceptance and confirmation; frank discussion of the protégé's anxieties and fears; and friendship. Mentoring has become a popular technique for developing younger employees, so much so that claims like 'everyone needs a mentor' (Clutterbuck, 2004) are taken seriously.

Many studies suggest that people who have been mentored enjoy better salaries and promotion rates, at least under some circumstances. Allen et al. (2004) and Underhill (2006) have both provided helpful meta-analyses of the relevant literature. They report that in studies that directly compared people who had received mentoring with those who had not, receipt of mentoring showed a small but statistically significant association with earnings and promotions, and a slightly bigger one with career satisfaction. Among those who received mentoring, similar findings were reported for the extent to which the mentor provided career support (see above). The provision of psychosocial support was associated with career and job satisfaction but not with earnings and promotions. The extent to which the mentor was reported to have provided the career benefits of mentoring was associated with both provisions. The benefits of mentoring seem stronger when the mentoring is informal (i.e. it happens spontaneously) rather than formal, where it happens because there is a mentoring scheme that people have to participate in (Chao et al., 1992).

Research methods in focus

Who is a mentor?

Haggard et al. (2011) have discussed the organisational mentoring literature with a particular focus on how a mentor is defined. That might sound a little obscure, but in fact it is very important. They demonstrate that the many studies evaluating the impact of mentoring define a mentor in quite different ways, and that this probably has effects on what those studies find. For example, many definitions of a mentor strongly imply that someone is a mentor if they have provided the career functions of mentoring for the protégé. Therefore it would not be a surprise if people who say they have had a mentor report more career success than those who have not. Other definitional differences concern whether the mentor is assumed to be a more senior member of the organisation, whether he or she can be the protégé's supervisor as well as mentor, and whether the mentor can be someone outside the organisation. Eby et al. (2013) among others also point out that much mentoring research is cross-sectional, which means it is especially difficult to establish whether being mentored makes successful people or being successful makes you attractive to mentors (which it does). There is also the problem of common method variance, since in many studies either the mentor or the protégé provide all the data, which means that their assumptions about the effects of mentoring may simply be translated into the data. A good example of a study that avoids many of these methodological problems is Chun et al. (2012), where 111 matched mentor and protégé pairs in a Korean organisation provided data on three occasions. In order to avoid common method variance, one party's perceptions of the quality of the relationship were used to predict the outcomes (such as organisational commitment) experienced by the other party.

Although interest in mentoring seems to be very long-lasting, related concepts have also received more attention in recent years. For example, some work psychologists earn their living by offering *coaching*, usually to managers. Coaching may simply be a new word for the same activities as mentoring, but it may also signal a shift to a more performance-focused approach where the emphasis is more on improving quality of work now than on long-term career or general psychological well-being. There is also a move towards considering how networks of people, not just one mentor, can help in career development (Higgins and Thomas, 2001; Molloy, 2005). In fact it is possible that people who report having a mentor also have a broad social network, the members of which contribute to the person's development (Blickle et al., 2009). This could mean either that the mentor acts as a source of new contacts, or that having a mentor is simply a sign of a proactive approach to engaging others in one's development. The first possibility would mean that mentoring still played a key (mediating) role, but the second would suggest that having a mentor in itself does not contribute greatly to career development.

Key learning point

Despite limitations in much of the research, it seems that mentoring has potential benefits for all parties involved. However, it is not easy to achieve those benefits with an organised mentoring scheme.

Gender differences in career success

As the Ng et al. and Judge et al. studies imply, when women's career success is assessed on conventional objective criteria of salary progression and promotion, there is generally bad news (see also Alkadry and Tower, 2006, for further evidence of this). Also it is common to see reports in the general and professional press of inequalities between women and men, especially at higher levels of organisational and professional hierarchies. For example, in the UK, the average male in an executive role earned a basic salary of £40,325 over the 12 months to August 2012, compared to £30,265 for a female in the same type of role. Although female junior executives earned marginally more (£363) than males at junior levels for the second year running (£21,491 compared to £21,128), the gender pay gap remained substantial at the opposite end of the executive career ladder. Female directors earned an average basic salary of £127,257, which is £14,689 less than the male director average of £141,946 (Chartered Management Institute, 2013: 4).

In a well-designed and influential study, Stroh et al. (1992) found that women members of a large sample of American managers, who were comparable to men in education, qualifications, experience, proportion of family income generated and willingness to relocate, still suffered from slightly less good salary progression than the men. Furthermore, Lam and Dreher (2004) found that the men gained much more in salary by moving between employing organisations than women did. Schneer and Reitman (1995) found that women MBA graduates, up to 18 years after obtaining their degree, earned on average 19 per cent less than their male counterparts. Even among women who have 'made it', there appears to be some disadvantage relative to men. Lyness and Thompson (2000) found that senior women reported more difficulty getting geographical mobility opportunities, and more concern that they did not fit the dominant culture. Lyness and Schrader (2004) examined announcements of senior job moves in the *Wall Street Journal*, and found that women's moves typically involved smaller changes of role than men's, which might well inhibit their subsequent earning power. A common theme among these and other studies is that objective differences between women and men in years of relevant experience, demonstrable skills etc. could not account for the gender differences.

Key learning point

Barriers to objective career success for women are greater than for men, though the gap seems to be decreasing somewhat. On the other hand, subjective career success seems to be about equal for men and women.

Point of integration

The disadvantages faced by women relative to men in achieving objective career success are likely to be due partly to perceptions of leadership roles and behaviour as being more characteristic of male stereotypes than female ones. Yet there is no evidence that men are better leaders than women – if anything it's the reverse (see Chapter 12).

One way in which women's careers have traditionally differed from men's is, of course, their likelihood of being interrupted by childbearing and childrearing, and by the fact that in most households a woman does more of the childcare and housework than a man, no matter what her employment situation. The presence of two people in a household pursuing careers (usually called dual-career couples) adds extra stresses for both partners, but again these seem to fall more on the woman than on the man (Cooper and Lewis, 1993). A variety of measures designed to help people with family responsibilities are used by some employers, and in general there is increasing attention paid to issues of work–life balance (see Wilkinson and Redman, 2013: Chapter 15, for a review of organisational practices to support work–life balance). Human resource practices include annualised working hours, which people can distribute through the year as they wish (within certain fairly broad limits), and career breaks where people can suspend their career with the organisation for several years, normally in order to make a start on raising a family. During that time they must report for refresher training for a small number of weeks per year. These may look like expensive schemes, but what evaluation evidence there is suggests that they are cost-effective for organisations because they help to retain skilled labour (the costs of lost expertise, and finding good-quality replacement staff can be enormous). On the other hand, there is some feeling that people who make use of the scheme may find that their subsequent progress is handicapped by others perceiving that they are not really serious about their career. Judiesch and Lyness (1999) reported that leaves of absence for family responsibilities were almost always taken by women not men, and that leaves result in fewer subsequent promotions and smaller salary increases. Furthermore, these disadvantages can be very long-lasting: 25 years or more (Reitman and Schneer, 2005). From the perspective of gender power relations, it might even be argued that the effect of measures to help work–life balance is to keep women in the workforce, but in a subordinate position and still able to look after the home and family tasks that men don't want to do (Loretto and Vickerstaff, 2015).

Point of integration

Organisational policies to assist women and men to have fulfilling careers while also honouring other parts of their lives are relevant to the reduction of work stress and the promotion of personal well-being and development (Chapter 10).

Key learning point

Despite claims that careers have become more flexible, it seems that taking career breaks is still costly and that women have somewhat more difficulty in achieving objective career success than men do.

Improving your career success

An assumption behind the notions of boundaryless and protean careers is that individuals have the power to influence what happens to them, and to steer their own careers. However, many of the variables shown in Figure 13.4 might suggest otherwise. If personality and cognitive ability are quite stable, the implication is that there isn't much a person can do to change them, or indeed the sociodemographic variables. How these can be taken into account by organisations in managing careers is discussed earlier in this chapter. Organisational sponsorship is somewhat more under personal control, but also presumably partly dependent upon organisational policies and practices. A person's human capital seems more readily open to change by his or her own actions. Even so, some aspects of capital, such as education and international experience, may be constrained by a person's ability, family circumstances and so on. All this serves to highlight that the rhetoric of boundaryless and protean careers may be a little too optimistic about individuals' capacity to influence their own fate.

Still, it would be discouraging to think of ourselves as helpless! The human capital variables in the Ng et al. study do give us some clues about how we can influence our career success, and it is probably not surprising that putting work first in your life and working long hours tends to help. Whether you want to do that is another question. The concept of *career competencies* is potentially useful to individuals in enhancing their career success. DeFillippi and Arthur (1996) suggested that three kinds of competence might be especially helpful in an era of boundaryless careers. 'Knowing why' concerns a person's insight into his or her career motivations and abilities. 'Knowing whom' concerns developing and using social contacts (i.e. accumulating career capital). 'Knowing how' refers to specific skills and abilities relating to one's job and career. Although some research suggests that these might be useful constructs (Eby et al., 2003), at present they are poorly defined and measured. A somewhat stronger taxonomy of competencies is offered by Kuijpers and Scheerens (2006), who suggest career development ability, reflection on capacities, reflection on motives, work exploration, career control and networking. More recently, Akkermans et al. (2012) have developed a set of six career competencies: reflection on motivation, reflection on qualities, networking, self-profiling, work exploration, and career control. Based on this framework, they developed the Career Competencies Questionnaire (CCQ).

Prominent in discussions of career success is the concept of *social capital*. Its prominence is based on the 'common-sense' idea that who you know is at least as important as what you know, which is reflected in the 'knowing whom' concept mentioned above. In fact, perhaps career success is best seen as a fundamentally social process (see Figure 13.5 for a suggested model of how social processes might work). Social capital refers to the social resources that a person can access and utilise. In work settings, Forret and Dougherty (2001, 2004) have identified five kinds of behaviour that can enhance social capital: socialising, engaging in professional activities, maintaining contacts, participation in home community and increasing one's visibility at work. Of course, some people will find these things easier to do than others. This is partly a matter of

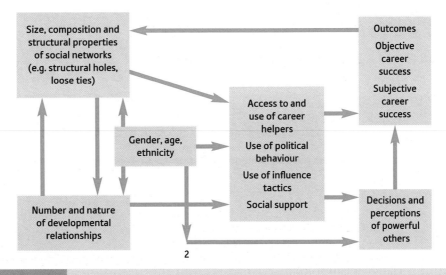

Figure 13.5   The social processes of career success

personality, but also of social position. Bosley et al. (2009) analyse the roles of informal career helpers in enhancing a person's career success. For example, a person may act as a *witness*, giving another individual feedback on their skills and perhaps boosting their self-confidence. Or they may be an *intermediary*, approaching people with power on behalf of the person they are helping.

Other research in this area has used social network analysis to describe a person's social network. This maps out who an individual knows, how well and in what ways they know them and whether those people know each other. The most influential study in this tradition is by Seibert et al. (2001) who investigated the extent to which features of respondents' social networks affected career success. Two features were of particular interest. *Structural holes* referred to the extent to which an individual's contacts did *not* know each other (i.e. there were holes in the network) and the number of *weak ties* reflected the extent to which the person had many contacts they knew slightly, rather than a few they knew well. Social network theory suggests that the most effective networks have both of these properties because they allow the person to access many different perspectives without getting too attached to any of them. Seibert and colleagues found that the number of weak ties and structural holes both predicted the number of contacts at higher levels a person had, which in turn influenced their career satisfaction (but interestingly not so much their salary and promotions). Again, though, we must be careful when talking about cause and effect. Although Seibert and colleagues developed a sophisticated theory and tested it carefully, their data were cross-sectional. Also, they were drawn from a sample of US university graduates, most of whom were working in corporate settings, so the findings may be somewhat context-specific.

Key learning point

Developing and using our career competences and social networks may be the most useful things to focus on in improving our own career success.

The cleaner who soared all the way to the board

Karen Hester had no thought of becoming a manager when she started a cleaning job at Adnams, the British brewer based in the seaside town of Southwold. "I wanted evening work, so my children wouldn't miss out during the day," she says. Twenty-six years on, she runs Adnams' entire operations and is about to join its board.

Her potential was spotted after she became a purchasing clerk simply because she needed to change her hours when her children started school. In her new role, she met Andy Wood, now chief executive but then supply chain head. Impressed by how she project managed the purchase of his company car, he asked about her background. When he discovered she had qualified to drive heavy goods vehicles as a 17-year-old army recruit, and gained two promotions in record time, he persuaded her to join the transport division and became her mentor.

"Karen wasn't an obvious model for a future business leader, but she displayed a tenacity, an inquisitiveness and willingness to learn that marked her out," Mr Wood says.

Individuals with underused talents – even if not on the scale of Ms Hester's latent abilities – exist in all walks of life. But many organisations struggle to judge people on their true merits.

First, talented employees with unconventional backgrounds may have to overcome the unconscious bias of superiors to reach senior roles. Even if we try to be "neutral judges", says Francesca Gino, a professor at Harvard Business School, we tend to view people with whom we feel some affinity – whether because of education, gender, ethnicity or some lesser connection – more favourably.

Likewise, as institutions, businesses may create barriers for individuals who do not fulfil stereotypical expectations. A case in point is

fast-tracking graduates over other employees. Executives "must be bright enough" to do the job, as John Mervyn-Smith, chief psychologist at UK-based talent consultancy eg. 1 observes. But he adds that qualities such as energy and drive, emotional maturity, ability to solve problems and learn quickly – at which Ms Hester excelled – are often better predictors of successful leadership than academic qualifications.

What can businesses do to find potential that may be hiding in plain sight, especially if the individuals concerned may not think promotion is for them and so do not put themselves forward?

Creating a variety of routes into senior roles helps. Having previously concentrated on honing the leadership skills of executives near the top of the organisation, Vodafone has introduced a career development programme, known internally as "Retail Spine". The initiative spots promising shop floor employees and equips them with skills and experience they will need to become general managers and advance into the top jobs.

Candidates nominate themselves or are put forward by a manager to be assessed for potential to think strategically, manage through influence and adapt to change. "By taking people out of their day-to-day role and looking at them from a broader perspective, we aim to spot potential early and pull people up through the organisation," says Jenni Heyes, who runs Vodafone's employee training and development operations.

Another approach is to encourage employees with thoughts on how to improve the business, wherever they are in the pecking order, to pitch for resources to put their ideas into action. At L'Oréal 33-year-old James Taylor has spent three years managing a £4m IT project to improve planning and forecasting processes. He had the idea while working as an account manager in the UK consumer products division and entered an internal innovation competition. Now he is about to begin a global role, at director level, at L'Oréal's The Body Shop. "The project gave me exposure to senior managers across Europe ... and [an opportunity to show] what I was capable of achieving," he says.

Having taken an unusual route herself, Ms Hester says she keeps a weather eye open for untapped potential, taking particular care not to typecast people. "I never assume the warehouse-worker in blue trousers and a blue top isn't capable of doing the same role as the person in the shirt and chinos," she says.

 Source: Financial Times, adapted from story posted by Alicia Clegg, 5 January 2015 (accessed 9 July 2015)

Suggested exercise

List the factors that can affect career success that are highlighted in this article. Where do they fit in Ng et al. (2005) classification of predictors of success?

Career choice

Psychologists have long been interested in how people choose an occupation, and how they can be helped to do so effectively. Here the term career is usually taken to mean occupation or line of work. The task of identifying, measuring and matching a person's characteristics and those of an occupation is 'core business' for applied psychology, so a great deal of effort has been devoted to the endeavour over many decades. Three basic requirements of effective career choice were proposed long ago by Frank Parsons (1909: 5, described in Sharf, 1992: Chapter 2):

1   A clear understanding of ourselves, our attitudes, abilities, interests, ambitions, resource limitations and their causes.

2   A knowledge of the requirements and conditions of success, advantages and disadvantages, compensation, opportunities and prospects in different lines of work.

3   True reasoning on the relations of these two groups of facts.

This nicely describes the nature of the task, but does not in itself help people to do it well. We now examine psychologists' attempts to take things further. An excellent overview of some of this work can be found in Savickas (2007).

John Holland's theory

Over many years John Holland developed an influential theory of career choice (e.g. Holland, 1997). In the course of his work as a careers counsellor in the USA, Holland thought he could discern six pure types of vocational personality. He also felt that he could see the roots of these types in traditional personality theory. He developed his concepts and measures of them. Subsequent work has sought to validate these, and to test Holland's hypotheses about career choice (see below). Very briefly, Holland's six personality types are as follows:

1   *Realistic*: outdoor-type. Tends to like, and be good at, activities requiring physical strength and/or coordination. Not keen on socialising.

2   *Investigative*: interested in concepts and logic. Tends to enjoy, and be good at, abstract thought. Often interested in the physical sciences.

3   *Artistic*: tends to use imagination a lot. Likes to express feelings and ideas. Dislikes rules and regulations. Enjoys music, drama, art.

4   *Social*: enjoys the company of other people, especially in affiliative (i.e. helping, friendly) relationships. Tends to be warm and caring.

5   *Enterprising*: also enjoys the company of other people, but mainly to dominate or persuade rather than help them. Enjoys action rather than thought.

6   *Conventional*: likes rules and regulations, structure and order. Usually well-organised, not very imaginative.

Holland proposed that the types can be arranged in a hexagon in the order described above to express their similarity to each other (see Figure 13.6). This ordering is usually referred to as RIASEC. Each type is placed at a corner of the hexagon. Types on opposite corners of the hexagon (i.e. three corners apart) are in many senses opposites. Types on adjacent corners (e.g. *realistic* and *conventional*) are quite similar to each other. Nobody exactly matches any single type, but nevertheless each of us resembles some types more than others. In fact, Holland suggests that people are most usefully described in terms of the three types they resemble most, in descending order of similarity. Hence, for example, for an ISE person, the *investigative* type comes closest to describing them, the *social* type comes next and *enterprising* third. Holland proposed that occupations can also be described in terms of the six types. He has argued that any environment exerts its influence through the people in it. Hence occupations are described in terms of the people in them, again using the three most prevalent types in descending order. In the USA, Holland's classification of occupations has been widely applied in, for example, the *Dictionary of Holland Occupational Codes* (Gottfredson and Holland, 1996).

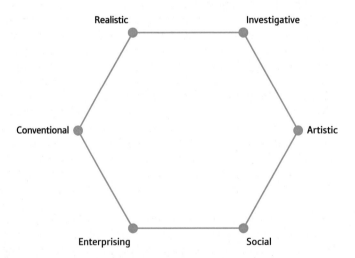

| Figure 13.6 | Holland's six types of vocational personality |

Key learning point

John Holland has identified six vocational personality types. These types map on to different occupations.

Some of Holland's main theoretical propositions (see Holland, 1997: 67–8) are as follows:

- People find environments satisfying when environmental patterns resemble their own personality patterns. This situation (often referred to as *congruence*) encourages stability of behaviour because people receive a lot of reinforcement of their already-preferred styles. Congruence also tends to enable a person to perform well in their work.

- Incongruent interactions stimulate change in behaviour. A person may seek a more congruent environment, remake the present one or change to become more congruent in behaviour and/or perceptions.

- An environment expels incongruent people, seeks new congruent ones or changes its demands on inhabitants.

Holland has said he is irritated by what he sees as a lack of attention to the more dynamic social–psychological elements of his theory. However, his fundamental hypothesis is relatively straightforward and states that people will be most satisfied, and most successful, in occupations that are congruent with (i.e. match) their personality. Thus Holland's theory reflects a well-established tradition in work psychology: the matching of person and work, with the assumption that both are fairly stable over time. The large volume of research on this and other aspects of Holland's theory has been reviewed by Nauta (2010) and Arnold (2004), among others. Several conclusions can be drawn.

First, Holland's vocational personality types are a reasonably good reflection of basic personality dimensions identified in more general psychology, as indeed they should be.

Second, the hexagonal arrangement, while not a perfect representation of the relative similarities of the types, is nevertheless a good approximation for most of the voluminous data collected using Holland's measures (Tracey and Rounds, 1993). At the very least, it looks as if the circumplex arrangement of the types (that is, they can be positioned on a circle in a certain order) is accurate. Third, and somewhat contrary to the second point above, the hexagonal arrangement may not be very generalisable across cultures. Although Leong et al. (1998) argued that their data from India did match the hexagon quite well, their conclusion looks rather optimistic. For example, E and R were quite similar, which might be expected in an economy where agriculture plays quite a big role in the everyday lives of much of the population. In China, Long and Tracey (2006) found that a plausible interpretation of the types was as three pairs: R/I, A/S and E/C. These could approximate to science, arts/humanities and business respectively, and may partly be a consequence of relatively early specialisation in parts of the Chinese education system.

Fourth and finally, there is some evidence that congruence is correlated with satisfaction and success, but it is surprisingly weak (about .25 according to Spokane et al., 2000, and less than that according to Young et al., 1998). Even when the correlation is observed, we cannot be sure that congruence leads to satisfaction and success, although Donohue (2006) found that people can increase their congruence either by shifting to another occupation or by adjusting their interests over time.

What might be the problems and limitations of defining congruence as the match between the vocational personality of an individual and that of the typical individual in an occupation? On what other basis might congruence be measured?

Arnold (2004) analysed 14 possible reasons for the weak or non-existent correlations between congruence and satisfaction/performance outcomes. He grouped these under three general headings: problems with the theory; problems with research on the theory; and the nature of 21st-century careers. He concluded that the following three factors, all to do with the theory and research (not so much with the nature of 21st-century careers), were most likely to be responsible:

1　Holland's theory and measures do not adequately reflect some aspects of the person (for example, the values/anchors discussed earlier in this chapter). If aspects of the person other than those Holland includes are partly responsible for satisfaction and/or performance, then we can expect the Holland measure to show relatively weak correlations.

2　Similarly, measures of the environment might miss significant features, and in any case what is most appropriately construed as the 'environment'? Is it occupation, employing organisation, work group, industry or what? In fairness to Holland, in his occupations finder he differentiates to some extent between the same occupation in different contexts (e.g. clinical psychologist versus organisational psychologist). However, this differentiation does not always occur, and in any case may not reflect the kinds of distinction that matter to some people. Is being a management accountant in a heavy engineering company the same as being a management accountant in a charity, for example?

3　Measures of congruence are weakened by the above two factors, and by the fact that many of them lose too much of the available data. For example, congruence indices based on three-letter codes ignore scores on the other three career-related personality types. McLarnon et al. (2015) suggest that clustering people on the basis of their overall pattern of scores is more helpful than simply listing the top three. They tried this out with Canadian students and found eight sub-groups, the largest of which tended to score low on all six Holland types – surely significant information for career decision-making and guidance.

Congruence between person and environment, as defined in Holland's theory, is less good at predicting a person's satisfaction in an occupation than might be expected.

Holland's approach to personality assessment is a little unusual. He has developed the *Self-Directed Search* (SDS) (see http://www.self-directed-search.com/), which asks the respondent about their preferred activities, reactions to occupational titles, abilities, competencies and even daydreams. People can score their own SDS, establish their three-letter code, and then examine an 'occupations finder' to check which occupations might be appropriate for them. There is also a 'leisure activities finder' for people who are seeking congenial spare-time pursuits. They are encouraged to try various permutations of their three-letter code, especially if their three highest scores are of similar magnitude. All of this is unusual in a number of respects. First, it is rare for questions about both abilities and interests to be included in a vocational guidance instrument. Second, the SDS is deliberately transparent – people can see what it is getting at (Reardon and Lenz, 1998). Third, it is rare for psychologists to allow the people they assess to score and interpret their own data. Holland feels that most people simply need reassurance that their career ideas are appropriate, and that the SDS generally provides this much more quickly and cheaply than careers counselling.

More generally, there are many tests of occupational interests on the market – some paper-and-pencil, many available on the Web. Few have such a strong theoretical and empirical basis as Holland's. One that does is the *Strong Interest Inventory* (Harmon et al., 1994), which has been revised to reflect the Holland types. Data from it have contributed to the classification of occupations in Holland's terms.

Key learning point

Holland's self-directed search makes it easy for a person to see for him- or herself what occupations appear to be most suitable.

Theories such as Holland's describe the *content* of actual and ideal decisions, but not the *process*. How can a person make an effective career decision? Several factors are relevant.

Knowledge of self and occupations

According to Parsons (1909, see above), in order to make sound career decisions, a person needs to have an accurate view of their own strengths and weaknesses, values, likes and dislikes. Numerous exercises and techniques are available for this, some in published books that aim to provide a complete practical guide to making and implementing career decisions (e.g. Bolles, 2008; Lees, 2007) and others home-grown in (for example) college careers services. Most are designed to help people to examine systematically their experiences in the work setting and outside it, in order to arrive at the most accurate and complete self-assessment that their past experience allows. Research has suggested that people are not necessarily very accurate in their perceptions of their abilities (Church, 1997), though with practice and by careful comparison with other people, they can improve (Mabe and West, 1982; Miller, 2007).

Hall's notion of the protean career discussed earlier in this chapter stresses the importance of being guided by a clear sense of self, but also being flexible enough to change it somewhat in response to experience and the opportunities and constraints of the labour market. This is a departure from the usual psychologists' idea that individual differences are relatively fixed after a fairly early age. Hall also stresses the importance of 'psychological success' in building up a person's identity as a competent person. Objectively verifiable success in tasks leads to greater self-confidence and self-esteem, which in turn encourages the person to take on more challenging tasks, which can lead to more success, and so on.

Again, there are many workbooks that give guidance on how to find out about occupations (e.g. Hopson and Scally, 2000; Bolles, 2008). Apart from reading published information, methods include talking to a person in that occupation, and 'shadowing' such a person for a period of time in order to see what they actually do. Emphasis is placed on avoiding stereotypes of occupations, and ensuring that one pays attention not only to positions one might ultimately occupy in an occupation, but also to those one will have to fill on the way. Often it is surprisingly difficult for people to relate what they know about occupations to what they know about self (Nathan and Hill, 2006). This is especially the case when a person is trying to choose between fairly similar occupations. As we have seen above with John Holland's theory, one advantage of the better-developed vocational measures is that they do describe people and occupations in the same language, but even then there are usually several occupations to which the person seems well suited. It is the choice between these which is often difficult.

Becoming aware of self and of the world of work requires *exploration*. Blustein (1997: 261) defined career (or vocational) exploration as 'encompassing those activities, directed towards enhancing the knowledge of the self and the external environment, that an individual engages in to foster progress in career development'. In early theorising, career exploration was seen as a life stage that occurs in adolescence and early adulthood (Super, 1957; see also next section), or as a stage in the career decision-making process (Tiedeman and O'Hara, 1963), again typically associated with youth. More recent approaches (e.g. Flum and Blustein, 2000) have construed exploration somewhat differently. They see it as a set of activities that a person can (and probably should) engage in throughout life. Also, a key outcome of exploration is the construction and reconstruction of self-identity. It is not just about getting a job or choosing an occupation. Instead, exploration can be intrinsically motivated behaviour, performed for its own sake and as an expression of an individual's autonomy and curiosity. Notice that this is highly consistent with the idea that in the protean career a key developmental task is to get the right balance between identity and adaptability. Not surprisingly, career exploration can have a positive effect on career decision-making (Zikic and Klehe, 2006). However, like congruence in John Holland's theory, the effects are sometimes weaker than one would expect (e.g. Cheung and Arnold, 2014). This may be because people who engage in a lot of exploration take time to digest what they find out, and its benefits therefore take longer to become apparent than most research projects can accommodate.

Key learning point

Good awareness of self and the world of work is often a consequence of willingness to engage in exploration, and a cause of successful career decisions.

Career decision-making processes

It tends to be assumed that (i) being decided about an occupation is a good thing and (ii) careers advisors and others can help people only if they know why they are undecided. The first assumption in particular can be challenged. Arnold (1990) argued that career decidedness contributed to psychological well-being only during the transition from education to work, not before. Earl and Bright (2007) found that being decided might be helpful during that transition, but having a clear sense of self was more so. Perhaps a lot depends on how a person reaches their decision. Here the long-established concept of *identity status* (Marcia, 1966) is relevant. Marcia suggested that among young people there are four possible patterns in the development of sense of self:

1   *diffusion*: general vagueness;
2   *foreclosure*: dealing with uncertainty by making quick and early decisions;

3   *moratorium*: deliberately waiting and seeing;

4   *identity achievement*: a clear sense of self based on experience and reflection.

In the context of career decision-making, it seems likely that decisions made as a consequence of foreclosure may be somewhat inappropriate, and based more on a need for certainty than careful consideration of the match between self and career. In this case decidedness would probably not be a good thing. Conversely, someone in a state of moratorium may be undecided about a career choice, but purposefully so. This person doesn't feel ready to decide: they are not avoiding the issue, nor are they rushing to a premature conclusion. In this case, not being decided seems appropriate.

As a consequence of the second assumption described above, many attempts have been made to identify and analyse the different causes and types of career indecision. Various factors have been suggested, including lack of information about one's own interests or abilities, lack of information about the world of work, having two or more equally attractive choices, social pressure (e.g. from parents), lack of self-confidence, decision-making anxiety, home–work tensions and habitual indecision (see for example Brown and Rector, 2008). Other researchers have focused on decision-making styles (Harren, 1979), most notably including rational (logical conscious processing of information), intuitive (unconscious information-processing and 'gut feel') and dependent (reliance on others). Arguing that neither the indecision nor the styles approach tells the whole story, Gati et al. (2010) drew on both to develop a questionnaire for profiling career decision-making called the Career Decision-Making Profile (CDMP). They came up with eleven dimensions which collectively represent a person's career decision-making profile, as shown in Table 13.6.

Despite the intention to use the overall profile of a person's scores in helping him or her make good career decisions, Gadassi et al. (2012) examined it dimension by dimension to see whether one end of each was more adaptive than the other, and if so which. Based on statistical relationships with measures of career decidedness and of decision-making difficulty, they found that comprehensive information-gathering, internal locus of control, absence of procrastination, fast decision-making, and low dependence on others were all consistently beneficial. On the other hand, aspiration for an ideal occupation, willingness to compromise and consulting with others were not associated one way or the other with

Table 13.6	Decision-making profiles

Information-gathering (comprehensive versus minimal): the thoroughness with which the person collects and organises relevant information

Information-processing (analytic versus holistic): whether the person deals with information in terms of its components, or as a whole

Locus of control (internal versus external): the extent to which the person believes they control their occupational future

Effort invested (much versus little): the amount of time and energy the person puts into the decision-making process

Procrastination (high versus low): the degree to which the person avoids or delays starting the decision-making process

Speed of making the final decision (high versus low): how long the person takes to decide once the relevant information has been collected

Consulting with others (frequent versus rare): the extent to which the person consults with others at various stages of the process

Dependence on others (high versus low): the extent to which the person looks to other people to make decisions on their behalf

Desire to please others (high versus low): the extent to which the person tries to satisfy the expectations of others

Aspiration for an ideal occupation (high versus low): the extent to which the person strives for an occupation that is a perfect fit

Willingness to compromise (much versus little): the extent to which the person is willing to be flexible about their preferred alternative when they encounter difficulties

Source: Adapted with permission from Gadassi et al., 2012: 612–13.

decidedness or decision-making difficulty. Probably most of these findings are unsurprising, but nevertheless the CDMP seems a helpful tool for self-assessment and for careers counsellors in developing effective decision-making.

Key learning point

The nature of a person's approach to decision-making, his/her identity development to date and his/her knowledge of self and world of work are all likely to affect how successful his or her career decision-making is.

Development of career preferences during early life

Career choices in early adulthood are not made at one point in time. They reflect a young person's cognitive development and experiences during childhood. Gottfredson (1981, 1996) has developed an influential theory of how this happens. According to her, very young children cannot distinguish between reality and fantasy, and their occupational choices are influenced by size and power, so they might say they want to be a wizard or an elephant when they grow up. By about age six, a child becomes aware of gender roles, and will select occupations based on that alone. By nine or ten, the child realises that different jobs have different statuses in society, and will want to aspire to the highest possible given his or her family's social class. For many middle-class boys, this is when aspirations to be a train driver or a postman are abandoned. According to Gottfredson, it is not until early teens that an emerging sense of abilities, interests and values (i.e. what most of this section of the chapter has been about) begins to influence occupational preferences, though Schultheiss et al. (2005) found that this awareness is sometimes apparent in younger children.

Gottfredson has a lot to say about career compromise, because occupational preferences are frequently not attainable, or at least not easily. Note also that compromise also features in Gati's CDMP described above. Controversially, Gottfredson argues that when a young person has to compromise, he or she most readily gives up the match with self-concept, then prestige and finally gender compatibility. This is especially marked when the need for compromise is severe, i.e. attainable occupations are a long way from the ideal preference. Wee (2014) found some support for the idea that gender typing is the last resort, but not that prestige sits in between interests and gender type when compromises are needed. Sinclair et al. (2014) found evidence that compromise is at least partly a social process, because in her study the more close friends of the same gender a young person had, the more likely they were to compromise with a gender-stereotyped occupational choice.

According to Super's (1957) theory of career development, during their mid to late teens, most people are in a **career stage** he referred to as *exploration*. This stage has three substages, as follows:

1   *Crystallisation*: becoming clear about one's self-concept and identity.
2   *Specification*: on the basis of that self-concept, choosing a suitable line of work.
3   *Implementation*: finding ways of getting into that line of work.

This is, of course, a logical ordering, but it is surprisingly easy to try to do them in the wrong order, and end up confused. Of course, this assumes, contrary to Gottfredson, that career choices are made on the basis of self-concept.

The perils of career decision-making

With the retirement age rising to 67 by 2026–28, young people will soon work for 50 years or more. I realise that choosing the profession I want to follow – and the A-levels and university courses that will get me there – is a decision of paramount importance. But I can't help thinking that it's too much for an inexperienced 17-year-old to make.

What you want to be when you grow up requires careful thought: we need time to learn about and consider all the options. But the rush to get good grades – and the fact that our grades heavily influence what we can and can't do – means that some students make hurried, expedient decisions, which may not be for the best in the long-term.

Pressure is piled on young people to choose qualifications for a career they want now but will wait five years to get. GCSEs came and went in a blur. Then I was preparing for the next hurdle – A-levels. As soon as these were under way, I found myself on the busy road of university open days, prospectuses and student finance talks. In the midst of all of this, employers expect you to be building relevant work experience. And none of this can be easily undone – if I suddenly find that being a doctor is the only career for me but I don't have any science A-levels, I face a long hard trip back through education.

The higher education system doesn't help much either. Universities often demand top grades and experience for certain courses. In the crush to get all this sorted, it's hard to find the time to consider your options.

It's not like there's no support out there. There is, but sometimes it can be as much of a curse as a blessing. Vast amounts of guidance have introduced me to the various career routes I could take. But, on the flip side, the variety of careers that I've become aware of has left me, and doubtless many others, even more uncertain of which I want to pursue. While it's better to be over-informed than uninformed, at the tender age of 17, I've been bombarded with numerous options. But telling me about the many options – while piling on the pressure to make a snappy decision – isn't really helping.

With students choosing careers that may not suit them, a worrying scenario could emerge: we could be stuck in careers like round pins in square holes. This is detrimental for the students because reconsidering a career is an enormous decision. But it's also detrimental for employers who will struggle to keep excellent students interested in careers that they no longer want.

The majority of us do not know what we want to do when we finish education – let alone when we're halfway through. And the few who do know what they want often rethink their choice as they develop and grow. Who I am now isn't who I might be in the future, and the education and recruitment system needs to give us the space and time to make the right career choices.

Source: Guardian newspaper online, article by Abigail Lane (17 year-old student at a school in Hertfordshire, England). Posted 26 July 2013. http://www.theguardian.com/careers/young-people-take-career-decisions-too-early (accessed 16 July 2015).

Suggested exercises

1   Consider how the factors mentioned by Abigail Lane might impair effective career decision-making, using the material in this section of the chapter.

2   To what extent do you think taking a questionnaire like the Self-Directed Search which asks you about your interests, skills and preferences can provide an effective shortcut to a good decision for someone in Abigail's position?

3   Do you think the situation is as much of a problem as she portrays?

On the move: stages, ages and job transitions

Stages

In the middle part of the 20th century several attempts were made to map out the whole of a person's career or life in terms of a series of age-linked stages, each with its own characteristics. Brief mention of Super has already been made above. As well as the exploration stage, he suggested subsequent stages as follows:

- *Establishment*: Perhaps after one or two false starts, the person finds a career field, and makes efforts to prove their worth in it. Typical ages: 25–44.

- *Maintenance*: The concern now is to hold onto the niche one has carved for oneself. This can be a considerable task, especially in the face of technological changes and vigorous competition from younger workers. Typical ages: 45–64.

- *Disengagement*: Characterised by decreasing involvement in work and a tendency to become an observer rather than a participant. Typical ages: 65+.

In his later writing, Super loosened up the links between stages and ages somewhat, and called them concerns rather than stages, which people could be pre-occupied by at any age. He also identified six roles people typically perform in Western societies: homemaker, worker, citizen, leisurite, student and child. The importance of each of these roles in a person's life can rise and fall over time. Also, at any given time, a person can be at different stages (exploration, establishment etc.) in different roles. These insights do not in themselves create a theory, but they do help people to consider their lives in a systematic way (Super, 1990). Some self-assessment devices such as the Adult Career Concerns Inventory (Super et al., 1985; Perrone et al., 2003) and the Salience Inventory (Super and Nevill, 1985) have been developed to assist in this process.

Levinson and colleagues (1978) and Levinson and Levinson (1996) developed another influential theory based on stages, or 'seasons' of life as Levinson called them. In this theory, periods of stability of purpose (when a person knows what he or she is trying to achieve) alternate with transitional times when the key elements of a person's life are under review, and changes of direction are more likely. Unlike Super, Levinson stayed with the idea that these seasons are closely linked with age – within two or three years either way he thought. The *midlife transition* (ages 40–45) identified by Levinson has often been considered the most significant aspect of his work. He argued that lifestyle is reappraised at this age, often with considerable urgency and emotion – so much so, that it is sometimes referred to as the 'midlife crisis'. People realise that their life is probably at least half over and this concentrates their minds on what they should be doing with the rest of it. In the eyes of their children they are now symbols of authority, old-timers. Physical signs of ageing become unmistakable. There are by now clear indications of whether or not earlier career ambitions will be achieved. These factors can lead to substantial life changes: for example, a change of career or a change of spouse. Alternatively, a commitment to the current lifestyle may be reaffirmed, and increased effort put into it. Despite the popularity of the midlife crisis concept, there is in fact little evidence that men generally find it an especially troubling time (Lawrence, 1980).

Super and Levinson's theories, and other similar ones, developed from post-Freudian analyses of the experiences and struggles people face as they go through life. Especially influential here was Erikson (1968, 1980). Erikson proposed that we journey through eight stages of psychosocial development, each with its key developmental task that must be tackled before the person is ready to move forward. A key task that many people face in the middle and later parts of their career is to pass on something of themselves and their achievements to future generations. This is often termed *generativity*.

Taken at face value, these approaches to adult development have implications for career management in organisations. If people are going to work effectively, the needs and concerns of their life stage should be taken into account. Therefore, in early adulthood, people must be given the opportunity to integrate themselves into an organisation and/or career, and demonstrate their worth to themselves and others. This may involve special efforts to give the newcomer significant work assignments and social support. In mid-career, it may be necessary to provide opportunities for some people to retrain, perhaps in the light of a midlife reappraisal. They could also be given opportunities to allow them to keep up to date in their chosen field. It may also be helpful to give people in their mid- to late career a chance to act as mentor or guide to younger employees (see Mentoring as a means to enhance career success, above) – this is, after all, a way of handing on one's accumulated wisdom and thereby making a lasting impression.

Key learning point

Career stage theories attempt to paint the 'big picture' of people's lives. This is difficult to do in a way that fits most people without being so general that it tells us nothing we don't know already. Stages are also of dubious relevance in an era of volatile careers and lives.

Much has changed since the time these theories were developed. As noted above, many people think that work has become much less predictable, with more changing of jobs and occupations. Inevitable questions arise about whether the stages have to be tackled in the order listed, whether it really is impossible to successfully tackle one stage without having successfully tackled the previous one, and whether recycling through the stages has become the norm now that more people have to remake occupational decisions during their careers. As Hall (1986: Chapter 4) pointed out, it is difficult to identify what career stage a person is in, especially if, for example, they enter a career relatively late in life. Most importantly, these stage theories are all vulnerable to the accusation that they really only reflect the lives of middle-class males in Western countries in the mid- to late-20th century. As Sullivan and Crocitto (2007: 283) put it:

> The intent of the early developmental career theories ... was to describe the work life of the typical post-World War II professional. At that time, the average employee was a man who worked for one or two organisations until retirement, while his wife was at home caring for their children.

Bardwick (1980) and Gallos (1989), among others, argued that women focus more on attachment and affiliation in their development, in contrast to men, who emphasise separateness and achievement. Nevertheless, although some developmental issues are more problematic for women than for men, Levinson and Levinson (1996) argued that the same underlying concerns arise at the same ages for both sexes. So whereas for a man the age 30 transition might focus mainly on occupational concerns, for a woman it might concern whether and when to have children. The issues are different but the theme of fine-tuning the direction of one's life is the same (Roberts and Newton, 1987). Still, even if these traditional stage theories are applicable to women, they may nevertheless not be the best potentially available. O'Neil and Bilimoria (2005) conducted an in-depth study of 60 women. They suggested that their careers could be divided into three quite long phases:

1   *Phase 1: idealistic achievement*: Emphasis on personal control, career satisfaction and achievement, and positive impact on others. Typically in the woman's 20s and early 30s.

2   *Phase 2: pragmatic endurance*: Doing what has to be done, while managing multiple relationships and responsibilities. Less personal control; more dissatisfaction, especially with organisations and managers. Typically in the woman's mid-30s to late 40s.

3   *Phase 3: re-inventive contribution*: To organisations, families and communities, without losing sight of self. Careers as learning opportunities and a chance to make a difference to others. Typically from around age 50 onwards.

Gersick and Kram (2002) reported a small-scale but intensive study with women aged 45–55 working for a large American financial company. Their conclusions were somewhat similar to those of O'Neil and Bilimoria (2005), but the view of mid-career was somewhat more positive.

Key learning point

Women and men tend to have different developmental paths. Traditional career stage theory reflects men's perspectives better than women's.

Age

Relative to stages, age has the advantage that it is a continuous variable: that is, it increases in tiny steps (by the minute if one wants to be that precise). This means that change and difference that emerge gradually over time can be spotted and it is not necessary to define when and how one stage ends and another begins. Of course, this does not necessarily mean that the relationship between a variable and age is linear. For example, there is some evidence that well-being and job satisfaction fall a little in midlife before rising again thereafter (Warr, 1992). The obvious measure of age is chronological. Indeed, at first it is hard to think of any other way of measuring it. However, in principle at least, age can also be functional (what a person can do relative to population norms), or organisational (how long a person has been in the organisation), or socially defined for example in terms of family stage, so that someone who was born 30 years ago could be the same 'age' as someone born 50 years ago if they both have children aged (say) 12 and 10 (Kooij et al., 2008). In the 21st century, lives are longer and perhaps more varied in form than ever before, so these alternative conceptions of age may be important. It is also sometimes necessary to consider age in conjunction with other variables. So, for example, women's age seems to have more impact on how they are perceived and on their career prospects than men's age does on their prospects (Lincoln and Allen, 2004). In the UK, this has been illustrated by high-profile cases of women TV presenters taking legal action against their employers for being dropped from prominent programmes.

Despite the fact that relationships between age and other variables are not necessarily linear, most people are interested in linear trends with age. These are less easy to be sure of than it might seem. If we find that 60 year olds and 30 year olds differ in a number of ways, is this because of the difference in age, or is it because of generational differences (i.e. were they always different?). Interestingly, the literature on generations (always a popular topic with the media) and age seem to proceed in parallel, with little cross-referencing (Dries et al., 2008). Even more complicated, is there an interaction between age and events, such that, for example, a recession affects older people in different ways from younger ones? It is often argued that older people find it harder to get a new job than younger ones do, and this might be even more the case when jobs are hard to find (Conen et al., 2011).

From the literature on ageing and work (e.g. Kooij et al., 2011; Salthouse, 2010; Truxillo et al., 2012), the following can be concluded. In general, there is no correlation between age and work performance. Younger workers tend to have higher fluid intelligence, which is raw abstract reasoning power, whereas older workers have more crystallised intelligence, which means accumulated knowledge and know-how. Younger workers tend to be interested in making their reputation, acquiring new skills and making progress, whereas older workers tend to put more emphasis on using the skills they already have and contributing to the collective good, perhaps by developing others (generativity again). Stereotypes of older workers tend to be negative (Posthuma and Campion, 2009), particularly around unwillingness to change, learn new skills and expend energy. This is partially compensated for by perceptions of high loyalty and reliability.

Key learning point

Capabilities and motives at work vary somewhat with age, with the mental agility of younger people and the wisdom and experience of older people tending to cancel each other out in determining performance in most jobs.

Of course, there is also a lot of variability between workers of the same age. For example, it has been shown that older workers' attitudes to learning and change depend partly on their Future Time Perspective (FTP) (Zacher and Frese, 2009). Some older people are still orientated towards the future, and they are more open to new learning. It seems that an exclusive emphasis on holding on to past gains (Super's maintenance stage) is not healthy for older workers, and that continuing development is an important buffer against poor psychological health (Arnold and Clark, 2015). Research on lifespan development (Baltes and Baltes, 1990; Zacher and Frese, 2011) has recommended that older people should compensate for declining fluid intelligence by using so-called SOC strategies, which are *Selection* (restricting one's range of activities to a smaller number of important domains, such as focusing on just a few main job activities); *Optimisation* (increasing one's development reserves and maximising one's capabilities, for example participating in training for updating key skills); *Compensation* (using pragmatic strategies or external aids in order to compensate developmental losses, for example by telling people what tasks you feel most able to take on).

Moving between jobs

Most people's careers are partly defined by moves between jobs, or as they are called in the jargon of work psychology, 'work-role transitions'. If asked about our career history, we are likely to talk about moves we have made, when and why. On the other side of the same coin, if a person has stayed in a job for a very long time, he or she often seems to feel it is necessary to explain why. Work-role transitions can take many different forms, including getting one's first job after full-time education, getting a promotion, making a lateral move to gain experience, changing occupations, moving into or out of unemployment, and retirement. The ease or difficulty with which a transition is navigated depends on many things, including some more general features of life events such as whether the move is desirable to the person, whether it is experienced by a lot of people so that there is an opportunity to learn from them, whether it is occurring at an expected and socially approved time in one's career, and whether it happens due to a trauma such as major injury (Haynie and Shepherd, 2011).

Models of job mobility (Forrier et al., 2009; Ng et al., 2007) have attempted to explain how, when and why people move. This is affected by macro-economic, organisational/institutional and personal factors, and although we usually think of job moves as voluntary, sometimes of course they are imposed on a person, for example redundancy. From an organisational point of view, mobility can be thought of as employee turnover (Hom et al., 2012), which often means the unwanted loss of people. Some models of mobility have tended to assume that a person stays in a job unless and until they are unhappy with it, which rather ignores the possibility that some people move for future prospects, with their ability to do so depending on their 'movement capital' as Forrier et al. call it – that is, their personal attributes and experiences that make them attractive in alternative jobs. **Embeddedness** in social groups in and out of work also affects people's willingness to move (Jiang et al., 2012).

Exercise 13.4	A work-role transition

Last month, Harry Brown (a UK national) started his new job as quality manager in the UK data-processing centre of Round the World Bank. Harry had previously been long-serving manager of a branch of the bank in Singapore, where he had lived for many years. He is 48 years old, and ever since the financial crisis of 2008–9 he has felt very insecure in his employment. The bank's major reductions in workforce size, especially among the over 50s, have been all too obvious. Harry is keeping his current grade and employment conditions but his relocation package is much less generous than he has been used to. The bank gave Harry fully a year's notice of his redeployment back to the UK but only recently has he found out what his new job would be. It is a new role that nobody has done before. Although he has been involved in quality issues before, Harry is fairly inexperienced in the quality area and he does not know the details of what his new job will involve. In general terms he has always expected a job move at about this age, because the bank often moves people approaching 50 to keep them interested and make space for younger employees to move into new roles. Harry has not lived in the UK for more than 20 years, and is more comfortable in Asia than Europe these days, but he feels he must accept this move because the alternative might be redundancy and Harry does not want that. People have been rather reluctant to talk to Harry about this move, being unsure about whether to congratulate him on getting a new role, or sympathise with him for being shunted to one side.

Suggested exercise

What are the likely consequences of the features of this transition for Harry's adjustment and performance in his new job?

Just as whole careers have been divided into stages (see above), so have individual work-role transitions. Nicholson (1990) proposed the *transition cycle* shown in Figure 13.7, with four phases: preparation, encounter, adjustment and stabilisation. The phases are distinct from each other, but also inter-dependent: that is, what happens in one phase has implications for others. Nicholson also argued that sometimes the stabilisation phase is not reached before a person moves on. Although the cycle is most obviously applicable to individuals, it can also apply to organisations as they prepare for, encounter and adjust to their newcomers.

Although often overlooked, the *preparation* phase is important. This is the time when expectations about a future job are formed, and there is at least the opportunity to get ready for a new role, though not everyone takes full advantage of it. If a job move happens suddenly or unexpectedly with little notice, this may have negative implications for *encounter*. Research carried out many years ago established that both individual and organisation can develop inflated expectations of each other as they both attempt to sell themselves to the other party (Vroom and Deci, 1971). This can be countered by use of a realistic job preview (RJP), where the organisation tries to portray the job(s) to which it is recruiting in a balanced way, including the less attractive features as experienced by people who have done it before. This not only helps newcomers know what to expect, it also leads them to feel more committed to the organisation because of its honesty (Earnest et al., 2011).

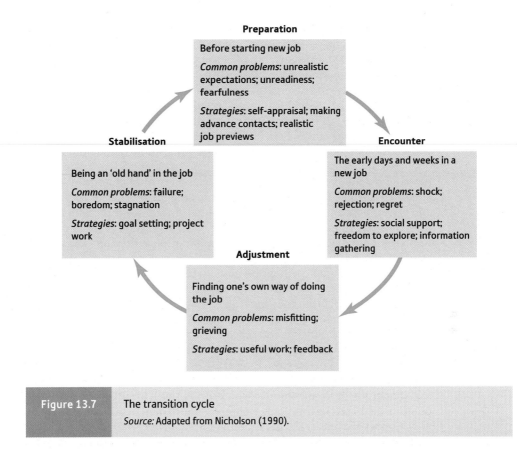

Figure 13.7	The transition cycle
	Source: Adapted from Nicholson (1990).

From an individual's point of view, a key aspect of the preparation phase is searching for a job. If that activity is not successful, then perhaps no transition will take place at all. There has been extensive research on the process of job search (see Van Hoye and Saks, 2008; Wanberg et al., 2012). It is clear that job search often requires both skill and persistence, with a determination not to be discouraged. In general a focused strategy where a person searches for jobs and/or employers from a carefully screened and limited range produces the most success in terms of getting a satisfying job. An exploratory strategy, where the searcher is more open to different possibilities, tends to produce more offers but less satisfaction with them. A haphazard strategy, where the person has no clear idea of what he or she is looking for is not surprisingly the least successful. As implied by the superiority of focused job search strategies, it is important to engage in preparatory search where information about possible jobs is gathered, before engaging in active search where employers are approached and jobs applied for. Use of informal job sources usually produces better results than formal ones, though it is not clear why. Perhaps more proactive and employable people have the courage to make direct approaches to employers and have a good range of contacts who can tip them off about opportunities (the 'knowing whom' competency described earlier), or perhaps these informal sources give a more realistic idea than formal job advertisements about what the job is like, thus encouraging a good match between person and job.

Stop and consider

What job search strategy would you say you have tended to use most? What have been the consequences? Apart from the strategy you use, how skilfully do you think you applied that strategy?

In the *encounter and adjustment* phases, it is important that newcomers seek feedback on their behaviour and performance, and observe and learn from what they see around them (Anseel et al., 2015). However, much of the attention in this phase has been on how organisations deal with newcomers, and in particular how they socialise them so that they become effective members of the organisation. Socialisation means learning to perform in ways deemed appropriate, establishing good relationships with others, understanding and being able to operate with the organisation's politics, goals, language and history (Chao et al., 1994). Van Maanen and Schein (1979) distinguished between institutionalised and individualised ways of socialising people, and their analysis has been built upon in a lot of subsequent research (e.g. Perrot et al., 2014). Where an organisation uses institutionalised tactics, newcomers experience structured training and learning opportunities together as a group and often separate from other organisational members. There is a clearly defined timetable and career plan, and the newcomers tend to learn from people who have already done the roles the newcomers will do, and who are considered good representatives by the organisation's senior managers. Individualised socialisation is the opposite: ambiguous timings of assignments, on-the-job haphazard learning from a range of people and relative isolation from other newcomers (perhaps because there aren't any).

Not surprisingly, newcomers generally prefer institutionalised socialisation because this enables them to feel that they are being valued and that the organisation knows what it is doing. They therefore feel more committed to the organisation and more inclined to stay in it (Allen and Meyer, 1990). It is also suggested that institutionalised socialisation enables people to develop strong social networks (a social capital perspective, Ellis et al., 2015) and to reduce uncertainty (a stress perspective, Fang et al., 2011). However, this may overlook the possibility that individualised socialisation might in fact be a deliberate strategy by an organisation, and that it might produce newcomers who learn to think for themselves and deal with different points of view and the inevitable ambiguity that sometimes occurs (Ashforth and Saks, 1996). Also, Cooper-Thomas et al. (2011) point out that people who have been through a few transitions before are likely to be active participants in the socialisation process rather than passive recipients of it. So, for example, they may seek opportunities to do work that is already familiar to them in order to demonstrate their competence at an early stage.

Key learning point

Both individuals and organisations can do a lot in both the preparation and encounter phases to ensure that newcomers' entry to organisations is successful.

Summary

Careers concern the sequence of jobs people hold, and the attitudes and behaviours associated with them. Labour market and organisational changes have made the careers experienced by many people less predictable than they once were. One approach to this is for individuals to take control and responsibility for their own careers, and psychologists have analysed the skills and attributes needed to do this. It is increasingly recognised that choices frequently have to be re-made later in careers, and that between choices many significant developments can occur. Much career development theory and practice therefore attempts to identify people's concerns at different ages and stages of their lives, though research on career choice still tends to treat it as a choice of a type of work made by young people on the basis of their relatively static personal characteristics. Psychologists have produced helpful theories for understanding different types of people and different types of job. They have also produced some practical ways in which individuals can improve their own choice of occupation. There is also useful guidance concerning what helps people be successful in their careers, and in recent years psychologists have produced many insights about what career success might mean apart from promotion and pay increases. In general, career theory tends to reflect men's perspectives better than women's. It is based on men's lives and men's values, paying insufficient attention to the different patterns of women's lives and the greater barriers that they face to some types of career success. Given the increasing frequency of job changes, there is also a lot of attention paid to how transitions from one job to another can be managed, especially regarding effective job search by individuals and the socialisation tactics used by organisations. Some organisations attempt to manage the career development of their employees beyond initial socialisation. A number of techniques can be used to achieve this, including mentoring, careers counselling and development centres. The value and success of interventions is hard to assess and they depend on many different organisational factors other than the quality of the intervention.

Closing case study) **Charity careers**

There was a time when charities had to rely on inspired volunteers and passionate but not necessarily well-qualified individuals for their employment base.

In recent years, this has changed and today entering the non-profit sector at graduate level is an increasingly competitive business.

For a start, the profile of the charitable sector has been rising rapidly. With figures such as Bill Gates and international celebrities such as Angelina Jolie championing causes, the sector is of intense interest to the new generation of cause-driven graduates.

'The 20-somethings and early 30-somethings are more interested in making a difference than making a fortune,' says Gib Bulloch, director of Accenture Development Partnerships, a non-profit arm of Accenture that sends select staff to work for non-profit groups in developing countries.

'They've been growing up with these issues and they want something different out of their career.'

Moreover, non-profit groups are becoming more professional and effective than their predecessors and offering better salaries. 'Charities are recognising the value of people with different skill sets,' says Salvatore

LaSpada, chief executive of the UK-based Institute for Philanthropy. 'They realise they need to pay for that, so salaries are going up.'

They are also looking for a new level of skills and experience in the people they consider as employees. 'The big change is that whereas before it was dominated by passion-driven but not necessarily well-managed organisations, now they're more strategic, more skilfully using public communications and placing more emphasis on benchmarking and evaluation,' says Mr LaSpada.

For graduates, this means securing the kinds of charity jobs to which they aspire is becoming even harder. Zoe Perrott, team manager at Eden Brown, the recruitment consultancy, has been working with the charity sector for seven years. She says jobs in non-profit organisations have always been highly sought-after by graduates.

The majority of responses to Eden Brown's advertisements for non-profit jobs are from graduates, according to Ms Perrott. 'About 50 per cent have masters degrees and a lot of them are from Cambridge and Oxford,' she says. 'I've always found the sector incredibly popular with graduates. We get always about 300 CVs for every advert.'

▶

▶

As a result, graduates hoping to pursue a career in the non-profit sector may have to start by taking low-ranking positions and be prepared to progress slowly through the sector. 'So we might not necessarily get them their dream job but we'll give them an opportunity to go into a charity network and they then work their way up through an organisation,' says Ms Perrott.

This, however, requires some tough conversations with students. 'When they're idealistic, it's very difficult,' she says. 'They come in with all these wonderful ideas but they have to start at the bottom and be prepared to do anything and everything.'

Adding to the competition is the fact that, as more business people make the switch from the corporate world to the non-profit sector, charities have an expanding pool of talented and experienced recruits from which to hire their more senior staff.

Even so, the non-profit sector is approaching a leadership deficit, with baby boomers starting to retire. Mr LaSpada argues that, as a result, non-profit organisations will need to get better at helping young employees rise up through the organisation.

Some of the larger non-profit organisations are starting to do so. The United Nations World Food Programme, for example, has a career management framework, supported by a new IT system, that brings together its recruitment and staff development initiatives designed not only to hire people but also to establish what they are interested in and find them assignments that will prepare them for future positions in the organisation.

Addaction, the leading UK drug and alcohol treatment charity, offers learning and development opportunities as well as a chance to gain professional accreditations through organisations such as the Open College Network and the Open University, with which the charity offers a Leading for Results training course for managers.

The UK's Charities Aid Foundation, which promotes the effectiveness of charities and social enterprises, has in-house training facilities. 'A great way to retain talented staff is not only to move them up the ladder within the organisation,' says Mr LaSpada, 'but also to provide them with lifelong learning opportunities.'

 Source: 'Charities: Passion and skills in aid of a good cause', *Financial Times*, 13 October 2008 2 (Murray, S.) © Sarah Murray. With permission

Suggested exercises

1 According to this article, what career anchors might be well-suited to work in charities? Are these changing and if so, how?
2 What role do career management interventions play in charities' attempts to manage their human resources? Could this role be expanded, and if so, how?
3 In what ways does this article portray bureaucratic forms of career, and in what ways does it portray other forms?

Test your learning

Short-answer questions

1 Describe the reasons why careers are more difficult to manage than they used to be.
2 What are the distinguishing features of protean and boundaryless careers?
3 According to Schein, what is a career anchor? List at least six of the anchors Schein proposed.
4 List some of the available criteria for assessing objective and subjective career success.
5 Define mentoring and describe how it can contribute to career success.
6 What vocational personality types have been identified by John Holland, and how are they related to each other?
7 List three limitations of Holland's theory.

8   Name and define eight techniques that organisations can use to manage the careers of employees.

9   List five ways in which people can differ in the way they go about career decision-making.

10 Suggest three reasons why career stage theories have gone out of fashion.

11 Describe two key research findings that show how women are at a disadvantage relative to men in their careers.

Suggested assignments

1   Critically examine the extent to which careers are less predictable and faster moving than they were a generation ago.

2   Critically analyse the extent to which the concepts of the boundaryless career and the protean career are advancing our understanding of careers.

3   What does research evidence tell us about the most effective things that people can do to increase their career success?

4   Examine the extent to which John Holland's theory has improved our understanding of careers.

5   To what extent do older workers and younger workers have different work values and capabilities? Why might differences exist?

6   Critically examine what individuals and organisations can do before and during transitions to ensure that the early months in a new job go well.

Relevant websites

A good example of a site geared to helping people manage their own careers (especially internationally mobile ones) is http://www.expatica.com. It gives information about the current job market in various countries, and also advice about how to present oneself effectively across cultures, and survive and prosper when starting a new job in an unfamiliar culture.

A website to make you think about careers in diverse ways is Career-learning at http://www.hihohiho.com/. Run by UK careers expert Bill Law, it has articles and debates about the nature of careers and how they can be managed by individuals, employers and governments.

John Holland's Self-Directed Search career choice questionnaire has its own website at http://www.self-directed-search.com/. You can take a version of the SDS and see what your scores suggest about appropriate occupations for you. Beware: it does cost, though not very much. You get an on-screen report which will probably suggest more possible occupations than you expected.

CareerLab, http://www.careerlab.com/free.htm, is a US-based site that offers a huge range of advice, information and job opportunities. This includes some free articles by 'The Career Advisor'.

Another good example of a self-help all-purpose careers site is http://content.monster.co.uk/ (see the Career Advice section, but there is a variety of relevant information on the www.monster.co.uk website). You can find advice about many aspects of managing your career, as well as information about various occupations. It's primarily geared to the USA, but travels relatively well.

To understand more about how age works against women's career prospects more than men's see http://www.theguardian.com/media/2013/may/15/female-tv-presenters-ageism-sexism

Suggested further reading

Full details for all references are given in the list at the end of this book.

1 *The Handbook of Career Studies* (Sage, 2007), edited by Hugh Gunz and Maury Peiperl, is an excellent collection of chapters which together provide a wide-ranging set of perspectives on theoretical and practical aspects of careers.

2 Inkson et al.'s *Understanding Careers*, second edition (Sage, 2014), provides a somewhat more in-depth analysis of most of the issues mentioned in this chapter, and also has a section on practical career management for individuals, counsellors and human resource managers.

3 Jon Briscoe and colleagues have edited a book called *Careers Around the World*, (Routledge, 2012a) which describes some findings of a major international study of how people in different parts of the world experience careers.

4 *Managing Careers* by Yehuda Baruch (Pearson Education, 2003), although quite old now, provides a thorough analysis of organisational aspects of careers, especially global organisations.

CHAPTER 14

Understanding organisational change and culture

LEARNING OBJECTIVES

After studying this chapter, you should be able to:

1 place the different approaches to change within a wider framework;

2 identify the two main approaches to organisational change;

3 describe and compare the strengths and weaknesses of the main approaches to change;

4 understand the role of culture both as an objective of, and a constraint on, change programmes;

5 identify the respective roles of managers, employees and change agents;

6 understand the difference between open-ended change and closed change;

7 appreciate how the main approaches view employee involvement and resistance;

8 explain how the different approaches view 'political' behaviour;

9 list the main reasons why change projects fail.

Opening case study   Serco set to clear out senior UK team

Serco, which runs air-traffic control towers, prisons and hospitals worldwide, is expected to clear out its senior UK management as part of a sweeping overhaul aimed at rebuilding its troubled relationship with the British government after a clutch of high-profile contract failures. Outside experts warn, however, that the outsourcer will struggle to turn its culture around in the three months given by the UK government to transform "corporate practices" or face exclusion from bidding for public sector contracts. "You can't change a culture in three months," says Andre Spicer, professor of organisational behaviour at Cass Business School.

Serco is facing an investigation into all its British government contracts after claims that it overcharged on electronic tagging for offenders. It has also been referred to the City of London police after being accused of altering records on the transport of prisoners. Serco employs 122,000 staff in 30 countries but about a quarter of its £4.9bn annual revenues come from work with the UK government, so the group has a powerful incentive to act quickly.

Its planned management changes are expected to include the departure of Jeremy Stafford, chief executive of the UK and Europe division for the past three years. The group has also brought in a variety of advisers: Ernst & Young is examining management processes and identifying why front-line staff decided to make a false record of information on key contracts. Ethical Learning Group, a US company, is delivering a new code of conduct and ethics, which has already been taught to 1,300 staff and will be transferred to its 122,000 employees worldwide over the next few years. A "crisis management" task force, led by the chairman Alastair Lyons, has been established with about 60 staff, with some helping PwC carry out the electronic tagging audit, trawling through emails and helping to find any evidence of overbilling on other government contracts. Serco has also appointed Lord Gold, a senior City lawyer, to conduct a review of its business practices.

This burst of activity has already taken up half the period set by the government deadline. While an underlying shift in business behaviour is unlikely to be completed in the six weeks remaining, experts say, there is still time for Serco to show that it is changing its ways. "Ultimately they could go for a few small wins rather than something grandiose and fuzzy – maybe two or three changes that could make their processes better in some ways," Prof Spicer says. Julian Birkinshaw, professor of strategy and entrepreneurship at London Business School, agrees there are improvements Serco should be able to make. "You are trying to change the behaviour of tens of thousands of people but you're not trying to change everything, just certain specific behaviours," he said. "Almost certainly Serco will tighten formal procedures and review the processes around which additional charges get pushed to clients."

Yet this sort of procedural change as managers exert more control can hinder a longer-term cultural shift. Prof Birkinshaw says: "This [type of change] has a couple of debilitating consequences. It is disempowering and alienating to the rank and file, because the company is saying 'We can't trust you' as even relatively minor matters go back to the controllers."

 Source: Adapted from 'Serco set to clear out senior UK team', *Financial Times*, 18 October 2013, p. 25 (Plimmer, G. and Smith, A.)

Introduction

The above case study illustrates three key aspects of organisational change. First, no matter how successful an organisation has been, there comes a point where there is a need for change, often of a dramatic nature. Second, where the existing leaders have been in post for many years, a change of leadership is often accompanied by attempts to change the organisation's culture. In the case of Serco, this is being driven by concerns raised by its biggest customer – the British government. Lastly, just because there is a need to change culture, this does not mean that it will be welcomed by all or lead to success, especially given Andre Spicer's concerns about the very short timescale. Indeed, as many writers have noted, change projects fail far more often than they succeed (Burnes, 2011).

Change confronts managers with a major dilemma. On the one hand, the majority of change efforts appear to fail; on the other, if organisations do not change, they will eventually go out of business. As Turner and Crawford (1999) noted, managers have two prime tasks, managing their organisations so that they meet the needs of their stakeholders today, and reshaping their organisations in order to meet the needs of their stakeholders in the future. This is a delicate balancing act: if the wrong changes are made or if they are made at the wrong time or in an inappropriate manner, organisations may lose the ability to meet their obligations today and not develop the capabilities to meet them in future either. Therefore, the ability to identify the right changes and implement them successfully is a prime task facing managers. This applies to all forms of change. Whether change is small-scale or large-scale, strategic or operational, culture-centred or technology-focused, it needs to be planned and implemented effectively. This chapter provides a critical review of the main approaches to planning and implementing change that have been developed since the 1950s. It begins by examining the importance and complexity of organisational change and illustrates this with an examination of organisational culture. From this, it is argued that an understanding of the theory and practice of change management is crucial to organisational effectiveness and success. The chapter then goes on to review the two main approaches to organisational change: the planned approach and the emergent approach. It is shown that the planned approach, which was developed by Kurt Lewin in the 1940s and forms the core of organisational development (OD), views organisational change as essentially a process of moving from one stable behavioural state to another (through a series of iterative steps or phases). However, it will be seen that the emergent approach, which came to the fore in the 1980s, starts from the assumption that change is a continuous, open-ended and unpredictable process of aligning and realigning an organisation to its changing environment. Advocates of the emergent approach argue that it is more suitable to the turbulent environment in which firms now operate and that, unlike the planned approach, it recognises the need for organisations to align their internal practices and behaviour with changing external conditions. However, it will also be shown that the emergent approach, while strong on theory, does not provide organisations with a practical alternative to OD. This is one of the reasons why there has been a resurgence of interest in OD over the last decade.

The review of these two approaches will reveal that, despite the large body of literature devoted to the topic of change management, and the many tools and techniques available to change agents, there is considerable disagreement regarding the most appropriate approach. In an effort to bring clarity to the issue, the chapter concludes by presenting a *framework for change* which shows that neither the emergent nor planned approach is suitable for all situations and circumstances. Instead, it is maintained that approaches to change tend to be situation-specific and that the potential exists for organisations to influence the constraints under which they operate in order to exercise choice over what to change and how to change.

The importance of change management

Change management would not be considered particularly important if products and markets were stable and organisational change was rare. However, that is not the case, nor has it ever been so. Change is an ever-present feature of organisational life, though many leading management thinkers such as Tom Peters (1997, 2006) and Rosabeth Moss Kanter (1997, 2008) do argue that the pace, magnitude and necessity of change have increased significantly over time.

Certainly, over the last 30 years, there has been much evidence that the prevalence of change is increasing (Burnes, 2014; Carnall, 2003; Coulson-Thomas and Coe, 1991; Cummings and Worley, 2001; Ezzamel et al., 1994; Jones et al., 2006; Kotter, 2008; McKinsey & Company, 2008; Senturia et al., 2008; Wheatley, 1992; Worrall and Cooper, 1997, 1998). Despite the increasing prevalence of change, it is debatable whether such a level of change actually brings benefits to organisations or to those who work in them. Indeed, there is considerable evidence to show that approximately 70 per cent of change efforts fail to achieve their objectives (Beer and Nohria, 2000; Burnes, 2011; Jones et al., 2006). Though this may seem a staggering rate of failure, studies of business process re-engineering (BPR) have shown failure rates of 70 per cent (Coombs and Hull, 1994; Hammer and Champy, 1993; Huczynski and Buchanan, 2001; Short and Venkatraman, 1992) and studies of total quality management (TQM) have revealed failure rates as high as 90 per cent (Kearney, 1992; Cruise O'Brien and Voss, 1992; Economist Intelligence Unit, 1992; Crosby, 1979; Whyte and Witcher, 1992; Witcher, 1993; Zairi et al., 1994). Therefore, even well-established change initiatives, for which a great deal of information, advice and assistance are available to organisations, are no guarantee of success. This is perhaps why managers list their ability (or inability) to manage change as the number one obstacle to the increased competitiveness of their organisations (Rigby and Bilodeau, 2011).

Key learning point

Effective organisational change is crucial to an organisation's competitiveness but, despite the plethora of advice available, the majority of change programmes appear to fail.

There are many reasons why change management programmes fail (Burnes and Jackson, 2011; Hoag et al., 2002; Huczynski and Buchanan, 2001; Kotter, 1996). Though some of these are specific to the particular organisations concerned, many relate to the inadequacy or inappropriateness of the various recipes for change that are available to organisations (Burnes, 2014). In addition, it needs to be recognised that change, even in quite small organisations, is a complex process whose consequences can be difficult to predict. Perhaps the prime example of this is culture change. Since the early 1980s, most organisations have come to believe that culture has a key role to play in achieving competitiveness (Chatman and Cha, 2003; Industrial Society, 1997; Jones et al., 2006). Not surprisingly, therefore, a global survey by Bain & Company (Rigby and Bilodeau, 2011) found that 89 per cent of senior managers saw culture as important as a strategy for business success. To understand and illustrate why change is so complex, the following section will examine organisational culture.

Changing organisational culture

There is widespread agreement that managers and employees do not perform their duties in a value-free vacuum (Brown, 1998). Their work and the way it is done are governed, directed and tempered by an organisation's culture – the particular set of values, beliefs, customs and systems unique to that organisation. From this perspective, culture is seen as the 'glue' which holds organisations together (Van den Berg and Wilderom, 2004). Though this view has been around for many years (see Blake and Mouton, 1969; Turner, 1971; Eldridge and Crombie, 1974), it was only in the 1980s and 1990s that academics and practitioners became obsessed with culture (Fleming, 2013). It was through the work of writers such as Peters and Waterman (1982) and Deal and Kennedy (1982) that culture (rather than factors such as structure, strategy or politics) came to be regarded as central to organisational success. Indeed, Hansen and Wernerfelt (1989) reported that organisational factors (i.e. culture) were twice as important in explaining the variance in profit as economic factors. So influential has this view become that, as Wilson (1992) observed, culture has come to be seen as the great 'cure-all' for the majority of organisational ills.

As Brown (1998) noted, there are many different definitions of organisational culture. Perhaps the most widely accepted definition is that offered by Eldridge and Crombie (1974: 78), who stated that culture refers 'to the unique configuration of norms, values, beliefs, ways of behaving and so on, that characterise the manner in which groups and individuals combine to get things done'. Culture defines how those in the organisation should behave in a given set of circumstances. It affects all, from the most senior manager to the humblest porter. Their actions are judged by themselves and others in relation to expected modes of behaviour. Culture legitimises certain forms of action and proscribes other forms.

There have been a number of attempts to identify and categorise the constituent elements of culture (e.g. Schein, 1985; Hofstede, 1990). Based on an analysis of the different definitions of culture, Cummings and Huse (1989: 421) produced a composite model of culture (see Figure 14.1), comprising four major elements existing at different levels of awareness:

1   *Basic assumptions.* At the deepest level of cultural awareness are unconscious, taken-for-granted assumptions about how organisational problems should be solved. They represent non-confrontable and non-debatable assumptions relating to the environment, as well as about the nature of human nature, human activity and human relationships.

2   *Values.* The next higher level of awareness includes values about what ought to be in organisations. Values tell members what is important in the organisation and what they need to pay attention to.

3   *Norms.* Just below the surface of cultural awareness are norms guiding how members should behave in particular situations. These represent unwritten rules of behaviour.

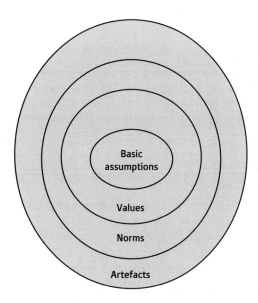

| Figure 14.1 | The major elements of culture |

4   *Artefacts*. At the highest level of cultural awareness are the artefacts and creations that are visible manifestations of the other levels of cultural elements. These include observable behaviours of members, as well as the structures, systems, procedures, rules and physical aspects of the organisation.

However, while the various hierarchical models of culture elements are useful, we should always remember that, as Brown (1995: 8–9) notes, 'actual organisational cultures are not as neat and tidy as the models seem to imply'.

As well as the numerous attempts to define organisational culture, there have also been a number of attempts to categorise the various types of culture (e.g. Deal and Kennedy, 1982; Quinn and McGrath, 1985). Perhaps the best-known typology of culture, and the one that has been around the longest, is that developed by Handy (1979) from Harrison's (1972) work on 'organisation ideologies'. Handy (1986: 188) observed that '[t]here seem to be four main types of culture':

1   *Power culture*. This is frequently found in small entrepreneurial organisations such as some property, trading and finance companies. Such a culture is associated with a web-like structure with one or more powerful figures at the centre: it is these figures that wield control.

2   *Role culture*. This is appropriate to bureaucracies, and organisations with mechanistic, rigid structures and narrow jobs. Such cultures stress the importance of procedures and rules, hierarchical position and authority, security and predictability. In essence, role cultures create situations in which those in the organisation stick rigidly to their job description (role), and any unforeseen events are referred to the next layer up in the hierarchy.

3   *Task culture*. This is job- or project-orientated culture where the onus is on getting the job in hand (the task) done rather than there being a prescribed way of doing things. Such types of culture are appropriate to organically structured organisations where flexibility and teamworking are encouraged. Task cultures create situations in which speed of reaction, integration and creativity are more important than adherence to particular rules or procedures, and where position and authority are less important than the individual contribution to the task in hand.

4   *Person culture*. This is a rare form of culture where the individual and his or her wishes are the central focus. It is associated with a minimalistic structure, the purpose of which is to assist those individuals who choose to work together. Therefore, a person culture can be characterised as a cluster or galaxy of individual 'stars'.

One of the most widely used tools for assessing culture is the Organisational Culture Inventory (OCI) (Jones et al., 2006: 18). Instead of seeking to predefine the main forms of culture, the developers of the OCI used statistical analysis of large sets of OCI data to identify three clusters of similar cultures. These were:

1   *Constructive cultures*. Cultures in which members are encouraged to interact with others and approach tasks in ways that will help them to meet their higher-order satisfaction needs (includes achievement, self-actualisation, humanistic-encouraging and affiliative cultures).

2   *Passive/defensive cultures*. Cultures in which members believe that they must interact with people in defensive ways that will not threaten their own security (includes approval, conventional, dependent and avoidance cultures).

3   *Aggressive/defensive cultures*. Cultures in which members are expected to approach tasks in forceful ways to protect their status and security (includes oppositional, power, competitive and perfectionist cultures).

The various attempts to provide a universal categorisation of culture types do have their critics, especially among those who point to the influence of the host society on organisational cultures (Hofstede, 1980, 1990). Perhaps the most extensive and in-depth attempt to unravel the vagaries of national culture has been the GLOBE (Global Leadership and Organisational Behaviour Effectiveness) study. The study comprises some 17,000 leaders in over 950 organisations in 62 countries and involves over 200 academic coordinators (Chhokar et al., 2007; Javidan and Dastmalchian, 2009). From this research, Gupta et al. (2002: 14–15) concludes that it is necessary to recognise that national cultures do play a significant role in shaping organisational behaviour. However, while the culture of each organisation within a particular country will be influenced by its societal culture, it will also be influenced by a range of other factors, such as its history, past leadership, industry and technology (Allaire and Firsirotu, 1984; Brown, 1998). Therefore, important as it is to classify national cultures, it is just as important, if not more so, to classify types of organisational culture. In this respect, Handy's categorisation of types of culture is very useful, in that it takes us beyond vague generalisations and gives us a picture of differing cultures.

Key debate

Can culture be changed?

As Burnes (2014) notes, the debate over how to define and describe culture only has significant implications for how organisations operate and are managed if culture can be influenced or changed by managers. However, as Martin (1992, 2002) maintains, the literature on culture and the extent to which it can be changed is extensive and confusing with little apparent agreement.

There are those, such as Barratt (1990: 23) who claim that 'values, beliefs and attitudes are learnt, can be managed and changed and are potentially manipulable by management'. Others support this view, arguing that it is possible to change or manage a culture by choosing the attitudes and behaviours that are required, identifying the norms or expectations that either promote or impede them, and then taking action to create the desired effect (Brown, 1998; Burke, 2011; O'Reilly, 1989). Therefore, there is a body of opinion that sees culture as something that can be managed and changed. There are also many, many organisations which, for a variety of reasons, have decided that their existing culture is inappropriate or even detrimental to their competitive needs and, therefore, must be changed (Jones et al., 2006; Peters and Waterman, 1982; Raz, 2009; Rigby and Bilodeau, 2011).

On the other hand, Filby and Willmott (1988) questioned the notion that management has the capacity to control culture. They point out that this ignores the way in which an individual's values and beliefs are conditioned by experience outside the workplace (e.g. through exposure to the media, through social activities, as well as through previous occupational activities). Hatch (1997: 235) is also very dubious about attempts to change organisational culture:

Do not think of trying to manage culture. Other people's meanings and interpretations are highly unmanageable. Think instead of trying to culturally manage your organisation, that is, manage your organisation with cultural awareness of the multiplicity of meanings that will be made of you and your efforts.

A further concern expressed by a number of writers relates to the ethical issues raised by attempts to change culture (Van Maanen and Kunda, 1989; Willmott, 1995). This concern is succinctly articulated by Watson (1997: 278) who concludes that:

Employers and managers engaging in these ways with issues of employees' self-identities and the values through which they judge the rights and wrongs of their daily lives must be a matter of serious concern. To attempt to mould cultures – given that culture in its broad sense provides the roots of human morality, social identity and existential security – is indeed to enter 'deep and dangerous waters'.

A third group of writers seem to take a position somewhere in between those who see culture as something that is amenable to managerial choice and those who see it as unalterable. These writers appear to agree that culture as a whole cannot be changed but argue that certain key elements, such as norms of behaviour, can

▶

▶

be influenced by management (Chatman and Cha, 2003; Schein, 1985). This viewpoint is summed up by Meek (1988: 469–70) who argues that,

> Culture as a whole cannot be manipulated, turned on or off, although it needs to be recognised that some [organisations] are in a better position than others to intentionally influence aspects of it.

Ogbonna and Harris (2002) have labelled these three groups of writers as the optimists, the pessimists and the realists. As the labels might imply, Ogbonna and Harris tend to believe that the realists have the best of the argument; culture as a whole cannot be changed but it is possible to intentionally and successfully change key elements of it.

There is plenty of evidence that many organisations underestimate the difficulties involved in attempting to change their culture and this leads to a high level of failure (Brown, 1998). As Jones et al. (2006: 45) observe, many culture change programmes fail because they 'ignored two critical factors: the need to generate valid data on which to base a diagnosis of change requirement, and a clear line of sight to performance outcomes'.

These comments echo the views of one of the leading writers on culture, Schein (1985). He cautions organisations to be wary of rushing into culture change programmes. He believes that before any attempt is made to change an organisation's culture, it is first necessary to understand the nature of its existing culture and how this is sustained. According to Schein, this can be achieved by analysing the values that govern behaviour and uncovering the underlying and often unconscious assumptions that determine how those in the organisation think, feel and react. His approach, therefore, is to treat the development of culture as an adaptive and tangible learning process. Schein emphasises the way in which an organisation communicates its culture to new recruits, how assumptions are translated into values and how values influence behaviour. Schein seeks to understand the mechanisms used to propagate culture, and how new values and behaviours are learned. Once these mechanisms are revealed, he argues, they can then form the basis of a strategy to change the organisation's culture: the argument is that change is likely to fail if it does not start with such an analysis.

In a synthesis of the literature on organisational culture, Hassard and Sharifi (1989: 11) proposed a similar approach to Schein's. In particular, they stressed the crucial role of senior managers:

> Before a major [cultural] change campaign is commenced, senior managers must understand the implications of the new system for their own behaviour: and senior management must be involved in all the main stages preceding change. In change programmes, special attention must be given to the company's 'opinion leaders'.

As we can see, most observers see organisational culture as being complex and difficult to understand. However, even among those who believe it can be changed, few appear to believe that such a change is easy or without dangers. This is perhaps why so many organisations have found successful culture change so difficult to achieve (Brown, 1998; Cummings and Worley, 2001; De Witte and van Muijen, 1999). Indeed, it is the fact that organisations are not machines but very complex social systems that makes any form of change potentially hazardous.

Key learning point

Organisational culture may be crucial to an organisation's performance but it is also difficult to understand and change.

Women stuck in executive slow lane

A man who starts his career with a FTSE 100 company is four and a half times more likely to reach the executive committee than his female counterpart, says research that questions the assumptions on which companies base gender diversity policies. Companies need to rethink their organisational culture rather than make "piecemeal fixes" if they want to achieve gender parity, according to the study for the 30% Club, backed by the chairmen of 70 of Britain's largest businesses. It argues that companies' diversity policies tend to involve helping women to adapt rather than making fundamental changes to corporate practices. It also identifies differences in the way men's and women's careers develop.

The findings come amid concern that women's progress in the workforce may be slowing or even stalling. The research for the 30% Club is being carried out by YSC, a business psychology consultancy, and KPMG, the advisory firm. Early findings were disclosed yesterday. "Men and women are different – equally intelligent but we behave differently and are motivated by different things," said Helena Morrissey, chief executive of Newton Investment Management and founder of the club, which aims to boost the proportion of women on boards to 30 per cent. KPMG found on average FTSE 100 companies had 21 per cent female representation on executive committees and that a quarter had achieved 30 per cent. YSC found that women's ambition, unlike men's, tended not to show itself until they reached executive level – and that companies should not rule them out early as candidates for top jobs. Women tended to make more sideways career moves, which could give them broader experience. It found that women with young families depended on the relationship with their line manager to find an arrangement to balance work and home life. Investment in training line managers could make as much difference as formal female development programmes, sponsoring, mentoring and executive coaching. It urged companies to use wider performance measures, reflecting the fact that women were stronger in "values-based leadership" compared with a more commercial male approach.

"It's not about what women need to do differently, it's about how organisations need to think about what needs to be done differently," said Rachel Short, a YSC director. She added: "Women are assimilating and adapting to a male culture. They are doing that by working superhard. They are seen as grafting, ethical, organised and time-efficient." Women felt under pressure to "network like mad" to get promoted, she said, when in fact many were already outperforming colleagues.

 Source: From 'Women stuck in executive slow lane', *Financial Times,* 11 December, 2013, p 22 (Groom, B)

Suggested exercises

1 Drawing on the discussion of culture in this chapter, discuss the pros and cons of the following statement: 'Companies need to rethink their organisational culture rather than make "piecemeal fixes" if they want to achieve gender parity'.
2 Using Cummings and Huse's model of culture (Figure 14.1), identify which aspects of an organisation's culture would need to change in order to promote greater workforce diversity.
3 What difficulties might an organisation encounter in changing its culture to promote workforce diversity and how might these be overcome?

Despite the adverse experience of many organisations, change, of an increasingly radical form, seems to be the order of the day, as the Serco case study at the beginning of this chapter shows. Some organisations look to management gurus such as Charles Handy (1994), Rosabeth Moss Kanter (2008), John Kotter (1996) and Tom Peters (2006) for their salvation. Others seek the assistance of management consultants such as McKinsey, Bain & Company and KPMG?. However, whether organisations seek outside advice and assistance or rely on their own competence, they cannot expect to achieve successful change unless those responsible for managing it understand the different approaches on offer and can match them to their circumstances and preferences. On this basis, understanding the theory and practice of change management is not an optional extra but an essential prerequisite for survival. However, as the following examination of the two main approaches to change management will show, this is by no means an easy or straightforward exercise.

Stop to consider

From your reading so far, what appear to be the main reasons behind the high failure rates of organisational change? Given these reasons, what are the key issues that need to be covered by theories of change in order to help organisations achieve greater success when implementing change?

The planned approach to organisational change

The founding father of **planned change** was Kurt Lewin (Burnes, 2004a, 2007). He used the term to distinguish change that was consciously embarked upon and planned by an organisation, as opposed to types of change that might come about by accident, by impulse or which might be forced on an organisation (Marrow, 1977). Therefore, 'planned', in this case, does not mean that someone sits down in advance and writes a detailed plan, rather it means that the organisation pro-actively identifies an area where it believes change is required and undertakes a process to evaluate and, if necessary, bring about change. Among those advocating planned change, a variety of different models of change management have arisen over the years. Nevertheless, the planned approach to change is most closely associated with the practice of organisational development (OD), and lies at its core. According to French and Bell (1995: 1–2):

> Organisation development is a unique organisational improvement strategy that emerged in the late 1950s and early 1960s . . . [It] has evolved into an integrated framework of theories and practices capable of solving or helping to solve most of the important problems confronting the human side of organisations. Organisation development is about people and organisations and people in organisations and how they function. OD is also about planned change, that is getting individuals, teams and organisations to function better.

Underpinning OD is a set of values, assumptions and ethics that emphasise its humanistic–democratic orientation and its commitment to organisational effectiveness. These values have been articulated by many writers over the years (Conner, 1977; Warwick and Thompson, 1980; Gellerman et al., 1990). Hurley et al. (1992) found there were five clear values that OD practitioners espoused:

1   empowering employees to act;
2   creating openness in communications;
3   facilitating ownership of the change process and its outcomes;
4   the promotion of a culture of collaboration;
5   the promotion of continuous learning.

> ### Point of integration
>
> Leaders and managers are often tasked with delivering change. Several leadership theories include factors thought to be linked to effective change management. One example is transformational leadership (see Chapter 12).

Within the OD field, there are a number of major theorists and practitioners who have contributed their own models and techniques to its advancement (e.g. Argyris, 1962; Beckhard, 1969; French and Bell, 1973; Blake and Mouton, 1976). However, despite this, there is general agreement that OD grew out of, and became the standard bearer for, Kurt Lewin's pioneering work on behavioural science in general, and his development of planned change in particular (Burnes, 2004a, 2007; Burnes and Cooke, 2012). Lewin was a prolific theorist, researcher and practitioner in interpersonal, group, intergroup and community relationships. Out of this, he developed his planned model of change. Planned change has four individual elements – field theory, group dynamics, action research and the three-step model – and though they are often treated as separate themes of his work, Lewin saw them as a unified whole with each element supporting and reinforcing the others (Burnes, 2004a). This can be seen by examining these four elements of his work in turn.

Field theory

Lewin's field theory argues that behaviour is derived from the totality of co-existing and interdependent forces which impinge on a person or group and which make up the 'life space' or 'field' in which the behaviour takes place (Burnes and Cooke, 2013a). Lewin's view was that if one could identify, plot and establish the potency of these forces, then it would be possible not only to understand why individuals, groups and organisations behave as they do, but also what forces would need to be diminished or strengthened in order to bring about change. A key belief of Lewin's was that, in general, change could only be effective if people embarked on it of their own free will and could make informed choices about whether and what to change (Burnes, 2004a, 2007). Therefore, individuals and groups had to be involved in identifying and changing their own life space or field. The theoretical foundations of this approach lie in gestalt-field theory: this stresses that change can only successfully be achieved by helping individuals and groups to reflect on and gain new insights into their situation, i.e. field (Smith et al., 1982). Though field theory is now probably the least understood element of Lewin's work, because of its potential to map the forces impinging on an individual, group or organisation, it underpinned the other elements of his work (Marrow, 1969).

Group dynamics

Lewin was the first psychologist to write about 'group dynamics' and the importance of the group in shaping the behaviour of its members (Bargal et al., 1992). Indeed, Lewin's (1939: 165) definition of a 'group' is still generally accepted: 'it is not the similarity or dissimilarity of individuals that constitutes a group, but interdependence of fate'. Group dynamics stresses that group behaviour, rather than that of individuals, should be the main focus of change (Dent and Goldberg, 1999). Lewin (1947b) maintained that it is fruitless to concentrate on changing the behaviour of individuals because the individual in isolation is constrained by group pressures to conform. Consequently, the focus of change must be at the group level and should concentrate on factors such as group norms, roles, interactions and socialisation processes to create 'disequilibrium' and change (Schein, 1988). As with field theory, Lewin stressed the need to involve staff in any changes. Indeed, Lewin often used the terms group dynamics and participative management interchangeably.

Point of integration

There is a great deal of research about the processes that influence the behaviour of team members. Not all of it is conducted during periods of change, but clearly change processes mean that team members have to make and implement lots of decisions. We also know that team processes do not always lead to good decision-making and effective performance (see Chapter 11).

Research methods in focus

Action research as a means of implementing change

This model was designed by Lewin as a collective approach to solving social and organisational problems. Although often seen as American in origin, parallel developments were taking place at the Tavistock Institute in the UK at the same time (Burnes and Cooke, 2013b), and used to improve managerial competency and efficiency in the coal industry. Since then it has acquired a strong following on both sides of the Atlantic (French and Bell, 1984).

In an organisational setting, an action research project usually comprises three distinct groups: the organisation (in the form of one or more senior managers), the subject (people from the area where the change is to take place) and the change agent (a consultant who may or may not be a member of the organisation). These three distinct entities form a *learning community* in and through which the research is carried out, and by which the organisation's problem is solved (Heller, 1970).

Action research is a two-pronged process. First, it emphasises that change requires action (i.e. something needs to happen), and is directed at achieving this. Second, it recognises that successful action is based on research – a process of *learning* – that allows those involved to analyse the situation correctly, identify all the possible alternative solutions (hypotheses) and choose the one most appropriate to the situation at hand (Bennett, 1983).

Although action research is highly regarded as an approach to managing change (Cummings and Huse, 1989), it is Lewin's three-step model of change that lies at the core of planned change.

Key learning point

Action research is concerned as much with individual and group learning as it is with achieving change.

The three-step model of change

In developing this model, Lewin (1947a: 228) noted that:

A change towards a higher level of group performance is frequently short lived; after a 'shot in the arm', group life soon returns to the previous level. This indicates that it does not suffice to define the objective of a planned change in group performance as the reaching of a different level. Permanency at the new level, or permanency for a desired period, should be included in the objective.

A successful change project, Lewin (1947b) argued, should involve three iterative steps:

1   unfreezing the present level;
2   moving to the new level;
3   refreezing the new level.

It should be recognised that these three steps do not form a linear sequence, but comprise an iterative process of revisiting and reviewing each step until common understanding and agreement have been reached.

Step 1 recognises that before new behaviour can be successfully adopted, the old has to be discarded. Only then can the new behaviour become accepted. Central to this approach is the belief that the will of the change adopter (the subject of the change) is important, both in discarding the old, 'unfreezing' and then 'moving' to the new.

Unfreezing usually involves reducing those forces maintaining the group's behaviour at its present level. According to Rubin (1967), unfreezing requires some form of confrontation meeting or re-education process for those involved. The essence of these activities is to enable those concerned to become convinced of the need for change. Unfreezing clearly equates with the research element of action research, just as step 2, moving, equates with the action element.

Moving, in practice, involves acting on the results of step 1. That is, having analysed the present situation, identified options and selected the most appropriate, action is then necessary to move to the more desirable state of affairs. This involves developing new behaviours, values and attitudes through changes in organisational structures and processes. The key task is to ensure that this is done in such a way that those involved do not, after a short period, revert to the old ways of doing things.

Refreezing is the final step in the three-step model and represents, depending on the viewpoint, either a break with action research or its logical extension. Refreezing seeks to stabilise the organisation at a new state of equilibrium in order to ensure that the new ways of working are relatively safe from regression. It is frequently achieved through the use of supporting mechanisms that positively reinforce the new ways of working; these include organisational culture, norms, policies and practices (Cummings and Huse, 1989).

The three-step model provides a general framework for understanding the process of organisational change. However, the three steps are relatively broad and, for this reason, have been further developed in an attempt to enhance the practicable value of this approach.

Phases of planned change

In attempting to elaborate upon Lewin's three-step model, writers have expanded the number of steps or phases. Lippitt et al. (1958) developed a seven-phase model of planned change, while Cummings and Huse (1989), not to be outdone, produced an eight-phase model. However, as Cummings and Huse (1989: 51) point out, 'the concept of planned change implies that an organisation exists in different states at different times and that planned movement can occur from one state to another'. Therefore, in order to understand planned change, it is not sufficient merely to understand the processes that bring about change; there must also be an appreciation of the states that an organisation must pass through in order to move from an unsatisfactory present state to a more desired future state.

Bullock and Batten (1985) developed an integrated, four-phase model of planned change based on a review and synthesis of over 30 models of planned change. Their model describes planned change in terms of two major dimensions: change phases, which are distinct states an organisation moves through as it undertakes planned change; and change processes, which are the methods used to move an organisation from one state to another.

The four change phases, and their attendant change processes, identified by Bullock and Batten are as follows:

1   *Exploration phase.* In this state members of an organisation have to explore and decide whether they want to make specific changes in its operations and, if so, commit resources to planning the changes. The change processes involved in this phase are: becoming aware of the need for change; searching for outside assistance (a consultant/ facilitator) to assist with planning and implementing the changes; and establishing a contract with the consultant which defines each party's responsibilities.

2   *Planning phase.* Once the consultant and the organisation have established a contract, then the next state, which involves understanding the organisation's problem or concern, begins. The change processes involved in this are: collecting information in order to establish a correct diagnosis of the problem; establishing change goals and designing the appropriate actions to achieve these goals; and getting key decision-makers to approve and support the proposed changes.

3   *Action phase.* In this state, an organisation implements the changes derived from the planning. The change processes involved are designed to move an organisation from its current state to a desired future state, and include: establishing appropriate arrangements to manage the change process and gaining support for the actions to be taken; and evaluating the implementation activities and feeding back the results so that any necessary adjustments or refinements can be made.

4   *Integration phase.* This state commences once the changes have been successfully implemented. It is concerned with consolidating and stabilising the changes so that they become part of an organisation's normal, everyday operation and do not require special arrangements or encouragement to maintain them. The change processes involved are: reinforcing new behaviours through feedback and reward systems and gradually decreasing reliance on the consultant; diffusing the successful aspects of the change process throughout the organisation; and training managers and employees to monitor the changes constantly and seek to improve upon them.

According to Cummings and Huse (1989), this model has broad applicability to most change situations. It clearly incorporates key aspects of many other change models and, especially, it overcomes any confusion between the processes (methods) of change and the phases of change – the sequential states that organisations must go through to achieve successful change.

Point of integration

There is considerable debate about the effectiveness of primary interventions to tackle work-related stress (see Chapter 10). Some argue that this is because it requires careful management of change processes in order to ensure that primary interventions result in good outcomes for employee well-being.

Key learning point

Both the three-step and the phases models view change as a sequential activity involving a beginning, a middle and an end.

The focus of Bullock and Batten's model, just as with Lewin's, is change at individual and group level. However, OD practitioners have recognised, as many others have, that '[o]rganisations are being reinvented; work tasks are being reengineered; the rules of the marketplace are being rewritten; the fundamental nature of organisations is changing' (French and Bell, 1995: 3–4), and, therefore, OD has to adapt to these new conditions and broaden its focus out beyond individual and group behaviour.

From organisation development to organisation transformation

OD is now a global movement with its own regulatory bodies, to which OD practitioners have to belong, its own recognised qualifications, a host of approved tools and techniques and its own ethical code of practice (Burnes, 2014). The members of this profession, whether employed in academic institutions, consultancy practices or private and public organisations, exist to provide consultancy services. As with any profession or trade, unless they provide their customers with what they want, they will soon go out of business. This became evident from the 1970s onwards with organisations becoming more focused on value for money from OD initiatives, and as response practitioners began to take over from academics in developing new approaches to change (Burnes and Cooke, 2012). Therefore, to appreciate the current role and approach of planned change, it is necessary to say something of how OD has responded to the changing needs of its customers.

The original focus of OD was on work groups within an organisational setting rather than organisations in their entirety, and it was primarily concerned with the human processes and systems within organisations. However, as French and Bell (1995) and Cummings and Worley (2001) noted, from the 1970s there has been a major shift of focus within the OD field from improving group effectiveness to transforming organisations. This move to 'transformational' OD stems from three key developments:

1   With the rise of the job design movement in the 1960s, and particularly the advent of sociotechnical systems theory, OD practitioners came to recognise that they could not solely concentrate on the work of groups and individuals in organisations, but that they needed to look at other and wider systems. Gradually, OD has adopted an open systems perspective that allows it to look at organisations in their totality and within their environments.

2   OD practitioners have broadened their perspective to include organisational culture. Given that OD had always recognised the importance of group norms and values, it is a natural progression to translate this into an interest in organisational culture in general.

3   The increasing use of organisation-wide approaches to change, such as culture change programmes, coupled with increasing turbulence in the environment in which organisations operate (e.g. their marketplace and the broader national and global economy), have drawn attention to the need for OD to become involved in transforming organisations in their totality rather than focusing on changes to their constituent parts.

While these major additions to the OD repertoire are understandable, the danger is that they appear to be moving away from the commitment to individual involvement and learning that has, traditionally, been espoused by OD practitioners. This can be seen from the following five-step approach to culture change advocated by Cummings and Huse (1989: 428–30):

1   *A clear strategic vision*. Effective cultural change should start from a clear vision of the firm's new strategy and of the shared values and behaviour needed to make it work. This vision provides the purpose and direction for cultural change.

2   *Top management commitment*. Cultural change must be managed from the top of the organisation. Senior managers and administrators need to be strongly committed to the new values and the need to create constant pressure for change.

3   *Symbolic leadership.* Senior executives must communicate the new culture through their own actions. Their behaviours need to symbolise the kind of values and behaviours being sought.

4   *Supporting organisational changes.* Cultural change must be accompanied by supporting modifications in organisational structure, human resource systems, information and control systems and management style. These organisational features can help to orientate people's behaviours to the new culture.

5   *Organisational membership.* One of the most effective methods for changing culture is to change organisational membership. People can be selected in terms of their fit with the new culture, and provided with an induction clearly indicating desired attitudes and behaviour. Existing staff who cannot adapt to the new ways may have their employment terminated.

Not only does Cummings and Huse's approach exclude all but senior staff from being involved in decisions about what to change and how to implement it, but also those who are deemed not to 'fit' the new culture can have their employment terminated. This was part of the growing tendency in the 1980s and 1990s for top managers to focus less on people-orientated values and more on 'the bottom line and/or the price of stock . . . [Consequently] some executives have a "slash and burn" mentality' (French and Bell, 1995: 351). Clearly, this tendency is not conducive to the democratic and humanistic values traditionally espoused by OD practitioners. Instead, the emphasis is on the change consultant as a provider of expertise that the organisation lacks. The consultant's task is not only to facilitate but also to provide solutions. The danger in this situation is that the learner (the change adopter) becomes a passive recipient of external and, supposedly, objective data: one who has to be directed to the 'correct' solution (Cummings and Worley, 2001). This has led a number of key writers to question whether OD has lost its way as its practices have moved away from its original values (Bradford and Burke, 2004; Greiner and Cummings, 2004; Worley and Feyerherm, 2003).

As can be seen, for better or ill, the 1980s and 1990s saw attempts by many in the OD movement to shift its emphasis from planned, participative change and towards a far more organisation- and system-wide perspective on change.

Exercise 14.2   Working with suppliers

When Nissan established its British car-assembly operation in the mid-1980s, it recognised that UK component suppliers fell far short of Japanese standards of quality, reliability and cost. As one means of helping suppliers to improve their capability, it established a Supplier Development Team (SDT). The aim of the SDT was to help suppliers to develop their business to the stage where they can meet Nissan's performance requirements.

Though the assistance given by the SDT to suppliers is in effect free consultancy, this is not philanthropy on Nissan's part. Nissan believes that unless its suppliers achieve world-class performance standards, it cannot produce world-beating cars. Therefore, in helping its suppliers, Nissan is helping itself.

The SDT approach is to work cooperatively with suppliers to help them identify areas for improvement, and then to assist them to develop and monitor improvement plans. The basic elements of the SDT's approach are as follows:

- Suppliers are at liberty to choose whether or not to invite the SDT into their plant.
- The SDT begins by explaining to senior managers within suppliers that its objective is to help them to develop a continuous improvement philosophy.
- The SDT seeks to train and guide a supplier's personnel to undertake change projects for themselves, rather than doing the work for them.
- The SDT insists that staff in the area where change is to take place are involved.

- The SDT seeks to promote trust, cooperation and teamworking within suppliers.
- The SDT's own members are extremely well trained and proficient and, consequently, are able to win the confidence of the people with whom they work.
- The SDT seeks to ensure that those who carry out the improvement get the credit and praise for it, rather than seeking to take the credit itself.

It would be misleading to give the impression that Nissan was in any way 'soft' on suppliers. As Sir Ian Gibson, Nissan's then Managing Director, stated: 'Co-operative supply relationships are not an easy option, as many imagine, but considerably harder to implement than traditional buyer–seller relationships'.

Source: Adapted from Lloyd et al. (1994).

Suggested exercises

1   To what extent does Nissan's approach to supplier development fit in with the planned approach to change?

2   How does the philosophy promoted by Nissan's SDT compare to Lewin's own underlying philosophy of change?

3   Is the SDT approach compatible with 'transformational' OD?

4   What effect might a supplier's organisational culture have on the longer-term success of the SDT approach?

Planned change: summary and criticisms

Planned change is an iterative, cyclical process involving diagnosis, action and evaluation, and further action and evaluation. It is an approach that recognises that once change has taken place, it must be self-sustaining (i.e. safe from regression). The purpose of planned change is to improve the effectiveness of the human side of the organisation. Central to planned change is the emphasis placed on the collaborative nature of the change effort: the organisation, both managers and recipients of change, and the consultant jointly diagnose the organisation's problem and jointly plan and design the specific changes. Underpinning planned change, and indeed the origins of the OD movement as a whole, is a strong humanist and democratic orientation and an emphasis on organisational effectiveness (Burnes, 2004a, 2007). This fits in well with its gestalt-field orientation, seeing change as a process of learning which allows those involved to gain or change insights, outlooks, expectations and thought patterns. This approach seeks to provide change adopters with an opportunity to 'reason out' their situation and develop their own solutions (Bigge, 1982).

However, the advent of more organisation-wide approaches, which seem to have shifted the focus of OD away from its original focus on the human side of the organisation, coupled with a more hostile business environment, appear to be eroding the values that Lewin and the early pioneers of OD saw as being central to successful change (Bradford and Burke, 2004; Greiner and Cummings, 2004; Worley and Feyerherm, 2003).

As might be expected, these developments in OD, as well as newer perspectives on organisations, have led many to question not only particular aspects of the planned approach to change but also the utility and practicality of the approach as a whole. The main criticisms levelled against the planned approach to change are as follows.

First, as Wooten and White (1999: 8) observe, 'Much of the existing OD technology was developed specifically for, and in response to, top-down, autocratic, rigid, rule-based organisations operating in a somewhat predictable and controlled environment.' This may account for the assumption by many proponents of OD that, as Cummings and Huse (1989: 51) pointed out, 'an organisation exists in different states at different times and that planned movement can occur from one state to another'. However, from the 1980s onwards in particular, an increasing number of writers argued that, in the turbulent and chaotic world in which we live, such assumptions are increasingly tenuous and that organisational change is more a continuous and open-ended process than a set of discrete and self-contained events (Nonaka, 1988; Peters, 1989; Garvin, 1993; Stacey, 2003).

Second, and on a similar note, a number of writers have criticised the planned approach for its emphasis on incremental and isolated change and its inability to incorporate radical, transformational change (Miller and Friesen, 1984; Hatch, 1997; Schein, 1985; Dunphy and Stace, 1993).

Third, the planned approach is based on the assumption that common agreement can be reached, and that all the parties involved in a particular change project have a willingness and interest in doing so. This assumption appears to ignore organisational conflict and politics, or at least assumes that problem issues can be easily identified and resolved which, as Pfeffer (1992), among many others, has shown, is not always the case.

Fourth, it assumes that one type of approach to change is suitable for all organisations, all situations and all times. Stace and Dunphy (2001) show that there is a wide spectrum of change situations, ranging from fine-tuning to corporate transformation, and an equally wide range of ways of managing these, ranging from collaborative to coercive. Though planned change may be suitable to some of these situations, it is clearly much less applicable to situations where more directive approaches may be required, such as when a crisis, requiring rapid and major change, does not allow scope for widespread involvement or consultation. This has led Dunphy and Stace (1993: 905) to argue that:

> Turbulent times demand different responses in varied circumstances. So managers and consultants need a model of change that is essentially a 'situational' or 'contingency model', one that indicates how to vary change strategies to achieve 'optimum fit' with the changing environment.

Leading OD advocates, as might be expected, dispute these criticisms and point to the way that planned change has tried to incorporate issues such as power and politics and the need for organisational transformation (Burnes and Cooke, 2012; French and Bell, 1995; Cummings and Worley, 1997). Also, as Burnes (2004a) argues, there is a need to draw a distinction between Lewin's original analytical approach to planned change and the more recent prescriptive and practitioner-orientated approaches of OD practitioners. Nevertheless, even taking these points into account, it has to be recognised that planned change was never intended to be applicable to all change situations and it was certainly never meant to be used in situations where rapid, coercive and/or wholesale change was required.

Key learning point

The main criticism of the planned approach is that it is not suitable for open-ended and unpredictable situations.

Stop to consider

You will have read a number of criticisms of the planned change approach. However, what might be the merits of the planned change approach? Can it be used in some ways, in some circumstances, to help organisations implement change better? If so, under what circumstances might it be most useful?

The emergent approach to organisational change

The planned approach to change is relatively well developed and understood, and is supported by a coherent body of literature, methods and techniques. The emergent approach, on the other hand, though it has now been around in various forms since the 1980s, lacks an agreed set of methods and techniques. The proponents of the emergent approach to change view it from differing perspectives and tend to focus on their own particular concerns. Therefore, they are a much less coherent group than the advocates of planned change. Rather than being united by a shared belief, they tend to be distinguished by a common disbelief in the efficacy of planned change.

Buchanan and Storey (1997: 127) maintain that the main criticism of planned change is its 'attempt to impose an order and a linear sequence to processes that are in reality messy and untidy, and which unfold in an iterative fashion with much backtracking and omission'. For proponents of the emergent approach, change is a continuous, dynamic and contested process that emerges in an unpredictable and unplanned fashion. As Weick (2000: 237) states:

> Emergent change consists of ongoing accommodations, adaptations, and alternations that produce fundamental change without a priori intentions to do so. Emergent change occurs when people reaccomplish routines and when they deal with contingencies, breakdowns, and opportunities in everyday work. Much of this change goes unnoticed, because small alternations are lumped together as noise in otherwise uneventful inertia.

The rationale for the emergent approach stems, according to Hayes (2002: 37), from the belief that:

> the key decisions about matching the organisation's resources with opportunities, constraints and demands in the environment evolve over time and are the outcome of cultural and political processes in organisations.

Pettigrew (1990a, 1990b) has argued that the planned approach is too prescriptive and does not pay enough attention to the need to analyse and conceptualise organisational change. He maintains that it is essential to understand the context in which change takes place. In particular he emphasises:

■ the interconnectedness of change over time (i.e. change events have causes and consequences that are linked to each other in a complex way);

■ how the context of change shapes, and is shaped by, action;

■ the multicausal and non-linear nature of change (i.e. many things impact on change, and the change process is a complex one, rather than one that takes place in a simple predictable sequence).

Pettigrew (1987) argues that change needs to be studied across different levels of analysis and different time periods. This is because organisational change cuts across functions, spans hierarchical divisions and has no neat starting or finishing point; instead it is a 'complex analytical, political, and cultural process of challenging and changing the core beliefs, structure and strategy of the firm' (Pettigrew, 1987: 650).

Advocates of the emergent approach, therefore, stress the developing and unpredictable nature of change. They view change as a process that unfolds through the interplay of multiple variables (context, political processes and consultation) within an organisation. In contrast to what he sees as the preordained certainty of planned change, Dawson (1994) adopted a processual approach to change. The processual approach views organisations and their members as shifting coalitions of individuals and groups with different interests, imperfect knowledge and short attention spans. Change, under these conditions, is portrayed as a pragmatic process of trial and error, aimed at achieving a compromise between the competitive needs of the organisation and the objectives of the various warring factions within the organisation.

Advocates of **emergent change** who adopt the processual approach tend to stress that there can be no simple prescription for managing organisational transitions successfully, owing to temporal and contextual factors (Pettigrew, 1997). Dawson (2003) sees change as:

> a complex ongoing dynamic in which the politics, substance and context of change all interlock and overlap, and in which our understanding of the present and expectations of the future can influence our interpretation of past events, which may in turn shape our experience of change.

Key learning point

The emergent approach challenges the view that organisations are rational entities and seeks to replace it with a view of organisations as comprising moving coalitions of different interest groups.

The rationale for the emergent approach stems from the belief that change should not and cannot be solidified, or seen as a series of linear events within a given period of time; instead, it is viewed as a continuous process. Dawson (1994) sees change as a period of organisational transition characterised by disruption, confusion and unforeseen events that emerge over long timeframes. Even when changes are operational, they will need to be constantly refined and developed in order to maintain their relevance.

From this perspective, Clarke (1994) suggested that mastering the challenge of change is not a specialist activity facilitated or driven by an expert, but an increasingly important part of every manager's role. To be effective in creating sustainable change, according to McCalman and Paton (1992), managers will need an extensive and systemic understanding of their organisation's environment, in order to identify the pressures for change and to ensure that, by mobilising the necessary internal resources, their organisation responds in a timely and appropriate manner. Dawson (1994) claimed that change must be linked with the complexity of changing market realities, the transitional nature of work organisation, systems of management control and redefined organisational boundaries and relationships. He emphasises that, in today's business environment, one-dimensional change interventions are likely to generate only short-term results and heighten instability rather than reduce it.

As can be seen, though they do not openly state it, advocates of emergent change tend to adopt a contingency perspective. For them, it is the uncertainty of the environment that makes planned change inappropriate and emergent change appropriate. Stickland (1998: 76) extends this point by raising a question that many of those studying organisational change appear not to acknowledge: 'To what extent does the environment drive changes within a system [i.e. organisation] and to what extent is the system in control of its own change processes?' Finstad (1998: 721) puts this issue in a wider context by arguing that 'the organisation is . . . the creator of its environment and the environment is the creator of the organisation'.

This reciprocal relationship between an organisation and its environment clearly has profound implications for how managers in organisations conceptualise and manage change. It also serves to emphasise that a key competence for organisations is the ability to scan the external environment in order to identify and assess the impact of trends and discontinuities (McCalman and Paton, 1992; Stickland, 1998). This includes exploring the full range of external variables, including markets and customers, shareholders, legal requirements, the economy, suppliers, technology and social trends. This activity is made more difficult by the changing and arbitrary nature of organisation boundaries: customers can also be competitors; suppliers may become partners; and employees can be transformed into customers, suppliers or competitors.

Changes in the external environment require appropriate responses within organisations. Appropriate responses, according to the supporters of the emergent approach, should promote extensive and deep understanding of strategy, structure, systems, people, style and culture. The organisation also needs an understanding of how these factors can function either as sources of inertia that can block change, or alternatively, as levers to encourage an effective change process (Pettigrew, 1997; Dawson, 2003). A major development in this respect is the move to adopt a 'bottom-up' rather than 'top-down' approach to initiating and implementing change. This is based on the view that the pace of environmental change is so rapid and complex that it is impossible for a small number of senior managers effectively to identify, plan and implement the necessary organisational responses. The responsibility for organisational change is therefore, out of necessity, becoming more devolved.

Point of integration

Participation and involvement in decision-making feature heavily in theories of work-related stress and the associated stress-management interventions. These have emerged from a large amount of research showing that perceived control and autonomy at work can have a positive impact on employee well-being. Emergent change emphasises devolving some control over change to employees.

Key learning point

'While the primary stimulus for change remains those forces in the external environment, the primary motivator for how change is accomplished resides with the people within the organisation' (Benjamin and Mabey, 1993: 181).

Supporters of the emergent approach identify five features of organisations that either promote or obstruct success: cultures, structures, organisational learning, managerial behaviour, and power and politics.

Organisational culture

Earlier in this chapter, it was argued that organisational culture is a complex and contentious subject which can be seen both as a constraint on, and as an object of, change. In looking at culture from the emergent perspective, Johnson (1993: 64) has taken the view that the strategic management of change is 'essentially a cultural and cognitive phenomenon' rather than an analytical, rational exercise. Clarke (1994) stated that the essence of sustainable change is to understand the culture of the organisation that is to be changed. If proposed changes contradict cultural biases and traditions, it is inevitable that they will be difficult to embed in the organisation.

In a similar vein, Dawson (1994) suggested that attempts to realign internal behaviours with external conditions require change strategies that are sensitive to the culture of the organisation. Organisations, he points out, must be aware that the change process is lengthy, potentially dangerous and demands considerable reinforcement if culture change is to be sustained against the inevitable tendency to regress to old behaviours. Clarke (1994) also stressed that change can be slow, especially where mechanisms that reinforce old or inappropriate behaviour (such as reward, recruitment and promotion structures) continue unchallenged. In addition, if these reinforcement mechanisms are complemented by managerial behaviour that promotes risk aversion and fear of failure, a climate where people are willing to propose or undertake change is unlikely. Accordingly, as Clarke (1994: 94) suggested, 'Creating a culture for change means that change has to be part of the way we do things around here, it cannot be bolted on as an extra.' Therefore, for many proponents of the emergent approach to change, if an appropriate organisational culture does not exist, it is essential that one is created.

However, not all its proponents take this view. Beer et al. (1993) suggested that the most effective way to promote change is not by directly attempting to influence organisational behaviour or culture. Instead, they advocate restructuring organisations in order to place people in a new organisational context, which imposes new roles, relationships and responsibilities upon them. This, they believe, *forces* new attitudes and behaviours upon people. Wilson (1992: 91) also warns against attempting to use culture to promote change, claiming that:

> to effect change in an organisation simply by attempting to change its culture assumes an unwarranted linear connection between something called organisational culture and performance. Not only is this concept of organisational culture multi-faceted, it is also not always clear precisely how culture and change are related, if at all, and, if so, in which direction.

It is apparent that, while the emergent approach recognises the importance of culture to organisational change, there is a split between two groups of experts:

1   those who believe an appropriate culture can be created, where one does not exist; and

2   those who believe that attempting to change culture is something an organisation does at its peril.

Key learning point

Several authors propose that cultural change is at the heart of the organisational change process – but there is some debate about whether it is wise to make deliberate attempts to change culture.

Organisational structure

This is seen as playing a crucial role in defining how people relate to each other and in influencing the momentum for change (Huczynski and Buchanan, 2001; Dawson, 2003; Kotter, 1996; Hatch, 1997). Therefore, an appropriate organisational structure can be an important lever for achieving change. However, both the informal and formal aspects of organisational structure need to be recognised if structure is to be used to effect change.

The case for developing more appropriate organisational structures in order to facilitate change very much follows the arguments of the contingency theorists (Child, 1984). Those favouring an emergent approach to change point out that the last 30 years have witnessed a general move to create flatter organisational structures. The aim of this has been to increase organisational responsiveness by devolving authority and responsibility (Senior, 2002). As Kotter (1996: 169) remarks, the case for such structural changes is that, 'An organisation with more delegation, which means a flat hierarchy, is in a far superior position to manoeuvre than one with a big, change-resistant lump in the middle.'

There is an increasing trend for organisations to position themselves to respond rapidly to changing conditions by breaking down internal barriers, disseminating knowledge and developing synergy across functions. Organisations that have done this have been called *network organisations* or, to use Handy's (1989) term, 'federal' organisations. Snow et al. (1993) suggested that the semi-autonomous nature of each part of a network reduces the need for, and erodes, the power of centrally managed bureaucracies. This, in turn, leads to change and adaptation being driven from the *bottom up* rather than from the top down. They further argue that the specialisation and flexibility required to cope with globalisation, intense competition and rapid technological change can only be achieved by loosening (i) the ties between the various parts of the organisation and its 'centre' and (ii) the control that the centre of the organisation has over its various parts.

Key learning point

Adopting an emergent approach to change may require organisations to move towards radically different structures and cultures.

Organisational learning

For advocates of the emergent approach, learning plays a key role in preparing people for, and allowing them to cope with, change (Bechtold, 1997; Senge, 2000). Put simply, this learning is 'the capacity of members of an organisation to detect and correct errors and to seek new insights that would enable them to make choices that better produce outcomes that they seek' (Martin, 2000: 463). In many instances, a willingness to change only stems from the feeling that there is no other option. Therefore, as Wilson (1992) suggests, change can be precipitated by making impending crises real to everyone in the organisation (or perhaps even engineering crises) or encouraging dissatisfaction with current systems and procedures. The latter is probably best achieved through the creation of mechanisms by managers that allow staff to become familiar with the marketplace, customers, competitors, legal requirements etc. in order to recognise the pressures for change.

Point of integration

Organisational learning is a much broader topic than training – but it often involves the development of new knowledge and skills. This means theories widely used in the design and delivery of training are also often relevant as components of organisational learning.

Clarke (1994) and Nadler (1993) suggested that individual and organisational learning stems from effective top-down communication and the promotion of self-development and confidence. In turn, this encourages the commitment to, and shared ownership of, the organisation's vision, actions and decisions that are necessary to (i) respond to the external environment and (ii) take advantage of the opportunities it offers. Additionally, as Pugh (1993) pointed out, in order to generate the need and climate for change, people within organisations need to be involved in the diagnosis of problems and the development of solutions. Carnall (2003) took this argument further, maintaining that organisational effectiveness can be achieved and sustained only through learning from the experience of change.

Clarke (1994: 156) believed that involving staff in change management decisions was so important because it was 'stimulating habits of criticism and open debate', enabling them to challenge existing norms and question established practices. This, in turn, creates the opportunity for innovation and radical change. Benjamin and Mabey (1993) argued that such questioning of the status quo is the essence of bottom-up change. They consider that, as employees' learning becomes more valued and visible, then rather than managers putting pressure on staff to change, the *reverse* occurs. The new openness and knowledge of staff put pressure on managers to address fundamental questions about the purpose and direction of the organisation, questions which previously they might have avoided. Consequently, as Easterby-Smith et al. (2000) and Tsang (1997) suggest, organisational learning is neither an easy nor an uncontentious option for organisations. There is also a great diversity of opinion as to what it is and how it can be promoted, which makes organisational learning a more difficult concept to apply than many of its supporters acknowledge (Burnes et al., 2003).

Key learning point

The emergent approach highlights the importance of employees in stimulating and influencing the change process.

Managerial behaviour

The traditional view of organisations sees managers as directing and controlling staff, resources and information. However, the emergent approach to change requires a radical change in managerial behaviour. Managers are expected to operate as facilitators and coaches who, through their ability to span hierarchical, functional and organisational boundaries, can bring together and motivate teams and groups to identify the need for, and achieve, change (Mabey and Mayon-White, 1993).

To be effective in this new role, Clarke (1994) believed that managers would require knowledge of, and expertise in, strategy formulation, human resource management, marketing/sales and negotiation/conflict resolution. However, the key to success, the decisive factor in creating a focused agenda for organisational change is, according to Clarke (1994), managers' own behaviour. If managers are to gain the commitment of others to change, they must first be prepared to challenge their own assumptions, attitudes and mindsets so that they develop an understanding of the emotional and intellectual processes involved (Boddy and Buchanan, 1992).

Point of integration

Contemporary theories of leadership (see Chapter 12) include considerable coverage of the complex and multifaceted demands placed on leaders by the challenges presented by collaborative change processes. It may also be that such processes demand high levels of cognitive ability and specific personality traits (Chapter 3), favourable attitudes to employee collaboration (Chapter 11) and a tolerance for ambiguity (Chapter 10).

For supporters of the emergent approach, the essence of change is the move from the familiar to the unknown. In this situation, it is essential for managers to be able to tolerate risk and cope with ambiguity. Pugh (1993) took the view that, in a dynamic environment, open and active communication with those participating in the change process is the key to coping with risk and ambiguity. This is echoed by Clarke's (1994: 172) assertion that because 'top-down, unilaterally imposed change does not tend to work, bottom-up, early involvement and genuine consultation' are essential to achieving successful change. This, in turn, requires managers to facilitate open, organisation-wide communication via groups, individuals and formal and informal channels.

An organisation's ability to gather, disseminate, analyse and discuss information is, from the perspective of the emergent approach, crucial for successful change. The reason for this, as Wilson (1992) argued, is that to effect change successfully, organisations need consciously and proactively to move forward incrementally. Large-scale change and more formal and integrated approaches to change (such as TQM) can quickly lose their sense of purpose and relevance for organisations operating in dynamic and uncertain environments. If organisations move towards their strategic vision on the basis of many small-scale, local-ised incremental changes, managers have a key role to play. They must ensure that those concerned, which could (potentially) be the entire workforce, have access to and are able to act on all the available information. Also, by encouraging a collective pooling of knowledge and information in this way, a better understanding of the pressures and possibilities for change can be achieved: this should then enable managers to improve the quality of strategic decisions (Buchanan and Boddy, 1992a, 1992b; Quinn, 1993).

As well as ensuring the free flow of information, managers must also recognise and be able to cope with resistance to change, and political intervention in it. They will, especially, need to acquire and develop a range of interpersonal skills that enable them to deal with individuals and groups who seek to block change, or manipulate change, for their own benefit (Buchanan and Boddy, 1992a, 1992b).

Point of integration

Theories of training design and delivery provide a great deal of information about how these managerial skills may be best developed (Chapter 9).

In addition, supporting openness, reducing uncertainty and encouraging experimentation can be powerful mechanisms for promoting change (Mabey and Mayon-White, 1993). In this respect, Coghlan (1993) and McCalman and Paton (1992) advocated the use of OD tools and techniques (such as transactional analysis, teamwork, group problem-solving, role playing etc.), which have long been used in planned change programmes. However, there is an enormous and potentially confusing array of these; Mayon-White (1993) and Boddy and Buchanan (1992) argued that managers have a crucial role to play in terms of identifying and applying the appropriate tools and techniques. The main objective in deploying such tools and techniques is to encourage shared learning through teamwork and cooperation. It is this that provides the framework and support for the emergence of creative solutions and encourages a sense of involvement, commitment and ownership of the change process (Carnall, 2003; McCalman and Paton, 1992).

Nevertheless, it would be naive to assume that everyone will want to work, or be able to function effectively, in such situations. The cognitive and behavioural changes necessary for organisational survival may be too large for many people, including and perhaps especially managers. An important managerial task will, therefore, be to identify sources of inertia, assess the skill mix within their organisation and, most of all, consider whether their own managerial attitudes and styles are appropriate.

The emergent approach requires a major change in the traditional role of managers. In future they will need to be facilitators and coaches rather than initiators and directors.

Power and politics

Although the advocates of emergent change tend to view power and politics from differing perspectives, they all recognise their importance and that they have to be managed if change is to be effective. Dawson (1994: 176), for example, concludes that: 'The central argument is that it is important to try and gain the support of senior management, local management, supervisors, trade unions and workplace employees.' Pettigrew et al. (1992: 293) state that: 'The significance of political language at the front end of change processes needs emphasising. Closures can be labelled as redevelopments. Problems can be re-coded into opportunities with . . . broad positive visions being articulated to build early coalitions.' However, in an era in which political 'spin' is increasingly recognised and questioned, the effectiveness and integrity of such 'political language' are debatable. Kanter et al. (1992: 508) argue that the first step to implementing change is coalition-building: 'involve those whose involvement really matters . . . Specifically, seek support from two general groups: (1) power sources and (2) stakeholders.' In a similar vein, Nadler (1993) advocates the need to shape the political dynamics of change so that power centres develop that support the change rather than block it. Senior (2002), drawing on the work of Nadler (1993), proposes four steps organisations need to take to manage the political dynamics of change:

Step 1   Ensure, or develop, the support of key power groups.

Step 2   Use leader behaviour to generate support for the proposed change.

Step 3   Use symbols and language to encourage and show support for the change.

Step 4   Build in stability by using power to ensure that some things remain the same.

Though power and politics can play an influential role in managing change, other factors, such as culture, also play an influential role.

Important though power and politics are in the change process, as Hendry (1996) and Pugh (1993) argue, they are not the be all and end all of change and it is important not to focus on these to the exclusion of other important factors. Nevertheless, the focus placed on the political dynamics of change does serve to highlight the need for those who manage change to be aware of and control this dimension of the change process.

Earlier in this chapter we asked you to consider the merits of the planned change approach. Now we would like you to do the opposite with the emergent approach to change. What might be the criticisms of the emergent approach to change? In what circumstances might it not be helpful to organisations seeking to implement change better? Try to do this for yourself before moving on to the next section.

Nuclear meltdowns are bad for returns

Tepco's struggle with its tsunami-damaged Fukushima nuclear power plant reminds us of last year's "black swan": BP's struggle with the Gulf of Mexico oil spill. One year has passed since what Barack Obama called the US's "environmental 9/11". Why dwell on what is already in the rear-view mirror? Having looked in-depth at the Gulf of Mexico crisis, we see some parallels between the two events. With corporate disasters apparently increasing in frequency, understanding a pattern that may have wider significance is clearly relevant to investors. One common driver of such disasters is regulatory failure. Lack of support for regulators from government and corporate political influence played a significant role in ineffective regulation of offshore drilling in the US. Some are suggesting it is also true for Fukushima: according to WikiLeaks, in 2006 the government overturned a court order to close a nuclear power plant because of safety risks related to serious earthquakes. And a Financial Times report highlighted that the "System bred Tepco's cosy links to watchdogs".

Both companies have experienced what sociologists call "organisational learning disabilities". A narrow conception of risk also played a big part in allowing these events

to happen: in BP's case relying on fatality data as a proxy indicator for process safety and for Tepco, being inadequately prepared for the risk of severe earthquakes. BP's leadership was noted for its unwavering focus on cost-cutting, while it also had incontrovertible evidence of weak process safety culture. Clearly Tepco's approach to managing this dilemma will need to be closely investigated. A weak concern for negative externalities seems to be a common feature in these two high impact industries. Both deepwater oil and gas and nuclear have been promoted as good for energy independence. But as events have shown, the full costs of a serious accident are not integrated into cost-benefit analyses, partly because of the assumption that costs will be socialised.

Collectively, and without conscious intent, investors play an important role in shaping the path to these "preventable surprises". Shareholder value fundamentalism puts pressure on companies to deliver quarterly returns, leading to M&A and outsourcing without adequate emphasis on integration and oversight, or a short-cut approach to the extension of nuclear plant lifespan. The lack of attention to safety issues by sell-side analysts has been well documented by leading behavioural finance specialists.

 Source: 'Nuclear meltdowns are bad for returns', *Financial Times,* 2 May 2011, p. 6 (Le Floc'h, M and Thamatheram, R)

Suggested exercises

1 What is meant by the term 'organisational learning disabilities' and how might these lead to disasters such as occurred at the Fukushima nuclear power plant and Deepwater Horizon?
2 How might organisational learning prevent such disasters?
3 What changes would an organisation need to make to adopt organisational learning and what obstacles might it encounter?

Emergent change: summary and criticisms

The proponents of emergent change are a somewhat disparate group who tend to be united more by their scepticism regarding planned change than by a commonly agreed alternative. Nevertheless, there does seem to be some agreement regarding the main tenets of emergent change, which are:

■ Organisational change is a continuous process of 'experiment' and adaptation aimed at matching an organisation's capabilities to the needs and dictates of a dynamic and uncertain environment.

■ Though this is best achieved through a multitude of (mainly) small-scale incremental changes, over time these can lead to a major reconfiguration and transformation of an organisation.

■ The role of managers is not to plan or implement change. Instead it is to create or foster an organisational structure and climate that encourages and sustains experimentation and risk-taking, and to develop a workforce that will take responsibility for identifying the need for change and implementing it.

■ Although managers are expected to become facilitators rather than doers, they also have the prime responsibility for developing a collective vision or common purpose which gives direction to their organisation, and within which the appropriateness of any proposed change can be judged.

■ The key organisational activities that allow these elements to operate successfully are: information-gathering – about the external environment and internal objectives and capabilities; communication – the transmission, analysis and discussion of information; and learning – the ability to develop new skills, identify appropriate responses and draw knowledge from their own and others' past and present actions.

Though not always stated openly, the case for an emergent approach to change is based on the assumption that all organisations operate in a turbulent, dynamic and unpredictable environment. Therefore, if the external world is changing in a rapid and uncertain fashion, organisations need to be continually scanning their environment in order to adapt and respond to changes. Because this is a continuous and open-ended process, the planned approach to change is seen as inappropriate given the unpredictable nature of the environment that organisations exist within. To be successful, changes need to emerge locally and incrementally in order to respond to and take advantage of environmental threats and opportunities.

Presented in this fashion, there is certainly an apparent coherence and validity to the emergent approach. However, it is a fragile coherence and its validity can be challenged. As far as coherence is concerned, some proponents of emergent change, especially Dawson (1994) and Pettigrew and Whipp (1993), clearly approach it from the processual perspective on organisations. However, it is not clear that Wilson (1992) and Buchanan and Boddy (1992a, 1992b) would fully subscribe to this view. In the case of Clarke (1994) and Carnall (2003), it is clear that they do not take a processual perspective. Partly, this is explained by the fact that some of these writers (especially Wilson, 1992; Pettigrew and Whipp, 1993; Dawson, 1994) are attempting to understand and investigate change from a critical perspective, while others (notably Carnall, 2003; Boddy and Buchanan, 1992; Buchanan and Boddy, 1992a, 1992b; Clarke, 1994) are more concerned to provide practical guidance and tools for managing change successfully. Nevertheless, these differing objectives and perspectives do put a question mark against the coherence of the emergent approach.

The validity or general applicability of the emergent approach to change depends to a large extent on whether or not one subscribes to the view that all organisations operate in a dynamic and unpredictable environment to which they continually have to adapt. Burnes (2014) produced substantial evidence that not all organisations face the same degree of environmental turbulence and that, in any case, it is possible to manipulate or change environmental constraints. This does not necessarily invalidate the emergent approach as a whole, but it does indicate that for some organisations, the planned approach to change may be both appropriate and effective in their particular circumstances.

Obviously, the above issues raise a question mark regarding the emergent approach; however, even without reservations regarding its coherence and validity, there would still be serious criticisms of this approach. For example, a great deal of emphasis is given to creating appropriate organisational cultures; but many writers have questioned whether this is either easy or indeed possible (Filby and Willmott, 1988; Meek, 1988). Indeed, as mentioned earlier, even Wilson (1992) was sceptical about the case for viewing culture as a facilitator of change. Similar points can be made regarding the 'learning organisation' approach. As Whittington (1993: 130) commented:

> The danger of the purely 'learning' approach to change, therefore, is that . . . managers [and others] may actually recognise the need for change, yet still refuse to 'learn' because they understand perfectly well the implications for their power and status. Resistance to change may not be 'stupid'. . . but based on a very shrewd appreciation of the personal consequences.

A variant of this criticism relates to the impact of success on managerial learning. Miller (1993: 119) observed that, while managers generally start out by attempting to learn all they can about their organisation's environment, over time, as they gain experience, they 'form quite definite opinions of what works and why' and as a consequence tend to limit their search for information and knowledge. So experience, especially where it is based on success, may actually be a barrier to learning, in that it shapes the cognitive structures by which managers, and everyone else, see and interpret the world. As Nystrom and Starbuck (1984: 55) observed:

> What people see, predict, understand, depends on their cognitive structures . . . [which] manifest themselves in perceptual frameworks, expectations, world views, plans, goals . . . myths, rituals, symbols . . . and jargon.

This brings us neatly to the topic of the role of managers. As the above quotations indicate, they may neither welcome nor be able to accept approaches to change that require them to challenge and amend their own beliefs, especially where such approaches run counter to their experience of 'what works and why'. It is in such situations that managers may seek to use their power and political influence in an adverse manner.

Advocates of the emergent approach have undoubtedly provided a valuable contribution to our understanding of change by highlighting the neglect of these important issues. However, they have also been criticised for overstating their case. Hendry (1996: 621) argues that: 'The management of change has become . . . overfocused on the political aspects of change', while Collins (1998: 100), voicing concerns of his own and of other researchers, argues that:

> in reacting to the problems and critiques of [the planned approach], managers and practitioners have swung from a dependence on under-socialised models and explanations of change and instead have become committed to the arguments of, what might be called, over-socialised models of change.

Another and important point which needs to be considered is that, though the emergent approach offers valuable insights and guidance, it does not appear to be as universally applicable as its advocates imply. The focus of emergent change tends to be the organisation and its major subsystems rather than individuals and groups per se. It is also the case that, both implicitly and explicitly, the emergent approach advocates cooperative change rather than coercive or confrontational change. Though this is to be applauded, it is clear that there are many situations where change is pushed through in a rapid and confrontational manner (see Edwardes, 1983; Grinyer et al., 1988; Dunphy and Stace, 1992; Franklin, 1997). In addition, it is the case that the emergent approach is specifically founded on the assumption that organisations operate in a dynamic environment that requires continuous, coherent and, over time, large-scale change. It is, then, by its own definition, not applicable to organisations operating in stable environments or to those seeking to achieve a large-scale and rapid transition from one fixed state to another. In addition, as mentioned above, if the possibility exists to manipulate environmental variables and constraints to avoid having to undertake radical change, managers may perceive this as a more attractive or viable option.

The final criticism of emergent change is that it is strong on analysis and weak on practice (Burnes, 2014). Certainly, if one looks at the foregoing examination of emergent change, it does appear to be very global and lacking in the many specific and practical tools and techniques for its application which can be found in most OD textbooks (see for example Cummings and Worley, 2001; French and Bell, 1995). This is a point acknowledged by Dawson (2011: 128), one of the major figures in the development of the processual approach, who states that the problem with such research is:

> on the one hand, the inability of this type of study to produce anything of 'practical' value (in the form of systematic predictive capabilities) and, on the other hand, the tendency for studies to produce guidelines that undermine their theoretical foundations through outlining rather banal lists of ingredients on how best to manage change.

In effect, the emergent approach is theoretically rigorous, but lacks practical relevance, and its attempts to address this weakness have tended both to be simplistic and undermine its theoretical strength. This is why emergent change appears to have failed in its attempts to become the dominant approach to organisational change and OD once again seems to be in the ascendency, as the following will show (Burnes, 2014).

Key learning point

Though the emergent approach to change has apparent advantages over the planned approach, an examination of it reveals that there are question marks over its coherence, validity and applicability.

The renaissance of OD

For OD, the 1980s and 1990s were difficult times. Yet, despite the torrent of criticism and self-doubt, the 1990s saw two major developments which led to renewed support for Lewin and OD. First, a new generation of scholars started to take a critical and surprisingly supportive interest in the work of Kurt Lewin. In 1992 the *Journal of Social Issues* (48, 2) published a special issue to mark (belatedly) the centenary of Lewin's birth in 1890. This brought Lewin's work to a new generation and argued that it was still highly relevant to the needs of organisations and society at large, claiming that 'psychology as a field has moved much closer to Lewin's worldview than it was during his lifetime' (Bargal et al., 1992: 4). Other writers have also made claims for the continuing relevance of Lewin's work (Boje et al., 2011; Burnes and By, 2012; Burnes and Cooke, 2012, 2013a; Coghlan and Jacobs, 2005). Burnes (2004a), in a re-appraisal of planned change, also observed that many of Lewin's critics appear to have misread, or perhaps even not read, his work, which has generated a simplistic and misleading picture of Lewin's contribution to the field. Therefore, while many in the OD community were busy questioning its purpose and values, other scholars, often from outside the community, were rehabilitating Lewin and OD.

The second development, or rather continuing development, was that OD did not stand still. OD practices were increasingly being incorporated into HRM and Human Resource Development (HRD), creating strong overlaps between the three areas (Grieves and Redman, 1999; Ruona and Gibson, 2004), and the internationalisation of OD continued apace (Burnes and Cooke, 2012). Also, long-standing OD bodies became increasingly international in their membership and outlook, such as the OD Network, the OD Institute, the International Organisation Development Association and the NTL Institute; and newer bodies have been created, including the Asia OD Network. Some, though, have questioned whether OD is still growing in its traditional markets (Alban, 2003). However, the issue here may be that while some organisations, especially the big consultancies, have shied away from the term OD, they have not necessarily shied away from its practice (see, for example, Human Synergistics International's 'Planned Culture Change' programme which appears to draw on core OD practices; Jones et al., 2006). One can also see this rebadging with some scholar-practitioners who use labels such as 'Long March' (Kanter et al., 1992) and 'Theory O' (Beer and Nohria, 2000) for approaches which have a distinctly OD flavour.

Therefore, as can be seen, while the emergent approach has been losing ground, OD has been experiencing something of a renaissance.

Organisational change: approaches and choices

A framework for change

As Stickland (1998: 14) remarks:

> the problem with studying change is that it parades across many subject domains under numerous guises, such as transformation, development, metamorphosis, transmutation, evolution, regeneration, innovation, revolution and transition to name but a few.

As this chapter has shown, there are two dominant and, in the main, quite different approaches to managing change – the planned and the emergent. However, despite their contributions to assisting organisations to manage change more effectively, as has been indicated, they do not cover the full spectrum of change events organisations encounter. Indeed, given the vast array of types of organisation – operating in different industries and different countries – and the enormous variety of change situations – ranging from small to large, from technical to people – and all stages in between, *it would be surprising if just two approaches could encompass all these situations*. Nevertheless, the important point is not to be able to categorise the variety of change situations per se, but to provide a framework that matches types of change situations with the appropriate ways of managing them.

Key learning point

Recent approaches to change place a great deal of emphasis on the situation that the organisation is in, rather than arguing for the effectiveness of a particular approach to change across a variety of different organisations faced with situations and challenges.

This, of course, is no small task. Dunphy and Stace (1992), for example, identify four approaches to managing change based on the degree to which employees are involved in planning and executing change, as follows: collaborative, consultative, directive and coercive. They also argue that consultative and directive approaches tend to dominate, except where rapid organisational transformations are required, when more coercive approaches come into play.

Point of integration

The way that change is planned and executed can have a significant impact on employee attitudes (Chapter 6) and well-being (Chapter 10). This may be one of the reasons why rapid coercive organisational change can sometimes be linked to problems with employee well-being and satisfaction.

Kotter (1996) takes a different view, seeing the overall direction of change as being decided by senior managers, but its implementation being the responsibility of empowered managers and employees at all levels. Storey (1992) takes yet another tack. He identifies two key dimensions. The first concerns the degree of collaboration between the parties concerned: varying from change that is unilaterally constructed by management, to change brought about by some form of joint agreement with those involved. The second dimension concerns the form that change takes: ranging from change that is introduced as a complete package, to change comprising a sequence of different individual initiatives.

We could cover many pages in this fashion, listing the various ways of managing change that writers have identified. However, the key issues are: how can these approaches be classified and what determines which approach an organisation should take and in what circumstances?

In addressing these questions, Burnes (2014) constructed *a framework for change* (see Figure 14.2) comprising four quadrants, each of which has a distinct focus in terms of change. The top half of the figure, quadrants 1 and 2, represents situations where organisations need to make large-scale, organisation-wide changes to either their culture or structure. The need for these changes may be caused by the organisation's environment being turbulent or the environment may become turbulent due to the organisation's structure/culture being inappropriate. The bottom half of the figure, quadrants 3 and 4, represents situations

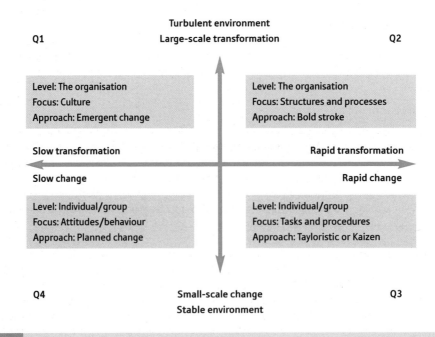

	Turbulent environment	
Q1	Large-scale transformation	Q2
Level: The organisation Focus: Culture Approach: Emergent change		Level: The organisation Focus: Structures and processes Approach: Bold stroke
Slow transformation		Rapid transformation
Slow change		Rapid change
Level: Individual/group Focus: Attitudes/behaviour Approach: Planned change		Level: Individual/group Focus: Tasks and procedures Approach: Tayloristic or Kaizen
Q4	Small-scale change Stable environment	Q3

Figure 14.2   A framework for change

where organisations need to make relatively small-scale and localised adjustments to the attitudes and behaviours or tasks and procedures of individuals and groups. Such changes must be sustained and, therefore, it is crucial to ensure that the post-change environment is stable. As can be seen, the left-hand side of the figure, quadrants 1 and 4, represents situations where the main focus of change is the human side of the organisation, i.e. cultural and attitudinal/behavioural change. As argued above, these sorts of changes are likely to be best achieved through a relatively slow, participative approach, rather than a rapid and directive or coercive one. The right-hand side of Figure 14.2 represents situations where the primary focus is on achieving changes to the technical side of the organisation, i.e. structures, processes, tasks and procedures. These types of changes tend to be less participative in nature and relatively more rapid in their execution.

Key learning point

The nature of the change process required can be better understood by looking at the size of the change required, its intended outcomes and the organisational context of change.

Taking each of the quadrants in turn: quadrant 1 identifies situations where the culture of an organisation is no longer appropriate for the environment in which the organisation is operating. For such relatively large-scale initiatives, where the main focus is culture change at the level of the entire organisation or large parts of it, the emergent approach (e.g. Kanter et al.'s **Long March**: Kanter et al., 1992), which emphasises both the collaborative and political dimensions of change, is likely to be most appropriate. Although the organisation may be operating in a turbulent environment and, therefore, individual elements of the cultural change may be rapid, the overall cultural transformation is likely to be a slow process.

Quadrant 2 relates to situations where the focus is on achieving major changes in structures and processes at the level of the entire organisation (e.g. Kanter et al.'s **Bold Stroke**). Situations where such changes are required arise for a variety of reasons. It may be that an organisation finds itself in serious trouble and needs to respond quickly to realign itself with its environment. Alternatively, it may be that an organisation is not experiencing a crisis, but that it perceives that it will face one unless it restructures itself to achieve a better fit with its environment. In such cases, it may not be possible or advisable to change the structure slowly or on a piecemeal basis and, therefore, a major and rapid reorganisation is necessary. Because it involves the entire organisation or major components of it, this is likely to be driven by the centre and to be the focus of a political struggle, given that major structural changes are usually accompanied by major shifts in the distribution of power. Therefore, the new structure will be imposed from the top in a directive or even coercive way, depending on the balance between winners and losers.

Quadrant 3 presents a different picture. This represents situations where change is aimed at the individual and group level rather than at the level of the entire organisation. The aim is to improve the performance of the areas involved through changes to the technical side of the organisation. Such changes tend to be relatively small-scale and piecemeal and with few (if any) implications for behaviour and attitudes. A key objective is to ensure the predictability and stability of the performance of the areas involved but at a higher level. How these changes are managed will depend on the culture of the organisation. In a traditional, bureaucratic organisation, a Tayloristic approach may be adopted, i.e. specialist managers and engineers will identify the 'best way of working' and impose it. In a more participative culture, such as a Japanese company, a more collaborative approach may be appropriate, such as a *Kaizen* initiative that brings together a team comprising workers and specialists. But either is possible and both can be achieved in a relatively speedy fashion.

Finally, quadrant 4 covers relatively small-scale initiatives whose main objective is performance improvement through attitudinal and behavioural change at the individual and group level. As in the case of quadrant 3, a key objective is to ensure the predictability and stability of the performance of the people involved, but at a higher level. In such situations, planned change, with its emphasis on collaboration and participation, is likely to be the most appropriate approach. However, because of the focus on behavioural and attitudinal change, the process may be relatively slow.

Of course, it could be argued that, at the organisational level, it is difficult to identify situations that involve solely cultural changes or involve solely structural changes. A similar comment could be made with regard to attitudinal/behavioural change and changes to tasks and procedures at the individual/group level. Such comments are valid to an extent, but the real issue is to identify the main focus of the change.

For example, writers such as Tom Peters (1997) and Rosabeth Moss Kanter (1989) argue for structural change in order to promote the cultural change they see as necessary for organisations to survive in an increasingly complex world. Therefore, though they recommend significant structural changes, these are part of the process of culture change and not an end in themselves. John Kotter (1996) advocates the need for organisations to restructure themselves on a continual basis in order to meet the challenges of the future. At different times and in different areas, he believes that this can involve all of the types of change shown in Figure 14.2. There are also many cases, as Kotter argues, where an organisation already has an appropriate culture and where changes to its overall structure, and piecemeal changes to its component parts, are seen as working with and reinforcing the existing culture rather than leading to its replacement.

Consequently, the question of whether changes can be labelled as mainly structure-orientated or mainly people-orientated is partly a matter of sequencing: what does the organisation need to do first? It is also partly concerned with the extent to which environmental turbulence has a uniform effect across an organisation. The pioneering work of James Thompson (1967) identified that different parts of an organisation, by accident or design, could experience different levels of uncertainty. On this basis, it would be perfectly feasible for some parts of an organisation to be experiencing relatively low levels of uncertainty and concentrating on small-scale, piecemeal changes while at the same time the overall organisation was going through a process of rapid transformation.

Stop to consider

At this point in the chapter we are beginning to examine the merits of new approaches to understanding the change process. Earlier we asked you to consider the advantages and disadvantages of the planned and emergent approaches to change. Now take time to consider how successful these new approaches might be in overcoming the criticisms of the planned and emergent approaches. We also saw that the planned and emergent approaches had some strengths. Now consider whether these new approaches also have these same strengths.

Where does this leave us? Drawing on the work of Davenport (1993), we need to distinguish between initiatives that focus on fundamental attitudinal change and those aimed at fundamental structural change. As shown by Allaire and Firsirotu (1984), there is a strong relationship between organisational structures and organisational cultures, and so changes in one may require corresponding changes in the other. However, as they also showed, it is much easier and quicker to change structures than to change cultures. Consequently, we need to take into account the timescale for change.

Culture change, to be effective, is likely to be slow and involves incremental changes to the human side of the organisation. Also, because of its nature, it is likely to be participative and collaborative. Rapid change is only likely to be effective or necessary where the main changes are to structure, or where the organisation is in such trouble that delay is not an option (Beer and Nohria, 2000; Kanter et al., 1992). In the case of structural change, this may involve some consultation but is likely to have a large element of direction from the centre. In the latter case, where the organisation is in trouble because of the urgency of the situation, change is likely to be directive and, possibly, coercive.

There is one further point that needs to be noted, and that relates to how these various approaches can be used in combination. In a manner similar to Mintzberg's (1994) definition of 'umbrella' strategies, Pettigrew et al. (1992: 297) write of instances where change is both 'intentional and emergent'. Storey (1992) identifies the need for change projects whose outlines are decided at corporate level with little or no consultation, but whose implementation comprises an inter-related series of change initiatives, some or all of which could be the product of local cooperation and consultation. Kotter (1996) takes a similar perspective. He sees strategic change as comprising a series of large and small projects aimed at achieving the same overall objectives but which are begun at different times, can be managed differently and vary in nature.

Buchanan and Storey (1997) also hint at this when criticising planned change for attempting to impose order and a linear sequence to processes that are untidy, messy, multilevel and multifunction, and that develop in an iterative and backtracking manner. This is also identified by Kanter et al. (1992) when speaking of Long Marches and Bold Strokes. They argue that Bold Strokes often have to be followed by a whole series of smaller-scale changes over a more extended timescale in order to embed the changes brought about by the Bold Stroke. Beer and Nohria (2000) are even more explicit in arguing for the use of Theory E (comparable to Kanter et al.'s Bold Stroke) and Theory O (comparable to Kanter et al.'s Long March) in tandem. Similarly, Burnes (2004b) has also shown that major change projects that involve both structural and cultural change can successfully utilise both planned and emergent approaches. Consequently, when we attempt to understand, analyse or influence major change projects, we should not see them as being managed solely in a cooperative fashion or solely in a coercive fashion. Instead, they may have elements of both but at different levels, at different times and be managed by different people. They may also, indeed probably will, unfold in an unexpected way, which will require rethinking and backtracking from time to time.

Key learning point

Change is a complex non-linear process. Attempts to better understand and manage change need to recognise this.

A framework for choice

As can be seen from Figure 14.2, what appears to be on offer is a menu approach to change whereby organisations, or more accurately those who manage them, can choose the approach that fits their circumstances. This conception of a multiplicity of approaches is in line with the call by Dunphy and Stace (1993: 905) for 'a model of change that is essentially a "situational" or "contingency model", one that indicates how to vary strategies to achieve "optimum fit" with the changing environment'. However, does this mean that organisations have no choice about which approach to use? We have identified situations where these various approaches seem appropriate or not, but does that mean they cannot be used in other situations and does that mean that the context cannot be changed? Supposing organisations whose management prefer a cooperative approach find themselves seriously out of alignment with their environment: is their only option rapid and coercive structural change? Or, alternatively, where managers prefer a more directive, less participative style, are they compelled to adopt a more participative style and culture?

These questions revolve around two issues. The first issue concerns the extent to which an organisation can influence the forces driving it to change in one direction or another. If we accept that the speed and nature of the changes that organisations are required to make are dependent upon the nature of the environment in which they are operating, then choice will relate to the extent that organisations can influence, manipulate or recreate their environment to suit their preferred way of working. Over recent years, there has been growing support for those who argue that organisations can influence their environment, either to stabilise or to destabilise it (Morgan, 1997; Hatch, 1997; Burnes, 2014). If this is the case, then the important question is not just how organisations can do this, but whether, finding themselves in trouble, they have the *time* to influence their environment.

Point of integration

Contingency approaches are also found in leadership theories, but these are more focused on everyday interactions with employees. Nevertheless, these share several features of contingency models of change.

This leads on to the second issue – to what extent and for how long can an organisation operate with structures, practices and cultures that are out of line with its environment? The answer to this question revolves around Child's (1972) concept of *equifinality*. Sorge (1997: 13) states that equifinality 'quite simply means that different sorts of internal arrangements are perfectly compatible with identical contextual or environmental states'. Put more simply, there are different ways to achieve the same end result. This does not imply that any structure is suitable for any environment. What it does suggest, though, is that total alignment between structure and environment is not always necessary. The duration for which this non-alignment is sustainable will clearly vary with the degree of non-alignment and the circumstances of the organisation in question; however, at the very least, it does offer organisations the potential to stave off realignment for some time during which they can influence or change their circumstances. It follows that Figure 14.2 depicts not only a framework for change but also a framework for choice.

It follows that the debate between planned change and emergent change is too narrow. It is too narrow in the sense that there are other approaches to change that organisations have available to them; in particular it tends to ignore the more coercive and directive approaches to change that, in many organisations, may be more prevalent than more cooperative ones. It is also too narrow in the sense that it assumes that change is unidirectional, i.e. is driven by the environment. People in organisations do have the opportunity to make choices about what to change, how to change and when to change. This does not mean that all organisations will exercise such choices or that those that do will be successful. Nor does it mean that choice is not severely constrained. However, it does mean that those who do not recognise that choice exists may be putting themselves in a worse competitive position than those who do.

Key learning point

To understand change we need to consider the influence of the environment and the choices that are made by those involved in the change process.

Key learning point

Just as organisations have choice in terms of what to change, they also have choice in what approach they adopt to change.

Summary

This chapter began by examining the importance of organisational change, especially in relation to culture. It then went on to examine the merits, drawbacks and appropriateness of the planned and emergent approaches to change which have dominated the theory and, to a large extent, the practice of organisational change over the past 60 years. It has been argued that just as change comes in all shapes and sizes, so too do models or approaches to change. Therefore, instead of portraying the argument regarding the most appropriate approach to change as a contest between the merits of the planned and emergent approaches, a change framework has been developed (see Figure 14.2) which provides an overview of the range of change situations and approaches organisations face or are offered, and the types of situations in which they can best be applied.

It has also been argued that the environment and other organisational constraints can be manipulated or subject to managerial choice. Consequentially, some organisations will find that the organisational adjustments required to accommodate their position on the environment continuum coincide with the dominant view in the organisation of how it should operate. In that case, whether the approach to change adopted is planned or emergent, directive or cooperative, it will fit in with both how the organisation wishes to operate and the needs of the environment. Some organisations will, obviously, find that the dominant view internally of how they should operate is out of step with what is required to align or realign them with their environment. Such organisations face a number of choices ranging from whether to attempt to change their structures, cultures or style of management to accommodate the environment, or whether to attempt to manipulate the environment and other constraints so as to align them more closely with the dominant view within the organisation of how it should operate. Still further, there will be other organisations that face severe problems either because they failed to respond quickly enough or in an appropriate manner to changes in their environment, or because the environment moved too rapidly for an incremental approach to respond adequately. Nevertheless, by showing that a more conducive environment can be brought about, the framework also provides those who wish to promote more cooperative approaches to change with the means to argue their case in situations where previously more directive and coercive measures appeared to be the only option.

The concept of a change framework that allows approaches to change to be matched to environmental conditions and organisational constraints is clearly attractive. The fact that it incorporates the potential for managers, and others, to exercise some choice or influence over their environment and other constraints allows the model to move beyond the limitations of mechanistic and rational perspectives on organisations, and into the heartland of organisational reality.

Closing case study

Culture change at XYZ Construction

Background: XYZ Construction employs 500 staff and is part of a Europe-based multinational enterprise. Its main business is the provision of specialist services to major construction projects. XYZ operates in a highly competitive and at times hostile and aggressive environment. Disputes between contractors and subcontractors can become bitter and frequently end in litigation, though there have been a number of attempts over the last decade to create better relationships. Relationships within organisations were also less than friendly. Up to 1996, XYZ had been run by an autocratic managing director who was feared by his colleagues and who treated the company as his own personal fiefdom. His style of management was not liked and many felt that it was counter-productive but, as one manager commented, 'You didn't challenge him, you didn't put your head above the parapet, or he'd make life hell for you.' When he retired, the parent company took the view that XYZ was underperforming and that much of this was due to poor management and a lack of cooperation within the company. His replacement was appointed with the remit to improve the performance of the company and develop its managerial competency. This he did to great effect. Over a four-year period, he transformed the operation, culture and structure of the organisation.

Focusing on people and performance: The new managing director was appointed in 1996. He had trained as an engineer at XYZ but had then left and worked for a number of other companies in the construction industry. Construction is a close-knit industry, however, and he still knew XYZ and its staff quite well. He came with a reputation as an enlightened manager who could deliver performance improvements. The construction industry was notorious for the antagonistic relations between the main contractors and subcontractors such as XYZ, who specialise in one aspect of the construction process. The managing director recognised, however, that the industry was attempting to change, and conflict was being replaced by 'partnership' initiatives – contractors and subcontractors working in a more cooperative and team-based manner. The managing director also recognised that external partnerships needed internal partnerships and teamworking if they were to be successful. In turn this would require a new style of participative management in XYZ. Therefore, the managing director set out not just to upgrade XYZ's management but to undertake a root-and-branch overhaul of the company's operations and culture.

As a first step in creating better relationships among managers, he broadened out the Senior Management Team to include key staff who were not directors. In what had been a very hierarchical and status-conscious company, this was a significant change. The managing director knew that the staff in the company, particularly at a senior level, were experienced and competent people. He believed it was in the company's interest to retain staff rather than replace them. However, he also believed that they would need to change their attitudes and behaviours and upgrade their managerial skills if the company was to achieve the changes he believed were necessary. His strategy for transforming the company rested on carrying out two crucial activities in parallel: to introduce new practices and techniques into the company in order to provide a better service to customers (and thus improve the company's overall performance), and to change attitudes and behaviours within the company, especially those of managers. He did not see these as being separate activities or programmes: he saw them as being linked. New practices, such as customer care and customer partnering, were not mere technical exercises. They required behavioural changes and new managerial skills. Therefore, the managing director wanted to create a change programme whereby any change designed to improve the organisation's performance, whether it be new skills, new techniques or whatever, also had to promote and reinforce behavioural and culture change. The converse was also the case: any effort designed to change culture or behaviour also had to have the objective of improving the organisation's performance.

Between 1996 and 2000, the company undertook a series of organisational, management and staff development initiatives designed collectively to transform the organisation's performance and culture. The main initiatives were as follows:

Date	Event
June 1996	New managing director appointed
August 1996	Kaizen phase 1
October 1996	Customer care programme launched
March 1997	Investors in People launched
April 1997	Kaizen phase 2
September 1997	Customer care programme extended to construction sites
January 1998	Construction supervisors' new role launched
June 1998	New Senior Management Team formed
November 1998	Kaizen phase 3
March 1999	Site-based trainers appointed
June 1999	XYZ culture redefined
July 1999	Leadership and behaviours review

The managing director's first initiative was to introduce a small-scale Kaizen programme. Kaizen is a Japanese technique for achieving small-scale improvements through teamwork. The managing director saw his Kaizen initiative as delivering four benefits: it would show the organisation that improvements could be achieved on a quick low-cost/no-cost basis; it would promote teamworking; it would give managers confidence to delegate to and empower their staff; and it would allow both staff and managers to acquire new skills. In a traditional company such as XYZ, it was not easy to introduce new ideas and new ways of working, especially where managers might perceive them as a threat. But the managing director made it clear he was committed to this initiative and that it had to work. Over the next few years the Kaizen approach was rolled out throughout the organisation.

The next initiative, in October 1996, was a customer care programme. This was designed to engender a positive view of customers by promoting joint teamworking. In an industry where antagonism between customers and suppliers (contractor and subcontractors) was the order of the day, where settling disputes through the courts was almost a standard practice, it was never going to be easy to promote customer care. The managing director knew, however, that the future of the company depended on working with customers to understand what they wanted and to give it to them. Once again, this initiative was a combination of organisational change and management development; but, much more than the Kaizen initiative, it was also central to changing the culture of the organisation. It began with a few key customers and a few key managers, but such was its perceived success that a year later it was extended to the actual construction sites.

Other initiatives were introduced over the next few years, including Investors in People, and a redesigning of the construction supervisors' role to ensure that the post-holders possessed the skills, competencies and behaviours necessary to work closely with customers and staff under the new regime. Once again, this was designed to achieve a combination of aims, including changes to working practices, the upgrading of managerial competency on the construction sites, and the promotion and development of a more team-based culture in the organisation.

▶

▶
By the end of 1999, the managing director felt the company had made sufficient changes to its behaviour and practices to believe its culture was very different from when he took over in 1996. However, he felt that the new culture needed to be formalised and consolidated. Therefore, he initiated a company-wide review of each manager's leadership abilities and behaviours in order to ensure they were compatible with and promoted the new culture.

Suggested exercises

1   Use the framework for change shown in Figure 14.2 to analyse and identify the form of change or changes described in the XYZ case study.

2   To what extent and why can the changes in how XYZ now operates be seen as a cultural change?

3   Does the XYZ case study represent an example of emergent change, or of an ad hoc approach to culture change?

Test your learning

Short-answer questions

1   What was Kurt Lewin's main contribution to the development of organisational change?

2   How does Bullock and Batten's phases of change model differ from Lewin's three-step model?

3   What are the main advantages of the planned approach?

4   What are the main disadvantages of the planned approach?

5   What are the key components of the emergent approach?

6   How does the emergent approach view the role of organisational culture?

7   What are the main advantages of the emergent approach?

8   What are the main disadvantages of the emergent approach?

9   What are the main arguments for linking organisational culture to organisational performance?

10 What are the arguments for and implications of seeing organisations as 'societies in miniature'?

11 Explain the main components of organisational culture.

12 What are the practical benefits of the framework for change shown in Figure 14.2?

13 What factors should managers take into account, and why, when choosing an approach to change?

14 In what ways might an organisation influence its environment?

Suggested assignments

1   To what extent can it be said that, in today's rapidly changing world, the planned approach to change is no longer relevant?

2   Discuss the proposition that the emergent approach is nothing more than an attempt to provide an intellectual justification for allowing managers to adopt an ad hoc approach to change.

3   Describe and discuss the planned and emergent approaches' view of the role of managers.

4   Critically evaluate the differences between the optimists', pessimists' and realists' approach to culture.

5   What are the main constraints on organisations when deciding on which approach to change to adopt?

6   In what ways can the framework for change, shown in Figure 14.2, be used to increase managerial choice?

Relevant websites

Most of the big management consultancies have websites which contain free articles, reports and other material on organisational change. For example, see www.mckinsey.com and www.ibm.com.

A significant proportion of academic work on organisational change is published in the *Journal of Change Management* – http://www.tandfonline.com/toc/rjcm20/current. If you are a student at a university, there is a good chance that your university subscribes to this journal, in which case you will probably be able to download articles free of charge. A free sample copy can be requested.

Suggested further reading

Full details for all references are given in the list at the end of this book.

1   Bernard Burnes's *Managing Change*, sixth edition (Pearson, 2014), provides a comprehensive review of the development of organisations and organisational change. It expands on this chapter and contains 14 detailed case studies of major change projects.

2   Bernard Burnes and Bill Cooke's 2012 article, 'The past, present and future of organisation development: Taking the long view', *Human Relations*, 65(11), 1395–429, provides a comprehensive review of the history and current state of OD.

3   Thomas G. Cummings and Christopher G. Worley's *Organization Development and Change*, 10th edition (Cengage Learning, 2013) provides a comprehensive guide to planned change and OD.

4   Karl Weick's 'Emergent change as a universal in organisations', in Beer and Nohria (eds), *Breaking the Code of Change* (Harvard Business School Press, 2000) provides a good overview of the case for emergent change.

5   Patrick Dawson's *Reshaping Change: A processsual perspective* (Routledge, 2003) examines, as the title states, the processual perspective on change which, for many people, lies at the core of the arguments for emergent change.

CHAPTER 15

The psychology of dispersed work

LEARNING OBJECTIVES

After studying of this chapter, you should be able to:

1 identify the core features of dispersed working;

2 describe some of the challenges related to dispersed working and technology-mediated communications;

3 be aware of the relevant theories and literature that help to explain these challenges;

4 develop recommendations on how to design more effective dispersed collaborations.

Opening case study

Working from a distance

More and more people are now working remotely, but what happens to team dynamics when colleagues are based hundreds – or even thousands – of miles apart? It's hard enough for people to work as a team when they are based in the same building. But for a virtual team of IT developers at Eli Lilly the challenges were much greater.

The 15-strong team was split across a larger group in the centre-west of Germany (Giessen) and two smaller satellites: one in north-east Germany (Berlin) and one in London, England. An added complication was that team members communicated with each other in English, which for many was a second language.

Small wonder, then, that despite the team's shared professional background there were misunderstandings – especially when the software developers used email to convey complex information to each other. Task coordination also became a problem as new members arrived. With role boundaries not always clearly defined and the added problem of distance, uncertainty arose as to who was supposed to carry out activities such as updating the project database. Some tasks fell in the cracks because team members assumed that someone else was dealing with them.

The team responded to these problems by clarifying and modifying individuals' roles. Team-building events also helped cement working relations between colleagues based at the different locations. As one software developer said, the larger group at Giessen all knew each other well, but communications between those working at different sites could initially be a bit cold and impersonal. The team-building events, which were held around three times a year and included workshops and meetings, as well as fun activities such as go-karting, helped break the ice, and over time led to improved communications between team members. Telephone conversations between those who had met several times began to include the social chat that goes on between people who really are part of the same team. However, there were a number of other problems that needed to be addressed.

The software developers needed to liaise with customers throughout Eli Lilly's European sites. A misunderstanding between a German developer and a Spanish customer illustrates the problem. When the customer took delivery of a product she had ordered, it turned out that there had been confusion about some of the system requirements and their cost. This was partly because of the difficulty of exchanging information about complex technical issues via telephone or email. It didn't help that the customer did not share the developer's technical know-how and that they had been communicating in English, which was neither party's first language.

The IT developers also ran into difficulties when dealing with the UK-based 'server management' team, which was responsible for putting software onto the appropriate server – for example, for testing or development purposes. The development team blamed the server team for causing delays and could not understand why it took them so long to put new software on the right server, while the server team did not understand what the developers' priorities were. Their only communication was via a database, which meant that the development team did not know who was working on their request or what its status was – they just had to wait. One of the developers said that the main problem was that they did not know any of the server team and did not understand how they worked. He pointed out that if the server team had been in the next room, it wouldn't have been such a problem as they could have just gone in and asked them how they were getting on with the work.

▶

▶   Our interviews with people in 32 different organisations who were involved in dispersed working suggest that the experience of the Eli Lilly team is typical of the growing number of people who are now collaborating with remote colleagues.

Some of these colleagues may work from home, from multiple locations, such as their cars or client offices, while others may work in a traditional office, but in a different country or region. The flexibility of these arrangements is often hailed as a good thing as it means that people are no longer constrained by where they live. Working with remote colleagues can bring diverse expertise and different local knowledge bases together, and this can have a positive impact on innovation and team effectiveness. However, lack of a common context can also create tensions.

When people work in the same place they can often get away with less than best practice, because there is a shared social system to paper over any cracks. Such colleagues usually understand each other because they come from the same or similar organisational and national backgrounds. Face-to-face communication, whether in meetings or informal corridor chats, enables them to check whether they have understood each other and put right any misunderstandings before they cause too much damage.

The organisations we studied generally agreed that the human and organisational aspects of dispersed teamworking hampered effectiveness more than any inadequacies with the technology used to keep remote workers in touch with each other.

This makes it doubly important to stick to good practice and adopt a structured and planned approach to dispersed working. The dispersed nature of the work and reliance on communications technologies exacerbates many of the problems that can occur in any working environment. Those who manage dispersed teams therefore need to be aware of these issues and make sure they are prepared to deal with them.

Source: Adapted from Carolyn Axtell, Jo Wheeler, Malcolm Patterson and Anna Leach (now Meachin), 'From a distance', *People Management*, 25 March 2004, pp. 39–40.

Suggested exercises

As you study this chapter, consider the following issues:

1   How might this organisation (and others) enhance the effectiveness of their dispersed teams?

2   What interventions might help to tackle the two specific problems identified in this case study?

3   Now consider some topics outside of this chapter in your answer. For example, how might selection and training be used to address some of the issues raised by this case study?

Introduction

Recent developments in information and communication technologies have transformed the way we work and play. Since the Internet was privatised and opened for commercial use in the early 1990s it has become integral to the way we live and work, providing opportunities for (among other things) finding information, buying products, downloading music and communicating with others (Okin, 2005). Personal computers (PCs) are almost ubiquitous in the workplace, and technologies are becoming increasingly mobile with tablet PCs and smartphones becoming ever more popular and laptops getting smaller and lighter. These mobile technologies allow employees more flexibility over the location in which they work and offer the potential to be contacted and to conduct work in a range of places such as cafés, trains, hotel rooms or at home. E-mail has also transformed the way we work, allowing written communication and attached documents to be delivered to the other side of the world about as quickly as they can be delivered to the neighbouring desk. Advances in tele-conferencing and video-conferencing enable group meetings to occur, with people attending from different locations without having to travel.

Such advances in technology mean that employees no longer have to be located at the main company office, or be in the same location as their colleagues. When coupled with the increase in globalisation, this means that more and more collaborative work is being done at a distance (dispersed collaboration) via communications technologies (Duarte and Snyder, 2001). Most organisations now use some form of dispersed working. A whole range of work activities are conducted in this way from software development and aircraft design to marketing and management. Such work may cross time zones, national borders and different organisations. As such, established theories relating to topics such as team-work, work design, employee stress and leadership may need to be re-evaluated in this new context. Rather than scatter the discussion of these important topics throughout the text, we have chosen to explore these issues in some depth in this single chapter.

In the following sections we consider dispersed collaboration in more detail. First, we will consider the core features of dispersed collaborations, and look at how they impact upon the work that employees do, their well-being and the interactions that employees have with each other. Later in this chapter, we examine what actions need to be taken with regard to setting up and designing these ways of working.

Core features of dispersed collaborations

Dispersion

The defining feature of a dispersed collaboration is that colleagues are split across different locations. These locations may be few or many in number, separated by only a few, or a few thousand, miles. While some people may have fellow collaborators available at their own loca-tion, others may not. Thus, different collaborations may have different levels of dispersion: this has major implications for communications and their functioning in relation to their reliance on technology, the time zones and national (and cultural) boundaries they cross.

Technology-mediated communication

Most immediately, the obvious problem about dispersion is that at least some colleagues are not working together face to face and so have to collaborate and interact via communica-tions technologies (such as telephone, e-mail, instant messaging, teleconferencing). While co-located teams also use technologies such as e-mail to communicate with each other, the key difference when colleagues are located at a distance is the increased reliance on these technologies. There is less opportunity for face-to-face interaction or chance meetings at the water cooler when colleagues are distributed far and wide, and so technology-mediated communication becomes the dominant method of interaction.

Theoretical perspectives on technology mediation

A key concern when thinking about technology-mediated communications is that these technologies may be limited in their ability to convey certain types of information. This is the view taken by theories that place emphasis on the filtering out of social cues in such technologies. For instance, media richness theory (Daft and Lengel, 1986) proposes that there are objective characteristics of communications media which determine their ability to carry 'rich' information (i.e. that which contains social, non-verbal and feedback cues) and thus determine the suitability of those media for certain tasks. For instance, text-based communications like e-mail might be considered a relatively 'lean' medium: recipients of the message do not have the benefit of hearing the sender's voice-tone or seeing their facial expressions to help them understand the message. Moreover, there is typically a long gap between delivering a message and receiving feedback. The telephone, however, is relatively 'rich' as a communication medium as voice-tone, hesitation and other auditory cues can be transmitted and these can be immediately heard and responded to by the receiver (thus providing fast feedback). Face-to-face communication is considered the richest due to the high level of visual and auditory cues available.

The lack of social cues in 'lean media' can be problematic for the development of mutual understanding and good relations. Sproull and Kiesler's (1986) 'lack of social context cues' hypothesis proposes a possible mechanism for this and argues that the lack of social cues available in text-based media increases participant anonymity. They argue that the result is that participants pay less attention to themselves and others, resulting in a state of 'deindividuation'. The concept of deindividuation is argued to occur because in text-based electronic communications 'individuating' cues (those cues which give everyone a distinctive character, such as tone of voice, appearance, pace of speech, expression of emotion etc.) are greatly reduced, rendering the participants relatively anonymous. This state is characterised by feeling less embarrassed or self-conscious as well as more impersonal and task-focused. People become less inhibited, which can result in reduced politeness and increased hostility and intolerance (e.g. an employee typing something in an e-mail that they would not say to the recipient face to face or over the telephone). As a result of this, relationship development can be impeded.

Key learning point

Some communications media have the capacity to deliver more social cues than others, with face-to-face communication having the richest array of cues available, with text-based media being lean in comparison.

While some research supports these theories, media richness and lack of social context cues approaches have been criticised for: (i) being too technologically deterministic; (ii) not considering the impact of the many cues remaining in the media; (iii) not considering the possibilities of people adapting to the technology and adapting the technology to their needs. For instance, channel expansion theory (Carlson and Zmud, 1999) proposes that even a 'lean', text-based message can be perceived as 'richer' if the people using it have experience and are familiar with (i) the communications channel/technology; (ii) the topic in the message; (iii) the organisational context; and (iv) the communication partner. For example, we might not be offended by a short e-mail message if we know the sender is busy and has a habit of writing brief messages regardless of the length of the message you have sent them.

In a similar vein, Joseph Walther (1992) proposed the social information processing (SIP) hypothesis, which states that despite there being less social information available via text-based media like e-mail, users adapt to using the social information that is available (although processing these cues is slower than face-to-face interaction). Indeed, in support of this, Walther and colleagues have found that with the social cues that are available in text-based media (such as time taken to receive a response, the style or content of the message), strong relationships can develop but they take longer to grow (e.g. Walther, 1993). The impersonal and task-focused communications suggested by the lack of social context cues hypothesis might therefore only be expected in very short term computer-mediated collaborations.

However, other research has also found that even very early on in the communication process, few differences are found between relations in some face-to-face and computer-mediated groups (e.g. Walther and Burgoon, 1992). It also appears that relations can sometimes be more positive when computer mediated than when face to face (Walther, 1995). One reason for this might be that if people expect there to be lots of future interaction right from the start, communication is likely to become positive and stimulate close working collaborations almost immediately (Walther, 1994).

Another explanation for these sorts of effects is offered by the social identification/deindividuation (SIDE) model (Lea and Spears, 1992; Spears and Lea, 1994). Earlier we examined the idea that deindividuation depersonalises communication. However, according to SIDE, deindividuation results in attention being shifted away from a focus on individual differences and towards a group identity. The limited cues that are available in the communications media (such as the department where the sender of the e-mail works) take on relatively greater importance such that stereotypical impressions of communication partners are developed. A common group identity may be inferred from these impressions which can promote immediate attraction (e.g. if you know that the sender of an e-mail works with people that you know and like then your attitudes towards those people may influence your view of the individual sender).

Walther also extended his SIP theory to develop the 'hyperpersonal perspective' (Walther, 1996) to take account of the more intense relationships that can develop via communications technology. Again, it is argued that the limited cues available electronically (which may be selectively revealed by the communication partners for purposes of impression management) take on relatively greater importance. For instance, if a remote colleague sends a speedy response to an initial e-mail, they might create the impression of being efficient and responsive. These cues may contribute disproportionately to impressions of that remote colleague in the absence of any evidence to the contrary (especially when a long-term relationship is expected and there is a shared social identity). As a result, impressions of others can become exaggerated and 'idealised'. This effect, however, may not be very stable. For instance, one study of student teams (Walther et al., 2001) found that after hyperpersonal relations had developed via communications technology, showing photographs of team members reduced affection and affiliation within the team, as they revealed individual difference information that disrupted group identity. Thus, while relations developed exclusively across communications technology may be very positive at first, they are based on limited (and perhaps biased) information. This means that they may be rather fragile in nature.

Key learning point

Although there are fewer social cues available in text-based communications media like e-mail, this does not necessarily result in less positive social relations. However, these relations may be more unrealistic and fragile.

Relationship and performance outcomes

These technology characteristics, along with the dispersion of team members, can have a profound impact on the relationship and performance outcomes of dispersed collaborations. For instance, as a result of the lack of social cues it can take longer to develop trust with distant colleagues. Trust has been highlighted as an important factor in dispersed teams, and has been found to be related to various team outcomes such as team cohesion and task efficiency. Low trust, on the other hand, is often associated with excessive monitoring, duplication of effort and less willingness to share knowledge. Perhaps due to the difficulties of developing social relations at a distance, some studies have found that trust development is related to task accomplishment more than to social relationships (see Mitchell and Zigurs' 2009 review). So, if team members produce good work and stick to deadlines this can enhance task-related trust, even if more affective trust, based on social ties, is harder to develop. Dispersed teams have also been found to experience more conflict, particularly task conflict involving different and conflicting opinions about ways of completing the task. However, a review of the literature suggests that such task conflict is less evident in long-term teams within organisations than in short-term teams in experimental studies (Ortiz de Guinea et al., 2012).

Sharing knowledge and making decisions when colleagues are dispersed can also be a challenge. Knowledge-sharing difficulties seem to persist even in longer-term teams – although they are worse in teams that are only working together for a limited period (Ortiz de Guinea et al., 2012). Moreover, as a result of having less information about remote colleagues, individuals may not be aware of the diversity of knowledge within the team unless it is explicitly identified and communicated. Decision-making via text-based media is likely to be inefficient and less than optimal due to the time it takes to read, type and send messages. As a result, issues might not be discussed fully and decisions could be made based on less than full information. Decisions can also be prone to bias when the identity and status of other contributors is known. Evidence suggests a reliance on text-based media results in lower decision-making effectiveness unless there is unlimited time and anonymous contributions (see Baltes et al., 2002, for a review).

The potential for misunderstandings is also an important issue to consider as a result of the lack of social cues and also because of the different norms, values and knowledge bases of the different members in a diverse team. In this situation, dispersed colleagues may not have a common understanding or shared language in relation to their task. Therefore colleagues may interpret particular messages using different knowledge bases and may erroneously assume they have understood them the same way (Krauss and Fussell, 1990). For example, one employee may receive an e-mail about last month's sales figures and view it as an 'information update', while another employee might see it as positive (or negative) feedback from management. Moreover, given the lack of feedback cues and false assumptions made, misunderstandings can take some time to come to light.

Of course, there are positive outcomes related to dispersed work, which suggests that people can indeed adapt well to this way of working. For instance, telework (where employees are working away from the main office – usually from home) has been found to be related to higher job satisfaction, performance ratings and lower work–family conflict (Gajendran and Harrison, 2007). Moreover, it has been argued that people have found ways to cope with the lack of social cues in text-based technologies, such as by using emoticons and by choosing different media for different types of messages (Derks et al., 2008).

However, there does seem to be some variation in the findings which suggests that outcomes may depend on a range of moderating factors such as the nature of the task, the organisational context or culture, the duration of the collaboration, familiarity between participants and the extent of dispersion/reliance on communications technologies. In relation to the level of dispersion, it is certainly unusual to have a team that is completely distributed (with every member at a different location, and 100 per cent technology-mediated communication) and it is also unusual these days to have a team that is 100 per cent face to face. Most collaborations are likely to sit somewhere on a continuum between these two extremes. Some studies suggest that there might be an optimum level for dispersed work, where higher levels of reliance on communications technologies are associated with lower team effectiveness (e.g. Gibson and Gibbs, 2006; Schweitzer and Duxbury, 2010). Another study suggests a tipping point where having to rely on computer-mediated technology for more than 90 per cent of the team's activities is detrimental for team outcomes (Johnson et al., 2009). When considering the outcomes of teleworking from home, studies suggest that approximately two to two and a half days a week is about optimum for teleworker satisfaction while also allowing teleworkers to maintain social relations with colleagues (Gajendran and Harrison, 2007; Golden, 2006; Golden and Veiga, 2005). So it may be that the main challenges arise at higher levels of dispersion and reliance on communications technologies.

On the other hand, longer-term or established teams in organisations may have fewer problems with dispersed working, especially if familiarity among team members is already high. Assudini (2011) found within ongoing dispersed teams in a US-based marketing company that familiarity through prior working relationships determined the perceived absence of mutual knowledge gaps in the teams. She argues that familiarity with the team members and the task creates redundant knowledge structures, which have the potential to bridge gaps between dispersed team members. She concludes that dispersion itself is not the key factor in determining outcomes, but rather it is about familiarity. The findings of this research lend support to theories and approaches that focus on the role of human adaptation to dispersed work.

Key learning point

The outcomes of dispersed collaborations are likely to depend on a range of moderating factors, in particular: the type of task, the context in which the work is taking place, the duration of the collaboration, the familiarity between participants, as well as the extent of dispersion/reliance on communications technologies.

Well-being outcomes

As mentioned previously, the lack of social cues and information about distant others can result in a state of deindividuation characterised by less inhibited, more aggressive online interactions. These unpleasant interactions, if they continue in the long term, can have a negative impact on an employee's well-being. In a study that compared work-based bullying both online and offline (face to face), it was found that the effect of 'cyber-bullying' had a more severe impact on employee satisfaction and well-being (Best and Coyne, 2010). Cyber-bullying is thought to have this stronger effect because with traditional, face-to-face bullying, there is relief and escape when one leave's the office. Cyber-bullying can follow the victim to their home computer and to almost anywhere on their mobile technologies. There is also the chance of it being repeated (through repeat viewings). The perpetual nature of cyber-bullying can result in feelings of powerlessness and helplessness, which in turn have negative consequences for well-being.

E-mail overload is another source of demands to which dispersed workers might be susceptible. Rennecker and Derks (2013) propose that e-mail overload consists of *information overload* (when processing demands of information received exceeds information-processing capacity); *work overload* (when volume of messages requiring response exceeds time available to do so); and *social overload* (from the diversity of e-mail interactions that exceed personal interaction capacity). Such overload can result in inefficiency, confusion and stress. Interruptions from incoming e-mails can add to productivity losses by distracting the worker from the focal task. Of course, this demand is also going to be evident in those who do not practise dispersed working, but when most of an individual's communication is done via technology this effect may be even more pronounced.

Another way that dispersed working can impact on employee well-being is via its impact on work–life balance. A good thing about modern communications technologies is that they can provide a lot of flexibility. This flexibility can give people the ability to work at a location that suits them and depending on the hours that an employee needs to be available, can also give them the flexibility to work at a time that suits their other commitments. So, if a busy parent needs to pick children up from school and then carry on working at home when the children have gone to bed, they can do that. Working from home can enable employees to deal with household issues (such as waiting for a delivery, hanging the washing out to dry during their lunch break) while at the same time having a productive work day away from office interruptions. This ability to integrate home and work can have a positive effect on work–life balance. When employees feel in control of where, when and how they work, this can have a positive effect on their well-being (Kossek et al., 2006).

Point of integration

Work–life balance and bullying are well-established sources of work-related stress (Chapter 10), but much of the work in this area focuses on traditional work environments rather than dispersed working.

Key debate

Flexibility or extended demands?

Does the flexibility offered by dispersed working come at a cost? Being contactable anytime, anywhere can lead to excessive work hours and the lack of ability to psychologically detach and recover from work. Organisational pressures and norms can play a role here as expectations of continual availability can make employees feel compelled to respond to e-mails sent outside of normal work hours. This can lead to feelings of reduced control and stress. In a diary study of smartphone users, Derks and Bakker (2014) found that intensive smartphone use outside of normal working hours was related to higher work–family interference (in other words, work demands interfering with family time) on a daily basis. In turn, this was related to higher levels of burnout. Furthermore, there was a stronger relationship between work–home interference and exhaustion for intensive smartphone users compared to less intensive users. This might be because intensive smartphone use extends the exposure to work demands and thus prevents adequate recovery from work. Moreover, in this particular study, the sample were provided with smartphones by their organisation, which may have given them a stronger sense of obligation to remain available and a reduced sense of control, which could have heightened the negative impact on well-being.

Key learning point

Although there are positive effects related to the flexibility and pervasiveness of modern communications technologies, these advantages can also have a downside for well-being in relation to overload and intrusion into non-work time.

Designing for dispersion

As a result of the issues described above, there is a need to consider how dispersed collaborations should be designed and implemented. Particular attention needs to be paid to the human and organisational issues, as it is these, rather than the technology itself, that tend to be the most difficult to deal with. However, the characteristics of the technology (i.e. limited cues) can exacerbate these problems. Some of the important considerations in planning for a dispersed team are outlined below (and summarised in Figure 15.1).

Preparation

In line with the design of any product, spending time on the preparation stages before implementation is crucial. It is particularly important to spend time thinking about and preparing for the human and organisational implications and not just the technology. There needs to be a clear identification of a mission (i.e. what the collaborators are going to do) and how they are going to do it: a clearly understood statement of direction is required (Duarte and Snyder, 2001).

Point of integration

The processes involved in designing dispersed work share some common ground with the processes that need to be followed in any other work environment (see Chapters 7, 8 and 10). But there are some important differences that are highlighted in this section.

Some forethought is also required on how the task will be completed and the context in which it will be done (its functional/organisational/national context). Contextual issues

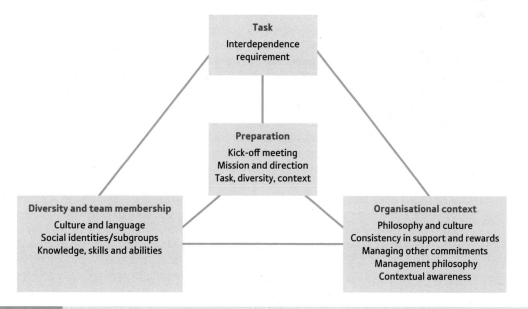

| Figure 15.1 | Designing for dispersion |

concern the membership of the collaboration (and its diversity) as well as the organisational processes and structures (such as organisational philosophy, reward structures, management style). It is often advised that dispersed teams try to have an initial face-to-face kick-off meeting to develop a shared vision, a shared understanding of the task and agreed methods for working. Such meetings can also help to develop relationships between distant collaborators and a greater awareness of what is involved in dispersed working. Being aware of the challenges of dispersed work and preparing for these help to alleviate problems later on. Consideration of the interaction between these factors is also advised in preparations (e.g. how the diversity of the team will have implications for how the task is managed). The following sections therefore outline the task, membership and contextual issues that need to be considered in the design of dispersed collaborations.

Key learning point

When designing a dispersed collaboration, preparation is key. The human and organisational issues are particularly important: just planning the technology alone is likely to lead to failure.

The task

The type of task is likely to influence the ease with which the dispersed colleagues can conduct their work and so should be considered within the design of a dispersed collaboration. Of particular concern for dispersed teams is the extent to which close collaboration between distant members is necessary. Tasks vary in terms of the level of interdependence required (the extent to which co-workers rely on each other's skills and outputs to complete the task) and information requirements (e.g. cognitive, behavioural or emotional). Media richness and lack of social context cues approaches suggest that complex tasks that require a high level of information exchange, coordinated effort, consensus, negotiation, ambiguity or emotion are not suitable for 'leaner' technologies such as e-mail: instead they might require richer media (preferably face to face). Simple, routine, independent and non-emotive tasks are considered to be suited to less rich technologies (e.g. Riopelle et al., 2003). This line of reasoning has led many commentators to advocate that dispersed collaborations should be designed for independence (working within rather than across locations) and that where interdependence cannot be avoided, then face-to-face meetings should be encouraged (e.g. Eppinger, 2001).

The problem with this line of reasoning is that such a practice might not be possible if the skills of distant colleagues are required to complete the task. Moreover, such division can enhance subgroup formation and conflict because it removes some of the ties across locations (see the next section on diversity). Interdependence and connectivity across locations might help to increase cohesion and trust within the team, particularly in the early stages of the task. Consistent with this idea, Hertel and colleagues (2004) found in a field study of dispersed teams that task interdependence was strongly related to team effectiveness in the first year of the team's life. However, once the team was established task interdependence had little impact on effectiveness. This finding suggests that it might be worth tolerating the initial process and coordination losses of high interdependence because it allows good relations to develop in the group. Interdependence can then be reduced once solid relations have developed.

It might also be the case that the team will adapt to using less rich communications media, particularly once a common language and understanding have been developed. For instance, a study of rocket engine design engineers found that at least some ambiguous tasks (such as clarifying and changing project objectives or specifications, learning about unfamiliar parts of the concept, and understanding design concerns of other team members) could be conducted via collaborative technology rather than face to face (Majchrzak et al., 2000). This was thought to be due to the common language and understanding that had been developed in earlier face-to-face meetings. The existence of a common language and understanding might mean that if interdependence is used in a mature dispersed collaboration, process losses might be less of a problem (at least for some types of task). Thus, in terms of task design for dispersed collaborations, it might be prudent to design tasks that encourage initial interdependence, but this can be relaxed later for tasks that do not adapt well to the less rich media.

Key learning point

There is a tension between designing for 'interdependent' work and designing for 'independent' work. Interdependent work can help to develop relations at a distance and people may adapt to using the leaner media. However, designing for independent work can help to reduce the process and coordination losses that occur when collaborating at a distance.

Diversity and team membership

One of the reasons organisations employ dispersed collaborations is to take advantage of expertise from different functions, organisations and countries. This means that such collaborations may be quite diverse. Thus, a further complication for dispersed collaborations is the addition of 'culture': the different values, assumptions and expectations that guide human behaviour. The shared values and beliefs of a culture are expressed in their norms, which shape the attitudes, behaviours and expectations about what is appropriate behaviour.

Point of integration

Dispersed working means that interactions are very likely to occur between people from different organisational and national cultures. The concept of a single, or homogenous culture (see Chapter 14) might not fit well with the reality of dispersed working.

In a dispersed team there may be national cultural differences between colleagues as well as differences in organisational culture and functional/professional culture which will affect the norms they operate under. These differences need to be understood and dealt with if the collaborators are to work together successfully (Duarte and Snyder, 2001). The different members of the collaboration may have different expectations and ways of doing things that are not compatible across the group. Moreover, there may be differences in language (not just between national languages but different uses of language across professions and even organisations). Therefore, the different cultural and language perspectives may lead those in the collaboration to make different assumptions and develop different understandings about the same information. Such variation could lead to norm violations where one group is surprised or annoyed by the behaviour of another (see Moser and Axtell, 2013 for a review on norms in dispersed work).

Diversity can affect team relations because it is harder to develop a shared social identity if other collaborators in the group are considered to be different (cf. Tajfel, 1981). Of relevance to dispersed teams is that location may form the basis of social identities since those at the same site are likely to share more attributes (e.g. nationality, language, organisational culture) with each other than with team members at other locations. This can lead to the development of dividing lines or 'faultlines' (cf. Lau and Murnighan, 1998) between locations splitting them into subgroups, resulting in greater conflict and lower trust between subgroups. Such processes are likely to result in performance losses, especially when the differences between the locations are greater. Polzer and colleagues (2006) found experimental support for the negative impact of these faultlines, with the effects being strongest when there were two subgroups of equal size and when there was national homogeneity within each subgroup. The effect was weakest when teams were fully dispersed (with each person at a different location) because subgroups could not form on the basis of shared location. In another experimental study, the perception of faultlines was found to be reduced by using personal weblogs to share information about the leisure activities of team members because this information facilitated social attraction (Chiu and Staples, 2013). This, in turn, also promoted greater exchange, discussion, integration of task-relevant information and better decision-process quality. Therefore, sharing personal information is likely to help reduce subgroup formation and enhance performance as long as the information shared is attractive to the other team members.

Overall, we might conclude that while there are advantages to having diverse knowledge available, the diversity associated with dispersion can lead to process problems as a result of subgroup formation and different norms, values and expectations. This has implications for the skills requirements of dispersed team members. While it is obviously important to ensure that the relevant professional, task-work- and teamwork-related knowledge, skills and abilities are held among team members, dispersed team members also require good 'tele-cooperation' skills which include interpersonal trust, persistence, self-management, creativity and intercultural skills (see Hertel et al., 2006, and Chapter 11).

Point of integration

The skills needed to work well in a dispersed team overlap somewhat with the skills required to work effectively in other types of teams (see Chapter 11). There are also some skills that are particularly important in dispersed working.

Thus, the selection of dispersed colleagues should not only focus on their technical expertise and skills but also on their ability to communicate and work within a multidisciplinary and multicultural environment. Where possible these collaborations should also be designed so that they are not split into distinct locational subgroups. In addition, efforts should be made to build relations across the potential faultlines (e.g. by highlighting and focusing on similarities across locations, promoting the use of weblogs to share information about each other and by maintaining a high level of communication across different sites).

Key learning point

Distant colleagues may be thought of as 'different', which might lead to subgroup formation. This can be problematic for collaborative relationships and so efforts need to be made to build strong relationships across locations and select members with strong 'tele-cooperation' skills.

Organisational context

The organisational structure(s) and processes within which the dispersed collaboration is located is also likely to have a profound impact on team functioning. For instance, Rennecker (2002) found that the local rhythms, relationships, rules, politics and resources at the different locations affected the contributions that members in each location made to the team.

First, the general organisational philosophy and culture is likely to have an impact on the success of the team. For instance, organisations that focus on technology rather than people may find their dispersed collaborations are less successful (Cramton and Webber, 2005). This is because their collaborations are likely to be structured around the technological systems rather than the social systems: yet what is required for success is *joint* optimisation of the technical and social systems (cf. socio-technical theory, Cherns, 1976). Moreover, people and organisational skills might be overlooked in a technically orientated organisational environment but these skills are particularly crucial to the success of dispersed collaborations (Kirkman et al., 2002).

Another way in which organisational culture can have an impact on dispersed workers is via the organisational norms and expectations about availability and responsiveness. In some organisations, employees feel increasingly obliged to respond immediately to work-related messages, irrespective of time of day. This has been especially so since the advent of mobile technologies like the smartphone, with smartphone users reporting increased work pressure and inability to 'switch off' from work (Jarvenpaa and Lang, 2005). However, having a personal **boundary management** strategy that favours the separation of work and family has been found to be related to well-being among teleworkers (Kossek et al., 2006). Thus, maintaining this boundary and having an organisation that supports this strategy is likely to be increasingly important given the prevalence of mobile digital technologies. Allowing employees to have control over where, when and how they work can enhance well-being, but also being able to psychologically detach and relax after work hours is an important process which allows recovery and promotes well-being. Overall, then, it is important to ensure that the organisational philosophy, culture and norms are suitable for dispersed work and that expectations are reasonable.

Second, there is a need to ensure consistency across locations in terms of reward structures, availability of communications technologies and managerial support. For instance, differences in access to technology and communication transmission speeds were found to have a detrimental impact on dispersed student team functioning in a study by Cramton (2001). These differences in access led to feelings of isolation and being 'out of synch' with the rest of the team (see the Closing case study for more detail). Moreover, if reward structures are different at different locations (which might be more likely when collaborating across organisational boundaries) then this may give rise to feelings of inequality. In dispersed collaborations, team-based incentives and rewards might be appropriate for encouraging cooperation. In contrast, individual skill-based rewards might help to stimulate the development of the necessary skills for working at a distance (Lawler, 2003). Indeed, some support has been found for the effectiveness of team-based recognition in dispersed collaborations (Hertel et al., 2004).

Third, another concern is how obligations towards the dispersed collaboration will coincide with other commitments within the organisation. For instance, there may be conflicts between commitments to the local site and commitments to distant colleagues: these conflicts can have a large impact on employee contributions to the dispersed collaboration (Axtell et al., 2004a). When collaborations cross multiple organisational units, functional groups or even different organisations these challenges may become more severe. In particular, being a member of multiple teams may be particularly challenging due to the increased demands on team members' attention. A study in a large multinational company found a positive effect of multiple team membership on a team's performance, but this effect was attenuated by high levels of dispersion (Cummings and Haas, 2012). So while there was a positive effect of having these experienced members on the team (who bring their insights and learning from other projects) there seems to be a point where the *attention costs* of having members spread across multiple locations and multiple teams outweighs the benefits. Thus, managers need to think carefully about what level of multiple team membership is optimal for the individuals and the tasks they are conducting. Moreover, good boundary management skills are required to maintain organisational support and resources across multiple organisational and team boundaries (Hertel et al., 2005).

Fourth, there are different ways that the collaboration could be managed. Because they cannot see their dispersed subordinates, managers might try to control them by closely monitoring (e.g. using electronic performance data). This type of activity might be particularly evident when dispersed colleagues are conducting relatively routine tasks and in industries that already monitor employees (call centres are one such example – see Valsecchi, 2006). However, the types of behaviours that tend to be observed electronically are rather limited (e.g. log-on/log-off, length of call, work rate) and such monitoring can be quite stressful for the employees (Hertel et al., 2005). In the absence of such monitoring capabilities, managers might instead attempt to control employees through formal coordination mechanisms such as detailed project plans, deadlines, formal handover points and clear task specifications (Hinds and Bailey, 2003).

Point of integration

Much of the research on leadership is focused on face-to-face interaction (Chapter 12). In dispersed working there are different challenges for leaders, and these may influence their choice of leadership behaviours.

An alternative approach is to manage by trust rather than control. This type of approach emphasises the commitment of employees and allows them the autonomy to self-manage and regulate their own actions (Bell and Kozlowski, 2002). The task of management then becomes one of (participatively) setting goals and monitoring outcomes rather than processes. This type of management philosophy was examined by Hertel et al. (2004) who found a relationship between team perceptions of quality of goal-setting and managers' ratings of dispersed team effectiveness (good-quality goal-setting being linked to team effectiveness). Thus, trust and control may not be mutually exclusive philosophies. Many studies have found that having formal team controls (such as goal-setting and deadlines) in place can help to increase trust because such measures reduce uncertainty (e.g. Crisp and Jarvenpaa, 2000; Walther and Bunz, 2005). Thus it may be necessary to find a balance between trust and control when managing dispersed collaborations (Axtell et al., 2004a).

Finally, an important issue in dispersed collaborations is that of 'contextual awareness', i.e. an awareness of the organisational context and situation that the distant colleague is in. People are generally very aware of the situation they themselves are in and the influence that this has on their own behaviour, but tend to underestimate the influence of the situation on other people's behaviour. When judging the cause of another person's actions people tend to overestimate the influence that the other person's disposition has on their behaviour. This is called 'the fundamental attribution error' (Ross, 1977). In part, this is due to the lack of awareness of the situation the other person is in: this effect is likely to be exacerbated in dispersed teams where the other person (and their situation) is at a distance and not visible or readily accessible (Cramton, 2002). Without this contextual awareness the few cues available via communications technologies are likely to be the only ones that are used when making attributions about remote colleagues (e.g. that they did not reply to an e-mail). Therefore this behaviour may be attributed to them being lazy or rude (Cramton, 2001). A dispositional attribution is made that fails to consider the situation the remote person is in (e.g. that they are extremely busy or they did not receive the message because their technology is not working). Naturally, such negative attributions can cause relational problems.

However, Cramton and her colleagues have found that ensuring that communication partners are aware of the other person's situation can reduce these attribution errors (Cramton et al., 2007). Also situational explanations can help repair relations after transgressions have occurred (such as a team member missing a deadline) if accompanied with expressions of respect and concern about the impact of this behaviour on other members (Cramton and Wilson, 2002). This research shows how important it is that dispersed collaborators learn about each other's contexts and are aware of the situation their dispersed colleagues are in. Mechanisms for doing this might include arranging visits to each other's locations, having online biographies and weblogs about team members which include information on their work–life context and ensuring that contextual issues are mentioned in other communications.

Key learning point

It is important not to forget the organisational context in which the dispersed collaboration is going to operate when setting up and designing it. Features such as the culture, reward structures, other organisational obligations, management philosophy and level of awareness of distant colleague's organisational contexts are all likely to have an impact on success.

Summary

More and more people are working remotely as a result of increased globalisation and advances in communications technologies. Certain challenges arise for colleagues working in this way, such as the variation in the ability of different communications technologies to transmit certain 'rich' information, which can hamper relationship formation. However, people may adapt to using such media and the expectation of future communications, familiarity with team members and development of common group identities can help to override the negative impacts of leaner media. Other challenges include the impact on well-being from the inability to detach and recovery from work when using mobile technologies or working from home. When setting up such collaborations choices need to be made about whether colleagues work interdependently across sites or independently (within site) and how to manage the diversity in the team and the organisational context in which the collaborators work. Preparation is key when designing such collaborations. Ignoring the human and social aspects and just focusing on the technical issues is bound to lead to failure.

Closing case study

The importance of 'mutual knowledge'

Catherine Cramton (2001) studied a set of 13 internationally dispersed student project teams. Each team had six members with two pairs of students at two different US universities and one pair at a university located either in Canada, Australia or Portugal. Some of the students who participated were international exchange students and so there was a variety of nationalities involved. The project spanned a seven-week period.

Cramton found that failures of mutual knowledge were the most important problem faced by the teams. She identified:

1 Failure to communicate and retain contextual information about distant colleagues, for example the timing of the spring break was different at different universities, so some team members disappeared without warning, while their distant colleagues were working on things and requiring their input.

2 Unevenly distributed information, for example sometimes an e-mail or information was sent to only part of the team, which led to different perspectives on the task developing at the different locations.

3 Differences in speed of access to information, for example some students had 24-hour access to e-mail whereas others only had access when at their university. When using chat facilities, it was also noted that the Australian members seemed to be lagging behind in the discussion such that the exchanges between the American students kept being interrupted by messages from the Australians which referred to subjects from which they had already moved on. This caused tension and frustration within the team as the Australians' contributions were seemingly ignored because they were 'out of synch' with the rest of the team.

4 Difficulty communicating and understanding the salience of information, for example when writing an e-mail students tended to assume that what was salient to them in the message would be salient to others (students would differ in which topics they thought were most prominent).

5 Difficulty interpreting the meaning of silence – silence could mean all sorts of things from agreement, disagreement, indifference, away for a few days, too busy to respond, having technical problems, didn't realise a response was required etc.

These difficulties tended to result in negative 'dispositional' attributions about remote colleagues (e.g. that they were lazy, aggressive or rude) and had a negative impact on relationships and team functioning.

Suggested exercises

1 What does Catherine Cramton's research tell us about how dispersed collaborations should be designed and managed within organisations?

2 Consider the setting for, and the participants in, this research. To what extent can we use the findings to provide guidance to commercial organisations? Which findings do you think might be most likely to transfer to organisations, and which might not?

Test your learning

Short-answer questions

1 Describe the different theoretical viewpoints regarding the impact of technology-mediated communications on dispersed working.
2 What factors contribute to relationship outcomes in dispersed collaborations?
3 What are the key areas to focus on when designing for dispersion?

Suggested assignments

1 The CEO of a large multinational organisation tells you he has ensured he has the most up-to-date technology for collaboration across the different sites of his organisation. He feels that as long as the technology is right, the human and organisational factors will not be a problem. Drawing on the relevant literature in this area, write a report that will convince this CEO that these human and organisational factors are important and should be considered.
2 A team of employees is made up of people who work in different parts of the same building. Because of a company restructuring, half of the team members move out of the building to a new site 50 kilometres away. The team of employees still work together on the same set of tasks. What are the problems that might occur during this change? What could be done to prevent these problems from happening or to minimise their impact?
3 What can psychological theory and research tell us about the relationship, performance and well-being challenges of dispersed collaborations?

Relevant website

Virtual Teams: teams developed and/or operated over the Internet/Web: http://www.managementhelp.org/grp_skll/virtual/virtual.htm

Suggested further reading

Full details for all references are given in the list at the end of this book.

The four texts listed here all provide more detailed reviews of the issues discussed in this chapter. Virtual working raises a variety of issues in addition to the study of remote working. Therefore reading the Hislop et al. reference would be a good starting point, followed by one of the two other works cited.

1 Axtell et al. (2004a) 'Virtual teams: collaborating across distance'.
2 Derks and Bakker (eds) (2013) *The Psychology of Digital Media at Work* (Psychology Press).
3 Hertel et al. (2005) 'Managing virtual teams: A review of current empirical research'.
4 Hislop et al. (2008) 'The challenge of remote working'.

GLOSSARY OF TERMS

Action research   A form of research that concentrates on solving practical problems in collaboration with the people and organisations experiencing them. For example in organisational change this is an iterative process aimed at improving organisational performance, and it involves three equal parties acting in concert: the organisation, its employees and a change agent.

Adjustment   The extent and ways in which a person is able to function effectively and happily in their environment.

Advanced manufacturing technology   Computer-controlled machinery that can perform sophisticated production activities once appropriately programmed.

Agreeableness   A positive orientation towards others, sympathetic, eager to help – preferring collaboration to conflict.

Alarm reaction   When an individual's defence mechanisms become active.

Alienation   A state of being where a person does not feel that they are in touch with their true self, nor do they experience fulfilling relationships with others.

Alternative hypothesis   The hypothesis that is the alternative to the null hypothesis. The alternative hypothesis essentially proposes that 'something is going on' in the data. That is, that two or more groups of people do differ on a psychological variable, or that two or more variables are correlated with each other. Also called the experimental hypothesis.

Analysis of variance   A statistical technique used to test whether two or more samples have significantly different mean scores on one or more variables.

Antecedents   Events that precede the occurrence of behaviour. In (non-behaviourist) approaches they may be seen to *cause* the behaviour.

Anxiety   See **Neuroticism**.

Archival data   Research information obtained from written, computerised or audio-visual sources that exist independent of the research.

Assessee   Person whose behaviour is being assessed by an assessor (either in an interview, performing a work sample task or on the job).

Assessment centre   An assessment process that involves multiple exercises and multiple assessors to rate an assessee's performance on a series of job-related competencies.

Assessor Person who is observing and assessing a target person's behaviour for the purposes of assessing whether they are performing, or are likely to be able to perform, a role effectively.

Associative phase The second phase of skill acquisition, when the learner begins to combine the actions needed to produce skilled performance.

Attitude A regularity in an individual's feelings, thoughts and predispositions to act towards some aspect of their environment.

Attribution The explanation a person constructs for the nature or behaviour of another person.

Autonomous phase The final phase of skill acquisition, when performance becomes increasingly polished. To some degree, performance is automatic and control relies less and less on memory or attention.

Autonomy at work (control) When individuals feel that they have some influence and control over their jobs.

Behavioural indicator A description of an observable behaviour related to a specific competency.

Behaviourally anchored rating scales (BARS) Rating scales that use anchors that describe specific behaviour. The behaviours provide anchors for a spread (good–poor) of performance standards and are derived from a systematic development procedure.

Behaviourism An approach to psychology that concentrates on the external (to the person) conditions under which behaviour is exhibited and the observable consequences of behaviour.

Behaviourist tradition The approach that focuses on behaviour, rather than thoughts and emotions.

Behaviour-modelling training An approach to training in which models are reinforced for engaging in the intended behaviour.

Behaviour modification Application of reinforcement principles to strengthen desired behaviour patterns at work.

Belongingness The psychological need to feel part of a group, organisation or other collective endeavour.

Bias A psychological assessment procedure is biased if consistent errors of prediction (or classification) are made for members of a particular subgroup.

Biodata Life history information about candidates, usually collected with the aid of a structured questionnaire. Criterion-related validity for biodata is explored by examining statistical links between biodata items and criterion measures.

Bold Strokes These are major and rapid change initiatives which are imposed on an organisation from the top in a directive rather than participative manner.

Boundary management The way individuals use strategies to either segment (separate) or integrate work and non-work activities (e.g. use of a personal smartphone to check work e-mails after work hours would be an example of integration).

Boundaryless career A term given to careers that cross boundaries, for example between employers and job functions.

Brainstorming A technique for generating ideas which involves people thinking of as many things as possible that might be relevant to a given problem, however far-fetched their ideas may seem.

British Psychological Society (BPS)   The governing body for psychologists in the UK.

Bullying   Negative acts towards a person where the perpetrator has more power than the victim. The definition of bullying is complex (see Chapter 10) and this glossary definition is intended to capture just a couple of the main points discussed in the research.

Bureaucratic career   The term given by Kanter to a career characterised by predictable upwards movement within one organisation and/or occupation.

Call centres   Work environments where computer and telephone-based technologies are used to distribute incoming calls from customers or clients to available staff.

Career   The sequence of employment-related positions, roles, activities and experiences encountered by a person.

Career anchor   The set of self-perceived skills, interests, motives and values that form a basis for a person's career preferences, and which they would not give up, even if required to make a difficult choice.

Career choice   The selection made by a person of an area of work or sequence of work roles that they intend to pursue.

Career decision-making   The psychological processes involved in making a career choice.

Career development   The changes and adjustments experienced by a person as a consequence of a career choice.

Career exploration   The process of investigating oneself and the world of work in order to assist in career decision-making and career management.

Career management   The techniques and strategies used by individuals and organisations in seeking to optimise careers.

Careers counselling   An interpersonal process that enables people to recognise and utilise their resources to make career-related decisions and manage career-related problems.

Career stage   A period of time in a person's career characterised by a particular set of concerns or motives.

Career success   The extent to which a person's career is achieving the goods that matter to the person and/or society as a whole.

Change agent   An internal or external facilitator whose role is to guide an organisation through a process of change.

Charisma   A set of attributes of leaders and/or their relationships with subordinates where the leader demonstrates and promotes a sense of pride and mission through personal example.

Chartered Psychologist (C. Psychol.)   Title conferred by the BPS recognising the qualifications and experience of psychologists in the UK. Appropriately qualified work psychologists may also use the title Chartered Occupational Psychologist.

Chi-square   A statistical technique used to test whether two or more groups of people differ in the frequency with which their members fall into different categories.

Coaching   A form of development where one person advises and demonstrates to another on how to improve their work performance.

Cognitive ability   Also referred to as intelligence or general mental ability. Refers to the capacity of individuals to process information and use the information to behave effectively (including the capacity to learn from experience).

Cognitive phase The first phase of skill acquisition, when the learner is developing knowledge about the task but lacks the procedural skill to carry it out.

Cognitive psychology The branch of basic psychology that concerns the study of human perception, memory and information-processing.

Cognitive resource theory (CRT) A theory of leadership proposed by Fred Fiedler which focuses on how the cognitive resources (e.g. intelligence, knowledge) of leaders influence group performance in situations of varying stress and leader control.

Cognitive task analysis (CTA) An analysis of the underlying cognitive skills and processes required for performing a task.

Cohort effect Lasting differences in psychological functioning between people born in different eras.

Common method variance The extent to which people's scores on two or more psychological variables are related solely because the variables were assessed using the same research method.

Competency The specific behaviour patterns (including knowledge, skills and abilities) a job holder is required to demonstrate in order to perform the relevant job tasks with competence.

Competency analysis A person- or worker-orientated approach to job analysis that focuses on identifying the relevant knowledge, skills and abilities relevant to a specific job role.

Concurrent validity A form of criterion-related validity in which data on the predictor and criterion are obtained at the same time.

Conditions of worth In phenomenological approaches to personality, conditions of worth are the conditions under which other people are prepared to value us as a person.

Congruence In John Holland's theory, congruence is the extent to which a person's vocational personality matches their work environment.

Conscientiousness A predisposition to prefer active control and organisation. A conscientious person will like to be purposeful and well organised and see life in terms of tasks to be accomplished.

Conservation of resources (COR) A theory of stress that proposes that individuals are motivated to obtain, protect and develop psychological resources (e.g. knowledge, social support, control) and tangible resources (e.g. work equipment, money). These help them to meet demands they are currently facing or may face in the future. Loss or the threat of loss of resources can be a cause of stress.

Consideration An aspect of leadership style which reflects the extent that the leader demonstrates trust of subordinates, respect for their ideas and consideration of their feelings.

Construct validity An indication of the extent to which the test or procedure measures the psychological construct that it is intended to measure.

Content analysis A technique for analysing qualitative data that sorts the data, or parts of it, into different categories according to its content.

Content theories of motivation Theories which concentrate on what motivates people, rather than how motivation works. Contrast with **Process theories of motivation**.

Content validity A form of validity based on a logical analysis of the extent to which a test or procedure embodies a representative sample of the behaviour from the domain being measured.

Contextual awareness   An awareness of the situation that another person (e.g. a colleague) finds themselves in.

Contingency   This is present if reinforcement (or punishment) is given only when specific behaviour precedes it.

Contingency model   An approach to organisation design which rejects any universal best way and instead views organisation structures as being dependent (i.e. contingent) on the particular combination of situational variables each organisation faces. The main situational variables cited in the literature are environment, technology and size.

Contingency theories of leadership   These are theories of leadership that focus on how features of the situation determine what is the most effective leadership style.

Control group   In an experiment investigating the impact of one or more interventions, the control group of research subjects does *not* experience an intervention. This group provides a comparison with groups which do experience an intervention.

Core job characteristics   The five aspects of jobs suggested by Hackman and Oldham as being essential in influencing satisfaction, motivation and job performance. The five are: skill variety, task identity, task significance, autonomy and feedback.

Core self-evaluations (CSEs)   A cluster of individual differences including self-esteem, self-efficacy, emotional stability and locus of control that exhibit trait-like qualities but that may also be altered through experiences. There is evidence linking high CSEs with various positive outcomes including well-being and work performance.

Correlation   A statistical technique used to test whether scores obtained from one sample on two variables are associated with each other, such that as scores on one variable increase, scores on the other either increase (positive correlation) or decrease (negative correlation).

Counterproductive work behaviour   Act that result in harm to the employing organisation or to one's work colleagues. Examples include stealing, persistent lateness, verbal abuse towards clients or colleagues and spreading rumours.

Creativity   The generation of new and original ideas (contrast with **Innovation**).

Criterion-related validity   The extent to which a predictor (e.g. a selection test score) is related to a criterion (e.g. work performance). In personnel selection, high criterion-related validity indicates that a selection measure gives an accurate indication of candidates' performance on the criterion.

Critical incident technique (CIT)   A technique developed by Flanagan (1954), still widely used, to obtain information about jobs by concentrating on specific examples (incidents) of outstandingly good or poor performance.

Critical psychological states   The three immediate psychological effects of the core job characteristics, as proposed by Hackman and Oldham. The three are: experienced meaningfulness of the work, experienced responsibility for outcomes of the work, and knowledge of the actual results of work activities.

Cross-sectional research   Research where data are collected at only one point in time.

Cross-validation   A research technique where a piece of research is repeated on a second sample to see if the same results as first time are obtained.

Culture   The human-generated part of the environment that is transmitted across time and generations and leads to people within that culture developing shared meanings; culture gives people 'standard operating procedures' or ways of doing things.

Dark Triad   A cluster of three personality traits: narcissism, Machiavellianism and psychopathy, thought to be linked to malevolent behaviour. The impact of these on leadership behaviour is one example of its relevance to work psychology.

Decision-making style   A person's normal or habitual way of going about making decisions.

Declarative knowledge   Factual knowledge that may be stated or made explicit.

Defence mechanisms   In the psychoanalytic approach to personality, these are the methods we use to deal with intrapsychic conflicts that provoke anxiety.

Demand characteristics   Features of experiments that convey clues to subjects about the hypotheses being investigated.

Democratic leadership   A leader style that encourages self-determination, equal participation and active deliberation by group members.

Dependent variable   The variable on which the impact of one or more independent variables is investigated in an experiment.

Developmental psychology   The branch of basic psychology that concerns how people develop and change throughout their life.

Development centre   A career management intervention where assessment centre methods are used to identify individual development needs and formulate development plans.

Differential validity   This would exist if there was conclusive evidence that a selection procedure had different levels of criterion-related validity for different subgroups of the population.

Discourse analysis   A technique for analysing qualitative data where the aim is to interpret what is said or written in the light of how the speaker or writer might be trying to present themselves.

Dispersed collaboration   When people working together on a task are spread across different locations.

Dispositional characteristics   An individual's behavioural preferences, linked to personality.

Distributive justice   Perceptions of equal treatment of different people.

Diversity   A general term given to the ways in which members of a workplace or labour force differ from one another (see also **Managing diversity**).

Effect evaluation (or outcome evaluation)   A test of whether an intervention has resulted in change to important variables (e.g. increased performance). See also **Process evaluation**.

Effect size   The magnitude of an association between scores on one or more variables, or of the differences in mean scores between two or more samples.

Ego   In the psychoanalytic approach to personality, the ego is the part of the psyche that seeks to channel id impulses in socially acceptable ways.

e-learning   The use of ICT to shape the learning environment and deliver education and training interventions.

Electronic monitoring   There are different forms of electronic monitoring, which involve computers and recording instruments to observe and record an employee's performance over time. Examples include using computer programs to record the keystrokes made by an employee, or everything that is said to customers.

Embeddedness   The factors that work together to motivate an employee to stay with an organisation (as distinct from the factors that could be linked to their intention to leave).

Emergent change   This is a bottom-up and open-ended approach that views organisations as constantly having to adjust to changing environmental circumstances.

Emotional instability   See **Neuroticism**.

Emotional intelligence (EI)   A set of characteristics and styles that is thought to enable a person to utilise intellect, emotion and awareness of other people in their day-to-day behaviour.

Emotional labour   The psychological effort that goes into a job that requires the worker to manage their emotions often in response to others' (e.g. customers') displays of emotions.

Employee assistance programme (EAP)   Usually refers to a counselling service provided for employees, most often by outside providers.

Empowerment   A human resource management technique that (i) increases employee involvement in (and responsibility for) decision-making and quality management, and (ii) encourages employees to learn a wide range of skills to ensure their capacity to make an effective contribution to organisational performance.

Engagement   Absorption in work, often because it is fulfilling and enjoyable.

Equal opportunities   The attempt to ensure that all people, no matter what their group memberships, are given a fair chance to succeed in the workplace.

Equity theory   An approach to motivation which argues that people are motivated to achieve an equitable (fair) return for their efforts in comparison with other people.

Ergonomics (human factors integration)   The application of what we know about human psychology and physiology to the design of tasks, work environments and wider organisational systems that are integral to the use of work equipment.

Ethics   Rules of conduct that protect the well-being, dignity and other interests of people who participate in the research of work psychologists and/or use their services.

Ethnic identity   A person's image of self in terms of cultural, national or racial characteristics (see also **Ethnicity**).

Ethnicity   A person's cultural, national or racial group membership (see also **Ethnic identity**).

Evidence-based management (EBMgt)   The use of a combination of good-quality evidence from various sources (not just research) to inform advice and decision-making.

Exhaustion   When one's adaptive mechanisms collapse.

Expectancy   In expectancy theory, expectancy is the extent to which a person believes that they have the ability to perform certain behaviours.

Expectancy theory   An approach to motivation that focuses on the rational decision-making processes involved in choosing one course of action from alternatives.

Experiment   A research design in which the researcher controls or manipulates one or more independent variables in order to investigate their effect on one or more dependent variables.

Experimental group   The group of subjects in an experiment which experiences one or more interventions in an investigation of the impact of those interventions.

Experimental hypothesis   See **Alternative hypothesis**.

External validity   The extent to which one can be sure that some specific training will generalise and bring about results for subsequent groups of trainees or settings.

Extrinsic motivation   The motivation to perform a task derived from rewards that are not part of the task itself (e.g. money, status). Contrast with **Intrinsic motivation**.

Extroversion   A personality factor characterised by lively, sociable, excitable and gregarious behaviour.

Face validity   A very weak form of validity based on the extent to which a test or procedure appears to measure a particular construct.

Factor analysis   A statistical technique used to identify key factors that underlie relationships between variables.

Faith validity   A blind acceptance by users of the extent to which a selection tool is valid.

Fight or flight reaction   Individuals will choose whether to stay and fight or try to escape when confronting extreme danger or stress.

Flow   A state of extremely high level of engagement in enjoyment of a task in which performance is of a high standard, seems effortless despite the high level of skill involved, and time passes almost unnoticed.

Forced-choice questions   A question response format that requires ('forces') respondents to choose between alternatives. It is sometimes used in personality questionnaires to prevent people from endorsing multiple responses in an attempt to present themselves in a positive way to others (see **Social desirability effect**).

Framing bias   The impact on decision-making of the way the problem is expressed – for example either in terms of its potential losses or its potential gains.

Freudian slip   When a person accidentally says something that reflects their unconscious desires.

Functional job analysis (FJA)   An approach to job analysis that uses a standardised language and concentrates on the tasks (rather than skills) required for the job.

Fundamental attributional error   The tendency to attribute our own behaviour to more situational causes (e.g. circumstances, behaviour of others) than internal causes (e.g. personality, intentions), while doing the opposite when observing the behaviour of other people.

'g'   See **Cognitive ability**.

General mental ability   See **Cognitive ability**.

Goal commitment   In goal-setting theory, goal commitment is the extent to which a person is determined to achieve a goal.

Goal-setting theory   This approach to motivation concentrates on how goals (performance targets) can affect a person's work strategies and performance.

Grounded theory   Theory that develops during the process of data collection in a research project, and which influences data collection later in the same project.

Group   Two or more people who are perceived by themselves and others as a social entity.

Group polarisation   A phenomenon where the decision of a group after discussion is more extreme than the original preferences of individual group members.

Groupthink   A failure of group decision-making identified by Irving Janis, where the motivation of group members to seek agreement with each other exceeds their motivation to conduct a thorough and open analysis of the situation.

Haptic display   A device that presents information in a form that can be detected by our sense of touch (e.g. a vibrating alert on our mobile phone).

Hawthorne studies   A series of investigations of work behaviour conducted at the Hawthorne factory of the Western Electric Company near Chicago, USA in the 1920s.

Heuristics   General rules that people use to guide their decision-making about complex problems.

Hierarchical task analysis (HTA)   A procedure for identifying the tasks involved in a job, which proceeds to increasingly detailed task units. Task breakdown ceases when predetermined criteria are satisfied, ensuring that the analysis is sufficiently detailed for the purpose in mind.

Human-centred design (HCD)   The process of designing tasks and equipment for humans that is guided by knowledge of the end-users' needs and capabilities.

Humanism   See **Phenomenological approach to research**.

Human–machine interface (HMI)   The fit between the skills, knowledge and ability of the user and the controls and displays of the machine.

Human Systems Integration (HSI)   The name often given to the specification, design and development of equipment, and its subsequent use, that takes careful account of the needs and capabilities of the users of the equipment.

id   In the psychoanalytic approach to personality, the id is the part of the psyche that consists of basic instincts and drives.

Incremental validity   The importance of a variable in addition to other variables already accounted for.

Independent variable   A variable that is manipulated or controlled in an experiment in order to examine its effects on one or more dependent variables.

Initiating structure   Sometimes called structure, this is an aspect of leadership style that reflects the extent to which the leader plans, organises and monitors the work of their group.

Innovation   The successful development of new ideas.

Instrumentality   In expectancy theory, instrumentality is the extent to which a person believes that performing certain behaviours will lead to a specific reward.

Intelligence   See **Cognitive ability**.

Interactional justice   This has two components: interpersonal refers to the extent to which people are treated with dignity, courtesy and respect; informational concerns the extent to which relevant information is shared with employees.

Internal validity   The extent to which one can be confident that a specific training programme (rather than some other possible cause) has brought about changes in trainees.

Interpretative phenomenological analysis (IPA)   An approach to the collection and analysis of qualitative data. It emphasises the impact that both researcher and participant interpretations of the world have on the data collected and the results of the analysis.

Interviewing   Research method where the researcher asks questions face to face or on the telephone with one or more subjects.

Intrinsic motivation   The motivation to perform a task for rewards that are part of the task itself (e.g. interest, challenge). Contrast with **Extrinsic motivation**.

Introversion   A personality factor characterised by a lack of enthusiasm for the company of others and a low-key, risk-averse and unexcitable approach.

Job analysis   Procedures (there is more than one way to do a job analysis) for producing systematic information about jobs, including the nature of the work performed, position in the organisation and relationships of the job holder with other people.

Job characteristics model   The name given to Hackman and Oldham's theory (see also **Core job characteristics** and **Critical psychological states**).

Job components inventory (JCI)   A job analysis technique developed in the UK (Banks et al., 1983) which can provide profiles of the skills required for the job in question.

Job redesign   Collective name given to techniques designed to increase one or more of the variety, autonomy and completeness of a person's work tasks.

Job satisfaction   A pleasurable or positive emotional state arising from the appraisal of one's job or job experiences.

Joint cognitive system (JCS)   Where work activities, workers' competencies and work equipment/technology function in an integrated way to facilitate the achievement of work goals.

Knowledge management   A general term given to the attempt by organisations to ensure that the learning, information and experience possessed by individuals or subgroups is made available to all members.

Laissez-faire leadership   A leadership style in which the leader remains very uninvolved and passive.

Latent structure   For example, of work performance and personality. Personality theorists have identified five broad factors of personality that they argue encapsulate the underlying structure of personality. Certain work psychologists argue that there is a similar latent structure to work performance that comprises the underlying components common to all work roles.

Leader   The person who is appointed, elected or informally chosen to direct and coordinate the work of others in a group.

Leader–member relations   Defined as a feature of the situation in Fiedler's contingency theory of leadership, this refers to the extent to which leader and subordinates have relationships characterised by respect and mutual trust.

Learning data   Data that are concerned with the extent to which specific skills and knowledge have been attained.

Learning goal orientation   An approach people may take to a task where their main concern is to increase their level of competence on the task. Contrast with **Performance goal orientation**.

Learning organisation   An organisation that has systems and processes in place to encourage individual learning, and ensure that it is passed on and shared by different organisational members and groups. The learning is focused on helping the organisation achieve its goals.

Least preferred co-worker (LPC)   In Fiedler's contingency theory, LPC refers to the leader's attitude towards the subordinate they like least. This attitude is assumed to reflect the leader's general orientation towards others at work.

Life stage   A period of time in a person's life characterised by a particular set of concerns or motives.

Likert scaling   A method of measuring attitudes where people respond by indicating their opinion on a dimension running from (for example) 'strongly agree' at one end to 'strongly disagree' at the other.

Locus of control   The degree to which the individual feels that they have substantial control over events (internality) or little control over events (externality).

Longitudinal research   Research where data are collected at two or more points in time, usually months or years apart.

Long Marches   Change initiatives that comprise a series of small-scale, local, incremental changes which have little overall effect in the short term but over the long term can transform an organisation.

Managerial grid   Put forward by Blake and Mouton, this is a simple aid to assessing leadership style, based on the leader's person and task orientation.

Managing diversity   The process of ensuring that all members of a workforce are treated in a way that respects their individuality, group memberships and capacity to make a contribution.

Media richness   This is the theory that some ways of communicating contain more contextual information than others, and that this contextual information has an impact on how people interpret the communication.

Mediator variable   A variable that acts as a link in the relationship between two other variables (i.e. it is the 'bridge' that forges the relationship between two variables).

Mentoring   An approach to development in which an experienced mentor is paired with a less experienced colleague to offer career advice, support and assistance in the development of new skills.

Meta-analysis   A statistical technique for aggregating data from a number of different studies in order to establish overall trends.

Mixed methods   The use of different methods, often both qualitative and quantitative, in a single piece of research. If done effectively this mixing of methods can strengthen the research.

Moded displays   Displays that give the user access to information as it is needed, rather than displaying all the information all of the time.

Modelling   The process by which one person demonstrates certain behaviours which are then learned, and may be performed, by observers.

Moderator variable   A variable that alters the strength of the relationship between two other variables.

Motivation   The factors which determine the effort, direction and persistence of a person's behaviour.

Multiple intelligences   The notion that there is a range of quite separate human abilities (contrast to **Cognitive ability**).

Multiple regression   A statistical technique used to identify which of two or more variables are most strongly correlated with another variable (usually called the criterion variable).

Multi-source feedback (MSF)   A system of collecting performance feedback from multiple sources, usually including self, manager, subordinates, colleagues and possibly clients or customers.

Myers-Briggs Type Indicator (MBTI)   A measure of personality differences between people in terms of a set of four different dichotomies.

National culture   The set of values, assumptions and beliefs that are dominant in the population of a particular country.

Need   A biologically based desire that is activated by a discrepancy between actual and desired states.

Need for achievement   The desire to carry out a task as well and as quickly as possible.

Negative reinforcement   This is not punishment. Negative reinforcers increase the probability of the preceding behaviour when they are removed from the situation (for example, putting up an umbrella takes away the rain).

Negotiation   The process of attempting to resolve, through discussion, differences of opinion between two or more individuals or groups.

Networking   The development and maintenance of social contacts in order to increase one's learning access to information and opportunity, and to help others do the same.

Neuroticism   A predisposition to be tense and anxious. Sometimes referred to as emotional instability, or anxiety.

New technology   A generic label used to describe any form of computer-based technology.

Normal distribution   The term given to a particular distribution of scores on a variable where the distribution curve is symmetrical about the mean, with unit area and unit standard deviation.

Null hypothesis   The null hypothesis essentially proposes that 'nothing is happening' in the data. That is, that the variables measured are not correlated, or that there are no differences in mean scores between groups of people.

Openness to experience   A tendency to be curious about inner (psychological) and outer worlds with a willingness to entertain novel ideas and unconventional values.

Organisational analysis   Aims to understand where training activities fit into the wider organisational systems and how they relate to organisational strategy.

Organisational behaviour modification   A systematic approach to influencing the behaviour of people in organisations which is based on the principles of conditioning.

Organisational citizenship behaviour (OCB)   Discretionary behaviour by employees that is not explicitly requested or expected by employers, but which helps to promote effective organisational functioning.

Organisational commitment   The relative strength of an individual's identification with and involvement in an organisation.

Organisational culture   The distinctive norms, beliefs, principles and ways of behaving that combine to give each organisation its distinctive character.

Organisational development (OD)   The application of behavioural science knowledge to the planned creation and reinforcement of organisational strategies, structures and processes.

Organisational justice   An approach to motivation that focuses on the extent to which people perceive that rewards are distributed fairly in their organisation, and that the process of deciding reward allocation is fair.

Organisational learning   The ability of an organisation to develop and utilise knowledge in order to create and sustain competitive advantage.

Organisational politics   Interpersonal processes used by people in an organisation to enhance or maintain their reputation.

Participant observation   Research method where the researcher observes events, and perhaps asks the people involved about them, while also participating in the events.

Participants   People who contribute data in a research project (they are also sometimes called respondents or subjects, though the latter term is discouraged nowadays as being too impersonal).

Perceived behavioural control   In the theory of planned behaviour, perceived behavioural control concerns the extent to which a person believes that they can perform the behaviour required in a given situation.

Performance appraisal   A process whereby a manager (usually) observes the performance of an employee, records evidence and feeds back to them about how their performance relates to others in the group and whether it meets expected standards.

Performance goal orientation   An approach to a task where people's main concern is to demonstrate their competence to themselves and other people. Contrast with **Learning goal orientation**.

Performance-related pay (PRP)   Where some or all of a person's pay is based on how successfully they produce results in their work.

Personal identity   Aspects of our self-concept that reflect us as individuals, differentiated from others, even those in the same social group as we are (contrast with **Social identity**).

Personality psychology   The branch of basic psychology that concerns how and why people differ from each other psychologically.

Person analysis   Involves identifying who needs training and what kind of training they need.

Person–job fit   The extent to which a person's skills, interests and needs are consistent with the requirements and rewards of their work.

Person–organisation fit   A term used to describe the extent to which an individual's values, interests and behaviour fit with the culture of an organisation as a whole rather than a specific role or task.

Person specification   A representation of the demands of a job translated into human terms (i.e. a statement of the attributes needed for successful job performance).

Phases of change   These are distinct states through which an organisation moves as it undertakes planned change.

Phenomenological research   See **Social constructionist research**.

Physiological needs   The desire to avoid hunger, thirst and other unpleasant bodily states.

Physiological psychology   The branch of basic psychology that concerns the relationship between brain and body.

Planned behaviour   A theory which attempts to explain how and when attitudes determine intentions and behaviour.

Planned change   This is a generic term for approaches to change that have predetermined goals and a distinct starting and finishing point.

Position analysis questionnaire (PAQ)   A questionnaire-based procedure for job analysis which produces information about the major job elements involved, broken down into six divisions.

Position power   In Fred Fiedler's contingency theory, position power refers to the extent to which a leader is able, by virtue of their position in the organisation, to influence the rewards and punishments received by subordinates.

Positive well-being   This concept defines well-being as something that is more than just the absence of ill-health. For example, a worker may obtain pleasure from their work and develop a sense of purpose from the tasks they are engaged in.

Positivist research   In contrast to social constructionist research, positivist research takes the view that human behaviour, thoughts and feelings are substantially influenced by objectively measurable factors which exist independent of the researchers and people being researched.

Power-as-control theory   Developed by Fiske (2001), this theory seeks to explain why powerful people at work stereotype less powerful people. Fiske identifies three reasons: managing large numbers of people means that individuals need to exert considerable cognitive effort, powerful people already have resources therefore have less need to overcome stereotypes, and those in positions of power may have personal characteristics that make them less likely to individuate those lower in a hierarchy.

Practical intelligence   A view of intelligent behaviour that focuses on real-world activity, rather than controlled behaviour assessed by conventional intelligence testing.

Pragmatic science   The use of rigorous scientific methods to investigate and tackle important problems.

Predictive validity   A form of criterion-related validity in which data on the criterion are obtained after data on the predictor.

Predictor   A term sometimes used to refer to a selection procedure, on the grounds that a selection procedure is intended to predict candidates' job performance.

Pre-experimental design   Study design (e.g. one-shot, post-only data) that does not control for major threats to validity. The results of such designs cannot be interpreted with any certainty since many factors could have been involved in causing the observed outcomes. This design may be useful for case studies.

Primary interventions   Tackling the source of a problem.

Procedural justice   An individual's perception that the process they have been through (e.g. selection) was well designed, appropriate and well managed.

Procedural knowledge   The kind of knowledge that provides a basis for skilful performance; knowledge of how to do something that may be difficult to articulate.

Process evaluation   An examination of the factors that have an impact on the effects of an intervention, i.e. the focus is on why something brought about change. Contrast with **Effect evaluation**.

Process theories of motivation   Approaches to motivation that focus on how motivation works, rather than what motivates behaviour. Contrast with **Content theories of motivation**.

Processual approach   An approach to change that sees organisations as shifting coalitions of individuals and groups with different interests and aims, imperfect knowledge and short attention spans.

Professional career   The term given by Kanter to a career where work is primarily specialised and progress is derived from increasing challenge, competence development and personal reputation rather than promotion up a hierarchy.

Pseudo-transformational leadership   The adoption and use of transformational leadership behaviour but with a self-serving motive on the part of the leader.

Purposeful work behaviour   An integrated theory of motivation. It proposes that personality and job characteristics interact to determine what makes work meaningful for people and this, in turn, is linked to their work motivation. Personality is linked to what people strive for in their work: the motivational power of different job characteristics varies according to individual differences.

Psychoanalytic tradition   The approach to psychology that focuses on unconscious drives and conflicts as determinants of behaviour.

Psychological capital (PsyCap)   A cluster of individual differences including hope, self-efficacy, optimism and resilience, sometimes referred to as the 'positive psychological core'. These can be developed and have been linked to various positive outcomes for the individual.

Psychological contract   An individual employee's beliefs about the rights and obligations of both sides in the employment relationship.

Psychological flexibility   The extent to which a person uses thinking strategies that bring them into contact with the present moment. It is a cluster of psychological processes that help the individual to recognise and accept their thoughts in a non-judgemental way, thus allowing them to focus on goal-directed activities.

Psychology   Sometimes defined as the science of mental life, psychology concerns the systematic study of behaviour, thoughts and emotions.

Psychometric tests   Standardised procedures (often using pen and paper or delivered online) embodying a series of questions (items) designed to assess key cognitive or personality dimensions. Must have acceptable levels of validity and reliability to be of value.

Punishment   In the behaviourist approach to personality, punishment is the occurrence of an unpleasant stimulus or the removal of a pleasant stimulus following a specific behaviour.

Qualitative data   Information expressed in the form of words or images, rather than numbers.

Qualitative overload   Work that is too difficult for an individual.

Qualitative research   Research design where the researcher aims to obtain a detailed picture of the way in which a limited number of people interpret one or more aspects of their world, normally using words rather than numbers.

Quantitative data   Information expressed in the form of numbers.

Quantitative overload   Having too much work to do.

Quasi-experimental research design   Study design that has some, but not all, of the features needed for a perfect experimental design. Such designs are often used in field settings.

Questionnaire   A written list of questions designed to obtain information about a person's life history, beliefs, attitudes, interests, values or self-concept.

Random sample   A number of people selected from a population in such a way that everyone in that population had an equal chance of being selected.

Range restriction   This arises when a limited range of scores (rather than when the full population range) is present in a sample. It can occur when the sample is biased in some way, for example selection scores are available only for people who were given jobs.

Reaction data   Data that are concerned with how trainees react to the training they have been given.

Realistic job preview   A technique used in recruitment where an organisation presents a balanced view of a job to applicants rather than only its good points. This can be done using written materials, videos or even a day or two's experience of the job itself.

Reciprocal determinism   The complex interaction between situational, personal and behavioural variables.

Reinforcement   In the behaviourist approach to personality, reinforcement is the occurrence of a pleasant stimulus (positive reinforcement) or the removal of an unpleasant stimulus (negative reinforcement) following a specific behaviour.

Reliability   An indicator of the consistency which a test or procedure provides. It is possible to quantify reliability to indicate the extent to which a measure is free from error.

Relocation   A job move within an organisation to a different location that requires a move of home.

Repertory grid technique   A method of collecting data about the way individuals view the world. It is often used to gather the views of experts, for example when analysing what constitutes effective job performance.

Resilience   Many definitions mention the positive adaptation of individuals to adversity. This adaptation helps people to cope better with difficulties they encounter in the future. The definition is still the cause of some debate.

Respondent   A term often given to a person who provides data in psychological research, particularly a survey research sample.

Retirement   There is no single accepted definition of retirement. For most people it is the time when, having experienced a number of years of work, they withdraw from the labour market and do not intend to re-enter it.

Role ambiguity   Unclear picture of the nature of the job, its objectives, responsibilities, etc.

Role conflict   When an individual is torn by conflicting job demands.

Role innovation   The extent to which a person seeks to change the nature of their job.

Safety needs   The desire to avoid physical or psychological danger.

Sample   A number of people drawn from a defined population (e.g. all people; all females; all sales managers).

Sampling error   Fluctuations in observed results that arise when small samples are used. Any small sample may contain some unrepresentative cases, but if the sample is small these cases may have an unduly large influence on the results.

Schema   In the social cognitive tradition in psychology, a schema is an organised set of beliefs and expectations held by a person.

Science   A branch of knowledge based upon systematically collected data under controlled conditions.

Scientific management   Also called Taylorism, this is an approach to management that emphasises management control, simplification and standardisation of work activities and purely financial incentives.

Scientist-practitioner   A person who integrates research and practice to good effect.

Script   In the social cognitive tradition in psychology, a script is an expected sequence of events that a person associates with a particular type of situation.

Secondary intervention   Helping employees to develop skills that will enable them to cope better with a problem (e.g. stress management training).

Selection ratio   An indication of the number of positions available compared with the number of candidates. Ten candidates for every post would give a selection ratio of 1:10, i.e. 0.1.

Self-actualisation   The need to fulfil one's potential: to develop and express one's capacities.

Self-awareness   The capacity to know and understand one's own characteristics, motives and values.

Self-categorisation theory   A theory that proposes that we define who we are by placing ourselves into categories, and these categories are often social groups. We seek to defend our identity when threatened. Similar to **Social identity theory**.

Self-concept   The total set of beliefs a person holds about themselves.

Self-development   An approach to staff development that places primary responsibility for identifying development needs and taking action to deal with them on the individual employee.

Self-efficacy   A person's own belief in their own ability, skills, knowledge, etc.

Self-regulation   The strategies a person uses to monitor and direct their behaviour in pursuit of a goal.

Servant leadership   An approach to leadership that portrays the leader as a helpful facilitator of others' efforts, rather than a dominant agenda-setter.

Situational interviews   A form of structured interview in which key work situations (identified through job analysis) are used to provide a basis for questioning and assessing job candidates.

Situational judgement test (SJT)   A selection test that requires candidates to decide how they would behave in response to a situation described in the test. Often the test would also require the candidates to give details of the reasoning that led to their decision.

Situational leadership theory   A theory of leadership that proposes that the maturity of subordinates dictates the style a leader should adopt.

Social approach   A 'common-sense' approach to motivation that argues that a person is motivated to establish and maintain meaningful social relationships.

Social cognitive theory   A theory that developed from behaviourist origins and sees the behaviourist view as incomplete, rather than wrong. In social cognitive theory internal cognitive processes (e.g. expectancies about what might happen) and external (social/situational) factors play a key role in determining behaviour.

Social cognitive tradition   The tradition in psychology that emphasises how we process information in a social context.

Social constructionist research   Research based on the assumption that there are few objective facts about the social world, and that it is therefore necessary to focus on people's subjective interpretations rather than objectively verifiable causal laws. Sometimes called **phenomenological research**.

Social desirability effect   The effect that occurs when a person provides biased information because of their desire to provide responses that they believe will be looked upon favourably by others. For example, more people break the speed limit when driving than admit to it when asked (even if they are not being asked by a police officer!).

Social identity   Aspects of our self-concept that reflect the general characteristics of people in the same social groups as we are, and which differentiate us from members of other groups (contrast with **Personal identity**).

Social identity theory   A theory that suggests we define ourselves largely in terms of our membership of social groups, and often tend to value our own group more than others. Similar to **Self-categorisation theory**.

Socialisation   The processes by which the person learns and adopts the behaviours, attitudes and values expected in their role.

Social loafing   The process where some members of a group do not contribute their share of effort, but still obtain the rewards of group membership.

Social psychology   The branch of basic psychology that concerns how the social world affects the behaviour, thoughts and emotions of individuals and groups.

Social support   Refers to informal and formal relationships which can help the individual to explore and deal with stress.

Socio-cognitive   An approach to attitudes which stresses how they are encoded in a person's memory and what functions they serve for the person.

Solomon four-group design   An experimental design that can be used to evaluate the impact of an intervention. The design uses a number of control groups to help rule out alternative explanations for change and therefore isolate the impact of the intervention.

Standard deviation   A measure of how much variability around the mean there is in a set of numerical data.

Statistical power   A measure of the probability that a statistically significant effect will be observed in a sample of given size if such an effect does actually exist in the population from which the sample is drawn.

Statistical significance   The probability of rejecting the null hypothesis on the basis of data obtained from a sample when it is in fact true for the population from which the sample is drawn. Psychologists are normally only willing to reject the null hypothesis if there is, at most, a 1 in 20 chance of it being true.

Stereotype   A generalised belief about what people in a particular group are like.

Strategic decision   A decision that affects the overall goals, aims or mission of an organisation.

Stress   The unpleasant, and potentially damaging, emotional state that arises when a person perceives that the demands placed upon them exceed the resources available to them to cope with those demands.

Stressor   The source of the stress; the cause or underlying reasons why an employee may show stress symptoms or disease.

Structural approaches to stress   Theories of stress that focus on describing the aspects of work that are the likely sources of stress.

Structural equation modelling   A method of data analysis that can be used to examine quantitative data when there are likely to be multiple and complex relationships between the variables in the study.

Structured observation   A research method where the researcher remains uninvolved in events, but records what occurs using a predetermined system.

Subjective norm   In the theory of planned behaviour, subjective norm is a combination of the (perceived) opinions of other people and the person's motivation to comply with them.

Superego   In the psychoanalytic tradition in psychology, the superego is the part of the psyche that concerns moral values, or conscience.

Survey   Research design where a sample of respondents/subjects provides data in a standard form on one or more variables.

Systematic review   A way of reviewing a body of research that is highly rigorous. It involves applying the principles of best practice in research design and data analysis to the evaluation of published research.

Target audience description (TAD)   The characteristics of the users of equipment that are considered during human-centred design.

Task analysis   Involves determining what important tasks need to be performed and the KSAs that an individual requires in order to perform them.

Team   A group of people who work together towards group objectives.

Team-building   Techniques designed to enhance the effectiveness of a new or established team.

Team roles   The functions that need to be fulfilled by team members if the team is to be effective.

Technology-mediated communications   The use of the telephone, Internet, e-mail (etc.) as means of communicating.

Teleworking   Working from a remote location using information and communication technologies (ICTs).

Tertiary intervention   An intervention designed to help employees who have already been damaged in some way by their work (e.g. workplace counselling).

Theories of learning   Theories that represent ideas about how learning occurs; they feed into training practice by identifying the most appropriate methods of instruction.

Theory X   A 'common-sense' approach to motivation that views people as untrustworthy, to be motivated by financial reward and punishment.

Theory Y   A 'common-sense' approach to motivation that views people as inherently trustworthy and responsible, to be motivated by challenge and responsibility.

Three-step model   This model views change as a planned and finite process which proceeds through three stages: unfreezing, moving and refreezing.

Three-stratum theory of cognitive ability   John B. Carroll's theory that intelligence can be understood by thinking of it as having three levels (strata) with clusters of similar abilities at the lower two levels. The levels are: general intellectual ability (see also 'g'); broad factors (e.g. memory, decision speed) and specific factors (e.g. memory span, reaction time).

Thurstone scaling   A method of measuring attitudes where statements are graded in terms of their extremity of agreement or disagreement with a particular attitude.

Total quality management (TQM)   A strategic and organisation-wide approach to quality which is associated with Japanese manufacturing organisations.

Training   Organised efforts to provide employees with structured opportunities to learn and develop within their work role.

Training design   Relates to the content of the training programme and includes decisions about what information is presented to trainees and how it is presented.

Training evaluation   Considers the validity of training programmes by assessing the extent to which the training objectives have been achieved.

Training objectives (TOs)   These define what the training needs to achieve and can include individual and organisational-level objectives.

Trait   A dimension upon which people differ psychologically. Traits are stable over time. This is in contrast to a state which is transient.

Trait-factor analytic approach   An approach to individual differences that uses factor analysis to identify the major structural dimensions (traits) of personality.

Trait tradition   The tradition in psychology that emphasises stable differences between people in their position on various personality dimensions.

Transactional leadership   A leadership style originally identified by Burns (1978), in which the leader uses rewards for good performance and tends to maintain existing work methods unless performance goals are not being met.

Transactional theories of stress   Theories of stress that focus on describing the psychological processes that lead to the experience of negative emotions.

Transformational leadership   Another leadership style originally identified by Burns (1978), this refers to the extent to which a leader articulates a clear vision and mission, while treating individuals on their merits and encouraging free thinking.

Transition   A relatively permanent move from one environment to another experienced by a person. The sequence of phases a person goes through in adjusting to a new job.

Triarchic theory of intelligence   The theory that there are three facets of intelligence: analytical, creative and practical.

t-Test   A statistical technique used to test whether two samples have significantly different mean scores on a variable.

Type I error   This occurs when the null hypothesis is erroneously rejected on the basis of research data.

Type II error   This occurs when the alternative hypothesis is erroneously rejected on the basis of research data.

Type III error   This occurs when a researcher erroneously concludes that an intervention is ineffective when it was the implementation of the intervention that was faulty.

Unconditional positive regard (UPR)   In the phenomenological tradition in psychology, unconditional positive regard is the acceptance of one person by another, irrespective of their behaviour.

Underemployment   A situation that arises when a person has a job but for some reason the job does not fulfil their current needs. It includes, but is not limited to, working fewer hours and getting paid less than one desires or being in employment that is insufficiently stimulating or engaging. It can also include working in a job that is perceived by the individual as not being intellectually, physically or emotionally challenging or demanding enough.

Utility (financial)   A procedure for estimating the financial gain that may be derived from the improved job performance that is obtained from better personnel selection.

Valence   In expectancy theory, valence is the subjective value a person attaches to a particular reward.

Validation study   A test of whether a prediction developed from a theory or model is supported by data. A common use of this concept in work psychology is the validation of selection tests, i.e. whether the result of the selection test is related to subsequent job performance.

Validity   A general term indicating the extent to which a test or procedure measures what it is intended to measure.

Vitamin model   This model proposes that working conditions behave like vitamins in that some are beneficial in the 'correct doses', too little of some causes problems, too much of some is 'toxic', etc.

Vroom–Jago theory of leadership   This theory assumes that leaders can vary the participativeness of their decision-making style according to the situation, and identifies key aspects of the situation.

'Wash-up' session   This is a meeting of the assessors at the end of an assessment centre. In the wash-up the ratings for each assessee are discussed and an overall rating made.

Wellness programme   A company-wide programme to promote employee health, both physical and psychological.

Work–life balance/integration   A general term often applied to the examination of the impact of work on other aspects of a person's life (and vice versa).

Work-role transition   Any move between jobs, into a job or out of one, or any substantial change in work duties.

Work sample tests   Personnel assessment procedures that require candidates to conduct tasks that are sampled from the job(s) in question.

REFERENCES

Abele, A.E. and Spurk, D. (2009) 'How do objective and subjective career success interrelate over time?', *Journal of Occupational and Organizational Psychology*, 82(4), 803–24.

Abelson, R.P. (1981) 'Psychological status of the script concept', *American Psychologist*, 36, 715–29.

Ackoff, R.L. (1989) 'From data to wisdom', *Journal of Applied Systems Analysis*, 16, 3–9.

Adair, J.G. (1984) 'The Hawthorne effect: A reconsideration of the methodological artefact', *Journal of Applied Psychology*, 69, 334–45.

Adams, J.S. (1965) 'Inequity in social exchange', in L. Berkowitz (ed.), *Advances in Experimental Social Psychology*, vol. 2. New York: Academic Press.

Agho, A.O., Mueller, C.W. and Price, J.L. (1993) 'Determinants of employee job satisfaction: An empirical test of a causal model', *Human Relations*, 46, 1007–27.

Agho, A.O., Price, J.L. and Mueller, C.W. (1992) 'Discriminant validity of measures of job satisfaction, positive affectivity and negative affectivity', *Journal of Occupational and Organizational Psychology*, 65, 185–96.

Aguinas, H. and Kraiger, K. (2009) 'Benefits of training and development for individuals and teams, organisations and society', *Annual Review of Psychology*, 60, 451–74.

Ahlstrom, L., Grimby-Ekman, A., Hagberg, M. and Dellve, L. (2010) 'The work ability index and single-item question: Associations with sick leave, symptoms, and health – a prospective study of women on long-term sick leave', *Scandinavian Journal of Work Environment and Health*, 36, 404–12.

Ahlstrom, V. and Longo, K. (2003) *Human Factors Design Standard (HF-STD-001)*. Atlantic City International Airport, NJ: Federal Aviation Administration, William J. Hughes Technical Centre.

Aiello, J.R. and Kolb, K.J. (1995) 'Electronic performance monitoring and social context: Impact on productivity and stress', *Journal of Applied Psychology*, 80, 339–53.

Ajzen, I. (1991) 'The theory of planned behaviour', *Organisational Behaviour and Human Decision Processes*, 50, 179–211.

Ajzen, I. (2001) 'Nature and operation of attitudes', *Annual Review of Psychology*, 24, 1251–63.

Ajzen, I. and Fishbein, M. (1980) *Understanding Attitudes and Predicting Social Behaviour*. Englewood Cliffs, NJ: Prentice Hall.

Ajzen, I. and Fishbein, M. (2000) 'Attitudes and the attitude–behaviour relation: Reasoned and automatic process', in W. Stroebe and M. Hewstone (eds), *European Review of Social Psychology*. Chichester: John Wiley.

Ajzen, I. and Madden, J.T. (1986) 'Prediction of goal-directed behaviour: Attitudes, intentions, and perceived behavioural control', *Journal of Experimental Social Psychology*, 22, 453–74.

Akgün, A.E., Lynn, G.S. and Byrne, J.C. (2003) 'Organisational learning: A socio-cognitive framework', *Human Relations*, 56, 839–68.

Akkermans, J., Brenninkmeijer, V., Huibers, M. and Blonk, R.W. (2012) 'Competencies for the contemporary career: Development and preliminary validation of the Career Competencies Questionnaire', *Journal of Career Development*, 83, 245–67.

Alban, B. (2003) 'The future', in M. Wheatley, R. Tannenbaum, P.Y. Griffin and K. Quade (eds), *Organisation Development at Work: Conversations on the values, applications and future of OD*. San Francisco, CA: Pfeiffer.

Aldag, R.J. and Fuller, S.R. (1993) 'Beyond fiasco: A reappraisal of the groupthink phenomenon and a new model of group decision processes', *Psychological Bulletin*, 113, 533–52.

Alderfer, C.P. (1972) *Existence, Relatedness and Growth: Human needs in organisational settings*. New York: Free Press.

Alimo-Metcalfe, B. and Alban-Metcalfe, J. (2005) 'Leadership: Time for a new direction?', *Leadership*, 1, 51–71.

Alkadry, M.G. and Tower, L.E. (2006) 'Unequal pay: The role of gender', *Public Administration Review*, November–December, 888–98.

Allaire, Y. and Firsirotu, M.E. (1984) 'Theories of organisational culture', *Organisation Studies*, 5(3), 193–226.

Allen, N.J. and Hecht, T.D. (2004) 'The "Romance of Teams": Towards an understanding of its psychological underpinnings and implications', *Journal of Occupational and Organizational Psychology*, 77(4), 439–61.

Allen, N.J. and Meyer, J.P. (1990) 'The measurement and antecedents of affective, continuance and normative commitment to the organisation', *Journal of Occupational Psychology*, 63, 11–18.

Allen, T.D. and Eby, L.T. (2008) *The Blackwell Handbook of Mentoring: A multiple perspectives approach*. Oxford: Blackwell Publishing.

Allen, T.D., Eby, L.T. and Poteet, M.L. (2004) 'Career benefits associated with mentoring for protégés: A meta-analysis', *Journal of Applied Psychology*, 89, 127–36.

Alliger, G.M. and Janak, E.A. (1997) 'Kirkpatrick's levels of training criteria thirty years later', *Personnel Psychology*, 41, 63–105.

Allison, T., Cooper, C.L. and Reynolds, P. (1989) 'Stress counselling in the workplace – the Post Office experience', *The Psychologist*, 2, 384–8.

Allport, G.W. (1937) *Personality: A psychological interpretation*. New York: Holt, Rinehart and Winston.

Amabile, T.M. (1988) 'A model of creativity and innovation in organisations', *Research in Organisational Behavior*, 10(1), 123–67.

Ambrose, M.L. and Kulik, C.T. (1999) 'Old friends, new faces: Motivation research in the 1990s', *Journal of Management*, 25, 213–92.

American Society for Training and Development (2013) *State of the Industry Report*. Accessed at: http://www.astd.org/Publications/Research-Reports

Amundsen, S. and Martinsen, Ø.L. (2014) 'Self–other agreement in empowering leadership: Relationships with leader effectiveness and subordinates' job satisfaction and turnover intention', *The Leadership Quarterly*, 25, 784–800.

Anastasi, A. (1988) *Psychological Testing*, New York: Macmillan.

Ancona, D. and Bresman, H. (2007) *X-Teams: How to build teams that lead, innovate, and succeed*. Harvard: Harvard Business School Press.

Anderson, J.R. (1983) *The Architecture of Cognition*. Cambridge, MA: Harvard University Press.

Anderson, J.R. (1987) 'Skill acquisition: Compilation of weak-method problem solutions', *Psychological Review*, 94, 192–210.

Anderson, N. (2003) 'Applicant and recruiter reactions to new technology in selection: A critical review and agenda for future research', *International Journal of Selection and Assessment*, 11(2–3), 121–36.

Anderson, N. and Prutton, K. (1993) 'Occupational psychology in business: Strategic resource or purveyor of tests?', *The Occupational Psychologist*, 20, 3–10.

Anderson, N. and Sleap, S. (2004) 'An evaluation of gender differences on the Belbin Team Role Self-Perception Inventory', *Journal of Organisational and Occupational Psychology*, 77, 429–37.

Anderson, N. and Witvliet, C. (2008) 'Fairness reactions to personnel selection methods: An international comparison between the Netherlands, the United States, France, Spain, Portugal, and Singapore', *International Journal of Selection and Assessment*, 16(1), 1–13.

Anderson, N., Born, M. and Cunningham-Snell, N. (2001a) 'Recruitment and selection: Applicant perspectives and outcomes', in N. Anderson, D.S. Ones, H.K. Sinangil and C. Viswesvaran (eds), *Handbook of Industrial, Work and Organisational Psychology*. Thousand Oaks, CA: Sage Publications.

Anderson, N., Herriot, P. and Hodgkinson, G.P. (2001b) 'The practitioner–researcher divide in Industrial, Work and Organisational (IWO) psychology: Where are we now, and where do we go from here?', *Journal of Occupational and Organizational Psychology*, 74, 391–411.

Anderson, N., Lievens, F., van Dam, K. and Born, M. (2006) 'A construct-driven investigation of gender differences in a leadership-role assessment centre', *Journal of Applied Psychology*, 91, 555–66.

Anderson, N.R. and West, M.A. (1998) 'Measuring climate for work group innovation: Development and validation of the team climate inventory', *Journal of Organisational Behaviour*, 19, 235–58.

Anderson, V. (2007) *The Value of Learning: A new model of value and evaluation*. London: Chartered Institute of Personnel Development.

Annett, J. and Duncan, K.D. (1967) 'Task analysis and training design,' *Occupational Psychology*, 41, 211–21.

Annett, J., Duncan, K.D., Stammers, R.B. and Grey, M.J. (1971) *Task Analysis*. Department of Employment Information Training Paper 6. London: HMSO.

Anseel, F., Beatty, A.S., Shen, W., Lievens, F. and Sackett, P.R. (2015) 'How are we doing after 30 years? A meta-analytic review of the antecedents and outcomes of feedback-seeking behaviour', *Journal of Management*, 41, 318–48.

April, K., Macdonald, R. and Vriesendorp, S. (2000) *Rethinking Leadership*. Cape Town: University of Cape Town Press.

Argote, L., Ingram, P., Levine, J.M. and Moreland, R.L. (2000) 'Knowledge transfer in organisations: Learning from the experience of others', *Organisational Behaviour and Human Decision Processes*, 82(1), 1–8.

Argyris, C. (1960) *Understanding Organisational Behaviour*. Homewood, IL: Dorsey.

Argyris, C. (1962) *Interpersonal Competence and Organisational Effectiveness*. Homewood, IL: Irwin.

Argyris, C. (1964) *Integrating the Individual and the Organisation*. Chichester: John Wiley.

Armitage, C.J. and Conner, M. (2001) 'Efficacy of the theory of planned behaviour: A meta-analytic review', *British Journal of Social Psychology*, 40, 471–99.

Arnold, J. (1990) 'From education to job markets', in S. Fisher and C.L. Cooper (eds), *On the Move: The psychological effects of change and transition*. Chichester: John Wiley.

Arnold, J. (1996) 'The psychological contract: A concept in need of closer scrutiny?', *European Journal of Work & Organisational Psychology*, 5, 511–20.

Arnold, J. (2002) 'Tensions between assessment, grading and development in development centres: A case study', *International Journal of Human Resource Management*, 13(6), 975–91.

Arnold, J. (2004) 'The congruence problem in John Holland's theory of vocational decisions', *Journal of Occupational and Organizational Psychology*, 77, 95–113.

Arnold, J. and Clark, M. (2015) 'Running the penultimate lap of the race: A multi-method analysis of growth, generativity, career orientation and personality amongst men in mid/late career', *Journal of Occupational and Organizational Psychology*. In press.

Arnold, J. and Cohen, L. (2008) 'The psychology of careers in industrial-organisational settings: A critical but appreciative analysis', in G.P. Hodgkinson and J.K. Ford (eds), *International Review of Industrial/Organisational Psychology*, vol. 23. Chichester: Wiley.

Arnold, J. and Cohen, L. (2013) 'Careers in organisations', in W.B. Walsh, M.L. Savickas, and P.J. Hartung (eds), *Handbook of Vocational Psychology*, 4th edition. Mahwah, NJ: Erlbaum.

Arnold, J. and Mackenzie Davey, K. (1999) 'Graduates' work experiences as predictors of organisational commitment, intention to leave, and turnover: Which experiences really matter?', *Applied Psychology: An International Review*, 48(2), 211–38.

Aronsson, G. and Gustafsson, K. (2005) 'Sickness presenteeism: Prevalence, attendance-pressure factors, and an outline of a model for research', *Journal of Occupational and Environmental Medicine*, 47, 958–66.

Aronsson, G., Gustafsson, K. and Dallner, M. (2000) 'Sick but yet at work. An empirical study of sickness presenteeism', *Journal of Epidemiology and Community Health*, 54, 502–9.

Arthur, M. (2014) 'The boundaryless career at 20: Where do we stand, and where can we go?', *Career Development International*, 19, 627–40.

Arthur, M.B. (2008). Examining contemporary careers: A call for interdisciplinary inquiry. *Human Relations*, 61(2), 163–186.

Arthur, M.B. and Rousseau, D.M. (1996) 'The boundaryless career as a new employment principle', in M.B. Arthur and D.M. Rousseau (eds), *The Boundaryless Career: A new employment principle for a new organisational era*. Oxford: Oxford University Press.

Arthur, M.B., Inkson, K. and Pringle, J.K. (1999) *The New Careers, Individual Action and Economic Change*. London: Sage.

Arthur, W. Jr, Day, E.A. and Woehr, D.J. (2008) 'Mend it, don't end it: An alternate view of assessment centre construct-related validity evidence', *Industrial and Organisational Psychology*, 1, 105–11.

Arthur, W. Jr, Bennett, W.J., Edens, P. and Bell, S.T. (2003) 'Effectiveness of training in organisations: A meta-analysis of design and evaluation features', *Journal of Applied Psychology*, 88, 234–45.

Arvey, R.D. and Murphy, K.R. (1998) 'Performance evaluation in work settings', *Annual Review of Psychology*, 49, 141–68.

Arvey, R.D., Carter, W.G. and Buerkley, D.K. (1991) 'Job satisfaction: Dispositional and situational influences', in C.L. Cooper and I.T. Robertson (eds), *International Review of Industrial and Organisational Psychology*, 6. Chichester: John Wiley.

Aryee, S., Walumbwa, F.O., Mondejar, R. and Chu, C.W. (2015) 'Accounting for the influence of overall justice on job performance: Integrating self-determination and social exchange theories', *Journal of Management Studies*, 52, 231–52.

Ashforth, B.K. and Saks, A.M. (1996) 'Socialisation tactics: Longitudinal effects on newcomer adjustment', *Academy of Management Journal*, 39, 149–78.

Ashkanasy, N. and Jackson, C. (2001) 'Organisational culture and climate', in N. Anderson, D. Ones, H.K. Sinangil and C. Viswesvaran (eds), *Handbook of Industrial, Work and Organisational Psychology*, vol. 2. London: Sage.

Ashkanasy, N.M. and Tse, B. (2000) 'Transformational leadership as management of emotion: A conceptual review', in N.M. Ashkanasy, C.E. Härtel and W.J. Zerbe (eds), *Emotions in the Workplace: Research, theory, and practice*, 221–35. Westport, CT: Quorum Books/Greenwood Publishing Group.

Ashmos, D.P., Duchon, D., McDaniel, R.R. Jr and Huonker, J.W. (2002) 'What a mess! Participation as a simple managerial rule to "complexify" organisations', *Journal of Management Studies*, 39(2), 189–206.

Ashton, D. and Felstead, A. (2000) 'From training to lifelong learning: The birth of the knowledge society?', in J. Storey (ed.) *Human Resource Management: A critical text*. London: Thomson Learning.

Assudini, R.H. (2011) 'Role of familiarity in affecting knowledge gaps in geographically dispersed work', *IEEE Transactions on Professional Communication*, 54, 314–32.

Atwater, L.E., Brett, J.F. and Charles, A.C. (2007) 'Multisource feedback: Lessons learned and implications for practice', *Human Resource Management*, 46, 285–307.

Atwater, L.E., Ostroff, C., Yammarino, F.J. and Fleenor, J.W. (1998) 'Self–other agreement: Does it really matter?', *Personnel Psychology*, 51, 577–98.

Austin, J.T. and Crespin, T.R. (2006) 'Problems of criteria in industrial and organisational psychology: Progress, problems and prospects', in W. Bennett Jr, C.E. Lance and D.J. Woehr (eds), *Performance Measurement: Current perspectives and future challenges*. London: Lawrence Erlbaum Associates.

Avery, R.E., Smillie, L.D. and Fife-Schaw, C.R. (2015) 'Employee achievement orientations and personality as predictors of job satisfaction facets', *Personality and Individual Differences*, 76, 56–61.

Avolio, B.J., Gardner, W.L., Walumba, F.O., Luthans, F. and May, D.R. (2004) 'Unlocking the mask: A look at the process by which authentic leaders impact follower attitudes and behaviours', *The Leadership Quarterly*, 15, 810–23.

Axtell, C., Fleck, S. and Turner, N. (2004a) 'Virtual teams: collaborating across distance', in C.L. Cooper and I.T. Robertson (eds), *International Review of Industrial and Organisational Psychology*, vol. 19. Chichester: John Wiley.

Axtell, C., Wheeler, J., Patterson, M. and Leach, A. (2004b) 'From a distance', *People Management*, 10(6), 39–40.

Baas, M., De Dreu, C.K. and Nijstad, B.A. (2008) 'A meta-analysis of 25 years of mood-creativity research: Hedonic tone, activation, or regulatory focus?', *Psychological Bulletin*, 134(6), 779–806.

Baay, P.E., de Ridder, D.T.D., Eccles, J.S., van der Lippe, T.D. and van Aken, M.A.G. (2014) 'Self-control trumps work motivation in predicting job search behaviour', *Journal of Vocational Behaviour*, 85, 443–51.

Bacon, N. and Hoque, K. (2010) 'Union representation and training: The impact of Union Learning Representatives and the factors influencing their effectiveness', *Human Relations*, 64(3), 387–413.

Baglioni, A.J. Jr and Cooper, C.L. (1988) 'A structural model approach towards the development of a theory of the link between stress and mental health', *British Journal of Medical Psychology*, 61, 87–102.

Bailey, C. and Fletcher, C. (2002) 'The impact of multiple source feedback on management development: Findings from a longitudinal study', *Journal of Organisational Behaviour*, 23, 853–67.

Bain, P., Watson, A., Mulvey, G., Taylor, P. and Gall, G. (2002) 'Taylorism, targets and the pursuit of quantity and quality by call-centre management', *New Technology, Work and Employment*, 17, 170–85.

Bainbridge, L. (1987) 'Ironies of automation', in J. Rasmussen, K. Duncan and J. Leplat (eds), *New Technology and Human Error*, 271–83. Chichester: John Wiley.

Bakker, A.B. and Demerouti, E. (2007) 'The job demands-resources model: State of the art', *Journal of Managerial Psychology*, 22, 309–28.

Bakker, A.B. and Demerouti, E. (2008) 'Towards a model of work engagement', *Career Development International*, 13, 209–23.

Bakker, A.B. and Demerouti, E. (2013) 'The spillover-crossover model', in J. Grzywacs and E. Demerouti (eds), *New Frontiers in Work and Family Research*. Hove, Sussex: Psychology Press.

Bakker, A.B. and Sanz-Vergel, A.I. (2013) 'Weekly work engagement and flourishing: The role of hindrance and challenge job demands', *Journal of Vocational Behaviour*, 83, 397–409.

Bakker, A.B., Demerouti, E. and Sanz-Vergel, A.I. (2014) 'Burnout and work engagement: The JD-R approach', *Annual Review of Organisational Psychology and Organisational Behaviour*, 1, 389–411.

Bakker, A.B., Demerouti, E. and Schaufeli, W.B. (2003) 'Dual processes at work in a call centre: An application of the job demands–resources model', *European Journal of Work & Organisational Psychology*, 12, 393–428.

Bal, P.M., De Lange, A.H., Jansen, P.G.W. and Van der Velde, M.E.G. (2008) 'Psychological contract breach and job attitudes: A meta-analysis of age as a moderator', *Journal of Vocational Behaviour*, 72, 143–58.

Bal, P.M., De Lange, A.H., Jansen, P.G.W. and Van Der Velde, M.E.G. (2013) 'A longitudinal study of age-related differences in reactions to psychological contract breach', *Applied Psychology: An International Review*, 62, 157–81.

Baldwin, T.T. (1992) 'Effects of alternative modelling strategies on outcomes of interpersonal-skills training', *Journal of Applied Psychology*, 77, 147–54.

Baldwin, T.T. and Ford, J.K. (1988) 'Transfer of training: A review and directions for future research', *Personnel Psychology*, 41, 63–105.

Ball, J., Maben, J., Murrells, T., Day, T. and Griffiths, P. (2014) *12-hour Shifts: Prevalence, views and impact*. National Nursing Research Unit, King's College London.

Baltes, P.B. and Baltes, M.M. (1990) 'Psychological perspectives on successful ageing: The model of selective optimisation with compensation', *Successful Ageing: Perspectives from the Behavioural Sciences*, 1, 1–34.

Baltes, B.B., Dickinson, M.W., Sherman, M.P., Bauer, C.C. and La Ganke, S. (2002) 'Computer mediated communication and group decision making: A meta-analysis', *Organisational Behaviour and Human Decision Processes*, 87, 156–79.

Bambra, C., Egan, M., Thomas, S., Petticrew, M. and Whitehead, M. (2007) 'The psychosocial and health effects of workplace restructuring. 2. A systematic review of task restructuring interventions', *Journal of Epidemiology and Community Health*, 61, 1028–37.

Bandura, A. (1977a) 'Self-efficacy: Towards a unifying theory of behavioural change', *Psychological Review*, 84, 191–215.

Bandura, A. (1977b) *Social Learning Theory*. Englewood Cliffs, NJ: Prentice Hall.

Bandura, A. (1982) 'The self-efficacy mechanism in human agency', *American Psychologist*, 37, 122–47.

Bandura, A. (1986) *Social Foundations of Thought and Action: A social cognitive theory*. Englewood Cliffs, NJ: Prentice Hall.

Bandura, A. (1997) *Self-efficacy: The exercise of control*. New York: Freeman.

Bankins, S. (2015) 'A process perspective on psychological contract change: Making sense of, and repairing, psychological contract breach and violation through employee coping actions', *Journal of Organisational Behaviour*, 36(8), 1071–95.

Banks, M.H. (1988) 'Job components inventory', in S. Gael (ed.), *Job Analysis Handbook*. New York: John Wiley.

Banks, M.H., Jackson, P.R., Stafford, E.M. and Warr, P.B. (1983) 'The job components inventory and the analysis of jobs requiring limited skill', *Personnel Psychology*, 36, 57–66.

Bannai, A. and Tamakoshi, A. (2014) 'The association between long working hours and health: A systematic review of epidemiological evidence', *Scandinavian Journal of Work, Environment and Health*, 40, 5–18.

Barclay, W.B., Chapman, J.R. and Brown, B.L. (2013) 'Underlying factor structure of Schein's career anchor model', *Journal of Career Assessment*, 21, 451–70.

Barczak, G., Lassk, F. and Mulki, J. (2010) 'Antecedents of team creativity: An examination of team emotional intelligence, team trust and collaborative culture', *Creativity and Innovation Management*, 19, 332–45.

Bardwick, J. (1980) 'The seasons of a woman's life', in D. McGuigan (ed.), *Women's Lives: New theory, research and policy*. Ann Arbor, MI: University of Michigan.

Bargal, D., Gold, M. and Lewin, M. (1992) 'The heritage of Kurt Lewin – Introduction', *Journal of Social Issues*, 48, 3–13.

Barker, R.A. (1997) 'How can we train leaders if we do not know what leadership is?', *Human Relations*, 50(4), 343–62.

Barling, J., Wade, B. and Fullagar, C. (1990) 'Predicting employee commitment to company and union: Divergent models', *Journal of Occupational Psychology*, 63, 49–61.

Barnes, C. (1991) *Disabled People in Britain: A case for anti-discrimination legislation*. London: C. Hurst and Co. Ltd.

Barnes-Farrell, J.L. (2001) 'Performance appraisal: Person perception, processes and challenges', in M. London (ed.), *How People Evaluate Others in Organisations*. London: LEA.

Barnes-Farrell, J.L., Davies-Schrils, K., McGonagle, A. et al. (2008) 'What aspects of shiftwork influence off-shift well-being of healthcare workers?', *Applied Ergonomics*, 39, 589–96.

Barnett, B.J. and Wickens, C.D. (1988) 'Display proximity in multicue information integration: The benefits of boxes', *Human Factors*, 30, 15–24.

Bar-On, R. (1997) *The Emotional Intelligence Inventory (EQ-i): Technical manual*. Toronto: Multi-Health Systems.

Bar-On, R. (2000) 'Emotional and social intelligence: Insights from the Emotional Quotient Inventory', in R. Bar-On and J.D.A. Parker (eds), *The Handbook of Emotional Intelligence*. San Francisco, CA: Jossey-Bass.

Baron, R.M. and Kenny, D.A. (1986) 'The moderator–mediator variable distinction in social psychological research: Conceptual, strategic and statistical considerations', *Journal of Personality and Social Psychology*, 51, 1173–82.

Barratt, E.S. (1990) 'Human resource management: Organisational culture', *Management Update*, 2(1), 21–32.

Barreto, M.E., Ryan, M.K. and Schmitt, M.T. (2009) *The Glass Ceiling in the 21st Century: Understanding barriers to gender equality*. New York: American Psychological Association.

Barrick, M.R., Mount, M.K. and Li, N. (2013) 'The theory of purposeful work behaviour: The role of personality, higher-order goals, and job characteristics', *Academy of Management Review*, 38, 132–53.

Barrick, M.R., Shaffer, J.A. and DeGrassi, S.W. (2009) 'What you see may not be what you get: Relationships among self-presentation tactics and ratings of interview and job performance', *Journal of Applied Psychology*, 94(6), 1394–411.

Barsk, A. (2008) 'Understanding the ethical cost of organisational goal-setting: A review and theory development', *Journal of Business Ethics*, 81, 63–81.

Bartram, D. (2005) 'The great eight competencies: A criterion-centric approach to validation', *Journal of Applied Psychology*, 90, 1185–203.

Baruch, Y. (2003) *Managing Careers*. Harlow: Pearson Education.

Baruch, Y. (2004) 'Transforming careers – from linear to multidirectional career paths: Organisational and individual perspective', *Career Development International*, 9, 58–73.

Baruch, Y. and Peiperl, M.A. (2000) 'Career management practices: An empirical survey and theoretical implications', *Human Resource Management*, 39, 347–66.

Bass, B.M. (1985) *Leadership and Performance: Beyond expectations.* New York: Free Press.

Bass, B.M. (1997) 'Does the transactional–transformational leadership paradigm transcend organisational and national boundaries?', *American Psychologist*, 52(2), 130–9.

Bass, B.M. and Avolio, B.J. (1994) *Improving Organisational Effectiveness Through Transformational Leadership.* Thousand Oaks, CA: Sage.

Bass, B.M. and Stogdill, R.M. (1990) *Handbook of Leadership*, vol. 11. New York: Free Press.

Bateman, T. and Strasser, S. (1984) 'A longitudinal analysis of the antecedents of organisational commitment', *Academy of Management Journal*, 27, 95–112.

Bates R.A. and Holton E.F. (2005) 'Computerised performance monitoring: A review of research issues', *Human Resource Management Review*, 5, 267–88.

Bauer, T.N. and Erdogan, B. (2011) 'Organisational socialisation: The effective onboarding of new employees' in S. Zedeck (ed.), *Handbook of Industrial and Organisational Psychology*, vol. 3. Washington, DC: American Psychological Association.

Beal, D.J., Cohen, R.R., Burke, M.J. and McLendon, C.L. (2003) 'Cohesion and performance in groups: Meta-analytic clarification of construct relations', *Journal of Applied Psychology*, 88, 989–1004.

Beaujean, A.A. (2005) 'Heritability of cognitive abilities as measured by mental chronometric tasks: A meta-analysis', *Intelligence*, 33, 187–201.

Bechtold, B.L. (1997) 'Chaos theory as a model for strategy development', *Empowerment in Organisations*, 5(4), 193–201.

Beck, A.T. (1996) *BDI-II, Beck Depression Inventory.* Boston, MA: Harcourt Brace.

Beck, J.S. (1995) *Cognitive Therapies: Basics and beyond.* New York: Guilford.

Beck, R.C. (1983) *Motivation: Theory and principles.* Englewood Cliffs, NJ: Prentice Hall.

Becker, T.E., Billings, R.S., Eveleth, D.M. and Gilbert, N.L. (1996) 'Foci and bases of employee commitment: Implications for job performance', *Academy of Management Journal*, 39, 464–82.

Beckhard, R. (1969) *Organisation Development: Strategies and models.* Reading, MA: Addison-Wesley.

Beehr, T.A. (1995) *Psychological Stress in the Workplace.* London: Routledge.

Beehr, T.A., Bowling, N.A. and Bennett, M.M. (2010) 'Occupational stress and failures of social support: When helping hurts', *Journal of Occupational Health Psychology*, 15, 45–59.

Beer, M. and Nohria, N. (eds) (2000) *Breaking the Code of Change.* Boston, MA: Harvard Business School Press.

Beer, M., Eisenstat, R.A. and Spector, B. (1993) 'Why change programmes don't produce change', in C. Mabey and B. Mayon-White (eds), *Managing Change*, 2nd edition. London: Open University/Paul Chapman Publishing.

Belbin, R.M. (1981) *Management Teams: Why they succeed or fail.* London: Heinemann.

Belbin, R.M. (1993a) *Team Roles at Work: A strategy for human resource management.* Oxford: Butterworth-Heinemann.

Belbin, R.M. (1993b) 'A reply to the Belbin Team Role Self-Perception Inventory by Furnham, Steele and Pendleton', *Journal of Organisational and Occupational Psychology*, 66, 259–60.

Belbin, R.M. (2000) *Beyond the Team.* Oxford: Butterworth-Heinemann.

Bell, B.S. and Kozlowski, S.W.J. (2002) 'A typology of virtual teams: Implications for effective leadership', *Group and Organisation Management*, 27, 14–49.

Bell, S.T. (2007) 'Deep-level composition variables as predictors of team performance: A meta-analysis', *Journal of Applied Psychology*, 92, 595–615.

Bem, D.J. (1972) 'Self-perception theory', *Advances in Experimental Social Psychology*, 6, 1–62.

Benders, J., Huijgen, F. and Ulricj, P. (2001) 'Measuring group work: Findings and lessons from a European survey', *New Technology, Work and Employment*, 16(3), 204–17.

Benjamin, G. and Mabey, C. (1993) 'Facilitating radical change', in C. Mabey and B. Mayon-White (eds), *Managing Change*, 2nd edition. London: Open University/Paul Chapman Publishing.

Bennett, R. (1983) *Management Research*, Management Development Series no. 20. Geneva: International Labour Office.

Bennett, W., Lance, C.E. and Woehr, D.J. (2006) *Performance Measurement: Current perspectives and future challenges*. London: Lawrence Erlbaum Associates.

Benoliel, P. and Somech, A. (2014) 'The health and performance effects of participative leadership: Exploring the moderating role of the Big Five personality dimensions', *European Journal of Work & Organisational Psychology*, 23, 277–94.

Bentley, R.J., Kavanagh, A., Krnjacki, L. and LaMontagne, A.D. (2015) 'A longitudinal analysis of changes in job control and mental health', *American Journal of Epidemiology*, Advance Access published 1 July 2015, DOI: 10.1093/aje/kwv046.

Bergman, M.E., Drasgow, F., Donovan, M.A. and Henning, J.B. (2006) 'Scoring situational judgment tests: Once you get the data, your troubles begin', *International Journal of Selection and Assessment*, 14, 223–35.

Bernin, P. and Theorell, T. (2001) 'Demand-control-support among female and male managers in eight Swedish companies', *Stress and Health*, 17(4), 231–43.

Berridge, J. and Cooper, C.L. (1993) 'Stress and coping in US organisations: The role of the Employee Assistance Programme', *Work & Stress*, 7, 89–102.

Berridge, J., Cooper, C.L. and Highley-Marchington, C. (1997) *Employee Assistance Programmes and Workplace Counselling*. Chichester: John Wiley.

Berry, C.M., Clark, M.A. and McClure, T.K. (2011) 'Racial/ethnic differences in the criterion-related validity of cognitive ability tests: A qualitative and quantitative review', *Journal of Applied Psychology*, 96, 881.

Berry, C.M., Cullen, M.J. and Meyer, J.M. (2014) 'Racial/ethnic subgroup differences in cognitive ability test range restriction: Implications for differential validity', *Journal of Applied Psychology*, 99, 21–37.

Berry, C.M., Sackett, P.R. and Landers, R.N. (2007) 'Revisiting interview–cognitive ability relationships: Attending to specific range restriction mechanisms in meta-analysis', *Personnel Psychology*, 60(4), 837–74.

Bertolino, M. and Steiner, D.D. (2007) 'Fairness reactions to selection methods: An Italian study', *International Journal of Selection and Assessment*, 15(2), 197–205.

Bertua, C., Anderson, N. and Salgado, J.F. (2005) 'The predictive validity of cognitive ability tests: A UK meta-analysis', *Journal of Occupational and Organizational Psychology*, 78, 387–410.

Best, L. and Coyne, I. (2010) 'The relationship between workplace cyberbullying and well-being: A comparison with traditional bullying'. Paper presented at the 7th International Conference on Workplace Bullying and Harassment, Cardiff, June 2010.

Bettenhausen, K.L. (1991) 'Five years of group research: What we have learned and what needs to be addressed', *Journal of Management*, 17, 345–81.

Beugelsdijk, S. and Smeets, R. (2008) 'Entrepreneurial culture and economic growth', *American Journal of Economics and Sociology*, 67, 915–39.

Bhave, D.P. (2014) 'The invisible eye? Electronic performance monitoring and employee job performance', *Personnel Psychology*, 67, 605–35.

Bickley, P.G., Keith, T.Z. and Wolfe, L.M. (1995) 'The three-stratum theory of cognitive abilities: Test of the structure of intelligence across the life span', *Intelligence*, 20, 309–28.

Bigge, L.M. (1982) *Learning Theories for Teachers*. Aldershot: Gower.

Billings, C.E. (1997) *Aviation Automation: The search for a human-centred approach*. Mahwah, NJ: LEA.

Binnewies, C., Sonnentag, S. and Mojza, E.J. (2009) 'Feeling recovered and thinking about the good sides of one's work', *Journal of Occupational Health Psychology*, 14, 243–56.

Birdi, K., Allan, C. and Warr, P. (1997) 'Correlates and perceived outcomes of four types of employee development activity', *Journal of Applied Psychology*, 82(6), 845–57.

Birdi, K., Clegg, C., Patterson, M., Robinson, A., Stride, C.B., Wall, T.D. and Wood, S.J. (2008) 'The impact of human resource management practices on company productivity: A longitudinal study', *Personnel Psychology*, 61, 467–501.

Blackler, F. (1982) 'Organisational psychology', in S. Canter and D. Canter (eds), *Psychology in Practice*. Chichester: John Wiley.

Blackler, F. and Brown, C. (1986) 'Alternative models to guide the design and introduction of the new information technologies into work organisations', *Journal of Occupational Psychology*, 59, 287–314.

Blake, R.R. and Mouton, J.S. (1964) *The Managerial Grid*. Houston, TX: Gulf Publishing.

Blake, R.R. and Mouton, J.S. (1969) *Building a Dynamic Corporation Through Grid Organisation Development*. Reading, MA: Addison-Wesley.

Blake, R.R. and Mouton, J.S. (1976) *Organisational Change by Design*. Austin, TX: Scientific Methods.

Blanchard, K., Zigarmi, P. and Zigarmi, D. (2013) *Leadership and the One Minute Manager: Increasing effectiveness through Situational Leadership® II*. New York: William Morrow.

Blanchard, P.N. and Thacker, J.W. (2007) *Effective Training: Systems, strategies, and practices*, 3rd edition. Upper Saddle River, NJ: Pearson Prentice Hall.

Blasi, J.R. and Kruse, D.L. (2006) 'U.S. high performance work practices at century's end', *Industrial Relations*, 45(4), 547–87.

Blass F.R., Brouer R.L., Perrewé P.L. et al. (2007) 'Politics understanding and networking ability as a function of mentoring: The roles of gender and race', *Journal of Leadership and Organisational Studies*, 14, 93–105.

Blickle, G., Witzki, A. and Schneider, P.B. (2009) 'Self-initiated mentoring and career success: A predictive field study', *Journal of Vocational Behaviour*, 74, 94–101.

Bloom, M. (1999) 'The performance effects of pay dispersion on individuals and organisations', *Academy of Management Journal*, 42, 25–40.

Blume, B.D., Ford, J.K., Baldwin, T.T. and Huang, J.L. (2010) 'Transfer of training: A meta-analytic review', *Journal of Management*, 36, 1065–105.

Blustein, D.L. (1997) 'A context-rich perspective of career exploration across the life roles', *Career Development Quarterly*, 45, 260–74.

Bobko, P. and Roth, P.L. (2013) 'Reviewing, categorizing, and analyzing the literature on Black–White mean differences for predictors of job performance: Verifying some perceptions and updating/correcting others', *Personnel Psychology*, 66(1), 91–126.

Böckerman, P., Bryson, A. and Ilmakunnas, P. (2012) 'Does high involvement management improve worker wellbeing?', *Journal of Economic Behaviour and Organisation*, 84, 660–80.

Boddy, D. and Buchanan, D. (1992) *Take the Lead: Interpersonal skills for change agents*. London: Prentice-Hall.

Bodenhausen, G.V. and Macrae, C.N. (1996) 'The self-regulation of intergroup perception: Mechanisms and consequences of stereotype suppression', in C.N. Macrae, M. Hewstone and C. Stangor (eds), *Foundations of Stereotypes and Stereotyping*. New York: Guilford Press.

Boehm, J.K. and Kubzansky, L.D. (2012) 'The heart's content: The association between positive psychological well-being and cardiovascular health', *Psychological Bulletin*, 138, 655–91.

Boje, D.M., Burnes, B. and Hassard, J. (eds) (2011) *The Routledge Companion to Organisational Change*. London: Routledge.

Bolino, M.C. and Turnley, W.H. (2008) 'Old faces, new places: Equity theory in cross-cultural contexts', *Journal of Organisational Behaviour*, 29, 29–50.

Bolles, R.N. (2008) *What Colour is Your Parachute? 2009: A practical manual for job-hunters and career changers*. Berkeley, CA: Ten Speed Press.

Bolton, G.E., Katok, E. and Ockenfels, A. (2004) 'How effective are electronic reputation mechanisms? An experimental investigation', *Management Science*, 50, 1587–602.

Bond, F.W. and Bunce, D. (2001) 'Job control mediates change in a work reorganisation intervention for stress reduction', *Journal of Occupational Health Psychology*, 6, 290–302.

Bond, F.W., Flaxman, P.E. and Bunce, D. (2008) 'The influence of psychological flexibility on work redesign: Mediated moderation of a work reorganisation intervention', *Journal of Applied Psychology*, 93, 645–54.

Bond, F.W., Flaxman, P.E. and Loivette, S. (2006) *A Business Case for the Management Standards for Stress*. Norwich, UK: Her Majesty's Stationery Office, Research Reports.

Bond, F.W., Lloyd, J. and Guenole, N. (2013) 'The work-related acceptance and action questionnaire (WAAQ): Initial psychometric findings and their implications for measuring psychological flexibility in specific contexts', *Journal of Occupational and Organizational Psychology*, 86, 331–47.

Bonde, J.P.E. (2008) 'Psychosocial factors at work and risk of depression: A systematic review of the epidemiological evidence', *Occupational and Environmental Medicine*, 438–45.

Boniwell, I. and Henry, J. (2007) 'Developing conceptions of well-being: Advancing subjective, hedonic and eudamonic theories', *Social Psychological Review*, 9, 3–18.

Bono, J.E. and Ilies, R. (2006) 'Charisma, positive emotions and mood contagion', *The Leadership Quarterly*, 17, 317–34.

Bono, J.E. and Judge, T.A. (2003) 'Self-concordance at work: Towards understanding the motivational effects of transformational leaders', *Academy of Management Journal*, 46, 554–71.

Booher, H.R. (1997) *Human Factors Integration: Cost and Performance Benefits on Army Systems (ARL-CR-341)*. Aberdeen Proving Ground, MD: Army Research Laboratory.

Booher, H.R. and Minninger, J. (2003) 'Human systems integration in army systems acquisition', in H.R. Booher (ed.), *Handbook of Human Systems Integration*. Hoboken, NJ: Wiley.

Boring, E.C. (1923) 'Intelligence as the tests test it', *New Republic*, 35, 35–7.

Borman, W.C. and Motowidlo, S.J. (1997) 'Task performance and contextual performance: The meaning for personnel selection', *Human Performance*, 10, 99–109.

Borman, W.C., Hanson, M.A., Oppler, S.H., Pulakos, E.D. and White, L.A. (1993) 'Role of early supervisory experience in supervisor performance', *Journal of Applied Psychology*, 78(3), 443–9.

Bosley, S., Arnold, J. and Cohen, L. (2009) 'How other people shape our careers: A typology drawn from career narratives', *Human Relations*, 62, 1487–520.

Bouchard, T.J. and McGue, M. (1990) 'Genetic and rearing environmental influences on adult personality: An analysis of adopted twins reared apart', *Journal of Personality*, 58, 263–92.

Bowler, M.C. and Woehr, D.J. (2006) 'A meta-analytic evaluation of the impact of dimension and exercise factors on assessment centre ratings', *Journal of Applied Psychology*, 91, 1114–24.

Bowling, N.A., Alarcon, G.M., Bragg, C.B. and Hartman, M.J. (2015) 'A meta-analytic examination of the potential correlates and consequences of workload', *Work & Stress*, 29, 95–113.

Bowling, N.A., Beehr, T.A. and Lepisto, L.R. (2006) 'Beyond job satisfaction: A five-year prospective analysis of the dispositional approach to work attitudes', *Journal of Vocational Behaviour*, 69, 315–30.

Bradford, D.L. and Burke, W.W. (2004) 'Introduction: Is OD in crisis?', *Journal of Applied Behavioural Science*, 40(4), 369–73.

Brannick, M.T., Levine, E.L. and Morgeson, F.P. (2007) *Job and Work Analysis: Methods, research, and applications for human resource management*. Chicago: Sage.

Brayfield, A.H. and Rothe, H.F. (1951) 'An index of job satisfaction', *Journal of Applied Psychology*, 35, 307–11.

Brebels, L., De Cremer, D. and Van Dijke, M. (2014) 'Using self-definition to predict the influence of procedural justice on organisational-, interpersonal-, and job/task-orientated citizenship behaviour', *Journal of Management*, 40, 731–63.

Breckler, S.J. (1984) 'Empirical validation of affect, behaviour and cognition as distinct attitude components', *Journal of Personality and Social Psychology*, 47, 1191–205.

Breslow, L. and Buell, P. (1960) 'Mortality from coronary heart disease and physical activity of work in California', *Journal of Chronic Diseases*, 11, 615–25.

Breukelen, W., Van der Vlist, R. and Steensma, H. (2004) 'Voluntary employee turnover: Combining variables from the "traditional" turnover literature with the theory of planned behaviour', *Journal of Organisational Behaviour*, 25, 893–914.

Briner, R.B., Denyer, D. and Rousseau, D.M. (2009) 'Evidence-based management: Concept clean-up time?', *Academy of Management Perspectives*, 23, 19–32.

Briner, R.B., Robertson, I., Patterson, F., Anderson, N., Dietmann, A., Cassell, C. and Kandola, B. (2010) 'Occupational psychology in a changing world', *The Psychologist*, 23, 892–99.

Briscoe, J.P. and Hall, D.T. (2006) 'The interplay of boundarylessness and protean careers: Combinations and implications', *Journal of Vocational Behaviour*, 69, 4–18.

Briscoe, J.P., Hall, D.T. and Frautschy DeMuth, R.L. (2006) 'Protean and boundaryless careers: An empirical exploration', *Journal of Vocational Behaviour*, 69, 30–47.

Briscoe, J.P., Hall, D.T. and Mayrhofer, W. (2012a) *Careers Around the World*. London: Routledge.

Briscoe, J.P., Henagan, S.C., Burton, J.P. and Murphy, W.M. (2012b) 'Coping with an insecure employment environment: The differing roles of protean and boundaryless career orientations', *Journal of Vocational Behaviour*, 80, 308–16.

British Psychological Society (2009) *Code of Ethics and Conduct*. Leicester: BPS.

British Psychological Society (2014) *Standards for the Accreditation of Masters and Doctoral Programmes in Occupational Psychology*. Leicester: BPS.

Brodbeck, F.C., Frese, M., Akerblom, S., Audia, G., Bakacsi, G., Bendova, H. et al. (2000) 'Cultural variation of leadership prototypes across 22 European countries', *Journal of Occupational and Organizational Psychology*, 73, 1–29.

Brough, P., O'Driscoll, M.P., Kalliath, T.J., Cooper, C.L. and Poelmans, S.A. (2009) *Workplace Psychological Health: Current research and practice*. Cheltenham: Edward Elgar.

Brown, A. (1995) *Organisational Culture*. London: Pitman.

Brown, A. (1998) *Organisational Culture*, 2nd edition. Harlow: FT/Prentice Hall.

Brown, K.G. (2005) 'An examination of the structure and nomological network of trainee reactions: A closer look at "smile sheets"', *Journal of Applied Psychology*, 90, 991–1001.

Brown, M.E. and Treviño, L.K. (2006) 'Ethical leadership: A review and future directions', *Leadership Quarterly*, 17, 595–616.

Brown, M.E., Treviño, L.K. and Harrison, D.A. (2005) 'Ethical leadership: A social learning perspective for construct development and testing', *Organisational Behaviour and Human Decision Processes*, 97, 117–34.

Brown, S.D. and Rector, C.C. (2008) 'Conceptualising and diagnosing problems in vocational decision making', *Handbook of Counselling Psychology*, 4, 392–407.

Brun, J. and Lamarche, C. (2006) *Assessing the Costs of Work Stress*. Université Laval, Quebec, Canada. Available online at: http://www.cgsst.com/stock/eng/doc272-806.pdf.

Brunner, E. (2007) 'Biology and health inequality', *PLoS Biol*, Nov; 5(11): e267.

Brunwasser, S.M., Gillham, J. and Kim, E.S. (2009) 'A meta-analytic review of the Penn Resiliency Program's effect on depressive symptoms', *Journal of Consulting and Clinical Psychology*, 77, 1042–54.

Bryman, A. (1992) *Charisma and Leadership in Organisations*. London: Sage.

Bryman, A. (2001) *Social Research Methods*. Oxford: Oxford University Press.

Bryman, A. (2006) 'Integrating quantitative and qualitative research: How is it done?', *Qualitative Research*, 6, 97–113.

Buchanan, D. and Boddy, D. (1992a) *The Expertise of the Change Agent*. London: Prentice Hall.

Buchanan, D. and Boddy, D. (1992b) *Take the Lead: Interpersonal skills for change agents*. London: Prentice Hall.

Buchanan, D.A. and Storey, J. (1997) 'Role-taking and role-switching in organisational change: The four pluralities', in I. McLoughlin and M. Harris (eds), *Innovation, Organisational Change and Technology*. London: International Thompson.

Buck, J.R. (1983) 'Visual displays', in B.H. Kantowitz and R.D. Sorkin (eds), *Human Factors: Understanding People-System Relationships*. New York: Wiley.

Bullock, R.J. and Batten, D. (1985) 'It's just a phase we're going through: A review and synthesis of OD phase analysis', *Group and Organisation Studies*, 10, 383–412.

Bunce, D. (1997) 'What factors are associated with the outcome of individual-focused worksite stress management interventions?', *Journal of Occupational and Organizational Psychology*, 70, 1–17.

Bureau of Labor Statistics (2005) 'Charting the U.S. Labor market in 2005', report retrieved from: http://www.bls.gov/cps/labor2005/ (accessed 21 October 2015).

Burgoyne, J.G. (1999) 'Design of the times: A new model for the learning organisation', *People Management*, June, 38–44.

Burke, R.J. and Cooper, C.L. (2008) *The Long Work Hours Culture: Causes, consequences and choices*. Bingley: Emerald Press.

Burke, W.W. (2011) 'A perspective on the field of organisation development and change: The Zeigarnik effect', *Journal of Applied Behavioral Science*, 47, 143–67.

Burnes, B. (1989) *New Technology in Context*. Aldershot: Gower.

Burnes, B. (2004a) 'Kurt Lewin and the planned approach to change: A re-appraisal', *Journal of Management Studies*, 41(6), 977–1002.

Burnes, B. (2004b) *Managing Change*, 4th edition. Harlow: FT/Prentice Hall.

Burnes, B. (2007) 'Kurt Lewin and the Harwood Studies: The foundations of OD', *Journal of Applied Behavioural Science*, 43(2), 213–31.

Burnes, B. (2011) 'Introduction: Why does change fail and what can we do about it?', *Journal of Change Management*, 11, 445–50.

Burnes, B. (2014) *Managing Change*, 6th edition. Harlow: Pearson.

Burnes, B. and By, R.T. (2012) 'Leadership and change: The case for greater ethical clarity', *Journal of Business Ethics*, 108(2), 239–52.

Burnes, B. and Cooke, B. (2012) 'The past, present and future of organisation development: Taking the long view', *Human Relations*, 65, 1395–429.

Burnes, B. and Cooke, B. (2013a) 'Kurt Lewin's field theory: A review and re-evaluation', *International Journal of Management Reviews*, 15, 408–25.

Burnes, B. and Cooke, B. (2013b) 'The Tavistock's 1945 invention of Organisation Development: Early British business and management applications of social psychiatry', *Business History*, 55, 768–89.

Burnes, B. and Jackson, P. (2011) 'Success and failure in organisational change: An exploration of the role of values', *Journal of Change Management*, 11, 133–62.

Burnes, B., Cooper, C. and West, P. (2003) 'Organisational learning: The new management paradigm?', *Management Decision*, 41(5), 443–51.

Burns, J.M. (1978) *Leadership*. New York: Harper and Row.

Byrne, D.E. (1971) *The Attraction Paradigm*. London: Academic Press.

Campbell, D.T. and Stanley, J.C. (1963) *Experimental and Quasi-Experimental Designs for Research*. Chicago, IL: Rand McNally.

Campbell, J.P. (1990) 'Modelling the performance prediction problem in industrial organisational psychology', in M.D. Dunnette and L.M. Hough (eds), *Handbook of Industrial and Organisational Psychology*, 2nd edition, vol. 1. Palo Alto, CA: Consulting Psychologists Press.

Campbell, J.P. (2012) 'Behaviour, performance, and effectiveness in the 21st century', in S. Kozloski (ed.) *The Oxford Handbook of Organisational Psychology*. New York: Oxford University Press.

Campbell, J.P., Gasser, M.B. and Oswald, F.L. (1996) 'The substantive nature of job performance variability', in K.R. Murphy (ed.), *Individual Differences and Behaviour in Organisations*. San Francisco, CA: Jossey-Bass.

Campbell, J.P., McCloy, R.A., Oppler, S.H. and Sager, C.E. (1993) 'A theory of performance', in N. Schmitt and W. Borman (eds), *Personnel Selection in Organisations*. San Francisco, CA: Jossey-Bass.

Campion, M.A., Fink, A.A., Ruggeberg, B.J., Carr, L., Phillips, G.M. and Odman, R.B. (2011) 'Doing competencies well: Best practices in competency modelling', *Personnel Psychology*, 64, 225–62.

Cannon, W.B. (1929) *Bodily Changes in Pain, Hunger, Fear and Rage*. New York: Appleton.

Cannon-Bowers, J.A. and Salas, E. (2001) 'Reflections on team cognition', *Journal of Organisational Behaviour*, 22, 195–202.

Caplan R.D., Cobb, S., French J.R.P., Van Harrison, R. and Pinneau, S.R. (1975) *Job Demands and Worker Health*. Cincinnati, OH: National Institute for Occupational Safety and Health.

Caplan, R.D., Cobb, S., French, J.R.P., Van Harrison, R. and Pinneau, S.R. (1980) *Job Demands and Worker Health*. Ann Arbor: University of Michigan Institute of Social Research.

Card, S., Moran, T.P. and Newell, A. (1980) 'The keystroke-level model for user performance with interactive systems', *Communications of the ACM*, 23, 396–410.

Carlson, J.R. and Zmud, R.W. (1999) 'Channel expansion theory and the experiential nature of media richness perceptions', *Academy of Management Journal*, 42, 153–70.

Carmeli, A., Schaubroeck, J. and Tishler, A. (2011) 'How CEO empowering leadership shapes top management team processes: Implications for firm performance', *The Leadership Quarterly*, 22, 399–411.

Carnall, C.A. (2003) *Managing Change in Organisations*, 4th edition. Harlow: FT/Prentice-Hall.

Carr, A. (2011) *Positive Psychology: The science of happiness and human strengths*. Hove, Sussex: Routledge.

Carroll, J.B. (1993) *Human Cognitive Abilities: A survey of factor-analytic studies*. Cambridge: Cambridge University Press.

Carter, M., Thompson, N., Crampton P., Morrow, G., Burford, B., Gray, C. and Illing, J. (2013) 'Workplace bullying in the UK NHS: A questionnaire and interview study on prevalence, impact and barriers to reporting', *BMJ Open*, 3:e002628.

Cartwright, S. and Cooper, C.L. (1997) *Managing Workplace Stress*. London: Sage.

Carver, C.S., Scheier, M.F. and Weintraub, J.K. (1989) 'Assessing coping strategies: A theoretically based approach', *Journal of Personality and Social Psychology*, 56, 267–83.

Cascio, W.F. and Aguinis, H. (2008) 'Staffing twenty-first-century organisations', *Academy of Management Annals*, 2, 133–65.

Cassell, C. (2000) 'The business case and the management of diversity', in M.J. Davidson and R.J. Burke (eds), *Women in Management*. London: Sage.

Cassell, C. and Symon, G. (2004) *Essential Guide to Qualitative Methods in Organisational Research*. London: Sage.

Cassidy, T. and Lynn, R. (1989) 'A multifactorial approach to achievement motivation: The development of a comprehensive measure', *Journal of Occupational Psychology*, 62, 301–12.

Cattell, R.B. (1965) *The Scientific Analysis of Personality*. Harmondsworth: Penguin.

Cattell, R.B. and Cattell, H.E.P. (1995) 'Personality structure and the new fifth edition of the 16PF', *Educational and Psychological Measurement*, 55, 926–37.

Cattell, R.B., Eber, H.W. and Taksuoka, M.M. (1970) *Handbook for the Sixteen Personality Factor Questionnaire*. Windsor: National Foundation for Educational Research.

Cavendish, C. (2013) *The Cavendish Review: An independent review into healthcare assistants and support workers in the NHS and social care settings*. London: Department of Health.

Cerasoli, C.P., Nicklin, J.M. and Ford, M.T. (2014) 'Intrinsic motivation and extrinsic incentives jointly predict performance: A 40-year meta-analysis', *Psychological Bulletin*, 140, 980–1008.

Cervone, D. and Mischel, W. (eds) (2002) *Advances in Personality Science*. New York: Guilford Press.

Chaney, L. and Martin, J. (2013) *Intercultural Business Communication*, 3rd edition. Harlow: Pearson Higher Ed.

Chao, G.T., O'Leary-Kelly, A.M., Wolf, S., Klein, H.J. and Gardner, P.D. (1994) 'Organisational socialisation: Its content and consequences', *Journal of Applied Psychology*, 79, 730–43.

Chao, G.T., Walz, P.M. and Gardner, P.D. (1992) 'Formal and informal mentorships – a comparison on mentoring functions and contrast with nonmentored counterparts', *Personnel Psychology*, 45(3), 619–36.

Chapman, D.S., Uggerslev, K.L. and Webster, J. (2003) 'Applicant reactions to face-to-face and technology-mediated interviews: A field investigation', *Journal of Applied Psychology*, 88(5), 944–53.

Chapman, M. (2000) '"When the entrepreneur sneezes, the organisation catches a cold": A practitioner's perspective on the state of the art in research on the entrepreneurial personality and the entrepreneurial process', *European Journal of Work and Organisational Psychology*, 9, 97–101.

Chartered Management Institute (2013) *Women in Management: Tackling the talent pipeline*. London: CMI.

Chase, B. and Karwowski, W. (2003) 'Advanced manufacturing technology', in D. Holman, T.D. Wall, C.W. Clegg, P. Sparrow and A. Howard (eds), *The New Workplace*. Chichester: John Wiley.

Chatman, J.A. and Cha, S.E. (2003) 'Leading by leveraging culture', *California Management Review*, 45, 20–34.

Chen, C., Gustafson, D.H. and Lee, Y. (2002) 'The effect of a quantitative decision aid – analytic hierarchy process – on group polarisation', *Group Decision and Negotiation*, 11, 329–44.

Cheng, E.W.L and Hampson, I. (2008) 'Transfer of training: A review and new insights', *International Journal of Management Reviews*, 10, 327–41.

Cherns, A.B. (1976) 'The principles of sociotechnical design', *Human Relations*, 29, 783–92.

Cherns, A.B. (1987) 'Principles of sociotechnical design revisited', *Human Relations*, 40, 153–62.

Cheung, R. and Arnold, J. (2014) 'The impact of career exploration on career development among Hong Kong Chinese university students', *Journal of College Student Development*, 55(7), 732–48.

Chhokar, J.S., Brodbeck, F.C. and House, R.J. (eds) (2007) *Culture and Leadership Across the World: The GLOBE book of in-depth studies of 25 societies*. Mahwah, NJ: Lawrence Erlbaum Associates.

Chiaburu, D.S., Oh, I.S., Berry, C.M., Li, N. and Gardner, R.G. (2011) 'The five-factor model of personality traits and organisational citizenship behaviours: A meta-analysis', *Journal of Applied Psychology*, 96, 1140–66.

Chiang, C.-F. and Jang, S. (2008) 'An expectancy model for hotel employee motivation', *International Journal of Hospitality Management*, 27, 313–22.

Chida, Y. and Steptoe, A. (2008) 'Positive psychological well-being and mortality: A quantitative review of prospective observational studies', *Psychosomatic Medicine*, 70, 741–56.

Child, J. (1972) 'Organisational structure, environment and performance: The role of strategic choice', *Sociology*, 6(1), 1–22.

Child, J. (1984) *Organisation*. Cambridge: Harper and Row.

Chiocchio, F. and Essiembre, H. (2009) 'Cohesion and performance: A meta-analytic review of disparities between project teams, production teams, and service teams', *Small Group Research*, 40, 382–400.

Chiu, Y. and Staples, D.S. (2013) 'Reducing faultlines in geographically dispersed teams: Self-disclosure and task elaboration', *Small Group Research*, 44, 498–531.

Choi, D., Oh, I.-S. and Colbert, A.E. (2015) 'Understanding organisational commitment: A meta-analytic examination of the roles of the five-factor model of personality and culture', *Journal of Applied Psychology*, 100, 1542–67.

Christian, M.S., Edwards, B.D. and Bradley, J.C. (2010) 'Situational judgment tests: Constructs assessed and a meta-analysis of their criterion-related validities', *Personnel Psychology*, 63, 83–117.

Christiansen, N., Sliter, M. and Frost, C.T. (2014) 'What employees dislike about their jobs: Relationship between personality-based fit and work satisfaction', *Personality and Individual Differences*, 71, 25–9.

Christie, A., Barling, J. and Turner, N. (2011) 'Pseudo-transformational leadership: Model specification and outcomes', *Journal of Applied Social Psychology*, 41, 2943–84.

Chun, J.U., Sosik, J.J. and Yun, N.Y. (2012) 'A longitudinal study of mentor and protégé outcomes in formal mentoring relationships', *Journal of Organisational Behaviour*, 33, 1071–94.

Church, A.H. (1997) 'Managerial self-awareness in high-performing individuals in organisations', *Journal of Applied Psychology*, 82(2), 281–92.

Cialdini, R.B. and Trost, M.R. (1998) 'Social influence: Social norms, conformity, and compliance', in D.T. Gillbert, S.T. Fiske and G. Lindzey (eds), *The Handbook of Social Psychology*, vols 1 and 2, 4th edition. Boston: McGraw-Hill.

CIPD (2007) *Absence Management. Annual survey report.* London: CIPD.

CIPD (2011) *Managing Careers for Organisational Capability.* London: CIPD.

CIPD (2012) *Measuring, Reporting and Costing Sickness Absence.* Available at: http://www.cipd.co.uk/NR/rdonlyres/3A208F80-3484-4CE7-B8DD-907FFE660850/0/Wellbeing_sample_chapter_02.pdf.%20S%C3%B3tt%20%C3%BEann%2012 (accessed 8 August 2014).

Clarke, A., Oswald, A. and Warr, P. (1996) 'Is job satisfaction U-shaped in age?', *Journal of Occupational and Organizational Psychology*, 69, 57–81.

Clarke, L. (1994) *The Essence of Change.* London: Prentice Hall.

Clarke, M. (2013) 'The organisational career: Not dead but in need of redefinition', *International Journal of Human Resource Management*, 24, 684–703.

Clarke, S. and Cooper, C.L. (2004) *Managing the Safety Risk of Workplace Stress.* London: Routledge.

Cleary, T.S. and Shapiro, S.I. (1996) 'Abraham Maslow and Asian psychology', *Psychologia*, 39, 213–22.

Clegg, C. and Spencer, C. (2007) 'A circular and dynamic model of the process of job design', *Journal of Occupational and Organizational Psychology*, 80, 321–39.

Clegg, S. and Cooper, C.L. (2009) *The Sage Handbook of Organisational Behaviour: Macro approaches.* California and London: Sage.

Clevenger, J., Pereira, G.M., Wiechmann, D., Schmitt, N. and Harvey, V.S. (2001) 'Incremental validity of situational judgment tests', *Journal of Applied Psychology*, 86, 410–17.

Clinton, M.E. and Guest, D.E. (2014) 'Psychological contract breach and voluntary turnover: Testing a multiple mediation model', *Journal of Occupational and Organizational Psychology*, 87, 200–7.

Clutterbuck, D. (2004) *Everyone Needs a Mentor*, 4th edition. London: CIPD.

Coch, L. and French, J.R.P. (1948) 'Overcoming resistance to change', *Human Relations*, 1, 512–32.

Coghlan, D. (1993) 'In defence of process consultation', in C. Mabey and B. Mayon-White (eds), *Managing Change*, 2nd edition. London: Open University/Paul Chapman Publishing.

Coghlan, D. and Jacobs, C. (2005) 'Kurt Lewin on re-education; Foundations for action research', *Journal of Applied Behavioural Science*, 41, 444–57.

Cohen, J. (1977) *Statistical Power Analysis for the Behavioural Sciences.* London: Academic Press.

Cohen, J., Cohen, P., West, S. and Aiken, L. (2003) *Applied Multiple Regression/Correlation Analysis for the Behavioural Sciences*, 3rd edition. Mahwah, NJ: Lawrence Erlbaum Associates.

Cohen, S., Miller, G.E. and Rabin, B.S. (2001) 'Psychological stress and antibody response to immunisation: A critical review of the human literature', *Psychosomatic Medicine*, 63, 7–18.

Collins, D. (1998) *Organisational Change*. London: Routledge.

Colquitt, J.A., Conlon, D.E., Wesson, M.J., Porter, C.O. and Ng, K.Y. (2001) 'Justice at the millennium: A meta-analytic review of 25 years of organisational justice research', *Journal of Applied Psychology*, 86, 425–45.

Colquitt, J.A., Greenberg, J. and Scott, B.A. (2005) 'Organisational justice: Where do we stand?', in J. Greenberg and J.A. Colquitt (eds), *Handbook of Organisational Justice*. Mahwah, NJ: Lawrence Erlbaum.

Colquitt, J.A., LePine, J.A. and Noe, R.A. (2000) 'Toward an integrative theory of training motivation: A meta-analytic path analysis of 20 years of research', *Journal of Applied Psychology*, 85, 678–707.

Communications Directorate, South West Thames Regional Health Authority (1993) *Report of the Inquiry into the London Ambulance Service* (February 1993). London: Communications Directorate, South West Thames Regional Health Authority.

Conen, W.S., Henkens, K. and Schippers, J.J. (2011) 'Are employers changing their behaviour towards older workers? An analysis of employers' surveys 2000–2009', *Journal of Ageing and Social Policy*, 23, 141–58.

Conger, J.A. and Kanungo, R.N. (1998) *Charismatic Leadership in Organisations*. London: Sage.

Conger, J.A., Kanungo, R.N. and Menon, S.T. (2000) 'Charismatic leadership and follower effects', *Journal of Organisational Behaviour*, 21(7), 747–67.

Conn, S. and Rieke, M. (eds) (1994) *16PF-5. Technical Manual*. Champaign, IL: Institute for Personality and Ability Testing.

Conner, P.E. (1977) 'A critical enquiry into some assumptions and values characterising OD', *Academy of Management Review*, 2(1), 635–44.

Conte, J.M. (2005) 'A review and critique of emotional intelligence measures', *Journal of Organisational Behaviour*, 26, 433–40.

Conway, J.M. and Huffcutt, A.I. (1997) 'Psychometric properties of multisource performance ratings: A meta-analysis of subordinate, supervisor, peer and self-ratings', *Human Performance*, 10, 331–60.

Conway, N. and Briner, R.B. (2005) *Understanding Psychological Contracts at Work: A critical evaluation of theory and research*. Oxford: Oxford University Press.

Conway, N. and Coyle-Shapiro, J.A.M. (2012) 'The reciprocal relationship between psychological contract fulfilment and employee performance and the moderating role of perceived organisational support and tenure', *Journal of Occupational and Organizational Psychology*, 85, 277–99.

Conway, N., Guest, D. and Trenberth, L. (2011) 'Testing the differential effects of changes in psychological contract breach and fulfilment', *Journal of Vocational Behaviour*, 79, 267–76.

Cook, M. (2004) *Personnel Selection: Adding value through people*, 4th edition. London: Wiley.

Cook, M. (2009) *Personnel Selection: Adding value through people*, 5th edition. Oxford: Wiley-Blackwell.

Cook, T.D. and Campbell, D.T. (1979) *Quasi-experimentation: Design and analysis issues for field settings*. Chicago, IL: Rand McNally.

Cook, T.D. and Shadish, W.R. (1994) 'Social experiments: Some developments over the past fifteen years', *Annual Review of Psychology*, 45, 545–79.

Cook, T.D., Campbell, D.T. and Peracchio, L. (1990) 'Quasi experimentation', in M.D. Dunnette and L.M. Hough (eds), *Handbook of Industrial and Organisational Psychology*. Palo Alto, CA: Consulting Psychologists Press.

Cooke, B., Mills, A.J. and Kelley, E.S. (2005) 'Situating Maslow in Cold War America', *Group and Organisation Management*, 30, 129–52.

Coombs, R. and Hull, R. (1994) 'The best or the worst of both worlds: BPR, cost reduction and the strategic management of IT'. Paper presented to the OASIG Seminar on Organisation Change through IT and BPR: Beyond the Hype, September, London.

Cooper, C.L. and Cartwright, S. (1994) 'Healthy mind; healthy organisation – a proactive approach to occupational stress', *Human Relations*, 47, 455–71.

Cooper, C.L. and Lewis, S. (1993) *The Workplace Revolution: Managing today's dual career families.* London: Kogan Page.

Cooper, C.L. and Quick, J. (1999) *Stress and Strain.* Oxford: Health Press.

Cooper, C.L. and Sadri, G. (1991) 'The impact of stress counselling at work', in P.L. Perrewe (ed.), *Handbook of Job Stress* (special issue), *Journal of Social Behaviour and Personality*, 6, 411–23.

Cooper, C.L., Dewe, P. and O'Driscoll, M. (2001) *Organisational Stress: A review and critique of theory, research and application.* London: Sage.

Cooper, C.L., Sloan, S. and Williams, S. (1987) *Occupational Stress Indicator.* Windsor: NFER/ Nelson.

Cooper, C.L., Sloan, S. and Williams, S. (1988) *Occupational Stress Indicator: The manual.* Windsor: NFER/Nelson.

Cooper-Thomas, H., Anderson, N. and Cash, M. (2011) 'Investigating organisational socialisation: A fresh look at newcomer adjustment strategies', *Personnel Review*, 41, 41–55.

Coopey, J. and Hartley, J. (1991) 'Reconsidering the case for organisational commitment', *Human Resource Management Journal*, 1, 18–32.

Corr, P.J. and Gray, J.A. (1996) 'Attributional style as a personality factor in insurance sales performance in the UK', *Journal of Occupational and Organizational Psychology*, 69, 83–7.

Costa, P.T. and McCrae, R.R. (1992) *The NEO PI-R Professional Manual.* Odessa, FL: Psychological Assessment Resources Inc.

Costa, P.T. and McCrae, R.R. (2006) *Revised NEO Personality Inventory (NEO PI-R) Manual* (UK edition). Oxford: Hogrefe.

Costa, P.T., Zonderman A.B. and McCrae R.R. (1991) 'Personality, defence, coping, and adaptation in older adulthood', in E.M. Cummings, A.L. Greene and K.K. Karraker (eds), *Life-span Development Psychology: Perspectives on stress and coping.* Hillsdale, NJ: Laurence Erlbaum Associates.

Coulson-Thomas, C. and Coe, T. (1991) *The Flat Organisation.* London: British Institute of Management.

Courtney, A.J. and Chow, H.M. (2001) 'A study of the discriminability of shape symbols by foot', *Ergonomics*, 44, 328–38.

Cox, T. (1993) *Stress Research and Stress Management: Putting theory to work.* Sudbury: HSE Books.

Cox, T., Griffiths, A.J., Barlow, C.A., Randall, R.J., Thomson, L.E. and Rial-Gonzalez, E. (2000) *Organisational Interventions for Work Stress.* Sudbury: HSE Books.

Cox, T., Karanika, M., Griffiths, A. and Houdmont, J. (2007) 'Evaluating organisational-level work stress interventions: Beyond traditional methods', *Work & Stress,* 21, 348–68.

Cox, T., Randall, R. and Griffiths, A. (2002) *Interventions to Control Stress at Work in Hospital Staff.* Sudbury: HSE Books.

Coyne, I. (2010) 'Bullying in the workplace', in C.P. Monks and I. Coyne (eds), *Bullying in Different Contexts.* Cambridge: Cambridge University Press.

Coyne, I., Seigne, E. and Randall, P. (2000) 'Predicting workplace victim status from personality', *European Journal of Work and Organisational Psychology,* 9, 335–50.

Crail, M. (2007) 'Assessment centres are worth the high cost', *Personnel Today,* 8(21), 49.

Cramton, C.D. (2001) 'The mutual knowledge problem and its consequences for dispersed collaboration', *Organisation Science,* 12, 246–371.

Cramton, C.D. (2002) 'Attribution in distributed teams', in P. Hinds and S. Kiesler (eds), *Distributed Work.* Cambridge, MA: MIT Press.

Cramton, C.D. and Webber, S.S. (2005) 'Relationships among geographic dispersion, team processes and effectiveness in software development work teams', *Journal of Business Research,* 58, 758–65.

Cramton, C.D. and Wilson, J.M. (2002) 'Explanation and judgement in distributed groups: An interactional justice perspective'. Paper presented at the Academy of Management Conference, Denver, CO.

Cramton, C.D., Orvis, K.L. and Wilson, J.M. (2007) 'Situation invisibility and attribution in distributed collaborations', *Journal of Management,* 33, 525–46.

Crandall, B., Klein, G. and Hoffman, R.R. (2006) *Working Mind: A practitioner's guide to cognitive task analysis.* Cambridge, MA: MIT Press.

Crawford, E.R., LePine, J.A. and Rich, B.L. (2010) 'Linking job demands and resources to employee engagement and burnout: A theoretical extension and meta-analytic test', *Journal of Applied Psychology,* 95, 834–48.

Creed, P.A., King, V., Hood, M. and McKenzie, R. (2009) 'Goal orientation, self-regulation strategies and job-seeking intensity in unemployed adults', *Journal of Applied Psychology,* 94, 806–13.

Crisp, C.B. and Jarvenpaa, S.L. (2000) 'Trust over time in global virtual teams'. Research paper at the Academy of Management Meeting, Toronto, Canada, 2000.

Croft, A. and Schmader, T. (2012) 'The feedback withholding bias: Minority students do not receive critical feedback from evaluators concerned about appearing racist', *Journal of Experimental Social Psychology,* 48, 1139–44.

Cronbach, L.J. (1970) *Essentials of Psychological Testing.* New York: Harper and Row.

Cronin, M.A., Weingart, L.R. and Todorova, G. (2011) 'Dynamics in groups: Are we there yet?', *The Academy of Management Annals,* 5, 571–612.

Cropanzano, R. and Stein, J.H. (2009) 'Organisational justice and behavioural ethics', *Business Ethics Quarterly,* 19, 193–233.

Cropanzano, R., Bowen, D.E. and Gilliland, S.W. (2007) 'The management of organisational justice', *Academy of Management Perspectives*, 21(4), 34–48.

Cropanzano, R., Byrne, Z.S., Bobocel, D.R. and Rupp, D.E. (2001) 'Moral virtues, fairness heuristics, social entities and other denizens of organisational justice', *Journal of Vocational Behaviour*, 58, 164–209.

Crosby, P.B. (1979) *Quality is Free*. New York: McGraw-Hill.

Cruise O'Brien, R. and Voss, C. (1992) *In Search of Quality*. Working Paper. London: London Business School.

Csikszentmihalyi, M. (1990) *Flow: The Psychology of Optimal Experience*. New York: Harper and Row.

Csikszentmihalyi, M. (1999) 'If we are so rich, why aren't we happy?', *American Psychologist*, 54, 821–7.

Cummings, J.N. and Haas, M.R., (2012) 'So many teams, so little time: Time allocation matters in geographically dispersed teams', *Journal of Organisational Behaviour*, 33, 316–41.

Cummings, T. and Cooper, C.L. (1979) 'A cybernetic framework for the study of occupational stress', *Human Relations*, 32, 395–419.

Cummings, T.G. and Huse, E.F. (1989) *Organisation Development and Change*. St Paul, MN: West.

Cummings, T.G. and Worley, C.G. (1997) *Organisation Development and Change*, 6th edition. Cincinnati, OH: South-Western College Publishing.

Cummings, T.G. and Worley, C.G. (2001) *Organisation Development and Change*, 7th edition. Cincinnati, OH: South-Western College Publishing.

Cummings, T.G. and Worley, C.G. (2013) *Organisation Development and Change*, 10th edition. Stamford, CT: Cengage Learning.

Currie, G. and Kerrin, M. (2003) 'Human resource management and knowledge management: Enhancing knowledge sharing in a pharmaceutical company', *International Journal of Human Resource Management*, 14(6), 1027–45.

Daft, R.L. and Lengel, R.H. (1986) 'Organisational information requirements, media richness and structural design', *Management Science*, 32, 554–71.

Dai, G., De Meuse, K. and Peterson, C. (2010) 'Impact of multisource feedback on leadership competency development: A longitudinal field study', *Journal of Managerial Issues*, 22, 197–219.

Dambrin, C. (2004) 'How does telework influence the management–employee relationship?', *International Journal of Human Resource Development and Management*, 4, 358–74.

Daniels, K.J., Boocock, J.G., Glover, J., Hartley, R. and Holland, J. (2009) 'An experience sampling study of learning, affect and the demand control support model', *Journal of Applied Psychology*, 94, 1003–17.

Danziger, N., Rachman-Moore, D. and Valency, R. (2008) 'The construct validity of Schein's career anchors orientation inventory', *Career Development International*, 13, 7–19.

Darr, W. and Johns, G. (2008) 'Work strain, health and absenteeism', *Journal of Occupational Health Psychology*, 13, 293–318.

Davenport, T.H. (1993) *Process Innovation: Re-engineering Work through IT*. Boston, MA: Harvard Business School Press.

Davies, I.K. (1972) *The Management of Learning*. London: McGraw-Hill.

Davis, F.D. and Yi, M.Y. (2004) 'Improving computer skill training: Behaviour modelling, symbolic mental rehearsal, and the role of knowledge structures', *Journal of Applied Psychology*, 89, 509–23.

Dawson, P. (1994) *Organisational Change: A Processual Approach*. London: Paul Chapman Publishing.

Dawson, P. (2003) *Reshaping Change: A processual perspective*. London: Routledge.

Dawson, P. (2011) 'The contribution of the processual approach to the theory and practice of organisational change', in D.M. Boje, B. Burnes and J. Hassard (eds), *The Routledge Companion to Organisational Change*. London: Routledge.

Day, D.V., Zaccaro, S.J. and Halpin, S.M. (2014) *Leader Development for Transforming Organisations: Growing leaders for tomorrow*. Abingdon, Oxon: Routledge.

De Cuyper, N., Mauno, S., Kinnunen, U. and Mäkikangas, A. (2011) 'The role of job resources in the relation between perceived employability and turnover intention: A prospective two-sample study', *Journal of Vocational Behaviour*, 78, 253–63.

De Hoogh, A.H.B. and Den Hartog, D.N. (2008) 'Social responsibility, ethical leadership and performance', *Leadership Quarterly*, 19, 297–311.

De Hoogh, A.H.B., Den Hartog, D.N., Koopman, P.L., Thierry, H., Van den Berg, P.T., Van der Weide, J.G. and Wilderom, C.P.M. (2004) 'Charismatic leadership, environmental dynamism and performance', *European Journal of Work and Organisational Psychology*, 13(4), 447–71.

De Hoogh, A.H.B., Den Hartog, D.N., Koopman, P.L., Thierry, H., Van den Berg, P.T., Van der Weide, J.G. and Wilderom, C.P.M. (2005) 'Leader motives, charismatic leadership and subordinates' work attitude in the profit and voluntary sector', *Leadership Quarterly*, 16(1), 17–35.

de Jonge, J. and Dormann, C. (2006) 'Stressors, resources and strain at work: A longitudinal test of the triple-match principle', *Journal of Applied Psychology*, 91, 1359–74.

De Lange, A.H., Taris, T.W., Kompier, M.A.J., Houtman, I.L.D. and Bongers, P.M. (2003) '"The very best of the millennium": Longitudinal research and the demand-control-(support) model', *Journal of Occupational Health Psychology*, 8, 282–305.

de Meijer, L.A. and Born, M.P. (2009) 'The situational judgement test: Advantages and disadvantages', *Online readings in testing and assessment, International Test Commission*. Available at http://www.intestcom.org/Publications/ORTA

De Menezes, L.M. and Kelliher, C. (2011) 'Flexible working and performance: A systematic review of the evidence for a business case', *International Journal of Management Reviews*, 13, 452–74.

De Treville, S. and Antonakis, J. (2006) 'Could lean production job design be intrinsically motivating? Contextual, configurational and levels-of-analysis issues', *Journal of Operations Management*, 24, 99–123.

De Vos, A. and Dries, N. (2013) 'Applying a talent management lens to career management: The role of human capital composition and continuity', *International Journal of Human Resource Management*, 24, 1816–31.

De Vos, A., Dewettinck, K. and Buyens, D. (2009) 'The professional career on the right track: A study on the interaction between career self-management and organisational career management in explaining employee outcomes', *European Journal of Work and Organisational Psychology*, 18, 55–80.

De Vries, R.E., Pathak, R.D. and Paquin, A.R. (2011) 'The paradox of power sharing: Participative charismatic leaders have subordinates with more instead of less need for leadership', *European Journal of Work and Organisational Psychology*, 20, 779–804.

De Witte, K. and van Muijen, J.J. (1999) 'Organisational culture: Critical questions for researchers and practitioners', *European Journal of Work and Organisational Psychology*, 8(4), 583–95.

De Witte H., Verhofstadt, E. and Omey, E. (2007) 'Testing Karasek's learning and strain hypotheses on young workers in their first job', *Work & Stress*, 21, 131–41.

Deal, T. and Kennedy, A. (1982) 'Culture: A new look through old lenses', *Journal of Applied Behavioural Science*, 19(4), 497–507.

Dean, J.W. Jr and Sharfman, M.P. (1996) 'Does decision process matter? A study of strategic decision-making effectiveness', *Academy of Management Journal*, 39, 368–96.

Dean, M.A., Roth, P.L. and Bobko, P. (2008) 'Ethnic and gender subgroup differences in assessment centre ratings: A meta-analysis', *Journal of Applied Psychology*, 93, 685–91.

Deci, E.L. and Ryan, R.M. (1980) 'The empirical exploration of intrinsic motivational processes', in L. Berkowitz (ed.), *Advances in Experimental Social Psychology*, vol. 13. New York: Academic Press.

Defence Science and Technology Office (DSTO) (2010) *Human Systems Integration is Worth the Money and Effort! The argument for the application of human systems integration processes in defence capability acquisition.* Canberra, ACT: Department of Defence.

DeFillippi, R.J. and Arthur, M.B. (1996) 'Boundaryless contexts and careers: A competency-based perspective', in M.B. Arthur and D.M. Rousseau (eds), *The Boundaryless Career: A new employment principle for a new organisational era.* Oxford: Oxford University Press.

Dekker, S.W.A. and Woods, D.D. (2002) 'MABA-MABA or abracadabra? Progress on human-automation coordination', *Cognition, Technology and Work*, 4, 240–4.

Demerouti, E., Bakker, A.B., Nachreiner, F. and Schaufeli, W.B. (2001) 'The job demands resources model of burnout', *Journal of Applied Psychology*, 86, 499–512.

Demir, A., Ulusoy, M. and Ulusoy, M.F. (2003) 'Investigation of factors influencing burnout levels in professional and private lives of nurses', *International Journal of Nursing Studies*, 40, 807–27.

Den Hartog, D.N., De Hoogh, A.H.B. and Keegan, A.E. (2007) 'Belongingness as a moderator of the charisma–OCB relationship', *Journal of Applied Psychology*, 92(4), 1131–9.

Den Hartog, D.N., House, R.J., Hanges, P.J., Ruiz-Quintanilla, S.A. and Dorfman, P.W. (1999) 'Culture-specific and cross-culturally generalizable implicit leadership theories: Are attributes of charismatic/transformational leadership universally endorsed?', *Leadership Quarterly*, 10, 219–57.

Den Hartog, D.N., Van Muijen, J.J. and Koopman, P.L. (1997) 'Transactional versus transformational leadership: An analysis of the MLQ', *Journal of Occupational and Organizational Psychology*, 70, 19–34.

DeNeve, K.M. and Cooper, H. (1998) 'The happy personality: A meta-analysis of 137 personality traits and subjective well-being', *Psychological Bulletin*, 124, 197–229.

Dent, E.B. and Goldberg, S.G. (1999) 'Challenging resistance to change', *Journal of Applied Behavioural Science*, 35, 25–41.

Department for Work and Pensions (2014) *Press release: Older People's Day: 1 million in work over 65: 3 years since end of default retirement age*. https://www.gov.uk/government/news/older-peoples-day-1-million-in-work-over-65-3-years-since-end-of-default-retirement-age

Department of Defence (1999) *Department of Defence Design Criteria Standard: Human Engineering (MIL-STD-1472F)*. Ft Belvoir, VA: US Department of Defence 1947b7 Program Office.

Derks, D. and Bakker, A.B. (eds) (2013) *The Psychology of Digital Media at Work*. Hove, Sussex: Psychology Press.

Derks, D. and Bakker, A.B. (2014) 'Smartphone use, work–home interference, and burnout: A diary study on the role of recovery', *Applied Psychology: An International Review*, 63, 411–40.

Derks, D., Fischer, A.H. and Bos, A.E.R. (2008) 'The role of emotion in computer-mediated communication: A review', *Computers in Human Behaviour*, 24, 766–85.

Derogatis, L.R. and Melisaratos, N. (1983) 'The brief symptom inventory: An introductory report', *Psychological Medicine*, 13, 595–605.

DeRue, D.S., Nahrgang, J.D., Wellman, N.E.D. and Humphrey, S.E. (2011) 'Trait and behavioural theories of leadership: An integration and meta-analytic test of their relative validity', *Personnel Psychology*, 64, 7–52.

DeShon, R.P. and Gillespie, J.Z. (2005) 'A motivated action theory account of goal orientation', *Journal of Applied Psychology*, 90, 1096–127.

DeVaro, J., Li, R. and Brookshire, D. (2007) 'Analysing the job characteristics model: New support from a cross-section of establishments', *International Journal of Human Resource Management*, 18, 986–1003.

Devine, D.J. and Philips, J.L. (2001) 'Do smarter teams do better? A meta-analysis of cognitive ability and team performance', *Small Group Research*, 32(5), 507–33.

Devine, P.G. (1989) 'Stereotypes and prejudice: Their automatic and controlled components', *Journal of Personality and Social Psychology*, 56, 5–18.

DeYoung, C.G., Quilty, L.C. and Peterson, J.B. (2007) 'Between facets and domains: 10 aspects of the Big Five', *Journal of Personality and Social Psychology*, 93(5), 880–96.

Diamantopoulos, A. and Schlegelmilch, B. (1997) *Taking the Fear out of Data Analysis*. London: Dryden Press.

Diaper, D. and Stanton, N.A. (eds) (2004) *The Handbook of Task Analysis for Human–Computer Interaction*. Mahwah, NJ: Lawrence Erlbaum Associates.

Dick, P. (2004) 'Discourse analysis', in C. Cassell and G. Symon (eds), *Essential Guide to Qualitative Methods in Organisational Research*. London: Sage.

Dick, P. and Hyde, R. (2006) 'Consent as resistance, resistance as consent: Re-reading part-time professionals' acceptance of their marginal positions', *Gender, Work and Organisation*, 13(6), 543–64.

Dickson, M.W., Den Hartog, D.N. and Mitchelson, J.K. (2003) 'Research on leadership in a cross-cultural context: Making progress, and raising new questions', *Leadership Quarterly*, 14(6), 729–68.

Diehl, M. and Stroebe, W. (1987) 'Productivity loss in brainstorming groups: Towards the solution of a riddle', *Journal of Personality and Social Psychology*, 53, 497–509.

Digman, J.M. (1990) 'Personality structure: Emergence of the five-factor model', *Annual Review of Psychology*, 41, 417–40.

Dipboye, R.L. (2005) 'The selection/recruitment interview: Core processes and contexts', in A. Evers, N. Anderson and O. Voskuijl (eds), *The Blackwell Handbook of Personnel Selection*. Malden, MA: Blackwell Publishing.

Dipboye, R.L., Macan, T. and Shahani-Denning, C. (2012) 'The selection interview from the interviewer and applicant perspectives: Can't have one without the other', *The Oxford Handbook of Personnel Assessment and Selection*, 323–53.

Direnzo, M.S., Greenhaus, J.H. and Weer, C.H. (2015) 'Relationship between protean career orientation and work–life balance: A resource perspective', *Journal of Organisational Behaviour*, 36, 538–60.

Dollinger, S.J., Burke, P.A. and Gump, N.W. (2007) 'Creativity and values', *Creativity Research Journal*, 19(2–3), 91–103.

Donald, I., Taylor, P., Johnson, S., Cooper, C., Cartwright, S. and Robertson, S. (2005) 'Work environments, stress and productivity: An examination using ASSET', *International Journal of Stress Management*, 12, 409–23.

Donaldson-Feilder, E., Yarker, J. and Lewis, R. (2008) 'Management competencies for preventing and reducing stress at work', in J. Houdmont and S. Leka (eds), *Occupational Health Psychology: European Perspectives on Research, Education and Practice*, vol. III. Nottingham, UK: European Academy of Occupational Health Psychology and Nottingham University Press.

Donnellan, M.B., Oswald, F.L., Baird, B.M. and Lucas, R.E. (2006) 'The mini-IPIP scales: Tiny-yet-effective measures of the Big Five factors of personality', *Psychological Assessment*, 18(2), 192–203.

Donohue, R. (2006) 'Person-environment congruence in relation to career change and career persistence', *Journal of Vocational Behavior*, 68(3), 504–15.

Dorfman, P., Javidan, M., Hanges, P., Dastmalchian, A. and House, R. (2012) 'GLOBE: A twenty year journey into the intriguing world of culture and leadership', *Journal of World Business*, 47, 504–18.

Dormann, C. and Zapf, D. (2001) 'Job satisfaction: A meta-analysis of stabilities', *Journal of Organisational Behaviour*, 22, 483–504.

Dries, N. (2013) 'The psychology of talent management: A review and research agenda', *Human Resource Management Review*, 23(4), 272–85.

Dries, N., Pepermans, R. and Carlier, O. (2008) 'Career success: Constructing a multidimensional model', *Journal of Vocational Behaviour*, 73, 254–67.

Duarte, D.L. and Snyder, N.T. (2001) *Mastering Virtual Teams: Strategies, tools and techniques that succeed*, 2nd edition. San Francisco, CA: Jossey-Bass.

Duckworth, A.L., Quinn, P.D., Lynam, D.R., Loeber, R. and Stouthamer-Loeber, M. (2011) 'Role of test motivation in intelligence testing', *Proceedings of the National Academy of Sciences*, 108, 7716–20.

Dunham, R., Grube, J.A. and Castañeda, M.B. (1994) 'Organisational commitment: The utility of an integrative definition', *Journal of Applied Psychology*, 79, 370–80.

Dunphy, D. and Stace, D. (1992) *Under New Management: Australian organisations in transition*. Roseville, NSW, Australia: McGraw-Hill.

Dunphy, D. and Stace, D. (1993) 'The strategic management of corporate change', *Human Relations*, 46(8), 905–18.

Dweck, C.S. (1986) 'Motivational processes affecting learning', *American Psychologist*, 41, 1040–8.

Dweck, C.S. and Elliott, E.S. (1983) 'Achievement motivation', in E.M. Hetherington (ed.), *Socialisation, Personality, and Social Development*. New York: Wiley.

Dwyer, D.J. and Ganster, D.C. (1991) 'The effects of job demands and control on employee attendance and satisfaction', *Journal of Organisational Behaviour*, 12, 595–608.

Eagly, A. and Carli, L. (2003) 'The female leadership advantage: An evaluation of the evidence', *Leadership Quarterly*, 14, 807–34.

Eagly, A.H., Karau, S.J. and Makhijani, M.G. (1995) 'Gender and the effectiveness of leaders: A meta-analysis', *Psychological Bulletin*, 117, 125–45.

Earl, J. and Bright, J. (2007) 'The relationship between career decision status and important work outcomes', *Journal of Vocational Behaviour*, 71, 233–46.

Earley, C.P. (1989) 'Social loafing and collectivism: A comparison of the United States and the People's Republic of China', *Administrative Science Quarterly*, 34, 565–81.

Earnest, D.R., Allen, D.G. and Landis, R.S. (2011) 'Mechanisms linking realistic job previews with turnover: A meta-analytic path analysis', *Personnel Psychology*, 64, 865–97.

Easterby-Smith, M., Crossan, M. and Nicolini, D. (2000) 'Organisational learning: Debates past, present and future', *Journal of Management Studies*, 37(6), 783–96.

Easterby-Smith, M., Thorpe, R. and Jackson, P. (2012) *Management Research: An introduction*, 4th edition. London: Sage.

Easterby-Smith, M., Thorpe, R. and Lowe, A. (2002) *Management Research: An introduction*, 2nd edition. London: Sage.

Eby, L.T., Allen, T.D., Hoffman, B.J., Baranik, L.E., Sauer, J.B., Baldwin, S. and Evans, S.C. (2013) 'An interdisciplinary meta-analysis of the potential antecedents, correlates, and consequences of protégé perceptions of mentoring', *Psychological Bulletin*, 139, 441–76.

Eby, L.T., Butts, M. and Lockwood, A. (2003) 'Predictors of success in the era of the boundaryless career', *Journal of Organisational Behaviour*, 24, 689–708.

Eby, L.T., Freeman, D.M., Rush, M.C. and Charles, L.E. (1999) 'Motivational bases of affective organisational commitment: A partial test of an integrative theoretical model', *Journal of Occupational and Organizational Psychology*, 72, 463–83.

Economist Intelligence Unit (1992) *Making Quality Work: Lessons from Europe's leading companies*. London: Economist Intelligence Unit.

Eden, M. and Chisholm, R.F. (1993) 'Emerging varieties of action research', *Human Relations*, 46, 121–42.

Edkins, G.D. (2002) 'A review of the benefits of aviation human factors training', *Human Factors Aerospace Safety*, 2, 201–16.

Edwardes, M. (1983) *Back from the Brink*. London: Collins.

Edwards, J.A., Webster, S., Van Laar, D. and Easton, S. (2008) 'Psychometric analysis of the UK Health and Safety Executive's Management Standards work-related Stress Indicator Tool', *Work & Stress*, 22, 96–107.

Edworthy, J. and Patterson, R.D. (1985) 'Ergonomic factors in auditory warnings', in I.D. Brown, R. Goldsmith, K. Coombes and M.A. Sinclair (eds), *Ergonomics International 85*. London: Taylor and Francis.

Effelsberg, D., Solga, M. and Gurt, J. (2014) 'Getting followers to transcend their self-interest for the benefit of the company: Testing a core assumption of transformational leadership theory', *Journal of Business Psychology*, 29, 131–43.

Egan, M., Bambra, C., Petticrew, M. and Whitehead, M. (2008) 'Reviewing evidence on complex social interventions: Appraising implementation in systemic reviews of the health effects of organisational-level workplace interventions', *Journal of Epidemiology and Community Health*. Published online 21 August 2008, DOI:10.1136/jech.2007.07.1233.

Einarsen, S. (1999) 'The nature and causes of bullying at work', *International Journal of Manpower*, 20, 16–27.

Einarsen, S. and Mikkelsen, E.G. (2003) 'Individual effects of exposure to bullying at work', in S. Einarsen, H. Hoel, D. Zapf and C.L. Cooper (eds), *Bullying and Emotional Abuse in the Workplace: International perspectives in research and practice*. London: Taylor and Francis.

Einarsen, S., Raknes, B.I. and Matthiesen, S.B. (1994) 'Bullying and harassment at work and their relationship to work environment quality: An explanatory study', *European Journal of Work and Organisational Psychology*, 5, 185–201.

Eisenberger, R., Rhoades, L. and Cameron, J. (1999) 'Does pay for performance increase or decrease perceived self-determination and intrinsic motivation?', *Journal of Personality and Social Psychology*, 77(5), 1026–40.

Eldridge, J.E.T. and Crombie, A.D. (1974) *A Sociology of Organisations*. London: George Allen and Unwin.

Ellemers, N., Spears, R. and Doosji, B. (2002) 'Self and social identity', *Annual Review of Psychology*, 53, 161–86.

Elliot, A.J. and Harackiewicz, J.M. (1996) 'Approach and avoidance achievement goals and intrinsic motivation: A mediational analysis', *Journal of Personality and Social Psychology*, 70, 461–75.

Elliot, A.J., Shell, M.M., Henry, K.B. and Maier, M.A. (2005) 'Achievement goals, performance contingencies, and performance attainment: An experimental test', *Journal of Educational Psychology*, 97, 630.

Ellis, A.M., Bauer, T.N., Mansfield, L.R., Erdogan, B., Truxillo, D.M. and Simon, L.S. (2015) 'Navigating uncharted waters: Newcomer socialisation through the lens of stress theory', *Journal of Management*, 41, 203–35.

Elo, A.-L., Ervasti, J. and Mattila, P. (2008) 'Evaluation of an organisational stress management program in a municipal public works organisation', *Journal of Occupational Health Psychology*, 13, 10–23.

Elsbach, K.D. and Hargadon, A.B. (2006) 'Enhancing creativity through "mindless" work: A framework of workday design', *Organisation Science*, 17, 470–83.

Ely, R.J. and Thomas, D.A. (2001) 'Cultural diversity at work: The effects of diversity perspectives on work group processes', *Administrative Science Quarterly*, 46, 229–73.

Embrey, D.E. (1986) 'SHERPA: A systematic human error reduction and prediction approach'. Paper presented at the International Meeting on Advances in Nuclear Power Systems, Knoxville, Tennessee.

Emmerling, R.J. and Goleman, D. (2003) 'Emotional intelligence: Issues and common misunderstandings', The Consortium for Research on Emotional Intelligence in Organisations Issues in EI (www.eiconsortium.org).

Employee Assistance Professionals Association (EAPA) (2003) *EAPA Standards and Professional Guidelines for Employee Assistance Programs*. Arlington, VA: Employee Assistance Professionals Association.

Endsley, M.R. (1988) 'Design and evaluation for situation awareness enhancement', in *Proceedings of the Human Factors Society 32nd Annual Meeting*. Santa Monica, CA: Human Factors Society.

Eppinger, S.D. (2001) 'Innovation at the speed of information', *Harvard Business Review*, January, 149–60.

Erez, M. (1986) 'The congruence of goal-setting strategies with sociocultural values and its effect on performance', *Journal of Management*, 12, 585–92.

Erez, M. and Somech, A. (1996) 'Is group productivity loss the rule or the exception? Effects of culture and group-based motivation', *Academy of Management Journal*, 39, 1513–37.

Erikson, E.H. (1968) *Identity, Youth and Crisis*. New York: W.W. Norton.

Erikson, E.H. (1980) *Identity and the Life Cycle*. New York: W.W. Norton.

Eurofound (2012) *Fifth European Working Conditions Survey*. Luxembourg: Publications Office of the European Union.

European Agency for Safety and Health at Work (EU-OSHA) (2014) *Calculating the Costs of Work-related Stress and Psychosocial Risk*. Luxembourg: Publications Office of the European Union.

Evers, A., Anderson, N. and Voskuijl, O. (eds) (2005) *The Blackwell Handbook of Personnel Selection*. Oxford: Blackwell Publishing.

Ewen, R.B. (2010) *An Introduction to Theories of Personality*, 7th edition. Hove, Sussex: Psychology Press.

Eysenck, H.J. (1967) *The Biological Basis of Personality*. Springfield, IL: Charles C. Thomas.

Eysenck, H.J. and Eysenck, S.B.G. (1964) *Manual of the Eysenck Personality Inventory*. London: University of London Press.

Ezzamel, M., Green, C., Lilley, S. and Willmott, H. (1994) *Change management: Appendix 1 – A review and analysis of recent changes in UK management practices*. Manchester: Financial Services Research Centre, UMIST.

Fang, R., Duffy, M.K. and Shaw, J.D. (2011) 'The organisational socialisation process: Review and development of a social capital model', *Journal of Management*, 37, 127–52.

Faragher, E.B., Cass, M. and Cooper, C.L. (2005) 'The relationship between job satisfaction and health: A meta-analysis', *Occupational and Environmental Medicine*, 62, 105–12.

Farr, J.L., Hofman, D.A. and Ringenbach, K.L. (1993) 'Goal orientation and action control theory: Implications for industrial and organisational psychology', in I.T. Robertson and C.L. Cooper (eds), *International Review of Industrial and Organisational Psychology*, vol. 8. Chichester: John Wiley.

Feldman, D.C. and Bolino, M.C. (2000) 'Career patterns of the self-employed: Career motivations and career outcomes', *Journal of Small Business Management*, 38, 53–67.

Ferguson, E. and Patterson, F. (1998) 'The Five Factor Model of personality: Openness as a distinct but related construct', *Personality and Individual Differences*, 24, 1–4.

Fernando, W.D.A. and Cohen, L. (2014) 'Respectable femininity and career agency: Exploring paradoxical imperatives', *Gender, Work and Organisation*, 21, 149–64.

Ferrie, J. (2004) 'Work, stress and health', *Occupational Health Review*, 111, 26–28.

Ferrie, J.A., Shipley, M.J., Newman, K., Stansfeld, S.A. and Marmot, M. (2005) 'Self-reported job insecurity and health in the Whitehall II study: Potential explanations of the relationship', *Social Science and Medicine*, 60, 1593–602.

Ferris, G.R. and King, T.R. (1991) 'Politics in human resources decisions: A walk on the dark side', *Organisational Dynamics*, 20, 59–71.

Ferris, P. (2004) 'A personal view: A preliminary typology of organisational response to allegations of workplace bullying: See no evil, speak no evil', *British Journal of Guidance and Counselling*, 32, 389–95.

Fevre, R., Lewis, D., Robinson A. and Jones, T. (2011) *Insight into Ill-treatment in the Workplace*. Cardiff: Cardiff School of Social Sciences.

Fiedler, F.E. (1967) *A Theory of Leadership Effectiveness*. New York: McGraw-Hill.

Fiedler, F.E. (1995) 'Cognitive resources and leadership performance', *Applied Psychology: An International Review*, 44, 5–28.

Field, A. (2009) *Discovering Statistics Using SPSS*. London: Sage.

Filby, I. and Willmott, H. (1988) 'Ideologies and contradictions in a public relations department', *Organisation Studies*, 9(3), 335–51.

Fine, S.A. and Cronshaw, S.F. (1999) *Functional Job Analysis: A foundation for human resources management*. Hove, Sussex: Psychology Press.

Fine, S.A. and Wiley, W.W. (1974) 'An introduction to functional job analysis', in E.A. Fleishman and A.R. Bass (eds), *Studies in Personal and Industrial Psychology*. Homewood, IL: Dorsey Press.

Finegan, J.E. (2000) 'The impact of person and organisational values on organisational commitment', *Journal of Occupational and Organizational Psychology*, 73, 149–69.

Finke, R.A., Ward, T.B. and Smith, S.M. (1992) *Creative Cognition: Theory, research, and applications*. Cambridge, MA: MIT Press.

Finkelstein, S. (1992) 'Power in top management teams: Dimensions, measurement and validation', *Academy of Management Journal*, 35, 505–38.

Finstad, N. (1998) 'The rhetoric of organisational change', *Human Relations*, 51, 717–40.

Fisher, D.M. (2014) 'A multilevel cross-cultural examination of role overload and organisational commitment: Investigating the interactive effects of context', *Journal of Applied Psychology*, 99, 723–36.

Fisher, S.G., Hunter, T.A. and Macrosson, W. (2001) 'A validation study of Belbin's team roles', *European Journal of Work and Organisational Psychology*, 10(2), 121–44.

Fiske, S.T. (2001) 'Effects of power on bias: Power explains and maintains individual, group and societal disparities', in A.Y. Lee-Chai and J.A. Bargh (eds), *The Use and Abuse of Power: Multiple perspectives on the causes of corruption*. New York: Taylor and Francis.

Fitts, P.M. (1962) 'Factors in complex skill training', in R. Glaser (ed.), *Training Research and Education*. New York: John Wiley.

Flanagan, J.C. (1954) 'The critical incident technique', *Psychological Bulletin*, 51, 327–58.

Flaxman, P.E. and Bond, F.W. (2010) 'Worksite stress management training: Moderated effects and clinical significance', *Journal of Occupational Health Psychology*, 15, 347–58.

Flaxman, P.E., Menard, J., Bond, F. and Kinman, G. (2012) 'Academics' experiences of a respite from work: Effects of self-critical perfectionism and preservative cognition on post-respite well-being', *Journal of Applied Psychology*, 97, 854–65.

Fleishman, E.A. (1969) *Leadership Opinion Questionnaire Manual*. Henley-on-Thames: Science Research Associates.

Fleming, P. (2013) '"Down with Big Brother!": The End of "Corporate Culturalism"?', *Journal of Management Studies*, 50, 474–96.

Fletcher, C. (2008) *Appraisal, Feedback and Development: Making performance review work*, 4th edition. Oxford: Routledge.

Fletcher, C. (2015) 'Using 360-degree feedback as a development tool', in K. Kraiger, J. Passmore, N. Rebelo dos Santos and S. Malvezzi (eds), *The Psychology of Training, Development and Performance Improvement*. Chichester: Wiley.

Fletcher, D. and Sarkar, M. (2013) 'Psychological resilience: A review and critique of definitions, concepts, and theory', *European Psychologist*, 18, 12–23.

Flum, H. and Blustein, D.L. (2000) 'Reinvigorating the study of vocational exploration: A framework for research', *Journal of Vocational Behaviour*, 56, 380–404.

Flynn, F.J. and Schaumberg, R.L. (2012) 'When feeling bad leads to feeling good: Guilt-proneness and affective organisational commitment', *Journal of Applied Psychology*, 97, 124–33.

Foley, B. and Cox, A. (2013) 'Work organisation and innovation – Case study: Nottingham University Hospitals NHS Trust, UK', Dublin: European Foundation for the Improvement of Living and Working Conditions.

Folger, R. (1977) 'Distributive and procedural justice: Combined impact on "voice" and improvement on experienced inequity', *Journal of Personality and Social Psychology*, 35, 109–19.

Folger, R., Rosenfield, D., Grove, J. and Corkran, L. (1979) 'Effects of "voice" and peer opinions on responses to inequity', *Journal of Personality and Social Psychology*, 37, 2253–61.

Forbes, D.P. and Milliken, F.J. (1999) 'Cognition and corporate governance: Understanding boards of directors as strategic decision-making groups', *Academy of Management Review*, 24(3), 489–505.

Ford, M.T. and Wooldridge, J.D. (2012) 'Industry growth, work role characteristics, and job satisfaction: A cross-level mediation model', *Journal of Occupational Health Psychology*, 17, 492–504.

Ford, M.T., Cerasoli, C.P., Higgins, J.A. and Decesare, A.L. (2011) 'Relationships between psychological, physical, and behavioural health and work performance: A review and meta-analysis', *Work & Stress*, 25, 185–204.

Ford, M.T., Heinen, B.A. and Langkamer, K.L. (2007) 'Work and family satisfaction and conflict: A meta-analysis of cross-domain relations', *Journal of Applied Psychology*, 92, 57–80.

Forret, M.L. and Dougherty, T.W. (2001) 'Correlates of networking behaviour for managerial and professional employees', *Group and Organisation Management*, 26, 283–311.

Forret, M.L. and Dougherty, T.W. (2004) 'Networking behaviours and career outcomes: Differences for men and women?', *Journal of Organisational Behaviour*, 25, 419–37.

Forret, M.L., Sullivan, S.E. and Mainiero, L.A. (2010) 'Gender role differences in reactions to unemployment: Exploring psychological mobility and boundaryless careers', *Journal of Organisational Behaviour*, 31, 647–66.

Forrier, A., Sels, L. and Stynen, D. (2009) 'Career mobility at the intersection between agent and structure: A conceptual model', *Journal of Occupational and Organizational Psychology*, 82, 739–59.

Fortin, M. (2008) 'Perspectives on organisational justice: Concept clarification, social context integration, time and links with morality', *International Journal of Management Reviews*, 10, 93–126.

Fotaki, M., Long, S. and Schwartz, H.S. (2012) 'What can psychoanalysis offer organisation studies today? Taking stock of current developments and thinking about future directions', *Organisation Studies*, 33, 1105–20.

Fox, M., Dwyer, D. and Ganster, D. (1993) 'Effects of stressful job demands and control on physiological and attitudinal outcomes in a hospital setting', *Academy of Management Journal*, 36, 289–318.

Francis, R. QC (2013) *Report of the Mid Staffordshire NHS Foundation Trust Public Inquiry*. http://www.midstaffspublicinquiry.com/sites/default/files/report/Executivesummary.pdf

Franklin, B. (1997) *Newszak and News Media*. London: Arnold.

Fransella, F. and Bannister, D. (1977) *Manual for Repertory Grid Technique*. London: Academic Press.

Frayne, C.A. and Geringer, J.M. (2000) 'Self-management training for improving job performance: A field experiment involving salespeople', *Journal of Applied Psychology*, 85, 361–72.

Fredrickson, B.L. (1998) 'What good are positive emotions?', *Review of General Psychology*, 2, 300–19.

Fredrickson, B.L. and Joiner, T. (2002) 'Positive emotions trigger upwards spirals towards emotional well-being', *Psychological Science*, 13, 172–5.

Fredrickson, B.L., Tugade, M.M., Waugh, C.E. and Larkin, G.R. (2003) 'What good are positive emotions in crises? A prospective study of resilience and emotions following the terrorist attacks on the United States on September 11th, 2001', *Journal of Personality and Social Psychology*, 84, 365–76.

French, J.R.P. and Caplan, R.D. (1972) 'Organisational stress and individual strain', in A. Marrow (ed.), *The Failure of Success*. New York: AMACOM.

French J.R.P., Caplan R.D. and Van Harrison, R. (1982) *The Mechanisms of Job Stress and Strain*. New York: Wiley.

French, M.T., Dunlap, L.J., Roman, P.M. and Steele, P.D. (1997) 'Factors that influence the use and perceptions of employee assistance programs at six worksites', *Journal of Occupational Health Psychology*, 2, 312–24.

French, W.L. and Bell, C.H. (1973) *Organisation Development*. Englewood Cliffs, NJ: Prentice-Hall.

French, W.L. and Bell, C.H. (1984) *Organisation Development*, 4th edition. Englewood Cliffs, NJ: Prentice-Hall.

French, W.L. and Bell, C.H. (1995) *Organisation Development*, 5th edition. Englewood Cliffs, NJ: Prentice-Hall.

Frese, M. and Beimel, S. (2003) 'Action training for charismatic leadership: Two evaluations of studies of a commercial training module on inspirational communication of a vision', *Personnel Psychology*, 56, 671–97.

Frese, M., Fay, D., Hilburger, T., Leng, K. and Tag, A. (1997) 'The concept of personal initiative: Operationalization, reliability and validity in two German samples', *Journal of Occupational and Organisational Psychology*, 70, 139–62.

Freud, S. (1960) *The Psychopathology of Everyday Life*. London: Hogarth (first published 1901).

Fried, Y. and Ferris, G.R. (1987) 'The validity of the job characteristics model: A review and meta-analysis', *Personnel Psychology*, 40, 287–322.

Friedman, R.A. and Krackhardt, D. (1997) 'Social capital and career mobility: A structural theory of lower returns to education for Asian employees', *Journal of Applied Behavioural Science*, 33, 316–34.

Frink, D.D. and Ferris, G.R. (1998) 'Accountability, impression management and goal setting in the performance evaluation process', *Human Relations*, 51, 1259–83.

Frone, M.R. (2002) 'Work–family balance', in J.C. Quick and L.E. Tetrick (eds), *Handbook of Occupational Health Psychology*. Washington, DC: American Psychology Association.

Fryer, D. (1998) 'Labour market disadvantage, deprivation and mental health', in P. Drenth and H. Thierry (eds), *Handbook of Work and Organisational Psychology*, vol. 2. Hove, Sussex: Psychology Press/Erlbaum.

Furnham, A., Hyde, G. and Trickey, G. (2014) 'Do your dark side traits fit? Dysfunctional personalities in different work sectors', *Applied Psychology: An International Review*, 63, 589–606.

Furnham, A., Kirkcaldy, B.D. and Lynn, R. (1994) 'National attitudes to competitiveness, money and work among young people: First, second and third world differences', *Human Relations*, 47(1), 119–32.

Furnham, A., Steele, H. and Pendleton, D. (1993) 'A psychometric assessment of the Belbin Team-Role Self-Perception Inventory', *Journal of Occupational and Organizational Psychology*, 66, 245–57.

Gadassi, R., Gati, I. and Dayan, A. (2012) 'The adaptability of career decision-making profiles', *Journal of Counselling Psychology*, 59, 612–22.

Gagné, M. and Deci, R.E. (2005) 'Self-determination theory and work motivation', *Journal of Organisational Behaviour*, 26, 331–62.

Gagné, M., Forest, J., Vansteenkiste, M., Crevier-Braud, L., Broeck, A.V.D., Aspeli, A.K. et al. (2014) 'The Multidimensional Work Motivation Scale: Validation evidence in seven languages and nine countries', *European Journal of Work and Organisational Psychology*, 24, 178–96.

Gajendran, R.J. and Harrison, D.A. (2007) 'The good, the bad, and the unknown about telecommuting: Meta-analysis of psychological mediators and individual consequences', *Journal of Applied Psychology*, 92, 1524–41.

Gallos, J.V. (1989) 'Exploring women's development: Implications for career theory, practice and research', in M.B. Arthur, D.T. Hall and B.S. Lawrence (eds), *Handbook of Career Theory*. Cambridge: Cambridge University Press.

Gardner, H. (1983) *Frames of Mind: The theory of multiple intelligences.* New York: Basic Books.

Gardner, H. (1995) 'Reflections on multiple intelligences', *Phi Delta Kappan*, 77, 200–8.

Gardner, H. (2003) 'Higher education for the era of globalisation', *The Psychologist*, 16, 520–1.

Gardner, W.L. and Avolio, B.J. (1998) 'The charismatic relationship: A dramaturgical perspective', *Academy of Management Review*, 23, 32–58.

Garvin, D.A. (1993) 'Building a learning organisation', *Harvard Business Review*, July–August, 78–91.

Gastil, J. (1994) 'A definition and illustration of democratic leadership', *Human Relations*, 47, 953–75.

Gati, I., Landman, S., Davidovitch, S., Asulin-Peretz, L. and Gadassi, R. (2010) 'From career decision-making styles to career decision-making profiles: A multidimensional approach', *Journal of Vocational Behaviour*, 76, 277–291.

Gaver, W.W. (1989) 'The SonicFinder: An interface that uses auditory icons', *Human Computer Interaction*, 4, 67–94.

Gawron, V.J. (2000) *Human Performance Measures Handbook.* Mahwah, NJ: Lawrence Erlbaum Associates.

Gelfand, M.J., Erez, M. and Aycan, Z. (2007) 'Cross-cultural organisation psychology', *Annual Review of Psychology*, 58, 479–514.

Gellerman, W., Frankel, M.S. and Ladenson, R.F. (1990) *Values and Ethics in Organisational and Human Dystems Development: Responding to dilemmas in professional life.* San Francisco, CA: Jossey-Bass.

Gemmill, G. and Oakley, J. (1992) 'Leadership: An alienating social myth?', *Human Relations*, 45, 113–29.

George, J.M. and Jones, G.R. (1997) 'Experiencing work: Values, attitudes and moods', *Human Relations*, 50, 393–416.

Georgellis, Y., Lange, T. and Tabvuma, V. (2012) 'The impact of life events on job satisfaction', *Journal of Vocational Behaviour*, 80, 464–73.

Gersick, C. and Kram, K.E. (2002) 'High-achieving women at midlife: An exploratory study', *Journal of Management Enquiry*, 11, 104–27.

Geurts, S.A.E. and Demerouti, E. (2003) 'Work/non-work interface: A review of theories and findings', in M. Schabracq, J. Winnubst and C.L. Cooper (eds), *Handbook of Work and Health Psychology*. Chichester: John Wiley and Sons.

Geyer, A. and Steyrer, J.M. (1998) 'Transformational leadership and objective performance in banks', *Applied Psychology: An International Review*, 47, 397–420.

Gibson, C.B. and Gibbs, J.L. (2006) 'Unpacking the concept of virtuality: The effects of geographic dispersion, electronic dependence, dynamic structure, and national diversity of team innovation', *Administrative Science Quarterly*, 51, 451–95.

Gibson, C.B. and Zellmer-Bruhn, M.E. (2002) 'Minding your metaphors: Applying the concept of teamwork metaphors to the management of teams in multicultural contexts', *Organisational Dynamics*, 31, 101–16.

Gibson, C.B., Gibbs, J.L., Stanko, T.L., Tesluk, P. and Cohen, S.G. (2011) 'Including the "I" in virtuality and modern job design: Extending the job characteristics model to include the moderating effect of individual experiences of electronic dependence and copresence', *Organisation Science*, 22, 1481–99.

Giga, S.I., Hoel, H. and Lewis, D. (2008) *The Costs of Workplace Bullying*. London: Unite the Union/Department for Business, Enterprise and Regulatory Reform.

Giga, S.I., Noblet, A.J., Faragher, B. and Cooper, C.L. (2003) 'The UK perspective: A review of research on organisational stress management interventions', *Australian Psychologist*, 38, 158–64.

Gilliland, S.W. (1993) 'The perceived fairness of selection systems – an organisational justice perspective', *Academy of Management Review*, 18(4), 694–734.

Gimeno, D., Amick III, B., Barrientos-Gutiérrez, T. and Mangione, T.W. (2009) 'Work organisation and drinking: An epidemiological comparison of two psychosocial work exposure models', *International Archives of Occupational and Environmental Health*, 82, 305–17.

Gioia, D.A. and Longenecker, C.O. (1994) 'Delving into the dark side: The politics of executive appraisal', *Organisational Dynamics*, 22, 47–58.

Gioia, D.A. and Manz, C.C. (1985) 'Linking cognition and behaviour: A script processing interpretation of vicarious learning', *Academy of Management Review*, 10, 527–39.

Gist, M.E. (1989) 'The influence of training methods on self-efficacy and idea generation among managers', *Personnel Psychology*, 42, 787–805.

Gittleman, M., Horrigan, M. and Joyce, M. (1998) '"Flexible" workplace practices: Evidence from a nationally representative survey', *Industrial and Labour Relations Review*, 52(1), 99–115.

Glazer, S. and Beehr, T.A. (2005) 'Consistency of implications of three role stressors across four countries', *Journal of Organisational Behaviour*, 26, 467–87.

Glomb, T.M., Duffy, M.K., Bono, J.E. and Yang, T. (2011) 'Mindfulness at work', *Research in Personnel and Human Resources Management*, 30, 115–57.

Goffin, R.D. and Gellatly, I.R. (2001) 'A multi-rater assessment of organisational commitment: Are self-report measures biased?', *Journal of Organisational Behaviour*, 22, 437–51.

Goh, S.C. (2002) 'Managing effective knowledge transfer: An integrative framework and some practice implications', *Journal of Knowledge Management*, 6(1), 23–30.

Goldberg, D.P. and Williams, P. (1988) *The User's Guide to the General Health Questionnaire*. Slough: NFER/Nelson.

Goldberg, L.R. (1999) 'A broad-bandwidth, public domain, personality inventory measuring the lower-level facets of several five-factor models', *Personality Psychology in Europe*, 7, 7–28.

Golden, T.D. (2006) 'The role of relationships in understanding telecommuter satisfaction', *Journal of Organisational Behaviour*, 27, 319–40.

Golden, T.D. and Veiga, J.F. (2005) 'The impact of extent of telecommuting on job satisfaction: Resolving inconsistent findings', *Journal of Management*, 31, 301–18.

Goldstein, I. and Ford, K. (2001) *Training in Organisations: Needs assessment, development, and evaluation*, 4th edition. Belmont, CA: Wadsworth Publishing.

Goleman, D. (1995) *Emotional Intelligence*. New York: Bantam Books.

Goleman, D. (1998) *Working with Emotional Intelligence*. New York: Bantam Books.

Goleman, D. (2001) 'An EI-based theory of performance', in C. Cherniss and D. Goleman (eds), *The Emotionally Intelligent Workplace*. San Francisco, CA: Jossey-Bass Wiley.

Gottfredson, G. and Holland, J.L. (1996) *Dictionary of Holland Occupational Codes*, 3rd edition. Odessa, FL: Psychological Assessment Resources Inc.

Gottfredson, L.S. (1981) 'Circumscription and compromise: A developmental theory of occupational aspirations', *Journal of Counselling Psychology*, 28, 545.

Gottfredson, L.S. (1996) 'Gottfredson's theory of circumscription and compromise', in D. Brown, L. Brookes and associates (eds), *Career Choice and Development*, 3rd edition. San Francisco: Jossey-Bass.

Gottfredson, L.S. (2002) '*g*: Highly general and highly practical', in R.J. Sternberg and E.L. Grigorenko (eds), *The General Factor of Intelligence: How general is it?* Mahwah, NJ: Erlbaum.

Grandjean, E. and Kroemer, K.H.E. (1997) *Fitting the Task to the Human: A textbook of occupational ergonomics*, 5th edition. London: Taylor and Francis.

Grant, A.M. (2007) 'Relational job design and the motivation to make a prosocial difference', *Academy of Management Review*, 32, 393–417.

Grant, S. and Langan-Fox, J. (2007) 'Personality and the occupational stressor–strain relationship: The role of the Big Five', *Journal of Occupational Health Psychology*, 12, 20–33.

Graves, L.M. and Powell, G.N. (1988) 'An investigation of sex discrimination in recruiters' evaluations of actual applicants', *Journal of Applied Psychology*, 73, 20–9.

Greenberg, J. (2001) 'Setting the justice agenda: Seven unanswered questions about "What, Why and How"', *Journal of Vocational Behaviour*, 58, 210–19.

Greenberg, J. and Colquitt, J.A. (eds) (2013) *Handbook of Organisational Justice*. New York: Psychology Press.

Greene, J.C., Caracelli, V.J. and Graham, W.F. (1989) 'Towards a conceptual framework for mixed methods evaluation designs', *Educational Evaluation and Policy Analysis*, 11, 255–74.

Greenhaus, J.H. (1971) 'An investigation of the role of career salience in vocational behaviour', *Journal of Vocational Behaviour*, 1, 209–16.

Greenhaus, J.H. and Beutell, N.J. (1985) 'Sources and conflict between work and family roles', *Academy of Management Review*, 10, 76–88.

Greenhaus, J.H. and Parasuraman, S. (1999) 'Research on work, family and gender: Current status and future directions', in G.N. Powell (ed.), *Handbook of Gender and Work*. Thousand Oaks, CA: Sage.

Greenhaus, J.H., Parasuraman, A. and Wormley, W.M. (1990) 'Effects of race on organisational experiences, job performance evaluations and career outcomes', *Academy of Management Journal*, 33, 64–86.

Greenleaf, R.K. (1977) *Servant leadership: A journey into the nature of legitimate power and greatness*. Westfield, IN: Greenleaf Centre for Servant Leadership.

Greenwald, A.G., McGhee, D.E. and Schwartz, J.L.K. (1998) 'Measuring individual differences in implicit cognition: The implicit association test', *Journal of Personality and Social Psychology*, 74, 1464–80.

Greiner, L.E. and Cummings, T.G. (2004) 'Wanted: OD more alive than dead!', *Journal of Applied Behavioural Science*, 40(4), 374–91.

Grieves, J. and Redman, T. (1999) 'Living in the shadow of OD: HRD and the search for identity', *Human Resource Development International*, 2, 81–102.

Griffeth, R.W., Horn, P.W. and Gaertner, S. (2000) 'Meta-analysis of antecedents and correlates of employee turnover: Update, moderator tests and research implications for the next millennium', *Journal of Management*, 26, 463–76.

Griffin, M.A., Neal, A. and Parker, S.K. (2007) 'A new model of work role performance: Positive behaviour in uncertain and interdependent contexts', *Academy of Management Journal*, 50, 327–47.

Griffin, R.W. and Bateman, T.S. (1986) 'Job satisfaction and organisational commitment', in C.L. Cooper and I.T. Robertson (eds), *International Review of Industrial and Organisational Psychology*. Chichester: John Wiley.

Griffiths, A. (1999) 'Organisational interventions: Facing the limits of the natural science paradigm', *Scandinavian Journal of Work, Environment and Health*, 25, 589–96.

Griffiths, A., Cox, T., Karanika, M., Khan, S. and Tomás, J.M. (2006) 'Work design and management in the manufacturing sector: Development and validation of the Work Organisation Assessment Questionnaire', *Occupational and Environmental Medicine*, 63, 669–75.

Grinyer, P.H., Mayes, D.G. and McKiermon, P. (1988) *Sharpbenders: The secrets of unleashing corporate potential*. Oxford: Blackwell.

Gross, J.J. and John, O.P. (2003) 'Individual differences in two emotion regulation processes: Implications for affect, relationships, and well-being', *Journal of Personality and Social Psychology*, 85(2), 348–62.

Grugulis, I. (2007) *Skills, Training and Human Resource Development*. Basingstoke: Palgrave Macmillan.

Grzywacz, J.G. and Marks, N.F. (2000) 'Reconceptualising the work–family interface: An ecological perspective on the correlates of positive and negative spillover between work and family', *Journal of Health Psychology*, 5, 111–26.

Gubler, M., Arnold, J. and Coombs, C. (2014a) 'Organisational boundaries and beyond: A new look at the components of a boundaryless career orientation', *Career Development International*, 19, 641–67.

Gubler, M., Arnold, J. and Coombs, C. (2014b) 'Reassessing the protean career concept: Empirical findings, conceptual components, and measurement', *Journal of Organisational Behaviour*, 35, 23–40.

Gubrium, J. and Holstein, J. (1997) *The New Language of Qualitative Method*. Oxford: Oxford University Press.

Guchait, P., Ruetzler, T., Taylor, J. and Toldi, N. (2013) 'Understanding the pros and cons of video interviewing: A qualitative study to understand applicant perspective', *Proceeding: Travel and Tourism Research Association (TTRA)*, Kansas City, Missouri, USA, 20–22.

Guest, D. (1998) 'Is the psychological contract worth taking seriously?', *Journal of Organisational Behaviour*, 19, 649–64.

Guest, D.E. (1997) 'Human resource management and performance: A review and research agenda', *International Human Resource Management*, 8, 263–76.

Guilford, J.P. (1996) 'Intelligence: 1965 model', *American Psychologist*, 21(1), 20.

Guion, R.M. (1965) *Personnel Testing*. New York: McGraw-Hill.

Gunnell, D., Platt, S. and Hawton, K. (2009) 'The economic crisis and suicide', *British Medical Journal*, 338, 1456–7.

Gunz, H.P. and Peiperl, M. (2007) *The Handbook of Career Studies*. Thousand Oaks, CA: Sage.

Gupta, V., Hanges, P.J. and Dorfman, P. (2002) 'Cultural clusters: Methodology and findings', *Journal of World Business*, 37, 11–15.

Gürbüz, S., Şahin, F. and Köksal, O. (2014) 'Revisiting of Theory X and Y: A multilevel analysis of the effects of leaders' managerial assumptions on followers' attitudes', *Management Decision*, 52, 1888–906.

Gutek, B. (1995) *The Dynamics of Service: Reflections on the changing nature of customer/ provider interactions*. San Francisco, CA: Jossey-Bass.

Gutek, B., Searle, S. and Klewpa, L. (1991) 'Rational versus gender role explanations for work/family conflict', *Journal of Applied Psychology*, 76, 560–8.

Guzzo, R.A. and Dickson, M.W. (1996) 'Teams in organisations: Recent research on performance and effectiveness', *Annual Review of Psychology*, 47, 307–38.

Haar, J.M., Russo, M., Suñe, A. and Ollier-Malaterre, A. (2014) 'Outcomes of work–life balance on job satisfaction, life satisfaction and mental health: A study across seven cultures', *Journal of Vocational Behaviour*, 85, 361–73.

Hackman, J.R. (1990) *Groups that Work (and Those that Don't): Creating conditions for effective teamwork*. San Francisco, CA: Jossey-Bass.

Hackman, J.R. (2002) *Leading Teams: Setting the stage for great performance*. Boston, MA: Harvard Business School Press.

Hackman, J.R. and Oldham, G.R. (1976) 'Motivation through the design of work: Test of a theory', *Organisational Behaviour and Human Performance*, 16, 250–79.

Hackman, J.R. and Oldham, G.R. (1980) *Work Redesign*. Reading, MA: Addison-Wesley.

Haggard, D.L., Dougherty, T.W., Turban, D.B. and Wilbanks, J.E. (2011) 'Who is a mentor? A review of evolving definitions and implications for research', *Journal of Management*, 37, 280–304.

Halbesleben, J.R.B. and Wheeler, A.R. (2008) 'The relative roles of engagement and embeddedness in predicting job performance and intention to leave', *Work & Stress*, 22, 242–56.

Hall, D.T. (1976) *Careers in Organisations*. Glenview, IL: Scott, Foresman.

Hall, D.T. (1986) 'Breaking career routines: Midcareer choice and identity development', in D.T. Hall (ed.), *Career Development in Organisations*. London: Jossey-Bass.

Hall, D.T. (2002) *Careers In and Out of Organisations*. Thousand Oaks, CA: Sage Publications.

Hall, D.T. and Chandler, D.E. (2005) 'Psychological success: When the career is a calling', *Journal of Organisational Behaviour*, 26, 155–76.

Hall, D.T. and Nougaim, K. (1968) 'An examination of Maslow's need hierarchy in an organisational setting', *Organisational Behaviour and Human Decision Processes*, 3, 12–35.

Halvor Teigen, K. (1986) 'Old truths or fresh insights? A study of students' evaluations of proverbs', *British Journal of Social Psychology*, 25, 43–9.

Hammer, M. and Champy, J. (1993) *Re-engineering the Corporation*. London: Nicolas Brealey.

Hammond, M.M., Neff, N.L., Farr, J.L., Schwall, A.R. and Zhao, X. (2011) 'Predictors of individual-level innovation at work: A meta-analysis', *Psychology of Aesthetics, Creativity, and the Arts*, 5, 90.

Handy, C. (1979) *Gods of Management*. London: Pan.

Handy, C. (1986) *Understanding Organisations*. Harmondsworth: Penguin.

Handy, C. (1989) *The Age of Unreason*. London: Arrow.

Handy, C. (1994) *The Empty Raincoat*. London: Hutchinson.

Hanisch, K.A. (1994) 'Reasons people retire and their relations to attitudinal and behavioural correlates in retirement', *Journal of Vocational Behaviour*, 45, 1–16.

Hansemark, O.C. (2003) 'Need for achievement, locus of control and the prediction of business start-ups: A longitudinal study', *Journal of Economic Psychology*, 24, 301–19.

Hansen, G.S. and Wernerfelt, B. (1989) 'Determinants of firm performance: The relative importance of economic and organisational factors', *Strategic Management Journal*, 10, 399–411.

Hanson, M.A. and Borman, W.C. (2006) 'Citizenship performance: An integrative review and motivational analysis', in W. Bennett, Jr, C.E. Lance and D.J. Wohr (eds), *Performance Measurement: Current Perspectives and Future Challenges*. London: Lawrence Erlbaum Associates.

Harari, M.B., Rudolph, C.W. and Laginess, A.J. (2015) 'Does rater personality matter? A meta-analysis of rater Big Five performance rating relationships', *Journal of Occupational and Organizational Psychology*, 88, 387– 414.

Harley, B. (2001) 'Team membership and the experience of work in Britain: An analysis of the WERS98 data', *Work, Employment and Society*, 15(4), 721–42.

Harmon, L.W., Hansen, J.C., Borgen, F.H. and Hammer, A.L. (1994) *Strong Interest Inventory: Applications and technical guide*. Stanford, CA: Stanford University Press.

Harren, V.A. (1979) 'A model of career decision making for college students', *Journal of Vocational Behaviour*, 14, 119–33.

Harris, C., Daniels, K. and Briner, R. (2003) 'A daily diary study of goals and affective well-being at work', *Journal of Occupational and Organizational Psychology*, 76, 401–10.

Harris, D. (2004) 'Head down display design', in D. Harris (ed.), *Human Factors for Civil Flight Deck Design*. Aldershot: Ashgate.

Harris, D. (2011) *Human Performance on the Flight Deck*. Aldershot: Ashgate.

Harris, D. and Harris, F.J. (2004) 'Predicting the successful transfer of technology between application areas: A critical evaluation of the human component in the system', *Technology in Society*, 26, 551–65.

Harris, D. and Thomas, L. (2005) 'The contribution of industrial and organisational psychology to safety in commercial aircraft', in G. Hodgkinson and K. Ford (eds), *International Review of Industrial and Organisational Psychology*. London: John Wiley.

Harris, D., Stanton, A., Marshall, A., Young, M.S., Demagalski, J.M. and Salmon, P. (2005) 'Using SHERPA to predict design-induced error on the flight deck', *Aerospace Science and Technology*, 9(6), 525–32.

Harris, M.M. (2013) *Handbook of Research in International Human Resource Management*. London: Lawrence Erlbaum Associates.

Harrison, D.A. (2007) 'What's the difference? Diversity constructs as separation, variety or disparity in organisations', *Academy of Management Review*, 32, 1199–228.

Harrison, D.A., Newman, D.A. and Roth, P.L. (2006) 'How important are job attitudes? Meta-analytic comparisons of integrative behavioural outcomes and time sequences', *Academy of Management Journal*, 49, 305–25.

Harrison, R. (1972) 'How to describe your organisation', *Harvard Business Review*, 50, September–October.

Hart, P.M. and Cooper, C.L. (2001) 'Occupational stress: Towards a more integrated framework', in N. Anderson, D.S. Ones, H.K. Sinangil and C. Viswesvaran (eds), *Handbook of Work, Industrial and Organisational Psychology*, vol. 2. London: Sage.

Harter, J.K., Schmidt, F.L. and Hayes, T.L. (2002) 'Business-unit-level relationship between employee satisfaction, employee engagement and business outcomes: A meta-analysis', *Journal of Applied Psychology*, 87, 268–79.

Haslam, S.A. (2004) *Psychology in Organisations: The social identity approach*, 2nd edition. London: Sage.

Haslam, S.A., Powell, C. and Turner, J.C. (2000) 'Social identity, self-categorisation, and work motivation: Rethinking the contribution of the group to positive and sustainable organisational outcomes', *Applied Psychology: An International Review*, 49, 319–39.

Haslam, S.A., Reicher, S.D. and Platow, M.J. (2011) *The New Psychology of Leadership: Identity, influence and power*. Abingdon: Psychology Press.

Haslam, S.A., Wegge, J. and Postmes, T. (2009) 'Are we on a learning curve or a treadmill? The benefits of participative group goal setting become apparent as tasks become increasingly challenging over time', *European Journal of Social Psychology*, 39, 430–46.

Hassard, J. and Sharifi, S. (1989) 'Corporate culture and strategic change', *Journal of General Management*, 15(2), 4–19.

Hatch, M.J. (1997) *Organisation Theory: Modern, symbolic and postmodern perspectives*. Oxford: Oxford University Press.

Hauff, S., Richter, N.F. and Tressin, T. (2015) 'Situational job characteristics and job satisfaction: The moderating role of national culture', *International Business Review*, 24, 710–23.

Hausknecht, J.P. and Holwerda, J.A. (2013) 'When does employee turnover matter? Dynamic member configurations, productive capacity, and collective performance', *Organisation Science*, 24, 210–25.

Hausknecht, J.P., Day, D.V. and Thomas, S.C. (2004) 'Applicant reactions to selection procedures: An updated model and meta-analysis', *Personnel Psychology*, 57, 639–83.

Hausknecht, J.P., Sturman, M.C. and Roberson, Q.M. (2011) 'Justice as a dynamic construct: Effects of individual trajectories on distal work outcomes', *Journal of Applied Psychology*, 96, 872–80.

Hayes, J. (2002) *The Theory and Practice of Change Management*. Basingstoke: Palgrave.

Haynie, J.M. and Shepherd, D. (2011) 'Towards a theory of discontinuous career transition: Investigating career transitions necessitated by traumatic life events', *Journal of Applied Psychology*, 96, 501–24.

Health and Safety Executive (1999) *Initial Advice Regarding Call Centre Working Practices*. Sheffield: HSE.

Heaney, C., Israel, B., Schurman, S., Barker, E., House, J. and Hugentobler, M. (1993) 'Industrial relations, work stress reduction and employee well-being: A participatory action research investigation', *Journal of Organisational Behaviour*, 14, 495–510.

Heller, F. (1970) 'Group feed-back analysis as a change agent', *Human Relations*, 23(4), 319–33.

Heller, F. (1989) 'Human resource management and the socio-technical approach', in G. Bamber and R. Lansbury (eds), *New Technology: International perspectives on human resources and industrial relations*. London: Unwin Hyman.

Heller, F.A., Drenth, P., Koopman, P. and Rus, V. (1988) *Decisions in Organisations: A three-country comparative study*. London: Sage.

Hellervik, L.W., Hazucha, F. and Schneider, R.J. (1992) 'Behaviour change: Models, methods, and a review of evidence', in M.D. Dunnette and L.M. Hough (eds), *Handbook of Industrial and Organisational Psychology*. Palo Alto, CA: Consulting Psychologists Press.

Hellgren, J. and Sverke, M. (2003) 'Does job insecurity lead to impaired well-being or vice versa? Estimation of cross-lagged effects using latent variable modelling', *Journal of Organisational Behaviour*, 24, 215–36.

Hemp, P. (2004) 'Presenteeism at work: At work – but out of it', *Harvard Business Review*, 83, 49–58.

Hendey, N. and Pascall, G. (2001) *Disability and Transition in Adulthood: Achieving independent living*. London: Pavilion Publishing.

Hendry, C. (1996) 'Understanding and creating whole organisational change through learning theory', *Human Relations*, 48(5), 621–41.

Heraclides A., Chandola T., Witte, D.R. and Brunner, E.J. (2009) 'Psychosocial stress at work doubles the risk of type 2 diabetes in middle-aged women: Evidence from the Whitehall II study', *Diabetes Care*, 32, 2230–5.

Hermelin, E. and Robertson, I.T. (2001) 'A critique and standardisation of meta-analytic validity coefficients in personnel selection', *Journal of Occupational and Organizational Psychology*, 74, 153–77.

Hermelin, E., Lievens, F. and Robertson, I.T. (2007) 'The validity of assessment centres for the prediction of supervisory performance ratings: A meta-analysis', *International Journal of Selection and Assessment*, 15, 405–11.

Herriot, P. (1992) *The Career Management Challenge: Balancing individual and organisational needs*. London: Sage.

Herriot, P. and Pemberton, C. (1995) *New Deals*. Chichester: John Wiley.

Hersey, P. and Blanchard, K. (1982) *Management of Organisational Behaviour*, 4th edition. Englewood Cliffs, NJ: Prentice Hall.

Hertel, G., Geister, S. and Konradt, U. (2005) 'Managing virtual teams: A review of current empirical research', *Human Resource Management Review*, 15, 69–95.

Hertel, G., Konradt, U. and Orlikowski, B. (2004) 'Managing distance by interdependence: Goal setting, task interdependence and team-based rewards in virtual teams', *European Journal of Work and Organisational Psychology*, 13, 1–28.

Hertel, G., Konradt, U. and Voss, K., (2006) 'Competencies for virtual teamwork: Development and validation of the web-based selection tool for members of distributed teams', *European Journal of Work and Organisational Psychology*, 15, 477–505.

Herzberg, F. (1966) *Work and the Nature of Man*. Cleveland, OH: World Publishing.

Hewstone, M., Ruibin, M. and Willis, H. (2002) 'Intergroup bias', *Annual Review of Psychology*, 53, 575–604.

Hiemstra, A.M., Derous, E., Serlie, A.W. and Born, M.P. (2012) 'Fairness perceptions of video resumes among ethnically diverse applicants', *International Journal of Selection and Assessment*, 20(4), 423–33.

Higgins, M.C. and Thomas, D.A. (2001) 'Constellations and careers: Towards understanding the effects of multiple developmental relationships', *Journal of Organisational Behaviour*, 22, 223–47.

Hilton, J.L. and Von Hippel, W. (1996) 'Stereotypes', *Annual Review of Psychology*, 47, 237–71.

Hinds, P. and Bailey, D. (2003) 'Out of sight, out of sync: Understanding conflict in distributed teams', *Organisation Science*, 14, 615–32.

Hinkle, L.E. (1973) 'The concept of stress in the biological social sciences', *Stress Medicine*, 1, 31–48.

Hirsh, W. and Jackson, C. (2004) *Managing Careers in Large Organisations*. London: The Work Foundation.

Hirsh, W., Jackson, C. and Jackson, C. (1995) *Careers in Organisations: Issues for the future*, IES report 287. Brighton: Institute for Employment Studies.

Hislop, D., Axtell, C. and Daniels, K. (2008) 'The challenge of remote working', in S. Cartwright and C. Cooper (eds), *The Oxford Handbook of Personnel Psychology*. Oxford: Oxford University Press.

Ho, C. and Spence, C. (2008) *The Multisensory Driver*. Aldershot: Ashgate.

Hoag, B.G., Ritschard, H.V. and Cooper, C.L. (2002) 'Obstacles to effective organisation change: The underlying reasons', *Leadership and Organisation Development Journal*, 23(1), 6–15.

Hobfoll, S.E. (1989) 'Conservation of resources: A new attempt at conceptualising stress', *American Psychologist*, 44, 513–24.

Hodgkinson, G.P. (2003) 'The interface of cognitive and industrial, work and organisational psychology', *Journal of Occupational and Organizational Psychology*, 76, 1–25.

Hodgkinson, G.P. and Healey, M.P. (2008) 'Cognition in organisations', *Annual Review of Psychology*, 59, 387–417.

Hodgkinson, G.P. and Herriot, P. (2002) 'The role of psychologists in enhancing organisational effectiveness', in I.T. Robertson, M. Callinan and D. Bartram (eds), *Organisational Effectiveness: The role of psychology*. Chichester: Wiley.

Hodgkinson, G.P., Bown, N.J., Maule, A.J., Glaister, K.W. and Pearman, A.D. (1999) 'Breaking the frame: An analysis of strategic cognition and decision-making under uncertainty', *Strategic Management Journal*, 20(10), 977–85.

Hoegl, M. and Gemuenden, H.G. (2001) 'Teamwork quality and the success of innovative projects: A theoretical concept and empirical evidence', *Organisation Science*, 12(4), 435–49.

Hoel, H., Einarsen, S. and Cooper, C.L. (2003) 'Organisational effects of bullying', in S. Einarsen, H. Hoel, D. Zapf and C.L. Cooper (eds), *Bullying and Emotional Abuse in the Workplace: International perspectives in research and practice*. London: Taylor and Francis.

Hoffman, A.J. and Scott, L.D. (2003) 'Role stress and career satisfaction among registered nurses by work shift patterns', *Journal of Nursing Administration*, 33, 337–42.

Hoffman, B., Lance, C.E., Bynum, B. and Gentry, W.A. (2010) 'Rater source effects are alive and well after all', *Personnel Psychology*, 63, 119–51.

Hoffman, B.J. and Woehr, D.J. (2006) 'Examining the relationship between person-organisation fit and behavioural outcomes: A quantitative review', *Journal of Vocational Behaviour*, 3, 389–99.

Hoffman, L.R. and Maier, N.R.F. (1961) 'Quality and acceptance of problem solutions by members of homogeneous and heterogeneous groups', *Journal of Abnormal and Social Psychology*, 62, 401–7.

Hofmann, S.G., Asnaani, A., Vonk, I.J.J., Sawyer, A.T. and Fang, A. (2012) 'The efficacy of Cognitive Behavioural Therapy: A review of meta-analyses', *Cognitive Therapy and Research*, 36, 427–40.

Hofstede, G. (1980) *Culture's Consequences: International differences in work-related values.* London: Sage.

Hofstede, G. (1990) 'The cultural relativity of organisational practices and theories', in D.C. Wilson and R.H. Rosenfeld (eds), *Managing Organisations: Text, readings and cases.* London: McGraw-Hill.

Hofstede, G. (2001) *Culture's Consequences*, 2nd edition. London: Sage.

Hogan, R. (2009) *Hogan Development Survey Manual.* Tulsa, OK: Hogan Assessment Systems.

Holland, J.L. (1997) *Making Vocational Choices: A theory of vocational personalities and work environment*, 3rd edition. Odessa, FL: Psychological Assessment Resources Inc.

Hollenbeck, J.R., Beersma, B. and Shouten, M.E. (2012) 'Beyond team types and taxonomies: A dimensional scaling conceptualization for team description', *Academy of Management Review*, 37, 82–106.

Hollnagel, E. (1999) 'From function allocation to function congruence', in S.W.A Dekker and E. Hollnagel (eds), *Coping With Computers in the Cockpit.* Aldershot: Ashgate.

Hollnagel, E. (ed.) (2003) *Handbook of Cognitive Task Design.* Mahwah, NJ: Lawrence Erlbaum Associates.

Hollnagel, E. (2007) 'Flight decks and free flight: Where are the system boundaries?', *Applied Ergonomics*, 38, 409–16.

Holman, D. (2003) 'Call centres', in D. Holman, T.D. Wall, C.W. Clegg, P. Sparrow and A. Howard (eds), *The New Workplace.* Chichester: John Wiley.

Holman, D. (2005) 'Call centres', in D. Holman, T.D. Wall, C.W. Clegg, P. Sparrow and A. Howard (eds), *The Essentials of the New Workplace: A Guide to the Human Impact of Modern Working Practices.* Chichester: John Wiley.

Holman, D. (2013) 'Job types and job quality in Europe', *Human Relations*, 66, 475–502.

Holman, D., Chissick, C. and Totterdell, P. (2002) 'The effects of performance monitoring and emotional labour on well-being in call centres', *Motivation and Emotion*, 26, 57–81.

Holman, D.J., Axtell, C.M., Sprigg, C.A., Totterdell, P. and Wall, T.D. (2010) 'The mediating role of job characteristics in job redesign interventions: A serendepitous quasi-experiment', *Journal of Organisational Behaviour*, 31, 84–105.

Holman, D.J., Wall, T.D., Clegg, C.W., Sparrow, P. and Howard, A. (eds) (2004) *The Essentials of the New Workplace: A guide to the human impact of modern working practices.* Chichester: John Wiley and Sons.

Hom, P.W., Mitchell, T.R., Lee, T.W. and Griffeth, R.W. (2012) 'Reviewing employee turnover: Focusing on proximal withdrawal states and an expanded criterion', *Psychological Bulletin*, 138, 831–58.

Hopson, B. and Scally, M. (2000) *Build Your Own Rainbow: A workbook for career and life management.* London: Management Books.

Horwitz, S.K. and Horwitz, I.B. (2007) 'The effects of team diversity on team outcomes: A meta-analytic review of team demography', *Journal of Management*, 33, 987–1015.

Houdmont, J. (2013) 'UK police custody officers' psychosocial hazard exposures and burnout', *Policing: An International Journal of Police Strategies and Management*, 36, 620–35.

Houdmont, J. and Leka, S (eds). (2010) Contemporary Occupational Health Psychology: Global perspectives on research and practice. Chichester: Wiley-Blackwell.

Houdmont, J., Randall, R., Kerr, R. and Addley, K. (2013) 'Psychosocial risk assessment in organisations: Concurrent validity of the brief version of the Management Standards Indicator Tool', *Work & Stress*, 27, 403–12.

Hough, L.M. and Furnham, A. (2003) 'Use of personality variables in work settings', in W.C. Borman, D.R. Ilgen, R.J. Klimoski and I.B. Weiner (eds), *Handbook of Psychology*. Hoboken, NJ: John Wiley.

Hough, L.M. and Ones, D.S. (2001) 'The structure, measurement, validity and use of personality variables in industrial, work, and organisational psychology', in N. Anderson, D.S. Ones, H.K. Sinangil and C. Viswesvaran (eds), *Handbook of Industrial, Work and Organisational Psychology*, vol. 1. London: Sage.

Hough, L.M. and Oswald, F.L. (2000) 'Personnel selection: Looking forward to the future – remembering the past', *Annual Review of Psychology*, 51, 631–64.

House, R.J. and Baetz, M.L. (1979) 'Leadership: Some empirical generalisations and new research directions', in B.M. Staw (ed.), *Research in Organisational Behaviour*, vol. 1. Greenwich, CT: JAI Press.

House, R.J., Hanges, P.J., Javidan, M., Dorfman, P.W. and Gupta, V. (eds) (2004) *Culture, Leadership, and Organisations: The GLOBE study of 62 societies*. London: Sage.

House, R.J., Hanges, P.J., Ruiz-Quintanilla, S.A., Dorfman, P.W., Javidan, M., Dickson, M. and Gupta, V. (1999) 'Cultural influences on leadership and organisations: Project GLOBE', in W.H. Mobley (ed.), *Advances in Global Leadership*. Stanford, CN: JAI Press.

House, R.J., Spangler, W.D. and Woycke, J. (1991) 'Personality and charisma in the US Presidency: A psychological theory of leader effectiveness', *Administrative Science Quarterly*, 36, 364–96.

Huczynski, A. and Buchanan, D. (2001) *Organisational Behaviour*, 4th edition. Harlow: FT/Prentice Hall.

Huffcutt, A.I. and Culbertson, S.S. (2010) 'Interviews', in S. Zedeck (ed.), *APA Handbook of Industrial and Organisational Psychology*. Washington, DC: American Psychological Association.

Huffcutt, A.I. and Roth, P.L. (1998) 'Racial group differences in employment interview evaluations', *Journal of Applied Psychology*, 83, 179–89.

Huffcutt, A.I., Conway, J.M., Roth, P.L. and Stone, N.J. (2001) 'Identification and meta-analytic assessment of psychological constructs measured in employment interviews', *Journal of Applied Psychology*, 86, 897–913.

Huffcutt, D., Allen, I., Conway, J.M., Roth, P.L. and Klehe, U.C. (2004) 'The impact of job complexity and study design on situational and behavior description interview validity', *International Journal of Selection and Assessment*, 12(3), 262–73.

Huffman, A.H., Culbertson, S.S., Wayment, H.A. and Irving, L.H. (2015) 'Resource replacement and psychological well-being during unemployment: The role of family support', *Journal of Vocational Behaviour*, 89, 74–82.

Hull, C.L. (1952) *A Behaviour System*. New Haven, CT: Yale University Press.

Hülsheger, U.R., Alberts, H.J.E.M., Feinholdt, A. and Lang, J.W.B. (2013) 'Benefits of mindfulness at work: The role of mindfulness in emotion regulation, emotional exhaustion, and job satisfaction', *Journal of Applied Psychology*, 98, 310–25.

Hülsheger, U.R., Anderson, N. and Salgado, J. (2009) 'Team-level predictors of innovation at work: A comprehensive meta-analysis spanning three decades of research', *Journal of Applied Psychology*, 94, 1128–45.

Hülsheger, U.R., Feinholdt, A. and Nübold, A. (2015) 'A low-dose mindfulness intervention and recovery from work: Effects on psychological detachment, sleep quality, and sleep duration', *Journal of Occupational and Organizational Psychology*, 88, 464–89.

Human Factors National Advisory Committee for Defence and Aerospace (2003) *Gaining Competitive Advantage through Human Factors: A guide for the civil aerospace industry*. London: Department of Trade and Industry.

Humphrey, S.E., Nahrgang, J.D. and Morgeson, F.P. (2007) 'Integrating motivational, social and contextual work design features: A meta-analytic summary and theoretical extension of the work design literature', *Journal of Applied Psychology*, 92, 1332–56.

Hunt, E. (2011) 'Where are we? Where are we going? Reflections on the current and future state of research on intelligence', *Handbook of Intelligence*. New York: Cambridge University Press.

Hunter, J.E. and Schmidt, F.L. (2004) *Methods of Meta-analysis: Correcting error and bias in research findings*, 2nd edition. Thousand Oaks, CA: Sage.

Hunter, J.E., Schmidt, F.L. and Le, H. (2006) 'Implications of direct and indirect range restriction for meta-analysis methods and findings', *Journal of Applied Psychology*, 91, 594–612.

Hurley, R.F., Church, A.H., Burke, W.W. and Van Eynde, D.F. (1992) 'Tension, change and values in OD', *OD Practitioner*, 29, 1–5.

Hurst, J., Skinner, D. and Worrall, L. (2009) *The 24/7 Work/Life Balance Survey 2009*. Keele: University of Keele Work/Life Balance Centre.

Huseman, R.C., Hatfield, J.D. and Miles, E.W. (1987) 'A new perspective on equity theory: The equity sensitivity construct', *Academy of Management Review*, 12, 222–34.

Hutchins, E. (1995a) *Cognition in the Wild*. Cambridge, MA: MIT Press.

Hutchins, E. (1995b) 'How a cockpit remembers its speeds', *Cognitive Science*, 19, 265–88.

Iaffaldano, M.T. and Muchinsky, P.M. (1985) 'Job satisfaction and job performance: A meta-analysis', *Psychological Bulletin*, 97, 251–73.

Ibarra, H. (1995) 'Race, opportunity, and diversity of social circles in managerial networks', *Academy of Management Journal*, 18, 673–703.

Igbaria, M. and Baroudi, J. J. (1993) 'A short-form measure of career orientations: A psychometric evaluation', *Journal of Management Information Systems*, 131–54.

Ilgen, D.R., Hollenbeck, J.R., Johnson, M. and Jundt, D. (2005) 'Teams in organisations: From input–process–output models to IMOI models', *Annual Review of Psychology*, 56, 517–43.

Industrial Society (1997) *Culture Change: Managing best practice 35*. London: Industrial Society.

Inkson, K., Dries, N. and Arnold, J. (2014) *Understanding Careers*, 2nd edition. London: Sage.

Inkson, K., Gunz, H., Ganesh, S. and Roper, J. (2012) 'Boundaryless careers: Bringing back boundaries', *Organisation Studies*, 33, 323–40.

International Standards Organisation (1999) *ISO 13407: Human-centred Design Processes for Interactive Systems*. Geneva: International Organisation for Standardisation.

Isenberg, D.J. (1986) 'Group polarisation: A critical review and meta-analysis', *Journal of Personality and Social Psychology*, 50, 1141–51.

Ivancevich, J.M. and Matteson, M.T. (1980) *Stress and Work*. Glenview, IL: Scott, Foresman and Co.

Ivancevich, J.M., Matteson, M.T., Freedman, S.M. and Phillips, J.S. (1990) 'Worksite stress management interventions', *American Psychologist*, 45, 252–61.

Jackson, B.J. (2001) *Management Gurus and Management Fashions: A dramatistic enquiry*. London: Routledge.

Jackson, S.E. (1983) 'Participation in decision-making as a strategy for reducing job-related strain', *Journal of Applied Psychology*, 68, 3–19.

Jackson, S.E. and Joshi, A. (2001) 'Research on domestic and international diversity in organisations: A merger that works?', in N. Anderson, D. Ones, H. Sinangil and C. Viswesvaran (eds), *Handbook of Industrial, Work and Organisational Psychology*, vol. 2. London: Sage.

Jahoda, M. (1979) 'The impact of unemployment in the 1930s and the 1970s', *Bulletin of the British Psychological Society*, 32, 309–14.

Janis, I.L. (1972) *Victims of Groupthink*. Boston, MA: Houghton Mifflin.

Janis, I.L. (1982a) *Groupthink*. Boston, MA: Houghton Mifflin.

Janis, I.L. (1982b) 'Counteracting the adverse effects of concurrence – seeking in policy planning groups: Theory and research perspectives', in H. Brandstatter, J.H. Davis and G. Stocker-Kreichgauer (eds), *Group Decision Making*. London: Academic Press.

Janssens, M. and Zanoni, P. (2005) 'Many diversities for many services: Theorising diversity (management) in service companies', *Human Relations*, 58, 311–40.

Janz, J.T. (1989) 'The patterned behaviour description interview: The best prophet of the future is the past', in R.W. Eder and G.R. Ferris (eds), *The Employment Interview: Theory, research and practice*. London: Sage.

Jarvenpaa, S. and Lang, K. (2005) 'Managing the paradoxes of mobile technology', *Information Systems Management Journal*, 22, 7–23.

Jarvis, W.B.G. and Petty, R.E. (1996) 'The need to evaluate', *Journal of Personal and Social Psychology*, 70, 172–94.

Javidan, M. and Dastmalchian, A. (2009) 'Managerial implications of the GLOBE project: A study of 62 societies', *Asia Pacific Journal of Human Resources*, 47, 41–58.

Javidan, M., Dorfman, P.W., de Luque, M.S. and House, R.J. (2006) 'In the eye of the beholder: Cross-cultural lessons in leadership from project GLOBE', *Academy of Management Perspectives*, 20, 67–90.

Jehn, K.A., Northcraft, G.B. and Neale, M.A. (1999) 'Why differences make a difference: A field study of diversity, conflict, and performance of workgroups', *Administrative Science Quarterly*, 44, 741–63.

Jenkinson, J.C. (1997) *Mainstream or Special? Educating students with disabilities*. London: Routledge.

Jiang, K., Liu, D., McKay, P.F., Lee, T.W. and Mitchell, T.R. (2012) 'When and how is job embeddedness predictive of turnover? A meta-analytic investigation', *Journal of Applied Psychology*, 97, 1077.

Johansen, V., Aronsson, G. and Marklund, S. (2014) 'Positive and negative reasons for sickness presenteeism in Norway and Sweden: A cross-sectional survey', *BMJ Open*, 4, e004123.

Johns, G. (1993) 'Constraints on the adoption of psychology-based personnel practices: Lessons from organisational innovation', *Personnel Psychology*, 46, 596–602.

Johns, G. (1994) 'How often were you absent? A review of the use of self-reported absence data', *Journal of Applied Psychology*, 79, 574–91.

Johns, G. (2001) 'In praise of context', *Journal of Organisational Behaviour*, 22, 31–42.

Johns, G. (2006) 'The essential impact of context on organisational behaviour', *Academy of Management Review*, 31, 386–408.

Johns, G. (2010) 'Presenteeism in the workplace: A review and research agenda', *Journal of Organisational Behaviour*, 31, 519–42.

Johns, G. (2011) 'Attendance dynamics at work: The antecedents and correlates of presenteeism, absenteeism, and productivity loss', *Journal of Occupational Health Psychology*, 16, 483–500.

Johnson, C.W. (2001) 'A case study in the integration of accident reports and constructive design documents', *Reliability Engineering and Systems Safety*, 71(3), 311–26.

Johnson, G. (1993) 'Processes of managing strategic change', in C. Mabey and B. Mayon-White (eds), *Managing Change*, 2nd edition. London: Open University/Paul Chapman Publishing.

Johnson, J. and Hall, E. (1988) 'Job strain, work place social support and cardiovascular disease: A cross-sectional study of a random sample of the working population', *American Journal of Public Health*, 78, 1336–42.

Johnson, J.W. and Ferstl, K.L. (1999) 'The effects of interrater and self–other agreement on performance improvement following upwards feedback', *Personnel Psychology*, 52(2), 271–303.

Johnson, P. and Cassell, C. (2001) 'Epistemology and work psychology: New agendas', *Journal of Occupational and Organizational Psychology*, 74, 125–43.

Johnson, S., Cooper, C., Cartwright, S., Donald, I., Taylor, P.J. and Millet, C. (2005) 'The experience of work-related stress across occupations', *Journal of Management*, 20, 178–87.

Johnson, S.K., Bettenhausen, K. and Gibbons, E. (2009) 'Realities of working in virtual teams: Affective and attitudinal outcomes of using computer mediated communication', *Small Group Research*, 40, 623–49.

Joiner, T.A. (2007) 'Total quality management and performance: The role of organisation support and co-worker support', *International Journal of Quality and Reliability Management*, 24, 617–27.

Jones, Q., Dunphy, D., Fishman, R., Larne, M. and Canter, C. (2006) *In Great Company: Unlocking the secrets of cultural transformation*. Sydney, Australia: Human Synergistics.

Joseph, D.L. and Newman, D.A. (2010) 'Emotional intelligence: An integrative meta-analysis and cascading model', *Journal of Applied Psychology*, 95(1), 54–78.

Judge, T.A. (2009) 'Core self-evaluations and work success', *Current Directions in Psychological Science*, 18, 58–62.

Judge, T.A. and Bono, J.E. (2000) 'Five-factor model of personality and transformational leadership', *Journal of Applied Psychology*, 85(5), 751–65.

Judge, T.A. and Hulin, C.L. (1993) 'Job satisfaction as a reflection of disposition: A multiple source causal analysis', *Organisational Behaviour and Human Decision Processes*, 56, 388–421.

Judge, T.A. and Kammeyer-Mueller, J.D. (2007) 'Personality and career success', in H.P. Gunz and M. Peiperl (eds), *Handbook of Career Studies*. London: Sage.

Judge, T.A. and Piccolo, R. (2004) 'Transformational and transactional leadership: A meta-analytic test of their relative validity', *Journal of Applied Psychology*, 89, 755–68.

Judge, T.A., Bono, J.E., Ilies, R. and Gerhardt, M.W. (2002) 'Personality and leadership: A qualitative and quantitative review', *Journal of Applied Psychology*, 87, 765–80.

Judge, T.A., Cable, D.M., Boudreau, J.W. and Bretz, R.D. (1995) 'An empirical investigation of the predictors of career success', *Personnel Psychology*, 48, 485–519.

Judge, T.A., Colbert, A.E. and Ilies, R. (2004a) 'Intelligence and leadership: A quantitative review and test of theoretical propositions', *Journal of Applied Psychology*, 89, 542–52.

Judge, T.A, Ilies, R. and Zhang, Z. (2012) 'Genetic influences on core self-evaluations, job satisfaction, and work stress: A behavioural genetics mediated model', *Organisational Behaviour and Human Decision Processes*, 117, 208–20.

Judge, T.A., Piccolo, R.F. and Ilies, R. (2004b) 'The forgotten ones? The validity of consideration and initiating structure in leadership research', *Journal of Applied Psychology*, 89, 36–51.

Judge, T.A., Piccolo, R.F. and Kosalka, T. (2009) 'The bright and dark sides of leader traits: A review and theoretical extension of the leader trait paradigm', *Leadership Quarterly*, 20, 855–75.

Judge, T.A., Rodell, J.B., Klinger, R.L., Simon, L.S. and Crawford, E.R. (2013) 'Hierarchical representations of the five-factor model of personality in predicting job performance: Integrating three organising frameworks with two theoretical perspectives', *Journal of Applied Psychology*, 98, 875.

Judge, T.A., Thoreson, C.J., Bono, J.E. and Patton, G.K. (2001) 'The job satisfaction–job performance relationship: A qualitative and quantitative review', *Psychological Bulletin*, 127, 376–407.

Judiesch, M.K. and Lyness, K.S. (1999) 'Left behind? The impact of leaves of absence on managers' career success', *Academy of Management Journal*, 42, 641–51.

Jung, C.G. (1933) *Psychological Types*. New York: Harcourt, Brace and World.

Jurgensen, C.E. (1978) 'Job preferences (What makes a job good or bad?)', *Journal of Applied Psychology*, 63, 267–76.

Kandola, B. (2009) *The Value of Difference: Eliminating bias in organisations*. Oxford: Pearn Kandola.

Kandola, B. and Fullerton, J. (1994) *Managing the Mosaic: Diversity in action*. London: Institute for Personnel and Development.

Kandola, R. (1995) 'Managing diversity: New broom or old hat?', in C.L. Cooper and I.T. Robertson (eds), *International Review of Industrial and Organisational Psychology*, vol. 10. Chichester: John Wiley.

Kanfer, R. and Ackerman, P.L. (1989) 'Motivation and cognitive abilities: An integrative/ aptitude–treatment interaction approach to skill acquisition', *Journal of Applied Psychology*, 74, 657–90.

Kanfer, R. and Ackerman, P.L. (2002) 'Non-ability influences on volition during skill training'. Paper presented as part of the symposium: New directions in research on motivational traits, Society for Industrial and Organisational Psychology 17th Annual Conference, Toronto.

Kanning, U.P., Grewe, K., Hollenberg, S. and Hadouch, M. (2006) 'From the subjects' point of view – reactions to different types of situational judgment items', *European Journal of Psychological Assessment*, 22, 168–76.

Kanter, R.M. (1989) *When Giants Learn to Dance: Mastering the challenges of strategy, management, and careers in the 1990s*. London: Unwin.

Kanter, R.M. (1997) *World Class: Thriving locally in the global economy*. New York: Simon and Schuster.

Kanter, R.M. (2008) 'Transforming giants', *Harvard Business Review*, 86, 43–52.

Kanter, R.M., Stein, B.A. and Jick, T.D. (1992) *The Challenge of Organisational Change: How companies experience it and leaders guide it*. New York: Free Press.

Kanungo, R.N. (2001) 'Ethical values of transactional and transformational leaders', *Canadian Journal of Administrative Sciences*, 18, 257–65.

Karagonlar, G., Eisenberger, R. and Aselage, J. (2015) 'Reciprocation wary employees discount psychological contract fulfilment', *Journal of Organisational Behaviour*, Published online first DOI: 10.1002/job.2016.

Karasek, R. (1979) 'Job demands, job decision latitude and mental strain: Implications for job redesign', *Administrative Science Quarterly*, 24, 285–306.

Karasek, R. and Theorell, T. (1990) *Healthy Work: Stress, productivity and the reconstruction of working life*. New York: Basic Books.

Karasek, R., Brisson, C., Kawakami, N., Houtman, I., Bongers, P. and Amick, B. (1998) 'The Job Content Questionnaire (JCQ): An instrument for internationally comparative assessments of psychosocial job characteristics', *Journal of Occupational Health Psychology*, 3, 322–55.

Kark, R., Shamir, B. and Chen, G. (2003) 'The two faces of transformational leadership: Empowerment and dependency', *Journal of Applied Psychology*, 88, 246–55.

Karpinski, A. and Hilton, J.L. (2001) 'Attitudes and the Implicit Association Test', *Journal of Personality and Social Psychology*, 81, 774–88.

Kawakami, N., Schunichi, A., Kawashima, M., Masumoto, T. and Hayashi, T. (1997) 'Effects of work-related stress reduction on depressive symptoms among Japanese blue-collar workers', *Scandinavian Journal of Work, Environment and Health*, 23, 54–9.

Kearney, A.T. (1992) *Total Quality: Time to take off the rose-tinted spectacles*. Kempston: IFS.

Keashly, L. (2001) 'Interpersonal and systemic aspects of emotional abuse at work: The target's perspective', *Violence and Victims*, 16, 233–68.

Keashly, L. and Jagatic, K. (2003) 'US perspectives on workplace bullying', in S. Einarsen, H. Hoel, D. Zapf and C. Cooper (eds), *Bullying and Emotional Abuse in the Workplace: International perspectives, research and practice*. London: Taylor and Francis.

Keenan, T. (1995) 'Graduate recruitment in Britain: A survey of selection methods used by organisations', *Journal of Organisational Behaviour*, 16, 303–17.

Keller, A.C. and Semmer, N.K. (2013) 'Changes in situational and dispositional factors as predictors of job satisfaction', *Journal of Vocational Behaviour*, 83, 88–98.

Kelly, G.A. (1951) *The Psychology of Personal Constructs*, vols 1 and 2. New York: Norton.

Kelly, G.A. (1955) *The Psychology of Personal Constructs*. New York: Norton.

Kelly, J.E. (1993) 'Does job redesign theory explain job re-design outcomes?', *Human Relations*, 45, 753–74.

Kemp, N.J., Wall, T.D., Clegg, C.W. and Cordery, J.L. (1983) 'Autonomous work groups in a greenfield site: A comparative study', *Journal of Occupational Psychology*, 56, 271–88.

Kerr, N.L. and Bruun, S.E. (1983) 'Dispensability of member effort and group motivation losses: Free-rider effects', *Journal of Personality and Social Psychology*, 44, 78–94.

Kerr, N.L. and Tindale, R.S. (2004) 'Group performance and decision making', *Annual Review of Psychology*, 55, 623–55.

Kersley, B., Alpin, C., Forth, J., Bryson, A., Bewley, H., Dix, G. and Oxenbridge, S. (2005) *Inside the Workplace: First findings from the 2004 Workplace Employment Relations Survey*. London: Department of Trade and Industry.

Kessler, S.R., Spector, P.E., Chang, C.H. and Parr, A.D. (2008) 'Organisational violence and aggression: Development of the three-factor violence climate survey', *Work & Stress*, 22, 108–24.

Kiazad, K., Seibert, S.E. and Kraimer, M.L. (2014) 'Psychological contract breach and employee innovation: A conservation of resources perspective', *Journal of Occupational and Organizational Psychology*, 87, 535–56.

Kidd, J.M. (2006) *Understanding Career Counselling*. London: Sage.

Kiesler, C.A. (1971) *The Psychology of Commitment*. New York: Academic Press.

Kim, S. and Gefland, M.J. (2003) 'The influence of ethnic identity on perceptions of organisational recruitment', *Journal of Vocational Behaviour*, 63, 396–416.

Kinder, A., Hughes, R. and Cooper C.L. (2008) *Employee Well-being Support: A workplace resource*. Chichester: John Wiley.

King, N. (1992) 'Modelling the innovation process: An empirical comparison of approaches', *Journal of Occupational and Organizational Psychology*, 65, 89–100.

King, N. (2004a) 'Using interviews in qualitative research', in C. Cassell and G. Symon (eds), *Essential Guide to Qualitative Methods in Organisational Research*. London: Sage.

King, N. (2004b) 'Using templates in the thematic analysis of text', in C. Cassell and G. Symon (eds), *Essential Guide to Qualitative Methods in Organisational Research*. London: Sage.

King, Z. (2004) 'Career self-management: Its nature, causes and consequences', *Journal of Vocational Behaviour*, 65, 112–33.

King, Z., Burke, S. and Pemberton, J. (2005) 'The "bounded" career: An empirical study of human capital, career mobility and employment outcomes in a mediated labour market', *Human Relations*, 58, 981–1007.

Kinicki, A.J., Prussia, G.E. and McKee Ryan, F.M. (2000) 'A panel study of coping with involuntary job loss', *Academy of Management Journal*, 43, 90–100.

Kipnis, D., Schmidt, S.M. and Wilkinson, I. (1980) 'Intraorganisational influence tactics: Explorations in getting one's way', *Journal of Applied Psychology*, 65, 440–52.

Kirkman, B.L., Rosen, B., Gibson, C.B., Tesluk, P.E. and McPherson, S.O. (2002) 'Five challenges to virtual team performance: Lessons from Sabre Inc.', *Academy of Management Executive*, 16, 67–79.

Kirkpatrick, D.L. (1967) 'Evaluation of training', in R.L. Craig and L.R. Bittel (eds), *Training and Development Handbook*. New York: McGraw-Hill.

Kirwan, B. and Ainsworth, L.K. (eds) (1992) *A Guide To Task Analysis*. London: Taylor and Francis.

Kivimäki, M., Jokela, M., Nyberg, S. et al. (2015) 'Long working hours and risk of coronary heart disease and stroke: A systematic review and meta-analysis of published and unpublished data for 603 838 individuals', *The Lancet*, published online: http://dx.doi.org/10.1016/S0140-6736(15)60295-1

Kivimäki, M., Virtanen, M., Elovainio, M., Kouvonen, A., Väänänen, A. and Vahtera, J. (2006) 'Work stress in the aetiology of coronary heart disease – a meta-analysis', *Scandinavian Journal of Work, Environment and Health*, 32, 431–42.

Klehe, U.C. and Latham, G. (2006) 'What would you do – really or ideally? Constructs underlying the behavior description interview and the situational interview in predicting typical versus maximum performance', *Human Performance*, 19(4), 357–82.

Klein, C., Diaz-Granados, D., Salas, E., Le, H., Burke, C.S., Lyons, R. and Goodwin, G.F. (2009) 'Does team building work?', *Small Group Research*, 40, 181–222.

Klein, H.J., Noe, R.A. and Wang, C. (2006) 'Motivation to learn and course outcomes: The impact of delivery mode, learning goal orientations and perceived barriers and enablers', *Personnel Psychology*, 59, 665–702.

Kleinman, M. and Klehe, U.C. (2011) 'Selling oneself: Construct and criterion-related validity of impression management in structured interviews', *Human Performance*, 24, 29–46.

Klimoski, R.J. and Donahue, L.M. (2001) 'Person perception in organisations: An overview of the field', in M. London (ed.), *How People Evaluate Others in Organisations*. London: LEA.

Kline, P. (1993) *An Easy Guide to Factor Analysis*. London: Routledge.

Kline, P. (1999) *Handbook of Psychological Testing*, 2nd edition. London: Sage.

Kline, P. (2000) *The New Psychometrics: Science, psychology and measurement*. London: Routledge.

Kluger, A. and Tikochinsky, J. (2001) 'The error of accepting the "theoretical" null hypothesis: The rise, fall and resurrection of commonsense hypotheses in psychology', *Psychological Bulletin*, 127, 408–23.

Kluger, A.N. and DeNisi, A. (1996) 'The effects of feedback interventions on performance: A historical review, a meta-analysis, and a preliminary feedback intervention theory', *Psychological Bulletin*, 119, 254–84.

Koenig, A.M., Eagly, A.H., Mitchell, A.A. and Ristikari, T. (2011) 'Are leader stereotypes masculine? A meta-analysis of three research paradigms', *Psychological Bulletin*, 137, 616–42.

Kompier, M., Geurts, S., Grundemann, R., Vink, P. and Smulders, P. (1998) 'Cases in stress prevention: The success of a participative and stepwise approach', *Stress Medicine*, 14, 155–68.

Kompier, M.A.J. and Kristensen, T.S. (2001) 'Organisational work stress interventions in a theoretical, methodological and practical context', in J. Dunham (ed.), *Stress in the Workplace: Past, present and future*. London: Whurr.

König, C.J., Klehe, U.C., Berchtold, M. and Kleinmann, M. (2010) 'Reasons for being selective when choosing personnel selection procedures', *International Journal of Selection and Assessment*, 18, 17–27.

Konrad, A.M. (2003) 'Defining the domain of workplace diversity scholarship', *Group and Organisation Management*, 28, 4–17.

Konradt, U., Warszta, T. and Ellwart, T. (2013) 'Fairness perceptions in web-based selection: Impact on applicants' pursuit intentions, recommendation intentions, and intentions to reapply', *International Journal of Selection and Assessment*, 21, 155–69.

Konstantinou, E. and Fincham, R. (2011) 'Not sharing but trading: Applying a Maussian exchange framework to knowledge management', *Human Relations*, 64, 823–42.

Kooij, D., De Lange, A., Jansen, P. and Dikkers, J. (2008) 'Older workers' motivation to continue to work: Five meanings of age: A conceptual review', *Journal of Managerial Psychology*, 23, 364–94.

Kooij, D.T., De Lange, A.H., Jansen, P.G., Kanfer, R. and Dikkers, J S. (2011) 'Age and work-related motives: Results of a meta-analysis', *Journal of Organisational Behaviour*, 32, 197–225.

Kopelman, R.E., Greenhaus, J.H. and Connolly, T.F. (1983) 'A model of work, family and inter-role conflict: A construct validation study', *Organisational Behaviour and Human Performance*, 32, 198–215.

Körner, A., Reitzle, M. and Silbereisen, R.K. (2012) 'Work-related demands and life satisfaction: The effects of engagement and disengagement among employed and long-term unemployed people', *Journal of Vocational Behaviour*, 80, 187–96.

Kornhauser, A. (1965) *Mental Health of the Industrial Worker*. Chichester: John Wiley.

Korunka, C., Kubicek, B., Prem, R. and Cvitan, A. (2012) 'Recovery and detachment between shifts, and fatigue during a twelve hour shift', *Work*, 41, 3227–33.

Kossek, E., Ruderman, M., Braddy, P. and Hannum, K. (2012) 'Work-nonwork boundary management profiles: A person-centred approach', *Journal of Vocational Behaviour*, 81, 112–28.

Kossek, E.E., Lautsch B.A. and Eaton, S.C. (2006) 'Telecommuting, control, and boundary management: Correlates of policy use and practice, job control, and work–family effectiveness', *Journal of Vocational Behaviour*, 68, 347–67.

Kossek, E.E., Pichler, S.M., Meece, D. and Barratt, M.E. (2008) 'Family, friend and neighbour child care providers and maternal well-being in low income systems: An ecological and social perspective', *Journal of Occupational and Organizational Psychology*, 81, 369–91.

Kotter, J.P. (1996) *Leading Change*. Boston, MA: Harvard Business School Press.

Kotter, J.P. (2008) *A Sense of Urgency*. Boston, MA: Harvard Business Press.

Kovjanic, S., Schuh, S.C. and Jonas, K. (2013) 'Transformational leadership and performance: An experimental investigation of the mediating effects of basic needs satisfaction and work engagement', *Journal of Occupational and Organizational Psychology*, 86, 543–55.

Kozlowski, S. and Ilgen, D. (2006) 'Enhancing the effectiveness of work groups and teams', *Psychological Science in the Public Interest*, 7(3), 77–124.

Kozlowski, S.W.J., Gully, S.M., Brown, K.G., Salas, E., Smith, E.M. and Nason, E.R. (2001) 'Effects of training goals and goal orientation traits on multidimensional training outcomes and performance adaptability', *Organisational Behavior and Human Decision Processes*, 85, 1–31.

Kraiger, K. and Ford, J.K. (1985) 'A meta-analysis of ratee race effects in performance ratings', *Journal of Applied Psychology*, 70, 56–65.

Kraiger, K., Ford, J. and Salas, E. (1993) 'Application of cognitive, skill-based, and affective theories of learning outcomes to new methods of training evaluation', *Journal of Applied Psychology*, 78, 311–28.

Kraiger, K., Passmore, J., Rebelo dos Santos, N. and Malvezzi, S. (2015) *The Psychology of Training, Development and Performance Improvement*. Chichester: John Wiley.

Krajewski, H.T., Goffin, R.D., McCarthy, J.M., Rothstein, M.G. and Johnston, N. (2006) 'Comparing the validity of structured interviews for managerial-level employees: Should we look to the past or focus on the future?', *Journal of Occupational and Organizational Psychology*, 79(3), 411–32.

Kram, K.E. (1985) *Mentoring at Work: Developmental relationships in organisational life*. Glenview, IL: Scott Foresman.

Krauss, R. and Fussell, S.R. (1990) 'Mutual knowledge and communicative effectiveness', in J. Galegher, R. Kraut and C. Egido (eds), *Intellectual Teamwork: Social and technological foundations of cooperative work*. Hillsdale, NJ: Lawrence Erlbaum Associates.

Kray, L.J. and Shirako, A. (2011) 'Stereotype threat in organisations: Its scope, triggers, and possible interventions', in M. Inzlicht and T. Schmader (eds), *Stereotype Threat: Theory, process, and application*, 173–88. New York: Oxford University Press.

Krieger, T., Zimmermann, J., Huffziger, S., Ubl, B., Diener, C., Kuehner, C. and Grosse Holtforth, M. (2014) 'Measuring depression with a well-being index: Further evidence for the validity of the WHO Well-Being Index (WHO-5) as a measure of the severity of depression', *Journal of Affective Disorders*, 156, 240–4.

Krueger, J. (1991) 'Accentuation effects and illusory change in exemplar-based category learning', *European Journal of Social Psychology*, 21, 37–48.

Kuijpers, M. and Scheerens, J. (2006) 'Career competencies for the modern career', *Journal of Career Development*, 32, 303–19.

Kuncel, N.R. and Sackett, P.R. (2014) 'Resolving the assessment centre construct validity problem (as we know it)', *Journal of Applied Psychology*, 99, 38.

Kuper, H. and Marmot, M. (2008) 'Job strain, job demands, decision latitude and risk of coronary heart disease within the Whitehall II study', *Journal of Epidemiology and Community Health*, 57, 147–53.

Kuper, H., Hemingway, M. and Marmot, M. (2002) 'Systematic review of prospective cohort studies of psychosocial factors in the etiology and prognosis of coronary heart disease', *Seminars in Vascular Medicine*, 2(3), 267–314.

Lam, S.S.K. and Dreher, G.F. (2004) 'Gender, extra-firm mobility and compensation attainment in the United States and Hong Kong', *Journal of Organisational Behaviour*, 25, 791–805.

Lambert, L.S. (2011) 'Promised and delivered inducements and contributions: An integrated view of psychological contract appraisal', *Journal of Applied Psychology*, 96, 695–712.

Lambert, L.S., Tepper, B.J., Carr, J.C., Holt, D.T. and Barelka, A.J. (2012) 'Forgotten but not gone: An examination of fit between leader consideration and initiating structure needed and received', *Journal of Applied Psychology*, 97, 913–30.

Lamm, H. and Trommsdorf, G. (1973) 'Group versus individual performance on tasks requiring ideational proficiency (brainstorming)', *European Journal of Social Psychology*, 3, 361–87.

LaMontagne, A.D. and Keegel, T. (2012) *Reducing Stress in the Workplace: An evidence review full report.* Melbourne, Australia: Victorian Health Promotion Foundation.

LaMontagne, A.D., Keegel, T., Louie, A.M., Ostrey, A. and Landsbergis, P.A. (2007) 'A systematic review of the job-stress intervention evaluation literature, 1990-2005', *International Journal of Occupational and Environmental Health*, 13, 268–80.

Lance, C.E. (2008) 'Why assessment centres do not work the way they are supposed to', *Industrial and Organisational Psychology*, 1, 84–97.

Landers, R.N., Sackett, P.R. and Tuzinski, K.A. (2011) 'Retesting after initial failure, coaching rumours, and warnings against faking in online personality measures for selection', *Journal of Applied Psychology*, 96, 202–10.

Landy, F.J. (1989) *The Psychology of Work Behaviour*, 4th edition. Homewood, IL: Brooks/Cole Publishing Co.

Lankau M.J. and Scandura, T.A. (2002) 'An investigation of personal learning in mentoring relationships: Content, antecedents, and consequences', *Academy of Management Journal*, 45, 779–90.

Lansisalmi, H., Piero, J.-M. and Kivimäki, M. (2004) 'Grounded theory in organisational research', in C. Cassell and G. Symon (eds), *Essential Guide to Qualitative Methods in Organisational Research*. London: Sage.

Larson, C.E. and LaFasto, F.M.J. (1989) *Teamwork: What must go right/what can go wrong.* London: Sage.

Latane, B., Williams, K. and Harkins, S. (1979) 'Many hands make light the work: The causes and consequences of social loafing', *Journal of Personality and Social Psychology*, 37, 822–32.

Latham, G.P. (2007) *Work Motivation: History, theory, research and practice.* London: Sage.

Latham, G.P. and Piccolo, R.F. (2012) 'The effect of context-specific versus nonspecific subconscious goals on employee performance', *Human Resource Management*, 51, 511–23.

Latham, G.P. and Pinder, C.C. (2005) 'Work motivation theory and research at the dawn of the twenty-first century', *Annual Review of Psychology*, 56, 485–516.

Latham, G.P., Skarlicki, D., Irvine, D. and Siegal, J.P. (1993) 'The increasing importance of performance appraisals to employee effectiveness in organisational settings in North America', in C.L. Cooper and I.T. Robertson (eds), *International Review of Industrial and Organisational Psychology*, vol. 8. Chichester: John Wiley.

Lau, D.C. and Murnighan, J.K. (1998) 'Demographic diversity and faultlines: The compositional dynamics of organisational groups', *Academy of Management Review*, 23, 325–40.

Lawler, E.E., III (2003) 'Pay systems for virtual teams', in C.B. Gibson and S.G. Cogen (eds), *Virtual Teams that Work: Creating conditions for effective virtual teams.* San Francisco: Jossey-Bass.

Lawrence, B.S. (1980) 'The myth of the mid-life crisis', *Sloan Management Review*, 4, 35–49.

Lazarus, R.S. (1966) *Psychological Stress and Coping Process*. New York: McGraw-Hill.

Lazarus, R.S. and Folkman, S. (1984) *Stress, Appraisal and Coping*. New York: Springer Publications.

Le, H., Oh, I.S., Robbins, S.B., Ilies, R., Holland, E. and Westrick, P. (2011) 'Too much of a good thing: Curvilinear relationships between personality traits and job performance', *Journal of Applied Psychology*, 96, 113.

Lea, M. and Spears, R. (1992) 'Paralinguistic and social perception in computer-mediated communication', *Journal of Organisational Computing*, 2, 321–41.

Lee, K. and Ashton, M.C. (2004) 'The HEXACO Personality Inventory: A new measure of the major dimensions of personality', *Multivariate Behavioural Research*, 39, 329–58.

Lee, T.W. and Mitchell, T.R. (1994) 'An alternative approach: The unfolding model of voluntary employee turnover', *Academy of Management Review*, 19, 51–89.

Lees, J. (2007) *How to Get a Job You'll Love*. Maidenhead: McGraw-Hill.

Lefkowitz, J. (1994) 'Sex-related differences in job attitudes and dispositional variables: Now you see them...', *Academy of Management Journal*, 37, 323–49.

Lehman, D.R., Chiu, C.Y. and Schaller, M. (2004) 'Psychology and culture', *Annual Review of Psychology*, 55, 689–714.

Leka, S. and Houdmont, J. (eds) (2010) *Occupational Health Psychology*. Oxford: Wiley-Blackwell.

Leon, F.R. (1981) 'The role of positive and negative outcomes in the causation of motivational forces', *Journal of Applied Psychology*, 66, 45–53.

Leonard, N.H., Beauvois, L.L. and Scholl, R.W. (1999) 'Work motivation: The incorporation of self-concept-based processes', *Human Relations*, 52, 969–98.

Leong, F., Austin, J. and Sakaran, U. (1998) 'An evaluation of cross-cultural validity of Holland's theory: Career choices by workers in India', *Journal of Vocational Behaviour*, 52, 441–55.

Lester, S.W., Kickul, J.R. and Bergmann, T.W. (2007) 'Managing employee perceptions of the psychological contract over time: The role of employer social accounts and contract fulfilment', *Journal of Organisational Behaviour*, 28, 191–208.

Levashina, J. and Campion, M.A. (2007) 'Measuring faking in the employment interview: Development and validation of an interview faking behavior scale', *Journal of Applied Psychology*, 92(6), 1638–56.

Levashina, J., Hartwell, C.J., Morgeson, F.P. and Campion, M.A. (2014) 'The structured employment interview: Narrative and quantitative review of the research literature', *Personnel Psychology*, 67, 241–93.

Levine, E.L., Ash, R.A. and Bennett, N. (1980) 'Exploratory comparative study of four job analysis methods', *Journal of Applied Psychology*, 65(5), 524–35.

Levinson, D.J. with Darrow, C.N., Klein, E.B., Levinson, M.H. and McKee, B. (1978) *Seasons of a Man's Life*. New York: Knopf.

Levinson, D.J. with Levinson, J. (1996) *The Seasons of a Woman's Life*. New York: Knopf.

Lewin, K. (1939) 'When facing danger', in G.W. Lewin (ed.), *Resolving Social Conflict*. London: Harper and Row.

Lewin, K. (1945) 'The Research Centre for Group Dynamics at Massachusetts Institute of Technology', *Sociometry*, 8, 126–36.

Lewin, K. (1946) 'Action research and minority problems', *Journal of Social Issues*, 2, 34–6.

Lewin, K. (1947a) 'Frontiers in group dynamics', in D. Cartwright (ed.), *Field Theory in Social Science*. London: Social Science Paperbacks.

Lewin, K. (1947b) 'Group decisions and social change', in T.M. Newcomb and E.L. Hartley (eds), *Readings in Social Psychology*. New York: Henry Holt.

Lewis, K.M. (2000) 'When leaders display emotion: How followers respond to negative emotional expression of male and female leaders', *Journal of Organisational Behaviour*, 21, 221–34.

Lewis, S. and Arnold, J. (2012) 'Organisational career management techniques in the UK retail buying and merchandising community', *International Journal of Retail and Distribution Management*, 40, 451–70.

Lewis, S. and Cooper, C.L. (2005) *Work–Life Integration: Case studies in organisational change*. Chichester and New York: John Wiley and Sons.

Lewis, T. (2011) 'Assessing social identity and collective efficacy as theories of group motivation at work', *International Journal of Human Resource Management*, 22, 963–80.

Li, A. and Cropanzano, R. (2009) 'Do East Asians respond more/less strongly to organisational justice than North Americans? A meta-analysis', *Journal of Management Studies*, 46, 787–805.

Li, N., Chiaburu, D.S., Kirkman, B.L. and Xie, Z. (2013) 'Spotlight on the followers: An examination of moderators of relationships between transformational leadership and subordinates' citizenship and taking charge', *Personnel Psychology*, 66(1), 225–60.

Libbrecht, N., Lievens, F., Carette, B. and Côté, S. (2014) 'Emotional intelligence predicts success in medical school', *Emotion*, 14, 64–73.

Licht, M.H. (1997) 'Multiple regression and correlation', in L.G. Grimm and P.R. Yarnold (eds), *Reading and Understanding Multivariate Statistics*. Washington, DC: American Psychological Association.

Liden, R.C., Wayne, S.J., Kraimer, M.L. and Sparrowe, R.T. (2003) 'The dual commitments of contingent workers: An examination of contingents' commitment to the agency and the organisation', *Journal of Organisational Behaviour*, 24, 609–25.

Lievens, F. and Harris, M.M. (2003) 'Research on Internet recruitment and testing: Current status and future directions', in C.L. Cooper and I.T. Robertson (eds), *International Review of Industrial and Organisational Psychology*, vol. 18. Chichester: John Wiley.

Lievens, F. and Patterson, F. (2011) 'The validity and incremental validity of knowledge tests, low-fidelity simulations, and high-fidelity simulations for predicting job performance in advanced-level high-stakes selection', *Journal of Applied Psychology*, 96, 927–40.

Lievens, F. and Sackett, P.R. (2006) 'Video-based versus written situational judgment tests: A comparison in terms of predictive validity', *Journal of Applied Psychology*, 91(5), 1181–8.

Lievens, F., Buyse, T. and Sackett, P.R. (2005) 'The operational validity of a video-based situational judgment test for medical college admissions: Illustrating the importance of matching predictor and criterion construct domains', *Journal of Applied Psychology*, 90, 442–52.

Lievens, F., Peeters, H. and Schollaert, E. (2008) 'Situational judgement tests: A review of recent research', *Personnel Review*, 37, 426–41.

Lincoln, A.E. and Allen, M.P. (2004) 'Double jeopardy in Hollywood: Age and gender in the careers of film actors, 1926–1999', *Sociological Forum*, 19, 611–31.

Linley, A.P. (2006) 'Coaching research: Who? what? where? when? why?', *International Journal of Evidence Based Coaching and Mentoring*, 4, 1–7.

Lippitt, R., Watson, J. and Westley, B. (1958) *The Dynamics of Planned Change*. New York: Harcourt, Brace and World.

Littrell, L.N., Salas, E., Hess, K.P., Paley, M. and Riedel, S. (2006) 'Expatriate preparation: A critical analysis of 25 years of cross-cultural training research', *Human Resource Development Review*, 5, 355–88.

Liu, D., Zhang, S., Wang, L. and Lee, T.W. (2011) 'The effects of autonomy and empowerment on employee turnover: Test of a multilevel model in teams', *Journal of Applied Psychology*, 96, 1305–16.

Livi, S., Alessandri, G., Caprara, G.V. and Pierro, A. (2015) 'Positivity within teamwork: Cross-level effects of positivity on performance', *Personality and Individual Differences*, 85, 230–5.

Lloyd, A., Dale, B. and Burnes, B. (1994) 'Supplier development: A study of Nissan Motor Manufacturing (UK) and its suppliers', *Proceedings of the Institution of Mechanical Engineers Part D: Journal of Automobile Engineering*, 208, 63–8.

Lobban, R.K., Husted, J. and Farewell, V.T. (1998) 'A comparison on the effect of job demand, decision latitude, role and supervisory style on self-reported job satisfaction', *Work & Stress*, 12, 337–50.

Locke, E.A. (1976) 'The nature and causes of job satisfaction', in M.D. Dunnette (ed.), *Handbook of Industrial and Organisational Psychology*. Chicago, IL: Rand McNally.

Locke, E.A. (1995) 'The micro-analysis of job satisfaction: Comments on Taber and Alliger', *Journal of Organisational Behaviour*, 16, 123–5.

Locke, E.A. (2000) 'Motivation, cognition and action: An analysis of studies of task goals and knowledge', *Applied Psychology: An International Review*, 49, 408–29.

Locke, E.A. (2005) 'Why emotional intelligence is an invalid concept', *Journal of Organisational Behaviour*, 26, 425–31.

Locke, E.A. and Latham, G.P. (1990) *A Theory of Goal-setting and Task Performance*. Englewood Cliffs, NJ: Prentice Hall.

Locke, E.A. and Latham, G.P. (2002) 'Building a practically useful theory of goal setting and task motivation: A 35-year odyssey', *American Psychologist*, 57, 705–17.

Locke, E.A. and Latham, G.P. (2004) 'What should we do about motivation theory? Six recommendations for the twenty-first century', *Academy of Management Review*, 29, 388–403.

Locke, E.A., Shaw, K.N., Saari, L.M. and Latham, G.P. (1981) 'Goal setting and task performance 1969–1980', *Psychological Bulletin*, 90, 125–52.

London, M. (2001a) 'The great debate: Should multi-source feedback be used for administration or development only?', in D. Bracken, C. Timmreck and A. Church (eds), *The Handbook of Multi-source Feedback*. San Francisco, CA: Jossey-Bass.

London, M. (2001b) *How People Evaluate Others in Organisations*. London: Lawrence Erlbaum.

London, M. and Smither, J.W. (1995) 'Can multi-source feedback change perceptions of goal accomplishment, self-evaluations and performance related outcomes? Theory-based applications and directions for research', *Personnel Psychology*, 48, 803–39.

London, M. and Tornow, W.W. (1998a) *Maximising the Value of 360-degree Feedback*. Greensboro, NC: Centre for Creative Leadership.

London, M. and Tornow, W.W. (1998b) 'Introduction: 360-degree feedback – more than a tool!', in M. London and W.W. Tornow (eds), *Maximising the Value of 360-degree Feedback*. Greensboro, NC: Centre for Creative Leadership.

Long, L. and Tracey, T.J. (2006) 'Structure of RIASEC scores in China: A structural meta-analysis', *Journal of Vocational Behaviour*, 68, 39–51.

Longenecker, C.O., Gioia, D.A. and Sims, H.P., Jr (1987) 'Behind the mask: The politics of employee appraisal', *Academy of Management Executive*, 1: 183–93.

Lord, R.G. and Maher, K.J. (1991) *Leadership and Information Processing*. Boston, MA: Routledge.

Loretto, W. and Vickerstaff, S. (2015) 'Gender, age and flexible working in later life', *Work, Employment and Society*, 29, 233–49.

Lowman, R.L. (2012) 'The scientist-practitioner consulting psychologist', *Consulting Psychology Journal: Practice and Research*, 64, 151–6.

Luthans, F. and Kreitner, R. (1975) *Organisational Behaviour Modification*. Glenview, IL: Scott-Foresman.

Luthans, F., Avey, J.B. and Patera, J.L. (2008) 'Experimental analysis of a web-based training intervention to develop positive psychological capital', *Academy of Management Learning and Education*, 7, 209–21.

Lyness, K.S. and Schrader, C.A. (2004) 'Moving ahead or just moving? An examination of gender differences in senior corporate management appointments', *Group and Organisation Management*, 31, 651–76.

Lyness, K.S. and Thompson, D.E. (2000) 'Climbing the corporate ladder: Do female and male executives follow the same route?', *Journal of Applied Psychology*, 85(1), 86–101.

Lyons, S.T., Schweitzer, L., & Ng, E.S. (2015). How have careers changed? An investigation of changing career patterns across four generations. *Journal of Managerial Psychology*, 30(1), 8–21.

Lyubomirsky, S. (2007) *The How of Happiness: A new approach to getting the life you want*. London: Penguin Books.

Lyubomirsky, S. (2013) *The Myths of Happiness*. London: Penguin Books.

Lyubomirsky, S., King, L.A. and Diener, E. (2005) 'The benefits of frequent positive affect: Does happiness lead to success?', *Psychological Bulletin*, 131, 803–55.

Mabe, P.A. and West, S.G. (1982) 'Validity of self-evaluation of ability: A review and meta-analysis', *Journal of Applied Psychology*, 67, 280–96.

Mabey, C. (1986) *Graduates into Industry*. Aldershot: Gower.

Mabey, C. (2001) 'Closing the circle: Participant views of a 360-degree feedback programme', *Human Resource Management Journal*, 11, 41–54.

Mabey, C. and Mayon-White, B. (1993) *Managing Change*, 2nd edition. London: Open University/Paul Chapman Publishing.

Mabey, C. and Ramirez, M. (2005) 'Does management development improve organisational productivity? A six country analysis of European firms', *International Journal of Human Resource Management*, 16, 1067–82.

Macan, T. (2009) 'The employment interview: A review of current studies and directions for future research', *Human Resource Management Review*, 19(3), 203–18.

MacLeod, D. and Brady, C. (2008) *The Extra Mile: How to Engage Your People to Win*. Harlow: Pearson Education.

Maier, N.R.F. and Solem, A.R. (1952) 'The contribution of a discussion leader to the quality of group thinking: The effective use of minority opinions', *Human Relations*, 5, 277–88.

Majchrzak, A., Rice, R.E., King, N., Malhotra, A. and Ba, S.L. (2000) 'Computer mediated inter-organisational knowledge sharing: Insights from a virtual team innovating using a collaborative tool', *Information Resources Management Journal*, 13(1), 44–53.

Makin, P., Cooper, C.L. and Cox, C. (1996) *Organisations and the Psychological Contract*. Leicester: British Psychological Society.

Malone, J.C. and Cruchon, N.M. (2001) 'Radical behaviourism and the rest of psychology'. A review/précis of Skinner's *About Behaviourism*', *Behaviour and Philosophy*, 29, 31–57.

Maltarich, M.A., Nyberg, A.J. and Reilly, G. (2010) 'A conceptual and empirical analysis of the cognitive ability–voluntary turnover relationship', *Journal of Applied Psychology*, 95, 1058–70.

Marcia, J.E. (1966) 'Development and validation of ego-identity status', *Journal of Personality and Social Psychology*, 3, 551–8.

Mark, G.M. and Smith, A.P. (2008) 'Stress models: A review and suggested new direction', in J. Houdmont and S. Leka (eds), *Occupational Health Psychology: European perspectives on research, education and practice*, vol. III. Nottingham: Nottingham University Press.

Marks, M.A., Sabella, M.J., Burke, C.S. and Zaccaro, S.J. (2002) 'The impact of cross-training on team effectiveness', *Journal of Applied Psychology*, 87, 3–13.

Marrow, A.J. (1969) *The Practical Theorist: The life and work of Kurt Lewin*. New York: Teachers College Press.

Marrow, A.J. (1977) *The Practical Theorist: The life and work of Kurt Lewin*. New York: Teachers College Press.

Martin, J. (1992) *Cultures in Organisations: Three perspectives*. Oxford: Oxford University Press.

Martin, J. (2002) *Organisational Culture: Mapping the terrain*. London: Sage.

Martin, R. (2000) 'Breaking the code of change: Observations and critique', in M. Beer and N. Nohria (eds), *Breaking the Code of Change*. Boston, MA: Harvard Business School Press.

Maslach, C. and Jackson, S.E. (1981) 'The measurement of experienced burnout', *Journal of Occupational Behaviour*, 2, 99–113.

Maslow, A.H. (1943) 'A theory of motivation', *Psychological Review*, 50, 370–96.

Maslow, A.H. (1954) *Motivation and Personality*. New York: Harper and Row.

Mathieu, C., Neumann, C.S., Hare, R.D. and Babiak, P. (2014) 'A dark side of leadership: Corporate psychopathy and its influence on employee well-being and job satisfaction', *Personality and Individual Differences*, 59, 83–8.

Mathieu, J.E. and Zajac, D.M. (1990) 'A review and meta-analysis of the antecedents, correlates and consequences of organisational commitment', *Psychological Bulletin*, 108, 171–94.

Matrix (2013) *Economic analysis of workplace mental health promotion and mental disorder prevention programmes and of their potential contribution to EU health, social and economic policy objectives*, Executive Agency for Health and Consumers, Specific Request EAHC/2011/Health/19 for the Implementation of Framework Contract EAHC/2010/Health/01; http://ec.europa.eu/health/mental_health/docs/matrix_economic_analysis_mh_promotion_en.pdf

Matthews, G. and Deary, I.J. (1998) *Personality Traits*. New York: Cambridge University Press.

Matthews, G., Deary, I.J. and Whiteman, M.C. (2003a) *Personality Traits*, 2nd edition. Cambridge: Cambridge University Press.

Matthews, G., Zeidner, M. and Roberts, R. (2003b) *Emotional Intelligence: Science and myth*. Cambridge, MA: MIT Press.

Maume, D.J. (1999) 'Glass ceilings and glass escalators: Occupational segregation and race and sex differences in managerial promotions', *Work and Occupations*, 26, 483–509.

Maurer, S.D., Sue-Chan, C. and Latham, G.P. (1999) 'The situational interview', in R.W. Eder and M.M. Harris (eds), *The Employment Interview Handbook*. London: Sage.

Maurer T.J., Solamon, J.M. and Lippstreu, M. (2008) 'How does coaching interviewees affect the validity of a structured interview?', *Journal of Organisational Behaviour*, 29, 355–71.

Mayer, J.D. and Salovey, P. (1997) 'What is emotional intelligence?', in P. Salovey and D.J. Sluyter (eds), *Emotional Development and Emotional Intelligence: Educational implications*. New York: Basic Books.

Mayer, J.D., Caruso, D. and Salovey, P. (1999) 'Emotional intelligence meets traditional standards for an intelligence', *Intelligence*, 27, 267–98.

Mayer, J.D., Perkins, D., Caruso, D.R. and Salovey, P. (2001) 'Emotional intelligence and giftedness', *Roeper Review*, 23(3), 131–7.

Mayer, J.D., Salovey, P. and Caruso, D.R. (2000) 'Emotional intelligence as zeitgeist, as personality, and as a mental ability', in R. Bar-On and J.D.A. Parker (eds), *Handbook of Emotional Intelligence*. San Francisco, CA: Jossey-Bass.

Mayon-White, B. (1993) 'Problem-solving in small groups: Team members as agents of change', in C. Mabey and B. Mayon-White (eds), *Managing Change*, 2nd edition. London: Open University/Paul Chapman Publishing.

Maznevski, M.L. (1994) 'Understanding our differences: Performance in decision-making groups with diverse members', *Human Relations*, 47(5), 531–52.

McCall, M.W. (2010) 'Recasting leadership development', *Industrial and Organisational Psychology*, 3, 3–19.

McCalman, J. and Paton, R.A. (1992) *Change Management: A guide to effective implementation*. London: Paul Chapman Publishing.

McClelland, D.C. (1961) *The Achieving Society*. Princeton, NJ: Van Nostrand.

McClough, A.C. and Rogelberg, S.G. (2003) 'Selection in teams: An exploration of the teamwork knowledge, skills and ability test', *International Journal of Selection and Assessment*, 11(1), 56–66.

McCormick, E.J. and Sanders, M.S. (1992) *Human Factors in Engineering and Design*, 7th edition. New York: McGraw Hill.

McCormick, E.J., Jeanneret, P. and Meacham, R.C. (1972) 'A study of job characteristics and job dimensions as based on the position analysis questionnaires', *Journal of Applied Psychology*, 36, 347–68.

McCrae, R.R. and Costa, P.T. (1990) *Personality in Adulthood*. New York: Guilford Press.

McCrae, R.R. and Costa, P.T. (1997) 'Personality trait structure as a human universal', *American Psychologist*, 52, 509–16.

McDaniel, M.A. (2005) 'Big-brained people are smarter: A meta-analysis of the relationship between *in vivo* brain volume and intelligence', *Intelligence*, 33, 337–46.

McDaniel, M.A. and Nguyen, N.T. (2001) 'Situational judgment tests: A review of practice and constructs assessed', *International Journal of Selection and Assessment*, 9, 103–13.

McDaniel, M.A., Hartman, N.S., Whetzel, D.L. and Grubb, W.L. III (2007) 'Situational judgment tests, response instructions and validity: A meta-analysis', *Personnel Psychology*, 60, 63–91.

McDaniel, M.A., Morgeson, F.P., Finnegan, E.B., Campion, M.A. and Braverman, E.P. (2001) 'Use of situational judgment tests to predict job performance: A clarification of the literature', *Journal of Applied Psychology*, 86, 730–40.

McEachan, R.R.C., Conner, M., Taylor, N.J. and Lawton, R.J. (2011) 'Prospective prediction of health-related behaviours with the Theory of Planned Behaviour: A meta-analysis', *Health Psychology Review*, 5, 97–144.

McEntire, L., Dailey, L., Osburn, H. and Mumford, M. (2006) 'Innovations in job analysis: Development and application of metrics to analyse jobs', *Human Resource Management Review*, 16(3), 310–23.

McFarlin, D.B. and Sweeney, P.D. (1992) 'Distributive and procedural justice as predictors of satisfaction with personal and organisational outcomes', *Academy of Management Journal*, 35, 626–37.

McGrath, J.E. (1964) *Social Psychology: A brief introduction*. New York: Holt, Rinehart and Winston.

McGrath, J.E. (1984) *Groups: Interaction and performance*. Englewood Cliffs, NJ: Prentice Hall.

McGregor, D. (1960) *The Human Side of Enterprise*. New York: McGraw-Hill.

McHugh, M.F. (1991) 'Disabled workers: Psychosocial issues', in M.J. Davidson and J. Earnshaw (eds), *Vulnerable Workers*. Chichester: John Wiley.

McKay, P. and McDaniel, M.A. (2006) 'A re-examination of black–white mean differences in work performance: More data, more moderators', *Journal of Applied Psychology*, 91, 531–54.

McKee-Ryan, F.M. and Harvey, J. (2011) '"I have a job, but...": A review of underemployment', *Journal of Management*, 37, 962–96.

McKee-Ryan, F.M., Virick, M., Prussia, G.E., Harvey, J. and Lilly, J.D. (2009) 'Life after the layoff: Getting a job worth keeping', *Journal of Organisational Behaviour*, 30, 561–80.

McKinsey and Company (2008) 'Creating organisational transformations', *The McKinsey Quarterly*, July, 1–7. Available at: www.mckinseyquarterly.com

McLarnon, M.J., Carswell, J.J. and Schneider, T.J. (2015) 'A case of mistaken identity? Latent profiles in vocational interests', *Journal of Career Assessment*, 23, 166–85.

McLeod, P.L., Baron, R.S., Marti, M.W. and Yoon, K. (1997) 'The eyes have it: Minority influence in face-to-face and computer-mediated group discussion', *Journal of Applied Psychology*, 82, 706–18.

Meek, V.L. (1988) 'Organisational culture: Origins and weaknesses', *Organisation Studies*, 9(4), 453–73.

Meichenbaum, D. (1996) *Treating Adults with Post-traumatic Stress Disorder*. Waterloo, ON, Canada: Institute Press.

Meier, L.L., Semmer, N.K., Elfering, A. and Jacobshagen, N. (2008) 'The double meaning of control: Three-way interactions between internal resources, job control and stressors at work', *Journal of Occupational Health Psychology*, 13, 244–58.

Meindl, J.R., Ehrlich, S.B. and Dukerich, J.M. (1985) 'The romance of leadership', *Administrative Science Quarterly*, 30, 78–102.

Melamed, S., Ben-Avi, I., Luz, J. and Green, M.S. (1995) 'Objective and subjective work monotony: Effects on job satisfaction, psychological distress and absenteeism in blue-collar workers', *Journal of Applied Psychology*, 80, 29–42.

Melchers, K.G., Lienhardt, N., Von Aarburg, M. and Kleinmann, M. (2011) 'Is more structure really better? A comparison of frame-of-reference training and descriptively anchored rating scales to improve interviewers' rating quality', *Personnel Psychology*, 64, 53–87.

Mellor, N., Arnold, J. and Gelade, G. (2009) *The Effects of Transformational Leadership on Employees' Absenteeism in Four UK Public Sector Organisations*. Norwich: HSE Books.

Mento, A.J., Steel, R.P. and Karren, R.J. (1987) 'A meta-analytic study of the effects of goal setting on task performance: 1966–1984', *Organisational Behaviour and Human Decision Processes*, 39, 52–83.

Meriac, J.P., Hoffman, B.J., Woehr, D.J. and Fleisher, M.S. (2008) 'Further evidence for the validity of assessment centre dimensions: A meta-analysis of the incremental criterion-related validity of dimension ratings', *Journal of Applied Psychology*, 93, 1042–52.

Meyer, J. (2001) 'Action research', in N. Fulop, P. Allen, A. Clarke and N. Black (eds), *Studying the Organisation and Delivery of Health Services: Research methods*. London: Routledge.

Meyer, J.P., Allen, N.J. and Smith, C.A. (1993) 'Commitment to organisations and occupations: Extension and test of a three-component conceptualization', *Journal of Applied Psychology*, 78, 538–51.

Meyer, J.P., Paunonen, S.V., Gellatly, I.R., Goffin, R.D. and Jackson, D.N. (1989) 'Organisational commitment and job performance: It's the nature of the commitment that counts', *Journal of Applied Psychology*, 74, 152–6.

Meyer, J.P., Stanley, D.J., Herscovitch, L. and Topolnytsky, L. (2002) 'Affective, continuance and normative commitment to the organisation: A meta-analysis of antecedents, correlates and consequences', *Journal of Vocational Behaviour*, 61, 20–52.

Mikkelsen, E.G. and Einarsen, S. (2001) 'Bullying in Danish work-life: Prevalence and health correlates', *European Journal of Work and Organisational Psychology*, 10, 393–413.

Miles, E.W. and Clenney, E.F. (2012) 'Extremely difficult negotiator goals: Do they follow the predictions of goal-setting theory?', *Organisational Behaviour and Human Decision Processes*, 118, 108–15.

Millar, M.G. and Tesser, A. (1989) 'The effects of affective–cognitive consistency and thought on attitude–behaviour relations', *Journal of Experimental Social Psychology*, 25, 189–202.

Miller, D. (1993) 'The architecture of simplicity', *Academy of Management Review*, 18(1), 116–38.

Miller, D. (2001) 'Reexamining teamwork and team performance', *Small Group Research*, 32(6), 745–66.

Miller, D. and Friesen, P.H. (1984) *Organisations: A quantum view*. Englewood Cliffs, NJ: Prentice Hall.

Miller, G.A. (1966) *Psychology: The science of mental life*. Harmondsworth: Penguin.

Miller, M.J. (2007) 'Examining the degree of congruency between a traditional career intervention and an online self-assessment exercise', *Journal of Employment Counselling*, 44, 11–16.

Millette, V. and Gagné, M. (2008) 'Designing volunteers' tasks to maximise motivation, satisfaction and performance: The impact of job characteristics on volunteer engagement', *Motivation and Emotion*, 32, 11–22.

Millward, L.J. (2006) 'The transition to motherhood in an organisational context: An interpretative phenomenological analysis', *Journal of Occupational and Organizational Psychology*, 79, 315–34.

Milner, A., Page, A. and LaMontagne, A.D. (2014) 'Cause and effect in studies on unemployment, mental health and suicide: A meta-analytic and conceptual review', *Psychological Medicine*, 44, 909–17.

Miner, J.B. (2003) 'The rated importance, scientific validity, and practical usefulness of organisational behaviour theories: A quantitative review', *Academy of Management Learning and Education*, 2, 250–68.

Ministry of Defence (2000) *Overview of Target Audience Descriptions*. London: Ministry of Defence.

Ministry of Defence (2001) *Human Factors Integration (HFI): Practical guidance for IPTs*. London: Ministry of Defence.

Ministry of Defence (2008) *Human Factors for Designers of Systems: Defence Standard 00-250*. London: MOD. Also available at http://everyspec.com/DEF-STAN/

Ministry of Defence, Human Factors Integration Defence Technology Centre (2006) *Cost Arguments and Evidence for Human Factors Integration*. London: Ministry of Defence.

Mintzberg, H. (1983) *Power In and Around Organisations*. Englewood Cliffs, NJ: Prentice Hall.

Mintzberg, H. (1994) *The Rise and Fall of Strategic Planning*. London: Prentice Hall.

Mischel, W. (1968) *Personality Assessment*. New York: John Wiley.

Mitchell, A. and Zigurs, I. (2009) 'Trust in virtual teams: Solved or still a mystery', *The Data Base for Advances in Information Systems*, 40, 61–83.

Mitchell, R.J. and Williamson, A.M. (2000) 'Evaluation of an 8-hour versus a 12-hour shift register on employees at a power station', *Applied Ergonomics*, 31, 83–93.

Mobley, W.H., Horner, S.O. and Hollingsworth, A.T. (1978) 'An evaluation of precursors of hospital employee turnover', *Journal of Applied Psychology*, 63, 408–14.

Mohr, R.D. and Zoghi, C. (2008) 'High-involvement work design and job satisfaction', *Industrial and Labour Relations Review*, 61, 275–96.

Mohrman, S.A., Cohen, S.G. and Mohrman, A.M. Jr (1995) *Designing Team-based Organisations: New forms for knowledge work*. San Francisco, CA: Jossey-Bass Wiley.

Molloy, J.C. (2005) 'Development networks: Literature review and future research', *Career Development International*, 10, 536–47.

Montano, D., Hoven, H. and Siegrist, J. (2014) 'Effects of organisational-level interventions at work on employees' health: A systematic review', *BMC Public Health*, 14, 135–44.

Moore, C., Gunz, H. and Hall, D.T. (2007) 'Tracing the historical roots of career theory in management and organisation studies', in H. Gunz and M. Peiperl (eds), *Handbook of Career Studies*, 13–38. London: Sage.

Moran, C.M., Diefendorff, J.M., Kim, T.Y. and Liu, Z.Q. (2012) 'A profile approach to self-determination theory motivations at work', *Journal of Vocational Behaviour*, 81, 354–63.

Morey, J.C., Simon, R., Jay, G.D., Wears, R.L., Salisbury, M., Dukes, K.A. and Berns, S.D. (2002) 'Error reduction and performance improvement in the emergency department through formal teamwork training: Evaluation results of the MedTeams project', *Health Services Research*, 37, 1553–81.

Morgan, G. (1997) *Images of Organisation*, 2nd edition. London: Sage.

Morgeson, F.P. and Campion, M.A. (2002) 'Minimising trade-offs when redesigning work: Evidence from a longitudinal quasi-experiment', *Personnel Psychology*, 55, 589–612.

Morgeson, F.P. and Dierdorff, E.C. (2011) 'Work analysis: From technique to theory', *APA Handbook of Industrial and Organisational Psychology*, 2, 3–41.

Morgeson, F.P. and Humphrey, S.E. (2006) 'The Work Design Questionnaire (WDQ): Developing and validating a comprehensive measure for assessing job design and the nature of work', *Journal of Applied Psychology*, 91, 1321–39.

Morgeson, F.P., Campion M.A., Dipboye R.L., Hollenbeck J.R., Murphy, K. and Schmitt, N. (2007a) 'Reconsidering the use of personality tests in personnel selection contexts', *Personnel Psychology*, 60, 683–729.

Morgeson, F.P., Campion, M.A., Dipboye, R.L., Hollenbeck, J.R., Murphy, K. and Schmitt, N. (2007b) 'Are we getting fooled again? Coming to terms with limitations in the use of personality tests for personnel selection', *Personnel Psychology*, 60, 1029–49.

Morgeson, F.P., Spitzmuller, M., Garza, A.S. and Campion, M.A. (2014) 'Pay Attention! The liabilities of respondent experience and carelessness when making job analysis judgments', *Journal of Management*, 0149206314522298.

Morita, M. (2001) 'Have the seeds of Japanese teamworking taken root abroad?', *New Technology, Work and Employment*, 16(3), 178–90.

Morley, F.J.J. and Harris, D. (1994) 'Terrain and vertical navigation displays to enhance situational awareness: A user-centred iterative design approach'. Paper presented to the Royal Aeronautical Society Conference on Controlled Flight into Terrain, 8 November 1994, London.

Morrell, K., Loan-Clarke, J. and Wilkinson, A. (2001) 'Unweaving leaving: The use of models in the management of employee turnover', *International Journal of Management Reviews*, 3, 219–44.

Morrell, K., Loan-Clarke, J. and Wilkinson, A. (2004) 'The role of shocks in employee turnover', *British Journal of Management*, 15, 335–49.

Morris, J.A. and Feldman, D.C. (1996) 'The dimensions, antecedents and consequences of emotional labour', *Academy of Management Review*, 21, 986–1010.

Morrow, P.C. (2011) 'Managing organisational commitment: Insights from longitudinal research', *Journal of Vocational Behaviour*, 79, 18–35.

Moscoso, S. and Salgado, J.F. (2004) '"Dark side" personality styles as predictors of task, contextual, and job performance', *International Journal of Selection and Assessment*, 12(4), 356–62.

Moscovici, S. (1985) 'Social influence and conformity', in G. Lindzey and E. Aronson (eds), *The Handbook of Social Psychology*, 3rd edition. New York: Random House.

Moscovici, S. and Mugny, G. (1983) 'Minority influence', in P.B. Paulus (ed.), *Basic Group Processes*. New York: Springer-Verlag.

Moser, K. and Schuler, H. (1989) 'The nature of psychological measurement', in P. Herriot (ed.), *Assessment and Selection in Organisations*. Chichester: John Wiley.

Moser K.S. and Axtell, C. (2013) 'The role of norms in virtual work: A review and agenda for future research', *Journal of Personnel Psychology*, 12, 1–6.

Mowday, R., Steers, R. and Porter, L. (1979) 'The measurement of organisational commitment', *Journal of Vocational Behaviour*, 14, 224–47.

Mowday, R.T. (1991) 'Equity theory predictions of behaviour in organisations', in R.M. Steers and L.W. Porter (eds), *Motivation and Work Behaviour*, 5th edition. New York: McGraw-Hill.

Mullen, B. and Copper, C. (1994) 'The relation between group cohesiveness and performance: An integration', *Psychological Bulletin*, 115, 210–27.

Murphy, G.C. and Athanasou, J.A. (1999) 'The effect of unemployment on mental health', *Journal of Occupational and Organizational Psychology*, 72, 83–99.

Murphy, K. and Cleveland, J. (1995) *Understanding Performance Appraisal: Social organisational and goal-based perspectives.* London: Sage.

Murphy, L.R. (1988) 'Workplace interventions for stress reduction and prevention', in C.L. Cooper and R. Payne (eds), *Causes, Coping and Consequences of Stress at Work*. Chichester: John Wiley.

Murphy, L.R. and Sauter, S.L. (2003) 'The USA perspective: Current issues and trends in the management of work stress', *Australian Psychologist*, 38, 151–7.

Murphy, P.R. and Jackson, S.E. (1999) 'Managing work role performance: Challenges for twenty-first century organisations and their employees', in D.R. Ilgen and E.D. Pulakos (eds), *The Changing Nature of Performance: Implications for staffing, motivation and development*. San Francisco, CA: Jossey-Bass.

Murray, H.J. (1938) *Explorations in Personality*. Oxford: Oxford University Press.

Musek, J. (2007) 'A general factor of personality: Evidence for the Big One in the five-factor model', *Journal of Research in Personality*, 41(6), 1213–33.

Myors, B., Lievens, F., Schollaert, E., Van Hoye, G., Cronshaw, S.F., Mladinic, A. et al. (2008) 'International perspective on the legal environment for selection', *Industrial and Organisational Psychology: Perspectives on Science and Practice*, 1, 206–46.

Nadler, D.A. (1993) 'Concepts for the management of strategic change', in C. Mabey and B. Mayon-White (eds), *Managing Change*, 2nd edition. London: Open University/Paul Chapman Publishing.

Nagy, M.S. (2002) 'Using a single-item approach to measure facet job satisfaction', *Journal of Occupational and Organizational Psychology*, 75, 77–86.

Namie, G. (2014) *2014 WBI U.S. Workplace Bullying Survey*. www.workplacebullying.org

Nathan, R. and Hill, L. (2006) *Career Counselling*, 2nd edition. London: Sage.

Nauta, M.M. (2010) 'The development, evolution, and status of Holland's theory of vocational personalities: Reflections and future directions for counseling psychology', *Journal of Counseling Psychology*, 57(1), 11–22.

Neal, A., Yeo, A. and Xiao, T. (2012) 'Predicting the form and direction of work role performance from the Big 5 model of personality traits', *Journal of Organisational Behaviour*, 33, 175–92.

Neisser, U. (1976) *Cognition and Reality*. San Francisco: W.H. Freeman and Co.

Nemanich, L.A. and Keller, R.T. (2007) 'Transformational leadership in an acquisition: A field study of employees', *The Leadership Quarterly*, 18, 49–68.

Nemeth, C.J. (1986) 'Differential contributions of majority and minority influence', *Psychological Review*, 93, 23–32.

Nemeth, C.J. (2010) *Minority Influence Theory. IRLE Working Paper No. 218-10*. http://www. irle.berkeley.edu/workingpapers/218-10.pdf

Nemetz, P.L. and Christensen, S.L. (1996) 'The challenge of cultural diversity: Harnessing adversity of views to understand multiculturalism', *Academy of Management Review*, 21, 434–62.

Ng, K.Y. and Van Dyne, L. (2001) 'Individualism–collectivism as a boundary condition for effectiveness of minority influence in decision making', *Organisational Behaviour and Human Decision Processes*, 84(2), 198–225.

Ng, T. and Feldman, D.C. (2009) 'Re-examining the relationship between age and voluntary turnover', *Journal of Vocational Behaviour*, 74, 283–94.

Ng, T., Eby, L.T., Sorensen, K.L. and Feldman, D.C. (2005) 'Predictors of objective and subjective career success: A meta-analysis', *Personnel Psychology*, 58, 367–408.

Ng, T., Sorensen, K. and Eby, L.T. (2006) 'Locus of control at work: A meta-analysis', *Journal of Organisational Behaviour*, 27, 1057–87.

Ng, T.W. and Feldman, D.C. (2014) 'Subjective career success: A meta-analytic review', *Journal of Vocational Behaviour*, 85, 169–79.

Ng, T.W. and Sorenson, K.L. (2008), 'Towards a further understanding of the relationships between perceptions of support and work attitudes', *Group and Organisation Management*, 33, 243–68.

Ng, T.W., Sorensen, K.L., Eby, L.T. and Feldman, D.C. (2007) 'Determinants of job mobility: A theoretical integration and extension', *Journal of Occupational and Organizational Psychology*, 80, 363–86.

Ng, T.W.H. (2015) 'The incremental validity of organisational commitment, organisational trust, and organisational identification', *Journal of Vocational Behaviour*, 88, 154–63.

Ng, T.W.H. and Feldman, D.C. (2010) 'Idiosyncratic deals and organisational commitment', *Journal of Vocational Behaviour*, 76, 419–27.

Ng, T.W.H., Feldman, D.C. and Lam, S.S.K. (2010) 'Psychological contract breaches, organisational commitment, and innovation-related behaviours: A latent growth modelling approach', *Journal of Applied Psychology*, 95, 744–51.

Nicholson, N. (1990) 'The transition cycle: Causes, outcomes, processes and forms', in S. Fisher and C. Cooper (eds), *On the Move: The psychology of change and transition*. Chichester: Wiley.

Nicholson, N. and de Waal-Andrews, W. (2005) 'Playing to win: Biological imperatives, self-regulation and trade-offs in the game of career success', *Journal of Organisational Behaviour*, 26, 137–54.

Nicholson, N. and West, M.A. (1988) *Managerial Job Change: Men and women in transition*. Cambridge: Cambridge University Press.

Nielsen, K. (2013) 'Review article: How can we make organisational interventions work? Employees and line managers as actively crafting interventions', *Human Relations*, 66, 1029–50.

Nielsen, K. and Abildgaard, J. (2012) 'The development and validation of a job crafting measure for use with blue collar workers', *Work and Stress*, 26, 365–84.

Nielsen, K. and Abildgaard, J.S. (2013) 'Organisational interventions: A research-based framework for the evaluation of both process and effects', *Work & Stress*, 27, 278–97.

Nielsen, K., Abildgaard, J.S. and Daniels, K. (2014) 'Putting context into organisational intervention design: Using tailored questionnaires to measure initiatives for worker well-being', *Human Relations*, 67, 1537–60.

Nielsen, K. and Cleal, B. (2010) 'Predicting flow at work: Investigating the activities and job characteristics that predict flow states at work', *Journal of Occupational Health Psychology*, 15, 180–90.

Nielsen, K. and Daniels, K. (2012) 'Enhancing team leaders' daily well-being and proactive behaviours during organisational change: A randomised, controlled study', *Human Relations*, 65, 1207–31.

Nielsen, K. and Randall, R. (2012) 'The importance of employee participation and perceptions of changes in procedures in a teamworking intervention', *Work & Stress*, 26, 91–111.

Nielsen, K. and Randall, R. (2013) 'Opening the black box: A framework for evaluating organisational-level occupational health interventions', *European Journal of Work and Organisational Psychology*, 22, 601–17.

Nielsen, K., Randall, R. and Albertsen, K. (2007) 'Participants' appraisals of process issues and the effects of stress management interventions', *Journal of Organisational Behaviour*, 28, 793–810.

Nielsen, K., Randall, R. and Christensen, K.B. (2010) 'A longitudinal field study of the effects of team manager training', *Human Relations*, 63, 1719–41.

Nielsen, K., Randall, R. and Christensen, K.B. (2015) 'Do different training conditions facilitate team implementation? A quasi-experimental mixed methods study', *Journal of Mixed Methods Research*, online first DOI: 10.1177/1558689815589050.

Nielsen, K., Randall, R., Yarker, J. and Brenner, S.-O. (2008a) 'The effects of transformational leadership on followers' perceived work characteristics and well-being: A longitudinal study', *Work & Stress*, 22, 16–32.

Nielsen, K., Yarker, J., Brenner, S.-O., Randall, R. and Borg, V. (2008b) 'The importance of transformational leadership style for the well-being of employees working with older people', *Journal of Advanced Nursing*, 63, 465–75.

Nijholt, J.J. and Benders, J. (2010) 'Measuring the prevalence of self-managing teams: Taking account of defining characteristics', *Work, Employment and Society*, 24, 375–85.

NIOSH (1993) *A National Strategy for the Prevention of Psychological Disorders in the Workplace*. Cincinnati, OH: NIOSH.

NIOSH and Sauter, S., Murphy, L., Colligan, M., Hurrel, J., Scharf, F., Sinclair, R., Grubb, P., Goldenhar, L., Alterman, T., Johnston, J., Hamilton, A. and Tisdale, J. (1999) *Stress at Work*. Available at: http://www.cdc.gov/niosh/docs/99-101/

Nisbett, R. and Wilson, T. (1977) 'Telling more than we know: Verbal reports on mental processes', *Psychological Review*, 84, 231–59.

Nisbett, R.E., Aronson, J., Blair, C., Dickens, W., Flynn, J., Halpern, D.F. and Turkheimer, E. (2012) 'Group differences in IQ are best understood as environmental in origin', *American Psychologist*, 67(6), 503–4.

Nixon, A.E., Mazzola, J.J., Bauer, J., Krueger, J.R. and Spector, P.E. (2011) 'Can work make you sick? A meta-analysis of the relationships between job stressors and physical symptoms', *Work & Stress*, 25, 1–22.

Noe, R.A. (2012) *Employee Training and Development*, 6th edition. New York: McGraw Hill.

Nonaka, I. (1988) 'Creating organisational order out of chaos: Self-renewal in Japanese firms', *Harvard Business Review*, November–December, 96–104.

Nonaka, I. (1994) 'A dynamic theory of organisational knowledge creation', *Organisation Science*, 5, 14–37.

Norman, D.A. (1993) *Things That Make Us Smart*. New York: Perseus Books.

Northouse, P.G. (2015) *Leadership*, 7th edition. London: Sage.

Noyes, J. (2001) *Designing for Humans (Psychology at Work)*. Hove, Sussex: Psychology Press.

Noyes, J.M., Starr, A.F and Kazem, M.L.N. (2004) 'Warning system design in civil aircraft', in D. Harris (ed.), *Human Factors for Civil Flight Deck Design*. Aldershot: Ashgate.

Nystrom, P.C. and Starbuck, W.H. (1984) 'To avoid crises, unlearn', *Organisational Dynamics*, 12, 53–65.

Nytrø, K., Saksvik, P.Ø., Mikkelsen, A., Bohle, P. and Quinlan, M. (2000) 'An appraisal of key factors in the implementation of occupational stress interventions', *Work & Stress*, 14, 213–25.

O'Driscoll, M.P. and Brough, P. (2010) 'Work organisation and health', in S. Leka and J. Houdmont (eds), *Occupational Health Psychology: A key text*. Chichester: Wiley-Blackwell.

O'Neil, D.A. and Bilimoria, D. (2005) 'Women's career development phases: Idealism, endurance and reinvention', *Career Development International*, 10, 168–89.

O'Reilly, C. (1989) 'Corporations, culture and commitment', *California Management Review*, 31, 9–24.

O'Reilly, C.A. and Caldwell, D.F. (1985) 'The impact of normative social influence and cohesiveness on task perceptions and attitudes: A social information-processing approach', *Journal of Occupational Psychology*, 58, 193–206.

Oerlemans, W.G.M. and Bakker, A.B. (2014) 'Burnout and daily recovery: A day reconstruction study', *Journal of Occupational Health Psychology*, 19, 303–14.

Offerrmann, L.R. and Gowing, M.K. (1990) 'Organisations of the future', *American Psychologist*, 45, 95–108.

Office for National Statistics (2014) *Labour Market Statistics, March 2014*. London: ONS.

Ogbonna, E. and Harris, L.C. (2002) 'Managing organisational culture: Insights from the hospitality industry', *Human Resource Management Journal*, 12(1), 33–53.

Okin, J.R. (2005) *The Technology Revolution: The not-for-dummies guide to the impact, perils and promise of the internet*. Winter Harbour, ME: Ironbound Press.

Oliver, M. (1990) *The Politics of Disablement*. London: Macmillan.

Olkkonen, M.E. and Lipponen, J. (2006) 'Relationships between organisational justice, identification with organisation and work unit and group-related outcomes', *Organisational Behaviour and Human Decision Processes*, 100, 202–15.

Ones, D.S. (2005) 'Personality at work: Raising awareness and correcting misconceptions', *Human Performance*, 18(4), 389–404.

Ones, D.S. and Viswesvaran, C. (2003) 'Job-specific applicant pools and national norms for personality scales: Implications for range-restriction corrections in validation research', *Journal of Applied Psychology*, 88(3), 570–7.

Ones, D.S., Dilchert, S., Viswesvaran, C. and Judge, T.A. (2007a) 'In support of personality assessment in organisational settings', *Personnel Psychology*, 60, 995–1027.

Ones, D.S., Viswesvaran, C. and Dilchert, S. (2007b) 'Cognitive ability in personnel selection decisions', in A. Evers, O. Voskuijl and N. Anderson (eds), *Handbook of Selection*. Oxford: Blackwell.

Oostrom, J.K., Van Der Linden, D., Born, M.P. and Van Der Molen, H.T. (2013) 'New technology in personnel selection: How recruiter characteristics affect the adoption of new selection technology', *Computers in Human Behaviour*, 29, 2404–15.

Organ, D.W. (1988) *Organisational Citizenship Behaviour: The good soldier syndrome*. Lexington, MA: Lexington.

Organ, D.W. (1997) 'Organisational citizenship behaviour: It's construct clean-up time', *Human Performance*, 10, 85–98.

Ortiz de Guinea, A., Webster, J. and Staples, D.S. (2012) 'A meta-analysis of the consequences of virtualness on team functioning', *Information and Management*, 49, 301–8.

Osborn, A.F. (1957) *Applied Imagination*, revised edition. New York: Scribner.

Oswald, F.L., Schmit, N., Kim, B.H., Ramsay, L.J. and Gillespie, M.A. (2004) 'Developing a biodata measure and situational judgment inventory as predictors of college student performance', *Journal of Applied Psychology*, 89, 187–207.

Palmer, S. and Cooper, C. (2007) *How to Deal with Stress*. London: Kogan Page.

Papadakis, V.M. and Barwise, P. (2002) 'How much do CEOs and top management matter in strategic decision-making?', *British Journal of Management*, 13(1), 83–95.

Parasuraman, R., Sheridan, T.B. and Wickens, C.D. (2000) 'A model for types and levels of human interaction with automation', *IEEE Transactions on Systems, Man and Cybernetics – Part A*, 30, 286–97.

Park, W. (2000) 'A comprehensive empirical investigation of the relationships among variables of the groupthink model', *Journal of Organisational Behaviour*, 21, 873–87.

Parker, B. and Chusmir, L.H. (1991) 'Motivation needs and their relationship to life success', *Human Relations*, 44, 1301–12.

Parker, L. and Bevan, S. (2011) *Good Work and Our Times: Report of the Good Work Commission*. London: The Work Foundation.

Parker, S.K. (2014) 'Beyond motivation: Job and work design for development, health, ambidexterity, and more', *Annual Review of Psychology*, 65, 661–91.

Parker, S.K., Wall, T.D. and Cordery, J.L. (2001) 'Future work design research and practice: Towards an elaborated model of work design', *Journal of Occupational and Organizational Psychology*, 74, 413–40.

Parkes, K.R. and Sparkes, T.J. (1998) *Organisational Interventions to Reduce Work Stress: Are they effective? A review of the literature*. Sudbury: HSE Books.

Parks, K.M. and Steelman, L.A. (2008) 'Organisational wellness programs: A meta-analysis', *Journal of Occupational Health Psychology*, 13, 58–68.

Parks, L. and Guay, R.P. (2009) 'Personality, values, and motivation', *Personality and Individual Differences*, 47(7), 675–84.

Parsons, F. (1909) *Choosing a Vocation*. Boston, MA: Houghton Mifflin.

Patrick, J. (1992) *Training: Research and practice*. London: Academic Press.

Patterson, F. (1999) *The Innovation Potential Indicator: Manual and user's guide*. Oxford: Oxford Psychologists Press.

Patterson, F. (2002) 'Great minds don't think alike? Person level predictors of innovation at work', *International Review of Industrial and Organisational Psychology*, 17, 115–44.

Patterson, F. (2004) 'Personal initiative and innovation', in C. Spielberger (ed.), *Encyclopaedia of Applied Psychology*. London: Elsevier.

Patterson, F. and Ferguson, E. (2007) *Selection into Medical Education and Training*. ASME monographs. Edinburgh: ASME.

Patterson, F., Baron, H., Carr, V., Plint, S. and Lane, P. (2009) 'Evaluation of three short-listing methodologies for selection into postgraduate training in general practice', *Medical Education*, 43, 50–7.

Patterson, F., Ferguson, E. and Thomas, S. (2008) 'Using job analyses to identify core and specific competencies for three secondary care specialties: Implications for selection and recruitment', *Medical Education*, 42, 1195–204.

Patterson, F., Ferguson, E., Lane, P., Farrell, K., Martlew, J. and Wells, A. (2000) 'A competency model for general practice: Implications for selection, training, and development', *British Journal of General Practice*, 50(452), 188–93.

Patterson, F., Ferguson, E., Norfolk, T. and Lane, P. (2005) 'A new selection system to recruit GP registrars: Preliminary findings from a validation study', *British Medical Journal*, 330, 711–14.

Patterson, F., Tavabie, A., Denney, M., Kerrin, M., Ashworth, V., Koczwara, A. and MacLeod, S. (2013) 'A new competency model for general practice: Implications for selection, training, and careers', *British Journal of General Practice*, 63(610), e331-8. DOI: 10.3399/bjgp13X667196.

Patterson, F., Zibarras, L., Kerrin, M., Lopes, S. and Price, R. (2014) 'Development of competency models for assessors and simulators in high-stakes selection processes', *Medical Teacher*, 36(12), 1082–5.

Patterson, F., Zibarras, L., & Ashworth, V. (2016). Situational judgement tests in medical education and training: Research, theory and practice: AMEE Guide No. 100. *Medical Teacher*, 38(1), 3–17.

Patterson, F., Knight, A., Dowell, J., Nicholson, S., Cousans, F., & Cleland, J. (2016). How effective are selection methods in medical education? A systematic review. *Medical Education*, 50(1), 36–60.

Paul, K.I. and Moser, K. (2006) 'Incongruence as an explanation for the negative mental health effects of unemployment: Meta-analytic evidence', *Journal of Occupational and Organizational Psychology*, 79, 595–621.

Paul, K.I. and Moser, K. (2009) 'Unemployment impairs mental health: Meta-analyses', *Journal of Vocational Behaviour*, 74, 264–82.

Paulus, P.B. (2000) 'Groups, teams, and creativity: The creative potential of idea-generating groups', *Applied Psychology: An International Review*, 49(2), 237–62.

Paustian-Underdahl, S.C., Walker, L.S. and Woehr, D.J. (2014) 'Gender and perceptions of leadership effectiveness: A meta-analysis of contextual moderators', *Journal of Applied Psychology*, 99, 1129–45.

Payne, S.C. and Huffman, A.H. (2005) 'A longitudinal investigation of the influence of mentoring on organisational commitment and turnover', *Academy of Management Journal*, 48, 158–68.

Pea, R.D. (1985) 'Beyond amplification: Using the computer to reorganise mental functioning', *Educational Psychologist*, 20, 167–82.

Pearlman, K. and Sanchez, J.I. (2010) 'Work analysis', in J.L. Farr and N.T. Tippins (eds), *Handbook of Employee Selection*, 74–98. New York: Routledge.

Peeters, M., Van Tuijl, H., Rutte, C. and Reymen, I. (2006) 'Personality and team performance: A meta-analysis', *European Journal of Personality*, 20, 377–96.

Pelled, L.H., Eisenhardt, K.M. and Xin, K.R. (1999) 'Exploring the black box: An analysis of work group diversity, conflict and performance', *Administrative Science Quarterly*, 44, 1–28.

Pendry, L.F. and Macrae, C.N. (1996) 'What the disinterested perceiver overlooks: Goal-directed social observation', *Personality and Social Psychology Bulletin*, 22, 249–56.

Perrone, K.M., Gordon, P.A. and Fitch, J.C. (2003) 'The adult career concerns inventory: Development of a short form', *Journal of Employment Counselling*, 40, 172–80.

Perrot, S., Bauer, T.N., Abonneau, D., Campoy, E., Erdogan, B. and Liden, R.C. (2014) 'Organisational socialisation tactics and newcomer adjustment: The moderating role of perceived organisational support', *Group and Organisation Management*, 39, 247–73.

Perry, N., Stevens, C. and Howell, C. (2006) 'Warning signal design: The effect of modality and iconicity on recognition speed and accuracy', *Proceedings of the 7th International Symposium of the Australian Aviation Psychology Association*, 9–12 November, 2006, Sydney, Australia.

Pervin, L.A. (1980) *Personality: Theory, assessment and research*, 3rd edition. New York: John Wiley.

Peters, L.H., Hartke, D.D. and Pohlmann, J.T. (1985) 'Fiedler's contingency theory of leadership: An application of the meta-analysis procedures of Schmidt and Hunter', *Psychological Bulletin*, 97, 274–85.

Peters, T. (1989) *Thriving on Chaos*. London: Pan.

Peters, T. (1997) *The Circle of Innovation: You can't shrink your way to greatness*. New York: Alfred A. Knopf.

Peters, T. (2006) *Re-imagine! Business excellence in a disruptive age*. London: Dorling Kindersley.

Peters, T. and Waterman, R.H. (1982) *In Search of Excellence: Lessons from America's best-run companies*. London: Harper and Row.

Peterson, M.F., Smith, P.B. and Tayeb, M.H. (1993) 'Development and use of English versions of Japanese PM leadership measures in electronics plants', *Journal of Organisational Behaviour*, 14, 251–67.

Petrides, K.V., Weinstein, Y., Chou, J., Furnham, A. and Swami, V. (2010) 'An investigation into assessment centre validity, fairness, and selection drivers', *Australian Journal of Psychology*, 62, 227–35.

Petrou, P., Demerouti, E., Peeters, M.C.W., Scahufeli, W.B. and Hetland, J. (2012) 'Crafting a job on a daily basis: Contextual correlates and the link to work engagement', *Journal of Organisational Behaviour*, 23, 1120–41.

Pettigrew, A. and Whipp, R. (1993) 'Understanding the environment', in C. Mabey and B. Mayon-White (eds), *Managing Change*, 2nd edition. London: Open University/Paul Chapman Publishing.

Pettigrew, A.M. (1987) 'Context and action in the transformation of the firm', *Journal of Management Sciences*, 24(6), 649–70.

Pettigrew, A.M. (1990a) 'Longitudinal field research on change: Theory and practice', *Organisational Science*, 3(1), 267–92.

Pettigrew, A.M. (1990b) 'Studying strategic choice and strategic change', *Organisational Studies*, 11(1), 6–11.

Pettigrew, A.M. (1997) 'What is a processual analysis?', *Scandinavian Journal of Management*, 13(40), 337–48.

Pettigrew, A.M., Ferlie, E. and McKee, L. (1992) *Shaping Strategic Change*. London: Sage.

Pettigrew, T.F. (1998) 'Intergroup contact theory', *Annual Review of Psychology*, 49, 65–85.

Petty, R.E. and Krosnick, J.A. (1992) *Attitude Strength: Antecedents and consequences*. Hillsdale, NJ: Lawrence Erlbaum.

Pfeffer, J. (1991) 'Organisation theory and structural perspectives on management', *Journal of Management,* 17, 789–803.

Pfeffer, J. (1992) *Managing with Power: Politics and influence in organisations*. Boston, MA: Harvard Business School Press.

Pierce, J.L., Jussila, I. and Cummings, A. (2009) 'Psychological ownership within the job design context: Revision of the job characteristics model', *Journal of Organisational Behaviour*, 30, 477–96.

Pierce, L. and Snyder, J.A. (2014) 'Unethical demand and employee turnover', *Journal of Business Ethics*, Published online: DOI: 10.1007/s10551-013-2018-2.

Pio, E. (2005) 'Knotted strands: Working lives of Indian women migrants in New Zealand', *Human Relations*, 58, 1277–300.

Plint, S. and Patterson, F. (2010) 'Identifying critical success factors for designing selection processes into postgraduate specialty training: The case of UK general practice', *Postgraduate Medical Journal*, 86, 323–7.

Podsakoff, N.P., LePine, J.A. and LePine, M.A. (2007) 'Differential challenge stressor–hindrance stressor relationships with job attitudes, turnover intentions, turnover and withdrawal behaviour: A meta-analysis', *Journal of Applied Psychology*, 92, 438–54.

Podsakoff, N.P., Podsakoff, P.M., MacKenzie, S.B., Maynes, T.D. and Spoelma, T.M. (2014) 'Consequences of unit-level organisational citizenship behaviours: A review and recommendations for future research', *Journal of Organisational Behaviour*, 35, 87–119.

Podsakoff, N.P., Whiting, S.W., Podsakoff, P.M. and Blume, B.D. (2009) 'Individual- and organisational-level consequences of organisational citizenship behaviours: A meta-analysis', *Journal of Applied Psychology*, 94, 122–41.

Polzer, J.T., Crisp, D.B., Jarvenpaa, S.L. and Kim, J.W. (2006) 'Extending the faultline model to geographically dispersed teams: How collocated subgroups can impair group functioning', *Academy of Management Journal*, 49, 679–92.

Port, R. and Patterson, F. (2003) 'Maximising the benefits of psychometric testing in selection', *Selection Development Review,* Special issue, Test Users Conference, 9(6), 6–11.

Posthuma, R.A. and Campion, M.A. (2009) 'Age stereotypes in the workplace: Common stereotypes, moderators, and future research directions', *Journal of Management*, 35, 158–88.

Posthuma, R.A., Morgeson, F.P. and Campion, M.A. (2002) 'Beyond employment interview validity: A comprehensive narrative review of recent research and trends over time', *Personnel Psychology*, 55, 1–81.

Potosky, D. and Bobko, P. (2004) 'Selection testing via the Internet: Practical considerations and exploratory empirical findings', *Personnel Psychology*, 57, 1003–34.

Potter, J. (1997) 'Discourse analysis as a way of analysing naturally occurring talk', in D. Silverman (ed.), *Qualitative Research: Theory, method and practice*. London: Sage.

Power, R. and Pluess, M. (2015) 'Heritability estimates of the Big Five personality traits based on common genetic variants', *Translational Psychiatry*, 5, e604. DOI: 10.1038/tp.2015.96.

Pratkanis, A.R. and Turner, M.E. (1994) 'Of what value is a job attitude? A socio-cognitive analysis', *Human Relations*, 47, 1545–76.

Pressman, R.S. (1992) *Software Engineering: A practitioner's approach*. New York: McGraw-Hill.

Pritchard, R.D. (1969) 'Equity theory: A review and critique', *Organisational Behaviour and Human Performance*, 4, 176–211.

Probst, G., Raisch, S. and Tushman, M.L. (2011) 'Ambidextrous leadership: Emerging challenges for business and HR leaders', *Organisational Dynamics*, 40, 326–34.

Procter, S. and Currie, G. (2002) 'How teamworking works in the Inland Revenue: Meaning, operation and impact', *Personnel Review*, 31(3), 304–19.

Proudford, K.L. and Smith, K.K. (2003) 'Group membership salience and the movement of conflict', *Group and Organisation Management*, 28, 18–44.

Pugh, D. (1993) 'Understanding and managing organisational change', in C. Mabey and B. Mayon-White (eds), *Managing Change*, 2nd edition. London: Open University/Paul Chapman Publishing.

Quick, J.C. and Quick, J.D. (1984) *Organisational Stress and Preventive Management*. New York: McGraw-Hill.

Quinn, J.B. (1993) 'Managing strategic change', in C. Mabey and B. Mayon-White (eds), *Managing Change*, 2nd edition. London: Open University/Paul Chapman Publishing.

Quinn, R.E. and McGrath, M.R. (1985) 'The transformation of organisational cultures: A competing values perspective', in P.J. Frost, L.F. Moore, M.R. Louis, C.C. Lundberg and J. Martin (eds), *Organisational Culture*. Newbury Park, CA: Sage.

Rafferty, A.E. and Griffin, M.A. (2006) 'Perceptions of organisational change: A stress and coping perspective', *Journal of Applied Psychology*, 91, 1154–62.

Ragins, B.R. (2010) 'Diversity and workplace mentoring relationships: A review and positive social capital approach' in T.D. Allen and L.T. Eby (eds), *The Blackwell Handbook of Mentoring: A multiple perspectives approach*, 281–300. Oxford: Wiley.

Rail Safety and Standards Board (2008) *Understanding Human Factors: A guide for the railway industry*. London: Rail Safety and Standards Board, available at: http://www.rssb.co.uk/Library/improving-industry-performance/2008-guide-understanding-human-factors-a-guide-for-the-railway-industry.pdf

Rajan, J. (1997) 'Interface design for safety critical systems', in F. Redill and J. Rajan (eds), *Human Factors in Safety Critical Systems*. London: Butterworth-Heinemann.

Randall, R. and Lewis, R. (2007) 'Stress management interventions', in E. Donaldson-Feilder (ed.), *Well-being and Performance*. London: CIPD.

Randall, R. and Sharples, D. (2012) 'The impact of rater agreeableness and rating context on the evaluation of poor performance', *Journal of Occupational and Organizational Psychology*, 85, 42–59.

Randall, R., Cox, T. and Griffiths, A. (2007) 'Participants' accounts of a stress management intervention', *Human Relations*, 60, 1181–209.

Randall, R., Griffiths, A. and Cox, T. (2005) 'Evaluating organisational stress-management interventions using adapted study designs', *European Journal of Work and Organisational Psychology*, 14, 23–41.

Randall, R., Nielsen, N. and Tvedt, S. (2009) 'The development of five scales to measure participants' appraisals of organisational-level stress management interventions', *Work & Stress*, 23, 1–23.

Rantanen, J., Metsäpelto, R.L., Feldt, T., Pulkkinen, L. and Kokko, K. (2007) 'Long-term stability in the Big Five personality traits in adulthood', *Scandinavian Journal of Psychology*, 48, 511–18.

Rasmussen, T.H. and Jeppesen, H.J. (2006) 'Teamwork and associated psychological factors: A review', *Work & Stress*, 20(2), 105–28.

Raub, S. and Robert, C. (2010) 'Differential effects of empowering leadership on in-role and extra-role employee behaviors: Exploring the role of psychological empowerment and power values', *Human Relations*, 63(11), 1743–70.

Rauch, A. and Frese, M. (2007) 'Let's put the person back into entrepreneurship research: A meta-analysis on the relationship between business owners' personality traits, business creation and success', *European Journal of Work and Organisational Psychology*, 16, 353–85.

Rauschenberger, J., Schmitt, N. and Hunter, J.E. (1980) 'A test of the need hierarchy concept by a Markov model of change in need strength', *Administrative Science Quarterly*, 25, 654–70.

Raven, J., Raven, J.C. and Court, J.H. (1996) *Raven's Progressive Matrices, Professional Manual*. Oxford: Oxford Psychologists Press.

Rayner, C., Hoel, H. and Cooper, C.L. (2002) *Workplace Bullying*. London: Taylor and Francis.

Rayton, B.A. and Yalabik, Z.Y. (2014) 'Work engagement, psychological contract breach and job satisfaction', *International Journal of Human Resource Management*, 25, 2382–400.

Raz, A.E. (2009) 'Transplanting management participative change, organisational development, and the Glocalization of corporate culture', *Journal of Applied Behavioural Science*, 280–304.

Reardon, R.C. and Lenz, J.G. (1998) *The Self-directed Search and Related Holland Career Materials: A practitioner's guide*. Odessa, FL: Psychological Assessment Resources Inc.

Rees, D. and Porter, C. (2001) *The Skills of Management*. London: Thomson Learning.

Reichers, A.E. (1985) 'A review and re-conceptualization of organisational commitments', *Academy of Management Review*, 10, 465–76.

Reilly, N.P., Bocketti, S.P., Maser, S.A. and Wennet, C.L. (2006) 'Benchmarks affect perceptions of prior disability in a structured interview', *Journal of Business and Psychology*, 20(4), 489–500.

Reiss, S. and Havercamp, S.M. (2005) 'Motivation in developmental context: A new method for studying self-actualization', *Journal of Humanistic Psychology*, 45, 41–53.

Reiter-Palmon, R., Sandall, D., Buboltz, C. and Nimps, T. (2006) 'Development of an O*NET web-based job analysis and its implementation in the US Navy: Lessons learned', *Human Resource Management Review*, 16(3), 294–309.

Reitman, F. and Schneer, J.A. (2005) 'The long-term negative impacts of managerial career interruptions – a longitudinal study of men and women MBAs', *Group and Organisation Management*, 30, 243–62.

Renko, M., Kroeck, K.G. and Bullough, A. (2012) 'Expectancy theory and nascent entrepreneurship', *Small Business Economics*, 39(3), 667–84.

Rennecker, J. and Derks, D. (2013) 'Email overload: Fine tuning the research lens', in D. Derks and A.B. Bakker (eds), *The Psychology of Digital Media at Work*. Hove, Sussex: Psychology Press.

Rennecker, J.A. (2002) 'The situated nature of virtual teamwork: Understanding the constitutive role of "place" in the enactment of virtual work configurations'. Paper presented at the Academy of Management Conference, Denver, CO.

Restubog, S.L.D., Bordia, P. and Bordia, S. (2011) 'Investigating the role of psychological contract breach on career success: Convergent evidence from two longitudinal studies', *Journal of Vocational Behaviour*, 79, 428–37.

Restubog, S.L.D., Bordia, P. and Tang, R.L. (2007) 'Behavioural outcomes of psychological contract breach in a non-western culture: The moderating role of equity sensitivity', *British Journal of Management*, 18, 376–86.

Restubog, S.L.D., Zagenczyk, T.J., Bordia, P., Bordia., S. and Chapman, G.J. (2015) 'If you wrong us, shall we not revenge? Moderating roles of self-control and perceived aggressive work culture in predicting responses to psychological contract breach', *Journal of Management*, 41, 1132–54.

Richardson, K.M. and Rothstein, H.R. (2008) 'Effects of occupational stress management programs: A meta-analysis', *Journal of Occupational Health Psychology*, 13, 69–93.

Richter, A.W., Dawson, J.F. and West, M.A. (2011) 'The effectiveness of teams in organisations: A meta-analysis', *International Journal of Human Resource Management*, 22, 2749–69.

Rigby, D. and Bilodeau, B. (2011) *Management Tools and Trends 2011*. Boston, MA: Bain and Company.

Riketta, M. (2008) 'The causal relation between job attitudes and performance: A meta-analysis of panel studies', *Journal of Applied Psychology*, 93, 472–81.

Riopelle, K., Gluesing, J.C., Baba, M.L., Britt, D., McKether, W., Montplaisir, L., Ratner, H. and Wagner, K.H. (2003) 'Context, task and the evolution of technology use in global virtual teams', in C.B. Gibson and S.G. Cohen (eds), *Virtual Teams that Work: Creating conditions for effective virtual teams*. San Francisco, CA: Jossey-Bass.

Roberts, B.W., Walton, K.E. and Viechtbauer, W. (2006) 'Patterns of mean-level change in personality traits across the life course: A meta-analysis of longitudinal studies', *Psychological Bulletin*, 132, 26–8.

Roberts, P. and Newton, P.M. (1987) 'Levinsonian studies of women's adult development', *Psychology and Ageing*, 2, 154–63.

Robertson, I.T. and Flint-Taylor, J. (2008) 'Leadership, psychological well-being and organisational outcomes', in S. Cartwright and C.L. Cooper (eds), *Oxford Handbook on Organisational Well-being*. Oxford: Oxford University Press.

Robertson, I.T. and Smith, M. (2001) 'Personnel selection', *Journal of Occupational and Organizational Psychology*, 74, 441–72.

Robertson, I.T., Cooper, C.L. and Jansen-Birch, A.J. (2012) 'Job and work attitudes, engagement and employee performance: Where does psychological well-being fit in?', *The Leadership and Organisation Development Journal*, 33, 224–32.

Robertson, I.T., Cooper, C.L., Sarkar, M. and Curran, T. (2015) 'Resilience training in the workplace from 2003 to 2014: A systematic review', *Journal of Occupational and Organizational Psychology*, 88, 533–62.

Robinson, D., Perryman, S. and Hayday, S. (2004) *The Drivers of Employee Engagement*. Brighton: Institute for Employment Studies.

Robinson, S.L. and Morrison, E.W. (2000) 'The development of psychological contract breach and violation: A longitudinal study', *Journal of Organisational Behaviour*, 21, 525–46.

Robinson, S.L. and Rousseau, D.M. (1994) 'Violating the psychological contract: Not the exception but the norm', *Journal of Organisational Behaviour*, 15, 245–59.

Roch, S.G., Woehr, D.J., Mishra, V. and Kieszcynska, U. (2012) 'Rater training revisited: An updated meta-analytic review of frame-of-reference training', *Journal of Occupational and Organizational Psychology*, 85, 370–95.

Rodrigues, R.A. and Guest, D. (2010) 'Have careers become boundaryless?', *Human Relations*, 63, 1157–75.

Roethlisberger, F.J. and Dickson, W.J. (1939) *Management and the Worker*. New York: John Wiley.

Rogers, C.R. (1970) *On Becoming a Person*. Boston, MA: Houghton Mifflin.

Rose, J.D. (2011) 'Diverse perspectives on the groupthink theory – a literary review', *Emerging Leadership Journeys*, 4, 37–57.

Rosenfeld, P., Giacalone, R.A. and Riordan, C.A. (2002) *Impression Management: Building and enhancing reputations at work*. London: Thomson Learning.

Rosenthal, R. and DiMatteo, M.R. (2000) 'Meta analysis: Recent developments in quantitative methods for literature reviews', *Annual Review of Psychology*, 52, 59–82.

Rosenthal, R. and Rosnow, R.L. (1984) *Essentials of Behavioural Research, Methods and Data Analysis*. New York: McGraw-Hill.

Ross, L. (1977) 'The intuitive psychologist and his shortcoming: Distortions in the attribution process', *Advances in Experimental Social Psychology*, 10, 174–220.

Rothmann, I. and Cooper, C.L. (2008) *Organisational Work Psychology*. London: Hodder Education.

Rotundo, M. and Sackett, P. (2002) 'The relative importance of task citizenship and counterproductive performance to global ratings of job performance: A policy-capturing approach', *Journal of Applied Psychology*, 87, 66–80.

Rousseau, D.M. (1990) 'New hire perceptions of their own and their employer's obligations: A study of psychological contracts', *Journal of Organisational Behaviour*, 11, 389–400.

Rousseau, D.M. (1995) *Psychological Contracts in Organisations*. London: Sage.

Rousseau, D.M. (1998) 'The "problem" of the psychological contract considered', *Journal of Organisational Behaviour*, 19, 665–71.

Rousseau, D.M. (2001) 'Schema, promise and mutuality: The building blocks of the psychological contract', *Journal of Occupational and Organizational Psychology*, 74, 511–42.

Rousseau, D.M. and Fried, Y. (2001) 'Location, location, location: Contextualising organisational research', *Journal of Organisational Behaviour*, 22, 1–13.

Rowan, J. (1998) 'Maslow amended', *Journal of Humanistic Psychology*, 28, 81–92.

Rowold, J. and Heinitz, K. (2007) 'Transformational and charismatic leadership: Assessing the convergent, divergent and criterion validity of the MLQ and the CKS', *The Leadership Quarterly*, 18, 121–33.

Rubin, I. (1967) 'Increasing self-acceptance: A means of reducing prejudice', *Journal of Personality and Social Psychology*, 5, 233–8.

Ruona, W.E. and Gibson, S.K. (2004) 'The making of twenty-first century HR: An analysis of the convergence of HRM, HRD and OD', *Human Resource Management*, 43, 49–66.

Rushton, J.P. and Irwing, P. (2008) 'A General Factor of Personality (GFP) from two meta-analyses of the Big Five: Digman (1997) and Mount, Barrick, Scullen and Rounds (2005)', *Personality and Individual Differences*, 45(7), 679–83.

Russ, T.L. (2011) 'Theory X/Y assumptions as predictors of managers' propensity for participative decision making', *Management Decision*, 49, 823–36.

Ryan, A.M. and Ployhart, R.E. (2014) 'A century of selection', *Annual Review of Psychology*, 65, 693–717.

Ryan, A.M., Chan, D., Ployhart, R.E. and Slade, L.A. (1999) 'Employee attitude surveys in a multinational organisation: Considering language and culture in assessing measurement equivalence', *Personnel Psychology*, 52, 37–58.

Ryan, R.M. and Deci, E.L. (2000) 'Intrinsic and extrinsic motivations: Classic definitions and new directions', *Contemporary Educational Psychology*, 25, 54–67.

Ryan, T.A. (1970) *Intentional Behaviour*. New York: Ronald Press.

Ryff, C.D. and Keyes, C.L.M. (1995) 'The structure of psychological well-being revisited', *Journal of Personality and Social Psychology*, 69, 719–27.

Rynes, S.L., Gerhart, B. and Minette, K.A. (2004) 'The importance of pay in employee motivation: Discrepancies between what people say and what they do', *Human Resource Management*, 43, 381–94.

Rynes, S.L., McNatt, D.B. and Bretz, R.D. (1999) 'Academic research inside organisations: Inputs, processes and outcomes', *Personnel Psychology*, 52, 869–98.

Sackett, P. and Lievens, F. (2008) 'Personnel selection', *Annual Review of Psychology*, 59, 16.1–16.32.

Sackett, P.R. (2011) 'Integrating and prioritising theoretical perspectives on applicant faking of personality measures', *Human Performance*, 24, 379–85.

Sackett, P.R. and Tuzinski, K.A. (2001) 'The role of dimensions and exercises in assessment centre judgements', in M. London (ed.), *How People Evaluate Others in Organisations*. London: LEA.

Sackett, P.R. and Yang, H. (2000) 'Correction for range restriction: An expanded typology', *Journal of Applied Psychology*, 85, 112–18.

Sackett, P.R., Borneman, M.J. and Connelly, B.S. (2008) 'High stakes testing in higher education and employment: Appraising the evidence for validity and fairness', *The American Psychologist*, 63, 215–27.

Sagie, A., Elizur, D. and Yamauchi, A. (1996) 'The structure and strength of achievement motivation: A cross-cultural comparison', *Journal of Organisational Behaviour*, 17, 431–44.

Saks, A.M., Gruman, J.A. and Cooper-Thomas, H. (2011) 'The neglected role of proactive behaviour and outcomes in newcomer socialisation', *Journal of Vocational Behaviour*, 79, 36–46.

Saksvik, P.Ø., Nytrø, K., Dahl-Jørgensen, C. and Mikkelsen, A. (2002) 'A process evaluation of individual and organisational occupational stress and health interventions', *Work & Stress*, 16, 37–57.

Salancik, G.R. and Pfeffer, J. (1977) 'An examination of need satisfaction models of job attitudes', *Administrative Science Quarterly*, 22, 427–56.

Salancik, G.R. and Pfeffer, J.C. (1978) 'A social information processing approach to job attitudes and task design', *Administrative Science Quarterly*, 23, 224–53.

Salanova, M., Del Líbano, M., Llorens, S. and Schaufeli, W.B. (2014) 'Engaged, workaholic, burned-out or just 9-to-5? Toward a typology of employee well-being', *Stress and Health*, 30, 1532–2998.

Salas, E., Diaz Granados, D., Klein, C., Burke, S., Stagl, K.C., Goodwin, G.F. and Halpin, S.M. (2008) 'Does team training improve team performance? A meta-analysis', *Human Factors*, 50, 903–33.

Salas, E., Tannenbaum, S.I., Kraiger, K. and Smith-Jentsch, K.A. (2012) 'The science of training and development in organisations: What matters in practice', *Psychological Science in the Public Interest*, 13, 74–101.

Salas, E., Wilson, K.A. and Burke, S. (2006) 'Does crew resource management training work? An update, an extension, and some critical needs', *Human Factors*, 48(2), 392–412.

Salgado, J. (2003) 'FFM and non-FFM personality predictors of work performance', *Journal of Occupational and Organisational Psychology*, 76, 323–46.

Salgado, J.F., Anderson, N., Moscoso, S., Bertua, C. and de Fruyt, F. (2003) 'International validity generalisation of GMA and cognitive abilities: A European Community meta-analysis', *Personnel Psychology*, 56, 573–605.

Salgado, J.F. and Táuriz, G. (2014) 'The Five-Factor Model, forced-choice personality inventories and performance: A comprehensive meta-analysis of academic and occupational validity studies', *European Journal of Work and Organisational Psychology*, 23, 3–30.

Salgado, J.F., Viswesvaran, C. and Ones, D. (2001) 'Predictors used for personnel selection: An overview of constructs, methods, techniques', in N. Anderson, D.S. Ones, H.K. Sinangil and C. Viswesvaran (eds), *Handbook of Industrial, Work and Organisational Psychology*. London: Sage.

Salin, D. (2003) 'Ways of explaining workplace bullying: A review of enabling, motivating and precipitating structures and processes in the work environment', *Human Relations*, 56, 1213–32.

Salomon, G. (1993) 'No distribution without individual's cognition: A dynamic interactional view', in G. Salomon (ed.), *Distributed Cognitions: Psychological and educational considerations*, 111–39. Cambridge: Cambridge University Press.

Salthouse, T.A. (2010) 'Selective review of cognitive ageing', *Journal of the International Neuropsychological Society*, 16, 754–60.

San Martin, A., Swaab, R.I., Sinaceur, M. and Vasiljevic, D. (2015) 'The double-edged impact of future expectations in groups: Minority influence depends on minorities' and majorities' expectations to interact again', *Organisational Behaviour and Human Decision Processes*, 128, 49–60.

Sanchez, J.I. and Levine, E.L. (2012) 'The rise and fall of job analysis and the future of work analysis', *Annual Review of Psychology*, 63, 397–425.

Sanders, M.S. and McCormick, E.J. (1993) *Human Factors in Engineering and Design*, 7th edition. New York: McGraw-Hill.

Savickas, M.L. (2007) 'Occupational choice', in H. Gunz and M. Peiperl (eds), *Handbook of Career Studies*, London: Sage.

Savickas, M.L. and Baker, D.B. (2005) 'The history of vocational psychology: Antecedents, origins and early development', in W.B. Walsh and M.L. Savickas (eds), *Handbook of Vocational Psychology*, 3rd edition. Mahwah, NJ: Erlbaum.

Sawilowsky, S.S. and Blair, R.C. (1992) 'A more realistic look at the robustness and type II error properties of the t-test to departures from population normality', *Psychological Bulletin*, 111, 352–60.

Scaife, M. and Rogers, Y. (1996) 'External cognition: How do graphical representations work?', *International Journal of Human-Computer Studies*, 45, 185–213.

Scarbrough, H. and Kinnie, N. (2003) 'Barriers to the development of teamworking in UK firms', *Industrial Relations Journal*, 34(2), 135–49.

Schaufeli, W.B., Salanova, M., González-Romá, V. and Bakker, A.B. (2002) 'The measurement of engagement and burnout: A two sample confirmatory factor analytic approach', *Journal of Happiness Studies*, 3, 71–92.

Schein, E.H. (1978) *Career Dynamics: Matching individual and organisational needs*. Reading, MA: Addison-Wesley.

Schein, E.H. (1985) *Organisational Culture and Leadership: A dynamic view*. San Francisco, CA: Jossey-Bass.

Schein, E.H. (1988) *Organisational Psychology*, 3rd edition. Englewood Cliffs, NJ: Prentice Hall.

Schein, E.H. (1992) *Organisational Culture and Leadership*, 2nd edition. San Francisco, CA: Jossey-Bass.

Schein, E.H. (1993) *Career Anchors: Discovering your real values*, revised edition. London: Pfeiffer and Co.

Schein, E.H. (1996) 'Career anchors revisited: Implications for career development in the 21st century', *Academy of Management Executive*, 10, 80–8.

Schein, V.E. (1975) 'The relationship between sex role stereotypes and requisite management characteristics among female managers', *Journal of Applied Psychology*, 60, 340–4.

Schein, V.E., Mueller, R., Lituchy, T. and Liu, J. (1996) 'Think manager – think male: A global phenomenon?', *Journal of Organisational Behaviour*, 17, 33–41.

Schippman, J.S., Ash, R.A., Carr, L., Hesketh, B., Pearlman, K., Battista, M. et al. (2000) 'The practice of competency modelling', *Personnel Psychology*, 53, 703–40.

Schlett, C. and Ziegler, R. (2014) 'Job emotions and job cognitions as determinants of job satisfaction: The moderating role of individual differences in need for affect', *Journal of Vocational Behaviour*, 84, 74–89.

Schmidt, F.L. and Hunter, J. (2004) 'General mental ability in the world of work: Occupational attainment and job performance', *Journal of Personality and Social Psychology*, 86, 162–73.

Schmidt, F.L. and Hunter, J.E. (1998) 'The validity and utility of selection methods in personnel psychology: Practical and theoretical implications of 85 years of research findings', *Psychological Bulletin*, 124, 262–74.

Schmidt, S., Roesler, U., Kusserow, T. and Rau, R. (2014) 'Uncertainty in the workplace: Examining role ambiguity and role conflict, and their link to depression – a meta-analysis', *European Journal of Work and Organisational Psychology*, 23, 91–106.

Schmitt, N. and Chan, D. (1998) *Personnel Selection: A theoretical approach*. Thousand Oaks, CA: Sage.

Schneer, J.A. and Reitman, F. (1995) 'The impact of gender as managerial careers unfold', *Journal of Vocational Behaviour*, 47, 290–315.

Schneider, B. (1987) 'The people make the place', *Personnel Psychology*, 40, 437–53.

Schneider, B., Ashworth, S.D., Higgs, A.C. and Carr, L. (1996) 'Design, validity and use of strategically focussed employee attitude surveys', *Personnel Psychology*, 49, 695–705.

Schneider, D.J. (1991) 'Social cognition', *Annual Review of Psychology*, 42, 527–61.

Schneider, S.C. and Dunbar, R.L.M. (1992) 'A psychoanalytic reading of hostile takeover events', *Academy of Management Review*, 17, 537–67.

Schneiderman, B. (1998) *Designing the User Interface*. Reading, MA: Addison-Wesley.

Schönpflug, W. (1993) 'Applied psychology: Newcomer with a long tradition', *Applied Psychology: An International Review*, 42, 5–30.

Schreurs, B., van Emmerik, H., Notelaers, G. and De Witte, H. (2010) 'Job insecurity and employee health: The buffering potential of job control and job self-efficacy', *Work & Stress*, 24, 56–72.

Schriesheim, C.A., Tepper, B.J. and Tetrault, L.A. (1994) 'Least preferred coworker score, situational control, and leadership effectiveness: A meta-analysis of contingency model performance predictions', *Journal of Applied Psychology*, 79, 561–73.

Schuler, R.S. and Jackson S.E. (eds) (2007) *Strategic Human Resource Management: A reader*. London: Blackwell.

Schultheiss, D.E.P., Palma, T.V. and Manzi, A.J. (2005) 'Career development in middle childhood: A qualitative inquiry', *The Career Development Quarterly*, 53, 246–62.

Schultz, D.P. and Schultz, S.E. (2001) *Theories of Personality*, 7th edition. Belmont, CA: Wadsworth/Thomson Learning.

Schulz-Hardt, S., Jochims, M. and Frey, D. (2002) 'Productive conflict in group decision making: Genuine and contrived dissent as strategies to counteract biased information seeking', *Organisational Behaviour and Human Decision Processes*, 88, 563–86.

Schwab, D.P., Olian-Gottlieb, J.D. and Heneman, H.G. (1979) 'Between subjects expectancy theory research: A statistical review of studies predicting effort and performance', *Psychological Bulletin*, 86, 139–47.

Schwartz, S.H. (1999) 'A theory of cultural values and some implications for work', *Applied Psychology: An International Review*, 48, 23–47.

Schweitzer, L. and Duxbury, L. (2010) 'Conceptualising and measuring the virtuality of teams', *Information Systems Journal*, 20, 267–95.

Scullen, S.E., Bergey, P.K. and Aiman-Smith, L. (2005) 'Forced distribution rating systems and the improvement of workforce potential: A baseline simulation', *Personnel Psychology*, 58, 1–32.

Scullen, S.E., Mount, M.K. and Goff, M. (2000) 'Understanding the latent structure of job performance ratings', *Journal of Applied Psychology*, 85, 956–70.

Sears, G.J. and Baba, V.V. (2011) 'Towards a multistage, multilevel theory of innovation', *Canadian Journal of Administrative Sciences/Revue Canadienne des Sciences de l'Administration*, 28, 357–72.

Secord, P.F. and Backman, C.W. (1969) *Social Psychology*. New York: McGraw-Hill.

Seibert, S.E., Kraimer, M.L. and Crant, J.M. (2001) 'What do proactive people do? A longitudinal model linking proactive personality and career success', *Personnel Psychology*, 54, 845–74.

Seibert, S.E., Kraimer, M.L., Holtom, B.C. and Pierotti, A.J. (2013) 'Even the best laid plans sometimes go askew: Career self-management processes, career shocks, and the decision to pursue graduate education', *Journal of Applied Psychology*, 98, 169–82.

Seijts, G.H. and Latham, G.P. (2001) 'The effect of learning, outcome and proximal goals on a moderately complex task', *Journal of Organisational Behaviour*, 22, 291–307.

Seijts, G.H. and Latham, G.P. (2012) 'Knowing when to set learning versus performance goals', *Organisational Dynamics*, 41, 1–6.

Seligman, M.E.P. and Csikszentmihalyi, M. (2000) 'Positive psychology: An introduction', *American Psychologist*, 55, 5–14.

Seligman, M.E.P., Steen, T.A., Park, N. and Petersen, C. (2005) 'Positive psychology progress: Empirical validation of interventions', *American Psychologist*, 60, 410–21.

Selye, H. (1946) 'The General Adaptation Syndrome and the diseases of adaptation', *Journal of Clinical Endocrinology*, 6, 117.

Senge, P. (2000) 'The puzzles and paradoxes of how living companies create wealth: Why single-valued objective functions are not quite enough', in M. Beer and N. Nohria (eds), *Breaking the Code of Change*. Boston, MA: Harvard Business School Press.

Senior, B. (2002) *Organisational Change*, 2nd edition. Harlow: FT/Prentice Hall.

Senior, B. and Swailes, S. (2007) 'Inside management teams: Developing a teamwork survey instrument', *British Journal of Management*, 18, 138–53.

Senturia, T., Flees, L. and Maceda, M. (2008) *Leading Change Management Requires Sticking to the PLOT*. London: Bain and Company.

Shah, S., Arnold, J. and Travers, C. (2004a) 'The impact of childhood on disabled professionals', *Children and Society*, 18, 194–206.

Shah, S., Travers, C. and Arnold, J. (2004b) 'Disabled and successful: Education in the life stories of disabled high achievers', *Journal of Research in Special Educational Needs*, 4, 122–32.

Shamir, B. and Howell, J.M. (1999) 'Organisational and contextual influences on the emergence and effectiveness of charismatic leadership', *The Leadership Quarterly*, 10, 257–83.

Shantz, A. and Latham, G.P. (2009) 'An exploratory field experiment of the effect of subconscious and conscious goals on employee performance', *Organisational Behaviour and Human Decision Processes*, 109, 9–17.

Sharf, R.F. (1992) *Applying Career Development Theory to Counselling*. Los Angeles, CA: Brooks/Cole.

Sharkey, P. (2010) 'The acute effect of local homicides on children's cognitive performance', *Proceedings of the National Academy of Sciences*, 107, 11733–8.

Sharma, P.N. and Kirkman, B.L. (2015) 'Leveraging leaders: A literature review and future lines of inquiry for empowering leadership research', *Group and Organisation Management*, 40, 193–237.

Shaw, J.B. and Barrett-Power, E. (1998) 'The effects of diversity on small work group processes and performance', *Human Relations*, 51(10), 1307–25.

Shaw, K. (2004) 'Changing the goal-setting process at Microsoft', *Academy of Management Executive*, 18(4), 139–42.

Shen, Y., Demel, B., Unite, J., Briscoe, J.P., Hall, D.T., Chudzikowski, K. et al. (2015) 'Career success across 11 countries: Implications for international human resource management', *International Journal of Human Resource Management*, 26(13), 1753–78.

Shepherd, A. (1976) 'An improved tabular format for task analysis', *Journal of Occupational Psychology*, 47, 93–104.

Shepherd, C. (2006) 'Constructing enterprise resource planning: A thoroughgoing interpretivist perspective on technological change', *Journal of Occupational and Organizational Psychology*, 79, 357–76.

Sheridan, T.B. and Verplank, W.L. (1978) *Human and Computer Control of Undersea Teleoperators*. Man-Machine Systems Laboratory Report. Cambridge, MA: MIT.

Shimazu, A., Sonnentag, S., Kubota, K. and Kawakami, N. (2012) 'Validation of the Japanese version of the Recovery Experience Questionnaire', *Journal of Occupational Health*, 54, 196–205.

Shimmin, S. and Wallis, D. (1994) *Fifty Years of Occupational Psychology in Britain*. Leicester: British Psychological Society.

Shipton, H.J., West, M.A., Parkes, C.L., Dawson, J.F. and Patterson, M.G. (2006) 'When promoting positive feelings pays: Aggregate job satisfaction, work design features and innovation in manufacturing organisations', *European Journal of Work and Organisational Psychology*, 15, 404–30.

Shirom, A., Gilboa, S.S., Fried, Y. and Cooper, C.L. (2008) 'Gender, age and tenure as moderators of work-related stressors' relationships with job performance: A meta-analysis', *Human Relations*, 61, 1371–98.

Sholihin, M., Pike, R., Mangena, M. and Li, J. (2011) 'Goal-setting participation and goal commitment: Examining the mediating roles of procedural fairness and interpersonal trust in a UK financial services organisation', *The British Accounting Review*, 43, 135–46.

Short, J.E. and Venkatraman, N. (1992) 'Beyond business process redesign: Redefining Baxter's business network', *Sloan Management Review*, Fall, 7–21.

Siegrist, J. (1996) 'Adverse health effects of high-effort/low-reward conditions', *Journal of Occupational Health Psychology*, 1, 27–41.

Siegrist, J., Dragano, N., Nyberg, S. et al. (2014) 'Validating abbreviated measures of effort-reward imbalance at work in European cohort studies: The IPD-Work consortium', *International Archives of Occupational and Environmental Health*, 87, 249–56.

Sikora, P., Moore, S., Greenberg, E. and Grunberg, L. (2008) 'Downsizing and alcohol use: A cross-lagged longitudinal examination of the spillover hypothesis', *Work & Stress*, 22, 51–68.

Silverman, D. (2001) *Interpreting Qualitative Data*, London: Sage.

Silvester, J. (2008) 'The good, the bad and the ugly: Politics and politicians at work', *International Review of Industrial and Organisational Psychology*, 23, 107–48.

Silvester, J. and Menges, C. (2011) *Political Mentoring: A Toolkit*. Swindon: Economic and Social Research Council. Available at: http://openaccess.city.ac.uk/444/2/Silvester%20%20Menges%20(2011)%20Political_Mentoring_Toolkit.pdf

Silvester, J. and Wyatt, M. (2016) 'Political effectiveness at work', in C. Viswesvaran, D.S. Ones, N. Anderson and H.K. Sinangil (eds), *Handbook of Industrial Work and Organisational Psychology*, 2nd edition, vol. 3. London: Sage.

Silvester, J., Anderson, N.R. and Patterson, F. (1999) 'Organisational culture change: An inter-group attributional analysis', *Journal of Occupational and Organizational Psychology*, 72, 1–23.

Silvester, J., Anderson-Gough, F.M., Anderson, N.R. and Mohammed, A.R. (2002) 'Locus of control, attributions and impression management in the selection interview', *Journal of Occupational and Organizational Psychology*, 75, 59–76.

Silvester, J., Patterson, F. and Ferguson, E. (2003) 'Comparing two attributional models of performance in retail sales: A field study', *Journal of Occupational and Organizational Psychology*, 76, 115–32.

Silvester, J., Wyatt, M. and Randall, R. (2014) 'Politician personality, Machiavellianism and political skill as predictors of performance ratings in political roles', *Journal of Occupational and Organizational Psychology*, 87, 268–79.

Silvia, P.J. (2008) 'Interest – the curious emotion', *Current Directions in Psychological Science*, 17(1), 57–60.

Simonton, D.K. (2004) *Creativity in Science: Chance, logic, genius, and Zeitgeist*. Cambridge, MA: Cambridge University Press.

Simpson, R. and Cohen, C. (2004) 'Dangerous work: The gendered nature of bullying in the context of higher education', *Gender, Work and Organisation*, 11, 163–86.

Sinclair, S., Carlsson, R. and Björklund, F. (2014) 'The role of friends in career compromise: Same-gender friendship intensifies gender differences in educational choice', *Journal of Vocational Behaviour*, 84, 109–18.

Singh, V. and Vinnicombe, S. (2000) 'What does "commitment" really mean?: Views of UK and Swedish engineering managers', *Personnel Review*, 29(1–2), 228–54.

Sitzman, T. and Ely, K. (2011) 'A meta-analysis of self-regulated learning in work-related training and educational attainment: What we know and where we need to go', *Psychological Bulletin*, 137, 421–42.

Sitzman, T.M., Kraiger, K., Stewart, D.W. and Wisher, R.A. (2006) 'The comparative effectiveness of web-based and classroom instruction: A meta-analysis', *Personnel Psychology*, 59, 623–64.

Sjöberg, S., Sjöberg, A., Näswall, K. and Sverke, M. (2012) 'Using individual differences to predict job performance: Correcting for direct and indirect restriction of range', *Scandinavian Journal of Psychology*, 53, 368–73.

Skakon, J., Nielsen, K., Borg, V. and Guzman, J. (2010) 'Are leaders' well-being, behaviours and style associated with the affective well-being of their employees? A systematic review of three decades of research', *Work & Stress*, 24, 107–39.

Skarlicki, D.P., Folger, R. and Tesluk, P. (1999) 'Personality as a moderator in the relationship between fairness and retaliation', *Academy of Management Journal*, 42, 100–8.

Skinner, B.F. (1971) *Beyond Freedom and Dignity*. New York: Knopf.

Slivinski, L.W. (2008) 'A test of the relative and incremental predictive validity associated with a set of paper-and-pencil test measures and a set of situational test measures within an assessment centre', *Dissertation Abstracts International: Section B: The Sciences and Engineering*, 68, 4878.

Smith, C.A., Organ, D.W. and Near, J.P. (1983) 'Organisational citizenship behaviour: Its nature and antecedents', *Journal of Applied Psychology*, 68, 653–63.

Smith, C.M., Tindale, R.S. and Dugoni, B.L. (1996) 'Minority and majority influence in freely interacting groups: Qualitative versus quantitative differences', *British Journal of Social Psychology*, 35, 137–49.

Smith, G. and Morris, P. (2015) 'Methods: Building confidence in confidence intervals', *The Psychologist*, 28, 476–79.

Smith, J.M. and Robertson, I.T. (1993) *The Theory and Practice of Systematic Personnel Selection*. London: Macmillan.

Smith, M., Beck, J., Cooper, C.L., Cox, C., Ottaway, D. and Talbot, R. (1982) *Introducing Organisational Behaviour*. London: Macmillan.

Smith, P.B., Misumi, J., Tayeb, M., Peterson, M. and Bond, M. (1989) 'On the generality of leadership style measures across cultures', *Journal of Occupational Psychology*, 62, 97–109.

Smith, P.C. and Kendall, L.M. (1963) 'Retranslation of expectations: An approach to the construction of unambiguous anchors for rating scales', *Journal of Applied Psychology*, 47, 149–55.

Smith, P.C., Kendall, L.M. and Hulin, C.L. (1969) *The Measurement of Satisfaction in Work and Retirement*. Chicago, IL: Rand-McNally.

Smither, J.W., London, M. and Reilly, R.R. (2005) 'Does performance improve following multi-source feedback? A theoretical model, meta-analysis and review of empirical findings', *Personnel Psychology*, 58, 33–66.

Sniehotta, F.F., Presseau, P. and Araújo-Soares, V. (2014) 'Time to retire the theory of planned behaviour', *Health Psychology Review*, 8, 1–7.

Snow, C., Miles, R. and Coleman, H. (1993) 'Managing 21st century network organisations', in C. Mabey and B. Mayon-White (eds), *Managing Change*, 2nd edition. London: Open University/Paul Chapman Publishing.

Solinger, O.N., van Olffen, W. and Roe, R.A. (2008) 'Beyond the three-component model of organisational commitment', *Journal of Applied Psychology*, 93, 70–83.

Sonnentag, S. and Fritz, C. (2015) 'Recovery from job stress: The stressor-detachment model as an integrative framework', *Journal of Organisational Behaviour*, 36, S72–S103. DOI: 10.1002/job.1924.

Sonnentag, S. and Niessen, C. (2008) 'Staying vigorous until work is over: The role of trait vigour, day-specific work experiences and recovery', *Journal of Occupational and Organizational Psychology*, 81, 435–58.

Sorge, A. (1997) 'Organisation behaviour', in A. Sorge and M. Warner (eds), *The IEBM Handbook of Organisational Behaviour*. London: International Thompson Business Press.

Spangler, W.D. (1992) 'Validity of questionnaire and TAT measures of need for achievement: Two meta-analyses', *Psychological Bulletin*, 112, 140–54.

Sparks, K., Cooper, C., Fried, Y. and Shirom, A. (1997) 'The effects of hours on work and health: A meta-analytic review', *Journal of Occupational and Organizational Psychology*, 70, 391–400.

Sparks, K., Faragher, B. and Cooper, C.L. (2001) 'Well-being and occupational health in the 21st century workplace', *Journal of Occupational and Organizational Psychology*, 74, 489–509.

Sparrow, P. (1999) 'Editorial', *Journal of Occupational and Organizational Psychology*, 72, 261–4.

Sparrow, P. and Hodgkinson, G.P. (2002) *The Competent Organisation: A psychological analysis of the strategic management process*. Milton Keynes: Open University Press.

Spearman, C. (1927) *The Abilities of Man: Their nature and measurement*. New York: Macmillan.

Spears, R. and Lea, M. (1994) 'Panacea or panopticon: The hidden power in computer-mediated communication', *Communication Research*, 21, 427–59.

Spector, P.E. (1985) 'Measurement of human service staff satisfaction: Development of the job satisfaction survey', *American Journal of Community Psychology*, 13, 693–713.

Spence, J.R. and Baratta, P.L. (2015) 'Performance appraisal and development', in K. Kraiger, J. Passmore, N. Rebelo dos Santos and S. Malvezzi (eds), *The Psychology of Training, Development and Performance Improvement*. Chichester: Wiley.

Spielberger, C.D., Gorsuch, R.C. and Lushene, R.E. (1970) *Manual for the State Trait Anxiety Inventory*. Paulo Alto, CA: Consulting Psychologists Press.

Spinelli, E. (1989) *The Interpreted World*. London: Sage.

Spokane, A.R., Meir, E.I. and Catalano, M. (2000) 'Person–environment congruence and Holland's theory: A review and reconsideration', *Journal of Vocational Behavior*, 57(2), 137–87.

Sproull, L. and Kiesler, S. (1986) 'Reducing social-context cues: Electronic mail in organisational communication', *Management Science*, 32, 1492–512.

Stace, D. and Dunphy, D. (2001) *Beyond the Boundaries: Leading and re-creating the successful enterprise*, 2nd edition. Sydney: McGraw-Hill.

Stacey, R.D. (2003) *Strategic Management and Organisational Dynamics: The challenge of complexity*. Harlow: FT/Prentice Hall.

Stahl, G.K., Maznevski, M.L, Voigt, A. and Jonsen, K. (2010) 'Unravelling the effects of cultural diversity in teams: A meta-analysis of research on multicultural work groups', *Journal of International Business Studies*, 41, 690–709.

Stamper, C.L. and Johlke, M.C. (2003) 'The impact of perceived organisational support on the relationship between boundary spanner role stress and work outcomes', *Journal of Management*, 29, 569–88.

Standish Group (1995) *The Standish Group Report*. Boston, MA: The Standish Group.

Stanford (2013) *The 2013 Coaching Survey*. http://www.gsb.stanford.edu/sites/default/files/2013-ExecutiveCoachingSurvey.pdf

Stangor, C., Lynch, L., Duan, C. and Glass, B. (1992) 'Categorisation of individuals on the basis of multiple social features', *Journal of Personality and Social Psychology*, 62, 207–18.

Stansfeld, S. and Candy, B. (2006) 'Psychosocial work environment and mental health: A meta-analytic review', *Scandinavian Journal of Work Environment and Health*, 32, 443–62.

Stanton, J.M. (2000) 'Reactions to employee performance monitoring: Framework, review and research directions', *Human Performance*, 13, 85–113.

Stanton, N.A. (2004) 'The psychology of task analysis today', in D. Diaper and N.A. Stanton (eds), *The Handbook of Task Analysis for Human–Computer Interaction*. Mahwah, NJ: Lawrence Erlbaum Associates.

Stanton, N.A., Harris, D., Salmon, P., Demagalski, J.M., Marshall, A., Young, M.S., Dekker, S.W.A. and Waldmann, T. (2006) 'Predicting design-induced pilot error using HET (Human Error Template): A new formal human error identification method for flight decks', *The Aeronautical Journal*, 110(February), 107–15.

Stanton, N.A., Salmon, P.M., Rafferty, L., Walker, G.H., Baber, C. and Jenkins, D.P. (2013) *Human Factors Methods: A practical guide for engineering and design*, 2nd edition. Aldershot: Ashgate.

Stauffer, J.M. and Buckley, M.R. (2005) 'The existence and nature of racial bias in supervisory ratings', *Journal of Applied Psychology*, 90, 586–91.

Staw, B.M., Bell, N.E. and Clausen, J.A. (1986) 'The dispositional approach to job attitudes: A lifetime longitudinal test', *Administrative Science Quarterly*, 31, 56–77.

Steel, P. and Konig, C. (2006) 'Integrating theories of motivation', *Academy of Management Review*, 31, 889–913.

Steers, R.M. and Mowday, R.T. (1981) 'Employee turnover and the post decision accommodation process', in B.M. Staw and L.L. Cummings (eds), *Research in Organisational Behaviour*. Greenwich, CT: JAI Press.

Steijn, B. (2001) 'Work systems, quality of working life and attitudes of workers: An empirical study towards the effects of team and non-teamwork', *New Technology, Work and Employment*, 16(3), 191–203.

Steiner, D.D. and Gilliland, S.W. (1996) 'Fairness reactions to personnel selection techniques in France and the United States', *Journal of Applied Psychology*, 81(2), 134–41.

Stern, L.R. (2004) 'Executive coaching: A working definition', *Consulting Psychology Journal: Practice and Research*, 56, 154–62.

Sternberg, R.J. (1985) *Beyond IQ: A triarchic theory of human intelligence*. Cambridge: Cambridge University Press.

Sternberg, R.J. (1995) 'A triarchic view of "cognitive resources and leadership performance"', *Applied Psychology: An International Review*, 44, 29–32.

Sternberg, R.J. (2006) 'The nature of creativity', *Creativity Research Journal*, 18(1), 87–98.

Sternberg, R.J., Forsythe, G.B., Hedlund, J., Horvath, J.A., Wagner, R.K., Williams, W.M., Snook, S.A. and Grigorenko, E. (eds) (2000) *Practical Intelligence in Everyday Life*. Cambridge: Cambridge University Press.

Sternberg, R.J., Reznitskaya, A. and Jarvin, L. (2007) 'Teaching for wisdom: What matters is not just what students know, but how they use it', *The London Review of Education*, 5(2), 143–58.

Stevens, C.K. and Gist, M. (1997) 'Effects of self-efficacy and goal orientation training on negotiation skill maintenance: What are the mechanisms?', *Personnel Psychology*, 50, 955–78.

Stevens, M.J. and Campion, M.A. (1994) 'The knowledge, skills and ability requirements for teamwork: Implications for human resource management', *Journal of Management*, 20, 503–30.

Stevens, M.J. and Campion, M.A. (1999) 'Staffing work teams: Development and validation of a selection test for teamwork settings', *Journal of Management*, 25, 207–28.

Stickland, F. (1998) *The Dynamics of Change: Insights into organisational transition from the natural world*. London: Routledge.

Stogdill, R.M. (1974) *Handbook of Leadership: A survey of theory and research*. New York: Free Press.

Storey, J. (1992) *Developments in the Management of Human Resources*. Oxford: Blackwell.

Stroh, L.K., Brett, J.M. and Reilly, A.H. (1992) 'All the right stuff: A comparison of female and male managers' career progression', *Journal of Applied Psychology*, 77, 251–60.

Sturges, J., Conway, N. and Liefooghe, A. (2010) 'Organisational support, individual attributes, and the practice of career self-management behavior', *Group and Organisation Management*, 35(1), 108–41.

Suliman, A.M. and Al-Shaikh, F.N. (2007) 'Emotional intelligence at work: Links to conflict and innovation', *Employee Relations*, 29(2), 208–20.

Sullivan, S. and Arthur, M.B. (2006) 'The evolution of the boundaryless career concept: Examining physical and psychological mobility', *Journal of Vocational Behaviour*, 69, 19–29.

Sullivan, S.E. and Crocitto, M. (2007) 'The developmental theories: A critical examination of their continuing impact on careers research', in H. Gunz and M. Peiperl (eds), *Handbook of Career Studies*. London: Sage.

Sundstrom, E., DeMuese, K.P. and Futrell, D. (1990) 'Work teams: Applications and effectiveness', *The American Psychologist*, 45, 120–33.

Super, D.E. (1957) *The Psychology of Careers*. New York: Harper and Row.

Super, D.E. (1990) 'A life-span, life-space approach to career development', in D. Brown and L. Brooks (eds), *Career Choice and Development*, 2nd edition. San Francisco, CA: Jossey-Bass.

Super, D.E. and Nevill, D.D. (1985) *The Salience Inventory*. Palo Alto, CA: Consulting Psychologists Press.

Super, D.E., Thompson, A.S. and Lindeman, R.H. (1985) *The Adult Career Concerns Inventory*. Palo Alto, CA: Consulting Psychologists Press.

Sutherland, V. and Cooper, C.L. (1987) *Man and Accidents Offshore*. London: Lloyd's.

Sverke, M., Hellgren, J. and Näswall, K. (2002) 'No security: A meta-analysis and review of job insecurity and its consequences', *Journal of Occupational Health Psychology*, 7, 242–64.

Swailes, S. and Aritzeta, A. (2006) 'Scale properties of the team role self-perception inventory', *International Journal of Selection and Assessment*, 14(3), 292–8.

Swain, A.D. and Guttman, H.E. (1983) *Handbook of Human Reliability Analysis with Emphasis on Nuclear Power Plant Application* (NUREG/CR-1278). Washington, DC: US Nuclear Regulatory Commission, Office of Nuclear Regulatory Research.

Swanson, V. and Power, K.G. (2001) 'Employees' perceptions of organisational restructuring: The role of social support', *Work & Stress*, 15, 161–78.

Swider, B.W., Boswell, W.R. and Zimmerman, R.D. (2011) 'Examining the job search– turnover relationship: The role of embeddedness, job satisfaction, and available alternatives', *Journal of Applied Psychology*, 96, 432–41.

Symon, G. and Cassell, C. (2012) *Qualitative Organisational Research: Core Methods and Current Challenges*. London: Sage.

Taber, T.D. and Alliger, G.M. (1995) 'A task-level assessment of job satisfaction', *Journal of Organisational Behaviour*, 16, 101–21.

Tajfel, H. (1981) *Human Groups and Social Categories*. Cambridge: Cambridge University Press.

Tajfel, H. and Turner, J. (1979) 'An integrative theory of intergroup conflict', in E.G. Austin and S. Worchel (eds), *The Social Psychology of Intergroup Relations*. Monterey, CA: Brooks-Cole.

Tams, S. and Arthur, M.B. (2007) 'Studying careers across cultures: Distinguishing international, cross-cultural and globalisation perspectives', *Career Development International*, 12, 86–98.

Tan, H.H. and Quek, B.C. (2001) 'An exploratory study on the career anchors of educators in Singapore', *Journal of Psychology*, 135, 527–45.

Tannenbaum, S.I. and Yukl, G.A. (1992) 'Training and development in work organisations', *Annual Review of Psychology*, 43, 399–441.

Taormina, R.J. and Gao, J.H. (2013) 'Maslow and the motivation hierarchy: Measuring satisfaction of the needs', *American Journal of Psychology*, 126, 155–77.

Taris, T.W. (2006) 'Burnout and objectively recorded performance: A critical review of 16 studies', *Work & Stress*, 20, 316–34.

Taris, T.W. and Schreurs, P.J.G. (2009) 'Well-being and organisational performance: An organisational-level test of the happy-productive worker hypothesis', *Work & Stress*, 23, 120–36.

Taris, T.W, Feij, J.A. and Capel, S. (2006) 'Great expectations and what comes of it: The effects of unmet expectations on work motivation and outcomes among newcomers', *International Journal of Selection and Assessment*, 14, 256–68.

Taylor, F.W. (1911) *Principles of Scientific Management*. New York: Harper.

Taylor, P J. and Small, B. (2002) 'Asking applicants what they would do versus what they did do: A meta-analytic comparison of situational and past behaviour employment interview questions', *Journal of Occupational and Organizational Psychology*, 75(3), 277–94.

Tetrick, L.E. and Winslow, C.J. (2015) 'Workplace stress management interventions and health promotion', *Annual Review of Organisational Psychology and Organisational Behaviour*, 2, 583–603.

Tett, R.P. and Christiansen N.D. (2007) 'Personality tests at the crossroads: A response to Morgeson, Campion, Dipboye, Hollenbeck, Murphy and Schmitt', *Personnel Psychology*, 60, 967–93.

Tett, R.P., Freund, K.A., Christiansen, N.D., Fox, K.E. and Coaster, J. (2012) 'Faking on self-report emotional intelligence and personality tests: Effects of faking opportunity, cognitive ability, and job type', *Personality and Individual Differences*, 52, 195–201.

Thomas, R.J. (1989) 'Blue collar careers: Meaning and choice in a world of constraints', in M. Arthur, D.T. Hall and B.S. Lawrence (eds), *Handbook of Career Theory*. Cambridge: Cambridge University Press.

Thompson, E.R. (2008) 'Development and validation of an international English Big-Five mini-markers', *Personality and Individual Differences*, 45, 542–8.

Thompson, E.R. and Phua, F.T.T. (2012) 'A brief index of affective job satisfaction', *Group and Organisation Management*, 37, 275–307.

Thompson, G. and Vecchio, R.P. (2009) 'Situational leadership theory: A test of three theories', *The Leadership Quarterly*, 20, 837–48.

Thompson, J. (1967) *Organisations in Action*. New York: McGraw-Hill.

Thoresen, C.J., Kaplan, S.A., Barsky, A.P., Warren, C.R. and de Chermont, K. (2003) 'The affective underpinnings of job perceptions and attitudes: A meta-analytic review and integration', *Psychological Bulletin*, 129, 914–45.

Tiedeman, D.V. and O'Hara, R.P. (1963) *Career Development: Choice and adjustment*. New York: College Entrance Exam Board.

Tims, M. and Bakker, A.B. (2010) 'Job crafting: Towards a new model of individual job redesign', *South African Journal of Industrial Psychology*, 36, 1–9.

Tims, M., Bakker, A.B. and Xanthopoulou, D. (2011) 'Do transformational leaders enhance their followers' daily work engagement?', *The Leadership Quarterly*, 22, 121–31.

Tippins, N.T., Beaty, J., Drasgow, F., Gibson, W.M., Pearlman K., Segall D.O. et al. (2006) 'Unproctored Internet testing in employment settings', *Personnel Psychology*, 59, 189–225.

Tjosvold, D., Wedley, W.C. and Field, R.H.G. (1986) 'Constructive controversy, the Vroom–Yetton model, and managerial decision-making', *Journal of Occupational Behaviour*, 7, 125–38.

Toldi, N.L. (2011) 'Job applicants favour video interviewing in the candidate selection process', *Employment Relations Today*, 38, 19–27.

Tourish, D. (2013) *The Dark Side of Transformational Leadership*. London: Routledge.

Tourish, D. and Pinnington, A. (2002) 'Transformational leadership, corporate cultism and the spirituality paradigm: An unholy trinity in the workplace', *Human Relations*, 55, 147–72.

Tracey, J.B. and Hinkin, T.R. (1998) 'Transformational leadership or effective managerial practices', *Group and Organisational Management*, 23, 220–36.

Tracey, J.B., Tannenbaum, S.I. and Kavanaugh, M.J. (1995) 'Applying trained skills on the job: The importance of the work environment', *Journal of Applied Psychology*, 80, 239–52.

Tracey, T.J. and Rounds, S.B. (1993) 'Evaluating Holland's and Gati's vocational-interest models: A structural meta-analysis', *Psychological Bulletin*, 113, 229–46.

Trist, E.L. and Bamforth, K.W. (1951) 'Some social and psychological consequences of the long-wall method of coal getting', *Human Relations*, 4, 3–38.

Trompenaars, F. (1993) *Riding the Waves of Culture*. London: Economist Books.

Truxillo, D.M., Cadiz, D.M., Rineer, J.R., Zaniboni, S. and Fraccaroli, F. (2012) 'A lifespan perspective on job design: Fitting the job and the worker to promote job satisfaction, engagement, and performance', *Organisational Psychology Review*, 2, 340–60.

Tsang, E.W.K. (1997) 'Organisational learning and the learning organisation: A dichotomy between descriptive and prescriptive research', *Human Relations*, 50(1), 73–89.

Tsutsumi, A. and Kawakami, N. (2004) 'A review of empirical studies on the model of effort–reward imbalance at work: Reducing occupational stress by implementing a new theory', *Social Science and Medicine*, 59, 2235–59.

Tubré, T. and Collins, J. (2000) 'Jackson and Schuler (1985) revisited: A meta-analysis of the relationships between role ambiguity, role conflict and job performance', *Journal of Management*, 26, 155–69.

Tuckman, B.W. (1965) 'Development sequence in small groups', *Psychological Review*, 63, 384–99.

Tuller, H.M., Bryan, C.J., Heyman, G.D. and Christenfeld, N.J.S (2015) 'Seeing the other side: Perspective taking and the moderation of extremity', *Journal of Experimental Social Psychology*, 59, 18–23.

Turner, A.N. and Lawrence, P.R. (1965) *Industrial Jobs and the Worker*. Cambridge, MA: Harvard University Press.

Turner, B. (1971) *Exploring the Industrial Subculture*. London: Macmillan.

Turner, D. and Crawford, M. (1999) *Change Power: Capabilities that drive corporate renewal*. Sydney: Woodslane.

Turner, J.C. (1999) 'Some current themes in research on social identity and self-categorisation theories', in N. Ellemers, R. Spears and B. Doosje (eds), *Social Identity: Context, commitment, content*. Oxford: Blackwell.

Turner, J.C. and Onorato, R. (1999) 'Social identity, personality and the self-concept: A self-categorisation perspective', in T.R. Tyler, R. Kramer and O. John (eds), *The Psychology of the Social Self*. Hillsdale, NJ: Erlbaum.

Turner, N., Barling, J., Epitropaki, O., Butcher, V. and Milder, C. (2002) 'Transformational leadership and moral reasoning', *Journal of Applied Psychology*, 87, 304–11.

Tyson, S. and Ward, P. (2004) 'The use of 360-degree feedback techniques in the evaluation of management learning', *Management Learning*, 35, 202–23.

Tziner, A. (1985) 'How team composition affects task performance: Some theoretical insights', *Psychological Review*, 57, 1111–19.

UK Labour Force Survey (2012) *2012 Annual Survey of Hours and Earnings*. London: National Statistics.

Ulfvengren, P. (2003) 'Associability: A comparison of sounds in a cognitive approach to auditory alert design', *Human Factors and Aerospace Safety*, 3, 313–31.

Underhill, C.M. (2006) 'The effectiveness of mentoring programs in corporate settings: A meta-analytical review of the literature', *Journal of Vocational Behaviour*, 68, 292–307.

US Air Force (2009) *Air Force Human Systems Integration Handbook*. Washington, DC: US Government Printing Office. Retrieved from: http://www.wpafb.af.mil/shared/media/document/AFD-090121-054.pdf (accessed 19 October 2015).

US Nuclear Regulatory Commission (2002) *Human System Interface Review Design Guidelines (NUREG-0700 Rev. 2)*. Washington, DC: US Nuclear Regulatory Commission, Office of Nuclear Regulatory Research.

Väänänen, A., Tordera, N., Kivamäki, M., Kouvonen, A., Pentti, J., Linna, A. and Vahtera, J. (2008) 'The role of work group in individual sickness absence behaviour', *Journal of Health and Social Behaviour*, 49, 452–67.

Valsecchi, R. (2006) 'Visible moves and invisible bodies: The case of teleworking in an Italian call centre', *New Technology Work and Employment*, 22, 123–38.

Van den Berg, P. and Wilderom, C. (2004) 'Defining, measuring and comparing organisational culture', *Applied Psychology: An International Review*, 53, 575–82.

van den Heuvel, M., Demerouti, E. and Peeters, M.C.W. (2015) 'The job crafting intervention: Effects on job resources, self-efficacy, and affective well-being', *Journal of Occupational and Organizational Psychology*, 88, 511–32.

van der Aa, Z., Bloemer, J. and Henseler, J. (2012) 'Reducing employee turnover through customer contact centre job quality', *International Journal of Human Resource Management*, 23, 3925–41.

Van der Hek, H. and Plomp, H.N. (1997) 'Occupational stress management programmes: A practical overview of published effect studies', *Occupational Medicine*, 47, 133–41.

van der Klink, J.J.L., Blonk, R.W.B., Schene, A.H. and van Dijk, F.J.H. (2001) 'The benefits of interventions for work-related stress', *American Journal of Public Health*, 91, 270–6.

Van der Linden, D., te Nijenhuis, J. and Bakker, A.B. (2010) 'The general factor of personality: A meta-analysis of Big Five intercorrelations and a criterion-related validity study', *Journal of Research in Personality*, 44, 315–27.

Van Eerde, W. and Thierry, H. (1996) 'Vroom's expectancy models and work related criteria: A meta-analysis', *Journal of Applied Psychology*, 81, 575–86.

Van Harreveld, F., van der Plight, J., de Vries, N.K. and Andreas, S. (2000) 'The structure of attitudes: Attribute importance, accessibility, and judgement', *British Journal of Social Psychology*, 39, 363–80.

Van Hiel, A. and Mervielde, I. (2001) 'Preferences for behavioural style of minority and majority members who anticipate group interaction', *Social Behaviour and Personality*, 29(7), 701–10.

Van Hoye, G. and Lootens, H. (2013) 'Coping with unemployment: Personality, role demands, and time structure', *Journal of Vocational Behaviour*, 82, 85–95.

Van Hoye, G. and Saks, A.M. (2008) 'Job search as goal-directed behaviour: Objectives and methods', *Journal of Vocational Behaviour*, 73, 358–67.

Van Knippenberg, D. (2000) 'Work motivation and performance: A social identity perspective', *Applied Psychology: An International Review*, 49, 357–71.

Van Knippenberg, D. and Schippers, M.C. (2007) 'Work group diversity', *Annual Review of Psychology*, 58(1), 515–41.

Van Maanen, J. and Kunda, G. (1989) 'Real feelings: Emotional expression and organisational culture', in B. Staw and L. Cummings (eds), *Research in Organisational Behaviour*, vol. 11. Greenwich, CT: JAI Press.

Van Maanen, J. and Schein, E.H. (1979) 'Towards a theory of organisational socialisation', in B.M. Staw (ed.), *Research in Organisational Behaviour*, vol. 1. Greenwich, CT: JAI Press.

Van Mierlo, H., Rutte, C.G., Kompier, M. and Doorewaard, H. (2005) 'Self managing teamwork and psychological well-being: Review of a multilevel research domain', *Group and Organisation Management*, 30, 211–35.

van Steenbergen, E.F., Ellemers, N., Haslam, S.A. and Urlings, F. (2008) 'There is nothing either good or bad but thinking makes it so: Informational support and cognitive appraisal of the work–family interface', *Journal of Occupational and Organizational Psychology*, 81, 349–67.

van Veldhoven, M.J.P.M., Taris, T.W., de Jonge, J. and Broersen, S. (2005) 'The relationship between work characteristics and employee health and well being: How much complexity do we really need?', *International Journal of Stress Management*, 12, 3–28.

van Wanrooy, B., Bewley, H., Bryson, A., Forth, J., Freeth, S., Stokes, L. and Wood, S. (2014) *The 2011 Workplace Employment Relations Survey: First Findings*. London: Department for Business, Innovation and Skills.

Van Yperen, N.W., Hamstra, M.R. and Van der Klauw, M. (2011) 'To win, or not to lose, at any cost: The impact of achievement goals on cheating', *British Journal of Management*, 22(s1), S5–S15.

Vandenberg, R.J., Richardson, H.A. and Eastman, L.J. (1999) 'The impact of high involvement work processes on organisational effectiveness: A second-order latent variable approach', *Group and Organisation Management*, 24(3), 300–39.

Vandenberghe, C. and Bentein, K. (2009) 'A closer look at the relationship between affective commitment to supervisors and organisations and turnover', *Journal of Occupational and Organizational Psychology*, 82, 331–48.

VandeWalle, D.M., Cron, W.L. and Slocum, J.W. (2001) 'The role of goal orientation following performance feedback', *Journal of Applied Psychology*, 86, 629–40.

Vansteenkiste, M., Lens, W., De Witte, H. and Feather, N.T. (2005) 'Understanding unemployed people's job search behaviour, unemployment experience and well-being: A comparison of expectancy-value theory and self-determination theory', *British Journal of Social Psychology*, 44, 269–87.

Vansteenkiste, S., Verbruggen, M. and Sels, L. (2013) 'Being unemployed in the boundaryless career era: Does psychological mobility pay off?' *Journal of Vocational Behaviour*, 82, 135–43.

Vecchio, R.P. (1987) 'Situational leadership theory: An examination of a prescriptive theory', *Journal of Applied Psychology*, 72, 444–51.

Vecchio, R.P. (1990) 'Theoretical and empirical examination of cognitive resource theory', *Journal of Applied Psychology*, 75, 141–7.

Verkuyten, M. (1998) 'Attitudes in public discourse: Speakers' own orientations', *Journal of Language and Social Psychology*, 17(3), 302–22.

Vernon, H.M. (1948) 'An autobiography', *Occupational Psychology*, 23, 73–82.

Vernon, P.A., Petrides, K.V., Bratko, D. and Scherner, J.A. (2008) 'A behavioural genetic study of trait emotional intelligence', *Emotion*, 8, 635–42.

Villanova, P. and Bernardin, H.J. (1991) 'Performance appraisal: The means, motive and opportunity to manage impressions', in R.A. Giacalone and P. Rosenfeld (eds), *Applied Impression Management*. Newbury Park, CA: Sage Publications.

Vince, R. (2002) 'The politics of imagined stability: A psychodynamic understanding of change at Hyder plc', *Human Relations*, 55, 1189–208.

Vincente, K.J. (1999) *Cognitive Work Analysis: Towards safe, productive and healthy computer-based work*. Mahwah, NJ: Lawrence Erlbaum.

Viswesvaran, C., Schmidt, F. and Ones, D. (2005) 'Is there a general factor in ratings of job performance? A meta-analytic framework for disentangling substantive and error influences', *Journal of Applied Psychology*, 90, 108–31.

Vollrath, D.A., Sheppard, B.H., Hinsz, V.B. and Davis, J.H. (1989) 'Memory performance by decision-making groups and individuals', *Organisational Behaviour and Human Decision Processes*, 43, 289–300.

Vroom, V. (2000) 'Leadership and the decision-making process', *Organisational Dynamics*, 28, 82–94.

Vroom, V.H. (1964) *Work and Motivation*. Chichester: John Wiley.

Vroom, V.H. and Deci, E.L. (1971) 'The stability of post-decision dissonance: A follow-up study of the job attitudes of business school graduates', *Organisational Behaviour and Human Performance*, 6, 36–49.

Vroom, V.H. and Jago, A.G. (1988) *The New Leadership: Managing participation in organisations*. Englewood Cliffs, NJ: Prentice Hall.

Vroom, V.H. and Yetton, P.W. (1973) *Leadership and Decision Making*. Pittsburgh, PA: Pittsburgh Press.

Vyas, M.V. and Garg, A.X. (2012) 'Shift work and vascular events: Systematic review and meta-analysis', *BMJ*, 345: e4800. DOI: 10.1136/bmj.e4800.

Waddell, G. and Burton, K. (2006) *Is Work Good for your Health and Well-Being?* London: TSO.

Wahba, M.A. and Bridwell, L.B. (1976) 'Maslow reconsidered: A review of research on the need hierarchy theory', *Organisational Behaviour and Human Performance*, 15, 212–40.

Waldman, D.A. and Yammarino, F.J. (1999) 'CEO charismatic leadership: Levels-of-management and levels-of-analysis effects', *Academy of Management Review*, 24, 266–85.

Waldman, D.A., Ramirez, G.G., House, R.J. and Puranam, P. (2001) 'Does leadership matter? CEO leader attributes and profitability under conditions of perceived environmental uncertainty', *Academy of Management Journal*, 44, 134–43.

Walker, A. (1982) *Unqualified and Unemployed*. Basingstoke: Macmillan/National Children's Bureau.

Walker, A.G. and Smither, J.W. (1999) 'A five-year study of upwards feedback: What managers do with their results matters', *Personnel Psychology*, 52, 393–423.

Wall, T.D. (1982) 'Perspectives on job redesign', in J.E. Kelly and C.W. Clegg (eds), *Autonomy and Control in the Workplace*. London: Croom Helm.

Wall, T.D., Clegg, C.W. and Kemp, N.J. (1987) *The Human Side of Advanced Manufacturing Technology*. Chichester: John Wiley.

Wall, T.D., Cordery, J.L. and Clegg, C.W. (2002) 'Empowerment, performance and operational uncertainty: A theoretical integration', *Applied Psychology: An International Review*, 51, 146–69.

Walther, J.B. (1992) 'Interpersonal effects in computer-mediated interaction: A relational perspective', *Communication Research*, 19, 52–90.

Walther, J.B. (1993) 'Impression development in computer-mediated interaction', *Western Journal of Communication*, 57, 381–98.

Walther, J.B. (1994) 'Anticipated ongoing interaction versus channel effects on relational communication in computer-mediated interaction', *Human Communication Research*, 20, 473–501.

Walther, J.B. (1995) 'Relational aspects of computer-mediated communication: Experimental observations', *Organisation Science*, 6, 186–203.

Walther, J.B. (1996) 'Computer-mediated communication: Impersonal, interpersonal and hyperpersonal interaction', *Communication Research*, 23, 3–43.

Walther, J.B. and Bunz, U. (2005) 'The rules of virtual groups: Trust, liking and performance in computer-mediated communication', *Journal of Communication*, 55, 828–46.

Walther, J.B. and Burgoon, J.K. (1992) 'Relational communication in computer mediated interaction', *Human Communication Research*, 19, 50–88.

Walther, J.B., Slovacek, C. and Tidwell, L.C. (2001) 'Is a picture worth a thousand words? Photographic images in long-term and short-term virtual teams', *Communication Research*, 28, 105–34.

Walumbwa, F.O., Hartnell, C.A. and Oke, A. (2010) 'Servant leadership, procedural justice climate, service climate, employee attitudes, and organisational citizenship behaviour: A cross-level investigation', *Journal of Applied Psychology*, 95, 517–29.

Wanberg, C., Basbug, G., Van Hooft, E.A. and Samtani, A. (2012) 'Navigating the black hole: Explicating layers of job search context and adaptational responses', *Personnel Psychology*, 65, 887–926.

Wanberg, C.R., Kammeyer-Mueller, J. and Shi, K. (2001) 'Job loss and the experience of unemployment: International research and perspectives', in N. Anderson, D.S. Ones, H.K. Sinangil and C. Viswesvaran (eds), *Handbook of Work, Industrial and Organisational Psychology*, vol. 2. London: Sage.

Wang, G., Os, I.-S., Courtright, S.H. and Colbert, A.E. (2011) 'Transformational leadership and performance across criteria and levels: A meta-analytic review of 25 years of research', *Group and Organisational Management*, 36, 223–70.

Wang, G.P. and Lee, P.D. (2009) 'Psychological empowerment and job satisfaction: An analysis of interactive effects', *Group and Organisation Management*, 34, 271–96.

Wardwell, W., Hyman, I.M. and Bahnson, C.B. (1964) 'Stress and coronary disease in three field studies', *Journal of Chronic Disease*, 17, 73–4.

Warner, M. and Goodall, K. (2010) *Management Training and Development in China: Educating managers in a globalised economy*. Oxford: Routledge.

Warr, P. (1992) 'Age and occupational well-being', *Psychology and Ageing*, 7, 37–45.

Warr, P., Allan, C. and Birdi, K. (1999) 'Predicting three levels of training outcome', *Journal of Occupational and Organizational Psychology*, 72, 351–75.

Warr, P., Cook, J. and Wall, T. (1979) 'Scales for the measurement of some work attitudes and aspects of psychological well-being', *Journal of Occupational Psychology*, 52, 129–48.

Warr, P.B. (1987) *Work, Unemployment and Mental Health*. Oxford: Oxford University Press.

Warr, P.B. (2008) 'Work values: Some demographic and cultural correlates', *Journal of Occupational and Organizational Psychology*, 81, 751–75.

Warr, P.B. (2009) 'Environmental "vitamins", personal judgments, work values and happiness', in S. Cartwright and C.L. Cooper (eds), *The Oxford Handbook of Organisational Well-Being*. Oxford: Oxford University Press.

Warwick, D.P. and Thompson, J.T. (1980) 'Still crazy after all these years', *Training and Development Journal*, 34, 16–22.

Wasti, S.A. and Can, Ö. (2008) 'Affective and normative commitment to organisation, supervisor, and coworkers: Do collectivist values matter?', *Journal of Vocational Behaviour*, 73, 404–13.

Watson, D. and Pennebaker, J.W. (1989) 'Health complaints, stress, and distress: Exploring the central role of negative affectivity', *Psychological Review*, 96, 234–54.

Watson, D., Clark, L.A. and Tellegen, A. (1988) 'Development and validation of brief measures of positive and negative affect: The PANAS scales', *Journal of Personality and Social Psychology*, 54, 1063–70.

Watson, T.J. (1997) *Sociology, Work and Industry*, 3rd edition. London: Routledge.

Wayne, J.H., Casper, W.J., Matthews, R.A. and Allen, T.D (2013) 'Family-supportive organisation perceptions and organisational commitment: The mediating role of work–family conflict and enrichment and partner attitudes', *Journal of Applied Psychology*, 98, 606–22.

Webster, J. and Starbuck, W.H. (1988) 'Theory building in industrial and organisational psychology', in C.L. Cooper and I.T. Robertson (eds), *International Review of Industrial and Organisational Psychology*, vol. 3. Chichester: John Wiley.

Wee, S. (2014) 'Compromises in career-related decisions: Examining the role of compromise severity', *Journal of Counselling Psychology*, 61, 593–604.

Weekley, J.A. and Ployhart, R.E. (eds) (2006) *Situational Judgment Tests: Theory, measurement and application*. Mahweh, NJ: Lawrence Erlbaum.

Weick, K. (1996) 'Enactment and the boundaryless career: Organising as we work', in M.B. Arthur and D.E. Rousseau (eds), *The Boundaryless Career*. Oxford: Oxford University Press.

Weick, K.E. (2000) 'Emergent change as a universal in organisations', in M. Beer and N. Nohria (eds), *Breaking the Code of Change*. Boston, MA: Harvard Business School Press.

Weinberg, A. and Cooper, C.L. (2007) *Surviving the Workplace: A guide to emotional well-being*. London: Thomson.

Weinberg, A., Sutherland, V.J. and Cooper, C.L. (2010) *Organisational Stress Management: A strategic approach*. Basingstoke: Palgrave Macmillan.

Weirsma, U. and Latham, G.P. (1986) 'The practicality of behavioural expectation scales and trait scales', *Personnel Psychology*, 39, 619–28.

Welbourne, T.M., Cycyota, C.S. and Ferrante, C.J. (2007) 'Wall Street reaction to women in IPOs', *Group and Organisation Management*, 32, 524–47.

Welters, R., Mitchell, W. and Muysken, J. (2014) 'Self-determination theory and employed job search', *Journal of Economic Psychology*, 44, 34–44.

Werner, J.M. and Bolino, M.C. (1997) 'Explaining US courts of appeals decisions involving performance appraisal: Accuracy, fairness and validation', *Personnel Psychology*, 50, 1–24.

Wernimont, P.F. and Campbell, J.P. (1968) 'Signs, samples and criteria', *Journal of Applied Psychology*, 52, 372–6.

West, M.A. (1994) *Effective Teamwork*. Leicester: British Psychological Society.

West, M.A. (2001) 'The human team: Basic motivations and innovations', in. N. Anderson, D.S. Ones, H.K. Sinagil and C. Viswesvaran (eds), *Handbook of Industrial, Work and Organisational Psychology*. London: Sage.

West, M.A. (2002) 'Sparkling fountains or stagnant ponds: An integrative model of creativity and innovation implementation in work groups', *Applied Psychology: An International Review*, 51(3), 355–87.

West, M.A. and Farr, J.L. (1990) 'Innovation at work'. In M.A. West and J.L. Farr (eds), *Innovation and Creativity at Work: Psychological and organisational strategies*. Chichester: Wiley.

West, M.A. and Lyubovnikova, J. (2013) 'Illusions of team working in health care', *Journal of Health Organisation and Management*, 27, 134–42.

Westman, M., Etzion, D. and Gattenio, E. (2008) 'International business travels and the work–family interface: A longitudinal study', *Journal of Occupational and Organizational Psychology*, 81, 459–80.

Wexley, K.N. (1984) 'Personnel training', *Annual Review of Psychology*, 35, 519–51.

Wheatley, M. (1992) *The Future of Middle Management*. London: British Institute of Management.

Whetzel, D.L. and McDaniel, M.A. (2009) 'Situational judgment tests: An overview of current research', *Human Resource Management Review*, 19(3), 188–202.

Whetzel, D.L., McDaniel, M.A. and Nguyen, N.T. (2008) 'Subgroup differences in situational judgment test performance: A meta-analysis', *Human Performance*, 21(3), 291–309.

Whitfield, K. (ed.) (2009) *Employee Well-being and Working Life: Towards an evidence-based policy agenda*. An Economic and Social Research Council (ESRC)/Health and Safety Executive (HSE) public policy project report on a public policy seminar. Available at: http://www2.warwick.ac.uk/fac/soc/ier/publications/2009/whitfield_ed_2009_employee_well_being.pdf (accessed 3 August 2014).

Whitman, D.S., Van Rooy, D.L. and Viswesvaran, C. (2010) 'Satisfaction, citizenship behaviours, and performance in work units: A meta-analysis of collective construct relations,' *Personnel Psychology*, 63, 41–81.

Whitmore, J. (2004) *Coaching for Performance: Growing people, performance and purpose*, 3rd edition. London: Nicholas Brearley Publishing.

Whittington, R. (1993) *What is Strategy and Does it Matter?* London: Routledge.

Whyte, G. (1989) 'Groupthink reconsidered', *Academy of Management Review*, 14, 40–56.

Whyte, J. and Witcher, B. (1992) *The Adoption of Total Quality Management in Northern England*. Durham: Durham University Business School.

Wickens, C.D., Ververs, P.M. and Fadden, S. (2004) 'Head up displays', in D. Harris (ed.), *Human Factors for Civil Flight Deck Design*. Aldershot: Ashgate.

Widdowson, I. and Carr, J. (2002) *Human Factors Integration: Implementation in the onshore and offshore industries* (HSE Research Report 001). London: HSE Publications.

Wilk, S.L. and Cappelli, P. (2003) 'Understanding the determinants of employer use of selection methods', *Personnel Psychology*, 56(1), 103–24.

Wilkin, C.L. (2015) 'I can't get no job satisfaction: Meta-analysis comparing permanent and contingent workers', *Journal of Organisational Behaviour*, 34, 47–64.

Wilkinson, A. (1998) 'Empowerment theory and practice', *Personnel Review*, 27, 40–56.

Wilkinson, A.J. and Redman, T. (2013) *Contemporary Human Resource Management: Text and Cases,* 4th edition. Harlow: Pearson.

Williams, J.C. (1986) 'HEART: A proposed method for assessing and reducing human error'. Paper presented at the Ninth Advances in Reliability Technology Symposium, University of Bradford.

Williams, K., Harkins, S. and Latane, B. (1981) 'Identifiability as a deterrent to social loafing: Two cheering experiments', *Journal of Personality and Social Psychology*, 40, 303–11.

Williams, K.Y. and O'Reilly, C.A. (1998) 'Demography and diversity in organisations: A review of 40 years of research', *Research in Organisational Behaviour*, 20, 77–140.

Williams, R. (2002) *Managing Employee Performance: Design and implementation in organisations*. London: Thomson Learning.

Willig, C. (2008) *Introducing Qualitative Research in Psychology*, 2nd edition. Maidenhead: Open University Press.

Willmott, H. (1995) 'Strength is ignorance; slavery is freedom: Managing culture in modern organisations', *Journal of Management Studies*, 30, 511–12.

Willness, C.R., Steel, P. and Lee, K. (2007) 'A meta-analysis of the antecedents and consequences of workplace sexual harassment', *Personnel Psychology*, 60, 127–62.

Wilson, D.C. (1992) *A Strategy of Change: Concepts and controversies in the management of change*. London: Routledge.

Wilson, K.Y. (2010) 'An analysis of bias in supervisor narrative comments in performance appraisal', *Human Relations*, 63, 1903–33.

Winefield, A.H. (1995) 'Unemployment: Its psychological costs', in C.L. Cooper and I.T. Robertson (eds), *International Review of Industrial and Organisational Psychology*, vol. 10. Chichester: Wiley.

Winter, D.G. (2010) 'Why achievement motivation predicts success in business but failure in politics: The importance of personal control', *Journal of Personality*, 78, 1637–68.

Witcher, B. (1993) *The Adoption of Total Quality Management in Scotland*. Durham: Durham University Business School.

Woehr, D.J. and Huffcutt, A.I. (1994) 'Rater training for performance appraisal: A quantitative review', *Journal of Occupational and Organizational Psychology*, 67, 189–205.

Wong, C.S., Hui, C. and Law, K.S. (1998) 'A longitudinal study of the job perception–job satisfaction relationship: A test of the three alternative specifications', *Journal of Occupational and Organizational Psychology*, 71(2), 127–46.

Wood, W., Lundgren, S., Ouellette, J.A., Busceme, S. and Blackstone, T. (1994) 'Minority influence: A meta-analytic review of social influence processes', *Psychological Bulletin*, 115, 323–45.

Wooford, J.C., Goodwin, V.L. and Premack, S. (1992) 'Meta-analysis of the antecedents of personal goal level and of the antecedents and consequences of goals commitment', *Journal of Management*, 18, 595–615.

Wooten, K.C. and White, L.P. (1999) 'Linking OD's philosophy with justice theory: Postmodern implications', *Journal of Organisational Change Management*, 12, 7–20.

Worley, G.W. and Feyerherm, A.E. (2003) 'Reflections on the future of organisation development', *Journal of Applied Behavioural Science*, 39(1), 97–115.

Worrall, L. and Cooper, C.L. (1997) *The Quality of Working Life: The 1997 survey of managers' changing experiences*. London: Institute of Management.

Worrall, L. and Cooper, C.L. (1998) *The Quality of Working Life: The 1998 survey of managers' changing experiences*. London: Institute of Management.

Wright, P.M., O'Leary-Kelly, A.M., Cortina, J.M., Klein, H.J. and Hollenbeck, J. (1994) 'On the meaning and measurement of goal commitment', *Journal of Applied Psychology*, 79, 795–803.

Wright, T.A. and Cropanzano, R. (2004) 'The role of psychological well-being in job performance: A fresh look at an age-old quest', *Organisational Dynamics*, 33, 338–51.

Wright, T.A. and Staw, B.M. (1999) 'Affect and favourable work outcomes: Two longitudinal tests of the happy-productive worker thesis', *Journal of Organisational Behaviour*, 20, 1–23.

Wright, V. (1991) 'Performance-related pay', in F. Neale (ed.), *The Handbook of Performance Management*. London: CIPD.

Wrzesniewski, A. and Dutton, J.E. (2001) 'Crafting a job: Revisioning employees as active crafters of their work', *Academy of Management Review*, 26, 179–201.

Wu, C.-H. and Griffin, M.A. (2012) 'Longitudinal relationships between core self-evaluations and job satisfaction', *Journal of Applied Psychology*, 97, 331–42.

Wyatt, M. and Silvester, J. (2015) 'Reflections on the labyrinth: Investigating Black and minority ethnic leaders' career experiences', *Human Relations*, 68, 1243–69.

Wyatt, M.R., Pathak, S.B. and Zibarras, L.D. (2010) 'Advancing selection in an SME: Is best practice methodology applicable?', *International Small Business Journal*, 28, 258–73.

Wycoff, J. (2004) 'The big ten innovation killers and how to keep your innovation system alive and well', *Innovation Network*. Available at: www.knooppuntinnovatie.nl/documenten/TheBigTenInnovationKillers.pdf

Young, G., Tokar, D.M. and Subich, L.M. (1998) 'Congruence revisited: Do 11 indices differentially predict job satisfaction and is the relation moderated by person and situation variables?', *Journal of Vocational Behaviour*, 52, 208–23.

Young, M.S., Stanton, N.A. and Harris, D. (2007) 'Driving automation: Learning from aviation about design philosophies', *International Journal of Vehicle Design*, 45(3), 323–38.

Yukl, G.A. (2012) *Leadership in Organisations*, 8th edition. Upper Saddle River, NJ: Prentice Hall.

Yun, H., Kettinger, W. and Lee, C. (2012) 'A new open door: The smartphone's impact on work-to-life conflict, stress, and resistance', *Journal of Electronic Commerce*, 16, 121–52.

Yun, S., Faraj, S. and Sims, H.P. (2005) 'Contingent leadership and effectiveness of trauma resuscitation teams', *Journal of Applied Psychology*, 90, 1288–96.

Zacher, H. and Frese, M. (2009) 'Remaining time and opportunities at work: Relationships between age, work characteristics, and occupational future time perspective', *Psychology and Ageing*, 24, 487–93.

Zacher, H. and Frese, M. (2011) 'Maintaining a focus on opportunities at work: The interplay between age, job complexity, and the use of selection, optimisation, and compensation strategies', *Journal of Organisational Behaviour*, 32, 291–318.

Zairi, M., Letza, S. and Oakland, J. (1994) 'Does TQM impact on bottom line results?', *TQM Magazine*, 6(1), 38–43.

Zapata-Phelan, C.P., Colquitt, J.A., Scott, B.A. and Livingston, B. (2009) 'Procedural justice, interactional justice, and task performance: The mediating role of intrinsic motivation', *Organisational Behaviour and Human Decision Processes*, 108, 93–105.

Zapf, D. (1999) 'Organisational work group related and personal causes of mobbing/ bullying at work', *International Journal of Manpower*, 20, 70–85.

Zapf, D. (2002) 'Emotion work and psychological well-being: A review of the literature and some conceptual considerations', *Human Resource Management Review*, 12, 237–68.

Zapf, D. and Einarsen, S. (2003) 'Individual antecedents of bullying: Victims and perpetrators', in S. Einarsen, H. Hoel, D. Zapf and C.L. Cooper (eds), *Bullying and Emotional Abuse in the Workplace: International perspectives in research and practice*. London: Taylor and Francis.

Zeidner, M. and Endler, N.S. (1996) *Handbook of Coping: Theory, research, applications*. Oxford: John Wiley.

Zeidner, M., Roberts, R.D. and Matthews, G. (2008) 'The science of emotional intelligence: Current consensus and controversies', *European Psychologist*, 13, 64–78.

Zhao, H., Wayne, S.J., Glibkowski, B.C. and Bravo, J. (2007) 'The impact of psychological contract breach on work-related outcomes: A meta-analysis', *Personnel Psychology*, 60, 647–80.

Zhao, Z.J. and Chadwick, C. (2014) 'What we will do versus what we can do: The relative effects of unit-level NPD motivation and capability', *Strategic Management Journal*, 35, 1867–80.

Zhou, J. and Shalley, C.E. (2008) *Handbook of Organisational Creativity*. Hove, Sussex: Psychology Press.

Zhu, Y. and Akhtar, S. (2014) 'How transformational leadership influences follower helping behaviour: The role of trust and prosocial motivation', *Journal of Organisational Behaviour*, 35, 373–92.

Zibarras, L.D. and Patterson, F. (2015) 'The role of job relatedness and self-efficacy in applicant perceptions of fairness in a high-stakes selection setting', *International Journal of Selection and Assessment*, 23(4), 332–44.

Zibarras, L.D. and Woods, S.A. (2010) 'A survey of UK selection practices across different organisation sizes and industry sectors', *Journal of Occupational and Organizational Psychology*, 83, 499–511.

Zikic, J. and Klehe, U. (2006) 'Job loss as a blessing in disguise: The role of career exploration and career planning in predicting reemployment quality', *Journal of Vocational Behaviour*, 69, 391–409.

Zimmerman, R.D. (2008) 'Understanding the impact of personality traits on individuals' turnover decisions: A meta-analytic path model', *Personnel Psychology*, 61, 309–48.

Zsambok, C.E. and Klein, G. (1997) *Naturalistic Decision Making*. Mahwah, NJ: Lawrence Erlbaum.

INDEX

Note: **bold** page numbers denote glossary entries.